The Bed & Breakfast Guide 2007

GW00632188

37th edition
© Automobile Association Developments Limited 2006.
Automobile Association Developments Limited retains the copyright in the current edition © 2006 and in all subsequent editions, reprints and amendments to editions. The information contained in this directory is sourced from the AA's establishment database, AA Hotel Services. All rights reserved. No part of this publication may be reproduced, stored in a retrieval system, or transmitted in any form or by any means - electronic, photocopying, recording, or otherwise - unless the written permission of the publishers has been given beforehand. This book may not be sold, resold, hired out or otherwise disposed of by way of trade in any form of binding or cover other than that in which it is published, without the prior written consent of all relevant Publishers. The contents of this publication are believed correct at the time of printing. Nevertheless the Publisher cannot be held responsible for any errors or omissions or for changes in the details given in this guide or for the consequences of any reliance on the information provided in the same. This does not affect your statutory rights. Assessments of AA inspected establishments are based on the experience(s) of the hotel and restaurant inspectors on the occasion(s) of their visit(s), therefore the descriptions in this guide represent an element of subjective opinion that may not reflect a reader's own opinion on another occasion.

Please use the Reader's Report Form at the end of the guide or contact:
The Editor AA B&B Guide Fanum House Floor14
Basing View, Basingstoke, Hampshire RG21 4EA
lifestyleguides@theAA.com

Advertisement Sales: advertisingsales@theaa.com

Photographs in the gazetteer are provided by the establishments.
Typeset by Servis Filmsetting Ltd, Manchester
Printed by Printer Industria Grafica, Barcelona

Published by AA Publishing, which is a trading name of Automobile Association Developments Limited whose registered office is:
Fanum House, Basing View, Basingstoke, Hampshire RG21 4EA
Registered number 1878835
A CIP catalogue record for this book is available from the British Library.
ISBN-10: 0 7495 4918 1
ISBN-13: 978 0 7495 4918 1
A02831

Maps prepared by the Cartography Department of The Automobile Association.
Maps © Automobile Association Developments Limited 2006.

This product includes mapping data licensed from Ordnance Survey ® with the permission of the Controller of Her Majesty's Stationery Office. © Crown copyright 2006. All rights reserved. Licence number 399221.

This product includes mapping based upon data licensed from Ordnance Survey of Northern Ireland ® reproduced by permission of the Chief Executive, acting on behalf of the Controller of Her Majesty's Stationery Office. © Crown copyright 2006. Permit number 60016.

Republic of Ireland mapping based on Ordnance Survey Ireland Permit number MP000106. © Ordnance Survey Ireland and Government of Ireland.

Contents

Using the guide

❶ Each country is listed in alphabetical order by county then town/village. The Channel Islands and Isle of Man follow the England section and the Scottish islands follow the rest of Scotland. Establishments are listed alphabetically in descending order of Stars then Diamonds.

The map page number refers to the atlas at the back of the guide and is followed by the National Grid Reference. To find the town/village, read the first figure across and the second figure vertically within the lettered square. You can find routes at **theAA.com**, see page 8 or **AAbookings.ie**.

Farmhouse entries also have a six-figure National Grid Reference, which can be used with Ordnance Survey maps or www.ordsvy.gov.uk. We also show the name of the proprietor, as often farms are known locally by their name.

❷ **Establishment classification and designator** See pages 6 and 10. Five Star and Five Diamond establishments are highlighted as Premier Collection, and they are listed on page 16.

If the establishment's name is shown in italic, then details have not been confirmed by the proprietor for this edition.

Rosettes ❀ The AA's food award, see page 9.

Egg cups ⬓ and pies 3 These symbols indicate that, in the experience of the inspector, either breakfast or dinner exceeded the required level for the rating achieved by the establishment.

e indicates bed and breakfast for up to £30 (€44) per person per night. Remember, prices can change during the currency of the guide.

In the Republic of Ireland, GH refers to Guest Houses, and T&C to the Town and Country Homes Association, an umbrella organisation for B&Bs that are officially recognised by Bord Failte and have six rooms or less.

❸ **E-mail address** and **website** Website addresses are included where they have been specified by the establishment. Such websites are not under the control of The Automobile Association Developments Limited, who cannot accept any responsibility or liability in respect of any and all matters whatsoever relating to such websites.

❹ Distances in **directions** are given are in miles (m) and yards (yds), or kilometres (km) and metres in the Republic of Ireland.

4

---

❷ ◆◆◆◆ ❦

Poletrees Farm *(SP660160)*

Ludgershall Rd HP18 9TZ
❸ ☎ 011844 238276 ▤ 01844 238276 Mrs Cooper
e-mail: poletrees.farm@virgin.net
❹ *Dir* S off A41 signed Ludgerhall/Brill, after railway bridge 0.5m on left

The 15th-century farmouse has a wealth of exposed beams and the bedrooms are in converted outbuildings. There is a welcoming wood burning stove in the lounge and the cosy dining room is the setting for wholesome breakfasts.

❼ **Facilities** 4 Annexe en suite (4 GF) ⊗ FTV TVB tea/coffee ✶ Cen ht TVL 110 acres beef sheep **Prices** S fr £35.40; d £60.70✳ **LB**
❾ **Parking** 6 **Notes**

---

❺ Establishments choose to include a photograph.

❻ Description.

❼ **FACILITIES** For key to symbols and abbreviations see opposite.

The final stage (Part III) of the **Disability Discrimination Act** (access to Goods and Services) came into force in 2004. This means that service providers may have to consider making adjustments to their premises. For further information see **disability.gov.uk/dda**. Ground-floor rooms are noted under FACILITIES. The establishments in this guide should all be aware of their responsibilities under the Act. Always phone in advance to ensure that the establishment you have chosen has appropriate facilities. See also **holidaycare.org.uk**.

The number of letting bedrooms (**rms**), or rooms with a bath or shower en suite are shown. Bedrooms that have a private bathroom (pri facs) adjacent may be included as en suite.

The number of bedrooms in an **annexe** of equivalent standard are also shown. Facilities may not be the same as in the main building.

The **no smoking** symbol by itself indicates a ban on smoking throughout the premises. If the establishment is only partly no smoking, the areas where smoking is not permitted are shown.

The **Smoking, Health and Social Care (Scotland) Act** came into force in March 2006 (clearingtheairscotland.com). The law bans smoking in no-smoking premises in Scotland, which includes guest houses and inns with two or more guest bedrooms. The proprietor can designate one or more bedrooms with ventilation systems where the occupants can smoke, but communal areas must be smoke-free. Communal areas include the interior bars and restaurants in pubs and inns. Similar laws covering England, Wales and Northern Ireland are due to come into effect during 2007.

Where, for example, **television in bedrooms** is shown TV4B, there is a television in four rooms.

Establishments that state **no dogs** may accept assist/guide dogs. Some places that accept dogs may restrict the size and breed and the rooms into which they can be taken. Check the conditions when booking.

No children - children cannot be accommodated, or a minimum age may be specified, e.g. No children 4 yrs means no children under four years old.

Establishments with special facilities for children (**ch fac**) may include a babysitting service or baby-intercom system, playroom or playground, laundry facilities, drying and ironing facilities, cots, high chairs and special meals. If you have very young children, check before booking.

If **Dinner** is shown, you may have to order in advance. Last d is the last order time for dinner.

No coaches is published in good faith from details supplied by the establishment. Inns have well-defined legal obligations towards travellers; in the event of a query the customer should contact the proprietor or local licensing authority.

Additional facilities such as lifts or any leisure activities available are also listed.

❽ PRICES Charges are per night:
  S bed and breakfast per person;
  D bed and breakfast for two people sharing a room.
  The euro € is the currency of the Republic of Ireland.

Prices are indications only, so check before booking. Some places may offer free accommodation to children provided they share their parents' room.

LB indicates that Short or Leisure Breaks are available. Contact the establishment for details.

❾ The number of **parking** spaces available.

❿ NOTES Establishments are open all year unless **Closed** dates/months are shown.

Some places are open all year but offer a restricted service (rs) in low season. If the text does not say what the restricted services are you should check before booking.

Civ Wed 50 The establishment is licensed for civil weddings and can accommodate 50 guests for the ceremony.

⊜ shows that **credit/debit cards are not accepted**, but check when booking. Where credit cards are accepted there may be an extra charge.

Key to symbols

★ ♦ ♦	Classification (see page 6)
⊛	AA Rosette award (see page 9)
A	Associate entry (see page 7)
U	Unclassified rating (see page 7)
★	Rating from VisitWales/VisitScotland (see page 7)
◖	Inn
❤	Farmhouse
☎	Phone number
▤	Fax number
⏚	Breakfast exceeds quality requirements at Star/Diamond rating
⊖	Dinner exceeds quality requirements at Star/Diamond rating
▦	Member of the Blue Book Consortium (Republic of Ireland)
s	Single room
d	Double room (2 people sharing)
fmly	Family bedroom
GF	Ground-floor bedroom
◇	Bed and breakfast for up to £30 per person per night (single)
LB	Short or leisure breaks
＊	2006 prices
Cen ht	Full central heating
ch fac	Special facilities for children
TVL	Lounge with television
TVB	Television in bedrooms
STV	Satellite television
⊜	Credit cards not accepted
tea/coffee	Tea and coffee facilities
Conf 60	Conference facilities available and number of delegates
Last d	Last time dinner can be ordered
rms	bedrooms in main building
Etr	Easter
fr	From
rs	Restricted service
⊗	No Smoking
✖	No dogs
⊘	Heated indoor pool
⊸	Heated outdoor pool
⊘	Unheated indoor pool
⊸	Unheated outdoor pool
↳	Croquet
⊶	Tennis
⌁	Golf

AA inspected guest accommodation

The AA inspects and classifies more than 4000 guest houses, farmhouses and inns for its Guest Accommodation Scheme, under common quality standards agreed among the AA, VisitBritain, VisitScotland and VisitWales.

AA recognised establishments pay an annual fee according to the classification and the number of bedrooms. The classification is not transferable if an establishment changes hands.

The AA presents several awards within the B&B scheme, from **AA Landlady of the Year**, which showcases the very finest hospitality in the country, to the **Guest Accommodation of the Year** awards, presented to establishments in Scotland, Ireland, Wales and England. See pages 12 and 14 for this year's winners.

Stars & Diamonds

The AA Stars and Diamonds classify guest accommodation at five levels of quality, from one at the simplest, to five offering the highest quality. From inspections in 2006, **Stars** replaced the Diamond classification, though the parallel one to five ratings indicate similar levels of quality (see page 10). To obtain a higher rating the establishment must provide enhanced quality standards across all areas with emphasis on:

■ Cleanliness and housekeeping
■ Hospitality and service
■ Quality and condition of bedrooms, bathrooms and public rooms
■ Food quality

Establishments applying for AA recognition are visited by one of the AA's qualified accommodation inspectors as a **mystery guest**. Inspectors stay overnight to make a thorough test of the accommodation, food, and hospitality. After paying the bill, the following morning they identify themselves and ask to be shown round the premises. The inspector completes a full report, resulting in a recommendation for the appropriate Star or Diamond award. After this first visit, the establishment will receive an annual visit to check that standards are maintained. If it changes hands, the new owners must re-apply for classification, as standards can change.

Guests can expect to find the following minimum standards at all levels:

■ Pleasant and helpful welcome and service, and sound standards of housekeeping and maintenance
■ Comfortable accommodation equipped to modern standards
■ Bedding and towels changed for each new guest, and at least weekly if the room is taken for a long stay.
■ Adequate storage, heating, lighting and comfortable seating
■ A sufficient hot water supply at reasonable times
■ A full cooked breakfast. (If this is not provided, the fact must be advertised and a substantial continental breakfast must be offered.)

♦ Red Diamonds highlight the best establishments within the three, four and five Diamond ratings.

B&B

Many B&Bs and guest houses offer a very high standard of accommodation and personal level of service. Under the new Star classification, B&B accommodation is provided in a private house run by the owner and with no more than six guests. There may be restricted access particularly in the late morning and the afternoon, so do check when booking.

Guest House

A Star-rated Guest House provides for more than six paying guests and usually offers more services than a B&B, for example dinner, by staff as well as the owner.

Some Diamond-rated guest houses include the word 'hotel' in their name, though they cannot offer all the services required for the AA hotel Star rating (for example evening meals).

London prices tend to be higher than outside the capital, and normally only bed and breakfast is provided, although some establishments do provide a full meal service.

❤ Farmhouse

A farmhouse usually provides good value B&B or guest-house accommodation and excellent home cooking on a working farm or smallholding. Sometimes the land has been sold and only the

house remains, but many are working farms and some farmers are happy to allow visitors to look around, or even to help feed the animals. However, you should always exercise care and never leave children unsupervised. Although the directory entry states the acreage and the type of farming, do check when booking to make sure that it matches your expectations. The farmhouses are listed under towns or villages, but do ask for directions when booking.

◀ Inn

Traditional inns often have a cosy bar, convivial atmosphere, and good beer and pub food. Those listed in the guide will provide breakfast in a suitable room, and should also serve light meals during licensing hours. The character of the properties vary according to whether they are country inns or town establishments. Check before you book, including arrival times as these may be restricted to opening hours.

🏠 Restaurant with Rooms

These restaurants offer overnight accommodation with the restaurant being the main business and open to non-residents. The restaurant usually offers a high standard of food and service at least five nights a week.

U Unclassified entries

These establishments joined the AA Guest Accommodation Scheme too late for a full inspection to take place. For up-to-date information on these and other new establishments check **theAA.com**.

A Associate entries

These establishments have been inspected and rated by the RAC, VisitBritain, VisitScotland or VisitWales. In Northern Ireland the Tourist Board inspects but does not give ratings. The RAC, VisitBritain, VisitScotland and VisitWales have joined the AA scheme on a marketing only basis. A limited entry for these places appears in the guide, with a rating under their Notes, while descriptions for these establishments appear on **theAA.com**.

Find it with theAA.com

Click on to the AA website, **theAA.com**, to find AA listed guest houses, hotels, pubs and restaurants – some 12,000 establishments – the **AA Route Planner and Map Finder will help you find the way**.

Search for a Hotel/B&B or a Pub/Restaurant by location or establishment name and then scroll down the list of establishments for the interactive map and local routes.

To use the **Route Planner** on the Home page, simply enter your postcode and the establishment postcode given in this guide and click **Get route**. Check your details and then you are on your way.

Discover new horizons with Britain's largest travel publisher

AA

Useful information

AA Rosette awards

From around 40,000 restaurants, the AA awards Rosettes to some 1800 as the best in the UK

◉
Excellent local restaurants serving food prepared with care, understanding and skill, using good quality ingredients.

◉◉
The best local restaurants, which aim for and achieve higher standards and better consistency, and where a greater precision is apparent in the cooking. There will be obvious attention to the selection of quality ingredients.

◉◉◉
Outstanding restaurants that demand recognition well beyond their local area.

◉◉◉◉
Among the very best restaurants in the British Isles, where the cooking demands national recognition.

◉◉◉◉◉
The finest restaurants in the British Isles, where the cooking compares with the best in the world.

Booking

Book as early as possible, particularly for the peak holiday period (early June to the end of September) and for Easter and other public holidays. In some parts of Scotland the skiing season is also a peak holiday period.

Some establishments only accept weekly bookings from Saturday, and some require a deposit on booking.

Prices

Minimum and maximum prices are shown for one (s) and two people (d) per night and include a full breakfast. If dinner is also included this is indicated in brackets (including dinner).

Prices in the guide include VAT (and service where applicable), except the Channel Islands where VAT does not apply.

Where proprietors have been unable to provide us with their 2007 charges we publish the 2006 price as a rough guide (shown by an asterisk *). Where no prices are given, please make enquiries direct.

Cancellation

If you have to cancel a booking, let the proprietor know at once. If the room cannot be re-let you may be held legally responsible for partial payment; you could lose your deposit or be liable for compensation, so consider taking out cancellation insurance.

Food and drink

Some guest houses provide evening meals, ranging from a set meal to a full menu. Some even have their own restaurant. You may have to

arrange dinner in advance, at breakfast, or on the previous day, so do ask when booking.

If you book on bed, breakfast and evening meal terms, you may find that the tariff includes only the set menu. If there is a carte you may be able to order from this and pay a supplement.

On Sundays, many establishments serve the main meal at midday, and provide only a cold supper in the evening. In some parts of Britain, particularly in Scotland, high tea (i.e. a savoury dish followed by bread and butter, scones and cakes) is sometimes served instead of or as an alternative to dinner. The last time at which high tea or dinner may be ordered on weekdays is shown, but this may vary at weekends.

Star quality for
AA accommodation

The AA has introduced new quality standards for inspected accommodation. This follows extensive consultation by the inspection organisations (VisitBritain, VisitScotland, VisitWales and the AA) with consumers and the hospitality industry in order to make the rating systems for hotels and guest accommodation easier to understand. The development of these new quality standards has also been supported by the government.

From January 2006 each inspection organisation will use the same standard procedures to determine the new Star rating of any inspected establishment. Ratings range from one to five **Stars**, with five the highest, and guests can be confident that, for example, a three Star guest house anywhere in the UK and Ireland will offer consistent quality and facilities.

In order to achieve a **one Star** rating an establishment must meet certain minimum entry requirements, including:

- A cooked breakfast, or substantial continental option is provided.

- The proprietor and/or staff are available for your arrival, departure and at all meal times.

- Once registered, you have access to the establishment at all times unless previously notified.

- All areas of operation meet minimum quality requirements for cleanliness, maintenance and hospitality as well as facilities and the delivery of services.

- A dining room or similar eating area is available unless meals are only served in bedrooms.

Our research shows that **quality** is very important to visitors. To obtain a higher Star rating, an establishment must provide increased quality standards across all areas, with particular emphasis in five key areas: cleanliness, hospitality, breakfast, bedrooms

and bathrooms. There are also particular requirements in order for an establishment to achieve three, four or five Stars, for example:

Three Stars and above - access to both sides of all beds for double occupancy.

Three Stars and above - bathrooms/shower rooms cannot be used by the proprietor.

Three Stars and above (from January 1 2008) - there is a washbasin in every guest bedroom (either in the bedrooms or the en suite/private facility).

Four Stars (from January 1 2008) - half of bedrooms must be en suite or have private facilities.

Five Stars (from January 1 2008) - all bedrooms must be en suite or have private facilities.

Not all establishments have been inspected under the new quality standards in time for the 2007 edition of the AA B&B Guide, and so many are still rated with Diamonds (see page 6). However, you can be sure these inspected guest houses still offer very good comfort, hospitality and value for money.

Along with the Star ratings, six discriptive **designators** have been introduced. The proprietors, in discussion with our inspectors, choose which designator best describes their establishment. There are five **descriptive** designators:

■ **B&B** A private house run by the owner with accommodation for no more than six paying guests.

■ **Guest House** Run on a more commercial basis than a B&B, the accommodation provides for more than six paying guests and there are usually more services; for example staff as well as the owner may provide dinner.

■ **Farmhouse** The B&B or guest house accommodation is part of a working farm or smallholding.

■ **Inn** The accommodation is provided in a fully licensed establishment. The bar will be open to non-residents and can provide food in the evenings.

■ **Restaurant with Rooms** This is a destination restaurant offering overnight accommodation, with dining being the main business and open to non-residents. The restaurant should offer a high standard of food and restaurant service at least five nights a week. A liquor licence is necessary and there is a maximum 12 bedrooms.

Guest Accommodation Any establishment that meets the minimum entry requirements is eligible for this general category.

So when an AA inspector has visited a property, and evaluated all the aspects of the accommodation for comfort, facilities, attention to detail and presentation, you can be confident the Star rating will allow you to make the right choice for an enjoyable stay.

AA Guest Accommodation of the year

Every year we ask our inspectors to nominate those establishments they feel come closest to the ideal of what a B&B should be. They consider location, food standards and quality of furnishings and fittings, as well as charm and hospitality. From a shortlist of around 20, one is selected from each country in the guide.

England

Fulready Manor
Ettington, Warwickshire

Nothing is too much trouble for Maureen and Malcolm Spencer. After running a guest house in nearby Stratford-upon-Avon for more than 20 years, they built Fulready Manor five years ago. Already the Cotswold stone is mellowing and the gardens are thriving, making the house look comfortable within the 120 acres of arable farmland that includes a lake. The family's experience in interior design, fine art and antiques makes the inside equally memorable, including a king-size leather sleigh bed, a richly carved four-poster and antique mahogany furniture. The breakfast award is a richly deserved and Maureen really does believe in guests making themselves at home.

Scotland

Tigh Na Leigh Guesthouse
Alyth, Perth & Kinross

Tigh Na Leigh is Gaelic for House of the Doctor or Physician, and it certainly is an excellent prescription for rest and relaxation. Chris and Bettina Black have an easy friendliness and always extend the warmest of welcomes to their lovingly restored Victorian house in the heart of the delightful town of Alyth. They have seamlessly combined quality antique and contemporary furnishings with the original character, while the en suites have super showers and spa baths. There is a choice of stylish lounges, and delicious evening meals and breakfasts are enjoyed the spacious conservatory-dining room overlooking the lovely garden.

Wales

Radford House
Caerleon, Newport

The difference is in the detail at Radford House. This elegant Grade II listed Georgian house has been superbly renovated to incorporate sumptuous bathrooms and modern comforts. The bedrooms have wonderful beds and quality linen, flat-screen televisions, and stylish soft furnishings, while fresh flowers, fridges with fresh milk, fruit and bottled water, an extensive range of teas, home-made biscuits, robes and luxurious toiletries complete the winning formula. Downstairs the spacious drawing room has a roaring log fire on cool evenings, while the selection of hot and cold dishes uses the best of local produce.

Ireland

Ashlee Lodge
Blarney, Co Cork

Anne and John O'Leary's purpose-built guest house stands in tranquil grounds in the village of Tower, close to Blarney and only a short drive from Cork city. Their superb guest rooms provide a break from the ordinary, decorated with elegance in mind, and some bedrooms come with whirlpool baths. The beautiful area is a golfing paradise and tee times can be booked at many of the nearby courses, or else just unwind in the sauna or the outdoor hot tub. Best of all is Anne's home baking and cooking, which make the extensive breakfast and dinner menus truly special.

AA Landlady of the Year 2006

From left: Kate Mylrea, winner Lilwen McAllister, and Beth Cruickshank

The annual AA Landlady of the Year award - LOTY - recognises the vital role played by guest houses, farmhouses and inns in the tourist industries of the UK and Ireland. It celebrates the hard work, endless patience and good humour of those dedicated people who strive to make your stay both pleasant and memorable.

Lilwen McAllister, from Pontfaen in Pembrokeshire, was crowned AA Landlady of the Year 2006 at the annual awards lunch at Tylney Hall in Hampshire. Lilwen has been a finalist three times, most recently in 2005. A resident of the Gwaun Valley all her life, she has run Erw-Lon Farm guest house for 29 years and been married to farming husband Bernard for 38 years. As a young married couple she supplemented their farming income by opening a bed & breakfast, combining her love of the area with the pride she has in her home.

AA inspectors are at a loss to know how she finds time to manage a wonderful guest house as well as farming, organist at her local church, and running the parish magazine. The undercover judge that stayed at the farmhouse commented: 'The building is very impressive but more significant is the wonderful personality of the hostess, who dominates this working farmhouse with her contagious humour and warmth.' Lilwen won a Villeroy & Boch dinner service to honour the event.

Beth Cruickshank from Arden House near Linlithgow, West Lothian, and **Kate Mylrea** from Manor Farm Oast near Rye, East Sussex were worthy runners up. Beth and Kate each received a Villeroy & Boch cutlery set, and all finalists received an engraved Villeroy & Boch decanter.

Each year AA inspectors nominate 100 landladies and landlords from over 4000 B&Bs featured in the **AA Bed & Breakfast Guide**, and after a tough selection process, which includes mystery phone calls and an overnight stay from an undercover judge, 20 finalists are selected. Now in its 13th year, the LOTY award is about the people who run the establishments, celebrating their hard work, patience and good humour, and is a testament to the increasingly high standards the industry is striving for.

The LOTY top twenty

Winner
Lilwen McAllister
Erw-Lon Farm, Fishguard, Pembrokeshire

Runner-up
Beth Cruickshank
Arden House, Linlithgow, West Lothian

Runner-up
Kate Mylrea
Manor Farm Oast, Rye, East Sussex

Rachael Abraham
*North Wheddon Farm, Wheddon Cross,
Somerset*

Lauraine Awdry
Penmachno Hall, Betws-y-Coed, Conwy

Gill Bridges
Polraen Country House, Looe, Cornwall

Angela Dallyn
Bulleigh Park Farm, Newton Abbot, Devon

Oneil Edwards & Michael Hubbard
Plantation House, Holt, Norfolk

Irene England
Crubenbeg House, Newtonmore, Highland

Helen Goaman
East Dyke Farmhouse, Clovelly, Devon

Daphne Gwilliam
Dryslade Farm, Coleford, Gloucestershire

Diane Hickling
*Woodside Farm, Near Barkestone-le-Vale,
Leicestershire*

Lynn Laughton
Clifton Farm, Westow, North Yorkshire

Judy Mairs
Woodlands, Glossop, Derbyshire

Karen & Michael Orchard
Highcliffe House, Lynton, Devon

Richard Paxton
Westbourne Guest House, Inverness, Highland

Dee Pennington
*West Vale Country House, Hawkshead,
Cumbria*

Jane Rothery
Quinhay Farmhouse, Petersfield, Hampshire

Annie Walker
The Manse B&B, Eastbourne, East Sussex

Laura Wood
Mulberry House, Torquay, Devon

A big smile from the LOTY winners; inset Lilwen McAllister

★ ★ ★ ★ ★
Premier Collection

These guest houses, farmhouses and inns awarded five Stars or Diamonds
by the AA represent the highest standards in quality and guest care

ENGLAND

BERKSHIRE

NEWBURY
Hamstead Holt Farm

SULHAMSTEAD
The Old Manor

BUCKINGHAMSHIRE

CHESHAM
Braziers Well

CAMBRIDGESHIRE

CHIPPENHAM
The Old Bakery

ELY
Springfields

CHESHIRE

CHESTER
Chester Stone Villa Hotel

MALPAS
Tilston Lodge

CORNWALL &
ISLES OF SCILLY

DRYM
Drym Farm

FALMOUTH
Dolvean House

FOWEY
The Old Quay House Hotel

LOOE
The Beach House
St Aubyn's Guest House

NEWQUAY
Corisande Manor Hotel

PADSTOW
Cross House Hotel
The Old Cabbage Patch
St Ervan Manor

PENZANCE
Chy-an-Mor
Ennys
The Summerhouse

PERRANUTHNOE
Ednovean Farm

POLPERRO
Trenderway Farm

ST AUSTELL
Anchorage House
Highland Court Lodge
Lower Barn
Wisteria Lodge

ST BLAZEY
Nanscawen Manor House
Penarwyn House

ST IVES
Jamies
Porthglaze
Primrose Valley Hotel

CUMBRIA

AMBLESIDE
Drunken Duck Inn

BORROWDALE
Hazel Bank Country House

BRAMPTON
The Hill On The Wall

CARTMEL
Hill Farm

CARLISLE [CATLOWDY]
Bessiestown Country Guest House

CONISTON
Coniston Lodge Hotel
Wheelgate Country Guest House

CROSTHWAITE
The Punchbowl Inn At Crosthwaite

HAWKSHEAD
West Vale Country House

KESWICK
The Grange Country House

KIRKBY STEPHEN
Brownber Hall Country House

KIRKCAMBECK
Cracrop Farm

LORTON
New House Farm
Winder Hall Country House

MILLOM
Underwood Country Guest House

NEAR SAWREY
Ees Wyke Country House
Sawrey House Country Hotel &
    Restaurant

NEWBY BRIDGE
The Knoll Country House

WINDERMERE
The Beaumont
The Howbeck
Low House

BOWNESS-ON-WINDERMERE
Oakbank House

WORKINGTON
Falconwood

DERBYSHIRE

ASHBOURNE
Omnia Somnia
Turlow Bank

BELPER
Dannah Farm Country House Ltd

BUXTON
Buxton's Victorian Guest House
Grendon Guest House

HOPE
Underleigh House

NEWHAVEN
The Smithy

WESTON UNDERWOOD
Park View Farm

WIRKSWORTH
The Old Manor House

DEVON

AXMINSTER
Kerrington House
Lea Hill

BAMPTON
The Bark House

BARNSTAPLE
Halmpstone Manor

BOVEY TRACEY
Brookfield House

CHAGFORD
Parford Well

CHILLATON
Tor Cottage

DARTMOUTH
Barrington House
Nonsuch House

EXETER
Galley Fish & Seafood Restaurant
    with Rooms

HONITON
West Colwell Farm

HORNS CROSS
The Round House

LUSTLEIGH
Woodley House

LYDFORD
Moor View House

LYNMOUTH
Bonnicott House
The Heatherville
Sea View Villa

LYNTON
Highcliffe House
Victoria Lodge

MORETONHAMPSTEAD
Gate House

NEWTON ABBOT
Castle Dyke House

POSTBRIDGE
Lydgate House

SIDMOUTH
The Old Farmhouse
The Salty Monk

SOUTH MOLTON
Kerscott Farm

TEIGNMOUTH
Thomas Luny House

TIVERTON
Hornhill Farmhouse
Rhode Farm House

TORQUAY
Colindale Hotel
Cranborne House
Millbrook House Hotel
Mulberry House

TOTNES
The Durant Arms

UMBERLEIGH
Eastacott Barton

YARCOMBE
The Belfry Country Hotel

DORSET

BLANDFORD FORUM
Portman Lodge

BOURNEMOUTH
The Balincourt Hotel

BRIDPORT
Roundham House Hotel

CHRISTCHURCH
Druid House
The Lord Bute Hotel & Restaurant
Seawards

DORCHESTER
B & B @ Poundbury
The Casterbridge Hotel
Little Court
Yalbury Cottage Hotel & Restaurant

FARNHAM
Farnham Farm House

FRAMPTON
Frampton House

IWERNE COURTNEY OR SHROTON
The Cricketers

SHERBORNE
Munden House

WEYMOUTH
Chandlers Hotel

DURHAM, CO

DARLINGTON
Clow Beck House

ESSEX

CHIPPING ONGAR
Diggins Farm

WIX
Dairy House Farm

GLOUCESTERSHIRE

BLOCKLEY
Lower Brook House

CHELTENHAM
Cleeve Hill House
Georgian House

CHIPPING CAMPDEN
The Malt House

GUITING POWER
Guiting Guest House

STONEHOUSE
The Grey Cottage

STOW-ON-THE-WOLD
Rectory Farmhouse

STROUD
Hunters Lodge

WINCHCOMBE
Isbourne Manor House

GREATER LONDON

RICHMOND UPON THAMES
Doughty Cottage

ALTRINCHAM
Ash Farm Country House

LITTLEBOROUGH
Hollingworth Lake Bed & Breakfast

HAMPSHIRE

ANDOVER
Old Fullerton Station

BROCKENHURST
The Cottage Hotel

FORDINGBRIDGE
Cottage Crest

LYMINGTON
The Olde Barn

LYNDHURST
Rufus House

MILFORD ON SEA
Ha'penny House

RINGWOOD
Little Forest Lodge

SOUTHAMPTON
Riverside Bed & Breakfast

SWAY
The Nurse's Cottage

WINCHESTER
Orchard House

HEREFORDSHIRE

LEOMINSTER
Ford Abbey

LEOMINSTER
Hills Farm

MOCCAS
Moccas Court

ROSS-ON-WYE
Trecilla Farm

ISLE OF WIGHT

BONCHURCH
Winterbourne Country House

CHALE
Chale Bay Farm

GODSHILL
Godshill Park Farm House

SHANKLIN
Foxhills

KENT

CANTERBURY
Magnolia House
Thanington Hotel

DEAL
Sutherland House Hotel

FARNINGHAM
Beesfield Farm

FOLKESTONE
Hotel Relish

HAWKHURST
Southgate-Little Fowlers

IVYCHURCH
Olde Moat House

MAIDSTONE
Goldings
Ringlestone House

MARDEN
Merzie Meadows

ROYAL TUNBRIDGE WELLS
Alconbury Guest House
Danehurst House

LANCASHIRE
PRESTON
The Park Restaurant Hotel
WHITEWELL
The Inn at Whitewell
YEALAND CONYERS
The Bower

LEICESTERSHIRE
KEGWORTH
Kegworth House
SHEPSHED
The Grange

LINCOLNSHIRE
LINCOLN
Bailhouse & Mews
Minster Lodge
MARKET RASEN
Blaven
NORMANTON
La Casita
STAMFORD
Rock Lodge

LONDON
N4
Mount View
SW3
L'Hotel

MERSEYSIDE
SOUTHPORT
Cambridge Town House Hotel

NORFOLK
BLAKENEY
Blakeney House
HINDRINGHAM
Field House
HOLT
Plantation House
NORTH WALSHAM
Whitehouse Farm
NORWICH
Catton Old Hall
SHERINGHAM
Bench Mark House
SWANTON ABBOT
Pheasant Cottage
THURSFORD
Holly Lodge

WALCOTT
Holly Tree Cottage

NORTHAMPTONSHIRE
STANWICK
The Courtyard

NORTHUMBERLAND
BERWICK-UPON-TWEED
High Steads
CORNHILL-ON-TWEED
Ivy Cottage
HEXHAM
Montcoffer Bed & Breakfast
ROTHBURY
The Orchard House
WOOLER
The Old Manse

NOTTINGHAMSHIRE
HOLBECK
Browns
NOTTINGHAM
Greenwood Lodge City Guest House

OXFORDSHIRE
BECKLEY
Lower Farm
BURFORD
Burford House
Jonathans at the Angel
HENLEY-ON-THAMES
Lenwade
Milsoms Hotel
Thamesmead House Hotel
OXFORD
Burlington House Hotel Ltd
STADHAMPTON
The Crazy Bear Hotel

SHROPSHIRE
BRIDGNORTH
The Albynes
CHURCH STRETTON
Willowfield Guest House
Rectory Farm
CLUN
Birches Mill
IRONBRIDGE
The Library House
LLANFAIR WATERDINE
The Waterdine
LUDLOW
Bromley Court B & B
Line Farm

SHREWSBURY
The Catherine Of Aragon Suite

SOMERSET
BATH
Apsley House Hotel
Athole House
The Ayrlington
Bamboo Gardens
Cheriton House
Dorian House
Haydon House
Kennard Hotel
Monkshill Guest House
Paradise House Hotel
Villa Magdala Hotel
BEERCROCOMBE
Whittles Farm
CHARD
Bellplot House & Thomas's
  Restaurant
Higher Beetham Farm
CHEDDAR
Batts Farm
DULVERTON
Tarr Farm Inn
DUNSTER
Dollons House
FROME
Lullington House
The Place To Stay
ILMINSTER
The Old Rectory
NETHER STOWEY
Castle of Comfort County House
SOMERTON
Lydford House
WELLS
Beaconsfield Farm
Riverside Grange
WINCANTON
Rectory Farm House
WITHYPOOL
Kings Farm
YEOVIL
Little Barwick House Ltd

STAFFORDSHIRE
BURTON UPON TRENT
Dovecliff Hall Hotel
CHEADLE
The Grange

CHEDDLETON
Choir Cottage and Choir House

TAMWORTH
Oak Tree Farm

SUFFOLK

BEYTON
Manorhouse

BURY ST EDMUNDS
Clarice House

FRESSINGFIELD
Chippenhall Hall

HADLEIGH
Edge Hall

KEDINGTON
The White House

LAVENHAM
Lavenham Priory

STOWMARKET
Bays Farm

WOODBRIDGE
Long Springs B&B

YAXLEY
The Bull Auberge

SURREY

FARNHAM
Bentley Mill

SUSSEX, EAST

BATTLE
Farthings Farm

EASTBOURNE
The Manse B & B
Ocklynge Manor

HALLAND
Tamberry Hall

HASTINGS & ST LEONARDS
Parkside House
Stream House

HERSTMONCEUX
Wartling Place

LEWES
Nightingales

RYE
The Benson
Jeake's House
Little Orchard House
Manor Farm Oast
The Old Vicarage Guest House

SUSSEX, WEST

ARUNDEL
Arundel House Restaurant & Rooms

CHICHESTER
West Stoke House
Royal Oak Inn

HORSHAM
Random Hall

MIDHURST
Rivermead House
Park House Hotel
York House Rooms

ROGATE
Mizzards Farm

WARWICKSHIRE

ETTINGTON
Fulready Manor

GREAT WOLFORD
The Old Coach House

NUNEATON
Leathermill Grange Country Guest
House

STRATFORD–UPON–AVON
Cherry Trees

WEST MIDLANDS

BIRMINGHAM
Westbourne Lodge

WILTSHIRE

BOX
Spinney Cross
White Smocks

BRADFORD-ON-AVON
Bradford Old Windmill
Widbrook Grange

CALNE
Chilvester Hill House

DEVIZES
Blounts Court Farm

LACOCK
At the Sign of the Angel

PURTON
The Old Farmhouse

WHITLEY
The Pear Tree Inn

WORCESTERSHIRE

BEWDLEY
Number Thirty

BROADWAY
Mill Hay House

YORKSHIRE, EAST RIDING OF

BEVERLEY
Burton Mount Country House

BRIDLINGTON
Marton Grange

YORKSHIRE, NORTH

AMPLEFORTH
Shallowdale House

BEDALE
Mill Close Farm

GRASSINGTON
Ashfield House Hotel
Grassington Lodge

HARROGATE
Ruskin Hotel

HAWES
Rookhurst Country House

HELLIFIELD
Ribblecote Manor

PICKERING
The Moorlands Country House Hotel

RAMSGILL
Yorke Arms

RIPON
Mallard Grange

THIRSK
Spital Hill

YORK
Alexander House

YORKSHIRE, SOUTH

SHEFFIELD
Westbourne House Hotel

ISLE OF MAN

PORT ST MARY
Aaron House

RAMSEY
The River House

SCOTLAND

ARGYLL & BUTE

BOWMORE
The Harbour Inn & Restaurant

CARDROSS
Kirkton House

HELENSBURGH
Lethamhill

OBAN
Blarcreen House

CITY OF EDINBURGH

EDINBURGH
Dunstane House Hotel
Elmview
Kew House

Premier Collection

Kildonan Lodge Hotel
The Lodge Hotel
The Stuarts
Violet Bank House
The Witchery by the Castle

DUMFRIES &
GALLOWAY
CASTLE DOUGLAS
Craigadam
Smithy House
DUMFRIES
Wallamhill House
ESKDALEMUIR
Hart Manor
KIRKCUDBRIGHT
Baytree House
THORNHILL
Gillbank House

EAST LOTHIAN
EAST LINTON
Kippielaw Farmhouse
GULLANE
Faussetthill House

FIFE
ST ANDREWS
The Paddock

HIGHLAND
AVIEMORE
The Old Minister's House
BALLACHULISH
Ballachulish House
Craiglinnhe House
BRORA
Glenaveron
COLBOST
The Three Chimneys &
  The House Over-By
DAVIOT
The Lodge-Daviot Mains
DORNOCH
2 Quail Restaurant and Rooms
FORT WILLIAM
Ashburn House
Distillery House
The Grange
GRANTOWN-ON-SPEY
An Cala Guest House
INVERNESS
Ballifeary Guest House
Moyness House

Trafford Bank
KINGUSSIE
The Cross at Kingussie
Osprey Hotel
MELVICH
The Sheiling Guest House

PERTH & KINROSS
ALYTH
Tigh Na Leigh Guesthouse
PITLOCHRY
Easter Dunfallandy House

RENFREWSHIRE
LOCHWINNOCH
East Lochhead

SCOTTISH BORDERS
COLDSTREAM
Ruthven House
JEDBURGH
The Spinney
MELROSE
Fauhope House

SOUTH AYRSHIRE
DUNURE
Dunduff Farm

STIRLING
STRATHYRE
Creagan House

WEST LOTHIAN
EAST CALDER
Ashcroft Farmhouse
LINLITHGOW
Arden House

WALES
CARMARTHENSHIRE
ST CLEARS
Coedllys Country House

CEREDIGION
ABERAERON
Harbourmaster Hotel
ABERYSTWYTH
Awel-Deg

CONWY
BETWS-Y-COED
Tan-y-Foel Country House
CONWY
The Old Rectory Country House
Sychnant Pass House

LLANDUDNO
Abbey Lodge
Bryn Derwen
RHOS-ON-SEA
Plas Rhos

DENBIGHSHIRE
CORWEN
Bron-y-Graig

GWYNEDD
DOLGELLAU
Tyddynmawr Farmhouse
PORTHMADOG
Tyddyn Du Farm Holiday Suites

ISLE OF ANGLESEY
MENAI BRIDGE
Wern Farm

MONMOUTHSHIRE
MONMOUTH
Hendre Farm House
SKENFRITH
The Bell at Skenfrith
WHITEBROOK
The Crown at Whitebrook

NEWPORT
CAERLEON
Radford House
REDWICK
Brickhouse Country Guest House
ST BRIDES WENTLOOGE
The Inn at the Elm Tree

PEMBROKESHIRE
SOLVA
Lochmeyler Farm Guest House
TREFIN
Awel-Mor Bed & Breakfast

POWYS
BRECON
Canal Bank
BUILTH WELLS
The Drawing Room
CAERSWS
The Talkhouse
CRICKHOWELL
Glangrwyney Court
WELSHPOOL
Moors Farm B&B

NORTHERN IRELAND
DOWN
DOWNPATRICK
Pheasants' Hill Country House
NEWTOWNARDS
Ballynester House
Edenvale House
LONDONDERRY
COLERAINE
Greenhill House
TYRONE
DUNGANNON
Grange Lodge

REPUBLIC OF IRELAND
CARLOW
CARLOW
Barrowville Town House
CLARE
BALLYVAUGHAN
Drumcreehy Guesthouse
Rusheen Lodge
DOOLIN
Ballyvara House
LAHINCH
Moy House
CORK
BLARNEY
Ashlee Lodge
CORK
Lancaster Lodge
FERMOY
Ballyvolane House
KINSALE
The Old Bank House
Perryville House
SCHULL
Rock Cottage
SHANAGARRY
Ballymaloe House
YOUGHAL
Ahernes
DONEGAL
LAGHEY
Coxtown Manor
DUBLIN
DUBLIN
Aberdeen Lodge

Blakes Townhouse
Brownes Hotel
Glenogra Guest House
Harrington Hall
Merrion Hall
Pembroke Town House
GALWAY
CLIFDEN
Byrne Mal Dua House & Restaurant
CRAUGHWELL
St Clerans Manor House
GALWAY
Killeen House
KERRY
BALLYBUNION
Cashen Course House
CASTLEGREGORY
The Shores Country House
DINGLE
Castlewood House
Dingle Benners Hotel
Emlagh House
Gormans Clifftop House & Restaurant
Heatons Guest House
Milltown House
Pax House
KENMARE
Sallyport House
KILLARNEY
Earls Court House
Fairview Guest House
Foleys Town House
Kathleens Country House
Old Weir Lodge
KILLORGLIN
Carrig House Country House & Restaurant
KILDARE
ATHY
Coursetown Country House
LAOIS
PORTLAOISE
Ivyleigh House
LIMERICK
GLIN
Glin Castle
KILMALLOCK
Flemingstown House

LOUTH
CARLINGFORD
Beaufort House
MAYO
CONG
Ballywarren House
SLIGO
ENNISCRONE
Seasons Lodge
TIPPERARY
THURLES
The Castle
Inch House Country House & Restaurant
WATERFORD
BALLYMACARBRY
Glasha Farmhouse
Hanoras Cottage
CAPPOQUIN
Richmond House
DUNGARVAN
Powersfield House
DUNGARVAN
The Castle Country House
Sliabh gCua Farmhouse
WATERFORD
Foxmount Country House
Sion Hill House & Gardens
WEXFORD
CAMPILE
Kilmokea Country Manor & Gardens
GOREY
Woodlands Country House
ROSSLARE HARBOUR
Churchtown House
WICKLOW
BRAY
Pine Cottage
DUNLAVIN
Rathsallagh House
KILTEGAN
Barraderry House

England

Hidcote Manor Garden,
Gloucestershire

England

BEDFORDSHIRE

ASTWICK
MAP 12 TL23

♦♦♦ ◫

Tudor Oaks Lodge

Taylors Rd SG5 4AZ ☎ 01462 834133 ▤ 01462 834133
e-mail tudoroakslodge@aol.com
Dir On A1 N, 1m past junct 10

The 16th-century house has been renovated to provide open-plan
public areas serving real ales and imaginative food. The smart, well-
equipped bedrooms surround an attractive courtyard and there is
ample private parking.

Facilities 13 en suite (13 GF) ⊘ in 4 bedrooms ⊘ in area of dining
room ⊘ in 1 lounge TVB tea/coffee Direct dial from bedrooms ✕
Cen ht No children 10yrs Dinner Last d 10pm **Prices** S £52-£62.50;
D £67-£87✳ **Conf** Max 30 Thtr 30 Class 20 Board 12 **Parking** 200
See advertisement on page 25

BEDFORD
MAP 12 TL04

♦♦♦♦ ⍟ ⊜ ◫

Knife & Cleaver

The Grove, Houghton Conquest MK45 3LA
☎ 01234 740387 ▤ 01234 740900
e-mail info@knifeandcleaver.com
web www.knifeandcleaver.com
Dir 5m S of Bedford off A6, opp village church

In a pleasant village setting, this relaxing inn consists of a cosy bar and
an elegant conservatory-restaurant. Interesting dishes are
complemented by a good wine list. Bedrooms, located in a garden
annexe, come in a variety of styles, all comfortably appointed and well
equipped; the de luxe rooms are particularly good.

Facilities 9 annexe en suite (1 fmly) (9 GF) ⊘ in 2 bedrooms
⊘ in dining room STV TVB tea/coffee Direct dial from bedrooms Cen ht
No coaches Dinner Last d 9.30pm **Prices** S £59-£69; D £59-£84✳
Conf Max 12 Thtr 16 Class 8 Board 12 Del from £64.50 ✳ **Parking** 35
Notes Closed 27-30 Dec rs Sun evening

♦♦♦

Hertford House Hotel ◇

57 De Parys Av MK40 2TR
☎ 01234 350007 & 354470 ▤ 01234 353468
e-mail carlo@noto.powernet.co.uk
web www.hertfordhousehotel.co.uk
Dir Off N end of High St near swimming pool

Located in a residential avenue within easy walking distance of the
town centre, this detached house provides a range of bedrooms,
some suitable for family use. Guests can relax in public areas, which
include a comfortable guest lounge and a spacious dining room
overlooking the pretty rear garden.

Facilities 20 rms (18 en suite) (4 fmly) (4 GF) ⊘ TVB tea/coffee ✕
Licensed Cen ht TVL **Prices** S £30-£40; D £50-£60✳ **Conf** Max 30
Parking 14 **Notes** rs 24 Dec-2 Jan room only

HARROLD
MAP 11 SP95

Ⓤ ◫

The Muntjac

71 High St MK43 7BJ ☎ 01234 721500 ▤ 01234 721672
e-mail russell@themuntjac.co.uk
Dir A428 (Lavendon) turn onto Harrold Rd, The Muntjac is on the
right hand side opposite butcher shop

At the time of going to press the rating for this establishment had not
been confirmed. Please check the AA website www.theAA.com for up-
to-date information.

Facilities 4 en suite (4 GF) ⊘ TVB tea/coffee ✕ Cen ht Dinner
Last d 9.30pm **Prices** S £35-£40; D £48-£54; (room only) ✳
Parking 7

MARSTON MORETAINE
MAP 11 SP94

♦♦♦♦ ◮

Twin Lodge

Lower Shelton Rd, Lower Shelton MK43 0LP
☎ 01234 767597 ▤ 01234 767597
e-mail pwillsmore@waitrose.com
Dir Off A421 into Lower Shelton

Facilities 4 rms (3 en suite) (1 pri facs) (1 fmly) ⊘ TVB tea/coffee ✕
Cen ht TVL No coaches **Prices** S £30-£35✳ **Parking** 5 **Notes** ⊜

SANDY
MAP 12 TL14

♦♦♦♦♦ ◮ ❧

Highfield Farm *(TL166515)*

Tempsford Rd SG19 2AQ ☎ 01767 682332 Mrs Codd
e-mail margaret@highfield-farm.co.uk
Dir 1.5m N of Sandy, driveway off E side of A1

Facilities 7 en suite 3 annexe en suite (2 fmly) (5 GF) ⊘ TVB tea/coffee
Cen ht TVL 300 acres arable **Prices** S £55-£65; D £65-£75✳ **LB Parking** 12

BERKSHIRE

ALDERMASTON
MAP 05 SU56

♦♦♦♦ ⬛

Hinds Head

Wasing Ln RG7 4LX ☎ 0118 971 2194 🖷 0118 971 4511
e-mail hindshead@accommodating-inns.co.uk
web www.accommodating-inns.co.uk/hindshead.html
Dir On A340 in village centre at minirdbt

The former coaching inn, dating from the 17th and 18th centuries, is a prominent feature in the village centre. Enjoyable freshly prepared meals are available in the popular bar and dining areas, which retain many original features. Bedrooms come in a variety of styles and are situated in the main building or annexe.

Facilities 11 en suite 4 annexe en suite (1 fmly) (6 GF) ⊗ in bedrooms ⊗ in area of dining room TVB tea/coffee Direct dial from bedrooms ✕ Cen ht Dinner Last d 9pm **Prices** S £67.50; D £80✳ **Parking** 30

BOXFORD
MAP 05 SU47

♦♦♦

White Hart Cottage ◇

Westbrook RG20 8DN ☎ 01488 608410
e-mail g.jones-parry@newbury.net
Dir A4 onto B4000, through Wickham, right to Boxford. House 0.25m down Westbrook on right

Guests are ensured of a friendly welcome at this pretty cottage, peacefully located in the delightful village of Boxford. Newbury and the M4 are both just a short drive away. Bedrooms are attractively appointed and guests have access to a small TV lounge. A hearty breakfast is served at the large kitchen table.

Facilities 3 rms (1 en suite) (2 pri facs) ⊗ TV2B tea/coffee ✕ Cen ht TVL No children No coaches **Prices** S £25-£35✳ **Parking** 6 **Notes** ☺

[U] ♥

High Street Farm Barn (SU424714)

RG20 8DD ☎ 01488 608783 Mr & Mrs Boden
e-mail nboden@uk2.net
Dir B4000 from Newbury, through Wickham Heath. Take 1st right signed Boxford. Farm first on left opposite pub

At the time of going to press the rating for this establishment had not been confirmed. Please check the AA website www.theAA.com for up-to-date information.

Facilities 2 en suite (2 GF) ⊗ TVB tea/coffee Cen ht TVL 15 acres sheep **Prices** S £50; D £65✳ **Parking** 4 **Notes** ☺

BRACKNELL
MAP 05 SU86

★★★★ Farm House

Angel Farm (SU837712)

Monks Aly RG42 5PA
☎ 01344 455539 🖷 01344 484629 Mrs Muir
e-mail sj@angelfarm.co.uk
Dir Centre of Binfield, at rdbt turn onto Forest Rd signed Hurst. Turn right at 1st rdbt onto Wicks Green. Turn left onto Monks Alley, 3rd house on right

This alluringly named farmhouse is the home of delightful Mrs Muir and her equally welcoming canine friends. The accommodation has been stylishly and thoughtfully converted. Breakfast is taken around a large imposing dining table and includes home produced free-range eggs. Although close to the motorway network, the farm enjoys a tranquil country setting.

Facilities 2 rms (2 pri facs) (2 GF) ⊗ TVB tea/coffee ✕ Cen ht No children 10yrs 🦮 **Prices** D £50-£100✳ **Parking** 2 **Notes** rs Sat & Sun ☺

If the freedom to smoke or be in a non-smoking atmosphere is important to you, check the rules when you book

England

CHIEVELEY
MAP 05 SU47

★★★★ ◉◉ **Restaurant with Rooms**

The Crab at Chieveley
Wantage Rd RG20 8UE ☎ 01635 247550 🖷 01635 247440
e-mail info@crabatchieveley.com
Dir 1.5m W of Chieveley on B4494

The individually themed bedrooms at this former pub have been appointed to a very high standard and include a full range of modern amenities. Ground-floor rooms have a small private patio area complete with a hot tub. The restaurant is divided into a modern Fishbar brasserie area and a more formal dining area. Both offer an extensive and award-winning range of fish and seafood dishes.

Facilities 13 en suite (8 GF) STV TVB tea/coffee Direct dial from bedrooms Licensed No coaches Sauna Gymnasium Jacuzzi Hot tub Dinner Last d 10pm **Prices** S £100-£130; D £150-£170✶ **LB** **Conf** BC Max 40 Thtr 40 Class 40 Board 20 Del from £50 ✶ **Parking** 80 **Notes** Civ Wed 120

◆◆◆◆ Ⓐ

The Old Farmhouse
Downend Ln RG20 8TN ☎ 01635 248361
e-mail palletts@aol.com
Dir M4 junct 13, A34 N to Chieveley, 0.5m N of Chieveley in Downend

Facilities 1 en suite (1 fmly) (1 GF) ❷ STV TVB tea/coffee Cen ht TVL No coaches Discounted day membership of local health club **Prices** S £40-£45; D £70-£75✶ **Conf** Max 6 Thtr 6 Board 6 **Parking** 3 **Notes** ⊛

COOKHAM DEAN
MAP 05 SU88

★★★★ ◉◉ **Restaurant with Rooms**

The Inn on the Green
The Old Cricket Com SL6 9NZ
☎ 01628 482638 🖷 01628 487474
e-mail reception@theinnonthegreen.com
Dir A404 towards Marlow High St. Cross suspension bridge towards Bisham. 1st left into Quarry Wood Rd, right Hills Ln, right at Memorial Cross

A traditional English country inn set in rural Berkshire. Bedrooms are spacious and comfortable, with antique furnishings adding to the character. The building retains many traditional features including a wood panelled dining room and a bar with log fire. Food is imaginative and noteworthy and can be enjoyed outside in the garden or terrace in warmer months.

Facilities 9 en suite (4 GF) STV TVB tea/coffee Direct dial from bedrooms ✖ Last d 2.30pm **Prices** S £90-£130; D £110-£160✶ **LB** **Conf** BC Max 30 Thtr 30 Class 30 Board 30 **Parking** 50

EAST GARSTON
MAP 05 SU37

◆◆◆ ◖

The Queen's Arms Hotel
Newbury Rd RG17 7ET ☎ 01488 648757 🖷 01488 648642
e-mail info@queensarmshotel.co.uk
web www.queensarmshotel.co.uk

Situated in the famous Lambourn Valley, this character inn dates from the 18th century. The popular bar is a good choice for a pre-dinner drink while perusing the menus for either a bar snack or a more formal restaurant meal. Bedrooms have a more modern feel and some are located on the ground floor.

Facilities 6 en suite 4 annexe en suite (4 GF) ❷ in bedrooms ❷ in dining room ❷ in 1 lounge TVB tea/coffee Direct dial from bedrooms Cen ht No children 14yrs Dinner Last d 9.45pm **Conf** Max 20 Thtr 20 Class 20 Board 20 **Parking** 1

HUNGERFORD
MAP 05 SU36

◆◆◆◆ ◖

Crown & Garter
Great Com, Inkpen RG17 9QR ☎ 01488 668325
e-mail gill.hern@btopenworld.com
web www.crownandgarter.com
Dir 4m SE of Hungerford. Off A4 into Kintbury, opp corner stores onto Inkpen Rd, straight for 2m

Peacefully located in the attractive village of Inkpen, this charming 17th-century inn has a hop-draped bar where interesting well-prepared dishes are offered. The bedrooms, which are around a pretty garden, are attractively decorated in a country cottage style and are well equipped.

Facilities 8 annexe en suite (8 GF) ❷ in bedrooms ❷ in dining room TVB tea/coffee Cen ht No coaches Dinner Last d 9.30pm **Prices** S fr £55; d fr £80✶ **LB** **Parking** 40

◆◆◆◆ ◖

The Swan Inn
Craven Rd, Inkpen RG17 9DX
☎ 01488 668326 🖷 01488 668306
e-mail enquiries@theswaninn-organics.co.uk
web www.theswaninn-organics.co.uk
Dir 3.5m SE of Hungerford. S on Hungerford High St past railway bridge, left to Hungerford Common, right signed Inkpen

The delightful village inn dates from the 17th century and has open fires and beams in the bar, and the bonus of a smart restaurant.

continued

Bedrooms are generally spacious and furnished in keeping with the character of the building.

The Swan Inn

Facilities 10 en suite (2 fmly) ⊗ in bedrooms ⊗ in dining room ⊗ in 1 lounge TVB tea/coffee Direct dial from bedrooms ✻ Cen ht Organic farm shop Dinner Last d 9.30pm **Prices** S £60-£65; D £80-£95✲ **Conf** Max 40 Class 40 Board 12 **Parking** 50 **Notes** Closed 25-26 Dec

Wasing

35 Sanden Cl RG17 0LA ☎ 01488 684127
e-mail derekpatsmalley@amserve.com
Dir *A338 High St onto Atherton Rd, left at T-junct onto Church Way, 2nd right onto Homefield, 1st left*

This friendly home is in a pleasant residential area close to the town centre. Bedrooms are available in a choice of sizes and provide comfortable and well-equipped accommodation. Breakfast is a delight and provides a good start to the day.

Facilities 3 rms (2 GF) ⊗ in bedrooms ⊗ in dining room ⊗ in 1 lounge tea/coffee ✻ Cen ht TVL **Notes** Closed 19 Dec-2 Jan ⊗

Beacon House ◇

Bell Ln, Upper Gn, Inkpen RG17 9QJ
☎ 01488 668640 ◳ 01488 668640
e-mail l.g.cave@classicfm.net
web www.beaconhouseinkpen.co.uk
Dir *4m SE of Hungerford. Off A4 S into Kintbury, left onto Inkpen Rd, 1m over x-rds, right to common, 3rd left after Crown & Garter pub*

This large house is set in peaceful countryside and has been owned by the same family for many years. Bedrooms, comfortably furnished, overlook fields and there is a spacious lounge. Fresh produce from the

continued

garden features in the carefully prepared meals, while hospitality is warm and genuine.

Facilities 3 rms ⊗ TVB Cen ht TVL No coaches Art Studio & Gallery Dinner Last d 4pm **Prices** S fr £28; d fr £56 LB **Parking** 6 **Notes** ⊗

HURLEY   MAP 05 SU88

★★★★ ◉◉ **Restaurant with Rooms**

Black Boys Inn

Henley Rd SL6 5NQ ☎ 01628 824212
e-mail info@blackboysinn.co.uk
web www.blackboysinn.co.uk
Dir *1m W of Hurley on A4130*

This 16th-century inn has been restored to provide stylish contemporary accommodation with modern en suites. Extra facilities include DVD players and complimentary Internet access. Imaginative food and interesting wines are served in the bar-restaurant, where local produce and fresh fish are prominent.

Facilities 8 annexe en suite (5 GF) ⊗ TV available tea/coffee ✻ Cen ht No children 12yrs No coaches Dinner Last d 9pm **Prices** D £65-£75✲ **Conf** Max 10 Board 10 **Parking** 40 **Notes** Closed 24 Dec-9 Jan

NEWBURY   MAP 05 SU46

Premier Collection

♦♦♦♦♦ 🚭 ❦

Hamstead Holt Farm *(SU396664)*

Kintbury Holt RG20 0DD
☎ 01488 657259 ◳ 01488 657393 Mr & Mrs Hawkins
e-mail hamsteadholt@aol.com
web www.hamsteadholtfarm.com
Dir *4m SW of Newbury. Off A4 S into Kintbury, 1st left onto Newbury St & Holt Rd to Hamstead Marshall, 1st farm on left*

The original stable blocks of the farm have been converted to provide an idyllic rural retreat. The bedrooms are furnished to a high standard, and are in a self-contained wing with a sitting room, kitchen and dining area. Breakfast is a memorable serving of tasty treats.

Facilities 3 annexe en suite (1 GF) ⊗ TVB tea/coffee ✻ Cen ht Fishing 65 acres Sheep/Beef/Livery **Prices** S £50-£60; D £65-£70 LB **Parking** 3 **Notes** Closed 23 Dec-3 Jan ⊗

♦♦♦♦ ◧

Dolphin Inn

113 Bartholomew St RG14 5DT
☎ 01635 232425 ◳ 01635 230356
e-mail room@dolphin-inns.com
Dir *Off A339 at Sainsburys/police station rdbt towards town centre/Kennet Centre, signs for council offices, inn opp*

A warm welcome and attentive service are assured at this renovated 17th-century coaching inn, located within easy walking distance of the historic centre. Thoughtfully furnished bedrooms feature smart modern bathrooms, and spacious public areas include an attractive conservatory-restaurant.

Facilities 4 en suite ⊗ in bedrooms ⊗ in area of dining room ⊗ in 1 lounge STV FTV TVB tea/coffee Direct dial from bedrooms ✻ Cen ht No children 16yrs Dinner Last d 9pm **Prices** S £39.99-£60; D £39.99-£70✲ LB **Conf** Max 50 Thtr 50 Class 50 Board 40 **Parking** 20

NEWBURY continued

◆◆◆◆

55 Chapel Street

RG18 4JS ☎ 01635 861000 🖥 01635 862067
e-mail bandb@pwapublicity.co.uk
Dir A4 W into Thatcham, 250yds past Little Szechaun on left

This self-contained bedroom is in the heart of Thatcham, just a stroll from a selection of pubs, restaurants and shops. With a comfortable lounge and dining area, longer-stay guests will appreciate the spacious accommodation. A continental breakfast can be served in your room, or a full English in the dining room.

Facilities 1 en suite ⊗ STV TVB tea/coffee ✹ Cen ht TVL No children No coaches **Prices** S £45; D £50 **Parking** 1 **Notes** 🐾

◆◆◆◆

Pilgrims Guest House

Oxford Rd RG14 1XB ☎ 01635 40694 🖥 01635 44873
e-mail normaofpilgrims@aol.com
web www.pilgrimsnewbury.co.uk
Dir Off Waitrose A4 rdbt onto B4494 towards Wantage, 0.5m on left

Located close to the town centre, this smartly presented house appeals for business and leisure. The stylish bedrooms have modern bathrooms, and some rooms are in a new annexe. Hearty breakfasts are served in the bright dining room. Large car park.

Facilities 13 rms (9 en suite) 4 annexe en suite (1 fmly) (3 GF) ⊗ in 5 bedrooms ⊗ in dining room TVB tea/coffee ✹ Cen ht **Prices** S £40-£50; D £50-£60✳ **Parking** 17 **Notes** Closed 24 Dec-2 Jan 🐾

◆◆◆

The Limes Guest House

368 London Rd RG14 2QH
☎ 01635 33082 🖥 01635 580023
e-mail s.j.sweeney@btinternet.com
web www.limesguesthouse.co.uk
Dir On A4 between Newbury & Thatcham

Built in 1910, the Edwardian house is convenient for Newbury and Thatcham, and Newbury Racecourse is only 1m away. The en suite bedrooms are individually decorated and the large garden is a highlight. Wireless Internet access and ample parking are available.

Facilities 20 en suite (2 fmly) (9 GF) ⊗ in 9 bedrooms ⊗ in dining room STV TVB tea/coffee Direct dial from bedrooms ✹ Licensed Cen ht TVL Dinner Last d 7.30pm **Parking** 20 **Notes** Closed 25 Dec-1 Jan

◆◆◆

Rookwood Farm House

Stockcross RG20 8JX ☎ 01488 608676 🖥 01488 657961
e-mail charlotte@rookwoodfarmhouse.co.uk
Dir 2m W of Newbury. Junct A4 & A34 onto B4000, 0.75 m to Stockcross, 1st right signed Woodspeen, bear left, 1st on right

This delightful farmhouse with wonderful views is still a family home. Bedrooms are attractively presented and feature fine pieces of furniture. The coach house has a kitchen and sitting room. During the summer visitors can enjoy the beautiful gardens and outdoor pool.

continued

Rookwood Farm House

Facilities 1 en suite 2 annexe en suite (1 fmly) ⊗ TVB tea/coffee ✹ Cen ht TVL No coaches ⊰ 🗘 **Prices** S £50; D £70✳ **Conf** Max 12 Board 12 Del from £120 ✳ **Parking** 3

PANGBOURNE MAP 05 SU67

◆◆◆◆

Weir View House

9 Shooters Hl RG8 7DZ ☎ 0118 984 2120 🖥 0118 984 3777
e-mail info@weirview.co.uk
web www.weirview.co.uk
Dir A329 N from Pangbourne, after minirdbt under rail bridge, opp Swan pub

A warm welcome is guaranteed at this delightful house, situated in the village of Pangbourne overlooking the River Thames. The spacious modern bedrooms have been finished to a very high standard and the thoughtful extras including a well-stocked minibar. A continental breakfast is served in the bright and airy dining room, and freshly cooked meals can be delivered to your room from the pub across the road.

Facilities 9 en suite (6 fmly) (3 GF) ⊗ TVB tea/coffee Direct dial from bedrooms ✹ Cen ht TVL **Prices** D £75-£90✳ **Parking** 10 **Notes** Closed 23 Dec-1 Jan

READING MAP 05 SU77

◆◆◆◆ 🍴

The New Inn

Chalkhouse Gn Road, Kidmore End RG4 9AU
☎ 0118 972 3115 🖥 0118 977 4733
e-mail thenewinn@4cinns.co.uk

This delightful village inn successfully combines traditional charm with stylish sophistication. The popular bar offers real ales and a selection

continued

England

of snacks, while more formal meals are available in the restaurant. Bedrooms are modern and peaceful and some have their own patios and balconies.

Facilities 6 en suite (3 fmly) (3 GF) ⊘ STV TVB tea/coffee Direct dial from bedrooms ✗ Cen ht No coaches Dinner Last d 9:30pm **Parking** 50

◆◆◆

Chestnuts Bed & Breakfast

Basingstoke Rd, Spencers Wood RG7 1AA
☎ 0118 988 6171 & 07903 956397
e-mail chestnuts4bb@hotmail.com
Dir M4 junct 11, A33 for Basingstoke, next rdbt onto B3349 Three Mile Cross, over white-spot rdbt, Chestnuts 1m on left between chemist & bakery

This detached Georgian house is convenient for the business parks of Reading, just 1.5m from the M4 and with easy access to the M3. The non-smoking house provides spacious bedrooms, warm hospitality, a good breakfast, and off-road parking.

Facilities 3 rms ⊘ TVB tea/coffee ✗ Cen ht No children 16yrs No coaches **Prices** S £35-£40; D £50-£55✳ **Parking** 4 **Notes** ⊛

SONNING   MAP 05 SU77

◆◆◆◆ ◀

Bull Inn

High St RG4 6UP ☎ 0118 969 3901 ▤ 0118 969 7188
e-mail bullinn@accommodating-inns.co.uk
web www.accommodating-inns.co.uk/bullinn.html
The 16th-century village inn stands opposite St Andrew's Church. The Bull now offers high quality accommodation and a delightfully relaxed atmosphere in the character bars where blackboards display an extensive range of home-cooked dishes.

Facilities 5 en suite (1 fmly) ⊘ in bedrooms ⊘ in area of dining room STV TVB tea/coffee Direct dial from bedrooms ✗ Cen ht TVL Dinner Last d 9pm **Parking** 14

SULHAMSTEAD   MAP 05 SU66

Premier Collection

◆◆◆◆◆

The Old Manor

Whitehouse Gn RG7 4EA
☎ 0118 983 2423 ▤ 0118 983 6262
e-mail rags-r@theoldmanor.fsbusiness.co.uk
Dir M4 junct 12, A4 W, left for Theale Station, over railway, over river, right after 0.4km. Continue for 1km and turn left at x-rds & Old Manor entrance on left

A warm welcome awaits you at this fine manor house, set in 10 acres of well-kept gardens and grounds and close to the M4. Bedrooms are elegantly furnished; one has a four-poster bed and a spa bath. Afternoon tea can be taken in the drawing room, and good food and a complimentary glass of wine are offered at dinner.

Facilities 3 en suite ⊘ ✗ Cen ht TVL No children 8yrs No coaches ♨ Bowls Volley ball Dinner Last d previous day **Prices** S £40; D £80 **Parking** 8 **Notes** Closed 23 Dec-2 Jan ⊛

THEALE   MAP 05 SU67
See **Sulhamstead**

WINDSOR   MAP 06 SU97

◆◆◆

Clarence Hotel

9 Clarence Rd SL4 5AE ☎ 01753 864436 ▤ 01753 857060
e-mail enquiries@clarence-hotel.co.uk
web www.clarence-hotel.co.uk
Dir M4 junct 6, dual-carriageway to Windsor, left at 1st rdbt onto Clarence Rd

This Grade II listed Victorian house is in the heart of Windsor. Space in some rooms is limited, but all are well maintained and offer excellent value for money. Facilities include a lounge with a well-stocked bar, and a steam room. Breakfast is served in the dining room overlooking attractive gardens.

Facilities 20 en suite (6 fmly) (2 GF) ⊘ in dining room TVB tea/coffee Licensed Cen ht TVL Sauna Steam room **Prices** S £45-£68; D £55-£79 **Parking** 4

◆◆◆

Netherton Hotel

96 St Leonards Rd SL4 3DA
☎ 01753 855508 & 855510 ▤ 01753 621267
e-mail netherton@btconnect.com
Dir M4 Junct 6 towards Staines. After 2nd roundabout turn left at traffic lights.

This attractive family-run Edwardian house is in a quiet residential area, just a short walk from the town centre. There is a small lounge and breakfasts are served in a separate dining room. The smart, pine-furnished bedrooms offer a good range of facilities. Parking off road is a bonus.

Facilities 12 en suite (5 fmly) (2 GF) ⊘ TVB tea/coffee Direct dial from bedrooms ✗ Cen ht TVL **Parking** 13

If you have to cancel a booking, let the proprietor know immediately

WINDSOR continued

Trooper

97 St Leonards Rd SL4 3BZ
☎ 01753 670123 📄 01753 670124
e-mail trooper@accommodating-inns.co.uk
web www.accommodating-inns.co.uk
Dir M4 junct 6, towards Windsor, 2nd exit onto Goslar Way, left at lights, 200yds on left

At the time of going to press the rating for this establishment had not been confirmed. Please check the AA website www.theAA.com for up-to-date information.

Facilities 5 en suite 4 annexe en suite (2 fmly) (3 GF) ⊘ in bedrooms ⊘ in dining room TVB tea/coffee ✖ Cen ht No children 14yrs Dinner Last d 9.15pm **Conf** Thtr 25 Class 25 Board 18 **Parking** 9 **Notes** rs 25 Dec (no food)

BRISTOL

BRISTOL   MAP 04 ST57

◆◆◆◆ ⊜

Westfield House

37 Stoke Hill, Stoke Bishop BS9 1LQ
☎ 0117 962 6119 📄 0117 962 6119
e-mail admin@westfieldhouse.net
web www.westfieldhouse.net
Dir 2m NW of city centre in Stoke Bishop

A genuine welcome is assured at this friendly, family-run guest house in a quiet location on the edge of Durdham Downs. The very well-equipped bedrooms offer high levels of quality and comfort. Home-cooked dinners are available by arrangement, and in summer they can be enjoyed on the patio overlooking the large rear garden.

Facilities 3 en suite ⊘ TVB tea/coffee Direct dial from bedrooms ✖ Cen ht TVL No children 11yrs No coaches ⌘ Dinner 9.30pm **Prices** S £55-£79; D £85-£99✳ LB **Conf** Max 10 **Parking** 5

◆◆◆◆

Downlands House

33 Henleaze Gdns, Henleaze BS9 4HH
☎ 0117 962 1639 📄 0117 962 1639
e-mail mjdownlands@blueyonder.co.uk
web www.downlandshouse.co.uk
Dir 2m NW of city centre off A4018. M5 junct 17, signs Westbury-on-Trym/City Centre, pass private girls schools, Henleaze Gdns on left

This elegant Victorian property is convenient for Durdham Downs, Clifton village and Bristol Zoo. The attractive bedrooms have lots of extra touches, there is a smart lounge, and breakfast is served in either the conservatory or the stylish dining room.

Facilities 10 rms (7 en suite) (1 fmly) (1 GF) ⊘ TVB tea/coffee Cen ht TVL No coaches **Prices** S £38-£52; D £60-£75✳ LB

◆◆◆◆

Downs Edge

Saville Rd, Stoke Bishop BS9 1JA
☎ 0117 968 3264 & 07885 866463 📄 0117 968 7063
e-mail welcome@downsedge.com
Dir M5 junct 17, onto A4018, 4th rdbt right onto B4054 Parrys Ln, 1st left onto Saville Rd, 3rd right onto Hollybush Ln, left after 2nd speed ramp

Downs Edge has a quiet but convenient setting on the edge of Bristol's famous Durdham Downs. The well-equipped bedrooms are nicely furnished and there is an elegant lounge. Breakfast is a variety of hot and cold dishes served around one large table.

Facilities 4 en suite 3 annexe en suite ⊘ in bedrooms ⊘ in dining room ⊘ in lounges TVB tea/coffee ✖ Cen ht No children 6yrs No coaches **Prices** S £52-£58; D £75-£78✳ **Parking** 8 **Notes** Closed Xmas/New Year

◆◆◆◆

Greenlands

BS39 4ES ☎ 01275 333487 📄 01275 331211
For full entry see **Stanton Drew (Somerset)**

◆◆◆◆ ✿

Valley Farm (ST595631)

Sandy Ln BS39 4EL
☎ 01275 332723 & 07799 768161 📄 01275 332723
Mr & Mrs Keel
e-mail highmeade.gardens@virgin.net
For full entry see **Stanton Drew (Somerset)**

◆◆◆◆

Westbury Park Hotel

37 Westbury Rd, Westbury-on-Trym BS9 3AU
☎ 0117 962 0465 📠 0117 962 8607
e-mail westburypark@btconnect.com
web www.westburypark-hotel.co.uk
Dir M5 junct 17, onto A4018, 3.5m opp gates of Badminton School

Situated by the famous Durdham Downs, the attractive Victorian property offers pleasant accommodation with all modern comforts. Drinks are available from a small bar in the lounge, and at breakfast a choice of cooked dishes is served in the stylish dining room.

Facilities 8 en suite (2 fmly) ⊗ in bedrooms ⊗ in dining room TVB tea/coffee Direct dial from bedrooms Licensed Cen ht No coaches
Prices S £40-£50; D £65-£70✳ **Parking** 4

◆◆◆

Mayfair Lodge

5 Henleaze Rd, Westbury-On-Trym BS9 4EX
☎ 0117 962 2008 📠 0117 962 2008
e-mail mayfairlodge@blueyonder.co.uk
Dir M5 junct 17, A4018, after 3rd rdbt onto Henleaze Rd, Lodge 50yds on left

The charming Victorian house is in a residential area close to Durdham Downs and Bristol Zoo. Mayfair Lodge has well-equipped bedrooms of varying sizes and a relaxed, friendly atmosphere. Breakfast is served at separate tables in the bright dining room, and off-road parking is available behind the property.

Facilities 9 rms (6 en suite) ⊗ TVB tea/coffee ✕ Cen ht No children 5yrs No coaches **Prices** S £32-£50; D £65-£70✳ **Parking** 6
Notes Closed Xmas & New Year

◆◆◆

Shirehampton Lodge Hotel

62-64 High St, Shirehampton BS11 0DJ
☎ 0117 907 3480 📠 0117 907 3481
Dir M5 junct 18, B4054 to Shirehampton for 1m, premises on left above Alldays shop, entrance up ramp

Situated above shops, this imaginatively converted warehouse offers easy access to the motorway and the city centre. The modern bedrooms are thoughtfully equipped for business and leisure, and there is a well-furnished lounge-dining room.

Facilities 12 en suite (3 fmly) STV TVB tea/coffee Licensed Cen ht LB
Parking 10

◆◆◆

Washington Hotel

11-15 St Pauls Rd, Clifton BS8 1LX
☎ 0117 973 3980 📠 0117 973 4740
e-mail washington@cliftonhotels.com
Dir A4018 into city, right at lights opp BBC, house 200yds on left

This large terrace house is within walking distance of the city centre and Clifton village. The bedrooms, many refurbished, are well equipped for business guests. Public areas include a modern reception lounge and a bright basement breakfast room. The property has secure parking and a rear patio garden.

continued

Facilities 46 rms (40 en suite) (4 fmly) (10 GF) ⊗ in 13 bedrooms ⊗ in dining room ⊗ in lounges STV TVB tea/coffee Direct dial from bedrooms Licensed Cen ht Reduced rate pass for local health club
Prices S £35-£64; D £57-£84 **Parking** 20 **Notes** Closed 23 Dec-3 Jan

◆◆◆

Willow Tree ◇

7 Waterdale Cl BS9 4QN
☎ 0117 962 9560 📠 0117 962 8607
Dir A38 Filton rdbt onto B4056 Southmead Rd, 1.5m to end B4056, Willow Tree opp police station

This modern establishment is in a residential area convenient for the city centre, universities and local amenities. The neatly furnished bedrooms are light and airy, and the breakfast room overlooks the garden.

Facilities 8 rms (4 en suite) (1 pri facs) (2 fmly) (2 GF) ⊗ TVB tea/coffee ✕ Cen ht No coaches **Prices** S £30-£35; D £55-£60✳
Parking 6 **Notes** 🐾

◆◆◆ 🅰

Basca House ◇

19 Broadway Rd, Bishopston BS7 8ES ☎ 0117 942 2182
Dir A38 Gloucester Rd onto Berkeley Rd, 1st left onto Broadway Rd

Facilities 4 rms ⊗ TVB tea/coffee ✕ Cen ht TVL No coaches
Prices S fr £28; d fr £46✳ **Notes** Closed Xmas & New Year 🐾

◆◆◆ 🅰

Downs View

38 Upper Belgrave Rd, Clifton BS8 2XN
☎ 0117 973 7046 📠 0117 973 8169
e-mail bookings@downsviewguesthouse.co.uk
Dir M5 junct 17, signs for zoo, on left after 5m, just before zoo

Facilities 16 rms (9 en suite) (1 fmly) (2 GF) ⊗ in bedrooms ⊗ in dining room ⊗ in lounges TVB tea/coffee ✕ Cen ht
Prices S £45-£55; D £60-£70✳ **Notes** Closed Xmas & New Year

◆◆◆ 🅰

Highcliffe Hotel

Wellington Ter, Clevedon BS21 7PU
☎ 01275 873250 📠 01275 873572
e-mail highcliffehotel@aol.com
web www.highcliffehotel.com
Dir SW of Bristol, on Clevedon seafront

Facilities 20 en suite (2 fmly) (4 GF) ⊗ in bedrooms ⊗ in dining room TVB tea/coffee Direct dial from bedrooms Licensed Cen ht TVL Dinner Last d 8.45pm **Prices** S £47.50-£55; D £60-£70✳ LB **Conf** Thtr 80 Class 60 Board 60 **Parking** 12

England

EASTON-IN-GORDANO ♦♦♦ MAP 04 ST57

The Tynings B & B
Martcombe Rd BS20 0QE ☎ 01275 372608
Dir M5 junct 19, A369 towards Bristol (signed Clifton), house 0.5m
on right opp Rudgleigh Inn

Located just a short drive from the M5, this popular guest house offers
comfortable bedrooms and a relaxed atmosphere. There is a television
lounge and a car park, and meals are available at the pleasant local pub.
Facilities 6 rms (3 en suite) (4 fmly) ⊘ TVB tea/coffee ✗ Cen ht TVL
No coaches **Prices** S £35-£40; D £45-£50✲ **Parking** 8 **Notes** Closed
Xmas/New Year ⊛

BUCKINGHAMSHIRE

AMERSHAM MAP 06 SU99

★★ Bed & Breakfast

Morningside
Piggots Orch HP7 0JG ☎ 01494 721134
Dir A413 onto A355, B&B 20yds on right.

A warm welcome is assured at this private home located a short walk
from the old town. Thoughtfully furnished bedrooms are equipped
with lots of thoughtful extras and breakfast is taken at one table in the
attractive pine-furnished dining room, or conservatory during the
warmer months.
Facilities 2 rms (2 pri facs) (1 fmly) ⊘ TVB tea/coffee ✗ Cen ht
Parking 2 **Notes** ⊛

♦♦♦♦

Pond Cottage
Village Rd, Coleshill HP7 0LH
☎ 01494 728177 ▤ 01494 728177
e-mail pondcott@msn.com
web www.pondcottagecoleshill.co.uk
Dir 2m S of Amersham. Off A355/A404 into Coleshill

A warm welcome is guaranteed at this charming cottage, set in a rural
location near major routes. The well-appointed bedrooms have a
wealth of thoughtful extras, and delicious breakfasts are served around
a communal table.
Facilities 3 rms (1 en suite) (1 pri facs) (1 fmly) ⊘ TVB tea/coffee ✗
Cen ht TVL No coaches **Prices** D £60-£75✲ **Parking** 3

Ⓤ

Glory Farm Cottage
Fagnall Ln, Winchmore Hill HP7 0PQ ☎ 01494 727598
e-mail frangfc@btinternet.com
Dir A355 turn at Mulberry Bush to Winchmore Hill x-rds. Left past
Potters, located 8th on right.

At the time of going to press the rating for this establishment had not
been confirmed. Please check the AA website www.theAA.com for up-
to-date information.
Facilities 2 rms (1 en suite) (1 pri facs) ⊘ TVB tea/coffee Cen ht TVL
No coaches **Parking** 3 **Notes** ⊛

AYLESBURY ♦♦♦ MAP 11 SP81

Brickwall Farm Cottage
Mill Ln, Weston Turville HP22 5RG ☎ 01296 612656
e-mail accommodation@brickwallfarmcottage.co.uk
Dir 3m SE of Aylesbury, junct B4544 & Mill Ln

Expect a warm welcome and attentive service at this charming
establishment. Original features have been lovingly restored and a
hearty breakfast is served in the bright dining area. Bedrooms have a
homely feel and are well equipped, including broadband Internet
access.
Facilities 4 rms (1 en suite) (1 pri facs) ⊘ STV TVB tea/coffee ✗
Cen ht No children 2yrs No coaches **Prices** S fr £35; D £60-£75
Parking 6 **Notes** ⊛

BRILL MAP 11 SP61

♦♦♦ ⍩

Poletrees Farm *(SP660160)*
Ludgershall Rd HP18 9TZ
☎ 01844 238276 ▤ 01844 238276 Mrs Cooper
e-mail poletrees.farm@virgin.net
Dir S off A41 signed Ludgershall/Brill, after railway bridge 0.5m on
left

Located between the villages of Ludgershall and Brill, this 15th-century
farmhouse retains many original features including a wealth of
exposed beams. The bedrooms are in converted outbuildings, and a
lounge with a welcoming wood-burning stove is available in addition
to the cosy dining room, the setting for wholesome breakfasts.
Facilities 4 annexe en suite (4 GF) ⊘ FTV TVB tea/coffee ✗ Cen ht
TVL 110 acres beef sheep **Prices** S fr £35.40; d fr £60.70✲ LB
Parking 6

CHALFONT ST GILES MAP 06 SU99

♦♦♦♦ ⬛

The Ivy House
London Rd HP8 4RS ☎ 01494 872184 ▤ 01494 872870
e-mail enquiries@theivyhouse-bucks.co.uk
web www.theivyhouse-bucks.co.uk
Dir 1.5m N of Chalfont on A413

This lovely, late 18th-century freehouse lies in the heart of the Chiltern
Hills with superb views of the surrounding countryside. The carefully

continued

appointed public rooms include a very well-stocked bar with at least four cask ales, and a wide selection of wines and malt whiskies. A worthy, ever-changing menu is available in the bar or the non-smoking restaurant in the adjoining coach house. The stylish bedrooms vary in size and each is thoughtfully equipped.

Facilities 5 en suite ⊘ in bedrooms ⊘ in area of dining room ⊘ in 1 lounge STV TVB tea/coffee ✖ Cen ht Golf 18 Dinner Last d 9:30pm **Prices** S fr £75; d fr £95✱ **LB Conf** Max 25 Thtr 25 Class 25 Board 25 **Parking** 45

CHESHAM
MAP 06 SP90

Premier Collection

◆◆◆◆◆ 🏛

Braziers Well

Oak Ln, Braziers End HP5 2UL
☎ 01494 758956 & 07860 317762
e-mail info@brazierswell.co.uk
web www.brazierswell.co.uk
Dir *From Chesham N off A416 signed Bellingdon/Cholesbury, after 5m sharp left bend, Braziers Well 100yds on right*

Peacefully located within an unspoiled rural community, this impressive detached house provides a spacious, thoughtfully furnished bedroom with a wealth of homely extras and a smart modern shower room. Imaginative breakfasts, using quality produce, are served in an attractive conservatory-dining room and a warm welcome is assured.

Facilities 1 en suite (1 GF) ⊘ TVB tea/coffee ✖ Cen ht No children 16yrs No coaches table tennis **Parking** 4 **Notes** 🚭

DENHAM
MAP 06 TQ08

◆◆◆◆ ☕ ◀▌

The Falcon Inn

Village Rd UB9 5BE ☎ 01895 832125
e-mail falcon.inn@btconnect.com
Dir *Off A40 into village centre*

The 18th-century inn stands in the heart of the picturesque village, opposite the green. The bedrooms, with smart shower rooms en suite, are well equipped and display original features. Carefully prepared dishes and a good selection of wines are available for lunch and dinner in the cosy restaurant.

Facilities 3 en suite ⊘ in bedrooms ⊘ in dining room TVB tea/coffee ✖ Cen ht No children 10yrs Dinner Last d 9.30pm **Prices** S £50-£75; D £70-£95✱ **LB**

DINTON
MAP 05 SP71

◆◆◆

Wallace *(SP770110)*

HP17 8UZ ☎ 01296 748660 ▤ 01296 748851 Mrs Cook
e-mail jackiecook@wallacefarm.freeserve.co.uk
Dir *Off A418 signed Dinton/Ford, 1st left signed Upton, farm on right*

Located between Aylesbury and Thame, this farm supports the Rare Breeds Survival Trust and many unusual species of animal and fowl are found in abundance. The 16th-century house retains many original features and has a great deal of charm. Bedrooms are equipped with thoughtful extras and a comfortable sitting room is available.

Facilities 3 rms (2 en suite) (1 pri facs) (1 fmly) ⊘ in bedrooms ⊘ in dining room TV2B tea/coffee ✖ Cen ht TVL 24 acres beef cattle sheep **Prices** S £41; D £52-£54✱ **Parking** 6

FARNHAM COMMON
MAP 06 SU98

◆◆◆◆

Penn Lodge

33 Mayflower Way SL2 3TU
☎ 01753 643594 & 07736 955069 ▤ 01753 643594
e-mail pennlodge@hotmail.com
Dir *Off A355 onto Temple Wood Ln, 1st left onto Mayflower Way, 100yds on left*

This delightful guest house in a quiet residential area provides a warm welcome. The refurbished bedrooms vary in size and have a good range of facilities, and wireless broadband Internet access is available. Breakfast is served in the dining room overlooking the gardens.

Facilities (1 fmly) (1 GF) ⊘ in bedrooms ⊘ in dining room TVB tea/coffee ✖ Cen ht TVL No coaches **Prices** S fr £45; d fr £65✱ **Parking** 5 **Notes** Closed 24 Dec-15 Jan 🚭

GAYHURST
MAP 11 SP84

◆◆◆

Mill Farm ⬦ *(SP852454)*

MK16 8LT
☎ 01908 611489 & 07714 719640 ▤ 01908 611489
Mrs Adams
e-mail adamsmillfarm@aol.com
Dir *B526 from Newport Pagnell, 2.5m left onto Haversham Rd, Mill Farm 1st on left*

Within easy reach of Newport Pagnell and the M1, this traditional farmhouse has a peaceful setting with wonderful views over farmland. Bedrooms are decorated in a homely style and have a host of thoughtful extras. The sumptuous lounge-dining room is enhanced with fine antiques.

Facilities 3 rms (2 en suite) 1 annexe en suite (1 fmly) (1 GF) ⊘ in 1 bedrooms ⊘ in dining room ⊘ in 1 lounge TVB tea/coffee Cen ht TVL ⚬ Fishing Riding 🏓 Rough shooting Trout & Coarse fishing 550 acres mixed **Prices** S £25-£30; D £45-£55 **Parking** 13 **Notes** 🚭

England

HIGH WYCOMBE MAP 05 SU89

◆◆◆◆
Best Western Alexandra Hotel
Queen Alexandra Rd HP11 2JX
☎ 01494 463494 🖹 01494 463560
e-mail reservations@alexandra-hotel.co.uk
Dir M40 junct 4, A404 towards town centre, left at bottom of Marlow
Hill, 200yds opp hospital

This modern guest house, with secure parking, is in residential road
close to the hospital, within easy walking distance of the town centre.
Light snacks and bar drinks are available, and a full breakfast is served
in the modern restaurant. The contemporary bedrooms have smart
bathrooms.

Facilities 28 en suite (8 GF) 🚭 in 23 bedrooms 🚭 in dining room
🚭 in lounges FTV TVB tea/coffee Direct dial from bedrooms ✖
Licensed Cen ht TVL No coaches Dinner Last d 8.30pm
Prices S £95-£100; D £100-£109✷ **Conf** Max 15 Thtr 15 Board 12 Del
from £130 ✷ **Parking** 28

◆◆◆◆
Squirrel House
129 New Rd, Booker HP12 4RH ☎ 01494 520709
e-mail margaret_m_doherty@hotmail.com
Dir M40 junct 4, A4010, over 3 minirdbts, B&B on right by lights

A warm welcome is guaranteed at this guest house with a home from
home atmosphere. Within easy reach of the motorway, this is a good
base for exploring the area. Hearty breakfasts are served in the
attractive lounge-dining room.

Facilities 2 rms (1 en suite) (1 pri facs) 🚭 STV TVB tea/coffee ✖
Cen ht TVL No coaches **Prices** S £39; D £55✷ **Parking** 5 **Notes** 🚭

◆◆◆
Clifton Lodge Hotel
210 West Wycombe Rd HP12 3AR
☎ 01494 440095 & 529062 🖹 01494 536322
e-mail sales@cliftonlodgehotel.com
web www.cliftonlodgehotel.com
Dir A40 from town centre towards Aylesbury, on right after BP
station & opp phone box

Located west of the town centre, this long-established hotel provides a
range of bedrooms, popular with a regular commercial clientele.

continued

Public areas include an attractive conservatory-dining room and a cosy
lounge. Ample parking behind the property.

Facilities 32 rms (20 en suite) (1 fmly) (7 GF) 🚭 in dining room
🚭 in lounges TVB tea/coffee Direct dial from bedrooms ✖ Licensed
Cen ht TVL Dinner Last d 8.45pm **Prices** S £55-£89; D £65-£110✷ **LB**
Conf Max 30 Thtr 30 Class 20 Board 15 **Parking** 28

CAMBRIDGESHIRE

ALCONBURY MAP 12 TL17

◆◆◆◆ 🍴
Manor House Hotel
20 Chapel St PE28 4DY ☎ 01480 890423 🖹 01480 891663
e-mail stayatmanorhouse@aol.com
Dir In village centre

This popular inn was originally the 16th-century manor house. The
accommodation has been refurbished to provide cheerful, well-
equipped bedrooms, some with four-poster beds. Public rooms
include a cosy, well-stocked bar with open fires, and a more formal
dining area.

Facilities 5 en suite 1 annexe en suite (6 fmly) 🚭 in bedrooms
🚭 in dining room 🚭 in 1 lounge TVB tea/coffee Direct dial from
bedrooms ✖ Cen ht TVL Dinner Last d 8.45pm **Parking** 25 **Notes** rs
25 Dec (limited opening)

BOXWORTH MAP 12 TL36

◆◆◆◆ 🍴
The Golden Ball Hotel
High St CB3 8LY ☎ 01954 267397 🖹 01954 267497
e-mail info@goldenballhotel.co.uk
Dir In village centre

The Golden Ball is a delightful 17th-century thatched inn with a
modern accommodation annexe. The bedrooms are well appointed
and each bathroom has a bath and power shower. The inn is very
popular for its restaurant, pub meals and real ales, and service is
helpful and friendly.

Facilities 11 en suite (1 fmly) (9 GF) 🚭 TVB tea/coffee Direct dial from
bedrooms ✖ Cen ht Dinner Last d 9.15pm **Prices** S £64.50-£99.50;
D £74.50-£115✷ **LB Conf** Max 20 **Parking** 75

BURWELL MAP 12 TL56

◆◆◆◆ 🄰
The Meadow House ◇
2A High St CB5 0HB ☎ 01638 741926 🖹 01638 741861
e-mail hilary@themeadowhouse.co.uk
web www.themeadowhouse.co.uk
Dir A14 at Stow-cum-Quy onto B1102 to Burwell, Meadow House on
left opposite phone box

Facilities 7 rms (4 en suite) (4 fmly) (2 GF) 🚭 TVB tea/coffee Cen ht
No coaches **Prices** S £25-£30; D £50-£60✷ **Parking** 16 **Notes** 🚭

England

CAMBRIDGE MAP 12 TL45

♦♦♦♦

Finches Bed & Breakfast

144 Thornton Rd CB3 0ND ☎ 01223 276653
e-mail enquiry@finches-bnb.com
web www.finches-bnb.com
Dir 2m NW of city centre off A1307

The friendly and attentive hosts offer a home from home north-west of the city centre. The stylish bedrooms vary in size and have a wealth of extras, and hearty breakfasts are served at a communal table in the cosy breakfast room.

Facilities 3 en suite (2 GF) ⊘ TVB tea/coffee ✖ Cen ht No coaches Golf **Prices** S £45-£50; d fr £60✳ **Parking** 3 **Notes** ⊕

♦♦♦♦ ⌂

The Gate Lodge

2 Hinton Rd, Fulbourn CB1 5DZ
☎ 01223 881951 ▤ 08700 513050
e-mail bandb@thegatelodge.freeservers.com
Dir 5m E of Cambridge. W side of Fulbourn village opp Bakers Arms pub

This restful, lovingly restored guest house is in a sleepy village not far from Cambridge and the M11. The spacious bedrooms are well appointed with useful extras including Internet connections and some with freeview and DVD facilities. Breakfast is a feature, served round a large oak table in the attractive dining room.

Facilities 4 rms (1 en suite) (2 pri facs) (2 fmly) ⊘ FTV TVB tea/coffee ✖ Cen ht ♪ **Prices** S £50-£65; D £70-£85✳ **Parking** 5 **Notes** ⊕

♦♦♦♦

Acorn Guest House

154 Chesterton Rd CB4 1DA
☎ 01223 353888 ▤ 01223 350527
e-mail info@acornguesthouse.co.uk
web www.acornguesthouse.co.uk
Dir 0.5m NE of city centre

Located close to the ring road and city centre, this attractive, yellow-brick house has been carefully extended and renovated by the friendly owners to provide homely accommodation. Tasty English breakfasts are served in the cosy dining room.

Facilities 10 en suite (1 fmly) ⊘ TVB tea/coffee Direct dial from bedrooms ✖ Cen ht TVL **Parking** 7

See advertisement on this page

♦♦♦♦

Aylesbray Lodge

5 Mowbray Rd CB1 7SR
☎ 01223 240089 ▤ 01223 528678
e-mail stay@aylesbray.com
web www.aylesbray.com
Dir 1.5m SE of city centre on A1134

A warm welcome is assured at this family-run guest house. The en suite bedrooms are well equipped, each with a modern shower room, and two rooms have attractive four-poster beds. Tasty English breakfasts are served in the elegant dining room and a lounge is available.

Facilities 6 en suite (1 fmly) (1 GF) ⊘ STV TVB tea/coffee Direct dial from bedrooms ✖ Cen ht TVL **Parking** 6

England

CAMBRIDGE continued

◆◆◆◆

Hamden

89 High St, Cherry Hinton CB1 9LU
☎ 01223 413263 🗐 01223 245960
Dir 3m SE of city centre off A1134 to Cherry Hinton

Expect a warm welcome at this small, family-run guest house, which is just a short drive from the city centre. The pleasant bedrooms are generally quite spacious and equipped with many thoughtful extras. Public rooms include a large kitchen-dining room where breakfast is served at individual tables.

Facilities 3 en suite (1 fmly) (2 GF) ⊗ TVB tea/coffee Direct dial from bedrooms 🐾 Cen ht No children 10yrs No coaches **Prices** S £40-£45; D £60-£65✳ **LB** **Parking** 6

See advertisement on opposite page

◆◆◆◆

Rose Bungalow ◇

68 High St, Great Wilbraham CB1 5JD
☎ 01223 882385 & 07876 426271
e-mail rose.bungalow@btinternet.com
web www.rosebungalow.co.uk
Dir 6m E of Cambridge in Great Wilbraham centre

The attractive bungalow with pretty gardens stands in a quiet village very close to the park and ride for Cambridge and the Imperial War Museum. The comfortable bedrooms contain many thoughtful extras and the nutritious breakfast is a speciality. Off-road parking.

Facilities 2 rms (1 en suite) (1 pri facs) (2 GF) ⊗ TVB tea/coffee 🐾 Cen ht No children 10yrs No coaches Golf 18 **Prices** S £28-£30; D £55-£60 **Parking** 2 **Notes** 🖂

◆◆◆◆

Rose Corner ◇

42 Woodcock Cl, Impington CB4 9LD
☎ 01223 563136 🗐 01223 233886
e-mail wsalmon.rosecorner@virgin.net
web www.rose-corner.co.uk
Dir 4m N of Cambridge. A14 junct 32, B1049 N into Impington, off Milton Rd

The detached property is in a quiet cul-de-sac in the popular village of Impington, north of the city. Its spacious bedrooms are carefully furnished and thoughtfully equipped, and breakfast is served in the comfortable lounge-dining room overlooking the rear gardens.

Facilities 5 rms (3 en suite) ⊗ TVB tea/coffee 🐾 Cen ht TVL No coaches **Prices** S £25-£28; D £50-£60✳ **Parking** 5

◆◆◆◆ 🅰

Alexander Bed & Breakfast

56 St Barnabas Rd CB1 2DE ☎ 01223 525725
e-mail enquiries@beesley-schuster.co.uk
web www.beesley-schuster.co.uk
Dir From railway station onto Station Rd, 1st left onto Tenison Rd, 2nd lights right onto St Barnabas Rd, B&B on right

Facilities 2 en suite (2 GF) ⊗ TVB tea/coffee 🐾 Cen ht No children 5yrs No coaches **Prices** S £35-£60; D £50-£75✳ **Parking** 1 **Notes** 🖂

◆◆◆

Alpha Milton

61-63 Milton Rd CB4 1XA
☎ 01223 311625 🗐 01223 565100
e-mail welcome@alphamiltonguesthouse.co.uk
Dir 0.5m NE of city centre

The Alpha Milton is in a residential area just a short walk from the city centre. The attractive lounge-dining room overlooks the rear garden, and the pleasant bedrooms are have a good range of facilities.

Facilities 8 rms (6 en suite) (1 pri facs) (2 fmly) (2 GF) ⊗ TV6B tea/coffee 🐾 Cen ht TVL **Parking** 6

◆◆◆

Ashtrees Guest House

128 Perne Rd CB1 3RR ☎ 01223 411233 🗐 01223 411233
e-mail ashtrees@cscuk.net
web www.ashtreesguesthouse.co.uk
Dir 1.5m SE of city centre on A1134

Service is informal, cheerful and helpful at Ashtrees, and the en suite bedrooms come in a variety of styles and sizes. A continental or cooked breakfast is served at individual tables in the pleasant breakfast room. Some private parking behind the property.

Facilities 5 en suite (1 fmly) (2 GF) ⊗ TVB tea/coffee Cen ht **Parking** 5

◆◆◆

Benson House

24 Huntingdon Rd CB3 0HH
☎ 01223 311594 🗐 01223 311594
e-mail bensonhouse@btconnect.com
Dir 0.5m NW of centre on A604

The popular guest house is well placed for the city centre and New Hall and Fitzwilliam colleges. Its pleasant bedrooms vary in size and style and are well equipped. Limited private parking behind the property.

Facilities 5 rms (4 en suite) (1 pri facs) (1 GF) ⊗ TVB tea/coffee 🐾 Cen ht No children 12yrs No coaches **Prices** D £60-£70✳ **Parking** 5

Brooklands

95 Cherry Hinton Rd CB1 7BS
☎ 01223 242035 📠 01223 242035
e-mail michelle@brooklandsguesthouse.co.uk
Dir *1m SE of city centre off A1307*

Located close to the ring road, this renovated Edwardian terrace house offers well-equipped homely bedrooms. Freshly cooked breakfasts are served in the cosy dining room and a sauna is available. Limited free parking is available nearby.

Facilities 5 en suite (1 fmly) ⊘ STV TVB tea/coffee Direct dial from bedrooms Cen ht No coaches Snooker Sauna **Parking** 5

Dykelands

157 Mowbray Rd CB1 7SP
☎ 01223 244300 📠 01223 566746
e-mail dykelands@fsbdial.co.uk
web www.dykelands.com
Dir *1.5m SE of city centre on A1134*

The large detached house is in a mainly residential area near Addenbrooke's Hospital. It offers well-equipped and comfortable accommodation, and breakfast is served in the cosy dining room. There is also a small lounge. Private parking at the front of the house.

Facilities 9 rms (7 en suite) (3 fmly) (2 GF) ⊘ TVB tea/coffee Cen ht No coaches **Prices** S £40-£56; D £46-£56 **Parking** 7

Fairways ◇

143 Cherry Hinton Rd CB1 7BX
☎ 01223 246063 📠 01223 248306
e-mail michaelslatter@btconnect.com
web www.fairwaysguesthouse.com
Dir *1m SE of city centre off A1307*

The large Victorian house provides well-equipped bedrooms convenient for the city centre and the ring road. Many of the rooms have attractive, handcrafted pine furniture, and the en suite rooms have modern showers. Breakfast is served in the ground-floor dining room.

Facilities 16 rms (9 en suite) (3 fmly) (4 GF) ⊘ TVB tea/coffee ✈ Cen ht **Prices** S £28-£40; D £50-£68 **Parking** 20 **Notes** Closed 22 Dec-2 Jan

See advertisement on this page

England

CAMBRIDGE continued

◆◆◆

Hamilton Hotel ◇

156 Chesterton Rd CB4 1DA
☎ 01223 365664 ▤ 01223 314866
e-mail hamiltonhotel@talk21.com
web www.hamiltonhotelcambridge.co.uk
Dir 1m NE of city centre, off A1134 ring road

Just a short walk from the city centre, the Hamilton has pleasant bedrooms with a good range of facilities. The relaxing public areas include a restaurant-bar, where evening meals and snacks are available.

Facilities 25 rms (19 en suite) (4 fmly) ⊗ in dining room TVB tea/coffee Direct dial from bedrooms ✹ Licensed Cen ht No coaches Dinner Last d 8pm **Prices** S £28-£55; D £50-£70✶ **Parking** 20 **Notes** Closed 25 & 26 Dec

◆◆◆

Lynwood House ◇

217 Chesterton Rd CB4 1AN
☎ 01223 500776 ▤ 01223 300552
e-mail info@lynwood-house.co.uk
web www.lynwood-house.co.uk
Dir M11 N junct 13, A1303 towards city centre, left at minirdbt, house 1m on left

Located close to the river and central attractions, this well-maintained guest house provides a range of practically equipped bedrooms, some of which have modern shower rooms en suite. Wholesome breakfasts are served in the cosy dining room and a warm welcome is assured.

Facilities 8 rms (5 en suite) (2 fmly) (3 GF) ⊗ TVB tea/coffee Cen ht No children 12yrs No coaches **Prices** S £28-£55; D £55-£75✶ **Parking** 3

If you book on bed, breakfast and evening meal terms, you may find that the tariff includes only the set menu

◆◆◆

Southampton

7 Elizabeth Way CB4 1DE
☎ 01223 357780 ▤ 01223 314297
e-mail southamptonhouse@telco4u.net
web www.southamptonguesthouse.com
Dir 0.5m E of city centre

The proprietors provide a friendly service at the 19th-century terrace house, which is on the inner ring road, just a short walk from the Grafton Centre. The property has well-equipped bedrooms, and a comprehensive English breakfast is served.

Facilities 5 en suite (3 fmly) (1 GF) ⊗ TVB tea/coffee Direct dial from bedrooms ✹ Cen ht **Prices** S £35-£45; D £48-£58✶ **Parking** 8 **Notes** ⊗

Ⓤ

26 High Street

Great Shelford CB2 5EH ☎ 01223 843275
Dir A10 onto A1301. Great Shelford High St. Approx 1.5m right at war memorial

At the time of going to press the rating for this establishment had not been confirmed. Please check the AA website www.theAA.com for up-to-date information.

Facilities 2 rms (1 fmly) ⊗ TVB tea/coffee ✹ Cen ht No coaches ⅃Ꝺ **Notes** Closed Nov-Mar ⊗

CHIPPENHAM   MAP 12 TL66

◆◆◆◆◆ ⇔

The Old Bakery

22 High St CB7 5PP ☎ 01638 721185 ▤ 01638 721185
e-mail joycemgrimes@aol.com
web www.the-old-bakery.co.uk
Dir A11 onto B1085 into village centre

Set in beautiful gardens, this delightful Grade II listed Tudor house has been restored to retain its original character. The bedrooms are well appointed and the spacious public rooms include an inviting lounge, a conservatory and a snooker room. Carefully prepared meals are served in the beamed dining room around an enormous elm table. The Old Bakery is non-smoking.

Facilities 3 en suite ⊗ TVB tea/coffee ✹ Cen ht TVL No children 12yrs No coaches Pool Table **Prices** S £40-£45; D £80-£95 **Parking** 5 **Notes** Closed Xmas & New Year

ELY

MAP 12 TL58

◆◆◆◆◆

Springfields

Ely Rd, Little Thetford CB6 3HJ
☎ 01353 663637 ▤ 01353 663130
e-mail springfields@talk21.com
Dir 1m S of Ely on A10

The elegant home stands within landscaped gardens and an orchard, just 1m from Ely. The attractive and very well-appointed ground-floor bedrooms look out to the rear gardens, home to a variety of wild birds. Fresh flowers, luxurious beds with starched linen, and a host of useful extras ensure a memorable visit. A freshly cooked breakfast is served at a large communal table in the dining room.

Facilities 3 en suite (3 GF) ⊛ TVB tea/coffee ✹ Cen ht No children 12yrs No coaches Golf 18 **Prices** S £65; D £65✳ LB **Parking** 6 **Notes** Closed Dec ⊛

◆◆◆◆ ⊛ ⏚ ⊜ ◖

Anchor

Sutton Gault CB6 2BD ☎ 01353 778537 ▤ 01353 776180
e-mail anchorinn@popmail.bta.com
web www.anchor-inn-restaurant.co.uk
Dir 6m W of Ely. Sutton Gault signed off B1381 at S end of Sutton

Located beside the New Bedford River with stunning country views, the 17th-century inn has original features enhanced by period furniture. The spacious bedrooms are equipped with lots of thoughtful extras, and service by the friendly young team is helpful and attentive.

Facilities 4 en suite (2 fmly) ⊛ FTV TVB tea/coffee Direct dial from bedrooms ✹ Cen ht No coaches Dinner Last d 9pm **Prices** S £55-£89.50; D £65-£149.50✳ LB **Parking** 16 **Notes** Closed 26 Dec

◆◆◆◆ ♥

Hill House (TL589817)

9 Main St, Coveney CB6 2DJ
☎ 01353 778369 ▤ 01353 778369 Mrs Nix
e-mail info@hillhousefarm-ely.co.uk
Dir 3m W of Ely in Coveney centre

A warm welcome is assured at this Victorian farmhouse situated in an unspoiled fenland village. Bedrooms are individually decorated and well appointed, and breakfast, which includes local bacon and sausages, is served in the elegant dining room. There is also a cosy lounge.

Facilities 3 en suite (1 GF) ⊛ TVB tea/coffee ✹ Cen ht No children 12yrs 240 acres arable **Prices** D £56-£58 LB **Parking** 6 **Notes** Closed Xmas

◆◆◆

Castle Lodge Hotel

50 New Barns Rd CB7 4PW
☎ 01353 662276 ▤ 01353 666606
e-mail castlelodgehotel@supanet.com
Dir Off B1382 Prickwillow Rd NE from town centre

Located within easy walking distance of the cathedral, this extended Victorian house offers well-equipped bedrooms in a variety of sizes. Public areas include a traditionally furnished dining room and a comfortable air-conditioned bar-lounge. Service is friendly and helpful.

Facilities 11 rms (6 en suite) (2 fmly) ⊛ in dining room TVB tea/coffee Direct dial from bedrooms ✹ Licensed Cen ht TVL No coaches Dinner Last d 9pm **Prices** S £32.50; D £75✳ **Conf** Max 40 Board 40 **Parking** 6

◆◆◆

Clare Farm House ◈

Main St, Witchford CB6 2HQ ☎ 01353 664135
e-mail seymour8@aol.com
Dir 2m SW of Ely in Witchford centre

This attractive home is in a fenland village near Ely. You can expect friendly and helpful service, and freshly cooked breakfasts served around a large table in the pleasant dining room. Bedrooms vary in style and size, and most are quite spacious; two rooms share one general bathroom.

Facilities 4 rms (2 en suite) ⊛ TVB tea/coffee ✹ Cen ht No children 12yrs No coaches **Prices** S £25-£30; D £50-£60✳ **Parking** 6 **Notes** ⊛

◆◆◆

The Nyton Hotel

7 Barton Rd CB7 4HZ ☎ 01353 662459 ▤ 01353 666217
e-mail nytonhotel@yahoo.co.uk
Dir From S, A10 into Ely on Cambridge Rd, pass golf course, 1st right

Set in 2 acres of mature gardens, this family-run establishment offers comfortable bedrooms in a range of sizes and styles. The pleasant public rooms include a wood-panelled restaurant, a smart bar, and a conservatory-lounge overlooking the gardens. Meals are available in the dining room and informal light meals are served in the lounge bar.

Facilities 10 en suite (3 fmly) (2 GF) ⊛ in bedrooms ⊛ in dining room TVB tea/coffee Direct dial from bedrooms ✹ Licensed Cen ht TVL Golf Dinner Last d 6.30pm **Prices** S £45-£50; D £75-£80✳ LB **Conf** Max 40 Board 40 **Parking** 25 **Notes** Civ Wed 100

England

ELY continued

♦♦♦ ⌨

Red Lion

47 High St, Stretham CB6 3JQ
☎ 01353 648132 ▤ 01353 648327
e-mail info@redlion-stretham.co.uk
Dir 4.5m S of Ely. Off A10 into Stretham

The 17th-century village inn has accommodation in the main house or in a modern annexe. Public areas include two bustling bars, one with satellite television, and the larger lounge bar encompassing a family conservatory-restaurant.

Facilities 5 en suite 6 annexe en suite (3 fmly) (3 GF) ⊗ in bedrooms ⊗ in dining room ⊗ in lounges TVB tea/coffee Cen ht TVL Dinner Last d 9pm **Prices** S fr £40; d fr £40; (room only) ✳ **Parking** 14

♦♦♦ 🅰

Bury House

11 Main St, Little Downham CB6 2ST
☎ 01353 698766 & 07748 378198 ▤ 01353 698089
Dir 2m NW of Ely on B1411 in Little Downham
Facilities 2 rms (1 fmly) ⊗ TVB tea/coffee ✖ Cen ht TVL No coaches **Prices** d fr £50✳ **Parking** 3 **Notes** ⊛

HILTON
MAP 12 TL26

♦♦♦♦ ⌨

Prince of Wales

Potton Rd PE28 9NG ☎ 01480 830257 ▤ 01480 830257
Dir A14 onto B1040 towards Biggleswade, 2m into village, Prince of Wales on left

The popular village inn offers a choice of cosy traditional bars serving good food and real ales. The en suite bedrooms vary in size and come well equipped.

Facilities 4 en suite TVB tea/coffee Direct dial from bedrooms ✖ Cen ht No children 5yrs Pool Table Dinner Last d 8.45pm **Parking** 12

HUNTINGDON
MAP 12 TL27

♦♦♦ ☕ ⌨

The Three Horseshoes

Moat Ln, Abbots Ripton PE28 2PD
☎ 01487 773440 ▤ 01487 773440
e-mail abbotsripton@aol.com
web www.thethreehorseshoes.com
Dir 3m N of Huntingdon. Off B1090 in Abbots Ripton

The thatched village inn has been extended to provide bedrooms with modern facilities in converted outbuildings, and a restaurant serving fine food. Cask-conditioned beers, log fires, and a super local atmosphere characterise the main bar.

Facilities 3 en suite 2 annexe en suite (1 fmly) (4 GF) ⊗ in bedrooms ⊗ in dining room TVB tea/coffee ✖ Cen ht No coaches Dinner Last d 9.30pm **Prices** S £55; D £70✳ **Parking** 80

KIMBOLTON
MAP 12 TL16

♦♦♦♦

Apothecary

1 St Andrews Ln PE28 0HN ☎ 01480 860352
e-mail pippataylor@dsl.pipex.com
Dir Off High St next to church

This 16th-century former pharmacy stands next to the village church with its renowned Tiffany window. The smart bedrooms are thoughtfully equipped and breakfast is served at a large table in the delightful dining hall, which retains original stone floors and exposed beams.

Facilities 3 rms (2 en suite) (1 pri facs) (3 fmly) ⊗ TVB tea/coffee ✖ Cen ht No coaches **Prices** S £35-£60; d £50-£65 **Notes** ⊛

KIRTLING
MAP 12 TL65

♦♦♦ 🍃

Hill Farm Guest House ◇ (TL685585)

CB8 9HQ ☎ 01638 730253 ▤ 01638 731957 Mrs Bailey
Dir 0.5m NW of Kirtling

Located on arable land south of Newmarket, in the heart of horse-breeding country, this 400-year-old property retains many original features. Public areas are furnished in keeping with the building's character, and hearty breakfasts are served at a family table in the elegant dining room.

Facilities 3 rms (2 en suite) ⊗ TVB tea/coffee Direct dial from bedrooms Cen ht TVL ♞ Games room 500 acres arable **Prices** S £30; D £55✳ **LB Parking** 15 **Notes** ⊛

PETERBOROUGH

MAP 12 TL19

◆◆◆

Aaron Park Hotel

109 Pk Road PE1 2TR ☎ 01733 564849 🖹 01733 564855
e-mail aaronparkhotel@yahoo.co.uk
Dir A1 onto A1139 to junct 5, to city centre on Boongate, over rdbt onto Crawthorne Rd, over lights, next left

Family service is both friendly and helpful at this Victorian house, which is in a tree-lined avenue just a short walk from the city centre and cathedral. Bedrooms come in a variety of styles and sizes; each room is nicely presented and has a good range of modern facilities. Freshly cooked breakfasts are carefully presented and provide a good start to the day.

Facilities 10 en suite (3 fmly) (2 GF) ⊗ STV TVB tea/coffee ✕ Cen ht
No coaches **Prices** S £47; D £59✻ **Parking** 8 **Notes** Closed Xmas

ST NEOTS

MAP 12 TL16

◆◆◆◆

Agden Hill Farm

Agden Gn, Great Staughton PE19 5EX
☎ 01480 869424 🖹 01480 860996
Dir 4.5m NW of St Neots off B645

Dating from the 18th century, this extended farmhouse stands amid 100 acres of arable farmland near Grafham Water, well known for its wildlife, fishing, sailing and cycling. The charming proprietors provide a very warm welcome, making every effort to put you at ease, while providing helpful service and good food. There are spacious lounges, a stylish dining room, and the bedrooms vary in style. Smoking is allowed only in one lounge and the property is not suited to young children.

Facilities 2 rms 2 annexe en suite (2 GF) ⊗ in bedrooms ⊗ in dining room TV3B tea/coffee ✕ Cen ht TVL No children 11yrs No coaches
Dinner Last d 9.30pm **Prices** D £70-£85 **LB** **Conf** Max 10 Class 10
Board 8 **Parking** 20 **Notes** ⊠

STETCHWORTH

MAP 12 TL65

◆◆◆◆

The Old Mill

Mill Ln CB8 9TR ☎ 01638 507839
e-mail gbell839@aol.com
Dir In village centre off Tea Kettle Ln

Situated in a delightful village, the accommodation comprises a thoughtfully equipped, self-contained flat sleeping four, with a small kitchen, quality pine furniture and a DVD player. Access is via a private staircase leading to a sun terrace overlooking mature gardens. Breakfast is served at a large communal table in the main house.

Facilities 1 annexe en suite ⊗ in bedrooms TVB tea/coffee ✕ TVL
No coaches **Parking** 2 **Notes** ⊠

TOFT

MAP 12 TL35

◆◆◆◆

Orchard Farmhouse *(TL362561)*

56 Comberton Rd CB3 7RY
☎ 01223 262309 🖹 01223 263979 Jane Tebbit
e-mail tebbit.bxb.toft@talk21.com
Dir B1046 to Toft. Opposite road to Harwick

This imposing traditional farmhouse has a delightful village setting amid well-nurtured grounds. Bedrooms are spacious and much care has gone into furnishing them. A cosy lounge comes complete with a television and a large selection of reading material, while a hearty, freshly made breakfast can be enjoyed in the conservatory in fine weather.

Facilities 3 en suite ⊗ TVB tea/coffee ✕ Cen ht TVL Golf 🐾
Prices S £35-£45; D £55-£65✻ **Parking** 5 **Notes** Closed 24-25 Dec ⊠

WILBURTON

MAP 12 TL47

◆◆◆◆

Sharps Farm

Twentypence Rd CB6 3PU
☎ 01353 740360 🖹 01353 740360
e-mail sharpsfarm@yahoo.com
web www.sharpsfarm.co.uk
Dir Off A1123 in Wilburton onto B1049 for 0.3m, signed on left after s-bend

Sharps Farm lies in substantial grounds south of Wilburton. A warm welcome is assured at the family home and you are encouraged to walk in the pastures and visit the horses. Tasty, freshly prepared breakfasts are served around one large communal table in the conservatory-style dining room.

Facilities 3 rms (2 en suite) (1 pri facs) (1 fmly) (2 GF) ⊗ in bedrooms
⊗ in dining room ⊗ in lounges TVB tea/coffee ✕ Cen ht No coaches
Dinner Last d 5pm **Parking** 6 **Notes** ⊠

England

WILLINGHAM
MAP 12 TL47

U

Willingham House

50 Church St CB4 5HT ☎ 01954 260606 🖷 01954 260603
e-mail info@cimcol.com
web www.cimcol.com
Dir *From A14 at junct 29, turn onto B1050 to Willingham*

At the time of going to press the rating for this establishment had not been confirmed. Please check the AA website www.theAA.com for up-to-date information.

Facilities 16 en suite 6 annexe en suite (7 GF) ⊗ in bedrooms ⊗ in area of dining room ⊗ in 1 lounge TVB tea/coffee Direct dial from bedrooms ✱ Licensed Cen ht TVL Pool Table Dinner Last d 9.30pm **Prices** S £50-£110; D £68-£135✳ **LB** **Conf** Max 40 Thtr 40 Class 23 Board 24 **Parking** available

CHESHIRE

AUDLEM
MAP 15 SJ64

♦♦♦♦ ♥

Little Heath Farm ◇ *(SJ663455)*

CW3 0HE ☎ 01270 811324 Mrs Bennion
e-mail hilaryandbob@ukonline.co.uk
Dir *Off A525 in village onto A529 for 0.3m*

The 200-year-old brick farmhouse retains much original character, including low beamed ceilings. The traditionally furnished public areas include a cosy sitting room and a dining room where you dine family style. The refurbished bedrooms are stylish, and the friendly proprietors create a relaxing atmosphere.

Facilities 3 en suite (1 fmly) ⊗ TVB tea/coffee Cen ht TVL 50 acres beef dairy mixed. Dinner Last d 10am **Prices** S £28-£35; D £50-£60 **LB** **Conf** Max 10 Board 10 Del from £70 **Parking** 6 **Notes** Closed Xmas & New Year ⊠

Book as early as possible, particularly in the peak holiday period

BURWARDSLEY
MAP 15 SJ55

♦♦♦♦ ♥

Sandhollow Farm B&B *(SJ511563)*

Harthill Rd CH3 9NU ☎ 01829 770894 Mr & Mrs Stafford
e-mail paul.kickdrum@tiscali.co.uk

The converted farmhouse has spectacular views of the Cheshire plain and Welsh hills. Bedrooms have been carefully renovated and there is a comfortable lounge with a log fire. Substantial breakfasts using organic, home-made and local produce are served in the adjoining dining room with views across the garden and surrounding countryside.

Facilities 3 en suite (1 GF) ⊗ TVB tea/coffee ✱ Cen ht No children 12yrs 2 acres Non-Working **Prices** S £45; D £60✳ **LB** **Parking** 4 **Notes** Closed Xmas & annual holiday

CHESTER
MAP 15 SJ46
See also **Malpas**

★★★ Inn

George & Dragon

1 Liverpool Rd CH2 1AA
☎ 01244 380714 🖷 01244 390694
e-mail 7783@greeneking.co.uk
Dir *100yds from Northgate St fountains rdbt and the city centre*

This large, busy and popular pub is within easy reach of the city centre. It provides modern accommodation and a variety of bedrooms. A wide choice of food is served throughout the day and evening in the bar.

Facilities 14 en suite (3 fmly) STV TVB tea/coffee ✱ No children Pool Table Dinner Last d 9pm **Prices** S £43-£53; D £85-£95✳ **LB** **Parking** 16

★★★ Inn

Oaklands ◇

93 Hoole Rd CH2 3NB ☎ 01244 345528 🖷 01244 322156
e-mail 7878@greeneking.co.uk
Dir *A56 into Chester, Hoole Rd, 0.5m on left*

This busy and popular pub is convenient for the city centre and the M56 Motorway. It provides modern accommodation, and a wide range of food is available in the open-plan bar and dining area.

Facilities 14 rms (12 en suite) (1 fmly) (4 GF) TVB tea/coffee ✱ TVL No children No coaches Dinner Last d 9pm **Prices** S £25-£40; D £55; (room only) ✳ **LB** **Conf** Max 18 Board 18 **Parking** 40

England

Premier Collection

♦♦♦♦♦

Chester Stone Villa Hotel

Stone Pl, Hoole Rd CH2 3NR
☎ 01244 345014 📠 01244 345015
e-mail enquiries@stonevillahotel.co.uk
web www.stonevillahotel.co.uk
Dir 0.5m NE of city centre off A56 Hoole Rd

The attractive stone property offers stylish en suite bedrooms, all thoughtfully equipped. Freshly cooked breakfasts are served in the elegant dining room, and there is a small lounge area and a private car park. Attentive friendly service is a highlight.

Facilities 10 en suite (4 fmly) (3 GF) ⊗ STV FTV TVB tea/coffee Direct dial from bedrooms ✖ Cen ht No coaches **Prices** S £45-£50; D £70-£80✱ LB **Parking** 10

♦♦♦♦♦ 🅰

Mitchell's of Chester

28 Hough Gn CH4 8JQ ☎ 01244 679004 📠 01244 659567
e-mail mitoches@dialstart.net
web www.mitchellsofchester.com
Dir 1m SW of city centre. A483 onto A5104, 300yds on right in Hough Green

Facilities 7 en suite (2 fmly) (1 GF) ⊗ in bedrooms ⊗ in dining room TVB tea/coffee ✖ Cen ht TVL No coaches **Prices** S £40-£48; D £65-£70 LB **Parking** 5 **Notes** Closed 21-29 Dec

♦♦♦♦

Alton Lodge Hotel

78 Hoole Rd CH2 3NT ☎ 01244 310213 📠 01244 319206
e-mail reception@altonlodge.co.uk
web www.altonlodge.co.uk
Dir M53 junct 12, A56 into Chester, house 0.5m on right opp playing field

This renovated and extended Edwardian property is between the ring road and the city centre. The lodge-style bedrooms are thoughtfully equipped and furnished with quality pine furniture. The bright public areas include a comfortable bar-lounge and an attractive dining room. Dinner is available Monday to Thursday.

Facilities 4 en suite 13 annexe en suite (2 fmly) ⊗ in bedrooms ⊗ in dining room TVB tea/coffee Direct dial from bedrooms ✖ Licensed Cen ht TVL No coaches Dinner Last d 9pm **Prices** S £68-£98; D £98-£128✱ LB **Parking** 22 **Notes** Closed Xmas/New Year rs Fri-Sun (bar & restaurant closed)

♦♦♦♦

Cheltenham Lodge

68 Hoole Rd, Hoole CH2 3NL ☎ 01244 346767
Dir 1m NE of city centre on A56, opp All Saints Church

The small guest house lies midway between the city centre and M53. Its attractive modern bedrooms, which include some on the ground floor and a family room, are well equipped, and a substantial breakfast is served in the smart dining room.

continued

Facilities 5 en suite (2 fmly) ⊗ in 3 bedrooms ⊗ in dining room ⊗ in lounges TVB tea/coffee ✖ Cen ht **Parking** 5 **Notes** Closed 23 Dec-7 Jan 🐾

♦♦♦♦

Golborne Manor

Platts Ln, Hatton Heath CH3 9AN
☎ 01829 770310 & 07774 695268 📠 01829 770370
e-mail info@golbornemanor.co.uk
web www.golbornemanor.co.uk
Dir 5m SE of Chester. Off A41 onto Platts Ln, 400yds on left

The elegant Edwardian house stands in beautiful gardens with spectacular views across open countryside. Accommodation is in spacious bedrooms with either brass bedsteads or a richly carved antique Arabian bed. Breakfast is served around a large table in the dining room, and there is also a comfortable lounge.

Facilities 3 en suite (1 fmly) ⊗ TVB tea/coffee ✖ Cen ht 🏓 table tennis Dinner **Conf** Max 10 **Parking** 6 **Notes** rs wknds 🐾

♦♦♦♦

Green Gables

11 Eversley Pk CH2 2AJ ☎ 01244 372243 📠 01244 376352
e-mail perruzza_d@hotmail.com
Dir Off A5116 Liverpool Rd signed Countess of Chester Hospital, right at 3rd pedestrian lights to Eversley Park

The attractive Victorian house, set in pretty gardens, is in a quiet residential area close to the city centre. The well-equipped bedrooms include a family room, and there is a choice of sitting rooms. The bright breakfast room is strikingly decorated.

Facilities 2 en suite (1 fmly) ⊗ TVB tea/coffee Direct dial from bedrooms ✖ Cen ht TVL **Prices** S £36-£52; D £52✱ **Parking** 10 **Notes** 🐾

CHESTER continued

◆◆◆◆
Greenwalls B & B
Whitchurch Rd, Waverton CH3 7PB
☎ 01244 336799 & 332124 📠 01244 332124
e-mail jmitchellgreenwalls@hotmail.com
Dir 3m SE of city centre on A41 near Waverton

Greenwalls is an attractive Victorian home with many original features, and is a good base for business or leisure, being near the Chester park and ride. The spacious bedrooms are well equipped and the comfortable lounge has a log fire. Hearty breakfasts featuring home-made bread are served in the attractive dining room.

Facilities 2 rms (1 en suite) (1 pri facs) (1 GF) ⊗ TVB tea/coffee 🦮 Cen ht TVL No children 5yrs No coaches Golf 18 **Parking** 8

◆◆◆◆
Lavender Lodge ◇
46 Hoole Rd CH2 3NL ☎ 01244 323204 📠 01244 329821
e-mail bookings@lavenderlodge.co.uk
web www.lavenderlodge.com
Dir 1m NE of city centre on A56, opp All Saints' Church

A warm welcome is assured at this smart late Victorian house located within easy walking distance of central attractions. The bedrooms are equipped with thoughtful extras and have modern bathrooms. Quality breakfasts are served in the attractive dining room.

Facilities 5 en suite (2 fmly) ⊗ TVB tea/coffee 🦮 Cen ht
Prices S £30-£40; D £65-£80✱ LB **Parking** 7 **Notes** Closed 24 Dec-2 Jan

◆◆◆◆
The Mount
Lesters Ln, Higher Kinnerton CH4 9BQ
☎ 01244 660275 📠 01244 660275
e-mail major@mountkinnerton.freeserve.co.uk
web www.bandbchester.com
Dir 6m SW of Chester. A5104 W over A55, 1st left towards Higher Kinnerton

The Mount is an elegant Victorian house set in extensive grounds and gardens. Bedrooms and public areas are furnished with fine period pieces and have a host of thoughtful extras. The friendly hosts provide a relaxing atmosphere, and the house is convenient for exploring Chester and north Wales.

Facilities 3 en suite ⊗ TVB tea/coffee 🦮 Cen ht No children 12yrs No coaches ⚬ 🐾 **Parking** 10 **Notes** Closed 22 Dec-6 Jan 🐾

◆◆◆◆
The Rowton Poplars Hotel
Whitchurch Rd, Rowton CH3 6AF
☎ 01244 333010 📠 01244 333020
e-mail val@rowtonpoplars.co.uk
Dir 2m SE of Chester. A55 onto A41 for Whitchurch, premises before filling station

The stylish Victorian house has been converted into a friendly, family-run establishment convenient for visiting Chester. Bedrooms are well equipped and downstairs there is a comfortable lounge and a bar. Dinner is available by arrangement and meals are served in the attractive dining room.

Facilities 8 en suite (4 fmly) ⊗ in 6 bedrooms ⊗ in area of dining room ⊗ in lounges TVB tea/coffee Direct dial from bedrooms Licensed Cen h TVL Dinner Last d 8.15pm **Prices** S £55-£65; D £65-£75 LB
Conf Max 18 **Parking** 30

See advertisement on opposite page

◆◆◆◆
Summerhill Bed & Breakfast ◇
4 Greenfield Ln, Hoole Village CH2 2PA
☎ 01244 400020 & 400334
e-mail capricorn@taurusuk.net
Dir 1.5m NE of city centre. A56 onto A41, 1st right

Summerhill is a converted Edwardian house with comfortable, well-equipped accommodation. The helpful owners provide a friendly atmosphere and hearty breakfasts in the attractive dining room.

Facilities 4 en suite (1 fmly) ⊗ TVB tea/coffee 🦮 Cen ht No children 8yrs No coaches **Prices** S £26-£30; D £56-£70✱ LB **Parking** 4

◆◆◆
Chester Brooklands
8 Newton Ln CH2 3RB ☎ 01244 348856 📠 01244 348856
e-mail enquiries@chester-bandb.co.uk
web www.chester-bandb.co.uk
Dir M53 junct 12, A56 towards city, 1m right onto Newton Ln, B&B o right

Located in a mainly residential area close to Hoole village centre, this well-presented house has been carefully renovated to provide a rang of thoughtfully furnished bedrooms with modern shower rooms en suite. Breakfast is served in the attractive dining room and a warm welcome is assured.

Facilities 5 en suite (1 fmly) ⊗ TVB tea/coffee 🦮 Cen ht
Prices S £42-£70; D £55-£80✱ LB **Parking** 5

◆◆◆
Chester House ◇
44 Hoole Rd, Hoole CH2 3NL
☎ 01244 348410 📠 01244 348856
e-mail chesterhouse@chester-bandb.co.uk
web www.chester-bandb.co.uk/chester-house
Dir 1m NE of city centre on A56

The small guest house lies on the eastern approach to the city. The smart bedrooms are well equipped and there is a light, attractive breakfast room.

continue

Facilities 8 en suite (3 fmly) (4 GF) ⊗ TVB tea/coffee ✱ Cen ht
Prices S £30-£44; D £45-£65 **LB** **Parking** 5

◆◆◆

The Glann Hotel
Stone Pl CH2 3NR ☎ 01244 344800
e-mail reception@theglannhotel.co.uk
Dir 0.5m NE of city centre off A56 Hoole Rd

Located in a quiet cul-de-sac in the fashionable Hoole district, this renovated Victorian house has a range of thoughtfully furnished bedrooms with modern shower rooms. Comprehensive breakfasts are served in the spacious dining room, which includes a lounge bar section. Large private car park.

Facilities 10 rms (9 en suite) (2 fmly) (1 GF) ⊗ in 8 bedrooms ⊗ in dining room ⊗ in lounges TVB tea/coffee ✱ Licensed Cen ht TVL No coaches **Parking** 10

◆◆◆

Glen Garth
59 Hoole Rd CH2 3NJ ☎ 01244 310260 🖷 01244 310260
e-mail glengarth@chester63.fsnet.co.uk
Dir 0.5m NE of city centre on A56

Situated within easy walking distance of the city, the family-run Glen Garth provides well-equipped bedrooms and hearty breakfasts served in the pleasant rear dining room. Friendly, attentive service is a strength here.

Facilities 5 rms (3 en suite) (2 pri facs) (3 fmly) ⊗ TVB tea/coffee ✱ Cen ht No coaches **Prices** D £50-£75✱ **LB** **Parking** 5 **Notes** 🚭

CHOLMONDELEY   MAP 15 SJ55

◆◆◆ 🍽 🍷

Cholmondeley Arms
SY14 8HN ☎ 01829 720300 🖷 01829 720123
e-mail guy@cholmondeleyarms.co.uk
Dir On A49 x-rds near Cholmondeley Castle

Complete with raftered ceilings and open fires, this former village school has been renovated to provide spacious public areas furnished in rustic style, the setting for imaginative food and good wines. Bedrooms are in a separate house, once the headmaster's residence.

Facilities 6 en suite (1 fmly) (3 GF) ⊗ in bedrooms ⊗ in area of dining room ⊗ in 1 lounge TVB tea/coffee Direct dial from bedrooms Cen ht Dinner Last d 10pm **Parking** 60

England

CONGLETON

MAP 16 SJ86

◆◆◆◆ ◧

Egerton Arms Hotel

Astbury village CW12 4RQ
☎ 01260 273946 📠 01260 277273
e-mail egertonastbury@totalise.co.uk
Dir 1.5m SW of Congleton off A34, by St Mary's Church

This traditional country inn stands opposite the church in the pretty
village of Astbury. The creative, good-value menus in the bars and
restaurant attract a strong local following, and the bedrooms have
been refurbished to provide high standards of comfort and facilities.

Facilities 6 en suite ⊛ in bedrooms ⊛ in dining room ⊛ in 1 lounge
TVB tea/coffee ✖ Cen ht No coaches Golf & fishing can be arranged
Dinner Last d 9pm **LB** **Conf** Max 40 Thtr 40 Class 30 Board 20
Parking 100

◆◆◆◆ **A**

Sandhole Farm

Hulme Walfield CW12 2JH
☎ 01260 224419 📠 01260 224766
e-mail veronica@sandholefarm.co.uk
Dir 2m N of Congleton on A34, left down drive

Facilities 2 en suite 15 annexe en suite (3 fmly) (7 GF) ⊛ TVB
tea/coffee Direct dial from bedrooms Cen ht TVL **Prices** S £52-£55;
D £62-£65✱ **Conf** Thtr 160 Class 80 Board 50 **Parking** 50 **Notes** rs wk
at Xmas (self-catering only) Civ Wed 150

KNUTSFORD

MAP 15 SJ77

◆◆◆◆

The Hinton

Town Ln, Mobberley WA16 7HH
☎ 01565 873484 📠 01565 873484
e-mail the.hinton@virgin.net
Dir 1m NE on B5085 in Mobberley

This well-proportioned house offers a range of comfortable bedrooms
with thoughtful extras. Comprehensive breakfasts, and dinners by
arrangement, are served in the attractive dining room and a lounge is
available.

Facilities 6 en suite (1 fmly) ⊛ FTV TVB tea/coffee ✖ Licensed
Cen ht No coaches Dinner Last d Morning **Prices** S fr £44; d fr £58✱
Parking 8

◆◆◆◆

Old Vicarage

Moss Ln, Over Tabley WA16 0PL
☎ 01565 652221 📠 01565 755918
e-mail normaweston@aol.com
Dir 2m NW of Knutsford. M6 junct 19, A556 N, right after Little Chef
onto Moss Ln

The Old Vicarage is a charming 19th-century house set in 2 acres of
landscaped wooded grounds and gardens. Bedrooms are attractively
furnished, and there is a golf practice area and croquet lawn.

Facilities 4 en suite (1 fmly) (1 GF) ⊛ TVB tea/coffee ✖ Licensed
Cen ht TVL No children 12yrs Arrangements with 2 golf courses Last
d 9pm **Prices** S £52; D £68✱ **Parking** 50 **Notes** Closed 2-18 Jan

◆◆◆◆ ◧

The Dog Inn

Well Bank Ln, Over Peover WA16 8UP
☎ 01625 861421 📠 01625 864800
e-mail info@doginn-overpeover.co.uk
web www.doginn-overpeover.co.uk
Dir 4m SE of Knutsford. Off A50 at Whipping Stocks 2m to Peover
Heath

Nestling in Cheshire countryside, the front of the popular 18th-century
inn is adorned with hanging baskets and tubs. The attractive
bedrooms have many extras, while the lounge bar and restaurant offer
a wide selection of ales and an extensive all-day menu using local
produce.

Facilities 6 en suite ⊛ TVB tea/coffee Direct dial from bedrooms ✖
Cen ht Pool Table Dinner Last d 9pm **Prices** S £45-£60; D £75-£80✱
Parking 80

◆◆◆◆ ⊜

Laburnum Cottage

Knutsford Rd, Mobberley WA16 7PU
☎ 01565 872464 📠 01565 872464
Dir 1m NE of Knutsford on B5085 towards Mobberley

Set in attractive gardens, the cottage-style property is within easy reach
of the M6, M56 and Manchester Airport. The attractive bedrooms are
thoughtfully equipped, and imaginative and carefully prepared
evening meals are available by arrangement. There is also a
comfortable lounge.

Facilities 5 en suite ⊛ TVB tea/coffee Cen ht TVL No coaches Dinner
Last d 3pm **Parking** 6

◆◆◆◆

Rose Cottage Guest House

Newton Hall Ln, Mobberley WA16 7LL
☎ 01565 872430 📠 01565 880014
e-mail info@rose-cottage-guesthouse.com
web www.rose-cottage-guesthouse.com
Dir 3m NE of Knutsford. B5085 E through Mobberley, at Bird in
Hand pub left onto Newton Hall Ln, 0.5m on right

Standing in extensive mature gardens on the outskirts of Mobberley,
the Victorian house offers bedrooms with thoughtful extras in a
extension. Comprehensive breakfasts are served in an attractive
lounge-dining room overlooking a wildlife pond.

Facilities 3 en suite (2 GF) ⊛ TVB tea/coffee ✖ Cen ht No children
12yrs No coaches Fishing **Prices** S £49; D £59✱ **LB** **Parking** 10
Notes Closed 24 Dec-1 Jan

continued

England

LOWER WITHINGTON

MAP 15 SJ86

Jolly Tree Farm (SJ802709)

Holmes Chapel Rd SK11 9DT
☎ 01477 571257 ▤ 01477 571257 Mrs Venables
Dir Situated on main A535 Holmes Chapel Rd, directly in front of Jodrell Bank

At the time of going to press the rating for this establishment had not been confirmed. Please check the AA website www.theAA.com for up-to-date information.

Facilities 3 en suite (1 fmly) ⊗ TVB tea/coffee ✗ Cen ht TVL
90 acres Beef, sheep & poultry **Prices** S £35-£40; D £55-£70✳ **LB**
Parking 3 **Notes** ⊛

MACCLESFIELD

MAP 16 SJ97

See also **Rainow**

◆◆◆ A

Penrose Guest House ◇

56 Birtles Rd, Whirley SK10 3JQ
☎ 01625 615323 & 0776 545 3226 ▤ 01625 432284
e-mail pb@penroseguesthouse.co.uk
web www.penroseguesthouse.co.uk
Dir 1.5m W of town centre. A537 W to Broken Cross, onto Fallibroome Rd, left onto Priory Ln, 1st left

Facilities 3 rms ⊗ TVB tea/coffee ✗ Cen ht No children 7yrs
No coaches Golf 18 **Prices** S £25-£35; D £50-£70✳ **LB Parking** 5

MALPAS

MAP 15 SJ44

Premier Collection

◆◆◆◆ ▣

Tilston Lodge

Tilston SY14 7DR ☎ 01829 250223 ▤ 01829 250223
Dir 3m NW of Malpas in Tilston village

This impressive Victorian hunting lodge stands in 16 acres of rolling orchards and pasture, which are home to rare breeds of sheep and poultry. The spacious bedrooms are furnished with fine period pieces and a wealth of thoughtful extras. Ground-floor areas overlook immaculate gardens, and a choice of lounges is available in addition to the elegant dining room, the setting for memorable breakfasts.

Facilities 3 en suite (1 fmly) ⊗ TVB tea/coffee ✗ Cen ht TVL
No coaches ♨ Hot tub **Prices** S £45-£50; D £70-£80 **LB Parking** 8
Notes ⊛

◆◆◆◆ ❦

Hampton House ◇ (SJ505496)

Stevensons Ln, Hampton SY14 8JS
☎ 01948 820588 ▤ 01948 820588 Mrs Sarginson
e-mail enquiries@hamptonhousefarm.co.uk
Dir 2m NE of Malpas. Off A41 onto Cholmondeley Rd, next left

Parts of this house are reputed to date from 1600. It is located on a quiet dairy farm and offers thoughtfully appointed accommodation and a warm welcome.

Facilities 3 rms (1 en suite) (2 pri facs) ⊗ tea/coffee ✗ Cen ht TVL
No children 14yrs 180 acres Dairy **Prices** S £30-£35; D £50-£60✳
Parking 10 **Notes** ⊛

◆◆◆◆ ❦

Millmoor Farm ◇ (SJ518475)

Nomansheath SY14 8DY ☎ 01948 820304 Mrs Chesters
e-mail bookings@millmoorfarm.co.uk
Dir 2m E of Malpas. Off A41 into No Mans Heath, left at minirdbt in village, farm signed after 0.5m

Set in attractive gardens on a beef and dairy farm near Nomansheath, parts of this modernised farmhouse date from the late 17th century. Bedrooms include one with a four-poster bed and some within a cottage, used also for self-catering. The attractive lounge-dining room has a welcoming log fire in the cooler months.

Facilities 3 rms (2 en suite) (1 pri facs) ⊗ TVB tea/coffee Cen ht
Fishing 270 acres dairy & beef Dinner Last d noon **Prices** S £25-£30;
D £44-£50✳ **LB Conf** Max 12 Board 12 **Parking** 11 **Notes** ⊛

A

Mill House & Granary ◇

Mill House, Higher Wych SY14 7JR
☎ 01948 780362 ▤ 01948 780566
e-mail angela@videoactive.co.uk
web www.millhouseandgranary.co.uk
Dir 3m S of Malpas. A41 onto B5395, next left by bus shelter, Mill House 1m on left

Facilities 3 rms (2 en suite) ⊗ in dining room TVB tea/coffee ✗
Cen ht TVL No coaches Dinner Last d 6pm **Prices** S £25-£30;
D £44-£50✳ **Parking** 6 **Notes** ★★★ Closed Dec ⊛

England

NANTWICH
MAP 15 SJ65

See also **Wybunbury**

★★★★ Guest House
Oakland House
252 Newcastle Rd, Blakelow, Shavington CW5 7ET
☎ 01270 567134
e-mail enquiries@oaklandhouseonline.co.uk
Dir 2m E of Nantwich. Off A500 into Shavington, house 500yds W of village

Oakland House offers a friendly and relaxed atmosphere. Bedrooms, some of which are in a separate chalet, are attractively furnished and well equipped. There is a spacious sitting room and a modern conservatory overlooks the pretty garden and Cheshire countryside. A substantial breakfast is served around one large table.

Facilities 3 en suite 6 annexe en suite (1 fmly) (6 GF) ⊗ TVB tea/coffee Cen ht TVL No coaches **Prices** S £34-£39; D £49-£54✱ LB **Parking** 13

NORTHWICH
MAP 15 SJ67

◆◆◆

The Coachman
286 Chester Rd, Hartford CW8 1QU
☎ 01606 871359 📠 01606 871359
e-mail coachmanhotel1@aol.com
web www.the-coachman.co.uk
Dir On A559 1m SW of centre of Hartford Village

Located on the outskirts of Hartford village near the railway station, this renovated inn provides cosy lounge areas and serves food during the day. The thoughtfully equipped, pine-furnished bedrooms are in converted stables and one has been adapted for easier access.

Facilities 5 en suite (1 fmly) (5 GF) ⊗ in bedrooms ⊗ in area of dining room ⊗ in 1 lounge TVB tea/coffee ✖ Cen ht No coaches Pool Table Dinner Last d 6pm **Prices** D £40-£50; (room only) ✱ **Parking** 50

Please mention the AA B&B Guide when booking your stay

RAINOW
MAP 16 SJ97

◆◆◆◆ ♥

Common Barn Farm B & B (SJ965764)
Smith Ln SK10 5XJ
☎ 01625 574878 & 07779 816098 Mrs Cooper
e-mail g_greengrass@hotmail.com
web www.cottages-with-a-view.co.uk
Dir Through Rainow on B5470 towards Whaley Bridge, turn right into Smith Ln, B&B 0.5m on right

Located high in the Peninnes and straddling the border of Cheshire and the Peak district, this brand new barn conversion provides a popular destination for walkers. Bedrooms are spacious and stylish and all bathrooms offer modern power showers. A conservatory lounge encourages total relaxation while enjoying stunning views. Hearty breakfasts are as memorable as the warmth of welcome. A coffee shop during the day provides light snacks and home-baked fare.

Facilities 5 annexe en suite (1 fmly) (3 GF) ⊗ TVB tea/coffee ✖ Cen ht TVL Fishing Clay pigeon shooting on request 250 acres Sheep **Prices** S fr £35; d fr £56 **Conf** Max 25 **Parking** 30

TARPORLEY
MAP 15 SJ5◼

★★★ 🅰 Inn
Foresters Arms
92 High St CW6 0AX ☎ 01829 733151 📠 01829 730020
e-mail stuart@forestersarms.fsbusiness.co.uk
Dir Off A49 into village centre

Facilities 5 rms (4 en suite) ⊗ TVB tea/coffee ✖ Licensed Cen ht No children 10yrs No coaches Pool Table Dinner Last d 8.30pm **Prices** S £37.50; D £50✱ **Parking** 20

◆◆◆◆

Alvanley Arms Inn
Forest Rd, Cotebrook CW6 9DS ☎ 01829 760200
web www.alvanleyarms.co.uk
Dir 2m NE of Tarporley on A49 in Cotebrook

Records show that there has been a pub on this site since the 16th century, and renovations have uncovered original beams in some of the stylish, well-equipped bedrooms. Wide-ranging menus are available in the cosy bars, and the adjoining Shire Horse Centre and Countryside Park is popular with families. Delamere Forest Park and Oulton Park race circuit are nearby.

continue

Facilities 7 en suite ⊕ in bedrooms ⊕ in dining room TVB tea/coffee ✗ Cen ht No coaches free entry to Shire Horse Centre for residents Dinner Last d 9pm **Prices** S £40-£55; D £70-£80✳ **Parking** 70

♦♦♦♦ ❦

Haycroft ◇ (SJ554573)

Peckforton Hall Ln, Spurstow CW6 9TF
☎ 01829 260389 Mr Spencer
e-mail richard.a.spencer@talk21.com
web www.haycroftfarm.co.uk
Dir 4m S of Tarporley. Off A49 at Spurstow x-rds onto Peckforton Hall Lane, 100yds right at x-rds, farm at end

Haycroft is a traditional house on a working farm. The comfortable accommodation is carefully decorated and well equipped, and hearty breakfasts are served in the beamed dining room with its wood-burning stove. There is also a comfortable lounge and an attractive garden.

Facilities 3 rms (1 fmly) (1 GF) ⊕ TVB tea/coffee Cen ht TVL 166 acres Mixed **Prices** S £30-£40; d fr £57.50 **Parking** 6

♦♦♦♦

Hill House Farm

Rushton CW6 9AU ☎ 01829 732238 📠 01829 733929
e-mail rayner@hillhousefarm.fsnet.co.uk
web www.hillhousefarm.info
Dir 1.5m E of Tarporley. Off A51/A49 to Eaton, continue E for Rushton, right onto The Hall Ln, farm 0.5m

This impressive brick farmhouse stands in very attractive gardens within 14 acres of rolling pastureland. The stylish bedrooms have en suites or private facilities, and there is a spacious lounge and a traditionally furnished breakfast room. The proprietors are especially friendly.

Facilities 3 en suite (1 fmly) ⊕ TVB tea/coffee Cen ht TVL No coaches **Prices** S £35-£40; D £60-£65✳ **LB** **Parking** 6 **Notes** Closed Xmas & New Year

TATTENHALL   MAP 15 SJ45

♦♦♦♦ ❦

Ivy Farm ◇ (SJ452555)

Ivy Farm, Coddington CH3 9EN
☎ 01829 782295 📠 01829 782583 Mrs Arden
Dir 3m SW of Tattenhall. Off A534 through Clutton to Coddington, farm opp fenced pond

This impressive creeper-clad 18th-century farmhouse stands in beautiful Cheshire countryside and is a convenient base for visiting

continued

north Wales and Chester. It has well-equipped bedrooms and comfortably furnished public areas. You can expect warm hospitality and good hearty breakfasts.

Facilities 3 rms (2 en suite) (1 fmly) ⊕ TVB tea/coffee ✗ Cen ht 75 acres beef **Prices** S £30; D £50-£55✳ **Parking** 6 **Notes** Closed Xmas & New Year ⊠

WARMINGHAM   MAP 15 SJ76

♦♦♦♦ ⬛

The Bear's Paw Hotel

School Ln CW11 3QN ☎ 01270 526317 & 526342
e-mail enquiries@thebearspaw.co.uk
Dir Off A530/A533, in village centre opp church

The very friendly inn offers a wide choice of well-prepared dishes in the restaurant, while the well-equipped bedrooms are generally spacious. The Bear's Paw is in a peaceful location in central Cheshire.

Facilities 12 en suite (1 fmly) ⊕ in dining room ⊕ in 1 lounge FTV TVB tea/coffee Direct dial from bedrooms ✗ Cen ht No coaches Pool Table Dinner Last d 9-9.30pm **Prices** S £60; D £75✳ **Parking** 60

WILMSLOW
See **Manchester Airport (Greater Manchester)**

WINSFORD   MAP 15 SJ66

♦♦♦ Ⓐ

The Winsford Lodge

85-87 Station Rd CW7 3DE
☎ 01606 862008 📠 01606 591822
e-mail winsfordlodge@aol.com
web www.winsfordlodge.co.uk
Dir Off A54 at rdbt by Winsford station onto Station Rd

Facilities 3 en suite 8 annexe en suite (2 fmly) (7 GF) ⊕ in bedrooms ⊕ in dining room ⊕ in lounges TVB tea/coffee ✗ Licensed Cen ht TVL No coaches Dinner Last d 11am **Prices** S £35-£39; D £45-£49; (room only) ✳ **Parking** 15

WYBUNBURY   MAP 15 SJ64

♦♦♦ ❦

Lea Farm ◇ (SJ717489)

Wrinehill Rd CW5 7NS
☎ 01270 841429 📠 01270 841030 Mrs Callwood
e-mail jean@leafarm.freeserve.co.uk
Dir 1m E of Wybunbury village church on unclassified road

The working dairy farm is surrounded by delightful gardens and beautiful Cheshire countryside. The spacious bedrooms have modern facilities, and the cosy lounge features a small snooker table. Hearty breakfasts are served in the attractive dining room, which looks out over the garden with resident peacocks.

Facilities 3 rms (2 en suite) (1 fmly) ⊕ TVB tea/coffee Cen ht TVL Fishing Pool Table 150 acres Dairy & beef **Prices** S £28-£32; D £48-£52 **Parking** 24 **Notes** ⊠

England

CORNWALL & ISLES OF SCILLY

BISSOE MAP 02 SW74

U

Higher Bissoe Cottage
TR4 8SX ☎ 01872 864668 🖹 01872 863398

At the time of going to press the rating for this establishment had not been confirmed. Please check the AA website www.theAA.com for up-to-date information.

Facilities 2 rms (1 en suite) (1 pri facs) ⊗ TVB Cen ht No children 12yrs No coaches **Notes** Closed Dec-Etr

BODMIN MAP 02 SX06

★★★ Guest Accommodation
Mount Pleasant Farm ◇
Mount PL30 4EX ☎ 01208 821342
e-mail info@mountpleasantcottages.co.uk
Dir A30 from Bodmin towards Launceston for 4m, right signed Millpool, continue 3m

Set in 10 acres, this is a wonderfully peaceful base from which to explore the delights of Cornwall. Originally a farmhouse dating back to the 17th-century, there is something here for all the family with extensive facilities including a games room and a heated swimming pool. The cosy bedrooms are well furnished, while public areas include a spacious sun lounge and extensive gardens. Breakfast, served in the well-appointed dining room, features local produce and is a highlight of a stay.

Facilities 6 en suite (3 fmly) ⊗ TVB tea/coffee ✖ Cen ht ch fac No coaches 🖹 Pool Table Games room Dinner Last d 10pm previous day **Prices** S £25-£35; D £50-£70 **LB** **Parking** 8 **Notes** 🐾

U

The Stables
The Stables at Welltown, Cardinham PL30 4EG
☎ 01208 821316 🖹 01208 821673
e-mail rogerdellaba@hotmail.com

At the time of going to press the rating for this establishment had not been confirmed. Please check the AA website www.theAA.com for up-to-date information.

Facilities 2 en suite ⊗ TVB tea/coffee ✖ Cen ht No coaches **Parking** 2 **Notes** 🐾

U

Tranack
26 Castle St PL31 2DU ☎ 01208 269095
e-mail sandrambutler@onetel.com
Dir A30 to St Petrocs church, 2nd exit at minirdbt, 1st right, 1st left, 150yds on left

At the time of going to press the rating for this establishment had not been confirmed. Please check the AA website www.theAA.com for up-to-date information.

Facilities 2 en suite ⊗ TV1B tea/coffee ✖ Cen ht No coaches **Notes** 🐾

BOSCASTLE MAP 02 SX09

◆◆◆◆

Old Coach House
Tintagel Rd PL35 0AS ☎ 01840 250398 🖹 01840 250346
e-mail parsons@old-coach.demon.co.uk
Dir In village at junct B3266 & B3263

Over 300 years old, the Old Coach House has lovely views over the village and rolling countryside. The pleasant bedrooms are well equipped and include two rooms on the ground floor. A hearty breakfast is served in the conservatory, which overlooks the well-kept garden.

Facilities 8 en suite (2 fmly) (2 GF) ⊗ TVB tea/coffee Cen ht TVL No coaches **Prices** S £38-£48; D £40-£48 **LB** **Parking** 9 **Notes** Closed Xmas

◆◆◆◆

Tolcarne House Hotel
Tintagel Rd PL35 0AS ☎ 01840 250654 🖹 01840 250654
e-mail crowntolhouse@eclipse.co.uk
Dir In village at junct B3266 & B3263

You are assured of a warm welcome at this substantial Victorian residence, set in delightful grounds and gardens at the top of the village. The stylish bedrooms have many extras, and there is a lounge with an open fire and a separate cosy bar. Evening meals, by arrangement, are served in the elegant dining room.

Facilities 8 en suite ⊗ in 4 bedrooms ⊗ in dining room TVB tea/coffee No children 10yrs No coaches ⏛ large garden Dinner Last d 5pm **Prices** S £44-£46; D £66-£81✳ **Parking** 15 **Notes** Closed Dec-Feb

◆◆◆◆ 🅰

Lower Meadows
Penally Hill PL35 0HF ☎ 01840 250570
e-mail stay@lowermeadows.co.uk
web www.lowermeadows.co.uk
Dir A39 onto B3266 to Boscastle. Lower Meadows opp Coweb Inn

Facilities 5 en suite ⊗ TVB tea/coffee ✖ Cen ht TVL No children 12yrs No coaches **Prices** S £35.50-£39.50; D £51-£59✳ **LB** **Parking** 5 **Notes** Closed 22-28 Dec

Pencarmol ♦♦♦

5 Penally Ter, The Harbour PL35 0HA
☎ 01840 250435 & 07791 076852
e-mail info@pencarmol.co.uk
Dir From A39, Atlantic Highway, take road signed Boscastle.

This lovely cottage has super views of the harbour and dramatic cliffs. The friendly proprietors are most welcoming and attentive. There is a lovely garden and car parking is available. Bedrooms are compact and provide a good range of facilities. Breakfast, features mackerel freshly caught when available.

Facilities 3 en suite (1 fmly) ⊘ TVB tea/coffee Cen ht TVL No coaches **Prices** D £50-£60✱ LB **Parking** 3 **Notes** Closed 25-26 Dec ⊠

BUDE
MAP 02 SS20

★★★ Bed & Breakfast

Maymyo

46 Kings Hl EX23 8QH ☎ 01288 355019
Dir A39 onto A3073. B&B 0.5m on left after bend.

This refurbished ground-floor home is within walking distance of the town, canal and beaches. Guests are assured of a warm welcome, and in addition to the lounge-breakfast room the sunroom leads to a decking area and the garden beyond.

Facilities 2 rms (1 en suite) (2 GF) ⊘ TVB ✻ Cen ht TVL No coaches **Notes** ⊠

Bangors Organic ♦♦♦♦

Poundstock EX23 0DP ☎ 01288 361297 🖹 01288 361508
e-mail info@bangorsorganic.co.uk
Dir 4m S of Bude on A39, left towards Week Orchard, house on right

Located a few miles south of Bude, this renovated Victorian establishment offers elegant accommodation with a good level of comfort. The bathrooms are spacious and luxurious. Breakfast, featuring organic, local and home-made produce, is served in the pleasant dining room, which is open to the public as a tea room from mid morning until early evening. The establishment is Certified Organic by the Soil Association.

Facilities 2 en suite ⊘ TVB tea/coffee ✻ Licensed Cen ht TVL No children 13yrs No coaches Dinner **Prices** D £76-£100✱ LB **Parking** 2

Fairway House ♦♦♦♦ ◇

8 Downs View EX23 8RF ☎ 01288 355059
e-mail enquiries@fairwayguesthouse.co.uk
Dir N through town to Flexbury, brown tourist signs to Downs View from golf course

Genuine hospitality and attentive service await you at this delightful Victorian terrace property, which overlooks the golf course and is close to the beach and town centre. The comfortable bedrooms are of a high standard and have many thoughtful extra facilities. A hearty breakfast, using local produce, is served at separate tables.

Facilities 7 rms (5 en suite) (1 fmly) ⊘ TVB tea/coffee ✻ Cen ht **Prices** S £23-£36; D £44-£55✱ LB **Notes** Closed Dec-Jan ⊠

Bude Haven Hotel ♦♦♦♦ ◇

Flexbury Av EX23 8NS ☎ 01288 352305 🖹 01288 352662
e-mail enquiries@budehavenhotel.com
web www.budehavenhotel.com
Dir 0.5m N of Bude in Flexbury village centre

This charming, refurbished Edwardian property is in a quiet area within easy walking distance of Bude centre and Crooklets Beach. Bedrooms are bright and airy, and the restaurant offers an interesting menu at dinner. You can also relax in the lounge or the bar.

Facilities 10 en suite (1 fmly) ⊘ TVB tea/coffee ✻ Licensed Cen ht TVL No coaches Hot tub Dinner Last d 9pm **Prices** S £26.50-£35; D £53-£70 ✱ LB **Parking** 6

Cliff Hotel ♦♦♦♦

Maer Down, Crooklets Beach EX23 8NG
☎ 01288 353110 & 356833 🖹 01288 353110
web www.cliffhotel.co.uk
Dir A39 through Bude, left at top of High St, pass Somerfields, 1st right between golf course, over x-rds, premises at end

Overlooking the sea from a clifftop location, this friendly and efficient establishment provides spacious, well-equipped bedrooms. Public areas include a bar and lounge and an impressive range of leisure facilities. Delicious dinners and tasty breakfasts are available in the attractive dining room.

Facilities 15 en suite (15 fmly) (8 GF) ⊘ in 8 bedrooms ⊘ in dining room TVB tea/coffee Direct dial from bedrooms Licensed Cen ht TVL No coaches ▢ ⚲ Gymnasium Pool Table ⚓ Bowling green Canal fishing Dinner Last d 6pm **Prices** S £39.60-£46.20; D £66-£77✱ LB **Parking** 18 **Notes** Closed Nov-Mar

Pencarrol ♦♦♦♦ ◇

21 Downs View EX23 8RF ☎ 01288 352478
e-mail pencarrolbude@aol.com
Dir 0.5m N of Bude. N from Bude into Flexbury village

This cosy guest house is only a short walk from Bude centre and Crooklets Beach, and has glorious views over the golf course. Bedrooms are attractively furnished and there is a first-floor lounge. Breakfast is served at separate tables in the dining room.

Facilities 7 rms (3 en suite) (2 pri facs) (2 fmly) (2 GF) ⊘ TVB tea/coffee ✻ Cen ht TVL No coaches **Prices** S £23-£27; D £52-£60✱ LB **Notes** Closed Dec ⊠

England

BUDE continued

◆◆◆◆

Stonepark

Marine Dr, Widemouth Bay EX23 0DE
☎ 01288 361469 & 07974 940420
e-mail info@stonepark-widemouth.co.uk
Dir 3m S of Bude, turn off the A39, 2nd Widemouth Bay Coastal route rd

A warm welcome awaits you at this detached bungalow with distant views of the rugged coastline and the sea. Just a short walk from the beach and the South West Coast Path, this is an ideal centre from which to explore the surrounding area. The bedrooms are comfortable and equipped with numerous thoughtful extra facilities.
Facilities 2 en suite (2 fmly) (2 GF) ⊗ TVB tea/coffee ✕ Cen ht No coaches ♨ **Prices** S £35-£40; D £40-£60✶ LB **Parking** 12
Notes Closed 14 Dec-14 Jan ⊛

CALLINGTON   MAP 03 SX36

◆◆◆◆ 🄰

Woodpeckers

Rilla Mill PL17 7NT ☎ 01579 363717
e-mail alisonmerchant@virgin.net
Dir A30 towards Bodmin. At Launceston follow B3254 towards Liskeard, at x-rds straight across to North Hill, turn left for Rilla Mill, B&B on left
Facilities 3 en suite ⊗ STV TVB tea/coffee ✕ Cen ht No coaches Dinner Last d 10am **Parking** 7 **Notes** ⊛

◆◆◆

Green Pastures Bed & Breakfast ◇

Longhill PL17 8AU ☎ 01579 382566
e-mail greenpast@aol.com
Dir 0.5m E of Callington on A390 to Tavistock
Located on the southern side of Kit Hill, this friendly and homely establishment has panoramic views across the Tamar valley and distant views of Dartmoor. The modern bungalow stands in 5 acres of land, where Shetland ponies contentedly graze. Bedrooms are comfortably furnished and there is a large lounge.
Facilities 3 rms (2 en suite) (1 pri facs) (3 GF) ⊗ TVB tea/coffee ✕ Cen ht No children 18yrs No coaches **Prices** S £27.50-£30; D £50-£55✶ LB **Parking** 8 **Notes** ⊛

CAMBORNE   MAP 02 SW64

◆◆◆ ◖

The Pendarves Inn

Carnhell Gn TR14 0NB ☎ 01209 832116
e-mail info@pendarves.co.uk
web www.pendarves.co.uk
Dir A30 onto A3047 Camborne West. Signs to Connor Downs, left to Carnhell Green

This country inn on the outskirts of the town welcomes travellers and locals alike. Bedrooms are decorated in peaceful colours and have contemporary furnishings. Lunch and dinner include a good choice of freshly cooked dishes, and the bar offers a good selection of ales, wines and spirits.
Facilities 3 en suite ⊗ in bedrooms ⊗ in dining room ⊗ in 1 lounge TVB tea/coffee ✕ Cen ht No children 16yrs No coaches Dinner Last d 9pm **Prices** S £40; D £55✶ LB **Conf** Max 20 Del £75 ✶ **Parking** 7

CAMELFORD   MAP 02 SX18

◆◆◆◆

Kings Acre

PL32 9UR ☎ 01840 213561 ▤ 01840 213561
e-mail webmaster@kings-acre.com
Dir 0.5m NW of Camelford on B3266

This friendly house is convenient for the coast and country. The cosy bar has a fire in cooler months, and the bedrooms are attractively decorated. A hearty Cornish breakfast is served in the dining room and a vegetarian option is available.
Facilities 3 en suite (3 GF) ⊗ FTV TVB tea/coffee ✕ Licensed Cen ht TVL No children 13yrs No coaches Sauna Hot tub Arts suite Walking machine Last d 6pm **Prices** S £40; D £90-£95✶ LB **Parking** 5
Notes Closed Xmas

◆◆◆

Silvermoon

La End PL32 9LE ☎ 01840 213736 ▤ 01840 213736
e-mail silvermoonbandb-jennymetters@hotmail.com
Dir A39 S to Camelford, right at 1st x-rds onto Lane End, 2nd property on right

A warm welcome awaits you at Silvermoon, situated on the edge of the town within easy reach of Bodmin Moor and Tintagel Castle, and convenient for the Eden Project. Cyclists and walkers are welcome. Bedrooms are well equipped with two on the ground floor. You can relax in the pretty garden.
Facilities 3 en suite (2 GF) ⊗ TVB tea/coffee ✕ Cen ht TVL No coaches **Prices** D £50-£55✶ LB **Parking** 5 **Notes** ⊛

CAWSAND
MAP 03 SX45

♦♦♦

Wringford Down Hotel
Hat Ln PL10 1LE ☎ 01752 822287
e-mail a.molloy@virgin.net
web www.cornwallholidays.co.uk
Dir *A374 onto B3247, pass Millbrook, right towards Cawsand & sharp right, 0.5m on right*

This family-run establishment has a peaceful location near Rame Head and the South West Coast Path, and is particularly welcoming to families. There is a nursery, swimming pool, games room, and gardens with play areas. A range of rooms, and some suites and self-catering units are available. Breakfast and dinner are served in the bistro.

Facilities 7 en suite 5 annexe en suite (9 fmly) (4 GF) ⊘ TVB tea/coffee Licensed Cen ht TVL No coaches 🔌 ☃ Pool Table Table tennis Bar billiards Dinner Last d 8pm **Prices** S £40-£47.50; D £60-£85✳ LB **Conf** Max 40 Thtr 40 Class 20 Board 20 **Parking** 20 **Notes** Civ Wed 100

CRACKINGTON HAVEN
MAP 02 SX19

♦♦♦ ◀▆

Coombe Barton ◈
EX23 0JG ☎ 01840 230345 🖨 01840 230788
e-mail info@coombebarton.co.uk
Dir *Off A39 to village & beach*

Overlooking the beach and surrounded by rugged cliffs, this long-established, family-run inn is popular with locals and visitors alike. An impressive range of Cornish real ales and a large selection of meals are available, and booking is advised for the popular Sunday carvery. The attractive bedrooms are well equipped.

Facilities 6 rms (4 en suite) (1 fmly) ⊘ in bedrooms ⊘ in dining room ⊘ in lounges FTV TV5B tea/coffee Cen ht Pool Table Dinner Last d 9.30pm **Prices** S £30-£58; D £50-£96✳ LB **Conf** Thtr 70 Class 50 Board 40 **Parking** 25

CRANTOCK
MAP 02 SW76

♦♦♦♦

Carrek Woth
West Pentire Rd TR8 5SA ☎ 01637 830530
Dir *W from Crantock village towards West Pentire*

Many guests return to this friendly, family-run house where hospitality and service are keynotes. Carrek Woth takes its name from the Cornish for Goose Rock, which can be seen in Crantock Bay. Bedrooms, on the ground floor, are neatly furnished and some have good views. The first-floor lounge looks toward Newquay and the sea. Breakfast is served in the attractive dining room, where Sunday lunch is also available.

Facilities 6 en suite (1 fmly) (6 GF) ⊘ TVB tea/coffee Licensed Cen ht TVL No coaches **Prices** S fr £37; d fr £60 LB **Parking** 6 **Notes** ⊛

If the freedom to smoke or be in a non-smoking atmosphere is important to you, check the rules when you book

England

DRYM
MAP 02 SW63

Premier Collection

◆◆◆◆◆ 🛏

Drym Farm
Drym, Nr Leedstown TR14 0NU ☎ 01209 831039
e-mail drym_farm@onetel.com
web www.drymfarm.co.uk
Dir Off B3302 at Leedstown to Drym, house on right after Drym
House on left

This delightful granite house stands in mature grounds and gardens
within a lush, secluded valley. Friendly hospitality provides a relaxing
environment. Bedrooms are simply but carefully furnished, with an
emphasis on good linen and comfort. There is a cosy lounge, and the
lovingly prepared breakfasts use local and organic produce.

Facilities 3 rms (2 pri facs) ⊗ TVB tea/coffee ✖ Cen ht No coaches
Prices S £45-£55; D £70-£85 LB **Parking** 6 **Notes** ➆

FALMOUTH
MAP 02 SW83

★★★★ Guest Accommodation

Swanpool House ❖
Swanpool TR11 5BB
☎ 01326 316501 & 07974 311075 📠 01326 316501
e-mail brain@swanpoolhouse.fsnet.co.uk
Dir A39 to Falmouth. Follow signs for Swanpool Lake/Beach.
Swanpool House is situated on unnamed lane near lake.

Located within walking distance of Falmouth's lovely beach, this smart,
light and airy accommodation is quietly placed. Public rooms are
unnecessary as all bedrooms are suites, offering good levels of
comfort; one even has a private upper floor terrace where you can sit
and enjoy the sea view. Breakfast is a range of choices pleasantly
served in the dining area of your room.

Facilities 3 en suite (1 fmly) (2 GF) ⊗ ✖ Cen ht TVL No coaches
Prices S £30-£40; D £60-£80 LB **Parking** 8 **Notes** ➆

Premier Collection

◆◆◆◆◆

Dolvean House
50 Melvill Rd TR11 4DQ ☎ 01326 313658 📠 01326 313995
e-mail reservations@dolvean.co.uk
web www.dolvean.co.uk
Dir On A39 near town centre & docks

The charm and peace of this fine Victorian house is enhanced by the
proprietors' hospitality and attentive service. The elegant bedrooms
come with many thoughtful extras, there is an inviting lounge, and
delicious home-cooked breakfasts are served in the spacious dining
room at individual tables.

Facilities 10 en suite (2 GF) ⊗ TVB tea/coffee ✖ Licensed Cen ht
TVL No children 12yrs No coaches **Prices** S fr £35; d fr £70✳ LB
Parking 10 **Notes** Closed Xmas

◆◆◆◆

Prospect House
1 Church Rd, Penryn TR10 8DA
☎ 01326 373198 📠 01326 373198
e-mail stay@prospecthouse.co.uk
web www.prospecthouse.co.uk
Dir Off A39 at Treluswell rdbt onto B3292, past Crosskeys pub & over
lights, after 50yds right through white gates next to phone box

Situated close to the waterside, Prospect House is an attractive
building, which was built for a ship's captain around 1820. The original
charm of the house has been carefully maintained. The attractive
bedrooms are well equipped. A comfortable lounge is available, and
freshly cooked breakfasts are served in the elegant dining room.

Facilities 3 en suite ⊗ TVB tea/coffee Cen ht TVL No coaches Dinner
Last d 9.30pm **Prices** S £35-£37.50; D £65-£70✳ LB **Parking** 4

If you have to cancel a booking, let the
proprietor know immediately

Book as early as possible, particularly
in the peak holiday period

◆◆◆◆

The Rosemary ◇

22 Gyllyngvase Ter TR11 4DL ☎ 01326 314669
e-mail therosemary@tiscali.co.uk
web www.therosemary.co.uk
Dir A39 Melvill Rd signed to beaches & seafront, right onto
Gyllyngvase Rd, 1st left

In a pleasant central location with splendid views over Falmouth Bay,
this is a friendly and comfortable place to stay. The attractive
bedrooms are thoughtfully equipped and some have sea views. You
can relax in the lounge with a drink from the well-stocked bar, and
there is a sun deck in the pretty garden, facing the sea.

Facilities 10 en suite (4 fmly) ⊗ TVB tea/coffee Licensed Cen ht TVL
No coaches garden with sundeck & sea views **Prices** S £30-£34;
D £60-£68✷ **Parking** 3 **Notes** Closed Nov-Jan

See advertisement on this page

◆◆◆◆

Carmelle Lodge Hotel

59 Melvill Rd TR11 4DF ☎ 01326 311344
Dir On A39 near town centre & docks

The proprietor of this pleasant house provides comfortable and
spacious accommodation and a friendly atmosphere. Bedrooms are
attractively decorated and well equipped. There is a smart lounge and
terrace overlooking the well-tended garden, ample parking and a small
bar. Breakfast is served in the stylish dining room.

Facilities 12 en suite (3 fmly) (2 GF) ⊗ in bedrooms ⊗ in dining room
TVB tea/coffee Licensed Cen ht TVL No coaches Dinner Last d 5pm
Parking 12 **Notes** Closed Nov-Mar

◆◆◆◆

Cotswold House Hotel ◇

49 Melvill Rd TR11 4DF ☎ 01326 312077
e-mail info@cotswoldhousehotel.com
Dir On A39 near town centre & docks

The smart Victorian house has splendid sea views and is just a short
walk from the town. The atmosphere is relaxed, the bar is popular,
and the lounge provides a good level of comfort. Breakfast is served
in the dining room, and dinner, featuring home-cooked dishes, is
available by arrangement.

Facilities 10 en suite (1 fmly) (1 GF) ⊗ FTV TVB tea/coffee ✗
Licensed Cen ht TVL Dinner Last d noon **Prices** S £28-£37; D £56-£70✷
LB **Parking** 10

◆◆◆◆

Esmond House ◇

5 Emslie Rd TR11 4BG ☎ 01326 313214
e-mail esmondhouse@btopenworld.com
Dir Off A39 Melvill Rd left onto Emslie Rd

The friendly and comfortable Edwardian house is just a short easy
walk from the beach. Bedrooms vary in size and some have sea views;
the rooms are on the first and second floors. A hearty, freshly cooked
breakfast is served in the spacious, traditionally furnished front room
with large bay windows.

Facilities 6 en suite (1 fmly) ⊗ TVB tea/coffee ✗ Cen ht No coaches
Prices S £25-£30; D £28-£35✷ LB **Notes** Closed 20 Dec-2 Jan

◆◆◆◆

Gayhurst

10 Pennance Rd TR11 4EA ☎ 01326 315161
e-mail jfjgriffin@yahoo.co.uk
web www.falmouth-gayhurst.co.uk
Dir A39 towards town centre, at end of Western Ter right at minirdbt
onto Pennance Rd

Many guests return to this friendly home, located in a quiet residential
area close to the beaches. The spacious bedrooms are comfortably
appointed, and some have sea views. Freshly cooked breakfasts are
served in the bright dining room, which overlooks the attractive garden.

Facilities 5 en suite (1 fmly) ⊗ TVB tea/coffee ✗ No children 5yrs
Prices S £35✷ **Parking** 5 **Notes** Closed Nov-Etr

FALMOUTH continued

♦♦♦♦

Hawthorne Dene Guest House

12 Pennance Rd TR11 4EA
☎ 01326 311427 📠 01326 311994
e-mail enquiries@hawthornedenehotel.co.uk
web www.hawthornedenehotel.com
Dir A39 towards town centre, at end of Western Ter right at minirdbt onto Pennance Rd

The picture windows in the lounge, dining room and many of the bedrooms of this late Victorian house look out over the sea. Cuisine is a feature, and dishes focus on the best of local and organic produce. A log fire burns in winter in the comfortable lounge. Sign language is understood.

Facilities 10 en suite (1 fmly) (1 GF) ⊗ TVB tea/coffee ✖ Licensed Cen ht No coaches Dinner Last d 8.30pm **Prices** S £35-£45; D £70-£80 **LB Parking** 7

♦♦♦♦

Ivanhoe ◇

7 Melvill Rd TR11 4AS ☎ 01326 319083
e-mail info@ivanhoe-guesthouse.co.uk
web www.ivanhoe-guesthouse.co.uk
Dir On A39 near town centre & docks

You are made to feel most welcome at this charming Edwardian house, where the relaxed atmosphere makes for an enjoyable stay. Bedrooms are thoughtfully equipped, anf the cheerful breakfast room is an uplifting venue for an impressive range of choices, including vegetarian dishes and local produce.

Facilities 6 rms (4 en suite) (1 GF) ⊗ TVB tea/coffee ✖ Cen ht TVL No children 5yrs No coaches **Prices** S £22-£26; D £50-£60 **LB Parking** available **Notes** 🐾

♦♦♦♦

Melvill House ◇

52 Melvill Rd TR11 4DQ ☎ 01326 316645
e-mail melvillhouse@btconnect.com
Dir On A39 near town centre & docks

Well situated for the beach, the town centre and the National Maritime Museum on the harbour, Melvill House is a family-run establishment with a relaxed atmosphere. Some bedrooms have four-poster beds, and breakfast is served in the smart dining room. Ample parking.

Facilities 7 en suite (2 fmly) (1 GF) ⊗ TVB tea/coffee ✖ Cen ht TVL No coaches **Prices** S £24-£27; D £50-£54✱ **LB Parking** 8

♦♦♦♦

Rosemullion ◇

Gyllyngvase Hill TR11 4DF
☎ 01326 314690 📠 01326 210098
e-mail gail@rosemullionhotel.demon.co.uk

This pleasant, friendly property is recognisable by its mock-Tudor exterior. Bedrooms, some on the ground floor, are comfortably furnished, and service and hospitality are strengths. Breakfast, served in the panelled dining room, is freshly cooked, and there is a well-appointed lounge.

Facilities 13 rms (11 en suite) (3 GF) ⊗ TVB tea/coffee ✖ Cen ht No children No coaches **Prices** S £30-£40; D £53-£64✱ **LB Parking** 18 **Notes** Closed 23-29 Dec 🐾

♦♦♦♦

Tudor Court Hotel ◇

55 Melvill Rd TR11 4DF ☎ 01326 312807 📠 01326 312807
e-mail enquiries@tudorcourthotel.com
Dir On A39 near town centre & docks

The mock Tudor accommodation offers bright, well-equipped bedrooms, some having delightful sea views. There is a lounge-bar, which is furnished with comfortable seating. The dining room, where a full English breakfast is served, overlooks the attractive garden.

Facilities 9 rms (8 en suite) (1 pri facs) (1 fmly) ⊗ TVB tea/coffee ✖ Licensed Cen ht TVL No coaches **Prices** S £28-£32; D £55-£65 **Parking** 9

♦♦♦♦

Westcott Hotel ◇

Gyllyngvase Hill TR11 4DN
☎ 01326 311309 📠 01326 212041
e-mail info@westcotthotel.co.uk
Dir A39 from Truro to Falmouth. Gyllyngvase Hill on right 600yds before Princess Pavillion

Please note that this establishment has recently changed hands. This attractive house is in a pleasant location close to Gyllyngvase beach and is within walking distance of the town. Bedrooms are well maintained and some have sea views. Hearty, freshly cooked breakfasts are served in the airy dining room.

Facilities 10 en suite ⊗ TVB tea/coffee ✖ Licensed Cen ht TVL No children 12yrs **Prices** S £30-£35; D £60-£80✱ **LB Parking** 9

◆◆◆
Lyonesse
17 Western Ter TR11 4QN
☎ 01326 313017 & 07739 554655
e-mail keith.botfield@btopenworld.com
Dir On A39, Dracaena Av onto Western Ter

The welcoming, family-run Lyonesse has a pleasant location in a leafy terrace close to the town centre and the beach and harbour. The bright bedrooms come in a variety of sizes.

Facilities 5 rms (4 en suite) (1 pri facs) (4 fmly) (1 GF) ⊗ TVB tea/coffee ✖ Cen ht No coaches **Prices** S £23-£31; D £49-£54✳
Notes Closed 23 Dec-2 Jan

◆◆◆
The Observatory
27 Western Ter TR11 4QL ☎ 01326 314509
Dir On A39, Dracaena Av onto Western Ter

This interesting house is a pleasant place to stay close to the town and harbour, and the proprietors are very friendly. Bedrooms come in a range of sizes, and freshly cooked breakfasts, with vegetarian options, are served in the dining room. Parking available.

Facilities 6 en suite (2 fmly) (3 GF) ⊗ TVB tea/coffee ✖ Cen ht
Prices D £50✳ **LB** **Parking** 6 **Notes** ✆

◆◆◆
Penwarren
3 Avenue Rd TR11 4AZ ☎ 01326 314216
e-mail penwarren@btconnect.com

Penwarren is in the heart of Falmouth, not far from Gyllyngvase beach. Service is attentive and thoughtful, and the fresh accommodation comes with considerate extras. Breakfast is served in the dining room and there is also a cosy lounge.

Facilities 7 rms (6 en suite) (1 fmly) ⊗ TVB tea/coffee ✖ Cen ht TVL
Prices S £24-£30; D £48-£60✳ **LB** **Parking** 7

◆◆◆
Trevoil
25 Avenue Rd TR11 4AY
☎ 01326 314145 & 07966 409782 ▤ 01326 314145
e-mail alan.jewel@btconnect.com
Dir Off A39 Melvill Rd left onto Avenue Rd, B&B 150yds from Maritime Museum

Located within walking distance of the town centre, the friendly Trevoil has a comfortable and relaxed environment. Breakfast is enjoyed in the light, pleasant dining room.

Facilities 8 rms (4 en suite) (3 fmly) (1 GF) ⊗ in dining room TVB tea/coffee Cen ht **Parking** 6

Ⓤ
The Bosanneth
Gyllyngvase Hill TR11 4DW
☎ 01326 314649 ▤ 01326 314649
e-mail bosanneth@fsbdial.co.uk

At the time of going to press the rating for this establishment had not been confirmed. Please check the AA website www.theAA.com for up-to-date information.

Facilities 8 en suite ⊗ in bedrooms ⊗ in dining room TVB tea/coffee ✖ Cen ht No children 15yrs No coaches Dinner Last d 4pm
Prices S £30-£35; D £60-£70✳ **LB** **Parking** 7 **Notes** Closed Oct-Feb ✆

Ⓤ
Falmouth Rose
7 Fenwick Rd TR11 4DR ☎ 01326 210024
e-mail info@falmouthroseguesthouse.co.uk
web www.falmouthroseguesthouse.co.uk
Dir From town centre towards end of Western Ter, right onto Fenwick Rd, house at end

At the time of going to press the rating for this establishment had not been confirmed. Please check the AA website www.theAA.com for up-to-date information.

Facilities 3 en suite (1 fmly) ⊗ TVB tea/coffee ✖ Cen ht TVL
No children 12yrs **Prices** D £50-£70✳ **Parking** 4

FLUSHING
MAP 02 SW83

◆◆◆
Trefusis Barton Farmhouse B & B
(SW815341)
TR11 5TD
☎ 01326 374257 & 07866 045646 ▤ 01326 374257
Mrs Laity
e-mail trefusisbarton@aol.com
Dir Off A39 towards Carclew, follow signs to Mylor Bridge, left at minirdbt, signs to B&B

This working farm is easily reached high above the village of Flushing. The friendly home is convenient for a relaxing break or for touring, and the comfortable bedrooms have many thoughtful extras. Breakfast is served at the farmhouse kitchen table, fresh from the Aga.

Facilities 3 en suite (1 GF) ⊗ TVB tea/coffee ✖ Cen ht 400 acres Dairy/Arable **Prices** S £32.50-£50; D £50-£60 **Parking** 6 **Notes** ✆

England

FOWEY
MAP 02 SX15

★★★★★ ◉◉ **Restaurant with Rooms**

The Old Quay House
28 Fore St PL23 1AQ ☎ 01726 833302 🖷 01726 833668
e-mail info@theoldquayhouse.com
web www.theoldquayhouse.com
Dir M5 junct 31 onto A30 to Bodmin. Then A389 through town &
B3269 to Fowey

Looking out across Fowey's busy waterway from the end of steep and
winding streets, Old Quay House offers very stylish bedrooms, some
with harbour views. The old quay itself is where you dine or take
drinks; the cuisine is accomplished, and breakfast is also noteworthy.

Facilities 12 en suite STV TVB tea/coffee Direct dial from bedrooms ✘
Licensed No children 12yrs No coaches Dinner Last d 9pm
Prices S £130-£210; D £160-£210✳ **LB Notes** Civ Wed 100

◆◆◆◆ ◧

King of Prussia
Town Quay PL23 1AT ☎ 01726 833694 🖷 01726 834902
Dir A390 onto A3082 into Fowey, one-way system to Town Quay

This atmospheric, family-run inn takes its name from an infamous
local smuggler who operated around nearby Prussia Cove. The smart
bedrooms have wonderful estuary views. Good home-cooked meals
and snacks are available in the convivial bar, and hearty breakfasts are
served in the dining room.

Facilities 6 en suite (4 fmly) ⊗ in bedrooms ⊗ in dining room STV
TVB tea/coffee ✘ Cen ht No coaches Pool Table Dinner Last d 9.30pm

◆◆◆◆

Trevanion
70 Lostwithiel St PL23 1BQ ☎ 01726 832602
e-mail alisteve@trevanionguesthouse.co.uk
web www.trevanionguesthouse.co.uk
Dir A3082 into Fowey, down hill, left onto Lostwithiel St, Trevanion
on left

This 16th-century merchant's house provides comfortable
accommodation within easy walking distance of the historic town
centre and is convenient for visiting The Eden Project. A hearty,
farmhouse-style cooked breakfast, using local produce, is served in the
attractive dining room and other menu options are available.

Facilities 5 rms (4 en suite) (1 pri facs) (2 fmly) (1 GF) ⊗ TVB
tea/coffee Cen ht No coaches Dinner Last d morning **Prices** S £35-£45;
D £50-£65✳ **LB Parking** 5 **Notes** 🐾

GOLDSITHNEY
MAP 02 SW53

◆◆◆◆ ◧

The Trevelyan Arms ◇
Fore St TR20 9JH ☎ 01736 710453
e-mail cusickgeorge@hotmail.com
web www.trevelyanarms.com
Dir Off A394, 5m from Penzance at rdbt signed Goldsithney,
Trevelyan Arms 0.5m on right

Locals and visitors alike appreciate the convivial environment at this
pleasant inn. Now refurbished, it has a cosy bar and a separate
restaurant serving appetising home-made dishes. The stylish
bedrooms are well equipped.

Facilities 2 en suite (1 fmly) ⊗ in bedrooms ⊗ in area of dining room
⊗ in 1 lounge TVB tea/coffee Cen ht Pool Table Dinner Last d 8.30pm
Prices S £30-£35; D £50-£60✳ **LB Conf** Max 12 Board 12 **Parking** 5

◆◆◆

Penleen
South Rd TR20 9LF ☎ 01736 710633
e-mail jimblain@penleen.com
web www.penleen.com
Dir Off main street in village

Penleen is a quiet home close to Penzance and Mount's Bay. The
friendly proprietors ensure you have a comfortable stay. The lounge
overlooks an attractive garden and freshly cooked breakfasts are
served in the dining room. Bedrooms come with a good range of
facilities.

Facilities 2 rms (1 en suite) (1 pri facs) ⊗ TVB tea/coffee ✘ Cen ht
No children 8yrs No coaches **Prices** S £35-£40; D £50-£55 **Parking** 2
Notes Closed 17 Dec-4 Jan 🐾

GORRAN
MAP 02 SW94

◆◆◆◆ 🖥 🐾

Tregerrick Farm B & B (SW992436)
PL26 6NF ☎ 01726 843418 🖷 01726 843418 Mrs Thomas
e-mail fandc.thomas@btconnect.com
web www.tregerrickfarm.co.uk
Dir 1m NW of Gorran. B3273 S from St Austell, right after Pentewan
Sands campsite to The Lost Gardens of Heligan, continue 3m, farm
on left

Near many attractions, the family-run Victorian farmhouse offers a
high standard of accommodation in peaceful countryside. Two of the

continued

attractive bedrooms are in the main house, the other is in a self-contained, two-bedroom suite. Delicious breakfasts, featuring home-made breads and preserves, are served around the large dining table.

Facilities 2 en suite 2 annexe rms (2 annexe pri facs) (1 fmly) (2 GF) ⊗ TVB tea/coffee ✻ Cen ht TVL No children 4yrs 280 acres arable, beef Last d 5pm **LB Parking** 4

GORRAN HAVEN
MAP 02 SX04

★★★ Bed & Breakfast

Bumble Bees

Foxhole Ln PL26 6JP ☎ 01726 842219
e-mail bamford@foxhole.vispa.com
Dir Take B3273, before Mevagissey turn right to Gorran Haven. At beach turn right onto Foxhole Lane

A warm, friendly welcome is offered at this small bed & breakfast perched on a hillside overlooking the rooftops of the village. The small harbour, beach and rugged coastline are just a short walk down the hill. A home from home atmosphere prevails and each of the bedrooms has a bathroom across the hallway. A hearty breakfast, featuring home-made bread, marmalade and preserves, is served in the kitchen-breakfast room, which has a glorious view.

Facilities 2 en suite (2 GF) ⊗ TVB tea/coffee ✻ Cen ht TVL No coaches **Parking** 4 **Notes** ⊗

GRAMPOUND
MAP 02 SW94

◆◆◆

Perran House ◇

Fore St TR2 4RS ☎ 01726 882066 🖷 01726 882936
Dir On A390 halfway between St Austell & Truro

Convenient for Truro or St Austell, Perran House dates from the 17th century and offers brightly decorated and coordinated bedrooms equipped with modern facilities. Breakfast is served in the airy dining room and there is ample off-road parking.

Facilities 5 rms (3 en suite) ⊗ TVB tea/coffee ✻ Cen ht No coaches **Prices** S £20; D £45✳ **Parking** 8

GWEEK
MAP 02 SW72

◆◆◆ ❤

Barton Farm ◇ (SW692279)

TR13 0QH ☎ 01326 572557 Mrs Jenkin
e-mail bartonfarm@talk21.com
Dir Off A394 at Manhay x-rds towards Gweek. After 1m at Boskenwyn left at junct & farm 150yds on left

This dairy farm near Gweek has been in the same family for four generations. The proprietors' warm hospitality brings guests back year after year. Scrumptious breakfasts are served in the traditionally furnished dining room.

Facilities 3 rms (1 pri facs) ⊗ tea/coffee ✻ TVL 178 acres beef dairy **Prices** S £22.50-£25; D £40-£50✳ **Parking** 5 **Notes** Closed Dec-Jan ⊗

HAYLE
MAP 02 SW53

◆◆◆◆ 🍴

Calize Country House

Prosper Hill, Gwithian TR27 5BW
☎ 01736 753268 🖷 01736 753268
e-mail jillywhitaker@firenet.uk.net
Dir 2m NE of Hayle. B3301 in Gwithian at Red River Inn, house 350yds up hill on left

The refurbished establishment has superb views of the sea and countryside, and is well located for the beaches and coves of West Penwith, and the many gardens in the area. The attentive proprietors provide a most welcoming environment and invite you to share their comfortable lounge, which has a log-burning fire during cooler months. Enjoyable breakfasts featuring delicious home-made fare are served around a communal table with sea views.

Facilities 4 en suite ⊗ TVB tea/coffee ✻ Cen ht TVL No children 12yrs No coaches **Prices** S £40-£55; D £70-£90✳ **Parking** 6 **Notes** ⊗

Always confirm details with the
establishment when booking

England

HELSTON
MAP 02 SW62

See also **St Keverne**

Premier Collection

◆◆◆◆◆ ≘

Drym Farm
Drym, Nr Leedstown TR14 0NU ☎ 01209 831039
e-mail drym_farm@onetel.com
web www.drymfarm.co.uk
For full entry see **Drym**

HESSENFORD
MAP 03 SX35

◆◆◆ ◖

Copley Arms
PL11 3HJ ☎ 01503 240209 🖷 01503 240766
e-mail reservations@smallandfriendly.co.uk
Dir On A387 in village

The popular village inn is just a short drive from Plymouth, and is a good base for exploring east Cornwall. Its smart bedrooms have good levels of quality, and the extensive bar menu incorporates daily specials. Alfresco dining is popular on summer evenings. There is ample parking.

Facilities 5 annexe rms (4 en suite) (1 annexe pri facs) (1 fmly) ⊛ in bedrooms ⊛ in dining room STV TVB tea/coffee ✗ Cen ht Dinner Last d 8.45pm **Parking** 40

LANLIVERY
MAP 02 SX05

◆◆◆◆

The Barns ◈
Lower Pennant PL30 5DD ☎ 01208 873977
e-mail lowerpennant@aol.com
Dir Off A390, to Lanlivery church, left at Crown Inn towards Luxulyan, right at x-rds, entrance on left

The Barns is set in an attractive garden and is ideal for a quiet break, or for easy access to the coast and surrounding countryside. The comfortable bedroom with private lounge offers a peaceful and smoke-free environment. The proprietors are friendly and attentive.

Facilities 1 rms (1 pri facs) (1 GF) ⊛ TVB tea/coffee ✗ Cen ht No children 12yrs No coaches **Prices** S £30-£35; D £50-£60 LB **Parking** 3 **Notes** Closed 18 Dec-14 Jan ⊛

If you book on bed, breakfast and evening meal terms, you may find that the tariff includes only the set menu

◆◆◆ ◖

The Crown Inn
PL30 5BT ☎ 01208 872707 🖷 01208 871208
e-mail thecrown@wagtailinns.com
web www.wagtailinns.com
Dir Signed off A390, 2m W of Lostwithiel. Pub 0.5m down lane into village, opp church

This characterful inn has a long history, reflected in its worn flagstone floors, beams and open fireplaces. Dining is a feature and the menus offer a wide choice of fresh fish, local produce and interesting dishes. The bedrooms are more contemporary and are impressively appointed.

Facilities 2 en suite 2 annexe en suite (2 GF) ⊛ TVB tea/coffee Dinner Last d 9pm **Prices** D £39.95-£69.95✳ LB **Parking** 51

LAUNCESTON
MAP 03 SX38

◆◆◆◆ ◗ ✿

Hurdon ◈ (SX333828)
PL15 9LS ☎ 01566 772955 Mrs Smith
Dir A30 onto A388 to Launceston, at rdbt exit for hospital, 2nd right signed Trebullett, premises 1st on right

Genuine hospitality is assured at this delightful 18th-century granite farmhouse. The bedrooms are individually furnished and decorated, and equipped with numerous extras. The delicious dinners, by arrangement, use only the best local produce, and include home-made puddings and farm-fresh clotted cream.

Facilities 6 en suite (1 fmly) (1 GF) ⊛ TVB tea/coffee ✗ Cen ht TVL 400 acres mixed Dinner Last d 4.30pm **Prices** S £25-£30; D £46-£54✳ **Parking** 10 **Notes** Closed Nov-Apr ⊛

◆◆◆◆ ❦
Bradridge Farm *(SX328938)*

PL15 9RL ☎ 01409 271264 🖷 01409 271331 Mrs Strout
e-mail Angela@BradridgeFarm.co.uk
Dir *5.5m N of Launceston. Off B3254 at Ladycross sign for Boyton, Bradridge 2nd farm on right after Boyton school*

The late Victorian farmhouse stands in glorious countryside on the border of Devon and Cornwall. The well-presented bedrooms have numerous thoughtful extras, and the Aga-cooked breakfasts feature farm-fresh eggs.

Facilities 4 rms (3 en suite) (1 fmly) ⊗ TVB tea/coffee Cen ht TVL Fishing 250 acres arable/beef/sheep/hens **Parking** 5 **Notes** Closed Nov-Feb

◆◆◆◆
Tyne Wells House ◇

Pennygillam PL15 7EE ☎ 01566 775810
e-mail btucker@IC24.net
Dir *0.6m SW of town centre. Off A30 onto B3254 Pennygillam rdbt, house off rdbt*

Situated on the outskirts of the town, Tyne Wells House has panoramic views over the countryside. A relaxed and friendly atmosphere prevails and the cosy bedrooms are neatly furnished. A hearty breakfast is served in the dining room, which overlooks the garden. Evening meals are available by arrangement.

Facilities 3 rms (2 en suite) (1 pri facs) (1 fmly) ⊗ TVB tea/coffee ★ Cen ht No coaches Dinner Last d 11am **Prices** S £27-£32; D £45-£52 LB **Parking** 4 **Notes** 🖾

◆◆◆◆ ❦
Withnoe Farm ◇ *(SX347333)*

Tavistock Rd PL15 9LG
☎ 01566 772523 & 07743 793427 Mrs Colwill
Dir *On A388 towards Plymouth, opp route sign Tavistock (B3362) 13, Liskeard (A390) 19 and Plymouth (A38) 24*

A warm welcome is assured at this farmhouse, which has spectacular views over open countryside and is convenient for the A30. The attractive accommodation is spacious and very comfortable. A delicious breakfast is provided in the dining room around a large family table, and the views are breathtaking.

Facilities 3 rms (2 en suite) (1 fmly) ⊗ TVB tea/coffee ★ Cen ht TVL 20 acres **Prices** S £25-£30; D £48-£54✳ **Parking** 6 **Notes** Closed Dec-Jan 🖾

◆◆◆ 🅰
Oakside Farm Bungalow ◇

Oakside, South Petherwin PL15 7JL ☎ 01566 86733
Dir *3m SW of Launceston. A30 W, 1st left after passing under Kennards House (A395) flyover*

Facilities 3 rms (2 en suite) (1 pri facs) (3 GF) ⊗ TVB tea/coffee ★ Cen ht TVL No coaches **Prices** S £25; D £45-£50✳ **Parking** 6 **Notes** 🖾

LISKEARD   MAP 02 SX26

◆◆◆◆ ❦
Tregondale *(SX294643)*

Menheniot PL14 3RG
☎ 01579 342407 🖷 01579 342407 Mrs Rowe
e-mail tregondalefarm@btconnect.com
web www.tregondalefarm.co.uk
Dir *3m E of Liskeard. Off A38 or A390 to Menheniot, 0.7m N of village, signed*

Located in a peaceful valley, the working farm offers individually decorated bedrooms with thoughtful extras. Attention to detail is the hallmark here and every effort is made to ensure a comfortable stay. Delicious meals, using home-grown produce, are served in the airy dining room. Convenient for The Eden Project.

Facilities 3 en suite ⊗ TVB tea/coffee ★ Cen ht TVL No children 5yrs ⚘ 200 acres arable beef mixed sheep Dinner **Prices** S £35-£40; D £56-£70✳ LB **Parking** 3

◆◆◆◆
Great Trethew Manor ◇

Horningtops PL14 3PY ☎ 01503 240663 🖷 01503 240695
e-mail great_trethew_manor@yahoo.com
Dir *3m SE of Liskeard. Off A38 onto B3251*

Set in attractive wooded grounds, the family-run establishment provides a range of comfortable rooms. There is a bar, and the spacious restaurant with log fires offers an impressive choice of freshly prepared dishes featuring local fish and game.

Facilities 12 en suite (2 fmly) ⊗ in bedrooms ⊗ in dining room ⊗ in 1 lounge TVB tea/coffee ★ Licensed Cen ht TVL ⚘ Fishing Riding ⏉ Pony Trekking Dinner Last d 9pm **Prices** S £30-£45; D £50-£75✳ LB **Parking** 30

England

LISKEARD continued

◆◆◆◆
Redgate Smithy

Redgate, St Cleer PL14 6RU ☎ 01579 321578
e-mail enquiries@redgatesmithy.co.uk
web www.redgatesmithy.co.uk
Dir 3m NW of Liskeard. Off A30 at Bolventor/Jamaica Inn onto St
Cleer Rd for 7m, B&B just past x-rds

This 200-year-old converted smithy is on the southern fringe of Bodmin
Moor near Golitha Falls. The friendly accommodation offers smart
bedrooms with many extra facilities. There are several dining choices
nearby, and freshly cooked breakfasts are served in the conservatory.

Facilities 3 rms (2 en suite) (1 pri facs) ⊗ TVB tea/coffee Cen ht
No children 12yrs No coaches **Prices** d fr £60 **LB Parking** 3
Notes Closed Xmas & New Year ✉

◆◆◆◆
Trecarne House

Penhale Grange, St Cleer PL14 5EB
☎ 01579 343543 📠 01579 343543
e-mail trish@trecarnehouse.co.uk
Dir B3254 N from Liskeard to St Cleer. Right at Post Office, 3rd left
after church, 2nd right, house on right

A warm welcome awaits you at this large family home, peacefully
located on the edge of the village. The stylish and spacious bedrooms,
which have magnificent country views, feature pine floors and have
many thoughtful extras. The buffet-style breakfast offers a wide choice,
which can be enjoyed in the dining room and conservatory
overlooking rolling countryside.

Facilities 3 en suite (2 fmly) ⊗ TVB tea/coffee ✖ Cen ht TVL
No coaches Snooker Table tennis Trampoline **Prices** S £45-£55;
D £66-£99✳ **LB Parking** 6

◆◆◆
Elnor ◇

1 Russell St PL14 4BP ☎ 01579 342472 📠 01579 345673
e-mail Elnor@btopenworld.com
Dir Off A38 from Plymouth into town centre, house on right opp
Dairy Centre

This friendly, well-established guest house is close to the town centre
and railway station, and is just a short drive from Bodmin Moor.
Bedrooms are neatly presented and well equipped, and some are on
the ground floor. A cosy lounge and a small bar are available.

Facilities 6 rms (4 en suite) 3 annexe en suite (3 fmly) (4 GF)
⊗ in bedrooms ⊗ in dining room TVB tea/coffee Direct dial from
bedrooms ✖ Licensed Cen ht TVL No coaches **Prices** S £24-£28;
D £44-£52✳ **Parking** 7 **Notes** ✉

◆◆◆
Moor Gate

Higher Rd, Pensilva PL14 5NJ ☎ 01579 362386
e-mail sylvia@doney.co.uk
Dir B3254 N from Liskeard for 4m, right to Pensilva, Moor Gate on
right

Having excellent country views, this friendly house stands in attractive
grounds on the edge of the pleasant village of Pensilva, perfect for a
quiet break. The attractive bedrooms are well equipped, and freshly
cooked breakfasts are served in the lounge overlooking the garden.

Facilities 2 rms (1 en suite) (1 pri facs) ⊗ TVB tea/coffee ✖ Cen ht
No coaches **Parking** 4 **Notes** ✉

LIZARD   MAP 02 SW71

◆◆◆◆
Penmenner House

Penmenner Rd TR12 7NR ☎ 01326 290370
Dir A3083 into Lizard, right at green to sea, last house on right

Interesting tales abound at this Victorian house, which has a splendid
coastal setting. A friendly welcome is assured and the comfortable
bedrooms, some having sea views, are equipped with modern
facilities. Excellent home-cooked dinners, by arrangement, feature
fresh and local ingredients.

Facilities 6 rms (5 en suite) ⊗ TVB tea/coffee ✖ Licensed Cen ht
No coaches Dinner Last d 4pm **Parking** 10

LOOE — MAP 02 SX25

★★★ Bed & Breakfast

The Old Malt House

West Looe Hill PL13 2HE ☎ 01503 264976
e-mail oldmalt@tiscali.co.uk

A short level stroll from the harbour, the Old Malt House dates back to 1650 and is very convenient for all of Looe's amenities. The cosy bedrooms are well equipped and are approached via an external stone stairs, while a hearty breakfast is served in the ground-floor dining room.

Facilities 3 en suite ⊗ TVB tea/coffee ✖ Cen ht No children No coaches **Parking** available **Notes** ⊗

★★★ Inn

The Ship Inn

Fore St PL13 1AD ☎ 01503 263124 ◈ 01503 263624
e-mail reservations@smallandfriendly.co.uk
web www.smallandfriendly.co.uk

This lively family pub in the very heart of bustling East Looe has a local following. A wide range of popular dishes is served at lunch times and during the evenings, with light refreshments available throughout the day.

Facilities 8 en suite (1 fmly) ⊗ in bedrooms ⊗ in dining room ⊗ in 1 lounge STV TVB tea/coffee ✖ Cen ht TVL Pool Table Dinner Last d 9pm

Premier Collection

◆◆◆◆◆ ⌂

The Beach House

Marine Dr, Hannafore PL13 2DH
☎ 01503 262598 ◈ 01503 262298
e-mail enquiries@thebeachhouselooe.com
Dir *From Looe W over bridge, left to Hannafore & Marine Dr, on right after Tom Sawyer Tavern*

This peaceful property has panoramic sea views and is just a short walk from the harbour, restaurants and town. Some rooms have been refurbished with stylish hand-made furniture, and the bedrooms are well equipped and have many extras. Hearty breakfasts are served in the first-floor dining room, a good start for the South West Coast Path that goes right by the house.

The Beach House

Facilities 6 rms (4 en suite) (2 pri facs) (4 GF) ⊗ TVB tea/coffee ✖ Cen ht No children 12yrs No coaches **Prices** D £80–£110✳ **Parking** 6

◆◆◆◆ ⌂ ⌂

Barclay House

St Martin's Rd PL13 1LP ☎ 01503 262929 ◈ 01503 262632
e-mail info@barclayhouse.co.uk
Dir *0.5m N of Looe bridge on junct A387 & B3253*

Barclay House stands in 6 acres of grounds overlooking Looe harbour and is within walking distance of the town. The thoughtfully furnished bedrooms have modern facilities, and there is a sitting room, a spacious bar, a terrace where you can enjoy an aperitif during the summer, and a light and airy restaurant serving freshly prepared food. A heated swimming pool is also available.

Facilities 10 en suite (1 fmly) ⊗ STV TVB tea/coffee Direct dial from bedrooms ✖ Licensed Cen ht No coaches ⌇ **Prices** S £40–£67.50; D £80–£130 **LB** **Parking** 20 **Notes** Closed 22-27 Dec, 2 wks mid Jan

England

LOOE continued

◆◆◆◆ 😋 ❦

Bay View Farm ◇ (SX282548)

St Martins PL13 1NZ
☎ 01503 265922 🖹 01503 265922 Mrs Elford
Dir 2m NE of Looe. Off B3253 for Monkey Sanctuary, farm signed

The renovated and extended bungalow has a truly spectacular location with ever-changing views across Looe Bay. The bedrooms have many thoughtful extras. Add a genuine Cornish welcome, tranquillity and great food, and it's easy to see why guests are drawn back to this special place.

Facilities 2 en suite (2 GF) ⊗ TVB tea/coffee ✖ Cen ht TVL No children 5yrs 56 acres Mixed shire horses Dinner Last d 4pm **Prices** S £27-£30; D £50-£55✳ LB **Parking** 3 **Notes** 😋

◆◆◆◆ ❦

Bucklawren Farm ◇ (SX278540)

St Martin-by-Looe PL13 1NZ
☎ 01503 240738 🖹 01503 240481 Mrs Henly
e-mail bucklawren@btopenworld.com
web www.bucklawren.com
Dir 2m NE of Looe. Off B3253 to Monkey Sanctuary, 0.5m right to Bucklawren, farmhouse 0.5m on left

The spacious 19th-century farmhouse stands in 450 acres of farmland just 1m from the beach. The attractive bedrooms, including one on the ground floor, are well equipped, and the front-facing rooms have spectacular views across fields to the sea. Breakfast is served in the dining room, and tempting home-cooked evening meals are available at the nearby Granary Restaurant.

Facilities 6 en suite (3 fmly) (1 GF) ⊗ TVB tea/coffee ✖ Cen ht TVL No children 5yrs 450 acres arable/beef **Prices** S £30-£40; D £54-£61 LB **Parking** 6 **Notes** Closed Nov-Feb

◆◆◆◆ ❦

Polgover Farm (SX277586)

Widegates PL13 1PY ☎ 01503 240248 Mrs Wills
e-mail enquiries@polgoverfarm.co.uk
web www.polgoverfarm.co.uk
Dir 4m NE of Looe. A38 S onto B3251 & B3252, B&B 0.5m on right

This attractive house stands in farmland with fine views and is a peaceful place to stay. The welcoming proprietors ensure you feel at home. Bedrooms are thoughtfully equipped and hearty breakfasts are served in the very pleasant lounge.

Facilities 3 rms (2 en suite) (1 pri facs) ⊗ TVB tea/coffee ✖ Cen ht TVL No children 12yrs 93 acres Arable/Sheep **Prices** D £55-£60✳ LB **Parking** 9 **Notes** Closed Nov-Feb 😋

◆◆◆◆ 😋

South Trelowia Barns ◇

Widegates PL13 1QL ☎ 01503 240709
e-mail madley.cornwall@virgin.net
Dir A387 W from Hessenford, 1m left signed Trelowia, 0.75m down lane on right

Set in a very peaceful rural location, this home offers a relaxing environment and is full of character. The proprietors provide a warm welcome and make you feel at home. The comfortable bedrooms have lots of extra facilities. Cooking is accomplished and features home-grown and local produce.

Facilities 2 en suite 1 annexe en suite (2 fmly) ⊗ TV2B tea/coffee Cen ht TVL No coaches Dinner Last d 10.30am **Prices** S £25-£45; D £46-£50✳ LB **Parking** 6 **Notes** 😋

◆◆◆◆ 🍴 😋

Trehaven Manor

Station Rd PL13 1HN ☎ 01503 262028 🖹 01503 265613
e-mail enquiries@trehavenhotel.co.uk
web www.trehavenhotel.co.uk
Dir In East Looe between railway station & bridge. Hotel drive adjacent to The Globe PH

Run by a charming family, the former rectory has a stunning location with magnificent views of the estuary. Many of the attractive bedrooms have views, and all are particularly well equipped. There is also a cosy lounge bar. Dinner, by arrangement, specialises in Oriental cuisine, and breakfast features traditional fare; both meals are memorable.

Facilities 7 en suite (1 fmly) (1 GF) ⊗ TVB tea/coffee ✖ Licensed Cen ht TVL No coaches Dinner Last d 11am **Parking** 8

◆◆◆◆

Tresco

Dawn Rd, Hannafore PL13 2DS ☎ 01503 265981
e-mail enquiries@trescolooe.co.uk
web www.trescolooe.co.uk
Dir From Looe W over bridge, left to Hannafore & Marine Dr, right at Tom Sawyers Tavern, 20yds right onto Hannafore Ln, at No Through Road sign left onto Dawn Rd

This lovely 1930s house stands high above Hannafore Point and has a truly wonderful outlook. The vistas and warm hospitality ensure an

continued

England

enjoyable stay, and the bedrooms combine comfort and quality; some rooms have either a balcony or a patio. The breakfast menu offers a good choice of freshly prepared dishes with sea views.

Tresco

Facilities 3 en suite ⊘ TVB tea/coffee ✗ Cen ht No children 12yrs No coaches **Prices** D £64-£76✳ **LB Parking** 3 **Notes** Closed Nov-Mar

♦♦♦♦ 🍽

Woodlands

St Martins Rd PL13 1LP ☎ 01503 264405
Dir *0.5m N of Looe bridge on B3253*

The charming Victorian country house looks over woodland and the Looe estuary, and is within walking distance of the harbour and beaches. The cosy bedrooms are well equipped, and public rooms include a lounge and the elegant dining room where dinner is served by arrangement.

Facilities 5 rms (4 en suite) ⊘ TVB tea/coffee ✗ Licensed Cen ht TVL No children 7yrs No coaches Dinner Last d breakfast **Prices** D £60-£80✳ **LB Parking** 6 **Notes** Closed Dec-Jan

♦♦♦♦

Coombe Farm

Widegates PL13 1QN ☎ 01503 240223
e-mail coombe_farm@hotmail.com
web www.coombefarmhotel.co.uk
Dir *3.5m E of Looe on B3253 just S of Widegates*

Set in 10 acres of grounds and gardens, Coombe Farm has a friendly atmosphere. The bedrooms are in a converted stone barn, and are comfortable and spacious. Each has a dining area, with breakfast delivered to your room. Additional facilities include an outdoor heated swimming pool.

Coombe Farm

Facilities 3 annexe en suite (1 fmly) (3 GF) ⊘ STV TVB tea/coffee Direct dial from bedrooms No coaches ❊ **Prices** S £45-£55; D £68-£78✳ **Parking** 20

♦♦♦♦

Dovers House

St Martins Rd PL13 1PB ☎ 01503 265468
e-mail twhyte@btconnect.com
web www.dovershouse.co.uk
Dir *1.5m NE of Looe bridge on B3253*

This non-smoking home stands in attractive grounds a short drive from the lively town centre. The charming proprietors ensure you feel welcome and the spacious bedrooms are very well equipped. A hearty breakfast is served in the conservatory.

Facilities 4 en suite (1 fmly) ⊘ TVB tea/coffee ✗ Cen ht No children 8yrs No coaches **Prices** D £55-£65✳ **Parking** 4 **Notes** Closed 21-27 Dec

♦♦♦♦

The Old Bridge House Hotel ◇

The Quay PL13 2BU ☎ 01503 263159 🖷 01503 263159
e-mail mail@theoldbridgehouse.com
Dir *From Looe W over bridge, sharp left, house on right*

This pleasant property lies alongside the harbour and looks across small boats and yachts to East Looe. The well-equipped bedrooms come in a range of sizes, and you can enjoy the views from the small lounge bar. Hearty breakfasts are served in the dining room, which also overlooks the harbour.

Facilities 9 en suite (3 fmly) ⊘ TVB tea/coffee ✗ Licensed Cen ht No children 2yrs No coaches **Prices** S £30-£40; D £60-£80 **LB Notes** Closed 25 Dec

♦♦♦♦

Panorama Hotel

Hannafore Rd PL13 2DE ☎ 01503 262123 🖷 01503 265654
e-mail enquiries@looe.co.uk
web www.looe.co.uk
Dir *A387 W over Looe bridge, left onto Hannafore Rd*

The Panorama certainly lives up to its name, with spectacular views over the bay and harbour from the comfortable bar and the balconies of some rooms. All bedrooms are well furnished and equipped with many extras.

Facilities 8 en suite 1 annexe en suite (5 fmly) ⊘ in bedrooms ⊘ in dining room TVB tea/coffee ✗ Licensed Cen ht TVL No children 5yrs No coaches **Parking** 6

continued

England

LOOE continued

◆◆◆◆

Polraen Country House

Sandplace PL13 1PJ ☎ 01503 263956
e-mail enquiries@polraen.co.uk
web www.polraen.co.uk
Dir 2m N of Looe at junct A387 & B3254

The 18th-century stone house, formerly a coaching inn, nestles in the peaceful Looe valley. The charming hosts provide friendly service in a relaxed atmosphere, and bedrooms and public areas are stylish and well equipped. The licensed bar, lounge and dining room overlook the garden, and there are facilities for children. Excellent evening meals features local produce. Gill Bridges is a top-twenty finalist for AA Landlady of the Year 2006.

Facilities 5 en suite (2 fmly) ✪ STV FTV TVB tea/coffee ✖ Licensed Cen ht TVL Dinner Last d 5pm **Prices** S £45-£76; D £64-£76✳ **LB** **Conf** Max 20 Thtr 20 Class 20 Board 20 **Parking** 20 **Notes** Closed 25-27 Dec rs Nov-Feb (dinner by prior arrangement)

◆◆◆◆ ❦

Tremaine Farm ◇ (SX194558)

Pelynt PL13 2LT ☎ 01503 220417 Mrs Philp
e-mail rosemary@tremainefarm.co.uk
Dir 5m NW of Looe. B3359 N from Pelynt, left at x-rds

Convenient for Fowey, Looe and Polperro, this pleasant working farm offers a comfortable stay. The proprietors provide friendly hospitality and attentive service, and the spacious bedrooms are well equipped. A hearty breakfast is served in the dining room and there is a particularly pleasant lounge. This is a non-smoking house.

Facilities 2 rms (1 en suite) (1 pri facs) (2 fmly) ✪ TVB tea/coffee ✖ Cen ht TVL No children 4yrs 300 acres Arable/Sheep **Prices** S £27-£30; D £54-£60 **LB** **Notes** ✉

◆◆◆

Little Harbour

Church St PL13 2EX ☎ 01503 262474
e-mail littleharbour@btinternet.com

Little Harbour is almost on Looe's harbour, in the historic old town, and parking is available. The proprietors are friendly and attentive. The bedrooms are well appointed and attractively decorated. Breakfast is served freshly cooked in the dining room.

Facilities 5 en suite (1 fmly) ✪ FTV TVB tea/coffee Cen ht No children 12yrs **Prices** D £40-£60 **LB** **Parking** 3 **Notes** ✉

◆◆◆

Seaview

Portuan Rd, Hannafore PL13 2DW ☎ 01503 265837
e-mail sharon@seaviewlooe.fsworld.co.uk
Dir W over Looe bridge, 1st left to Hannafore, 1st right after Tom Sawyers Inn, turn left, 6th house on right

This pleasant home offers a warm welcome and many guests return here. Bedrooms, some with sea/harbour views, are cosy and attractively decorated. Just a few steps from the harbour, there is limited parking on site but a public car park at the harbour edge. Hearty breakfasts are served in the dining room, and Seaview is a short stroll from Looe's many restaurants.

Facilities 3 rms (2 en suite) (1 pri facs) ✪ in dining room ✪ in lounges TVB tea/coffee ✖ Cen ht **Prices** D £44-£60✳ **LB** **Notes** Closed 19-29 Dec ✉

Ⓤ

St Johns Court ◇

East Cliff PL13 1DE ☎ 01503 262301
e-mail enquiries@stjohnscourt.com
Dir Past Looe Station, through Main St, left next to 'Ship Inn'. B&B 200yds on left.

At the time of going to press the rating for this establishment had not been confirmed. Please check the AA website www.theAA.com for up-to-date information.

Facilities 7 en suite (2 fmly) ✪ TVB tea/coffee ✖ Cen ht TVL No coaches **Prices** S £25-£40; D £55-£62✳ **Parking** 3

Always confirm details with the
establishment when booking

LOSTWITHIEL

MAP 02 SX15

◆◆◆ ❦

Hartswell Farm *(SX119597)*

St Winnow PL22 0RB
☎ 01208 873419 🖹 01208 873419 Mrs Jordan
e-mail hartswell@connexions.co.uk
web www.connexions.co.uk/hartswell
Dir 1m E of Lostwithiel. S off A390 at Downend Garage, farm 0.25m
up hill on left

The 17th-century farmhouse has a wonderfully peaceful setting, and
offers generous hospitality and a homely atmosphere. The cosy
bedrooms look across rolling countryside, and breakfast includes tasty
eggs fresh from the farm.

Facilities 3 rms (2 en suite) (1 pri facs) ⊗ TV1B tea/coffee 🐾 Cen ht
TVL No children 6yrs River cruises with proprietor when staying 5 days
52 acres beef mixed **Prices** S £32-£42; D £52-£68 LB **Parking** 3 **Notes** ⊛

◆◆◆ ▣

The Ship Inn Lerryn

Lerryn PL22 0PT ☎ 01208 872374 🖹 01208 872614
e-mail enquires@theshipinnlerryn.co.uk
Dir 3m SE of Lostwithiel in Lerryn village

This 17th-century village inn offers a warm welcome on the banks of
the River Fowey. Bedrooms vary in size but all are comfortably
appointed. Local ales and freshly prepared dishes using local produce
feature in the bar and restaurant.

Facilities 7 en suite (1 fmly) (3 GF) ⊗ in bedrooms ⊗ in dining room
TV5B tea/coffee Direct dial from bedrooms Cen ht No coaches Pool
Table Dinner Last d 9.30pm **Prices** S £60-£80✳ LB

MANACCAN

MAP 02 SW72

Ⓤ

The Hen House

Tregarne TR12 6EW ☎ 01326 280236
e-mail henhouseuk@aol.com
Dir B3293 left into Newtown, right at T-junct. After 2.3m, take left
fork, then 1st right, last house

At the time of going to press the rating for this establishment had not
been confirmed. Please check the AA website www.theAA.com for up-
to-date information.

Facilities 1 en suite 1 annexe en suite (2 GF) ⊗ TVB tea/coffee Cen ht
No children 12yrs No coaches Tai-Chi Reiki Reflexology healing
Prices S £50; D £75✳ LB **Parking** 5

MARAZION

MAP 02 SW53

◆◆◆◆

Glenleigh Hotel

Higher Fore St TR17 0BQ ☎ 01736 710308
e-mail info@marazionhotels.com
Dir Off A394 to Penzance, opp the Fire Engine Inn

This proud granite house has an elevated position with wonderful
views towards St Michael's Mount. The welcoming proprietors have

owned this house for more than 30 years and many guests return.
Dinner, by arrangement, is served in the comfortable dining room and
features fresh local produce whenever possible.

Facilities 9 en suite (1 fmly) (1 GF) ⊗ TVB tea/coffee 🐾 Licensed
Cen ht TVL No children 3yrs No coaches Dinner Last d noon LB
Parking 9 **Notes** Closed Nov-Mar ⊛

◆◆◆

Blue Horizon ◈

Fore St TR17 0AW ☎ 01736 711199
e-mail holidaybreaksmarazion@freeola.com
web www.holidaybreaksmarazion.co.uk
Dir E end of village centre

Located in the heart of the market town, the rear of the Blue Horizon
is almost at the waters edge, and has superb sea views from its
garden, some of the bedrooms and the breakfast room. The
atmosphere is laid back, and additional facilities (charged) include a
laundry room, sauna cabin and barbeque. Ample parking is available.

Facilities 6 rms (5 en suite) (1 pri facs) (2 GF) ⊗ TVB tea/coffee 🐾
TVL No coaches Sauna Spa cabin with hot tub **Prices** S £30;
D £55-£65✳ LB **Parking** 7 **Notes** Closed Nov-5 Jan

MAWGAN PORTH

MAP 02 SW86

◆◆◆◆ Ⓐ

Bedruthan House Hotel ◈

St Eval PL27 7UW ☎ 01637 860346
e-mail reception@bedruthanhousehotel.co.uk
Dir From A30 follow airport signs. Past airport turn right onto B3276.
Follow Padstow signs 2m.

Facilities 6 rms (5 en suite) (1 pri facs) 2 annexe en suite (5 fmly)
(2 GF) ⊗ in 4 bedrooms ⊗ in dining room ⊗ in lounges TVB
tea/coffee 🐾 Licensed Cen ht TVL No coaches Dinner Last d 8pm
Prices S £26-£30; D £52-£60✳ LB **Parking** 11

MEVAGISSEY

MAP 02 SX04

◆◆◆◆ ❦

Kerryanna *(SX008453)*

Treleaven Farm, Valley Rd PL26 6SA
☎ 01726 843558 🖹 01726 843558 Mrs Hennah
e-mail enquiries@kerryanna.co.uk
web www.kerryanna.co.uk
Dir B3273 into village, turn right by bowling green

Located on the peaceful outskirts of the fishing village, Kerryanna
stands in 2 acres of gardens and looks across countryside to the sea.
The attractive bedrooms are comfortably furnished, with one room on
the ground floor. There are three cosy lounges, a swimming pool and
a putting green.

Facilities 6 en suite (1 GF) ⊗ TVB tea/coffee 🐾 Cen ht No children
12yrs ⭼ ⚲ 40 acres non-working **Prices** D £68-£70✳ LB **Parking** 6
Notes Closed Nov-Feb

continued

England

MEVAGISSEY continued

♦♦♦♦

The Anchorage

Portmellon Rd PL26 6PH ☎ 01726 844412 📠 01726 844412
e-mail lee@anchorage4u.co.uk
web www.anchorage4u.co.uk
Dir *B3273 to Mevagissey, through one-way system, left at Ship Inn & signs to Portmellon & Gorran Haven, 1st left, Anchorage 0.5m on left*

Perching on the cliff overlooking the bay towards Chapel Point, this charming home dates from the late 18th century and provides comfortable, well-appointed accommodation. Bedrooms are spacious, light and have lovely sea views. Breakfast is served around one large table in the lounge-dining room and features home-made bread, marmalade and preserves.

Facilities 3 rms (2 en suite) (1 pri facs) ⊗ TVB tea/coffee ✖ Cen ht TVL No children 12yrs No coaches **Prices** D £60-£75 **LB** **Parking** 3 **Notes** Closed 22 Dec-mid Feb 🚭

♦♦♦♦

Mevagissey House

Vicarage Hl PL26 6SZ ☎ 01726 842525 📠 01726 842266
e-mail helen@mevagissey.net
Dir *500yds N of village centre. B3273 to Mevagissey, after Pentewan left at x-rds on top of hill, right at small rdbt, B&B on right*

This non-smoking house has an enviable location high above the town with splendid views. There is ample parking and it is only a short walk to the harbour. The comfortable bedrooms are well appointed, and breakfast features quality local produce, and eggs supplied by the resident hens.

Facilities 2 en suite (1 fmly) ⊗ in bedrooms ⊗ in dining room ⊗ in lounges TVB tea/coffee ✖ Cen ht No children 7yrs No coaches **Parking** 6 **Notes** Closed Dec

♦♦♦♦ ❦

Treleaven (SX008454)

Valley Rd PL26 6RZ ☎ 01726 842413 Mrs Hennah
e-mail stay@treleaven.co.uk
web www.treleaven.co.uk
Dir *Entering Mevagissey turn right at foot of hill, farm lane between playing park & football pitch*

Treleaven is a peaceful base for touring or visiting The Eden Project. From its elevated position there are lovely views across the countryside to Mevagissey and the sea. There is a licensed bar, and

continued

---

leisure facilities include an outdoor pool, an 18-hole putting green and a games area.

Treleaven

Facilities 8 en suite (1 fmly) ⊗ TVB tea/coffee ✖ Licensed Cen ht No children 10yrs ⤷ Pool Table ⚑ Games room 50 acres mixed Dinner Last d 5.30pm **Parking** 8 **Notes** Closed 15 Dec-7 Jan

♦♦♦

Headlands Hotel

Polkirt Hl PL26 6UX ☎ 01726 843453
e-mail headlandshotel@talk21.com
Dir *One-way through village & ascend towards Port Mellon, Headlands on right*

Set on an elevated position with spectacular views over the bay, this family-run establishment offers friendly service and comfortable accommodation. The colourful bedrooms are well equipped, with many having sea views. Public rooms include a stylish lounge bar and dining room.

Facilities 14 rms (12 en suite) (1 fmly) (4 GF) ⊗ in bedrooms ⊗ in dining room TVB tea/coffee ✖ Licensed Cen ht No coaches **Prices** S £37.50-£55; D £85-£90 **LB** **Parking** 10

♦♦♦ ◼

The Ship

Fore St PL26 6UQ ☎ 01726 843324 📠 01726 844368
e-mail reservations@smallandfriendly.co.uk
Dir *B3273 S from St Austell to Mevagissey, in central square*

The 400-year-old Ship Inn stands in the centre of the delightful fishing village. The popular bar, with low beams, flagstone floors and a strong nautical feel, offers a choice of menu or blackboard specials. The pine-furnished bedrooms are attractively decorated. Car park nearby.

Facilities 5 en suite (2 fmly) ⊗ in dining room TVB tea/coffee ✖ Cen ht Dinner Last d 9pm

♦♦♦ ◪

The Rising Sun Inn

Portmellon Cove PL26 6PL ☎ 01726 843235
e-mail cliffnsheila@tiscali.co.uk
web www.risingsunportmellon.co.uk
Dir *Onto narrow coast road S from Mevagissey into Portmellon Cove, inn on left*

Facilities 7 en suite ⊗ in dining room TVB tea/coffee Licensed Dinner Last d 9pm **Prices** S £45-£60; D £60-£90✳ **Parking** 50 **Notes** Closed Nov-Feb

MITCHELL

MAP 02 SW85

◆◆◆◆

The Beeches

Tredinnick Farm TR8 4PW ☎ 01872 510729
e-mail thebeeches2@btopenworld.com
Dir *1m N of village. A30 onto A3076, property on left*

Located near the A30, this light and airy establishment is well situated for touring Cornwall. The atmosphere is relaxed and friendly, and each bedroom, including one on the ground floor, has a cosy television area. Breakfast is served in the conservatory overlooking the rear garden.

Facilities 2 en suite (1 GF) ⊘ FTV TVB tea/coffee ✖ Cen ht No coaches **LB** **Parking** 3 **Notes** ⊠

MOUSEHOLE

MAP 02 SW42

★★★★ ◉◉ **Restaurant with Rooms**

The Cornish Range Restaurant with Rooms

6 Chapel St TR19 6BD ☎ 01736 731488
e-mail info@cornishrange.co.uk
Dir *Follow coast road through Newlyn into Mousehole. Along harbour past Ship Inn, turn sharp right, then left, located on right*

This is a memorable place to eat and stay. Stylish rooms, with delightful Cornish hand-made furnishings, and attentive, friendly service create a relaxing environment. Interesting and accurate cuisine relies heavily on local freshly landed fish and shellfish, as well as local meat and poultry, and the freshest fruit and vegetables.

Facilities 3 en suite TVB tea/coffee Licensed Dinner Last d 9pm
Prices D £100✳ **Notes** Closed 26 Dec & 1 Jan, Mon & Tue in winter

◆◆◆◆ ◖▮

Ship Inn

TR19 6QX ☎ 01736 731234 🖹 01736 732259
e-mail reservations@smallandfriendly.co.uk
Dir *Off B3315 into village*

This smart harbourside inn is full of charm, and friendly locals and staff provide a relaxed atmosphere. Many bedrooms have views over the harbour and across Mount's Bay towards the Lizard peninsula. Fresh Newlyn fish and shellfish feature in the restaurant and in the bar.

Facilities 6 en suite ⊘ TVB tea/coffee ✖ Cen ht ch fac No coaches Dinner Last d 9pm

MULLION

MAP 02 SW61

◆◆◆◆ ☙

Colvennor Farmhouse *(SW683219)*

Cury TR12 7BJ ☎ 01326 241208 Mrs Royds
e-mail colvennor@aol.com
Dir *A3083 Helston-Lizard, across rdbt at end of airfield, next right to Cury/Poldhu Cove, continue 1.4m, farm on right at top of hill*

The friendly proprietors ensure a comfortable stay at this Grade II listed property, which dates from the 17th century. Set in extensive

continued

tranquil grounds, the house is a good base for touring the Lizard peninsula. Freshly cooked breakfasts are served in the dining room.

Colvennor Farmhouse

Facilities 3 en suite (1 GF) ⊘ TVB tea/coffee ✖ Cen ht No children 10yrs **Prices** S £32-£36; D £50-£56 **LB** **Parking** 4 **Notes** Closed Dec & Jan ⊠

NEWQUAY

MAP 02 SW86

★★★★ ⒶGuest Accommodation

Pine Lodge ◈

91 Henver Rd TR7 3DJ ☎ 01637 850891 🖹 01637 877804
e-mail enquiries@pinelodgehotel.co.uk
Dir *A3059 towards Newquay across double rdbt, B&B on right past crossing.*

Facilities 12 en suite (4 fmly) (3 GF) ⊘ in bedrooms ⊘ in dining room ⊘ in 1 lounge TVB tea/coffee ✖ Licensed Cen ht TVL ↘ Pool Table Dinner Last d 8pm **Prices** S £29-£35; D £58-£70✳ **LB** **Parking** 14 **Notes** Closed 18 Dec-14 Feb

Premier Collection

◆◆◆◆◆ ⊛ ⊜

Corisande Manor Hotel

Riverside Av, Pentire TR7 1PL
☎ 01637 872042 🖹 01637 874557
e-mail relax@corisande.com
web www.corisande.com
Dir *Off A392 in Pentire*

This attractive manor house has a tranquil setting tucked away on the side of an estuary. The friendly proprietors provide attentive and skilled service. Bedrooms, many with superb views, are decorated and furnished with imagination and individuality. Freshly prepared dishes are offered from a daily changing menu, supported by a lovingly compiled wine list of considerable merit.

Facilities 9 en suite ⊘ in 2 bedrooms ⊘ in dining room ⊘ in lounges TVB tea/coffee Direct dial from bedrooms Licensed Cen ht No coaches Dinner Last d 6pm **Prices** D £150-£178✳ **LB** **Parking** 19 **Notes** Closed Oct-Apr

England

NEWQUAY continued

◆◆◆◆ ▶

Degembris ◇ (SW852568)

St Newlyn East TR8 5HY
☎ 01872 510555 📠 01872 510230 Mrs Woodley
e-mail kathy@degembris.co.uk
Dir 3m SE of Newquay. A30 onto A3058 towards Newquay, 3rd left to St Newlyn East & 2nd left

This delightful Grade II listed 16th-century farmhouse is convenient for The Eden Project and Newquay, and the warm hospitality and farmhouse breakfasts are highlights. The well-appointed bedrooms have lovely country views, as does the inviting sitting room.

Facilities 5 rms (3 en suite) (1 fmly) ⊗ TVB tea/coffee ✖ Cen ht TVL Farm trail 165 acres arable **Prices** S £28-£30; D £60-£64 **LB Conf** Max 12 **Parking** 8 **Notes** Closed Xmas

◆◆◆◆

Chynoweth Lodge ◇

1 Eliot Gdns TR7 2QE ☎ 01637 876684 📠 01637 876684
e-mail chynowethlodge@btconnect.com
Dir A30 onto A392 into Newquay. Right onto A3058 Trevemper Rd/Edgecombe Av, 4th left, 2nd road on right

A friendly, family home set in a peaceful location close to Tolcarne beach and the town's attractions. The comfortable bedrooms are pleasantly equipped. There is a spacious lounge and adequate parking. Dinner, by arrangement, is served in summer.

Facilities 9 en suite (4 fmly) (3 GF) ⊗ TVB tea/coffee Cen ht TVL No coaches Dinner Last d 9.30am **Prices** S £24-£30; D £48-£80✱ **LB Parking** 10 **Notes** ⊗

◆◆◆◆

Kallacliff Hotel ◇

12 Lusty Glaze Rd TR7 3AD ☎ 01637 871704
e-mail kallacliffhotel@btconnect.com
Dir 0.5m NE of town centre. A3058 to Newquay, right off Henver Rd onto Lusty Glaze Rd, 350yds on right

This popular establishment is in a peaceful area close to the South West Coast Path. There are stunning views of the Atlantic from the bar and the breakfast dining room, and some of the attractive bedrooms also have sea views. Beaches and eateries are just a stroll away.

Facilities 8 en suite (3 fmly) (2 GF) ⊗ TVB tea/coffee ✖ Licensed Cen ht TVL No coaches **Prices** D £60-£74✱ **LB Parking** 10

◆◆◆◆

Kellsboro Hotel

12 Henver Rd TR7 3BJ ☎ 01637 874620
e-mail kellsborohotel@btconnect.com
web www.kellsborohotel.co.uk
Dir In town on A3058 Henver Rd near Lusty Glaze Beach

Convenient for the town and beaches, this spacious property offers good hospitality. There is a large bar and games area, and the indoor pool is popular. Well-cooked traditional dinners are served in the attractive dining room.

Facilities 16 en suite (6 fmly) (2 GF) ⊗ in bedrooms ⊗ in dining room ⊗ in 1 lounge TVB tea/coffee Licensed Cen ht TVL No coaches ⛱ Pool Table Dinner Last d at breakfast **Prices** S £31-£41; D £52-£72✱ **LB Parking** 12 **Notes** Closed Nov

◆◆◆◆

Priory Lodge Hotel ◇

30 Mount Wise TR7 2BN ☎ 01637 874111 📠 01637 851803
e-mail fionapocklington@tiscali.co.uk
Dir At lights in town centre onto Berry Rd, right onto B3282 Mount Wise, 0.5m on right

A stroll from the town centre and beaches, this pleasant property provides an impressive range of facilities. The bedrooms are spacious, and some have a balcony and sea view. Dinner is a good range of choices, including vegetarian. Entertainment is provided in the bar most summer evenings.

Facilities 22 rms (20 en suite) 6 annexe en suite (13 fmly) (1 GF) ⊗ in bedrooms ⊗ in dining room ⊗ in lounges TVB tea/coffee Direct dial from bedrooms ✖ Licensed Cen ht TVL ⛱ Sauna Solarium Pool Table Video machines Outdoor jacuzzi Dinner Last d 7.30pm **Prices** S £30-£38; D £70-£76✱ **LB Parking** 30 **Notes** Closed 11-22 Dec & 4 Jan-early Mar

◆◆◆◆

Windward Hotel

Alexandra Rd, Porth Bay TR7 3NB
☎ 01637 873185 📠 01637 851400
e-mail enquiries@windwardhotel.co.uk
web www.windwardhotel.co.uk
Dir 1.5m NE of town centre. A3508 towards Newquay, right onto B3276 Padstow road, 1m on right

Windward is pleasantly located almost on Porth Beach and is convenient for the airport. It offers spectacular views, friendly hospitality, and a pleasant bar and terrace for relaxing. The spacious bedrooms, some with a balcony, and many with sea views, are well equipped, and the feature breakfast is served in the restaurant overlooking the beach.

Facilities 12 en suite (1 fmly) (2 GF) ⊗ TVB tea/coffee ✖ Licensed Cen ht TVL No coaches **Prices** S £49-£69; D £79-£99✱ **Conf** Max 12 **Parking** 12 **Notes** Closed Dec-Feb

The Pippin Guesthouse ◇

2 Godolphin Way TR7 3BU ☎ 01637 873979
e-mail thepippins@btinternet.com
web www.thepippinguesthouse.co.uk
Dir *A3058 to Newquay (Henver Rd), 1st right after double rdbt*

This family-run establishment is just a short walk from Newquay's
north beaches. The environment is friendly, the accommodation clean,
and the comfort is like home. Hearty, freshly cooked dinners and
breakfast are served in the light and airy dining room, which overlooks
the well-tended rear garden.

Facilities 7 rms (5 en suite) (2 pri facs) (1 fmly) (4 GF) ⊗ TVB
tea/coffee ✗ Cen ht TVL No children 2yrs Dinner Last d 10am
Prices S £24.50-£29.50; D £49-£59✳ **LB** **Parking** 8 **Notes** ⊠

The Three Tees Hotel

21 Carminow Way TR7 3AY
☎ 01637 872055 🗎 01637 872055
e-mail greg@3tees.co.uk
web www.3tees.co.uk
Dir *A30 onto A392 Newquay. Right at Quintrell Downs rdbt signed
Newquay (Porth), over double minirdbt & 3rd right*

Located in a quiet residential area just a short walk from the town and
beach, this friendly family-run accommodation is comfortable and well
equipped. There is a lounge, bar and a sun lounge. Breakfast is served
in the dining room, where snacks are available throughout the day.
Light snacks are available in the bar during the evenings.

Facilities 8 rms (7 en suite) (1 pri facs) 1 annexe en suite (4 fmly)
(2 GF) ⊗ TVB tea/coffee Licensed Cen ht TVL No coaches
Prices D £50-£70✳ **LB** **Parking** 11 **Notes** Closed Nov-Feb

Wenden

11 Berry Rd TR7 1AU ☎ 01637 872604 🗎 01637 872604
e-mail wenden@newquay-holidays.co.uk
web www.newquay-holidays.co.uk
Dir *In town centre off seafront Cliff Rd, near station*

The family-run guest house offers bright, modern accommodation
near the beach and the town centre. Bedrooms have been carefully
designed to make best use of space, and each is individually styled.
Breakfast, served in the stylish dining room, is a filling start to the day.

Facilities 7 en suite ⊗ in dining room TVB tea/coffee ✗ Cen ht
No children 16yrs No coaches **Prices** D £40-£60✳ **LB** **Parking** 5

The Croft Hotel

37 Mount Wise TR7 2BL ☎ 01637 871520 🗎 01637 871520
e-mail info@the-crofthotel.co.uk
web www.the-crofthotel.co.uk
Dir *A392, centre of town opp Towan Beach, at corner of Mount Wise
and Mayfield Rd*

Located just minutes from the town centre and beach, this
accommodation is comfortable and the friendly host creates a homely
atmosphere. A full English breakfast is served in the informal bar-dining
room, and enjoyable home-cooked dinners are available by arrangement.

Facilities 8 rms (6 en suite) (2 pri facs) (4 fmly) ⊗ in bedrooms
⊗ in dining room ⊗ in lounges TVB tea/coffee Licensed Cen ht Dinner
Last d Breakfast **Prices** D £45-£70✳ **LB** **Parking** 7

Dewolf Guest House ◇

100 Henver Rd TR7 3BL ☎ 01637 874746
e-mail holidays@dewolfguesthouse.com
Dir *In town on A3058 Henver Rd near sports centre*

Making you feel welcome and at home is the priority here. The
bedrooms in the main house are bright and well equipped, and there
are two chalets behind the establishment. The cosy lounge has pictures
and items that reflects the host's interest in wildlife. Dinner is available
by arrangement. Dewolf is just a short walk from Porth Beach.

Facilities 4 en suite 2 annexe en suite (2 fmly) (3 GF) ⊗ TVB
tea/coffee Licensed Cen ht TVL No coaches **Prices** S £22-£40;
D £44-£80✳ **LB** **Parking** 6

Pencrebar

4 Berry Rd TR7 1AT ☎ 01637 872037
e-mail enquiries@pencrebar.com
Dir *In town centre off seafront Cliff Rd, near station*

Please note that this establishment has recently changed hands. The
Pencrebar offers spacious, well-equipped rooms near the beach.
Breakfast is served in an attractive dining room, and the lounge-bar and
evening meals are available in high season. Parking is available.

Facilities 7 en suite (2 fmly) ⊗ in bedrooms ⊗ in dining room TVB
tea/coffee ✗ Licensed Cen ht TVL Parking charged in peak season
Dinner Last d 11am **Prices** D £40-£70✳ **LB** **Parking** 5 **Notes** Closed
Xmas rs Oct/May ⊠

Rolling Waves ◇

Alexandra Rd, Porth TR7 3NB
☎ 01637 873236 🗎 01637 873236
e-mail enquiries@rollingwaves.co.uk
Dir *A3059 onto B3276 into Porth, past beach, opp pitch & putt on right*

The friendly proprietors are most attentive and many guests return to
this peaceful establishment on an elevated position away from the
bustle of Newquay, overlooking Porth Beach. Dinner is available and
there are panoramic views from the bar.

Facilities 9 rms (8 en suite) (2 fmly) (5 GF) ⊗ TVB tea/coffee ✗
Licensed Cen ht TVL No coaches Dinner Last d 3pm **Prices** S £21-£28;
D £46-£60✳ **LB** **Parking** 9 **Notes** Closed 19-28 Dec

England

NEWQUAY continued

◆◆◆

Tir Chonaill Lodge ◇

106 Mount Wise TR7 1QP ☎ 01637 876492
e-mail tirchonailhotel@talk21.com
web www.tirchonaill.co.uk
Dir A392 into Newquay, last rdbt right onto Mount Wise

Expect a warm at the long-established and family-owned Tir Chonaill Lodge, situated close to the beaches and the town centre. Some of the neat bedrooms have wonderful views across town to the sea, and the wholesome dinners and ample breakfasts are sure to satisfy.

Facilities 9 en suite (9 fmly) (1 GF) ⊗ TVB tea/coffee Licensed Cen ht TVL **Prices** S £30-£50; D £50-£80✴ **LB** **Parking** 10

[U]

Meadow View

135 Mount Wise TR7 1QR ☎ 01637 873132
e-mail meadowview135@hotmail.com
Dir From A30 onto A39 to Quintrell Downs. Follow road into Newquay to Mountwise, Meadow View is on left before rdbt to Pentire

At the time of going to press the rating for this establishment had not been confirmed. Please check the AA website www.theAA.com for up-to-date information.

Facilities 7 en suite (2 fmly) ⊗ TVB tea/coffee ✕ Cen ht No coaches **Prices** D £40-£56✴ **LB** **Parking** 7 **Notes** Closed 7 Nov-mid Feb ⊛

[U]

Tregarthen Guest House

1 Arundel Way TR7 3BB ☎ 01637 873554 📠 01637 873554
e-mail info@tregarthen.co.uk
web www.tregarthen.co.uk
Dir From A30 at Indian Queens onto A392 to Quintnell Down. At rdbt turn right on Henvor Rd, over rdbt, then 2nd turning on right.

At the time of going to press the rating for this establishment had not been confirmed. Please check the AA website www.theAA.com for up-to-date information.

Facilities 5 en suite 2 annexe en suite (2 fmly) (6 GF) TVB tea/coffee Direct dial from bedrooms Cen ht Dinner Last d 11am **Prices** S £35-£45; D £44-£70✴ **LB** **Parking** 7 **Notes** Closed Xmas rs Oct-Jun ⊛

PADSTOW   MAP 02 SW97
See also **St Wenn**

Premier Collection

★★★★★ ⊛⊛⊛ **Restaurant with Rooms**

St Ervan Manor

The Old Rectory, St Ervan PL27 7TA ☎ 01841 540255
e-mail info@stervanmanor.co.uk
Dir 4m S of Padstow. A39 onto B3274 for Padstow, 2.5m left & signs to St Ervan Manor

The proprietors of this former Victorian rectory are at the cutting edge for providing good food and relaxed accommodation. They provide a pleasant Cornish welcome, a tranquil environment and professional service. Cuisine is very much to the fore, heavily reliant on fresh and local produce; there's a choice of tasting menus and an impressive wine selection too. The Garden Suite cottage has a bedroom, bathroom and a lounge.

Facilities 5 rms (4 en suite) (1 pri facs) 1 annexe en suite ⊗ TVB tea/coffee ✕ Licensed Cen ht No children 14yrs No coaches Dinner Last d 9pm **Prices** S £100-£185; D £140-£245✴ **Parking** 16 **Notes** Closed 19 Dec-19 Jan

Premier Collection

◆◆◆◆◆ ⌂

Cross House Hotel

Church St PL28 8BG ☎ 01841 532391 📠 01841 533633
e-mail info@crosshouse.co.uk
Dir A389 into town, one way past church, sharp left 50yds

A friendly and relaxed atmosphere prevails at this delightful Grade II listed Georgian house, which is a short walk from the picturesque harbour. The stylish bedrooms and bathrooms are spacious and complemented by an impressive range of accessories. Two sumptuous lounges are available and the premises are licensed. A choice of full English or continental breakfast is served in the cosy dining room.

Facilities 6 en suite 5 annexe en suite (3 fmly) (2 GF) ⊗ TVB tea/coffee Direct dial from bedrooms ✕ Licensed Cen ht No coaches **Prices** D £70-£125✴ **LB** **Parking** 4

◆◆◆◆◆

The Old Cabbage Patch

Trevone Rd, Trevone Bay PL28 8QX
☎ 01841 520956 ▤ 01841 520956
e-mail info@theoldcabbagepatch.co.uk
Dir 2m W of Padstow. Off B3276 into Trevone village centre

A warm welcome is assured at this charming, modern bungalow near the centre of Trevone. The well-equipped bedrooms are comfortable and stylishly decorated. Hearty, freshly cooked breakfasts are served in the dining room, which includes a sunny conservatory. Ample parking available.

Facilities 2 en suite (2 GF) ⊗ STV TVB tea/coffee ✘ Cen ht
No children 18yrs No coaches **Prices** D £80-£95✳ LB **Parking** 10
Notes Closed 31Oct-Mar

◆◆◆◆◆ 🄰

Woodlands Country House

Treator PL28 8RU ☎ 01841 532426 ▤ 01841 533353
e-mail info@woodlands-padstow.co.uk
Dir 1m W of Padstow on B3276

Facilities 9 en suite (1 fmly) (2 GF) ⊗ in bedrooms ⊗ in dining room
⊗ in 1 lounge TVB tea/coffee Direct dial from bedrooms Licensed
Cen ht TVL No coaches 🏓 table tennis **Prices** D £78-£132✳ LB
Parking 10 **Notes** Closed 16 Dec-1 Feb

◆◆◆◆

The Old Mill House

PL27 7QT ☎ 01841 540388 ▤ 01841 540406
e-mail enquiries@theoldmillhouse.com
web www.theoldmillhouse.com
Dir A389 between Wadebridge & Padstow, in centre of Little Petherick

Situated in an Area of Outstanding Natural Beauty, the Old Mill House is a 16th-century corn mill with attractive secluded gardens beside a gentle stream. Guests enjoy an English breakfast or a four-course dinner in the mill room where the mill wheel still turns.

Facilities 7 en suite ⊗ TVB tea/coffee Direct dial from bedrooms ✘
Licensed Cen ht TVL No children 14yrs No coaches Dinner Last
d 8.30pm **Prices** S £75-£115; D £75-£115✳ **Parking** 20 **Notes** Closed
Nov-Jan

◆◆◆◆

Penjoly Cottage

Padstow Rd PL28 8LB ☎ 01841 533535 ▤ 01841 532313
e-mail penjoly.padstow@btopenworld.com
Dir 1m S of Padstow. Off A389 near Padstow Holiday Park

Standing in extensive grounds, this is a good base for exploring north Cornwall. Bedrooms are carefully decorated and complemented with an impressive range of extras. Attention to detail is a hallmark throughout public areas. Breakfast is served in the attractive dining room or conservatory, and a lounge is also available.

Facilities 3 en suite (3 GF) ⊗ STV TVB tea/coffee ✘ Cen ht TVL
No children 16yrs No coaches **Prices** D £65-£73✳ LB **Parking** 10
Notes ⊛

◆◆◆◆

Rick Stein's Cafe

10 Middle St PL28 8AP ☎ 01841 532700 ▤ 01841 532942
e-mail reservations@rickstein.com
Dir A389 into town, one way past church, 3rd right

Another Rick Stein success story, this lively cafe by day, restaurant by night, offers good food, quality accommodation, and is just a short walk from the harbour. Three rooms are available, all quite different but sharing high standards of cosseting comfort. Friendly and personable staff complete the picture.

Facilities 3 en suite (1 fmly) ⊗ in dining room TVB tea/coffee Direct
dial from bedrooms Licensed Cen ht No coaches Dinner Last d 9.30pm
Prices D £90-£110✳ LB **Notes** rs 24-26 Dec & 1 May

◆◆◆◆

Roselyn

20 Grenville Rd PL28 8EX
☎ 01841 532756 ▤ 01841 532756
e-mail padstowbbroselyn@bushinternet.com
web www.padstowbbroselyn.co.uk
Dir After Welcome to Padstow sign, Grenville Rd 1st left

This charming small guest house is in a quiet residential area just a 10-minute walk from the centre of the delightful fishing village. The owners provide warm hospitality, and smartly furnished and well-equipped bedrooms. A good choice of breakfast options is available.

Facilities 3 en suite (1 fmly) ⊗ TVB tea/coffee ✘ Cen ht No coaches
Prices S £40-£45; D £60-£65✳ LB **Parking** 5 **Notes** rs Xmas ⊛

◆◆◆◆

Trevone Beach House

PL28 8QX ☎ 01841 520469 ▤ 01841 520469
e-mail info@trevonebeach.co.uk
Dir 1.5m W of Padstow. Off B3276 at windmill to Trevone, on left before beach car park

This friendly house is just a short walk from the beautiful sandy beach at Trevone Bay. Bedrooms, some on the ground floor, are light and airy and well equipped. There are two comfy lounges and a cosy bar, and imaginative home-cooked meals are served in the dining room.

Facilities 9 en suite (2 fmly) (2 GF) ⊗ TVB tea/coffee Licensed Cen ht
Dinner Last d 2pm **Prices** S £31-£35; D £68-£78✳ LB **Conf** Max 20
Class 20 Board 20 **Parking** 11 **Notes** rs Nov-Mar

England

PADSTOW continued

@@@ U ≧ ⊜

The Seafood Restaurant

Riverside PL28 8BY ☎ 01841 532700 ⧉ 01841 532942
e-mail reservations@rickstein.com

Dir A38 towards Newquay, then A389 towards Padstow. After 3m, right at T-junct, follow signs for Padstow town centre. Restaurant on left

At the time of going to press the rating for Rick Stein's Seafood Restaurant had not been confirmed. Please check the AA website www.theAA.com for up-to-date information.

Facilities 14 en suite 6 annexe en suite (6 fmly) (3 GF) ⊗ in bedrooms STV TVB tea/coffee Direct dial from bedrooms Licensed Cen ht No coaches No children 3yrs Dinner Last d 10pm **Prices** D £120-£250✻ **LB Conf** Max 50 Thtr 50 Board 18 **Parking** 12 **Notes** rs May & Dec

PENZANCE   MAP 02 SW43

★★★ Inn

The Swordfish Inn

The Strand, Newlyn TR18 5HN ☎ 01736 362830
e-mail info@swordfishinn.co.uk

Situated in the very heart of the fishing village of Newlyn, the Swordfish was totally renovated during 2005. The spacious en suite bedrooms are well appointed, as are the shower rooms. A popular drinking venue for locals and tourists alike.

Facilities 4 en suite TVB tea/coffee ✘ Cen ht

Premier Collection

◆◆◆◆◆

Chy-an-Mor

15 Regent Ter TR18 4DW
☎ 01736 363441 ⧉ 01736 363441
e-mail reception@chyanmor.co.uk
web www.chyanmor.co.uk

Dir A30 to Penzance, at railway station follow road along harbour front onto Promenade Rd, pass Jubilee Pool, right at Stanley Hotel

This elegant Grade II listed Georgian house has been refurbished to provide high standards throughout. Bedrooms are individually designed and equipped with thoughtful extras, and many have spectacular views of Mount's Bay. The spacious lounge has similar views, and tasty breakfasts are served in the dining room.

Facilities 10 en suite (2 fmly) (3 GF) ⊗ TVB tea/coffee ✘ Cen ht No children 10yrs No coaches **Prices** S £34-£43; d fr £58✻ **Parking** 12 **Notes** Closed Nov-Jan rs Feb

Premier Collection

◆◆◆◆◆ ≧ ✿

Ennys Farm (SW559328)

Trewhella Ln, St Hilary TR20 9BZ
☎ 01736 740262 ⧉ 01736 740055 Miss Charlton
e-mail ennys@ennys.co.uk
web www.ennys.co.uk

For full entry see **St Hilary**

Premier Collection

◆◆◆◆◆ @@ ≧ ⊜

The Summerhouse

Cornwall Ter TR18 4HL ☎ 01736 363744 ⧉ 01736 360959
e-mail reception@summerhouse-cornwall.com
web www.summerhouse-cornwall.com

Dir A30 to Penzance, at railway station follow road along harbour front onto Promenade Rd, pass Jubilee Pool, right after Queens Hotel, Summerhouse 30yds on left

This house, in a delightful residential location close to the seafront and harbour, is decorated in a Mediterranean style. The walled garden also reflects the theme, with sub-tropical plantings and attractive blue tables and chairs; dinner and drinks are served here on summer evenings. Expect warm hospitality and attentive service. Fresh local produce is simply prepared to provide memorable dishes on the daily changing menu.

Facilities 5 en suite ⊗ in bedrooms ⊗ in dining room TVB tea/coffee ✘ Licensed Cen ht TVL No children 13yrs No coaches Dinner **Prices** D £90-£110✻ **LB Parking** 6 **Notes** Closed Nov-Feb

◆◆◆◆ ≧

Blue Seas ◇

13 Regent Ter TR18 4DW ☎ 01736 364744
e-mail blueseas@ukonline.co.uk

Dir A30 to Penzance, at railway station follow road along harbour front onto Promenade Rd. Opp Jubilee Bathing Pool, Regent Ter 2nd right

This comfortable house has great views of Mount's Bay. Convenient for the ferry and Scillies heliport, the Blue Seas is only a stroll from the town centre. Bedrooms are well equipped, the spacious lounge has books and magazines, and you can relax in the garden. Attractively presented and freshly prepared, breakfast features local and home-made produce.

continued

Blue Seas

Facilities 9 en suite (2 fmly) (3 GF) ⊘ TVB tea/coffee ✗ Cen ht No coaches **Prices** S £28-£35; D £56-£70✳ **LB Parking** 9 **Notes** Closed Dec-Jan

◆◆◆◆
Camilla House ◇

12 Regent Ter TR18 4DW ☎ 01736 363771 📠 01736 363771
e-mail enquiries@camillahouse.co.uk
web www.camillahouse.co.uk
Dir A30 to Penzance, at railway station follow road along harbour front onto Promenade Rd. Opp Jubilee Bathing Pool, Regent Ter 2nd right

The friendly proprietors at this attractive Grade II listed terrace house do their utmost to ensure a comfortable stay. Particularly suited to business guests, it is also a good base for touring. Wireless Internet access is available throughout the house, and there is also access to computers in the lounge. Bedrooms are attractive and many have delightful sea views.

Facilities 8 rms (7 en suite) (1 pri facs) (1 GF) ⊘ FTV TVB tea/coffee ✗ Licensed Cen ht TVL No coaches Free internet access in hotel Dinner Last d 9pm **Prices** S £28-£35; D £60-£79✳ **LB Parking** 6

◆◆◆◆
The Dunedin ◇

Alexandra Rd TR18 4LZ ☎ 01736 362652 📠 01736 360497
e-mail info@dunedinhotel.co.uk
web www.dunedinhotel.co.uk
Dir A30 to Penzance, at railway station along harbour front onto Promenade Rd, right onto Alexandra Rd, Dunedin on right

The house is in a tree-lined avenue just a stroll from the promenade and town centre. The friendly proprietors provide a relaxed atmosphere. Bedrooms are well equipped and smartly decorated to a high standard. There is a cosy lounge and hearty breakfasts are served in the dining room. *continued*

The Dunedin

Facilities 8 rms (8 pri facs) (2 fmly) (2 GF) ⊘ TVB tea/coffee ✗ Cen ht TVL **Prices** S £24-£32.50; D £48-£65✳ **LB Notes** Closed 19-28 Dec ⊛

◆◆◆◆
Lombard House Hotel

16 Regent Ter TR18 4DW
☎ 01736 364897 📠 01736 364897
e-mail lombardhouse@btconnect.com
web www.lombardhousehotel.com
Dir A30 to Penzance, at railway station along harbour front onto Promenade Rd. Opp Jubilee Bathing Pool, Regent Ter 2nd right

The house has a pleasant outlook across Mount's Bay towards Newlyn and Mousehole and is a convenient overnight stay for the Scillies. Bedrooms come in a range of sizes and are well equipped. There is a cosy lounge, and a large dining room where freshly cooked breakfasts are served.

Facilities 9 en suite (2 fmly) ⊘ TVB tea/coffee ✗ Cen ht TVL No coaches **Parking** 10

◆◆◆◆
The Old Vicarage

Churchtown, St Hilary TR20 9DQ
☎ 01736 711508 & 07736 101230 📠 01736 711508
e-mail johnbd524@aol.com
Dir 5m E of Penzance. Off B3280 in St Hilary

You are made to feel welcome at this friendly home. The spacious bedrooms are thoughtfully equipped, and there is a private bar-snooker room, a comfortable lounge and extensive gardens. The proprietors also run trekking and a horse-riding school.

Facilities 3 en suite (1 fmly) ⊘ in bedrooms ⊘ in dining room ⊘ in 1 lounge FTV TVB tea/coffee ✗ Licensed Cen ht TVL No coaches Riding Snooker **Prices** D £50-£70✳ **Parking** 8 **Notes** ⊛

England

PENZANCE continued

◆◆◆◆ ❦
Rose Farm (SW446290)
Chyanhal, Buryas Br TR19 6AN
☎ 01736 731808 📠 01736 731808 Mrs Lally
e-mail penny@rosefarmcornwall.co.uk
web www.rosefarmcornwall.co.uk
Dir 1.5m S of Penzance. Off A30 at Drift (behind phone box), 0.75m on left

Situated in peaceful countryside near Penzance, this working farm provides cosy accommodation with a genuine welcome and relaxed atmosphere. Bedrooms are attractively designed and well equipped, and some rooms have a private entrance. A hearty breakfast is served in the lounge-dining room at a refectory table.

Facilities 2 en suite 1 annexe en suite (1 fmly) (1 GF) ⊗ in bedrooms ⊗ in dining room TVB tea/coffee ✖ Cen ht Artist studio 23 acres beef **Prices** D £60-£70✳ **LB Parking** 8 **Notes** Closed 24-27 Dec

◆◆◆◆ 🅰
The Old Barn Bosulval ◇
Newmill TR20 8XA ☎ 01736 367742
e-mail info@laidback-trails.co.uk
Facilities 3 rms (1 en suite) ⊗ TVB tea/coffee ✖ Cen ht No coaches Golf 18 Guided walks Dinner Last d 24hrs before **Prices** S £30-£35; D £50-£60✳ **LB Parking** 3

◆◆◆
Estoril Hotel ◇
46 Morrab Rd TR18 4EX ☎ 01736 362468 📠 01736 367471
e-mail enquiries@estorilhotel.co.uk
web www.estorilhotel.co.uk
Dir A30 onto seafront road towards Newlyn, right before Queens Hotel onto Morrab Rd, 250yds on left

This family-run establishment is close to the centre of Penzance. Many return for the friendly welcome, and the well-equipped bedrooms, some with sea views, come in a choice of sizes. Freshly cooked breakfasts and a pleasant range of dinner dishes are served at separate tables in the dining room.

Facilities 9 en suite (2 fmly) ⊗ STV TVB tea/coffee ✖ Licensed Cen ht No coaches Dinner Last d 4pm **Prices** S £25-£35; D £50-£70✳ **LB Parking** 4

◆◆◆
Penmorvah Hotel ◇
61 Alexandra Rd TR18 4LZ ☎ 01736 363711 & 07875 675940
Dir A30 to Penzance, at railway station follow road along harbour front onto Promenade Rd. Right onto Alexandra Rd, Penmorvah on right

Situated in a quiet, tree-lined road just a short walk from the seafront and town centre, and convenient for the ferry port, the Penmorvah has a friendly and relaxing atmosphere. Bedrooms are well appointed and equipped with many thoughtful extras. Well-cooked breakfasts are served in the attractive dining room.

Facilities 8 en suite (2 fmly) (1 GF) ⊗ TVB tea/coffee Cen ht TVL **Prices** S £20-£27; D £40-£54

◆◆◆
Woodstock ◇
29 Morrab Rd TR18 4EZ ☎ 01736 369049 📠 01736 369049
e-mail info@woodstockguesthouse.co.uk
web www.woodstockguesthouse.co.uk
Dir From railway station, along seafront 0.6m, right at approach to Queens Hotel, Woodstock 200yds on right

This smart Victorian terrace house stands in well-tended gardens in a quiet residential area convenient for the town and seafront. The friendly proprietors provide attentive service. The smart bedrooms are well equipped and the beds are particularly comfortable. Hearty breakfasts are served in the dining room.

Facilities 8 rms (5 en suite) (1 fmly) (1 GF) ⊗ TVB tea/coffee No children 5yrs No coaches **Prices** S £24-£32; D £52-£64✳ **Notes** Closed Jan

◆◆◆
The Carlton ◇
Prom TR18 4NW ☎ 01736 362081 📠 01736 362081
e-mail carltonhotelpenzance@talk21.com
Dir From A30 follow signs for harbour & Newlyn. Hotel on right after rdbt

Situated on the pleasant promenade and having sea views from some of its rooms, the Carlton is an easy stroll from the town centre and amenities. Bedrooms are traditionally styled. The lounge and spacious dining room are both sea facing.

Facilities 12 rms (9 en suite) ⊗ in 9 bedrooms TVB tea/coffee ✖ TVL No coaches **Prices** S £25-£30; D £50-£60✳

♦♦♦
Coth'a Noweth

Catchall, Buryas Br TR19 6AQ ☎ 01736 810572

Dir On A30 past Penzance towards Land's End, 0.25m after B3283 to St Buryan

This charming granite house stands in delightful gardens bordered by a trout stream, and is convenient for the Minack Theatre and Land's End. A friendly welcome is assured. The attractive bedrooms are furnished with pine, and feature polished wood floors.

Facilities 4 rms (2 fmly) ⊗ in dining room ✱ Cen ht TVL No coaches **Prices** S fr £18; D £35-£39 **LB Parking** 8 **Notes** Closed Oct-start of Etr ⊠

♦♦♦
Mount Royal

Chyandour Cliff TR18 3LQ
☎ 01736 362233 🖨 01736 362233
e-mail mountroyal@btconnect.com
Dir Off A30 onto coast road into town

Part Georgian and part Victorian, the spacious Mount Royal has splendid views over Mount's Bay and is convenient for the town's attractions. The elegant dining room retains its original fireplace and ornate sideboard. Parking available.

Facilities 7 en suite (3 fmly) (1 GF) ⊗ FTV TVB tea/coffee ✱ Cen ht No coaches Pool Table **Prices** D £70-£75✳ **LB Parking** 10 **Notes** Closed Nov-Mar ⊠

♦♦♦
Mount View

Longrock TR20 8JJ ☎ 01736 710416 🖨 01736 710416
Dir Off A30 at Marazion/Penzance rdbt, 3rd exit signed Longrock. Hotel on right after pelican crossing

This Victorian inn, just a short walk from the beach and 0.5m from the Isles of Scilly heliport, is a good base for exploring west Cornwall. Bedrooms are well equipped. Breakfast is served in the dining room, and the bar is popular with locals. A dinner menu is available.

Facilities 5 rms (3 en suite) (2 fmly) ⊗ in dining room TVB tea/coffee Pool Table Dinner Last d 8.30pm **Prices** S £20-£27.50; D £40-£55 **Conf** Max 20 **Parking** 8

♦♦♦
Southern Comfort

Seafront, 8 Alexandra Ter TR18 4NX ☎ 01736 366333
Dir Follow seafront road 0.75m. At 1st rdbt continue along seafront for 0.25m, right after Lidl store, establishment clearly marked

This grand Victorian house is in a quiet location overlooking the bay and St Michael's Mount. A pleasant welcome awaits all guests, both tourist and business. Breakfast is served in the lower-ground dining room, and you can enjoy a drink either outside in summer or in the bar or lounge.

Facilities 12 en suite (2 fmly) ⊗ STV FTV TVB tea/coffee Licensed Cen ht TVL No coaches Dinner Last d noon **Prices** S £35-£45; D £60-£85✳ **LB Parking** 6 **Notes** ⊠

PERRANPORTH MAP 02 SW75

♦♦♦♦ 🄰
The Tides Reach

Ponsmere Rd TR6 0BW ☎ 01872 572188 🖨 01872 572188
e-mail jandf.boyle@virgin.net
web www.tidesreachhotel.com
Dir A30 onto B3285 to Perranporth. Onto St Piran's Rd, hotel 150yds along Ponsmere Rd on right

Facilities 9 rms (8 en suite) (1 pri facs) (1 fmly) (3 GF) ⊗ TVB tea/coffee ✱ Licensed Cen ht No children 5yrs No coaches Outdoor Hot Tub Dinner Last d 2pm **Prices** S £30-£35; D £60-£74✳ **LB Parking** 9

PERRANUTHNOE MAP 02 SW52

♦♦♦♦♦ 🛏 💗
Ednovean Farm (SW538295)

TR20 9LZ ☎ 01736 711883 Mr & Mrs Taylor
e-mail info@ednoveanfarm.co.uk
web www.ednoveanfarm.co.uk
Dir Off A394 Penzance-Helston towards Perranuthnoe at Dynasty Restaurant, farm drive on left on bend by post box

Tranquillity is guaranteed at this 17th-century farmhouse, which looks across countryside towards Mount's Bay. The bedrooms are individually styled and are most comfortable. The impressive Mediterranean style gardens are lovely to relax in. In addition to the sitting room, there is also a garden room and several patios. Breakfast is served at a magnificent oak table.

Facilities 3 en suite (3 GF) ⊗ TVB tea/coffee ✱ Cen ht No children 16yrs 22 acres grassland/horticultural **Prices** S fr £80; D £80-£100✳ **Parking** 4 **Notes** Closed 24-28 Dec & New Year

England

PERRANUTHNOE continued

◆◆◆◆

Ednovean House ◇

TR20 9LZ ☎ 01736 711071
e-mail clive@ednoveanhouse.co.uk
web www.ednoveanhouse.co.uk
Dir Off A394 at Perran x-rds between Penzance and Helston, 1st lane left, continue to end past farm

Ednovean House is in a tranquil location with spectacular views of Mount's Bay and St Michael's Mount. It is ideal for a relaxing break or for touring the area. The house has comfortable lounges, a bar, and well-tended gardens and terraces. Bedrooms are attractively decorated.

Facilities 7 en suite ⊗ tea/coffee Licensed Cen ht TVL No children 7yrs No coaches ♨ **Prices** S £28-£30; D £50-£78✱ **Parking** 12 **Notes** Closed Xmas & New Year

◆◆◆◆

Quilkyns Bed & Breakfast

1 St Pirans Way TR20 9NJ ☎ 01736 719141
e-mail paul@quilkyns.co.uk
Dir Off A394 into village, left onto St Pirans Way

Expect a friendly welcome at this family home. Quilkyns is in a quiet location convenient for the pleasant beach at Perran Sands or for the South West Coast Path. The spacious bedrooms are thoughtfully equipped and look across the garden to the sea.

Facilities 2 rms (1 en suite) (1 pri facs) (1 fmly) (2 GF) ⊗ TVB tea/coffee ✖ Cen ht No children 7yrs No coaches **Prices** S £35; D £50✱ **Parking** 2 **Notes** Closed Dec & Jan ⊛

◆◆◆ ◫

The Victoria Inn

TR20 9NP ☎ 01736 710309 ▤ 01736 719284
Dir Off A394 into village

Please note that this establishment has recently changed hands. The attractive and friendly inn, popular with locals and visitors alike, reputedly originates from the Middle Ages. Daily specials in the cosy bar or the dining room include local fish, while the bedrooms are small but well equipped.

Facilities 3 en suite ⊗ TVB tea/coffee ✖ No children 18yrs Dinner Last d 9pm **Prices** S £35; D £60✱ **Parking** 10 **Notes** Closed 2 wks Jan

POLPERRO   MAP 02 SX25

Premier Collection

◆◆◆◆◆ ❦

Trenderway (SX214533)

Pelynt PL13 2LY
☎ 01503 272214 ▤ 01503 272991 Mrs Tuckett
e-mail enquiries@trenderwayfarmholidays.co.uk
web www.trenderwayfarmholidays.co.uk
Dir A387 from Looe to Polperro, farm signed, onto 2nd signed turning

Warm hospitality is offered at this delightful 16th-century farmhouse, set in 300 acres of beautiful Cornish countryside. The stylish bedrooms (in the farmhouse or the adjacent barns) are luxuriously furnished and equipped. Hearty breakfasts, with free-range eggs from the farm, are served in the conservatory, or on the patio that looks across fields to the lakes beyond. In winter there is an open fire in the comfortable sitting room.

Facilities 2 en suite 4 annexe en suite (1 GF) ⊗ TVB tea/coffee ✖ Cen ht No children Fishing lakes 300 acres arable mixed sheep **Prices** S £35-£40 LB **Parking** 6 **Notes** Closed Xmas & New Year

◆◆◆◆ 🏛

Allhays Country Bed & Breakfast

Porthallow PL13 2JB ☎ 01503 273188
e-mail info@allhays.co.uk
Dir 2m from Looe on Polperro road, left signed Talland, 1m down lane

Built in the late 1930s, this spacious family home has a wonderful location with spectacular views over the rugged and unspoiled beauty of Talland Bay. A peaceful hideaway, the standard throughout is high with all bedrooms furnished with comfort and quality in mind. In addition to extensive gardens, public areas include a snug lounge and the conservatory. Imaginative breakfasts, using excellent local produce, are enjoyed against the scenic backdrop.

Facilities 3 en suite 1 annexe en suite (1 GF) ⊗ TVB tea/coffee ✗ Cen ht No children 10yrs No coaches **Prices** S £45-£75; D £70-£90✳ **Parking** 6 **Notes** Closed Dec

◆◆◆◆ ♥

Trenake Manor Farm *(SX190555)*

Pelynt PL13 2LT
☎ 01503 220835 📠 01503 220835 Mrs Philp
e-mail lorraine@cornishfarmhouse.co.uk
Dir 3.5m N of Polperro. A390 onto B3359 for Looe, 5m left at small x-rds

The welcoming 17th-century farmhouse is surrounded by countryside and is a good base for touring Cornwall. Bedrooms have considerate finishing touches and there is a comfortable lounge. Breakfast, using local produce, is enjoyed in the cosy dining room (you may just spot the milking cows quietly passing the end of the garden).

Facilities 3 en suite (1 fmly) ⊗ TVB tea/coffee Cen ht TVL 300 acres arable, dairy & beef **Prices** D £56-£60✳ **LB** **Parking** 10 **Notes** 🐾

◆◆◆◆ 🍽

Penryn House

The Coombes PL13 2RQ ☎ 01503 272157 📠 01503 273055
e-mail chrispidcock@aol.com
web www.penrynhouse.co.uk
Dir A387 to Polperro, at minirdbt left down hill into village (ignore restricted access). Hotel 200yds on left

Penryn House has a relaxed atmosphere and every effort is made to ensure a memorable stay. Bedrooms are neatly presented and reflect the character of the building. After a day exploring, enjoy a drink at the bar and relax in the comfortable lounge.

Facilities 12 rms (11 en suite) (1 pri facs) (3 fmly) ⊗ in bedrooms ⊗ in dining room TVB tea/coffee Direct dial from bedrooms Licensed No coaches **Prices** S £31-£35; D £62-£80 **LB** **Parking** 13

POLZEATH   MAP 02 SW97

◆◆◆

Seaways ◇

PL27 6SU ☎ 01208 862382
e-mail pauline@seaways99.freeserve.co.uk
Dir 250yds E of village centre

Seaways is just a short walk from the sandy beach popular with surfers and bathers. The house offers comfortable accommodation and a friendly environment, and an open fire burns in the cosy lounge on cooler evenings. Breakfast is served in a pleasant dining room.

Facilities 5 rms (3 en suite) (2 pri facs) (1 fmly) (1 GF) ⊗ TVB tea/coffee ✗ Cen ht TVL No coaches **Prices** S £27.50-£30; D £55-£60✳ **LB** **Parking** 5 **Notes** 🐾

PORTHCURNO   MAP 02 SW32

◆◆◆◆

The Porthcurno Hotel

The Valley TR19 6JX
☎ 01736 810119 & 07812 383221 📠 01736 810711
e-mail mail@porthcurnohotel.co.uk
web www.porthcurnohotel.co.uk
Dir Off B3315 for Porthcurno

You are assured of a friendly welcome and attentive service at the Porthcurno, set in the dramatic cove of Porthcurno, near the open-air Minack Theatre. The stylish dining room, with spectacular views, has a daily-changing menu using fresh local produce. Enjoy the sub-tropical gardens or take a drink on the balcony.

Facilities 8 en suite (1 fmly) (1 GF) ⊗ TVB tea/coffee ✗ Licensed Cen ht TVL No coaches Dinner Last d 8pm **Prices** S £50-£85; D £70-£110✳ **LB** **Conf** Max 28 **Parking** 16

PORTHLEVEN   MAP 02 SW62

◆◆◆◆ 🍴

Harbour Inn

Commercal Rd TR13 9JB ☎ 01326 573876 📠 01326 572124
e-mail reservations@smallandfriendly.co.uk
Dir In village by harbour

This pleasant harbourside inn is decked with flowers in summer. The spacious bars offer local beers, and there is a good choice of freshly cooked dishes. The smart contemporary bedrooms are very comfortable and well equipped, and many have harbour views.

Facilities 10 en suite (2 fmly) ⊗ in bedrooms ⊗ in dining room ⊗ in lounges STV FTV TVB tea/coffee Direct dial from bedrooms ✗ Cen ht TVL Pool Table Dinner Last d 9pm **Prices** S £35-£38; D £69-£70✳ **LB** **Conf** Max 20 **Parking** 10

PORT ISAAC

MAP 02 SW98

◆◆◆◆

The Corn Mill

Port Isaac Rd, Trelill PL30 3HZ ☎ 01208 851079
Dir *Off B3314, between Pendoggett and Trelill*

Dating from the 18th century, this mill has been lovingly restored to provide a home packed full of character. The bedrooms are individually styled and personal touches create a wonderfully relaxed and homely atmosphere. The farmhouse kitchen is the venue for a delicious breakfast.

Facilities 3 rms (2 en suite) (1 fmly) ⊗ TV1B tea/coffee Cen ht No coaches **Parking** 3 **Notes** Closed 24 Dec-5 Jan ⊠

PORTLOE

MAP 02 SW93

◆◆◆◆

Carradale ◇

TR2 5RB ☎ 01872 501508
e-mail theguesthouse.portlow@virgin.net
Dir *Off A3078 into Portloe, B&B 200yds from Ship Inn*

Carradale lies on the outskirts of the picturesque fishing village, a short walk from the South West Coast Path. It provides warm hospitality, a good level of comfort and well-equipped bedrooms. The upper-floor lounge has a television. Breakfast is served around a communal table in the pleasant dining room.

Facilities 2 en suite (1 fmly) (1 GF) ⊗ TV1B tea/coffee ✖ Cen ht TVL No coaches **Prices** S £30-£35; D £50-£55✱ **Parking** 5 **Notes** ⊠

PORTSCATHO

MAP 02 SW83

◆◆◆◆

Hillside House

8 The Square TR2 5HW ☎ 01872 580526
e-mail info@hillsidehouse-portscatho.co.uk
web www.hillsidehouse-portscatho.co.uk
Dir *In village centre*

Located in the centre of the quiet, picturesque seaside village, this establishment has been refurbished to a very high quality to provide stylish bedrooms and public areas. A continental breakfast is offered weekdays, while a traditional full English breakfast is available at weekends.

Facilities 6 en suite (1 fmly) ⊗ TVB tea/coffee Direct dial from bedrooms ✖ Cen ht No coaches **Parking** 3

PRAA SANDS

MAP 02 SW52

◆◆◆◆ 🕎

Gwynoon ◇

Chy-an-Dour Rd TR20 9SY ☎ 01736 763508
e-mail enquiries@gwynoon.co.uk
web www.gwynoon.co.uk
Dir *Off A394 at Germoe x-rds into village, 2nd left after Post Office, house on left*

Praa Sands is one of Cornwall's dazzling beaches. Gwynoon has excellent views from the front bedrooms, balcony and the well-tended gardens. Bedrooms are well furnished and have many extras. The hosts are very attentive and provide a peaceful atmosphere, and their enjoyable breakfasts feature fresh local produce.

Facilities 3 en suite (2 fmly) (1 GF) ⊗ TVB tea/coffee ✖ Cen ht No coaches **Prices** S £30; D £60 **Parking** 6 **Notes** ⊠

REDRUTH

MAP 02 SW64

★★ Inn

The Lanner Inn

The Square, Lanner TR16 6EH
☎ 01209 215611 🖷 01209 214065
e-mail enquiries@lannerinn.co.uk
web www.lannerinn.co.uk
Dir *Take Redruth exit from A30, follow Falmouth signs, Lanner is situated on the A393.*

This inn is ideal for those wanting a real pub atmosphere with a variety of real ales. Beside the bar, where friendly hospitality is extended to all, there is a snooker room and locals enjoy a game of darts. A full English breakfast is served in the bar-dining room.

Facilities 7 rms (4 en suite) (2 fmly) (1 GF) ⊗ in bedrooms ⊗ in dining room ⊗ in lounges TVB tea/coffee ✖ Cen ht No coaches **Parking** 16 **Notes** rs 23 Dec-1 Jan
See advertisement on opposite page

◆◆◆◆

Trewan House

Wheal Rose, Scorrier TR16 5DF
☎ 01209 890537 & 07771 915470
Dir *A30 onto A3047 at Scorrier. Right after pub, 1st left for Wheal Rose. Through village, sign on left Lansdown Park Homes, turn in at concrete pillars on right, 2nd house on right*

This accommodation stands in pretty gardens in a peaceful location,

continued

and you can expect quality, comfort and friendly hospitality. The ground-floor bedrooms are well equipped and finished with considerate extras. Hearty breakfasts are served around a communal table in the smart first-floor lounge-dining room.

Facilities 3 rms (1 en suite) (3 GF) TVB tea/coffee **⊀** Cen ht TVL No coaches **Parking** 6 **Notes** Closed Xmas & New Year 🚫

◆◆◆

Lansdowne Guest House ◇

Lansdowne House, 42 Clinton Rd TR15 2QE
☎ 01209 216002 📠 01209 216002
Dir A393 S from town centre, under railway bridge, pass library, 200yds on right

This detached Edwardian house, formerly owned by a tea merchant, is in a residential area within easy walking distance of the town centre and the railway station. The comfortable bedrooms are well equipped and a hearty breakfast is served in the cosy dining room.

Facilities 7 rms (3 en suite) (1 fmly) (1 GF) TVB tea/coffee **⊀** Cen ht No coaches **Prices** S £24-£35; D £48-£60✳ **Parking** 5

ROCHE   MAP 02 SW96

◆◆◆

Saffron Park ◇

Belowda PL26 8NL ☎ 01726 890105 & 07930 572536
e-mail saffron.park@btinternet.com
Dir 1.5m N of Roche. N off A30 onto minor road near junct B3274, signed Demelza/St Wenn

Saffron Park is midway between the north and south coasts and very convenient for The Eden Project. Friendly hospitality and attentive service are provided, and there is a comfortable lounge and pleasant bedrooms. A hearty breakfast is served in the dining room.

Facilities 2 en suite (1 fmly) TVB tea/coffee Cen ht TVL No coaches Sauna spa bath **Prices** S £25; D £50✳ **Parking** 5 **Notes** Closed 22 Dec-2 Jan 🚫

ROCK   MAP 02 SW97

◆◆◆◆ 🛏

The Gleneglos

Trewint Ln PL27 6LU ☎ 01208 862369 📠 01208 862797
e-mail franklin.gleneglos@btopenworld.com
web www.gleneglos.co.uk
Dir Turn off main street in Rock at x-rds

Located on the outskirts of the village, this Edwardian house offers well-equipped accommodation. Relax in the gardens in summer, or retreat to the cosy lounge with its open fire in winter. Breakfast, featuring local produce, is served in the pleasant dining room; the restaurant is open to non-residents for freshly prepared dinners.

Facilities 6 rms (5 en suite) (1 pri facs) (1 fmly) in 3 bedrooms in dining room in lounges TVB tea/coffee **⊀** Licensed Cen ht TVL No coaches Dinner Last d noon **Prices** D £62-£69✳ LB **Parking** 12 **Notes** Closed Dec rs Jan-Feb

◆◆◆

Roskarnon House Hotel

PL27 6LD ☎ 01208 862329 📠 01208 862785
The same family has run this property for over 45 years, which has fine views over the Camel estuary towards Padstow. Most of the traditionally furnished public rooms and bedrooms have impressive views.

Facilities 12 rms (10 en suite) (5 fmly) in bedrooms in dining room TVB tea/coffee **⊀** Licensed TVL No coaches Last d 8pm **Prices** S fr £35; d fr £70✳ LB **Parking** 16 **Notes** Closed Nov-Mar

RUAN MINOR   MAP 02 SW71

◆◆◆◆

The Coach House ◇

Kuggar TR12 7LY ☎ 01326 291044 📠 01326 291044
e-mail janmakin@aol.com
Dir 1m N of Ruan Minor in Kuggar village

This 17th-century house is close to Kennack Sands and Goonhilly Downs nature reserve. The friendly proprietors provide a warm welcome for their guests, who can relax in the spacious lounge-dining room where a fire burns in colder months. Bedrooms, two of which are in a converted stable block, are attractively decorated.

Facilities 3 en suite 2 annexe en suite (2 GF) STV TVB tea/coffee **⊀** Cen ht TVL No coaches **Prices** S £28-£30; D £56-£60✳ LB **Parking** 10 **Notes** Closed Xmas 🚫

England

ST AGNES
MAP 02 SW75

◆◆◆◆

Driftwood Spars Hotel

Trevaunance Cove TR5 0RT
☎ 01872 552428 & 553323 📠 01872 553701
e-mail driftwoodspars@aol.com
web www.driftwoodspars.com
Dir 0.5m N from village to Trevaunance Cove

The 18th-century inn was partly built from shipwreck timbers, hence the name. The attractive bedrooms, some in an annexe, are decorated in a bright seaside style and have many interesting features. Local produce served in the informal pub-dining area or in the restaurant ranges from hand-pulled beers to delicious smoked fish.

Facilities 9 en suite 6 annexe en suite (4 fmly) (5 GF) ⊗ in dining room ⊗ in 1 lounge TVB tea/coffee Direct dial from bedrooms Lift Cen ht TVL Snooker Pool Table Sea fishing Surfing Marine life Dinner Last d 9.30pm **Prices** S £41-£59; D £82-£94✳ **Conf** Max 20 Thtr 40 Class 40 Board 20 **Parking** 81 **Notes** Closed 24-25 Dec

◆◆

Penkerris ◇

Penwinnick Rd TR5 0PA ☎ 01872 552262 📠 01872 552262
e-mail info@penkerris.co.uk
web www.penkerris.co.uk
Dir A30 onto B3277 to village, 1st house on right after village sign

Set in gardens on the edge of the village, Penkerris is an Edwardian house with a relaxed atmosphere. The best possible use is made of space in the bedrooms, and home-cooked evening meals using local produce are served by arrangement. Ample parking is available.

Facilities 6 rms (3 en suite) (3 fmly) TVB tea/coffee Licensed TVL No coaches Dinner **Prices** S £22.50-£37.50; D £35-£55✳ **LB** **Parking** 9

ST AUSTELL
MAP 02 SX05
See also **Gorran Haven, Roche & St Blazey**

★★★★ Bed & Breakfast

Cooperage

37 Cooperage Rd, Trewoon PL25 5SJ
☎ 01726 70497 & 07854 960385
e-mail lyn.cooperage@tiscali.co.uk
web www.cooperagebb.co.uk
Dir 1m W of St Austell. On A3058 in Trewoon

Situated on the edge of the town, this late Victorian, semi-detached granite house has been renovated in a contemporary style. The comfortable bedrooms are well equipped and feature beautifully tiled en suites. You are assured of a friendly and relaxed welcome and the property is convenient for the numerous amenities and attractions locally. Cooperage is suitable for both business and leisure. Pets welcome by arrangement.

Facilities 4 rms (3 en suite) (1 pri facs) ⊗ TVB tea/coffee ✖ Cen ht No coaches **Prices** S £35; D £50-£60✳ **LB** **Parking** 6 **Notes** ⊛

Premier Collection

◆◆◆◆◆ 🏛 ⊟

Anchorage House

Nettles Cnr, Tregrehan Mills PL25 3RH ☎ 01726 814071
e-mail stay@anchoragehouse.co.uk
web www.anchoragehouse.co.uk
Dir 1m E of town centre off A390

This friendly house offers a luxury stay. The attractive bedrooms are spacious and furnished to high standards, with extra large beds, satellite television and numerous extra facilities. A lounge, conservatory and swimming pool are also available. Dinner, by arrangement, is served house-party style using the very best fresh Cornish produce. A wide choice is available at the buffet-style breakfast.

Facilities 4 en suite ⊗ STV FTV TVB tea/coffee ✖ Cen ht No children 16yrs No coaches ⊠ Sauna Gymnasium outdoor jacuzzi, spa treatments Dinner Last d 24hr **Prices** S £85-£115; D £110-£140 **Parking** 6 **Notes** Closed Dec-Feb

England

◆◆◆◆◆

Highland Court Lodge

Biscovey Rd, Biscovey, Par PL24 2HW
☎ 01726 813320 📄 01726 813320
e-mail enquiries@highlandcourt.co.uk
web www.highlandcourt.co.uk
Dir *2m E of St Austell. A390 E to St Blazey Gate, right onto Biscovey Rd, 300yds on right*

This friendly home has stunning views over St Austell Bay and is just over 1m from The Eden Project. Its impressive en suite bedrooms have luxurious fabrics and each room opens onto a private patio. There is a lounge with deep sofas, and the terrace shares the fine views. The local Cornish catch features strongly in the freshly prepared dinners, and like breakfast are not to be missed.

Facilities 3 en suite (2 fmly) (3 GF) ⊗ TVB tea/coffee ✖ Licensed Cen ht No coaches Dinner Last d 10am **Prices** D £90-£170✳ **LB** **Conf** Max 18 Class 18 Board 18 **Parking** 12

◆◆◆◆◆

Lower Barn

Bosue, St Ewe PL26 6EU ☎ 01726 844881
e-mail janie@bosue.co.uk
web www.bosue.co.uk
Dir *3.5m SW of St Austell. Off B3273 at x-rds signed Lost Gardens of Heligan, Lower Barn signed 1m on right*

The converted barn, tucked away in countryside with easy access to local attractions, has huge appeal. Warm colours create a Mediterranean feel, complemented by informal and genuine hospitality, and the bedrooms have a host of extras. Breakfast is served around a large table or on the patio deck overlooking the garden, which also has a hot tub.

Facilities 3 en suite (1 fmly) (1 GF) ⊗ TVB tea/coffee ✖ Cen ht No coaches Sauna Gymnasium Hot tub Dinner Last d lunchtime **Prices** S £70; D £100-£120 **LB** **Parking** 7 **Notes** Closed Jan

◆◆◆◆◆ ⊜

Wisteria Lodge

Boscundle, Tregrehan PL25 3RJ
☎ 01726 810800 📄 0871 661 6213
e-mail info@wisterialodgehotel.co.uk
web www.wisterialodgehotel.co.uk
Dir *1m E of town centre off A390*

You are made to feel very welcome at this delightful guest house set in a quiet location on the outskirts of town. The very well-equipped accommodation includes rooms on the ground floor and there is a comfortable sitting room. Skilfully prepared meals are served in conservatory-dining room, which overlooks the large garden.

Facilities 5 en suite (1 fmly) (2 GF) ⊗ STV TVB tea/coffee Direct dial from bedrooms ✖ Licensed Cen ht No children 12yrs No coaches Hot Tub Dinner Last d 1pm **Prices** D £90-£160✳ **Conf** Max 10 Board 10 **Parking** 5

See advertisement on page 85

◆◆◆◆

Highcroft Guest House

Highcroft, Truro Rd, Sticker PL26 7JA ☎ 01726 63549
e-mail highcroftbnb@virgin.net
Dir *2m SW of St Austell. Off A390 S into Sticker, pass Hewas Inn, B&B at top of hill*

Highcroft is pleasantly located in a quiet village, and the attentive proprietors make you feel at home. The comfortable bedrooms are impressively appointed and have a range of thoughtful facilities. The freshly cooked breakfast is a highlight, served in the dining room that opens on to a decked area.

Facilities 3 en suite (1 GF) ⊗ TVB tea/coffee ✖ Cen ht No children 10yrs No coaches **Prices** D £54-£66✳ **LB** **Parking** 6 **Notes** ⊛

ST AUSTELL continued

◆◆◆◆

Hunter's Moon

Chapel Hl, Polgooth PL26 7BU
☎ 01726 66445 ▤ 01726 66445
e-mail richard.scott77@virgin.net
Dir *1.5m SW of town centre. Off B2373 into Polgooth, pass village shop on left, 1st right*

Hunter's Moon lies in a quiet village just a few miles from Heligan and within easy reach of The Eden Project. Service is friendly and attentive and the bedrooms are well equipped for business and leisure. There is a conservatory-lounge and a pretty garden to enjoy during warmer weather. Breakfast is served in the cosy dining room and the nearby village inn serves freshly prepared meals.

Facilities 4 en suite (2 fmly) ☺ TVB tea/coffee ✖ Cen ht No children 14yrs No coaches **Prices** S £38-£44; D £56-£64 **Parking** 5 **Notes** ✉

◆◆◆◆

Sunnyvale Bed & Breakfast ◇

Hewaswater PL26 7JF ☎ 01726 882572
e-mail jmuden@aol.com
Dir *4m SW of St Austell. Off A390 in Hewas Water*

This house has pleasant gardens in a peaceful location, and the very friendly proprietor makes you feel most welcome. The smart bedrooms have an extensive range of facilities and there is also a sitting area.

Facilities 2 annexe en suite (2 GF) ☺ TVB tea/coffee ✖ Cen ht No children 16yrs No coaches **Prices** S £30-£35; D £56-£60 **Parking** 4 **Notes** ✉

◆◆◆◆

The Elms

14 Penwinnick Rd PL25 5DW
☎ 01726 74981 ▤ 01726 74981
e-mail sue@edenbb.co.uk
web www.edenbb.co.uk
Dir *A390 W from St Austell, The Elms 200yds on right, junct Pondhu Rd*

Well located for The Eden Project or for touring Cornwall, this accommodation offers a relaxed and friendly environment for leisure and business. Bedrooms, one with a four-poster bed, are well equipped and there is an inviting lounge. Breakfast is served in the conservatory dining room, and home-cooked dinners are available by arrangement.

Facilities 3 en suite ☺ TVB tea/coffee ✖ Cen ht TVL No coaches Dinner Last d noon **Prices** S £35-£50; D £60-£70✶ **LB Parking** 3

◆◆◆◆

Polgreen Farm ◇

London Apprentice PL26 7AP ☎ 01726 75151
e-mail polgreen.farm@btclick.com
web www.polgreenfarm.co.uk
Dir *1.5m S of St Austell. Off B3273, turn left entering London Apprentice & signed*

Guests return regularly for the friendly welcome at this peaceful accommodation located just south of St Austell. The spacious and well-equipped bedrooms are divided between the main house and an adjoining property, and each building has a comfortable lounge. Breakfast is served in a pleasant conservatory overlooking the garden.

Facilities 3 rms (2 en suite) (1 pri facs) 4 annexe en suite (1 fmly) (1 GF) ☺ TVB tea/coffee ✖ Cen ht TVL No coaches **Prices** S £25-£35; D £48-£58✶ **LB Parking** 8 **Notes** ✉

◆◆◆◆ 🐾

Poltarrow (SW998518)

St Mewan PL26 7DR
☎ 01726 67111 📠 01726 67111 Mrs Nancarrow
e-mail enquire@poltarrow.co.uk
Dir 1.5m W of town centre. Off A390 to St Mewan, pass school, 2nd farm on left after 0.5m

Set in 45 acres of gardens and pasture, this delightful traditional farmhouse retains many original features, including open fires. The attractive bedrooms are comfortably furnished and decorated with style. Breakfast, cooked on an Aga, is served in the conservatory-dining room overlooking the gardens. An impressive indoor pool is available.

Facilities 3 en suite 2 annexe en suite (1 fmly) ⊘ TVB tea/coffee 🐾 Cen ht TVL No children 5yrs 🎣 Fishing Pool Table 45 acres mixed
Parking 10 **Notes** Closed 16 Dec–5 Jan

◆◆◆◆

Rashleigh Arms

Quay Rd, Charlestown PL25 3NX
☎ 01726 73635 📠 01726 67133
e-mail rashleigharms@smallandfriendly.co.uk
Dir 0.5m SE of town in Charlestown. Signed off A390 rdbt

The harbour village and former port of Charlestown is very popular as a film location, and the Rashleigh Arms adds to the character of the place. Its quality bedrooms are light and airy and well equipped, and the bars offer a range of eating options, from bar snacks to a carvery or from the carte.

Facilities 8 en suite (1 fmly) ⊘ in bedrooms ⊘ in dining room TVB tea/coffee 🐾 Cen ht Pool Table Dinner Last d 9pm **Prices** S fr £49; d fr £68✳ LB **Parking** 120

◆◆◆◆

Sunnycroft ◇

28 Penwinnick Rd PL25 5DS
☎ 01726 73351 📠 01726 879409
e-mail info@sunnycroft.net
web www.sunnycroft.net
Dir 600yds SW of town centre on A390

The 1930s house is convenient for The Eden Project and just a short walk from the town centre. Its bright bedrooms offer good levels of comfort, and ground-floor rooms are available. Substantial tasty breakfasts are served in the smart dining room.

Facilities 5 en suite 2 annexe en suite (1 fmly) (3 GF) ⊘ TVB tea/coffee Cen ht No coaches Cycle hire **Prices** S £25–£35; D £50–£65✳ LB **Parking** 7

◆◆◆

Spindrift Guesthouse

London Apprentice PL26 7AR ☎ 01726 69316
e-mail enquiries@spindrift-guesthouse.co.uk
web www.spindrift-guesthouse.co.uk
Dir 1.5m S of St Austell on B3273

This comfortable accommodation is within easy reach of The Eden Project and The Lost Gardens of Heligan. The well-equipped bedrooms, one on the ground floor, have pleasant views of either the garden or across the valley to the woods. A full cooked or continental breakfast is served in either the dining room of the suite or the reception-dining area.

Facilities 2 rms (1 en suite) (1 pri facs) (2 fmly) (1 GF) ⊘ TVB tea/coffee 🐾 Cen ht TVL No coaches **Prices** D £50–£70✳ LB **Parking** 6 **Notes** Closed Xmas & New Year ⊘

England

ST AUSTELL continued

◆◆◆

T'Gallants

6 Charlestown Rd, Charlestown PL25 3NJ
☎ 01726 70203 ▤ 01726 70203
Dir 0.5m SE of town off A390 rdbt signed Charlestown

Please note that this establishment has recently changed hands. The fine Georgian house partly dates from 1630. It overlooks the historic port of Charlestown, with its fleet of square-rigged sailing ships. Bedrooms are generally spacious and well maintained, and one has a four-poster bed and views of the port. Breakfast, served at separate tables, often features smoked haddock from the local smokehouse.

Facilities 7 rms (6 en suite) (1 pri facs) ⊛ TVB tea/coffee ✖ Cen ht TVL No coaches **Prices** S fr £45; D £60-£75✱

ST BLAZEY   MAP 02 SX05

Premier Collection

◆◆◆◆◆ 🏛

Penarwyn House

PL24 2DS ☎ 01726 814224 ▤ 01726 814224
e-mail mrussell@fsbdial.co.uk
web www.penarwyn.co.uk
Dir A390 W through St Blazey, left at 2nd speed camera, house past school

The impressive house stands in tranquil surroundings close to main routes, The Eden Project and many attractions. Painstakingly restored, the spacious house offers a host of facilities, and the bedrooms are particularly comfortable and delightfully appointed. Breakfast is another highlight, and along with the proprietor's most welcoming hospitality provide a memorable stay.

Facilities 3 en suite ⊛ FTV TVB tea/coffee ✖ Cen ht No children 10yrs No coaches 3/4 size snooker table **Prices** S £79-£100; D £88-£112✱ LB **Parking** 6 **Notes** Closed 21 Dec-9 Jan

Premier Collection

◆◆◆◆◆

Nanscawen Manor House

Prideaux Rd, Luxulyan Valley PL24 2SR ☎ 01726 814488
e-mail keith@nanscawen.com
web www.nanscawen.com
Dir A390 W to St Blazey, right after railway, Nanscawen 0.75m on right

This renovated manor house originates from the 14th century and provides a high standard of accommodation, with elegant bedrooms and bathrooms with spa baths. There are extra touches throughout to pamper you, a spacious lounge with a well-stocked honesty bar, and 5 acres of pleasant gardens with splendid woodland views. Breakfast, served in the conservatory, features fresh local produce.

Facilities 3 en suite ⊛ FTV TVB tea/coffee Direct dial from bedrooms ✖ Cen ht No children 12yrs No coaches 🐾 Whirlpool spa **Prices** D £96-£120✱ **Parking** 8

ST COLUMB MAJOR   MAP 02 SW96

◆◆◆◆ 🏛

Larkrise Barn

Quoit TR9 6HY ☎ 01637 880425 & 07974 388206
Dir 0.5m SE of village. Off A39 rdbt at village E towards Quoit

The converted barn stands within tranquil countryside with good access to the buzzing resorts of Newquay and Padstow. The hosts are very welcoming and invite you to share their lounge. The spacious bedroom is well equipped, and the freshly prepared breakfast, featuring local produce whenever possible, is served in the kitchen-dining room, or outside on the terrace on sunny days.

Facilities 1 rm (1 pri facs) ⊛ TVB tea/coffee ✖ Cen ht TVL No children No coaches LB **Parking** 4 **Notes** 🐾

ST GENNYS

MAP 02 SX19

★★★★ Guest House

Bears & Boxes Country Guest House ◇

Penrose, Dizzard EX23 0NX ☎ 01840 230318
e-mail rwfrh@btinternet.com
web www.bearsandboxes.com

Dir At Wainhouse Corner A39 follow signs to Crackington Haven. After 0.75m turn right signed Millook and Dizzard. Bears and Boxes 2.5m on left.

Dating in part from the mid 17th century, Bears and Boxes is a small, family-run guest house situated 500yds from the South West Coast Path. You are welcomed with a tray of tea and home-made cake and the caring owners are always around to help and advise about the locality. The cosy bedrooms have numerous thoughtful extras, and evening meals, using the very best of local ingredients and cooked with flair, are served by arrangement.

Facilities 3 en suite 1 annexe rms (1 annexe pri facs) (1 fmly) (1 GF) ⊗ FTV TVB tea/coffee Cen ht TVL No coaches Dinner Last d noon **Prices** S £29.50-£35; D £59-£70✳ **Parking** 6

ST HILARY

MAP 02 SW53

Premier Collection

◆◆◆◆◆ 🏠 💗

Ennys (SW559328)

Trewhella Ln TR20 9BZ
☎ 01736 740262 🖳 01736 740055 Miss Charlton
e-mail ennys@ennys.co.uk
web www.ennys.co.uk

Dir 1m N of B3280 Leedstown-Goldsithney road at end of Trewhella Ln

Set off the beaten track, this 17th-century manor house is a perfect
continued

place to unwind. A friendly welcome awaits you, and a complimentary afternoon tea is laid out in the kitchen. Ennys retains much original character and the rooms are impressively furnished. A delightful Cornish breakfast is served in the dining room, using a wealth of fresh local ingredients and home-produced fresh eggs.

Facilities 3 en suite 2 annexe en suite (2 fmly) (1 GF) ⊗ TVB tea/coffee 🛪 Cen ht No children 3yrs ⚡ ⚡ 20 acres Non-working **Prices** S £60-£100; D £80-£105✳ **Parking** 8 **Notes** Closed Nov-15 Mar

ST IVES

MAP 02 SW54

★★★★ Guest Accommodation

Headland House ◇

Headland Rd, Carbis Bay TR26 2NS ☎ 01736 796647
e-mail headland.house@btconnect.com

Dir A30 onto A3074 towards St Ives. At Carbis Bay turn right to Porthepta Rd, Headland Rd is 3rd on right.

This Victorian establishment has been sensitively refurbished to provide comfortable, well-equipped accommodation. Some of the bedrooms have a lovely sea view. The local railway station and beach are just a stroll away. There is a small bar-lounge and a traditional English breakfast is served in the sea-facing dining room-library. During the summer months you can enjoy a cool drink on the decked patio or lawn.

Facilities 7 rms (5 en suite) (1 fmly) ⊗ TVB tea/coffee 🛪 Licensed Cen ht TVL No coaches **Prices** S £25-£28; D £56-£68✳ **LB** **Parking** 7

★★ Bed & Breakfast

Making Waves

3 Richmond Pl TR26 1JN ☎ 01736 793895
e-mail simon@making-waves.co.uk

Dir Signed from A30, located above Trewyn Gardens.

Centrally located with the harbour just a short walk away, this Victorian terrace property is fully vegan, with freshly squeezed juices and home-made muesli featuring on the breakfast menu. Breakfast is served around one large table in the lounge-dining room. The host has an environmental approach and this is reflected in the accommodation, which has been renovated using organic paints and reclaimed materials. One bedroom has stunning views of the bay.

Facilities 3 rms (1 fmly) (1 GF) ⊗ tea/coffee 🛪 Cen ht TVL No coaches Dinner Last d 10am **Parking** 1 **Notes** rs Oct-Mar ⊠

Premier Collection

◆◆◆◆◆ 🏠

Jamies

Wheal Whidden, Carbis Bay TR26 2QX ☎ 01736 794718
e-mail info@jamiesstives.co.uk
web www.jamiesstives.co.uk

Dir A3074 to Carbis Bay, onto Pannier Ln, 2nd left

Accomplished hosts Felicity and Jamie provide a most pleasant home at this attractive Cornish villa, which has been thoughtfully renovated and stylishly appointed. Bedrooms are spacious and comfortable, all have sea views, and lots of thoughtful extras are provided. Breakfast is a feature and is served in the elegant dining room at a large round table.

Facilities 3 en suite (1 GF) ⊗ TVB tea/coffee 🛪 Cen ht No children 12yrs No coaches **Prices** S £60-£90; D £80-£90 **LB** **Parking** 4 **Notes** Closed 20 Dec-6 Jan ⊠

England

ST IVES continued

Premier Collection

◆◆◆◆◆ 🏛

Porthglaze

Steeple Ln TR26 2AY ☎ 01736 799409
e-mail info@porthglaze.co.uk
Dir A3074 to St Ives, left at Cornish Arms, left onto Steeple Ln, Porthglaze 500yds on left

Porthglaze is in a quiet residential area just a stroll from St Ives and Carbis Bay. You are made to feel relaxed and at home, and the impressive choice at breakfast is memorable. The spacious bedrooms are particularly well equipped, and there is also a pleasant garden. Parking is available.

Facilities 2 en suite (2 GF) ⊗ TVB tea/coffee ✝ Cen ht TVL No children 14yrs No coaches **Parking** 4

Premier Collection

◆◆◆◆◆ 🏛

Primrose Valley Hotel

Primrose Valley, Porthminster Beach TR26 2ED
☎ 01736 794939 📠 01736 794939
e-mail info@primroseonline.co.uk
web www.primroseonline.co.uk
Dir A3074 to St Ives, 25yds after town sign right onto Primrose Valley, left under bridge, along beach front, turn left back under bridge, property on left

St Ives is just a short walk from this friendly, family-run establishment close to Porthminster Beach. The atmosphere is light and airy and modernisation provides a good level of comfort. Some bedrooms have balconies with stunning views. There is a lounge and bar area, and dinner is available. Breakfast features local produce and home-made goodies.

Facilities 10 en suite (2 fmly) ⊗ TVB tea/coffee ✝ Licensed Cen ht TVL No coaches Dinner Last d 6.30pm **Prices** D £80-£195✳ **LB** **Parking** 10 **Notes** Closed Dec-Jan rs Low season

◆◆◆◆

Borthalan

Off Boskerris Rd, Carbis Bay TR26 2NQ
☎ 01736 795946 📠 01736 795946
e-mail borthalanhotel@btconnect.com
web www.borthalan-hotel.co.uk
Dir A3074 into Carbis Bay, right onto Boskerris Rd, 1st left onto cul-de-sac

Borthalan has a convenient location with good parking. A short walk from Carbis Bay station, you can travel the 3-minute journey to St Ives car free. The friendly proprietors provide a relaxing and welcoming environment, and well-equipped bedrooms. There is a cosy lounge and an attractive garden, and breakfast is served in the bright dining room.

Facilities 7 en suite ⊗ TVB tea/coffee ✝ Licensed Cen ht TVL No children 12yrs No coaches **Prices** D £75-£90✳ **Parking** 7 **Notes** Closed 20-28 Dec

◆◆◆◆

Glanmor

The Belyars TR26 2BX ☎ 01736 795613
e-mail margaret@glanmor.net
Dir A3074 to St Ives, left at Porthminster Hotel & up Talland Rd

The relaxed and friendly atmosphere at the Glanmor draws guests back time after time. It is just a short walk from the town centre and beaches, and offers attractive, well equipped bedrooms. There is a comfortable lounge and conservatory, and the pretty landscaped gardens have seating for warm sunny days. Carefully prepared breakfasts are served in the light and airy dining room.

Facilities 6 en suite (3 fmly) (1 GF) ⊗ TVB tea/coffee ✝ Licensed Cen ht TVL No coaches **Parking** 6 **Notes** 🚭

◆◆◆◆ 🏛

Pebble Private Hotel ◇

4 Parc Av TR26 2DN ☎ 01736 794168
e-mail info@pebble-hotel.co.uk
Dir A3074 to St Ives, left at NatWest bank, left at minirdbt, pass car park, house 150yds on right

The welcoming proprietors ensure you feel relaxed at this stylish, impeccably maintained house with spectacular views over St Ives Bay. Breakfast is an impressive choice, including vegetarian, and local produce is used whenever possible. The accommodation is well equipped and there is an inviting lounge.

Facilities 6 en suite (1 fmly) ⊗ FTV TVB tea/coffee ✝ Licensed Cen ht TVL No coaches **Prices** S £30-£42; D £60-£88✳ **LB Parking** 6

Rathlena

6 Higher Trewidden Rd TR26 2DP ☎ 01736 798882
e-mail evelyn@rathlena.fsnet.co.uk
web www.rathlena.com

A short walk downhill from this elevated location leads to the centre of St Ives. All rooms have a private terrace, and most have a sea view. There is a spacious lounge and another smaller cosy lounge. Breakfast is served around a grand communal table in the dining room.

Facilities 3 en suite ✖ TVB tea/coffee ✖ Cen ht TVL No children 12yrs No coaches **Parking** 3 **Notes** Closed 20 Dec-1 Feb ✖

◆◆◆◆ ☕

Regent Hotel

Fernlea Ter TR26 2BH ☎ 01736 796195 📠 01736 794641
e-mail keith@regenthotel.com
web www.regenthotel.com
Dir In town centre, near bus & railway station

This popular and attractive property stands on an elevated position convenient for the town centre and seafront. The Regent has well-equipped bedrooms, some with spectacular sea vistas, and the comfortable lounge also has great views. The breakfast choices, including vegetarian, are excellent.

Facilities 9 rms (7 en suite) ✖ TVB tea/coffee ✖ Cen ht TVL No children 16yrs No coaches 25% discount on golfers fees
Prices S £32.50-£33.50; D £70-£95✱ **LB Parking** 12

Bay View ◇

Headland Rd, Carbis Bay TR26 2NX
☎ 01736 796469 & 07834 722962 📠 01736 796469
e-mail sandie@bayview1.freeserve.co.uk
web www.bayview-hotel.co.uk
Dir A3074 into Carbis Bay, 1st right onto Porthrepta Rd, 3rd right into Headland Rd

Located close to the beach and within easy reach of St Ives, this friendly home offers pleasant bedrooms with comfortable furnishings. The large lounge contains games and books and there is also a conservatory-lounge. The bar-dining room serves traditional home-cooked hearty breakfasts.

Facilities 9 en suite (1 fmly) (6 GF) ✖ TVB tea/coffee ✖ Licensed Cen ht TVL No children 5yrs bicycle hire **Prices** S £29-£36; D £54-£68✱ LB **Parking** 7 **Notes** Closed 24-28 Dec

◆◆◆◆ ☕

Chy Roma

2 Seaview Ter TR26 2DH ☎ 01736 797539 📠 01736 797539
e-mail jenny@omshanti.demon.co.uk
web www.connexions.co.uk/chyroma
Dir A3074 into St Ives, fork left at Porthminster Hotel, 1st left, 1st right, down slope 2nd guest house on left

This friendly home is quietly tucked away and its attentive proprietors offer genuine hospitality. The smart bedrooms are comfortably appointed, and some have pleasant views of the harbour and St Ives Bay. Substantial, freshly prepared breakfasts are served in the lounge-dining room. Some parking is available.

Facilities 6 en suite (2 fmly) ✖ TVB tea/coffee Cen ht TVL No children 5yrs No coaches Dinner **Parking** 5 **Notes** ✖

◆◆◆◆ ✿

Coombe Farmhouse *(SW514360)*

TR27 6NW ☎ 01736 740843 Ms Pester
e-mail coombefarmhouse@aol.com
web www.coombefarmhouse.com
Dir 1.5m W of Lelant. Off A3074 to Lelant Downs

Built of sturdy granite, this early 19th-century farmhouse has a delightful location tucked away at the southern foot of Trencrom Hill, yet convenient for St Ives. The comfortable bedrooms are attractively decorated. There is a cosy lounge and substantial breakfasts, featuring farm-fresh eggs, are served in the dining room overlooking the garden.

Facilities 3 rms (2 en suite) (1 pri facs) ✖ tea/coffee ✖ Cen ht TVL No children 12yrs 15 acres Non-working **Prices** S £32; D £64-£72✱ **Parking** 3 **Notes** Closed Dec ✖

◆◆◆◆

Edgar's

Higher Stennack TR26 2HA
☎ 01736 796559 📠 01736 796559
e-mail stay@chy.co.uk
web www.chy.co.uk
Dir 0.5m W of town centre on B3306, opp Leach Pottery

High standards of comfort are provided at this friendly, family-run guest house. Public areas are spacious and include a bar and a lounge, and bedrooms, some on the ground floor, are well equipped. Bar snacks are available and breakfast, served in the dining room, includes home-made preserves.

Facilities 8 en suite (2 fmly) (4 GF) ✖ TVB tea/coffee ✖ Licensed Cen ht TVL No coaches **Prices** S £39; D £58-£90✱ LB **Parking** 8 **Notes** Closed Nov-Feb

England

ST IVES continued

◆◆◆◆

Fairfield House ◇

Porthrepta Rd, Carbis Bay TR26 2NZ ☎ 01736 793771
e-mail info@fairfieldhouse.net
Dir A3074 to Carbis Bay, right towards station, 0.25m on right

The Edwardian house is near beautiful Carbis Bay beach and a short drive, train ride or coastal walk to St Ives. Bedrooms are well equipped and some have spectacular sea views. During summer there is a pleasant garden in which to relax, and at colder times the lounge has a log-burning fire. The breakfast menu offers a good choice in the light dining room, which also has sea views.

Facilities 6 rms (4 en suite) (1 GF) ⊗ TVB tea/coffee ✗ Cen ht TVL No children No coaches **Prices** S £25-£32; D £56-£64✱ **LB Parking** 5

◆◆◆◆

Fernhill

St Ives Rd, Carbis Bay TR26 2JT
☎ 01736 795620 ▤ 01736 795620
e-mail fernhill@connexions.co.uk
Dir A3074 through Carbis Bay, Fernhill on right after newsagent

The pleasant house is in a quiet area near Carbis Bay station. The spacious bedrooms, some on the ground floor, are well equipped and some have spectacular views to Godrevy lighthouse. Hearty breakfasts are served in the dining room. Parking available.

Facilities 10 en suite (3 fmly) (4 GF) ⊗ TVB tea/coffee ✗ Cen ht No coaches **Prices** D £60-£80✱ **LB Parking** 10

◆◆◆◆

Kynance

The Warren TR26 2EA ☎ 01736 796636
e-mail enquiries@kynance.com
Dir A3074 into town centre, sharp right before bus/coach station onto railway station approach road, Kynance 20yds on left

The charming Kynance lies just yards from the picturesque harbour and Porthminster Beach. Its attractive bedrooms are well equipped and some have superb views, and the varied choice at breakfast includes a vegetarian option.

Facilities 6 rms (5 en suite) (1 pri facs) ⊗ TVB tea/coffee ✗ Cen ht TVL No children 7yrs No coaches **Prices** D £56-£64✱ **Parking** 5 **Notes** Closed Nov-end Mar

◆◆◆◆

The Mustard Tree

Sea View Meadows, St Ives Rd, Carbis Bay TR26 2JX
☎ 01736 795677
e-mail enquiries@mustard-tree.co.uk
Dir A3074 to Carbis Bay, The Mustard Tree on right opp Methodist church

Please note that this establishment has recently changed hands. Set in delightful gardens and having sea views, the attractive house is just a short drive from the centre of St Ives. Alternatively, the coastal path leads from Carbis Bay to St Ives. The pleasant bedrooms are very

continued

comfortable and have many extra facilities, and the attentive proprietors provide a friendly, relaxing atmosphere. A splendid choice is offered at breakfast, with vegetarian or continental options.

Facilities 7 rms (6 en suite) (1 pri facs) (1 fmly) (4 GF) ⊗ TVB tea/coffee ✗ Cen ht TVL No coaches Last d 10am **Prices** S £36; D £62-£74✱ **Conf** Max 13 **Parking** 7

◆◆◆◆ ▣

The Old Vicarage Hotel

Parc-an-Creet TR26 2ES ☎ 01736 796124
e-mail holidays@oldvicaragehotel.com
web www.oldvicaragehotel.com
Dir Off A3074 in town centre onto B3306, 0.5m right into Parc-an-Creet

The former Victorian rectory stands in secluded gardens in a quiet part of St Ives and is convenient for the seaside, town and the Tate. The bedrooms have modern facilities, and a good choice of local produce is offered at breakfast, plus home-made yoghurt and preserves.

Facilities 7 en suite (4 fmly) ⊗ in bedrooms ⊗ in dining room ⊗ in 1 lounge TVB tea/coffee Licensed Cen ht TVL No coaches ⚲ **Prices** S £51; D £68✱ **Parking** 12 **Notes** Closed Oct-Etr

◆◆◆◆

The Palms

17 Ayr Ter TR26 1ED ☎ 01736 793659 ▤ 01736 793659
e-mail info@thepalmsstives.co.uk
web www.thepalmsstives.co.uk
Dir B3074 into town, left onto Gabriel St, right at minirdbt, left at top of hill, Palms 200yds on right

The Palms is within walking distance (not level) of the town and beaches and the hosts are friendly and helpful. The cosy bedrooms have sofas for relaxation, and freshly prepared breakfasts are served in the pleasant dining room. Some parking is available.

Facilities 5 rms (3 en suite) (2 pri facs) ⊗ TVB tea/coffee ✗ Cen ht No children 14yrs No coaches **Prices** D £50-£70✱ **Parking** 3 **Notes** Closed 30 Nov-27 Dec

◆◆◆◆

The Pondarosa

10 Porthminster Ter TR26 2DQ
☎ 01736 795875 ▤ 01736 797811
e-mail pondarosa.hotel@talk21.com
Dir A3074 towards town, fork left at Porthminster Hotel & follow road to left bend, 1st left, Pondarosa on right

The family-run Pondarosa provides a relaxing and friendly environment in a pleasant location with views over the town. There is a comfortable lounge and a stylish bar, and bedrooms are attractively decorated in pleasant colours and fabrics. Breakfast is served in the ground-floor dining room. Good parking.

Facilities 9 rms (8 en suite) (4 fmly) ⊗ TVB tea/coffee ✗ Licensed Cen ht TVL **Parking** 17

England

Porthminster View ◇

13 Draycott Ter TR26 2EF
☎ 01736 795850 🖹 01736 796811
e-mail enquiry@porthminster.com
web www.porthminster.com
Dir A3074 entering town, 300yds past Ford station right onto Draycott Ter

Built about 1896, this relaxed, family-friendly establishment was formerly home to the local stationmaster. It stands high above Porthminster Beach and has spectacular views. The bedrooms are thoughtfully equipped. The well-appointed lounge has many books and videos, and the portions at breakfast are generous.

Facilities 6 en suite (1 fmly) ⊗ TVB tea/coffee ✖ Cen ht TVL No children 11yrs No coaches **Prices** S £30-£35; D £60-£70✳ **Parking** 1

The Rookery

8 The Terrace TR26 2BL ☎ 01736 799401
e-mail therookerystives@hotmail.com
Dir A3074 through Carbis Bay, right fork at Porthminster Hotel, The Rookery 500yds on left

This friendly establishment stands on an elevated position overlooking the town and sandy beach. The attractive bedrooms, with one on the ground floor, are well equipped and offer a good level of comfort. Breakfast is served in the first-floor dining room at separate tables.

Facilities 6 en suite (1 GF) ⊗ STV TVB tea/coffee ✖ Cen ht No children 7yrs No coaches **Parking** 6

St Dennis

6 Albany Ter TR26 2BS ☎ 01736 795027 🖹 01736 795027
e-mail stdennis007@btopenworld.com
Dir A3074 to St Ives, pass St Ives Motor Co on right, continue down hill, Albany Ter 1st left, signed Edward Hain Hospital

St Dennis is a friendly and comfortable place to stay. Breakfast, featuring mostly organic produce, is carefully prepared and presented, and includes vegetarian options. Bedrooms are attractively decorated and have many thoughtful touches. Parking is available.

Facilities 3 en suite ⊗ FTV TVB tea/coffee ✖ Cen ht No children 12yrs No coaches **Prices** D £58-£72✳ **Parking** 5 **Notes** Closed Nov-Feb

Skidden House Hotel

Skidden Hill TR26 2DU ☎ 01736 796899 🖹 01736 798619
e-mail skiddenhousehotel@tiscali.co.uk
web www.skiddenhouse.com
Dir A3074 to St Ives, 1st right after bus/railway station

Skidden House is in the heart of town and is reputed to have formerly been a jail, brothel and a pub, as well as St Ives' oldest hotel. The accommodation is now much more comfortable and welcoming, with pleasant, well-equipped rooms. Some parking is available.

Facilities 7 en suite (4 fmly) (2 GF) ⊗ TVB tea/coffee Direct dial from bedrooms ✖ Licensed Cen ht TVL No coaches **Prices** S £38-£45; D £76-£90✳ **LB** **Parking** 4

The Sloop Inn

The Wharf TR26 1LP ☎ 01736 796584 🖹 01736 793322
e-mail sloopinn@btinternet.com
web www.sloop-inn.co.uk
Dir On St Ives harbour by middle slipway

This attractive, historic inn has an imposing position on the harbour. Each of the bedrooms has a nautical name, many with pleasant views, and all have impressive modern facilities. A good choice of dishes is offered at lunch and dinner in the atmospheric restaurant-bar.

Facilities 16 rms (13 en suite) (5 fmly) (1 GF) ⊗ in 2 bedrooms ⊗ in area of dining room TVB tea/coffee ✖ Cen ht No coaches Dinner Last d 9.30pm **Prices** D £82-£92✳ **LB**

Book as early as possible, particularly in the peak holiday period

England

ST IVES continued

◆◆◆◆

Tregony

1 Clodgy View TR26 1JG ☎ 01736 795884
e-mail info@tregony.com
web www.tregony.com
Dir A3074 tnto St Ives, left at NatWest onto B3306, right at minirdbt up Bullans Ln, right at T-junct, over junct, house 100yds on right

Set high above the town with spectacular sea views, the attractive home is close to Tate St Ives and the town centre. The welcoming owners provide a homely atmosphere and attractive bedrooms, and freshly cooked breakfasts are served in the pleasant dining room with views.

Facilities 5 rms (4 en suite) (1 pri facs) (2 fmly) ⊗ TVB tea/coffee ✕ Cen ht No children 3yrs **Prices** D £56-£68✳

◆◆◆◆

Tregorran Hotel

Headland Rd, Carbis Bay TR26 2NU ☎ 01736 795889
e-mail book@carbisbay.com
web www.carbisbay.com
Dir Right at Carbis Bay to beach, along Porthrepta Rd, last right onto Headland Rd, Tregorran halfway along

There are wonderful views of Carbis Bay and St Ives from the friendly, family-run Tregorran. Relax by the pool, in the garden or in the pleasant bar, and there is also a comfortable lounge, and a games room and a gym. Breakfast is served in the airy dining room with superb views.

Facilities 18 en suite (5 fmly) (4 GF) ⊗ in bedrooms ⊗ in dining room TVB tea/coffee Licensed Cen ht TVL No coaches ⁓ Gymnasium Pool Table Games room **Prices** S £32-£47; D £64-£94 LB **Parking** 20 **Notes** Closed Nov-Etr

◆◆◆◆ 🏠

Treliska ◇

3 Bedford Rd TR26 1SP ☎ 01736 797678 ▤ 01736 797678
e-mail info@treliska.com
web www.treliska.com
Dir A3074 to St Ives, fork at Porthminster Hotel into town, at T-junct facing Barclays Bank left onto Bedford Rd, house on right

This friendly home is close to the seafront, restaurants and galleries. The attractive bedrooms have contemporary features, and the bathrooms are particularly smart. Enjoyable, freshly cooked Cornish breakfasts are served in the lounge-dining room.

continued

Facilities 5 en suite ⊗ FTV TVB tea/coffee ✕ Cen ht No children 10yrs No coaches **Prices** S £30-£35; D £56-£70✳ **Notes** 🐾

◆◆◆◆

Woodside Hotel

The Belyars TR26 2DA ☎ 01736 795681
e-mail woodsidehotel@btconnect.com
Dir A3074 to St Ives, left at Porthminster Hotel onto Talland Rd, 1st left onto Belyars Ln, Woodside 4th on right

This attractive house is in a peaceful location overlooking St Ives Bay. The friendly proprietors provide a welcoming and relaxing environment, and the bedrooms, some with sea views, come in a range of sizes. Hearty breakfasts are served in the dining room, and there is a comfortable lounge and a well-stocked bar.

Facilities 10 en suite (3 fmly) ⊗ TVB tea/coffee ✕ Licensed Cen ht TVL No children 5yrs No coaches ⁓ Pool Table **Prices** S £36-£51; D £72-£108✳ LB **Parking** 12

◆◆◆◆ 🅰

Beechwood House

St Ives Rd, Carbis Bay TR26 2SX
☎ 01736 795170 ▤ 01736 795170
e-mail beechwood@carbisbay.wanadoo.co.uk
Dir From A30 onto A3074 signed for St Ives. Through Lelant to Carbis Bay, past Costcutter shop on left

Facilities 8 en suite (2 fmly) (3 GF) ⊗ TVB tea/coffee ✕ Cen ht TVL **Prices** D £50-£60✳ LB **Parking** 8

◆◆◆

The Hollies

4 Talland Rd TR26 2DF
☎ 01736 796605 & 793495 ▤ 01736 796605
e-mail theholliesstives@aol.com
Dir A3074 Trelyon Av to St Ives, left at Porthminster Hotel, 500yds bear left, bear left again, 3rd property on right

The Hollies has an elevated position with fine views, and is within eas walking distance of town and harbour. Some of the homely bedrooms have sea views, and families are particularly welcome. A hearty breakfast is served in the pleasant dining room.

Facilities 10 en suite (4 fmly) ⊗ TVB tea/coffee ✕ Cen ht TVL No children 3yrs **Prices** S £41-£56; D £52-£80✳ LB **Parking** 10 **Notes** Closed Xmas

◆◆◆

Thurlestone Hotel ◇

St Ives Rd, Carbis Bay TR26 2RT ☎ 01736 796369
e-mail anna.monkman@virgin.net
Dir A3074 to Carbis Bay, pass convenience store on left, 0.25m on left next to newsagents

The granite chapel built in 1843 now offers pleasant modern accommodation. The friendly proprietors provide a comfortable environment, and many guests return regularly. There is a cosy loung bar, and some of the well-equipped bedrooms have sea views.

Facilities 9 en suite (4 fmly) (1 GF) ⊗ TVB tea/coffee ✕ Licensed Cen ht TVL **Prices** S £23-£30; D £46-£60✳ LB **Parking** 5

England

◆◆◆

27 The Terrace

TR26 2BP ☎ 01736 797450 📠 01736 793623

Dir *On A3074 near town centre*

Well located with splendid views across the harbour and St Ives Bay, the family-run property offers parking for all guests. Bedrooms are spacious and many have sea views, and a bar is available during the summer. Hearty breakfasts are served in the dining room.

Facilities 7 en suite (2 fmly) (2 GF) ⊗ TVB tea/coffee ✘ Licensed Cen ht TVL No coaches **Prices** S £28-£40; D £56-£70✳ **Parking** 9

◆◆◆

Atlantic

8 Atlantic Ter TR26 1JQ ☎ 01736 793957

e-mail mail@atlantichouse.org.uk

Dir *In town centre via A3306 Fore St*

Situated on the hill above Tate St Ives, the Atlantic has sea views from all rooms. The property is beside a car park and within walking distance of the town's beaches. Bedrooms are well equipped, and a hearty breakfast featuring home-made bread is served in the pleasant front dining room around two large tables.

Facilities 3 en suite ⊗ TVB tea/coffee ✘ Cen ht **Prices** S £27-£45; D £50-£65✳ LB **Notes** 🐾

◆◆◆

Channings Hotel

3 Talland Rd TR26 2DF ☎ 01736 799500 📠 01736 799500

e-mail channings@tinyworld.co.uk

Dir *A3074 into St Ives, fork left at Porthminster Hotel, 1st left & 1st left again onto Talland Rd, Channings on right*

This friendly, family-run establishment occupies an elevated position in a quiet residential area. Many of the bedrooms have impressive views over St Ives Bay, and there is an attractive lounge and bar. Traditional dishes are served at breakfast and dinner in the comfortable dining room.

Facilities 10 en suite (4 fmly) ⊗ TVB tea/coffee ✘ Licensed Cen ht TVL Dinner Last d 2pm **Parking** 9 **Notes** Closed Dec-Jan rs Nov, Feb-Mar

◆◆◆

Horizon

5 Carthew Ter TR26 1EB ☎ 01736 798069

Having an elevated position, this family home has pleasant sea views and is within walking distance to the town centre and beaches. The host welcomes you as a friend and creates a most homely atmosphere. Bedrooms, some with wonderful views, are attractive and there is a comfortable lounge. A traditional English cooked breakfast is served around a communal table. Dinner, available by arrangement, is served house-party style.

Facilities 3 en suite ⊗ TV available ✘ Cen ht TVL No children No coaches Dinner Last d 10am **Parking** 2 **Notes** Closed Nov-Apr 🐾

◆◆◆

Norway House

Norway Sq TR26 1NA ☎ 01736 795678

e-mail stives-norwayhouse@tiscali.co.uk

Dir *Just back from The Old Lifeboat subway, above the Sloop carpark.*

Located in the historic heart of St Ives, this pleasant house is tucked away, close to the galleries, shops and beaches. Rooms are pleasantly appointed and have a good range of facilities, and some have sea views. Breakfast is served in the ground floor dining room, and parking is available.

Facilities 3 rms (2 en suite) (1 pri facs) ⊗ in bedrooms ⊗ in dining room ⊗ in lounges TVB tea/coffee Cen ht No children 7yrs No coaches LB **Parking** 2 **Notes** 🐾

◆◆◆

Portarlington

11 Parc Bean TR26 1EA ☎ 01736 797278 📠 01736 797278

e-mail info@Portarlington.co.uk

web www.portarlington.co.uk

This pleasant home is convenient for the town, beaches and Tate St Ives. The friendly proprietors have long welcomed guests to their home and many return a regularly. Bedrooms are well furnished and some have sea views. There is a comfortable lounge, and enjoyable breakfasts are served in the attractive dining room.

Facilities 4 en suite (3 fmly) ⊗ TVB tea/coffee ✘ Cen ht TVL No children 3yrs No coaches **Parking** 4 **Notes** Closed Nov-Jan 🐾

◆◆◆ ▥

The Queens Hotel

High St TR26 1RR ☎ 01736 796468 📠 01736 799621

e-mail info@queenshotelstives.co.uk

web www.queenshotelstives.co.uk

Dir *A3074 to town centre*

The refurbished property offers a relaxed atmosphere and pleasant accommodation close to the beach and attractions. Lunch and dinner feature seafood and daily specials, and the stylish bar has a good selection of wines, beers and spirits.

Facilities 5 en suite (1 fmly) TVB tea/coffee ✘ Cen ht No coaches Dinner Last d 8.45pm

◆◆◆

St Margaret's Guest House

3 Parc Av TR26 2DN ☎ 01736 795785

e-mail btrevena@aol.com

web www.stmargaretsguesthouse.co.uk

Dir *A3074 to town, left onto Gabriel St & The Stennack, left onto Parc Av*

Guests feel comfortable at St Margaret's, with its panoramic views of the town and bay, and just a short walk from the sandy beaches. Breakfast is served in a pleasant dining room and dinner is available by arrangement. There is a cosy bar-television room.

Facilities 4 en suite (1 fmly) ⊗ TVB tea/coffee No coaches Dinner Last d 8pm LB **Parking** 3

England

ST IVES continued

Ⓤ

Godrevy

Trelyon Av TR26 2AA ☎ 01736 799257 & 07989 131833
e-mail lynne.godrevy@btinternet.com
Dir On main road into St Ives, on right after coastguard cottages

At the time of going to press the rating for this establishment had not been confirmed. Please check the AA website www.theAA.com for up-to-date information.

Facilities 2 en suite ⊗ TVB tea/coffee ✗ Cen ht No children No coaches **Prices** D £60-£75✴ **LB Parking** 2 **Notes** ⊛

Ⓤ

Lamorna Lodge Hotel

Boskerris Rd, Carbis Bay TR26 2NG ☎ 01736 795967
e-mail lamorna@tr26.wanadoo.co.uk
Dir A30 onto A3074 turn right after playground in Carbis Bay. Hotel 200mtrs

At the time of going to press the rating for this establishment had not been confirmed. Please check the AA website www.theAA.com for up-to-date information.

Facilities 9 en suite (4 fmly) (2 GF) ⊗ TVB tea/coffee ✗ Licensed Cen ht No coaches Dinner Last d 5pm **Parking** 9 **Notes** Closed 5 Nov-8 Apr ⊛

Ⓤ

Penlee International Guest House ◇

St Ives Rd, Carbis Bay TR26 2SX ☎ 01736 795497
e-mail enquiries@penleeinternational.co.uk
web www.penleeinternational.co.uk
Dir A30 onto A3074, 75yds after Carbis Bay sign on left, left onto Polmennor Dr, 1st left into car park

At the time of going to press the rating for this establishment had not been confirmed. Please check the AA website www.theAA.com for up-to-date information.

Facilities 9 rms (8 en suite) (3 fmly) ⊗ TVB tea/coffee ✗ Licensed Cen ht TVL No children Pool Table **Prices** S fr £25; D £50-£60✴ **LB Parking** 6

Ⓤ

Rivendell Guest House

7 Porthminster Ter TR26 2DQ
☎ 01736 794923 ▤ 01736 794923
e-mail rivendellstives@aol.com
Dir A30 onto A3074, left at junct, left again & up hill, over road, 50yds on right

At the time of going to press the rating for this establishment had not been confirmed. Please check the AA website www.theAA.com for up-to-date information.

Facilities 7 rms (6 en suite) (1 pri facs) (1 fmly) ⊗ TV available tea/coffee ✗ Cen ht TVL No coaches Dinner Last d noon **Parking** 5

Ⓤ

Wheal-e-Mine Bed & Breakfast

9 Belmont Ter TR26 1DZ ☎ 01736 795051 ▤ 01736 795051
e-mail whealemine@btinternet.com
Dir A3074 into town. Left at library x-rds, right at rdbt. Left at top of hill.

At the time of going to press the rating for this establishment had not been confirmed. Please check the AA website www.theAA.com for up-to-date information.

Facilities 3 rms (2 en suite) (1 pri facs) (1 fmly) ⊗ TVB tea/coffee ✗ Cen ht No children 14yrs No coaches **Prices** D £46-£56✴ **LB Parking** 3 **Notes** Closed Nov-Mar ⊛

ST JUST (NEAR LAND'S END)　MAP 02 SW33

♦♦♦ ◉

Wellington Hotel

Market Sq TR19 7HD ☎ 01736 787319 ▤ 01736 787906
e-mail wellingtonhotel@msn.com
Dir 6m W of Penzance

This friendly inn in busy Market Square offers comfortable accommodation and is popular with locals and visitors alike. Bedrooms are spacious and well equipped, and home-cooked food and local ales in the well-stocked bar make for a pleasant stay.

Facilities 5 en suite 6 annexe en suite (4 fmly) (3 GF) ⊗ in 1 bedrooms ⊗ in dining room TVB tea/coffee Cen ht Pool Table Dinner Last d 9pm **Conf** Max 20

ST KEVERNE　MAP 02 SW72

♦♦♦

Gallen-Treath Guest House ◇

Porthallow TR12 6PL ☎ 01326 280400 ▤ 01326 280400
e-mail gallentreath@btclick.com
Dir 1.5m N of St Keverne in Porthallow

Gallen Treath has super views over countryside and the sea from its elevated position above Porthallow. Bedrooms are individually decorated and feature many personal touches. You can relax in the large, comfortable lounge complete with balcony. Hearty breakfasts (and dinners by arrangement) are served in the bright dining room.

Facilities 5 rms (4 en suite) (1 fmly) (1 GF) ⊗ in bedrooms ⊗ in dining room TVB tea/coffee Licensed Cen ht TVL Dinner Last d noon **Prices** S £23-£28; D £46-£56✴ **Parking** 6 **Notes** ⊛

ST KEW　MAP 02 SX0?

♦♦♦♦

Tremoren

PL30 3HA ☎ 01208 841790 ▤ 01208 841031
Dir A39 SW to St Kew highway, right by garage, left at Red Lion pub 0.25m left after sharp right bend, 2nd entrance on right

This 200-year-old stone barn has been converted and extended to provide good quality accommodation comprising a double and a twin bed room. There is a choice of sitting rooms and an elegant dining room, where expertly prepared dinners are available by arrangement. The house stands in extensive gardens on the outskirts of the village.

Facilities 3 rms (1 en suite) (1 GF) ⊗ STV TVB tea/coffee ✗ Cen ht TV No children 8yrs No coaches Dinner Last d 8pm **Parking** 10 **Notes** ⊛

ST MAWGAN

MAP 02 SW86

♦♦♦♦ ◧

The Falcon

TR8 4EP ☎ 01637 860225 🖷 01637 860884
e-mail enquiries@thefalconinn-newquay.co.uk
web www.thefalconinn-newquay.co.uk
Dir In village centre

The delightful early 19th-century inn stands opposite the village church
in a quiet wooded valley. It is popular with locals and has a friendly
atmosphere, with warming log fires. Bedrooms vary in size and are
well equipped. There is a good choice for lunch and dinner, including
local fish and cheeses.

Facilities 2 en suite ⊗ in bedrooms ⊗ in dining room TVB tea/coffee
Direct dial from bedrooms Cen ht Games room/children's play room in
garden Dinner Last d 8.45-9.15pm **Prices** D £68-£74✳ **Parking** 12

ST NEOT

MAP 02 SX16

♦♦♦♦ ⊖ ◧

London

St Neot PL14 6NG ☎ 01579 320263 🖷 01579 321642
e-mail lon.manager@ccinns.com
Dir In village next to church

The team at the London Inn provide a friendly welcome. Dating from
the 18th century, this was the first coaching inn stop from Penzance to
London. The charming public areas have beams and flagstone floors,
and there is also a skittle alley. The bedrooms have modern facilities.

Facilities 3 en suite ⊗ in bedrooms ⊗ in dining room TVB tea/coffee
✖ Dinner Last d 9pm **Parking** 14

ST WENN

MAP 02 SW96

♦♦♦ ♥

Treliver Farm (SW981656)

Treliver PL30 5PQ
☎ 01726 890286 🖷 01726 890286 Mrs Tucker
e-mail jenny@tucker600.freeserve.co.uk
Dir 1m NE of St Wenn. A30 onto B3274, right to St Wenn, through
village to T-junct

This working farm is in lovely countryside with good access to
Padstow and Newquay, and lies near the Saints Way path. Hospitality
is very friendly, and the spacious bedrooms are particularly well
appointed. There is also a lounge. Dinner, by arrangement, and
breakfast, are hearty and satisfying affairs.

continued

Facilities 2 en suite (1 fmly) (2 GF) ⊗ TVB tea/coffee ✖ Cen ht TVL
90 acres Beef Dinner Last d 11am **Prices** S £37; D £54 **Parking** 5
Notes ⊠

SALTASH

MAP 03 SX45

♦♦♦♦ ◧

The Crooked Inn

Stoketon Cross, Trematon PL12 4RZ
☎ 01752 848177 🖷 01752 843203
e-mail info@crooked-inn.co.uk
Dir 1.5m NW of Saltash. A38 W from Saltash, 2nd left to Trematon,
sharp right

The friendly animals that freely roam the courtyard add to the relaxed
country style of this delightful inn. The spacious bedrooms are well
equipped, and freshly cooked dinners are available in the bar and
conservatory. Breakfast is served in the cottage-style dining room.

Facilities 18 annexe rms (15 en suite) (5 fmly) (7 GF) ⊗ in 7 bedrooms
⊗ in area of dining room ⊗ in 1 lounge TVB tea/coffee Cen ht ✂
Childrens play area Dinner Last d 9.30/10pm Fri/Sat **Conf** Max 60
Parking 45

See advertisement on this page

England

SALTASH continued

◆◆◆◆

Weary Friar Inn

Pillaton PL12 6QS ☎ 01579 350238 ▤ 01579 350238
web www.wearyfriar.co.uk
Dir 5m NW of Saltash. Off A388 into Pillaton

Well located for touring east Cornwall and west Devon, the extended
inn stands next to the medieval village church and is popular with
locals and tourists. There are open fires, a wealth of beams, homely
bedrooms, and a good choice of imaginative food.

Facilities 13 en suite (3 fmly) ⊗ TVB tea/coffee ✶ Cen ht TVL Dinner
Last d 9pm **Prices** S fr £45; D £60-£90✻ **Conf** Max 45 **Parking** 30

◆◆◆ ◖

The Holland Inn

Callington Rd, Hatt PL12 6PJ
☎ 01752 844044 ▤ 01752 849701
e-mail hollandinn@myopal.net
web www.hollandinn.co.uk
Dir 2m NW of Saltash on A388

The popular country inn provides spacious and comfortable
accommodation in countryside near the A38. The attractive bedrooms
are in an annexe. The wide choice for lunch and dinner includes a
carvery, and a good selection of ales and wines is available at the bar.

Facilities 30 en suite (5 fmly) (30 GF) ⊗ in 11 bedrooms ⊗ in dining
room ⊗ in 1 lounge FTV TVB tea/coffee Direct dial from bedrooms ✶
Cen ht Pool Table Dinner Last d 9.30pm **Prices** S £52.50-£57.50;
D £60-£65✻ **LB** **Conf** Max 20 Del £87.50 ✻ **Parking** 30

SCILLY, ISLES OF (ST MARY'S)   MAP 02 SV91

Premier Collection

◆◆◆◆◆ Ａ

Amaryllis

Buzza Hill TR21 0NQ ☎ 01720 423387
e-mail earlsamaryllis@aol.com
Dir Situated at Buzza Hill, 10 min walk from High Town.

Facilities 3 en suite ⊗ TVB tea/coffee ✶ Licensed Cen ht TVL
No children 12yrs No coaches Dinner **Prices** D £115-£132✻ **LB**
Notes Closed Nov-mid Mar ⊜

◆◆◆◆

Crebinick House

Church St TR21 0JT ☎ 01720 422968
e-mail aa@crebinick.co.uk
web www.crebinick.co.uk
Dir Crebinick House 500yds from quay through Hugh Town. Airport
bus to Crebinick House

Many guests return to this friendly, family-run house close to the town
centre and seafront. The granite Crebinick dates from 1760 and its
smart bedrooms, with two on the ground floor, are well equipped.
There is a quiet lounge for relaxing.

Facilities 6 en suite (2 GF) ⊗ TVB tea/coffee ✶ Cen ht TVL
No children 10yrs No coaches **Prices** D £66-£80✻ **Notes** Closed
Nov-Mar ⊜

SEATON   MAP 03 SX35

◆◆◆◆

Smugglers Inn

Treunnick Ln PL11 3JD
☎ 01503 250646 & 01503 220078 ▤ 01503 220078
web www.the-smugglers-inn.co.uk
Dir A387 to Hessonford, onto B3247 Downderry Rd for 2m

Close to the fishing port of Looe, this friendly inn has an enviable
location close to the waters edge. The attractive bedrooms are
pleasantly appointed. Entertainment features in the bar on certain
nights of the week, and the menu has a wide range of choices,
including a children's menu.

Facilities 5 en suite (2 fmly) ⊗ in bedrooms ⊗ in dining room TVB
tea/coffee ✶ Cen ht Pool Table Dinner Last d 9pm **Parking** available

SENNEN   MAP 02 SW32

◆◆◆◆

Mayon Farmhouse

TR19 7AD ☎ 01736 871757
e-mail enquiries@mayonfarmhouse.co.uk
Dir A30 into Sennen, driveway opp Post Office

You receive a genuine welcome at this 19th-century granite former
farmhouse. About 1m from Land's End, it has country and distant
coastal views. The attractive bedrooms are well equipped, and an
imaginative choice is offered at breakfast. An on-site beauty room,
providing a range of holistics treatments, is exclusively available for
guests

Facilities 3 en suite (1 fmly) ⊗ TVB tea/coffee ✶ Cen ht TVL
No children 8yrs No coaches Beauty Treatment Room **Prices** S £40-£50;
D £56-£70 **LB** **Parking** 20 **Notes** ⊜

England

TINTAGEL
MAP 02 SX08

♦♦♦♦

Pendrin Guest House ◇
Atlantic Rd PL34 0DE ☎ 01840 770560
e-mail pendrin@tesco.net
web www.pendrinhouse.co.uk
Dir Through village, pass entrance to Tintagel Castle, last house on right before Headlands caravan site

Located close to coastal walks, castle and the town centre, this Victorian house provides comfortable accommodation with most rooms having sea or country views. Delicious evening meals, using quality fresh ingredients, are available by arrangement, and there is a cosy lounge.

Facilities 9 rms (4 en suite) (1 pri facs) (2 fmly) (1 GF) ☻ TVB tea/coffee ✖ Cen ht TVL No coaches Dinner Last d 6pm **Prices** S £22; D £44-£50✳ **LB** **Parking** 6 **Notes** Closed Dec-13 Feb

♦♦♦♦ ⬛

Port William Inn
Trebarwith Strand PL34 0HB
☎ 01840 770230 ▤ 01840 770936

The Port William has a splendid cliff location just south of Tintagel, with sea views from the attractive bedrooms. The spacious bar-restaurant has a conservatory and outside area, where the extensive menu can be enjoyed with the spectacular scenery.

Facilities 8 en suite (1 fmly) ☻ in bedrooms ☻ in area of dining room ☻ in 1 lounge TVB tea/coffee Cen ht Pool Table Dinner Last d 8.45pm **Conf** Max 100 Thtr 100 Class 50 Board 50 **Parking** 45 **Notes** Civ Wed 50

♦♦♦♦ ⬛

The Cottage Teashop
Bossiney Rd PL34 0AH ☎ 01840 770639
Dir Off A30, 2m past Launceston junct onto A395. Follow signs to Camelford then Tintagel

Facilities 3 en suite 1 annexe en suite (1 GF) ☻ TVB tea/coffee Licensed Cen ht No children 10yrs No coaches **Prices** D £46-£60✳ **LB** **Parking** 4 **Notes** Closed 25-26 Dec

TORPOINT
MAP 03 SX45

♦♦♦♦ ⬛

Edgcumbe Arms
Cremyll PL10 1HX ☎ 01752 822294 ▤ 01752 822014
e-mail edgcumbe-arms@btconnect.com
Dir B3237 to Cremyll

Situated within the 800-acre Mount Edgcumbe Park Estate at the mouth of the River Tamar, this characterful inn has wonderful views across Plymouth Sound. The spacious bedrooms offer good standards of comfort, and tasty food is served in the flagstoned bar.

Facilities 6 en suite (2 fmly) ☻ in bedrooms ☻ in dining room ☻ in 1 lounge TVB tea/coffee ✖ Cen ht Dinner Last d 9pm **Conf** Max 10 **Parking** 10 **Notes** Civ Wed 40

See advertisement on this page

TREBARWITH
MAP 02 SX08

♦♦♦♦

Upton Farm
PL33 9DG ☎ 01840 770225 ▤ 01840 770337
e-mail ricardo@dorich.co.uk
Dir A39 onto B3314, through Delabole. Atlantic garage on left, sharp right onto Treligga Downs Rd, 0.5m right at T-junct, farm 1m on right

Having unrivalled sea views over Trebarwith, this attractive house has a rural location close to the South West Coast Path and is convenient for good local dining. Expect a combination of warm hospitality and smart accommodation. Breakfast, featuring local produce and home-made muesli, is served in the conservatory-dining room around one large table.

Facilities 3 en suite ☻ TVB tea/coffee ✖ Cen ht No children 8yrs No coaches table tennis in games room & small snooker table **Prices** D £75-£85 **Conf** Max 40 **Parking** 4 **Notes** ⬛

England

TRURO
MAP 02 SW84

★★★★ **Guest House**

Bissick Old Mill

Ladock TR2 4PG ☎ 01726 882557
e-mail enquiries@bissickoldmill.plus.com
Dir B3275 towards Ladock village centre, turn left just after Falmouth Arms pub

This charming mill, family run, dates back some 300 years. Low beams, stone walls and an impressive fireplace all contribute to its character. Equally inviting are the hospitality and breakfast menu for a range of hot dishes freshly prepared for a memorable aspect to any stay.

Facilities 3 en suite 1 annexe en suite (1 GF) ⊘ TVB tea/coffee Direct dial from bedrooms ✖ Cen ht No coaches **Prices** S £45-£55; D £60-£80 **LB Parking** 6

★★ **Bed & Breakfast**

Riverside Bed and Breakfast ◇

Newham Rd TR1 2SU ☎ 01872 276952
e-mail judy.cull@tiscali.co.uk
Dir 1m S of city centre. Off A39/A390 onto Newham Rd

Set in grounds, this family-run guest house is just a ten-minute level walk from the city centre. The homely bedrooms are well equipped, and a full English breakfast, featuring local produce whenever possible, is served around a communal table in the traditional dining room.

Facilities 2 rms (1 en suite) ⊘ TVB tea/coffee ✖ Cen ht No children 12yrs No coaches Dinner Last d 3pm **Prices** S £25-£40; D £40-£60 **Parking** 2 **Notes** ⊛

◆◆◆◆

Bickford House

29 Green Cl TR1 2DD ☎ 01872 272747
e-mail chrissie@bickfordhouse.co.uk
web www.bickfordhouse.co.uk
Dir 0.5m S of town centre off A390 Green Ln ring road

The refurbished accommodation is in a residential area near the city centre. The atmosphere is homely and welcoming, and the bright bedrooms range from traditional style to the more contemporary, and are finished with many considerate extras. A choice of cooked or continental breakfast is served in the pleasant dining room.

Facilities 2 en suite ⊘ TVB tea/coffee ✖ Cen ht No children 15yrs No coaches **Prices** S fr £35; d fr £50✳ **Parking** 2 **Notes** ⊛

◆◆◆◆

Bodrean Manor Farm (SW851480)

Trispen TR4 9AG
☎ 01872 273227 ◻ 01872 273225 Mrs Marsh
web www.bodreanmanorfarm.co.uk
Dir 3m NE of Truro. A30 onto A39 towards Truro, left after Trispen village signed Frogmore & Trehane, farm driveway 100yds

This friendly house with attractive gardens stands in peaceful countryside convenient for Truro. Bedrooms are thoughtfully and extensively equipped, and the bathrooms are well provisioned with soft towels and toiletries. The home-cooked breakfast is a feature.

Facilities 3 rms (2 en suite) (1 pri facs) (1 fmly) ⊘ TVB tea/coffee ✖ Cen ht TVL 230 acres Dairy **Prices** S £35-£40; D £50-£55✳ **LB Parking** 6 **Notes** ⊛

◆◆◆◆

Manor Cottage

Tresillian TR2 4BN ☎ 01872 520212
e-mail man.cott@boltblue.com
Dir 2.5m NE of Truro on A390

This charming property is a good base for exploring the region and attractions such as The Eden Project and The Lost Gardens of Heligan. The stylish conservatory-restaurant, open Thursday to Sunday evenings, offers British cuisine using local produce. The attractive guest rooms are comfortably appointed with period furniture.

Facilities 5 rms (2 en suite) (1 pri facs) (1 fmly) ⊘ in 1 bedrooms ⊘ in dining room TVB tea/coffee ✖ Licensed Cen ht No coaches Dinner Last d 9pm **Parking** 9 **Notes** Closed 24-26 Dec

◆◆◆◆

Oxturn House

Ladock TR2 4NQ ☎ 01726 884348 ◻ 01726 884248
e-mail oxturnhouse@hotmail.com
web www.oxturnhouse.co.uk
Dir 6m NE of Truro. B3275 into Ladock, onto lane opp Falmouth Arms, up hill 200yds, 1st right after end 30mph sign, Oxturn on right

A friendly welcome is assured at this large family house, set slightly above the village and close to a pub and several dining venues. Bedrooms are spacious and a pleasant lounge is available. In summer you can enjoy the country views from the patio. Hearty breakfasts are served in the dining room.

Facilities 2 rms (1 en suite) (1 pri facs) ⊘ TVB tea/coffee ✖ Cen ht TVL No children 12yrs No coaches **Prices** D £52-£62✳ **Parking** 4 **Notes** Closed Dec-mid Jan ⊛

◆◆◆◆

Trevispian Vean ◇ (SW850502)

St Erme TR4 9AT ☎ 01872 279514 Mr & Mrs Dymond
Dir 3m N of Truro. A30 onto A39 for Truro, 2nd left in Trispin, 0.5m sharp left, farm 500yds on left

This busy, family-run farm is a good base for exploring the area. You are assured of a friendly welcome and many guests return regularly. Freshly cooked farmhouse breakfasts are served in the spacious dining room at separate tables.

continued

Trevispian Vean

Facilities 5 en suite (1 fmly) ⊗ TV3B tea/coffee ✯ TVL Fishing Snooker Pool Table Table tennis 300 acres arable/pigs **Prices** S £25-£28; D £50-£56✶ LB **Parking** 20 **Notes** Closed Oct-Mar ⊛

◆◆◆◆

Woodsedge ◇

10 Gig Ln, Carnon Downs TR3 6JS
☎ 01872 870269 & 07812 738656
Dir *3m S of Truro. Off A39 at Carnon Downs rdbt onto Gig Ln, house on left at x-rds*

This small and friendly house, pleasantly located in a quiet residential area in Carnon Downs, offers a warm welcome and is a comfortable place to stay. Breakfast, served in the cosy lounge-dining room, is a hearty start to the day.

Facilities 2 rms (1 en suite) (1 pri facs) ⊗ TVB tea/coffee ✯ Cen ht No children 9yrs No coaches **Prices** S £25-£27; D £50-£54✶ LB **Parking** 1 **Notes** Closed Xmas wk ⊛

◆◆◆◆ A

The Townhouse Rooms

20 Falmouth Rd TR1 2HX
☎ 01872 277374 ▤ 01872 241666
e-mail info@trurotownhouse.com
web www.trurotownhouse.com
Dir *500yds S of city centre*

Facilities 9 en suite 3 annexe en suite (2 GF) ⊗ TVB tea/coffee Licensed Cen ht No coaches **Prices** S £35-£45; D £55-£65✶ LB **Parking** 12

See advertisement on this page

◆◆◆

Gwarnick Cottage

St Allen TR4 9QU ☎ 01872 540377
e-mail jon17bet23price@btinternet.com
Dir *B3284 from Truro to Shortlanesend, right fork opp Old Plough Inn, 2nd right signed St Allen. Cottage 1st on right*

This quiet home is tucked away in lush countryside, only 10 minutes from Truro. The proprietors are very friendly and you are made to feel most welcome. Breakfast is freshly cooked and is served in the lounge that looks onto the attractive garden with its busy bird table.

Facilities 2 rms ⊗ TVB tea/coffee ✯ Cen ht TVL No children 10yrs No coaches **Prices** D £44✶ LB **Parking** 2 **Notes** Closed Oct-Mar ⊛

◆◆◆

Gwel-Tek Lodge Guest House

41 Treyew Rd TR1 2BY ☎ 01872 276843 ▤ 01872 242574
e-mail rooms@gweltek.co.uk
Dir *0.5m W of town centre on A39, opp Truro City Football Club*

The house has undergone much refurbishment. Bedrooms, with one on the ground floor, are well equipped, and a full English breakfast is served in the cosy dining room. Dinner is available by arrangement.

Facilities 7 en suite (2 fmly) (1 GF) ⊗ TVB tea/coffee ✯ Cen ht No coaches Dinner Last d noon **Prices** S £35-£45; D £55-£65✶ LB **Parking** 5

England

TRURO continued

◆◆◆
Spires
45 Treyew Rd TR1 2BY ☎ 01872 277621
Dir *0.5m W of town centre on A39, opp Truro City Football Club*

This comfortable and friendly home is just a short drive from the city centre, or a walk for the more energetic. Bedrooms are spacious and one room has a splendid view of the city and cathedral. Breakfast is served in the cosy dining room, and there is a pub-restaurant nearby.

Facilities 2 rms (1 en suite) (1 pri facs) (1 fmly) ☺ TVB tea/coffee ✗ Cen ht No coaches **Prices** S £30-£35; D £45-£52✳ **Parking** 2 **Notes** ⊛

◆◆◆
Cliftons
46 Tregolls Rd TR1 1LA ☎ 01872 274116 ▤ 01872 274116
e-mail cliftonsbandb@hotmail.com
Dir *0.5m NE of city centre on A390*

The comfortable accommodation is in relaxed surroundings within walking distance of the city centre. Bedrooms, some on the ground floor, have considerate extras and there is also a lounge. The breakfast menu offers a good choice of dishes in the bright dining room.

Facilities 6 en suite (1 fmly) (1 GF) ☺ TVB tea/coffee ✗ Cen ht TVL No coaches **Prices** S £33-£35; D £53-£56 **Parking** 6

◆◆◆ ❦
Polsue Manor Farm *(SW858462)*
Tresillian TR2 4BP
☎ 01872 520234 ▤ 01872 520616 Mrs Holliday
e-mail geraldineholliday@hotmail.com
Dir *2m NE of Truro. Farm entrance on A390 at S end of Tresillian*

The 190-acre sheep farm is in peaceful countryside a short drive from Truro. The farmhouse provides a relaxing break from the city, with hearty breakfasts and warm hospitality. The spacious dining room has pleasant views and three large communal tables, and there is also a lounge.

Facilities 5 rms (2 en suite) (3 fmly) (1 GF) ☺ tea/coffee TVL 190 acres mixed/sheep/horses/working **Prices** S £25-£32; D £46-£54 LB **Parking** 5 **Notes** Closed 21 Dec-2 Jan

◆◆◆
The Terrace
2 Coronation Ter TR1 3HJ ☎ 01872 274514
e-mail theterracecornwall@hotmail.co.uk
Dir *Opposite railway station*

Located just a short distance from the city centre and near the railway station, this well-cared for Victorian property offers clean and bright accommodation. A freshly prepared traditional English breakfast is served in the pleasant dining room at the rear of the house.

Facilities 3 rms ☺ TVB tea/coffee ✗ Cen ht No children 8yrs **Prices** S £25-£28; D £50-£55✳ **Notes** ⊛

ⓤ
Far Views
Tregoose Barton, Tresithick, Carnon Downs TR3 6JW
☎ 07899 848787
e-mail farviews@virgin.net

At the time of going to press the rating for this establishment had not been confirmed. Please check the AA website www.theAA.com for up-to-date information.

Facilities 2 rms (2 GF) ☺ TVB tea/coffee Cen ht TVL No coaches **Prices** D £50✳ **Parking** available **Notes** ⊛

TYWARDREATH
MAP 02 SX05

◆◆◆◆
Elmswood
Tehidy Rd PL24 2QD ☎ 01726 814221 ▤ 01726 814399
Dir *In village opp St Andrews Church*

Elmswood is a fine Victorian house, where many return for the warm welcome. Bedrooms have quality furnishings and many extra facilities, and the attractive dining room, lounge and bar overlook a beautiful garden. Home-cooked dinners using local produce are available by arrangement.

Facilities 7 rms (6 en suite) (1 fmly) (1 GF) ☺ in bedrooms ☺ in dining room TVB tea/coffee ✗ Licensed Cen ht TVL No coaches Dinner Last d noon **Prices** S £25-£40; D £46-£60✳ **Parking** 8 **Notes** Closed Dec-Jan ⊛

VERYAN
MAP 02 SW93

◆◆◆◆
Elerkey
Elerkey House TR2 5QA ☎ 01872 501261 ▤ 01872 501354
e-mail enquiries@elerkey.co.uk
Dir *In village, 1st left after church & water gardens*

This peaceful home is surrounded by attractive gardens in a tranquil village. The resident proprietors and their family provide exemplary hospitality and many guests return time and again. The pleasant bedrooms have many considerate extras.

Facilities 4 en suite (1 fmly) ☺ TVB tea/coffee Direct dial from bedrooms ✗ Cen ht No coaches **Prices** S £36.50-£37.50; D £53-£55✳ LB **Parking** 5 **Notes** Closed Xmas/New Year rs 15 Dec-Jan (by arrangement only)

England

◆◆◆◆ ☕ ◄

The New Inn

TR2 5QA ☎ 01872 501362 ▤ 01872 501078
e-mail jack@newinn-veryan.fsnet.co.uk
Dir In village centre

Popular with visitors and locals, the New Inn is a good base for
touring the Roseland peninsula. Bedrooms are brightly decorated and
have thoughtful extras. Dining is an enjoyable experience: fresh local
produce graces much of the menu and the changing specials.

Facilities 3 rms (2 en suite) (1 pri facs) ⊗ in bedrooms ⊗ in dining
room TVB tea/coffee 🐾 Cen ht No children 14yrs No coaches Dinner
Last d 9pm

WADEBRIDGE   MAP 02 SW97
See also **St Kew & St Wenn**

★★★ Inn

The Molesworth Arms

Molesworth St PL27 7DP
☎ 01208 812055 ▤ 01208 814254
e-mail info@moleswortharms.co.uk
*Dir A30 through Bodmin, then take A389 to Wadebridge. Over old
bridge, right at rdbt, then 1st left*

Situated in a pedestrian area of the town, this 16th-century former
coaching inn is a popular base for exploring the area. The comfortable
bedrooms retain their original character. In addition to the wide range
of snacks and meals served in the lively bar, the Courtyard Restaurant
offers a comprehensive carte with daily specials.

Facilities 16 rms (14 en suite) (2 fmly) STV TVB tea/coffee Direct dial
from bedrooms TVL Dinner **Prices** S £45-£52.50; D £75-£87.50✱ **LB**
Conf BC Thtr 60 Class 50 Board 40 **Parking** 16

◆◆◆◆ ◄

Swan Hotel ◇

9 Molesworth St PL27 7DD
☎ 01208 812526 ▤ 01208 816479
e-mail reservations@smallandfriendly.co.uk
Dir In town centre near bridge

The popular traditional inn is in the centre of the town and has
beamed ceilings and wood-panelled walls. The pleasant bedrooms are
well equipped, and bar meals are available at lunch and dinner. There
is a delightful function room.

Facilities 6 en suite (1 fmly) ⊗ in bedrooms ⊗ in dining room
⊗ in 1 lounge TVB tea/coffee 🐾 Cen ht Dinner Last d 9pm
Prices S £30-£45; D £60-£70✱ **LB** **Conf** Max 80 Thtr 80 Class 60 Board 30

WENDRON   MAP 02 SW63

★★★ Bed & Breakfast

Carthew B & B

Carthew TR13 0JA ☎ 01209 832203 ▤ 01209 832882
e-mail rmatt55349@aol.com
*Dir From A30 take B3297 signed Helston/Scorrier, 2m past
Fourlanes, signed on right*

This barn conversion is set within 4 acres of pastureland and is
continued

surrounded by beautiful countryside. The smart modern bedrooms
are on the ground floor separate from the main house and have their
own front entrance from the car park. There is a lounge-snooker room
and during the summer the decked terrace overlooks tranquil green
fields. A full English breakfast is served in the pleasant cottage dining
room.

Facilities 2 annexe en suite (2 fmly) (2 GF) ⊗ TVB tea/coffee 🐾
Cen ht TVL No coaches Pool Table **Prices** S £45; D £45✱ **LB**
Parking 10 **Notes** ⊗

CUMBRIA

ALSTON   MAP 18 NY74
See also **Cowshill (Co Durham)**

◆◆◆◆

Greycroft ◇

Middle Pk, The Raise CA9 3AR ☎ 01434 381383
e-mail mail@greycroft.co.uk
web www.greycroft.co.uk
*Dir A686 SW from Alston, over river, 2nd junct right, 1st left signed
Ward Way/Middle Park, Greycroft 200yds on right*

This bungalow stands in well-tended and colourful gardens just
outside the town, and looks out over the fells. The two ground-floor
bedrooms are comfortably furnished and there is a lounge. A
generous breakfast is served in the spacious dining room with picture
windows. Expect a warm welcome and helpful service.

Facilities 2 en suite (1 fmly) (2 GF) ⊗ TVB tea/coffee 🐾 Cen ht TVL
No coaches **Prices** S £28-£36; D £56-£60✱ **LB** **Parking** 3 **Notes** Closed
Xmas & New Year ⊗

◆◆◆◆

Lowbyer Manor Country House

Hexham Rd CA9 3JX ☎ 01434 381230 ▤ 01434 381425
e-mail stay@lowbyer.com
Dir A686 from Penrith pass South Tynedale Railway on left, turn right

Located on the edge of the village, this Grade II listed Georgian
property retains many original features, which are highlighted by the
furnishings and decor. Cosy bedrooms are filled with a wealth of
thoughtful extras and day rooms include an elegant dining room, a
comfortable lounge and bar equipped with memorabilia.

Facilities 9 en suite (1 fmly) ⊗ TVB tea/coffee Licensed Cen ht
No coaches **Prices** S £33-£45; D £66-£80✱ **LB** **Parking** 9

AMBLESIDE   MAP 18 NY30

Premier Collection

★★★★★ ◉◉ Inn

Drunken Duck

Barngates LA22 0NG ☎ 015394 36347 🖷 015394 36781
e-mail info@drunkenduckinn.demon.co.uk
web www.drunkenduckinn.co.uk
Dir B5285 S from Ambleside towards Hawkshead, 2.5m signed right,
0.5m up hill

This 400-year-old coaching inn has been stylishly modernised to offer a
high standard of accommodation. Superior rooms are in a courtyard
house looking over private gardens and a tarn. The bar retains its
original character and is the hub of the inn. Fresh local produce
features on the imaginative bar menus and in the cosy restaurant. The
onsite brewery ensures a fine selection of ales.

Facilities 8 en suite 3 annexe en suite ⊘ in bedrooms ⊘ in dining room
TVB Direct dial from bedrooms 🐾 Cen ht No coaches Fishing Dinner
Last d 9pm **Parking** 40

★★★ Guest House

Haven Cottage Guest House ◇

Rydal Rd LA22 9AY ☎ 015394 33270
e-mail enquiries@amblesidehavencottage.co.uk
web www.amblesidehavencottage.co.uk
Dir On A591, 150yds after police station

A warm welcome along with home baking and refreshments are
served on arrival. Claire and Tim create a definite home from home.
The well-presented property offers off-road parking on the edge of
Ambleside. Very good breakfast; see how many puzzles you can work
out.

Facilities 7 rms (5 en suite) (2 fmly) ⊘ TVB tea/coffee 🐾 Cen ht
No children 8yrs No coaches **Prices** S £25-£35; D £50-£70✳ **LB** **Parking** 6

◆◆◆◆

The Fisherbeck Hotel

Lake Rd LA22 0DH ☎ 015394 33215 🖷 015394 33600
e-mail email@fisherbeckhotel.co.uk
web www.fisherbeckhotel.co.uk

Set on the southern approach to the town, this well-presented and
friendly establishment offers a high standard of accommodation. Many
of the spacious, modern bedrooms have fine views. There is a choice

of lounges, where refreshments are served, and the split-level
breakfast room provides many interesting dishes.

Facilities 18 en suite (2 fmly) (4 GF) ⊘ TVB tea/coffee Direct dial from
bedrooms 🐾 Licensed Cen ht TVL Use of nearby leisure club, free
fishing available **Prices** S £33-£69; D £50-£110 **LB** **Parking** 20
Notes Closed 24 Dec-24 Jan

◆◆◆◆

Lake House Hotel

Waterhead Bay LA22 0HD
☎ 015394 32360 🖷 015394 31474
e-mail info@lakehousehotel.co.uk
Dir Exit M6 signed A591, Ambleside. Pass Ambleside sign, continue
past lights, 1st right

Set on a hillside with lake views, this delightful house has very stylish
accommodation and a homely atmosphere. The bedrooms are all
individual in style. Dinner is available at the nearby sister property with
complimentary transport, and leisure facilities are available there too.
Breakfast is an interesting and substantial cold buffet.

Facilities 12 en suite (3 fmly) (2 GF) ⊘ TVB tea/coffee 🐾 Licensed
Cen ht TVL No coaches **Prices** S £99-£139; D £99-£139✳ **LB** **Conf** Max
32 Thtr 32 Class 12 Board 30 Del from £110 ✳ **Parking** 12
Notes Civ Wed 40

◆◆◆◆

Riverside

Under Loughrigg LA22 9LJ
☎ 015394 32395 🖷 015394 32440
e-mail info@riverside-at-ambleside.co.uk
web www.riverside-at-ambleside.co.uk
Dir A593 from Ambleside to Coniston, over stone bridge, right onto
Under Loughrigg Ln, Riverside 150yds left

A friendly atmosphere prevails at this refurbished Victorian house,
situated on a quiet lane by the River Rothay, below Loughrigg Fell.
Bedrooms, all with lovely views, are very comfortable, stylishly
furnished and feature homely extras; some have spa baths. A log-
burning stove warms the lounge in winter. The garden has seating for
morning and evening sun.

Facilities 6 en suite (1 fmly) ⊘ TVB tea/coffee 🐾 Licensed Cen ht
TVL No children 5yrs No coaches Fishing Jacuzzi **Prices** S £50-£60;
D £66-£96✳ **LB** **Parking** 15 **Notes** Closed Xmas & New Year

continued

◆◆◆◆

Wateredge Inn

Waterhead Bay LA22 0EP
☎ 015394 32332 📄 015394 31878
e-mail rec@wateredgeinn.co.uk
web www.wateredgeinn.co.uk
Dir On A591, at Waterhead, 1m S of Ambleside. Wateredge situated at end of promenade by lake

This modern inn has an idyllic location on the shore of Windermere at Waterhead Bay. The pretty bedrooms are particularly smart and generally spacious, and all offer a high standard of quality and comfort. The airy bar-restaurant opens onto attractive gardens, which have magnificent lake views. There is also a comfortable lounge, bar and dining area.
Facilities 15 en suite 6 annexe en suite (3 fmly) (3 GF) ⊗ in 1 bedrooms ⊗ in area of dining room ⊗ in lounges TVB tea/coffee Cen ht Complimentary membership to nearby leisure club Dinner Last d 9pm **Prices** S £40-£65; D £80-£140✳ **LB Parking** 40

◆◆◆◆

Ambleside Lodge ◇

Rothay Rd LA22 0EJ ☎ 015394 31681 📄 015394 34547
e-mail hmd@ambleside-lodge.com
web www.ambleside-lodge.com

Located close to the centre of the historic market town, this Grade II listed 18th-century residence has a peaceful atmosphere. The stylish accommodation includes bedrooms with antique and contemporary pieces, including four-poster beds. Attentive, personal service is provided.
Facilities 18 en suite (8 GF) ⊗ TVB tea/coffee Licensed Cen ht No coaches Pass to local leisure facilities. **Prices** S £30-£40; D £70-£140✳ LB **Parking** 20

◆◆◆◆

Brathay Lodge

Rothay Rd LA22 0EE ☎ 015394 32000
e-mail brathay@globalnet.co.uk
web www.brathay-lodge.com
Dir One-way system in town centre, Lodge on right opp church

Brathay Lodge is a high-amenity, limited-service accommodation. The traditional property has been refurbished in a bright contemporary style, and the pine-furnished bedrooms are mainly very spacious; some share a communal balcony and some ground-floor rooms have their own entrance. All rooms have spa baths. The self-service continental breakfast can be taken in the informal lounge or in your bedroom.
Facilities 17 en suite 4 annexe en suite (3 fmly) (6 GF) ⊗ TVB tea/coffee Cen ht TVL use of Langdale Country Club **Prices** S £45-£95; D £65-£142✳ **LB Parking** 23

◆◆◆◆

Cherry Garth Hotel

Old Lake Rd LA22 0DH ☎ 015394 33128 📄 015394 33885
e-mail reception@cherrygarth.com
Dir A591 N into Ambleside, over lights, B&B 800yds on right

Set on the southern approach to the town, this detached house stands in well-landscaped gardens with views of Loughrigg Fell and Wetherlam. Bedrooms offer a range of styles, are spacious and have modern fittings. Traditional Lakeland breakfasts are served in the lounge-breakfast room overlooking the front garden.
Facilities 12 en suite (2 fmly) (3 GF) ⊗ TVB tea/coffee Licensed Cen ht **Prices** S £35-£55; D £70-£110✳ **LB Parking** 14

England

AMBLESIDE continued

◆◆◆◆

Easedale Lodge

Compston Rd LA22 9DJ ☎ 015394 32112
e-mail enquiries@easedaleambleside.co.uk
web www.easedaleambleside.co.uk
Dir On one-way system N through Ambleside, corner Compston Rd overlooking bowling & putting greens

A very warm welcome awaits you at this centrally located Victorian guest house. Bedrooms are all well equipped, featuring homely extras, and breakfast is served in the cosy dining room. There is a stylish lounge and private parking is available.

Facilities 7 rms (5 en suite) (2 pri facs) (1 fmly) ⊗ TVB tea/coffee ✕ Cen ht No children 12yrs No coaches Reduced day membership at Langdale Country Club **Prices** D £60-£80✱ LB **Parking** 7 **Notes** Closed Xmas

◆◆◆◆

Elterwater Park

Skelwith Br LA22 9NP ☎ 015394 32227
e-mail enquiries@elterwater.com
web www.elterwater.com
Dir A593 from Ambleside to Coniston, 1m past Skelwith Bridge Hotel, layby on right fronts estate road to Elterwater Park, signed at gate

This traditional Lakeland house stands high on the hills above Langdale and has spectacular views. The attractive bedrooms, including a ground-floor room, are comfortably furnished and well equipped. Evening meals are available by arrangement in the dining room that also has a small lounge area, and there is a useful drying room too.

Facilities 4 en suite 1 annexe en suite (1 GF) ⊗ TVB tea/coffee ✕ Licensed Cen ht No children 10yrs No coaches Dinner Last d Previous day **Prices** S £40-£46; D £60-£72✱ **Parking** 8 **Notes** 🖾

◆◆◆◆ 🏠

Kent House

Lake Rd LA22 0AD ☎ 015394 33279
e-mail mail@kent-house.com
web www.kent-house.com
Dir From town centre, by Post Office on one-way system 300yds on left on terrace above main road

From its elevated location overlooking the town, this Lakeland house offers comfortable, well-equipped accommodation with attractive

bedrooms. Traditional breakfasts featuring the best of local produce are served at individual tables in the elegant dining room.

Facilities 5 rms (4 en suite) (1 pri facs) (2 fmly) ⊗ TVB tea/coffee Direct dial from bedrooms ✕ Cen ht TVL No coaches **Prices** S £40-£50; D £56-£90 **LB** **Parking** 2 **Notes** Closed 24-25 Dec

◆◆◆◆

The Rysdale ◇

Rothay Rd LA22 0EE ☎ 015394 32140 🖨 015394 33999
e-mail info@rysdale.f9.co.uk
Dir A591 into Ambleside, one-way system to A593, Rysdale on right

The comfortable Edwardian house is only a stroll from the town centre and overlooks the church and the park. The friendly proprietors offer attractive, well-equipped bedrooms and most have superb mountain views, as does the smart dining room. The cosy lounge has a fireplace and a well-stocked bar.

Facilities 9 rms (7 en suite) (2 pri facs) (2 fmly) ⊗ TVB tea/coffee ✕ Cen ht No children 5yrs No coaches **Prices** S £28-£35; D £60-£90✱ **Parking** 1 **Notes** Closed 23-29 Dec 🖾

◆◆◆◆

Wanslea Guest House ◇

Low Fold, Lake Rd LA22 0DN
☎ 015394 33884 🖨 015394 33884
e-mail information@wanslea.co.uk
Dir On S side of town, opp garden centre

Located between the town centre and lakeside pier, this Victorian house provides a range of thoughtfully furnished bedrooms, some of which are individually themed and have spa baths. Comprehensive breakfasts are served in the spacious dining room and a cosy lounge is available.

continued

continued

Facilities 8 en suite (2 fmly) ⊗ FTV TVB tea/coffee Cen ht TVL
No children 6yrs No coaches **Prices** S £29-£50; D £58-£90✳ LB
Notes Closed 23-26 Dec

◆◆◆◆

Claremont House

Compston Rd LA22 9DJ ☎ 015394 33448
e-mail enquiries@claremontambleside.co.uk
web www.claremontambleside.co.uk
Dir On one-way system, Claremont House after church

Facilities 6 en suite (2 fmly) (1 GF) ⊗ TVB tea/coffee Cen ht
No coaches **Prices** D £55-£64

◆◆◆◆

The Old Vicarage

Vicarage Rd LA22 9DH ☎ 015394 33364 ▤ 015394 34734
e-mail the.old.vicarage@kencomp.net
web www.oldvicarageambleside.co.uk
Dir In town centre. Off Compston Rd onto Vicarage Rd

Facilities 10 en suite (3 fmly) (2 GF) ⊗ in bedrooms ⊗ in dining room
⊗ in 1 lounge TVB tea/coffee Cen ht TVL ▣ Sauna Pool Table Hot tub
Prices S £52.50-£85; d fr £85✳ LB **Parking** 15

◆◆◆

Meadowbank Guest House ◇

Meadowbank, Rydal Rd LA22 9BA ☎ 015394 32710
e-mail enquiries@meadowbank.org.uk
Dir On the A591 on the northern edge of town.

Set in secluded grounds on the edge of Ambleside, this substantial
family-run house offers well-equipped accommodation. Most
bedrooms blend bright modern furnishings and decor with the
character features of the property. The cosy lounge has Internet
access, and traditional hearty breakfasts are served at individual tables
in the large airy dining room. Cyclists are especially welcome.

Facilities 7 rms (6 en suite) (1 pri facs) (1 fmly) (1 GF) ⊗ TVB
tea/coffee Cen ht TVL No coaches **Prices** S £26-£38; D £32-£76✳
Parking 8

Ⓤ

Broadview Guest House ◇

Lake Rd LA22 0DN ☎ 015394 32431
e-mail enquiries@broadviewguesthouse.co.uk
web www.broadviewguesthouse.co.uk
Dir On A591 south side of Ambleside, opposite Garden Centre

At the time of going to press the rating for this establishment had not
been confirmed. Please check the AA website www.theAA.com for up-
to-date information.

Facilities 6 rms (3 en suite) (1 pri facs) ⊗ TVB tea/coffee ✖ Cen ht
No coaches **Prices** S £30-£70; D £40-£80✳ LB

◆◆◆◆

Bongate House ◇

Bongate CA16 6UE ☎ 017683 51245 & 51423
e-mail information@bongatehouse.co.uk
Dir 0.5m from town centre on B6542 signed Brough

This Georgian house dating from 1740 stands in landscaped gardens.
A friendly and relaxed atmosphere prevails, and hearty breakfasts are
served in the spacious dining room. Bedrooms are thoughtfully
furnished with lots of homely extras. A comfortable lounge is
available.

Facilities 8 rms (5 en suite) (4 fmly) ⊗ in bedrooms ⊗ in dining room
TVB tea/coffee Cen ht TVL Riding ⚑ ⚒ **Prices** S £22.50; D £45-£52✳
LB **Parking** 10 **Notes** rs Nov-Feb ⊠

◆◆◆◆

Hall Croft ◇

Dufton CA16 6DB ☎ 017683 52902
e-mail r.walker@leaseholdpartnerships.co.uk
Dir Dufton signed from A66 near Appleby, B&B at bottom of village
green

Standing at the end of a lime-tree avenue, Hall Croft, built in 1882, has
been restored to its original glory. Bedrooms are comfortably
proportioned, traditionally furnished and well equipped. Breakfasts,
served in the lounge-dining room, are substantial and include home-
made produce. The lovely garden has views of the Pennines.

Facilities 3 rms (2 en suite) (1 pri facs) ⊗ TVB tea/coffee Cen ht
No coaches **Prices** S fr £28; d fr £50 **Parking** 3 **Notes** Closed 24-26 Dec
⊠

◆◆◆ ◗

The Dukes Head Hotel

Front St CA4 9PB ☎ 016974 72226
e-mail info@dukeshead-hotel.co.uk
web www.dukeshead-hotel.co.uk
Dir In village centre opp Post Office

Located in the peaceful village close to the River Eden, the Dukes
Head offers comfortable accommodation with a warm friendly
atmosphere. There is a relaxing lounge bar with open fires, and a wide
choice of meals is available either here or in the restaurant.

Facilities 5 rms (3 en suite) (2 pri facs) ⊗ in 5 bedrooms ⊗ in dining
room TV4B Cen ht Fishing Dinner Last d 9pm **Prices** S fr £38.50; d fr
£58.50✳ LB **Parking** 20 **Notes** Closed 25 Dec

England

BAMPTON

MAP 18 NY51

◆◆◆ 🏠

Mardale Inn

CA10 2RQ ☎ 01931 713244
e-mail info@mardaleinn.co.uk
web www.mardaleinn.co.uk
Dir M6 junct 39, onto A6 to Shap, left to Bampton (through Bampton Grange)

This owner-run 18th-century village inn lies in spectacular countryside close to Haweswater in the Lake District, and is just a short drive south from Penrith. The homely pub has a welcoming fire in the lounge bar, and home-cooked meals are served every evening and at weekend lunchtimes. The bedrooms are carefully finished and comfortably equipped. This is a non-smoking establishment.

Facilities 3 rms (2 en suite) (1 pri facs) (1 fmly) ⊗ TVB tea/coffee Cen ht Dinner Last d 7.45pm **Prices** S £49; D £67✴ LB **Notes** Closed Jan

BARROW-IN-FURNESS

MAP 18 SD26

◆◆◆◆ 🅰

King Alfred Hotel ◇

Ocean Rd, Walney Island LA14 3DU
☎ 01229 474717 📠 01229 476181
e-mail kingalfred@walney4.fsnet.co.uk
Dir 1m W of town centre. A590 to Isle of Walney, left at x-rds after Walney bridge onto Ocean Rd

Facilities 6 en suite (1 fmly) ⊗ in area of dining room TVB tea/coffee ✘ Licensed Cen ht Pool Table Bowling green Dinner **Prices** S fr £30; d fr £60 **Parking** 60

BEETHAM

MAP 18 SD47

◆◆◆◆ 🏠

Wheatsheaf Hotel

LA7 7AL ☎ 015395 62123 📠 015395 64840
e-mail wheatbeeth@aol.com
web www.wheatsheafbeetham.com
Dir Off A6 into village centre, next to parish church

This delightful historic inn has an idyllic setting in the heart of this unspoiled village. The stylish bedrooms have a host of thoughtful extras, and the modern bathrooms are spacious and well equipped. A wide choice of bar meals and more adventurous dishes are served in the bar areas and upstairs dining room. Staff are friendly.

continued

Facilities 6 en suite (1 fmly) ⊗ TVB tea/coffee ✘ Cen ht Dinner Last d 8.30pm **Prices** S £55-£65; D £75-£95 LB **Conf** Max 70 Thtr 30 Class 30 Board 30 Del from £75 ✴ **Parking** 40 **Notes** Closed Xmas & 8-18 Jan

BOOT

MAP 18 NY10

◆◆◆◆ 🏠

Brook House Inn

CA19 1TG ☎ 01946 723288 📠 01946 723160
e-mail stay@brookhouseinn.co.uk
web www.brookhouseinn.co.uk
Dir In village centre. 500yds NE of Dalegarth Station

Located in the heart of Eskdale, this impressive inn dates from the early 18th century and has been renovated to offer comfortable accommodation with smart modern bathrooms for weary walkers and travellers. Wholesome meals using local produce are served in the traditionally furnished dining room or attractive bar, the latter featuring real ales and country memorabilia.

Facilities 7 en suite (2 fmly) ⊗ in bedrooms ⊗ in dining room ⊗ in lounges TVB tea/coffee ✘ Cen ht Dinner Last d 8.30pm **Prices** S £46.50-£48.50; D £68-£72✴ LB **Conf** Max 35 **Parking** 24

BORROWDALE

MAP 18 NY21

Premier Collection

★★★★★ ⊛ **Guest House**

Hazel Bank Country House

Rosthwaite CA12 5XB ☎ 017687 77248 📠 017687 77373
e-mail enquiries@hazelbankhotel.co.uk
web www.hazelbankhotel.co.uk
Dir B5289 to Rosthwaite, signed opp village

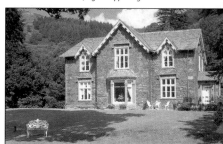

Set on an elevated position surrounded by 4 acres of well-tended lawns and woodland, this Victorian residence has magnificent views of Borrowdale. Bedrooms are well proportioned, thoughtfully equipped and carefully decorated. Four-course dinners, cooked with imagination and skill, and excellent breakfasts are served in the delightful dining room. Service is attentive and the hospitality makes you feel very much at home.

Facilities 8 en suite (2 GF) ⊗ TVB tea/coffee ✘ Licensed Cen ht No children 12yrs No coaches 🍴 Dinner Last d 3pm **Prices** S £65-£95; (incl. dinner) **Parking** 12

BOWNESS-ON-WINDERMERE

See **Windermere**

BRAITHWAITE

MAP 18 NY22

◆◆◆◆ 😐 📶

The Royal Oak

Braithwaite CA12 5SY ☎ 017687 78533 📄 017687 78533
e-mail tpfranks@hotmail.com
web www.tp-inns.co.uk
Dir *In Braithwaite centre*

The pretty village inn has delightful views of Skiddaw and Barrow, and is a good base for tourists and walkers. Some of the well-equipped bedrooms are furnished with four-poster beds. Hearty meals and traditional Cumbrian breakfasts are served in the restaurant, and there is an atmospheric, well-stocked bar.

Facilities 10 en suite (1 fmly) ⊗ in bedrooms ⊗ in dining room STV TVB tea/coffee Cen ht ⚲ local golf available and bowling green Dinner Last d 9pm **Prices** S £37-£39.50; D £60-£79✳ LB **Parking** 20

See advertisement on page 121

BRAMPTON

MAP 21 NY56

See also **Castle Carrock, Gilsland & Kirkcambeck**

Premier Collection

◆◆◆◆◆

The Hill On The Wall

Gilsland CA8 7DA ☎ 016977 47214 📄 016977 47214
e-mail info@hadrians-wallbedandbreakfast.com
web http://hadrians-wallbedandbreakfast.com
Dir *A69 into Gilsland & follow brown tourist signs for Birdoswald, The Hill on the Wall 0.5m on right*

Overlooking Hadrian's Wall, this elegant house was originally built in the 16th century as a fortified farmhouse. The spacious bedrooms are well equipped, and the lounge is comfortably furnished and stocked

continued

with books and games. Breakfast, using good local produce, is served in the smart dining room (dinner by arrangement).

Facilities 3 rms (2 en suite) (1 pri facs) (1 GF) ⊗ TVB tea/coffee 🦅 Cen ht TVL No children 10yrs No coaches Dinner Last d 24hrs
Prices S £40-£50; D £66✳ LB **Parking** 8 **Notes** ✉

BRAMPTON continued

♦♦♦♦ ◨

The Blacksmiths Arms

Talkin Village CA8 1LE
☎ 016977 3452 & 42111 📠 016977 3396
e-mail blacksmithsarmstalkin@yahoo.co.uk
web www.blacksmithstalkin.co.uk
Dir B6413 from Brampton to Castle Carrock, after level crossing 2nd left signed Talkin

Dating from the early 19th century and used as a smithy until the 1950s, this friendly village inn offers good home-cooked fare and real ales, with two Cumbrian cask beers always available. Bedrooms are well equipped, and three are particularly smart. An extensive menu and daily specials are offered in the cosy bar lounges or the smart, panelled Old Forge Restaurant.

Facilities 5 en suite 3 annexe en suite (2 fmly) (3 GF) ☉ in bedrooms ☉ in dining room ☉ in lounges TVB tea/coffee Direct dial from bedrooms ✖ Cen ht No coaches Dinner Last d 9pm **Prices** S £40-£50; D £55-£65 **Parking** 20

See advertisement on page 107

♦♦♦♦

Hullerbank

Talkin CA8 1LB ☎ 016977 46668 📠 016977 46668
e-mail info@hullerbank.freeserve.co.uk
Dir B6413 from Brampton for 2m, over railway & after golf club left to Talkin, onto Hallbankgate Rd & signs to Hullerbank

Dating from 1635, Hullerbank is a delightful farmhouse set in well-tended gardens, convenient for Hadrian's Wall and the Lake District. Bedrooms are comfortably proportioned, attractively decorated and well equipped. There is a cosy ground-floor lounge with an inglenook fireplace, and traditional hearty breakfasts are served in the dining room.

continued

Facilities 3 rms (2 en suite) (1 pri facs) ☉ TVB tea/coffee ✖ Cen ht TVL No children 12yrs No coaches **Prices** S £35-£40; D £56-£58 **Parking** 6 **Notes** Closed Dec-Jan

BRIGSTEER
MAP 18 SD48

♦♦♦♦ ▤ ▭ ◨

The Wheatsheaf

LA8 8AN ☎ 015395 68254
e-mail wheatsheaf@brigsteer.gb.com
web www.brigsteer.gb.com
Dir Off A591 signed Brigsteer, Wheatsheaf at bottom of hill

Lying in a peaceful hamlet to the west of Kendal, the Wheatsheaf offers attractive, well-equipped en suite bedrooms, all of which have been refurbished to offer modern comforts. There is a cosy, well-stocked bar, and a charming dining room where delicious home-cooked fare is served at individual tables.

Facilities 3 en suite ☉ TVB tea/coffee ✖ Cen ht No coaches Dinner Last d 9pm **Parking** 25

BROUGHTON-IN-FURNESS
MAP 18 SD28

See also **Millom**

★★★ Bed & Breakfast

Fair View

LA20 6ES ☎ 01229 716992
e-mail joycefairview@aol.com
Dir 500yds W of village centre near junct A595 & A593

With a countryside location close to the western fringe of the Lake District, this large country house offers comfortable, well proportioned and maintained bedrooms, each with a shower room en suite and thoughtful extras. The cosy lounge has an open fireplace and Sky television. Breakfast is served in the pleasant dining room.

continued

Facilities 3 en suite ⊗ TVB tea/coffee ✖ Cen ht TVL Dinner Last d 12 noon **LB** **Parking** 10

CALDBECK
MAP 18 NY34

♦♦♦♦ ♥

Swaledale Watch Farm ◇ (NY309396)

Whelpo CA7 8HQ ☎ 016974 78409 🖹 016974 78409
Mr & Mrs Savage
e-mail nan.savage@talk21.com
web www.swaledale-watch.co.uk
Dir 1m SW of Caldbeck on B5299

This attractive farmhouse, set within its own nature reserve, is in a peaceful location with a backdrop of picturesque fells. The en suite bedrooms are spacious and well equipped; two rooms are in an adjacent converted farm building and share a comfortable sitting room. Traditional hearty breakfasts are served in the attractive dining room overlooking the garden, with views to the fells.

Facilities 2 en suite 2 annexe en suite (2 fmly) (4 GF) ⊗ TVB tea/coffee ✖ Cen ht TVL 100 acre Nature Reserve, badger watching evenings 150 acres Sheep **Prices** S fr £28; d fr £50✳ **Parking** 8 **Notes** Closed 24-26 Dec 😊

CARLISLE
MAP 18 NY35
See also **Brampton & Castle Carrock**

Premier Collection

♦♦♦♦♦ 🏠 ♥

Bessiestown Country Guest House

(NY457768)

CA6 5QP ☎ 01228 577219 & 577019 🖹 01228 577219
Mr & Mrs Sisson
e-mail info@bessiestown.co.uk
web www.bessiestown.co.uk
For full entry see **Catlowdy**

♦♦♦♦ 🍴

Angus Hotel & Almonds Bistro

14-16 Scotland Rd CA3 9DG
☎ 01228 523546 🖹 01228 531895
e-mail hotel@angus-hotel.co.uk
web www.angus-hotel.co.uk
Dir 0.5m N of city centre on A7

Situated just north of the city, this family-run establishment is ideal for business and leisure. A warm welcome is assured and the accommodation is well equipped. Almonds Bistro provides enjoyable food and home baking, and there is also a lounge and a large meeting room.

Facilities 11 en suite (2 fmly) ⊗ in bedrooms ⊗ in dining room TVB tea/coffee Direct dial from bedrooms Licensed Cen ht No coaches Dinner Last d 9pm **Prices** S £40-£50; D £57-£67 **LB** **Conf** Max 25 Thtr 25 Class 16 Board 16

♦♦♦♦

Cambro House ◇

173 Warwick Rd CA1 1LP
☎ 01228 543094 🖹 01228 543094
e-mail davidcambro@aol.com
Dir M6 junct 43, onto Warwick Rd, 1m on right before St Aidan's Church

This smart Victorian house is close to the town centre and motorway. The beautifully refurbished and spacious bedrooms are smartly appointed and thoughtfully equipped. A hearty Cumbrian breakfast is served in the cosy morning room.

Facilities 3 en suite (1 GF) ⊗ TVB tea/coffee ✖ Cen ht No children 5yrs No coaches **Prices** S £30; D £45-£50✳ **LB** **Parking** 2

♦♦♦♦

Howard House

27 Howard Pl CA1 1HR
☎ 01228 529159 & 512550 🖹 01228 512550
e-mail howardhouse@bigfoot.com
Dir M6 junct 43, towards city centre, past church on right, pedestrian crossing & 1st right

This late-Victorian house is located in a quiet tree-lined street close to the city centre. The smart bedrooms are brightly decorated. Public areas include an inviting lounge and a smart dining room. Guests interested in family history will enjoy chatting to Mr Fisher who specialises in genealogy.

Facilities 6 rms (3 en suite) (2 fmly) ⊗ in dining room TVB tea/coffee ✖ Cen ht TVL

England

CARLISLE continued

◆◆◆◆
No1 Guest House ◇
1 Etterby St CA3 9JB ☎ 01228 547285 & 07899 948711
e-mail enquiries@number1guesthouse.net
Dir M6 junct 44, right at 7th lights onto Etterby St, house 1st on left

This small friendly guest house is on the north side of the city within walking distance of the centre. The attractive, well-equipped en suite bedrooms consist of a double, a twin-bed and a single room. Hearty traditional breakfasts featuring the best of local produce are served in the ground-floor dining room.

Facilities 3 en suite ⊗ TVB tea/coffee ✖ Cen ht No coaches Dinner Last d 10am **Prices** S £25-£30✳ **LB** **Parking** 1

◆◆◆
Craighead ◇
6 Hartington Pl CA1 1HL
☎ 01228 596767 & 593801 📠 01228 593801
Dir M6 junct 43, through 4 lights, then 4th turn on right

This smartly presented Grade II listed Victorian town house is only a short walk from the city centre. All bedrooms are individually styled and families are catered for. Breakfast is served at two separate tables in the period-style sitting room.

Facilities 5 rms (1 en suite) (1 fmly) ⊗ TVB tea/coffee Cen ht TVL No coaches **Prices** S £21-£22; D £40-£42 **Notes** rs 25-26 Dec & 1 Jan ⊛

◆◆◆
Kenilworth Guest House ◇
34 Lazonby Ter, London Rd CA1 2PZ
☎ 01228 526179 📠 01228 526179
e-mail reception@kenilworth-guesthouse.co.uk
Dir M6 junct 42, towards city centre, 1.5m on left opp television mast

Built at the end of the 19th century, this friendly family home at the end of a terrace has been upgraded to offer attractive and well-equipped accommodation. Kenilworth is a good base for touring: it is on the main bus route just 1.5m from the city centre, and is convenient for the Lake District, Gretna and Scotland. Secure parking is available.

Facilities 5 en suite (1 fmly) ⊗ TVB tea/coffee ✖ Cen ht TVL No coaches **Prices** S £30; d fr £50✳ **LB** **Parking** 4

CARTMEL MAP 18 SD37

Premier Collection

◆◆◆◆◆ 🛋 ❦
Hill Farm (SD367792)
LA11 7SS
☎ 015395 36477 📠 015395 36636 Mrs Foulerton
e-mail hillfarmbb@btinternet.com
Dir Exit village centre signed Cartmel Village Store, follow cul-de-sac signs then signs to Hill Farm

Hill Farm, dating from 1539, stands on an elevated position on the edge of the village famous for its sticky toffee pudding. The farmhouse has been renovated to provide comfortable accommodation with

continued

---

original character, and the attractive bedrooms are thoughtfully equipped with many extra touches. The comfortable lounge has log fires, and delicious freshly cooked breakfasts are served at a large table in the dining room.

Facilities 3 en suite ⊗ in bedrooms ⊗ in dining room ⊗ in 1 lounge TVB tea/coffee ✖ Cen ht TVL No children 5yrs Solarium 6 acres **Prices** S £35-£40; D £40-£45✳ **LB** **Parking** 3 **Notes** Closed Nov-Jan ⊛

CASTLE CARROCK MAP 18 NY55

★★★★ ◉ Restaurant with Rooms
The Weary at Castle Carrock
Castle Carrock CA8 9LU
☎ 01228 670230 & 670089 📠 01228 670089
e-mail relax@theweary.com
web www.theweary.com
Dir Turn of A69 onto B6143 immediate left. Continue for 4m, T-junct turn left. Hotel 1m on right in centre of village

Dating from 1740 but transformed over the past four years, the stylish restaurant with rooms offers bedrooms brimming with modern gadgets; the bathrooms have televisions built into the bath/shower areas. The restaurant opens into the walled garden area in the summer months. Hospitality is very strong.

Facilities 5 en suite STV TVB tea/coffee Direct dial from bedrooms ✖ Licensed TVL No coaches Dinner Last d 9pm **Prices** S £65-£85; D £95-£135✳ **LB** **Parking** 8

◆◆◆ ❦
Gelt Hall Farm ◇ (NY542554)
CA8 9LT ☎ 01228 670260 📠 01228 670260 Mrs Annie Robinson
e-mail robinson@gelthall.fsnet.co.uk
Dir B6413 to Castle Carrock, farm in village centre

This working farmhouse retains much of its original 17th-century character. The cheerful bedrooms are traditionally furnished and overlook the farmyard. Breakfast is served at communal table in the cosy lounge, and warm hospitality is a particular feature.

Facilities 3 rms (1 en suite) (1 fmly) ⊗ TV2B tea/coffee ✖ TVL 400 acres beef dairy sheep mixed **Prices** S £25-£27✳ **Parking** 7 **Notes** ⊛

CATLOWDY MAP 21 NY47

Premier Collection

◆◆◆◆◆ 🛋 ❦
Bessiestown Country Guest House
(NY457768)
CA6 5QP ☎ 01228 577219 & 577019 📠 01228 577219
Mr & Mrs Sisson
e-mail info@bessiestown.co.uk
web www.bessiestown.co.uk
Dir On B6318 in Catlowdy

The owners have welcomed guests to this delightful farmhouse for the past 30 years. The stylish bedrooms, with refurbished bathrooms, include family rooms and the luxury Dovecote Suite, which has a king-size four-poster bed, separate dressing room and a spa bath. There is

continued

a choice of lounges and a heated indoor swimming pool. Freshly prepared dinners and hearty breakfasts with home-made bread and preserves are served in the smart dining room.

Bessiestown Country Guest House

Facilities 5 en suite (1 fmly) (2 GF) ⊗ TVB tea/coffee ✖ Licensed Cen ht TVL 🐾 140 acres sheep Dinner Last d 4pm **Prices** S £45-£49 **LB** **Parking** 10

COCKERMOUTH
MAP 18 NY13

◆◆◆◆ 🏠 🐓

Highside Farmhouse *(NY163292)*

Embleton CA13 9TN ☎ 01768 776893 🖹 01768 776893
Mr & Mrs Winstanley
e-mail enquiries@highsidefarmhouse.co.uk
web www.highsidefarmhouse.co.uk
Dir A66 Keswick to Cockermouth, left at sign Lorton/Buttermere, left at T-junct. 300yds turn right opp church, farm at top of hill

True to its name, this 17th-century farmhouse stands over 600 feet up Ling Fell with breathtaking views across to the Solway Firth and Scotland. Add warm hospitality, great breakfasts, an inviting lounge-dining room with open fire in winter, and pine-furnished bedrooms, and the trip up the narrow winding road is well worth it.

Facilities 2 en suite ⊗ TVB tea/coffee Cen ht No children 10yrs 2 acres non working **Prices** S £36-£40; D £56-£60✱ **Parking** 2 **Notes** 🚭

◆◆◆◆ 🏠

Croft Guest House

6/8 Challoner St CA13 9QS
☎ 01900 827533 & 07717 053342
e-mail info@croft-guesthouse.com
Dir In town centre off Main St

Croft Guest House, one of the town's oldest buildings, lies in the heart of Cockermouth. It has been carefully upgraded to offer generally spacious, stylish accommodation. Bedrooms are well equipped and retain some original features. There is a cosy ground-floor lounge next to the spacious dining room, where delicious breakfasts from the extensive blackboard menu are served at individual tables.

Facilities 6 en suite (1 fmly) ⊗ TVB tea/coffee Cen ht No coaches **Parking** 5 **Notes** Closed Jan

◆◆◆◆ 🖙

Rose Cottage

Lorton Rd CA13 9DX ☎ 01900 822189 🖹 01900 822189
e-mail bookings@rosecottageguest.co.uk
Dir A5292 from Cockermouth to Lorton/Buttermere, Rose Cottage on right

This former inn is on the edge of town and has been refurbished to provide attractive, modern accommodation. The smart, well-equipped en suite bedrooms include a self-contained studio room with external access. There is a cosy lounge and the delicious home-cooked dinners are a highlight.

Facilities 6 en suite 1 annexe en suite (2 fmly) (3 GF) ⊗ TVB tea/coffee Licensed Cen ht Dinner Last d 5pm **Prices** S £40-£60; D £60-£90 **LB** **Parking** 12 **Notes** Closed 7-29 Feb rs 24-27 Dec

CONISTON
MAP 18 SD39

Premier Collection

◆◆◆◆◆ 🏠 🖙

Coniston Lodge Hotel

Station Rd LA21 8HH ☎ 015394 41201 🖹 015394 41201
e-mail info@coniston-lodge.com
Dir Off A593 x-rds near filling station up hill onto Station Rd

Coniston Lodge stands in mature gardens and is adorned with artistic touches, collectables and beautiful fresh and dried flower arrangements. An open staircase leads to the lounge (with a balcony overlooking the gardens) and the dining room. The well-proportioned bedrooms are in an extension on columns above the car park. Breakfasts are memorable, as are dinners (by arrangement).

Facilities 6 en suite ⊗ TVB tea/coffee Direct dial from bedrooms ✖ Licensed Cen ht No children 10yrs No coaches Dinner Last d 10am **Prices** S £49.50-£64.50; D £92-£109✱ **LB** **Parking** 9

England

CONISTON continued

◆◆◆◆◆

Wheelgate Country House Hotel

Little Arrow LA21 8AU ☎ 015394 41418 ▤ 015394 41114
e-mail enquiry@wheelgate.co.uk
Dir 1.5m S of Coniston, on W side of road

Dating from the 17th century, this charming farmhouse has original oak beams, panelling and low ceilings. An intimate bar, laundry facilities and a comfortable lounge with open fire are provided. There are impressive views over the well-tended gardens and the beautiful Lakeland countryside. A warm welcome can be expected.

Facilities 4 en suite 1 annexe en suite ⊗ TVB tea/coffee ✕ Licensed Cen ht No children 8yrs No coaches Free membership of Health Club with swimming pool **Prices** S £36-£39; D £62-£78✱ **LB Parking** 5

CROSTHWAITE   MAP 18 SD49

◆◆◆◆◆

The Punchbowl Inn at Crosthwaite

Lyth Valley LA8 8HR ☎ 015395 68237 ▤ 015397 68875
e-mail info@the-punchbowl.co.uk
Dir E end of village beside church

Located in the stunning Lyth valley alongside the village church, the historic inn has been renovated to provide excellent standards of comfort and facilities. Its sumptuous bedrooms have a wealth of thoughtful extras, and imaginative food is available in the elegant restaurant or in the rustic-style bar with open fires. A warm welcome and professional service is assured.

Facilities 9 en suite ⊗ TVB Direct dial from bedrooms ✕ Cen ht No coaches Dinner Last d 9pm **Prices** D £130-£250 **Parking** available
See advertisement on opposite page

◆◆◆◆

Crosthwaite House ◇

LA8 8BP ☎ 015395 68264 ▤ 015395 68264
e-mail bookings@crosthwaitehouse.co.uk
web www.crosthwaitehouse.co.uk
Dir A590 onto A5074, 4m right to Crosthwaite, 0.5m turn left

Having stunning views across the Lyth valley, this friendly Georgian house is a tranquil haven. Bedrooms are spacious and offer a host of
continued

thoughtful extras. The reception rooms include a comfortable lounge and a pleasant dining room with polished floorboards and individual tables.

Facilities 6 en suite ⊗ TVB tea/coffee Licensed Cen ht TVL No coaches Dinner Last d 5pm **Prices** S £25-£27.50; D £50-£55 **Parking** 10
Notes Closed mid Nov-Dec rs early Nov & Feb-Mar ⊛

DALTON-IN-FURNESS   MAP 18 SD27

◆◆◆◆

Park Cottage

Pk LA15 8JZ ☎ 01229 462850
e-mail nicholson.parkcottage@quista.net
web www.parkcottagedalton.co.uk
Dir Off rdbt junct A590 & A595 signed Dalton, 200yds sharp right down hill 0.5m. Private road on right before level crossing, 0.5m on right

A very warm welcome awaits you at this cottage set in peaceful grounds. Bedrooms are comfortably proportioned and have many thoughtful touches. There is also a cosy lounge with a log-burning stove. Hearty breakfasts are freshly prepared and served in the dining room with views of woodland.

Facilities 3 en suite (1 fmly) ⊗ TVB tea/coffee Cen ht TVL Dinner Last d 11am **Parking** 6 **Notes** Closed 31 Dec-Jan ⊛

GILSLAND   MAP 21 NY66

◆◆◆◆

Bush Nook ◇

Upper Denton, Gilsland CA8 7AF
☎ 016977 47194 ▤ 016977 47194
e-mail info@bushnook.co.uk
web www.bushnook.co.uk
Dir 6.5m NE of Brampton. Off A69 signed Spadeadam, Birdoswald, Bush Nook

Located in open countryside, this converted farmhouse offers comfortable bedrooms, split between the main house and the barn, with many original features. Other guest areas include the spacious breakfast room, cosy lounge and impressive conservatory leading out to a large, well maintained garden. Particularly popular with walkers and cyclists, a warm welcome is given to all.

Facilities 6 en suite ⊗ TVB tea/coffee ✕ Licensed Cen ht No coaches Dinner Last d noon **Prices** S £28-£40; D £56-£80 **LB Parking** 6

GRANGE-OVER-SANDS
MAP 18 SD47

♦♦♦♦
Elton House Bed & Breakfast
Windermere Rd LA11 6EQ
☎ 015395 32838 📠 015395 32838
e-mail info@eltonprivatehotel.co.uk
Dir A590 onto B5277 signed Grange-over-Sands, pass railway station, right at T-junct, 100yds on left

Friendly, attentive service is assured at this attractive Victorian house, just a stroll from the town. There are well-equipped bedrooms, with two on the ground floor, and the spacious lounge has a stunning feature fireplace.

Facilities 7 rms (5 en suite) (1 fmly) (2 GF) ⊗ TVB tea/coffee Licensed Cen ht TVL No coaches **Prices** S £34-£36; D £52-£56 **LB** **Parking** 5 **Notes** Closed Nov-Feb 🐾

♦♦♦♦
Mayfields
3 Mayfield Ter, Kents Bnk Road LA11 7DW
☎ 015395 34730 📠 015395 34730
Dir M6 junct 36, take A590 to Meathop rdbt, turn for Lindale. Left in Lindale at small rdbt to Grange, 1m S past rail station & just past the fire station

This small guest house overlooking the bay offers a friendly welcome. Bedrooms are individually decorated and equipped with thoughtful extras. Hearty breakfasts and tasty lunches and dinners are served in the attractive dining room, and there is also a comfy lounge.

Facilities 3 rms (2 en suite) (1 pri facs) ⊗ TVB tea/coffee ✕ Licensed Cen ht TVL No coaches Dinner Last d 6.30pm **LB** **Parking** 4 **Notes** Closed 21 Dec-6 Jan 🐾

GRASMERE
MAP 18 NY30

♦♦♦♦
Silverlea
Easedale Rd LA22 9QE ☎ 015394 35657 📠 015394 35657
e-mail info@silverlea.com
Dir Easedale Rd opp village green, Silverlea 300yds on right

Please note that this establishment has recently changed hands. A friendly welcome is assured at this ivy-clad stone house, just a short walk from the village. Delicious home-cooked meals using fresh produce are served in the cosy cottage dining room. Bedrooms, some having their own sitting area, are fresh in appearance and very comfortable.

Facilities 4 en suite (1 fmly) ⊗ TVB tea/coffee ✕ Cen ht No children 1yrs No coaches use of local country club Dinner Last d 12 hrs prior **Parking** 5 **Notes** Closed Dec-Jan 🐾

♦♦♦♦ Ⓐ
Lake View Country House
Lake View Dr LA22 9TD ☎ 015394 35384
e-mail michelleking@buryend.freeserve.co.uk
Dir A591 into Grasmere, left at minirdbt onto Stock Ln. Pass car park on right, sharp left onto Lake View Dr, house at end

Facilities 4 en suite (2 fmly) (1 GF) ⊗ TVB tea/coffee Cen ht No children 6yrs No coaches Fishing **Prices** D £80-£98 **LB** **Parking** 8

GRIZEDALE
MAP 18 SD39

♦♦♦♦
Grizedale Lodge The Hotel in the Forest
LA22 0QL ☎ 015394 36532 📠 015394 36572
e-mail enquiries@grizedale-lodge.com
web www.grizedale-lodge.com
Dir From Hawkshead signs S to Grizedale, Lodge 2m on right

Set in the heart of the tranquil Grizedale Forest Park, this charming establishment provides particularly comfortable bedrooms, some with four-poster beds and splendid views. Hearty breakfasts are served in the attractive dining room, which leads to a balcony for relaxing on in summer.

Facilities 8 en suite (1 fmly) (2 GF) ⊗ TVB tea/coffee Licensed Cen ht No coaches Dinner Last d 8.30pm **Conf** Max 10 **Parking** 20

HAWKSHEAD
See also **Near Sawrey**

MAP 18 SD39

Premier Collection

♦♦♦♦♦ ⊛⊛ 🍺 ☕

West Vale Country House

Far Sawrey LA22 0LQ ☎ 015394 42817 📠 015394 45302
e-mail enquiries@westvalecountryhouse.co.uk
web www.westvalecountryhouse.co.uk
Dir *Cross Windemere by car ferry at Bowness, B5285 for 1.25m to
Far Sawrey, West Vale on left leaving village*

West Vale Country House is on the edge of the beautiful village of Far
Sawrey, and has delightful views across the vale to Grizedale Forest.
All the bedrooms have been furnished to a high standard, and there is
a lounge and an elegant dining room, where traditional breakfasts and
dinners are served at individual tables. Dee Pennington is a top-twenty
finalist for AA Landlady of the Year 2006.

Facilities 7 en suite (1 fmly) ⊗ TVB tea/coffee ✈ Licensed Cen ht
No children 12yrs Membership of local leisure club Dinner Last d 5.30pm
Prices S £70-£78; D £116-£134✳ **LB Parking** 8

Premier Collection

♦♦♦♦♦ 🍺 ☕

Ees Wyke Country House

LA22 0JZ ☎ 015394 36393
e-mail mail@eeswyke.co.uk
web www.eeswyke.co.uk
For full entry see **Near Sawrey**

♦♦♦♦

Sawrey Ground

Hawkshead Hill LA22 0PP ☎ 015394 36683
e-mail mail@sawreyground.com
Dir *B5285 from Hawkshead, 1m to Hawkshead Hill, sharp right after
Baptist chapel, signs to Tarn Hows for 0.25m. Sawrey Ground on right*

Set in the heart of the Lake District, this charming 17th-century
farmhouse has a superb setting on the doorstep of Tarn Hows. The
flagstone entrance hall leads to a sitting room with a beamed ceiling,
where an open fire burns on winter nights. Hearty breakfasts featuring
fresh fruit and home-baked bread are served in the dining room. The
traditional bedrooms are furnished in pine and oak.

Sawrey Ground

Facilities 3 en suite ⊗ TVB tea/coffee ✈ Cen ht No children 8yrs
No coaches **Prices** D £60-£70✳ **Parking** 6 **Notes** ⊠

♦♦♦ 🍺

Kings Arms Hotel

LA22 0NZ ☎ 015394 36372 📠 015394 36006
e-mail info@kingsarmshawkshead.co.uk
web www.kingsarmshawkshead.co.uk
Dir *In main square*

A traditional Lakeland inn set in the heart of a conservation area. The
cosy, thoughtfully equipped bedrooms retain much character and are
traditionally furnished. A good choice of freshly prepared food is
available in the lounge bar and the neat dining room.

Facilities 9 rms (8 en suite) (3 fmly) ⊗ in dining room TVB tea/coffee
Direct dial from bedrooms Cen ht Fishing Dinner Last d 9.30pm
Prices S £36-£45; D £62-£80 **LB Parking** available **Notes** Closed 25 Dec

HELTON

MAP 18 NY52

♦♦♦♦

Beckfoot Country House

CA10 2QB ☎ 01931 713241 📠 01931 713391
e-mail info@beckfoot.co.uk
Dir *M6 junct 39, A6 through Shap & left to Bampton. Through
Bampton Grange and Bampton, house 2m on left*

This delightful Victorian country house stands in well-tended gardens
surrounded by beautiful open countryside, yet is only a short drive
from Penrith. Bedrooms are spacious and particularly well equipped,
and the four-poster room is impressive. Public areas include an
elegant drawing room, where guitar workshops are occasionally held, and
an oak-panelled dining room and a television lounge.

Facilities 7 en suite (1 fmly) ⊗ in bedrooms ⊗ in dining room STV
TVB tea/coffee Licensed Cen ht TVL No coaches Play area for children.
Prices S £35-£45✳ **LB Conf** Max 20 **Parking** 12 **Notes** Closed Dec-Feb

continued

KENDAL

MAP 18 SD59

See also **Brigsteer**

♦♦♦♦

Burrow Hall Country Guest House ◇

Plantation Br LA8 9JR ☎ 01539 821711 ▤ 01539 821711
e-mail info@burrowhall.fsnet.co.uk
web www.burrowhall.co.uk
Dir On A591 between Kendal and Windermere, 1.5m on right after Crook rdbt

Dating from 1648, this charming country house has been restored to provide comfortable, modern accommodation. Some of the en suite bedrooms have lovely views of the fells, and all are neatly furnished and well equipped. Guests have a separate entrance to a comfortable lounge and the breakfast room.

Facilities 4 en suite ⊗ TVB tea/coffee ✘ Cen ht TVL No children 12yrs No coaches **Prices** S £25-£35; D £50-£65✳ **Parking** 8 **Notes** Closed 23-26 Dec

♦♦♦♦ 🅰

The Glen ◇

Oxenholme LA9 7RF ☎ 01539 726386 ▤ 01539 724434
e-mail greenintheglen@btinternet.com
web www.glen-kendal.co.uk
Dir 2m S of Kendal. B6254 to Oxenholme, past railway station, driveway on right up hill

Facilities 6 en suite (2 fmly) (1 GF) ⊗ TVB tea/coffee Cen ht No coaches hot tub **Prices** S £30-£45; D £50-£67✳ **Parking** 10 **Notes** Closed 31 Dec

♦♦♦ 🕮

Gilpin Bridge

Br End, Levens LA8 8EP ☎ 015395 52206 ▤ 015395 52444
e-mail info@gilpinbridgeinn.co.uk
Dir M6 junct 36, 10m on A5074, 100yds from A590

Situated just outside Levens, this modern Tudor-style inn offers a creative and appealing bar and restaurant menu. The bedrooms offer comfortable accommodation, and there is a games room, a function suite, and an outside playground for children.

Facilities 10 en suite (1 fmly) ⊗ in bedrooms ⊗ in dining room ⊗ in lounges TVB tea/coffee ✘ Cen ht Pool Table Childrens outside play area Dinner Last d 9pm **Prices** S £45; D £65-£80✳ **LB** **Conf** Max 80 Thtr 80 Class 60 Board 60 **Parking** 100

♦♦♦

Millers Beck Country Guest House ◇

Stainton LA8 0DU ☎ 015395 60877 ▤ 015395 60877
e-mail millersbeck@aol.com
Dir M6 junct 36, A65, 1st left signed Crooklands/Endmoor, Millers Beck 3.5m on right

The delightful sound of cascading water can be heard from this converted 16th-century corn mill. Situated in countryside close to Kendal, this charming property offers cosy, modern bedrooms. Public areas include a choice of two comfortable gallery lounges, with hearty breakfasts served in the conservatory-dining room.

Facilities 3 en suite ⊗ in bedrooms ⊗ in dining room ⊗ in 1 lounge TVB tea/coffee ✘ Cen ht TVL No coaches **Prices** S £26-£30; D £48-£52✳ **LB** **Parking** 4 **Notes** Closed Jan 🐾

KESWICK

MAP 18 NY22

See also **Lorton & Mungrisdale**

★★★★ Guest House

Hazelwood Guesthouse ◇

Chestnut Hill CA12 4LR ☎ 017687 73496
e-mail info@hazelwoodkeswick.com
web www.hazelwoodkeswick.com
Dir On junct of Ambleside & Penrith roads.

Ideally located on the edge of town and having private parking. Hospitality is warm and a traditional Lakeland welcome awaits. Gardens enhance the property with views down into Keswick and onto the fells.

Facilities 6 rms (5 en suite) (1 pri facs) (1 fmly) ⊗ TVB tea/coffee ✘ Cen ht No coaches **Prices** S £30-£50; D £45-£60✳ **LB** **Parking** 6

England

Premier Collection

◆◆◆◆◆

Grange Country House

Manor Brow, Ambleside Rd CA12 4BA ☎ 017687 72500
e-mail info@grangekeswick.com
web www.grangekeswick.com
Dir A591 from Keswick towards Windermere, 0.5m 1st right, house 200yds on right

This stylish Victorian residence stands in beautiful gardens just a stroll from the town centre. It offers a relaxed atmosphere and professional service. The spacious bedrooms are well equipped, and some have beams and mountain views. Spacious lounges and ample parking are available, and the proprietors are keen to give advice on walks and local activities.

Facilities 10 en suite ⊗ TVB tea/coffee Direct dial from bedrooms ✸ Licensed Cen ht No children 7yrs No coaches **Prices** S £36-£51; D £72-£92 **LB** **Parking** 11 **Notes** Closed 2 Nov-5 Mar

◆◆◆◆

Dalegarth House Country Hotel

Portinscale CA12 5RQ ☎ 017687 72817 ▤ 017687 72817
e-mail allerdalechef@aol.com
Dir Off A66 to Portinscale, pass Farmers Arms, 100yds on left

The friendly family-run establishment stands on an elevated position in the village of Portinscale, and has fine views from the well-tended garden. The attractive bedrooms are well equipped, and there is a peaceful lounge, a well-stocked bar, and a spacious dining room where the resident owner-chef produces hearty breakfasts and delicious evening meals.

continued

Facilities 10 en suite (1 fmly) (2 GF) ⊗ TVB tea/coffee ✸ Licensed Cen ht TVL No children 5yrs No coaches Dinner Last d 6pm
Prices S £33-£37; D £66-£74✳ **LB** **Parking** 14

◆◆◆◆

Honister House

1 Borrowdale Rd CA12 5DD
☎ 017687 73181 ▤ 0870 120 2948
e-mail honisterhouse@btconnect.com
web www.honisterhouse.co.uk
Dir 300yds S of town centre, off Market Sq onto Borrowdale Rd

This vibrant family home is one of the oldest properties in Keswick, dating from the 18th century, and has attractive, well-equipped bedrooms. The friendly proprietors Sue and Phil are keen fell walkers and cyclists, and can help plan a pleasant day by the lakes or in the hills. They also support sustainable tourism, and use the highest quality local, organic and Fair Trade produce as much as possible.

Facilities 3 en suite (2 fmly) ⊗ TVB tea/coffee ✸ Cen ht No coaches
Prices S £40-£70; D £60-£80✳ **LB** **Parking** 3

◆◆◆◆

Howe Keld Lakeland Hotel

5-7 The Heads CA12 5ES ☎ 017687 72417 ▤ 017687 72417
e-mail david@howekeld.co.uk
web www.howekeld.co.uk
Dir From town centre towards Borrowdale, right opp main car park, 1st on left

Modern accommodation is offered at this friendly, well-run property close to the town and lake. Bedrooms are smartly decorated and furnished, and the first-floor lounge has spectacular views of the fells. Breakfast is a highlight, with local and home-made produce featuring on the menu.

Facilities 15 en suite (3 fmly) (2 GF) ⊗ TVB tea/coffee Licensed Cen ht No coaches **Prices** S £35; D £70✳ **LB** **Parking** 9 **Notes** Closed Xmas & Jan

◆◆◆◆

Parkfield

The Heads CA12 5ES ☎ 017687 72328
e-mail enquiries@parkfieldkeswick.co.uk
Dir A66 2nd exit to Keswick & left. At T-junct left to minirdbt, right & right again into The Heads

Overlooking Hope Park, Parkfield is a late 19th-century building that has been renovated to provide well-equipped accommodation. There

continued

is an elegant lounge and a charming dining room where delicious breakfasts include the best of local produce. The atmosphere is relaxed and hospitality is second to none.

Facilities 6 en suite (1 GF) ⊗ TVB tea/coffee ✖ Cen ht No children 16yrs No coaches **Prices** S £45; D £60-£64✱ **Parking** 8 **Notes** Closed Dec-Jan

◆◆◆◆

Amble House

23 Eskin St CA12 4DQ ☎ 017687 73288
e-mail info@amblehouse.co.uk
web www.amblehouse.co.uk
Dir *400yds SE of town centre. Off A5271 Penrith Rd onto Greta St & Eskin St*

An enthusiastic welcome awaits you at this Victorian mid-terrace house, close to the town centre. The thoughtfully equipped bedrooms have coordinated decor and are furnished in pine. Healthy breakfasts are served in the attractive dining room.

Facilities 5 en suite ⊗ TVB tea/coffee ✖ Cen ht No children 14yrs No coaches **Prices** S £25-£45; D £50-£60✱ **LB** **Notes** Closed 24-26 Dec

◆◆◆◆

Avondale

20 Southey St CA12 4EF ☎ 017687 72735
e-mail enquiries@avondaleguesthouse.com
web www.avondaleguesthouse.com
Dir *A591 towards town centre, left at war memorial onto Station St, sharp left onto Southey St, Avondale 100yds on right*

Expect efficient and friendly service at this pristine terrace house just a short walk from the town centre. Bright, modern, well-equipped bedrooms come in a variety of sizes. The cosy lounge has a collection of books and there is an airy dining room.

Facilities 6 en suite ⊗ TVB tea/coffee ✖ Cen ht No children 12yrs No coaches **Prices** S £28-£32; D £56-£64

◆◆◆◆

Badgers Wood

30 Stanger St CA12 5JU ☎ 017687 72621 🖷 017687 72621
e-mail enquiries@badgers-wood.co.uk
web www.badgers-wood.co.uk
Dir *In town centre off A5271 Main St*

A warm welcome awaits you at this delightful Victorian terrace house, located in a quiet area close to the town centre. The smart bedrooms

continued

are nicely furnished and well equipped, and the attractive breakfast room at the front of the house overlooks the fells. The house is non-smoking and vegetarians are gladly catered for.

Facilities 6 en suite ⊗ TVB tea/coffee ✖ Cen ht No children 12yrs No coaches **Prices** S £29; D £58 **Notes** Closed 3-31 Jan ⊗

◆◆◆◆

Charnwood **

6 Eskin St CA12 4DH ☎ 017687 74111 & 07711 773925
e-mail sue@excite.com
Dir *400yds SE of town centre. Off A5271 Penrith Rd onto Greta St & Eskin St*

This Grade II listed Victorian house is close to the town centre. Beautifully decorated and furnished in keeping with the period of the building, the individually styled bedrooms are well equipped. Delicious breakfasts (and home-cooked dinners by arrangement) are served in the spacious and stylish dining room. A comfortable lounge is available during summer.

Facilities 5 en suite (3 fmly) ⊗ TVB tea/coffee ✖ Licensed Cen ht No children 5yrs No coaches Dinner Last d 10am **Notes** Closed 24-25 Dec

◆◆◆◆

Claremont House

Chestnut Hill CA12 4LT ☎ 017687 72089
e-mail claremonthouse@btinternet.com
web www.claremonthousekeswick.co.uk
Dir *A591 N onto Chestnut Hill, Keswick. Pass Manor Brow on left, Claremont House 100yds on right*

This attractive and well-maintained family home was built in the mid 19th century and stands in mature grounds overlooking the town. The smart en suite bedrooms are well equipped, and the airy dining room has good views towards the fells.

Facilities 6 en suite ⊗ TVB tea/coffee ✖ Cen ht No children 12yrs **Prices** S £40-£70; D £46-£70✱ **LB** **Parking** 6 **Notes** Closed 23-27 Dec ⊗

◆◆◆◆

Craglands

Penrith Rd CA12 4LJ ☎ 017687 74406 & 07702 217017
e-mail craglands@msn.com
Dir *0.5m E of Keswick centre on A5271 Penrith Rd at junct A591*

This stylish Victorian house occupies an elevated position within walking distance of the town centre. The good-value accommodation provides attractive well-equipped bedrooms, and delicious hearty breakfasts are served in the ground-floor dining room.

Facilities 7 rms (5 en suite) ⊗ TVB tea/coffee ✖ Cen ht No children 8yrs No coaches **Prices** S £28-£37.50; D £58-£75 **LB** **Parking** 6

England

♦♦♦♦

Cragside ◇

39 Blencathra St CA12 4HX
☎ 017687 73344 📠 017687 73344
e-mail wayne-alison@cragside39blencathra.fsnet.co.uk
web http://cragside-keswick.mysite.wanadoo-members.co.uk
Dir A591 Penrith Rd into Keswick, under railway bridge, 2nd left

Expect warm hospitality at this guest house located within easy walking distance of the town centre. The attractive bedrooms are well equipped, and many have fine views of the fells. Hearty Cumbrian breakfasts are served in the breakfast room, which overlooks the small front garden. Visually or hearing impaired guests are catered for, with Braille information, televisions with teletext, and a loop system installed in the dining room.

Facilities 4 en suite (2 fmly) ⊗ TVB tea/coffee Cen ht No coaches
Prices S £30; D £44

♦♦♦♦

Dorchester House

17 Southey St CA12 4EG ☎ 017687 73256
e-mail dennis@dorchesterhouse.co.uk
Dir 200yds E of town centre. Off A5271 Penrith Rd onto Southey St, 150yds on left

A warm welcome awaits you at this guest house, just a stroll from the town centre and its amenities. The comfortably proportioned, well-maintained bedrooms offer pleasingly coordinated decor. Hearty breakfasts are served in the attractive ground-floor dining room. This is a non-smoking establishment.

Facilities 8 rms (7 en suite) (2 fmly) ⊗ TVB tea/coffee ✗ Cen ht
No coaches

♦♦♦♦

Eden Green ◇

20 Blencathra St CA12 4HP
☎ 017687 72077 📠 017687 80870
e-mail enquiries@edengreenguesthouse.com
web www.edengreenguesthouse.com
Dir A591 Penrith Rd into Keswick, under railway bridge, 2nd left, house 500yds on left

This mid-terrace house, faced with local stone, offers well-decorated and furnished bedrooms, some suitable for families and some with fine views of Skiddaw. Traditional English and vegetarian breakfasts are served in the neat breakfast room, and packed lunches can be provided on request.

Facilities 6 en suite (1 fmly) (1 GF) ⊗ TVB tea/coffee ✗ Cen ht
No children 8yrs **Prices** S £25-£30; D £50-£60✶ LB

♦♦♦♦

Goodwin House ◇

29 Southey St CA12 4EE ☎ 017687 74634
e-mail enquiries@goodwinhouse.co.uk
web www.goodwinhouse.co.uk
Dir 200yds E of town centre. Off A5271 Penrith Rd onto Southey St, house at x-rds with Church St

Built in 1890, this appealing house is on the corner of an attractive terrace, just a stroll from the town centre. The bedrooms, which vary in size and style, are attractively decorated and well equipped.

Facilities 6 en suite ⊗ TVB tea/coffee ✗ Cen ht No children 12yrs
No coaches **Prices** S £30-£35; D £56-£70✶ **Notes** Closed 25 Dec ✉

♦♦♦♦

Greystones ◇

Ambleside Rd CA12 4DP ☎ 017687 73108
e-mail greystones@keslakes.freeserve.co.uk
Dir A591 from Keswick for Windermere, 1st right Manor Brow, Greystones 0.5m on right

Greystones is just a short walk from the town centre. The spacious, individually styled bedrooms are thoughtfully equipped and some have stunning views of the fells. The proprietors offer friendly hospitality and attentive service, and freshly cooked breakfasts are served in the dining room at individual tables.

Facilities 8 rms (7 en suite) (1 pri facs) ⊗ TVB tea/coffee ✗ Cen ht
No children 10yrs No coaches **Prices** S £26-£35; D £52-£64✶ LB
Parking 7 **Notes** Closed Dec

♦♦♦♦

Hall Garth ◇

37 Blencathra St CA12 4HX
☎ 017687 72627 📠 017687 72627
e-mail tracyhallgarth@aol.com
web www.keswickguesthouse.co.uk
Dir 500yds E of town centre. Off A5271 Penrith Rd onto Southey St & 2nd left

This welcoming, family-run guest house is in a peaceful residential area within walking distance of the town centre. The modern bedrooms are attractive and well equipped. The pretty breakfast room on the ground floor is the setting for hearty Cumbrian breakfasts.

Facilities 4 en suite ⊗ TVB tea/coffee Cen ht **Prices** S £25-£35;
D £45-£50

♦♦♦♦

Hazelmere ◇

Crosthwaite Rd CA12 5PG
☎ 017687 72445 📠 017687 74075
e-mail info@hazelmerekeswick.co.uk
web www.hazelmerekeswick.co.uk
Dir Off A66 at Crosthwaite rdbt (A591 junct) for Keswick, Hazelmere 400yds on right

This large Victorian house is only a short walk from Market Square and within walking distance of Derwentwater and the local fells. The attractive bedrooms are comfortably furnished and well equipped.

continue.

Hearty Cumbrian breakfasts are served at individual tables in the ground-floor dining room, which has delightful views.

Facilities 6 en suite (1 fmly) ⊗ TVB tea/coffee Cen ht No children 8yrs No coaches **Prices** S £28-£30; D £56-£66✱ **LB Parking** 7

♦♦♦♦

Hedgehog Hill Guest House ◇

18 Blencathra St CA12 4HP ☎ 01768 774386
e-mail aa@hedgehoghill.co.uk
web www.hedgehoghill.co.uk
Dir Exit A66 towards Keswick, turn left after 1.1m at Millfield House, then 1st right. B&B 150yds on left.

Expect warm hospitality at this Victorian terrace house. Hedgehog Hill is convenient for the town centre, many walks and local attractions and is totally non-smoking. Bedrooms are comfortably equipped and offer thoughtful extras. Hearty breakfasts are served in the light and airy dining room with vegetarians well catered for.

Facilities 6 rms (4 en suite) ⊗ TVB tea/coffee ✖ Cen ht No children 12yrs No coaches **Prices** S £23; D £52-£56✱

♦♦♦♦

The Hollies ◇

Threlkeld CA12 4RX ☎ 017687 79216 ▤ 017687 79216
e-mail info@theholliesinlakeland.co.uk
web www.theholliesinlakeland.co.uk
Dir 3m E of Keswick. Off A66 into Threlkeld, The Hollies opp village hall

Built in 1900 using local stone, The Hollies is an impressive detached property in the heart of Threlkeld. Lying at the foot of Blencathra, it is on the coast-to-coast walk, and the sea-to-sea cycle route. The attractive bedrooms are well equipped, and hearty breakfasts served in the dining room feature the best of local produce.

Facilities 4 en suite ⊗ STV TVB tea/coffee Cen ht No coaches **Prices** S £28-£35; D £56✱ **LB Parking** 6 **Notes** ⊠

♦♦♦♦

Keswick Park Hotel ◇

33 Station Rd CA12 4NA ☎ 017687 72072 ▤ 017687 74816
e-mail reservations@keswickparkhotel.com
web www.keswickparkhotel.com
Dir 200yds NE of town centre. Off A5271 Penrith Rd onto Station Rd

A friendly welcome awaits you at this comfortable Victorian house, situated within a short walking distance of the town centre. Bedrooms

continued

are mostly of a good size, and have homely extras. The breakfast room is in two sections, one with a good outlook, and there also is a cosy bar. Fine days can be enjoyed sitting on the front garden patio.

Facilities 16 en suite (2 fmly) ⊗ TVB tea/coffee Direct dial from bedrooms ✖ Licensed Cen ht No coaches **Prices** S £28-£32; D £56-£66✱ **LB Parking** 8

England

♦♦♦♦
Rickerby Grange Hotel

Portinscale CA12 5RH ☎ 017687 72344 📠 017687 75588
e-mail stay@rickerbygrange.co.uk
web www.rickerbygrange.co.uk
Dir *1m W of Keswick. Off A66 into Portinscale, 2nd right after Farmer Arms*

Built at the end of the 19th century by a local farmer, this small, friendly guest house is in the village of Portinscale. Bedrooms are comfortably proportioned and brightly decorated, with one on the ground floor. The bright spacious dining room has an adjoining bar and lounge area, and traditional breakfasts (and dinner by arrangement) are served at individual tables. Large private car park.

Facilities 10 rms (9 en suite) (1 pri facs) (2 fmly) (1 GF) ⊛ TVB tea/coffee Direct dial from bedrooms Licensed Cen ht No children 5yrs No coaches Dinner Last d 6pm **Prices** S £35-£40; D £70-£76✳ LB **Parking** 15 **Notes** Closed Jan

♦♦♦♦
Skiddaw Grove Country House ◇

Vicarage Hill CA12 5QB ☎ 017687 73324 📠 017687 73324
e-mail skiddawgrove@hotmail.com
Dir *Off A66 at Crosthwaite rdbt into Keswick, sharp right onto Vicarage Hill, house 50yds on left*

The house stands in lovely gardens 500yds north-west of the town in the quiet village of Great Crosthwaite. It has an outdoor pool and magnificent views of Skiddaw. Bedrooms are thoughtfully equipped, and there is a cosy lounge with a bar.

Facilities 5 en suite (1 fmly) ⊛ TVB tea/coffee ✖ Cen ht No coaches ⚲ Table tennis **Prices** S £28-£35; D £56-£70✳ LB **Parking** 6 **Notes** ✉

♦♦♦♦
Sunnyside ◇

25 Southey St CA12 4EF ☎ 017687 72446
e-mail enquiries@sunnysideguesthouse.com
web www.sunnysideguesthouse.com
Dir *200yds E of town centre. Off A5271 Penrith Rd onto Southey St, Sunnyside on left*

This stylish guest house is in a quiet area close to the town centre. All bedrooms have been refurbished to a high standard, including a family room, and are comfortably furnished and well equipped. There is a spacious lounge with plenty of books and magazines. Breakfast is served at individual tables in the airy dining room. Private parking is available.

Facilities 7 rms (6 en suite) (1 pri facs) (1 fmly) ⊛ TVB tea/coffee ✖ Cen ht TVL No coaches Dinner Last d am **Prices** S £28-£32; D £56-£64✳ **Parking** 8

♦♦♦♦
Tarn Hows ◇

3-5 Eskin St CA12 4DH ☎ 017687 73217 📠 017687 73217
e-mail info@tarnhows.co.uk
web www.tarnhows.co.uk
Dir *500yds SE of town centre. Off A5271 Penrith Rd onto Greta St & Eskin St*

This attractive and well-maintained house consists of two interconnecting stone-clad houses, recognisable in summer by the colourful garden and hanging baskets. Bedrooms vary in size and style, and are smartly furnished. Hearty Cumbrian breakfasts are served at individual tables in the spacious dining room.

Facilities 8 rms (6 en suite) (2 pri facs) ⊛ TVB tea/coffee ✖ Cen ht TVL No children 6yrs No coaches Dinner Last d on booking **Prices** S £29.50-£31.50; D £54-£68✳ LB **Parking** 8

♦♦♦♦
Winchester Guest House ◇

58 Blencathra St CA12 4HT
☎ 017687 73664 📠 017687 73664
e-mail lyn.dave@winchesterguesthouse.com
web www.winchesterguesthouse.co.uk
Dir *A66 onto A591 Penrith Rd into Keswick. Under railway bridge, 2nd left, house on Wordsworth St junct*

This friendly, family-run guest house, built in the 1870s, is within walking distance of the town centre. The en suite bedrooms are attractive and well equipped, and tasty Cumbrian breakfasts are served at individual tables in the ground-floor dining room.

Facilities 7 rms (6 en suite) (1 fmly) ⊛ TVB tea/coffee ✖ Cen ht No children 10yrs No coaches **Prices** S £20; D £50✳

♦♦♦♦
Paddock Guest House

Wordsworth St CA12 4HU
☎ 017687 72510 📠 017687 72510
e-mail val@thepaddock.info
web www.thepaddock.info
Dir *500yds E of town centre. Off A5271 Penrith Rd onto Wordsworth St, The Paddock on right*

Facilities 6 en suite (1 fmly) ⊛ TVB tea/coffee ✖ Cen ht TVL No children 5yrs No coaches **Prices** D £46-£52✳ LB **Parking** 5

♦♦♦♦
Sandon Guesthouse ◇

13 Southey St CA12 4EG ☎ 017687 73648
e-mail enquiries@sandonguesthouse.com
Dir *200yds E of town centre. Off A5271 Penrith Rd onto Southey St*

Facilities 6 rms (5 en suite) (1 pri facs) ⊛ TVB tea/coffee ✖ Cen ht No children 4yrs No coaches **Prices** S £25-£30; D £50-£60✳ **Notes** Closed Xmas ✉

◆◆◆◆
Watendlath
15 Acorn St CA12 4EA ☎ 017687 74165 📠 017687 74165
e-mail info@watendlathguesthouse.co.uk
Dir 350yds SE of town centre. Off A5271 Penrith Rd onto Southey St, left onto Acorn St
Facilities 4 en suite (2 fmly) ⊗ TVB tea/coffee ✱ Cen ht
Prices D £45-£54✱ **Notes** Closed 15-26 Dec 🐾

◆◆◆ 🍴
The Mill Inn
CA11 0XR ☎ 017687 79632 📠 017687 79632
e-mail info@the-millinn.co.uk
For full entry see **Mungrisdale**

◆◆◆
Brierholme
21 Bank Street CA12 5JZ ☎ 017687 72938
e-mail enquiries@brierholme.co.uk
web www.brierholme.co.uk
Dir On A591, 100yds from Post Office
The house is just a short walk from the main square. Bedrooms are traditionally furnished and thoughtfully equipped, and the rear rooms have lovely views of Skiddaw. The lounge looks over the town and surrounding peaks, and hearty breakfasts are served in the neat breakfast room.
Facilities 6 en suite (2 fmly) ⊗ TVB tea/coffee ✱ Cen ht No children
No coaches **Prices** D £52-£64 **LB** **Parking** 6

◆◆◆
Heatherlea
26 Blencathra St CA12 4HP ☎ 017687 72430
e-mail info@heatherlea-keswick.co.uk
Dir 300 yds E of town centre. Off A5271 Penrith Rd on Southey St & 2nd left
Please note that this establishment has recently changed hands. Just a stroll from the town centre, this end-of-terrace Victorian house provides well-equipped bedrooms. The proprietors give a friendly welcome, and substantial breakfasts are served in the dining room, which has lovely views of the surrounding fells.
Facilities 4 en suite (1 fmly) ⊗ TVB tea/coffee ✱ Cen ht No children
5yrs No coaches **Prices** S £30-£35; D £48-£52 **Notes** Closed
24 & 25 Dec 🐾

KIRKBY LONSDALE   MAP 18 SD67

◆◆
The Copper Kettle ◇
3-5 Market St LA6 2AU ☎ 015242 71714 📠 015242 71714
Dir In town centre, down lane by Post Office
Facilities 5 en suite (2 fmly) ⊗ TVB tea/coffee Licensed Dinner Last
d 9pm **Prices** S £26; D £39-£45✱ **LB** **Parking** 3 **Notes** Closed 2 wks
Jan, 1wk Nov

KIRKBY STEPHEN   MAP 18 NY70

◆◆◆◆◆
Brownber Hall Country House
Newbiggin-on-Lune CA17 4NX ☎ 01539 623208
e-mail enquiries@brownberhall.co.uk
web www.brownberhall.co.uk
Dir 6m SW of Kirkby Stephen. Off A685 signed Great Asby, 60yds right through gatehouse, 0.25m sharp left onto driveway
Having an elevated position with superb views of the surrounding countryside, Brownber Hall, built in 1860, has been restored to its original glory. The en suite bedrooms are comfortably proportioned, attractively decorated and well equipped. The ground floor has two lovely reception rooms, which retain many original features, and a charming dining room where traditional breakfasts, and by arrangement delicious dinners, are served. There is also a lift.
Facilities 6 en suite (1 GF) ⊗ TVB tea/coffee Lift Cen ht Dinner Last
d 24hrs in advance **Prices** S fr £35; d fr £60✱ **LB** **Conf** Max 20
Board 20 **Parking** 12

◆◆◆ ❦
Southview Farm ◇ *(NY785105)*
Winton CA17 4HS
☎01768 371120 & 07801 432184 📠 01768 371120
Mrs Marston
e-mail southviewwinton@hotmail.com
Dir 1.5m N of Kirkby Stephen. Off A685 signed Winton
A friendly family home, Southview lies in the centre of Winton village, part of a terrace with the working farm to the rear. Two well-proportioned bedrooms are available, and there is a cosy lounge-dining room where traditional breakfasts are served around one table.
Facilities 2 rms (2 fmly) ⊗ tea/coffee TVL 280 acres beef, dairy Dinner
Last d 8am **Prices** S £20; D £38✱ **Parking** 2 **Notes** 🐾

KIRKCAMBECK   MAP 21 NY56

◆◆◆◆◆ ❦
Cracrop *(NY521697)*
CA8 2BW ☎ 016977 48245 📠 016977 48333 Mrs Stobart
e-mail cracrop@aol.com
Dir B6318 N into Kirkcambeck, over bridge, left at B&B sign, 1m on right
Dating from 1847, this delightful, friendly farmhouse is part of a vibrant working farm. Set in colourful landscaped gardens, it offers spacious, carefully appointed bedrooms. There is an inviting lounge next to the traditional dining room where hearty breakfasts are served. Work off any over-indulgence in the well-equipped fitness room and sauna, or take a stroll in the lovely garden.
Facilities 3 en suite ⊗ TVB tea/coffee ✱ Cen ht TVL No children
10yrs Sauna Gymnasium Marked farm trail 485 acres arable beef/sheep
Parking 5

England

LORTON
MAP 18 NY12

Premier Collection

◆◆◆◆◆ ⇔

New House Farm
CA13 9UU ☎ 01900 85404 📠 01900 85478
e-mail hazel@newhouse-farm.co.uk
web www.newhouse-farm.co.uk
Dir 6m S of Cockermouth on B5289 between Lorton & Loweswater

A warm welcome awaits you at this restored Grade II listed 17th-century farmhouse, situated in Lorton Vale. The inviting public areas and bedrooms have been stylishly decorated to complement the original features. The bedrooms have thoughtful extras including home-baked biscuits; many have period-style beds and romantic bathrooms. The delicious daily changing, five-course dinner menu and the hearty breakfasts are highlights.

Facilities 3 en suite 2 annexe en suite (2 GF) ⊗ tea/coffee Licensed Cen ht No children 6yrs No coaches Hot spa in the garden Dinner Last d 5pm **Prices** S £67-£100; D £134-£138 **LB Conf** Max 12 **Parking** 30

Premier Collection

◆◆◆◆◆ ⛐ ⇔

Winder Hall Country House
CA13 9UP ☎ 01900 85107 📠 01900 85479
e-mail nick@winderhall.co.uk
web www.winderhall.co.uk
Dir A66 W from Keswick, at Braithwaite onto B5292 to Lorton, left at T-junct signed Buttermere, Winderhall 0.5m on right

Impressive Winder Hall dates from the 14th century. The lounge is luxuriously furnished and the elegant, spacious dining room is the venue for skilfully prepared meals using local produce. The smart,

individually styled bedrooms are thoughtfully equipped, and all are furnished with fine antiques or pine. Two rooms have beautiful four-poster beds.

Facilities 7 en suite (2 fmly) ⊗ TVB tea/coffee Direct dial from bedrooms ✗ Licensed Cen ht No coaches Fishing Complimentary leisure facilities at nearby hotel Dinner Last d 7pm **Conf** Max 25 Class 25 Board 25 **Parking** 10 **Notes** Closed 2-31 Jan Civ Wed 65

◆◆◆◆ ⛐ ⇔

Old Vicarage
Church Ln CA13 9UN ☎ 01900 85656
e-mail enquiries@oldvicarage.co.uk
web www.oldvicarage.co.uk
Dir B5292 onto B5289 N of Lorton. 1st left signed Church, house 1st on right

This delightful Victorian house offers spacious accommodation in the peaceful Lorton Vale, in the heart of the Lake District National Park. A converted barn offers two rooms with exposed stone walls, and is ideal for families with young children. Bedrooms in the main house are well equipped and have excellent views of distant mountains. Delicious home cooking is served in the bright dining room.

Facilities 6 rms (5 en suite) 2 annexe en suite (1 GF) ⊗ TVB tea/coffee ✗ Licensed Cen ht No coaches Dinner Last d 10am **Prices** S £48-£120; D £76-£130 **LB Parking** 12

LOWESWATER
MAP 18 NY12

◆◆◆◆ ⇔ ◖

Kirkstile Inn
CA13 0RU ☎ 01900 85219 📠 01900 85239
e-mail info@kirkstile.com
web www.kirkstile.com
Dir A66 onto B5292 into Lorton, left signed Buttermere. Signs to Loweswater, left signed Kirkstile Inn

This delightful 16th-century inn has breathtaking country views. It has a bar, an elegant restaurant, a choice of lounges and a beer garden. The attractive refurbished bedrooms retain their original character. Two spacious family suites are in an annexe, each with two bedrooms, a lounge and a bathroom.

Facilities 7 en suite 2 annexe en suite (2 fmly) (2 GF) ⊗ TV3B tea/coffee Cen ht TVL No coaches Dinner Last d 9pm **Prices** S £55-£79; D £73-£89✳ **LB Parking** 30 **Notes** Closed 25 Dec

continued

MAULDS MEABURN
MAP 18 NY61

◆◆◆◆ 🏠 ⟿

Meaburn Hill Farmhouse
CA10 3HN ☎ 01931 715168
e-mail kindleysides@btinternet.com
web www.cumbria-bed-and-breakfast.co.uk
Dir M6 junct 39 signed Shap, after 4m turn right for Crosby
Ravensworth. Turn left to Maulds Meaburn, 1st on left after cattle grid

This 16th-century Westmorland longhouse is in the picturesque
Lyvennet valley, 10 minutes from the M6. Annie Kindleysides, whose
family have worked the farm for many years, is a caring and attentive
host and provides great breakfasts and dinners by arrangement. There
are two lounges and the bedrooms are very homely, one having a
bath within the room, all full of character.
Facilities 3 en suite (1 fmly) ⊗ TV1B tea/coffee Cen ht TVL
No coaches 🍴 Dinner Last d at breakfast **Prices** S £45-£75; D £65-£80
LB Conf Thtr 12 Board 12 Del from £100 ✳ **Parking** 4 **Notes** Closed
3 Jan-1 Feb 🐾

MILLOM
MAP 18 SD18

Premier Collection

◆◆◆◆◆ ⟿

Underwood Country Guest House
The Hill LA18 5EZ ☎ 01229 771116 📠 01229 719900
e-mail Andrew.Miller@aggregate.com
Dir A595 onto A5093 through village, The Green & The Hill,
Underwood 0.5m after The Hill

A warm welcome is assured at this Victorian vicarage standing in
mature grounds overlooking the Duddon estuary and Whicham valley.
Bedrooms are well appointed and have a wealth of thoughtful extras.

continued

Imaginative dinners, using local produce, are served in an attractive
dining room and a two lounges are also available. Additional features
include a self-contained conference suite, an indoor swimming pool
and a tennis court.
Facilities 5 en suite ⊗ STV TVB tea/coffee Direct dial from bedrooms
🎯 Licensed Cen ht TVL No children 14yrs 🎱 ⚲ Sauna 🍴 Dinner Last
d 10.30am **Prices** S £35-£55; D £70-£110✳ **LB Conf** Max 18 Thtr 18
Class 18 Board 18 Del from £100 ✳ **Parking** 20

MUNGRISDALE
MAP 18 NY33

◆◆◆

The Mill Inn
CA11 0XR ☎ 017687 79632 📠 017687 79632
e-mail info@the-millinn.co.uk
Dir Off A66 into Mungrisdale

Having splendid views, this popular 16th-century inn stands beside a
tranquil stream with a woodland backdrop. The modern bedrooms
provide good levels of comfort and facilities. A wide selection of
home-cooked dishes is served in the spacious restaurant and bar, and
there is also a games room.
Facilities 6 rms (5 en suite) ⊗ in bedrooms ⊗ in dining room TVB
tea/coffee Cen ht ch fac Pool table Darts Dinner Last d 8.30pm
Parking 30 **Notes** Closed 25-26 Dec

NEAR SAWREY
MAP 18 SD39

Premier Collection

◆◆◆◆◆ 🏠 ⟿

Ees Wyke Country House
LA22 0JZ ☎ 015394 36393
e-mail mail@eeswyke.co.uk
web www.eeswyke.co.uk
Dir On B5285 on W side of village

A warm welcome awaits you at this elegant Georgian country house
with views over Esthwaite Water and the surrounding countryside. The
thoughtfully equipped bedrooms have been decorated and furnished
with care. There is a charming lounge with an open fire, and a
splendid dining room where a carefully prepared five-course dinner is
served. Breakfasts have a fine reputation due to the skilful use of local
produce.
Facilities 8 en suite (1 GF) ⊗ TVB tea/coffee Licensed Cen ht
No children 12yrs No coaches Dinner Last d noon **Prices** S £80-£108;
D £160-£180 **LB Parking** 12

England

NEAR SAWREY continued

Premier Collection

◆◆◆◆◆ ◉ ⊜

Sawrey House Country Hotel & Restaurant

LA22 0LF ☎ 015394 36387 🖷 015394 36010
e-mail enquiries@sawrey-house.com
web www.sawrey-house.com
Dir On B5285 in village

Set in 3 acres of gardens above Esthwaite Water and next door to Beatrix Potter's former home, Sawrey House dates from 1830. Most of the well-equipped bedrooms have delightful views, and the elegant lounge has deep sofas with a roaring fire in winter. Dinner is a highlight with imaginative dishes to choose from, and the substantial breakfasts show equal flair.

Facilities 12 en suite (1 fmly) (2 GF) ⊗ FTV TVB tea/coffee Direct dial from bedrooms Licensed Cen ht No children 10yrs Fishing 🎱 Dinner Last d 6pm **Prices** S £75-£80; D £150-£210; (incl. dinner) ✳ LB **Conf** Max 35 Thtr 25 Class 25 **Parking** 24 **Notes** Closed Jan rs Nov-Feb (wknds only) Xmas & New Year

◆◆◆◆

Buckle Yeat

LA22 0LF ☎ 015394 36446 & 36538
e-mail info@buckle-yeat.co.uk
Dir In village centre

Close to Beatrix Potter's former home, Buckle Yeat is mentioned in some of the author's well-known tales. This charming 200-year-old cottage retains many original features, including a beamed dining room where freshly cooked breakfasts and cream teas are served. Bedrooms are prettily decorated and there is an elegant lounge.

Facilities 7 rms (6 en suite) (1 pri facs) (1 fmly) (1 GF) ⊗ TVB tea/coffee Cen ht TVL No coaches **Prices** S £33-£35; D £66-£70✳ **Parking** 9

NEWBY BRIDGE　　　　MAP 18 SD38

Premier Collection

◆◆◆◆◆ 🍴 ⊜

The Knoll Country House

Lakeside LA12 8AU ☎ 015395 31347 🖷 015395 30850
e-mail enquiries@theknoll-lakeside.co.uk
Dir A590 to Newby Bridge, over rdbt, signed right for Lake Steamers, house 0.5m on left

This delightful Victorian house stands in a leafy dell on the western side of Windermere. Public areas have many original features, including an open fire in the cosy lounge. The attractive bedrooms vary in style and outlook, and are well maintained. Enthusiastic owners share the tasks - Tracey extends a very caring and natural welcome, and Jenny offers a good choice of excellent dishes at breakfast and dinner.

Facilities 8 en suite ⊗ TVB tea/coffee Direct dial from bedrooms 🐾 Licensed Cen ht TVL No children 16yrs No coaches Dinner Last d 4pm LB **Parking** 8 **Notes** Closed 24-26 Dec

◆◆◆◆

Hill Crest

Brow Edge LA12 8QP ☎ 015395 31766 🖷 015395 31986
e-mail enquiries@hillcrest.gbr.cc
Dir 1m SW of Newby Bridge. Off A590 onto Brow Edge Rd, house 0.75m on right

A warm welcome is offered at this well-kept family home. The stone house has stunning views and provides a quiet getaway, with attractive and thoughtfully equipped bedrooms. The pleasant lounge doubles as a breakfast room, where the menu makes good use of local produce.

Facilities 3 en suite (2 fmly) (1 GF) ⊗ TVB tea/coffee 🐾 Cen ht TVL No coaches Free use of health & fitness club **Prices** S £42-£48; D £60-£75 LB **Parking** 4 **Notes** Closed 22-26 Dec

◆◆◆◆

The Coach House ◇

Hollow Oak LA12 8AD ☎ 015395 31622
e-mail coachho@talk21.com
web www.coachho.com
Dir 2.5m W of Newby Bridge off A590 onto B5278 signed Cark & sharp left into car park

This converted coach house stands in delightful gardens south of Lake Windermere. The modern bedrooms are light and airy, and there is a cosy lounge. Breakfast is served a converted stable.

Facilities 3 rms (2 en suite) (1 pri facs) ⊗ tea/coffee 🐾 Cen ht TVL No children 10yrs No coaches **Prices** S £30-£32; D £50 LB **Parking** 3 **Notes** ⊜

◆◆◆◆
Lakes End
LA12 8ND ☎ 015395 31260 ▤ 015395 31260
e-mail info@lakesend.vispa.com
Dir On A590 in Newby Bridge, 100yds from rdbt

In a sheltered wooded setting away from the road, Lakes End is convenient for the coast and the lakes. The bedrooms have been thoughtfully furnished and equipped. Traditional English breakfasts are served, and delicious home-cooked evening meals can be provided by arrangement.

Facilities 4 en suite (1 fmly) ⊗ STV FTV TVB tea/coffee ✘ Licensed Cen ht No coaches Free use of local leisure club Dinner Last d 6pm **Prices** S £32.50-£35; D £55-£60✳ LB **Parking** 4

PENRITH   MAP 18 NY53

Premier Collection

◆◆◆◆◆ 🅰
Roundthorn Country House
Beacon Edge CA11 8SJ ☎ 01768 863952 ▤ 01768 864100
e-mail enquiries@roundthorn.co.uk
Dir 1.2m NE of town centre. Off A686 signed Roundthorn

Facilities 10 en suite (3 fmly) ⊗ in 8 bedrooms ⊗ in dining room ⊗ in 1 lounge TVB tea/coffee Direct dial from bedrooms ✘ Licensed Cen ht Dinner Last d 9.30pm **Prices** S £59-£65.50; D £85-£94.50✳ LB **Conf** Max 200 Thtr 200 Class 200 Board 50 Del from £105 ✳ **Parking** 60 **Notes** Civ Wed 100

◆◆◆◆
Brooklands ◇
2 Portland Pl CA11 7QN ☎ 01768 863395 ▤ 01768 863395
e-mail enquiries@brooklandsguesthouse.com
web www.brooklandsguesthouse.com
Dir From town hall onto Portland Place, 50yds on left

A friendly welcome awaits you at this delightful Victorian terrace house. Bedrooms are beautifully decorated and have furniture made by local craftsmen. There is a family room and a four-poster suite. A hearty breakfast is served at individual tables in the stylish dining room. A courtesy collection service from the railway or bus station is available by arrangement. This is a non-smoking establishment.

Facilities 7 en suite (2 fmly) ⊗ TVB tea/coffee ✘ Cen ht **Prices** S £30-£35; D £60-£70✳ LB **Parking** 2

◆◆◆◆
Beckfoot Country House
CA10 2QB ☎ 01931 713241 ▤ 01931 713391
e-mail info@beckfoot.co.uk
For full entry see **Helton**

◆◆◆◆
Brandelhow
1 Portland Pl CA11 7QN ☎ 01768 864470
e-mail enquiries@brandelhowguesthouse.co.uk
web www.brandelhowguesthouse.co.uk
Dir In town centre on one-way system, left at town hall

This friendly guest house is within easy walking distance of central amenities. The individually themed bedrooms are thoughtfully furnished and some are suitable for families. Breakfasts, using quality local produce, are served at in a Cumbria theme dining room overlooking the pretty patio garden.

Facilities 5 rms (3 en suite) (1 pri facs) (3 fmly) ⊗ TVB tea/coffee ✘ Cen ht No coaches **Notes** ⊜

◆◆◆◆
Glendale
4 Portland Pl CA11 7QN ☎ 01768 862579
e-mail glendaleguesthouse@yahoo.co.uk
Dir M6 junct 40, town centre signs. Pass castle, turn left before town hall

This friendly family-run guest house is part of a Victorian terrace only a stroll from the town centre. Bedrooms vary in size, but all are attractive and well equipped. Hearty breakfasts are served at individual tables in the charming ground-floor dining room. Drying facilities are available.

Facilities 7 rms (6 en suite) (1 pri facs) (4 fmly) ⊗ TVB tea/coffee Cen ht **Prices** S fr £35; d fr £55✳

◆◆◆◆ ◄
Queen's Head Inn
Tirril CA10 2JF ☎ 01768 863219 ▤ 017683 61841
e-mail bookings@queensheadinn.co.uk
Dir 2m S of Penrith. Off A6 into Tirril

Please note that this establishment has recently changed hands. This village inn, dating from 1719, has been extended to appeal to the modern traveller. It is home to the Tirril Brewery, an attraction for real-ale fans. Home-cooked food is served in the public areas.

Facilities 7 en suite ⊗ in bedrooms ⊗ in dining room TVB tea/coffee Cen ht No children 3-13yrs No coaches Pool Table Dinner Last d 9pm **Prices** S £35-£40; D £65-£70 **Parking** 40

England

PENRITH continued

◆◆◆

Abbey House

7 Victoria Rd CA11 8HR
☎ 01768 863414 & 07949 771548 📄 01768 863414
e-mail anne.abbeyhouse@aol.com
web www.abbeyhousebandb.co.uk
Dir M6 junct 40 take A66 E.

Located close to the centre of town, Abbey House offers a warm atmosphere and comfortable accommodation. Breakfast is served in the attractive downstairs dining room.

Facilities 4 en suite (1 fmly) (1 GF) ⊗ TVB tea/coffee ✖ Cen ht LB **Parking** 4 **Notes** ⊛

◆◆◆

Acorn Guest House

Scotland Rd CA11 9HL ☎ 01768 868696
e-mail stay@acorn-guesthouse.co.uk

The house, recently refurbished, is on the edge of the town and is popular with walkers and cyclists. Bedrooms are generally spacious and a substantial, freshly cooked breakfast is offered. Drying facilities are available.

Facilities 8 en suite (1 fmly) ⊗ TVB tea/coffee ✖ Licensed Cen ht **Prices** S £35-£39.50; D £59-£65✳ **Parking** 8 **Notes** ⊛

◆◆◆

Limes Country Guesthouse

Redhills, Stainton CA11 0DT
☎ 01768 863343 📄 01768 867190
e-mail jdhanton@aol.com
web www.members.aol.com/jdhanton/index.htm
Dir 1m SW of Penrith. M6 junct 40 onto A66 W, 0.5m left before Little Chef, signed

Convenient for touring the northern lakes, this impressive Victorian house stands in open countryside. The spacious bedrooms, some suitable for families, are traditionally furnished. There is a cosy lounge, which has plenty of games, books and magazines, and a dining room where substantial breakfasts and evening meals are served except in July and August.

Facilities 6 en suite (3 fmly) ⊗ in 4 bedrooms ⊗ in dining room ⊗ in lounges TVB tea/coffee ✖ Cen ht TVL No coaches Dinner Last d 3pm **Prices** S £35-£38; D £55-£60 LB **Parking** 7

◆◆◆ 🍴

Mardale Inn

CA10 2RQ ☎ 01931 713244
e-mail info@mardaleinn.co.uk
web www.mardaleinn.co.uk
For full entry see **Bampton**

POOLEY BRIDGE   MAP 18 NY42

◆◆◆◆

Elm House

High St CA10 2NH ☎ 017684 86334 📄 017684 86259
e-mail enquiries@stayullswater.co.uk
Dir B5320 into village, next to church

A friendly welcome awaits you at this delightful stone house, located on the edge of the village and within easy reach of Ullswater and the M6. The attractive bedrooms are thoughtfully equipped, and there is an inviting lounge. Interesting breakfasts are served in the smart dining room and conservatory, which looks on to the pretty rear garden.

Facilities 5 rms (4 en suite) (1 pri facs) ⊗ TVB tea/coffee ✖ Cen ht TVL No children 14yrs No coaches **Prices** D £50-£64✳ **Parking** 5 **Notes** Closed Xmas

RAVENSTONEDALE   MAP 18 NY70

◆◆◆ 🍴

The Kings Head

CA17 4NH ☎ 015396 23284
e-mail enquiries@kings-head.net
web www.kings-head.net
Dir Off A685 into village centre

This delightful village inn offers comfortably furnished bedrooms and public areas with much character. The bar, warmed by roaring log fires in the cooler months, attracts a mix of locals and visitors, while the extensive menu, featuring local produce whenever possible, is served either here or in the candlelit restaurant.

Facilities 3 rms (2 en suite) (1 pri facs) (1 fmly) ⊗ in bedrooms ⊗ in dining room TVB tea/coffee Cen ht Pool Table Dinner Last d 9pm **Conf** Max 30 Thtr 30 Board 20 **Parking** 10

See advertisement on opposite page

RYDAL
See **Ambleside**

ST BEES
MAP 18 NX91

◆◆◆ 🅰

Fairladies Barn
Main St CA27 0AD ☎ 01946 822718 🖹 01946 825838
e-mail info@fairladiesbarn.co.uk

Facilities 10 rms (8 en suite) (2 fmly) (4 GF) ⊘ TVB tea/coffee ✖ Cen ht ⚹ Squash **Parking** 20

SEASCALE
MAP 18 NY00

◆◆◆◆ 🏵 ➾

Cumbrian Lodge
Gosforth Rd CA20 1JG ☎ 019467 27309 🖹 019467 27158
e-mail cumbrianlodge@btconnect.com
web www.cumbrianlodge.com

Dir *Off A595 at Gosforth onto B5344 signed Seascale, B&B 2m on left*

A relaxed and friendly atmosphere prevails at this well-run licensed guest house, where well-prepared tasty dinners are a popular local attraction. Decor and fixtures are modern throughout, and the spacious bedrooms are well-equipped.

Facilities 6 en suite (1 fmly) ⊘ in bedrooms ⊘ in dining room STV TVB tea/coffee Direct dial from bedrooms ✖ Licensed Cen ht ⚹ Dinner Last d 9.30pm **Prices** S £72.50✳ **Parking** 15

SEDBERGH
MAP 18 SD69

◆◆◆◆

Cross Keys Temperance Inn
Cautley LA10 5NE ☎ 015396 20284 🖹 015396 21966
e-mail clowes@freeuk.com

Dir *4m NE of Sedbergh on A683*

Built in the 1732, this charming inn retains many original features. No alcohol is sold at this temperance inn, though you can bring your own to go with the ambitious home-cooked dishes. Bedrooms are traditionally presented and thoughtfully equipped, and the conservatory has delightful views of the dales.

Facilities 2 en suite (1 fmly) ⊘ tea/coffee Direct dial from bedrooms ✖ Cen ht Riding Dinner Last d 9pm **Prices** S £35; D £70✳ LB **Parking** 9

If the freedom to smoke or be in a non-smoking atmosphere is important to you, check the rules when you book

England

SHAP
MAP 18 NY51

◆◆◆◆

Brookfield ◇

CA10 3PZ ☎ 01931 716397 🖷 01931 716397
e-mail info@brookfieldshap.co.uk
Dir M6 junct 39, A6 towards Shap, 1st accommodation off motorway

Having a quiet rural location within easy reach of the M6, this inviting house stands in well-tended gardens. Bedrooms are thoughtfully appointed and well maintained. There is a comfortable lounge, and a small bar area next to the traditional dining room where substantial, home-cooked breakfasts and dinners are served at individual tables.

Facilities 4 rms (3 en suite) ⊗ TVB tea/coffee ✖ Licensed Cen ht TVL No children 12yrs No coaches Dinner Last d 6pm **Prices** S £30-£35; D £58-£60 **Conf** Max 20 **Parking** 20 **Notes** Closed Jan 🐾

TEBAY
MAP 18 NY60

◆◆◆◆ 🅰

Primrose Cottage ◇

Orton Rd CA10 3TL ☎ 01539 624791 & 07778 520930
e-mail primrosecottebay@aol.com
Dir M6 junct 38, right at rdbt, 1st house on right

Facilities 3 rms (1 en suite) (2 pri facs) (2 GF) ⊗ TVB tea/coffee Cen ht No coaches jacuzzi bath in one bedroom Dinner Last d 24hrs prior **Prices** S £30-£45; D £55-£60✳ **LB Parking** 8 **Notes** 🐾

◆◆◆ 🍴

Cross Keys

CA10 3UY ☎ 01539 624240 🖷 01539 624240
e-mail stay@crosskeys-tebay.co.uk
Dir M6 junct 38, A685 into village

Please note that this establishment has recently changed hands. Situated in the centre of the village, only a short drive from the motorway, this one-time coaching inn has original low-beamed ceilings and open fires. A wide selection of popular dishes is available in the bar and the smart dining room. The bedrooms are comfortably proportioned and traditionally furnished, with three attractive bedrooms in a converted barn at the rear.

Facilities 9 rms (6 en suite) (1 fmly) (6 GF) ⊗ in 3 bedrooms ⊗ in dining room TVB tea/coffee Cen ht TVL ✎ Fishing Pool Table Dinner Last d 9pm **Conf** Max 50 **Parking** 30

TEMPLE SOWERBY
MAP 18 NY62

◆◆◆ 🍃

Skygarth Farm ◇ (NY612261)

CA10 1SS ☎ 01768 361300 🖷 01768 361300 Mrs Robinson
e-mail enquire@skygarth.co.uk
Dir Off A66 at Temple Sowerby for Morland, Skygarth 500yds on right

Skygarth is just south of the village, 0.5m from the busy main road. The house stands in a cobbled courtyard surrounded by cowsheds and with gardens to the rear, where red squirrels feed. There are two well-proportioned bedrooms, and an attractive lounge where tasty breakfasts are served.

Facilities 2 rms (2 fmly) ⊗ FTV TVB tea/coffee ✖ Cen ht TVL 200 acres Mixed **Prices** S £25-£30; D £42-£48✳ **Parking** 4 **Notes** Closed Dec-Jan 🐾

THIRLMERE
MAP 18 NY31

◆◆◆ 🍃

Stybeck Farm Experience ◇ (NY319188)

CA12 4TN ☎ 017687 73232 Mr & Mrs Hodgson
e-mail stybeckfarm@farming.co.uk
web http://members.farmline.com/stybeckfarm
Dir On A591 near B5322 junct

A traditional farmhouse set below Lakeland fells and crags. Three bedrooms, one on the ground floor, are in the main house, while another two are in a nearby barn conversion. Both properties have their own dining room where hearty breakfasts are served.

Facilities 3 en suite 2 annexe en suite (1 GF) ⊗ TVB tea/coffee ✖ Cen ht TVL No children 5yrs 200 acres dairy mixed sheep working **Prices** S £29-£30; D £50-£60 **LB Parking** 5 **Notes** Closed 25 Dec 🐾

TROUTBECK (NEAR KESWICK) MAP 18 NY32

★★★★ Guest House

Lane Head Farm

CA11 0SY ☎ 017687 79220
e-mail b&b@laneheadfarm.co.uk
Dir On A66 between Penrith and Keswick, 8.7m from M6 junct 40

Dating from the 18th century, this converted farmhouse has a peaceful location with magnificent views. Bedrooms are comfortable, well equipped and two are furnished with four-poster beds. Public areas are well presented and include a lounge and spacious dining room. Meals are freshly prepared using local ingredients and hosts Chris and Julie give a warm welcome to all.

Facilities 7 en suite (1 GF) ⊗ TVB tea/coffee ✖ Licensed Cen ht No children 16yrs No coaches Dinner Last d 5pm **Prices** S £40-£47.50; D £55-£70✳ **Parking** 9 **Notes** Closed Jan

TROUTBECK   MAP 18 NY40
(NEAR WINDERMERE)

◆◆◆◆

Queens Head Hotel

Town Head LA23 1PW ☎ 015394 32174 ▤ 015394 31938
e-mail enquiries@queensheadhotel.com
web www.queensheadhotel.com
Dir A592 from Windermere for Penrith/Ullswater, Queens Head 2m on right

This 17th-century coaching inn has stunning views of the Troutbeck valley. The delightful bedrooms, several with four-poster beds, are traditionally furnished and equipped with modern facilities. Beams, flagstone floors, and a bar that was once an Elizabethan four-poster, provide a wonderful setting in which to enjoy imaginative food, real ales and fine wines.

Facilities 11 en suite 5 annexe en suite (2 GF) ⊗ in bedrooms ⊗ in dining room TVB tea/coffee ✖ Cen ht No coaches Dinner Last d 9pm **Prices** S £60-£77.50; D £100-£120✳ LB **Parking** 75 **Notes** Closed 25 Dec

Ⓤ

Broad Oak Country House

Bridge Ln LA23 1LA ☎ 015394 45566 ▤ 015394 88766
e-mail trev@broadoaksf9.co.uk
Dir Exit A591 junct 36 pass Windermere. Filing station on left, 1st right 0.5m

At the time of going to press the rating for this establishment had not

continued

been confirmed. Please check the AA website www.theAA.com for up-to-date information.

Facilities 11 en suite 3 annexe en suite (4 fmly) (4 GF) ⊗ STV TVB tea/coffee Direct dial from bedrooms Licensed Cen ht TVL Fishing ♨ ⚓ Shooting Dinner Last d 8.30pm **Prices** S £69.50-£155; D £99-£210✳ LB **Conf** Max 45 Thtr 45 Class 30 Board 30 Del from £120 ✳ **Parking** 42 **Notes** Civ Wed 200

ULVERSTON   MAP 18 SD27

◆◆◆◆

Church Walk House

Church Wk LA12 7EW ☎ 01229 582211
e-mail churchwalk@mchadderton.freeserve.co.uk
Dir Follow Town Centre sign at main rdbt, sharp right at junct opp Kings Arms, house opp Stables furniture shop

This Grade II listed 18th-century residence stands in the heart of the historic market town. Stylishly decorated, the accommodation includes attractive bedrooms with a mix of antiques and contemporary pieces. A peaceful atmosphere prevails with attentive service, and there is a small herbal garden and patio.

Facilities 3 rms (2 en suite) ⊗ tea/coffee Cen ht TVL No coaches **Prices** S fr £35; D £55-£60✳ LB **Notes** ⊛

WATERMILLOCK   MAP 18 NY42

◆◆◆◆ ⊜ ◧

Brackenrigg

CA11 0LP ☎ 017684 86206 ▤ 017684 86945
e-mail enquiries@brackenrigginn.co.uk
web www.brackenrigginn.co.uk
Dir 6m from M6. Onto A66 towards Keswick & A592 to Ullswater, right at lake & continue 3m

An 18th-century coaching inn with superb views of Ullswater and the surrounding countryside. Freshly prepared dishes and daily specials are served by friendly staff in the traditional bar and restaurant. The bedrooms include six attractive rooms in the stable cottages.

Facilities 11 en suite 6 annexe en suite (8 fmly) (3 GF) ⊗ in bedrooms ⊗ in dining room ⊗ in lounges TVB tea/coffee Cen ht Dinner Last d 9pm **Prices** S £33-£38; D £56-£99✳ LB **Conf** Max 48 Thtr 36 Class 12 Board 16 Del from £65 ✳ **Parking** 40

England

WHITEHAVEN
MAP 18 NX91

See also **St Bees**

★★★★ Guest House

Corkickle Guest House

1 Corkickle CA28 8AA ☎ 01946 692073 ▤ 01946 629073

Dir *A595 Whitehaven, pass BP station, turn right at lights, down hill, 2nd left after Chase Hotel, located at end of road.*

This delightful, beautifully maintained house has an elevated position at the end of a Georgian terrace fronted by a cobbled street. There is an inviting lounge and a smart dining room where breakfasts (and dinners by arrangement) are served around one large table. The well-equipped bedrooms are individually styled and smartly decorated.

Facilities 6 rms (4 en suite) (1 pri facs) ⊗ TVB tea/coffee ✘ Cen ht TVL No coaches **Prices** S £32-£34; D £48-£55✳ **LB** **Parking** 2

★★★★ Guest House

Glenfield Guest House

Back Corkickle CA28 7TS
☎ 01946 691911 & 07749 856784 ▤ 01946 694060
e-mail glenfieldgh@aol.com
web www.glenfield-whitehaven.co.uk
Dir *0.50m from town centre, on A5094 S.*

The imposing, family-run Victorian house is in a conservation area close to the historic town centre and harbour. Margaret and Andrew provide a relaxed environment with friendly but unobtrusive service, and this is a good start point for the Sea to Sea (C2C) cycle ride.

Facilities 6 en suite (2 fmly) ⊗ TVB tea/coffee Licensed Cen ht TVL No coaches Dinner Last d 7.30pm **Prices** S £32-£35; D £48-£55✳ **LB**

WINDERMERE
MAP 18 SD49

★★★★ Guest Accommodation

Holly-Wood Guest House

Holly Rd LA23 2AF ☎ 015394 42219
e-mail info@hollywoodguesthouse.co.uk
web www.hollywoodguesthouse.co.uk
Dir *On one-way system, left onto Ellerthwaite Road, then 1st left*

Located in a quiet residential area close to the town centre, the well-presented Victorian property has the benefit of off-road parking. The well-cooked breakfast using quality local ingredients is a good start to the day. Good hospitality and customer care is evident from the new proprietors.

Facilities 6 en suite (1 fmly) ⊗ TVB tea/coffee ✘ Cen ht No children 2yrs No coaches **Prices** S £45-£60; D £50-£66✳ **LB** **Parking** 3

◆◆◆◆◆

The Beaumont

Holly Rd LA23 2AF ☎ 015394 47075 ▤ 015394 88311
e-mail lakesbeaumont@btinternet.com
web www.lakesbeaumont.co.uk
Dir *On one-way system left onto Ellerthwaite Rd & 1st left*

A warm welcome awaits you at this smart traditional house, set in a peaceful location just a stroll from the town centre. Bedrooms, some with four-poster beds, are individually furnished to a high standard, as are the modern bathrooms. The spacious lounge has an honesty bar, and hearty breakfasts are served in the dining room.

Facilities 10 en suite (1 fmly) (5 GF) ⊗ TVB tea/coffee ✘ Licensed Cen ht TVL No children 12yrs Membership of Country Club **Prices** S £40-£60; D £65-£120✳ **LB** **Parking** 10

◆◆◆◆◆

The Howbeck

New Rd LA23 2LA ☎ 015394 44739
e-mail relax@howbeck.co.uk
Dir *A591 through Windermere town centre, left towards Bowness*

Please note that this establishment has recently changed hands. Howbeck is a delightful Victorian villa, convenient for the village and the lake. Bedrooms are well appointed and feature lovely soft furnishings, some with new luxurious spa baths. There is a bright lounge with Internet access, and an attractive dining room where

continued

continued

home-prepared dinners and hearty Cumbrian breakfasts are served at individual tables. This house is non-smoking.

Facilities 10 en suite (1 fmly) (3 GF) ⊘ TVB tea/coffee Licensed Cen ht No coaches Dinner Last d noon **Prices** D £63-£143✳ **LB Parking** 12

Premier Collection

◆◆◆◆◆
Low House

Cleabarrow LA23 3NA ☎ 015394 43156
e-mail info@lowhouse.co.uk
web www.lowhouse.co.uk
Dir A591 N past Kendal, 1st left B5284 signed Crook. After 5m, past Windermere Golf Club, 1st right signed Heathwaite, Low House on right

This delightful 17th-century house is in a quiet location just off the road that passes the golf club and a 25-minute country walk from Bowness. Restored to create a homely atmosphere, the bedrooms are well equipped and there are two lounges in addition to the breakfast room. An optional extra is the hire of the family's 1965 Bentley to visit local restaurants and attractions.

Facilities 3 en suite ⊘ TVB tea/coffee ✖ Cen ht No children 12yrs No coaches ♨ Dinner Last d 7pm **Prices** S £60-£70; D £90-£100✳ **LB Parking** 5

Premier Collection

◆◆◆◆◆ 🛏
Oakbank House Hotel

Helm Rd LA23 3BU ☎ 015394 43386 📠 015394 47965
e-mail enquiries@oakbankhousehotel.co.uk
web www.oakbankhousehotel.co.uk
Dir Off A591 through town centre into Bowness, Helm Rd 100yds on left after cinema

Oakbank House is just off the main street in Bowness overlooking Windermere and the fells beyond. Bedrooms are individually styled and very well equipped, and most have stunning lake views. There is an elegant lounge with a perpetual coffee pot, and delicious breakfasts are served at individual tables in the dining room.

Facilities 12 en suite (1 fmly) (2 GF) ⊘ TVB tea/coffee ✖ Licensed Cen ht Free membership to local country club **Prices** S £50-£98 **LB Parking** 14

◆◆◆◆ 🛏
Boston House

4 The Terrace LA23 1AJ ☎ 015394 43654
e-mail stay@bostonhouse.co.uk

This well-appointed and friendly guest house, which dates from the early 19th century, backs on to the A591 Kendal Rd and is a short walk from the station and town centre. Bedrooms are mostly spacious, individually decorated, with several having four-poster or canopied beds. There is a homely lounge and and an attarctive dining room with individual tables where innovative breakfasts are served

Facilities 4 rms (3 en suite) (1 pri facs) ⊘ TVB tea/coffee ✖ Cen ht TVL No children 12yrs No coaches **Prices** S £35-£43; D £70-£86 **LB Parking** 5 **Notes** Closed 24-31 Dec & 1Jan

◆◆◆◆
Dene House

Kendal Rd LA23 3EW ☎ 015394 48236 📠 015394 48236
e-mail denehouse@ignetics.co.uk
Dir 0.5m from Bowness on A5074 next to Burnside Hotel

A friendly welcome awaits you at this smart Victorian house, in a peaceful location just a short walk from the centre of Bowness. The elegant bedrooms are generally spacious, individually decorated and are particularly well equipped. Afternoon tea is served on the patio, which overlooks a well-tended garden. A car park is available.

Facilities 7 rms (5 en suite) (2 pri facs) (1 fmly) (1 GF) ⊘ TVB tea/coffee ✖ Cen ht TVL No coaches Free use of adjacent leisure centre **Parking** 7 **Notes** 🐾

◆◆◆◆
Fair Rigg

Ferry View LA23 3JB ☎ 015394 43941
e-mail stay@fairrigg.co.uk
web www.fairrigg.co.uk
Dir 0.5m S of village centre at junct A5074 & B5284

This late Victorian house has been refurbished to provide spacious accommodation, while retaining many original features. The elegant dining room and many of the bedrooms have delightful views up the lake to the mountains. Bedrooms are attractive and well equipped.

Facilities 6 en suite (1 GF) ⊘ TVB tea/coffee ✖ Cen ht No children 14yrs No coaches **Prices** S £40-£80; D £64-£84✳ **Parking** 6 **Notes** 🐾

◆◆◆◆
Newstead

New Rd LA23 2EE ☎ 015394 44485 📠 015394 88904
e-mail info@newstead-guesthouse.co.uk
web www.newstead-guesthouse.co.uk
Dir 0.5m from A591 between Windermere & Bowness

A family home set in landscaped gardens, this spacious Victorian house offers well-equipped accommodation. The attractive bedrooms retain original features such as fireplaces and include many thoughtful extra touches. There is a comfortable lounge and a smart dining room where freshly cooked breakfasts are served at individual tables.

Facilities 7 en suite (1 fmly) ⊘ TVB tea/coffee ✖ Cen ht No children 7yrs **Prices** S £40-£80; D £50-£90 **LB Parking** 10 **Notes** 🐾

England

WINDERMERE continued

♦♦♦♦
Belsfield House ◇

4 Belsfield Ter, Kendal Rd, Bowness-on-Windermere
LA23 3EQ ☎ 015394 45823 📠 015394 46913
e-mail enquiries@belsfieldhouse.co.uk
Dir *From A592 in Bowness, 1st left after minirdbt, left at St Martins Church onto Kendal Rd, house on right*

Situated in the heart of Bowness just a short walk from Windermere, this welcoming Victorian house offers good-value accommodation. The individually styled bedrooms are well equipped, some having lake views. There is a comfortable ground-floor lounge and traditional breakfasts are served in the dining room. Guests have free access to a local leisure complex.

Facilities 9 en suite (3 fmly) (1 GF) ⊗ in 5 bedrooms ⊗ in dining room ⊗ in lounges TVB tea/coffee ✗ Cen ht No coaches free use of Parklands country club **Prices** S £25-£35; D £50-£70 **LB** **Parking** 9

♦♦♦♦
Blenheim Lodge

Brantfell Rd, Bowness on Windermere LA23 3AE
☎ 015394 43440 📠 015394 43440
e-mail enquiries@blenheim-lodge.com
Dir *A591 Bowness village, left at minirdbt, 1st left & left again, house at top*

From its peaceful position above the town of Bowness, Blenheim Lodge has panoramic views over the lake. Bedrooms are traditionally furnished and some have four-poster or half-tester beds. There is a comfortable lounge and a pleasing dining room where hearty breakfasts are served at individual tables.

Facilities 11 rms (10 en suite) (1 pri facs) (2 fmly) (2 GF) ⊗ TVB tea/coffee ✗ Licensed TVL Free membership nearby private leisure facilities **Prices** S £40-£50; D £70-£110✳ **LB** **Parking** 11 **Notes** Closed 25-Dec rs 20-27 Dec

♦♦♦♦
Coach House

Lake Rd LA23 2EQ ☎ 015394 44494
e-mail enquiries@lakedistrictbandb.com
Dir *M6 junct 36, A590 then A591, in Windermere left towards Bowness. House 0.5m on right opp St Herberts Church*

Expect a relaxed and welcoming atmosphere at this stylish house, which has a minimalist interior with cosmopolitan furnishings. The attractive bedrooms are well equipped. There is a reception lounge, and a breakfast room where freshly prepared breakfasts feature the best of local produce.

Facilities 5 en suite (1 fmly) ⊗ TVB tea/coffee ✗ Licensed Cen ht No children 7yrs No coaches Membership of local Health Club **LB** **Parking** 5 **Notes** Closed 24-26 Dec

♦♦♦♦ ➾
The Coppice

Brook Rd LA23 2ED ☎ 015394 88501 📠 015394 42148
e-mail chris@thecoppice.co.uk
web www.thecoppice.co.uk
Dir *0.25m S of village centre on A5074*

This attractive detached house lies between Windermere and Bowness. There are colourful public rooms and bedrooms, and a restaurant serving freshly prepared local produce. The bedrooms vary in size and style and have good facilities.

Facilities 9 en suite (2 fmly) (1 GF) ⊗ TV8B tea/coffee Licensed Cen ht No coaches Private leisure club membership Dinner Last d 10am **Parking** 10

♦♦♦♦
The Fairfield Garden Guest House

Brantfell Rd, Bowness-on-Windermere LA23 3AE
☎ 015394 46565 📠 015394 46565
e-mail tonyandliz@the-fairfield.co.uk
Dir *Into Bowness town centre, turn opp St Martins Church & sharp left by Spinnery restaurant, house 200yds on right*

This welcoming house is in a quiet lane above the town and within walking distance of the lake and Bowness. Bedrooms are comfortably furnished and thoughtfully equipped. Public rooms include an inviting lounge with adjacent bar, and an attractive dining room overlook the landscaped gardens.

Facilities 10 rms (9 en suite) (2 fmly) (3 GF) ⊗ TVB tea/coffee Licensed Cen ht TVL ⅃ Dinner Last d 24hrs **Conf** Max 20 Thtr 20 Class 10 Board 12 **Parking** 9

England

◆◆◆◆

Fir Trees

Lake Rd LA23 2EQ ☎ 015394 42272 ▤ 015394 42512
e-mail enquiries@fir-trees.com
web www.fir-trees.co.uk
Dir *Off A591 through town, Lake Rd in 0.5m, Fir Trees on left after clock tower*

Located halfway between Windermere centre and the lake, this spacious Victorian house offers attractive and well equipped accommodation. Bedrooms are generously proportioned and have many thoughtful touches. Breakfasts, featuring the best of local produce, are served at individual tables in the smart dining room.

Facilities 9 en suite (2 fmly) (3 GF) ⊗ TVB tea/coffee 🐾 Free use of local country club (2 nights stay) Dinner Last d 10am
Prices S £30-£50; D £50-£88⁕ **LB** **Parking** 9

◆◆◆◆

Glencree Private Hotel

Lake Rd LA23 2EQ ☎ 015394 45822 & 0797 469714
e-mail h.butterworth@btinternet.com
web www.glencreelakes.co.uk
Dir *From town centre signs for Bowness & The Lake, Glencree on right after large wooded area on right*

Colourful hanging baskets and floral displays adorn the car park and entrance to Glencree, which lies between Windermere and Bowness. Bedrooms are brightly decorated and individually furnished. The attractive lounge, with an honesty bar, is next to the dining room where breakfast is served at individual tables.

Facilities 6 en suite (1 fmly) (1 GF) ⊗ TVB tea/coffee 🐾 Licensed Cen ht TVL No coaches Dinner Last d 2.30pm **Prices** S £35-£50; D £50-£90⁕ **LB** **Parking** 7

◆◆◆◆

Glenville House

Lake Rd LA23 2EQ ☎ 015394 43371 ▤ 015394 48457
e-mail mail@glenvillehouse.co.uk
Dir *Off A591 into Windermere, follow road for 0.5m, Glenville on right next to St John's Church*

This traditional Lakeland stone house has a relaxing and friendly atmosphere, and stands in well-tended gardens just a short walk from the town centre and the lake. Refreshments can be taken in the comfortable lounge, and breakfast is served in the cosy dining room. The attractive bedrooms are well appointed and mostly spacious.

Facilities 7 en suite (2 fmly) (1 GF) ⊗ TVB tea/coffee 🐾 Cen ht No coaches **Prices** D £78-£98⁕ **LB** **Parking** 7

◆◆◆◆

The Haven

10 Birch St LA23 1EG ☎ 015394 44017
e-mail thehaven.windermere@btopenworld.com
Dir *On A5074 enter one-way system, 3rd left onto Birch St*

Built from Lakeland slate and stone, this Victorian house is just a stroll from the town centre and shops. The bright, spacious bedrooms have en suite or private facilities, and one has a Victorian brass bed. A hearty Cumbrian breakfast is served in the well-appointed lounge-dining room.

Facilities 3 rms (2 en suite) (1 pri facs) (2 fmly) ⊗ TVB tea/coffee 🐾 Cen ht No children 7yrs No coaches **Prices** D £36-£70⁕ **LB** **Parking** 3

◆◆◆◆

High Fold Guesthouse

Troutbeck LA23 1PG ☎ 015394 32200 & 07717 804745
e-mail info@highfoldbedandbreakfast.co.uk
web www.highfoldbedandbreakfast.co.uk
Dir *A592 Windermere to Kirkstone. 2m on left for Troutbeck. Right at junct, 200yds turn right at White Cottage*

Occupying a blissfully quiet location on the hillside of this picturesque village, High Fold is set just off the road among a small cluster of buildings. Lovely views can be enjoyed from the pretty breakfast room and most of the bedrooms, which are on the first and second floors and are pleasantly appointed.

Facilities 6 en suite (1 fmly) ⊗ TVB tea/coffee 🐾 Cen ht No children 10yrs No coaches **Prices** D £60-£84⁕ **LB** **Parking** 6

◆◆◆◆

Laurel Cottage

St Martins Sq, Kendal Rd LA23 3EF
☎ 015394 45594 ▤ 015394 45594
e-mail enquiries@laurelcottage-bnb.co.uk
web www.laurelcottage-bnb.co.uk
Dir *Off A591 for Windermere & Bowness, at St Martins Church left onto Kendal Rd, cottage 30yds on left*

This attractive 17th-century cottage is in the centre of the town, very close to the lake and shops. The cosy bedrooms in the cottage have window seats, while spacious pine-furnished rooms are available in the Victorian part of the house.

Facilities 13 rms (11 en suite) (2 fmly) ⊗ TVB tea/coffee 🐾 Cen ht TVL No coaches Membership to local leisure clubs **Prices** S £26-£33; D £54-£90⁕ **LB** **Parking** 13

England

WINDERMERE continued

◆◆◆◆

The Old Court House

Lake Rd LA23 3AP ☎ 015394 45096
e-mail alison@theoch.co.uk
Dir On Windermere-Bowness road at junct Longlands Rd

A former Victorian police station and courthouse, this attractive property in the centre of Bowness was undergoing renovation at the time of inspection. Attractive pine-furnished bedrooms offer a good range of facilities. Freshly prepared breakfasts are served in the bright ground-floor dining room.

Facilities 6 en suite (2 GF) ⊗ TVB tea/coffee ✖ Cen ht No children 10yrs No coaches **Prices** S £30-£40; D £55-£75✱ **LB** **Parking** 6
Notes

◆◆◆◆

The Willowsmere

Ambleside Rd LA23 1ES
☎ 015394 43575 ▤ 015394 44962
e-mail info@thewillowsmere.com
web www.thewillowsmere.com
Dir On A591, 500yds on left after Windermere station, towards Ambleside

Willowsmere is a friendly, family-run establishment within easy walking distance of the town centre. It stands in a colourful, well-tended garden, with a patio and water feature to the rear. The attractive bedrooms are spacious, and there is a choice of inviting lounges and a well-stocked bar. Delicious breakfasts are served at individual tables in the stylish dining room.

Facilities 12 en suite (1 GF) ⊗ TVB tea/coffee Licensed Cen ht TVL No children 12yrs Free use of nearby swimming pool, gym
Prices S £35-£55; D £56-£106✱ **Parking** 15

◆◆◆◆

Woodlands Hotel

New Rd LA23 2EE ☎ 015394 43915 ▤ 015394 43915
e-mail enquiries@woodlands-windermere.co.uk
web www.woodlands-windermere.co.uk
Dir One-way system through town down New Rd towards lake, premises by war memorial clock

Comfortable bedrooms, welcoming hospitality and a relaxing atmosphere all ensure a memorable stay at Woodlands. Stylishly furnished to a high standard, public areas include a spacious lounge, a cosy bar and an attractive dining room that overlooks the neat rear garden.

Facilities 14 en suite (2 fmly) (3 GF) ⊗ TVB tea/coffee ✖ Licensed Cen ht No coaches Free facilities at local leisure/sports club Dinner
Parking 17

◆◆◆◆

Storrs Gate House

Longtail Hill LA23 3JD ☎ 015394 43272
e-mail enquiries@storrsgatehouse.co.uk
Dir At junct A592 & B5284, opp Windermere Marina
Facilities 6 en suite (2 GF) ⊗ STV TVB tea/coffee ✖ Licensed Cen ht TVL No children No coaches Dinner Last d 10.30am **Prices** D £60-£104
LB **Parking** 6

◆◆◆

St Johns Lodge

Lake Rd LA23 2EQ ☎ 015394 43078 ▤ 015394 88054
e-mail mail@st-johns-lodge.co.uk
web www.st-johns-lodge.co.uk
Dir On A5074 between Windermere & lake

Located between Windermere and Bowness, this large guest house offers a refreshingly friendly welcome. Bedrooms vary in size and style but all are neatly furnished. Freshly prepared traditional breakfasts, including vegetarian and vegan options, are served in the well-appointed basement dining room. Facilities include free Internet access.

Facilities 14 rms (12 en suite) (3 fmly) ⊗ TVB tea/coffee ✖ Cen ht No children 6yrs No coaches Facilities at private leisure club
Prices S £25-£40; D £40-£70 **LB** **Parking** 11

◆◆◆

Adam Place Guest House ◇

1 Park Av LA23 2AR ☎ 015394 44600 ▤ 015394 44600
e-mail adamplacewindermere@yahoo.co.uk
Dir Off A591 into Windermere, through town centre, left onto Ellerthwaite Rd & Park Av

Located in a mainly residential area within easy walking distance of the lake and town centre, this Victorian stone house has been renovated to provide homely bedrooms. Comprehensive breakfasts are served in the cosy dining room and there is a pretty patio garden.

continued

Adam Place Guest House

Facilities 5 en suite (2 fmly) ⊗ TVB tea/coffee ✲ Cen ht No children 6yrs **Prices** S £20-£34; D £40-£62

◆◆◆

Broadlands ◇

19 Broad St LA23 2AB ☎ 015394 46532
e-mail enquiries@broadlandsbandb.co.uk
Dir *From A591 follow one-way system, left onto Broad St after pedestrian crossing*

A friendly welcome is offered at this attractive house opposite the park and library and convenient for central amenities. Bedrooms are pleasantly coordinated and comfortably furnished, and freshly prepared breakfasts are served in the ground-floor dining room.

Facilities 5 en suite (2 fmly) ⊗ TVB tea/coffee ✲ Cen ht No children 12yrs No coaches **Prices** S £27-£30; D £48-£54✲ LB

◆◆◆ ◀

Eagle & Child Inn

Kendal Rd, Staveley LA8 9LP ☎ 01539 821320
e-mail info@eaglechildinn.co.uk
web www.eaglechildinn.co.uk
Dir *A591 from Kendal towards Windermere, sign for Staveley, pub 500yds on left*

Close to the beautiful Kentmere valley, this delightful village pub offers comfortable accommodation and good food. A choice of local cask ales can be enjoyed in either the tranquil riverside garden or the spacious bar. Breakfast is served in the Redmond Suite, which is available for functions.

Facilities 5 en suite (1 fmly) ⊗ in bedrooms ⊗ in area of dining room TVB tea/coffee ✲ Cen ht Local Leisure Club facilities can be arranged Dinner Last d 8.45pm **Conf** Max 60 Board 40 **Parking** 16

◆◆◆

Elim House ◇

Biskey Howe Rd LA23 2JP
☎ 015394 42021 📠 015394 43430
e-mail elimhouse@btopenworld.com
web www.elimhouse.co.uk
Dir *Left off A5074 150yds past police station, 1st house on left*

A short walk from the bustling village of Bowness and the lake, this attractive house has a colourful, well-kept garden. Bedrooms, some in an annexe, vary in size and style, but all offer sound levels of comfort. A hearty Cumbrian breakfast is served in the cheerful breakfast room.

Facilities 7 en suite 3 annexe en suite (1 fmly) ⊗ TVB tea/coffee ✲ No children 10yrs No coaches **Prices** S £30-£100; D £55-£120✲ LB **Parking** 7 **Notes** Closed 1-26 Dec rs Jan-Mar

◆◆◆

The Firgarth ◇

Ambleside Rd LA23 1EU
☎ 015394 46974 📠 015394 42384
e-mail thefirgarth@ktdinternet.com
Dir *On Windermere-Ambleside road, 0.25m on left past St Marys Church*

Situated on the main road between Windermere and Ambleside, this traditional guest house offers good-value accommodation. The attractive bedrooms are well appointed and thoughtfully equipped, and the rooms at the rear havea pleasant outlook. There is a cosy lounge and hearty breakfasts are served in the breakfast room.

Facilities 8 en suite (1 fmly) ⊗ TVB tea/coffee Cen ht No coaches **Prices** S £23-£35; D £42-£60 LB **Parking** 9

England

WINDERMERE continued

♦♦♦

Green Gables Guest House ◇

37 Broad St LA23 2AB ☎ 015394 43886
e-mail info@greengablesguesthouse.co.uk
Dir Off A591 into Windermere, 1st left after pelican crossing, B&B opp car park

Aptly named, Green Gables is a friendly guest house looking onto Elleray Gardens. Just a short walk from the centre, the house offers bright, fresh and well-appointed bedrooms. There is a comfortable bar-lounge, and substantial breakfasts are served in the spacious dining room.

Facilities 7 rms (4 en suite) (3 pri facs) (3 fmly) (1 GF) ⊗ in bedrooms ⊗ in dining room TVB tea/coffee ✗ Licensed Cen ht TVL No coaches **Prices** S £22-£30; D £45-£60✱ **LB Notes** Closed 23-27 Dec
See advertisement on page 135

WORKINGTON   MAP 18 NY02

Premier Collection

♦♦♦♦♦ ⌷

Falconwood

Moor Rd, Stainburn CA14 1XW ☎ 01900 602563
e-mail info@lakedistrict-bedandbreakfast.co.uk
Dir M6 Junct 44 to Keswick A66. Workington A595 to Whitehaven, turn right 0.25m to Stainburn

Having a peaceful setting, this welcoming house looks out to the Solway Firth towards Scotland and offers genuine hospitality. The bedrooms are attractive and thoughtfully equipped, and you are welcome to use the relaxing lounge. Ian's excellent dinners and hearty breakfasts are a highlight of any stay.

Facilities 2 en suite (2 GF) ⊗ TVB tea/coffee ✗ Licensed Cen ht TVL No children 14yrs No coaches Dinner Last d By arrangement **Prices** S £50; D £70✱ **LB Parking** 6

DERBYSHIRE

ALFRETON   MAP 16 SK45

♦♦♦ ❦

Oaktree Farm ◇ (SK385566)

Matlock Rd, Oakerthorpe, Wessington DE55 7NA
☎ 01773 832957 & 07732 549550 Mrs Prince
Dir 2m W of Alfreton. A615 W under railway bridge & past cottages, farmhouse on left

Set in 22 acres, including a fishing lake, chicken run and kitchen garden, this mellow-stone house provides thoughtfully equipped bedrooms with modern bathrooms. Breakfasts using the freshest ingredients are served in an attractive cottage-style dining room. The floral patio is pretty in summer.

Facilities 3 en suite ⊗ STV TVB tea/coffee ✗ Cen ht TVL Fishing 22 acres mixed **Prices** S £25-£27; D £45-£48✱ **Parking** 10 **Notes** ⊛

ALKMONTON   MAP 10 SK13

♦♦♦♦

The Courtyard

Dairy House Farm DE6 3DG
☎ 01335 330187 ▤ 01335 330187
e-mail michael@dairyhousefarm.org.uk
Dir 1.5m SE of Alkmonton. Off A50 at Foston, 3.5m up Woodyard Ln & Ashbourne Rd

Surrounded by open countryside, this is a delightful conversion of Victorian farm buildings in the Derbyshire Dales. The bedrooms are well furnished and thoughtfully equipped, and a hearty breakfast is provided in the bright dining room (dinner is available by arrangement). Two rooms have easier access.

Facilities 7 en suite (1 fmly) (7 GF) ⊗ TVB tea/coffee ✗ Cen ht No coaches Fishing **Prices** S £35-£40; D £58-£60✱ **LB Parking** 12 **Notes** Closed Xmas

If you have to cancel a booking, let the proprietor know immediately

England

ASHBOURNE
MAP 10 SK14

★★★★ Bed & Breakfast
Bank House
31 Church St DE6 1AE
☎ 01335 347079 & 07931 564985 📠 01335 347079
e-mail bankhouseashbourne@yahoo.co.uk
web www.janeboothroydbandb.co.uk
Dir In Ashbourne centre opp Methodist Church

This elegant period house, formally a bank, has been renovated to provide quality accommodation with modern facilities. Bedrooms, including a sumptuous four-poster suite, are equipped with a range of thoughtful extras and breakfast is served in the attractive kitchen-dining room. A spacious lounge is also available.

Facilities 3 en suite ⊘ TVB tea/coffee ✖ Cen ht No children 16yrs
Prices S £40-£50; D £60-£80✳ LB

★★★★ Bed & Breakfast
The Green at Hulland ◇
The Green, Hulland Village DE6 3EP
☎ 01335 370031 & 07970 281344
e-mail alison@thegreenathulland.co.uk
web www.thegreenathulland.co.uk
Dir 3m E of Ashbourne. On A517 opp turning to Hulland

The period house and adjoining cottage have been renovated to provide high standards of comfort and facilities. The homely pine-furnished bedrooms have smart modern bathrooms en suite, and comprehensive breakfasts are served at one table in the cosy dining room. A lounge is also available and a warm welcome is assured.

Facilities 2 rms (1 en suite) (1 pri facs) (1 fmly) ⊘ tea/coffee Cen ht TVL No coaches **Prices** S £27; D £54✳ LB **Parking** 3 **Notes** 🚭

★★★ Guest House
The Old Barn at Common End Farm
Com End Farm, Swinscoe DE6 2BW ☎ 01335 342342
e-mail commonendbarn@hotmail.co.uk
web www.commonendbarn.co.uk
Dir 4m W of Ashbourne. Off A52 at Swinscoe

The converted barn provides a range of pine-furnished bedrooms with modern shower rooms en suite. Breakfast is served in the cosy dining room and a lounge is available.

Facilities 6 en suite (2 fmly) (4 GF) ⊘ TVB tea/coffee ✖ Cen ht TVL
Prices d fr £60✳ LB **Parking** 10

♦♦♦♦♦ 🏛 🍴
Omnia Somnia
The Coach House, The Firs DE6 1HF ☎ 01335 300145
e-mail alan@omniasomnia.co.uk
web www.omniasomnia.co.uk
Dir 200yds S of town centre. Off station St onto Old Hill, 1st left onto The Firs & signed

Within easy walking distance of the town, this delightful house offers every comfort. Bedrooms are very well furnished and one is on the ground floor. Imaginative home-made dinners and substantial breakfasts are served in the delightful dining room overlooking the sloping garden. There is a cosy lounge.

Facilities 2 en suite (1 GF) ⊘ TVB tea/coffee ✖ Licensed Cen ht No children No coaches Dinner Last d 7pm **Prices** D £95-£105 LB **Parking** 2

♦♦♦♦♦
Turlow Bank
Hognaston DE6 1PW ☎ 01335 370299 📠 01335 370299
e-mail turlowbank@w3z.co.uk
web www.turlowbank.co.uk
Dir Off B5035 to Hognaston (signed Hognaston only), through village towards Hulland Ward, Turlow Bank 0.5m, look for clock tower

Nestling in delightful gardens on a superb elevated position close to Carsington Water, this extended 19th-century farmhouse provides high levels of comfort with excellent facilities. Bedrooms are equipped with many thoughtful extras and feature quality modern bathrooms. Comprehensive breakfasts, which include free-range chicken or duck eggs, are served at a family table in the cosy dining room. A spacious lounge is available, and the hospitality is memorable.

Facilities 2 en suite ⊘ tea/coffee ✖ Cen ht TVL No children 12yrs No coaches 🍴 **Prices** S £40-£50; D £65-£75 **Parking** 6 **Notes** Closed 25-27 Dec 🚭

England

ASHBOURNE continued

◆◆◆◆

Bramhall's ◇

6 Buxton Rd DE6 1EX ☎ 01335 346158
e-mail info@bramhalls.co.uk
web www.bramhalls.co.uk
Dir *From market square N onto Buxton Rd up hill, on left*

Located in the heart of the historic market town, this restaurant with rooms occupies a conversion of two cottages and an Edwardian house. It is popular for its imaginative food, attentive service and excellent value for money. Quality bedrooms are filled with thoughtful extras and a warm welcome is assured.

Facilities 10 rms (8 en suite) (1 fmly) (1 GF) ⊗ in bedrooms ⊗ in area of dining room ⊗ in 1 lounge TVB tea/coffee ✱ Licensed Cen ht No coaches Dinner Last d 9.30pm **Prices** S £30; D £60-£70 **Parking** 6 **Notes** Closed 1-14 Jan rs Nov-Mar

◆◆◆◆

Compton House ◇

27-31 Compton DE6 1BX ☎ 01335 343100
e-mail jane@comptonhouse.co.uk
web www.comptonhouse.co.uk
Dir *A52 from Derby into Ashbourne, across lights at bottom of hill, house 100yds on left opp garage*

Within easy walking distance of the central attractions, this conversion of three cottages has resulted in a house with good standards of comfort and facilities. Bedrooms are filled with homely extras and comprehensive breakfasts are served in the cottage-style dining room.

Facilities 5 en suite (2 fmly) (1 GF) ⊗ TVB tea/coffee Direct dial from bedrooms TVL No coaches **Prices** S £30-£35; D £48-£54 **LB Parking** 6

◆◆◆◆

Dove House B & B

Bridge Hill, Mayfield DE6 2HN ☎ 01335 343329
e-mail dovehouse2000@yahoo.com
Dir *1m W of Ashbourne. A52 onto B5032, B&B 300yds on right*

Peacefully located in Mayfield, this well-proportioned Victorian house has many original features, highlighted by the furnishings and decor. The comfortable bedroom has thoughtful extras and a spacious bathroom en suite. A lounge is also available.

Facilities 1 en suite ⊗ in bedrooms ⊗ in dining room ⊗ in 1 lounge tea/coffee ✱ Cen ht TVL No children No coaches Dinner Last d 1 day before **Prices** D £45-£55✳ **Parking** 1 **Notes** ⊚

◆◆◆◆ ✿

Mercaston Hall *(SK279419)*

Mercaston DE6 3BL ☎ 01335 360263 Mr & Mrs Haddon
e-mail mercastonhall@btinternet.com
Dir *Off A52 in Brailsford onto Luke Ln, 1m turn right at 1st x-rds, house 1m on right*

Located in a pretty hamlet, this medieval building retains many original features. Bedrooms are homely, and additional facilities include an all-weather tennis court and a livery service. This is a good base for visiting local stately homes, the Derwent valley mills and Dovedale.

Facilities 3 en suite ⊗ TVB tea/coffee Cen ht No children 12yrs ⚲ 60 acres mixed **Prices** S £38-£45; D £55-£66✳ **Parking** 3 **Notes** Closed Xmas ⊚

◆◆◆◆

Mona Villas Bed & Breakfast ◇

1 Mona Villas, Church Ln, Middle Mayfield DE6 2JS
☎ 01335 343773 🖷 01335 343773
e-mail info@mona-villas.fsnet.co.uk
web www.mona-villas.fsnet.co.uk
Dir *2.5m SW of Ashbourne. B5032 to Middle Mayfield, onto Church Ln, 400yds on right*

This well-furnished house overlooks open fields close to the village. The bedrooms are very well equipped and have good facilities. Substantial breakfasts are served in the bright dining room and hospitality is a major strength.

Facilities 3 en suite (1 GF) ⊗ TVB tea/coffee ✱ Cen ht No coaches **Prices** S £30-£35; D £45-£50✳ **LB Parking** 6 **Notes** ⊚

◆◆◆

Homesclose House

Stanton DE6 2DA ☎ 01335 324475
Dir *4m W of Ashbourne. Off A52 to Stanton village centre*

Stunning views of the surrounding countryside and manicured gardens are a feature of this beautifully maintained dormer bungalow, located within a pretty village. Bedrooms are filled with homely extras, and an attractive dining room with one family table is the setting for breakfast.

Facilities 3 rms (2 en suite) (1 fmly) (1 GF) ⊗ TVB tea/coffee Cen ht TVL No coaches **LB Parking** 4 **Notes** Closed Dec-Jan ⊚

◆◆◆ ◼

The Green Man Royal Hotel

10 Saint Johns St DE6 1GH
☎ 01335 345783 🖷 01335 346613
Dir *On A515 in town centre*

Located in the heart of the historic town, this 17th-century coaching inn preserves many original features, and bedroom furnishings recall a bygone age. Ground-floor areas include a cosy traditional bar and a music and games room, very popular at weekends. The inn has extensive function facilities.

continued

continued

Facilities 17 en suite (1 fmly) in area of dining room STV TVB tea/coffee Direct dial from bedrooms 🗡 Cen ht Pool Table Dinner Last d 9pm **Prices** S £40; D £60✳ **Conf** Max 250 Thtr 250 Class 150 Board 80 Del from £50 ✳ **Parking** 17 **Notes** Closed 25 Dec & 1 Jan

♦♦♦

Stone Cottage ◇

Green Ln, Clifton DE6 2BL
☎ 01335 343377 📠 01335 347117
e-mail info@stone-cottagefsnet.co.uk
web www.stone-cottage.fsnet.co.uk
Dir 1m from Ashbourne on A52 Leek-Uttoxeter. Left at sign for Clifton, 2nd house on right

A good base for touring and only a short drive from the town centre, this well-maintained stone house stands in pretty gardens and has homely bedrooms. Freshly cooked breakfasts are served in the attractive conservatory, and tourist information is available.

Facilities 3 en suite (1 fmly) STV TVB tea/coffee 🗡 Cen ht TVL No coaches Dinner Last d 9.30am **Prices** S £28-£38; D £45-£56✳ **Parking** 4 **Notes** Closed 25 Dec

♦♦ 🌱

Air Cottage Farm ◇ (SK142523)

Ilam DE6 2BD ☎ 01335 350475 Mrs Wain
Dir A515 from Ashbourne, left signed Thorpe/Dovedale/Ilam, in Ilam right at memorial stone to Alstonfield, right at 1st cattle grid gate

This 18th-century farmhouse has a magnificent elevated position with stunning views over countryside and Dovedale. It provides traditional standards of accommodation and is very popular with serious walkers, climbers and artists visiting this beautiful part of the Peak District.

Facilities 3 rms (3 GF) tea/coffee 🗡 Cen ht TVL 320 acres beef cattle sheep **Prices** S £23-£27; D £46-£54✳ **Parking** 4 **Notes** Closed Dec-Feb 📧

BAKEWELL   MAP 16 SK26

★★★ Inn
Castle Inn

Castle St DE45 1DU ☎ 01629 812103
web www.oldenglish.co.uk

A traditional Inn built in the 16th century and offering well-furnished bedrooms and extensive bars. A wide range of well-prepared dishes is available and real ales are served.

Facilities 4 annexe en suite TVB Direct dial from bedrooms No coaches Last d all day **Prices** S £60-£72.50; D £60-£72.50; (room only) ✳

♦♦♦♦

Avenue House

The Avenue DE45 1EQ ☎ 01629 812467
Dir Off A6 onto The Avenue, 1st house on right

Located a short walk from the town centre, this impressive Victorian house has original features complemented by the decor and furnishings. Bedrooms have many thoughtful extras and the modern bathrooms contain power showers. Hearty English breakfasts are served in the traditionally furnished dining room.

continued

Facilities 3 en suite TVB tea/coffee 🗡 Cen ht TVL No coaches **Prices** d fr £50✳ **Parking** 3 **Notes** 📧

♦♦♦♦

Bourne House

The Park, Haddon Rd DE45 1ET ☎ 01629 813274
web www.bournehousebakewell.co.uk
Dir 300yds S of town centre on A6, on left before park

This impressive former manse stands in mature gardens and overlooks the park close to the town centre. Bedrooms are spacious and lots of thoughtful extras enhance your comfort. Breakfast is served in an attractive period-furnished dining room and a warm welcome is assured.

Facilities 3 en suite TVB tea/coffee 🗡 Cen ht No children 7yrs No coaches **Prices** D £54-£60 **Parking** 5 **Notes** Closed Dec-Feb 📧

♦♦♦♦

Croft Cottages

Coombs Rd DE45 1AQ ☎ 01629 814101
e-mail croftco@btopenworld.com
Dir A619 E from town centre over bridge, right onto Station Rd & Coombs Rd

A warm welcome is assured at this Grade II listed stone building close to the River Wye and town centre. Thoughtfully equipped bedrooms are available in the main house or in an adjoining converted barn suite. Breakfast is served in a spacious lounge-dining room.

Facilities 3 rms (2 en suite) (1 pri facs) 1 annexe en suite (1 fmly) TVB tea/coffee Cen ht No coaches **Prices** D £54-£64 **LB** **Parking** 2 **Notes** 📧

♦♦♦♦

Holly Cottage

Pilsley DE45 1UH ☎ 01246 582245 📠 01246 582245
e-mail julie.hollycottage@tiscali.co.uk
Dir A619 from Baslow towards Buxton, follow signs for Chatsworth House

A warm welcome is assured at this mellow-stone cottage, part of a combined Post Office and shop within the conservation area of Pilsley, which is owned by the adjacent Chatsworth Estate. The cosy bedrooms feature a wealth of thoughtful extras, and comprehensive breakfasts, using quality local produce, are served in the attractive pine-furnished dining room.

Facilities 3 en suite TVB tea/coffee 🗡 Cen ht No coaches **Prices** S fr £40; d fr £50✳ **Notes** Closed 22 Dec-2 Jan

♦♦♦♦

Wyedale

Wyedale House, 25 Holywell DE45 1BA ☎ 01629 812845
Dir 500yds SE of town centre, off A6 Haddon Rd

Wyedale is close to the town centre and is ideal for relaxing or touring. Bedrooms, one of which is on the ground floor, are spacious and freshly decorated. Breakfast is served in the attractive dining room, overlooking the rear patio.

Facilities 3 en suite (1 fmly) (1 GF) TVB tea/coffee 🗡 Cen ht No coaches **Prices** D £50-£60 **Parking** 4 **Notes** Closed 31 Dec rs 24 Dec 📧

BAKEWELL continued

◆◆◆◆

Castle Cliffe Guest House

Monsal Head DE45 1NL
☎ 01629 640258 🖶 01629 640258
e-mail relax@castle-cliffe.com
web www.castle-cliffe.com
Dir *3m NW of Bakewell. On B6465 in Monsal Head, near Little Longstone*

Facilities 7 en suite (2 fmly) ⊘ TVB tea/coffee ✖ Licensed Cen ht TVL No coaches **Prices** S £40-£45; D £50-£70✳ **LB Parking** 10 **Notes** Closed 23-28 Dec

◆◆◆

Everton ◇

Haddon Rd DE45 1AW ☎ 01629 815028

Located opposite the park and a short walk from the centre, this large semi-detached house provides homely bedrooms and an attractive pine-furnished dining room, the setting for comprehensive breakfasts.

Facilities 3 rms (1 en suite) ⊘ TVB tea/coffee Cen ht ⚬ **Prices** S £30-£35; D £45-£55✳ **LB Parking** 6 **Notes** 🈲

◆◆◆ ⬛

George Hotel

Church St, Youlgreave DE45 1UW
☎ 01629 636292 🖶 01632 636292
Dir *3m S of Bakewell in Youlgreave, opp church*

The bars of the 17th-century George are popular with locals and tourists. Bedroom styles vary, and all have shower rooms en suite. Breakfast is served in the lounge bar, and a range of bar meals and snacks is available. A cash machine is also available.

Facilities 3 en suite (1 fmly) TVB tea/coffee Cen ht Fishing Dinner Last d 8.30pm **Prices** S fr £32; d fr £56✳ **Parking** 12 **Notes** 🈲

◆◆◆

Wyeclose

5 Granby Cft DE45 1ET ☎ 01629 813702 🖶 01629 813702
e-mail h.wilson@talk21.com
Dir *Off A6 Matlock St onto Granby Rd & Granby Croft*

Located in a quiet cul-de-sac in the town centre, this Edwardian house provides thoughtfully furnished bedrooms with smart modern bathrooms and an attractive dining room, the setting for comprehensive breakfasts. Original family art is a feature within the ground-floor areas.

Facilities 2 rms (1 en suite) (1 pri facs) ⊘ STV TVB tea/coffee ✖ Cen ht No children 8yrs No coaches **Prices** D £50✳ **Parking** 3 **Notes** Closed Xmas & New Year 🈲

BAMFORD

MAP 16 SK28

◆◆◆◆

The Outpost

Shatton Ln S33 0BG ☎ 01433 651400
e-mail aabest.enquires@theoutpost.info
web www.theoutpost.info
Dir *Off A6187 between Bamford & Hope opp High Peak Garden Centre, then 200yds on right*

In a sleepy location opposite a garden centre, this house offers large gardens, fine hospitality and excellent comfort. Superb breakfasts include home-made bread and preserves, served either in the dining room or the conservatory, and there is a splendid garden lounge. The Outpost is an ideal touring base.

Facilities 3 rms (1 en suite) ⊘ TVB tea/coffee ✖ Cen ht TVL No coaches **Prices** D £50-£60✳ **Parking** 3 **Notes** Closed 24 Dec-2 Jan 🈲

◆◆◆

Thornhill View ◇

Hope Rd, Bamford, Hope Valley S33 0AL ☎ 01433 651823
e-mail thornhill4bb@aol.com
Dir *Between Castleton & Hathersage A6187 corner of Thornhill Ln, 100yds Rising Sun Hotel.*

Comfortable accommodation set back from the main road running down the Hope Valley near to the Rising Sun. The compact bedrooms are well equipped, and Jo Fairbairn is a careful host.

Facilities 2 rms (1 en suite) (1 pri facs) (2 GF) ⊘ TVB tea/coffee ✖ Cen ht No coaches **Prices** S £25; D £50✳ **LB Parking** 8 **Notes** 🈲

◆◆◆

The White House ◇

Shatton Ln S33 0BG ☎ 01433 651487 🖶 01433 651487
Dir *A6187 Hathersage to Hope, left opp High Peak Garden Centre into Shatton, White House 250yds on left*

Set in a secluded lane among attractive gardens, this large detached family home offers spacious, nicely laid out bedrooms. Breakfast is served around a large communal table in the neat dining room, which overlooks the garden. The comfortable lounge has a television.

Facilities 5 rms ⊘ in bedrooms ⊘ in dining room TVB tea/coffee Cen ht TVL No coaches **Prices** S £25-£30; D £45-£50✳ **Parking** 4 **Notes** 🈲

BELPER

MAP 11 SK34

Premier Collection

♦♦♦♦♦ 🏠 🍽 💐

Dannah Farm Country House (SK314502)

Bowmans Ln, Shottle DE56 2DR

☎ 01773 550273 & 550630 📠 01773 550590 Mrs Slack

e-mail reservations@dannah.co.uk

web www.dannah.co.uk

Dir A517 from Belper towards Ashbourne, 1.5m right into Shottle after Hanging Gate pub on right, over x-rds & right

Located within the Chatsworth Estates at Shottle, on an elevated position with stunning views, this impressive Georgian house and outbuildings have been renovated to provide high standards of

continued

comfort and facilities. Original features are enhanced by quality decor and furnishings, and the bedrooms are filled with a wealth of thoughtful extras. One room has an outdoor hot tub. The Mixing Place restaurant is the setting for imaginative dinners and memorable breakfasts, which use the finest local produce.

Facilities 8 en suite (1 fmly) (2 GF) ✆ in bedrooms ✆ in dining room ✆ in 1 lounge TVB tea/coffee Direct dial from bedrooms ✖ Licensed Cen ht hot-tub, sauna 154 acres mixed Dinner Last d noon

Prices S £65-£100; D £100-£170❋ **LB Conf** Max 14 Thtr 14 Class 14 Board 14 Del £135 ❋ **Parking** 20 **Notes** Closed 24-26 Dec Civ Wed 50

See advertisement on this page

♦♦♦♦

Top Stable Cottage

Derbyhill House, Cross o'th Hands, Turnditch DE56 2LT

☎ 01773 550489

e-mail jane@derbyhill.co.uk

Dir 300/400yds south of the A517 at Cross o'th Hands. Derbyhill House on left after T-junct

Guests are warmly welcomed at this smart cottage, peacefully located a short drive from the Peak District, Matlock and Ashbourne. Adjoining the main house, the self-contained apartment is ideal for business and leisure. Accommodation comprises a spacious sitting-dining room with DVD, video and CD player, a well-equipped kitchen and an en-suite double bedroom.

Facilities 1 en suite ✆ ✖ Cen ht TVL No children No coaches **Parking** 2 **Notes** ✆

BELPER continued

◆◆◆◆ ⅋

Chevin Green Farm ◇ *(SK339471)*

Chevin Rd DE56 2UN ☎ 01773 822328 🖨 01773 822328
Mr & Mrs Postles
e-mail spostles@globalnet.co.uk
web www.chevingreenfarm.org.uk
Dir Off A6 opp Strutt Arms at Milford onto Chevin Rd, 1.5m on left

You can be sure of a warm welcome at this 300-year-old farm
overlooking the Derwent valley. Bedrooms are furnished with
thoughtful extras and smart modern bathrooms. There is a
comfortable lounge, and breakfast is served at separate tables in the
cosy dining room. Self-catering units are also available.

Facilities 6 en suite (1 fmly) (2 GF) ⊗ TVB tea/coffee ✖ Cen ht TVL
38 acres non-working **Prices** S £30-£35; D £50-£56✱ **Parking** 6
Notes Closed Xmas/New Year

◆◆◆

The Hollins ◇

45 Belper Ln DE56 2UQ ☎ 01773 823955
Dir A6 onto A517 W, over bridge, right onto Belper Ln, 300yds up hill

This immaculate house is a 10-minute walk from the town centre. The
bedrooms are equipped with many extras, and the dining room can
be used for evening work or take-away food. The full English breakfast
is a highlight.

Facilities 2 rms (1 fmly) ⊗ TVB tea/coffee ✖ Cen ht No children 4yrs
No coaches **Prices** S £28-£30; D £48-£50 **Parking** 1 **Notes** 🖼

BIRCH VALE   MAP 16 SK08

Ⓤ ◀

The Waltzing Weasel Inn

8 New Mills Rd SK22 1BT
☎ 01663 734402 🖨 01663 744397
e-mail w-weasel@zen.co.uk
web www.w-weasel.co.uk

At the time of going to press the rating for this establishment had not
been confirmed. Please check the AA website www.theAA.com for up-
to-date information.

Facilities 8 en suite (1 fmly) (2 GF) ⊗ in bedrooms ⊗ in dining room
TVB tea/coffee Cen ht Dinner Last d 9pm **Prices** S £48-£55;
D £75-£90✱ **LB Conf** Thtr 15 Class 12 Board 10 Del from £80 ✱
Parking 42

BONSALL   MAP 16 SK25

◆◆◆◆

Pig of Lead

Via Gellia Rd DE4 2AJ ☎ 01629 820040 🖨 01629 820040
e-mail pigoflead@aol.com
*Dir A6 Cromford onto A5012 Cromford Hill turn right onto Water Ln
for 0.3m.*

This delightful property dating back over two hundred years was once
an inn named after the measurement of lead mined locally. Only

continued

5 minutes from Matlock Bath, this is a good base for exploring the
area. The individually styled bedrooms are well appointed. A warm
welcome and hearty breakfasts featuring local produce are assured
here.

Facilities 3 en suite ⊗ TVB tea/coffee ✖ Cen ht No children 14yrs
No coaches **Prices** S £40; D £55✱ **Parking** 3 **Notes** 🖼

BRADWELL   MAP 16 SK18

◆◆◆◆ ◀

The Old Bowling Green Inn

Smalldale, Bradwell S33 9JQ
☎ 01433 620450 🖨 01433 620280
*Dir Off A623 onto B6049 to Bradwell. Onto Gore Ln by playing field
to Smalldale & inn*

Located in the unspoiled hamlet of Smalldale, this traditional inn is a
focal point within the community for its home-cooked food and real
ales. The attractive pine-furnished bedrooms are in a converted barn
and breakfasts feature own free-range eggs.

Facilities 6 en suite (3 GF) ⊗ in bedrooms ⊗ in dining room TVB
tea/coffee ✖ Cen ht Pool Table Dinner Last d 9pm **Prices** S £45-£55;
D £70-£75 **LB Parking** 40

BROUGH   MAP 16 SK18

◆◆◆◆ ◀

Travellers Rest ◇

Brough Ln Head S33 9HG
☎ 01433 620363 🖨 01433 623338
e-mail elliottstephen@btconnect.com
Dir On A6187/B6049 junct

On the main road approaching the village of Hope, this stone inn has
been refurbished to modern requirements. Open fires burn in the
winter in the bar, which is popular with locals, and a wide range of bar
food is also available. An excellent base for touring the Peak District.

Facilities 5 en suite ⊗ in bedrooms ⊗ in area of dining room TVB
tea/coffee Cen ht No coaches Dinner Last d 9pm **Prices** S £30-£40;
D £50-£70✱ **Parking** 50 **Notes** Closed 25 Dec rs Nov-Mar

BUXTON

MAP 16 SK07

Premier Collection

◆◆◆◆◆ ≣ ⊜

Grendon Guest House ◇

Bishops Ln SK17 6UN ☎ 01298 78831 🖹 01298 79257
e-mail grendonguesthouse@hotmail.com
web www.grendonguesthouse.co.uk
Dir 0.75m from Buxton centre, just off A53, St Johns Rd, turn before
Duke of York pub & lights leaving town

A warm welcome is assured at this non-smoking Edwardian house, set
in immaculate grounds just a short walk from the town centre. The
spacious, carefully furnished bedrooms are filled with thoughtful extras
and lots of local information. Stunning country views can be enjoyed
from the elegant lounge-dining room, where imaginative dinners are
served. The attractive breakfast roooom is the setting for
comprehensive breakfasts using local produce.

Facilities 4 rms (3 en suite) ⊗ TVB tea/coffee Cen ht TVL No children
10yrs No coaches Dinner Last d 6pm **Prices** S £30-£35; D £60-£85 **LB**
Parking 8 **Notes** Closed 3-20 Jan

Premier Collection

◆◆◆◆◆

Buxton's Victorian Guest House

3A Broad Wk SK17 6JE ☎ 01298 78759 🖹 01298 74732
e-mail buxtonvictorian@btconnect.com
web www.buxtonvictorian.co.uk
Dir Signs to Opera House, proceed to Old Hall Hotel. Right onto
Hartington Rd, car park 100yds on right

Standing in a prime position overlooking the Pavilion Gardens, this
delightfully furnished house has an interesting Victorian style.
Bedrooms are individually themed and have many thoughtful extras,
and a comfortable lounge is available. Excellent breakfasts are served
in the Oriental breakfast room and hospitality is first class.

Facilities 8 en suite (2 fmly) (1 GF) ⊗ TVB tea/coffee Cen ht
No children 4yrs No coaches **Prices** S £46-£74; D £64-£88✳ **LB**
Parking 8 **Notes** Closed 22 Dec-12 Jan

◆◆◆◆

The Grosvenor House

1 Broad Wk SK17 6JE ☎ 01298 72439 🖹 01298 214185
e-mail grosvenor.buxton@btopenworld.com
Dir In town centre

This Victorian house is centrally located overlooking the Pavilion
Gardens and Opera House. Bedrooms are carefully furnished and
have many thoughtful extras. There is a comfortable period-style
sitting room, and freshly prepared imaginative breakfasts are served in
the cosy dining room.

Facilities 8 en suite (1 fmly) ⊗ TVB tea/coffee Cen ht No coaches
Prices S £40-£50; D £55-£80✳ **LB** **Parking** 2 **Notes** Closed Xmas

◆◆◆◆

Oldfield

8 Macclesfield Rd SK17 9AH ☎ 01298 78264
e-mail aavril@oldfieldhousebuxton.co.uk
web www.oldfieldhousebuxton.co.uk
Dir On B5059 0.5m SW of town centre

Located on a leafy, mainly residential avenue within easy walking
distance of the centre, this impressive Victorian house provides
spacious bedrooms with modern en suites. Comprehensive breakfasts
are served in the bright dining room, and a cosy lounge is available.

Facilities 4 en suite (1 GF) ⊗ TVB tea/coffee Cen ht TVL
No children 5yrs No coaches **Prices** D £66-£74✳ **LB** **Parking** 7
Notes Closed Xmas & New Year

BUXTON continued

◆◆◆◆
Roseleigh Hotel

19 Broad Wk SK17 6JR ☎ 01298 24904 📠 01298 24904
e-mail enquiries@roseleighhotel.co.uk
web www.roseleighhotel.co.uk
Dir A6 to Safeway rdbt, onto Dale Rd, right at lights, 100yds left by Swan pub, down hill & right onto Hartington Rd

This elegant property has a prime location overlooking Pavilion Gardens, and quality furnishings and decor highlight the original features. Thoughtfully furnished bedrooms have smart modern shower rooms and a comfortable lounge is also available.

Facilities 14 rms (12 en suite) (2 pri facs) (1 GF) ⊘ TVB tea/coffee ✖ Cen ht No children 6yrs No coaches **Prices** S £33-£80; D £66-£80 **Parking** 9 **Notes** Closed 16 Dec-16 Jan

See advertisement on page 143

◆◆◆◆
Linden Lodge

31 Temple Rd SK17 9BA ☎ 01298 27591
e-mail info@lindentreelodge.co.uk
Dir Brown signs to Pooles Cavern, Temple Rd opp car park
Facilities 2 rms (1 en suite) (1 pri facs) ⊘ tea/coffee ✖ Cen ht TVL No children 5yrs No coaches **Prices** D £48-£52✳ **Parking** 3 **Notes** Closed 25 Dec-1 Jan 🚭

◆◆◆
Wellhead Farm

Wormhill SK17 8SL ☎ 01298 871023 📠 0871 236 0267
e-mail wellhead4bunkntrough@cbits.net
Dir Between Bakewell and Buxton. Off A6 onto B6049 signed Millers Dale/Tideswell & left to Wormhill

This 16th-century farmhouse is in a peaceful location, and has low beams and two comfortable lounges. The bedrooms, some with four-poster beds, come with radios, beverage trays and many thoughtful extras. The proprietors provide friendly and attentive hospitality in their delightful home.

Facilities 4 en suite (1 fmly) ⊘ in bedrooms ⊘ in dining room ⊘ in 1 lounge tea/coffee Cen ht TVL No coaches Dinner Last d 9am **Prices** S £40-£46; D £60-£68 **LB Parking** 4 **Notes** 🚭

◆◆◆
Old Manse ◇

6 Clifton Rd, Silverlands SK17 6QL ☎ 01298 25638
e-mail old_manse@yahoo.co.uk
web www.oldmanse.co.uk
Dir From A6 approach Buxton via Morrisons rdbt onto B5059 Dale Rd, 200yds before bridge right onto Peveril Rd & Clifton Rd

Close to the town centre, this large semi-detached house offers good-value accommodation with well-equipped bedrooms. There is a cosy sitting room, and the bar-dining room serves breakfast and set dinners.

Facilities 7 rms (6 en suite) (1 pri facs) (2 fmly) ⊘ TVB tea/coffee ✖ Licensed Cen ht No coaches Dinner Last d 4pm **Prices** S £20-£25; D £44-£52✳ **LB Parking** 4 **Notes** Closed 20-31Dec

CALVER   MAP 16 SK27

◆◆◆◆
Valley View

Smithy Knoll Rd S32 3XW ☎ 01433 631407
e-mail sue@a-place-2-stay.co.uk
web www.a-place-2-stay.co.uk
Dir A623 from Baslow into Calver, 3rd left onto Donkey Ln

This detached stone house is in the heart of the village. It is very well-furnished throughout and delightfully friendly service is provided. A hearty breakfast is served in the cosy dining room, which is well-stocked with local guide books.

Facilities 3 en suite (1 fmly) ⊘ TVB tea/coffee Cen ht No children 5yrs No coaches **Prices** S £45-£65; D £60-£90 **LB Parking** 6

CARSINGTON   MAP 16 SK25

◆◆◆◆
Henmore Grange

Hopton DE4 4DF ☎ 01629 540420 📠 01629 540420
e-mail henmoregrange@hotmail.com
web www.henmoregrange.co.uk
Dir B5035 into Hopton, Henmore Grange 2nd house on left

Located very close to Carsington Water, this restored stone farmhouse retains many original features. The spacious lounge is a feature with its stone fireplace and wood-burning stove. Breakfast is served in the farmhouse-style dining room, and the comfortable bedrooms are well-appointed. A good touring base with secure cycle storage.

Facilities 3 en suite ⊘ TVB tea/coffee ✖ Cen ht TVL No coaches **Prices** S £40-£60; d fr £60 **LB Parking** 8 **Notes** Closed 17-31 Dec 🚭

Book as early as possible, particularly in the peak holiday period

CASTLETON
MAP 16 SK18

See also **Hope**

◆◆◆◆

The Rising Sun Hotel

Thornhill Moor, Bamford S33 0AL
☎ 01433 651323 📠 01433 651601
e-mail info@the-rising-sun.org
web www.the-rising-sun.org
Dir On A625 from Sheffield to Castleton

Located at Thornhill Moor within the Hope Valley, this 18th-century inn has been renovated to provide high standards of comfort and facilities. Spacious luxury bedrooms offer quality furnishings and efficient modern bathrooms, and some have stunning views of the surrounding countryside. The staff are friendly and capable, and imaginative food is offered in the comfortable public areas.

Facilities 12 en suite (2 fmly) ⊗ in bedrooms ⊗ in area of dining room ⊗ in 1 lounge TVB tea/coffee Cen ht Dinner Last d 10pm **Conf** Max 200 Thtr 200 Class 200 Board 24 **Parking** 120 **Notes** Civ Wed 220

See advertisement under Preliminary Section

◆◆◆◆

The Peaks Inn

How Ln S33 8WJ ☎ 01433 620247 📠 01433 623590
e-mail info@peaks-inn.co.uk
web www.peaks-inn.co.uk
Dir In village centre

Located in the heart of Castleton, the Peaks Inn has been renovated to provide spacious, carefully furnished bedrooms with smart modern bathrooms en suite. Open-plan public areas offer character and comfort and there is an attractive beer garden.

Facilities 4 en suite ⊗ in bedrooms ⊗ in area of dining room ⊗ in 1 lounge TVB tea/coffee Direct dial from bedrooms 🍴 Cen ht TVL Dinner Last d 9pm **Prices** D £65-£90 **LB** **Parking** 40

◆◆◆

Losehill Hall

Peak District National Pk, Study Cen S33 8WB
☎ 01433 620373 📠 01433 620346
e-mail jackie.delaney@peakdistrict.gov.uk
web www.peakdistrict.org
Dir Signed off A6187 through Hope Valley

Located in 27 acres of mature gardens and farmland, this Grade II listed building has been a centre for environmental awarness for over 25 years. Study-style bedrooms have smart modern en suites, and the wholesome dinners feature fresh local produce. A comfortable lounge and a selection of meeting rooms are available.

Facilities 41 rms (40 en suite) (1 pri facs) (3 fmly) (3 GF) ⊗ 🍴 Licensed Cen ht TVL 27 acres of Victorian garden & parkland Dinner Last d day before **Prices** S £35; D £70✳ **LB** **Conf** Max 72 Del from £85 ✳ **Parking** 50 **Notes** Closed 19 Dec-4 Jan Civ Wed 120

CHESTERFIELD
MAP 16 SK37

◆◆◆◆ ☕

Hornbeam House

Mile Hill, Mansfield Rd, Hasland S41 0JN
☎ 01246 556851 & 07778 394735 📠 0870 052 1647
e-mail enquiries@hornbeamhouse4t.demon.co.uk
Dir M1 junct 29, A617 towards Chesterfield, 1.5m 1st exit turn left at top of slip road, 200yds turn right towards Hasland. Hornbeam House 0.75m on right

Convenient for the M1, Chesterfield and for touring, this large suburban detached house stands in substantial grounds. Attentive and helpful service is the hallmark, and fresh and healthy cooking is enjoyed at breakfast and dinner.

Facilities 2 en suite ⊗ tea/coffee 🍴 Cen ht TVL No coaches Dinner Last d 10am **Prices** S £35-£43; D £55-£71✳ **Conf** Max 12 **Parking** 3

CHESTERFIELD continued

♦♦♦♦ A

Bateman's Mill Country Hotel & Restaurant

Mill Ln, Old Tupton S42 6AE
☎ 01246 862296 ▤ 01246 865672
e-mail info@batemansmill.co.uk

Dir 6.5m S of Chesterfield. Off A61 at Clay Cross onto Holmgate Rd to Valley Rd & Mill Ln

Facilities 8 en suite (1 fmly) (4 GF) ⊗ in bedrooms ⊗ in dining room ⊗ in 1 lounge STV TVB tea/coffee Direct dial from bedrooms Licensed Cen ht Dinner Last d 9.30pm **Prices** S £65-£80; D £75-£80 **LB**
Conf Max 50 Thtr 50 Class 30 Board 30 Del from £100 ✳ **Parking** 50
Notes Closed 1st wk Jan

See advertisement on page 145

CROMFORD   MAP 16 SK25

U

Alison House

Intake Ln DE4 3RH ☎ 01629 822211 ▤ 01629 822316
e-mail alisonhouse@toch.org.uk

At the time of going to press the rating for this establishment had not been confirmed. Please check the AA website www.theAA.com for up-to-date information.

Facilities 15 en suite (1 fmly) ⊗ TVB tea/coffee Direct dial from bedrooms ✖ Licensed Cen ht TVL No coaches ◖ Dinner Last d 9pm
Conf Max 40 Thtr 40 Class 40 Board 40 **Parking** 30 **Notes** Civ Wed 50

DARLEY DALE   MAP 16 SK26

♦♦♦♦

Meadow House ◇

Dale Rd North DE4 2HX ☎ 01629 734324
Dir On A6 Matlock to Bakewell, on left

Located within a short distance of Matlock, this friendly, non-smoking house stands in grounds and is well furnished throughout. You can enjoy substantial tasty breakfasts in the cosy lounge-dining room.

Facilities 3 rms (2 en suite) (1 pri facs) (1 fmly) ⊗ TVB tea/coffee ✖ Cen ht No children 8yrs No coaches **Prices** S £30; D £46-£58✳
Parking 6 **Notes** ⌾

DERBY   MAP 11 SK33

See also **Belper & Melbourne**

♦♦♦

Chambers House ◇

110 Green Ln DE1 1RY ☎ 01332 746412
Dir In city centre opp Metro Cinema. Approach car park via Abbey St & Wilson St

Located a short walk from the centre, this impressive double-fronted Victorian house retains many original features. The attractive bedrooms are generally spacious, some having modern shower rooms en suite. A car park is available.

Facilities 10 rms (4 en suite) (2 fmly) (2 GF) ⊗ TVB tea/coffee ✖ TVL No coaches **Prices** S fr £28; d fr £58✳ **Parking** 6 **Notes** ⌾

♦♦♦

Rangemoor Park Hotel

67 Macklin St DE1 1LF ☎ 01332 347252 ▤ 01332 369319
e-mail res@rangemoorpark.freeserve.co.uk
Dir In city centre off Abbey St & Becket St

Located within easy walking distance of Pride Park Stadium, this commercial establishment has been in the same family ownership for 25 years, providing traditional standards of service and hospitality. A range of standard and executive bedrooms is offered and the spacious secure car park is an advantage.

Facilities 24 rms (13 en suite) (3 fmly) ⊗ in dining room TVB tea/coffee Direct dial from bedrooms Cen ht TVL **Parking** 37 **Notes** Closed Xmas & New Year

♦♦♦

The Rose & Thistle Guest House ◇

21 Charnwood St DE1 2GU
☎ 01332 344103 ▤ 01332 291006
Dir Close to Derby Royal Infirmary hospital

Just a short walk from the city centre, this Victorian terrace house is situated on the inner ring road. Rooms are pleasantly decorated and a warm welcome is provided. Breakfast is served in a light, modern dining room.

Facilities 8 rms (2 en suite) (5 fmly) (1 GF) ⊗ TVB tea/coffee ✖ Cen ht No coaches **Prices** S £25-£35; D £40-£50✳ **Notes** ⌾

ELTON   MAP 16 SK26

♦♦♦

Elton Guest House

Moor Ln DE4 2DA ☎ 01629 650217

Located within the heart of the village, the 17th-century former farmhouse has been renovated to provide spacious period-furnished bedrooms with four-poster beds. Comprehensive breakfasts are served in a pine-furnished dining room adorned with antique advertising memorabilia, which is open as a cafe at weekends. Self-catering cottages are also available.

Facilities 2 rms (2 pri facs) (1 fmly) ⊗ in dining room ⊗ in lounges TVB tea/coffee ✖ Cen ht No coaches **Parking** 6 **Notes** ⌾

continued

FROGGATT

MAP 16 SK27

◆◆◆◆

The Chequers Inn

S32 3ZJ ☎ 01433 630231 ▤ 01433 631072
e-mail info@chequers-froggatt.com
Dir On A625 between Sheffield & Bakewell

A very popular 16th-century inn offering an extensive range of well-cooked food. The bedrooms are comprehensively equipped with modern comforts and the hospitality is professional and sincere. A good location for touring Derbyshire.

Facilities 5 en suite ⊗ TVB tea/coffee Direct dial from bedrooms 🐾 Cen ht No coaches Dinner Last d 9.15pm **Prices** S £70-£95; D £70-£95※ LB **Parking** 45 **Notes** Closed 25 Dec

GLOSSOP

MAP 16 SK09

◆◆◆◆

Woodlands

Woodseats Ln, Charlesworth SK13 5DP ☎ 01457 866568
e-mail mairs@lineone.net
web www.woodlandshighpeak.co.uk
Dir 3m SW of Glossop. Off A626, 0.5m from Charlesworth towards Marple

This delightful Victorian house stands in well-tended grounds and offers very well-equipped and delightfully furnished bedrooms. There is a comfy lounge and a conservatory where very good breakfasts are served. Hospitality is a major strength here and Judy Mairs is a top-twenty finalist for AA Landlady of the Year 2006.

Facilities 3 rms (2 en suite) (1 pri facs) ⊗ TVB tea/coffee 🐾 Licensed Cen ht TVL No children 12yrs No coaches **Prices** S £40-£45; D £55-£65 **Parking** 6 **Notes** ⊠

◆◆◆◆ ❦

Rock Farm ♦ (SK027907)

Monks Rd SK13 6JZ
☎ 01457 861086 & 07780 670568 ▤ 01457 861086
Mrs Dennett
e-mail rockfarmbandb@btinternet.com
Dir Off A624 onto Monks Rd, signed Charlesworth. After 1m, Rock Farm on left, follow farm track past Higher Plainsteads Farm

The family home is located down a winding track, with spectacular views over Kinder Scout and the surrounding hills from all rooms.

Walkers, horses, and riders, as well as young families, are offered a particularly warm welcome. Fresh eggs are used at breakfast.

Facilities 2 rms ⊗ TVB tea/coffee Cen ht TVL Grazing & stabling for guests horses 6 acres non-working Dinner Last d notice required **Prices** S £30; D £50※ **Parking** 4 **Notes** ⊠

◆◆◆

Kings Clough Head Farm ♦

Back Rowarth SK13 6ED ☎ 01457 862668
e-mail kingscloughheadfarm@hotmail.com
Dir Monks Rd off A624 near Grouse Inn

Situated in the hills with stunning country views, this 18th-century stone house provides thoughtfully furnished bedrooms and a modern efficient bathroom. Breakfast is served at one table in an antique-furnished dining room and a warm welcome is assured.

Facilities 3 rms ⊗ TVB tea/coffee Cen ht TVL No coaches **Prices** S fr £25; d fr £46 **Parking** 4 **Notes** Closed Xmas ⊠

◆◆◆

The Old House ♦

Woodhead Rd, Torside SK13 1HU ☎ 01457 857527
e-mail oldhouse@torside.co.uk
Dir From A57 or A628 take B6105 for 3m, B&B between sailing club and hairpin bend.

Nestling on the slopes above a reservoir, this smallholding has superb views and offers all mod. cons, including a drying room for walkers on the Pennine Way. The oak beams and rough plastered walls date from the 17th century, and hospitality is warm.

Facilities 3 en suite (1 fmly) (1 GF) ⊗ in bedrooms ⊗ in dining room ⊗ in lounges tea/coffee Cen ht TVL No coaches **Prices** S £30-£50; D £50※ LB **Parking** 5 **Notes** ⊠

◆◆◆

Peakdale Lodge

49-53 High St East SK13 8PN
☎ 01457 854109 ▤ 01457 857080
Dir On A57 in town centre near leisure centre

This well-furnished guest house is in the centre of the town and offers friendly hospitality. Bedrooms have modern shower rooms and comprehensive breakfasts are served in the attractive dining room. A pretty rear patio garden is a feature during the summer.

Facilities 9 en suite (2 fmly) (1 GF) ⊗ in bedrooms ⊗ in dining room ⊗ in 1 lounge TVB tea/coffee Cen ht **Notes** ⊠

◆◆◆

White House Farm

Padfield SK13 1ET ☎ 01457 854695 ▤ 01457 854695
Dir A628 from Sheffield to Tintwistle, signed to Padfield

A 200-year-old farmhouse standing on the edge of Padfield village with fine views across Longdendale. The bedrooms are pleasantly furnished and breakfast is served around a large table in the dining room. There is a lounge and ample parking.

Facilities 1 rms 2 annexe rms (1 GF) ⊗ in 1 bedrooms ⊗ in dining room TVB tea/coffee Cen ht TVL No coaches **Parking** 10 **Notes** ⊠

continued

England

GREAT HUCKLOW
MAP 16 SK17

◆◆◆

The Queen Anne
SK17 8RF ☎ 01298 871246
e-mail mal@thequeenanne.net
Dir *Off A623 onto B6049 to Great Hucklow*

Set in the heart of this pretty village, the Queen Anne has been a licensed inn for over 300 years and the public areas retain many original features. The cosy bedrooms are in a separate building and have modern shower rooms en suite.

Facilities 2 annexe en suite (2 GF) ⊗ in bedrooms ⊗ in area of dining room ⊗ in 1 lounge TVB tea/coffee Cen ht Dinner Last d 8.30pm **Prices** D £60-£65✱ **Parking** 30

HARTINGTON
MAP 16 SK16

◆◆◆

Bank House ◇
Market Pl SK17 0AL ☎ 01298 84465
Dir *B5054 into village centre*

Bank House is a very well-maintained Grade II listed Georgian building and stands in the main square of this delightful village. Bedrooms are neat and fresh in appearance, and there is a comfortable television lounge. A hearty breakfast is served in the ground-floor cottage-style dining room.

Facilities 5 rms (3 en suite) (3 fmly) ⊗ TVB tea/coffee ✻ Cen ht TVL No coaches Dinner Last d noon **Prices** S £23-£30; D £44-£50✱ **LB** **Parking** 2 **Notes** Closed Xmas rs 22-28 Dec ⊠

HATHERSAGE
MAP 16 SK28

◆◆◆◆

Cannon Croft
Cannonfields S32 1AG ☎ 01433 650005
e-mail soates@cannoncroft.fsbusiness.co.uk
web www.cannoncroft.fsbusiness.co.uk
Dir *From George Hotel in village centre, 150yds W right onto single-track lane before bridge, Cannon Croft 130yds*

Set on the edge of the village with superb views of the surrounding countryside, this non-smoking home offers well-furnished and comprehensively equipped en suite bedrooms. An extensive choice of carefully prepared breakfasts is served in the conservatory-lounge. The enthusiastic hosts always offer a warm welcome.

continued

Facilities 3 en suite (1 fmly) (3 GF) ⊗ TVB tea/coffee ✻ Cen ht No children 12yrs No coaches sun terrace garden **Prices** S £48-£60; D £54-£65✱ **LB** **Parking** 5 **Notes** ⊠

◆◆◆◆ ♥

Hillfoot Farm *(SK226815)*
Castleton Rd S32 1EG ☎ 01433 651673 Mrs Wilcockson
e-mail hillfootfarm@hotmail.com
Dir *On A625 0.5m W from Hathersage on right*

This 16th-century former inn and tollhouse is at the end of an old packhorse route, and you can expect a welcome from the friendly dog. The house has been extended to offer spacious bedrooms and there is also a cosy lounge. Breakfast is served in the adjacent beamed dining room. This is a non-smoking establishment.

Facilities 4 en suite (1 fmly) (2 GF) ⊗ TVB tea/coffee ✻ Cen ht No children 12yrs **Prices** S £35-£60; D £52-£60✱ **LB** **Parking** 12 **Notes** ⊠

◆◆◆◆

Millstone
Sheffield Rd S32 1DA ☎ 01433 650258 ▤ 01433 651664
e-mail jerry@millstone.co.uk
web www.millstoneinn.co.uk
Dir *On A6187 from Sheffield, 0.5m before reaching Hathersage*

This timber and stone inn stands on an elevated position overlooking the Hope Valley. It offers modern, well-equipped bedrooms, and real ales and exciting food are served in the friendly bar. The smart Terrace fish restaurant offers fine dining with great views over the valley. Wireless Internet and free use of the local gym are benefits.

Facilities 7 en suite (2 fmly) ⊗ in bedrooms ⊗ in dining room ⊗ in 1 lounge TVB tea/coffee Direct dial from bedrooms Cen ht Gym membership free to guests Dinner Last d 9.30pm **Prices** S £45-£55✱ **LB** **Conf** Max 40 Thtr 40 Class 60 Board 40 **Parking** 80

◆◆◆◆ ◉ ⊟

The Plough Inn
Leadmill Br S32 1BA ☎ 01433 650319 ▤ 01433 651049
e-mail sales@theploughinn-hathersage.co.uk
Dir *1m SE of Hathersage on B6001. Over bridge, 150yds beyond at Leadmill*

This delightful 16th-century inn with beer garden has an idyllic location by the River Derwent. A selection of real ales and imaginative food is served in the spacious public areas, and original open fires and

continued

exposed beams have been preserved. The thoughtfully equipped, well-appointed bedrooms include two impressive suites.

Plough

Facilities 3 en suite 2 annexe en suite (1 GF) ⊗ TVB tea/coffee Direct dial from bedrooms ✻ Cen ht No coaches Dinner Last d 9.30pm LB **Parking** 50 **Notes** Closed 25 Dec

♦♦♦♦

The Scotsman's Pack Inn

School Ln S32 1BZ ☎ 01433 650253 📠 01433 650253
e-mail nickbeagriel@ukonline.co.uk
Dir *A625 into Heathersage, onto School Ln towards the church, Scotsmans Pack 100yds on right*

This comfortable inn on the edge of the village provides a wide range of well-prepared food. The bedrooms are compact, well-furnished and have been thoughtfully equipped, while the bar, which contains Little John's chair, is a great place to meet the locals. Hearty breakfasts are served in the separate dining room, and the staff are very friendly.

Facilities 5 en suite ⊗ in bedrooms ⊗ in area of dining room TVB tea/coffee Cen ht Dinner Last d 9pm **Prices** S fr £35; d fr £65 LB **Conf** Max 20 **Parking** 17

♦♦♦

Moorgate

Castleton Rd S32 1EH ☎ 01433 650293
Dir *On A6187 towards Hope, 100yds past George Hotel on right before railway bridge*

This large Victorian house stands in attractive gardens just a short walk from the village centre. Traditionally furnished, spacious bedrooms come with interesting books and original artwork. Breakfast is served in the lounge-dining room overlooking the delightful front garden.

Facilities 3 rms ⊗ TVB tea/coffee ✻ Cen ht No coaches **Parking** 3 **Notes** ⊛

♦♦♦♦

Spinney Cottage B&B ◇

Spinnerbottom SK22 1BL ☎ 01663 743230
Dir *A6 onto A6015 towards Hayfield, 2m turn left, 400yds on right*

Spinney Cottage lies a short distance from the picturesque village of Hayfield and is a good base for touring. Hospitality is warm, the attractive bedrooms are well equipped, and hearty breakfasts are served in the cottage-style dining room.

Facilities 3 rms (2 en suite) (1 pri facs) (1 fmly) ⊗ TVB tea/coffee ✻ Cen ht TVL No coaches **Prices** S £25; D £50✳ **Notes** Closed Xmas & New Year ⊛

Premier Collection

♦♦♦♦♦ 📖

Underleigh House

Off Edale Rd S33 6RF ☎ 01433 621372 📠 01433 621324
e-mail info@underleighhouse.co.uk
web www.underleighhouse.co.uk
Dir *From village church on A6187 onto Edale Rd, 1m left onto lane*

Situated at the end of a private lane amid glorious scenery, Underleigh House was converted from a barn and cottage that date from 1873, and now offers carefully furnished and attractive bedrooms with modern facilities. One room has a private lounge and others have access to the gardens. The very spacious lounge has comfortable chairs and a welcoming log fire. Memorable breakfasts are served at one large table in the dining room.

Facilities 6 en suite (2 GF) ⊗ TVB tea/coffee Direct dial from bedrooms Licensed Cen ht TVL No children 12yrs No coaches **Prices** S £50-£55; D £70-£90 LB **Parking** 6 **Notes** Closed Xmas, New Year & 8-31 Jan

Always confirm details with the establishment when booking

England

HOPE continued

♦♦♦♦

Stoney Ridge

Granby Rd, Bradwell S33 9HU ☎ 01433 620538
e-mail toneyridge@aol.com
web www.cressbrook.co.uk/hopev/stoneyridge
Dir *From N end of Bradwell onto Town Ln, left at x-rds, left onto Granby Rd*

This large, split-level bungalow stands in mature gardens at the highest part of the village and has extensive views. Hens and ducks roam freely and their fresh eggs add to the hearty breakfasts. Bedrooms are attractively furnished and thoughtfully equipped, and there is a spacious lounge and a superb indoor swimming pool.

Facilities 4 rms (3 en suite) (1 pri facs) ✆ in dining room TVB tea/coffee Cen ht TVL No children 10yrs No coaches ⌦ **Prices** S £40; D £65✱ **LB Parking** 3

♦♦♦ ❦

Round Meadow Barn ◇ (SK189836)

Parsons Ln S33 6RB
☎ 01433 621347 & 07836 689422 ▤ 01433 621347
Mr & Mrs Harris
e-mail rmbarn@bigfoot.com
Dir *Off A625 Hope Rd N onto Parsons Ln, over railway bridge, 200yds right into Hay barnyard, through gates, across 3 fields, house on left*

This converted barn, with original stone walls and exposed timbers, stands in open fields in the picturesque Hope Valley. The bedrooms are large enough for families and there are two modern bathrooms. Breakfast is served at one large table adjoining the family kitchen.

Facilities 4 rms (1 en suite) (1 fmly) ✆ TVB tea/coffee Golf Riding 4 acres non-working **Prices** S £30-£35; D £50-£60✱ **LB Parking** 8
Notes ✆

LONGFORD

MAP 10 SK23

♦♦♦♦

Russets ◇

Off Main St DE6 3DR ☎ 01335 330874 ▤ 01335 330874
e-mail geoffreynolan@btinternet.com
web www.russets.com
Dir *A516 in Hatton onto Sutton Ln, at T-junct right onto Long Ln, next right into Longford & right before phone box on Main St*

An indoor swimming pool is available at this beautifully maintained bungalow, which is in a peaceful location near Alton Towers. Bedrooms are well equipped and have smart modern bathrooms. Comprehensive breakfasts are served at a family table in the homely dining room, and a comfortable lounge is available.

Facilities 2 en suite (1 fmly) (2 GF) ✆ STV TVB tea/coffee Cen ht TVL No coaches ⌦ Gymnasium **Prices** S £30-£50; D £50✱ **Parking** 4
Notes Closed 3rd wk Dec-1st wk Jan ✆

MARSTON MONTGOMERY

MAP 10 SK13

★★★★ ◉ **Inn**

The Crown Inn

Riggs Ln DE6 2FF ☎ 01889 590541 ▤ 01889 591576
e-mail info@thecrowninn-derbyshire.co.uk
Dir *From A50, take A515 N towards Ashbourne. At Cubley, turn left to Marston Montgomery and left into village.*

This lovely inn stands at the heart of the peaceful village and provides modern bedrooms with informal dining in the bar and brasserie. Cooking shows much flair and imagination and the staff are friendly and caring.

Facilities 7 en suite (3 fmly) ✆ in bedrooms ✆ in dining room TVB tea/coffee ✖ Cen ht Pool Table Dinner Last d 9.30pm
Prices S £45-£50; D £55-£70✱ **Parking** 16 **Notes** Closed 25 Dec & 1 Jan rs Sun

MATLOCK

MAP 16 SK35

♦♦♦♦ ⇔

Holmefield

Dale Rd North, Darley Dale DE4 2HY ☎ 01629 735347
e-mail holmefieldguesthouse@btinternet.com
web www.holmefieldguesthouse.co.uk
Dir *Between Bakewell & Matlock on A6. 1m from Rowsley & Chatsworth Estate, 0.5m from Peak Rail*

Standing in mature grounds between Matlock and Bakewell, this elegant Victorian house has been furnished with flair to offer good levels of comfort and facilities. Imaginative dinners feature seasonal local produce, some from the Chatsworth Estate, and warm hospitality and attentive service are assured.

Facilities 4 en suite (2 fmly) ✆ TVB tea/coffee ✖ Cen ht No coaches Dinner Last d 11am **Parking** 4 **Notes** Closed 23 Dec-2 Jan

♦♦♦♦ ⌂

Yew Tree Cottage

The Knoll, Tansley DE4 5FP
☎ 01629 583862 & 07799 541903
e-mail enquiries@yewtreecottagebb.co.uk
web www.yewtreecottagebb.co.uk
Dir *1.2m E of Matlock. Off A615 into Tansley centre*

Located in Tansley village, this 18th-century cottage has been renovated to provide high standards of comfort while retaining original character. Memorable breakfasts are served in the elegant

continued

England

dining room and a cosy lounge is available. A warm welcome and attentive service are assured.

Yew Tree Cottage

Facilities 3 rms (1 en suite) (2 pri facs) ⊛ TVB tea/coffee ✻ Cen ht TVL No children No coaches Sauna **Prices** D £57-£70✳ **LB Parking** 3 **Notes** ⌨

◆◆◆◆

Brendon ◇

23 Snitterton Rd DE4 3LZ ☎ 01629 583310
Dir *Off A6 in Matlock by the Royal Bank of Scotland towards Snitterton, 7th house on left up hill*

Lots of local knowledge, well-equipped bedrooms and a healthy breakfast are the hallmarks of this friendly guest house. Decor throughout is bright and modern, and ample parking is available in the nearby car park.

Facilities 2 en suite ⊛ TVB tea/coffee ✻ Cen ht TVL No children 12yrs No coaches **Prices** S £30-£35; D £50-£54✳ **LB Notes** Closed Xmas & New Year ⌨

◆◆◆◆

Glendon ◇

Knowleston Pl DE4 3BU ☎ 01629 584732
Dir *Off A615 SE of town centre. Car park before Glendon B&B sign*

Non-smoking Glendon is set beside a park just a short walk from the town centre. The spacious bedrooms are pleasantly decorated and well equipped, and one is suitable for families. The comfortable third-floor lounge has lovely views over Bentley Brook and the local church.

Facilities 4 rms (2 en suite) (1 fmly) ⊛ TVB tea/coffee ✻ Cen ht TVL No children 3yrs No coaches **Prices** S £30-£35; D £50-£55✳ **Parking** 4 **Notes** Closed Dec ⌨

◆◆◆◆ ❦

Hearthstone Farm *(SK308583)*

Hearthstone Ln, Riber DE4 5JW
☎ 01629 534304 🖨 01629 534372 Mrs Gilman
e-mail enquiries@hearthstonefarm.co.uk
web www.hearthstonefarm.co.uk
Dir *A615 at Tansley 2m E of Matlock, turn opp Royal Oak towards Riber, at gates to Riber Hall left onto Riber Rd and 1st left onto Hearthstone Ln, farmhouse on left*

Situated on a stunning elevated location, this traditional stone farmhouse retains many original features and is stylishly decorated

throughout. Bedrooms are equipped with a wealth of homely extras and comprehensive breakfasts feature the farm's organic produce. There is a very comfortable lounge, and the farm animals in the grounds are an attraction.

Hearthstone Farm

Facilities 3 en suite ⊛ TVB tea/coffee Cen ht TVL 150 acres organic beef lamb pigs Dinner Last d 10am **Prices** S fr £40; d fr £130 **LB Parking** 6 **Notes** Closed Xmas & New Year ⌨

◆◆◆◆ ⌨

Hodgkinsons Hotel

150 South Pde, Matlock Bath DE4 3NR
☎ 01629 582170 🖨 01629 584891
e-mail enquiries@hodgkinsons-hotel.co.uk
Dir *On A6 in village centre*

This fine Georgian building was renovated in the Victorian period and has many interesting and unusual features. Bedrooms are equipped with fine antique furniture and a wealth of thoughtful extras. The elegant dining room is the setting for imaginative dinners and a comfortable lounge is available.

Facilities 8 en suite (1 fmly) ⊛ in 3 bedrooms ⊛ in dining room TVB tea/coffee Direct dial from bedrooms Licensed Cen ht No coaches garden Dinner Last d 8.30pm **Conf** Max 12 Thtr 12 Class 12 Board 12 **Parking** 5 **Notes** Closed 24-26 Dec

◆◆◆◆

Manor House

Wensley DE4 2LL
☎ 01629 734360 & 07831 583300 🖨 01629 734360
Dir *3m NW of Matlock. A6 onto B5057 signed Wensley, house signed on left 0.25m after Wensley sign*

Situated in 4 acres of immaculate landscaped grounds in the pretty village of Wensley, this mellow-stone Georgian cottage has many original features and is furnished with a great deal of style. Breakfast is served at one table in the cosy dining room, and a comfortable lounge and conservatory offer magnificent views of the surrounding countryside.

Facilities 2 rms ⊛ TVB tea/coffee ✻ Cen ht TVL No children 16yrs No coaches **Prices** S £35-£50; D £50-£60 **Parking** 6 **Notes** ⌨

continued

England

MATLOCK continued

◆◆◆◆

Mount Tabor House

Bowns Hill, Crich DE4 5DG
☎ 01773 857008 & 07813 007478 ▤ 01773 857008
e-mail mountabor@msn.com
Dir *Off A610 at Sawmills signed Crich, right at Market Place onto Bowns Hill. Driveway after chapel 200yds on right*

This former Victorian Methodist chapel has fine surroundings. The first floor is a spacious living-dining area, where dinner and breakfast are served at one table - leaded Gothic windows and a superb wrought-iron balcony look across the Amber Valley. Interesting meals are created from quality local and organic produce, with dietary needs willingly catered for. The two bedrooms have a useful range of facilities, and the larger room has a king-size antique pine bed.

Facilities 2 en suite (3 fmly) (1 GF) ⊗ TVB tea/coffee ✻ Cen ht
No children No coaches jacuzzi Dinner **Prices** D £72-£77 **Parking** 3
Notes Closed Xmas & New Year

◆◆◆◆

The Old Sunday School ◇

New St DE4 3FH ☎ 01629 583347 ▤ 01629 583347
e-mail davhpatrick@hotmail.com
Dir *Off A6 at Crown Sq up Bank Rd (steep) to Derby County Council Office car park, New St opp*

A warm welcome is assured at this converted Victorian chapel, built of mellow sandstone close to the centre. The homely bedroom has a modern shower room, and the spacious living area includes a period dining table, the setting for comprehensive breakfasts (and by arrangement imaginative dinners).

Facilities 1 en suite (1 fmly) ⊗ TVB tea/coffee ✻ Cen ht TVL
No coaches Dinner Last d 5pm **Prices** S £30; D £54 LB **Notes** ⊛

◆◆◆◆

Pear Tree Farm *(SK319572)*

Lea Main Rd, Lea Br DE4 5JN
☎ 01629 534215 & 07831 573688 ▤ 01629 534060
Mr & Mrs Barber
e-mail sue@derbyshirearts.co.uk
web www.derbyshirearts.co.uk
Dir *M1 junct 28, A38 S, A610 Ambergate, A6 Cromford. Turn right at lights, after 2m turn left at John Smedley Mills, 0.5m on left*

Set in 76 acres of woodland and pasture overlooking Lea Brook, this renovated farmhouse provides a range of thoughtfully furnished bedrooms, two of which have easier access. Comprehensive breakfasts are served in the oak-furnished dining room, and there is a spacious lounge with wood-burning stove and a separate art studio.

Facilities 8 en suite (1 fmly) (2 GF) ⊗ TVB tea/coffee ✻ Cen ht TVL
Studio (art based activities) 76 acres mixed, sheep Dinner Last d by prior
arrangement **Conf** Max 15 **Parking** 10

◆◆◆◆ ⊜

The Red Lion

Matlock Gn DE4 3BT ☎ 01629 584888
Dir *A632 from Matlock towards Chesterfield, car park 75yds on left*

This comfortable inn is a good base for exploring Matlock and the Derbyshire countryside. Each bedroom is furnished in quality pine. Public areas include a character bar with open fire and a restaurant offers a wide selection of meals.

Facilities 6 en suite (1 fmly) ⊗ in bedrooms ⊗ in dining room
⊗ in 1 lounge TVB tea/coffee ✻ Cen ht Pool Table Dinner Last d 9pm
Parking 20

◆◆◆◆

Woodside ◇

Stanton Lees DE4 2LQ ☎ 01629 734320 ▤ 01629 734320
e-mail derwentkk@potter8378.fsnet.co.uk
web www.stantonlees.freeserve.co.uk
Dir *4m NW of Matlock. A6 onto B5057 into Darley Bridge, opp pub right to Stanton Lees & right fork*

Located on an elevated position with stunning country views, this mellow-stone house has been renovated to provide high standards of comfort and facilities. The carefully decorated bedrooms come with a wealth of thoughtful extras, and ground-floor areas include a comfortable lounge and conservatory overlooking the garden, home to a variety of wild birds.

Facilities 3 en suite ⊗ FTV TVB tea/coffee ✗ Cen ht TVL No children 3yrs No coaches **Prices** S £30; D £48-£60✳ **Parking** 3 **Notes** ⊛

◆◆◆

Red House Carriage Museum ◇

Old Rd, Darley Dale DE4 2ER
☎ 01629 733583 ▤ 01629 733583
Dir *2m N of Matlock, left off A6, 200yds on left*

Located within a famous working carriage driving school and museum, this detached house provides homely and thoughtfully equipped bedrooms, one on the ground floor and in a former stable. Comprehensive breakfasts are served at a family table in the attractive dining room, and the comfortable lounge area overlooks spacious gardens.

Facilities 2 rms (1 en suite) 2 annexe en suite (1 fmly) (1 GF) ⊗ TVB tea/coffee ✗ Cen ht No coaches Carriage & horses trips/tuition **Prices** S £30-£40; D £65-£70 **Parking** 5 **Notes** ⊛

◆◆◆

Bradford Villa

26 Chesterfield Rd DE4 3DQ ☎ 01629 57147
Dir *On A632 towards Chesterfield, opp Lilybank Hydro-care home*

This non-smoking, semi-detached Victorian house is situated on an elevated position in neat gardens on the north edge of the town. Bedrooms are comfortably furnished and include one suitable for families. Small car park at rear.

Facilities 2 rms (1 en suite) (1 pri facs) (2 fmly) ⊗ TVB tea/coffee ✗ Cen ht No coaches **Parking** 4 **Notes** Closed 22 Dec-3 Jan ⊛

◆◆◆

Catered Cottage

Rose Cottage, Potters Hill, Wheatcroft DE4 5PH
☎ 01629 534727
e-mail cateredcottage@nutbeam.flyer.co.uk
web www.cateredcottage.com
Dir *5m SE of Matlock. Off A615 to South Wingfield, right onto Inns Lane/Potters Hill, premises 2m on right*

Located in an Area of Outstanding Natural Beauty, this pretty stone cottage with immaculate gardens has cosy, thoughtfully equipped bedrooms sharing two bathrooms. Breakfast (dinner by arrangement) is served round one table in the dining room with stunning country views. A comfortable lounge is available.

continued

Facilities 3 rms ⊗ ✗ Cen ht TVL No coaches Dinner Last d 7pm **Parking** 3 **Notes** Closed Feb

◆◆◆ ♈

Farley ◇ *(SK294622)*

Farley DE4 5LR
☎ 01629 582533 & 07801 756409 ▤ 01629 584856
Mrs Brailsford
e-mail eric.brailsford@btconnect.com
Dir *A6 Buxton/Bakewell 1st right after rdbt in Matlock. Right at top of hill, left up Farley Hill, 2nd farm on left*

You can expect a warm welcome at this traditional stone farmhouse. In addition to farming, the proprietors also breed dogs and horses. The bedrooms are pleasantly decorated and equipped with many useful extras. Breakfast is served round one large table (dinner is available by arrangement).

Facilities 2 en suite (2 fmly) ⊗ in bedrooms ⊗ in dining room ⊗ in 1 lounge TVB tea/coffee Cen ht TVL Riding 165 acres arable beef dairy Dinner Last d 5pm **Prices** S £25-£35; D £45-£50✳ **LB** **Parking** 8 **Notes** ⊛

◆◆◆ ◀

The Hollybush Inn

Grangemill DE4 4HU ☎ 01629 650300 & 07971 584266
Dir *Off A6 at Cromford onto B5012 for 4m*

A former drovers' inn, popular with locals and walkers, this 18th-century property is being renovated to provide thoughtfully equipped bedrooms, some of which are in converted stable blocks. The character public areas are the setting for wholesome food and real ales.

Facilities 3 rms (2 en suite) (1 pri facs) 6 annexe rms (6 annexe pri facs) (4 fmly) (2 GF) ⊗ in bedrooms ⊗ in dining room ⊗ in 1 lounge TV4B tea/coffee ✗ Cen ht TVL Pool Table Dinner Last d 9pm **Parking** 48 **Notes** ⊛

England

MATLOCK continued

◆◆◆ ▣

The Tavern at Tansley

Nottingham Rd, Tansley DE4 5FR
☎ 01629 57735 ▤ 01629 57840
e-mail enquiries@tavernattansley.co.uk
web www.tavernattansley.co.uk
Dir A615 towards Matlock, B&B on right after garden centre.

Identified by its colourful hanging baskets in the summer, this appealing inn provides a convenient base for touring. Wide-ranging menus make good use of fresh local ingredients while hearty breakfasts are served in the stylish restaurant. Staff are cheerful and service is attentive.

Facilities 3 en suite ⊗ in bedrooms ⊗ in dining room TVB tea/coffee Cen ht Golf Dinner Last d 9.15pm **Conf** Max 50 **Parking** 49

◆◆◆ ▣

Smithy Barn B & B

Smithy Barn, The Causeway S45 0DX
☎ 01246 590152 & 07808 292228
e-mail www.simon.oxspring@w3z.co.uk
Dir 3m NE of Matlock. On A632 in Kelstedge next to Kelstedge Inn
Facilities 2 en suite ⊗ TVB tea/coffee Cen ht No coaches Pool Table
Prices S fr £45; d fr £50✱ **Parking** 2 **Notes** ⊛

MELBOURNE

MAP 11 SK32

◆◆◆◆

The Coach House

69 Derby Rd DE73 8FE ☎ 01332 862338 ▤ 01332 695281
e-mail enquiries@coachhouse-hotel.co.uk
Dir Off B587 in village centre

Located in a conservation area and close to Donnington Park and East Midlands Airport, this traditional cottage has been restored to provide good standards of comfort and facilities. Bedrooms are thoughtfully furnished, and two are in converted stables. A lounge and secure parking are available.

Facilities 6 en suite (1 fmly) (3 GF) ⊗ in bedrooms ⊗ in dining room TVB tea/coffee ✖ Cen ht TVL No coaches **Prices** S £35-£39; D £55-£59 **Parking** 6

◆◆◆ ▣

The Melbourne Arms

92 Ashby Rd DE73 8ES ☎ 01332 864949 ▤ 01332 865525
e-mail info@melbournearms.co.uk
Dir 3m from East Midlands Airport

Well located for the airport and Donington Park, this Grade II listed inn provides modern, thoughtfully equipped bedrooms, one of which is in a converted outbuilding. Ground-floor areas include two bars, a coffee shop and an elegant Indian restaurant.

Facilities 7 en suite (1 fmly) ⊗ in bedrooms ⊗ in dining room TVB tea/coffee ✖ Cen ht TVL Bouncy Castle for children (weather permitting) Dinner Last d 11pm **Prices** S £35-£45; D £55-£60✱ **Conf** Max 25 Thtr 15 Class 15 Board 15 **Parking** 52

See advertisement on opposite page

NEWHAVEN

MAP 16 SK16

Premier Collection

◆◆◆◆◆ ≣ ⊜

The Smithy

SK17 0DT ☎ 01298 84548 ▤ 01298 84548
e-mail thesmithy@newhavenderbyshire.freeserve.co.uk
web www.thesmithybedandbreakfast.co.uk
Dir On A515 10m S of Buxton. Adjacent to Biggin Ln, entrance via private driveway opp Ivy House

Set in a peaceful location close to the Tissington and High Peak trails, the 17th-century drovers' inn and blacksmith's workshop have been carefully renovated. Bedrooms, which are in a former barn, are well equipped. Enjoyable breakfasts, which include free-range eggs and home-made preserves, are served in the forge, which features the original bellows to the vast open hearth. The resident owners provide excellent hospitality.

Facilities 4 en suite (1 fmly) (2 GF) ⊗ in bedrooms ⊗ in dining room TVB tea/coffee ✖ Cen ht TVL No coaches Dinner **Conf** Max 20 Thtr 15 Board 10 **Parking** 6 **Notes** Civ Wed 40 ⊛

RISLEY

MAP 11 SK43

◆◆◆◆

Braeside

113 Derby Rd DE72 3SS ☎ 0115 939 5885
e-mail bookings@braesideguesthouse.co.uk
web www.braesideguesthouse.co.uk
Dir M1 junct 25, signed Risley/Sandiacre. At x-rds left into Risley, 2nd cottage on left past Risley Park pub

The enthusiastic hosts of this delightful property offer a very warm welcome. Bedrooms, located in converted barns close to the house,

continued

are attractively appointed with many extras and set in extensive gardens. Breakfast is served in the conservatory, with superb views over open countryside. This is a non-smoking establishment.

Facilities 6 annexe en suite (2 fmly) (6 GF) ⊗ TVB tea/coffee ✘ Cen ht No coaches **Prices** S £45; D £60✱ **Parking** 10 **Notes** Closed 25-26 Dec

ROWSLEY
MAP 16 SK26

The Grouse and Claret

Station Rd DE4 2EB ☎ 01629 733233 ▤ 01629 735194
e-mail grouseandclaret.matlock@uk.mail.com
Dir M1 junct 28, A6 5m from Matlock, 3m from Bakewell

At the time of going to press the rating for this establishment had not been confirmed. Please check the AA website www.theAA.com for up-to-date information.

Facilities 8 en suite (2 fmly) ⊗ TVB tea/coffee ✘ Cen ht No coaches Dinner Last d 9pm **Prices** S £65; D £65✱ **Parking** 78

SWADLINCOTE
MAP 10 SK21

◆◆◆◆

Manor Farm

Coton In The Elms DE12 8EP
☎ 01283 760340 ▤ 01283 760340
Dir Off A38 for Walton-on-Trent & sign for Coton in the Elms, Manor Farm on right

This splendid traditional farmhouse retains its original staircase and many other interesting features. The spacious bedrooms are furnished with antiques. The farm is in a pleasant village, but not far from major roads for touring.

Facilities 3 en suite (1 fmly) ⊗ TVB tea/coffee ✘ Cen ht No coaches **Parking** 8 **Notes** ⊗

◆◆◆◆

Overseale House ◇

Acresford Rd, Overseal DE12 6HX
☎ 01283 763741 ▤ 01283 760015
e-mail oversealehouse@hotmail.com
web www.oversealehouse.co.uk
Dir On A444 between Burton upon Trent & M42 junct 11

Located in a village, this well-proportioned Georgian mansion, built for a renowned industrialist, retains many original features including a magnificent dining room decorated with ornate mouldings. The period-furnished ground-floor areas include a cosy sitting room, and bedrooms contain many thoughtful extras.

Facilities 4 en suite 1 annexe rms (3 fmly) (2 GF) ⊗ TVB tea/coffee Cen ht No coaches 3 acre garden **Prices** S £30-£35; D £50✱ **Conf** Max 14 Board 14 **Parking** 6 **Notes** ⊗

TIDESWELL
MAP 16 SK17

Topside ◇

7 Fountain St SK17 8JX ☎ 01298 872151
e-mail topsidebb@yahoo.co.uk
Dir From Anchor Inn/A623, South to Tideswell. 0.25m past Tideswell Church

Originally built in 1674 as a frame-knitter's workshop, this charming village guest house now provides warm hospitality in the heart of the Peak District. The bedrooms each have a shower room, and there is also a lounge/snug. Breakfast is served in the large family kitchen.

Facilities 2 en suite ⊗ TVB tea/coffee ✘ Cen ht TVL
Prices S £25-£30; D £45-£50✱ **Notes** ⊗

◆◆◆

Jaret House

Queen St SK17 8JZ ☎ 01298 872470 & 07779 412467
e-mail jarethouse@tesco.net
Dir In village centre opp Hills and Dales Tearooms

This Derbyshire cottage offers traditionally furnished bedrooms with shower rooms en suite. Friendly and attentive service is provided. The comfortable sitting room is warmed by a log fire during cooler months, and substantial freshly-prepared breakfasts are served in a cosy dining room.

Facilities 3 en suite (1 fmly) ⊗ TVB tea/coffee ✘ Cen ht TVL No coaches **Prices** S £25; D £50✱ **LB Notes** ⊗

England

TIDESWELL continued

♦♦♦

Poppies

Bnk Square SK17 8LA ☎ 01298 871083
e-mail poptidza@dialstart.net
Dir *On B6049 in village centre opp NatWest bank*

A friendly welcome is assured at this non-smoking house, located in the heart of a former lead-mining and textile community, a short walk from the 14th-century parish church. Bedrooms are homely and the excellent breakfast features good vegetarian options.

Facilities 3 rms (1 en suite) (1 fmly) ⊛ TVB tea/coffee Cen ht
No coaches Dinner Last d previous day **Prices** S £20.50-£30;
D £41-£50✳ **Notes** ⊛

WESTON UNDERWOOD   MAP 10 SK24

Premier Collection

♦♦♦♦♦ ❦

Park View Farm *(SK293425)*

DE6 4PA
☎ 01335 360352 & 07771 573 057 ▤ 01335 360352
Mrs Adams
e-mail enquiries@parkviewfarm.co.uk
Dir *6m NW of Derby off A38, 1.5m from Kedleston Hall*

An impressive Victorian farmhouse surrounded by beautiful gardens and 370 acres of arable land. Each bedroom has an antique four-poster bed, attractive decor, period furniture and a wealth of homely extras. Quality ornaments and art enhance the original features and ground-floor rooms include a spacious comfortable lounge and an elegant dining room.

Facilities 3 en suite ⊛ TVB tea/coffee ✸ Cen ht TVL No children 5yrs
370 acres Organic arable/sheep **Prices** S £50-£65; D £80-£85 LB
Parking 10 **Notes** Closed Xmas ⊛

WINSTER   MAP 16 SK26

♦♦♦♦ Ⓐ

Brae Cottage

East Bnk DE4 2DT ☎ 01629 650375
Dir *A6 onto B5057, driveway on right past pub*

Facilities 2 annexe en suite (1 fmly) (2 GF) ⊛ TVB tea/coffee Cen ht
No coaches **Prices** S £35-£46; D £46-£60✳ **Parking** 2 **Notes** ⊛

WIRKSWORTH   MAP 16 SK25

Premier Collection

★★★★★ Bed & Breakfast

The Old Manor House

Coldwell St DE4 4FB ☎ 01629 822502
e-mail ivan@spurrier-smith.fsnet.co.uk
Dir *From Derby B5023 towards Duffield/Matlock. Coldwell St turn right at Market Place.*

Located on the village edge, this impressive period house has been lovingly renovated to provide high standards of comfort and facilities.

continued

Quality furnishing and decor highlight the many original features and the spacious bedroom has a wealth of thoughtful extras.
Comprehensive breakfasts are served in the elegant dining room and a spacious drawing room is available.

Facilities 1 rm (1 pri facs) ⊛ TVB tea/coffee ✸ Cen ht No children
No coaches Pool Table ♨ **Parking** 1 **Notes** Closed Xmas & New Year ⊛

YOULGREAVE   MAP 16 SK26

♦♦♦

The Old Bakery

Church St DE45 1UR ☎ 01629 636887
Dir *Off A515/A6, in village centre*

Located in the heart of the unspoiled village, this former bakery has been renovated to provide a range of thoughtfully furnished bedrooms, one of which is in a converted barn. Breakfast is served in the original baker's shop and furnishings enhance the original features. This is a non-smoking establishment.

Facilities 2 rms 1 annexe en suite ⊛ ✸ Cen ht TVL No coaches
Prices S £28-£50 **Parking** 2 **Notes** Closed Xmas ⊛

DEVON

ASHBURTON   MAP 03 SX77
See also **Bickington**

♦♦♦♦

Greencott

Landscove TQ13 7LZ ☎ 01803 762649
Dir *3m SE of Ashburton. Off A38 at Peartree junct, Landscove signed on slip road, village green 2m on right, opp village hall*

Greencott has a peaceful village location and superb country views. The hosts extend a very warm welcome and a relaxed home from home atmosphere prevails. Service is attentive and caring and many guests return time and again. Bedrooms are attractive and very well equipped. Delicious country cooking is served around an oak dining table.

Facilities 2 en suite ⊛ in bedrooms ⊛ in dining room tea/coffee ✸
Cen ht TVL No coaches Dinner Last d by arrangement **Prices** S £21-£22;
D £42-£44 LB **Parking** 3 **Notes** Closed 25-26 Dec ⊛

♦♦♦♦ ⌂ ❦

Sladesdown Farm *(SX765684)*

Landscove TQ13 7ND ☎ 01364 653973 ▤ 01364 653973
Mr & Mrs Haddy
e-mail sue@sladesdownfarm.co.uk
Dir *2m S of Ashburton. Off A38 at Peartree junct, Landscove signed on slip road, left at 2nd x-rds, farm 100yds right*

Nestling amid 50 acres of tranquil pasture and well-tended gardens, yet near the A38, this modern farmhouse offers very spacious and attractive accommodation. A friendly atmosphere abounds, with relaxation assured either in the lounge or on the terrace in finer weather. You are welcome to wander across the land where a series of ponds have been created attracting wildlife. The hearty breakfast featuring delicious local and home-made produce is the perfect start to the day.

continued

Facilities 4 rms (2 en suite) (2 pri facs) ⊘ TVB tea/coffee ✗ Cen ht TVL No children 5yrs ⚓ 51 acres beef sheep **Prices** S £30-£35; D £56-£60 **Parking** 6 **Notes** ⊛

◆◆◆◆

Gages Mill ◇

Buckfastleigh Rd TQ13 7JW
☎ 01364 652391 📄 01364 652641
e-mail richards@gagesmill.co.uk
Dir Off A38 at Peartree junct, left at filling station, Gages Mill 500yds on left

Set in delightful grounds and well-tended gardens on the edge of Dartmoor National Park, Gages Mill is an attractive former wool mill originating from the 14th century. This family-run house offers a warm welcome and a home from home atmosphere. Breakfast is served in the dining room at individual tables, and there is a lounge where you can play games or watch television.

Facilities 7 en suite (1 fmly) (1 GF) ⊘ in bedrooms ⊘ in dining room ⊘ in 1 lounge tea/coffee ✗ Licensed Cen ht TVL No children 8yrs No coaches **Prices** S £26-£34; D £52-£68✳ **Parking** 7 **Notes** Closed 23 Oct-1 Mar ⊛

◆◆◆◆ ⬛

The Rising Sun

Woodland TQ13 7JT ☎ 01364 652544 📄 01364 654202
e-mail risingsun.hazel@btconnect.com
Dir Off A38 signed Woodland & Denbury, Rising Sun 1.5m on left

Please note that this establishment has recently changed hands. Peacefully situated in scenic countryside, this inn is just a short drive from the A38. A friendly welcome is extended to all guests, business, leisure and families alike. Bedrooms are comfortable and well equipped, and dinner and breakfast feature much local and organic

continued

produce. A good selection of home-made puddings, West Country cheeses, local wines and real ales are available.

Facilities 4 en suite (1 fmly) (2 GF) ⊘ in bedrooms ⊘ in dining room TVB tea/coffee Cen ht Dinner Last d 9.15pm **LB** **Parking** 40

◆◆◆◆ ⊜

West Down

Little Eastacombe EX37 9HP
☎ 01769 560551 📄 01769 560551
e-mail info@westdown.co.uk
Dir 0.5m from Atherington on B3227 to Torrington, turn right, 100yds on left

Set within 25 acres of lush countryside, this establishment is a good base for exploring the area. Peace and caring hospitality are assured. Bedrooms are equipped with a host of thoughtful extras, and every effort is made to ensure an enjoyable stay. A choice of homely lounges is available, and breakfast and scrumptious dinners are served in the sun lounge.

Facilities 3 en suite (1 GF) ⊘ TVB tea/coffee ✗ Cen ht TVL No coaches Dinner Last d 1pm **Prices** S £35-£40; D £60-£70 **LB** **Parking** 8 **Notes** ⊛

Premier Collection

◆◆◆◆◆ ▤ ⊜

Kerrington House

Musbury Rd EX13 5JR ☎ 01297 35333 📄 01297 35345
e-mail jreaney@kerringtonhouse.com
web www.kerringtonhouse.com
Dir 0.5m from Axminster on A358 towards Seaton, house on left

Set in landscaped gardens, this delightful house has been lovingly restored. The carefully decorated bedrooms are equipped with many thoughtful touches, and personal treasures adorn the light and airy drawing room. Dinner and breakfast are prepared with flair and imagination. The house is available with exclusive use for small house parties.

Facilities 5 en suite ⊘ TVB tea/coffee Direct dial from bedrooms ✗ Licensed Cen ht No coaches Dinner Last d 7pm **Conf** Max 12 Board 12 **Parking** 6

AXMINSTER continued

Premier Collection

◆◆◆◆◆

Lea Hill

Membury EX13 7AQ ☎ 01404 881881
e-mail reception@leahill.co.uk
web www.leahill.co.uk
Dir A30 W from Chard, 1m left signed Stockland, at x-rds right to
Membury, through village, pass church & Trout Farm, Lea Hill signed
on right

Lea Hill is set in 8 acres of tranquil grounds and gardens. The annexes
to the main house; a thatched Devon longhouse that dates from the
16th century or earlier, provide the accommodation. Bedrooms are
furnished to a high standard and offer a thoughtful range of extras.
Take tea on the terrace, or enjoy a game of golf on the six-hole
course. Breakfast is a highlight, with many local ingredients.

Facilities 2 en suite 2 annexe en suite ⊗ TVB tea/coffee Cen ht
No coaches Dinner Last d 24hrs prior **Prices** S £40-£55; D £60-£90✳ **LB**
Parking 20 **Notes** ⊗

◆◆◆◆ ❤

Pump Farm ◇ *(ST261955)*

Whitford EX13 7NN
☎ 01297 552798 ▤ 01297 552798 Mrs Loud
e-mail loud.pumpfarm@farmersweekly.net
web www.pumpfarmwhitford.co.uk
Dir Off A35 at Kilmington towards Whitford. Farmhouse on left at T-
junct in Whitford

Situated in a peaceful village between the A35 and Lyme Bay, this
attractive 15th-century thatched farmhouse features beams, wood
panelling and an inglenook fireplace. It is convenient for the beach
and coastal walks. The comfortable bedrooms are well appointed and
there is also a lounge. The farmhouse is non-smoking.

Facilities 2 en suite (1 fmly) ⊗ TVB tea/coffee ✗ Cen ht TVL
30 acres beef/organic **Prices** S £27; D £50-£55✳ **LB** **Parking** 4
Notes Closed Xmas ⊗

◆◆◆ ❤

Sellers Wood Farmhouse ◇ *(SY274941)*

Combpyne Rd, Musbury EX13 8SR ☎ 01297 552944
Mr & Mrs Pemberton
e-mail sellerswood@hotmail.com
web www.sellerswood.co.uk
Dir 3m SW of Axminster. Off A358 into Musbury village centre, onto
Combpyne Rd, 0.75m left onto driveway

Situated on the edge of Musbury with sweeping views over the Axe
valley to the cliffs of Beer, this delightful 16th-century farmhouse has a
wealth of beams and flagstone floors. Tasty farmhouse dinners using
home-grown vegetables are available by arrangement.

Facilities 4 rms (1 en suite) (1 pri facs) (2 fmly) ⊗ tea/coffee Cen ht
TVL ♨ 3 acres (small holding) Dinner Last d before 9am
Prices S £26-£34; D £52-£60 **LB** **Conf** Max 6 **Parking** 6 **Notes** ⊗

BAMPTON
MAP 03 SS92

Premier Collection

◆◆◆◆◆ ≜ ☕

The Bark House

Oakford Br EX16 9HZ ☎ 01398 351236
Dir 2m W of Bampton on A396

The charming Bark House lies in the Exe valley amid picturesque
countryside and pretty villages. The caring owners' unique blend of
pampering hospitality and service make you feel special, while the
house exudes character with its low beams, traditional furnishings and
log fires. Dinner is lovingly prepared from fresh local produce, and
breakfast, with many house specialities, is also memorable.

Facilities 5 rms (4 en suite) (1 pri facs) (1 fmly) ⊗ TVB Direct dial from
bedrooms Licensed Cen ht No coaches ♨ Dinner Last d 7.45pm
Prices S £50-£59.50; D £93-£119 **LB** **Parking** 15 **Notes** ⊗

◆◆◆◆ ☕ ❤

Newhouse Farm *(SS892228)*

EX16 9JE ☎ 01398 351347 Mrs Boldry
e-mail anne.boldry@btconnect.com
Dir 5m W of Bampton on B3227

Set in 42 acres of rolling farmland, this delightful farmhouse has a
friendly and informal atmosphere. The smart, rustic-style bedrooms
are well equipped with modern facilities, and imaginative and
delicious home-cooked dinners, using the best local produce, are
available by arrangement. Home-made bread and preserves feature at
breakfast.

Facilities 3 en suite (1 fmly) (1 GF) ⊗ TVB tea/coffee ✗ Cen ht
No children 10yrs Fishing 42 acres beef/sheep Dinner Last d 4pm
Prices D £56-£64 **LB** **Parking** 3 **Notes** Closed Xmas

BARNSTAPLE
MAP 03 SS53

Premier Collection

◆◆◆◆◆ ◉◉ ≜

Halmpstone Manor

Bishop's Tawton EX32 0EA
☎ 01271 830321 & 831003 ▤ 01271 830826
e-mail jane@halmpstonemanor.co.uk
web www.halmpstonemanor.co.uk
Dir 3m SE of Barnstaple. Off A377 E of river & rail bridges

The manor was mentioned in the Domesday Book and parts of the
later medieval manor house survive. Halmpstone Manor now provides
quality accommodation, personal service and fine cuisine. Delightful
day rooms include a spacious lounge complete with deep sofas and a
roaring fire, and a creative, daily changing menu is offered in the
elegant restaurant. Superb hospitality and excellent value make this a
great choice for a restful break.

Facilities 4 en suite ⊗ in bedrooms ⊗ in dining room ⊗ in lounges
TVB tea/coffee Licensed No coaches Dinner Last d 8pm
Prices D £100-£140✳ **Conf** Max 10 Thtr 10 Class 10 Board 10 Del £140
✳ **Parking** 12 **Notes** Closed Xmas & New Year

♦♦♦♦

Stoke House

Higher Davis Cl, Stoke Rivers EX32 7LD ☎ 01598 710542
e-mail info@stokehousedevon.co.uk
Dir *4m NE of Barnstaple. Off A399 signed Stoke Rivers, in village*

Stoke House has delightful views over the surrounding countryside yet is only a short drive from Barnstaple. The accommodation is friendly and relaxing, and you are most welcome to join the owners in the lounge to plan visits to nearby attractions. Bedrooms include welcome extras and one room is on the ground floor.

Facilities 3 en suite (1 GF) TVB tea/coffee ✖ Cen ht TVL
No children No coaches **Prices** D £50-£55✳ **LB Parking** 7
Notes Closed Nov-Mar

♦♦♦♦

Yeo Dale Hotel

Pilton Br EX31 1PG ☎ 01271 342954 🖷 01271 344530
e-mail stay@yeodalehotel.co.uk
Dir *A39 N from town centre over bridge, Yeo Dale on left after Pilton Park*

Please note that this establishment has recently changed hands. This elegant and deceptively spacious Georgian house is just a short walk from the town centre across the River Yeo. The well-furnished bedrooms are suitable for business and leisure, and a hearty breakfast is served in the stylish dining room.

Facilities 10 rms (9 en suite) (1 pri facs) (3 fmly) STV TVB tea/coffee ✖ Licensed Cen ht TVL No coaches

♦♦♦

Cresta ◇

26 Sticklepath Hill EX31 2BU
☎ 01271 374022 🖷 01271 374022
Dir *On A3215 0.6m W of town centre, top of hill on right*

Warm hospitality is provided at this detached property on the western outskirts of Barnstaple. The well-equipped bedrooms are comfortable and two are on the ground floor. A hearty breakfast is served in the dining room.

Facilities 6 rms (4 en suite) (2 fmly) (2 GF) in dining room TVB tea/coffee Cen ht No coaches **Prices** S £21; D £42✳ **Parking** 6

♦♦♦ 🐾

Rowden Barton ◇ (SS538306)

Roundswell EX31 3NP ☎ 01271 344365 Mrs Dallyn
Dir *2m SW of Barnstaple on B3232*

A warm welcome awaits you at Rowden Barton, a friendly and homely place. The two comfortable bedrooms share an adjoining bathroom, and both rooms have views of the surrounding countryside. Delicious breakfasts, featuring home-made bread and preserves, provide a fine start to the day.

Facilities 2 rms ✖ Cen ht TVL No children 12yrs 90 acres beef & sheep **Prices** S £20; D £40✳ **Parking** 4 **Notes** 📵

★★★ Inn

Anchor Inn

Fore St EX12 3ET ☎ 01297 20386 🖷 01297 24474
e-mail 6403@greeneking.co.uk
Dir *M5 junct 28, take A373 to Honiton, A375 towards Sidmouth, A3052 towards Lyme Regis. At Hangmans Stone take B3174 into Bear, Hotel along seafront*

Just a few steps from the beach, this popular harbourside inn offers smart, well-equipped bedrooms, many with the bonus of sea views. The atmosphere is convivial and welcoming with staff attentive and hospitable. A choice of bars is available and a smart restaurant area where local fish and seafood are specialities.

Facilities 8 rms (5 en suite) STV TVB tea/coffee ✖ Dinner Last d 9.30pm **Prices** S fr £50; d fr £85✳ **LB**

♦♦♦

Bay View ◇

Fore St EX12 3EE ☎ 01297 20489
Dir *Off A3052 to Beer & towards the sea, Bay View last building on left*

This delightful guest house is just a stone's throw from the beach in the centre of this charming fishing village. It is popular with walkers for its easy access to the South West Coast Path. Bedrooms are bright and comfortably furnished. During the day, snacks and light meals are available in the adjacent tea rooms.

Facilities 6 rms (2 en suite) (1 pri facs) 2 annexe en suite (1 fmly) TVB tea/coffee ✖ Cen ht **Prices** S £22-£52; D £44-£64 **Notes** Closed 18 Dec-10 Feb 📵

♦♦♦♦

Berry Mill House

Mill Ln EX34 9SH ☎ 01271 882990
e-mail enquiries@berrymillhouse.co.uk
web www.berrymillhouse.co.uk
Dir *Through Combe Martin, turn left at the bottom of the hill for house on left*

In a wooded valley on the edge of the village, this former grain mill is a 5-minute walk on the coastal path. You are assured of a warm reception from the owners, who obviously enjoy welcoming guests to their home. The freshly cooked breakfasts provide a substantial start to the day. Home-cooked evening meals are available by arrangement. Formerly known as Mill Park Country House.

Facilities 3 rms (2 en suite) (1 pri facs) TVB tea/coffee ✖ Licensed Cen ht TVL No children 12yrs No coaches ⏰ Dinner Last d 5pm **Prices** S £33.50-£38.50; D £53-£57✳ **LB Parking** 6 **Notes** Closed Nov & Xmas 📵

England

England

BICKINGTON (NEAR NEWTON ABBOT)

MAP 03 SX77

◆◆◆◆ ❦

Chipley Farm *(SX794726)*

TQ12 6JW ☎ 01626 821486 📠 01626 821486 Mrs Westcott
e-mail louisa@chipleyfarmholidays.co.uk
web www.chipleyfarmholidays.co.uk
Dir *0.6m SE of village centre. From village church onto lane, fork left, Chipley Farm on right*

A genuine welcome awaits you at this dairy farm. The hosts, with their pet dogs, make you feel like part of the family. Bedrooms, one with a four-poster bed, have modern facilities and many thoughtful extras. Dinner, by arrangement, and breakfast are enjoyed around a communal table in the dining room or in front of the Aga in the farmhouse kitchen.

Facilities 3 rms (1 en suite) (1 fmly) (2 GF) ⊗ TVB tea/coffee ✱ Cen ht TVL No children 3yrs painting lesson 160 acres Dairy/beef Dinner Last d previous day **Prices** D £55-£65✳ LB **Parking** 6 **Notes** ⊛

◆◆◆◆ ◼

Dartmoor Halfway Inn

TQ12 6JW ☎ 01626 821270 📠 01626 821820
Dir *Off A38 at Drumbridges rdb, signed Ilsington/Bickington, 3m left onto A383*

With medieval origins and a welcoming atmosphere, the inn is renowned for its extensive menu; food is served from breakfast until dinner. Comfortable, practically equipped accommodation is situated to the rear of the main building. As the name suggests, the inn is located half way between Newton Abbot and Ashburton.

Facilities 4 en suite (4 fmly) (4 GF) ⊗ in bedrooms ⊗ in dining room STV TVB tea/coffee Cen ht ♿ Dinner Last d 9pm **Parking** 80

BIDEFORD

MAP 03 SS42

See also **Westward Ho!**

◆◆◆◆

The Mount

Northdown Rd EX39 3LP ☎ 01237 473748 📠 01271 373813
e-mail andrew@themountbideford.fsnet.co.uk
web www.themount1.cjb.net
Dir *Bideford turning off A39, right after Rydon garage, premises on right after 600yds at minirdbt*

A warm welcome is assured at this delightful, centrally located Georgian property. Bedrooms are comfortably furnished and well equipped, and a ground-floor room is available for easier access. A hearty breakfast is served in the elegant dining room and there is a cosy sitting room.

Facilities 8 en suite (2 fmly) (1 GF) ⊗ TVB tea/coffee ✱ Licensed Cen ht No coaches **Prices** S £32-£35; D £64-£70 LB **Parking** 5

◆◆◆◆

Pines at Eastleigh

The Pines, Eastleigh EX39 4PA ☎ 01271 860561
e-mail pirrie@thepinesateastleigh.co.uk
Dir *A39 onto A386 signed East-The-Water. 1st left signed Eastleigh, 500yds next left, 1.5m to village, house on right*

Friendly hospitality is assured at this Georgian farmhouse set in 7 acres of gardens. Two of the comfortable bedrooms are in the main house, the remainder in converted barns around a charming courtyard, with a pretty pond and well. A delicious breakfast featuring local and home-made produce is served in the dining room, and a lounge and honesty bar are available.

Facilities 6 en suite (3 fmly) (4 GF) ⊗ TVB tea/coffee Direct dial from bedrooms Licensed Cen ht No children 9yrs No coaches ৹ Badminton, Link with outdoor activity centre **Prices** S £35-£45; D £75-£90✳ LB **Conf** Max 25 Thtr 20 Board 20 **Parking** 20

BOVEY TRACEY

MAP 03 SX87

Premier Collection

◆◆◆◆◆ 🏠

Brookfield House

Challabrook Ln TQ13 9DF
☎ 01626 836181 📠 01626 836182
e-mail brookfieldh@tinyworld.com
web www.brookfield-house.com
Dir *A382 to Bovey Tracey. Left at 1st rdbt, then right at T-junct. 300yds left onto Challabrook Ln, house 75yds on right*

Having panoramic views over Dartmoor, this charming Edwardian house is on the edge of the attractive town. Set in 2 acres of grounds, this is a perfect place for seclusion. The individually decorated bedrooms are comfortable and exceptionally well equipped, with the bonus of country views. Breakfast features local bacon and sausages, and home-made breads and preserves.

Facilities 3 rms (2 en suite) (1 pri facs) ⊗ TVB tea/coffee ✱ Cen ht No children 12yrs No coaches **Prices** S £45-£52; D £60-£74✳ LB **Parking** 6 **Notes** Closed Dec & Jan

◆◆◆◆ ◼

Cromwell Arms Hotel

Fore St TQ13 9AE ☎ 01626 833473 📠 01626 836873
e-mail reservations@smalland friendly.co.uk
Dir *In town centre*

Please note that this establishment has recently changed hands. This inn at the heart of the town dates from the 17th century. Rooms are stylish with quality furnishings, and two are suitable for families. There is a choice of dining in either the bar or restaurant and a non-smoking lounge is also available.

Facilities 12 en suite (2 fmly) ⊗ in bedrooms ⊗ in dining room STV TVB tea/coffee Direct dial from bedrooms ✱ Cen ht Dinner Last d 9.30pm **Prices** S fr £49.50; d fr £55✳ LB **Conf** Max 25 **Parking** 25

BRENDON

MAP 03 SS74

◆◆◆◆

Leeford Cottage ◇

EX35 6PS ☎ 01598 741279 ▤ 01598 741392
e-mail g.linley@virgin.net
web www.leefordcottage.com
Dir *4.5m E of Lynton. Off A39 at Brendon sign, cross packhorse bridges and village green, over x-rds, Leeford Cottage on left*

Situated in a quiet hamlet, this 400-year-old cottage has great character. The welcoming proprietors grow their own vegetables and rear hens, which provide the breakfast eggs. Bedrooms are cosy, there's a beamed lounge, and dinner is honest home cooking; no wonder guests return regularly.

Facilities 3 rms (1 en suite) (2 pri facs) ⊘ tea/coffee Cen ht TVL No coaches Dinner Last d 5pm **Prices** S £28-£29; D £47-£49✳ LB **Parking** 10 **Notes** Closed 3-31 Jan ⊛

BRIXHAM

MAP 03 SX95

◆◆◆

Harbour View Brixham ◇

65 King St TQ5 9TH ☎ 01803 853052 ▤ 01803 853052
Dir *A3022 to town centre/harbour, left at lights, right at T-junct, premises on right of inner harbour*

This comfortable house looks across the harbour towards Torbay. The friendly proprietors provide attractive, well-equipped accommodation, and there is a pleasant lounge area in the dining room. Breakfasts are traditional, well-cooked and appetising.

Facilities 8 rms (7 en suite) (1 pri facs) (1 fmly) ⊘ TVB tea/coffee ✖ Cen ht No coaches **Prices** S £29-£39; D £48-£62 LB **Parking** 7

BUCKFAST

MAP 03 SX76

◆◆◆

Furzeleigh Mill Country Hotel

Old Ashburton Rd TQ11 0JP ☎ 01364 643476
e-mail enquiries@furzeleigh.co.uk
web www.furzeleigh.co.uk
Dir *Off A38 at Dartbridge junct, right at end slip road, right opp Little Chef signed Ashburton/Prince Town (do not cross River Dart bridge), 200yds right*

The Grade II listed 16th-century converted corn mill stands in grounds and is a good base for touring Dartmoor. Spacious family rooms are available as well as a lounge and a bar. Meals are served in the dining room and use local produce.

Facilities 15 en suite (2 fmly) ⊘ in 6 bedrooms ⊘ in dining room ⊘ in 1 lounge TVB tea/coffee Licensed Cen ht TVL No children 8yrs No coaches Dinner Last d 8.10pm **Prices** S £31.50-£38; D £58-£68✳ LB **Parking** 32 **Notes** Closed 23 Dec-2 Jan

BUCKFASTLEIGH

MAP 03 SX76

★★★ Inn

Dartbridge Inn

Totnes Rd TQ11 0JR ☎ 01364 642214 ▤ 01364 643839
e-mail dartbridgeinn@oldenglishinns.co.uk
Dir *From A38 take A384 to Totnes, Hotel 250yds on left*

Situated close to the beautiful River Dart, this popular inn is ideally placed for exploring Dartmoor and south Devon. The atmosphere is friendly and relaxed with open fires and oak beams adding to the charm. Bedrooms are soundly appointed and an extensive menu is offered along with daily specials.

Facilities 10 en suite (1 fmly) TV available tea/coffee Direct dial from bedrooms Last d 9.30pm **Prices** S £55; D £80✳ LB **Conf** Max 150 Thtr 150 Class 75 Board 40 **Parking** 100

◆◆◆ ⌕

Kings Arms Hotel ◇

15 Fore St TQ11 0BT ☎ 01364 642341
Dir *In town centre opp tourist office & The Valiant Soldier*

This long-established, friendly and popular inn has been refurbished and now provides a well-appointed base from which to explore this picturesque area. Bedrooms are comfortably furnished, while public areas include a choice of bars, dining area and an attractive patio and garden.

Facilities 4 rms (1 en suite) ⊘ in bedrooms ⊘ in dining room TVB tea/coffee ✖ Dinner Last d 8.30pm **Prices** S £30-£35; D £50-£70✳ **Conf** Thtr 20 Class 14 Board 14 **Parking** 1

U

Kilbury Manor

Colston Rd TQ11 0LN ☎ 01364 644079 ▤ 01364 644697
e-mail visit@kilburymanor.co.uk
web www.kilburymanor.co.uk
Dir *Off A38 onto B3380 to Buckfastleigh, left onto Old Totnes Rd, at bottom turn right, Kilbury Manor on left*

At the time of going to press the rating for this establishment had not been confirmed. Please check the AA website www.theAA.com for up-to-date information.

Facilities 3 en suite (1 GF) ⊘ TVB tea/coffee ✖ Cen ht No coaches Dinner Last d am **Prices** S £35-£40; D £60-£70✳ **Parking** 5 **Notes** Closed 20 Dec-3 Jan ⊛

England

◆◆◆◆

Hansard House Hotel

3 Northview Rd EX9 6BY
☎ 01395 442773 📠 01395 442475
e-mail enquiries@hansardhotel.co.uk
web www.hansardhousehotel.co.uk
Dir B3178 to Budleigh Salterton

Refurbished Hansard House is quietly situated a short walk from the town centre. Many of the well-presented bedrooms have commanding views across the town to the countryside and estuary beyond; several are on the ground floor and have easier access. Enjoy a hearty and healthy breakfast in the spacious dining room, where by arrangement dinners are also served.

Facilities 12 en suite (1 fmly) (3 GF) ⊘ STV TVB tea/coffee Direct dial from bedrooms Licensed Lift Cen ht TVL Dinner Last d noon
Prices S £36-£42; D £75-£89✳ **LB** **Parking** 11

◆◆◆◆

Long Range Hotel

5 Vales Rd EX9 6HS ☎ 01395 443321 📠 01395 442132
e-mail info@thelongrangehotel.co.uk
Dir B3179 to Budleigh Salterton, left at lights, left at T-junct, 1st right & right again

This charming establishment has a relaxed and friendly atmosphere. Set in quiet surroundings, it is within walking distance of the town centre and the beach. Bedrooms are attractive , and there is a lounge and a conservatory-bar with lovely views, where you can enjoy a pre-dinner drink. Delightful home-cooked meals make good use of fresh local ingredients.

Facilities 7 rms (6 en suite) (1 pri facs) ⊘ TVB tea/coffee ✖ Licensed Cen ht TVL No coaches Dinner Last d 8.30pm **Prices** S £40-£42.50; D £75-£88✳ **LB** **Conf** Max 20 **Parking** 7

Premier Collection

◆◆◆◆◆

Parford Well

Sandy Pk TQ13 8JW ☎ 01647 433353
e-mail tim@parfordwell.co.uk
web www.parfordwell.co.uk
Dir A30 onto A382, after 3m left at Sandy Park towards Drewsteignton, house 50yds on left

Set in delightful grounds on the edge of Dartmoor, this attractive house is a restful and friendly home. Good quality and style are combined in the comfortable bedrooms. The lounge overlooks well-tended gardens, and breakfast is served at tables dressed with silver and crisp linen in one of two dining rooms. Carefully cooked, top local ingredients are hallmarks of a breakfast that's a perfect start for exploring the moors.

Facilities 3 rms (2 en suite) (1 pri facs) ⊘ ✖ Cen ht TVL No children 8yrs No coaches **Prices** S £40-£75; D £60-£75✳ **Parking** 4
Notes Closed Xmas 🐾

◆◆◆◆

Easton Court

Easton Cross TQ13 8JL ☎ 01647 433469 📠 01647 433654
e-mail stay@easton.co.uk
web www.easton.co.uk
Dir Off A30 at Whiddon Down rdbt onto A382 signed Moretonhampstead. House 3.5m on left at x-rds for Chagford

Set in Dartmoor National Park, the age of this picturesque house is reflected in the oak beams and deep granite walls. You can come and go via a separate entrance, and relaxation is obligatory, either in the lovely garden or in the snug lounge. The delightful bedrooms all have country views.

Facilities 5 en suite (2 GF) ⊘ TVB tea/coffee Direct dial from bedrooms Cen ht No children 10yrs No coaches **Parking** 5

If you book on bed, breakfast and evening meal terms, you may find that the tariff includes only the set menu

Book as early as possible, particularly in the peak holiday period

The Sandy Park Inn

TQ13 8JW ☎ 01647 433267
e-mail sandyparkinn@aol.com
Dir 1m NE of Chagford off A382

At the time of going to press the rating for this establishment had not been confirmed. Please check the AA website www.theAA.com for up-to-date information.

Facilities 5 rms (2 en suite) (3 pri facs) ⊗ in bedrooms ⊗ in dining room TVB tea/coffee Cen ht No coaches Fishing Dinner Last d 9pm **Parking** 4

CHALLACOMBE   MAP 03 SS64

Glebelands Farm ◇ (SS687405)

EX31 4TS ☎ 01598 763533 📠 01598 763533 Mr Hawkes
e-mail hawkes-glebelands@tiscali.co.uk
Dir Off B3358 at Four Cross Way for 1m

The modern farm bungalow nestles in the Challacombe valley and has glorious views of the surrounding countryside. Bedrooms are well equipped and you enjoy a hearty breakfast in the conservatory-dining room. A spacious lounge is also available.

Facilities 3 en suite (1 fmly) (3 GF) ⊗ TVB tea/coffee ✱ Cen ht 35 acres Beef and Sheep **Prices** S £27-£35; D £46 LB **Parking** 3

CHAWLEIGH   MAP 03 SS71

The Barn-Rodgemonts

Rodgemonts EX18 7ET ☎ 01769 580200
e-mail pyerodgemonts@btinternet.com
web www.devon-barn-accommodation.co.uk
Dir 1m NW of Chawleigh. Off A377 onto B3042 to Chawleigh, 1.5m left onto B3096 for Chulmleigh, 0.5m signed Chawleigh Week, fork left 250yds, Rodgemonts on right

Set in peaceful countryside, this attractive house offers friendly hospitality. Bedrooms are in the thatched, converted hay barn, each with views of the orchard from which the proprietors produce their own apple-juice, which features in the delightful breakfasts.

Facilities 2 en suite (1 fmly) ⊗ TVB tea/coffee Cen ht TVL No coaches **Prices** D £46-£56 LB **Parking** 3 **Notes** ⊠

CHERITON BISHOP   MAP 03 SX79

Holly Farm (SX767943)

EX6 6JD ☎ 01647 24616 & 07778 917 409 Mr Sears
e-mail graham.sears@lineone.net
Dir Off A30 into village, 2nd right signed Yeoford, farm 1m on left

Situated in beautiful countryside in the heart of Devon, yet convenient for the A30, this sheep farm and livery stables offers comfortable, practical accommodation. The spacious lounge has a television, a stereo and reading matter. The property is also available on a self-catering basis. Riding, golf, shooting and escorted tours of the moors can all be arranged.

continued

Facilities 3 rms (3 GF) ⊗ TV1B tea/coffee ✱ Cen ht TVL No children 2yrs ⊰ Riding can be arranged & tours of Dartmoor 50 acres sheep horses **Parking** 6 **Notes** ⊠

CHERITON FITZPAINE   MAP 03 SS80

Lower Burrow Coombe Farm (SS883054)

EX17 4JS ☎ 01363 866220 Mrs Kekwick
Dir M5 junct 27 to Tiverton, follow signs to Exeter. At Bickleigh take A3072 towards Crediton, 3m on right, sign for farm

At the time of going to press the rating for this establishment had not been confirmed. Please check the AA website www.theAA.com for up-to-date information.

Facilities 3 rms (1 pri facs) (1 fmly) ⊗ TVB tea/coffee ✱ Cen ht TVL 48 acres **Prices** D £44-£60✱ **Notes** Closed Oct-Mar ⊠

CHILLATON   MAP 03 SX48

Premier Collection

◆◆◆◆◆ 🏠

Tor Cottage

PL16 0JE ☎ 01822 860248 📠 01822 860126
e-mail info@torcottage.co.uk
web www.torcottage.co.uk
Dir A30 Lewdown exit through Chillaton towards Tavistock, 300yds after Post Office right signed Bridlepath No Public Vehicular Access to end

Tor Cottage, nestling in its own valley with 18 acres of grounds, provides an antidote to the frenetic pace of everyday life. Rooms are spacious and elegant; the cottage-wing bedroom has a separate sitting room, and the garden rooms have their own wood burners. The gardens are delightful, with a stream and heated outdoor pool. An exceptional range of dishes is offered at breakfast, which can be enjoyed either in the conservatory dining room or on the terrace.

Facilities 1 en suite 3 annexe en suite (3 GF) ⊗ TVB tea/coffee ✱ Cen ht TVL No children 16yrs No coaches ⊰ Riding, golf, fishing arranged locally Dinner **Prices** S fr £94; D £140-£150✱ LB **Parking** 8 **Notes** Closed 17 Dec-7 Jan

England

England

CHULMLEIGH
MAP 03 SS61

◆◆◆◆ ⌸

Old Bakehouse
South Molton St EX18 7BW
☎ 01769 580074 & 580137 📠 01769 580074
web www.colinandholly.co.uk
Dir A377 onto B3096 into village, left into South Molton St, 100yds on left

This 16th-century thatched house is situated in the centre of the town. The cosy licensed restaurant offers fixed-price menus featuring local produce; dishes are imaginative and made with care. Some of the charming bedrooms are located across a courtyard in the former village bakery.

Facilities 3 en suite 1 annexe en suite (1 fmly) (1 GF) ☺ TVB tea/coffee ✖ Licensed Cen ht No children 5yrs No coaches Dinner Last d 10am **Prices** S £38-£43; D £54-£62 LB

CLOVELLY
MAP 03 SS32

◆◆◆◆ 🏠 💜

East Dyke Farmhouse ◇ (SS312235)
East Dyke Farm, Higher Clovelly EX39 5RU
☎ 01237 431216 Mrs Goaman
e-mail steve.goaman@virgin.net
Dir A39 onto B3237 at Clovelly Cross rdbt, farm 500yds on left

Adjoining Clovelly's Iron Age hill fort, the working farm has glorious views across Bideford Bay in the distance. The farmhouse has a friendly atmosphere and offers coordinated bedrooms. A major attraction is the breakfast, where local produce and delicious home-made preserves are served around one large table. Helen Goaman is a top-twenty finalist for AA Landlady of the Year 2006. *continued*

Facilities 3 rms (2 en suite) (1 pri facs) ☺ in bedrooms ☺ in dining room TVB tea/coffee Licensed Cen ht TVL 300 acres Beef/Arable
Prices S £25-£30; D £50 **Parking** 6 **Notes** Closed 24-26 Dec 📵

◆◆◆◆

Fuchsia Cottage ◇
Burscott, Higher Clovelly EX39 5RR ☎ 01237 431398
e-mail curtis@fuchsiacottage.fslife.co.uk
web www.clovelly-holidays.co.uk
Dir From Clovelly Cross rdbt onto B3237, 0.75m right into Burscott (signed), establishment 300yds on right

Fuchsia Cottage is situated down a quiet country lane and is a good base for visiting the picturesque village of Clovelly. The modern house has stunning views over the surrounding countryside, and the comfortable bedrooms are delightfully decorated and have many extras. Two rooms are on the ground floor.

Facilities 4 rms (2 en suite) (2 GF) ☺ TVB tea/coffee ✖ Cen ht No coaches **Prices** S £20; D £50 **Parking** 3 **Notes** Closed 25-26 Dec 📵

COLEFORD
MAP 03 SS70

◆◆◆◆ ▮

The New Inn
EX17 5BZ ☎ 01363 84242 📠 01363 85044
e-mail enquiries@thenewinncoleford.co.uk
Dir Off A373 into Coleford

This 18th-century Grade II listed inn is full of character, with cob, thatch and beams. The chatty resident parrot, Captain, provides a unique welcome to all. Augmented by excellent local fish from Brixham, the varied menu offers a wide choice of interesting dishes, served alfresco in summer on the stream-side patio. Bedrooms are spacious with modern comforts enhancing the original architecture.

Facilities 6 en suite (1 fmly) (1 GF) ☺ in bedrooms ☺ in dining room TVB tea/coffee Direct dial from bedrooms ✖ Cen ht Dinner Last d 10pm **Prices** S £60-£70; D £75-£85✳ **Parking** 50 **Notes** Closed 25-26 Dec

COLYFORD
MAP 04 SY29

◆◆◆◆

Lower Orchard
Swan Hill Road EX24 6QQ ☎ 01297 553615
e-mail robin@barnardl.co.uk
Dir On A3052 in Colyford, between Lyme Regis & Sidmouth

This modern ranch-style family home looks over the Axe valley. The spacious ground-floor bedrooms are very well equipped. Breakfast is served in the lounge-dining room, which has patio doors leading to a private sun terrace, well-tended gardens and a splash pool. The owners are creating a motoring memories museum and a classic car showroom.

Facilities 2 rms (1 en suite) (1 pri facs) (2 GF) ☺ TVB tea/coffee Cen ht TVL No children No coaches ⚘ **Prices** S £40-£45; D £50-£60✳ **Parking** 3 **Notes** 📵

England

COMBE MARTIN
MAP 03 SS54

◆◆◆◆

Acorns Guest House ◇
2 Woodlands EX34 0AT ☎ 01271 882769 ▤ 01271 882769
e-mail info@acorns-guesthouse.co.uk
web www.acorns-guesthouse.co.uk
Dir *4m E of Ilfracombe. On A339 at W end of Combe Martin*

Facilities 8 rms (7 en suite) (1 pri facs) (1 fmly) ⊗ in bedrooms
⊗ in dining room TVB tea/coffee ✖ Licensed Cen ht TVL No coaches
Dinner Last d 5.30pm **Prices** S £27-£31; D £45-£55 LB **Parking** 8

CREDITON
MAP 03 SS80

◆◆◆◆

Fircroft
George Hill EX17 2DS ☎ 01363 774224
e-mail fircroftbb@talk21.com
Dir *Off W end of High St onto St Martin's Ln, over x-rds, 1st on right*

This delightful double-fronted Victorian family home is in a quiet
location with views over the market town below. It provides spacious,
thoughtfully equipped bedrooms for business and leisure. In warmer
weather you can relax in the south-facing gardens.

Facilities 2 en suite (2 fmly) ⊗ TVB tea/coffee ✖ Cen ht No coaches
Parking 6 **Notes**

CROYDE
MAP 03 SS43

◆◆◆◆ 🏠 🍽

The Whiteleaf
Croyde Rd EX33 1PN ☎ 01271 890266
Dir *On B3231 entering Croyde, on left at Road Narrows sign*

A warm family welcome awaits you at this attractive house within easy
walking distance of the pretty village and the sandy surfing beach.
Each of the well-equipped bedrooms has its own charm, and three
rooms have decked balconies. Ambitious and imaginative dinners,
using fresh seasonal produce, are served in the restaurant.

Facilities 5 en suite (2 fmly) ⊗ in 2 bedrooms ⊗ in dining room
⊗ in 1 lounge TVB tea/coffee Direct dial from bedrooms Licensed
Cen ht No coaches Dinner Last d 9pm **Prices** S £45-£50; D £66-£80✱
LB **Parking** 10

CULLOMPTON
MAP 03 ST00

◆◆◆◆ 🐾

Weir Mill Farm ◇ *(ST040108)*
Jaycroft, Willand EX15 2RE
☎ 01884 820803 ▤ 01884 820973 Mrs Parish
e-mail parish@weirmillfarm.freeserve.co.uk
Dir *M5 junct 27, B3181 to Willand. At Four Crossway rdbt left signed
Uffculme, 50yds 1st right onto Willand Moor Rd, after Lupin Way left
onto lane, Weir Mill is on the left*

Set in extensive farmland, this charming 19th-century farmhouse offers
comfortable accommodation with a relaxed and homely atmosphere.
The spacious bedrooms are attractively decorated and equipped with
an impressive range of thoughtful extras. A good choice is offered at
breakfast in the well-appointed dining room. The farmhouse is non-
smoking.

Facilities 3 rms (2 en suite) (1 pri facs) (1 fmly) ⊗ TVB tea/coffee ✖
Cen ht TVL 100 acres arable & beef **Prices** S £30; D £50 **Parking** 5
Notes

Ⓤ

Wishay Farm ◇
Trinity EX15 1PE ☎ 01884 33223 ▤ 01884 33223
e-mail wishayfarm@btopenworld.com
Dir *Cullompton Town Centre, right into Colbrook Ln, left &
immediate right 1.5m, straight across, farm 200yds on left*

At the time of going to press the rating for this establishment had not
been confirmed. Please check the AA website www.theAA.com for up-
to-date information.

Facilities 2 rms (1 en suite) (1 pri facs) (2 fmly) ⊗ TVB tea/coffee ✖
Cen ht TVL No coaches **Prices** S £25; D £42-£44✱ LB **Parking** 3

DARTMEET
MAP 03 SX67

◆◆◆◆ 🏠 🍽

Hunter's Lodge B & B ◇
PL20 6SG ☎ 01364 631173 & 07840 905624
e-mail mail@dartmeet.com
Dir *A38 at Ashburton onto B3357 to Dartmeet, Hunters Lodge 1st
right after bridge over Dart River*

Situated between the East and West Dart rivers, Hunter's Lodge stands
at the very heart of Dartmoor. The house offers splendid views and
the bedrooms are attractively presented. Dinner, available by
arrangement, features a wide range of fresh foods and local farm
produce. German, French and Spanish are spoken here.

Facilities 3 rms (2 en suite) 1 annexe en suite (1 fmly) ⊗ FTV TV1B
tea/coffee Cen ht No coaches Spa bath Dinner Last d 2 days prior
Prices S £25-£35; D £45-£70✱ LB **Parking** 6 **Notes** Closed 24-26 Dec

England

DARTMEET continued

♦♦♦

Brimpts Farm (SX668380)

PL20 6SG ☎ 01364 631450 📠 01364 631179 Miss Cross
e-mail info@brimptsfarm.co.uk
web www.brimptsfarm.co.uk
Dir *Dartmeet at E end of B3357, establishment signed on right at top of hill*

A popular venue for walkers and lovers of the outdoors, Brimpts is peacefully situated in the heart of Dartmoor and has been a Duchy of Cornwall farm since 1307. Bedrooms are simply furnished and many have views across Dartmoor. Dinner is served by arrangement. The sauna and spa are welcome facilities after a long day.

Facilities 10 en suite (2 fmly) (7 GF) ⊘ in bedrooms ⊘ in area of dining room ⊘ in 1 lounge TV1B tea/coffee Licensed Cen ht TVL Sauna Pool Table Abseiling, Climbing, Rafting, Hot tub 700 acres beef Dinner **Prices** S £30; D £48-£60✳ LB **Conf** Max 60 Thtr 60 Class 40 Board 25 Del from £71 ✳ **Parking** 50

If the freedom to smoke or be in a non-smoking atmosphere is important to you, check the rules when you book

DARTMOUTH MAP 03 SX85

Premier Collection

♦♦♦♦♦

Nonsuch House

Church Hill, Kingswear TQ6 0BX
☎ 01803 752829 📠 01803 752357
e-mail enquiries@nonsuch-house.co.uk
Dir *A3022 onto A379 2m before Brixham. Fork left onto B3205. Left up Higher Contour Rd, down Ridley Hill, house on bend*

This delightful Edwardian property has fabulous views across the Dart estuary. The marvellous hosts combine friendliness with unobtrusive service. Bedrooms are spacious and superbly appointed, each with a spectacular panorama of the harbour. Fresh, local ingredients are served at dinner, including top-quality meat and fish, along with farmhouse cheeses. Breakfast, on the patio in good weather, features freshly squeezed juice, local sausages and home-baked bread.

Facilities 3 en suite (1 GF) ⊘ TVB tea/coffee Cen ht No children 10yrs No coaches Dinner Last d 8pm **Prices** S £70-£95; D £95-£120✳ LB **Parking** 3

♦♦♦♦

Woodside Cottage

TQ9 7BL ☎ 01803 898164
e-mail stay@woodsidedartmouth.co.uk
web www.woodsidedartmouth.co.uk
Dir *Off A3122 to Dartmouth. After golf club brown sign right to house, sharp right, 0.5m on right*

This delightful and comfortable house lies in a scenic valley within easy reach of Dartmouth, and is ideal for walkers and for touring. The charming proprietors make you feel welcome, and provide attractive bedrooms. Local and organic produce, cooked on an Aga, and home-made marmalade and fresh eggs feature at breakfast.

continued

Facilities 3 en suite ⊗ TVB tea/coffee ✖ No children 18yrs
No coaches Concessions at Dartmouth Golf Club **Prices** D £70-£80✳
Parking 4 **Notes** Closed 25-26 Dec

◆◆◆◆

The Captain's House ◇

18 Clarence St TQ6 9NW ☎ 01803 832133
e-mail thecaptainshouse@aol.com
web www.captainshouse.co.uk
Dir B3122 into Dartmouth, Clarence St is parallel with the river

Dating from 1730, this charming house retains many original features and is only a short walk from the quayside and town centre. The attractive bedrooms are comfortable and well-equipped. Enjoyable breakfasts are served in the dining room and include local produce and a large selection of quality preserves.

Facilities 5 en suite ⊗ TVB tea/coffee ✖ Cen ht No children 5yrs
No coaches **Prices** S £30-£35; D £59-£76 LB

◆◆◆◆

The Cherub Inn

15 Higher St TQ6 9RB ☎ 01803 832482
e-mail cherubsnest4bb@aol.com
web www.cherubsnest.co.uk
Dir From Lower Dartmouth ferry along Lower St, left onto Smith St, left onto Higher St, 50yds on left

Dating from 1710, this former merchant's house, bedecked with flowers during the summer, is located in the very heart of historic Dartmouth. Full of character, the individually decorated bedrooms vary in size, but all are attractive and well-equipped. A choice of breakfasts is served in the cosy dining room.

Facilities 3 en suite ⊗ TVB tea/coffee Cen ht No children 10yrs
No coaches **Prices** S £45-£55; D £60-£75✳ LB

◆◆◆◆

Courtyard House

10 Clarence Hill TQ6 9NX ☎ 01803 835967
e-mail ronandgail@courtyard-house.co.uk

A relaxed atmosphere abounds at this enchanting house nestling in the picturesque and tranquil old town. Bedrooms are attractively decorated and comfortably furnished, and one has a four-poster bed. The house has excellent floral displays. Freshly cooked, substantial breakfasts are served in the bright dining room.

Facilities 1 en suite 3 annexe en suite ⊗ TVB tea/coffee ✖ Cen ht
No children 10yrs No coaches **Prices** S fr £40; D £65-£90✳ **Parking** 3
Notes Closed 20-27 Dec ⊛

◆◆◆◆

New Angel Rooms

51 Victoria Rd TQ6 9RT ☎ 01803 839425 🖺 01803 839567
e-mail reservations@thenewangel.co.uk

Just a level stroll from the acclaimed New Angel Restaurant, this terrace property offers very comfortable, contemporary accommodation, equipped with numerous extra facilities including a complimentary half bottle of Champagne. Breakfast is a feature, with freshly squeezed orange juice: specials such as eggs Benedict and scrambled eggs with smoked salmon are not to be missed.

Facilities 5 en suite (2 fmly) ⊗ TVB tea/coffee ✖ Cen ht No coaches
Dinner Last d 10pm **Prices** S £90-£110; D £90-£130✳ **Notes** Closed Jan

◆◆◆◆

Seale Arms

10 Victoria Rd TQ6 9SA ☎ 01803 832719 🖺 01803 839366
e-mail sealearms@hotmail.com
Dir A3122 into Dartmouth

The friendly Seale Arms is only a short walk from the quayside. Bedrooms are spacious and stylish, and are provided with a range of extras. The well-stocked bar is popular with locals and visitors alike, and offers a good selection of freshly cooked dishes. Breakfast is served in the dining room.

Facilities 4 en suite (2 fmly) ⊗ in bedrooms ⊗ in dining room
⊗ in 1 lounge TVB tea/coffee ✖ Cen ht TVL Pool Table Last d 9pm

◆◆◆◆

Warfleet Lodge

Warfleet TQ6 9BZ ☎ 01803 834352
Dir 0.5m S of town centre. From Dartmouth riverside B3205 to Warfleet, driveway on right

Just a 10-minute walk from the centre, Warfleet Lodge, built in 1870 and frequented by Edward VII, is a relaxing retreat from everyday life. With fine views over Warfleet creek and the River Dart, the accommodation is elegant and comfortable. Breakfast is a highlight, parking is a bonus, and pets are welcome.

Facilities 3 en suite TVB tea/coffee Cen ht No coaches
Prices D £80-£95✳ **Parking** 4 **Notes** ⊛

EXETER MAP 03 SX99

See also **Cheriton Bishop, Rockbeare, Silverton & Whimple**

Premier Collection

◆◆◆◆◆ ⊚ ⊜

Galley Fish & Seafood Restaurant with Rooms

41 Fore St EX3 0HU ☎ 01392 876078
e-mail fish@galleyrestaurant.co.uk
web www.galleyrestaurant.co.uk
Dir M5 junct 30, follow signs for Topsham, then signs to Quay. Restaurant behind Lighter Inn overlooking river

A tricky driveway is the first introduction to this nautical guest house. Described as cabins, the bedrooms have a maritime theme; all are reached via quite steep stairs as they are housed in a 17th-century cottage. One room is above the restaurant. All are exceptionally well-equipped with minibars and cable television. Breakfast is an extensive continental variety although cooked is served by request.

Facilities 2 en suite ⊗ STV TVB tea/coffee Direct dial from bedrooms ♆ Licensed Cen ht TVL No children 12yrs No coaches ⸼ Jacuzzi Hot tub Spa treatments Dinner Last d 9.30pm **Prices** S £87.50-£95; D £150-£250 **LB Parking** 4 **Notes** Closed Xmas-New Year

◆◆◆◆

St Andrews Hotel

28 Alphington Rd EX2 8HN
☎ 01392 276784 ▤ 01392 250249
e-mail standrewsexeter@aol.com
Dir M5 junct 31, follow signs for city centre & Marsh Barton along A377 Alphington road, property on left

Standards are high at this small friendly establishment, which has
continued

been owned by the same family for over 35 years. It stands within walking distance of the city centre. Bedrooms are continually being upgraded, and are equipped with modern comforts. Public rooms include a choice of sitting areas and a bright dining room where home cooking features on the menu.

Facilities 17 en suite (2 fmly) (1 GF) ⊗ FTV TVB tea/coffee Direct dial from bedrooms ♆ Licensed Cen ht No coaches Dinner Last d 8pm **Prices** S £45-£58; D £65-£76✳ **LB Conf** Max 10 Board 10 **Parking** 21 **Notes** Closed 24 Dec-1 Jan

◆◆◆◆

The Edwardian

30-32 Heavitree Rd EX1 2LQ
☎ 01392 276102 & 254699 ▤ 01392 253393
e-mail michael@edwardianexeter.co.uk
web www.edwardianexeter.co.uk
Dir M5 junct 29, right at lights signed city centre, on left after Exeter University School of Education

The new proprietors offer a warm welcome at this attractive Edwardian terrace property, which is within easy walking distance of the city centre. The bedrooms vary in size, are well presented, and offer a range of accessories. Breakfast is served in the spacious dining room and the inviting lounge offers comfort and relaxation.

Facilities 12 en suite (3 fmly) (3 GF) ⊗ TVB tea/coffee Direct dial from bedrooms Cen ht No coaches **Parking** 2

◆◆◆◆

Fairwinds Village House Hotel

Kennford EX6 7UD ☎ 01392 832911
e-mail fairwindshotbun@aol.com
Dir 4m S of Exeter. M5 junct 31, A38, 2m left for Kennford, house on left

A warm welcome is assured at this friendly, non-smoking establishment convenient for the coast, the moors and Exeter and Plymouth. Fairwinds is well suited for business and leisure, and home-cooked food can be enjoyed in the bright dining room next to the cosy bar.

Facilities 6 en suite (1 fmly) (3 GF) ⊗ TVB tea/coffee Direct dial from bedrooms ♆ Licensed Cen ht No coaches Dinner Last d 6.30pm **Prices** S £48-£50; D £64✳ **LB Parking** 8 **Notes** Closed mid Nov-early Jan rs early Jan-end Feb

England

The Gissons Arms

◆◆◆◆

Kennford EX6 7UD ☎ 01392 832444 🖹 01392 832444
e-mail enquiries@gissons.co.uk
Dir 4.5m S of city centre. Off A38 into Kennford village centre

Dating in part from the 15th century, this delightful inn offers well-equipped bedrooms, some with four-poster beds. The bars retain original character and have a relaxed atmosphere, and an extensive carvery, daily specials and tempting desserts are available.

Facilities 14 en suite (2 fmly) ⊗ in area of dining room TVB tea/coffee Direct dial from bedrooms Cen ht Dinner Last d 10pm **Prices** S £45; D £65✳ **LB** **Conf** Max 40 Thtr 50 Board 20 **Parking** 100 **Notes** rs 25-26 Dec eve

◆◆◆◆

Heath Gardens ◇

Broadclyst EX5 3HL ☎ 01392 462311
e-mail info@heathgardens.co.uk
web www.heathgardens.co.uk
Dir 5m NE of Exeter. From B3181 fork right at Broadclyst towards Whimple, 0.5m on left

Heath Gardens is a thatched 17th-century artisan's cottage situated on the outskirts of the village of Broadclyst. The National Trust's Killerton House is nearby. Accommodation is well presented and the spacious bedrooms overlook open countryside. There is adequate off-road parking to the side of the property.

Facilities 3 en suite (1 fmly) (1 GF) ⊗ TVB tea/coffee Cen ht No coaches **Prices** S £30; D £45-£50✳ **Parking** 6 **Notes** 🖾

◆◆◆◆ 🐾

Holbrook Farm ◇ *(SX991927)*

Clyst Honiton EX5 2HR
☎ 01392 367000 🖹 01392 367000 Mrs Glanvill
e-mail heatherglanvill@holbrookfarm.co.uk
web www.holbrookfarm.co.uk
Dir M5, A3052 for Sidmouth, pass Westpont (county showground) & Cat and Fiddle pub, 500yds left at Hill Pond caravans, B&B signed for 1m

This friendly, modern farmhouse stands in lush rolling countryside and has spectacular views. All bedrooms are on the ground floor, have their own entrance and offer bright and spacious accommodation. Breakfast features the best fresh local produce. Holbrook Farm is convenient for Exeter, the coast and moor, and there are popular inns and restaurants nearby.

Facilities 3 en suite (1 fmly) (3 GF) ⊗ TVB tea/coffee ✂ Cen ht 100 acres mixed **Prices** S £30-£45; D £50-£60 **LB** **Parking** 4

◆◆◆◆ 🐾

Mill Farm *(SX959839)*

Kenton EX6 8JR ☎ 01392 832471 Mrs Lambert
Dir A379 from Exeter towards Dawlish, over minirdbt by Swans Nest, farm 1.75m on right

Located just a short drive from the Powderham Estate, this imposing working farmhouse is surrounded by pastureland. Each of the spacious bedrooms is comfortably furnished and has coordinated decor; many rooms have views across the countryside. Breakfast is served in the sunny dining room and a lounge is also provided.

Facilities 5 en suite (3 fmly) ⊗ TVB tea/coffee ✂ Cen ht No children 6yrs 60 acres beef **Prices** S £32-£35; D £48-£50✳ **LB** **Parking** 12 **Notes** Closed Xmas 🖾

◆◆◆◆ 🐾

Rydon *(SX999871)*

Woodbury EX5 1LB
☎ 01395 232341 🖹 01395 232341 Mrs Glanvill
e-mail sallyglanvill@aol.com
Dir A376 & B3179 from Exeter into Woodbury, right before 30mph sign

Dating from the 16th century, this Devon longhouse has been run by the same family for eight generations. The farmhouse provides spacious bedrooms, which are equipped with many useful facilities and one has a four-poster bed. There is a television lounge and a delightful garden in which to relax. Breakfast is served in front of an inglenook fireplace.

Facilities 3 rms (2 en suite) (1 pri facs) (1 fmly) ⊗ tea/coffee Cen ht TVL 450 acres dairy **Prices** S £33-£45; D £60-£66✳ **LB** **Parking** 3

◆◆◆◆ 🅰

Raffles

11 Blackall Rd EX4 4HD ☎ 01392 270200 🖹 01392 270200
e-mail raffleshtl@btinternet.com
Dir M5, exit at Exeter services, follow signs for Middlemore & City Centre

Facilities 6 en suite (2 fmly) ⊗ in 4 bedrooms ⊗ in dining room STV TVB tea/coffee Licensed Cen ht TVL No coaches **Prices** S £38-£40; D £64-£68✳ **LB** **Parking** 6

England

◆◆◆

Culm Vale Country House

Culm Vale, Stoke Canon EX5 4EG
☎ 01392 841615 🖹 01392 841615
e-mail culmvale@hotmail.com
Dir *A396 from Exeter towards Tiverton, after Stoke Canon sign Culm Vale 5th property on right*

A warm welcome is extended at this impressive house situated on the edge of pretty Stoke Canon. Culm Vale is family run, full of character and it offers very spacious, comfortable accommodation. Breakfast, featuring eggs laid by the family's own hens, can be enjoyed in the grand dining room.

Facilities 3 rms (1 en suite) ⊗ TVB tea/coffee Cen ht No coaches
Prices S £35-£45; D £40-£50✱ **Parking** 3

◆◆◆ ▣

The Devon Arms

Fore St, Kenton EX6 8LD ☎ 01626 890213 🖹 01626 891678
e-mail devon.arms@ukgateway.net
Dir *5m S of Exeter. M5 junct 30, A379 towards Dawlish, Devon Arms in Kenton village centre*

The Devon Arms offers practically equipped, comfortable accommodation in the village of Kenton. The pub is popular with locals and tourists alike and has a skittle alley, pool and darts during winter. Traditional meals, as well as lighter options, are available in the bar-lounge.

Facilities 6 en suite (4 fmly) ⊗ in 3 bedrooms ⊗ in area of dining room TVB tea/coffee ✖ Cen ht No coaches Pool Table Dinner Last d 8.30pm
Prices S £33-£36; D £48-£58✱ **Parking** 22

◆◆◆

Dunmore Hotel

22 Blackall Rd EX4 4HE ☎ 01392 431643 🖹 01392 431643
e-mail Dunmorehtl@aol.com
Dir *M5 junct 29, through city centre, right at minirdbt, house on left*

Convenient for the city centre, Exeter College and the railway station, the Dunmore provides comfortable accommodation. The bedrooms are well presented, and many have been redecorated. Traditional English breakfasts are served in the dining room.

Facilities 9 rms (6 en suite) (4 fmly) (1 GF) ⊗ TVB tea/coffee ✖ Cen ht **Prices** S £32; D £44-£50✱ **LB**

◆◆◆

Park View Hotel ◇

8 Howell Rd EX4 4LG ☎ 01392 271772 🖹 01392 253047
e-mail enquiries@parkviewexeter.co.uk
Dir *M5 junct 29, A3015 to city centre & clock tower rdbt, 3rd exit Elm Grove, at T-junct left onto Howell Rd*

This friendly, family-owned guest house has a peaceful location overlooking Bury Meadow Park, close to the city centre. All bedrooms in this Grade II listed Georgian building are equipped with modern facilities. There is a comfortable sitting room, and breakfast is served in the bright and airy dining room.

Facilities 13 rms (9 en suite) (2 pri facs) (2 fmly) (1 GF) ⊗ in bedrooms ⊗ in dining room TVB tea/coffee Direct dial from bedrooms ✖ Cen ht TVL No coaches **Prices** S £26-£45; D £58-£68✱ **Parking** 6 **Notes** Closed Xmas-New Year

◆◆◆

Sunnymede ◇

24 New North Rd EX4 4HF
☎ 01392 273844 🖹 01392 273844
e-mail seldonsnnymds@aol.com
Dir *600yds N of cathedral. On one-way system pass Central Station in Queen St, at clocktower rdbt turn right, Sunnymede on left*

The Sunnymede has a central location in this historic city and is convenient for the college, shopping centre and attractions. A compact guest house, it offers comfortable, well-presented bedrooms, well suited for business or leisure. A good choice is available at breakfast. This is a no-smoking establishment.

Facilities 9 rms (5 en suite) (1 fmly) ⊗ TVB tea/coffee ✖ Cen ht TVL No coaches **Prices** S £25-£30; D £45-£50✱ **Notes** Closed 20 Dec-15 Jan

EXMOUTH   MAP 03 SY08

★★★★ **Guest Accommodation**

Barn

Foxholes Hill, Marine Dr EX8 2DF
☎ 01395 224411 🖹 01395 225445
e-mail info@barnhotel.co.uk
Dir *M5 junct 30- take A376 to Exmouth, then signs to seafront. At rdbt last exit into Foxholes Hill, located on right*

This Grade II-listed establishment has a prime location close to miles of sandy beaches. Equally pleasurable is the impeccable rear garden, which is sea facing and presents a terrace and swimming pool during

continued

the summer. Service is attentive and friendly. Spectacular sea views are enjoyed from most of the considerately equipped bedrooms and public rooms. Breakfast, featuring freshly squeezed juices and local produce is served in the pleasant dining room. An extensive dinner menu is also available.

Facilities 11 en suite (4 fmly) ⊗ TVB tea/coffee Direct dial from bedrooms ✱ Licensed Cen ht No coaches ⚹ ₤ ⅃ Dinner Last d 8pm **Prices** S £32-£49; D £64-£98⋇ **LB Parking** 30 **Notes** Closed 23 Dec-10 Jan

◆◆◆◆

The Devoncourt Hotel

16 Douglas Av EX8 2EX ☎ 01395 272277 📄 01395 269315
e-mail enquiries@devoncourt.com
web www.devoncourt.com
Dir M5/A376 to Exmouth, follow seafront to Maer Rd, right at T-junct

The Devoncourt stands in 4 acres of mature, subtropical gardens, sloping gently towards the sea and overlooking long sandy beaches. It offers extensive leisure facilities, and the smartly furnished bedrooms are exceptionally well equipped. Public areas are spacious and shared with timeshare owners. For meals you can choose between the informal bar or dining in the restaurant.

Facilities 10 en suite (1 fmly) ⊗ in dining room ⊗ in 1 lounge FTV TVB tea/coffee Direct dial from bedrooms ✱ Licensed Lift Cen ht TVL No coaches ⊡ ⚹ ✿ Snooker Sauna Solarium Gymnasium ₤ ⅃ Steam Room Vibrogym Dinner Last d 9pm **Prices** S £40-£70; D £65-£99; (room only) ⋇ **LB Parking** 50

GALMPTON   MAP 03 SX64

◆◆◆◆

Burton Farmhouse

TQ7 3EY ☎ 01548 561210 📄 01548 562257
e-mail anne@burtonfarm.co.uk
Dir Off A381 at Marlborough towards Galmpton & Hope Cove, 1m left onto lane

Facilities 15 rms (14 en suite) (6 fmly) (3 GF) ⊗ TVB tea/coffee ✱ Licensed Cen ht TVL Pool Table play area in garden Dinner Last d 24 hrs prior **Parking** 50

HALWILL JUNCTION   MAP 03 SS40

◆◆◆◆

Winsford Walled Garden

EX21 5XT ☎ 01409 221477
e-mail muddywellies@winsfordwalledgarden.co.uk
web www.winsfordwalledgarden.co.uk
Dir Off A3079, brown tourist signs from Halwill Junction for 1m

This very friendly home has a most notable and inspirational garden. Particularly interesting are the Victorian greenhouses, which have been restored to their original condition. Bedrooms are spacious and comfortable. Appetising, freshly-cooked breakfasts are served in the kitchen.

Facilities 2 en suite (2 GF) ⊗ TVB tea/coffee ✱ Cen ht TVL No children No coaches Historic Victorian walled garden **Prices** S £45; D £60⋇ **Parking** 18 **Notes** ⊛

HARTLAND   MAP 02 SS22

◆◆◆

Fosfelle ◇

EX39 6EF ☎ 01237 441273 📄 01237 441273
Dir A39 onto B3248, entrance 2m on right

Dating from the 17th century, this delightful manor house offers comfortable accommodation close to the village of Hartland. It stands in 6 acres of gardens with two fishing lakes. Enjoy pool or darts in the welcoming bar, and the restaurant offers a range of freshly prepared dishes.

Facilities 7 rms (4 en suite) (2 fmly) ⊗ in bedrooms ⊗ in area of dining room TV6B tea/coffee ✱ Licensed Cen ht TVL Fishing Pool Table Dinner Last d 9pm **Prices** S £30-£35; D £60-£70 **LB Parking** 20

HEMYOCK   MAP 03 ST11

◆◆◆

Orchard Lea

Culmstock Rd EX15 3RN
☎ 01823 680057 📄 01823 680057
e-mail anne@sworns.co.uk
Dir 0.8m W of Hemyock on B3391 to Culmstock

Well situated for touring Devon and Somerset, this family home has pleasant views over the surrounding countryside. The atmosphere is friendly and bedrooms, which are all on the ground floor, are equipped with considerate extras. Breakfast, featuring home-made and local produce, is served in the cosy lounge-dining room around a communal table. Dinner is available by arrangement.

Facilities 2 rms (2 pri facs) (2 GF) ⊗ TVB tea/coffee ✱ Cen ht No coaches volleyball in large garden, badminton Dinner Last d same morning **Prices** D £40-£46⋇ **Parking** 3 **Notes** Closed 24 Dec-2 Jan ⊛

England

◆◆◆◆ ❦

Leworthy Farm House ◈ (SS323012)

Lower Leworthy, Nr Pyworthy EX22 6SJ
☎ 01409 259469 📠 01409 259469 Mr & Mrs Jennings
e-mail leworthyfarmhouse@yahoo.co.uk
web www.leworthyfarmhouse.co.uk
Dir From Holsworthy onto Bodmin St towards North Tamerton, 4th left signed Leworthy/Southdown

Located in an unspoiled area of north Devon with 3 acres of gardens, meadows, a copse and a fishing lake, this delightful farmhouse provides bright, comfortable accommodation with numerous extra facilities. Dinner is available by arrangement and, like breakfast, is served in the large lounge-dining room.

Facilities 7 rms (6 en suite) (1 pri facs) (1 fmly) ❷ TVB tea/coffee ✖ TVL Fishing 3 acres non-working **Prices** S £27.50-£45; D £55-£65✱ **Parking** 8 **Notes** ❷

◆◆◆◆ ☕ 🍺

Bickford Arms

Brandis Cnr EX22 7XY ☎ 01409 221318 📠 01409 220085
e-mail info@bickfordarms.com
Dir On A3072, 4m from Holsworthy towards Hatherleigh

This light and airy inn offers style and comfort with a relaxed atmosphere. Bedrooms and bathrooms are attractively presented and well equipped. Lunch and a good choice of freshly prepared dinners are available in the spacious bar-restaurant, where an open fire burns in cooler months. On Friday and Saturday evenings, by reservations only, an a la carte is available in the dining room.

Facilities 5 en suite (1 fmly) ❷ in bedrooms ❷ in dining room ❷ in lounges TVB tea/coffee ✖ Cen ht No coaches Dinner Last d 9.30pm **Conf** Max 30 Thtr 40 Board 20 **Parking** 50

◆◆◆◆

Clawford Vineyard

Clawton EX22 6PN ☎ 01409 254177 📠 01409 254177
e-mail john.ray@clawford.co.uk
Dir A388 Holsworth to Launceston road, left at Clawton x-rds, 1.5m to T-junct, left, 0.5m left again

Situated in the peaceful Claw valley and having splendid views over fishing lakes and woods, this working cider orchard and vineyard offers spacious and comfortable bedrooms. There is a large lounge, a

well-stocked bar, a conservatory and a restaurant. Freshly cooked dishes are well prepared and attractively presented at dinner and breakfast. Self-catering apartments are also available, overlooking the lakes.

Facilities 11 en suite (7 fmly) ❷ TVB tea/coffee ✖ Licensed Cen ht TVL No children 6yrs Fishing Pool Table Coarse & game fishing Dinner Last d 9pm **Parking** 60

◆◆◆ ❦

The Hollies Farm Guest House

(SS371001)

Clawton EX22 6PN ☎ 01409 253770 & 07929 318033 Mr & Mrs Colwill
e-mail theholliesfarm@hotmail.com
Dir Off A388 at Clawton village & follow vineyard signs, the Hollies 2m in lane on left

This sheep and beef farm offers comfortable modern accommodation in a family atmosphere. There are pleasant views across the countryside from most bedrooms, and all of them are well appointed. Breakfast is served in the new conservatory and dinner is available by arrangement. There is also a barbecue area with a gazebo.

Facilities 3 en suite (3 fmly) ❷ TVB tea/coffee ✖ Cen ht TVL farm animals to see & touch 25 acres beef sheep Dinner Last d early morning LB **Parking** 6 **Notes** Closed 24-25 Dec ❷

Premier Collection

◆◆◆◆◆

West Colwell Farm

Offwell EX14 9SL ☎ 01404 831130 📠 01404 831769
e-mail westcolwell@tiscali.co.uk
Dir Off A35 to village, at church go downhill, farm 0.5m on right

Peacefully situated down a country lane in an Area of Outstanding Natural Beauty, West Colwell Farm offers stylish bedrooms in a converted dairy. The two rooms on the ground floor have direct access to their own terraces. Breakfast is served overlooking the wooded valley and fields in the split-level dining room, with a roaring log-buring stove in cooler months.

Facilities 3 en suite (2 GF) ❷ FTV TVB tea/coffee ✖ Cen ht No children 12yrs No coaches **Prices** S £45; D £70-£75✱ LB **Parking** 3 **Notes** Closed Xmas

◆◆◆◆ ❦

Courtmoor Farm (ST207068)

Upottery EX14 9QA ☎ 01404 861565 Mr & Mrs Buxton
e-mail courtmoor.farm@btinternet.com
web www.courtmoor.farm.btinternet.co.uk
Dir Off A30, 0.5m W of A30 & A303 junct, 4m from Honiton

This licensed farmhouse is set in attractive grounds, with stunning views over the Otter valley. All of the bedrooms share the views, and are spacious and well equipped. Dinner, by arrangement on weekdays, provides freshly cooked local produce. You have access to the leisure room, gym and sauna. Self-catering cottages are also available.

continued

continued

Facilities 3 en suite (1 fmly) ⊛ STV TVB tea/coffee ✖ Cen ht Fishing Sauna Gymnasium childrens play area & equipment 17 acres non-working Dinner Last d 10am **Prices** S £33-£35; D £50-£55✳ **Parking** 20 **Notes** Closed 20 Dec-1 Jan

◆◆◆◆

Atwell's at Wellington Farm ◇

Wilmington EX14 9JR ☎ 01404 831885
e-mail wilmington@btinternet.com
Dir 3m E of Honiton on A35 towards Dorchester, 500yds through Wilmington on left

Convenient for Honiton and the coast, this delightful Grade II listed 16th-century farmhouse is set in 5 acres of grounds, which also accommodates a rescue centre for animals including hens, a goat, sheep and horses of varying sizes (from Shire to Shetland). This friendly house offers comfortable accommodation, hearty breakfasts using fresh local produce and cream teas.

Facilities 3 rms (2 en suite) (1 GF) ⊛ TVB Cen ht TVL No coaches **Prices** S £18-£28; D £40-£46✳ **Parking** 10 **Notes** ⊠

◆◆◆◆

Ridgeway Farm ◇

Awliscombe EX14 3PY ☎ 01404 841331 🖹 01404 841119
e-mail jessica@ridgewayfarm.co.uk
Dir 3m NW of Honiton. A30 onto A373, through Awliscombe to end of 40mph area, right opp Godford Farm, farm 0.25m up narrow lane

This 18th-century farmhouse has a peaceful location on the slopes of Hembury Hill, and is a good base for exploring nearby Honiton and the east Devon coast. Renovations have brought the cosy accommodation to a high standard and the atmosphere is relaxed and homely. The proprietors and their pets assure a warm welcome.

Facilities 2 en suite ⊛ in bedrooms ⊛ in dining room TVB tea/coffee Cen ht TVL No coaches Dinner Last d morning **Prices** S £30-£34; D £52-£58 **LB** **Parking** 4 **Notes** ⊠

◆◆◆

Threshays ◇

Awliscombe EX14 3QB
☎ 01404 43551 & 07811 675800 🖹 01404 43551
e-mail threshays@tesco.net
Dir 2.5m NW of Honiton on A373

A converted threshing barn situated on a non-working farm, Threshays has wonderful views over open countryside. With tea and cake offered on arrival, this family-run establishment offers comfortable accommodation with a friendly atmosphere. The lounge-dining room is a light and airy setting for enjoying the good breakfasts. Ample parking is a bonus.

Facilities 2 rms (1 fmly) ⊛ tea/coffee ✖ Cen ht TVL No coaches **Prices** S £25; D £45 **Parking** 10 **Notes** ⊠

HORNS CROSS
MAP 03 SS32

Premier Collection

◆◆◆◆◆

The Round House

EX39 5DN ☎ 01237 451687 🖹 01237 451924
web www.the-round-house.co.uk
Dir A39 towards Bude, 0.5m past The Hoops Inn on the left

This charming converted barn stands in landscaped gardens within easy reach of Clovelly. You receive a warm welcome and a complimentary cream tea on arrival, which may be served in the lounge with exposed beams and an inglenook fireplace. Bedrooms are comfortable with numerous thoughtful extra facilities. A varied choice is offered at breakfast.

Facilities 3 en suite (1 fmly) (1 GF) ⊛ TVB tea/coffee ✖ Cen ht TVL No children 12yrs No coaches **Prices** S £40; D £60 **Parking** 8

HORRABRIDGE
MAP 03 SX56

◆◆◆◆ 🅰

Overcombe Guest House

Old Station Rd PL20 7RA
☎ 01822 853501 🖹 01822 853602
e-mail enquiries@overcombehotel.co.uk
Dir Signed 100yds off A386 at Horrabridge

Facilities 8 en suite (2 fmly) (2 GF) ⊛ TVB tea/coffee ✖ Licensed Cen ht TVL No children 2yrs No coaches **Prices** S £35-£40; D £58-£65 **Parking** 7 **Notes** Closed 25 Dec

See advertisement under TAVISTOCK

ILFRACOMBE
MAP 03 SS54

★★★★ Guest House

Lyncott House

56 St Brannocks Rd EX34 8EQ ☎ 01271 862425
web www.lyncotthouse.co.uk
Dir 0.5m S of town centre. On A361 opp Bicclescombe Park Rd

An elevated quality Victorian house offering spacious well equipped bedrooms with views across the valley. John and Carol offer a warm welcome and a relaxed and friendly atmosphere. The generous breakfast is a fine prelude to a day discovering Ilfracombe and Exmoor National Park. An evening meal is available upon request.

Facilities 5 en suite ⊛ TVB tea/coffee ✖ Cen ht No children 14yrs No coaches Dinner Last d 11am **Prices** S £35-£40; D £55-£80✳ **Parking** 5 **Notes** ⊠

England

ILFRACOMBE continued

★★★ Guest House
Avalon Ilfracombe ◇
6 Capstone Crs EX34 9BT
☎ 01271 863325 ▤ 01271 866543
e-mail ann_dudley_avalon@yahoo.co.uk
web www.avalon-hotel.co.uk
Dir A361 to Ilfracombe, right at first lights, at end of one-way system turn left & left again

This friendly, well-established guest house is near the centre of Ilfracombe and is within reach of beaches, spectacular coastal walks and Exmoor National Park. The bedrooms are well equipped including one on the ground floor; rooms to the rear of the property have magnificent sea views. Breakfast is served at separate tables in the well-appointed dining room, and free parking spaces are available a short distance from the house.

Facilities 9 en suite (3 fmly) (1 GF) ⊗ TVB tea/coffee No coaches Dinner Last d 2.30pm **Prices** S £25-£32; D £25-£60 **LB Notes** Closed Xmas, New Year & BHs

◆◆◆◆
Strathmore ◇
57 St Brannock's Rd EX34 8EQ
☎ 01271 862248 ▤ 01271 862248
e-mail peter@small6374.fsnet.co.uk
web www.strathmore.ukhotels.com
Dir A361 from Barnstaple to Ilfracombe, Strathmore 1.5m from Mullacot Cross entering Ilfracombe

Situated within walking distance of the town centre and beach, this charming Victorian property offers a very warm welcome. The attractive bedrooms are comfortably furnished, while public areas include a well-stocked bar, an attractive terraced garden, and an elegant breakfast room.

Facilities 8 en suite (3 fmly) ⊗ TVB tea/coffee Licensed Cen ht No coaches Last d 8.30pm **Prices** S £27-£35; D £50-£70✳ **LB Parking** 7

◆◆◆◆
Collingdale Hotel ◇
13 Larkstone Ter EX34 9NU
☎ 01271 863770 ▤ 01271 863867
e-mail info@collingdalehotel.co.uk
web www.collingdalehotel.co.uk
Dir E through Ilfracombe, on left past B3230 turning

Built in 1869, this friendly establishment is within easy walking distance of the town centre and seafront. The well-presented bedrooms, many with sea views, are equipped with modern facilities, and the comfortable lounge also has magnificent views over the sea. Dinner is available by arrangement and there is a cosy bar.

Facilities 9 rms (8 en suite) (1 pri facs) (3 fmly) ⊗ in bedrooms ⊗ in dining room ⊗ in lounges TVB tea/coffee ✖ Licensed TVL No coaches Dinner Last d 2pm **Prices** S £25-£37.50; D £50-£66✳ **LB**

◆◆◆◆
Marine Court Hotel
Hillsborough Rd EX34 9QQ ☎ 01271 862920
e-mail marinecourthtl@aol.com

This friendly, informal establishment offers comfortable accommodation opposite the Old Thatched Inn. The well-presented bedrooms vary in size and come with thoughtful extras, and freshly prepared evening meals are served in the spacious dining room. On-site and adjacent parking is a bonus.

Facilities 8 en suite (3 fmly) ⊗ in dining room TVB tea/coffee ✖ Licensed No coaches Dinner Last d 2pm **Parking** 5 **Notes** ⊜

◆◆◆◆
Norbury House ◇
Torrs Pk EX34 8AZ ☎ 01271 863888
e-mail info@norburyhouse.co.uk
web www.norburyhouse.co.uk
Dir A361 from Barnstaple, 1st lights turn left, 2nd lights left & left again into Torrs Park, Norbury House on right

Norbury House, built in 1870, is located on an quiet elevated position with views over the town and the sea in the distance. The contemporary interior includes well-equipped bedrooms, a conservatory-lounge and a cosy bar. Outside are terraced gardens with seating. Breakfast is served in the pleasant dining room and dinners are available by arrangement.

Facilities 6 en suite (4 fmly) ⊗ TVB tea/coffee Licensed Cen ht TVL No coaches Dinner Last d 5pm **Prices** S £30-£35; D £60-£70 **LB Parking** 6 **Notes** Closed Jan

♦♦♦♦

Varley House ◇

Chambercombe Pk EX34 9QW
☎ 01271 863927 📠 01271 879299
e-mail info@varleyhouse.co.uk
web www.varleyhouse.co.uk
Dir A399 to Combe Martin, right at swimming pool , around left corner, house on inside of right bend

Facilities 8 rms (7 en suite) (1 pri facs) (2 fmly) (1 GF) ⊗ in bedrooms ⊗ in dining room ⊗ in lounges TVB tea/coffee Licensed Cen ht TVL No children 5yrs No coaches Dinner Last d 4pm **Prices** S £29-£35; D £58-£70✳ **LB Conf** Max 20 **Parking** 8

♦♦♦

Dedes Hotel

1-3 The Promenade EX34 9BD
☎ 01271 862545 📠 01271 862234
e-mail jackie@dedes.fsbusiness.co.uk
Dir Entering Ilfracombe, signs to seafront, premises on right

Please note that this establishment has recently changed hands. The family-run Dedes offers comfortable accommodation on the seafront, with some rooms having sea views. You have a choice of dining options: carte and set menus in the formal restaurant, or a good choice of bar meals in the Wheel House bar.

Facilities 17 rms (12 en suite) (6 fmly) ⊗ in area of dining room TVB tea/coffee Licensed Cen ht TVL Clay pigeon shooting Dinner **Parking** 11 **Notes** Closed 23-26 Dec

♦♦♦

Langleigh Park House

Langleigh Pk EX34 8BG ☎ 01271 862158
e-mail info@langleigh.co.uk
web www.langleigh.co.uk
Dir Onto Church Hill at war memorial & end of Langleigh Rd, turn right, 1st left (Langleigh Park), 2nd left

Set in 14 acres just a 10-minute uphill walk from the town centre and beaches, the Victorian stone house looks over the sea and surrounding countryside. Some of the comfortable bedrooms have four-poster beds.

Facilities 8 rms (6 en suite) (2 fmly) ⊗ TV6B tea/coffee Cen ht TVL No coaches Pool Table Clay shooting, Mountain biking **Prices** S £45-£50; D £50-£64✳ **LB Parking** 8 **Notes** Closed Jan-Mar

U

The Harbour Lights ◇

26 Broad St EX34 9BL ☎ 01271 862778 📠 01271 863124
e-mail info@hlhar.co.uk
Dir From A361 follow signs to harbour, located at junct of Broad St and The Quay

At the time of going to press the rating for this establishment had not been confirmed. Please check the AA website www.theAA.com for up-to-date information.

Facilities 9 en suite (2 fmly) ⊗ in bedrooms ⊗ in area of dining room ⊗ in lounges TVB tea/coffee 🐾 Licensed No coaches Dinner Last d 9pm **Prices** S fr £25; D £72✳ **LB Notes** Closed Nov-Feb

---

JACOBSTOWE   MAP 03 SS50

♦♦♦♦

Higher Cadham *(SS585026)*

EX20 3RB ☎ 01837 851647 📠 01837 851410 Messrs Sallis
e-mail kingscadham@btopenworld.com
web www.highercadham.co.uk
Dir A386 onto A3072 for Jacobstowe, at junct turn left, sharp right after church & continue 0.5m

Guests return for the excellent hospitality and enjoyable food, and the location is great for cycling or walking breaks. Children will enjoy the animals and the large play area. Ground-floor bedrooms are available, two with easier access, and there is a comfortable lounge and bar.

Facilities 12 en suite (4 fmly) (4 GF) ⊗ TVB tea/coffee Licensed Cen ht TVL Nature Trail, Pets corner, Play area 120 acres beef & sheep Dinner Last d 5pm **Conf** Max 30 **Parking** 30 **Notes** Closed 21 Dec-10 Jan rs Sun

---

KINGSBRIDGE   MAP 03 SX74

♦♦♦♦ 🏠

Staunton Lodge

Emb Road TQ7 1JZ ☎ 01548 854542 📠 01548 854421
e-mail miketreleaven@msn.com
web www.stauntonlodge.co.uk
Dir A381 from Kingsbridge centre along estuary signed Dartmouth, Lodge 0.25m on left

The proprietors of this delightful house provide a friendly atmosphere and attentive service, ensuring a relaxing stay. Bedrooms are thoughtfully equipped and comfortably furnished. The waterside location provides pleasant views during the excellent breakfast, when freshly cooked local produce makes a memorable start to the day.

Facilities 2 rms (1 en suite) (1 pri facs) ⊗ STV TVB tea/coffee 🐾 Cen ht No children 8yrs No coaches **Prices** D £54-£60✳ **LB Parking** 4 **Notes** Closed 20 Dec-10 Jan rs Nov-19 Dec & 11 Jan-Feb

♦♦♦♦

Highwell House *(SX712457)*

Churchstow TQ7 3QP ☎ 01548 852131 Mrs Pope
e-mail highwellhouse@hotmail.com
web www.highwellhouse.co.uk
Dir Off A379 at Churchstow opp Church House Inn. 30yds right, house on right

Highwell House is a secluded country house set in extensive attractive gardens and has excellent country views. It is well situated for exploring the attractions and the beautiful coastline of the South Hams. The comfortable bedrooms are well equipped. In winter breakfast is served in the dining room and in summer in the conservatory.

Facilities 3 en suite (1 fmly) ⊗ TVB tea/coffee 🐾 Cen ht No children 14yrs 🐕 Woodland Walk, 2 acre garden 10 acres Sheep **Parking** 4 **Notes** Closed Dec-9 Mar

KINGSBRIDGE continued

♦♦♦♦

Ashleigh House

Ashleigh Rd TQ7 1HB ☎ 01548 852893
e-mail reception@ashleigh-house.co.uk
web www.ashleigh-house.co.uk
*Dir A381 from Kingsbridge in direction of Salcombe. Take 3rd left
going up hill, after rdbt, proceed to Ashleigh Rd, house on left*

Facilities 8 en suite (2 fmly) ⊗ in bedrooms ⊗ in dining room
⊗ in 1 lounge TVB tea/coffee Licensed Cen ht No coaches
Prices S £35-£38; D £50-£56✳ **LB Parking** 4 **Notes** Closed Dec-Jan

Ⓤ

Westpark Bed & Breakfast

Shute Hill, Malborough TQ7 3SF
☎ 01548 561831 ▤ 01548 561831
e-mail westpark@johnpauline.freeserve.co.uk
web http://mysite.freeserve.com/westpark
*Dir A381 Townsend Cross, right Collaton Rd, right lower town, left
Shute Hill, right at bottom*

At the time of going to press the rating for this establishment had not
been confirmed. Please check the AA website www.theAA.com for up-
to-date information.

Facilities 2 rms (1 en suite) (1 pri facs) (1 fmly) (2 GF) ⊗ TVB
tea/coffee ✖ **Notes** ⊛

LEWDOWN   MAP 03 SX48

♦♦♦♦ ⌂

Stowford House

EX20 4BZ ☎ 01566 783415 ▤ 01566 783415
e-mail alison@stowfordhouse.com
web www.stowfordhouse.com
Dir 1m E of Lewdown in Stowford village near church

The delightful Georgian country house in secluded gardens is a
tranquil base for exploring the area. Enjoy a varied choice at breakfast
in the smart dining room, and an elegant drawing room is available.
Light suppers (soup and sandwiches) are available on request. The
bedrooms have high standards of comfort and numerous extras.

Facilities 4 en suite ⊗ TVB tea/coffee ✖ Cen ht TVL No children
14yrs No coaches **Prices** S £43-£48; D £60-£68 **LB Parking** 5

LIFTON   MAP 03 SX38

★★★★ ⊛ Restaurant with Rooms

Tinhay Mill Guest House and Restaurant

Tinhay PL16 0AJ ☎ 01566 784201 ▤ 01566 784201
e-mail tinhay.mill@talk21.com
web www.tinhaymillrestaurant.co.uk
*Dir A30/A388 approach Lifton, restaurant at bottom of village on
right*

The former mill cottages are now a delightful restaurant with rooms of
much charm. Beams and open fireplaces set the scene, with

everything geared to ensure a relaxed and comfortable stay.
Bedrooms are spacious and well-equipped, with many thoughtful
extras. Cuisine is taken seriously here, using the best of local produce.

Facilities 3 en suite TVB Direct dial from bedrooms ✖ Licensed TVL
No children 12yrs No coaches Dinner Last d 9.30pm **Prices** S £45-£50;
D £65-£72✳ **LB Parking** 18

♦♦♦♦

The Old Coach House

The Thatched Cottage, Sprytown PL16 0AY
☎ 01566 784224 ▤ 01566 784334
e-mail tochsprytown@aol.com
web www.theoldcoach-house.co.uk
*Dir Off A30 through Lifton, 0.75m E to Sprytown x-rds, right to
Thatched Cottage in 100yds*

Set in a colourful cottage garden near the Cornwall border, the Old
Coach House provides a warm welcome. The comfortable bedrooms
have numerous extras, including a welcome basket. Hearty breakfasts,
served in the beamed dining room of the adjacent Thatched Cottage,
feature good local produce including vegetarian options.

Facilities 3 rms (3 fmly) (2 GF) ⊗ TVB tea/coffee Direct dial from
bedrooms ✖ No coaches **Parking** 6 **Notes** ⊛

LUSTLEIGH   MAP 03 SX78

★★★★ Guest Accommodation

Eastwrey Barton

Moretonhampstead Rd TQ13 9SN
☎ 01647 277338 ▤ 01647 277133
e-mail info@eastwreybarton.co.uk
*Dir On A382 between Bovey Tracey and Moretonhampstead, 4m
from A38*

Warm hospitality and a genuine welcome are hallmarks at this family-
run establishment, situated within the Dartmoor National Park. Built in
the 18th Century, the house retains many original features and has
lovely views across the Wray valley. Bedrooms are spacious and well
equipped, while public areas include a snug lounge warmed by a
crackling log fire. Breakfast and dinner are showcases for local
produce with an impressive wine list to accompany the latter.

Facilities 5 en suite (1 fmly) ⊗ TVB tea/coffee ✖ Licensed Cen ht
No children 10yrs No coaches Dinner Last d noon **Prices** S £47-£50;
D £64-£70✳ **Conf** Max 20 **Parking** 18

continued

Premier Collection

◆◆◆◆◆ 🏠

Woodley House

Caseley Hill TQ13 9TN ☎ 01647 277214 📄 01647 277126

Dir *Off A382 into village, at T-junct right to Caseley, house 2nd on left*

Set just a stroll from the village pub, church and tea room, Woodley House is a tranquil retreat with super views over rolling countryside. The hearty breakfast, featuring as many as 12 home-made preserves, home-baked bread and a vast range of cooked breakfast options, is enjoyed in the charming dining room. A good base for walkers, and dogs are welcome too.

Facilities 2 en suite ⊗ TVB tea/coffee Cen ht TVL No children 10yrs No coaches **Prices** S £48-£50; D £63-£65✶ **Parking** 3 **Notes** 😊

LYDFORD   MAP 03 SX58

Premier Collection

◆◆◆◆◆ 😊

Moor View House

Vale Down EX20 4BB ☎ 01822 820220 📄 01822 820220

Dir *1m NE of Lydford on A386*

Built about 1870, this charming house once changed hands over a game of cards. The elegant bedrooms are furnished with interesting pieces and retain many original features. Breakfast (dinner by arrangement) is served house-party style at a large oak table. The 2 acres of moorland gardens give access to Dartmoor.

Facilities 4 en suite ⊗ TVB tea/coffee 🗶 Licensed Cen ht TVL No children 12yrs No coaches 🏐 Bowls Dinner Last d 24 hrs prior LB **Parking** 15 **Notes** 😊

◆◆◆◆ 🐓

Downtown Farm B&B ◇ (SX522855)

EX20 4AX ☎ 01822 820210 & 07891 126817 Mr & Mrs P Strawbridge
e-mail downtownfarm@hotmail.com
web www.downtownfarm.co.uk

Dir *Off A30 S onto A386 signed Sourton, 4m right for Lydford, B&B 200yds on right*

The renovated 16th-century farmhouse has a delightful location on the edge of Dartmoor National Park. Set in 15 acres, the house is close to Lydford Gorge and within walking distance of country inns. Breakfast features home-grown produce when possible, including fresh eggs from farm hens. Self-catering cottages are also available.

continued

Facilities 3 en suite ⊗ TVB tea/coffee 🗶 Cen ht TVL No children 7yrs 🏐 Childrens outdoor area 12 acres sheep **Prices** S £25-£27; D £50-£54✶ LB **Parking** 22 **Notes** 😊

LYNMOUTH   MAP 03 SS74

See also **Brendon**

Premier Collection

◆◆◆◆◆ 🏠 😊

Sea View Villa

6 Summer House Path EX35 6ES
☎ 01598 753460 📄 01598 753496
e-mail reservations@seaviewvilla.co.uk
web www.seaviewvilla.co.uk

Dir *A39 from Porlock, 1st left after bridge, Sea View Villa on right 20yds along path opp church*

This charming Georgian villa, built in 1721, has been refurbished to a high standard by owners Steve Williams and Chris Bissex. Tucked away from the bustle of the main streets, the house provides elegant and peaceful accommodation. All bedrooms have thoughtful extras and impressive views of the harbour and sea. The proprietors' genuine hospitality assures a relaxed and comfortable stay. Dinner and breakfast are not to be missed.

Facilities 5 rms (3 en suite) (1 fmly) ⊗ TVB tea/coffee 🗶 Licensed Cen ht TVL No children 14yrs No coaches Beauty & Holistic treatments Dinner Last d 5pm **Prices** D £90-£110✶ LB **Notes** Closed Jan

Premier Collection

◆◆◆◆◆ 😊

Bonnicott House

Watersmeet Rd EX35 6EP ☎ 01598 753346
e-mail bonnicott@hotmail.com
Dir *A39 from Minehead over East Lyn River Bridge, left onto Watersmeet Rd, 50yds on right opp church*

Bonnicott House is set in attractive gardens with spectacular views over the harbour towards the sea and cliffs. Bedrooms, most with sea views, are very well equipped, with comfortable furnishings and thoughtful extra facilities. Dinner offers fresh local produce, imaginatively presented, and at breakfast hearty portions are served fresh from the Aga.

Facilities 8 rms (7 en suite) (1 pri facs) ⊗ TVB tea/coffee 🗶 Licensed Cen ht TVL No children 14yrs No coaches Dinner Last d noon **Prices** S £46-£86; D £64-£96✶ LB **Conf** Del from £130 ✶

England

LYNMOUTH continued

Premier Collection

◆◆◆◆◆ ⚏ ☞

The Heatherville

Tors Pk EX35 6NB ☎ 01598 752327 ⓘ 01598 752634
web www.heatherville.co.uk
Dir Off A39 onto Tors Rd, 1st left fork into Tors Park

Having a secluded and elevated south-facing position, the Heatherville has splendid views over Lynmouth and surrounding woodland. Lovingly restored over the last few years to a very high standard, the bedrooms and the lounge give a feeling of luxury, with the charm of a large country house. Enjoyable evening meals, by arrangement, feature organic and free-range produce whenever possible. There is also an intimate bar.

Facilities 6 en suite ⊘ TVB tea/coffee Licensed Cen ht No children 16yrs No coaches Dinner Last d breakfast **Prices** D £60-£80✳ LB **Parking** 7 **Notes** Closed Dec-Jan

◆◆◆◆

Orchard House Hotel

12 Watersmeet Rd EX35 6EP
☎ 01598 753247 ⓘ 01598 753855
e-mail bryn@lynmouthhotel.co.uk
web www.lynmouthhotel.co.uk
Dir On A39, W side of East Lyn river bridge, adjacent to car park and church

Expect a friendly welcome at Orchard House. The Grade II listed building is just a stroll from High St. Bedrooms are light and airy and have many considerate extras, and hearty breakfasts are served in the pleasant dining room. A cosy bar and a comfortable lounge are also available.

Facilities 6 rms (4 en suite) (2 pri facs) (2 fmly) ⊘ TVB tea/coffee ✻ Licensed Cen ht TVL No children 12yrs No coaches **Prices** S £35-£60; D £50-£60✳ LB **Notes** Closed mid Dec-mid Jan

◆◆◆◆ ☞

Rock House

Manor Grounds EX35 6EN
☎ 01598 753508 ⓘ 01598 753796
e-mail enquiries@rock-house.co.uk
web www.rock-house.co.uk
Dir On A39, at foot of Countisbury Hill right onto drive, pass Manor green/play area to Rock House

This Grade II listed house has a stunning location with breathtaking views at the harbour entrance. One of the attractive bedrooms is on the ground floor, while two have four-poster beds. You can dine either in the restaurant or in the spacious, comfortable bar

Facilities 8 en suite (1 GF) ⊘ in bedrooms ⊘ in dining room ⊘ in lounges TVB tea/coffee Licensed Cen ht TVL ✎ ♪ Dinner Last d 9pm **Prices** S £41; D £82-£88✳ LB **Parking** 8 **Notes** Closed 24-25 Dec

◆◆◆◆

Countisbury Lodge Hotel

6 Tors Pk, Countisbury Hill EX35 6NB ☎ 01598 752388
e-mail paulpat@countisburylodge.co.uk
Dir Off A39 Countisbury Hill just before Lynmouth centre, signed Countisbury Lodge

From its peaceful elevated position high above the town, this former Victorian vicarage has spectacular views of the harbour and countryside. The atmosphere is friendly and informal but with attentive service. The comfortable bedrooms are attractively decorated, and breakfast is served in the pleasant dining room. A cosy bar is also available.

Facilities 4 en suite (1 fmly) ⊘ TVB tea/coffee Licensed Cen ht TVL No coaches Dinner Last d noon **Prices** S £32-£36; D £50-£56✳ **Parking** 6

♦♦♦♦
Glenville House

2 Tors Rd EX35 6ET ☎ 01598 752202
e-mail tricia@glenvillelynmouth.co.uk
web www.glenvillelynmouth.co.uk
Dir *Off A39 at the bottom of Countisbury Hill, 200yds along Tors Rd*

A friendly welcome awaits you at this delightful Victorian house overlooking the East Lyn River. The attractive bedrooms feature coordinated furnishings, and traditional breakfasts are served at separate tables in the dining room. A comfortable first-floor lounge is also available, with river views and an attractive garden, where cream teas can be enjoyed in summer.

Facilities 6 rms (3 en suite) (1 pri facs) (1 GF) ⊗ tea/coffee ✖ Licensed Cen ht TVL No children 14yrs No coaches **Prices** S fr £27; D £54-£60✶ **LB Notes** Closed mid Nov-mid Feb 🐾

♦♦♦
Lorna Doone House

4 Tors Rd EX35 6ET ☎ 01598 753354 🖷 01598 763777
e-mail lornadoonehouselynmouth@fsmail.net
Dir *Off A39 at Lynmouth onto Tors Rd*

This refurbished Victorian property is just a short walk from the village centre. Bedrooms are equipped with considerate extras and there is a comfortable lounge. Breakfast is served in the attractive dining room at the front of the house.

Facilities 5 en suite (2 fmly) ⊗ TVB tea/coffee ✖ Cen ht TVL No coaches **Prices** S fr £36; D £58-£64✶ **LB Parking** 6 **Notes** Closed 15 Dec-Feb

[U]
River Lyn View

26 Watersmeet Rd EX35 6EP ☎ 01598 753501
e-mail riverlynview@aol.com
Dir *On A39, 200yds past St John's church on right*

At the time of going to press the rating for this establishment had not been confirmed. Please check the AA website www.theAA.com for up-to-date information.

Facilities 4 en suite (2 fmly) ⊗ TVB tea/coffee Cen ht TVL
Prices S £30-£35; D £47-£52✶

LYNTON
MAP 03 SS74
See also **Challacombe**

♦♦♦♦♦
Highcliffe House

Sinai Hill EX35 6AR ☎ 01598 752235 🖷 01598 753815
e-mail info@highcliffehouse.co.uk
web www.highcliffehouse.co.uk
Dir *Off A39 into Lynton, signs for Old Village, at pub turn right up steep hill, house 150yds on left*

Highcliffe House has stunning views of Exmoor and the coast, and across to south Wales. Built in the 1870s as a summer residence, this wonderful house is a good base for exploring the area. Bedrooms are
continued

spacious and elegant, likewise the lounges and candlelit conservatory restaurant with its spectacular outlook. Dinner, served Friday to Sunday, is an imaginative choice of home-made dishes. This is a non-smoking property. Karen and Michael Orchard are top-twenty finalists for AA Landlady of the Year 2006.

Highcliffe House

Facilities 6 en suite ⊗ TVB tea/coffee ✖ Licensed Cen ht TVL No children 14yrs No coaches Dinner Last d 11am (weekends only) **Prices** S £56-£66; D £72-£96✶ **LB Parking** 7 **Notes** Closed Dec-mid Feb

♦♦♦♦♦
Victoria Lodge

30-31 Lee Rd EX35 6BS ☎ 01598 753203
e-mail info@victorialodge.co.uk
Dir *Off A39 in village centre opp Post Office*

Please note that this establishment has recently changed hands. A warm welcome awaits you at this elegant 1880s villa in the heart of Lynton. Bedrooms are named after Queen Victoria's children and grandchildren, and the rich colours, feature coronets, half-testers and a four-poster bed reflect the style of the period.

Facilities 9 en suite ⊗ TVB tea/coffee ✖ Cen ht No children 11yrs No coaches **Prices** D £60-£90✶ **Parking** 6 **Notes** Closed Nov-23 Mar

♦♦♦♦
Pine Lodge

Lynway EX35 6AX ☎ 01598 753230
e-mail info@pinelodgelynton.co.uk
web www.pinelodgelynton.co.uk
Dir *500yds S of town centre off Lynbridge Rd opp Bridge Inn*

This attractive house, set in a secluded position with views of the wooded West Lyn valley, provides comfortable and friendly accommodation. Bedrooms are spacious and have many thoughtful extras. The lounge is particularly appealing and comfortable. Breakfast offers freshly cooked home-made dishes.

Facilities 6 en suite (2 GF) ⊗ TVB tea/coffee ✖ Licensed Cen ht No children 12yrs No coaches **Prices** S £24; D £48-£54✶ **LB Parking** 6 **Notes** Closed Nov-Jan

England

LYNTON continued

♦♦♦♦

North Walk House

North Wk EX35 6HY ☎ 01598 753372
e-mail northwalkhouse@btinternet.com
web www.northwalkhouse.co.uk
Dir In town centre, off Castle Hill by church down North Walk Hill, B&B on left

With fabulous views over the Bristol Channel to the Welsh coastline, North Walk House has been completely refurbished over the last year. You receive a friendly welcome from the owners, who are happy to advise on local walks. The contemporary bedrooms are well equipped, with rooms featuring DVDs and ironing equipment. Evening meals, by arrangement, use organic produce whenever possible.

Facilities 6 en suite (1 GF) ⊗ TVB tea/coffee ✱ Licensed Cen ht No children 14yrs No coaches Dinner Last d 5pm **Prices** S £42; D £76-£96✳ **LB** **Conf** Board 12 **Parking** 6

♦♦♦♦

St Vincent House Hotel & Restaurant

Castle Hl EX35 6JA ☎ 01598 752244 ▤ 01598 752244
e-mail welcome@st-vincent-hotel.co.uk
web www.st-vincent-hotel.co.uk
Dir Off Lynmouth Hill onto Castle Hill

Expect a warm welcome at this attractive Grade II listed house. The individually furnished bedrooms are well equipped, and an open fire burns in the charming drawing room during cooler months, the venue for a pre-dinner drink. Exmoor produce is used in the restaurant alongside signature dishes such as Provençal bouillabaisse and Noir de Noir Marquise, and classic Belgian beers.

Facilities 6 en suite ⊗ TVB tea/coffee ✱ Licensed Cen ht No children 8yrs No coaches Beauty therapy & Aromatherapy Dinner Last d 9pm **Prices** D £65✳ **LB** **Parking** 2 **Notes** Closed Jan-Etr

♦♦♦♦

Sinai House ◇

Lynway EX35 6AY ☎ 01598 753227 ▤ 01598 752663
e-mail enquiries@sinaihouse.co.uk
Dir A39 onto B3234 through town, pass church, house on right overlooking main car park

This Victorian residence has spectacular views over Lynton, Lynmouth and across the Bristol Channel. You are assured of a friendly welcome from the owners. Bedrooms are well furnished and the public rooms

continued

include a spacious, well-appointed lounge, a cosy bar and a smart dining room.

Facilities 8 rms (6 en suite) (2 pri facs) ⊗ TVB tea/coffee ✱ Licensed Cen ht TVL No children 12yrs No coaches **Prices** S £24-£28; D £54-£60 **LB** **Parking** 8 **Notes** Closed 15 Nov-28 Dec & 3 Jan-15 Feb

♦♦♦♦

Southcliffe ◇

34 Lee Rd EX35 6BS ☎ 01598 753328
e-mail info@southcliffe.co.uk
Dir Entering Lynton, Southcliffe opp Post Office

Situated in the main street, Southcliffe dates from Victorian times. The stylish bedrooms are comfortable and well equipped. In addition to the traditional cooked breakfast, non-meat eaters are well provided for. Similarly evening meals feature numerous vegetarian options and are served by arrangement.

Facilities 7 en suite ⊗ TVB tea/coffee ✱ Licensed Cen ht No children 14yrs No coaches Dinner Last d 10am **Prices** S £24-£32; D £48-£60✳ **Parking** 8 **Notes** Closed Nov-Feb

♦♦♦♦

Waterloo House ◇

Lydiate Ln EX35 6AJ ☎ 01598 753391
e-mail relax@waterloohousehotel.com
web www.waterloohousehotel.com
Dir A39 into Lynton, road bends to Lydiate Ln

This family-run Georgian property has abundant charm. Bedrooms are individually furnished and well equipped, and a choice of lounges is available. The atmosphere is convivial and relaxed, with every effort made to ensure an enjoyable stay. Authentic Thai cuisine is a feature in the elegant on-site restaurant Thai-Lyn.

Facilities 6 en suite (2 fmly) ⊗ TVB tea/coffee ✱ Licensed Cen ht TVL No children 10yrs No coaches Dinner Last d 9.30pm **Prices** S £25-£28; D £46-£70✳ **Parking** 3 **Notes** Closed mid Nov-mid Jan

♦♦♦♦ 🅰

Brendon House

Brendon EX35 6PS ☎ 01598 741206 ▤ 01598 741188
e-mail brendonhouse4u@aol.com
web www.brendonvalley.co.uk/brendonhouse4u.htm
Dir A39 towards Lynmouth, turn left signed Brendon, over bridge to green, B&B ahead

Facilities 5 en suite (1 fmly) ⊗ STV TVB tea/coffee Licensed Cen ht TVL Fishing Riding Dinner Last d 24hrs before **Prices** S £38; D £52-£60✳ **LB** **Parking** 7 **Notes** Closed Xmas 🐾

MARSH   MAP 04 ST21

◆◆◆◆

Cottage B & B ◇

EX14 9AJ ☎ 01460 234240
e-mail buttonstephens@btopenworld.com
web www.cottagemarsh.co.uk
Dir *A303 Ilminster to Honiton, left off dual-carrigeway, 1st right under bridge, 1st house on right*

Set in the beautiful Blackdown Hills on the border of Devon and Somerset, this accommodation has been refurbished to a high quality standard. Bedrooms are all at ground level, with walk-in shower rooms. Each room has its own entrance from the small courtyard where visitors, resident and non-resident, can sit in warmer weather and enjoy afternoon tea from the on-site tea room (seasonal afternoon opening times). Breakfast features eggs from the host's own chickens and local produce.

Facilities 4 en suite (4 GF) ⊗ TVB tea/coffee Cen ht No coaches
Prices S £25-£29.50; D £45-£49.50 **LB** **Parking** 4 **Notes** ⊗

MODBURY   MAP 03 SX65

◆◆◆ ▥

The White Hart Inn

Church St PL21 0QW ☎ 01548 831561 ▤ 01548 831265
e-mail whi.manager@ccinns.com
Dir *On A379 in village centre*

The village inn is well placed for exploring the picturesque South Hams and Dartmoor. A wide range of dishes is served in the spacious, contemporary public areas, and the bedrooms, varying in size, are equipped to a high standard.

Facilities 5 en suite ⊗ in bedrooms ⊗ in dining room ⊗ in 1 lounge
TVB tea/coffee ✱ Cen ht No coaches Dinner Last d 9pm **Conf** Max 100
Thtr 100 Class 80 Board 60 **Parking** available

MORETONHAMPSTEAD   MAP 03 SX78

★★★ Guest House

Cookshayes Country Guest House ◇

33 Court St TQ13 8LG ☎ 01647 440374 ▤ 01647 440374
e-mail cookshayes@aol.co.uk
web www.cookshayes.co.uk
Dir *A38 onto A382 to Moretonhampstead. Take B3212 towards Princetown. Cookshayes 400yds on left.*

A genuine welcome awaits you at this secluded Victorian house, a perfect base for exploring Dartmoor. Bedrooms are comfortably furnished and well appointed, and one has a four-poster bed. The smart dining room is the venue for scrumptious breakfasts and excellent dinners, where local produce is cooked with skill and enthusiasm. The cosy lounge overlooks an attractive garden.

Facilities 7 rms (5 en suite) (1 fmly) (1 GF) ⊗ in 4 bedrooms
⊗ in dining room ⊗ in lounges TVB tea/coffee Licensed Cen ht TVL
No children 5yrs No coaches Dinner **Prices** S £20-£25; D £40 £55✳ **LB**
Conf Max 16 Class 10 Board 10 **Parking** 10

◆◆◆◆◆ ⬯

Gate House

North Bovey TQ13 8RB ☎ 01647 440479 ▤ 01647 440479
e-mail gatehouseondartmoor@talk21.com
web www.gatehouseondartmoor.com
Dir *B3212 from Moretonhampstead to North Bovey*

The tranquil charm of this medieval Devon hall house, set in a beautiful conservation area, is enriched by the hospitality of the hosts and their splendid home cooking. The elegant bedrooms are furnished with coordinated fabrics and luxury beds. Meals are served house-party style and feature local speciality produce, while the aroma of freshly baked bread calls you to breakfast. An outdoor swimming pool is available in summer.

Facilities 3 rms (2 en suite) (1 pri facs) ⊗ TVB tea/coffee Cen ht
No children 15yrs No coaches ⤵ Last d by arrangement
Prices S £46-£48; D £70-£72 **LB** **Parking** 3 **Notes** ⊗

◆◆◆◆ ⬱

Hazlecott Bed & Breakfast ◇

Manaton TQ13 9UY
☎ 01647 221521 & 07800 994928 ▤ 01647 221405
e-mail hazelcott@dartmoordays.com
web www.dartmoordays.com
Dir *A38 onto A382 through Bovey Tracey to Manaton. Pass Kestor Inn, right at x-rds, 0.5m past church*

A delightful home from home is provided at this secluded house on the edge of Dartmoor. Rooms vary in size but all have superb views. Breakfasts are a feature, when local produce is used confidently. This is an ideal venue for ramblers.

Facilities 3 en suite (1 fmly) (1 GF) ⊗ TVB tea/coffee Licensed Cen ht
TVL No coaches Dinner Last d previous day **Prices** S £30-£40;
D £50-£75✳ **LB** **Parking** 6

England

England

MORETONHAMPSTEAD continued

◆◆◆◆

Moorcote

Chagford Cross TQ13 8LS ☎ 01647 440966
e-mail moorcote@smartone.co.uk
Dir A382 Chagford & Okehampton Rd from Moretonhampstead for 400yds. Past hospital, Moorcote is on right

Perched on a hill overlooking the town and surrounded by mature country gardens, this Victorian house is a good base for exploring Dartmoor and only a short walk from the town centre. Friendly owners Pat and Paul Lambert extend a warm welcome to their guests, many of whom return on a regular basis.

Facilities 4 en suite (2 fmly) ⊗ TVB tea/coffee ✖ Cen ht No children 5yrs No coaches **Prices** D £50-£54 **LB** **Parking** 6 **Notes** Closed Dec ⊛

◆◆◆◆ **A**

Great Sloncombe

TQ13 8QF ☎ 01647 440595 ▤ 01647 440595
e-mail hmerchant@sloncombe.freeserve.co.uk
Dir A382 from Moretonhampstead towards Chagford, 1.5m left at sharp double bend & farm 0.5m up lane

Facilities 3 en suite ⊗ TVB tea/coffee Cen ht No children 8yrs No coaches **Prices** D £60-£70 **Parking** 3 **Notes** ⊛

◆◆◆◆ **A** ❦

Great Wooston Farm ◇ (SX764890)

TQ13 8QA ☎ 01647 440367 ▤ 01647 440367 Mrs Cuming
e-mail info@greatwoostonfarm.com
web www.greatwoostonfarm.com
Dir Onto Lime St (opp library) for 1.5 m over cattle grid, fork left over 2nd cattle grid, 2nd house on right

Facilities 3 en suite ⊗ TVB tea/coffee ✖ Cen ht TVL No children 8yrs 320 acres mixed **Prices** S £56-£62; D £28-£31 **LB** **Parking** 3

NEWTON ABBOT   MAP 03 SX87
See also **Bickington & Widecombe in the Moor**

◆◆◆◆◆ ⌂

Castle Dyke House

Highweek Village TQ12 1QG ☎ 01626 367965
web www.castledykehouse.co.uk
Dir A38 onto A382, 1.9m right at left-hand bend signed Highweek, right at T-junct, 0.2m left onto driveway before bus layby

Castle Dyke is set in 2 acres of beautiful grounds, including a parterre and a herb garden, in a quiet village near Dartmoor. As the name suggests, the gardens feature the earthworks of a 12th-century motte and bailey castle with panoramic views of the coast and moors. Plenty of extras are provided in the comfortable bedrooms, and the delightful breakfast, featuring a range of local and home-made produce, is a highlight of any stay.

Facilities 3 en suite ⊗ TVB tea/coffee ✖ Cen ht TVL No children 12yrs No coaches **Parking** 8 **Notes** Closed 24 Dec-2 Jan ⊛

◆◆◆◆ ⌂ ❦

Bulleigh Park (SX860660)

Ipplepen TQ12 5UA
☎ 01803 872254 ▤ 01803 872254 Mrs Dallyn
e-mail bulleigh@lineone.net
web www.southdevonaccommodation.co.uk
Dir 3.5m S of Newton Abbot. Off A381 at Parkhill Cross by Jet station for Compton, continue 1m, signed

Bulleigh Park is a working farm producing award-winning Aberdeen Angus beef. Expect a friendly welcome at this family home set in glorious countryside, where the owner has won an award for green tourism by reducing the impact of the business on the environment. Breakfasts are notable for the wealth of fresh, local and home-made produce, and the porridge is cooked to a secret recipe. Angela Dallyn is a top-twenty finalist for AA Landlady of the Year 2006.

Facilities 2 en suite 1 annexe en suite ⊗ in bedrooms ⊗ in dining room ⊗ in 1 lounge FTV TVB tea/coffee ✖ Cen ht TVL Stabling available for own horse 60 acres beef, sheep **Prices** S £35-£40; D £66-£76 **LB** **Parking** 6

England

**◆◆◆◆ **

Chipley Farm (SX794726)

TQ12 6JW ☎ 01626 821486 📄 01626 821486 Mrs Westcott
e-mail louisa@chipleyfarmholidays.co.uk
web www.chipleyfarmholidays.co.uk
For full entry see **Bickington**

◆◆◆◆

Hazelwood Hotel

33A Torquay Rd TQ12 2LW
☎ 01626 366130 📄 01626 365021
Dir Off A380 Penn Inn rdbt into town, 750yds on right

The smart Hazelwood offers a friendly atmosphere just a stroll from
the town centre. It is a good base for business or leisure, and many
guests return regularly. The bedrooms are well equipped with
thoughtful extra touches and have attractive fabrics. Freshly prepared,
home-cooked dishes are served in the panelled dining room.

Facilities 8 rms (7 en suite) (1 pri facs) (2 GF) ⊗ in bedrooms
⊗ in dining room TVB tea/coffee Direct dial from bedrooms 🐾
Licensed Cen ht TVL No coaches Dinner Last d 5.30pm
Prices S £36-£41; D £54-£58 **Parking** 8

**◆◆◆◆ **

Sampsons Farm Hotel & Restaurant

Preston TQ12 3PP ☎ 01626 354913 📄 01626 354913
e-mail nigel@sampsonsfarm.com
web www.sampsonsfarm.com
Dir A380 onto B3195 signed Kingsteignton. Pass Ten Tors Inn on left
& 2nd right B3193 to Chudleigh. At rdbt 3rd exit, left after 1m

This attractive thatched 16th-century farmhouse stands in a quiet
location. Accommodation is provided in the main house and in
adjacent converted stables, and all rooms are well equipped. The
accomplished cuisine uses fresh local produce at dinner and breakfast.

Facilities 5 rms (2 en suite) 6 annexe en suite (2 fmly) ⊗ in bedrooms
⊗ in dining room TVB tea/coffee Direct dial from bedrooms Licensed Cen ht
No coaches Water colour classes Dinner Last d 9.15pm **Prices** S £50-£90;
D £60-£120✳ **LB Conf** Max 16 Class 20 Board 12 **Parking** 20

**◆◆◆ **

Moores Restaurant & Rooms ◇

6 Greenbank, High St EX10 0EB
☎ 01395 568100 📄 01395 568092
e-mail mooresrestaurant@aol.com
Dir On A3052 in village centre

This small restaurant offers very comfortable, practically furnished
bedrooms. You are assured of a friendly welcome and relaxed,
efficient service. Good quality, local ingredients produce imaginative
dishes, full of natural flavours, at lunch and dinner.

Facilities 3 rms (1 en suite) (2 fmly) ⊗ TVB tea/coffee 🐾 Licensed
Cen ht No coaches Dinner Last d 9.30pm **Prices** S £30-£40; D £40-£50
LB Conf Max 12 Board 12 **Notes** Closed 1st 2wks Jan

**◆◆◆◆ **

Pressland Country House

Hatherleigh EX20 3LW ☎ 01837 810871 📄 01837 810303
e-mail accom@presslandhouse.co.uk
web www.presslandhouse.co.uk
Dir 6m N of Okehampton on A386 towards Hatherleigh

A friendly welcome is assured at Pressland House, a delightful
Victorian property surrounded by landscaped gardens. The elegant
bedrooms have views over countryside and are provided with
excellent accessories. It is worth booking in advance for one of the
delicious dinners.

Facilities 4 rms (3 en suite) (1 pri facs) 2 annexe en suite (1 fmly)
(2 GF) ⊗ TVB tea/coffee 🐾 Licensed Cen ht TVL No children 12yrs
No coaches Dinner Last d 6pm **Prices** S £52-£77; D £60-£90✳ **LB**
Conf Thtr 12 Board 12 **Parking** 10 **Notes** Closed Dec-Feb

---

*If you book on bed, breakfast and evening
meal terms, you may find that the tariff
includes only the set menu*

OKEHAMPTON continued

◆◆◆◆

Week Farm *(SX519913)*

Bridestowe EX20 4HZ
☎ 01837 861221 🖺 01837 861221 Mrs Hockridge
e-mail margaret@weekfarmonline.com
web www.weekfarmonline.com
Dir 1m NE of Bridestowe. Off junct A30 & A386 towards Bridestowe,
fork right, right at x-rds to Week Farm

A delicious complimentary cream tea awaits you to this 17th-century
farmhouse. Surrounded by undulating countryside, the farm also has
three coarse fishing lakes. Traditional farmhouse breakfasts are
enjoyed in the dining room. The comfortable bedrooms are furnished
in traditional style; one ground-floor room has easier access.
Facilities 5 en suite (2 fmly) (1 GF) ⊗ TVB tea/coffee Cen ht TVL ⋌
Fishing 3 Coarse fishing lakes 180 acres sheep Devpm catte
Prices D £52-£56✳ LB **Conf** Max 12 **Parking** 10 **Notes** Closed 25 Dec

OTTERY ST MARY   MAP 03 SY19

◆◆

Fluxton Farm ◇

Fluxton EX11 1RJ ☎ 01404 812818 🖺 01404 814843
web www.fluxtonfarm.co.uk
Dir 2m SW of Ottery St Mary. B3174 W from Ottery over river, left,
next left to Fluxton

A haven for cat lovers, Fluxton Farm offers comfortable
accommodation with a choice of lounges and a large garden,
complete with pond and ducks. Set in peaceful farmland 4m from the
coast, this 16th-century longhouse has a wealth of beams and open
fireplaces.
Facilities 7 rms (6 en suite) (1 pri facs) (1 fmly) ⊗ in dining room
⊗ in lounges TVB tea/coffee Cen ht TVL No children 8yrs No coaches
Prices S £25.50-£27.50; D £50-£55✳ LB **Parking** 15 **Notes** rs Nov-Apr
⊛

PAIGNTON   MAP 03 SX86

◆◆◆◆

Aquamarine Hotel ◇

8 St Andrews Rd TQ4 6HA ☎ 01803 551193
e-mail aquahotel@aol.com
Dir Along Esplanade with sea on left, at minirdbt right onto Sands Rd,
St Andrews Rd 2nd left

The friendly proprietors give a warm welcome at the Aquamarine,
located just a short distance from the town centre and the seafront. A
comfortable lounge, small bar and a pleasant garden with decking are
available, and tasty home-cooked evening meals are served by
arrangement.
Facilities 9 en suite (3 fmly) ⊗ TVB tea/coffee ✖ Licensed Cen ht
TVL **Prices** S £22-£26; D £44-£52✳ LB **Parking** 4 **Notes** rs
19 Dec-18 Mar

◆◆◆◆

The Clydesdale

5 Polsham Pk TQ3 2AD ☎ 01803 558402
e-mail info@theclydesdale.co.uk
Dir Off A3022 Torquay Rd onto Lower Polsham Rd, 2nd right into
Polsham Park

Please note that this establishment has recently changed hands. The
proprietors warmly welcome you to their home with a splendid
garden, just a short walk from the town centre and seafront. Two
bedrooms are on the ground floor, and home-cooked evening meals
are available by arrangement; the home-made cakes are a speciality.
Facilities 7 en suite (1 fmly) (2 GF) ⊗ in dining room TVB tea/coffee
✖ Cen ht TVL No children 3yrs Free passes to local leisure centre
Dinner Last d noon LB **Parking** 5 **Notes** Closed 30 Nov-4 Jan

◆◆◆◆

Kingswinford Hotel

32 Garfield Rd TQ4 6AX ☎ 01803 558358
e-mail kingswinfordhotel@btconnect.com
web www.kingswinfordhotel.co.uk
Dir In town centre 250yds W of pier. Off A3022 over railway crossing
onto Torbay Rd, Garfield Rd 2nd left

This friendly establishment is just a level stroll from the beach and
pier. Accommodation is attractive, comfortable and non-smoking.
Breakfast is served in the pleasant dining room, and freshly prepared
home-cooked dinners are available during the summer by
arrangement.
Facilities 8 en suite (3 fmly) (1 GF) ⊗ TVB tea/coffee ✖ Cen ht TVL
No coaches Dinner Last d previous day

◆◆◆◆

Rosslyn Hotel

16 Colin Rd TQ3 2NR ☎ 01803 525578 🖹 01803 555450

Dir Left along seafront from Paignton town centre, road bends & Colin Rd on left

Rosslyn Hotel is an easy level stroll from the beach and town centre, and the friendly proprietors are most welcoming and attentive. Bedrooms are well equipped and comfortable, and dinner and breakfast are served in the beamed dining room, which has a cosy bar. You can relax in the inviting sitting room.

Facilities 9 rms (7 en suite) (2 fmly) ⊘ in 5 bedrooms ⊘ in dining room ⊘ in lounges TVB tea/coffee ✖ Licensed Cen ht TVL Dinner Last d noon **Parking** 10 **Notes** Closed Dec-Jan

◆◆◆◆

Bay Sands Hotel ◇

14 Colin Rd TQ3 2NR ☎ 01803 524877
e-mail enquiries@baysands.co.uk

Dir Off A3022 to Marine Drive on seafront, onto Colin Rd

Facilities 9 en suite ⊘ in 6 bedrooms ⊘ in dining room ⊘ in lounges FTV TVB tea/coffee ✖ Cen ht TVL No children 2yrs No coaches **Prices** S £20-£28; D £40-£56✱ **LB Parking** 9 **Notes** Closed Xmas/New Year

◆◆◆◆

Birchwood House Hotel ◇

33 St Andrews Rd TQ4 6HA
☎ 01803 551323 🖹 01803 409883
e-mail birchwoodhouse@aol.com

Dir Along seafront towards harbour, at rdbt right & 2nd left

Facilities 10 en suite (3 fmly) (4 GF) ⊘ in bedrooms ⊘ in dining room ⊘ in lounges TVB tea/coffee ✖ Licensed Cen ht TVL No children 5yrs Dinner Last d noon **Prices** S £25-£37; D £50-£74✱ **LB Parking** 7

◆◆◆◆

Earlston House Hotel ◇

31 St Andrew's Rd TQ4 6HA ☎ 01803 558355
e-mail earlstonhouse@aol.com
web www.earlstonhouse.co.uk

Dir From Paignton seafront at minirdbt onto Sands Rd, 2nd left onto St Andrew's Rd, hotel at brow of hill on left

Facilities 12 en suite (5 fmly) ⊘ in bedrooms ⊘ in dining room TV10B tea/coffee ✖ Licensed Cen ht TVL No coaches Dinner Last d 2pm **Prices** S £20-£26; D £40-£52✱ **LB Parking** 7 **Notes** Closed Nov-Jan

◆◆◆

Bay Cottage Hotel ◇

4 Beach Rd TQ4 6AY ☎ 01803 525729
e-mail info@baycottagehotel.co.uk

Dir Along B3201 Esplanade Rd past Paignton Pier, Beach Rd 2nd right

With easy level access to the beach, theatre and the shops, Bay Cottage offers friendly accommodation. In the bedrooms, the best possible use has been made of available space. Home-cooked

continued

dinners, by arrangement, are served in the pleasant pine-furnished dining room, and there is also a comfortable lounge.

Facilities 8 en suite (3 fmly) ⊘ in bedrooms ⊘ in dining room TVB tea/coffee Cen ht TVL No coaches Dinner Last d 9.30am **Prices** S £19-£25; D £38-£50✱ **LB Notes** Closed 20 Dec-3 Jan

◆◆◆

Park Hotel

Esp Road TQ4 6BQ ☎ 01803 557856 🖹 01803 555626
e-mail stay@parkhotel.me.uk

Dir On Paignton seafront, nearly opp pier

This large establishment has a prominent position on the seafront with excellent views of Torbay. The pleasant bedrooms are all spacious and available in a number of options, and several have sea views. Entertainment is provided on some evenings in the lounge. Dinner and breakfast are served in the spacious dining room, which overlooks the attractive front garden.

Facilities 47 rms (33 en suite) (5 fmly) (3 GF) ⊘ in bedrooms ⊘ in dining room ⊘ in 1 lounge TVB tea/coffee Licensed Lift Cen ht games room with 3/4 snooker table & table tennis Dinner Last d 6pm **Conf** Max 120 Board 12 **Parking** 35

◆◆◆

The Sealawn Hotel

Sea Front, 20 Esplanade Rd TQ3 3RT
☎ 01803 559031 🖹 01803 666285
e-mail sharondavies@sealawnhotel.wanadoo.co.uk

Dir On seafront between pier & cinema

Located on the seafront, the Sealawn is a pleasant place to stay. Bedrooms are comfortable and well equipped, and some are on the ground floor. Many have excellent views over the bay. Dinner is served in the lower ground-floor dining room where hearty portions are served at breakfast.

Facilities 12 en suite (3 fmly) (3 GF) ⊘ in dining room TVB tea/coffee Direct dial from bedrooms ✖ Licensed Cen ht TVL Dinner Last d 9.30pm **Prices** S £32-£35; D £54-£60✱ **LB Parking** 12

◆◆◆

Wentworth Hotel ◇

18 Youngs Park Rd, Goodrington TQ4 6BU
☎ 01803 557843
e-mail thewentworthhotel@blueyonder.co.uk

Dir Through Paignton on A378, 1m left at rdbt, sharp right onto Roundham Rd, right & right again onto Youngs Park Rd

Within 200yds of the beach, this Victorian house overlooks Goodrington Park and is convenient for many attractions and the town centre. The bedrooms are attractively decorated and well equipped, and feature many thoughtful extras. The traditional English breakfast is a tasty start to the day, and evening meals are available by arrangement. Additional facilities include a bar and a lounge.

Facilities 9 en suite (2 fmly) ⊘ in 7 bedrooms ⊘ in dining room ⊘ in lounges TVB tea/coffee Licensed Cen ht TVL No coaches Dinner Last d 24 hours prior **Prices** S £18-£27; D £36-£54✱ **LB Parking** 4

PARRACOMBE   MAP 03 SS64

◆◆◆

The Fox & Goose ◇

EX31 4PE ☎ 01598 763239 ▤ 01598 763621
Dir *Off A399 at Blackmoor Gate, after 1.5m turn left for Parracombe.
Bottom of hill, on left opp car park*

The Fox & Goose is a real village pub serving good food. Local meat
and game, along with locally landed fish feature on the blackboard
menus. The walls of the inn are adorned with memorabilia, and
guests are served breakfast in the comfort of their bedroom.

Facilities 1 en suite ⊛ in bedrooms ⊛ in dining room TVB tea/coffee
✖ Cen ht No coaches Dinner Last d 9pm **Prices** S £30-£45;
D £45-£60✳ **Parking** 10 **Notes** Closed 25 Dec

PLYMOUTH   MAP 03 SX45

★★★★ Guest Accommodation

Grosvenor

9 Elliot St, The Hoe PL1 2PP
☎ 01752 260411 ▤ 01752 668878
e-mail grosvenorhotel@btinternet.com
Dir *Off A38 for city centre & Barbican, left to Walrus, over junct on
left*

The Grosvenor is convenient for The Hoe, ferry port and the city's
attractions. Bedrooms are well equipped, with some family rooms, and
you can relax in the smart bar-lounge. A light meal/snack menu is
available at dinner in the pleasant dining room, where breakfast is also
served. Limited parking.

Facilities 28 en suite (3 fmly) (1 GF) ⊛ in dining room TVB tea/coffee
✖ Licensed Cen ht TVL Dinner Last d 8pm **Prices** S fr £35; d fr £50✳
Parking 6 **Notes** Closed 22 Dec-2 Jan

★★★ A Guest Accommodation

Tudor House ◇

105 Citadel Rd, The Hoe PL1 2RN
☎ 01752 661557 ▤ 01752 661557
Dir *Exit A38 towards city centre, onto A374 towards Continental Ferry
Port, left to Hoe and Citadel Rd.*

Facilities 8 rms (5 en suite) (1 fmly) (1 GF) ⊛ in 2 bedrooms
⊛ in dining room ⊛ in lounges TVB tea/coffee ✖ Licensed Cen ht
No coaches **Prices** S fr £18; D £40-£45✳ **Parking** 2 **Notes** Closed
23-31 Dec

◆◆◆◆

Berkeley's of St James

4 St James Pl East, The Hoe PL1 3AS
☎ 01752 221654 ▤ 01752 221654
e-mail enquiry@onthehoe.co.uk
Dir *Off A38 towards city centre, left at sign The Hoe, over 7 sets of
lights, left onto Athenaeum St, right to Crescent Av, 1st left*

Located in a quiet square close to The Hoe and just a short walk from
the city centre, this is a good choice for business and leisure.
Bedrooms are attractive and equipped with a number of thoughtful
extras. An enjoyable breakfast using organic and local produce,
whenever possible, is served in the dining room.
continued

Berkeley's of St James

Facilities 5 en suite (1 fmly) (1 GF) ⊛ TVB tea/coffee ✖ Cen ht
No coaches **Prices** S £38-£40; D £60-£65 **LB** **Parking** 3 **Notes** Closed
23 Dec-1 Jan

◆◆◆◆

The Cranbourne ◇

278-282 Citadel Rd, The Hoe PL1 2PZ
☎ 01752 263858 & 224646 ▤ 01752 263858
e-mail cran.hotel@virgin.net

This attractive Georgian terrace house has been extensively renovated,
and is just a short walk from The Hoe, The Barbican and the city
centre. Bedrooms are practically furnished and hearty breakfasts are
served in the elegant dining room. There is also a cosy bar.

Facilities 40 rms (28 en suite) (5 fmly) (1 GF) ⊛ in dining room TVB
tea/coffee Licensed Cen ht TVL **Prices** S £22-£40; D £44-£56✳ **Parking** 14

◆◆◆◆

The Dudley Hotel ◇

42 Sutherland Rd, Mutley PL4 6BN
☎ 01752 668322 ▤ 01752 673763
e-mail info@dudley-hotel.com
web www.dudley-hotel.com
Dir *A38 onto A386 to city centre, under railway bridge & left at rdbt
onto North Rd E, left at lights onto Houndiscombe Rd, left onto
Sutherland Rd*

Convenient for the city centre, railway station and university, the
Dudley offers comfortable and attractive accommodation. The
proprietor provides attentive service and the atmosphere is relaxed
and friendly. A good choice of dishes is served in the spacious dining
room at breakfast, including vegetarian options.

Facilities 6 rms (5 en suite) (1 pri facs) (2 fmly) ⊛ TVB tea/coffee ✖
Cen ht TVL **Prices** S £30-£35; D £49✳

◆◆◆◆

Jewell's

220 Citadel Rd, The Hoe PL1 3BB
☎ 01752 254760 ▤ 01752 254760
Dir *A38 towards city centre, follow sign for Barbican, then The Hoe.
Left at lights, right at top of road onto Citadel Rd. Jewell's 0.25m*

This smart, family-run guest house is only a short walk from The Hoe,
and is convenient for the city centre and the Barbican. Bedrooms
come with a wide range of extra facilities, and breakfast is served in
the pleasant dining room. Some secure parking is available.
continued

Facilities 10 rms (7 en suite) (5 fmly) ⊗ in bedrooms ⊗ in dining room TVB tea/coffee ✗ Cen ht **Parking** 3

◆◆◆
Caraneal ◇
12/14 Pier St, West Hoe PL1 3BS
☎ 01752 663589 ▤ 01752 663589
e-mail caranealhotel@hotmail.com
Dir *From A38 signs for city centre, signs for The Hoe & seafront, 1st right after Plymouth Dome*

Set within walking distance of the Hoe, city centre and attractions, the Caraneal offers stylish, well-equipped accommodation. Some rooms are on the ground floor and provide easier access. A comfortable lounge and a bar are available, and a full English breakfast is served in the dining room.

Facilities 9 en suite (1 fmly) (2 GF) ⊗ in bedrooms ⊗ in dining room TVB tea/coffee ✗ Cen ht TVL No coaches **Prices** S £30-£35; D £45-£50 **Parking** 2

◆◆◆
Four Seasons ◇
207 Citadel Rd East, The Hoe PL1 2JF ☎ 01752 223591
web www.fourseasonsguesthouse.co.uk
Dir *Off A38 for city centre & The Hoe*

Set opposite The Hoe and Barbican, this attractive house is tucked away within walking distance of the city's attractions. The friendly proprietors offer bedrooms with fresh bright colours and a restful, contemporary style. The freshly cooked breakfasts have good choices, including Cornish butter and Devonshire bacon.

Facilities 7 rms (5 en suite) (1 GF) ⊗ TVB tea/coffee Cen ht No coaches **Prices** S £30-£45; D £50-£60✳

◆◆◆
Devonshire ◇
22 Lockyer Rd, Mannamead PL3 4RL
☎ 01752 220726 ▤ 01752 220766
e-mail devonshiregh@blueyonder.co.uk
Dir *At Hyde Park pub on traffic island turn left onto Wilderness Rd. After 60yds turn left onto Lockyer Rd*

This comfortable Victorian house is located in a residential area close to Mutley Plain high street, from where there is a regular bus service to the city centre. The well-proportioned bedrooms are bright and attractive, and a comfy lounge is available. There is some parking.

continued

Facilities 10 rms (5 en suite) (4 fmly) (3 GF) ⊗ in 3 bedrooms ⊗ in dining room TVB tea/coffee ✗ Licensed Cen ht TVL **Prices** S £23-£40; D £40-£50✳ **LB Parking** 6

◆◆◆
Hotel Royal ◇
11 Elliot St, The Hoe PL1 2PP
☎ 01752 226222 & 0845 644 9474 ▤ 01752 226222
e-mail royal@hotels-plymouth.com
Dir *Off A38 for city centre & Pavilions, left onto Atheneum St & Elliot St*

Situated just a short walk from The Hoe, Barbican and city centre, this establishment is well located for business and leisure. The attractive bedrooms are have contemporary comforts, and a full cooked breakfast is served in the bright and cheerful dining room.

Facilities 14 rms (11 en suite) (5 fmly) ⊗ in 7 bedrooms ⊗ in dining room TVB tea/coffee Direct dial from bedrooms Cen ht **Prices** S £20-£30; D £40-£50✳ **Conf** Max 20 Thtr 20 Class 10 Board 16 **Parking** 3 **Notes** Closed 20 Dec-4 Jan

◆◆◆
The Lamplighter ◇
103 Citadel Rd, The Hoe PL1 2RN
☎ 01752 663855 & 07793 360815 ▤ 01752 228139
e-mail stay@lamplighterplymouth.co.uk
web www.lamplighterplymouth.co.uk
Dir *Near war memorial*

With easy access to The Hoe, Barbican and city centre, this comfortable guest house is a good base for leisure or business. Bedrooms, including family rooms, are light and airy and furnished to a consistent standard. Breakfast is served in the dining room, which has an adjoining lounge area.

Facilities 9 rms (7 en suite) (2 pri facs) (2 fmly) ⊗ in dining room TVB tea/coffee Cen ht TVL **Prices** S fr £30; D £42-£45✳ **Parking** 4

◆◆◆ Ⓐ
Brittany ◇
28 Athenaeum St, The Hoe PL1 2RQ
☎ 01752 262247 ▤ 01752 268843
e-mail enquiries@brittanyguesthouse.co.uk
web www.brittanyguesthouse.co.uk
Dir *A38 City Centre follow signs for Pavillions, bear left at minirdbt, turn left at lights*

Facilities 9 en suite (1 pri facs) (3 fmly) (1 GF) ⊗ TVB tea/coffee ✗ Cen ht No children 3yrs No coaches **Prices** S £30-£45; D £42-£49 **Parking** 6 **Notes** Closed 20 Dec-2 Jan

◆◆◆ Ⓐ
Chester House ◇
54 Stuart Rd, Pennycomequick PL3 4EE ☎ 01752 663706
e-mail info@chesterplymouth.co.uk
web www.chesterplymouth.co.uk
Dir *A38 onto A386 to City Centre, right at 1st rdbt, B&B 50yds on right*

Facilities 10 rms (4 en suite) (2 fmly) (3 GF) ⊗ TVB tea/coffee ✗ Cen ht TVL No coaches **Prices** S £22-£30; D £42-£45✳ **Parking** 6

England

PLYMOUTH continued

♦♦

West Hoe Guesthouse

26 Pier St, West Hoe PL1 3BT
☎ 01752 252006 & 07880 610252
e-mail carolehammett@hotmail.com
Dir *Signs to seafront or Barbican, pass The Dome, next right onto Pier St*

Set within walking distance of The Hoe, attractions and the Barbican, this small guest house offers friendly accommodation. Bedrooms are simply appointed in a range of sizes. A hearty breakfast is served in the lounge-dining room.

Facilities 3 rms (2 en suite) (2 fmly) (1 GF) ⊗ TVB tea/coffee Cen ht TVL No coaches **Prices** S £25-£30; D £40-£45✳ **LB Notes** 🐾

POSTBRIDGE   MAP 03 SX67

Premier Collection

♦♦♦♦♦

Lydgate House

PL20 6TJ ☎ 01822 880209 ▤ 01822 880202
e-mail lydgatehouse@email.com
web www.lydgatehouse.co.uk
Dir *B3212 SW into Postbridge, left down lane before bridge*

The house stands in 36 acres of moorland in a secluded valley with the East Dart River flowing through the grounds. The comfortable rooms and public areas are beautifully appointed, and enhanced with many extra facilities. Lunches, afternoon cream teas and dinner are available, and there is also a delightful lounge bar and a sun terrace.

Facilities 7 en suite (1 GF) ⊗ TVB tea/coffee Licensed Cen ht No children 16yrs No coaches Fishing Dinner Last d 6pm
Prices S £60-£65; D £110-£140 **Parking** 10 **Notes** Closed Nov-Feb

---

ROCKBEARE   MAP 03 SY09

♦♦♦ 🐾

Lower Allercombe Farm (SY048946)

EX5 2HD ☎ 01404 822519 ▤ 01404 822519 Ms Holroyd
e-mail susie@allercombe.fsnet.co
web www.lowerallercombefarm.co.uk
Dir *A30 at Daisy Mount onto B3180. After 200yds turn right to Allercombe. In 1m at Allercombe x-rds turn right , farm is 50yds on right*

Lower Allercombe dates from the 17th century and offers comfortable accommodation. The rural location is handy for the A30 and Exeter Airport, and is convenient for visiting local attractions. A self-catering cottage is also available.

Facilities 3 rms (1 en suite) (1 pri facs) (1 fmly) ⊗ in bedrooms ⊗ in dining room TVB tea/coffee Cen ht TVL 180 acres Horses Stud & cattle **Prices** S £30-£35; D £50-£65✳ **Parking** available **Notes** 🐾

♦♦♦

3 Cherry Tree Close

EX5 2HF ☎ 01404 822047
Dir *In village centre between bridge & church*

You are assured of a warm welcome at this homely establishment situated in a quiet cul-de-sac. The bedrooms, one of which looks over fields, are comfortable, and both are on the ground floor. The proprietor invites you to share the lounge, and breakfast is served in the kitchen-dining room.

Facilities 2 rms (2 GF) ⊗ tea/coffee 🐕 Cen ht TVL No children No coaches **LB Parking** 3 **Notes** Closed 23 Dec-4 Jan 🐾

SALCOMBE   MAP 03 SX73

♦♦♦♦

The Lodge Hotel

Higher Town, Malborough TQ7 3RN
☎ 01548 561405 ▤ 01548 561766
e-mail info@thelodge.uk.com
web www.lodge-churchills.co.uk
Dir *A381 from Kingsbridge to Salcombe. At Malborough turn opp petrol station, 1st right onto Lower Town Rd. Entrance 150yds on right*

Built around 1830, this attractive, friendly house is a peaceful and comfortable place to stay. The stylish bedrooms are light and airy with coordinated fabrics and furniture. Churchill's Bistro serves a range of imaginative dishes, alfresco during the summer. Freshly cooked breakfasts, made with local ingredients, are served in the conservatory.

Facilities 8 en suite (3 fmly) (2 GF) ⊗ in bedrooms ⊗ in dining room ⊗ in lounges TVB tea/coffee 🐕 Licensed Cen ht No coaches Dinner Last d 9pm **Prices** S £52-£130; D £72-£150 **Parking** 7

SAMPFORD COURTENAY   MAP 03 SS60

♦♦♦♦

Lower Trecott Farm

EX20 2TD ☎ 01837 880118
e-mail craig@trecott.fsnet.co.uk
Dir *A3072 W into village, left onto narrow lane, farm 0.25m on right*
Facilities 4 rms (1 en suite) (3 pri facs) (1 fmly) ⊗ tea/coffee 🐕 Cen ht TVL No coaches **Parking** 5 **Notes** 🐾

SEATON   MAP 04 SY29

♦♦♦♦

Beaumont

Castle Hill EX12 2QW ☎ 01297 20832
e-mail jane@lymebay.demon.co.uk
Dir *Off A3052 into Seaton to W end of seafront*

Quietly situated, this popular seafront guest house is close to the shops and just a few steps from the beach. Most of the spacious bedrooms have wonderful sea views, and a ground-floor room is also available. Breakfast is served in the light, airy dining room with Lyme Bay providing the scenic backdrop.

Facilities 5 en suite (2 fmly) (1 GF) ⊗ TVB tea/coffee Cen ht No coaches **Prices** D £55-£65✳ **Parking** 4 **Notes** Closed 21 Dec-3 Jan 🐾

♦♦♦♦
Mariners Hotel
East Walk Esp EX12 2NP ☎ 01297 20560
Dir *Off A3052 signed Seaton, B&B located on seafront*

Located on the seafront near the beach and cliff paths, this comfortable accommodation has a friendly and relaxed atmosphere. Bedrooms, some having sea views, are well equipped. The public rooms are light and airy, and the dining room, which is open to the public for lunch, afternoon teas and dinner, offers freshly prepared local produce.

Facilities 10 en suite (1 fmly) (1 GF) ⊘ TVB tea/coffee ✖ Licensed Cen ht No coaches Dinner Last d 3pm **Parking** 10

SHALDON	MAP 03 SX97

See **Teignmouth**

SIDMOUTH	MAP 03 SY18

See also **Ottery St Mary**

Premier Collection

♦♦♦♦♦ 🛡
The Old Farmhouse ◇
Hillside Rd EX10 8JG ☎ 01395 512284
Dir *A3052 from Exeter to Sidmouth, right at Bowd x-rds, 2m left at rdbt, left at minirdbt, next right, over hump-back bridge, bear right on the corner*

This beautiful 16th-century thatched farmhouse, in a quiet residential area just a stroll from the Esplanade and shops, has been lovingly restored. Bedrooms are attractive and the charming public rooms feature beams and an inglenook fireplace. The welcoming proprietors provide memorable dinners using traditional recipes and fresh local ingredients.

Facilities 3 en suite 4 annexe rms (3 en suite) (1 annexe pri facs) (1 fmly) (1 GF) ⊘ TV3B tea/coffee Licensed Cen ht TVL No children 8yrs No coaches Dinner Last d am **Prices** S £27-£32; D £54-£64❋ LB **Parking** 4 **Notes** Closed Nov-Feb

♦♦♦♦♦ ◉◉ 🛡
The Salty Monk
Church St, Sidford EX10 9QP ☎ 01395 513174
e-mail saltymonk@btconnect.com
Dir *On A3052 in Sidford opp church*

Set in the village of Sidford, this attractive property dates from the 16th century. Some of the well-presented bedrooms feature spa baths or special showers, and the ground-floor courtyard room has a king-size water bed. Meals are served in the restaurant, where the two owners both cook. They use fresh local produce to ensure that the food is of a high standard and thoroughly enjoyable.

Facilities 5 en suite (3 GF) ⊘ FTV TVB tea/coffee Licensed Cen ht No coaches Dinner Last d 9pm **Prices** S £60-£65; D £95-£150❋ LB **Conf** Max 14 Board 14 Del from £100 ❋ **Parking** 20 **Notes** Closed 2wks Nov & 3wks Jan

♦♦♦♦
Glendevon Hotel
Cotmaton Rd EX10 8QX ☎ 01395 514028
e-mail enquiries@glendevon-hotel.co.uk
web www.glendevon-hotel.co.uk
Dir *A3052 onto B3176 to minirdbt. Right, house 100yds on right*

Located in a quiet residential area just a short walk from the town centre and beaches, this stylish Victorian house offers neat bedrooms. You are assured of a warm welcome from the resident owners, who provide attentive service and wholesome home-cooked evening meals by arrangement. A lounge is available.

Facilities 8 en suite ⊘ TVB tea/coffee ✖ Licensed Cen ht No children No coaches Dinner Last d 9am LB **Notes** 🐾

♦♦♦♦ 🅰
Avalon Guest House
Vicarage Rd EX10 8UQ ☎ 01395 513443
e-mail owneravalon@aol.com
web www.avalonsidmouth.co.uk
Dir *From Exeter take A3052 at Sidford lights turn right. B&B is 1.3m on left.*

Facilities 4 en suite ⊘ FTV TVB tea/coffee ✖ Cen ht TVL No children 18yrs No coaches **Prices** D £54-£56❋ LB **Parking** 4 **Notes** Closed 10 Dec-15 Jan 🐾

England

◆◆◆

Bramley Lodge Guest House ◇

Vicarage Rd EX10 8UQ ☎ 01395 515710
e-mail haslam@bramleylodge.fsnet.co.uk
Dir 0.5m N of seafront on A375

You are assured of a warm welcome at this small, family-run guest house, a short level walk from the seafront. The neat bedrooms vary in size and each is equipped to a good standard. Home-cooked evening meals, including special diets, are available by arrangement.

Facilities 6 rms (5 en suite) (1 fmly) ⊗ FTV TVB tea/coffee Cen ht TVL No coaches Dinner Last d 1pm **Prices** S £27.50-£30; D £54-£60 **Parking** 6 **Notes** Closed Dec-Jan ⊠

◆◆

Enstone ◇

Lennox Av EX10 8TX ☎ 01395 514444
e-mail enstoneguesthouse@amserve.com
Dir A375 Vicarage Rd into Sidmouth, left onto Lennox Av

Situated in colourful gardens at the end of a quiet cul de sac, this family-run guest house is just 200yds from the town centre, and a short walk from the seafront. Bedrooms are neatly furnished, making the best use of the available space.

Facilities 5 rms (2 en suite) (1 fmly) (1 GF) ⊗ TVB tea/coffee ✖ Cen ht TVL No children 2yrs No coaches Dinner Last d 11am **Prices** S £20-£22; D £36-£52✳ LB **Parking** 5 **Notes** Closed Oct-Mar ⊠

U

The Groveside ◇

Vicarage Rd EX10 8UQ ☎ 01395 513406 ▤ 0870 224 6479
e-mail reservations@thegroveside.co.uk
Dir B3176, left at both rdbts, B&B 400yds on right.

At the time of going to press the rating for this establishment had not been confirmed. Please check the AA website www.theAA.com for up-to-date information.

Facilities 9 rms (7 en suite) (1 pri facs) ⊗ TVB tea/coffee ✖ Cen ht TVL No coaches Dinner Last d 4pm **Prices** S £27.50-£29.50; D £55-£59✳ LB **Parking** 8

◆◆◆

Hayne House

EX5 4HE ☎ 01392 860725 ▤ 01392 860725
e-mail haynehouse@ukonline.co.uk
web www.haynehouse-devon.co.uk
Dir Off A396 opp Ruffwell Hotel, right at fork, over 2 x-rds & right signed Hayne, 0.5m on left

Located in the peaceful Culm valley, the Georgian farmhouse offers homely accommodation, a friendly relaxed atmosphere and far-reaching views. A hearty breakfast is served around one large table, and sometimes dinner is available by arrangement. The country garden is filled with birdsong.

Facilities 2 rms (2 pri facs) (1 fmly) ⊗ tea/coffee ✖ TVL No coaches Dinner Last d 24hrs notice **Prices** D £48-£54 LB **Parking** 2 **Notes** Closed 15 Nov-23 Feb ⊠

◆◆◆◆

Higher Beneknowle Luxury B & B

TQ9 7LU ☎ 01364 649209 ▤ 01364 649203
e-mail trinadad48@aol.com
web www.higherbeneknowle.co.uk
Dir Off A38 at Marley Head, follow Avonwick/Totnes signs, left after Avon Inn, B&B 500yds on left

Nestling in a wooded valley in the South Hams near Dartmoor, Higher Beneknowle offers 17th-century charm with modern comforts. You are assured of the warmest of welcomes from the friendly owners. In the bedrooms, the very best use has been made of the available space, and the sitting and dining rooms are charmingly presented. Cordon Bleu dinners are served by arrangement.

Facilities 2 rms (1 en suite) (1 pri facs) ⊗ tea/coffee Cen ht TVL No coaches ⊀ hot air ballooning, horse riding Dinner Last d 7pm **Prices** S £45-£75; D £80-£100✳ LB **Parking** 4 **Notes** Closed 20 Dec-1 Apr ⊠

Premier Collection

◆◆◆◆◆ ⌇

Kerscott (SS793255)

Ash Mill EX36 4QG
☎ 01769 550262 ▤ 01769 550910 Mrs Sampson
e-mail kerscott.farm@virgin.net
web www.devon-bandb.co.uk
Dir 6m E of S Molton. A361 onto B3227, signed 1.5m

You are assured of a genuine warm welcome at this working beef and sheep farm on the edge of Exmoor National Park. Largely built in the 15th century, the property is full of character with original beams, sloping floors and inglenook fireplaces. Beautifully furnished throughout, the owners take great pride in their special corner of Devon. Dinner, by arrangement, uses home-grown produce whenever possible, and breakfast is just as hearty and memorable.

Facilities 3 en suite ⊗ TVB tea/coffee ✖ Cen ht No children 14yrs 110 acres beef, sheep Dinner Last d 24hrs prior **Prices** D £56-£60 LB **Parking** 4 **Notes** Closed Xmas & New Year ⊠

continued

♦♦♦♦

West Down Guest House (SS749259)

Whitechapel EX36 3EQ ☎ 01769 550839 Mrs S M Mason
e-mail westdown@hotmail.com

Dir Off M5 onto A361 at junct 27 & proceed towards Barnstaple. At
2nd rdbt (approx 25m) take 3rd exit signed Whitechapel, follow signs
to West Down

Set in 28 acres on the southern edge of Exmoor, West Down offers a
warm welcome and homely accommodation. Bedrooms are equipped
with many considerate extras. Using local produce whenever possible,
Sue's home-cooked dinners are available by arrangement. The restful
lounge has an open fire.

Facilities 3 en suite (1 fmly) ⊗ TVB tea/coffee ✹ Cen ht Fishing
28 acres non working Dinner Last d 24hrs notice **Parking** 10 **Notes** ✿

♦♦♦ ◼

Old Coaching Inn

Queen St EX36 3BJ ☎ 01769 572526

Dir Off A361 at rdbt signed to South Molton

There is a warm welcome at this popular inn in the bustling market
town. Bedrooms are soundly appointed, and the extensive menu in
the bar or restaurant provides a range of good value dishes. Additional
facilities include a large function room.

Facilities 10 en suite (2 fmly) ⊗ in dining room TVB tea/coffee ✹
Cen ht Pool Table Dinner Last d 9.30pm **Prices** S fr £35; d fr £60✳
Conf Max 100 Thtr 100 Class 100 Board 50 **Parking** 26

STOCKLAND   MAP 04 ST20

♦♦♦♦ ⊜ ◼

The Kings Arms Inn

EX14 9BS ☎ 01404 881361 📠 01404 881732
e-mail info@kingsarms.net
web www.kingsarms.net

Dir Off A30 NE of Honiton in village centre

A convivial atmosphere prevails at this attractive village inn, where staff
are helpful at all times. Bedrooms are spacious and comfortable, with
high quality en suites. Food is a highlight, with an extensive and
imaginative range of tempting home-made dishes. A garden is
available and ample parking too.

Facilities 3 en suite ⊗ in bedrooms ⊗ in dining room TVB tea/coffee
Direct dial from bedrooms Cen ht TVL Dinner Last d 9pm **Prices** S fr
£45; d fr £70✳ **Parking** 40 **Notes** Closed 25 Dec

STRETE   MAP 03 SX84

★★★★ Bed & Breakfast

Strete Barton Farmhouse

Totnes Rd TQ6 0RN ☎ 01803 770364 📠 01803 771182
e-mail info@stretebarton.co.uk

Dir From A38 take A384 to Totnes, onto A381/A3122 Dartmouth &
then A379 to Strete. B&B just below church.

This delightful 16th-century farmhouse has been refurbished to blend
stylish accommodation with original character. The village lies between
Dartmouth and Kingsbridge and has easy access to the natural beauty
of the South Hams. David and Veronica Worsley's ideas for Strete
continued

Barton were born of many years travelling and they have got it just
right.

Facilities 6 rms (4 en suite) (2 pri facs) (1 fmly) ⊗ TVB tea/coffee
Cen ht TVL No children 2yrs No coaches **Prices** S £40-£45; D £60-£80✳
LB **Parking** 4 **Notes** Closed 23-29 Dec

TAVISTOCK   MAP 03 SX47

♦♦♦♦♦ 🏠

Tor Cottage

PL16 0JE ☎ 01822 860248 📠 01822 860126
e-mail info@torcottage.co.uk
web www.torcottage.co.uk
For full entry see **Chillaton**

♦♦♦♦

April Cottage

12 Mount Tavy Road PL19 9JB ☎ 01822 613280

Dir A30 onto A386 to Tavistock, pass Kelly College, approaching
minirdbt April Cottage on right

Facilities 3 en suite (1 fmly) ⊗ TVB tea/coffee ✹ Cen ht TVL
No coaches Fishing Dinner Last d 5pm **Prices** S £40-£50; D £55-£64 LB
Parking 5 **Notes** ✿

♦♦♦

Sampford Manor ◇

Sampford Spiney PL20 6LH
☎ 01822 853442 📠 01822 855691
e-mail manor@sampford-spiney.fsnet.co.uk
web www.sampford-spiney.fsnet.co.uk

Dir B3357 towards Princetown, right at 1st x-rds. Next x-rds Warren
Cross left for Sampford Spiney. 2nd right, house below church

Once owned by Sir Francis Drake, this manor house is tucked away in
a tranquil corner of Dartmoor National Park. The family home is full of
character, with exposed beams and slate floors. A warm welcome is
assured and the freshly cooked breakfasts feature home-produced
eggs. Children, horses (stabling available) and dogs are welcome.

Facilities 3 rms (2 pri facs) (1 fmly) ⊗ in bedrooms ⊗ in dining room
TVB tea/coffee Cen ht No coaches Riding ♩♪ **Prices** S £27-£35;
D £45-£65✳ **Parking** 3 **Notes** Closed Xmas ✿

TAVISTOCK continued

◆◆◆

Coach House

PL19 8NS ☎ 01822 617515 📠 01822 617515
e-mail the-coachhouse@otterytavistock.fsnet.co.uk
web www.the-coachouse.co.uk
Dir *2.5m NW of Tavistock. A390 from Tavistock to Gulworthy Cross, right to Ottery village, 1st on right*

Dating from 1857, this building was constructed for the Duke of Bedford and converted by the current owners. Some bedrooms are on the ground floor and in an adjacent barn conversion. Dinner is available in the cosy dining room or the restaurant, which leads onto the south-facing garden.

Facilities 6 en suite 3 annexe en suite (4 GF) ⊘ in bedrooms ⊘ in dining room ⊘ in lounges TVB tea/coffee Direct dial from bedrooms Licensed Cen ht No children 5yrs Dinner Last d 9pm
Prices S £43; D £63 LB **Parking** 24

◆◆ ✿

Sowtontown Farm ◇ (SX513762)

Peter Tavy PL19 9JR ☎ 01822 810058 Mrs Clark
e-mail sowtontownfarm@msn.com
Dir *3m NE of Tavistock. Off A386 to Peter Tavy, over bridge, right, 2nd left, house on left*

Feel like one of the family at this Dartmoor smallholding with free-range chickens, sheep, ducks, dogs and a cat. There are great views all around to local churches and up to nearby Cox Tor. The home cooking is tasty and plentiful, with eggs from the resident hens, and pets can be accommodated by arrangement.

Facilities 3 rms (1 fmly) ⊘ in bedrooms TV2B tea/coffee ✗ 5 acres small holding Dinner Last d 8hrs notice **Prices** S £25; D £50✳
Parking 6 **Notes** Closed Xmas & New Year 🐾

TEIGNMOUTH   MAP 03 SX97

◆◆◆◆◆ 🏠

Thomas Luny House

Teign St TQ14 8EG ☎ 01626 772976
e-mail alisonandjohn@thomas-luny-house.co.uk
Dir *A381 to Teignmouth, at 3rd lights turn right to quay, 50yds turn left onto Teign St, after 60yds turn right through white archway*

Built in the late 18th century by marine artist Thomas Luny, this charming house offers unique and comfortable accommodation in the old quarter of Teignmouth. Bedrooms are individually furnished, and all are well equipped and have a good range of extras. An elegant drawing room with French windows leads into a walled garden with a terraced sitting area. A superb breakfast, featuring local produce, is served in the attractive dining room.

continued

Facilities 4 en suite ⊗ TVB tea/coffee Direct dial from bedrooms ✷
Licensed Cen ht No children 12yrs No coaches **Prices** S £57-£62;
D £70-£88✳ **LB Parking** 8

◆◆◆◆

Potters Mooring

30 The Green, Shaldon TQ14 0DN
☎ 01626 873225 📄 01626 872909
e-mail mail@pottersmooring.co.uk
web www.pottersmooring.co.uk
Dir A38 onto A380 signed Torquay, B3192 to Teignmouth & Shaldon,
over river signs to Potters Mooring

A former sea captain's residence dating from 1625, Potters Mooring
has been refurbished to provide charming accommodation of a very
high standard, including a four-poster room and a family-size cottage.
The friendly proprietors make every effort to ensure an enjoyable stay
and the Captain Potter's breakfast features tasty local produce.

Facilities 6 rms (5 en suite) (1 pri facs) (2 fmly) ⊗ TVB tea/coffee
Cen ht No coaches **Prices** S £35-£40; D £70-£80✳ **LB Parking** 8

TIVERTON
MAP 03 SS91

◆◆◆◆◆

Hornhill Farmhouse *(SS965117)*

Exeter Hill EX16 4PL
☎ 01884 253352 📄 01884 253352 Mrs Pugsley
e-mail hornhill@tinyworld.co.uk
web www.hornhill-farmhouse.co.uk
Dir Signs to Grand Western Canal, right fork up Exeter Hill.
Farmhouse on left at top of hill

Hornhill has a peaceful hilltop setting with panoramic views of the
town and the Exe valley. Elegant decor and furnishings enhance the
character of the farmhouse, which in part dates from the 18th century.
Bedrooms are beautifully equipped with modern facilities and there is
a lovely sitting room with a log fire. Meals are served at one large
table in the well-appointed dining room.

Facilities 3 rms (1 en suite) (2 pri facs) (1 GF) ⊗ TVB tea/coffee ✷
No children 12yrs ⚮ 75 acres beef sheep **Prices** S £32-£34; D £54-£56✳
Parking 5 **Notes** ⊜

◆◆◆◆◆ 🍷 ⊜ ✌

Rhode Farm House ◈ *(SS967102)*

Exeter Hill EX16 4PL ☎ 01884 242853 📄 01884 242853
Mr & Mrs Boulton
e-mail david@rhodefarmhouse.com
web www.rhodefarmhouse.com
Dir Signs to Grand Western Canal, right fork signed Exeter Hill,
farmhouse 3m on left

You receive a very warm welcome at Rhode Farm House. It stands in
5 acres with stables in the yard. Bedrooms are finished with many
considerate extras and there is an inviting lounge with a log fire for
cooler nights. A delicious breakfast, featuring local produce, is served
around a communal table in the dining room. Carefully prepared and
presented dinners are available by arrangement.

Facilities 2 en suite (2 fmly) ⊗ TVB tea/coffee ✷ Cen ht TVL
No children 4yrs Riding 4 acres Dinner Last d noon **Prices** S £30-£38.50;
D £50-£55✳ **Parking** 5

◆◆◆ ✌

Quoit-At-Cross ◈ *(ST923188)*

Stoodleigh EX16 9PJ
☎ 01398 351280 📄 01398 351351 Mrs Hill
Dir 3.5m N of Tiverton. A396 N for Bampton, 3.5m left over bridge
for Stoodleigh, farmhouse on junct

A friendly welcome is assured at this delightful stone farmhouse with
views over rolling countryside. The attractive bedrooms are well
furnished and have many extra facilities. A lounge and pretty garden
are available.

Facilities 3 en suite ⊗ TVB tea/coffee ✷ Cen ht TVL No children
160 acres organic mixed **Prices** S £27; D £54✳ **Parking** 3 **Notes** Closed
Dec-Apr ⊜

TORBAY
MAP 03 SX86

See **Brixham, Paignton and Torquay**

TORQUAY — MAP 03 SX96

★★★★ Guest House

Berkeley House

39 Babbacombe Downs Rd, Babbacombe TQ1 3LN
☎ 01803 322429
e-mail reception@berkeleyhouse.net
Dir *From Exeter join A38 keep left on A380 (Torquay). Follow signs for Babbacombe sea front*

Friendly hospitality awaits you at this very pleasant guest house, which is situated on the Babbacombe seafront. The bedrooms vary in size and style, but all are thoughtfully equipped. Three rooms including one on ground floor level, have sea views. Separate tables are provided in the dining room, where hearty breakfasts are served.

Facilities 5 en suite (1 fmly) (1 GF) ⊗ TVB tea/coffee 🐾 Cen ht No children 12yrs No coaches **Prices** S £40-£58; D £45-£63✱ **Parking** 4 **Notes** ⊛

★★★★ Guest House

The Marstan & Restaurant

Meadfoot Sea Rd TQ1 2LQ
☎ 01803 292837 📠 01803 299202
e-mail enquiries@marstanhotel.co.uk
Dir *A3022 to seafront, left onto A379 Torbay Rd & Babbacombe Rd, right onto Meadfoot Rd, Marstan on right*

The elegant mid 19th-century villa has recently changed hands and the new owners are making improvements to the accommodation. Hospitality and service are second to none, and every effort is made to create a relaxed and enjoyable atmosphere. Public areas include an impressive dining room, a bar and a comfortable lounge. Outdoors you can enjoy the heated swimming pool and hot tub in the pleasant garden.

Facilities 10 en suite (1 fmly) (3 GF) ⊗ FTV TVB tea/coffee Direct dial from bedrooms 🐾 Licensed Cen ht No coaches ⚓ Jacuzzi & special rates at health club Dinner Last d 7pm **Prices** S £50-£70; D £80-£130✱ **LB Conf** Max 12 Thtr 12 Class 12 Board 12 **Parking** 7

★★★ Guest House

Mariners Guest House ◇

35 Belgrave Rd TQ2 5HX ☎ 01803 291604
e-mail marinersguesthouse@btinternet.com
web www.marinerstorquay.co.uk
Dir *A380 onto A3022 to seafront, left onto Belgrave Rd, left at lights onto Lucius St, then 1st left*

This personally run guest house provides friendly hospitality and willing service. It is within easy reach of the town centre, and the modern bedrooms are being refurbished to a good standard. Separate tables are provided in the attractive breakfast room.

Facilities 6 en suite (2 fmly) (1 GF) ⊗ TVB tea/coffee 🐾 Cen ht No coaches **Prices** S £20-£30; D £40-£60✱ **Parking** 4

◆◆◆◆◆ 🛏

Colindale Hotel

20 Rathmore Rd, Chelston TQ2 6NY ☎ 01803 293947
e-mail rathmore@blueyonder.co.uk
web www.colindalehotel.co.uk
Dir *From Torquay station 200yds on left in Rathmore Rd*

Having attractive, well-tended gardens, the Colindale is in a quiet area close to the seafront. It is an elegant establishment and service is exemplary. Rooms, some with views over Torbay, are attractively coordinated, and memorable breakfasts are enjoyed in the relaxing dining room.

Facilities 8 rms (6 en suite) (2 pri facs) ⊗ in bedrooms ⊗ in dining room ⊗ in lounges TVB tea/coffee 🐾 Licensed Cen ht TVL No children 12yrs No coaches Dinner Last d 10.30am **Prices** S £35-£40; D £60-£75✱ **LB Parking** 6 **Notes** Closed Dec

◆◆◆◆◆ 🛏

Cranborne House

58 Belgrave Rd TQ2 5HY
☎ 01803 298046 & 294100 📠 01803 294100
e-mail info@cranbornehotel.co.uk
Dir *A380 into Torquay, head for seafront, on corner of Belgrave Rd and Falkland Rd*

Within easy walking distance of the town centre, seafront and harbour, this Victorian terrace property provides friendly, attentive service and superior accommodation. The attractive bedrooms are equipped with many useful facilities including hairdryers, dressing gowns, complimentary toiletries and silent fridges. In addition, there is an immaculately furnished sitting room and a smart dining room. Breakfast is memorable for the home-made muesli, fresh fruit salad and chutney.

Facilities 10 en suite (1 GF) ⊗ TVB FTV 🐾 Licensed Cen ht No children No coaches **Prices** S £40-£50; D £50-£80✱ **LB**

Premier Collection

◆◆◆◆◆

Millbrook House Hotel

1 Old Mill Rd, Chelston TQ2 6AP
☎ 01803 297394 ▤ 01803 297394
e-mail jeffandmandyshatford@hotmail.com
Dir *A380 onto A3022, pass Torre station onto Avenue Rd, right at lights onto Old Mill Rd*

Within easy walking distance of Torquay's attractions, the personally run Millbrook House has a friendly and relaxed atmosphere. The well-maintained bedrooms have many useful facilities; a king-size bed and a four-poster are available. Home-cooked evening meals are served by arrangement, featuring home-made soups and fresh vegetables.

Facilities 9 en suite (1 fmly) (2 GF) ⊗ TVB tea/coffee ✖ Licensed
Cen ht TVL No coaches Pool Table Dinner Last d noon
Prices S £25-£30; D £50-£70✶ LB **Parking** 8

Premier Collection

◆◆◆◆◆ ▤ ⇔

Mulberry House

1 Scarborough Rd TQ2 5UJ
☎ 01803 213639 & 07739 017744 ▤ 01803 213639
e-mail stay@mulberryhousetorquay.co.uk
Dir *From Torquay seafront onto Belgrave Rd, Scarborough Rd 1st right, house on corner*

This Grade II listed Victorian property is delightful gem set in a quiet residential area near the seafront. The attractive bedrooms have an abundance of charm, and creative, freshly prepared dishes are available in the restaurant. A cosy log fire burns on cooler evenings. Laura Wood is a top-twenty finalist for AA Landlady of the Year 2006.

Facilities 3 rms (2 en suite) (1 pri facs) (2 fmly) ⊗ FTV TVB tea/coffee
✖ Licensed Cen ht No coaches Dinner Last d 9.30pm
Prices S £40-£52; D £60-£80✶ LB **Notes** ⊛

◆◆◆◆

The Southbourne Villa

9 Cleveland Rd TQ2 5BD
☎ 01803 292960 ▤ 01803 291299
e-mail relax@thesouthbournevilla.co.uk
web www.thesouthbournevilla.co.uk
Dir *A3022 towards town centre, at Halfords right fork over lights onto Avenue Rd, Cleveland Rd 1st left, Villa at end*

Expect a warm welcome and a relaxed atmosphere at the Southbourne, located in the centre of town yet away from busy roads. There is a good standard of accommodation and you can unwind in the front lounge or in the bar.

Facilities 10 en suite (1 GF) ⊗ FTV TVB tea/coffee ✖ Licensed
Cen ht TVL No children 18yrs No coaches Open air hot tub spa
Prices S £50; D £70-£90✶ LB **Parking** 9

◆◆◆◆

Atlantis Hotel

68 Belgrave Rd TQ2 5HY ☎ 01803 292917 ▤ 01803 292917
e-mail info@atlantishotel.freeserve.co.uk
Dir *Signs to Torquay seafront, turn left, left at lights onto Belgrave Rd, over next lights, premises on left*

Convenient for the beach, theatre and conference centre, the Atlantis offers a thoughtfully equipped home from home. There is a well-stocked bar and a comfortable lounge, and the hearty breakfasts in the dining room are a tasty start to the day.

Facilities 11 rms (9 en suite) (7 fmly) ⊗ in bedrooms ⊗ in dining room
TVB tea/coffee ✖ Cen ht TVL **Prices** S £20-£40; D £40-£60 LB
Parking 3

◆◆◆◆

Aveland Hotel

Aveland Rd, Babbacombe TQ1 3PT
☎ 01803 326622 ▤ 01803 328940
e-mail avelandhotel@aol.com
web www.avelandhotel.co.uk
Dir *A379 into Babbacombe, off Babbacombe Rd onto Reddenhill Rd & right onto Carey Av, 2nd left*

Set in well-tended gardens in a peaceful area of Babbacombe, close to Cary Park and within easy walking distance of the town and downs, this family-run house offers warm and attentive service. The attractive bedrooms are well equipped, and a pleasant bar and two comfortable lounges are available. Hearing-impaired visitors are especially welcome, as both the proprietors are BSL signers. Evening meals and bar snacks are available by arrangement.

Facilities 10 en suite (3 fmly) ⊗ tea/coffee ✖ Licensed Cen ht TVL
No coaches Dinner Last d 5.30pm **Prices** S £25-£30; D £50-£60✶ LB
Parking 10

England

TORQUAY continued

◆◆◆◆
Babbacombe Hall Hotel
17 Manor Rd, Babbacombe TQ1 3JX
☎ 01803 325668 🖩 01803 325668
e-mail glyn.aida.rees@lineone.net
Dir A379 to Babbacombe, onto Manor Rd

This family-run establishment offers friendly and attentive service. The bedrooms are very well equipped and decorated in colourful styles, and there are many facilities. Dinner is a varied menu of traditional and Oriental dishes freshly prepared by the resident proprietors.

Facilities 7 en suite ⊘ in bedrooms ⊘ in dining room ⊘ in lounges TVB tea/coffee ✖ Licensed Cen ht TVL No coaches ⁺ Dinner Last d 4pm **Prices** D £50-£70 **LB** **Parking** 7

◆◆◆◆
Barclay Court Hotel
29 Castle Rd TQ1 3BB ☎ 01803 292791 🖩 01803 292791
e-mail barclaycourthotel@yahoo.co.uk
web www.barclaycourthotel.co.uk
Dir From Newton Abbot into Torquay follow Civic Offices signs, bear right at car park on right, sharp left after pedestrian crossing onto Castle Rd, premises up hill on right

The proprietors of this comfortable, family-run establishment provide a warm welcome and high standards in the bedrooms. Dinner is available by arrangement, and breakfast is enjoyed in the dining room overlooking the garden. There is also an attractive lounge and a spacious bar.

Facilities 5 en suite 9 annexe en suite (2 fmly) (4 GF) ⊘ TVB tea/coffee ✖ Licensed TVL No coaches Dinner Last d before noon **LB** **Parking** 8

◆◆◆◆
Belmont Hotel ◇
66 Belgrave Rd TQ2 5HY
☎ 01803 295028 🖩 01803 295028
e-mail belmont@murphytq2fsnet.co.uk
Dir Signs to town centre, right-hand lane in one-way system onto Belgrave Rd, Belmont before lights on right

Situated within walking distance of the seafront and town centre, this is an ideal base for exploring this ever-popular corner of Devon. Bedrooms have modern comforts, and the public rooms include a spacious lounge and an attractive dining room. The atmosphere is relaxed and welcoming and the proprietors are very helpful.

Facilities 10 rms (7 en suite) (1 pri facs) (3 fmly) ⊘ in 4 bedrooms ⊘ in dining room ⊘ in lounges TVB tea/coffee ✖ Cen ht TVL No coaches Dinner **Prices** S £17.50-£25; D £40-£70 **LB** **Parking** 2

◆◆◆◆
Coombe Court Hotel ◇
67 Babbacombe Downs Rd, Babbacombe TQ1 3LP
☎ 01803 327097 🖩 01803 327097
e-mail enquiries@coombecourthotel.co.uk
Dir Signs to St Marychurch & Babbacombe, through Hele, pass golf club & shops, 2nd left onto Babbacombe Downs Rd

Coombe Court is located in an attractive area on the seafront with beaches and coastal walks. A friendly welcome is extended to all. Bedrooms are comfortably furnished and include some with balconies and ground-floor rooms. In addition to the intimate bar, a choice of three lounges ensures there is ample space for relaxation.

Facilities 15 en suite (1 fmly) (2 GF) ⊘ TVB tea/coffee ✖ Licensed Cen ht TVL No children 10yrs No coaches Pool Table Dinner Last d 4.30pm **Prices** S £30-£43; D £60-£86✳ **Parking** 15 **Notes** Closed Nov-Feb

◆◆◆◆
Court Prior ◇
St Lukes Rd South TQ2 5NZ ☎ 01803 292766
e-mail courtprior@btconnect.com
Dir A380 to Torquay, at Halfords right at lights onto Avenue Rd to seafront, left at next lights up Sheddon Hill, second lights onto St Lukes Rd

Located in a quiet residential area within walking distance of the seafront and town centre, this charming house, built in 1860, offers comfortable accommodation. Rooms are spacious, well decorated and pleasantly furnished throughout. Traditional home-made dishes are served at dinner. There is also a large comfortable lounge.

Facilities 10 en suite (3 fmly) (2 GF) ⊘ in dining room TVB tea/coffee ✖ TVL No children 4yrs No coaches Dinner Last d 4pm **Prices** S £24-£26; D £48-£52✳ **LB** **Parking** 10

◆◆◆◆
The Cranmore ◇
89 Av Road TQ2 5LH ☎ 01803 298488
e-mail stay@thecranmore.co.uk
Dir A380 from Newton Abbot onto A3022, at Torre station right at lights, 200yds on left

This friendly, family-run guest house has a relaxed atmosphere and is convenient for the town centre and the seafront. The attractive bedrooms are well furnished, and a family room is available. Breakfast is served in the pleasant dining room and special dietary requirements can be catered for. Dinner is available by arrangement.

Facilities 6 en suite (1 fmly) ⊘ TVB tea/coffee ✖ Licensed Cen ht TVL No coaches Dinner Last d noon **Prices** S £27-£32; D £44-£60✳ **LB** **Parking** 4

◆◆◆◆
Crown Lodge ◇
83 Av Road TQ2 5LH ☎ 01803 298772 🖩 01803 291155
e-mail john@www.crownlodgehotel.co.uk
Dir A380 through Kingskerswell, over rbt & 3 sets traffic lights, right at Torre Station

Located within walking distance of the harbour and seafront and close to the town centre, Crown Lodge offers stylish and comfortable

continued

accommodation. Bedrooms have been refurbished to a high standard, each individually furnished with flair. A lounge is available, and the well-cooked breakfasts are a delight.

Facilities 5 en suite (1 fmly) (1 GF) ⊗ TVB tea/coffee ✖ Cen ht TVL No children 12yrs No coaches Dinner Last d at breakfast **Prices** S fr £30; D £50-£60 **LB Parking** 7

◆◆◆◆
Everglades Hotel

32 St Marychurch Rd TQ1 3HY
☎ 01803 295389 📠 01803 214357
e-mail enquiries@evergladeshotel.co.uk
Dir *A380 onto A3022 for town centre, 0.5m left at Courts onto Hele Rd, over rdbt onto Westhill Rd, right at lights onto St Marychurch Rd*

The Everglades offers comfortable accommodation and a warm welcome. The friendly proprietors are attentive and strive to ensure you feel at home. Well-appointed bedrooms feature a range of extras. There is a bright and spacious lounge, a sun terrace and a garden patio. Freshly cooked dinners are served in the airy dining room, with views over the town towards Torbay.

Facilities 10 en suite (2 fmly) ⊗ TVB tea/coffee Direct dial from bedrooms ✖ Licensed Cen ht No coaches Dinner Last d 5pm **LB Parking** 9 **Notes** Closed 23 Dec-2 Jan

◆◆◆◆
Glenorleigh

26 Cleveland Rd TQ2 5BE
☎ 01803 292135 📠 01803 213717
e-mail glenorleighhotel@btinternet.com
web www.glenorleigh.co.uk
Dir *A380 from Newton Abbot onto A3022, at Torre station lights right onto Avenue Rd & 1st left*

Located in a residential area, the Glenorleigh provides a range of smart bedrooms, some on the ground floor. With facilities such as a solarium, an outdoor pool and terrace, and a convivial bar, this family-run establishment is ideal for leisure or business.

Facilities 15 rms (14 en suite) (6 fmly) (7 GF) ⊗ in bedrooms ⊗ in dining room ⊗ in 1 lounge TVB tea/coffee ✖ Licensed Cen ht TVL No coaches ⤳ Solarium Pool Table Dinner Last d 2pm **Prices** S £32-£42; D £64-£84 **LB Parking** 10

◆◆◆◆
Harmony Hotel

67 Avenue Rdd TQ2 5LG ☎ 01803 293918
e-mail viv-cheryl@harmonyhotel.co.uk
web www.harmonyhotel.co.uk

This detached property is within walking distance of the seafront and town centre. Bedrooms, including ground-floor rooms, are attractively decorated. Facilities include a lounge, a bar and an ironing room. Ample off-road parking is a bonus, and dinner is available by arrangement.

Facilities 10 en suite (2 fmly) (4 GF) ⊗ in bedrooms ⊗ in dining room ⊗ in 1 lounge TVB tea/coffee ✖ Licensed Cen ht TVL No children 6yrs Dinner Last d 11am **Parking** 11

◆◆◆◆
Headland View

37 Babbacombe Seafront, Babbacombe TQ1 3LN
☎ 01803 312612
e-mail reception@headlandview.com
web www.headlandview.com
Dir *A379 S to Babbacombe, off Babbacombe Rd left onto Portland Rd & Babbacombe Downs Rd & seafront*

There are spectacular views of the bay and the Downs from the lounge and many of the bedrooms of Headland View. The attentive proprietors offer a friendly welcome, and several of the attractive bedrooms have balconies. Breakfast is memorable for the well-cooked quality ingredients.

Facilities 6 rms (4 en suite) (2 pri facs) ⊗ TVB tea/coffee ✖ Cen ht TVL No children 4yrs No coaches **Parking** 4 **Notes** Closed Dec-Feb ⊠

◆◆◆◆
Hotel Blue Conifer

Higher Downs Rd, The Seafront, Babbacombe TQ1 3LD
☎ 01803 327637
Dir *Signs for Babbacombe & seafront, premises 500yds from model village*

Surrounded by neat gardens and having splendid views across beaches to the bay, this attractive property provides a relaxed and friendly atmosphere. Bedrooms, many with sea views, are well-equipped and one is on the ground floor. Dinner is highly recommended.

Facilities 7 en suite (3 fmly) (1 GF) ⊗ TVB tea/coffee Cen ht No coaches Dinner Last d noon **Prices** S £31-£40; D £46-£68✳ **LB Parking** 9 **Notes** Closed Nov-Feb ⊠

England

TORQUAY continued

◆◆◆◆

Meadfoot Bay Guest House ◇

Meadfoot Sea Rd TQ1 2LQ
☎ 01803 294722 🗎 01803 214473
e-mail stay@meadfoot.com
Dir *A3022 to seafront, onto A379 & right onto Meadfoot Rd, 0.5m on right*

Please note that this establishment has recently changed hands. This elegant, spacious and well-cared for property offers a good level of comfort. The well-equipped bedrooms vary in size and style, and after a day exploring the area you can retreat to the lounge and the bar. Dinner, by arrangement, and breakfast are served in the pleasant dining room.

Facilities 20 en suite (1 fmly) (3 GF) ⊗ TVB tea/coffee ✖ Licensed Cen ht TVL Dinner Last d 6pm **Prices** S £30-£40; D £60-£80✱ **LB Parking** 15 **Notes** Closed Dec-Jan rs Nov-Feb

◆◆◆◆

Newton House ◇

31 Newton Rd, Torre TQ2 5DB
☎ 01803 297520 🗎 01803 297520
e-mail newtonhouse2004@yahoo.co.uk
Dir *From Torre station bear left at lights, Newton House 40yds on left*

You are assured of a warm welcome at Newton House, which is close to the town centre and the attractions. The attractive bedrooms, some at ground level, have thoughtful extras, and a lounge is available. Breakfast is enjoyed in the pleasant dining room.

Facilities 9 en suite (3 fmly) (5 GF) ⊗ TVB tea/coffee ✖ Cen ht No coaches **Prices** S £30-£35; D £45-£50✱ **LB Parking** 15

◆◆◆◆

Norwood Hotel ◇

60 Belgrave Rd TQ2 5HY
☎ 01803 294236 🗎 01803 294224
e-mail enquiries@norwoodhoteltorquay.co.uk
web www.norwoodhoteltorquay.co.uk
Dir *From Princess Theatre towards Paignton, 1st lights right onto Belgrave Rd, over x-rds, 3rd building on left*

You are assured of a warm welcome at this personally run property. Fronted by attractive floral displays, it is convenient for the town centre and most attractions, and the well-equipped accommodation includes

a family room. There is a comfortable lounge, and dinner and breakfast are served at separate tables in the pleasant dining room.

Facilities 10 en suite (5 fmly) (1 GF) ⊗ in 8 bedrooms ⊗ in dining room ⊗ in lounges TVB tea/coffee ✖ Licensed Cen ht TVL No coaches Dinner Last d noon **Prices** S £27-£45; D £40-£70✱ **LB Parking** 3

◆◆◆◆

Oscars Hotel

56 Belgrave Rd TQ2 5HY
☎ 01803 293563 🗎 01803 296685
e-mail stay@oscarshotel.co.uk
Dir *On Torquay seafront, off A379 Torbay Rd by abbey onto Belgrave Rd*

Oscars Hotel is within easy walking distance of the seafront and the shops. This attractive property offers comfortable, well-equipped accommodation, and a relaxed and friendly atmosphere prevails throughout. Breakfast is served in the basement dining room and home-cooked dinners are available by arrangement.

Facilities 14 en suite (1 GF) ⊗ TVB tea/coffee Direct dial from bedrooms ✖ Licensed Cen ht No children 12yrs No coaches Dinner Last d 2pm **Parking** 4

◆◆◆◆ 🅰

Grosvenor House Hotel ◇

Falkland Rd TQ2 5JP ☎ 01803 294110
e-mail aa@grosvenorhousehotel.co.uk
Dir *From Newton Abbot to Torquay, at Torre station right by Halfords, left at 2nd lights onto Falkland Rd*

Facilities 10 en suite (4 fmly) (3 GF) ⊗ in bedrooms ⊗ in dining room ⊗ in 1 lounge TVB tea/coffee ✖ Licensed Cen ht TVL Dinner Last d 4.30pm **Prices** S £22-£35; D £44-£70 **LB Parking** 7 **Notes** Closed Oct-Etr

◆◆◆◆ 🅰

Trelawney Hotel

48 Belgrave Rd TQ2 5HS ☎ 01803 296049
e-mail enquiries@trelawneyhotel.co.uk
Dir *A3022 onto Falkland Rd & 1st right, premises 250yds from beach*

Facilities 12 en suite (1 fmly) ⊗ TVB tea/coffee ✖ Licensed Cen ht TVL No children 14yrs No coaches Dinner Last d Breakfast **Prices** S £39-£45; D £48-£100✱ **LB Notes** Closed Dec

◆◆◆

Arran Lodge ◇

97 Av Road TQ2 5LH ☎ 01803 292273 🗎 01803 292273
e-mail linda@arranlodge.co.uk
Dir *A380 to Torquay, at Halfords right at lights onto Avenue Rd to seafront, Arran Lodge 50yds on left*

The proprietors at this pleasant and comfortable house offer a genuine welcome and treat you like friends. The attractive bedrooms are enhanced with numerous facilities. Dinner and breakfast are served in the light, pleasant dining room, where you can also relax in the evenings.

Facilities 6 en suite (2 fmly) (1 GF) ⊗ TVB tea/coffee ✖ Cen ht No coaches Dinner Last d 10am **Prices** S £20-£25; D £40-£50✱ **LB Parking** 3 **Notes** 🐾

England

◆◆◆

Burleigh House

25 Newton Rd TQ2 5DB ☎ 01803 291557
Dir *A380 to Torquay, 4th house on left past Torre station*

A warm welcome is extended at this comfortable establishment, just a short walk from the town centre and the seafront. The pleasant bedrooms have quality pine furnishings, and some rooms are on the ground floor. Secure parking is available.

Facilities 8 en suite (2 fmly) (4 GF) ⊗ TVB tea/coffee ⚡ Cen ht No coaches **LB** **Parking** 11 **Notes**

◆◆◆

Abberley Hotel ◇

100 Windsor Rd, Babbacombe TQ1 1SU
☎ 01803 392787 📠 01803 392787
e-mail stay@theabberleyhotel.co.uk
web www.theabberleyhotel.co.uk
Dir *A379 to Babbacombe, onto Reddenhill Rd to Windsor Rd T-junct*

The atmosphere is friendly and relaxed at this family-run property, set in a quiet residential area close to the town centre and a level stroll to the beaches and attractions. Two of the well-equipped bedrooms are on the ground floor. Breakfast is served in the cosy dining room and freshly prepared dinners are available by arrangement.

Facilities 7 en suite (2 fmly) (2 GF) ⊗ TVB tea/coffee Cen ht TVL No coaches Dinner Last d 5pm **Prices** S £25-£30; D £40-£50✳ **LB**

◆◆◆

Athina

8 Vansittart Rd, Torre TQ2 5BT ☎ 01803 297547
Dir *A380 S to Torquay, at Torre station lights left to town centre, 1st right*

The Athina is in a quiet residential area close to the centre and seaside attractions, and provides good-value accommodation. Rooms are spacious and comfortable and a cosy lounge is provided along with a car park. Traditional breakfasts served in the dining room provide an excellent start to the day.

Facilities 3 rms ⊗ in bedrooms ⊗ in dining room ⊗ in 1 lounge TVB tea/coffee ⚡ Cen ht TVL No children No coaches **LB** **Parking** 4 **Notes** Closed mid Oct-Feb

◆◆◆

Devonia Lodge

53 Av Road TQ2 5LG ☎ 01803 292723 📠 01803 292723
e-mail devonialodge@supanet.com
Dir *A3022, approach Torre station in right lane & onto Avenue Rd*

A warm welcome is extended at this friendly establishment just a stroll from the town centre and the seafront. Bedrooms are soundly appointed, with some rooms on the ground floor. A comfortable lounge is provided.

Facilities 6 en suite (3 fmly) (2 GF) ⊗ TVB tea/coffee ⚡ TVL No children 2yrs No coaches **Parking** 6

◆◆◆

Doogals Hotel

74 Belgrave Rd TQ2 5HY ☎ 01803 295966
e-mail tizturnip@aol.com
Dir *Town centre signs, pass police station on right, through small shopping area, premises on right*

This personally run guest house is convenient for the town centre and attractions. It provides friendly hospitality and well-equipped accommodation, which includes family rooms and bedrooms on the ground floor.

Facilities 7 en suite (2 fmly) (3 GF) ⊗ in 3 bedrooms ⊗ in dining room TVB tea/coffee ⚡ Cen ht TVL No coaches Dinner Last d noon **Parking** 4

◆◆◆

The Garlieston Guest House

5 Br Road TQ2 5BA ☎ 01803 294050
e-mail enquiries@thegarlieston.com
Dir *Newton Rd onto Avenue Rd towards seafront. Over lights, left onto Bampfylde Rd, house at Bridge Rd junct*

This small friendly guest house offers comfortable accommodation just a stroll from the seafront and is well located for the town centre. Bedrooms are neatly decorated and furnished.

Facilities 5 rms (5 pri facs) (1 fmly) (1 GF) ⊗ FTV TVB tea/coffee ⚡ Cen ht No coaches DVD players in all rooms Dinner Last d Jun-Aug by request **Notes** Closed 20-26 Dec

◆◆◆

Green Park Hotel

25 Morgan Av TQ2 5RR ☎ 01803 293618 📠 01803 293618
e-mail staygreenpark@hotmail.co.uk
Dir *From A3022 right lane Torre station, 2nd lights left onto Falkland Rd. Over next 2 lights, past Central Church & left onto Morgan Av*

Expect a warm welcome at this comfortable property close to the town centre. The attentive proprietors provide a relaxed, homely atmosphere, and the generous breakfasts are a pleasant start to the day. Home-cooked dinners are available by arrangement.

Facilities 8 rms (4 en suite) (3 fmly) (1 GF) ⊗ TVB tea/coffee ⚡ Licensed Cen ht No coaches Dinner Last d 11am **Parking** 7

◆◆◆

The Palms Hotel ◇

537 Babbacombe Rd TQ1 1HQ
☎ 01803 293970 📠 01803 298573
e-mail thepalmshotel@yahoo.co.uk
web www.palmshoteltorquay.co.uk
Dir *On A379, 300yds from Torquay Harbour opp Torwood Gardens*

The owners of Palms extend a very warm welcome. Family friendly, it offers comfortable accommodation, with books, games and videos available for children, and the cybercafe, well-stocked bar and bar meals are welcome facilities. Breakfast is served in the dining room overlooking Torwood Gardens.

Facilities 9 en suite (2 fmly) ⊗ in bedrooms ⊗ in area of dining room ⊗ in 1 lounge STV TVB tea/coffee Licensed Cen ht TVL No coaches Dinner Last d 6pm **Prices** S £25-£30; D £50-£60✳ **LB** **Parking** 4 **Notes** Closed 5 Jan-22 Feb

England

◆◆◆

Riviera Lodge Hotel

26 Croft Road TQ2 5UE ☎ 01803 292614 🖹 01803 211454
e-mail stay@hotels-torquay.com
web www.hotels-torquay.com
Dir From seafront left up Shedden Hill, Croft Rd 1st left

This establishment offers a relaxed atmosphere within walking distance of the promenade, shopping centre and the many attractions. Bedrooms vary in size, with the best use being made of available space; all rooms are well-equipped. There is a spacious bar and lounge area, and dinner, by arrangement, is a choice of dishes.

Facilities 20 en suite (2 fmly) ⊗ in bedrooms ⊗ in dining room ⊗ in 1 lounge TVB tea/coffee ✖ Licensed Cen ht TVL ⬞ Dinner Last d noon **Parking** 17

◆◆◆

Silverlands B&B ◇

27 Newton Rd TQ2 5DB ☎ 01803 292013
e-mail idnanij@aol.com
web www.silverlandshotel.co.uk
Dir A380 onto A3022 for Torquay, premises on left after Torre station lights

Convenient for the town centre and the beaches, this friendly establishment has a homely atmosphere. Some of the well-presented bedrooms are on the ground floor, and a hearty, freshly cooked breakfast is served in the dining room.

Facilities 9 rms (7 en suite) (2 pri facs) (3 fmly) (2 GF) ⊗ TVB tea/coffee ✖ Cen ht No coaches **Prices** S £20-£30; D £35-£48✱ **LB** **Parking** 13

◆◆◆

Stover Lodge Hotel ◇

29 Newton Rd TQ2 5DB ☎ 01803 297287 🖹 01803 297287
e-mail enquiries@stoverlodge.co.uk
web www.stoverlodge.co.uk
Dir Signs to Torquay town centre, at station/Halfords left onto lane, Lodge on left after lights

Located close to the town centre, the family-run Stover Lodge is relaxed and friendly. Children and babies are welcome, and a cot and high chair can be provided on request. Hearty breakfasts, with a vegetarian option, are served in the dining room. There is a garden to enjoy in summer.

Facilities 9 rms (8 en suite) (1 pri facs) (3 fmly) (2 GF) ⊗ TVB tea/coffee ✖ Cen ht No coaches **Prices** S £19-£35; D £42-£48 **LB** **Parking** 10

◆◆◆

Tyndale ◇

68 Av Road TQ2 5LF ☎ 01803 380888
Dir A380 onto A3022, pass Torre station onto Avenue Rd, 1st lights right onto Old Mill Rd & right into car park

Close to the seaside attractions and the town centre, this neatly presented house is only a short level walk from the railway station. Bedrooms are brightly decorated in a range of sizes. A comfortable lounge is provided and a freshly cooked, traditional British breakfast is served in the dining room.

Facilities 3 en suite (1 GF) ⊗ in dining room TVB tea/coffee Cen ht TVL No coaches **Prices** S £18; D £36 **LB** **Parking** 5 **Notes** ⊛

◆◆◆

Wayfarer ◇

37 Belgrave Rd TQ2 5HX ☎ 01803 299138
e-mail wayfarerbookings@aol.com
web www.wayfarertorquay.co.uk
Dir A380 onto A3022 to seafront, left, onto Belgrave Rd, left at lights onto Lucious St, 1st left to car park

The Wayfarer offers friendly accommodation convenient for the town centre and seaside attractions,. Bedrooms are equipped with ironing facilities. A hearty breakfast is served in the light and airy dining room.

Facilities 6 en suite (2 fmly) (1 GF) ⊗ TVB tea/coffee ✖ No coaches Dinner Last d breakfast same day **Prices** S £20-£30; D £35-£50✱ **Parking** 3 **Notes** ⊛

TOTNES MAP 03 SX86

See also **South Brent**

◆◆◆◆◆ ⌖

The Durant Arms

Ashprington TQ9 7UP ☎ 01803 732240

e-mail info@thedurantarms.com

web www.thedurantarms.com

Dir *A381 from Totnes for Kingsbridge, 1m left for Ashprington*

This delightful inn, the focal point of the picturesque village of Ashprington, offers comfortable bedrooms in the main building or annexe, which are very well appointed and attractively decorated. A range of carefully prepared dishes from blackboard menus can be enjoyed in the character bar or dining room, and local ales, juices and wines also feature.

Facilities 3 en suite 4 annexe rms (2 GF) ⊗ TV2B tea/coffee ✗ Cen ht TVL No children Dinner Last d 9.15pm **LB** **Conf** Max 20 Board 15 Del from £20 ✳ **Parking** 8

See advertisement on this page

◆◆◆◆◆ 🅰

The Old School House B&B

Blagdon Rd TQ3 3YA ☎ 01803 523011

e-mail abdy13@tiscali.co.uk

Dir *A380 onto A385 to Totnes, pass The Parkers Arms, right onto Blagdon Rd, Old School House 500yds on right*

Facilities 2 rms (1 en suite) (1 pri facs) ⊗ TVB tea/coffee ✗ Cen ht No children No coaches **Prices** D £70✳ **LB** **Parking** 4 **Notes** Closed Xmas & New Year 😂

◆◆◆◆

Corner Cottage

12 Cistern St TQ9 5SP ☎ 01803 864343

e-mail cornercottage.totnes@btinternet.com

web www.cornercottagetotnes.co.uk

Dir *A38 then A384/A385. At lights, right (A381). 3rd left, 1st house on left*

Located at the top end of High St and within walking distance of the railway station, this attractive Georgian cottage offers a friendly atmosphere. The comfortable bedrooms feature numerous facilities. Breakfast is served around a communal table and features local free-

range produce whenever possible. Free parking permits are provided for the car park nearby and throughout South Hams.

Facilities 3 en suite ⊗ TVB tea/coffee ✗ Cen ht No coaches **Prices** S fr £35; d fr £60✳ **Parking** available **Notes** 😂

◆◆◆◆

The Old Forge at Totnes

Seymour Pl TQ9 5AY ☎ 01803 862174 📠 01803 865385

e-mail enq@oldforgetotnes.com

Dir *From Totnes town centre cross river bridge & 2nd right*

Please note that this establishment has recently changed hands. Over 600 years old, this delightful property is close to the town centre and Steamer Quay. Bedrooms vary from spacious suites to cosy cottage-style, all of which have been equipped with thoughtful extras. Public areas include a conservatory overlooking the gardens, with a hot tub sensitively screened by exotic plants, and a comfortable lounge. Breakfast is a leisurely and enjoyable affair, served in the pleasant dining room.

Facilities 10 rms (9 en suite) (1 pri facs) (2 fmly) (2 GF) ⊗ TVB tea/coffee Direct dial from bedrooms ✗ Licensed Cen ht No coaches Spa bath **Prices** S £50-£70; D £60-£80✳ **LB** **Parking** 7

continued

TOTNES continued

◆◆◆◆

The Red Slipper

Stoke Gabriel TQ9 6RU ☎ 01803 782315
e-mail enquiries@redslipper.co.uk
web www.redslipper.co.uk
Dir Off A385 S to Stoke Gabriel. Hotel opp Church House Inn

An ideal base for exploring the South Hams or just for a relaxing break, this delightful 1920s house is hidden away in the picturesque village of Stoke Gabriel. The bedrooms have many extra facilities. Well-cooked dinners are served by arrangement, and feature local produce.

Facilities 3 en suite ⊘ TVB tea/coffee Licensed Cen ht TVL No coaches Dinner Last d 9am **Prices** S £32-£40; D £64-£70 **LB Parking** 4

◆◆◆◆

Steam Packet Inn

St Peter's Quay TQ9 5EW
☎ 01803 863880 📄 01803 862754
e-mail steampacket@buccaneer.co.uk
web www.thesteampacketinn-totnes.co.uk
Dir Off A38 at Totnes to Dartington & Totnes. Over 1st lights, pass railway station, signs for town centre at next rdbt. Over minirdbt, River Dart on left, inn 100yds on left

This friendly and popular riverside inn offers a warm welcome to visitors and locals alike. It has its own quay, and the public areas offer a choice of dining options, including the extensive waterside patio. Bedrooms are well equipped and comfortable, some have river views. Choices at lunch and dinner offer interesting, well-cooked dishes, while breakfast is a satisfying start to the day.

Facilities 4 en suite (1 fmly) ⊘ in bedrooms ⊘ in dining room TVB tea/coffee 🐾 Cen ht No coaches Dinner Last d 9pm **Prices** S fr £55; d fr £79.50✳ **LB Conf** Max 40 Thtr 40 Class 40 Board 20 Del £110 ✳ **Parking** 15

◆◆◆◆ 🅰

Four Seasons Guest House

13 Bridgetown TQ9 5AB ☎ 01803 862146 📄 01803 867779
e-mail ernestecornford@btinternet.com
Dir From minirdbt at bottom of Fore St over bridge, house 200yds on right

Facilities 7 en suite (1 fmly) (1 GF) ⊘ in 1 bedrooms ⊘ in dining room ⊘ in 1 lounge TVB tea/coffee Licensed Cen ht TVL Dinner **Parking** 6 **Notes** 🈑

Always confirm details with the establishment when booking

TWO BRIDGES   MAP 03 SX67

◆◆◆◆ ⊖

Cherrybrook Hotel

PL20 6SP ☎ 01822 880260
e-mail info@cherrybrookhotel.co.uk
Dir On B3212

Set amid dramatic scenery in the centre of Dartmoor, this family-run, non-smoking establishment offers friendly and attentive service. The bedrooms are pleasantly appointed, and there is a cosy bar and a lounge. The dinner menu includes local produce, and is a treat not to be missed.

Facilities 7 rms (6 en suite) (1 pri facs) (2 fmly) ⊘ TVB tea/coffee Licensed Cen ht No children 12yrs No coaches Dinner Last d 7pm **Prices** S £55-£59.50; D £110-£119; (incl. dinner) ✳ **LB Parking** 12

UMBERLEIGH   MAP 03 SS62

Premier Collection

◆◆◆◆◆ 🏠

Eastacott Barton

EX37 9AJ ☎ 01769 540545
e-mail stay@eastacott.com
web www.eastacott.com
Dir 1m E of Umberleigh. Off B3227 signed Eastacott, straight on at stone cross, Eastacott Barton 700yds on left

This large, stone-built former farmhouse has been restored to provide high quality, spacious and well-equipped accommodation, including three bedrooms in converted farm buildings. There is also a self-catering cottage. You have a choice of sitting rooms, and access to the extensive grounds and gardens. The house has a tranquil and picturesque location, with stunning views along the Taw valley.

continued

England

Facilities 2 en suite 3 annexe en suite ⊘ STV TVB tea/coffee Cen ht TVL No coaches Fishing Dinner **Prices** S £50-£95; D £70-£115✳ **LB** **Parking** 8

WESTWARD HO! MAP 03 SS42

◆◆◆◆

Culloden House

Fosketh Hl EX39 1UL ☎ 01237 479421 📠 08701 334359
e-mail enquiry@culloden-house.co.uk
web www.culloden-house.co.uk
Dir S of town centre. Off B3236 Stanwell Hill onto Fosketh Hill

This Victorian property stands on a wooded hillside with sweeping views over the beach and coast. Guests to this family-run house are assured a warm welcome and friendly atmosphere. A comfortable lounge with a wood burner is available.

Facilities 5 en suite (3 fmly) (1 GF) ⊘ TVB tea/coffee Cen ht TVL No coaches **Prices** S £35-£45; D £60-£70✳ **Parking** 5 **Notes** Closed Xmas

WHIMPLE MAP 03 SY09

◆◆◆◆◆ Ⓐ

Larkbeare Grange

Larkbeare, Talaton EX5 2RY
☎ 01404 822069 📠 01404 823746
e-mail stay@larkbeare.net
web www.larkbeare.net
Dir Off A30 at Daisymount signed Exmouth. Signs to Whimple, 0.25m right to Larkbeare, 0.5m left, entrance 1m on left

Facilities 3 en suite ⊘ TVB tea/coffee Direct dial from bedrooms ✘ Cen ht No coaches ℟ Dinner **Prices** S £70-£85; D £85-£105 **Conf** Max 12 Board 12 **Parking** 15

WIDECOMBE IN THE MOOR MAP 03 SX77

◆◆◆◆

Manor Cottage

TQ13 7TB ☎ 01364 621218
Dir A38, A382 to Bovey Tracey, left onto B3387 to Widecombe. Cottage with Post Office

Located in the centre of the village, this attractive cottage stands in a large and pleasant garden and has a lot of character. It offers friendly hospitality and spacious bedrooms. Breakfast is served in the cosy dining room and features good home cooking using fresh local produce.

Facilities 3 rms (1 en suite) ⊘ in bedrooms tea/coffee ✘ Cen ht TVL No children 15yrs No coaches **Prices** D £45-£55✳ **Parking** 3 **Notes** Closed Xmas 🖼

Please mention the AA B&B Guide when booking your stay

WINKLEIGH

MAP 03 SS60

◆◆◆◆

The Lymington Arms ◇

Lama Cross, Wembworthy EX18 7SA
☎ 01837 83772 & 83572 ▤ 01837 680074
Dir *2m NE of Winkleigh. A3124 to Winkleigh x-rds, E to Wembworthy*

This traditional inn has a well-deserved reputation for its convivial atmosphere. Accomplished cuisine makes excellent use of local produce in the bar and restaurant. After an enjoyable evening of good food and drink and good company, the homely bedrooms ensure a sound sleep.
Facilities 2 en suite ⊗ in bedrooms ⊗ in dining room TVB tea/coffee ✖ Cen ht TVL Dinner Last d 9.15pm **Prices** S £30; D £45-£50✳
Parking 30

◆◆◆◆

The Old Parsonage ◇

Ct Walk EX19 8JA ☎ 01837 83772 ▤ 01837 680074
e-mail tonypeel@fsbdial.co.uk
Dir *In village off A3124, behind parish church*

The Old Parsonage is a Grade II listed thatched house, dating in part from the 15th century, set in 2 acres of walled Victorian gardens next to the church. The bedrooms are individually designed and well appointed. Delicious breakfasts are served around a grand communal table in the dining room.
Facilities 3 en suite (1 GF) ⊗ TVB tea/coffee Cen ht No children 4yrs No coaches **Prices** S £30-£35; D £50-£60 **Parking** 4 **Notes** rs 25-26 Dec
⊠

WOOLACOMBE

MAP 03 SS44

◆◆◆◆

The Castle

The Esplanade EX34 7DJ ☎ 01271 870788 ▤ 01271 870812
e-mail the.castlehotel@amserve.net
Dir *A361 from Barnstaple to Ilfracombe, turn right at Woolacombe sign*

Built in 1898 in the style of a castle, this Victorian stone folly has stunning views over the bay. The attractive bedrooms are well equipped, and the lounge has a carved-wood ceiling and interesting panelling. There is also a lounge-bar, and breakfast is served in the elegant dining room.
Facilities 8 en suite (2 fmly) ⊗ in bedrooms ⊗ in dining room ⊗ in lounges TVB tea/coffee ✖ Licensed Cen ht TVL No children 5yrs No coaches **Parking** 8 **Notes** Closed Oct-Mar

◆◆◆◆

Sandunes

Beach Rd EX34 7BT ☎ 01271 870661
e-mail beaconhts@u.genie.co.uk
web www.sandwool.fsnet.co.uk
Dir *A361, turn left at Mullacott, cross onto B3343, property on right*

With outstanding views, and well located for the north Devon coast, this smart establishment offers light, airy, comfortable accommodation just a short walk from the shops and beach. Bedrooms are well equipped and some have a terrace where you can sit and soak up the sun. Breakfast is served at separate tables in the dining area, and there is also a pleasant lounge.
Facilities 4 en suite (2 GF) ⊗ TVB tea/coffee ✖ Cen ht TVL No coaches **Parking** 6 **Notes** Closed Xmas-New Year ⊠

YARCOMBE

MAP 04 ST20

Premier Collection

◆◆◆◆◆ ⊜

The Belfry Country Hotel

EX14 9BD ☎ 01404 861234 ▤ 01404 861579
e-mail stay@thebelfrycountryhotel.com
web www.thebelfrycountryhotel.com
Dir *A303 onto A30 signed Chard & Crewkerne, 2m on right opp church*

This 19th-century former village school is well situated for touring. The resident proprietors offer a warm welcome and have combined modern comforts with the original character. The extensive menu majors on local ingredients and careful cooking ensures maximum enjoyment; you make your selection in advance.
Facilities 6 en suite (2 GF) ⊗ TVB tea/coffee Direct dial from bedrooms ✖ Licensed Cen ht No children 13yrs No coaches Dinner Last d Previous day **Prices** S £55; D £80 LB **Parking** 8

YELVERTON

MAP 03 SX56

◆◆◆◆ ⊜

Harrabeer Country House Hotel

Harrowbeer Ln PL20 6EA ☎ 01822 853302
e-mail reception@harrabeer.co.uk
web www.harrabeer.co.uk
Dir *In village. Off A386 Tavistock Rd onto Grange Rd, right onto Harrowbeer Ln*

A warm welcome awaits you at this traditional Devon longhouse situated on the edge of Dartmoor. Providing an excellent base for
continued

exploring this beautiful area, the accommodation has modern comforts with a lounge, bar and a dining room overlooking the garden. There are also two self-catering units. Dinners are available by arrangement with special diets catered for.

Facilities 6 rms (5 en suite) (1 pri facs) (2 fmly) (1 GF) ⊘ TVB tea/coffee Direct dial from bedrooms Licensed Cen ht TVL No coaches Dinner Last d noon **Prices** S £48-£80; D £65-£95✳ **Conf** Max 20 Board 20 **Parking** 10 **Notes** Closed 3rd wk Dec, 2nd wk Jan

See advertisement on page 203

DORSET

ABBOTSBURY
MAP 04 SY58

◆◆◆

East Farm House *(SY578853)*

2 Rosemary Ln DT3 4JN
☎ 01305 871363 ▤ 01305 871363 Mrs Wood
e-mail wendy@eastfarmhouse.co.uk
web www.eastfarmhouse.co.uk
Dir B3157 W into Abbotsbury, Swan Inn on left, farmhouse 1st right onto Rosemary Ln

This unspoiled and charming farmhouse is in the centre of the pretty village and has been in the owner's family since 1729. The house has a homely atmosphere, traditionally furnished with much character and filled with memorabilia. Hearty, farmhouse-style dinners (by arrangement) are served in the lounge-dining room, where a log fire burns in winter.

Facilities 3 en suite ⊘ TVB tea/coffee Cen ht No children 14yrs 20 acres stud Dinner Last d breakfast **Parking** 3

ATHELHAMPTON
MAP 04 SY79

ⓤ

White Cottage

DT2 7LG ☎ 01305 848622
e-mail llindzpiper@aol.com

At the time of going to press the rating for this establishment had not been confirmed. Please check the AA website www.theAA.com for up-to-date information.

Facilities 2 rms (1 en suite) (1 pri facs) ⊘ tea/coffee ✖ Cen ht Fishing **Prices** D £60-£70✳ **Parking** 2 **Notes** Closed 23-26 Dec 🚭

BEAMINSTER
MAP 04 ST40

◆◆◆◆◆ 🅰 ❧

Watermeadow House *(ST535001)*

Bridge Farm, Hooke DT8 3PD
☎ 01308 862619 ▤ 01308 862619 Mrs Wallbridge
e-mail enquiries@watermeadowhouse.co.uk
web www.watermeadowhouse.co.uk
Dir Off A356 4m W of Maiden Newton signed Hooke. Left at x-rds signed Kingcombe, house 300yds on right

Facilities 2 rms (1 en suite) (1 pri facs) (1 fmly) ⊘ TVB tea/coffee ✖ Cen ht 280 acres dairy beef **Prices** S £30-£40; D £55-£60✳ LB **Parking** 6 **Notes** Closed Nov-Feb

BLANDFORD FORUM
MAP 04 ST80

◆◆◆◆◆

Portman Lodge

Whitecliff Mill St DT11 7BP
☎ 01258 453727 ▤ 01258 453727
e-mail enquiries@portmanlodge.co.uk
web www.portmanlodge.co.uk
Dir On NW end of Blandford's one-way system, to access follow signs from town centre to Shaftesbury & hospital

Built in the Victorian period and once used as a music school, this house now provides elegant accommodation and a genuine welcome. Carefully decorated and adorned with artefacts and pictures from the proprietors' extensive travels, the public rooms are spacious and inviting. Delicious dinners prepared with great skill are available by arrangement.

Facilities 3 en suite ⊘ TVB tea/coffee ✖ Cen ht No children 10yrs No coaches Dinner Last d noon **Prices** S £45-£50; D £65 **Parking** 6

◆◆◆◆

The Anvil Inn

Salisbury Rd, Pimperne DT11 8UQ
☎ 01258 453431 ▤ 01258 480182
e-mail info@anvilhotel.co.uk
Dir 2m NE of Blandford on A354 in Pimperne

Please note that this establishment has recently changed hands. Located in a village near Blandford, this 16th-century thatched inn provides a traditional country welcome with plenty of character. Bedrooms have been refurbished to high standards. Dinner is a varied selection of home-made dishes with a tempting variety of hand-pulled ales and wines by the glass.

Facilities 13 en suite (1 GF) ⊘ in bedrooms ⊘ in dining room STV TVB tea/coffee Direct dial from bedrooms Cen ht No coaches Dinner Last d 9.30pm **Prices** S £65-£70; D £85-£95✳ LB **Parking** 18

◆◆◆◆

St Martin's House

Whitecliff Mill St DT11 7BP
☎ 01258 451245 & 07748 887719
e-mail info@stmartinshouse.co.uk
Dir Off Market Place onto Salisbury St & left onto White Cliff Mill St, on right before traffic island

Dating from 1866, this restored property was once part of the chorister's house for a local church. The bedrooms are well equipped, and the hosts offer warm hospitality and attentive service. Breakfast, which features local and home-made items, is enjoyed around a communal table. Carefully prepared dinners are available by arrangement.

Facilities 2 rms (2 pri facs) (1 fmly) ⊘ TVB tea/coffee Cen ht No coaches Dinner Last d 24hrs before **Prices** S fr £40; d fr £60✳ **Parking** 3 **Notes** 🚭

England

BLANDFORD FORUM continued

♦♦♦
The Old Bakery
Church Rd, Pimperne DT11 8UB
☎ 01258 455173 & 07799 853784
e-mail jjtanners@hotmail.com
Dir 2m NE of Blandford. Off A354 into Pimperne village

Dating from 1890 and once, as the name suggests, the village bakery, this family home offers comfortable accommodation in a convenient location. Popular with business travellers, families can also be accommodated, with cots available. Substantial breakfasts featuring home-made bread and marmalade are served in the dining room.

Facilities 3 en suite (1 GF) ⊗ TVB tea/coffee Cen ht TVL No coaches Dinner Last d 9am **Prices** D £40-£60✳ **LB** **Parking** 2 **Notes** ⊛

♦♦♦ ❧
Pennhills Farmhouse ◈ *(ST819101)*
Sandy Ln, Shillingstone DT11 0TF
☎ 01258 860491 Mrs Watts
Dir 6.5m NW of Blandford. Off A357 at Shillingstone Post Office onto Gunn Ln, bear right to T-junct, left onto Lanchard Ln, B&B signed

Located in a quiet setting with far views over the surrounding countryside, this delightful, family-run farmhouse provides spacious rooms. The substantial English breakfast consists of home-produced items, served house-party style around one large table in the lounge-dining room, where an open fire burns during the winter.

Facilities 2 en suite (1 fmly) (1 GF) ⊗ TVB tea/coffee ✖ Cen ht TVL Walking 120 acres mixed **Prices** S fr £25; d fr £50✳ **Notes** Closed 22 Dec-3 Jan ⊛

♦♦♦
Weathervane Cottage
284 Bournemouth Rd, Charlton Marshall DT11 9NG
☎ 01258 453374 & 450193 📠 01258 453374
e-mail enquiries@weathervanes-direct.co.uk
Dir 2m S of Blandford on A350 in Charlton Marshall. 50yds N of church

This thatched 18th-century cottage offers comfortable accommodation. A hearty breakfast, including local produce, is served at a communal table overlooking the walled garden.

Facilities 3 rms (2 en suite) (1 pri facs) ⊗ TVB tea/coffee Cen ht No coaches **Parking** 3 **Notes** Closed 23 Dec-5 Jan

⑪
Church House
Church Rd, Shillingstone DT11 0SL ☎ 01258 860646
e-mail paul@chtours.demon.co.uk

At the time of going to press the rating for this establishment had not been confirmed. Please check the AA website www.theAA.com for up-to-date information.

Facilities 3 en suite ⊗ ✖ Cen ht TVL No coaches Dinner Last d previous day **Parking** 3 **Notes** Closed Xmas ⊛

BOURNEMOUTH
MAP 05 SZ09

★★★ Guest Accommodation
Burley Court
Bath Rd BH1 2NP
☎ 01202 552824 & 556704 📠 01202 298514
e-mail info@burleycourthotel.co.uk
Dir Leave A338 at St Pauls rdbt, take 3rd exit at next rdbt into Holdenhurst Rd. 3rd exit at next rdbt into Bath Rd, over crossing, 1st left

A large family-owned business that has been well established for many years. It's close to the East Cliff with good parking facilities, an outdoor swimming pool, and dinner is available in summer.

Facilities 38 en suite (8 fmly) (4 GF) ⊗ in 20 bedrooms ⊗ in dining room TVB tea/coffee Direct dial from bedrooms Licensed Lift Cen ht TVL ✦ Dinner **Prices** S £35-£49; D £70-£98✳ **LB** **Conf** Thtr 30 Class 15 Board 15 **Parking** 35 **Notes** Closed 30 Dec-14 Jan rs 15-31 Jan

★★★ Inn
Commodore ◈
Overcliff Dr, Southbourne BH6 3TD ☎ 01202 423150
e-mail 7688@greeneking.co.uk
web www.oldenglish.co.uk
Dir Exit A338 signed for Christchurch and Airport. Head towards Christchurch and then Southbourne Beaches.

Situated on the clifftop at Southbourne, the Commodore is adjacent to Fisherman's Walk. Popular with locals, the bar boasts spectacular views across Poole Bay and serves an extensive range of dishes. Bedrooms are due to be upgraded during 2006.

Facilities 10 en suite (1 fmly) ⊗ in 1 bedrooms ⊗ in dining room TVB tea/coffee ✖ Lift No children No coaches Dinner **Prices** S £20-£35; D £50; (room only) ✳ **LB** **Conf** Max 30 Thtr 30 Class 12 Board 20 Del from £72 ✳ **Parking** 12

Premier Collection
♦♦♦♦♦
Balincourt Hotel
58 Christchurch Rd BH1 3PF
☎ 01202 552962 📠 01202 552962
e-mail rooms@balincourt.co.uk
web www.balincourt.co.uk
Dir On A35 between Lansdowne & Boscombe Gardens, opp Lynton Court pub

The friendly Balincourt offers high standards of accommodation within easy reach of the town centre and beaches. The bedrooms are

continued

ndividually decorated and equipped with thoughtful facilities. There is
a lounge and a bar, and freshly prepared evening meals are available.

Balincourt Hotel

Facilities 12 en suite ⊗ TVB tea/coffee ✖ Licensed Cen ht TVL
No children 16yrs No coaches Dinner Last d 4pm **Prices** S £40-£70;
D £70-£80 **LB** **Conf** Max 20 **Parking** 11 **Notes** Closed Xmas

◆◆◆◆
Alexander Lodge ◇

21 Southern Rd, Southbourne BH6 3SR
☎ 01202 421662 📠 01202 421662
e-mail alexanderlodge@yahoo.com
Dir Southern Rd off Southbourne Overcliff near cliff lift

A warm welcome and high levels of service are assured at this
delightful family-run guest house, close to beaches and the town
centre. The comfortable bedrooms have many useful extras, and there
is a lounge and a bar. Evening meals are available by arrangement.

Facilities 6 en suite (2 fmly) ⊗ TVB tea/coffee ✖ Licensed Cen ht
TVL No coaches Dinner Last d 10am **Prices** S £25-£45; D £40-£66✶ **LB**
Conf Max 14 Thtr 14 **Parking** 7 **Notes** rs Xmas

◆◆◆◆
The Boltons Hotel

9 Durley Chine Rd South, West Cliff BH2 5JT
☎ 01202 751517
e-mail info@boltonshotel.co.uk
Dir A35/A338 onto B3066, 2nd rdbt right onto West Cliff Rd, Durly
Chine Rd South 2nd right

Located in a quiet position close to the town centre, this fine Victorian
property offers appealing public rooms, including a lounge, dining
room and a cosy bar. The secluded gardens contain a swimming pool.
The comfortable bedrooms vary in size and are well equipped and
furnished.

Facilities 13 en suite (2 fmly) (1 GF) ⊗ in bedrooms ⊗ in dining room
TVB tea/coffee Direct dial from bedrooms ✖ Licensed Cen ht ⚲
Parking 12 **Notes** Closed 24-26 Dec

◆◆◆◆
Cransley Hotel ◇

11 Knyveton Rd, East Cliff BH1 3QG
☎ 01202 290067 📠 07092 381721
e-mail info@cransley.com
web www.cransley.com
Dir Off A338 at St Pauls rdbt by ASDA store, over next rdbt, Knyveton
Rd 1st left

A warm welcome is assured at this delightful establishment,
convenient for major routes and rail links, the town centre and the
beach. By arrangement, traditional, home-cooked meals are served in
the south-facing dining room next to the elegant lounge, both having
a garden view.

Facilities 11 rms (10 en suite) (1 pri facs) (2 GF) ⊗ FTV TVB tea/coffee
✖ Cen ht TVL No children 14yrs No coaches Dinner Last d 2pm
Prices S £25-£35; D £50-£70✶ **Parking** 8

◆◆◆◆
Fielden Court Hotel

20 Southern Rd, Southbourne BH6 3SR
☎ 01202 427459 📠 01202 427459
e-mail enquiries@fieldencourthotel.co.uk
Dir A338 onto A3060, at 2nd rdbt onto Christchurch Rd, left at lights,
right onto Chestnut Av & Southern Rd

Please note that this establishment has recently changed hands. This
delightful guest house is close to the lift to the beach and provides
comfortable, well-equipped bedrooms. Home-cooked evening meals
are served by arrangement, and there is a charming lounge.

Facilities 8 en suite (1 fmly) ⊗ TVB tea/coffee ✖ Cen ht TVL Dinner
Last d 10am **Parking** 5

◆◆◆◆
The Maples ◇

1 Library Rd, Winton BH9 2QH ☎ 01202 529820
e-mail jeffreyhurrell@yahoo.co.uk
Dir Off A3060 Castle Ln West onto Wimborne Rd, The Maples 1m on
right after police station

A warm welcome awaits you at the Maples, which is just off Winton
High St. The atmosphere is friendly, and the bedrooms are quiet and
equipped with considerate extras. Breakfast is enjoyed in the pleasant
dining room around a communal table.

Facilities 2 en suite (1 fmly) ⊗ in dining room TVB tea/coffee ✖
Cen ht No children 7yrs No coaches **Prices** S £20-£30; D £40-£60
Parking 2 **Notes** 🐾

England

BOURNEMOUTH continued

◆◆◆◆

Rosscourt Guest Accommodation ◇

6 St Johns Rd, Boscombe BH5 1EL
☎ 01202 397537 🖹 01202 301039
e-mail enquiries@rosscourthotel.co.uk
Dir A338 signed to Kings Park, then signs for Boscombe. Left off Christchurch Rd onto St Johns Rd

A warm welcome is guaranteed at this central guest house, which is within easy reach of the beach, shops and many attractions. The attractive bedrooms, some of which are suitable for families, are comfortable and have been finished with many thoughtful extras. Home-cooked evening meals are available by arrangement.

Facilities 9 rms (7 en suite) (2 fmly) (1 GF) ⊗ TVB tea/coffee ✖ Cen ht TVL Dinner Last d 10am **Prices** S £30-£35; D £60-£70✱ **LB** **Parking** 11 **Notes** Closed 20-30 Dec rs 1/2wks Jan

◆◆◆◆

Thanet Hotel

2 Drury Rd, Alum Chine BH4 8HA ☎ 01202 761135
e-mail thanethotel_bournemouth@hotmail.com
Dir Signs for Alum Chine Beach. Hotel on corner Alumhurst Rd & Drury Rd

A warm welcome is assured at this delightful Edwardian house, located within easy walking distance of fashionable Westbourne and Alum Chine beach. The bedrooms are filled with many homely extras, and a lounge is available. Imaginative dinners and comprehensive breakfasts are served in the attractive dining room.

Facilities 8 rms (5 en suite) (1 fmly) ⊗ TVB tea/coffee ✖ Licensed Cen ht No children 7yrs Dinner Last d 4pm **LB** **Parking** 6 **Notes** Closed Nov-Mar

◆◆◆◆

Tudor Grange Hotel

31 Gervis Rd BH1 3EE
☎ 01202 291472 & 291463 🖹 01202 311503
web www.tudorgrangehotel.co.uk
Dir Signs for East Cliff

Set in well-maintained gardens, this fine Tudor-style house is located on the East Cliff close to the town centre. Bedrooms are well equipped and attractively decorated. The public areas have many interesting features, and include a lounge and bar in which to relax.

continued

208

Tudor Grange Hotel

Facilities 11 en suite (3 fmly) (1 GF) ⊗ in dining room ⊗ in lounges TVB tea/coffee Direct dial from bedrooms Licensed Cen ht TVL No coaches **Parking** 11 **Notes** Closed 24 Dec-2 Jan

◆◆◆◆

Westcotes House Hotel

9 Southbourne Overcliff Dr, Southbourne BH6 3TE
☎ 01202 428512
web www.westcoteshousehotel.co.uk
Dir 2m E of town centre. A35 onto B3059 & seafront road, 1m E of pie

The refurbished Westcotes House has spectacular views across Poole Bay. Situated on the quiet side of the town, it has well-equipped bedrooms, with one on the ground floor. There is a conservatory lounge and enjoyable home-cooked dinners are available by arrangement.

Facilities 6 en suite (1 GF) ⊗ TVB tea/coffee ✖ Cen ht TVL No children 10yrs No coaches Dinner Last d 5pm **Prices** S £40-£46; D £60-£72✱ **Parking** 6 **Notes** 🖂

◆◆◆◆

Whateley Hall Hotel

7 Florence Rd, Boscombe BH5 1HH
☎ 01202 397749 🖹 01202 397749
e-mail whateleyhall.hotel@virgin.net
Dir 1m E of Bournemouth centre. A338 onto A3049 Ashley Rd, right onto Christchurch Rd, left onto Sea Rd, 3rd right onto Florence Rd

The family-run Whateley Hall lies between Boscombe shopping centre and the beach, and is convenient for exploring the New Forest area. The brightly furnished bedrooms are well appointed, and there is a lounge and a bar. Dinner is available by arrangement.

Facilities 10 en suite (3 fmly) (2 GF) ⊗ TVB tea/coffee ✖ Licensed Cen ht TVL No children 8yrs No coaches Dinner Last d noon **Parking** 7

◆◆◆◆ 🅰

Blue Palms Hotel ◇

26 Tregonwell Rd, West Cliff BH2 5NS
☎ 01202 554968 🖹 01202 294197
e-mail bluepalmshotel@btopenworld.com
web www.bluepalmshotel.com
Dir Off A338 at Bournemouth West rdbt signed town centre, Triangle next rdbt onto Durley Chine Rd, at rdbt onto West Hill Rd, Tregonwell Rd 3rd left

Facilities 10 en suite (2 fmly) (2 GF) ⊗ in 4 bedrooms ⊗ in dining room ⊗ in lounges TVB tea/coffee ✖ Licensed Cen ht TVL No coaches Dinner Last d lunchtime **Prices** S £28-£35; D £56-£70✱ **LB** **Parking** 7

♦♦♦

Fenn Lodge ◇

1 Rosemount Rd, Alum Chine BH4 8HB
☎ 01202 761273 📄 01202 761273
e-mail fennlodge@btconnect.com
web www.fennlodge.co.uk
Dir A338 into Poole, at rdbt onto B3065 signed Alum Chime & Sandbanks. Left at lights, right at rdbt onto Alumhurst Rd, 3rd left

A warm welcome is assured at this family-run establishment, located within walking distance of Alum Chine and the beach. Bournemouth and Poole are just a short drive away. Bedrooms are comfortably furnished with many useful facilities, and there is a bar and a refurbished lounge.

Facilities 11 rms (10 en suite) (1 pri facs) (1 fmly) (1 GF) ✪ TVB tea/coffee ✗ Cen ht TVL No coaches **Prices** S £23.50-£29; D £47-£58 LB **Parking** 6 **Notes** Closed Nov-mid Mar

♦♦♦

Alum Grange Hotel

Burnaby Rd, Alum Chine BH4 8JF
☎ 01202 761195 & 07971 375130 📄 01202 760973
Dir B3065 The Avenue towards Canford Cliffs, left onto Tower Rd & Mountbatten Rd, over x-rds, 1st right

Located between Bournemouth and Poole, the spacious Alum Grange is only a stroll from the sandy Alum Chine beach. All bedrooms are brightly decorated and one room has a four-poster bed. A daily changing menu is served in the attractive dining room-lounge bar.

Facilities 14 en suite (7 fmly) (3 GF) ✪ in bedrooms ✪ in dining room ✪ in 1 lounge TVB tea/coffee Licensed Cen ht TVL No coaches Dinner Last d 4pm **Conf** Max 50 **Parking** 11

♦♦♦

Newlands Hotel ◇

14 Rosemount Rd, Alum Chine BH4 8HB
☎ 01202 761922 📄 01202 769872
e-mail newlandshotel@totalise.co.uk
web www.newlandshotel.com
Dir A338/A35 to Liverpool Victoria rdbt, exit for Alum Chine, left at lights, right at small rdbt onto Alumhurst Rd, 3rd left

Newlands is an attractive Edwardian house in a quiet area near Alum Chine beach and within easy driving distance of Bournemouth and Poole centres. It offers comfortable accommodation with wireless Internet access and there is an attractive garden.

Facilities 8 en suite (3 fmly) ✪ TVB tea/coffee ✗ Cen ht No coaches Wireless internet **Prices** S £25-£29; D £50-£58✱ LB **Parking** 8 **Notes** Closed Dec & Jan

♦♦♦

Pinedale Hotel ◇

40 Tregonwell Rd, West Cliff BH2 5NT
☎ 01202 553733 & 292702 📄 01202 553733
e-mail thepinedalehotel@btconnect.com
Dir A338 at Bournemouth West rdbt, signs to West Cliff, Tregonwell Rd is 3rd left after passing Wessex Hotel

This friendly guest house is enthusiastically run by two generations of the same family, and offers comfortable accommodation within a short walk of the seafront and attractions. The fresh-looking bedrooms are equipped with useful extras. There is also an attractive licensed bar and an airy dining room where you can enjoy wholesome home-cooked meals.

Facilities 15 rms (9 en suite) (1 fmly) ✪ in dining room ✪ in 1 lounge TVB tea/coffee ✗ Licensed TVL No coaches Dinner Last d 3pm **Prices** S £19-£36; D £38-£72✱ **Parking** 15

England

BOURNEMOUTH continued

♦♦♦

Tiffanys Hotel

31 Chine Crs, West Cliff BH2 5LB ☎ 01202 551424
e-mail tiffanyshotel@aol.com
Dir *Off Wessex Way A35/A338 at Bournemouth West rdbt signed West Cliffe, over next rdbt, right for Alum Chine & 1st right*

Located on the West Cliff, Tiffanys is an attractive detached property convenient for the town centre, beaches and attractions. It offers spacious, well-appointed bedrooms, some of which are on the ground floor. A cooked breakfast is served in the stylish dining room.

Facilities 15 en suite (2 fmly) ⊗ in 7 bedrooms ⊗ in dining room STV TVB tea/coffee ✖ Cen ht **Parking** 15

♦♦♦

Denewood Hotel

1 Percy Rd BH5 1JE
☎ 01202 394493 & 309913 🖹 01202 391155
e-mail res@denewood.co.uk
Dir *500yds NE of Boscombe Pier, signed*

Facilities 10 en suite (3 fmly) ⊗ STV TVB tea/coffee Licensed Cen ht TVL No coaches Solarium health & beauty salon **Parking** 14

BRIDPORT   MAP 04 SY49
See also **Chideock**

♦♦♦♦♦

Roundham House Hotel

Roundham Gdns, West Bay Rd DT6 4BD
☎ 01308 422753 🖹 01308 421500
e-mail cyprencom@compuserve.com
web www.roundhamhouse.co.uk
Dir *A35 into Bridport, at the Crown Inn rdbt take exit signed West Bay. Hotel 400yds on left*

The hosts here are invariably on hand to extend a warm welcome to their lovely home, which comes with well-tended gardens and views to the nearby coast. Bedrooms come in a variety of sizes and are all filled with useful extras. Public areas include a comfortable lounge and well-appointed dining room.

Roundham House Hotel

Facilities 8 rms (7 en suite) (1 fmly) ⊗ TVB tea/coffee Direct dial from bedrooms Licensed Cen ht No children 7yrs No coaches
Prices S £46-£55; D £76-£104✳ **Parking** 10 **Notes** Closed Jan-Feb

♦♦♦♦

Southcroft

Park Rd DT6 5DA ☎ 01308 423335
e-mail info@southcroftguesthouse.com
Dir *W of town centre off B3162 West Allington onto Park Rd*

The caring hosts do their utmost to ensure an enjoyable stay at Southcroft. The individually decorated bedrooms are spacious and feature home from home comforts as well as extras such as chocolates and bottled water. Breakfast is served around the kitchen table, overlooking the patio.

Facilities 3 rms (2 en suite) (1 pri facs) ⊗ STV TVB tea/coffee ✖ Cen ht No children No coaches **Prices** D £56-£64✳ **Parking** 1

♦♦♦♦

Britmead House

West Bay Rd DT6 4EG ☎ 01308 422941 & 07973 725243
e-mail britmead@talk21.com
web www.britmeadhouse.co.uk
Dir *1m S of town centre, off A35 onto West Bay Rd*

Britmead House is located south of Bridport, within easy reach of the town centre and West Bay harbour. Family-run, the atmosphere is friendly and the accommodation well-appointed and comfortable. Suitable for business and leisure, many guests return regularly. A choice of breakfast is served in the light and airy dining room.

Facilities 8 en suite (2 fmly) (2 GF) ⊗ TVB tea/coffee Cen ht TVL No coaches **Prices** S £40-£50; D £54-£70✳ LB **Parking** 12

continued

CASHMOOR

MAP 04 ST91

◆◆◆◆ 🖫

Cashmoor House ◇

DT11 8DN ☎ **01725 552339**
e-mail spencer@cashmoorhouse.co.uk
Dir On A354 Salisbury to Blandford, 3m S of Sixpenny Handley rdbt
just past Inn on the Chase

Situated halfway between Blandford and Salisbury, parts of Cashmoor
House date from the 17th century. The attractive property retains
much original character and has a warm farmhouse ambience.
Traditional Aga-cooked breakfasts, featuring home-made bread and
preserves, and eggs laid by the owners' hens, are served in the
beamed dining room. Suppers are available by arrangement.

Facilities 4 en suite (2 fmly) (2 GF) ⊗ TVB tea/coffee Cen ht TVL
No coaches Dinner Last d breakfast **Prices** S fr £30; d fr £45.50✳
Parking 8 **Notes** 🐾

CATTISTOCK

MAP 04 SY59

◆◆◆◆ 🍴

Fox & Hounds Inn

Duck St DT2 0JH ☎ **01300 320444** 📠 **01300 320444**
e-mail info@foxandhoundsinn.com
web www.foxandhoundsinn.com
Dir Signed from A37 Dorchester to Yeovil

This traditional village inn is quietly located not far from Dorchester
and is a delightful place from which to explore the attractions of
Dorset. Bedrooms are spacious and very well equipped, and the
public rooms offer real ales and a good choice of food in a relaxed
atmosphere.

Facilities 3 rms (2 en suite) (1 pri facs) (1 fmly) ⊗ in bedrooms
⊗ in dining room ⊗ in 1 lounge TVB tea/coffee Cen ht No coaches
Pool Table Skittle alley Dinner Last d 8.45pm **Prices** S fr £40; d fr £70✳
Parking 10 **Notes** rs Mon

CERNE ABBAS

MAP 04 ST60

◆◆◆

Purbeck Lodge

Lyons Gate DT2 7AZ ☎ **01300 345584**
Dir 3m N of Cerne Abbas. From A352 turn past Dittisham House,
next left, Lodge at top of drive

The Purbeck Lodge lies in a tranquil corner of Dorset. The modern
bedroom is contemporary in style and equipped to a high standard.
Home-cooked, two course evening meals are available by
arrangement.

Facilities 1 en suite (1 fmly) ⊗ STV TVB tea/coffee 🛏 Cen ht ch fac
No coaches Fishing Dinner Last d 10am **Prices** S £40; D £60✳ **LB**
Parking 2 **Notes** 🐾

CHICKERELL

MAP 04 SY68

★★★★ Guest Accommodation

The Turk's Head

8 East St DT3 4DS ☎ **01305 783093** 📠 **01305 786668**
e-mail mail@turksheadhotel.co.uk
Dir In village centre

The stone building dates back over 250 years, set in the village of
Chickerell just outside Weymouth. Family run, the popular restaurant
offers individually decorated, spacious bedrooms with many
accessories.

Facilities 6 en suite (2 fmly) ⊗ TVB tea/coffee Licensed Cen ht Dinner
Last d 9pm **Prices** S £59; D £79✳ **LB Conf** Max 14 Board 14
Parking 10

England

◆◆◆◆

Rose Cottage ◇

Main St DT6 6JQ ☎ 01297 489994 & 07980 400904
e-mail enquiries@rosecottage-chideock.co.uk
web www.rosecottage-chideock.co.uk
Dir On A35 in village centre

Located in the centre of the charming village, this 300-year-old cottage provides very well-appointed accommodation and a friendly welcome is assured. A delicious breakfast can be enjoyed in the renovated dining room which has many interesting features, and in finer weather you can relax in the pretty garden.

Facilities 2 en suite ⊗ FTV TVB tea/coffee ✈ Cen ht No coaches
Prices S £30-£35; D £50-£55✳ **LB Parking** 2 **Notes** ⊜

◆◆◆◆

Betchworth House

DT6 6JW ☎ 01297 489478 🖺 01297 489932
e-mail info@betchworthhouse.co.uk
web www.betchworthhouse.co.uk
Dir On A35 in village

There is a warm welcome and thoughtful and attentive service at this Grade II listed 19th-century house. Bedrooms, including one on the ground floor, are attractive and all feature numerous extra touches. Breakfast is served in the comfortable dining room, where a good choice of hot and cold options is provided. You can unwind in the garden and off-road parking is available.

Facilities 5 rms (3 en suite) (2 pri facs) (1 fmly) (1 GF) ⊗ TVB tea/coffee ✈ Cen ht No children 8yrs No coaches **Prices** S £35-£40; D £50-£55 **LB Parking** 5 **Notes** Closed Xmas

◆◆◆◆ 🅰

Warren House B&B ◇

DT6 6JW ☎ 01297 849996
e-mail kathy@warren-house.com
Dir A35 Chideock, turn by church signed North Chideock, parking signed 60mtrs

Facilities 4 en suite (2 fmly) ⊗ TVB tea/coffee ✈ Cen ht No coaches
Prices S £30; D £50✳ **Parking** 6 **Notes** Closed Xmas ⊜

Premier Collection

◆◆◆◆◆

Druid House

26 Sopers Ln BH23 1JE ☎ 01202 485615 🖺 01202 473484
e-mail reservations@druid-house.co.uk
web www.druid-house.co.uk
Dir A35 exit Christchurch main rdbt onto Sopers Ln, establishment on le▮

Overlooking the park, this delightful family-run establishment is just a stroll from High St, the Priory and the Quay. Bedrooms, some with balconies, are very comfortably furnished, and the many welcome extras include CD players. There is a pleasant rear garden and relaxin▮ lounge and bar areas.

Facilities 8 en suite (3 fmly) (4 GF) ⊗ in bedrooms ⊗ in dining room ⊗ in 1 lounge STV TVB tea/coffee Direct dial from bedrooms ✈ Licensed Cen ht No coaches **Parking** 8

Premier Collection

◆◆◆◆◆ ⍟⍟ ⊜

The Lord Bute Hotel & Restaurant

179-181 Lymington Rd, Highcliffe BH23 4JS
☎ 01425 278884 🖺 01425 279258
e-mail mail@lordbute.co.uk
web www.lordbute.co.uk
Dir A337 towards Highcliffe

The elegant Lord Bute stands directly behind the original entrance lodges of Highcliffe Castle close to the beach and historic town of Christchurch. Bedrooms have been finished to a very high standard with many thoughtful extras including spa baths and satellite television. Excellent food is available in the smart restaurant, and conferences and weddings are catered for.

continue

Facilities 9 en suite 4 annexe en suite (3 fmly) (6 GF) ⊗ in bedrooms ⊗ in dining room ⊗ in lounges FTV TVB tea/coffee Direct dial from bedrooms Licensed Cen ht No coaches Dinner Last d 9.45pm **Prices** D £98-£225✱ **LB Conf** Thtr 25 Class 15 Board 18 **Parking** 40

Premier Collection

◆◆◆◆◆ 🏠

Seawards

3 Avon Run Cl, Friars Cliff BH23 4DT
☎ 01425 273188 & 07811 934 059
e-mail seawards13@hotmail.com
web www.seawards13.plus.com
Dir A35 onto A337 towards Highcliffe, right towards Mudeford, down the Runway, onto Bure Ln, 2nd left onto Island Av, then 1st right, then right again

Set in a peaceful cul-de-sac just a stroll from the beach, Seawards offers home from home comfort in thoughtfully equipped bedrooms. For those not wanting to go to the beach there is a pretty, well-tended garden and one of the rooms has a conservatory. Breakfast offers plenty of choice and quality ingredients.

Facilities 2 en suite (2 GF) ⊗ STV TVB tea/coffee ✻ Cen ht TVL No children 5yrs No coaches Dinner Last d 6pm **Parking** 7 **Notes** Closed 21 Dec-14 Jan 🐾

◆◆◆◆

Beechcroft Place

106 Lymington Rd, Highcliffe BH23 4JX
☎ 01425 277171 & 07885 186015
e-mail b&b@unique-southcoast-uk.com
web www.unique-southcoast-uk.com
Dir On A337 opp Highcliffe Golf Club & beach

The proprietors are invariably on hand for their guests at this comfortable guest house set in a well-tended garden. The three suites each have a private entrance and a lounge with breakfast area. There is also an attractive conservatory-lounge. Breakfasts use organic produce whenever possible.

Facilities 3 en suite (3 GF) ⊗ TVB tea/coffee ✻ Cen ht TVL No children 18yrs No coaches Golf 9 **Prices** S £38-£48; D £58-£64✱ **LB Conf** Max 6 Thtr 6 Class 6 Board 6 **Parking** 3 **Notes** 🐾

◆◆◆◆

Windy Willums ◇

58 Island View Av BH23 4DS
☎ 01425 277046 & 07950 481433
e-mail enquiries@windywillums.co.uk
Dir A35 Somerford rdbt take A337 for Highcliffe, minirdbt last exit and left after Sandpiper pub

Just a stroll from Mudeford beach, the Willums is an ideal base for windsurfing, sailing or for exploring the New Forest. The garden is a feature; proprietor Julie was a finalist in the BBC Gardener of the Year competition in 2003.

Facilities 2 rms (1 en suite) (1 pri facs) (2 fmly) ⊗ TVB tea/coffee ✻ Cen ht No coaches Dinner Last d previous day **Prices** S £30-£50; D £50-£70✱ **LB Parking** 3 **Notes** 🐾

◆◆◆◆

Ashbourne

47 Stour Rd BH23 1LN ☎ 01202 475574 📠 01202 482905
e-mail ashcroft.b@hotmail.com
Dir A35 Christchurch to Bournemouth, left at lights onto Stour Rd, over lights, 4th house on right

Convenient for the historic market town of Christchurch, the scenic River Stour, the New Forest and nearby beaches, this delightful guest house provides a relaxed and friendly environment. Bedrooms and bathrooms are all neatly furnished and equipped with many extra facilities. Large cooked breakfasts are served in the bright dining room.

Facilities 7 rms (5 en suite) (1 fmly) ⊗ STV TVB tea/coffee ✻ Cen ht No coaches **Prices** S £35-£50; D £50-£60✱ **Parking** 6 **Notes** Closed Xmas & New Year 🐾

◆◆◆◆

Beautiful South

87 Barrack Rd BH23 2AJ
☎ 01202 568183 & 07958 597686
e-mail kevin.lovett1@ntlworld.com
web www.kevanddebbie.co.uk
Dir 0.25m from Christchurch town centre on A35, opp Pizza Hut at Bailey Bridge

The convenient location near to the main road on the outskirts of Christchurch makes this friendly guest house a good choice for leisure and business. Refurbished throughout, public areas and bedrooms are bright and inviting, and hearty dinners, by arrangement, can be enjoyed in the pleasant dining room.

Facilities 3 en suite (1 fmly) ⊗ TVB tea/coffee ✻ Cen ht No coaches Dinner Last d 10am **Parking** 4 **Notes** 🐾

◆◆◆◆

The Beech Tree

2 Stuart Rd, Highcliffe BH23 5JS
☎ 01425 272038 📠 01425 272038
Dir A337 Christchurch to New Milton for 2m, 1st right after lights in Highcliffe village

Convenient for the New Forest and the coast, this delightful guest house has bright bedrooms with many extra facilities. A cosy lounge is also available, and carefully presented breakfasts are served in the attractive dining room.

Facilities 6 en suite (2 GF) ⊗ TVB tea/coffee ✻ Cen ht TVL No children No coaches **LB Parking** 12 **Notes** 🐾

England

◆◆◆◆

Grosvenor Lodge ◇

53 Stour Rd BH23 1LN ☎ 01202 499008 📠 01202 486041
e-mail bookings@grosvenorlodge.co.uk
Dir *A35 from Christchurch to Bournemouth, at 1st lights left onto Stour Rd, house on right*

A friendly and popular guest house near the centre of this historic town. The bedrooms are brightly and individually decorated and have lots of useful extras. Hearty breakfasts are served in the cheerful dining room, and there is an extensive choice of local restaurants for lunch and dinner.

Facilities 7 en suite (4 fmly) (1 GF) ⊗ in bedrooms ⊗ in dining room TVB tea/coffee ✖ Cen ht **Prices** S £25-£45; D £50-£60✳ **LB** **Parking** 10

◆◆◆◆

The Rothesay

175, Lymington Rd, Highcliffe BH23 4JS ☎ 01425 274172
e-mail rothesayhotel.1@tiscali.co.uk
web www.rothesayhotel.net
Dir *A337 to Highcliffe towards The Castle, 1m on left*

Set on the edge of Highcliffe village, the Rothesay is a great base for exploring the Dorset-Hampshire coast. Highcliffe Castle is just a 5-minute walk, and there are clifftop walks and views to the Isle of Wight. The indoor pool is a real benefit, as are the pretty gardens and large car park.

Facilities 10 en suite 3 annexe en suite (6 GF) ⊗ TVB tea/coffee ✖ Licensed Cen ht TVL No children 12yrs ⬚ Sauna **Prices** S £35-£40; D £60-£100 **Parking** 18 **Notes** Closed 25 Dec & New Year

◆◆◆◆ ⬒

Sea Corner

397 Waterford Rd BH23 5JN
☎ 01425 272731 📠 01425 272077
e-mail marlene@seacorner.fsnet.co.uk
web www.seacorner-guesthouse.co.uk
Dir *A337 x-rds onto Waterford Rd, house on right*

Situated within walking distance of the shops and beaches, this appealing establishment is just a short drive from Highcliffe Castle, Christchurch and the New Forest. The stylish, spacious bedrooms are well equipped with many extra facilities. The proprietors also run the

delightful Italian restaurant on the ground floor where delicious evening meals are available.

Facilities 4 rms (3 en suite) TVB tea/coffee ✖ Licensed Cen ht No children 12yrs No coaches Dinner Last d 9.30am **Parking** 2

◆◆◆◆

Three Gables

11 Wickfield Av BH23 1JB
☎ 01202 481166 📠 01202 486171
e-mail rfgill@threegables.plus.com
web www.3gables-christchurch.co.uk
Dir *Rdbt top of High St, onto Sopers Ln, 1st left*

A short walk from the town and the Quay, Three Gables is a relaxed, family-run guest house with a home from home style. Guests are encouraged to join in the banter with the proprietors, especially at breakfast. Bedrooms include one on the ground floor with its own small patio.

Facilities 3 en suite (1 fmly) (1 GF) ⊗ STV TVB tea/coffee ✖ Cen ht TVL No children 5yrs No coaches **Prices** D £44-£60✳ **LB** **Parking** 5 **Notes** Closed Xmas & New Year ⬚

◆◆◆◆

White House

428 Lymington Rd, Highcliffe BH23 5HF
☎ 01425 271279 📠 01425 276900
e-mail thewhitehouse@themail.co.uk
web www.thewhitehouse-christchurch.co.uk
Dir *Off A35, signs to Highcliffe. After rdbt The White House 200yds on right*

This charming Victorian house is just a short drive from Highcliffe beach, the New Forest and the historic town of Christchurch. Comfortable, well-appointed accommodation is provided, and a generous, freshly cooked breakfast is served in the cosy dining room.

Facilities 6 rms (5 en suite) ⊗ TVB tea/coffee ✖ Cen ht TVL No coaches **Parking** 8

◆◆◆

Southern Comfort Guest House ◇

51 Stour Rd BH23 1LN ☎ 01202 471373
e-mail scomfortgh@aol.com
Dir *A338 onto B3073 towards Christchurch, 2m onto B3059 Stour R*

Convenient for Bournemouth, Christchurch and Southbourne, this practical and friendly guest house offers spacious bedrooms. Breakfast served in the bright lounge-dining room, is a relaxed affair with a good choice of hot items.

Facilities 3 en suite (3 fmly) ⊗ TVB tea/coffee ✖ Cen ht TVL No coaches **Prices** S £22.50-£30; D £45-£60✳ **LB** **Parking** 4 **Notes** ⬚

continued

◆◆◆ Stour Villa ◇

7 Stour Rd BH23 1LN ☎ 01202 483379 ▤ 01202 483379
e-mail stourvilla@hotmail.com
web www.stourvilla.co.uk
Dir A35 Christchurch to Bournemouth, left at lights onto Stour Rd,
Villa 150yds right

Stour Villa is well located for visiting the New Forest and local beaches,
being just a 5-minute walk from the town centre. The house is bright
and comfortable with a relaxed and friendly atmosphere, and the
bedrooms and bathrooms are neatly furnished. A substantial cooked
breakfast is served in the cosy dining room.

Facilities 6 en suite (2 fmly) ⊗ TVB tea/coffee ✖ Cen ht No children
5yrs No coaches **Prices** S £23.50-£30; D £47-£60✳ **LB Parking** 7
Notes 🌐

◆◆◆ Brantwood ◇

5 Stour Rd BH23 1LN ☎ 01202 473446
e-mail polly@brantwood-guesthouse.co.uk
Dir A35 Christchurch to Bournemouth, left at lights onto Stour Rd,
establishment over lights on right

A relaxed and friendly guest house where the new proprietors create a
home from home atmosphere. Bedrooms and bathrooms are well
decorated and comfortably furnished. The town centre is just a stroll
away and off-road parking is available.

Facilities 5 en suite (2 fmly) ⊗ TVB tea/coffee ✖ Cen ht No coaches
Prices S £27.50-£35; D £45-£55✳ **LB Parking** 5 **Notes** 🌐

◆◆◆ Bure Farmhouse

107 Bure Ln, Friars Cliff BH23 4DN ☎ 01425 275498
Dir A35 & A337 E from Christchurch towards Highcliffe, 1st rdbt right
into The Runway, farmhouse on left

Warm hospitality and an eclectic menu are keynotes at this guest
house. Bedrooms are bright, and a spacious lounge and bar are
available. Fresh, local produce is used extensively in the breakfast and
lunch, and in summer meals can be served in the secluded garden.

Facilities 3 en suite ⊗ TVB tea/coffee ✖ Cen ht No children 5yrs
No coaches **Parking** 3 **Notes** 🌐

◆◆◆ Fishermans Haunt

Winkton BH23 7AS ☎ 01202 477283 ▤ 01202 478883
e-mail fishermanshaunt@accommodating-inns.co.uk
web www.accommodating-inns.co.uk
Dir Follow B3347

Dating from 1673 and situated close to the River Avon, this
characterful inn is popular with anglers and walkers. Bedrooms, some
of which are suitable for families, offer comfortable accommodation
with many extras including satellite television. Real ales and
wholesome cuisine can be enjoyed in the spacious restaurant and
lounge bars, which have log fires in cooler months.

Facilities 3 en suite 14 annexe en suite (2 fmly) (6 GF) ⊗ in bedrooms
⊗ in dining room TVB tea/coffee Direct dial from bedrooms Cen ht
Fishing Dinner Last d 9pm **Parking** 70

Ⓤ Seapoint

121 Mudeford BH23 4AF ☎ 01425 279541 ▤ 01425 275715
web www.seapointb-b.com

At the time of going to press the rating for this establishment had not
been confirmed. Please check the AA website www.theAA.com for up-
to-date information.

Facilities 4 rms (2 en suite) (2 pri facs) (2 fmly) (4 GF) ⊗ TVB
tea/coffee ✖ Cen ht No coaches **Prices** D £45-£50✳ **LB Parking** 4
Notes 🌐

CORFE MULLEN   MAP 04 SY99

◆◆◆ Kenways ◇

90a Wareham Rd BH21 3LQ ☎ 01202 694655
e-mail eileen@kenways.com
web www.kenways.com
Dir 2m SW of Wimborne. Off A31 to Corfe Mullen. Over B3074 rdbt,
B&B 0.3m on right

Expect to be welcomed as one of the family at this homely guest
house between Wimborne Minster and Poole. The spacious bedrooms
are well provisioned with thoughtful extras, and breakfast is served in
the pleasant conservatory overlooking attractive gardens.

Facilities 3 rms (3 pri facs) (2 GF) ⊗ in bedrooms ⊗ in dining room
⊗ in lounges TVB tea/coffee Cen ht TVL No coaches Table Tennis
Snooker table **Prices** S £25-£30; D £60 **Parking** 4 **Notes** 🌐

CRANBORNE
MAP 05 SU01

◆◆◆◆ ⊚ ⊜

La Fosse at Cranborne

London House, The Square BH21 5PR ☎ 01725 517604
e-mail mac@la-fosse.com
web www.la-fosse.com
Dir *M27(W) onto A31 to Ringwood, left onto B3081 to Verwood & Cranborne*

Mac and Sue La Fosse have been welcoming guests to their charming home for over 20 years where the emphasis is on fine food and relaxation. A stay revolves around Mac's accomplished cooking in the attractive restaurant, and the bedrooms offer comfort and many thoughtful extras.

Facilities 3 en suite ⊗ in bedrooms ⊗ in dining room TVB tea/coffee Direct dial from bedrooms ✗ Licensed Cen ht No coaches Dinner Last d 9.30pm **Prices** S £42.50-£47.50; D £75-£86✳ **LB**

DORCHESTER
MAP 04 SY69
See also **Sydling St Nicholas**

★★★★ Bed & Breakfast

Baytree House Dorchester ◇

4 Athelstan Rd DT1 1NR ☎ 01305 263696
Dir *Situated on S side of Dorchester, 0.5m from town centre.*

A friendly, family-run bed and breakfast situated in the heart of Dorchester. The contemporary and spacious bedrooms offer high levels of comfort, and breakfast is farmhouse style in the kitchen-dining area. Parking available.

Facilities 3 en suite ⊗ TVB tea/coffee ✗ Cen ht **Prices** S £27-£30; D £53-£60✳ **LB** **Parking** 3 **Notes** ⊜

Premier Collection

◆◆◆◆◆

B & B @ Poundbury

37 Peverell Av East, Poundbury DT1 3RH
☎ 01305 250838 & 07759 667771
e-mail kathyandlenpaul@btopenworld.com
Dir *Off junct A35 & A37 onto B3150 for Dorchester town centre, left at 3rd rdbt & left*

Built in a traditional style, this large detached house is situated on the development overseen by HRH The Prince of Wales. The exceptionally well-equipped bedrooms are comfortable, and the hospitality is relaxed and welcoming. Breakfast is a variety of options, including eggs Benedict and the full cooked breakfast, along with home-made bread.

Facilities 2 rms (1 en suite) (1 pri facs) ⊗ TVB tea/coffee ✗ Cen ht No children No coaches **Prices** D £65-£80 **LB** **Parking** 3 **Notes** Closed 12 Dec-12 Jan rs Dec & Jan ⊜

Premier Collection

◆◆◆◆◆ ⌂

Casterbridge Hotel

49 High East St DT1 1HU
☎ 01305 264043 ▤ 01305 260884
e-mail reception@casterbridgehotel.co.uk
web www.casterbridgehotel.co.uk
Dir *In town centre, 75yds from town clock*

Within a short walk of the town centre, this Georgian property provides well-maintained and comfortable bedrooms, some of which are situated off a concealed courtyard annexe at the rear of the property; some ground-floor rooms available. Public areas consist of a bar-library, a drawing room, and a dining room and conservatory where a particularly good breakfast is provided.

Facilities 9 en suite 5 annexe en suite (1 fmly) (2 GF) ⊗ in 13 bedrooms ⊗ in dining room ⊗ in 1 lounge TVB tea/coffee Direct dial from bedrooms ✗ Licensed Cen ht No coaches **Prices** S £58-£78; D £95-£125✳ **LB** **Conf** Max 12 **Parking** 2 **Notes** Closed 24-26 Dec

Premier Collection

◆◆◆◆◆ ⌂

Little Court

5 Westleaze, Charminster DT2 9PZ
☎ 01305 261576 ▤ 01305 261359
e-mail info@littlecourt.net
web www.littlecourt.net
Dir *A37 from Dorchester, 0.25m right at Loders Garage, Little Court 0.5m on right*

Built in 1909 in the style of Lutyens, Little Court nestles in over 4 acres of attractive grounds and gardens. The property has been refurbished to a very high standard and the friendly proprietors are on hand to ensure a pleasant stay. A delicious breakfast, including home-grown produce, can be enjoyed in the stylish dining room.

Facilities 8 en suite ⊗ TVB tea/coffee ✗ Cen ht No coaches ⚲ ⨯ **Prices** S £69-£89; D £69-£89✳ **LB** **Conf** Max 30 Thtr 30 Class 20 Board 20 Del from £99 ✳ **Parking** 10

England

Premier Collection

♦♦♦♦♦

Yalbury Cottage Hotel & Restaurant

Lower Bockhampton DT2 8PZ ☎ 01305 262382
e-mail yalburyemails@aol.com
Dir *Off A35 past Thomas Hardys cottage, over x-rds, 400yds on left, past telephone box, opp village pump*

A fine country cottage with thatched roof and lots of character. The hosts are attentive and the atmosphere is relaxed. Bedrooms are homely, and you can enjoy a drink in the comfortable lounge before feasting on freshly prepared dishes from the daily fixed-price menu. The cosy beamed restaurant is open to the public for dinner.
Facilities 8 en suite (1 fmly) (6 GF) ⊗ in bedrooms ⊗ in dining room TVB tea/coffee Direct dial from bedrooms Licensed Cen ht No coaches Dinner Last d 9pm **Parking** 16

♦♦♦♦

Westwood House Hotel

29 High West St DT1 1UP
☎ 01305 268018 ▤ 01305 250282
e-mail reservations@westwoodhouse.co.uk
Dir *In town centre*

This fine, early 19th-century building on the western side of the town has been refurbished. Bedrooms are individually decorated in soft colours and there is a comfortable lounge. An impressive breakfast is served in the conservatory-dining room at the rear of the property.
Facilities 7 rms (5 en suite) (2 pri facs) (2 fmly) ⊗ TVB tea/coffee Direct dial from bedrooms ✖ Cen ht TVL No coaches **Prices** S £45-£55; D £65-£85 **LB**

♦♦♦♦ ❦

Yellowham Farmhouse (SY730330)

Yellowham Wood DT2 8RW
☎ 01305 262892 ▤ 01305 848155 Mrs K Birchenhough
e-mail mail@yellowham.freeserve.co.uk
web www.yellowham.freeserve.co.uk
Dir *1.5m NE of Dorchester, 500yds off A35*

Located north-east of Dorchester in the heart of Hardy Country, the farm stands amid fields and the tranquil 130 acres of Yellowham Wood. There are spectacular views, and the comfortable bedrooms are all on the ground floor. Thomas Hardy's Cottage and Puddletown Heath are only 0.5m to the south.

continued

Facilities 4 en suite (1 fmly) (4 GF) ⊗ TVB tea/coffee Cen ht No children 4yrs ⚭ 120 acres arable/horse breeding **Prices** S £42-£60; D £60-£70✶ **LB** **Parking** 8

Ⓤ

Beggars Knap

2 Weymouth Av DT1 1QS ☎ 01305 268191
e-mail beggarsknap@hotmail.co.uk

At the time of going to press the rating for this establishment had not been confirmed. Please check the AA website www.theAA.com for up-to-date information.

Facilities 3 en suite ⊗ TVB tea/coffee Cen ht TVL **Prices** S £39.50; D £60-£70✶

Ⓤ

Bramlies

107 Briport Rd DT1 2NH ☎ 01305 265778

At the time of going to press the rating for this establishment had not been confirmed. Please check the AA website www.theAA.com for up-to-date information.

Facilities 3 en suite (1 fmly) (1 GF) ⊗ TVB tea/coffee ✖ Cen ht No coaches **Prices** S fr £30; d fr £60✶ **LB** **Parking** available **Notes** ⊛

EVERSHOT   MAP 04 ST50

♦♦♦♦ ⊛ ⊜ ◀

The Acorn Inn

DT2 0JW ☎ 01935 83228 ▤ 01935 83707
e-mail stay@acorn-inn.co.uk
web www.acorn-inn.co.uk
Dir *0.5m off A37 between Yeovil and Dorchester, signed Evershot, Holywell*

This delightful 16th-century coaching inn stands in the heart of the village. Several of the bedrooms feature interesting four-poster beds, and all have been individually furnished. Public rooms retain many original features including oak panelling, open fires and flagstone floors. Fresh local produce is included on the varied menu.
Facilities 10 en suite (2 fmly) ⊗ in bedrooms ⊗ in dining room STV TVB tea/coffee Direct dial from bedrooms Cen ht TVL Pool Table Skittle alley Dinner Last d 9pm **Prices** S £75-£110✶ **LB** **Conf** Max 30 Thtr 30 Class 60 Board 30 **Parking** 40

England

FARNHAM
MAP 04 ST91

Premier Collection

◆◆◆◆◆ ❦

Farnham Farm House (ST952161)

DT11 8DG ☎ 01725 516254 🖹 01725 516306 Mr Benjafield
e-mail info@farnhamfarmhouse.co.uk
Dir Off A354 Thickthorn x-rds into Farnham, continue NW from
village centre T-junct, 1m bear right at sign

The country house, set in 350 acres of arable farmland, offers a high
level of quality, comfort and service. The atmosphere is friendly and the
accommodation charming and spacious. In the winter, a log fire burns in
the attractive dining room, where a delicious breakfast featuring local
produce is served and views across rolling countryside can be enjoyed.
Features include an outdoor pool and the Sarpenleana treatment room in
the converted stable.

Facilities 3 en suite (1 fmly) ⊛ TVB tea/coffee ✖ ⤢ ⏛ Natural
therapies centre 350 acres arable **Prices** S £50; D £70✳ **Parking** 7
Notes Closed 25-26 Dec ⊛

FONTMELL MAGNA
MAP 04 ST81

◆◆◆ ⊛ ⊜ ◼

The Crown Inn

SP7 0PA ☎ 01747 811441 & 812222 🖹 01747 811145
e-mail crowninnfm@hotmail.com
Dir In village centre

A traditional country inn where a friendly welcome is assured. Local
real ales are offered in the small bar, while the relaxing restaurant
serves a fine selection of carefully prepared dishes, with the emphasis
on local produce. Bedrooms vary in size but include welcome extras.

Facilities 5 rms (3 en suite) (1 pri facs) ⊛ in bedrooms ⊛ in dining
room ⊛ in lounges TVB tea/coffee Direct dial from bedrooms Cen ht
No children 9yrs No coaches Dinner Last d 9pm **Prices** S £39.50-£52;
D £75-£100✳ **LB Parking** 17

FRAMPTON
MAP 04 SY69

Premier Collection

◆◆◆◆◆ ⌂ ⊜

Frampton House

DT2 9NH
☎ 01300 320308 & 07785 391710 🖹 01300 321600
e-mail maynardryder@btconnect.com
Dir A356 into village, from green over bridge & left onto driveway
past houses

A truly delightful property located in a quiet village just outside of
Dorchester. The proprietors are naturally friendly and you are made to
feel instantly at home. The bedrooms, lounge and dining room offer
high standards of quality and comfort. Dinner, by arrangement, is
highly recommended.

Facilities 2 en suite ⊛ in bedrooms ⊛ in dining room TVB tea/coffee
✖ Cen ht No children 8yrs No coaches ⚲ Dinner **Prices** S fr £65; d fr
£85✳ **Parking** 8 **Notes** ⊛

HIGHCLIFFE
MAP 05 SZ29
For accommodation details see **Christchurch**

IWERNE COURTNEY OR SHROTON
See **Shroton** or **Iwerne Courtney**

LOWER ANSTY
MAP 04 ST70

◆◆◆◆ ⊜ ◼

The Fox Inn

DT2 7PN ☎ 01258 880328 🖹 01258 881440
e-mail fox@foxatansty.co.uk
Dir Off A354 at Millbourne St Andrew to Milton Abbas, signs to Ansty

This country inn is surrounded by delightful Dorset countryside. The
Fox started life over 250 years ago as the home of Charles Hall,
founder member of Hall and Woodhouse Brewery. The establishment
has the atmosphere of a traditional inn, with the emphasis on local
ales, delicious home-cooked meals and a friendly welcome.

Facilities 11 en suite (4 fmly) ⊛ in bedrooms ⊛ in dining room
⊛ in lounges TVB tea/coffee Direct dial from bedrooms ✖ Cen ht
No coaches Dinner Last d 9pm **Prices** D £80-£140✳ **LB Conf** Max 50
Parking 37 **Notes** Closed 25-26 Dec

LYME REGIS
MAP 04 SY39
See also **Axminster (Devon)**

◆◆◆◆

Old Lyme Guest House

29 Coombe St DT7 3PP ☎ 01297 442929
e-mail oldlyme.guesthouse@virgin.net
web www.oldlymeguesthouse.co.uk
Dir In town centre. Off A3052 Church St onto Coombe St

Comfort is a high priority at this delightful 18th-century, one-time post
office, which is just a short walk from the seafront. Bedrooms, which
vary in size, are all well equipped and include many thoughtful extras.
A wide choice is offered at breakfast, served in the cheerful dining
room.

Facilities 5 rms (4 en suite) (1 pri facs) (1 fmly) ⊛ TVB tea/coffee ✖
Cen ht TVL No children 5yrs No coaches **Prices** D £60-£65✳ **LB**
Notes ⊛

England

◆◆◆◆
Albany

Charmouth Rd DT7 3DP ☎ 01297 443066
e-mail albany@lymeregis.com
Dir *300yds NE of town centre on A3052*

Situated on the fringe of this popular town within easy walking distance of the seafront, this attractive house provides comfortable accommodation and a home from home atmosphere. Bedrooms are spacious, public rooms inviting, and you are welcome to use the garden. Breakfast, featuring local ingredients, is served in the smart dining room.

Facilities 6 en suite (1 fmly) (1 GF) TVB tea/coffee ✖ Cen ht TVL No children 5yrs No coaches **Prices** S £33-£38; D £58-£60✱ **Parking** 6 **Notes** ⊚

◆◆◆◆
Armada

8 Coombe St DT7 3PR ☎ 01297 445785
e-mail armadahouse@tiscali.co.uk

This accommodation is just a short level walk from the town and the famous Cobb. The individually styled bedrooms offer a good level of comfort and many considerate extras. The atmosphere is friendly and breakfast is served in the light and airy kitchen diner where you can watch the cook at work.

Facilities 3 en suite (1 GF) TVB tea/coffee ✖ Cen ht No children 16yrs No coaches Free parking permits for nearby car park
Prices D £65✱ LB **Notes** ⊚

◆◆◆◆
Dorset House

Pound Rd DT7 3HX ☎ 01297 442482 & 07971 296150
e-mail dorset@eclipse.co.uk

On the edge of the town centre, Dorset House is a Grade II listed building surrounded by sub-tropical plantings. The ground-floor bedrooms open onto a veranda, and each has its own front door. Breakfast is served in the main house around one large table, a varied selection of starters and a hearty, freshly cooked breakfast.

Facilities 3 en suite (3 GF) ⊚ TVB tea/coffee ✖ Cen ht No coaches LB **Parking** 5 **Notes** ⊚

◆◆◆◆
Manaton ◇

Hill Rd DT7 3PE ☎ 01297 445138
e-mail enquiries@manaton.net
web www.manaton.net
Dir *A35 onto A3052. At top of Broad St take right fork, then 1st road on right*

Located within comfortable walking distance of the Cobb and high street, this homely accommodation provides a friendly atmosphere. Bedrooms, some with a sea view, are comfortable and quiet. A full English breakfast is served in the pleasant dining room, which overlooks the rear garden.

Facilities 5 rms (4 en suite) (1 pri facs) (1 fmly) ⊚ TVB tea/coffee ✖ Cen ht TVL No coaches **Prices** S £25-£35; D £55-£65 LB **Parking** 6

◆◆◆◆
The Orchard Country Hotel

Rousdon DT7 3XW ☎ 01297 442972 ▤ 01297 443670
e-mail orchardrousdon@aol.com
web www.orchardcountryhotel.com
Dir *3m W Lyme Regis. Follow brown signs from Rousdon on A3052*

Located in the peaceful village of Rousdon and set in attractive orchard gardens, this friendly and comfortable establishment is a good base for exploring the area. The hop-on hop-off bus stop just outside provides a relaxed means to visit many of the local attractions. There is a spacious lounge, and breakfast is served in the pleasant dining room (freshly prepared dinners are available).

Facilities 11 en suite (1 GF) TVB tea/coffee ✖ Licensed Cen ht TVL No children 8yrs No coaches Dinner Last d 6pm **Prices** S £37-£47; D £66-£94✱ LB **Parking** 20 **Notes** Closed Nov-Mar

◆◆◆◆
The White House

47 Silver St DT7 3HR ☎ 01297 443420
e-mail whitehouselyme@btopenworld.co.uk
Dir *On B3165 Axminster-Lyme Regis road 50yds from A3052 junct*

This charming guest house dates from 1770 and is located in the centre of town, just a short walk from the beach. The comfortable, well-equipped bedrooms are cheerful and bright. There is a spacious lounge and an attractive dining room where hearty breakfasts are served.

Facilities 7 en suite ⊚ TVB tea/coffee Cen ht TVL No children 10yrs No coaches **Prices** D £56-£64✱ LB **Parking** 7 **Notes** Closed Xmas ⊚

◆◆◆ ⊜ ◖
Victoria Hotel

Uplyme Rd DT7 3LP ☎ 01297 444801 ▤ 01297 442949
e-mail info@vichotel.co.uk
Dir *On B3165 750yds from seafront*

The 1906 railway hotel is now a friendly guest house overlooking the picturesque town, Lyme Bay and the surrounding countryside. The bedrooms are neat, and the relaxing open-plan bar provides informal eating. More imaginative dishes are available in the restaurant with its large picture windows.

Facilities 7 en suite ⊚ in bedrooms ⊚ in dining room ⊚ in lounges TVB tea/coffee Cen ht Dinner Last d 9.30pm **Prices** S £35-£60; D £55-£70✱ LB **Conf** Max 30 Thtr 30 Class 20 Board 20 **Parking** 15 **Notes** Closed last 2wks Jan rs Mon

◆◆◆
Berrydown

Highcliff Rd DT7 3EW ☎ 01297 444448
Dir *Off the Sidmouth Rd (A3052) going in or out of Lyme Regis.*

Located at the top of Lyme Regis with pleasant views towards the sea, this welcoming accommodation offers two comfortable bedrooms including one on the ground floor. You are encouraged to use the pleasant rear garden with terrace seating. A carefully prepared breakfast is served in the conservatory.

Facilities 2 rms (2 pri facs) (1 GF) ⊚ TVB tea/coffee ✖ Cen ht No coaches **Parking** 4 **Notes** ⊚

England

LYME REGIS continued

U

Ware Barn B&B

Ware Ln, Ware Cross DT7 3EL
☎ 01297 442472 ▣ 01297 442472
e-mail info@kanta-enterprises.com
Dir 0.5m W of town centre off A3052

At the time of going to press the rating for this establishment had not been confirmed. Please check the AA website www.theAA.com for up-to-date information.

Facilities 4 en suite (2 fmly) ⊗ STV TVB tea/coffee ✗ Cen ht TVL
Prices S £45-£65; D £90-£150✻ **LB Parking** 12

MILTON ABBAS   MAP 04 ST80

◆◆◆ ❦

Fishmore Hill Farm ◇ *(ST799013)*

DT11 0DL ☎ 01258 881122 ▣ 01258 881122
Mr & Mrs Clarke
e-mail neal.clarke@btinternet.com
Dir Off A354 signed Milton Abbas, 3m left on sharp bend, up steep hill, B&B 1st left

This sheep farm and family home is surrounded by beautiful Dorset countryside and is close to historic Milton Abbey and a short drive from the coast. Bedrooms, which vary in size, are comfortable and finished with considerate extras. The atmosphere is friendly and relaxed. Breakfast is served in the smart dining room around a communal table.

Facilities 3 en suite ⊗ TVB tea/coffee ✗ Cen ht 50 acres Sheep and horses **Prices** S fr £27; d fr £54✻ **Parking** 4 **Notes** Closed Xmas & New Year ⊛

MOTCOMBE   MAP 04 ST82

◆◆◆◆ ▲

The Coppleridge Inn

SP7 9HW ☎ 01747 851980 ▣ 01747 851858
e-mail thecoppleridgeinn@btinternet.com
web www.coppleridge.com
Dir Motcombe off A350, 1m N of Shaftesbury. Enter village under railway bridge, 400yds right to Mere, inn 300yds on left

Facilities 10 en suite (2 fmly) (10 GF) ⊗ in area of dining room ⊗ in 1 lounge TVB tea/coffee Direct dial from bedrooms Licensed Cen ht TVL ⊶ Use of indoor pool in village Dinner Last d 9pm
Prices S £45; D £80✻ **LB Conf** Max 60 Thtr 60 Class 60 Board 30 Del from £71 ✻ **Parking** 100 **Notes** Civ Wed 80

PIDDLETRENTHIDE   MAP 04 SY79

◆◆◆◆ ◪

The Poachers Inn

DT2 7QX ☎ 01300 348358 ▣ 01300 348153
e-mail thepoachersinn@piddletrenthide.fsbusiness.co.uk
web www.thepoachersinn.co.uk
Dir 8m N from Dorchester on B3143, inn on left

The friendly, family-run inn combines original 16th-century character with contemporary style in the bar and dining areas. Home-cooked meals are a feature, and the smart, en suite bedrooms open onto a courtyard. In fine weather you can lounge round the swimming pool or relax in the garden.

Facilities 6 en suite 15 annexe en suite (3 fmly) (12 GF) ⊗ in bedrooms ⊗ in dining room TVB tea/coffee Direct dial from bedrooms Cen ht ⊶ Dinner Last d 9pm **LB Parking** 40
See advertisement on opposite page

U ◪

The Piddle Inn

DT2 7QF ☎ 01300 348468 ▣ 01300 348102
e-mail piddleinn@aol.com
web www.piddleinn.co.uk
Dir 7m N of Dorchester on the B3143 in middle of Piddletrenthide

At the time of going to press the rating for this establishment had not been confirmed. Please check the AA website www.theAA.com for up-to-date information.

Facilities 3 en suite (1 fmly) ⊗ in bedrooms ⊗ in dining room ⊗ in 1 lounge TVB tea/coffee Direct dial from bedrooms Cen ht TVL Pool Table Dinner Last d 9pm **Prices** S fr £45; d fr £70✻ **LB Parking** 15

POOLE   MAP 04 SZ09

◆◆◆◆

Acorns

264 Wimborne Rd, Oakdale BH15 3EF
☎ 01202 672901 ▣ 01202 672901
e-mail enquiries@acornsguesthouse.co.uk
web www.acornsguesthouse.co.uk
Dir On A35, 0.5m from town centre, opp Texaco station

You are assured of a warm welcome at the Acorns, located with easy access to the town, ferry terminal, business parks and attractions. The bedrooms are furnished to a high standard, and an English breakfast is served in the charming dining room. There is also a cosy lounge.
continued

Facilities 4 en suite (1 GF) TVB tea/coffee 🕇 Cen ht TVL No children 14yrs No coaches **Prices** D £50-£60 **LB Parking** 6 **Notes** Closed 23 Dec-1 Jan 🚭

◆◆◆◆

Blue Shutters

109 North Rd, Parkstone BH14 0LU ☎ 01202 748129
e-mail stay@blueshutters.co.uk
web www.blueshutters.co.uk
Dir 0.5m from Poole Park and Civic Centre buildings

The friendly, family-run Blue Shutters is close to the civic centre and offers brightly decorated, well-equipped bedrooms. Sound home-cooked meals are served in the well-presented dining room overlooking the attractive garden, and the lounge has bar facilities.

Facilities 7 en suite (2 fmly) (1 GF) in bedrooms in dining room in 1 lounge TVB tea/coffee 🕇 Cen ht TVL No children 5yrs No coaches **Prices** S £35-£40; d fr £58❋ **Parking** 7 **Notes** Closed 24 Dec-2 Jan

◆◆◆◆

Crystalz

465 Ringwood Rd, Parkstone BH12 4LX ☎ 01202 737219
Dir 2m N of town centre on B3068 Ringwood Rd, white bungalow up hill

This cosy bungalow is on the outskirts of the town close to major routes. Refurbishment has produced comfortable, well-appointed bedrooms, which are filled with useful extras. Freshly prepared breakfasts can be enjoyed in the inviting breakfast room.

Facilities 2 en suite (2 GF) TVB tea/coffee 🕇 Cen ht No children 14yrs No coaches **Prices** S £35-£40; D £50-£60❋ **Parking** 4 **Notes** 🚭

◆◆◆

Towngate

58 Wimborne Rd BH15 2BY ☎ 01202 668552
e-mail ayoun19@ntlworld.com
Dir B3093 from town centre, guest house on right

Expect a warm welcome at this central house, within walking distance of the town centre and harbour, and just a short drive from the ferry terminal. The well-equipped bedrooms are comfortable and nicely furnished.

Facilities 3 en suite in dining room TVB tea/coffee 🕇 Cen ht No children 10yrs No coaches **Prices** S £40-£45; D £55-£60 **Parking** 4 **Notes** Closed mid Dec-mid Jan 🚭

◆◆◆

The Burleigh ◇

76 Wimborne Rd BH15 2BZ
☎ 01202 673889 ▤ 01202 685283
Dir Off A35 onto A349

Suited to business and leisure, this well-kept house is close to the town centre and ferry terminal. The individually furnished bedrooms are of a good standard. Breakfast is served at separate tables and there is a small, attractive lounge.

Facilities 8 rms (4 en suite) (1 fmly) in bedrooms in dining room TVB tea/coffee Cen ht TVL **Prices** S £25-£34; D £45-£50❋ **Parking** 5

◆◆◆

Centraltown

101 Wimborne Rd BH15 2BP
☎ 01202 674080 ▤ 01202 674080
Dir From town centre onto A3093, Barclays International building on left, guest house 500yds

This friendly and well-maintained guest house is within easy reach of the town centre, ferry terminals, speedway and many other attractions. Bedrooms are attractive and equipped with many useful facilities. A full English breakfast is served in the bright cosy dining room.

Facilities 3 en suite (2 fmly) TVB tea/coffee 🕇 Cen ht No coaches **Parking** 6 **Notes** 🚭

◆◆◆

Harbour View ◇

157 Longfleet Rd BH15 2HS ☎ 01202 672421

This small, friendly and well-run guest house has fine views of Poole Harbour and Brownsea Island from its elevated position. The bright bedrooms are adequately furnished and equipped with modern en suites. Hearty, well-presented traditional choices are offered at breakfast in the cosy dining room.

Facilities 3 en suite TVB tea/coffee 🕇 Cen ht No children 5yrs No coaches **Prices** S £30-£35; D £50-£60❋ **Parking** 4 **Notes** 🚭

POOLE continued

◆◆◆

Lewina Lodge

225 Bournemouth Rd, Parkstone BH14 9HU
☎ 01202 742295 📠 01202 742295
e-mail lewinalodge@ntlworld.com
web www.lewinalodge.co.uk
Dir A35 Bournemouth to Poole, Lewina Lodge 400yds on right after Homebase

This family-run guest house is between Poole and Bournemouth, and Sandbanks beach is not far. The proprietors extend a warm welcome and the bedrooms are comfortable and practically furnished. Breakfast is enjoyed in the attractive dining room.

Facilities 5 rms (4 en suite) (2 fmly) (1 GF) ⊗ TVB tea/coffee ✖ Cen ht No coaches **Parking** 6

◆◆◆

Seacourt

249 Blandford Rd, Hamworthy BH15 4AZ
☎ 01202 674995
Dir Off A3049/A35 signed to Hamworthy

Within a short distance of the ferry port and town centre, this friendly establishment is well maintained and efficiently run. The comfortable bedrooms, some located on the ground floor, are all nicely decorated and equipped with useful facilities. Breakfast is served in the pleasant dining room at separate tables.

Facilities 5 rms (4 en suite) (1 pri facs) (1 fmly) (3 GF) ⊗ in 1 bedrooms TVB tea/coffee ✖ Cen ht No children 5yrs No coaches **Prices** S £37-£50; D £50 **Parking** 5 **Notes** 📵

◆◆

Holly House

97 Longfleet Rd BH15 2HP
☎ 01202 677839 📠 01202 461722
e-mail hol.house@tesconet.com
Dir Just off A35

Holly House is across the road from Poole Hospital and is well-situated for the town centre and the ferry terminal. It has a friendly and relaxed atmosphere. The comfortable bedrooms are simply furnished and are ideal for business or leisure.

Facilities 4 en suite (3 fmly) ⊗ TVB tea/coffee ✖ Cen ht TVL **Parking** 7 **Notes** Closed 20 Dec-5 Jan

PORTLAND   MAP 04 SY67

◆◆◆◆

Queen Anne House

2/4 Fortuneswell DT5 1LP
☎ 01305 820028 📠 01305 824389
e-mail margaretdunlop@tiscali.co.uk
Dir A354 to Portland then Fortuneswell. House on left 200yds past Royal Portland Arms

This delightful Grade II listed building is a charming and comfortable place to stay – just look at the Italianate gardens to the rear. Ideal for

continued

business and for leisure, Queen Anne House is close to the famous Chesil Beach, Portland Bill and Weymouth. Bedrooms are particularly attractive and pleasantly furnished. At breakfast there is a wide choice of options served around one large table.

Facilities 3 en suite ⊗ TVB tea/coffee ✖ Cen ht TVL No coaches **Prices** S £40-£45; D £60-£70 **Parking** 1 **Notes** 📵

◆◆◆

Alessandria Hotel

71 Wakeham Easton DT5 1HW
☎ 01305 822270 & 820108 📠 01305 820561
Dir Off A354

Alessandria Hotel provides compact but practically furnished bedrooms. Most have en suites and some have sea views. There is a dining room, in which breakfast is served, and a comfortable sitting room.

Facilities 15 rms (11 en suite) 1 annexe en suite (3 fmly) (2 GF) ⊗ TVB tea/coffee ✖ Licensed Cen ht TVL **Parking** 16

◆◆◆

Beach House

51 Chiswell DT5 1AW ☎ 01305 821155 & 07986 888514
Dir A354 to Portland, straight ahead into Chiswell, B&B 150yds on right.

Expect a warm welcome at this early Victorian property adjacent to Chesil Beach, part of the Dorset and East Devon World Heritage Site. Hearty breakfasts are served in the cosy dining room, and there is a comfy lounge. Beach House is a good base for sports facilities and for touring.

Facilities 5 rms (4 en suite) (1 pri facs) (2 fmly) ⊗ TVB tea/coffee ✖ Licensed Cen ht No coaches **Prices** S £40; D £60✹ LB **Parking** 10

◆◆◆

Portland Lodge ◇

Easton Ln DT5 1BW ☎ 01305 820265 📠 01305 860359
e-mail info@portlandlodge.com
Dir Signs to Easton/Portland Bill, rdbt at Portland Heights Hotel 1st right. Portland Lodge 200yds

Please note that this establishment has recently changed hands. Situated high on Portland Bill, this property is well located for exploring Weymouth and Chesil Beach. Bedrooms and bathrooms have been refurbished and provide good levels of comfort. A continental or full English breakfast is served at individual tables.

Facilities 24 en suite (9 fmly) (11 GF) ⊗ TVB tea/coffee ✖ Cen ht **Prices** S £30-£35; D £50-£60✹ **Parking** 50

England

POWERSTOCK
MAP 04 SY59

◆◆◆◆

Three Horseshoes Inn

DT6 3TF ☎ 01308 485328
e-mail info@threehorseshoesinn.com
web www.threehorseshoesinn.com
Dir *3m from Bridport. Powerstock signed off A3066 Bridport to Beaminster*

The Three Horseshoes overlooks rolling hills from its elevated position in the village. The unpretentious bar and cosy dining room appeal to locals and visitors alike, and a wide range of meals is available, with the emphasis on local and organic produce (when possible), cooked with care. The spacious bedrooms have considerate extras and provide comfort.

Facilities 1 en suite 2 annexe en suite (1 fmly) (2 GF) ⊗ in bedrooms ⊗ in dining room ⊗ in lounges FTV TVB tea/coffee Cen ht No coaches Dinner Last d 9pm **Prices** S £50; D £60-£80✱ LB **Parking** 25

PUNCKNOWLE
MAP 04 SY58

◆◆◆◆

Offley Bed & Breakfast

Looke Ln DT2 9BD ☎ 01308 897044 & 07792 624977
Dir *Off A35/B3157 into village centre. 250yds E of church*

With magnificent views over the Bride valley, this village house provides comfortable, quality accommodation. You are assured of a friendly welcome, and there are several local inns, one in the village just a stroll away.

Facilities 3 rms (1 en suite) ⊗ TV2B tea/coffee ✖ Cen ht TVL No coaches **Parking** 3 **Notes** ⊗

SHAFTESBURY
MAP 04 ST82

★★★★ ◉◉ **Restaurant with Rooms**

La Fleur de Lys Restaurant with Rooms

Bleke St SP7 8AW ☎ 01747 853717 ▤ 01747 853130
e-mail info@lafleurdelys.co.uk
Dir *0.25m off the junct of A30 with A350 at Shaftesbury towards Town centre*

Located just a short walk from the famous Gold Hill, this light and airy restaurant combines efficient service with a relaxed and friendly atmosphere. Bedrooms, which are suitable for both business and leisure, vary in size but all are well equipped, and are smartly furnished. A relaxing lounge and courtyard are available for afternoon tea or pre-dinner drinks.

Facilities 7 en suite (2 fmly) (1 GF) FTV TVB tea/coffee Direct dial from bedrooms ✖ Licensed No coaches Dinner Last d 10pm **Prices** S £65-£75; D £95-£110✱ **Conf** Max 12 Board 10 **Parking** 7

◆◆◆◆ ◉◉ ⌂

Wayfarers Restaurant

Sherborne Cswy SP7 9PX ☎ 01747 852821
Dir *2m W of Shaftesbury on A30*

Wayfarers lies within the Blackmore Vale in the heart of rural Dorset. Many guests return for the particularly well-equipped and luxurious bedrooms, and the delicious cuisine served in the 18th-century cottage restaurant. Breakfast is brought to a separate lounge area of your room.

Facilities 1 en suite ⊗ ✖ Licensed Cen ht No children 12yrs No coaches Dinner Last d 9pm **Prices** S £65; D £80 LB **Parking** 30 **Notes** rs 2 wks in Jun/Jul

SHERBORNE
MAP 04 ST61

Premier Collection

◆◆◆◆◆ ⌂

Munden House

Munden Ln, Alweston DT9 5HU
☎ 01963 23150 ▤ 01963 23153
e-mail admin@mundenhouse.demon.co.uk
web www.mundenhouse.demon.co.uk
Dir *3m SE of Sherborne. A352 onto A3030 to Alweston, pass village shop on right, 250yds on left at Oxfords Bakery sign*

Victorian Munden House has a peaceful location in the picturesque Blackmore Vale. Beautifully restored, the bedrooms and bathrooms are elegantly furnished. You are invited to use the luxurious sitting room to view the glorious surrounding countryside and the well-tended gardens. Memorable breakfasts are served in the impressive dining room.

Facilities 6 en suite 1 annexe en suite (2 GF) ⊗ TVB tea/coffee Direct dial from bedrooms ✖ Cen ht No coaches **Prices** S £45-£55; D £75-£95✱ **Conf** Max 30 **Parking** 20

◆◆◆◆

The Alders

Sandford Orcas DT9 4SB
☎ 01963 220666 ▤ 01963 220666
e-mail jonsue@btinternet.com
web www.thealdersbb.com
Dir *3m N of Sherborne. Off B3148 signed Sandford Orcas, near Manor House in village*

Located in the charming conservation area of Sandford Orcas and set in a lovely walled garden, this delightful property offers attractive, well-equipped bedrooms. There is a huge inglenook with a wood-burning fire in the comfortable sitting room, which features the owner's watercolours.

Facilities 3 en suite ⊗ TVB tea/coffee ✖ Cen ht TVL No coaches **Prices** D £48-£60✱ **Parking** 4 **Notes** ⊗

England

◆◆◆◆

The Green

Nether Compton DT9 4QB ☎ 01935 817993
web www.thegreenbandb.co.uk
Dir *2m W of Sherborne. Off A30 to Nether Compton, house near village church*

Standing alone at the back of the village green, the delightful, Grade II listed Ham stone house offers carefully furnished accommodation and freshly cooked breakfasts in the cosy sitting room. The village pub is only a short walk away.

Facilities 2 rms (1 pri facs) ⊗ ✂ Cen ht TVL No coaches
Prices D £55-£60✳ **Parking** 3 **Notes** Closed 20 Dec-5 Jan 🐾

◆◆◆◆ 🌱

Stowell Farm ◇ *(ST686223)*

Stowell DT9 4PE ☎ 01963 370200 Mrs Kingman
e-mail kingman@stowell-farm.freeserve.co.uk
Dir *5m NE of Sherborne. Off A357 to Stowell, farm next to church*

The 15th-century farmhouse stands in rolling countryside. You receive a friendly welcome and can look forward to a peaceful stay. Bedrooms are attractively furnished with comfortable beds, and have good views. The spacious bathrooms are equipped with showers and baths.

Facilities 2 rms (1 en suite) (1 pri facs) ⊗ TV1B tea/coffee ✂ TVL
Riding 240 acres dairy beef sheep **Prices** S £30; D £50-£54✳ LB
Parking 6 **Notes** Closed 20 Dec-2 Jan 🐾

◆◆◆ 🌱

Venn Farm ◇ *(ST684183)*

Milborne Port DT9 5RA
☎ 01963 250598 📠 01963 250598 Mrs Tizzard
Dir *3m E of Sherborne on A30 on edge of Milborne Port*

Set in a good location for exploring west Dorset, this farm specialises in training National Hunt racehorses. The individually furnished bedrooms are comfortable and bathrooms are fitted with power showers. A farmhouse breakfast is served in the lounge-dining room.

Facilities 3 en suite ⊗ in bedrooms ⊗ in dining room TVB tea/coffee ✂ Cen ht TVL Fishing 375 acres dairy/mixed/race horses **Prices** S fr £30; d fr £50✳ **Parking** 6 **Notes** Closed Xmas 🐾

◆◆◆

Cross House ◇

North St, Milborne Port DT9 5ET
☎ 01963 250032 & 07881 580130
e-mail cellwood@sherborne.org
Dir *3m E of Sherborne. Off A30 High St in Milborne Port*

This delightful family home stands in the centre of Milborne Port. You are welcomed into the kitchen to join the owners for breakfast straight from the Aga. Bedrooms are comfortable and compact, and there is a large comfortable lounge with a seasonal wood-burning fire.

Facilities 2 rms (2 pri facs) (2 fmly) ⊗ tea/coffee Cen ht TVL No coaches **Prices** S £25-£35✳ LB **Notes** 🐾

SHROTON OR IWERNE COURTNEY
MAP 04 ST81

Premier Collection

◆◆◆◆◆ ⊜ ◧

The Cricketers

Main St DT11 8QD ☎ 01258 860421 📠 01258 861800
Dir *Establishment signed from A350 Blandford-Shaftesbury road, 0.25m on village green*

Located in the sleepy village of Shroton, this is a real find, where friendly hospitality and attentive service assure a memorable stay. Accommodation is within the annexe garden room, refurbished to a high standard with many thoughtful extras. Dinner options range from bar snacks to interesting and tempting blackboard specials.

Facilities 1 en suite (1 GF) ⊗ in bedrooms ⊗ in dining room TVB tea/coffee ✂ Cen ht No coaches Pool Table Dinner Last d 9pm
Prices S £45-£50; D £70-£75✳ LB **Parking** 19

♦♦♦
Lattemere
Frog Ln DT11 8QL ☎ 01258 860115 📠 01258 860115
Dir Off A350 signed Shroton

Lattemere lies in a peaceful Dorset village. The owners are very attentive and friendly, and their home is comfortable, welcoming and filled with photographs and memorabilia. The two bedrooms are well appointed and thoughtfully equipped. Breakfast is served at a shared table in the lounge-dining room.

Facilities 2 rms (1 en suite) ⊗ TVB tea/coffee ✖ Cen ht No children 7yrs No coaches **Parking** 3 **Notes** ⊛

SIXPENNY HANDLEY   MAP 04 ST91

♦♦♦
Town Farm Bungalow
SP5 5NT ☎ 01725 552319 & 07885 407191 📠 01725 552319
e-mail townfarmbungalow@tiscali.co.uk
Dir A354 onto B3081 to Sixpenny Handley, bungalow 250yds on right

There are wonderful views of the surrounding countryside from all rooms of this delightful bungalow, where a very warm welcome and attentive service is guaranteed. Delicious breakfasts are served around one large table, and a wood-burning fire warms the cosy lounge in winter.

Facilities 3 rms (2 en suite) (3 GF) ⊗ TVB ✖ Cen ht TVL No children 12yrs No coaches **Prices** S £40-£60; D £50-£70✶ **Parking** 6 **Notes** ⊛

STURMINSTER NEWTON   MAP 04 ST71

♦♦♦♦ ⊜ ❦
Honeysuckle House (ST772102)
1995 Fifehead St Quintin DT10 2AP
☎ 01258 817896 & 07854 687415 Mrs Miller
Dir Off A357 up Glue Hill signed Hazelbury Bryan. Left after sharp bend, continue 2.5m

The young proprietors of this 400-acre dairy farm offer a particularly friendly welcome and ensure you are very well looked after. Bedrooms are comfortable and include welcome extras. Breakfasts are enormous, and be sure to book for dinner which is a real highlight.

Facilities 3 en suite (1 fmly) ⊗ in bedrooms ⊗ in dining room TVB tea/coffee Cen ht TVL ⬩ Fishing Riding 🐾 Pony rides, farm tours, children's tractor rides 400 acres Dairy Dinner Last d Previous day **Parking** 6 **Notes** Closed 22 Dec-2 Jan ⊛

♦♦♦♦
Northwood Cottages
2 Northwood Cottages, Manston DT10 1HD
☎ 01258 472666 📠 01258 473950
e-mail info@northwoodcottages.co.uk
web www.northwoodcottages.co.uk
Dir 3m NE of Sturminster. Off B3091 N onto Rams Hill (towards Todber), 3rd house on right

This rural property, dating from the late 19th century, is set in well-tended gardens on the edge of Blackmore Vale. The comfortable bedrooms and shower rooms are stylish and come with numerous facilities. A self-catering cottage is available and dinner is provided by arrangement.

Facilities 4 en suite (1 GF) ⊗ TVB tea/coffee ✖ Cen ht TVL No coaches Dinner Last d am **Prices** S £37-£45; D £64-£83✶ **LB** **Parking** 7

♦♦♦♦ ❦
Skylands Farm ◈ (ST749170)
Lower Rd, Stalbridge DT10 2SW ☎ 01963 362392
Mr & Mrs Nolder
e-mail alison@skylands.co.uk
Dir A357 in village, onto Lower Rd signed Marnhill/village hall. After 0.75m Skylands sign, drive on left before x-rds

Located on the edge of Blackmore Vale, this 17th-century farmhouse provides well-presented accommodation. The two bedrooms have private facilities. You can bring your own horse, and there is a BHS instructor on site.

Facilities 2 rms (2 pri facs) ⊗ TVB tea/coffee ✖ Cen ht TVL No children 12yrs Fishing Stables for guests horses 17 acres non-working **Prices** S £30-£35; D £60-£70✶ **Parking** 20 **Notes** ⊛

♦♦♦♦ 🍴 ⊜
Stourcastle Lodge
Goughs Cl DT10 1BU ☎ 01258 472320 📠 01258 473381
e-mail enquiries@stourcastle-lodge.co.uk
Dir Off town square opp cross

Tucked away off the market square, this charming 18th-century house stands in delightful gardens and offers warm hospitality. Bedrooms are spacious and well presented. A lounge, complete with crackling log fire, is also available. Satisfying, Aga-cooked meals are served at dinner and breakfast in the attractive dining room.

Facilities 5 en suite ⊗ TVB tea/coffee Direct dial from bedrooms ✖ Cen ht No children 18yrs No coaches Dinner Last d 7pm **Prices** S £50-£57; D £82-£96✶ **LB** **Parking** 8

England

STURMINSTER NEWTON continued

The Crown Inn
Marnhull DT10 1LN
☎ 01258 820224 & 821272 🖷 01258 821272
web www.thecrownatmarnhull.co.uk
Dir A30 onto B3092, pub 1.5m on right before St. Gregory's church.

At the time of going to press the rating for this establishment had not been confirmed. Please check the AA website www.theAA.com for up-to-date information.

Facilities 5 en suite (1 fmly) (1 GF) ⊗ TVB tea/coffee Direct dial from bedrooms Licensed Cen ht Dinner Last d 9.30pm

SWANAGE   MAP 05 SZ07

◆◆◆◆

The Castleton ◇
1 Highcliffe Rd BH19 1LW ☎ 01929 423972
e-mail stay@castletonhotel-swanage.co.uk
web www.castletonhotel-swanage.co.uk
Dir From town centre follow seafront towards Studland Rd, 110yds after leaving Promenade on right

Just a short walk from the town centre and beach, this establishment offers spacious, comfortable accommodation in a friendly environment. Breakfast is served in the dining room or conservatory area, and there is also a lounge.

Facilities 10 en suite (2 fmly) (1 GF) ⊗ TVB tea/coffee ✖ Cen ht TVL No children 6yrs No coaches **Prices** S £30-£50; D £60-£100✳ **Parking** 4 **Notes** 🐾

◆◆◆

Sandringham Hotel ◇
20 Durlston Rd BH19 2HX
☎ 01929 423076 🖷 01929 423076
e-mail silk@sandhot.fsnet.co.uk
Dir From centre follow signs for Durlston Country Park

This delightful property stands high above the town, close to the beach, and just 0.5m from the beautiful Durlston Country Park. It offers attractive, well-equipped bedrooms and comfortable public rooms, which include a conservatory-bar. Delicious home-cooked evening meals are available by arrangement.

Facilities 11 rms (9 en suite) (5 fmly) (1 GF) ⊗ in dining room TVB tea/coffee ✖ Licensed Cen ht TVL No coaches Dinner Last d 6pm **Prices** S £30-£40; D £60-£80 **LB** **Parking** 6 **Notes** Closed Xmas & New Year

SYDLING ST NICHOLAS   MAP 04 SY69

★★★★ Inn

The Greyhound Inn
26 High St DT2 9PD ☎ 01300 341303
e-mail info@thegreyhounddorset.co.uk
Dir Off A37 into village centre

Situated in a traditional English village complete with stream, the Greyhound offers stylish, well-equipped rooms, with three on the ground floor. Blackboards in the flagstone-floor bar offer an imaginative range of meals, served either in the restaurant or the bar. Relaxed and friendly, this inn is well located for exploring Hardy Country.

Facilities 6 en suite (3 fmly) (3 GF) ⊗ TVB tea/coffee ✖ Cen ht Dinner Last d 9.30pm **Prices** D £65-£85✳ **Conf** Max 40 Board 40 **Parking** 30

TARRANT MONKTON   MAP 04 ST90

◆◆◆◆ ◉ ➾ ◀

The Langton Arms
DT11 8RX ☎ 01258 830225 🖷 01258 830053
e-mail info@thelangtonarms.co.uk
Dir Off A354 in Tarrant Hinton to Tarrant Monkton, through ford, Langton Arms opp

Tucked away in this sleepy Dorset village, the Langton Arms offers stylish accommodation and is a good base for touring. Bedrooms, all situated at ground level in the modern annexe, are very well equipped. There is a choice of dining options, the relaxed bar-restaurant or the more formal Stables restaurant (open Wednesday to Saturday evenings and Sunday lunch time), which offers innovative and appetising dishes. Breakfast is served in the conservatory-dining room, just a few steps through the pretty courtyard.

Facilities 6 annexe en suite (6 fmly) (6 GF) ⊗ TVB tea/coffee Direct dial from bedrooms Pool Table Skittle Alley Dinner Last d 9.30pm **Prices** S £60; D £80✳ **LB** **Conf** Max 70 Class 70 Board 70 **Parking** 100 **Notes** Civ Wed 50

continued

VERWOOD

MAP 05 SU00

◆◆◆◆

Farleigh ◇

38 Dewlands Rd BH31 6PN

☎ 01202 826424 ▤ 01202 826424

e-mail jeanettehamp@waitrose.com

web www.users.waitrose.com/~jeanettehamp

Dir A31 onto B3081, 3m pass fire station, over rdbt, 1st left

There is a warm welcome at this dormer bungalow in this peaceful village near the New Forest. The attractive bedrooms are thoughtfully equipped and have stylish modern en suites, and a hearty breakfast is served in the smart dining room.

Facilities 2 en suite ⊗ TVB tea/coffee ✖ Cen ht No coaches **Prices** S £30-£40; D £50-£60✱ **LB Parking** 3 **Notes** ⊗

WAREHAM

MAP 04 SY98

◆◆◆◆

Hyde Cottage Bed & Breakfast

Furzebrook Rd, Stoborough BH20 5AX ☎ 01929 553344

e-mail hydecottbb@yahoo.co.uk

Dir Take A351 towards Swanage. Take Furzebrook/Blue Pool turning on 1st rdbt 200yds. B&B on right.

Easy to find, on the Corfe Castle side of Wareham, this friendly house has a great location. Bedrooms are large with lounge seating and are suitable for families, and are well equipped with extras such as fridges. Meals are served en famille in the dining area downstairs.

Facilities 3 en suite (2 fmly) (1 GF) ⊗ TVB tea/coffee Cen ht No coaches Dinner Last d Breakfast same day **Parking** 4 **Notes** Closed 24-27 Dec ⊗

◆◆◆

Luckford Wood House

East Stoke BH20 6AW ☎ 01929 463098 & 07737 742615 ▤ 01929 405715

e-mail johnbarnes@ukipemail.co.uk

web www.luckfordleisure.co.uk

Dir 3m W of Wareham. A352 from Wareham, 1.5m turn left onto B3070, 2nd right (Holme Lane), 1m at x-rds right onto Church Lane, 2nd right.

Rurally situated, this family home offers comfortable accommodation on the edge of woodland, and wildlife is in abundance. You are assured of a friendly welcome and breakfast is an extensive choice.

Facilities 4 rms (3 en suite) (3 fmly) (1 GF) ⊗ TVB tea/coffee Cen ht TVL No coaches **Prices** S £32-£50; D £55-£75✱ **LB Parking** 6 **Notes** ⊗

WEST LULWORTH

MAP 04 SY88

◆◆◆◆

West Coombe Farmhouse ◇

BH20 5PS ☎ 01929 462889 ▤ 01929 405863

e-mail westcoombefarmhouse@yahoo.co.uk

web www.westcoombefarmhouse.co.uk

Dir Off A352 at Wool onto B3071, 1.5m left into Coombe Keynes (signed), 1st house left after phone box

Located in the centre of the village, and just a short drive from Lulworth Cove, this delightful former farmhouse is a good base for exploring Hardy Country. Bedrooms are comfortably furnished with beautiful coordinated fabrics. A television lounge is available.

Facilities 3 rms (1 en suite) (1 pri facs) ⊗ tea/coffee ✖ Cen ht TVL No children 12yrs No coaches **Prices** S £25-£31; D £50-£62✱ **Parking** 5 **Notes** Closed Xmas ⊗

WEYMOUTH

MAP 04 SY67

See also **Portland**

★★★★ **Guest Accommodation**

The Pebbles Guest House

18 Kirtleton Av DT4 7PT ☎ 01305 784331 ▤ 01305 784331

e-mail info@pebblesguesthouse.co.uk

web www.pebblesguesthouse.co.uk

Situated in a quiet residential avenue and just a short walk from the seafront, this Victorian establishment provides a warm welcome and every effort is made to ensure an enjoyable and relaxing stay. Bedrooms are neatly presented with thoughtful extras and a ground-floor room is available. The refurbished dining room is the venue for satisfying breakfasts.

Facilities 8 rms (6 en suite) (1 fmly) (1 GF) ⊗ TVB tea/coffee ✖ Cen ht **Parking** 8

★★★ **Guest Accommodation**

Aztec House

4 Abbotsbury Rd DT4 0AE ☎ 01305 787803

e-mail elaine_miller@lineone.net

Dir From Dorchester take A354 to Westham rdbt turn left to Bride Port.

Just a short walk from the town centre and amenities, this well-presented establishment has much to offer. Bedrooms offer good levels of comfort and quality with cheery colour schemes. Public areas have similar qualities and include a relaxing lounge. Ample parking is available.

Facilities 6 rms (3 en suite) (1 pri facs) (1 fmly) ⊗ TVB tea/coffee ✖ Cen ht TVL No coaches **Parking** 7 **Notes** Closed 18 Dec-9 Jan ⊗

England

Premier Collection

◆◆◆◆◆

Chandlers Hotel

4 Westerhall Rd DT4 7SZ ☎ 01305 771341 ▤ 01305 830122
e-mail debbiesare@chandlershotel.com
web www.chandlershotel.com
Dir *500yds N of town centre, off A353 junct Esplanade & Greenhill*

A warm welcome awaits you at this stylishly refurbished Victorian property, set just 150yds from the beach. There is Internet access in all bedrooms, and small business meetings can be catered for in the contemporary-style public rooms. Breakfast is a wide choice, including a daily changing special. A spacious sitting room and a separate bar are also available.

Facilities 10 en suite (1 GF) ⊗ TVB tea/coffee ✖ Licensed Cen ht No children 14yrs No coaches **Prices** S £45-£75; D £75-£120✱ **Conf** Max 6 **Parking** 11

◆◆◆◆

Esplanade Hotel ◇

141 The Esplanade DT4 7NJ
☎ 01305 783129 ▤ 01305 783129
e-mail esplanadehotel@weymouth10.fsnet.co.uk
Dir *E end of Esplanade, opp pier bandstand*

Dating from 1835, this attractive Georgian property has public rooms, including a first-floor lounge, that all enjoy splendid sea views. A warm welcome is assured from the friendly owners. Bedrooms are particularly well furnished and attractively decorated, including many thoughtful extras. Some bedrooms have a sea view too.

Facilities 11 en suite (2 fmly) (2 GF) ⊗ TVB tea/coffee ✖ Cen ht TVL No children 4yrs No coaches **Prices** S £30-£42; D £50-£72✱ **LB** **Parking** 9 **Notes** Closed Nov-Jan & 1st 2wks Feb

◆◆◆◆

The Bay Guest House

10 Waterloo Pl DT4 7PE ☎ 01305 786289 ▤ 01305 786289
e-mail harrisbay@aol.com
web www.thebayguesthouse.co.uk
Dir *Weymouth seafront, from clock on esplanade with sea on right 200yds on left just before church*

This pleasant house has now been refurbished to provide comfortable and modern facilities. The proprietors are friendly and attentive, and

continued

many guests return regularly. Bedrooms come in a range of sizes and are pleasantly decorated in attractive colours. There is a cosy lounge and hearty breakfasts are served in the dining room.

Facilities 6 rms (4 en suite) (2 fmly) ⊗ TVB tea/coffee ✖ Cen ht No coaches **Parking** 8

◆◆◆◆

Bay View House

35 The Esplanade DT4 8DH
☎ 01305 782083 ▤ 01305 782083
web www.bayview-weymouth.co.uk
Dir *Hotel on seafront 100yds before ferry terminal*

An elegant, family-run Victorian house with views over Weymouth Bay. Located on the seafront, the property is well situated for the town centre and old harbour. Many guests return to enjoy the friendly hospitality of the resident proprietors.

Facilities 8 en suite (1 fmly) (1 GF) ⊗ TVB tea/coffee ✖ Cen ht TVL No coaches Solarium **Prices** S £35-£40; D £60-£70✱ **LB** **Parking** 13 **Notes** Closed Dec-1 Feb rs Feb-Mar

◆◆◆◆

Cavendish House

6 The Esplanade DT4 8EA ☎ 01305 782039
e-mail info@cavendishhousehotel.co.uk
web www.cavendishhousehotel.co.uk
Dir *Next to Condor Ferry Terminal & Pavilion Theatre, opp beach*

A warm welcome is assured at this delightful mid-terrace property at the end of The Esplanade close to the Pavilion Theatre. All bedrooms are well equipped and have views of either the beach and Weymouth Bay or the old harbour. Full English breakfasts are served at separate tables.

Facilities 8 en suite (2 fmly) ⊗ in dining room ⊗ in lounges TVB tea/coffee ✖ Cen ht TVL No coaches **Prices** D £50-£70✱ **LB** **Notes** Closed Xmas ▥

◆◆◆◆

Channel View ◇

10 Brunswick Ter, The Esplanade DT4 7RW
☎ 01305 782527
e-mail leggchannelview@aol.com
Dir *Off A353 The Esplanade onto Dorchester Rd, right onto Westerall Rd, 1st left at lights to Brunswick Ter*

Just off The Esplanade, this guest house is in a superb spot close to the beach and within walking distance of attractions. Bedrooms are on three floors and vary in size. Some have lovely views over the bay and all offer good levels of comfort and decor. You receive a warm welcome and breakfast is served in the well-appointed dining room.

Facilities 7 rms (5 en suite) (1 fmly) ⊗ TVB tea/coffee ✖ Cen ht TVL No coaches **Prices** S £24-£30; D £48-£60✱

◆◆◆◆

Kingswood Hotel

55 Rodwell Rd DT4 8QX
☎ 01305 784926 ▤ 01305 767984
e-mail robbie.f@virgin.net
Dir On A354 up hill towards Portland from inner harbour, on left after lights

Please note that this establishment has recently changed hands. Close to the old harbour, the family-friendly Kingswood is a convenient and relaxed accommodation. Bedrooms vary in size and most are spacious, some having distant sea views. In addition to a pleasant garden, there is a comfortable dining room with a wide choice of meals, and a bar.

Facilities 9 en suite (3 fmly) ⊗ in bedrooms ⊗ in dining room TVB tea/coffee ✖ Licensed Cen ht Pool Table Dinner Last d 9.30pm
Parking 25

◆◆◆◆

Letchworth Guest House ◇

5 Waterloo Pl, The Esplanade DT4 7NY
☎ 01305 786663 ▤ 01305 759203
e-mail letchworth.hotel@virginnet.co.uk
web www.letchworthweymouth.co.uk
Dir Off A31 at Bere Regis to Weymouth, signs to seafront & The Esplanade

Expect a warm welcome at this well-maintained, licensed guest house on the seafront. The bedrooms are brightly decorated and thoughtfully equipped, and there is also a cosy lounge.

Facilities 6 rms (4 en suite) (2 fmly) ⊗ in bedrooms ⊗ in dining room TVB tea/coffee ✖ Licensed TVL No children 5yrs No coaches
Prices S £25-£30; D £50-£64✳ **LB** **Parking** 6

◆◆◆◆

The Seaham

3 Waterloo Pl DT4 7NU ☎ 01305 782010
e-mail stay@theseaham.co.uk
web www.theseaham.co.uk
Dir Off A353 The Esplanade 200yds from St Johns Church

This well-presented establishment stands on the seafront close to the town centre. It's a good base for touring and offers attractive bedrooms with many useful extras. Generous breakfasts are served in the well-appointed dining room, which has an adjoining lounge.

Facilities 5 en suite ⊗ TVB tea/coffee ✖ Cen ht No children
No coaches **Prices** D £52-£76✳ **LB**

◆◆◆◆

Tamarisk Hotel

12 Stavordale Rd, Westham DT4 0AB
☎ 01305 786514 ▤ 01305 786556
e-mail hilary@tamariskhotel.co.uk
Dir A354 to Westham rdbt, 3rd exit to Bridport & sharp left

This well-organised establishment offers comfortable accommodation just a short walk from the harbour. Home-cooked breakfasts are served in the elegant dining room, and a small lounge is available. The pleasant bedrooms come in a range of sizes.

continued

Facilities 14 en suite (5 fmly) (1 GF) ⊗ in bedrooms ⊗ in dining room TVB tea/coffee ✖ Licensed Cen ht TVL No coaches **Parking** 19

◆◆◆◆

Upwater Barn

Sutton Rd, Sutton Poyntz DT3 6LW
☎ 01305 835710 ▤ 01305 835710
e-mail anderson@upwater.fsnet.co.uk
Dir From A353 signs to Sutton Poyntz, right at junct, Upwater Barn 200yds on right

This delightful, friendly property is ideal for a relaxing stay within a tranquil village setting. The stylish bedrooms are well equipped. In addition to lovely gardens, breakfast is served in the dining room overlooking the courtyard.

Facilities 2 rms (1 en suite) (1 pri facs) (1 GF) ⊗ TV available tea/coffee ✖ Cen ht ♨ **Prices** S £35-£45; D £60-£70✳ **LB** **Parking** 5 **Notes** ⊛

◆◆◆◆

Wenlock Hotel

107 The Esplanade DT4 7EE
☎ 01305 786674 & 0800 7813949
Dir On A353 The Esplanade near junct King St

The Wenlock offers a good standard of accommodation and a friendly atmosphere on the seafront, just a short walk from the station and town centre. The hosts are very attentive and always happy to help. The attractive bedrooms are well equipped and many have excellent views.

Facilities 10 rms (8 en suite) (2 fmly) ⊗ in 2 bedrooms ⊗ in dining room ⊗ in lounges TVB tea/coffee ✖ Cen ht No children 5yrs No coaches **Prices** S £35-£40; D £65-£70✳ **LB** **Notes** Closed end Oct-30 Dec, 3 Jan-Mar

◆◆◆

The Alendale Guest House

4 Waterloo Pl DT4 7NX ☎ 01305 788817 & 07799 111379
e-mail peter@thealendale.com
Dir From A353, B&B on right entering the Esplanade

Please note that this establishment has recently changed hands. This cosy guest house, located just 50yds from the beach, provides a warm, homely environment with easy access to the town centre, ferry terminals and places of interest. Bedrooms are well furnished and equipped with useful extras. Full English breakfasts are served at individual tables.

Facilities 5 en suite (3 fmly) ⊗ TVB tea/coffee ✖ Cen ht TVL
Prices S £31-£40; D £50-£60 ✳ **LB** **Parking** 6

England

WEYMOUTH continued

♦♦♦

Beachcomber ◇

6 Waterloo Pl DT4 7PD ☎ 01305 783078 ▤ 01305 768254
e-mail raycousins@beachcomberat6.co.uk
Dir On seafront 250yds from Jubilee Clock away from town

A warm welcome is assured at this friendly, family-run guest house close to the beach and within easy walking distance of the town centre and attractions. Bedrooms are cosy and well furnished, and there is a lounge. Tasty home-cooked evening meals are available by arrangement.

Facilities 8 rms (6 en suite) (2 fmly) ⊗ TVB tea/coffee ✗ Licensed Cen ht TVL No coaches Dinner Last d 10am **Prices** S £22-£32; D £44-£64✶ **LB** **Parking** 8

♦♦♦

Bedford House Hotel ◇

17 The Esplanade DT4 8DT
☎ 01305 786995 ▤ 01305 786995
Dir Along The Esplanade W towards harbour, turn right around amusement gardens (one-way), Bedford House on left

Known locally as the Bear House, because of the ever-growing collection of bears of every shape and description, Bedford House offers comfortable accommodation. You are assured of a friendly welcome and a relaxed atmosphere. Bedrooms are stylish, and the front-facing rooms are popular for their views over the bay, while rear-facing rooms look to the harbour.

Facilities 9 en suite (3 fmly) ⊗ in dining room ⊗ in lounges TVB tea/coffee ✗ Licensed Cen ht TVL No coaches **Prices** S £28-£35; D £50-£60✶ **LB** **Notes** Closed mid Nov-mid Feb ⊛

♦♦♦

Field Barn House ◇

44 Fieldbarn Dr, Southill DT4 0EE
☎ 01305 779140 & 07715 417270
Dir A354 to Weymouth, 1st rdbt 3rd exit, next rdbt 4th exit onto Southill/Fieldbarn Dr, house 300yds on right

Located on a residential estate on the outskirts of the town, yet only a short drive from the sandy beaches and town centre, this modern home is family run and provides comfortable accommodation. You share the lounge with the hosts and a full English breakfast is served at a communal table overlooking the well-tended rear garden.

Facilities 3 rms (1 fmly) ⊗ TVB ✗ Cen ht No children 3yrs No coaches **Prices** S £21; D £42✶ **LB** **Parking** 2 **Notes** Closed Dec ⊛

♦♦♦

Kimberley Guest House ◇

16 Kirtleton Av DT4 7PT ☎ 01305 783333 ▤ 01305 839603
e-mail kenneth.jones@btconnect.com
Dir Off A384 Weymouth road right onto Carlton Rd North, opp Rembrandt Hotel, Kirtleton Av on left

This friendly guest house is in a quiet residential area near the seafront. Bedrooms are well presented, and in addition to a hearty breakfast, traditional home-cooked meals using fresh local and seasonal produce are served by arrangement.

continued

Facilities 11 rms (7 en suite) (2 fmly) (1 GF) ⊗ TVB tea/coffee ✗ Cen ht No coaches Dinner Last d morning **Prices** S £18.50-£20.50; D £41-£45✶ **LB** **Parking** 8 **Notes** Closed 1-29 Dec ⊛

♦♦♦

Molyneux Guest House ◇

9 Waterloo Pl, The Esplanade DT4 7PD
☎ 01305 774623 & 07947 883235
e-mail stay@molyneuxguesthouse.co.uk
Dir A354 to Weymouth seafront, onto The Esplanade, The Molyneux on right

Located close to the seafront and beautiful beaches of Weymouth, this guest house offers a genuine welcome. Bedrooms are brightly decorated and there is a comfortable lounge. Breakfast is enjoyed in the smart dining room. Off-road parking to the rear is a bonus.

Facilities 6 rms (5 en suite) (1 fmly) (1 GF) ⊗ TVB tea/coffee ✗ Licensed Cen ht TVL Dinner Last d 10am **Prices** S £21-£28; D £42-£56✶ **LB** **Parking** 8 **Notes** ⊛

♦♦♦

Tara ◇

10 Market St DT4 8DD ☎ 01305 766235
Dir From Alexandra Gardens on The Esplanade right onto Belle Vue, right & left onto Market St

Neatly presented, this welcoming establishment is set just back from the seafront at the harbour end of town. Strictly non-smoking, the house provides a relaxed and friendly atmosphere. Bedrooms vary in size but all offer good levels of comfort. Home-cooked evening meals are served every day except Sundays.

Facilities 6 rms (1 fmly) ⊗ TVB tea/coffee ✗ Cen ht No children 4yrs No coaches Dinner Last d breakfast **Prices** S £18-£24; D £36-£48 **LB** **Notes** ⊛

♦♦♦

Trelawney Hotel

1 Old Castle Rd DT4 8QB
☎ 01305 783188 ▤ 01305 783181
e-mail trelawney-hotel@talk21.com
Dir From Harbourside follow Portland signs, Trelawney 700yds on left

This charming Victorian house stands amid attractive gardens in a quiet residential area a short walk from the town centre and beach. The friendly proprietors provide a comfortable environment, and many guests return regularly. Generous English breakfasts are offered

continued

in the light and airy dining room, and a comfortable lounge is available.

Facilities 8 en suite (3 fmly) ⊗ TVB tea/coffee 🛏 Licensed Cen ht TVL No children 5yrs No coaches ⚐ Putting green **Prices** S £45-£55; D £70-£80✱ **LB Parking** 13 **Notes** Closed Oct-Apr

◆◆◆

Wadham Guesthouse

22 East St DT4 8BN ☎ 01305 779640
Dir Off S end of A353 The Esplanade

The pleasant guest house offers a range of rooms in the town centre, and is a good base for touring or for a short stay. The comfortable bedrooms are attractively decorated, and home-cooked breakfasts are served in the ground-floor dining room. Parking permits are available.

Facilities 9 en suite (3 fmly) (1 GF) ⊗ in bedrooms ⊗ in dining room TVB tea/coffee 🛏 Cen ht TVL No children 4yrs No coaches Dinner Last d breakfast **Prices** S £23-£26; D £46-£52 **LB Notes** Closed Xmas

◆◆◆ 🅰

Weymouth Sands

5 The Esplanade DT4 8EA ☎ 01305 839022
e-mail enquiries@weymouthsands.co.uk
Dir A35 onto A354 signed for Ferry. Adjacent to Ferry Terminal

Facilities 9 rms (4 en suite) (1 pri facs) (1 fmly) ⊗ in dining room ⊗ in lounges TVB tea/coffee 🛏 Cen ht TVL No coaches **Prices** S £26; D £56-£60✱ **LB Notes** Closed Xmas

◆◆

Charlotte Guest House ◇

5 Commercial Rd DT4 7DW
☎ 01305 772942 & 07970 798425
e-mail charlotteGH1@aol.co.uk
Dir On A353 Esplanade, turn right at clock onto Kings St. 1st right at rdbt, then right onto Commercial Rd

A warm welcome is offered at this small renovated guest house within easy walking distance of the town's amienities. The breakfast room is light and airy and bedrooms vary in size.

Facilities 6 en suite (2 fmly) (1 GF) ⊗ in bedrooms ⊗ in lounges TVB tea/coffee Cen ht **Prices** S £25-£35; D £50-£60✱ **LB Parking** 3 **Notes**

◆◆

Ferndown Guest House ◇

47 Walpole St DT4 7HQ ☎ 01305 775228
e-mail odpjean@yahoo.co.uk
Dir Off A353 The Esplanade before Queen Victoria statue onto William St & Walpole St

Just a short walk from the seafront and the town centre, this neat, mid-terrace house provides comfortable accommodation. Rooms are simply furnished and pleasantly decorated, and downstairs there is a lounge-dining room for breakfast.

Facilities 6 rms (2 en suite) ⊗ in bedrooms ⊗ in dining room TVB tea/coffee 🛏 TVL No children 5yrs No coaches **Prices** S £18-£22; D £35-£45✱ **LB Notes** Closed Nov-Mar

WIMBORNE MINSTER   MAP 05 SZ09

◆◆◆◆

Ashton Lodge

10 Oakley Hill BH21 1QH
☎ 01202 883423 📄 01202 883423
e-mail ashtonlodge@ukgateway.net
web www.ashtonlodge.ukgateway.net
Dir Off A31 S of Wimborne onto A349 for Poole, left next rdbt signed Wimborne/Canford Magna, house 200yds on right

A warm welcome is assured at this delightful modern home, which provides comfortable bedrooms, stylishly furnished with coordinated decor and fabrics. All rooms are well equipped. Hearty breakfasts are served in the spacious dining room, which overlooks the well-maintained garden.

Facilities 5 rms (2 en suite) (1 pri facs) (2 fmly) ⊗ TVB tea/coffee 🛏 Cen ht TVL No coaches **Prices** S £34; D £58-£64✱ **LB Parking** 4 **Notes**

◆◆◆

Grove Lodge ◇

2 Grove Rd BH21 1BW ☎ 01202 882697
e-mail ruthebush@yahoo.co.uk
Dir A31 onto B3073, signs for town centre, after 3rd lights 1st left onto Grove Rd, 1st house on right

An Edwardian house offering comfortable accommodation close to the centre of this historic town. One bedroom has generous views of the secluded garden and a hearty breakfast can be enjoyed in the conservatory.

Facilities 2 rms (1 en suite) (1 pri facs) (1 fmly) (1 GF) ⊗ TVB tea/coffee 🛏 Cen ht No coaches **Prices** S £30-£35; D £50-£60✱ **Parking** 2 **Notes** Closed 21 Dec-2 Jan

◆◆ 🅰

The Albion Inn

19 High St BH21 1HR ☎ 01202 882492 📄 01202 639333
e-mail albioninn-wimborne@tiscali.co.uk
Dir Off town square opp Wimborne Minster

Facilities 4 rms (1 en suite) (1 fmly) ⊗ in bedrooms TVB tea/coffee Licensed Cen ht **Prices** D £50-£60 **Parking** 14

WINFRITH NEWBURGH MAP 04 SY88

◆◆◆

The Red Lion

DT2 8LE ☎ 01305 852814 📠 01305 851768

Dir On A352 N of village

Situated between Dorchester and Wareham, this traditional longhouse is surrounded by rolling countryside and is a good centre for touring. The Red Lion's characterful public areas offer an extensive range of dishes, and booking is essential at weekends. The comfortable bedrooms are well equipped.

Facilities 3 en suite ⊘ in bedrooms ⊘ in dining room TVB tea/coffee ✘ Cen ht No children 12yrs No coaches Dinner Last d 9.15pm **Prices** D £70-£80✷ **LB Parking** 70

WINTERBORNE WHITECHURCH MAP 04 ST80

◆◆◆◆

Shalom

Blandford Hill DT11 0AA ☎ 01258 881299
e-mail tranquillity@shalom2414.freeserve.co.uk
Dir On A354 5m SW from Blandford

A warm welcome awaits you at Shalom, situated in a village within an Area of Outstanding Natural Beauty. The comfortable modern house has attractive bedrooms enhanced with thoughtful extras. A delicious breakfast featuring organic and local produce is enjoyed in the dining room. Walkers and cyclists are welcome (garage for bicycles).

Facilities 2 rms (1 en suite) (1 pri facs) ⊘ TVB tea/coffee ✘ Cen ht No children No coaches **Prices** D £52-£56✷ **Parking** 3 **Notes** Closed Xmas & New Year 📧

CO DURHAM

BARNARD CASTLE MAP 19 NZ01

◆◆◆◆

Greta House

89 Galgate DL12 8ES ☎ 01833 631193 📠 01833 631193
e-mail gretahousebc@btclick.com
Dir 400yds NE of town centre on A67

Expect very warm hospitality at this spacious Victorian villa built in 1870. Greta House is convenient for the Bowes Museum, local antiques shops, High Force and Raby Castle, and is a truly comfortable home from home. Bedrooms come with a wealth of thoughtful extras, and memorable breakfasts are served in the elegant dining room.

Facilities 3 en suite ⊘ TVB tea/coffee ✘ Cen ht No children 5yrs No coaches **Prices** S £40-£45; D £60-£65✷ **Notes** 📧

◆◆◆◆

Homelands ◇

85 Galgate DL12 8ES ☎ 01833 638757
e-mail enquiries@homelandsguesthouse.co.uk
web www.homelandsguesthouse.co.uk
Dir 400yds NE of town centre on A67

A warm welcome awaits you at this central guest house. The Victorian property has been renovated to provide attractive and well-equipped bedrooms, and a hearty breakfast using local and home-made produce is served in the elegant dining room overlooking the garden. Light snacks are available in the stylish lounge.

Facilities 4 rms (3 en suite) (1 pri facs) 1 annexe en suite (1 GF) ⊘ TVB tea/coffee Direct dial from bedrooms ✘ Licensed Cen ht No children 5yrs No coaches **Prices** S £30-£40; D £58-£65 **Notes** Closed 23 Dec-2 Jan

◆◆◆◆

Wilson House ◇ (NZ081124)

Barningham DL11 7EB
☎ 01833 621218 📠 01833 621110 Mrs Lowes
e-mail helowes@tiscali.co.uk
Dir 5m SE of Barnard Castle. S off A66 at Greta Bridge to Barningham, 2nd farm on right

The attractive farmhouse, set in 475 acres among superb Pennine scenery, is an ideal retreat for a relaxing break. You can expect good home cooking, flexible bedrooms that are suitable for families, and can wander around the farm and enjoy the spectacular views.

Facilities 4 rms (2 en suite) (2 GF) ⊘ TVB tea/coffee ✘ Cen ht No children 3yrs 475 acres mixed livestock Dinner Last d 2pm **Prices** S £25-£30; D £45-£50✷ **LB Parking** 5 **Notes** Closed 30 Nov-1 Mar 📧

CHESTER-LE-STREET MAP 19 NZ25

◆◆◆◆

Waldridge Fell Guest House

Old Waldridge Village DH2 3RY ☎ 0191 389 1908
e-mail bbchesterlestreet@btinternet.com
Dir 1.5m SW of Chester. Off A167 at Chester Moor rdbt signed Waldridge, Left next rdbt, 0.75m on left

This former village chapel, renovated by the current owners, lies on the edge of the village and has fine views over the fells. The comfortable bedrooms are complemented by a lounge-dining room, where a substantial breakfast is served at one large table.

Facilities 6 en suite (2 fmly) (1 GF) ⊘ TVB tea/coffee ✘ Cen ht TVL No children 3yrs **Prices** S £35-£37; D £58-£60✷ **Parking** 8 **Notes** Closed Xmas & New Year 📧

COWSHILL

MAP 18 NY84

◆◆◆◆ ⊜ ♥

Low Cornriggs Farm ◇ (NY845413)

Cowshill-in-Weardale DL13 1AQ
☎ 01388 537600 & 07818 843159 🖹 01388 537777
Mrs Elliott
e-mail enquiries@lowcornriggsfarm.fsnet.co.uk
web www.alstonandkillhoperidingcentre.co.uk
Dir 0.6m NW of Cowshill on A689

Situated in the heart of Weardale close to Cumbria, this delightful
farmhouse has stunning views. Original stone and stripped pine
provide character, and excellent home-cooked dinners are offered
along with charming hospitality. Bedrooms are attractive and
thoughtfully equipped with many homely extras. There is a riding
stable available on the farm.

Facilities 3 en suite (1 fmly) ⊗ TVB tea/coffee ✖ Cen ht TVL Fishing
42 acres Hereford cows, pony Dinner Last d noon **Prices** S £30-£32;
D £48-£50 **LB** **Parking** 6

DARLINGTON

MAP 19 NZ21

See also **Aldbrough St John (Yorkshire, North)**

Premier Collection

◆◆◆◆◆ 🖹 ⊜ ♥

Clow Beck House (NZ281100)

Monk End Farm, Croft on Tees DL2 2SW
☎ 01325 721075 🖹 01325 720419 Mr & Mrs Armstrong
e-mail heather@clowbeckhouse.co.uk
web www.clowbeckhouse.co.uk
Dir 3m S of Darlington. In Croft-on-Tees on A167 follow brown tourist
signs to Clow Beck House

This impressive farmhouse has fabulous landscaped gardens,
including a gnome cricket match. The spacious bedrooms, housed in
traditional stone buildings, are very comfortable, well-equipped and
individually decorated in contemporary and Victorian themes. There is
a luxurious lounge in the main house, and imaginative meals using
home-grown and local produce are served in the dining room.

Facilities 13 annexe en suite (3 fmly) ⊗ in 4 bedrooms ⊗ in dining
room FTV TVB tea/coffee Direct dial from bedrooms ✖ Licensed
Cen ht TVL Fishing 2 acre award winning garden 90 acres mixed Dinner
Last d by arrangement **Prices** S £80; D £120 **Conf** Max 20 Class 20
Board 20 **Parking** 15 **Notes** Closed Xmas & New Year

◆◆◆◆

White Horse Hotel

Harrowgate Hill DL1 3AD
☎ 01325 382121 🖹 01325 355953
e-mail white-horse1@btconnect.com
Dir 2m N of Darlington on A167

Convenient for the A1(M), the White Horse provides a range of very
well-furnished bedrooms including family rooms. Comprehensive
buffet breakfasts are served in a spacious dining room, and extensive
conference facilities and an attractive lounge bar are available.

Facilities 40 en suite (3 fmly) (10 GF) ⊗ in 30 bedrooms ⊗ in dining
room ⊗ in 1 lounge TVB tea/coffee Direct dial from bedrooms Lift
Cen ht Dinner Last d 9pm **Conf** Max 150 Thtr 120 Class 50 Board 60
Parking 80

◆◆◆

Balmoral ◇

63 Woodland Rd DL3 7BQ
☎ 01325 461908 🖹 01325 461908
e-mail philip.marjorie.hawke@ntlworld.com
Dir 0.5m NW of town centre on A68 opp Memorial Hospital

The Victorian terrace house preserves its original wood panelling,
stained glass and intricate coving. Bedrooms come in a mix of styles
and sizes, and breakfast is served in the basement dining room, which
has a small lounge area. A kitchenette is also available.

Facilities 9 rms (5 en suite) (3 fmly) ⊗ TVB tea/coffee ✖ Cen ht
Prices S £27-£36; D £54✳ **Notes** Closed Xmas ⊜

DURHAM

MAP 19 NZ24

★★★★ 🅰 Guest House

Cathedral View Town House

212 Lower Gilesgate DH1 1QN ☎ 0191 386 9566
e-mail cathedralview@hotmail.com
Dir In town centre off A690 Gilesgate rdbt

Facilities 6 en suite (2 GF) ⊗ FTV TVB tea/coffee ✖ Cen ht TVL
No children 11yrs No coaches **Prices** S £60-£80; D £70-£90✳

◆◆◆◆

The Gables

10 South View, Middlestone Moor DL16 7DF
☎ 01388 817544
e-mail thegablesghouse@aol.com
Dir 6m S of Durham. Off A688 signed Spennymoor town centre,
then Middlestone Moor, 2nd lights left & 2nd right

A warm welcome awaits you at The Gables, which is in a quiet
residential area on the southern fringe of Spennymoor. The
immaculate house provides bright homely bedrooms, and light snacks
are available in the rooms.

Facilities 3 en suite (3 GF) ⊗ TVB tea/coffee Cen ht No children 12yrs
No coaches **Prices** S fr £38; d fr £58✳ **Parking** 6 **Notes** Closed
21 Dec-2 Jan

England

DURHAM continued

◆◆◆◆

Hillrise ◇

13 Durham Rd West, Bowburn DH6 5AU
☎ 0191 377 0302 🖹 0191 377 0898
e-mail enquiries@hill-rise.com
web www.hill-rise.com
Dir 4m SE of Durham. A1(M) junct 61 onto A177, Hillrise 300yds on left

Located in the village of Bowburn near the A1(M), this friendly house offers comfortable and well-equipped accommodation. Hearty breakfasts are served in the bright, airy dining room, and the inviting lounge has leather seating and a vast library of videotapes.

Facilities 5 en suite (2 fmly) (2 GF) ⊗ TVB tea/coffee ✱ Cen ht TVL No children 5yrs No coaches **Prices** S £30-£35; D £60-£70

◆◆◆◆ ⬛

The Old Mill

Thinford Rd, Metal Br DH6 5NX
☎ 01740 652928 🖹 01740 657230
e-mail office@theoldmill.uk.com
web www.theoldmill.uk.com
Dir 5m S of Durham. A1(M) junct 61, onto A688 S for 1.5m, left at rdbt & sharp right

This family-owned inn offers a friendly welcome. The stylish bedrooms are very well equipped, and the traditional bar offers a comprehensive list of wines and beer, and a very good selection of meals.

Facilities 8 en suite ⊗ in bedrooms ⊗ in area of dining room ⊗ in 1 lounge STV TVB tea/coffee Direct dial from bedrooms ✱ Cen ht Jacuzzi/Spa Dinner Last d 9pm **Conf** Max 40 Thtr 40 Class 40 Board 25 **Parking** 40

FIR TREE   MAP 19 NZ13

◆◆◆◆ ⬛

Duke of York Inn

DL15 8DG ☎ 01388 762848
e-mail suggett@firtree-crook.fsnet.co.uk
Dir On A68 in village

Nestled in a quiet village, the family-run inn is full of character and has a friendly atmosphere. The very comfortable bedrooms are spacious and carefully furnished, and the restaurant and bar offer an interesting choice of freshly prepared dishes. Original Mouseman Thompson oak furniture features in the bar and bar-lounge.

Facilities 5 en suite (1 fmly) (1 GF) ⊗ in bedrooms ⊗ in dining room ⊗ in lounges TVB tea/coffee Direct dial from bedrooms ✱ Cen ht No children 10yrs No coaches Dinner Last d 9pm **Prices** S fr £55; d fr £80✶ **LB Parking** 40

◆◆◆◆

Greenhead Country House Hotel

DL15 8BL ☎ 01388 763143 🖹 01388 763143
e-mail info@thegreenheadhotel.co.uk
web www.thegreenheadhotel.co.uk
Dir Off A68 at Fir Tree Inn E onto unclassified road

Set in the heart of rural Weardale, this traditional house was built in 1704. The spacious bedrooms, one with a four-poster bed, are carefully decorated and have homely extras. Public rooms include a beamed and stone-arched lounge with a well-stocked bar, and a stylish dining room.

Facilities 8 en suite (1 fmly) (2 GF) ⊗ TV7B tea/coffee ✱ Licensed Cen ht TVL No children 13yrs No coaches **Prices** S £60; D £75 **LB Parking** 20

HASWELL PLOUGH   MAP 19 NZ34

◆◆◆ 🅰

The Gables

Front St DH6 2EW ☎ 0191 526 2982 🖹 0191 526 2982
e-mail jmgables@aol.com
web www.thegables.co.uk
Dir On B1283 in village centre

Facilities 5 en suite (1 fmly) ⊗ in bedrooms ⊗ in dining room STV FTV TVB tea/coffee ✱ Licensed Cen ht TVL outdoor play area Dinner Last d 7.30pm **Prices** S £44-£50; D £58-£66✶ **Parking** 30

MIDDLETON-IN-TEESDALE   MAP 18 NY92

★★★★ 🅰 **Guest House**

Brunswick House

55 Market Pl DL12 0QH ☎ 01833 640393
e-mail enquiries@brunswickhouse.net
Dir On B6277 opp church
Facilities 5 en suite ⊗ TVB tea/coffee ✱ Licensed Cen ht No coaches Dinner Last d 7pm **Prices** S £38; D £58 **LB Parking** 5

STANLEY   MAP 19 NZ15

◆◆◆ ❦

Bush Blades Farm ◇ (NZ168533)

Harperley DH9 9UA ☎ 01207 232722 Mrs Gibson
Dir 2m W of Stanley. A693 W from Stanley for Consett, 0.5m right to
Harperley, farm 0.5m on right

The farmhouse stands on a peaceful plateau of farming land with very
good views. Well located for visiting Beamish and Durham, Bush
Blades has a friendly and relaxed atmosphere, and spacious,
traditionally furnished bedrooms.

Facilities 2 en suite (1 GF) ❷ in bedrooms ❷ in dining room TVB
tea/coffee ✱ Cen ht TVL No children 12yrs 50 acres sheep
Prices S £30; D £48 **Parking** 4 **Notes** Closed 20 Dec-2 Jan ❸

STOCKTON-ON-TEES   MAP 19 NZ41

◆◆◆◆

The Parkwood Hotel

64-66 Darlington Rd, Hartburn TS18 5ER ☎ 01642 587933
e-mail theparkwoodhotel@aol.com
web www.theparkwoodhotel.co.uk
Dir 1.5m SW of town centre. A66 onto A137 signed Yarm & Stockton
West, left at lights onto A1027, left onto Darlington Rd

A very friendly welcome awaits you at this family-run establishment.
The well-equipped en suite bedrooms come with homely extras, and
a range of professionally prepared meals are served in the cosy bar-
lounge, conservatory, or the attractive non-smoking dining room.

Facilities 5 en suite ❷ in bedrooms ❷ in dining room TVB tea/coffee
✱ Licensed Cen ht No coaches Dinner Last d 9.15pm **Parking** 36

◆◆◆

The Grange ◇

33 Grange Rd, Norton TS20 2NS ☎ 01642 552541
e-mail grangeguesthouse@tiscali.co.uk
Dir A19 onto A139 sliproad to Norton, over 1st rdbt with Red Lion
pub on right, 2nd left onto Grange Rd

Facilities 8 rms (4 en suite) ❷ STV TVB tea/coffee ✱ Cen ht
No coaches **Prices** S £25-£32✳ **Notes** Closed Xmas & New Year ❸

ESSEX

BILLERICAY   MAP 06 TQ69

◆◆◆

31 Mercer Road ◇

31 Mercer Rd CM11 1EP
☎ 01277 626547 ▤ 01277 657500
e-mail lyn@dean.fsbusiness.co.uk
Dir Off B1007 High St onto Norsey Rd, 1m left onto Mercer Rd

The charming detached property is on the outskirts of the town. The
individually decorated bedrooms are pleasantly furnished, and
breakfast is served around a large table in the elegant dining room.

Facilities 4 rms (1 en suite) ❷ TVB tea/coffee ✱ Cen ht No children
13yrs No coaches **Prices** S fr £25; d fr £50✳ **Parking** 3 **Notes** Closed
Xmas ❸

BRAINTREE   MAP 07 TL72

◆◆◆

Ambleside ◇

19 Warner Cl, Rayne CM77 6GX ☎ 01376 553605
e-mail janice.harrison@tesco.net
Dir Off A120

Expect a warm welcome at this small guest house on the outskirts of
town, and only a 20-minute drive from Stansted Airport. Bedrooms
are pleasantly decorated with coordinated fabrics and have many
thoughtful touches. Breakfast is served at a large communal table in
the kitchen-breakfast room.

Facilities 2 rms (2 pri facs) ❷ TVB tea/coffee ✱ Cen ht No coaches
Prices S £24; D £48 **Parking** 2 **Notes** Closed Xmas & New Year ❸

England

CHELMSFORD

MAP 06 TL70

◆◆◆◆

Boswell House Hotel

118/120 Springfield Rd CM2 6LF
☎ 01245 287587 📠 01245 287587
e-mail boswell118@aol.com
web www.boswellhousehotel.co.uk
Dir 500yds E of town centre. Signs to Riverside Ice & Leisure Centre, over river at junct Victoria Rd

Expect a warm welcome and attentive service from the caring hosts at this well-maintained house. The thoughtfully equipped bedrooms have well chosen pine furnishings and coordinated soft fabrics, and breakfast and dinner are served in the attractive dining room. Drinks can be enjoyed in the comfortable lounge bar.

Facilities 13 en suite (2 fmly) (4 GF) ⊗ in bedrooms ⊗ in dining room ⊗ in 1 lounge TVB tea/coffee Direct dial from bedrooms ✱ Licensed Cen ht TVL No coaches Dinner Last d 8.30pm **Prices** S £52-£55; D £65-£70✱ **Parking** 15 **Notes** Closed 24 Dec-4 Jan

◆◆◆

Beechcroft Private Hotel

211 New London Rd CM2 0AJ
☎ 01245 352462 & 250861 📠 01245 347833
e-mail enquiries@beechcrofthotel.com
Dir 0.5m SW of town centre. A12 onto A414, over 3 rdbts, left at 4th rdbt, on right after lights

The Beechcroft is just a short walk from the town centre. Bedrooms vary in size and style but all are pleasantly decorated and equipped with modern facilities. Breakfast is served at separate tables in the smart dining room and there is a cosy lounge.

Facilities 20 rms (13 en suite) (2 fmly) (6 GF) ⊗ in 10 bedrooms ⊗ in dining room TVB tea/coffee ✱ Cen ht TVL **Prices** S £40-£45; D £55-£65✱ **LB Parking** 14

CHIPPING ONGAR

MAP 06 TL50

Premier Collection

◆◆◆◆◆

Diggins Farm

Fyfield CM5 0PP ☎ 01277 899303 📠 01277 899015
Dir B184 N from Fyfield, right after Black Bull pub, farm 0.75m on left

This delightful Grade II listed 16th-century farmhouse stands amid open farmland in the Roding valley, and is only a short drive from Stansted Airport. The spacious bedrooms are carefully furnished and well equipped.

Facilities 2 rms (1 en suite) (1 pri facs) ⊗ TVB tea/coffee ✱ Cen ht No children 12yrs No coaches **Prices** S £30; D £50✱ **Parking** 20 **Notes** Closed 15 Dec-3 Jan 🐾

CLACTON-ON-SEA

MAP 07 TM11

★★★★ Guest House

Chudleigh

13 Agate Rd, Marine Pde West CO15 1RA
☎ 01255 425407 📠 01255 470280
e-mail reception@chudleighhotel.com
Dir Follow town centre/seafront & pier signs. Right at seafront, after lights at pier right into Agate Road

Conveniently situated for the seafront and shops, this immaculate property has been run by friendly Peter and Carol Oleggini for the last 30 years. Bedrooms are most attractive with coordinated decor and well chosen fabrics. Breakfast is served in the smart dining room and there is a cosy lounge with plush sofas.

Facilities 10 en suite (2 fmly) (2 GF) TVB tea/coffee Direct dial from bedrooms Licensed TVL No children 3yrs No coaches **Prices** S £41; D £60-£62✱ **LB Parking** 7

◆◆◆

The Sandrock

1 Penfold Rd, Marine Pde West CO15 1JN
☎ 01255 428215 📠 01255 428215
e-mail thesandrock@btinternet.com
web www.sandrockhotel.com
Dir A133 to seafront, right at pier, signed Sandrock, 2nd right

A warm welcome is offered at this Victorian property, which is just off the seafront and within easy walking distance of the town centre. The attractive bedrooms vary in size and style, are thoughtfully equipped, and some have sea views. Breakfast is served in the smart bar-restaurant and there is also a cosy lounge.

Facilities 9 en suite (1 fmly) (1 GF) ⊗ in 3 bedrooms ⊗ in dining room ⊗ in lounges TVB tea/coffee Licensed Cen ht TVL No coaches **Prices** S £35-£42; D £52-£59 **LB Parking** 5

◆◆◆

Adelaide Guesthouse Bed & Breakfast

24 Wellesley Rd CO15 3PP ☎ 01255 435628
e-mail adelaide_guesthouse@yahoo.co.uk
Facilities 4 rms (4 pri facs) (1 fmly) ⊗ in bedrooms ⊗ in dining room ⊗ in 1 lounge TVB tea/coffee ✱ Licensed Cen ht No coaches **Prices** S £35; D £40 **Parking** 3

COLCHESTER
See also **Nayland (Suffolk)**

MAP 13 TL92

◆◆◆◆

Fridaywood Farm

Bounstead Rd CO2 0DF ☎ 01206 573595 📄 01206 547011
e-mail lochorem8@aol.com
Dir *3m S of Colchester. Off B1026 at Layer-de-la Haye onto Malting Green Rd & Abberton Rd & Bounstead Rd*

The traditional farmhouse is surrounded by wooded countryside. Bedrooms are generally quite spacious, and each one is carefully furnished with well-chosen pieces, and equipped with many thoughtful touches. Public rooms include an elegant dining room where breakfast is served at a large communal table, and a cosy sitting room.

Facilities 2 en suite ⊗ TVB tea/coffee ✖ Cen ht No children 12yrs No coaches ✎ ⚬ **Prices** S £38-£45; D £55-£60✱ **Parking** 6 **Notes** ⊗

◆◆◆◆

Old Manse

15 Roman Rd CO1 1UR ☎ 01206 545154 📄 01206 545153
e-mail wendyanderson15@hotmail.com
web www.doveuk.com/oldmanse
Dir *High St onto East Hill, 1st left after castle, opp St James's Church*

Expect a warm welcome from the caring host at this Victorian house, situated just a short walk from the castle and High St. Bedrooms are carefully decorated with coordinated soft furnishings and equipped with many thoughtful touches. Breakfast is served at a large communal table in the attractive dining room and there is a comfortable lounge.

Facilities 3 rms (2 en suite) (1 pri facs) ⊗ TVB tea/coffee ✖ Cen ht No children 6yrs No coaches **Prices** S £35-£50; D £63-£70✱ **Parking** 1 **Notes** Closed 23-31 Dec ⊗

DEDHAM

MAP 13 TM03

◆◆◆◆ ⊜ ◀

The Sun Inn

High St CO7 6DF ☎ 01206 323351 📄 01206 323964
e-mail enquiries@thesuninndedham.com
Dir *In village centre opp church*

A charming 15th-century coaching inn situated in the centre of Dedham opposite the church. The carefully decorated bedrooms

feature four-poster and half tester beds, along with many thoughtful touches. The public rooms have a wealth of character with inglenook fires, oak beams and fine oak panelling.

Facilities 4 en suite ⊗ in bedrooms ⊗ in dining room TVB ✖ Cen ht Dinner Last d 10pm **Parking** 15 **Notes** Closed 25-28 Dec rs Sun evenings Oct-Mar Civ Wed 100

FEERING

MAP 07 TL82

◆◆◆◆ ⊜

Prested Hall

Prested Hall Chase CO5 9EE
☎ 01376 573399 📄 01376 572947
e-mail prestedhall@yahoo.co.uk
web www.prested.com
Dir *Off A12 at Kelvedon*

A Grade II listed 15th-century hall hidden down a long tree-lined avenue in 75 acres of parkland. The extensive public areas include a choice of lounges, library, dining room, and a conservatory, and leisure facilities feature two indoor 'real' tennis courts and a 20-metre pool. The carefully appointed bedrooms are generally spacious and well equipped.

Facilities 10 en suite (1 fmly) (1 GF) ⊗ TVB tea/coffee ✖ Licensed Cen ht TVL No coaches ▨ ✎ Sauna Solarium Gymnasium Steam room Dinner Last d 9.30pm **Conf** Max 60 Thtr 45 Class 24 Board 20 **Parking** 100 **Notes** Civ Wed 65

FELSTED

MAP 06 TL62

◆◆◆◆ ❦

Potash Farmhouse ◈ (TL686196)

Cobblers Gn, Causeway End Road CM6 3LX
☎ 01371 820510 Mr & Mrs Smith
e-mail jill@potashfarm.co.uk
web www.potashfarm.co.uk
Dir *B1417 S from Felsted, 0.5m left signed Cobbler's Green, farm signed 400yds on left*

A Grade II listed 15th-century house situated on the outskirts of Felsted amid extensive, half-moated mature gardens. There are original exposed beams and open fireplaces, and the bedrooms are carefully decorated and thoughtfully equipped. Public rooms include an attractive dining room, a comfortable lounge and a conservatory.

Facilities 3 rms ⊗ TVB tea/coffee ✖ Cen ht TVL No children 12yrs ⚬ 40 acres arable **Prices** S £30-£35; D £48-£50 **Parking** 6 **Notes** ⊗

continued

England

FRINTON-ON-SEA

MAP 07 TM22

♦♦♦

Uplands ◇

41 Hadleigh Rd CO13 9HQ
☎ 01255 674889 📠 01255 674889
e-mail info@uplandsguesthouse.co.uk
web www.uplandsguesthouse.com
Dir *B1033 into Frinton, over level crossing, Hadleigh Rd 3rd left, Uplands 250yds on left*

This large Edwardian house stands in a peaceful side road just a short walk from the shops and seafront. Bedrooms are pleasantly decorated and thoughtfully equipped with a good range of useful extras. Public rooms include a large lounge-dining room where breakfast is served at individual tables.

Facilities 4 rms (2 en suite) ⊗ TVB tea/coffee ✶ Cen ht TVL No coaches Dinner Last d 10am **Prices** S £20-£28; D £50-£56✶ **LB Parking** 4

GREAT DUNMOW

MAP 06 TL62

♦♦♦♦ ❦

Homelye Farm *(TL648225)*

Homelye Chase, Braintree Rd CM6 3AW
☎ 01371 872127 📠 01371 876428 Mr & Mrs Pickford
e-mail homelyebandb@btconnect.com
web www.homelyefarm.com
Dir *B1256 from Great Dunhow for Braintree, 1.5m up hill & left at water tower, farm at bottom of Homelye Chase*

Expect a warm welcome at this working farm situated in a peaceful rural location just a short drive from the town centre. The spacious bedrooms are in converted outbuildings; each one features exposed beams, coordinated fabrics and attractive pine furnishings. Breakfast is served at individual tables in the original farmhouse.

Facilities 14 en suite (1 fmly) (14 GF) ⊗ TVB tea/coffee ✶ Cen ht 113 acres arable **Prices** S £42.50-£45; D £60-£65 **Parking** 16 **Notes** Closed 24-27 Dec

HATFIELD HEATH

MAP 06 TL51

♦♦♦♦

Shrubbs Farm ◇

Sheering Rd CM22 7LL ☎ 01279 730332 📠 01279 739047
e-mail jennyliddell@yahoo.co.uk
Dir *0.5m SW of Hatfield Heath off B183*

Part of the arable working farm, this delightful farmhouse has a peaceful location within easy reach of Stansted Airport. Expect a warm welcome and lots of homey touches in the comfortable bedrooms. The hearty breakfast using quality local produce is a highlight.

Facilities 2 rms ⊗ TVB tea/coffee ✶ Cen ht TVL No coaches **Prices** S fr £27; D £54-£60✶ **Notes** Closed 19-31 Dec 🔄

♦♦♦♦ ▲

Marks Hall Farmhouse

Marks Hall, White Roding CM6 1RT
☎ 01279 876438 📠 01279 876236
e-mail jane@markshall.fsnet.co.uk
Dir *Off A1060 in White Roding onto Marks Hall Ln, between garage & Black Horse pub out of village, avenue of trees, farmhouse on right*

Facilities 4 rms (2 en suite) ⊗ in bedrooms ⊗ in dining room ⊗ in lounges TVB tea/coffee ✶ Cen ht TVL No coaches ♨ **Conf** Max 12 Board 12 **Parking** 6 **Notes** 🔄

♦♦♦ ❦

Lancasters Farm *(TL544149)*

Chelmsford Rd CM22 7BB
☎ 01279 730220 📠 01279 730220 Mrs Hunt
Dir *A1060 from Hatfield Heath for Chelmsford, 1m left on sharp right bend, through white gates*

You are made to feel at home at this delightfully spacious house, which is the heart of this large working arable farm close to Stansted Airport. Bedrooms vary in size and style but all are smartly decorated and thoughtfully equipped. Garaging arrangements can be made, as can transport to and from the airport.

Facilities 4 rms (1 en suite) ⊗ TVB tea/coffee ✶ Cen ht No children 12yrs 260 acres arable **Parking** 6 **Notes** Closed 14 Dec-14 Jan 🔄

LATCHINGDON

MAP 07 TL8

♦♦♦

Crouch Valley Motel

Burnham Rd CM3 6EX ☎ 01621 740770 📠 01621 743355
e-mail info@crouchvalley.com
web www.crouchvalley.com
Dir *In village off minirdbt at church, motel 600yds*

Situated in rural Essex, this modern motel offers comfortable, well-equipped chalet-style accommodation, with two rooms having easier access. Breakfast is served in the adjoining restaurant, and an interesting choice of dishes is available for dinner.

Facilities 10 en suite (8 fmly) (10 GF) ⊗ STV TVB tea/coffee Licensed Cen ht Dinner Last d 9.30pm **Prices** S £32.50-£50; D £47.50-£80; (room only) ✶ **LB Parking** 50

MALDON

MAP 07 TL8

★★★ Bed & Breakfast

Limburn House

Wycke Hill CM9 6SH ☎ 01621 851392 & 07840 926021
e-mail jabos@btinternet.com
Dir *From A12 onto A414, B&B 6.5m on right after Church.*

A smartly maintained detached property situated in landscaped grounds just off the A414. The bedrooms are in an adjoining annexe; each one has coordinated fabrics and many thoughtful touches. Breakfast is served in the lounge-dining room, which has a plush leather chesterfield and views of the surrounding countryside.

Facilities 3 rms (2 en suite) (1 pri facs) (1 fmly) (2 GF) ⊗ TVB tea/coffee ✶ Cen ht TVL No coaches Golf . **Parking** 6 **Notes** 🔄

MANNINGTREE   MAP 13 TM13

Premier Collection

◆◆◆◆◆ ❧

Dairy House Farm (TM148293)

Bradfield Rd CO11 2SR
☎ 01255 870322 📠 01255 870186 Mrs Whitworth
e-mail bridgetwhitworth@hotmail.com
web www.dairyhousefarm.info
For full entry see **Wix**

MAYLAND   MAP 07 TL90

🗓

Harmattan

7 Steeple Rd CM3 6EG ☎ 01621 740474 & 07981 809345
Dir 200yds past Mayland Mill pub on left

At the time of going to press the rating for this establishment had not been confirmed. Please check the AA website www.theAA.com for up-to-date information.

Facilities 2 rms (1 en suite) (1 pri facs) ⊗ TVB tea/coffee ✝ Cen ht
No children 4yrs No coaches **Prices** D £45-£50✳ **LB Parking** 10
Notes ⊛

RADWINTER   MAP 12 TL63

◆◆◆ 🅰

Hollingate B & B ◇

Radwinter End CB10 2UD
☎ 01799 599184 📠 01799 599632
e-mail enquiries@hollingate.co.uk
Dir B1053 through Radwinter, left at Plough x-rds, 1st right, left fork, &B 5th on left

Facilities 3 rms (2 en suite) ⊗ TVB tea/coffee ✝ Cen ht No children
10yrs No coaches **Prices** S £25-£30; D £45-£55 **Parking** 4 **Notes** ⊛

SAFFRON WALDEN   MAP 12 TL53

★★★ Bed & Breakfast

Warner's Farm

Top Rd, Wimbish Gn CB10 2XJ
☎ 01799 599525 & 07989 562316
e-mail nettymawson@aol.com
web www.warnersfarm.co.uk
Dir About 1.5m from B184, Saffron Walden to Thaxted Road.

Expect a warm welcome at this delightful property set in 5 acres of grounds and surrounded by open countryside. The comfortable bedrooms have a wealth of character; each one has coordinated fabrics and many thoughtful touches. Breakfast is served in the smart dining room and the lounge has an open fireplace.

Facilities 4 rms (2 en suite) (2 pri facs) ⊗ in bedrooms ⊗ in dining room ⊗ in 1 lounge TVB tea/coffee Cen ht TVL No children 10yrs No coaches ❅ Sauna Gymnasium Dinner Last d 8hrs notice **Parking** 13 **Notes** Closed Nov-Feb ⊛

◆◆◆◆ 🍺

The Cricketer's Arms

Rickling Gn CB11 3YG ☎ 01799 543210 📠 01799 543512
e-mail reservations@cricketers.demon.co.uk
web www.thecricketersarms.com
Dir Off B1383 at Quendon, premises 300yds opp cricket green

Parts of this refurbished inn, which overlooks Rickling village green, date from the 16th century. Real ales and imaginative food are available in the character bar and smart modern restaurant. In warm weather you can enjoy a drink on the landscaped decking area. Bedrooms, furnished in an understated colonial style, are well equipped.

Facilities 9 en suite (3 fmly) (2 GF) ⊗ in bedrooms ⊗ in dining room STV TVB tea/coffee Direct dial from bedrooms ✝ Cen ht Dinner Last d 9.30pm **Prices** S £65; D £95-£120✳ **Conf** Max 12 Board 12 **Parking** 40

◆◆◆◆

Rowley Hill Lodge

Little Walden CB10 1UZ ☎ 01799 525975 📠 01799 516622
e-mail rhlbandb@onetel.com
Dir 1.25m N of town centre on B1052. On left, establishment has three tall chimneys

Lovingly operated by the resident proprietors, this extended Victorian lodge stands in immaculate gardens. Bedrooms are well equipped and homely with pretty decor. Tasty English breakfasts are served at a family table in the elegant dining room, and a comfortable lounge is also available.

Facilities 2 en suite ⊗ TVB tea/coffee ✝ Cen ht TVL No coaches **Parking** 4 **Notes** ⊛

SOUTHEND-ON-SEA   MAP 07 TQ88

◆◆◆◆

Ilfracombe House Hotel

9-13 Wilson Rd SS1 1HG
☎ 01702 351000 📄 01702 393989
e-mail info@ilfracombehotel.co.uk
web www.ilfracombehotel.co.uk
Dir *A13 towards town centre, turn at Cricketers pub onto Milton Rd, 3rd left onto Cambridge Rd, 4th right. Car park in Alexandra Rd*

Ilfracombe House lies in Southend's conservation area, just a short walk from the cliffs, gardens and the beach. The public rooms include a dining room, lounge and a cosy bar, and the well-equipped bedrooms include deluxe options and three superb suites.

Facilities 20 en suite (3 fmly) (2 GF) ⊗ in 6 bedrooms ⊗ in dining room ⊗ in 1 lounge STV FTV TVB tea/coffee Direct dial from bedrooms Licensed Cen ht TVL Dinner Last d 7pm **Prices** S £44-£54; D £64-£84 **LB Parking** 9

◆◆◆

Terrace Hotel

8 Royal Ter SS1 1DY ☎ 01702 348143 📄 01702 348143
e-mail info@theterracehotel.co.uk
Dir *From pier up Pier Hill onto Royal Ter*

Set on a terrace above Western Esplanade, this comfortable guest house has an informal atmosphere. There is a cosy bar, and an elegant sitting room and breakfast room. The spacious, well-planned bedrooms consist of en suite front and rear-facing rooms, and front-facing rooms that share two bathrooms.

Facilities 9 rms (6 en suite) (2 fmly) ⊗ in 3 bedrooms ⊗ in dining room ⊗ in lounges TVB tea/coffee Cen ht TVL No coaches **Prices** S fr £29.60; d fr £44.65✳ **LB Notes** Closed 21 Dec-4 Jan

STANSTED AIRPORT   MAP 06 TL52

See also **Braintree & Bishops Stortford (Hertfordshire)**

◆◆◆◆

The White House

Smiths Gn CM22 6NR ☎ 01279 870257 📄 01279 870423
e-mail enquiries@whitehousestansted.co.uk
web www.whitehousestansted.co.uk
Dir *400yds E of Takeley village x-rds on corner of B1256 & Smiths Green*

This carefully refurbished family home, just 1m from Stansted Airport, combines original 16th-century features with modern comforts. The spacious bedrooms have large beds and luxurious bathrooms. Breakfast is served around one table in the farmhouse-style kitchen. A range of interesting dishes, using quality local ingredients, is available in a nearby inn under the same ownership.

Facilities 3 rms (2 en suite) (1 pri facs) (3 fmly) ⊗ TVB tea/coffee ✖ Cen ht No coaches Dinner Last d 10pm **Prices** S £60; D £65✳ **Parking** 6 **Notes** Closed 24-25, 31 Dec & 1 Jan

◆◆◆◆

Little Bullocks Farm

Hope End CM22 6TA ☎ 01279 870464 📄 01279 871430
e-mail julie@waterman-farm.demon.co.uk
Dir *M11 junct 8, B1256 to Takeley, over lights, 1st right to Hope End, left at triangle island, on left at bottom of lane*

Expect a friendly welcome at this pleasant, family-run guest house, which is situated in a peaceful rural location just a short drive from the M11 and Stansted Airport. The spacious bedrooms are cheerfully decorated, with coordinated soft furnishings and many thoughtful touches. Breakfast is served at individual tables in the smart dining room.

Facilities 4 en suite (2 fmly) (4 GF) ⊗ TVB tea/coffee ✖ Cen ht TVL No coaches **Prices** S £45-£55; D £50-£55✳ **Parking** 15 **Notes** ⊛

♦♦♦♦ ❦

Warish Hall Farm *(TL569222)*

CM22 6NZ ☎ 01279 870275 📠 01279 870571 Mr Brolly
e-mail warishbb@hotmail.com
Dir *Off B1256 towards Bambers Green, 0.5m on left*

The delightful Grade I listed moated manor house dates from the late 13th century. The property is set amid mature landscaped gardens and forms part of a 500 acre arable farm. Public rooms include a choice of lounges and breakfast is served in the smart dining room.

Facilities 2 en suite (1 fmly) ⊗ TVB tea/coffee Cen ht TVL ⚲ 📠 560 acres arable Dinner Last d Previous day **Prices** S £40-£45; D £50-£60✱ **Parking** 8 **Notes** ⊠

THAXTED   MAP 12 TL63

♦♦♦♦

Thaxted Bed & Breakfast

Totmans Farm, Dunmow Rd CM6 2LU
☎ 01371 830233 📠 01371 831545
e-mail stay@thaxtedandstanstedbandb.co.uk
web www.thaxtedandstanstedbandb.co.uk
Dir *On brow of B184 at S end of Thaxted*

There is a warm welcome at this charming property situated just a short drive from Stansted airport and close to major routes. The spacious, thoughtfully equipped bedrooms are in a converted outbuilding; each room has a separate lounge-dining area and a door to the communal west-facing conservatory.

Facilities 5 en suite (1 fmly) (1 GF) ⊗ TVB tea/coffee 🐾 Cen ht TVL No coaches **Prices** S £45-£50; D £60-£70✱ **LB** **Parking** 5

THORPE BAY   MAP 07 TQ98
See **Southend-on-Sea**

TOPPESFIELD   MAP 12 TL73

♦♦♦ ❦

Ollivers Farm *(TL754370)*

Toppesfield CO9 4LS
☎ 01787 237642 📠 01787 237602 Mrs Blackie
e-mail bandbolliversfarm@tesco.net
web www.essex-bed-breakfast.co.uk
Dir *A1017 N, left after White Hart pub in Gt Yeldham, right, farm 1.5m on left, last driveway before T-junct to village*

An impressive 16th-century farmhouse full of character set amid pretty landscaped gardens in a peaceful rural location. Bedrooms are pleasantly decorated and thoughtfully equipped. Public rooms have a wealth of original features including exposed beams and a huge open fireplace in the reception hall.

Facilities 2 rms (1 en suite) (1 pri facs) ⊗ TVB tea/coffee 🐾 No children 10yrs **Prices** D £55.60-£60✱ **Parking** 4 **Notes** Closed 23 Dec-1 Jan ⊠

WALTON ON THE NAZE   MAP 07 TM22

♦♦♦

Regency House

45 The Parade CO14 8AS
☎ 01255 676300 📠 01255 676300
e-mail enquiries@regency-hotel-uk.com
web www.regency-hotel-uk.com
Dir *On seafront near pier*

Situated on the seafront opposite the pier and the beach and just a short walk from the town centre. Bedrooms are pleasantly decorated and thoughtfully equipped; some rooms have lovely sea views. Public rooms include a cosy lounge bar and a smart dining room.

Facilities 8 en suite (3 fmly) ⊗ in bedrooms ⊗ in dining room TVB tea/coffee 🐾 Licensed Cen ht TVL No coaches **Notes** Closed 24-31 Dec

---

WESTCLIFF-ON-SEA   MAP 07 TQ88
See **Southend-on-Sea**

WITHAM   MAP 07 TL81

♦♦♦♦ ❦

The Granary *(TL847181)*

Clarks Farm, Cranes Ln, Kelvedon CO5 9AY
☎ 01376 570321 📠 01376 570321 Mr & Mrs Cullen
e-mail enquiries@thegranary.me.uk
web www.thegranary.me.uk
Dir *3m N of Witham. A12 N onto B1024 towards Kelvedon, 1st left & follow signs*

Clarks Farm is in open countryside on the outskirts of the quiet Essex town of Kelvedon. The spacious bedrooms are in converted farm buildings next to the main property, and each room is furnished in pine and equipped with many thoughtful touches. Breakfast is served at individual tables in the farmhouse.

Facilities 5 en suite (1 fmly) (5 GF) ⊗ TVB tea/coffee 🐾 Cen ht 370 acres arable **Prices** S £34-£70; D £55-£75✱ **Parking** 10

WIX   MAP 13 TM12

Premier Collection

♦♦♦♦♦ ❦

Dairy House Farm *(TM148293)*

Bradfield Rd CO11 2SR
☎ 01255 870322 📠 01255 870186 Mrs Whitworth
e-mail bridgetwhitworth@hotmail.com
web www.dairyhousefarm.info
Dir *Off A120 into Wix, turn at x-rds to Bradfield, farm 1m on left*

This Georgian house stands amid 700 acres of arable land, with stunning views of the surrounding countryside. Renovated in the Victorian period, it still retains original decorative tiled floors, moulded cornices and marble fireplaces. The spacious bedrooms are carefully furnished and equipped with many thoughtful touches. Breakfast is served in the elegant antique-furnished dining room and there is a cosy lounge.

Facilities 2 en suite ⊗ TVB tea/coffee 🐾 Cen ht TVL No children 12yrs 📠 700 acres arable, fruit **Prices** S £35-£38; D £53-£58✱ **Parking** 8 **Notes** ⊠

GLOUCESTERSHIRE

ALMONDSBURY
MAP 04 ST68

◆◆◆◆

Harts House
Gloucester Rd BS32 4JB ☎ 01454 625494 ▤ 01454 616665
e-mail alex@harts-house.co.uk
web www.harts-house.co.uk
Dir M5 junct 16, A38 to Thornbury, Harts House 1.5m, past Murco station

Situated in 10 acres of peaceful gardens and grounds, yet convenient for major routes, Harts House offers a warm welcome. Bedrooms are comfortably furnished and include some welcome extras. Breakfast is served around one large table, and on cooler evenings a log fire burns in the spacious, relaxing lounge.

Facilities 6 rms (4 en suite) (1 fmly) (2 GF) ⊗ TVB tea/coffee ✗ Cen ht TVL No children No coaches ⟐ **Prices** S fr £45; d fr £65✳ **LB** **Parking** 20

ALVINGTON
MAP 04 SO60

◆◆◆◆

Severn Lodge
Church Ln GL15 6BQ
☎ 01594 528289 & 07715 608690 ▤ 01594 528287
e-mail severnlodge@fsmail.net
Dir Off A48 in village centre by speed camera onto Church Ln, B&B 250yds on left

Spectacular views over the Severn estuary and a warm welcome from Mrs Winship and her equally friendly pets can be expected at this lovingly restored house. Public areas include a panelled library-lounge complete with snooker table, and the characterful dining room has memorable views.

Facilities 3 rms (1 en suite) (1 pri facs) ⊗ TV2B tea/coffee ✗ Cen ht TVL No children 6yrs No coaches Riding Snooker Stabling for 3 guest horses 2 Bicycles available **Parking** 6 **Notes** ⊜

ARLINGHAM
MAP 04 SO71

◆◆◆◆ ⊛⊛ ⊜ ◫

The Old Passage Inn
Passage Road GL2 7JR ☎ 01452 740547 ▤ 01452 741871
e-mail oldpassage@ukonline.co.uk
Dir A38 onto B4071 through Arlingham, inn by river

Standing on the site of an ancient river crossing, this former Victorian inn has a stunning location on the banks of the Severn. Renovation has resulted in stylish, lavishly equipped bedrooms, each with a unique colour scheme and personality. The restaurant specialises in excellent seafood and has a strong local following.

Facilities 3 en suite (1 fmly) ⊗ STV TVB tea/coffee Direct dial from bedrooms ✗ No coaches Dinner Last d 9pm **Prices** S £58-£68; D £88-£98✳ **Conf** Max 30 Board 10 Del £100 ✳ **Parking** 40 **Notes** Closed 24-31 Dec rs Sun & Mon evenings

BERKELEY
MAP 04 ST69

◆◆◆ ◫

The Malt House
22 Marybrook St GL13 9BA
☎ 01453 511177 ▤ 01453 810257
e-mail the-malthouse@btconnect.com
web www.themalthouse.uk.com
Dir A38 into Berkeley, at town hall follow road to right, premises on right past hospital & opp school

Well located for business and leisure, this family-run inn has a convivial atmosphere. Bedrooms are soundly appointed while public areas include a choice of bars, a skittle alley and an attractive restaurant. Local attractions include Berkeley Castle and the Slimbridge Wildfowl and Wetlands Trust.

Facilities 11 rms (9 en suite) (2 fmly) ⊗ in 9 bedrooms ⊗ in dining room ⊗ in 1 lounge TVB tea/coffee ✗ Cen ht Pool Table Skittle Alley Dinner Last d 9pm **Prices** S £35-£58; D £70-£75✳ **LB** **Parking** 30

BIBURY
MAP 05 SP10

◆◆◆◆

Cotteswold House
Arlington GL7 5ND ☎ 01285 740609 ▤ 01285 740609
e-mail enquiries@cotteswoldhouse.org.uk
web www.cotteswoldhouse.org.uk
Dir On B4425 500yds W of village centre

Convenient for exploring the Cotswolds, Cotteswold House offers a warm welcome and high levels of comfort and quality. The spacious bedrooms are equipped with thoughtful extras, and there is a cosy lounge with useful local information. This is a non-smoking establishment.

Facilities 3 en suite ⊗ TVB tea/coffee ✗ Cen ht No coaches **Prices** S £35-£45; D £52-£62✳ **LB** **Parking** 3

BIRDWOOD
MAP 10 SO71

◆◆◆ ◫

The Kings Head ◇
GL19 3EF ☎ 01452 750348 ▤ 01452 750348
Dir On A40 in village

This attractive roadside inn offers attractive, bright bedrooms, two of which have patios. The spacious public areas are themed with military

continued

memorabilia, and the cosy dining room is the setting for breakfast and popular bar meals.

Facilities 6 en suite (1 fmly) ⊘ in dining room TVB tea/coffee ✈ Cen ht TVL Golf 9 Pool Table Dinner Last d 9pm **Prices** S fr £30; d fr £46 **Conf** Max 70 **Parking** 100 **Notes** Closed 24-26 Dec

BLAKENEY
MAP 04 SO60

◆◆◆◆

Old Nibley Farmhouse ◇

Nibley Hill GL15 4DB ☎ 01594 516770 & 07989 575855
e-mail enquiries@oldnibleyfarmhouse.co.uk
Dir On A48 S of Blakeney, opp T-junct, signed Parkend

Dating back some 200 years, this former farmhouse has been imaginatively refurbished to provide accommodation of quality and character. Bedrooms and bathrooms are individually styled, with original features cleverly incorporated with modern comforts to great effect. The spacious beamed lounge features an impressive open fireplace. Breakfast (and dinner by arrangement) is served in the dining room using local produce whenever possible.

Facilities 4 rms (2 en suite) (1 GF) ⊘ tea/coffee Cen ht TVL No children 12yrs No coaches Dinner Last d 24hrs notice **Prices** S £30-£40; D £60-£80 **Parking** 4 **Notes** rs Nov-Dec

◆◆◆◆

Viney Hill Country

Lower Viney Hill GL15 4LT
☎ 01594 516000 📄 01594 516018
e-mail info@vineyhill.com
web www.vineyhill.com
Dir 2.5m from Lydney off A48 signed Viney Hill

Built in 1741, the house stands in mature gardens and has been renovated to provide homey accommodation. There is a choice of comfortable lounges, and a spacious dining room where breakfast (and dinner by arrangement) is served. This is a good base for exploring the Forest of Dean and the Wye valley.

Facilities 7 en suite (1 fmly) (1 GF) ⊘ TVB tea/coffee ✈ Licensed Cen ht TVL No coaches Dinner Last d 9am **Prices** D £50-£70✳ LB **Parking** 7 **Notes** Closed Xmas

BLOCKLEY
MAP 10 SP13

Premier Collection

◆◆◆◆◆

Lower Brook House

Lower St GL56 9DS ☎ 01386 700024 📄 01386 701400
e-mail info@lowerbrookhouse.com
web www.lowerbrookhouse.com
Dir In village centre

Dating from the 17th century, this enchanting house is a perfect place to relax. Genuine hospitality and attentive service are hallmarks and the bedrooms come in all shapes and sizes. Character abounds in the public areas, with beams, flagstone floors, a huge fireplace and deep stone walls. Enjoy an aperitif in the garden, followed by a skilfully prepared dinner, but leave room for the delicious breakfast.

Facilities 6 en suite ⊘ TVB tea/coffee ✈ Licensed Cen ht No children 10yrs Dinner Last d 9pm **Prices** S £80-£165; D £95-£165✳ **Parking** 8

◆◆◆◆

Arreton House

Station Rd GL56 9DT ☎ 01386 701077 📄 01386 701077
e-mail bandb@arreton.demon.co.uk
web www.arreton.demon.co.uk
Dir In village centre opp Great Western pub

With a mellow Cotswold-stone exterior, Arreton House dates from the 17th century and has genuine and hospitable proprietors. There is an engaging homeliness throughout with quality bedrooms filled with a wealth of thoughtful extras. Breakfasts using local and home-made produce are served in the cosy dining room or on the pretty patio.

Facilities 3 en suite ⊘ TVB tea/coffee ✈ Cen ht TVL No children 4yrs No coaches **Prices** S £40-£45; D £50-£56✳ LB **Parking** 6 **Notes** ⊜

BOURTON-ON-THE-WATER
MAP 10 SP12

◆◆◆◆

Coombe House

Rissington Rd GL54 2DT ☎ 01451 821966 📄 01451 810477
e-mail info@coombehouse.net
web www.coombehouse.net
Dir Off A429 through village, Coombe House past model village on left

A warm welcome is assured at this immaculate house set in a mature garden. Bedrooms are equipped with a wealth of homely extras and ground-floor rooms are available. Facilities include a comfortable lounge and sun terrace, and breakfast is served in the attractive breakfast room overlooking the flower-filled garden.

Facilities 6 en suite (2 GF) ⊘ TVB tea/coffee ✈ Cen ht TVL No children 12yrs No coaches **Prices** S £50-£65; D £65-£80✳ **Parking** 6 **Notes** rs Dec-Feb

◆◆◆◆

The Ridge Guest House

Whiteshoots Hill GL54 2LE
☎ 01451 820660 & 822448 📄 01451 822448
e-mail info@theridge-guesthouse.co.uk

Attention to detail and a generous welcome are the hallmarks of this large detached house, set in 2 acres of neat grounds. The attractive bedrooms are filled with a host of useful extras, part of the dedication to guest comfort. Breakfast is served in the pretty dining room.

Facilities 5 en suite (2 fmly) (2 GF) ⊘ TVB tea/coffee Cen ht No coaches ⏰ **Prices** S £35-£40; D £60-£75✳ **Parking** 12

BOURTON-ON-THE-WATER continued

◆◆◆◆
Whiteshoots Cottage B & B
Whiteshoots Hill GL54 2LE
☎ 01451 822698 & 07979 507229
e-mail whiteshootscottage@btinternet.com
web www.whiteshoots.co.uk
Dir On A429 0.5m SW of Bourton

A good touring base for the Cotswolds, this former cottage lies next to the ancient Fosse Way and is within walking distance of the village. A purpose-built extension offers three modern bedrooms, and a wholesome breakfast is served in the lounge-dining room.

Facilities 3 rms (3 pri facs) (1 fmly) (1 GF) ⊗ TVB tea/coffee ✖ No coaches **Parking** 10 **Notes** 🚭

◆◆◆
The Cotswold House ◇
Lansdowne GL54 2AR ☎ 01451 822373
e-mail meadowscotswoldhouse@btinternet.com
Dir Off A429 into Lansdowne & continue 0.5m to Cotswold House on right opp Paragon Garage

A warm welcome is assured at this well-maintained, mellow-stone house, just a short walk from the church and the attractions of this popular Cotswold village. Bedrooms are comfortably furnished, and one is a self-contained conversion of the former village telephone exchange, set within immaculate gardens.

Facilities 3 en suite 1 annexe en suite (1 fmly) ⊗ in dining room ⊗ in 1 lounge TVB tea/coffee ✖ Cen ht TVL No coaches
Prices S £30-£50; D £50-£65 **LB** **Parking** 5 **Notes** 🚭

◆◆◆
Strathspey
Lansdowne GL54 2AR ☎ 01451 810321 & 07889 491993
e-mail information@strathspey.org.uk
web www.strathspey.org.uk
Dir Off A429 into Lansdowne, 200yds on right

This friendly Edwardian-style cottage is just a short riverside walk from the charming village centre, perfume factory and the famous model village. Bedrooms are well presented with many useful extras, and substantial breakfasts are part of the caring hospitality.

Facilities 2 en suite 1 annexe en suite (1 fmly) (1 GF) ⊗ in 2 bedrooms ⊗ in dining room ⊗ in lounges TVB tea/coffee Cen ht TVL No coaches
Prices S fr £35; d fr £50✱ **LB** **Parking** 4 **Notes** 🚭

Ⓤ
Larks Rise
Old Gloucester Rd GL54 3BH
☎ 01451 822613 & 07884 438498
e-mail larks.rise@virgn.net
Dir A249 onto A436 (Old Gloucester Rd). Larks Rise is 1st driveway on left

At the time of going to press the rating for this establishment had not been confirmed. Please check the AA website www.theAA.com for up-to-date information.

Facilities 2 rms (1 en suite) (1 pri facs) (1 GF) ⊗ TVB tea/coffee ✖ Cen ht No children 12yrs No coaches **Parking** 6 **Notes** 🚭

CHELTENHAM   MAP 10 SO92

Premier Collection

◆◆◆◆◆
Cleeve Hill House
Cleeve Hill GL52 3PR ☎ 01242 672052 📠 01242 679969
e-mail info@cleevehill-hotel.co.uk
Dir 3m N of Cheltenham on B4632

Set on an elevated location north of Cheltenham, this elegant Edwardian house offers individually styled bedrooms, including a four-poster and a ground-floor room. Attention to detail is evident in the carefully chosen homey extras. The deep sofas, superb decor and soft furnishings in the spacious lounges provide a relaxed atmosphere. A bar service is available, and quality breakfasts are served in a conservatory that looks out over countryside to the Malvern Hills.

Facilities 8 en suite (1 GF) ⊗ TVB tea/coffee Direct dial from bedrooms ✖ Licensed Cen ht No children 6yrs No coaches **Parking** 10

Premier Collection

◆◆◆◆◆
Georgian House
77 Montpellier Ter GL50 1XA
☎ 01242 515577 📠 01242 545929
e-mail penny@georgianhouse.net
web www.georgianhouse.net
Dir M5 junct 11, A40 into town centre & onto Montpellier Ter, Georgian House on right after park

Dating from 1807, this elegant Georgian house is in the fashionable area of Montpellier. Renovation has resulted in delightful accommodation with quality and comfort throughout. Bedrooms are individually styled, with contemporary comforts cleverly interwoven with period furnishings. Warm hospitality and attentive service ensure a memorable stay.

Facilities 3 en suite ⊗ STV TVB tea/coffee Direct dial from bedrooms ✖ Cen ht No children 16yrs No coaches **Prices** S £55-£65; D £80-£90 **Parking** 2 **Notes** Closed Xmas & New Year

♦♦♦♦

Beaumont House

56 Shurdington Rd GL53 0JE
☎ 01242 223311 🖷 01242 520044
e-mail reservations@bhhotel.co.uk
web www.bhhotel.co.uk
Dir S side of town on A46 to Stroud

Built as a private residence, this popular establishment exudes genteel charm. Public areas include a large lounge, an elegant dining room that overlooks the garden, and a new conservatory. The spacious, well-equipped bedrooms are named after racehorses and those situated to the rear of the building have views of Leckhampton Hill.

Facilities 16 en suite (3 fmly) ⊘ STV FTV TVB tea/coffee Direct dial from bedrooms 🛪 Licensed Cen ht No children 5yrs No coaches Complimentary entrance to LA Fitness Dinner Last d 8.30pm
Prices S £56-£69; D £79-£149✳ LB **Parking** 16

♦♦♦♦

Butlers

Western Rd GL50 3RN ☎ 01242 570771 🖷 01242 528724
e-mail info@butlers-hotel.co.uk
web www.butlers-hotel.co.uk
Dir M5 junct 11, over 2 rdbts & 2 lights onto Landsdown Rd, left at next lights to end of Christchurch Rd, left at minirdbt onto Malvern Rd, Western Rd 2nd on the right

This elegant Regency house has a quiet location only a stroll from the Promenade, Montpellier and the town centre. Decor and furnishings are stylish, and the spacious, elegant bedrooms (named after butlers from literature and history) are extremely well equipped, and all have PCs. Public rooms include an inviting sitting room and a charming breakfast room that overlooks the delightful rear garden.

Facilities 6 en suite (2 fmly) (1 GF) ⊘ TVB tea/coffee Direct dial from bedrooms Licensed Cen ht TVL No children 5yrs No coaches Free wifi broadband **Prices** S £50-£65; D £75-£120✳ **Parking** 7

♦♦♦♦

Badger Towers at Beechworth Lawn

133 Hales Rd GL52 6ST ☎ 01242 522583 🖷 01242 574800
e-mail MrBadger@BadgerTowers.co.uk
web www.BadgerTowers.co.uk
Dir Off A40 London Rd onto Hales Rd, 0.5m on right

Located in the residential area of Battledown, close to the racecourse, town centre and GCHQ, this elegant Victorian house offers thoughtfully furnished bedrooms, a light and airy breakfast room, and a spacious lounge complete with piano. The well-cooked breakfasts, with an emphasis on local produce, are a satisfying start to the day.

Facilities 7 en suite (1 fmly) (2 GF) ⊘ FTV TVB tea/coffee Cen ht TVL No coaches **Prices** S £45-£55; D £60-£100 LB **Parking** 10

♦♦♦♦

The Battledown

125 Hales Rd GL52 6ST ☎ 01242 233881 🖷 01242 704219
e-mail battledown125@hotmail.com
Dir 0.5m E of town centre. A40 onto B4075, 0.5m on right

This elegant and well-proportioned Grade II listed house offers comfortable accommodation close to the town centre and racecourse. The refurbished bedrooms retain a homey feel, and the smart dining room is an attractive setting for breakfast.

Facilities 7 en suite (1 fmly) ⊘ TVB tea/coffee 🛪 Cen ht No coaches LB **Parking** 7 **Notes** Closed Xmas

♦♦♦♦

Cheltenham Lawn and Pitville Gallery ◇

5 Pittville Lawn GL52 2BE ☎ 01242 526638
e-mail anthea.miller@cheltenhamlawn.com
Dir From town centre onto A435 Evesham Rd, right onto Wellington Rd, Pittville Lawn 1st right

Quietly located on the edge of town in the attractive Pittville area, this Grade II listed Regency house with an art gallery offers well-equipped bedrooms with wireless Internet access. A spacious lounge is available and parking permits are provided. Breakfasts are totally vegetarian, using local organic produce when available and local free-range eggs.

Facilities 7 rms (5 en suite) (2 fmly) ⊘ TVB tea/coffee 🛪 Cen ht TVL No coaches **Prices** S £27-£45; D £70-£85✳ **Conf** Max 12 Class 12 **Notes** Closed Xmas & New Year

England

CHELTENHAM continued

◆◆◆◆

Moorend Park

Moorend Park Rd GL53 0LA
☎ 01242 224441 📠 01242 572413
e-mail moorendpark@freeuk.com
Dir On A46 1m S from centre

A warm welcome is extended at this elegant Victorian house, located a short distance from the town centre. All bedrooms are neatly presented, bright and spacious, and suitably equipped for business and leisure. Delicious breakfasts are served in the spacious dining room, and there is also a cosy bar and a peaceful reading lounge.

Facilities 9 en suite (2 fmly) ⊗ TVB tea/coffee Direct dial from bedrooms 🐾 Licensed Cen ht No coaches **Prices** S £56-£62; D £72-£92 **LB Conf** Max 25 Class 25 Board 25 **Parking** 20 **Notes** Closed Xmas/New Year

◆◆◆◆

White Lodge

Hatherley Ln GL51 6SH ☎ 01242 242347
e-mail pamela@whitelodgebandb.wanadoo.co.uk
Dir M5 junct 11, A40 to Cheltenham, 1st rdbt 4th exit Hatherley Ln, White Lodge 1st on right

Built around 1900, this friendly establishment is convenient for the M5. Bedrooms offer good levels of comfort and quality, and the extra facilities include fridges. The dining room looks out across extensive gardens, a pleasant backdrop to the enjoyable, tasty breakfast.

Facilities 3 en suite (1 GF) ⊗ FTV TVB tea/coffee Cen ht No coaches **Prices** S fr £35; d fr £50 **Parking** 6 **Notes** 🐾

◆◆◆◆

Wishmoor House

147 Hales Rd GL52 6TD ☎ 01242 238504 📠 01242 226090
e-mail wishmoor@hotmail.co.uk
Dir A40 onto B4075 Hales Rd signed Prestbury, Racecourse, Crematorium, 0.5m on right

A warm welcome is assured at this Victorian house, which is in a mainly residential area between the town centre and the racecourse. Original interior features are enhanced by the decor and the elegant dining room overlooks a pretty patio garden.

Facilities 10 rms (9 en suite) (1 pri facs) (1 fmly) ⊗ TVB tea/coffee 🐾 Cen ht No coaches **Conf** Thtr 10 Class 10 Board 10 **Parking** 8

◆◆◆

Hope Orchard ◇

Gloucester Rd, Staverton GL51 0TF
☎ 01452 855556 📠 01452 530037
e-mail info@hopeorchard.com
web www.hopeorchard.com
Dir A40 onto B4063 at Arlecourt rdbt, Hope Orchard 1.25m on right

Situated midway between Gloucester and Cheltenham, this is a good base for exploring the area. The comfortable bedrooms are next to the main house, all of which are on the ground floor and have their own separate entrances. There is a large garden and ample off-road parking is available.

Facilities 8 en suite (2 fmly) (8 GF) ⊗ FTV TVB tea/coffee Direct dial from bedrooms Cen ht No coaches **Prices** S £30-£38; D £60✱ **Parking** 10

◆◆◆

Clarence Court Hotel

Clarence Sq GL50 4JR ☎ 01242 580411 📠 01242 224609
e-mail enquiries@clarencecourthotel.co.uk
web www.clarencecourthotel.com

Situated in an attractive, tree-lined Georgian square, this property was once owned by the Duke of Wellington. Sensitive refurbishment is returning the building to its former glory with elegant public rooms reflecting a bygone age. Spacious bedrooms offer ample comfort and quality with many original features. The convenience of the peaceful location is a great asset, only a stroll from the town centre.

Facilities 21 rms (19 en suite) (3 fmly) (7 GF) ⊗ in 15 bedrooms ⊗ in area of dining room TVB tea/coffee Direct dial from bedrooms Licensed Cen ht **Parking** 21

◆◆◆

Lonsdale House ◇

Montpellier Dr GL50 1TX
☎ 01242 232379 📠 01242 232379
e-mail lonsdalehouse@hotmail.com
Dir Off A46 towards Stroud, 0.25m from town centre by Eagle Tower tall building

A warm welcome awaits you at this central guest house with private parking. This Regency property has been renovated and provides comfortable accommodation. Bedrooms range in size, with all featuring homey extras. Breakfast is served in the smart dining room, and a small lounge is available.

Facilities 9 rms (3 en suite) (1 pri facs) (3 fmly) ⊗ TVB tea/coffee 🐾 Cen ht No coaches **Prices** S £30-£44; D £55-£65✱ **Parking** 6

continued

♦♦♦
Montpellier Hotel
33 Montpellier Ter GL50 1UX
☎ 01242 526009 🖨 01242 579793
e-mail montpellierhotel@btopenworld.com
Dir M5 junct 11, A40 to rdbt at Montpellier, over rdbt & 100yds on right

The friendly and welcoming Montpellier forms part of an elegant Georgian terrace overlooking the municipal gardens. This fashionable area of town is convenient for shops, restaurants and amenities. Bedrooms are comfortably furnished with a range of practical extras and thoughtful touches.

Facilities 7 en suite (5 fmly) ⊘ in 3 bedrooms ⊘ in dining room FTV TVB tea/coffee Direct dial from bedrooms ✖ Licensed Cen ht TVL No coaches Dinner Last d 5pm **Prices** S £30-£50; D £45-£70✳ **LB** **Notes** ⊠

♦♦♦
Stray Leaves
282 Gloucester Rd GL51 7AG
☎ 01242 572303 🖨 01242 572303
e-mail strayleaves1@activemail.co.uk
Dir Next to railway station. Take rear entrance for access

This house is on a mainly residential road within easy walking distance of the railway station. The extended semi-detached house has a good selection of homely bedrooms, and public rooms include a lounge and modern dining room that overlook the pretty rear garden.

Facilities 4 en suite (2 fmly) (2 GF) ⊘ in dining room TVB tea/coffee ✖ Cen ht TVL No coaches Dinner Last d 9am **Prices** S £30-£50; D £50-£60✳ **LB** **Parking** 6

♦♦♦ 🅐
Cheltenham Guest House ◈
145 Hewlett Rd GL52 6TS
☎ 01242 521726 🖨 0871 661 4405
e-mail info@cheltenhamguesthouse.biz
Dir A40 London Rd into town, follow GH signs to hospital, Hewlett Rd on right after A&E

Facilities 9 rms (7 en suite) (1 fmly) ⊘ FTV TVB tea/coffee ✖ Cen ht No coaches **Prices** S £30-£40; D £55-£60✳ **Parking** 6

CHIPPING CAMPDEN   MAP 10 SP13
See also **Blockley**

★★★★ ⊛ ⊜ **Inn**
The Kings
The Square GL55 6AW ☎ 01386 840256 🖨 01386 841598
e-mail info@thekingscampden.co.uk
Dir In centre of town square

Located in the historic centre, this Grade II listed late Georgian inn is popular with visitors and locals alike, and the friendly and good-humoured staff contribute to the convivial buzz. Bedrooms offer ample comfort with period features and mod cons combining to stylish effect. Food is a highlight here, the menus offering a range of

flavour-packed dishes, complemented by a particularly good range of wines by the glass.

Facilities 14 en suite (2 fmly) ⊘ in bedrooms ⊘ in dining room TVB tea/coffee Direct dial from bedrooms Last d 2.30pm **Prices** S £75-£95; D £85-£165✳ **LB Conf** Thtr 30 Class 20 Board 20 **Parking** 8

Premier Collection

♦♦♦♦♦ 🏛
The Malt House
Broad Campden GL55 6UU
☎ 01386 840295 🖨 01386 841334
e-mail info@malt-house.co.uk
web www.malt-house.co.uk
Dir 0.8m SE of Chipping Campden in Broad Campden, by church

Formed from the village malt house and adjacent cottages, this beguiling house dates from the 16th century. Original features are mixed with contemporary comforts, and bedrooms have quality soft fabrics and period furniture. There is a choice of lounges, an elegant breakfast room, and a wonderful garden with a croquet lawn and relaxing seating. Dinner by arrangement for large parties only.

Facilities 4 en suite 3 annexe en suite (3 fmly) (1 GF) ⊘ TVB tea/coffee ✖ Licensed Cen ht TVL No coaches 🕸
Prices D £128-£150✳ **Conf** Max 8 Board 8 **Parking** 10 **Notes** Closed 22-28 Dec

♦♦♦♦
Bramley House
6 Aston Rd GL55 6HR ☎ 01386 840066 & 07855 760113
e-mail povey@bramleyhouse.co.uk
web www.bramleyhouse.co.uk
Dir Off High St onto B4081 towards Mickleton, house 0.5m opp cul-de-sac Grevel Ln & post box

A warm welcome and refreshment await you on arrival at Bramley House. With ample off-road parking and just a stroll from the centre of this popular market town, this friendly family home offers attractively coordinated accommodation, with many thoughtful extras. A delicious breakfast, featuring organic produce whenever possible, is served in the charming dining room.

Facilities 2 en suite ⊘ TVB tea/coffee ✖ Cen ht No children 12yrs No coaches **Prices** S £45-£50; D £55-£65✳ **Parking** 3 **Notes** Closed 16 Dec-Jan ⊠

continued

England

CHIPPING CAMPDEN continued

◆◆◆◆

Marnic House

Broad Campden GL55 6UR
☎ 01386 840014 & 841473 🖷 01386 840441
e-mail marnic@zoom.co.uk
Dir *B4081 to Chipping Campden & Broad Campden, Marnic on left entering village*

Located in immaculate gardens in the peaceful hamlet of Broad Campden, this very well-maintained mellow-stone house provides comfortable bedrooms filled with a wealth of homey extras. Imaginative breakfasts are taken at an antique oak table in the elegant dining room, and a spacious and relaxing lounge is available.

Facilities 3 en suite ⊘ TVB tea/coffee 🍴 Cen ht TVL No children 13yrs No coaches **Prices** S £48-£50; D £65-£70 **LB Parking** 4 **Notes** Closed 21 Dec-1 Jan 🖾

◆◆◆◆

Catbrook House

Catbrook GL55 6DE
☎ 01386 841499 & 07731 953365 🖷 01386 849248
e-mail m.klein@virgin.net
web www.chippingcampden.co.uk/catbrook.htm
Dir *B4081 into Chipping Campden, signs for Broad Campden until Catbrook House on right*

Having stunning rural views and just a short walk across meadows from the town centre, this mellow-stone house provides bedrooms filled with homey extras. Imaginative breakfasts are served in the comfortable, traditionally furnished dining room.

Facilities 3 rms (1 en suite) (2 pri facs) ⊘ TV2B tea/coffee 🍴 Cen ht No children 9yrs No coaches **Prices** S fr £40; d fr £50✱ **Parking** 3 **Notes** Closed Xmas 🖾

◆◆◆◆

Holly House

Ebrington GL55 6NL ☎ 01386 593213 🖷 01386 593181
e-mail hutsbybandb@aol.com
web www.hollyhousebandb.co.uk
Dir *B4035 from Chipping Campden towards Shipston on Stour, 0.5m left to Ebrington & signed*

Set in the heart of the pretty Cotswold village of Ebrington, this late Victorian house offers thoughtfully equipped accommodation. Bedrooms are housed in buildings that were formerly used by the local wheelwright, and offer level access, seclusion and privacy. Quality English breakfasts are served in the light and airy dining room. For other meals, the village pub is just a short walk away.

Facilities 2 en suite 1 annexe en suite (1 fmly) (2 GF) ⊘ TVB tea/coffee 🍴 Cen ht No coaches Last d am **Prices** S £40-£65; D £55-£65 **Parking** 5 **Notes** Closed Xmas 🖾

◆◆◆◆ ◧

Lygon Arms Hotel

High St GL55 6HB
☎ 01386 840318 & 840089 🖷 01386 841088
e-mail sandra@lygonarms.co.uk
web www.lygonarms.co.uk
Dir *In town centre near church*

Situated in the heart of this bustling town, the Lygon Arms originates from the 16th century. It is family run, and has an engaging atmosphere and a relaxed and cosy feel. Bedrooms offer a perfect blend of character and contemporary comforts. An extensive menu is served in the bar or dining rooms, and much of the food is locally sourced.

Facilities 6 en suite (1 fmly) ⊘ in bedrooms ⊘ in dining room TVB tea/coffee Direct dial from bedrooms 🍴 Dinner Last d 10pm **Parking** 10

◆◆◆◆ 🐾

Manor Farm *(SP124412)*

Weston Subedge GL55 6QH
☎ 01386 840390 & 07889 108812 🖷 0870 1640638
Mrs King
e-mail lucy@manorfarmbnb.demon.co.uk
web www.manorfarmbnb.demon.co.uk
Dir *2m NW of Chipping Campden. On B4632 in Weston Subedge*

A genuine welcome is extended at this 17th-century Cotswold-stone farmhouse. The welcome also extends to pets, and stabling is available by arrangement. Bedrooms are homely with thoughtful extras. Facilities include a lounge with a wood-burning stove, and an elegant dining room where mouth-watering breakfasts are served.

Facilities 3 en suite ⊘ FTV TVB tea/coffee Cen ht TVL Golf 18 800 acres arable, cattle, horses, sheep **Prices** S £40-£60; D £60✱ **LB Parking** 8

◆◆◆

Milliner's Barn

Church St, Weston Subedge GL55 6QT ☎ 01386 840285
e-mail bridget@millinersbarn.fsnet.co.uk
web www.millinersbarn.fsnet.co.uk
Dir *2m NW of Chipping Campden in Weston Subedge*

This converted 19th-century Cotswold-stone barn stands across the road from the family farmhouse. The bedroom is light and airy with lovely views across open fields, and breakfast is served at the kitchen table hot from the Aga. This is a non-smoking establishment.

Facilities 1 en suite (1 GF) ⊘ TVB tea/coffee 🍴 Cen ht No children No coaches **Prices** S £50-£60; D £60-£70✱ **Parking** 2 **Notes** 🖾

◆◆◆
Stonecroft Bed & Breakfast
Stonecroft, George Ln GL55 6DA ☎ 01386 840486
e-mail info@stonecroft-chippingcampden.co.uk
Quietly located in a residential area just a stroll from the High St, this well-maintained property offers relaxing accommodation. Guests have the key to their own entrance to come and go as they please. Breakfast is served around one large table in the compact but well-furnished dining room.

Facilities 3 en suite ⊗ TVB tea/coffee ✖ Cen ht No children 12yrs No coaches **Prices** S £45-£50; D £58-£60✳ **Parking** 2 **Notes** ⊛

◆◆
Green Cottage Bed & Breakfast
Green Cottage, Park Rd GL55 6EB ☎ 01386 841428
web www.greencottagebandb.co.uk
Dir B4081 into Chipping Campden. Left at t-junct on left passed Volunteer Inn.

This smart house stands in the heart of the town and has a pretty cottage garden. There are shops, pubs and restaurants nearby, and many pleasurable walks go from the doorstep.

Facilities 2 rms (2 pri facs) ⊗ ✖ Cen ht No children 10yrs No coaches **Prices** S £40; D £50 **Notes** rs 18 Oct-3 Nov ⊛

CHIPPING SODBURY
MAP 04 ST78

◆◆◆◆
The Moda Hotel
1 High St BS37 6BA ☎ 01454 312135 ▤ 01454 850090
e-mail enquiries@modahotel.com
web www.modahotel.com
Dir In town centre

This Grade II* listed Georgian house has an imposing position at the top of High St. It has been refurbished to provide modern bedrooms and comfortable public areas while retaining original features. Room facilities include satellite televisions and phones.

Facilities 7 en suite 3 annexe en suite (1 fmly) (3 GF) ⊗ STV TVB tea/coffee Direct dial from bedrooms Licensed Cen ht TVL No coaches Dinner **Prices** S £58.50-£62; D £75-£98✳ **LB** **Conf** Max 20 Thtr 10 Board 10

◆◆◆◆ Ⓐ
Rounceval House Hotel
Rounceval St BS37 6AR ☎ 01454 334410 ▤ 01454 314944
e-mail rouncevalhousehotel@tiscali.co.uk
Dir In town centre at W end of High St

Facilities 10 en suite (1 fmly) (1 GF) ⊗ in bedrooms ⊗ in dining room TVB tea/coffee Direct dial from bedrooms ✖ Licensed Cen ht TVL No coaches **Prices** S £69-£89; D £90-£110✳ **Parking** 7

CIRENCESTER
MAP 05 SP00

◆◆◆◆ ◉ ⊜ ◼
Hare & Hounds
Fosse-Cross, Chedworth GL54 4NN
☎ 01285 720288 & 720488 ▤ 01285 720488
e-mail stay@hareandhoundsinn.com
web www.hareandhoundsinn.com
Dir A419/A417 onto A429 Stow Rd. B&B by speed camera.

This traditional country inn built of Cotswold stone offers delicious home-cooked food in the garden, orangerie or one of the elegant dining rooms. The smart en suite bedrooms surround a peaceful courtyard.

Facilities 10 en suite (8 GF) ⊗ TVB tea/coffee Direct dial from bedrooms ✖ Cen ht Dinner Last d 9.30pm **Parking** 40

COLEFORD
MAP 04 SO51

◆◆◆◆
Chapel Cottage
3 Chapel Rd, Berry Hill GL16 7QY ☎ 01594 836547
e-mail chapelcottagefod@aol.com
Dir Off A4136 at Five Acres onto Park Rd. 1st left, B&B 200yds on left

This lovely 19th-century cottage is well situated for exploring the Forest of Dean. The welcome is genuine with every effort made to ensure a relaxing and comfortable stay. Bedrooms are attractively styled to a high standard with a host of thoughtful extras; the contemporary bathrooms are also of a high quality. Breakfast is a tasty and satisfying feast, served in the light and airy dining room.

Facilities 3 en suite ⊗ TVB tea/coffee ✖ Cen ht No coaches Dinner Last d prior notice needed **Prices** D £60✳ **Parking** 3 **Notes** ⊛

England

COLEFORD continued

◆◆◆◆ ❦

Dryslade Farm (SO581147)

English Bicknor GL16 7PA
☎ 01594 860259 ▤ 01594 860259 Mrs Gwilliam
e-mail daphne@drysladefarm.co.uk
Dir *3m N of Coleford. Off A4136 onto B4432, right towards English Bicknor, farm 1m*

You are warmly welcomed at this 184-acre working farm, which dates from 1780 and has been in the same family for almost 100 years. The en suite bedrooms are attractively furnished in natural pine and are well equipped. The lounge leads onto a conservatory where hearty breakfasts are served. Daphne Gwilliam is a top-twenty finalist for AA Landlady of the Year 2006.

Facilities 3 en suite (1 GF) ⊗ TVB tea/coffee Cen ht TVL 184 acres Beef **Prices** S £35-£40; D £52-£64 **LB Parking** 6 **Notes** 🐾

◆◆◆

Cor Unum ◇

Monmouth Rd, Edge-End GL16 7HB ☎ 01594 837960
e-mail antony@jones3649.freeserve.co.uk
Dir *On A4136 in village of Edge End*

A genuine welcome is assured at this comfortably appointed bungalow located in the heart of the Forest of Dean. Bedrooms are neatly furnished, and the lounge has wonderful views across the garden to the Welsh mountains. Breakfast, served in the cosy dining room, is a tasty and filling start to the day.

Facilities 2 rms (2 GF) ⊗ TVB tea/coffee Cen ht TVL No children Dinner Last d breakfast **Prices** S £23-£40; D £40-£80 **LB Parking** 1 **Notes** 🐾

COWLEY

MAP 10 SO91

Ⓤ ◧

The Green Dragon

Cockleford GL53 9NW ☎ 01242 870271
e-mail green-dragon@buccaneer.co.uk

At the time of going to press the rating for this establishment had not been confirmed. Please check the AA website www.theAA.com for up-to-date information.

Facilities 9 en suite (4 GF) ⊗ in bedrooms TVB tea/coffee Direct dial from bedrooms Cen ht Dinner Last d 10pm **Prices** S £57; D £75-£120✳ **LB Conf** Max 65 Thtr 65 Class 65 Board 65 **Parking** 11

DIDMARTON

MAP 04 ST88

◆◆◆◆ ◧ ◧

The Kings Arms

The Street GL9 1DT ☎ 01454 238245 ▤ 01454 238249
e-mail bookings@kingsarmsdidmarton.co.uk
Dir *In village centre*

Located on the fringes of the Beaufort Estate close to Westonbirt Arboretum, this 17th-century coaching inn has considerable charm, with original features cleverly interwoven with contemporary comforts. Local produce features on the imaginative menu, which can be enjoyed in either of the bars or the attractive restaurant. The comfortable bedrooms are light, bright and neatly presented.

Facilities 4 en suite ⊗ in bedrooms ⊗ in dining room ⊗ in 1 lounge TVB tea/coffee Direct dial from bedrooms ✗ Cen ht Boules pitch Dinner Last d 8.50pm **Prices** D £60-£80✳ **LB Conf** Max 30 Thtr 30 Class 20 Board 24 **Parking** 30

DYMOCK

MAP 10 SO73

◆◆◆◆

Woodcock's Farm

Kempley Gn GL18 2BN ☎ 01531 890156
web www.woodcocksfarm.co.uk
Dir *From M50 junct 3, turn right at Ross Golf Club, turn right at church after 2m, farm 0.5m on right.*

Peacefully located in delightful countryside, this relaxing farmhouse offers one large, comfortably furnished bedroom with a range of useful extras. Off-road parking is available and you are welcome to enjoy the surrounding gardens and the lounge. A number of pubs and restaurants are just a short drive away.

Facilities 1 en suite (1 fmly) ⊗ TVB tea/coffee ✗ Cen ht TVL No children 10yrs No coaches Horse riding **LB Parking** 3 **Notes** 🐾

FORD

MAP 10 SP02

◆◆◆◆ ◧ ◧

The Plough Inn

GL54 5RU ☎ 01386 584215 ▤ 01386 584042
e-mail info@theploughinnatford.co.uk
web www.theploughinnatford.co.uk
Dir *On B4077 in village*

This charming 16th-century inn retains many original features such as cobblestone walls, open fires and beamed ceilings. Many popular

continued

Cotswold towns and villages are within easy reach. Home-cooked food featuring local produce is a highlight. The attractive bedrooms are in a restored stable block across a courtyard, adjacent to the delightful beer garden.

Facilities 3 annexe en suite (2 fmly) ⊗ in bedrooms ⊗ in dining room TVB tea/coffee ✗ Cen ht Dinner Last d 9pm LB **Conf** Max 30 **Parking** 50

GLOUCESTER MAP 10 SO81

See also **Blakeney**

◆◆◆

Brookthorpe Lodge ◇

Stroud Rd, Brookthorpe GL4 0UQ
☎ 01452 812645 📄 01452 812645
e-mail enq@brookthorpelodge.demon.co.uk
Dir 3m S of Gloucester on A4173

Facilities 10 rms (6 en suite) (2 fmly) (3 GF) ⊗ TVB tea/coffee Licensed Cen ht TVL No coaches Dinner Last d 5pm **Prices** S £30-£40; D £55-£60✱ LB **Parking** 15

GUITING POWER MAP 10 SP02

Premier Collection

◆◆◆◆◆ ⊜

Guiting Guest House

Post Office Ln GL54 5TZ ☎ 01451 850470
e-mail info@guitingguesthouse.com
web www.guitingguesthouse.com
Dir In village centre

In keeping with all the surrounding houses, this engaging family home is built of mellow Cotswold stone. Comfortable bedrooms offer both individuality and charm, as do the stylish dining room and snug lounge. Breakfast (and dinner by arrangement) uses excellent local produce whenever possible.

Facilities 3 rms (2 en suite) (1 pri facs) 4 annexe rms (3 en suite) (1 annexe pri facs) (2 GF) ⊗ TVB tea/coffee Cen ht No coaches Dinner Last d 48hrs prior **Prices** S £38.50; D £72-£77✱ **Parking** 3

◆◆◆◆ ◀▮

The Hollow Bottom

Winchcombe Rd GL54 5UX
☎ 01451 850392 📄 01451 850945
e-mail hello@hollowbottom.com
web www.hollowbottom.com
Dir In village centre

Original features have been retained at this inn, located on the edge of this unspoiled Cotswold village and popular with followers of National Hunt racing. Rustic furniture and racing memorabilia add to the atmosphere, and real ales and good food are complemented by warm hospitality.

Facilities 4 en suite (1 fmly) (1 GF) ⊗ in bedrooms ⊗ in dining room TVB tea/coffee Cen ht Dinner Last d 9.30pm **Parking** 12

LAVERTON MAP 10 SP03

◆◆◆◆

Leasow House

Laverton Meadows WR12 7NA
☎ 01386 584526 📄 01386 584596
e-mail leasow@clara.net
web www.leasow.co.uk
Dir 2m SW of Broadway. Off B4632 towards Wormington, 500yds on right

Located in countryside to the south-west of Broadway, this 16th-century former farmhouse has been restored to provide high standards of comfort. Bedrooms have a wealth of extras and the attractive dining room is the setting for comprehensive breakfasts. There is also an elegant library-lounge and a warm welcome is assured.

Facilities 5 en suite 2 annexe en suite (2 fmly) (1 GF) ⊗ TVB tea/coffee Direct dial from bedrooms Cen ht No children 8yrs No coaches **Parking** 10 **Notes** Closed Xmas & New Year

LECHLADE ON THAMES
MAP 05 SU29

◆◆◆◆

Cambrai Lodge ◇

Oak St GL7 3AY ☎ 01367 253173 & 07860 150467
e-mail www.cambrailodge@btconnect.com
web www.cambrailodgeguesthouse.co.uk
Dir In town centre, off High St onto A361 Oak St

This delightful non-smoking house is just a stroll from the centre of the historic market town with its many pubs serving meals. Individually styled bedrooms, some in a pretty cottage across the garden, include a four-poster room and two ground-floor bedrooms. Breakfast is served in the conservatory overlooking the gardens.

Facilities 4 rms (2 en suite) 3 annexe en suite (1 fmly) (2 GF) ⊗ TVB tea/coffee Cen ht No coaches **Prices** S £30-£45; D £50-£65✱ **Parking** 12 **Notes** 🐾

LONGHOPE
MAP 10 SO61

◆◆◆◆ ❦

New House Farm B&B (SO685229)

Barrel Ln, Aston Ingham GL17 0LS
☎ 01452 830484 & 07768 354922 🖳 01452 830484
Ms Smith
e-mail scaldbrain@aol.com
Dir A40 onto B4222, Barrel Ln on right before Aston Ingham

Located in tranquil wooded countryside, this working farm is a good touring base on the Gloucestershire-Herefordshire border. Set in 65 acres, with plenty of sheep and cattle, the welcoming farmhouse will certainly appeal to nature lovers, and there is a comfortable lounge and bar. Breakfast is a good selection of carefully prepared local produce.

Facilities 3 en suite (1 fmly) ⊗ TVB tea/coffee 🎋 Cen ht TVL 🕯 65 acres Sheep woodland Dinner Last d day before **Prices** S £32-£45; D £50-£75✱ **LB** **Conf** Max 15 **Parking** 10 **Notes** rs Xmas & New Year

◆◆◆◆ ❦

The Old Farm (SO683206)

Barrel Ln GL17 0LR ☎ 01452 830252 Ms Rodger
e-mail lucy@the-old-farm.co.uk
Dir 1m N of Longhope. Off A40 N onto Barrel Ln, B&B 300yds on right

This former cider farm, just off the A40, offers some bedrooms in the main house and self-catering cottages in adjacent converted barns. The house has lots of character and the friendly host gives a warm welcome. There is a lounge, and breakfast, featuring home-made items and daily specials, is served in the cosy dining area. Pubs serving food are within walking distance.

Facilities 3 en suite (1 GF) ⊗ TVB tea/coffee Cen ht No children 12yrs 18 acres Mixed **Prices** S £31-£39; D £54-£65✱ **LB** **Parking** 6 **Notes** Closed 20 Dec-4 Jan

MINCHINHAMPTON
MAP 04 SO80

◆◆◆◆

Hyde Wood House

Cirencester Rd GL6 8PE ☎ 01453 885504 🖳 01453 885504
e-mail info@hydewoodhouse.co.uk
web www.hydewoodhouse.co.uk
Dir 1m E of Minchinhampton, house on right

Located within extensive mature grounds, this well-proportioned, mellow-stone house provides bedrooms filled with homey extras. Comprehensive breakfasts are served in the elegant dining room and a spacious comfortable lounge is available. A warm welcome is assured and afternoon tea includes delicious home-made cake.

Facilities 3 en suite ⊗ TVB 🎋 Cen ht TVL No children 14yrs No coaches **Prices** S £40-£50; D £60✱ **LB** **Parking** 6 **Notes** 🐾

England

MORETON-IN-MARSH
MAP 10 SP23

♦♦♦ 🅰

The Bell Inn
High St GL56 0AF ☎ 01608 651688 📠 01608 652195
e-mail keith.pendry@virgin.net
web www.bellinncotswold.com
Dir In town centre beside war memorial

Facilities 2 en suite 3 annexe en suite (3 fmly) (2 GF) ⊗ in area of
dining room TVB tea/coffee Direct dial from bedrooms Licensed Cen ht
Boule Dinner Last d 9pm

See advertisement on this page

NAILSWORTH
MAP 04 ST89

♦♦♦♦

Aaron Farm
Nympsfield Rd GL6 0ET ☎ 01453 833598 📠 01453 833626
e-mail aaronfarm@aol.com
Dir Off A46 at Nailsworth minirdbt onto Spring Hill & Nympsfield Rd.
Farm 1m on left at top of hill

Located on an elevated position on the rural outskirts of town, this
mellow-stone former farmhouse has been extended to provide
spacious bedrooms filled with thoughtful extras. Breakfasts, using local
produce, are served in the cosy dining room and a comfortable
lounge is available.

Facilities 3 en suite ⊗ TVB tea/coffee Cen ht No coaches **Prices** S £35;
D £50-£55 **Parking** 6 **Notes** 🚭

♦♦♦♦

Hazelwood
Church St GL6 0BP ☎ 01453 839304
e-mail karen@hazelwood.me.uk
web www.hazelwood.me.uk
Dir Off A46 in town centre onto A4014 Avening Rd, 1st right

Quietly located just a stroll from the centre of this interesting town,
Hazelwood offers a comfortable and relaxing base for exploring the
Cotswolds. The spacious bedrooms have many thoughtful extras, and
the pleasant garden and off-road parking are welcome benefits.

Facilities 3 rms (2 en suite) (1 pri facs) ⊗ TVB tea/coffee Cen ht
No children 12yrs No coaches **Prices** S £32-£38; D £50-£60 **Parking** 3
Notes 🚭

♦♦♦♦ ◉ ⊜

Heavens Above at The Mad Hatters Restaurant
3 Cossack Sq GL6 0DB ☎ 01453 832615 📠 01453 832615
e-mail mafindlay@waitrose.com
Dir In town centre. Off A46 onto Spring Hill, left onto Old Market

This engaging property lies in the heart of the delightful old mill town.
Genuine hospitality, attentive service and delicious organic food are
just some of the highlights. Above the attractive, bright restaurant are
three spacious, beautiful bedrooms. The thoughtful extra touches
more than compensate for the lack of televisions.

Facilities 3 rms (1 en suite) ⊗ tea/coffee ✖ Licensed Cen ht
No coaches Dinner Last d 9pm **Notes** 🚭

England

NAILSWORTH continued

♦♦♦♦

Highlands

Shortwood GL6 0SJ ☎ 01453 832591 📄 01453 833590

Dir *Off A46 rdbt in Nailsworth onto Nympsfield road, turn left, pass bus station, fork left at Brittania Inn, follow signs for Wallow Green, Highlands opp church*

This friendly guest house occupies a quiet elevated position on the outskirts of Nailsworth. The homely bedrooms are filled with stylish furniture and accessories, and there is a comfortable conservatory-lounge and an attractive breakfast dining room.

Facilities 3 en suite ⊗ TVB tea/coffee ✖ Cen ht TVL No children 8yrs No coaches **LB** **Parking** 3

NAUNTON

MAP 10 SP12

♦♦♦♦

Mill View

2 Mill View GL54 3AF ☎ 01451 850586 📄 01451 850970
e-mail ralph.boult@care4free.net
web www.millviewguesthousecotswolds.com
Dir *Off B4068 to E end of village*

Lying opposite a historic watermill, the house has been extended and modernised to provide every comfort. A warm welcome and attentive care are assured, and one bedroom is equipped for easier access. A good base for walkers or for touring Gloucestershire.

Facilities 3 en suite (1 GF) ⊗ TVB tea/coffee ✖ Cen ht TVL No coaches Dinner Last d 2pm **Prices** S £40-£55; D £55-£70 **LB** **Parking** 4 **Notes** 🐾

NEWENT

MAP 10 SO72

★★★★ ◉◉ **Restaurant with Rooms**

Three Choirs Vineyards

GL18 1LS ☎ 01531 890223 📄 01531 890877
e-mail info@threechoirs.com
web www.threechoirs.com
Dir *On B4215 North of Newent, follow brown tourist signs*

This thriving vineyard goes from strength to strength and is a wonderfully different place to stay. The restaurant, which overlooks the 100-acre estate, has a popular following thanks to well-executed dishes making good use of local produce. Spacious, high-quality bedrooms are equipped with many extras and each opens on to a private patio with wonderful views.

Facilities 8 annexe en suite (2 fmly) (8 GF) ⊗ TVB tea/coffee Direct dial from bedrooms ✖ Licensed Cen ht No coaches Wine tasting Vineyard Tours Dinner Last d 9pm **Prices** S £75-£115; D £95-£115✳ **LB** **Conf** Max 20 Thtr 20 Class 15 Board 20 Del from £125 ✳ **Parking** 8 **Notes** Closed 24 Dec-5 Jan Civ Wed 20

NEWNHAM

MAP 04 SO61

♦♦♦♦

Swan House Guest House ◇

Swan House, High St GL14 1BY
☎ 01594 516504 📄 01594 516177
e-mail stay@swanhousenewnham.co.uk
Dir *On A48 between Gloucester & Chepstow, on Newnham High St*

Please note that this establishment has recently changed hands. This Grade II listed house, dating in part from 1640, stands in the centre of this picturesque village. No two bedrooms are alike, but all present high standards of comfort and quality. Breakfast, and dinner by arrangement, are served in the cosy dining room with local produce used whenever possible. A lounge is also available, complete with honesty bar.

Facilities 5 en suite (1 fmly) (1 GF) ⊗ TVB tea/coffee Cen ht No coaches Dinner Last d 24hrs before **Prices** S £30-£35; D £60-£70✳ **LB** **Parking** 2

If you book on bed, breakfast and evening meal terms, you may find that the tariff includes only the set menu

England

NORTHLEACH

MAP 10 SP11

◆◆◆◆

Northfield Guest House

Cirencester Rd GL54 3JL
☎ 01451 860427 📄 01451 860427
e-mail nrthfield0@aol.com
Dir *Signed off A429 Northleach-Cirencester road, 1m from Northleach lights*

Located south of the historic town, this Cotswold-stone house offers homely bedrooms, two of which have direct access to the immaculate gardens. Tasty eggs from the contented resident hens feature at breakfast, and imaginative dinners are also available, served in the elegant dining room. A comfortable lounge is provided.

Facilities 2 en suite 1 annexe en suite (1 fmly) (3 GF) ⊗ TVB tea/coffee ✕ Cen ht TVL No coaches Dinner Last d 7pm
Prices S £45-£65; D £60-£80 **LB** **Parking** 10 **Notes** Closed 23-31 Dec

◆◆◆◆ ◉◉ ⊜ ◪

The Puesdown Inn

Compton Abdale GL54 4DN
☎ 01451 860262 📄 01451 861262
e-mail inn4food@btopenworld.com
web www.puesdown.cotswoldinns.com
Dir *3m W from Northleach on A40*

A friendly welcome awaits you at this long-established inn, a popular stop-off between Cheltenham and Oxford. The stylish modern restaurant is an enjoyable and informal environment for the accomplished cuisine. Individually designed bedrooms, which are accessed externally, have great appeal and offer high standards of contemporary quality.

Facilities 3 en suite (1 fmly) (3 GF) ⊗ in bedrooms ⊗ in dining room ⊗ in 1 lounge TVB tea/coffee ✕ Cen ht Golf 18 Dinner Last d 10.30pm
Prices D £85-£90✶ **LB** **Conf** Thtr 70 Class 20 Board 20 **Parking** 80

◆◆◆◆ ⊜ ◪

The Wheatsheaf Inn

West End GL54 3EZ ☎ 01451 860244 📄 01451 861037
e-mail info@wsan.co.uk
web www.wsan.co.uk
Dir *In village centre*

Originating from the 16th century, this late Georgian coaching inn is situated in the heart of the Cotswolds. The Wheatsheaf has a great atmosphere and is popular with locals and visitors. Wooden and stone floors and log fires provide charm, and the bedrooms offer good standards of comfort (some have king-size beds). The innovative menu uses quality local produce and fresh fish.

Facilities 8 en suite (1 fmly) ⊗ in bedrooms ⊗ in dining room TVB tea/coffee Direct dial from bedrooms ✕ Cen ht TVL Dinner Last d 9.30pm **Prices** S £50-£60; D £60-£80✶ **Conf** Thtr 22 Class 22 Board 22 Del from £80 ✶ **Parking** 20 **Notes** Civ Wed 150

NORTH NIBLEY

MAP 04 ST79

◆◆◆

Burrows Court

Nibley Gn, Dursley GL11 6AZ ☎ 01453 546230
e-mail burrowscourt@tesco.net
web www.burrowscourt.co.uk
Dir *Turn left off A38 signed Blanchworth, Stinchcombe and North Nibley. Opposite North Nibley sign*

Peacefully located on the edge of this pretty village, Burrows Court is a Grade II listed building. Full of period character, the house dates from the Regency period, with an 18th-century weaving mill. Bedrooms and public areas are furnished in traditional style with a homely atmosphere. Attractions close by include Berkeley Castle and Slimbridge Wildfowl Trust.

Facilities 6 en suite (1 fmly) (1 GF) ⊗ TVB tea/coffee Cen ht No coaches **Prices** S £35-£43; D £52-£64✶ **LB** **Parking** 20 **Notes** Closed Dec-Feb

England

OLD SODBURY

MAP 04 ST78

◆◆◆◆

The Sodbury House Hotel

Badminton Rd BS37 6LU ☎ 01454 312847 📠 01454 273105
e-mail sodburyhouse.hotel@virgin.net
Dir M4 junct 18, A46 N, 2m left onto A432 to Chipping Sodbury,
house 1m on left

This comfortably furnished 19th-century farmhouse stands in 6 acres
of grounds. The bedrooms, located on the ground floor and in
buildings adjacent to the main house, have many extra facilities.
Breakfast is a varied choice served in the spacious breakfast room.

Facilities 6 en suite 9 annexe en suite (2 fmly) (10 GF) ⊗ in bedrooms
⊗ in dining room ⊗ in 1 lounge TVB tea/coffee Direct dial from
bedrooms ✖ Cen ht TVL ⚬ Petanque **Prices** S £50-£56; D £70-£85
Conf Thtr 40 Class 25 Board 20 **Parking** 30 **Notes** Closed 24 Dec-3 Jan

PAINSWICK

MAP 04 SO80

◆◆◆◆ A

Cardynham House

The Cross GL6 6XX ☎ 01452 814006 📠 01452 812321
e-mail info@cardynham.co.uk
web www.cardynham.co.uk
Dir A46 into Painswick, at church onto Victoria Sq, house 100yds on
next junct

Facilities 9 en suite (3 fmly) (2 GF) TVB tea/coffee Direct dial from
bedrooms ✖ Licensed Cen ht No coaches 🏊 Indoor pool exclusive to
one room Dinner Last d 9.30pm (Tue-Sat) **Prices** S £50-£85;
D £69-£175✳ LB

ST BRIAVELS

MAP 04 SO50

◆◆◆◆ 🍴

Prospect Cottage

Lower Wye Valley Rd, Bigsweir GL15 6RR
☎ 01594 530566 📠 01594 530566
e-mail enquiries@prospectcottage.com
web www.prospectcottage.com
Dir A466 between Chepstow & Monmouth, 1m along track adjoining
Bigsweir Bridge traffic lights.

With a peaceful riverside location, this relaxing accommodation will
appeal to guests with an interest in wildlife. A variety of birds can be
observed from the comfortable balcony and there is also a well-

furnished lounge. Friendly and attentive service is a highlight of any
stay, as are the delicious home cooked dinners.

Facilities 3 rms (3 pri facs) ⊗ STV TVB tea/coffee ✖ Cen ht TVL
No children 11yrs No coaches Fishing Dinner Last d 48hrs prior
Prices S fr £45; d fr £60✳ **Parking** 8 **Notes** 🍴

◆◆◆◆

The Florence

Bigsweir GL15 6QQ ☎ 01594 530830 📠 01594 530830
e-mail enquiries@florencehotel.co.uk
Dir On A466 between Monmouth & Chepstow

Located on the Wye valley road, the Florence has delightful views
across the river and stands in over 5 acres of gardens and woodland
walks. Bedrooms come in a range of sizes and styles, with some in the
main house and others in an adjacent cottage. You can enjoy a cream
tea in the garden, a drink in the snug, and choose from a wide
selection of carefully prepared dishes at lunch and dinner.

Facilities 4 en suite 4 annexe en suite (1 fmly) (2 GF) ⊗ TVB
tea/coffee ✖ Licensed Cen ht No children 12yrs No coaches Fishing
Dinner Last d 6.30pm **Prices** S £42.50; D £85✳ LB **Conf** Max 12
Thtr 12 Class 12 Board 12 **Parking** 30

STONEHOUSE

MAP 04 SO80

Premier Collection

◆◆◆◆◆ 🍴 🍴

Grey Cottage

Bath Rd, Leonard Stanley GL10 3LU
☎ 01453 822515 📠 01453 822515
web www.greycottage.ik.com
Dir M5 junct 13, A419. After lights right for Leonard Stanley, left at T-
junct turn, Grey Cottage on right

This beautiful Victorian house stands in well-tended gardens and is
convenient for the Cotswolds and the M5. The friendly approach is at
the heart of the home from home feeling that is a highlight of any
stay here. Bedrooms are well appointed and have a host of extras.
Breakfast and dinner, served in the elegant dining room, are treats.

Facilities 3 rms (2 en suite) (1 pri facs) ⊗ in bedrooms ⊗ in dining
room ⊗ in 1 lounge TVB tea/coffee ✖ Cen ht TVL No children 10yrs
No coaches Dinner Last d on reservation **Prices** S £50-£55; D £60-£75
Parking 7 **Notes** rs May be closed for props holidays 🍴

continued

◆◆◆◆ ❦

Tiled House Farm ◇ *(SO817078)*

GL10 3DF ☎ 01453 822363 ▤ 01453 822363 Mrs Jeffery
e-mail TILEDHOUSEBB@aol.com
Dir *M5 junct 12, B4008 for Stonehouse, 2.5m left for Oxlynch*

Facilities 2 rms (1 en suite) (1 pri facs) (1 GF) ⊘ TVB tea/coffee ✖
Cen ht TVL No children 10yrs 90 acres Dairy **Prices** S £30; D £52-£58✳
Parking 3 **Notes** Closed Dec ⊛

STOW-ON-THE-WOLD

MAP 10 SP12

Premier Collection

◆◆◆◆◆

Rectory Farmhouse

Lower Swell GL54 1LH ☎ 01451 832351
e-mail rectory.farmhouse@cw-warwick.co.uk
Dir *B4068 from Stow-on-the-Wold signed Lower Swell, left before Golden Ball Inn onto private road, farmhouse at end of gravel driveway*

Located in the pretty hamlet of Lower Swell, this 17th-century former farmhouse has been renovated to provide comfortable accommodation with a host of thoughtful extras. Carefully chosen furnishings complement original features and you are assured of a warm welcome and genuine hospitality. Breakfast is served in the kitchen-dining room, or in summer, in the conservatory overlooking the gardens.

Facilities 2 en suite ⊘ TVB tea/coffee ✖ Cen ht TVL No children
16yrs No coaches **Prices** D £85-£90 **Parking** 6 **Notes** ⊛

◆◆◆◆

Crestow House

GL54 1JX ☎ 01451 830969 ▤ 01451 832129
e-mail Fsimonetti@btinternet.com
web www.crestow.co.uk
Dir *Junct A429 & B4068*

The beautiful Victorian manor house stands in peaceful grounds close to the town centre. The beautifully furnished bedrooms are thoughtfully equipped, and the spacious public rooms include an elegant drawing room, a conservatory, and a lovely morning room where hearty breakfasts are served around one large table. A heated outdoor swimming pool and a fitness room are also available.

Facilities 4 en suite ⊘ TVB tea/coffee ✖ Cen ht No children 15yrs
No coaches ⸙ Sauna Gymnasium **Parking** 4 **Notes** Closed Feb

◆◆◆◆ ⌂

The Mews

Fox Ln, Digbeth St GL54 1BN
☎ 01451 831633 & 07979 651644
e-mail enquiries@themewsfoxlane.co.uk
web www.themewsfoxlane.co.uk
Dir *Off Stow Sq onto Digbeth St, left after 2nd speed bump, The Mews on left*

Located down a quiet lane in this popular market town, the Mews offers an impressive standard of accommodation and a warm welcome. The one bedroom is spacious and brimming with generous extras. A delicious breakfast, which features quality local produce and home-made preserves, is enjoyed in the smart dining room.

Facilities 1 en suite (1 fmly) ⊘ TVB tea/coffee ✖ Cen ht TVL
No coaches **Prices** S £40-£50; D £60-£70 **Parking** 1 **Notes** Closed
Xmas, New Year & Feb ⊛

◆◆◆◆

Aston House

Broadwell GL56 0TJ ☎ 01451 830475
e-mail fja@netcomuk.co.uk
web www.astonhouse.net
Dir *A429 from Stow-on-the-Wold towards Moreton-in-Marsh, 1m right at x-rds to Broadwell, Aston House 0.5m on left*

Peacefully located on the edge of the village, this is a good base for exploring the Cotswolds. A genuine welcome is assured and every effort is made to provide a relaxed and enjoyable stay. Great care and attention is the hallmark here, with bedrooms equipped with many thoughtful extras such as electric blankets.

Facilities 3 rms (2 en suite) (1 pri facs) (1 GF) ⊘ TVB tea/coffee ✖
Cen ht No children 10yrs No coaches stairlift **Prices** D £58-£60
Parking 3 **Notes** Closed Nov-Feb ⊛

England

STOW-ON-THE-WOLD continued

◆◆◆◆ ⊜ ◼

Kings Head Inn & Restaurant

The Green, Bledington OX7 6XQ
☎ 01608 658365 📄 01608 658902
e-mail kingshead@orr-ewing.com
web www.kingsheadinn.net
Dir *4m SE off B4450*

Located on the delightful village green near the duck-populated river, this 16th-century inn has spacious public areas with characterful open fires, wobbly floors, beams and wood furnishings. The comfortable restaurant offers excellent dining and the bedrooms have been creatively decorated and well furnished; some rooms are in a converted annexe.

Facilities 6 en suite 6 annexe en suite (3 GF) ⊗ in bedrooms ⊗ in dining room ⊗ in 1 lounge FTV TVB tea/coffee Direct dial from bedrooms ✖ Cen ht TVL No coaches Dinner Last d 9pm Sun-Thur **Prices** S £55-£60; D £70-£125✱ **Parking** 24 **Notes** Closed 25-26 Dec

◆◆◆ ✔

Corsham Field Farmhouse *(SP217249)*

Bledington Rd GL54 1JH
☎ 01451 831750 📄 01451 832247 Mr Smith
e-mail farmhouse@corshamfield.co.uk
Dir *A436 from Stow-on-the-Wold for Chipping Norton, 1m fork right onto B4450 Bledington road, 1st farm on right*

This establishment, which has views of the surrounding countryside from its elevated position, is a popular choice with walking groups and families. The modern bedrooms are practically equipped and located within two separate houses. Enjoyable breakfasts are served in the spacious lounge-dining room. The local pub is just a short walk away and has a reputation for good food.

Facilities 7 rms (5 en suite) (3 fmly) (2 GF) ⊗ TVB tea/coffee ✖ Cen ht 100 acres arable **Prices** D £48-£60 **LB** **Parking** 10 **Notes** ⊛

◆◆◆

Limes

Evesham Rd GL54 1EJ ☎ 01451 830034 📄 01451 830034
e-mail thelimes@zoom.co.uk
Dir *500yds from village centre on A424*

Just a short walk from the village centre, this Victorian house provides a comfortable base from which to explore this beautiful area. Bedroom styles vary, with four-poster and a ground-floor room offered. A warm welcome is extended, and many guests return

continued

regularly. A spacious lounge is available and breakfast is served in the light and airy dining room.

Facilities 4 en suite 1 annexe en suite (1 fmly) (1 GF) ⊗ in bedrooms ⊗ in dining room STV TVB tea/coffee Cen ht TVL No coaches **Prices** S £35-£48; D £48-£52✱ **Parking** 4 **Notes** Closed Xmas/New Year ⊛

STROUD   MAP 04 SO80

◆◆◆◆

Hyde Crest

Cirencester Rd GL6 8PE ☎ 01453 731631
e-mail anthea@hydecrest.demon.co.uk
web www.hydecrest.co.uk
Dir *Off A419, 5m E of Stroud, signed Minchinhampton & Aston Down, house 3rd right opp Ragged Cot pub*

Hyde Crest lies on the edge of the picturesque Cotswold village of Minchinhampton. Bedrooms are carefully decorated and all are on the ground floor, each with private patios. Scrumptious breakfasts are served in the small lounge-dining room.

Facilities 3 en suite (3 GF) ⊗ TVB tea/coffee Cen ht TVL No children 10yrs No coaches **Prices** S £40; D £60✱ **Parking** 6 **Notes** rs Xmas & New Year (no meals available) ⊛

◆◆◆◆ ◮

Hillenvale ◈

The Plain, Whiteshill GL6 6AB
☎ 01453 753441 📄 01453 753441
e-mail bobsue@hillenvale.co.uk
web www.hillenvale.co.uk
Dir *A419 from Stroud to Cainscross, 3rd exit at rdbt, up hill to rdbt and & left up hill, The Plain opp church*

Facilities 3 en suite ⊗ TVB tea/coffee ✖ Cen ht TVL No coaches Dinner Last d 10am **Prices** S £30-£40; D £50-£60✱ **LB** **Parking** 4

◆◆◆

Downfield Hotel

134 Caincross Rd GL5 4HN
☎ 01453 764496 📄 01453 753150
e-mail info@downfieldhotel.co.uk
Dir *1m W on A419 from Stroud*

Located west of the town centre close to the M5, the long-established guest house is ideal for business and leisure. Bedrooms vary in style, and open-plan public areas include a comfortable lounge area,

continued

traditional restaurant, and a convivial bar offering a good range of wines by the glass.

Downfield Hotel

Facilities 21 rms (11 en suite) (4 fmly) ✦ in dining room TVB tea/coffee Direct dial from bedrooms Licensed Cen ht TVL Dinner Last d 8.15pm **Parking** 25

See advertisement on this page

George Inn

Frocester GL10 3TQ ☎ 01453 822302 📠 01453 791612
e-mail enquiries@georgeinn.fsnet.co.uk
web www.georgeinn.co.uk
Dir *M5 junct 13, A419 to Stroud, at rdbt take Easington exit to Frocester. Inn 400yds on right past railway bridge*

Located in the village of Frocester, this popular Georgian posting house retains many original features. Public areas include a superb function suite, while bedrooms offer ample space and comfort. The inn has a good reputation for food, real ale, and traditional hospitality.

Facilities 6 en suite (3 fmly) ✦ in bedrooms ✦ in dining room ✦ in lounges TVB tea/coffee ✖ Cen ht Boules Pitch Dinner Last d 9.30pm **Prices** S £40-£45; D £60-£65✶ **Conf** Thtr 60 Class 40 Board 25 **Parking** 30

TETBURY

MAP 04 ST89

◆◆◆◆

Tavern House

Willesley GL8 8QU ☎ 01666 880444
e-mail robertson@tavernhouse.co.uk
Dir *4m SW of Tetbury. A433 to Willesley, Tavern House set back from road*

Within easy reach of Bath and Bristol, this former staging post and inn, built of local stone, dates from the 17th century. Now restored, the
continued

smart accommodation has bedrooms with spacious en suites. Original features include oak beams, a fine open fireplace and a delightful walled garden.

Facilities 4 en suite ✦ in bedrooms ✦ in dining room ✦ in 1 lounge TVB tea/coffee Direct dial from bedrooms ✖ Licensed Cen ht No coaches Dinner Last d 9pm **Prices** S £45-£85; D £65-£90 **Parking** 12 **Notes** 🚭

◆◆◆

The Bedlodge

Folly Farm, Long Newton GL8 8XA
☎ 01666 502475 📠 01666 502358
e-mail info@gtb.co.uk
web www.gtb.co.uk
Dir *M4 junct 17, B4014 signed Tetbury, on right after Welcome to Tetbury sign*

The Bedlodge is located among rolling countryside just a 10-minute walk from Tetbury. The well-equipped bedrooms are next to a huge tithe barn with pleasant grounds, making this a popular venue for weddings. Breakfast is continental only and refrigerators are provided in the bedroom.

Facilities 16 en suite (2 fmly) (6 GF) ✦ TVB tea/coffee ✖ Cen ht ♫ **Conf** Max 180 Thtr 100 Class 64 Board 65 **Parking** 100 **Notes** Civ Wed 180

England

TEWKESBURY
MAP 10 SO83

◆◆◆◆ ❤

Alstone Fields Farm (SO977336)
Teddington Hands, Stow Rd GL20 8NG
☎ 01242 620592 Ms Rogers
e-mail janeandrobin@yahoo.co.uk
Dir M5 Junct 9. B46 towards Evesham. B4077 off Teddington Hands rdbt 1m right hand side.

A converted farm house set in 160 acres with superb gardens for relaxing in and magnificent views across the Cotswolds. This property is within easy reach of the M5 and close to many popular Cotswold villages. Well-appointed, comfortable bedrooms await you with a good range of extras. Breakfast is well cooked, with good use made of local free-range farm eggs and fresh produce, served in a delightful dining room with panoramic views.

Facilities 6 rms (5 en suite) (1 pri facs) (2 GF) ⊗ TVB tea/coffee ✖ Cen ht No children 12yrs 160 acres Mixed/Horses/Sheep **Prices** S £45; D £60✱ **Parking** 6 **Notes** Closed 25 Dec ⊛

◆◆◆

Willow Cottages
Shuthonger Common GL20 6ED
☎ 01684 298599 🖹 01684 298599
e-mail RobBrd1@aol.com
Dir 1m N of Tewkesbury, on A38, right hand side, or 1m S of M50 junct 1, on A38, left hand side

Located north of Tewkesbury in pretty countryside, this welcoming house offers homely bedrooms with efficient modern bathrooms and a cosy, pine-furnished breakfast room. An excellent base for work or pleasure.

Facilities 3 en suite (1 fmly) ⊗ in bedrooms ⊗ in dining room TVB tea/coffee Cen ht No coaches Dinner Last d noon **Prices** S £32-£35; D £54-£58 LB **Parking** 6 **Notes** ⊛

TIRLEY
MAP 10 SO82

◆◆◆ ❤

Town Street Farm ◇ (SO842291)
GL19 4HG
☎ 01452 780442 & 07762 166974 🖹 01452 780890
Mrs Warner
e-mail townstreetfarm@hotmail.com
Dir Off B4213 at Tirley x-rds for Chaceley, 1st farm on right

Surrounded by 500 acres of rolling farmland, this is a good base for exploring Gloucestershire. Bedrooms are spacious and comfortable with rural views. Hearty breakfasts are served in the conservatory and there are several pubs nearby. Facilities include a lounge and a tennis court.

Facilities 3 en suite (1 fmly) ⊗ in dining room ⊗ in lounges TVB tea/coffee Cen ht TVL ☌ 500 acres beef arable **Prices** S £30-£35; D £56-£60✱ **Parking** 6 **Notes** ⊛

WINCHCOMBE
MAP 10 SP02

★★★★ ⊛⊛ ≘ ☕ **Restaurant with Rooms**

Wesley House
High St GL54 5LJ ☎ 01242 602366 🖹 01242 609046
e-mail enquiries@wesleyhouse.co.uk
web www.wesleyhouse.co.uk
Dir In village centre

A 15th-century, half-timbered property named after John Wesley, founder of the Methodist Church, who stayed here while preaching in the town. A glass atrium has been added to cover the outside terrace, and the bedrooms are comfortably appointed. The lighting system changes colour to suit the mood required and to highlight floral creations by a world-renowned flower arranger.

Facilities 6 en suite ⊗ TVB tea/coffee Direct dial from bedrooms ✖ Licensed Cen ht Dinner Last d 2pm **Prices** S £110-£120; D £150-£200; (incl. dinner) ✱ LB **Notes** Closed 25-26 Dec rs Sun nights Civ Wed 60

England

Premier Collection

Isbourne Manor House

Castle St GL54 5JA ☎ 01242 602281 ▤ 01242 602281
e-mail felicity@isbourne-manor.co.uk
web www.isbourne-manor.co.uk
Dir On B4632 in village centre, onto Castle St & house on left before bridge

Tucked away in quiet gardens and bordered by the River Isbourne, this Grade II listed part-Georgian and part-Elizabethan house is just a short walk from Cotswold countryside and the town. The comfortable and elegant surroundings feature fine furnishings. Bedrooms are individual in character and attention to detail evident throughout. Breakfast uses local and home-made produce.

Facilities 3 rms (2 en suite) (1 pri facs) ⊗ TVB tea/coffee 🐾 Cen ht
No coaches **Prices** S £50-£70; D £70-£90✶ **LB** **Parking** 3 **Notes** Closed 25-26 Dec 🐾

◆◆◆◆ 🛏️ 🐾

Sudeley Hill Farm ◇ (SP038276)

GL54 5JB
☎ 01242 602344 ▤ 01242 602344 Mrs Scudamore
e-mail scudamore4@aol.com
Dir Off B4632 in Winchcombe onto Castle St, White Hart Inn on corner, farm 0.75m on left

Located on an 800-acre mixed arable and sheep farm, this 16th-century mellow-stone farmhouse is full of original features including open fires and exposed beams. Genuine hospitality is always on offer here with a relaxed atmosphere. The comfortable bedrooms are filled with thoughtful extras, and memorable breakfasts are served in the elegant dining room overlooking immaculate gardens.

Facilities 3 en suite (1 fmly) ⊗ in bedrooms ⊗ in dining room TVB tea/coffee 🐾 Cen ht TVL 800 acres sheep arable **Prices** S £30-£40; D £60-£65✶ **Parking** 10 **Notes** Closed Xmas 🐾

◆◆◆◆

Tally Ho Bed & Breakfast

20 Beckford Rd, Alderton GL20 8NL
☎ 01242 621482 & 07980 632375
e-mail tallyhobb@aol.com
Dir 3m NW of Winchcombe. Off B4077 into Alderton village

Convenient for the M5, this friendly establishment stands in a delightful quiet village. Bedrooms, including two on the ground floor,
continued

offer modern comforts and coordinated furnishings. Breakfast is served in the stylish dining room and the village pub is just a stroll away for dinner.

Facilities 3 en suite (1 fmly) (2 GF) ⊗ TVB tea/coffee Cen ht
No coaches **Prices** S £35; D £55-£60 **LB** **Parking** 3 **Notes** 🐾
See advertisement on this page

GREATER LONDON

BRENTFORD
See **London Plan 1 C3**

◆◆◆◆

Primrose House

56 Boston Gdns TW8 9LP ☎ 020 8568 5573
e-mail information@primrosehouse.com
web www.primrosehouse.com
Dir Off A3002 Boston Manor Rd near Boston Manor tube station

A warm welcome is assured at this delightful guest house, set in a quiet residential area convenient for central London and Heathrow by tube or road. The individually styled bedrooms are carefully appointed and feature numerous thoughtful extras. A continental breakfast is served in the dining room overlooking the garden.

Facilities 3 rms (2 en suite) ⊗ FTV TVB tea/coffee 🐾 Cen ht
No coaches **Prices** S £40-£50; D £55-£65 **Parking** 2

England

CRANFORD

See **London Plan 1 A3**
For accommodation details see **Heathrow Airport**

CROYDON

See **London Plan 1 F1**

★★★ 🅰 Guest Accommodation

Woodstock Hotel

30 Woodstock Rd CR0 1JR
☎ 020 8680 1489 🗎 020 8667 1229
e-mail woodstockhotel@tiscali.co.uk
web www.woodstockhotel.co.uk
Dir *At town centre rdbt exit A212, S Croydon onto Park Ln. Woodstock Rd 2nd left.*

Facilities 8 rms (2 en suite) (4 pri facs) (2 fmly) (3 GF) ⊗ TVB tea/coffee 🐾 Cen ht **Prices** S £40-£45; D £70 **LB Parking** 4

◆◆◆◆

Kirkdale Hotel

22 St Peters Rd CR0 1HD
☎ 020 8688 5898 🗎 020 8680 6001
e-mail reservations@kirkdalehotel.co.uk
Dir *A23 onto A232 W & A212 Lower Coombe St, 500yds right*

Close to the town centre, this Victorian property retains many original features. Public areas include a small lounge bar and an attractive breakfast room, and the bedrooms have good facilities. There is a sheltered patio for the summer.

Facilities 19 en suite (4 fmly) (6 GF) ⊗ in bedrooms ⊗ in area of dining room TVB tea/coffee Direct dial from bedrooms 🐾 Cen ht TVL **Prices** S £45-£72; D £65-£80✳ **Conf** Max 12 Thtr 12 Class 10 Board 18 **Parking** 12 **Notes** Closed Xmas & New Year

ENFIELD
MAP 06 TQ39

◆◆◆◆

Oak Lodge

80 Village Rd, Bush Hill Park EN1 2EU ☎ 020 8360 7082
e-mail oaklodge@fsmail.net
web www.oaklodgehotel.co.uk
Dir *1m S of Enfield on A105*

This charming establishment is located in a leafy suburb. Service and hospitality are particularly noteworthy, and the bedrooms come in a variety of styles and sizes, each individually furnished. A ground-floor room with easier access is available. Public areas are inviting and smartly furnished.

Facilities 7 en suite (1 fmly) (1 GF) ⊗ in bedrooms ⊗ in dining room TVB tea/coffee Direct dial from bedrooms Licensed Cen ht No coaches **Prices** S £79.50; D £89.50-£125✳ **Conf** Max 16 Class 16 Board 16 **Parking** 4

FELTHAM

See **London Plan 1 A2**
For accommodation details see **Heathrow Airport**

HARROW

See **London Plan 1 B5**

◆◆◆

Crescent Hotel

58-62 Welldon Crs HA1 1QR
☎ 020 8863 5491 🗎 020 8427 5965
e-mail Jivraj@crsnthtl.demon.co.uk
Dir *A312 onto Headstone Rd, 2nd right onto Hindes Rd, 1st right*

The family-run Crescent is in a quiet residential area in the heart of Harrow. The comfortable accommodation is well equipped with thoughtful extras and the public areas include a cosy lounge and an attractive breakfast room that looks over the large garden.

Facilities 21 rms (16 en suite) (2 fmly) ⊗ in dining room STV TVB tea/coffee Direct dial from bedrooms 🐾 Licensed Cen ht TVL **Parking** 8 **Notes** Closed Xmas

HARROW ON THE HILL

See **London Plan 1 B5**

◆◆◆

Old Etonian Hotel

36-38 High St HA1 3LL
☎ 020 8423 3854 & 8422 8482 🗎 020 8423 1225
e-mail info@oldetonian.com
Dir *In town centre. On B458 opp Harrow School*

Situated opposite the famous school, this friendly guest house is a delight. The redecorated bedrooms are attractive and well appointed. A continental breakfast is served in the dining room, which in the evening is home to a lively restaurant. On-road parking is available.

Facilities 9 en suite (1 GF) ⊗ in bedrooms FTV TVB tea/coffee Direct dial from bedrooms 🐾 Licensed Cen ht No coaches Dinner Last d 10.30pm **Prices** S £55-£65; D £70-£75✳ **Conf** Max 30 Thtr 20 Class 20 Board 20 Del £75 ✳ **Parking** 3

HAYES

See **London Plan 1 A3**
For accommodation details see **Heathrow Airport**

HEATHROW AIRPORT
See **London plan 1 A3**

◆◆◆◆

The Cottage
150-152 High St, Cranford TW5 9WB
☎ 020 8897 1815 📠 020 8897 3117
e-mail bermuthecottage@tinyworld.co.uk
Dir M4 junct 3, A312 towards Feltham, left at lights, left after 1st pub on left Jolly Gardner

This smart, family-run guest house has a peaceful location behind Cranford High St. It's just a short drive from Heathrow and is a good base for visiting Windsor Castle, Hampton Court and the attractions of west London. The attractive bedrooms, some across the garden and reached by a covered walkway, are thoughtfully equipped.
Facilities 17 en suite (2 fmly) (12 GF) ⊗ STV TVB tea/coffee ✖ Cen ht TVL **Parking** 18

See advertisement on this page

◆◆◆◆

Harmondsworth Hall
Summerhouse Ln, Harmondsworth UB7 0BG
☎ 020 8759 1824 & 07713 104229 📠 020 8897 6385
e-mail elaine@harmondsworthhall.com
web www.harmondsworthhall.com
Dir M4 junct 4, A3044 Holloway Ln onto Harmondsworth High St, left after Crown pub

Hidden away in the old part of Harmondsworth village, this delightful property has been restored and converted into a spacious guest house. It is well located for the airport and motorways. Breakfast is served in an attractive panelled dining room overlooking the gardens and there is a spacious lounge. The well-equipped bedrooms are all individually furnished.

continued

Facilities 10 en suite (4 fmly) (2 GF) ⊗ TVB tea/coffee Direct dial from bedrooms Licensed Cen ht TVL No coaches Dinner Last d by arrangement **Prices** S £55-£65; D £65-£75✱ **LB** **Conf** Max 25 Thtr 25 Class 25 Board 15 **Parking** 8

◆◆◆

Shepiston Lodge
31 Shepiston Ln UB3 1LJ
☎ 020 8573 0266 📠 020 8569 2536
e-mail shepistonlodge@aol.com
web www.shepistonlodge.co.uk
Dir M4 junct 4, 1st A408 rdbt onto Shepiston Ln, opp Great Western pub

Located close to Heathrow Airport, the Shepiston Lodge offers smart, well-equipped bedrooms. Public rooms include an informal bar, and a spacious dining room where freshly cooked breakfasts (and dinners by request) are served. Ample secure parking is available.

Facilities 22 en suite (2 fmly) (9 GF) ⊗ in 12 bedrooms ⊗ in dining room ⊗ in 1 lounge FTV TVB tea/coffee ✖ Licensed Cen ht TVL Dinner Last d 6pm **Prices** S £45; D £60✱ **Parking** 20

The Cottage
◆◆◆◆
150–152 HIGH STREET
CRANFORD, HOUNSLOW TW5 9WB
Tel: 020 8897 1815   Fax: 020 8897 3117

email: bermuthecottage@tinyworld.co.uk
web: www.cottageguesthouse-heathrow.co.uk

This beautiful property is a peacefully situated, family run guesthouse, often referred to as an oasis, it offers a taste of the idyllic Surrey countryside.

A very high standard of accommodation – very comfortable and spacious with high standard of housekeeping – all rooms ensuite.

The homely atmosphere extends to public areas – a stylish dining room opening onto a conservatory overlooking the picturesque landscaped garden.

Welcoming hosts are Pedro & Elena Bermudez

England

◆◆

Lampton

47 Lampton Rd TW3 1JG
☎ 020 8570 0056 ▤ 020 8577 1220
e-mail ppadda@talk21.com
web www.paddahotels.com
Dir *On A3005, 50yds from Hounslow Central tube station*

This guest house in the centre of Hounslow provides practical en suite accommodation. The breakfast area is quite compact and sometimes you may have to share a table.

Facilities 20 en suite (4 fmly) (4 GF) ⊛ in 10 bedrooms ⊛ in dining room ⊛ in lounges STV TVB tea/coffee Direct dial from bedrooms ✖ Cen ht ⚲ **Prices** S £40-£48; D £50-£60✳ **Parking** 13

◆◆ 🅰

Civic Guest House ◇

87/93 Lampton Rd TW3 4DP
☎ 020 8572 5107 ▤ 020 8814 0203
e-mail enquiries@civicguesthouse.freeserve.co.uk
web www.civicguesthouse.freeserve.co.uk
Dir *M4 junct 3, A306, left onto A4 towards Hounslow, right at BP station onto A3005 Jersey Rd, right at minirdbt, left at Blackhorse pub, house 0.5m on left*

Facilities 30 rms (16 en suite) (7 fmly) (11 GF) ⊛ STV TVB tea/coffee ✖ Cen ht **Prices** S £30-£40; D £45-£65✳ **Parking** 12

HOUNSLOW

See **London Plan 1 B2**
For accommodation details see under **Heathrow Airport**

ILFORD

See **London Plan 1 H5**

◆◆◆◆

Woodville

10-12 Argyle Rd IG1 3BQ
☎ 020 8478 3779 ▤ 020 8478 6282
e-mail cass@woodville-guesthouse.co.uk
Dir *250yds NW of Ilford station. Off A123 Cranbrook Rd onto York Rd, 2nd right*

Please note that this establishment has recently changed hands. This smart, family-run guest house has a quiet location within walking distance of the railway station with fast links to London. Bedrooms are well appointed and have attractive furnishings. There is a lounge and a bright dining room where hearty breakfasts are served.

Facilities 16 rms (6 en suite) (5 fmly) ⊛ in dining room STV TVB ✖ Cen ht **Parking** 11 **Notes** ⊛

ISLEWORTH

See **London Plan 1 B3**

◆◆◆ 🅰

The Swan

1 Swan St, Lower Sq TW7 6RJ
☎ 020 8847 4805 ▤ 020 8560 4835
Dir *A316 to St Margeret's rdbt, exit to Isleworth, opp Manns Bejing restaurant*

Facilities 5 en suite (1 fmly) ⊛ in bedrooms ⊛ in area of dining room ⊛ in 1 lounge TVB tea/coffee ✖ Licensed Cen ht TVL Pool Table LB **Parking** available

KENTON

See **London Plan 1 C5**

◆◆◆

Brent X Hotel

165 Preston Hill HA3 9UY
☎ 020 8904 9394 ▤ 020 8904 1155
e-mail info@brentxhotel.com
Dir *1m from Wembley stadium and arena*

This renovated house provides comfortable accommodation within easy reach of many attractions, including the new Wembley Stadium, which is visable from some rooms. Bedrooms feature modern decor and amenities, and public areas include a pleasant dining area where breakfast is served. Some off-road parking is available.

Facilities 19 rms (17 en suite) (1 fmly) (6 GF) ⊛ TVB tea/coffee Direct dial from bedrooms ✖ Cen ht No coaches **Prices** S £45-£50; D £50-£65 **Parking** 5

KINGSTON UPON THAMES
See **London Plan 1 C1**

◆◆◆◆

Chase Lodge Hotel
10 Park Rd, Hampton Wick KT1 4AS
☎ 020 8943 1862 📠 020 8943 9363
e-mail info@chaselodgehotel.com
web www.chaselodgehotel.com
Dir A308 onto A310 signed Twickenham, 1st left onto Park Rd

This delightful guest house is set in a quiet residential area, a short walk from Kingston Bridge. The individually decorated rooms vary in size and are all well-appointed and feature a range of useful extras. An attractive lounge-bar-restaurant is provided where lunch and dinner are served. On-road parking is available.

Facilities 6 en suite 5 annexe en suite (2 fmly) (4 GF) ⊘ STV TVB tea/coffee Direct dial from bedrooms Licensed Cen ht No coaches Dinner Last d 8pm **Prices** S £71-£79; D £71-£145 **LB** **Conf** Max 65 Thtr 50 Class 65 Board 30

NORTHWOOD
See **London Plan 1 A6**

◆◆◆

Frithwood House
31 Frithwood Av HA6 3LY
☎ 01923 827864 📠 01923 824720
e-mail frithwood_31@hotmail.com
Dir Off A4125 Watford Rd past RAF & NATO headquarters

This Edwardian property stands in a residential area close to the town centre. The quiet house offers an informal and relaxed environment. Bedrooms are decorated with a homely feel. A television lounge is

continued

available and breakfast is served communally in the kitchen dining room.
Facilities 12 en suite (4 fmly) (3 GF) ⊘ in bedrooms ⊘ in dining room STV TVB Direct dial from bedrooms 🅟 Cen ht TVL **Prices** S £42-£44; D £64-£66✳ **Parking** 10

RICHMOND (UPON THAMES)
See **London Plan 1 C2**

◆◆◆◆◆

Doughty Cottage
142A Richmond Hill TW10 6RN ☎ 020 8332 9434
e-mail mail@doughtycottage.com
Dir 0.5m S of town centre on B321, next to Richmond Hill Hotel

A warm welcome awaits you at this stunning house, set in an Italian walled garden, and having panoramic views from Richmond Hill over the river. Spacious, individually styled bedrooms are beautifully appointed with lots of thoughtful extra touches, some with their own private terrace or balcony. A substantial continental room-service breakfast is included.

Facilities 3 en suite (1 fmly) (2 GF) ⊘ STV TVB tea/coffee Cen ht Dinner **Prices** S £68-£90; D £80-£120✳ **Notes** Closed 24-25 Dec

◆◆◆

Hobart Hall Hotel
43-47 Petersham Rd TW10 6UL
☎ 020 8940 0435 📠 020 8332 2996
e-mail hobarthall@aol.com
Dir 200yds S of Richmond Bridge on A307

Built around 1690, the friendly establishment stands beside the River Thames close to Richmond Bridge. Many of the spacious bedrooms have river views and a good range of modern facilities. There is an impressive reception, a comfortable lounge, an attractive breakfast room, and a meeting room that overlooks the river.

Facilities 33 rms (18 en suite) (5 fmly) (3 GF) ⊘ in bedrooms ⊘ in dining room TVB tea/coffee Direct dial from bedrooms 🅟 Cen ht TVL **Parking** 14

Facilities 9 en suite ⊘ in dining room ⊘ in lounges TVB tea/coffee 🅟 Licensed Cen ht TVL No coaches **Prices** S £36; D £50✳ **Parking** 12

ROMFORD
MAP 06 TQ58

◆◆◆

Havering Guest House
2 Havering Rd RM1 4QU
☎ 01708 732302 & 07949 994105 ▤ 01708 732302
e-mail deethiara@yahoo.co.uk
Dir A12 onto B175, 1st bungalow on right

Expect a warm welcome at this friendly guest house just a short walk from the town centre and railway station. The attractive bedrooms have brightly coordinated furnishings and are thoughtfully equipped; a continental breakfast is placed in the refrigerator in each bedroom. Parking is available at the rear of the building.

Facilities 5 en suite (2 fmly) (5 GF) ⊗ in dining room ⊗ in lounges TVB tea/coffee ✖ Cen ht No coaches **Prices** S £40; D £48✻ **Parking** 7

SURBITON
See **London Plan 1 C1**

◆◆◆

Warwick Lodge
319-321 Ewell Rd KT6 7BX
☎ 020 8296 0516 & 8399 5837 ▤ 020 8296 0517
e-mail warwicklodge@yahoo.co.uk
web www.warwicklodge.co.uk
Dir A3 onto A240 towards Kingston, Warwick Lodge 0.5m on right before police station

Warwick Lodge is a smart guest house convenient for the A3. It offers a variety of rooms, many of which have been comfortably refurbished, with smart bathrooms.

Facilities 19 rms (12 en suite) (4 fmly) (6 GF) ⊗ in 7 bedrooms ⊗ in dining room ⊗ in lounges TVB tea/coffee Direct dial from bedrooms ✖ Cen ht **Prices** S £45-£65; D £65-£78✻ **Parking** 19

SUTTON
MAP 06 TQ26

★★★ Bed & Breakfast

Ashling Tara
50 Rosehill SM1 3EU
☎ 020 8641 6142 & 020 8296 9866 ▤ 020 8644 7872
e-mail info@ashlingtarahotel.com
web www.ashlingtarahotel.com

Situated only a few minutes from Sutton station, and a short walk from the town centre, this is a handy location for business travellers requiring access to the city. Bedrooms are generally spacious with comfortable easy chairs, and the landing has a communal seating area.

Facilities 9 en suite (2 fmly) (4 GF) ⊗ TVB tea/coffee ✖ Cen ht **Parking** 10

WEST DRAYTON
For accommodation details see **Heathrow Airport**

GREATER MANCHESTER

ALTRINCHAM
MAP 15 SJ78

Premier Collection

◆◆◆◆◆

Ash Farm Country House
Park Ln, Little Bollington WA14 4TJ
☎ 0161 929 9290 ▤ 0161 928 5002
e-mail jan@ashfarm97.fsnet.co.uk
web www.ashfarm.co.uk
For full entry see **Manchester Airport**

◆◆

Merton
12 Egerton Rd, Hale WA15 8EE ☎ 0161 980 6618
Dir M56 junct 6, A538 towards Hale, Egerton Rd 2m on right

Close to the attractive village of Hale, Merton offers comfortable accommodation and a friendly atmosphere. There is an attractive lounge where hearty breakfasts are also served.

Facilities 2 rms ⊗ TVB tea/coffee ✖ Cen ht TVL No coaches **Prices** S £24-£26; D £48✻ **Notes** 🐾

BOLTON
MAP 15 SD70

◆◆◆

Broomfield House
33-35 Wigan Rd, Deane BL3 5PX
☎ 01204 61570 ▤ 01204 650932
e-mail chris@broomfield.force9.net
Dir M61 junct 5, A58 to 1st lights, onto A676, premises on right

A friendly relaxed atmosphere prevails at the Broomfield, close to the motorway and west of the town centre. The bedrooms, some suitable for families, have modern facilities, and public areas include a bar and a lounge. The dining room offers good-value dinners and hearty breakfasts.

Facilities 20 en suite (2 fmly) (2 GF) ⊗ in 4 bedrooms ⊗ in dining room TVB tea/coffee Licensed Cen ht TVL Pool Table Dinner Last d 8pm **Prices** S fr £38; d fr £50✻ **Parking** 12

DIGGLE
MAP 16 SE00

★★ Bed & Breakfast

Sunfield Accommodation ◇
Diglea OL3 5LA ☎ 01457 874030
e-mail sunfield.accom@lineone.net
Dir From A670 Oldham to Huddersfield. Turn right towards Diggle Village, right Sam Rd to Diggle Hotel, follow signs for Diggle Ranges.

This friendly, family-run operation is located within easy reach of Manchester and the M62 and has wonderful views over the Pennine. Bedrooms are on the ground floor and pets are made welcome. Breakfast is served at one large table, and good pubs serving food can be found at the bottom of the lane.

Facilities 4 en suite (1 fmly) (4 GF) ⊗ FTV TVB tea/coffee Cen ht TVL No coaches **Prices** S £30-£35; D £45-£50✻ **Parking** 11 **Notes** 🐾

England

HYDE MAP 16 SJ99

◆◆◆ ✿

Needhams Farm (SJ968925)

Uplands Rd, Werneth Low, Gee Cross SK14 3AG
☎ 0161 368 4610 ▤ 0161 367 9106 Mr & Mrs Walsh
e-mail charlotte@needhamsfarm.co.uk

Dir A560 at Gee Cross onto Joel Ln, left onto Werneth Low Rd, 0.5m right onto Uplands Rd

This stone farmhouse has been restored to provide modern accommodation. The well-equipped bedrooms have many personal touches, and there is an open fire in the spacious lounge-dining room. Home cooking is served by arrangement and there is a small bar.

Facilities 7 rms (6 en suite) (1 pri facs) (1 fmly) ⊗ TVB tea/coffee Direct dial from bedrooms Licensed Cen ht TVL Golf 12 Riding 30 acres Non working Dinner Last d 8pm **Prices** S £25-£28; D £40-£44✳ **LB** **Parking** 14

LITTLEBOROUGH MAP 16 SD91

Premier Collection

◆◆◆◆◆

Hollingworth Lake Bed & Breakfast

164 Smithy Bridge Rd OL15 0DB ☎ 01706 376583

Dir M62 junct 21, brown signs to Hollingworth Lake Country Park, at T-junct onto small rdbt, right onto Smithy Bridge Rd, B&B 50yds on right

A warm welcome is assured at this delightful guest house only a short walk from the attractive Hollingworth Lake. Individually decorated bedrooms provide good levels of comfort and a range of thoughtful extras. The annexe accommodation is at the rear in beautiful gardens, and a hearty breakfast is served in the cosy dining room.

Facilities 3 rms (2 en suite) (1 pri facs) 2 annexe en suite (1 fmly) (2 GF) ⊗ TVB tea/coffee Cen ht No coaches **Prices** S £32.50; D £50✳ **Conf** Max 10 **Parking** 8

MANCHESTER MAP 15 SJ89

◆◆◆◆ Ⓐ

The Ascott

6 Half Edge Ln, Eccles M30 9GJ
☎ 0161 950 2453 ▤ 0161 661 7063
e-mail ascottmanchester@talk21.com
web www.ascotthotel.co.uk

Dir M602 junct 2, left onto Wellington Rd, 0.25m right onto Abbey Grove & left onto Half Edge Ln

Facilities 13 rms (8 en suite) (1 pri facs) (1 fmly) (4 GF) ⊗ in bedrooms ⊗ in dining room FTV TVB tea/coffee ✖ Cen ht TVL **Prices** S £45-£95; D £59-£120✳ **Parking** 12 **Notes** Closed Xmas

◆◆◆

The Mitre Hotel

Cathedral Gates M3 1SW
☎ 0161 834 4128 ▤ 0161 839 1646
e-mail paul.schnepper@btopenworld.com
Dir Within the grounds of Manchester Cathedral

This city centre property has an enviable location adjacent to Harvey Nichols, Selfridges, Manchester Cathedral and the MEN Arena. The traditionally furnished bedrooms are well equipped for business and for leisure, and there are conference facilities, two bars, and an attractive cafe.

Facilities 32 rms (26 en suite) (2 fmly) ⊗ in area of dining room STV TVB tea/coffee Direct dial from bedrooms ✖ Licensed Cen ht TVL Dinner **Conf** Max 80 Thtr 80 Class 50 Board 40

◆◆◆

New Central Hotel

144-146 Heywood St, off Cheetham Hill Rd M8 0DF
☎ 0161 205 2169 ▤ 0161 211 9299
e-mail info@newcentralhotel.com
Dir 1.5m N of city centre. Off A665 Cheetham Hill Rd opp Esso station onto Heywood St

Located within easy reach of the city, this refurbished property offer very good hospitality and modern bedrooms. There is a cosy lounge and secure parking, and ample breakfasts are served in the spacious dining room.

Facilities 9 rms (5 en suite) (3 fmly) ⊗ TVB tea/coffee ✖ Cen ht TVL No children 5yrs **Parking** 2

◆◆◆

Thistlewood Hotel

203 Urmston Ln, Stretford M32 9EF
☎ 0161 865 3611 ▤ 0161 866 8133
e-mail iain.campbell30@ntlworld.com
Dir M60 junct 7, A56 towards Stretford, left onto A5181 & Sandy Ln, left onto A5213

This grand Victorian house stands in attractive grounds in a residential area close to the M60, and within easy reach of Old Trafford football and cricket grounds, and the airport. The bedrooms are well equipped, and the public rooms, including a lounge, are spacious and comfortable.

◆◆◆ Ⓐ

Luther King House

Brighton Grove, off Wilmslow Rd M14 5JP
☎ 0161 224 6404 ▤ 0161 248 9201
e-mail reception@lkh.co.uk
web www.lkh.co.uk
Dir S of city centre opp Platt Fields park

Facilities 46 en suite (7 fmly) (6 GF) ⊗ STV TVB tea/coffee Direct dial from bedrooms ✖ Licensed Cen ht Pool Table Dinner Last d 8.30pm **Prices** S £36; D £44✳ **LB Conf** Max 125 Thtr 70 Class 70 Board 54 Del from £44.50 ✳ **Parking** 45 **Notes** Closed 24 Dec-2 Jan Civ Wed 125

England

MANCHESTER continued

♦♦

Clyde Mount Guest House ◇

866 Hyde Rd, Debdale Pk M18 7LH
☎ 0161 231 1515 📠 0161 231 1515
e-mail clydemount@hotmail.co.uk
Dir M60 Junct 24, 1m heading City Centre on A57 opposite Debdale Park.

Guest's are warmly welcomed at this value for money guest house, located just off the M60 and within easy reach of the city centre. Functionally furnished bedrooms are located either in the main property or in a separate house two doors away. Both houses offer private parking and a full cooked breakfast is served.

Facilities 5 rms (3 fmly) ⊗ in dining room TVB tea/coffee ✖ Cen ht No coaches **Prices** S £23; D £42; (room only) ✳ **Parking** 5

MANCHESTER AIRPORT MAP 15 SJ88

Premier Collection

♦♦♦♦♦

Ash Farm Country House

Park Ln, Little Bollington WA14 4TJ
☎ 0161 929 9290 📠 0161 928 5002
e-mail jan@ashfarm97.fsnet.co.uk
web www.ashfarm.co.uk
Dir Off A56 beside Stamford Arms

Ash Farm is an 18th-century farmhouse full of character. The atmosphere is welcoming and the accommodation is of high quality. Several of the rooms have fine period beds and all offer a very good range of extra facilities. There is an attractive lounge and a smart breakfast room with views over the valley.

Facilities 3 rms (2 en suite) ⊗ TVB tea/coffee Direct dial from bedrooms ✖ Licensed Cen ht No children 12yrs No coaches **Prices** S £49-£57; D £72-£79✳ **Parking** 6 **Notes** Closed 22 Dec-5 Jan

♦♦♦

Rylands Farm

Altrincham Rd SK9 4LT
☎ 01625 535646 & 548041 📠 01625 255256
e-mail info@rylandsfarm.com
web www.rylandsfarm.com
Dir M56 junct 6, A538 towards Wilmslow, house 1.5m on left after Wilmslow Moat House

Situated in pretty gardens and convenient for Manchester Airport, this property provides a range of bedrooms, some of which are well furnished and located in a separate building. Breakfast is served in the attractive conservatory-dining room, which also contains a comfortable lounge area with an honesty bar.

Facilities 3 en suite 6 annexe en suite (3 fmly) (3 GF) ⊗ TVB tea/coffee Licensed Cen ht TVL No coaches Dinner Last d 6pm **Prices** S fr £47.50; d fr £54.50 **Conf** Max 30 Class 30 **Parking** 15 **Notes** Closed 24-25 Dec & 31 Dec-1 Jan

MELLOR MAP 16 SJ98

♦♦♦♦ 🐾

The Moorfield Arms

Shiloh Rd SK6 5NE ☎ 0161 427 1580 📠 0161 427 1582
Dir 1m NE of Mellor. Off A6015 towards Mellor, right onto Shiloh Rd, B&B 0.3m on left

Located on an elevated position with stunning views of the surrounding countryside and Kinder Scout, this traditional house has been renovated and extended to provide spacious and comfortable public areas, and carefully furnished modern bedrooms in a converted barn.

Facilities 4 en suite (1 fmly) (3 GF) ⊗ in bedrooms ⊗ in area of dining room TVB tea/coffee ✖ Cen ht Dinner Last d 9.30pm **Prices** D £70-£90✳ **LB Conf** Max 90 Board 90 **Parking** 100

OLDHAM   MAP 16 SD90

◆◆◆◆
Essence of Asia Restaurant with Guest Rooms ◇
792-794 Huddersfield Rd, Austerlands OL4 3QB
☎ 0161 622 1234 ▤ 0161 622 1234
e-mail chondon-miah@hotmail.com
Dir 2m E of Oldham centre on A62

Please note that this establishment has recently changed hands. Surrounded by hills, the restaurant with rooms offers a wide choice of modern dishes and good honest hospitality. Bedrooms are stylish and well equipped, and there is a rear garden with decking.

Facilities 5 rms (4 en suite) (1 fmly) ⊗ in bedrooms ⊗ in dining room ⊗ in 1 lounge TVB tea/coffee ✖ Licensed Cen ht TVL No coaches Solarium Dinner Last d 10.30pm **Prices** S £40; D £60✳ **Conf** Max 40 Class 40 Board 40 **Parking** 11

◆◆◆◆ ◧
The Old Bell Inn
Huddersfield Rd, Delph OL3 5EG
☎ 01457 870130 ▤ 01457 876597
Dir On A62 Oldham-Huddersfield Rd, 100yds on left after x-rds

Situated near the centre of Delph, the stone inn dates from the 1770s and has been renovated by the present owners to provide well-equipped and carefully appointed accommodation. The pleasant public areas are very popular, particularly for the wide range of food available in the restaurant and the bar.

Facilities 14 en suite (3 fmly) ⊗ in dining room TVB tea/coffee Direct dial from bedrooms ✖ Dinner Last d 9.30pm **Prices** S £50-£70; D £85-£100✳ **Conf** Max 40 Thtr 40 Class 24 Board 30 **Parking** 21

ROCHDALE   MAP 16 SD81

◆◆◆◆ ▣
Fernhill Barn B&B and The Brow B&B ◇
Fernhill Ln, Lanehead OL12 6BW
☎ 01706 355671 ▤ 01706 868405
e-mail info@fernhillbarn.com

Dir On B6452 Rochdale Football Ground on right, follow road to T-junct, left up hill for 1m, left onto Fernhill Ln, B&B on left

Facilities 7 en suite (1 fmly) (5 GF) ⊗ FTV TVB tea/coffee Cen ht No coaches **Prices** S fr £27.50; d fr £39.95; (room only) ✳ **LB Conf** Del from £13.50 ✳ **Parking** 12

SALE   MAP 15 SJ79

◆◆◆◆
Brooklands Luxury Lodge ◇
208 Marsland Rd M33 3NE ☎ 0161 973 3283
Dir M60 junct 6, 1.5m on A6144 near Brooklands tram station

This long-established guest house is well located for Manchester Airport, the city centre, Old Trafford and the Trafford Centre. The comfortably furnished accommodation includes a host of thoughtful extras to provide a home from home. A complimentary breakfast is offered in all bedrooms, or a full English breakfast is available in the dining room.

Facilities 5 rms (4 en suite) (1 fmly) (3 GF) ⊗ FTV TVB tea/coffee ✖ Cen ht TVL No children 5yrs No coaches Whirlpool bath Dinner Last d 10am **Prices** S £30-£45; D £50-£60 **Parking** 7 **Notes** ⊠

STOCKPORT   MAP 16 SJ89

◆◆◆◆
Henry's ◇
204-206 Buxton Rd, Davenport SK2 7AE
☎ 0161 292 0202 ▤ 0161 355 6585
e-mail enquiries@henryshotel.com

Situated on the main road a short way from the town, this family-run guest house offers fine hospitality. The bedrooms are modern, well equipped, and a cosy lounge with Internet access is also provided.

Facilities 10 en suite (1 fmly) (2 GF) ⊗ TVB tea/coffee Cen ht TVL **Prices** S £25-£35; D £40-£50; (room only) ✳ **Parking** 24 **Notes** Closed 22 Dec-2 Jan

WIGAN   MAP 15 SD50

◆◆◆◆ ◧
The Beeches Hotel
School Ln, Standish WN6 0TD
☎ 01257 426432 & 421316 ▤ 01257 427503
e-mail mail@beecheshotel.co.uk
Dir M6 junct 27, A5209 into Standish on School Ln

Located a short drive from M6, this elegant Victorian house has been renovated to provide high standards of comfort. Bedrooms are equipped with homely extras, and public areas include spacious lounges, a popular brasserie, and a self-contained function suite.

Facilities 10 en suite (4 fmly) ⊗ in bedrooms ⊗ in dining room ⊗ in 1 lounge STV TVB tea/coffee Direct dial from bedrooms ✖ Cen ht Dinner Last d 9.45pm **Prices** S £40-£45; D £45-£50✳ **LB Conf** Max 120 Thtr 100 Board 40 **Parking** 120 **Notes** Civ Wed 60

HAMPSHIRE

ALRESFORD
MAP 05 SU53

See **New Alresford**

ALTON
MAP 05 SU73

★★★★ Guest House

Beech Barns Guest House

61 Wellhouse Rd, Beech GU34 4AQ

☎ 01420 85575 & 07759 723112 ▤ 01420 85575

e-mail timsiggs@yahoo.com

Dir *A339 towards Beech. Take 2nd right, Wellhouse Rd, continue for 0.5m, on left*

This well-appointed property is within easy reach of main routes. Set on the outskirts of Alton in grounds at the end of a quiet lane, there is no shortage of walking and cycling around this picturesque village location. The proprietors are welcoming and friendly, and bedrooms are smartly appointed in contemporary style with a good range of facilities. A separate lounge is available and dinner can be offered on request. Ample parking is available.

Facilities 9 en suite (2 fmly) (6 GF) ⊗ in bedrooms ⊗ in area of dining room ⊗ in 1 lounge TVB tea/coffee Cen ht TVL ℃ Dinner
Prices S £55-£80; D £80-£110✱ **LB** **Conf** Max 18 Class 18 Del from £100 ✱ **Parking** 12

◆◆◆◆ ❦

The Granary *(SU770397)*

Stubbs Farm, Kingsley GU35 9NR

☎ 01420 474906 ▤ 01420 474906 Mrs Stephens

e-mail info@stubbsfarm.co.uk

web www.stubbsfarm.co.uk

Dir *A31 at Alton onto B3004, 4.5m left to South Hay. 1m left at sign Stubbs Farm, 0.25m to farmhouse, The Granary on left*

Converted from a 17th-century barn, this delightful guest house offers a warm welcome. Individually decorated rooms, named after varieties of hops, look over the peaceful rural setting. Breakfasts are memorable, using plenty of local and organic produce. The on-site trout fishing lake is an added attraction.

Facilities 3 en suite ⊗ TVB tea/coffee Cen ht No children 12yrs Fishing 600 acres Mixed **Prices** S £50-£55; D £70-£75 **LB** **Parking** 6 **Notes** Closed Xmas & New Year

ANDOVER
MAP 05 SU34

Premier Collection

◆◆◆◆◆

Old Fullerton Station

Fullerton SP11 7JZ ☎ 01264 860202 ▤ 01264 860885

e-mail jane@oldfullertonstation.co.uk

web www.oldfullertonstation.co.uk

Dir *A303 onto A3057 signed Stockbridge for 3m, after Fullerton sign left onto track, through double gates on right*

Having a delightful location very close to the River Test, this interesting property was previously a train station. Large gardens, comfortable bedrooms and a friendly welcome are all provided at this relaxing

accommodation. There are good pubs and inns nearby, some of which are just a stroll away.

Facilities 2 en suite ⊗ TVB tea/coffee Cen ht TVL No children 8yrs No coaches Golf 18 Fishing **Prices** S £35-£45; D £60-£70✱ **Parking** 4

◆◆◆◆

Forest Edge

Andover Down SP11 6Lj ☎ 01264 364526

e-mail david@forest-edge.co.uk

web www.forest-edge.co.uk

Dir *From A303 take A3093 (Andover, Walworth). Turn onto B3400, Forest Edge is 1m on the right.*

Forest Edge is situated in beautiful Hampshire countryside a few miles from Andover and within easy reach of the A303 and M3. The property is set in extensive landscaped and eco-friendly gardens where you can relax or walk at your leisure.

Facilities 4 en suite (4 GF) ⊗ TVB tea/coffee Cen ht No coaches ⅃ Dinner Last d 7.30pm **Prices** S £40-£45; D £55-£60✱ **Conf** Max 10 **Parking** 4

◆◆◆◆

May Cottage

SP11 8LZ

☎ 01264 771241 & 07768 242166 ▤ 01264 771770

e-mail info@maycottage-thruxton.co.uk

web www.maycottage-thruxton.co.uk

Dir *3.5m W of Andover. Off A303 signed Thruxton (Village Only), opp George Inn*

Excellent customer care is assured at this 18th-century, part-thatched house, which stands in pretty gardens in the heart of the village. Fine art and furnishings enhance the original features, and bedrooms are filled with a wealth of thoughtful extras. Comprehensive breakfasts are served in the attractive dining room.

Facilities 3 en suite ⊗ STV TVB tea/coffee Cen ht TVL No coaches Golf course, Leisure facilities nearby **Prices** S £40-£55; D £65-£85 **LB** **Parking** 5 **Notes** ⊠

continued

England

◆◆◆◆
Tilehurst

Furzedown Ln, Amport SP11 8BW
☎ 01264 771437 🗎 01264 771437
e-mail orthtilehurst@aol.com
Dir *Off A303 W of Andover for Amport, right at T-junct, right at next T-junct. 4th house on left past St Marys Church*

Situated in the picturesque village of Amport, close to Thruxton race circuit, this delightful modern home provides comfortably furnished bedrooms with many thoughtful extras. You are welcome to use the attractive lounge and, in summer, the swimming pool and secluded gardens.

Facilities 3 en suite ⊘ TVB tea/coffee ✖ Cen ht No children 16yrs No coaches ⸙ Riding **Parking** 6 **Notes** 🐾

◆◆◆◆ 🅰
New House Bed & Breakfast ◇

Fullerton Rd, Wherwell SP11 7JS
☎ 01264 860817 🗎 01264 860817
e-mail enquire@newhousebedandbreakfast.com
Dir *A303 onto B3048 for Wherwell, past White Lion pub towards Fullerton, house 50yds on left from junct*

Facilities 3 rms (1 en suite) (2 fmly) ⊘ TVB tea/coffee ✖ Cen ht No coaches **Prices** S £30; D £50-£60✳ **Parking** 4 **Notes** Closed ?4-26 Dec 🐾

ASHURST   MAP 05 SU31

◆◆◆◆ 🅰
Forest Gate Lodge

161 Lyndhurst Rd SO40 7AW
☎ 023 8029 3026 🗎 023 8029 3026
web www.ukworld.net/forestgatelodge
Dir *On A35 in village*

Facilities 4 en suite (1 fmly) ⊘ TVB tea/coffee ✖ Cen ht No children 5yrs No coaches **Prices** D £50-£60✳ **LB** **Parking** 6 **Notes** 🐾

BASINGSTOKE   MAP 05 SU65
See also **Hook**

◆◆◆◆
Fernbank Hotel

4 Fairfields Rd RG21 3DR ☎ 01256 321191 🗎 01256 461476
e-mail availability@fernbankhotel.co.uk
Dir *M3 junct 6, 1st rdbt left, next rdbt right signed Fairfields, sharp left after Lamb pub on left, Fairfields Rd 2nd right*

The smart Fernbank is in a quiet residential area within walking distance of the town centre. Its comfortably furnished bedrooms are thoughtfully equipped and breakfast is served in the bright dining room. Car park to the rear.

Facilities 16 en suite (1 fmly) (3 GF) ⊘ in dining room ⊘ in lounges TVB tea/coffee Direct dial from bedrooms ✖ Licensed Cen ht No children 12yrs **Prices** S £72-£86; D £86-£96✳ **Parking** 16 **Notes** Closed 1 wk Xmas

◆◆◆◆
Hatchings

Woods Ln, Cliddesden RG25 2JF ☎ 01256 465279
Dir *2m S of town centre. Off A339 onto B3046 to Cliddesden, pass garage, next right*

This delightful house is in a pretty village convenient for Basingstoke and the M3. The comfortable bedrooms look out onto peaceful gardens and the extra touches are excellent. A hearty full English breakfast is served in the bedrooms, and cereals, bread, jams, fruit and biscuits are freely available.

Facilities 3 rms (1 en suite) (2 pri facs) (3 GF) ⊘ TVB tea/coffee Direct dial from bedrooms Cen ht No children 10yrs No coaches **Prices** S £38-£40; D £50-£55✳ **Parking** 10 **Notes** 🐾

BENTLEY   MAP 05 SU74

🆄
Green Farm

The Drift GU10 5JX ☎ 01420 23246 🗎 01252 737916
e-mail chris.powell@btopenworld.com
web www.greenfarm.org.uk
Dir *Take slip rd off A31 Farnham to Alton signposted Bentley. Take left at top and first right*

At the time of going to press the rating for this establishment had not been confirmed. Please check the AA website www.theAA.com for up-to-date information.

Facilities 1 rms (1 pri facs) 1 annexe en suite (1 fmly) (1 GF) ⊘ TV1B tea/coffee ✖ Cen ht TVL **Prices** D £70-£105✳ **Parking** 13 **Notes** 🐾

England

BISHOP'S WALTHAM
MAP 05 SU51

◆◆◆

Brent Villa
Winchester Rd SO32 1BD
☎ 01489 890188 ▤ 01489 890188

Convenient for Winchester, Southampton and Portsmouth, and close to Marwell Zoo, Brent Villa is suitable for business and leisure. Accommodation is spacious, attractive and very comfortable, and four-poster rooms are available. This is a non-smoking estasblishment.

Facilities 10 en suite (2 fmly) ⊗ TVB tea/coffee Direct dial from bedrooms ✖ Cen ht No coaches **Parking** 10

BRANSGORE
MAP 05 SZ19

◆◆◆◆ 🏛

Tothill House
Black Ln, off Forest Rd BH23 8EA
☎ 01425 674414 ▤ 01425 672235
Dir 0.75m NE of Bransgore centre

Built for an admiral in 1908, Tothill House stands in the southern part of the New Forest. The garden backs on to the forest, where deer, ponies and other wildlife are frequent visitors. The spacious bedrooms are furnished to a high standard, reflecting the character of the house. There is an elegant library, and a generous breakfast is served in the dining room.

Facilities 3 rms (2 en suite) (1 pri facs) ⊗ TVB tea/coffee ✖ Cen ht No children 16yrs No coaches **Prices** D £70-£80✳ **Parking** 6 **Notes** Closed Feb-Nov 🈂

BROCKENHURST
MAP 05 SU30

Premier Collection

◆◆◆◆◆

The Cottage Hotel
Sway Rd SO42 7SH ☎ 01590 622296 ▤ 01590 623014
e-mail enquiries@cottagehotel.org
web www.cottagehotel.org
Dir Off A337 opp Careys Manor Hotel onto Grigg Ln, 0.25m over x-rds, cottage next to war memorial

This 17th-century forester's cottage in the town centre is a good base for exploring the New Forest. The comfortable bedrooms are individually furnished and thoughtfully equipped, and there is a cosy

bar lounge with a fire, where tea can be served and a small selection of drinks is available.

Facilities 9 en suite (3 GF) ⊗ STV TVB tea/coffee ✖ Licensed Cen ht No children 10yrs **Prices** S £50-£90; D £50-£165✳ **LB** **Conf** Max 12 Thtr 12 Class 12 Board 12 **Parking** 14 **Notes** Closed Xmas

◆◆◆

Bridge House ◇
Lyndhurst Rd SO42 7TR
☎ 01590 623135 & 624760 ▤ 01590 623916
e-mail jmvb2@aol.com
Dir On A337, 3rd house on right as entering the village

Located between the town and Lymington River, this 18th-century house is well positioned for easy access to the surrounding New Forest. The comfortably furnished bedrooms are equipped with thoughtful extra facilities, and breakfast is a hearty affair.

Facilities 3 rms (1 en suite) (1 fmly) ⊗ TVB tea/coffee Cen ht No coaches ✆ **Prices** S £30-£45; d £60-£70✳ **LB** **Parking** 5 **Notes** Closed Xmas 🈂

◆◆◆

Crossings Cottage
Lyndhurst Rd SO42 7RL ☎ 01590 622478
e-mail lisa@crossings-brockenhurst.co.uk
Dir In centre just before rail crossing & opp cycle hire shop

Crossings is named due to its proximity to the town's station and level crossing. The friendly proprietor provides a warm welcome, and the rooms are comfortably furnished. Full English breakfasts are served at individual tables.

Facilities 3 rms ⊗ TVB tea/coffee ✖ Cen ht No coaches **Prices** D £48-£60 **LB** **Parking** 2 **Notes** Closed 24-26 Dec 🈂

◆◆◆

Seraya
8 Grigg Ln SO42 7RE ☎ 01590 622426
e-mail edwin.ward@btinternet.com
Dir Off A337 opp Careys Manor Hotel onto Grigg Ln, 500yds on corner Horlock Rd

Well placed for visiting the New Forest, and close to the centre of town with its good eateries, this delightful house offers attractive rooms with a broad selection of extra facilities. A hearty breakfast is served around the communal dining table.

Facilities 3 rms (1 en suite) ⊗ TVB tea/coffee Cen ht No coaches **Prices** D £50-£64✳ **LB** **Parking** 3 **Notes** 🈂

🅤

Little Heathers Guest House
13 Whitemoor Rd SO42 7QG ☎ 01590 623512
e-mail littleheathers@msn.com

At the time of going to press the rating for this establishment had not been confirmed. Please check the AA website www.theAA.com for up-to-date information.

Facilities 3 rms (2 en suite) (1 pri facs) (1 fmly) (3 GF) ⊗ TVB tea/coffee ✖ Cen ht No coaches **Prices** S fr £40; d fr £60✳ **Parking** 4 **Notes** 🈂

continued

BURLEY

MAP 05 SU20

◆◆◆◆

White Buck Inn

Bisterne Cl BH24 4AT ☎ 01425 402264 ◈ 01425 403588
e-mail whitebuckinn@accommodating-inns.co.uk
web www.accommodating-inns.co.uk
Dir Between A31 & A35, follow signs for Burley

Set in 3 acres of parkland in the heart of the New Forest, this delightful Inn offers comfortable accommodation in charming surroundings. Bedrooms, one of which has a four-poster bed, are finished to a very high standard with many thoughtful extras. A substantial choice of home-cooked meals are available in the spacious bar and restaurant.

Facilities 9 en suite (3 fmly) ⊗ in bedrooms ⊗ in dining room ⊗ in 1 lounge TVB tea/coffee Direct dial from bedrooms Cen ht Golf 18 Fishing Riding Dinner Last d 9pm **Conf** Max 15 Thtr 20 Class 15 Board 15 **Parking** 90 **Notes** Closed 24-26 Dec

CADNAM

MAP 05 SU31

◆◆◆◆

Walnut Cottage

Old Romsey Rd SO40 2NP
☎ 023 8081 2275 ◈ 023 8081 2275
Dir M27 junct 1, Cadnam rdbt onto A3090, Old Romsey Rd 1st left

This charming, mid 19th-century cottage is convenient for the New Forest or nearby business areas. The comfortable bedrooms are brightly decorated, and an inviting lounge is available. Hearty English breakfasts are enjoyed around a large table in the cosy dining room.

Facilities 3 rms (2 en suite) (1 pri facs) (1 GF) ⊗ TVB tea/coffee ✕ Cen ht TVL No children 14yrs No coaches **Prices** S £40; D £55✶ **Parking** 3 **Notes** Closed 24-26 Dec 🐾

DAMERHAM

MAP 05 SU11

◆◆◆◆

The Compasses Inn

Damerham SP6 3HQ
☎ 01725 518231 & 07795 096747 ◈ 01725 518880
e-mail info@compassesinn.net
web www.compassesinn.net
Dir In village centre

This friendly, 400-year-old traditional inn stands in a peaceful village near Salisbury and the New Forest. The comfortable bedrooms are
continued

pleasantly furnished and well-equipped, while the bars feature a selection of real ales and over 100 malt whiskies. Tasty meals are available at lunch and dinner.

Facilities 6 en suite (1 fmly) ⊗ in bedrooms ⊗ in dining room ⊗ in 1 lounge STV FTV TVB tea/coffee Direct dial from bedrooms Cen ht Pool Table Dinner Last d 9.30pm **Prices** S £39.50-£45; D £69-£80✶ **LB Parking** 30

DUMMER

MAP 05 SU54

◆◆◆

Tower Hill House

Tower Hill, Winchester Rd RG25 2AL
☎ 01256 398340 ◈ 01256 398340
e-mail martin_hyndman@ntlworld.com
web www.towerhill-guesthouse.co.uk
Dir M3 junct 7. Follow sign A30 Winchester. Take 2nd left turn, opposite signpost for North Waltham.

Well situated for the M3, while overlooking fields and countryside, this family-run property is in the pretty village of Dummer, just a short drive from Basingstoke. Bedrooms are simply, but comfortably furnished, and a well-made breakfast is served in the cheerful dining room.

Facilities 4 rms ⊗ TVB tea/coffee ✕ Cen ht No coaches **Prices** S £20-£35; D £50-£60✶ **Parking** 6 **Notes** 🐾

EASTLEIGH

MAP 05 SU41

◆◆◆◆ 🅰

Endeavour Guest House

40 Allbrook Hill, Allbrook SO50 4LY
☎ 023 8061 3400 ◈ 023 8061 4486
e-mail dcschauffeurs@btconnect.com
Dir M3 junct 12, A335 to rdbt, 1st exit to Allbrook Hill, house 250yds on right

Facilities 1 en suite (1 fmly) (1 GF) ⊗ STV TVB tea/coffee ✕ Cen ht TVL No coaches Fishing **Prices** S £40; D £55✶ **Parking** 2

EAST TYTHERLEY

MAP 05 SU22

★★★★ ◉◉ Inn

The Star at Tytherley

SO51 0LW ☎ 01794 340225 ◈ 01794 340678
e-mail info@starinn-uk.co.uk
Dir 1m S of East Tytherley

This charming coaching inn offers bedrooms in a purpose-built annexe, separate from the main pub. The spacious rooms have high levels of quality and comfort, and an outdoor children's play area is available. The inn has a loyal following of locals and visitors, drawn especially by the excellent food.

Facilities 3 annexe en suite (3 GF) ⊗ TVB tea/coffee Cen ht Dinner Last d 9pm **Prices** D £80-£100✶ **Conf** Max 30 Thtr 24 Class 24 Board 30 Del from £110 ✶ **Parking** 50

England

EMSWORTH
MAP 05 SU70

★★★★ Guest Accommodation

Hollybank House

Hollybank Ln PO10 7UN ☎ 01243 375502 ▤ 01243 378118
e-mail anna@hollybankhouse.com
Dir *From Emsworth central rdbt take B2148 for 1m. Turn right (Southleigh Rd) then 3rd left (Hollybank Lane). House at top*

The country house stands in a 10-acre woodland garden with a tennis court on the outskirts of Emsworth, and looks out to Chichester Harbour. Emsworth has a variety of restaurants, pubs and harbour walks.

Facilities 4 rms (3 en suite) (1 pri facs) (1 fmly) ⊗ TVB tea/coffee Cen ht ⌇ ♫ **Prices** S £40-£45; D £60-£75✳ **Parking** 85 **Notes** ⊠

★★★★ ◉◉◉ Restaurant with Rooms

36 on the Quay

47 South St PO10 7EG ☎ 01243 375592 & 372257

Occupying a prime position with far reaching views over the estuary, this 16th-century house is the scene for accomplished and exciting cuisine. The elegant restaurant has peaceful pastel shades, local art and crisp napery and glimpses of the bustling harbour. The contemporary bedrooms offer comfort and thoughtful extras.

Facilities 5 en suite TVB tea/coffee Licensed Dinner Last d 10pm **Prices** S £70-£90; D £95-£150✳ **LB** **Parking** 6 **Notes** Closed 3wks Jan, 1wk Oct

FAREHAM
MAP 05 SU50

◆◆◆◆

Springfield Hotel

67 The Avenue PO14 1PE ☎ 01329 828325
Dir *On A27 W of Fareham station*

This large, attractive 1930s house is surrounded by gardens. The spacious bedrooms have coordinated furnishings and are equipped with many useful extras. The elegant dining room overlooks the garden, as does the delightful lounge.

continued

Springfield Hotel

Facilities 6 en suite (1 fmly) ⊗ in bedrooms ⊗ in dining room TVB tea/coffee Direct dial from bedrooms ✕ Cen ht No coaches **Parking** 10 **Notes** Closed 21 Dec-1 Jan

◆◆◆

Travelrest - Solent Gateway

22 The Avenue PO14 1NS
☎ 01329 232175 ▤ 01329 232196
Dir *0.5m from town centre on A27. 500yds from railway station*

Situated just west of the town centre, the well-presented house is convenient for the ferry terminals and naval heritage sites. The comfortable bedrooms are spacious and well equipped, and one has a four-poster bed. Breakfast is served in the cosy conservatory-dining room and conference rooms are available.

Facilities 19 en suite (3 fmly) (6 GF) ⊗ in 10 bedrooms ⊗ in dining room FTV TVB tea/coffee Direct dial from bedrooms Cen ht Landscaped garden Dinner Last d 10pm **Prices** S £45-£60; D £49.50-£65; (room only) ✳ **Conf** Max 40 Thtr 30 Class 30 Board 30 **Parking** 27

◆◆ ▣

Catisfield Cottage ◇

1 Catisfield Ln PO15 5NW ☎ 01329 843301
Dir *Off A27 at Highlands Rd lights, Catisfield Ln 2nd left*

Facilities 6 rms (3 en suite) (1 fmly) ⊗ in 1 bedrooms ⊗ in dining room ⊗ in lounges TVB tea/coffee Cen ht TVL No coaches **Prices** S £22.50-£30; D £45-£55✳ **Parking** 6 **Notes** Closed 24 Dec-5 Jan ⊠

FARNBOROUGH

MAP 05 SU85

◆◆◆◆

Tudorwood Guest House

164 Farnborough Rd GU14 7JJ ☎ 01252 541123
e-mail info@tudorwood.net
Dir *Off A325 Farnborough Rd onto Sycamore Rd, next 3 left turns onto Cedar Rd, right onto Old Farnborough Rd*

A delightful Tudor-style house located close to the town centre. The individually decorated bedrooms are well appointed with a range of useful facilities. Public areas include a pleasant conservatory-lounge and an intimate dining room where home-cooked dinners are available. Ample parking is provided to the front of the property.

Facilities 2 en suite 4 annexe en suite (1 fmly) (4 GF) ⊗ TVB tea/coffee ✖ Cen ht TVL No coaches DVD library Dinner Last d 7pm **Prices** S £40-£55; D £55-£65✱ **Conf** Board 10 **Parking** 7 **Notes** Closed 24-29 Dec

◆◆◆

Amber Lodge ◇

101 Victoria Rd GU14 7PP
☎ 01252 371889 ▤ 01252 541880
e-mail enquiries@amberlodge.net
Dir *Off A325 Farnborough Rd at Clock House rdbt onto Victoria Rd, Amber Lodge 200yds on right after 2nd minirdbt*

Located near the town centre, this Victorian property offers comfortable, bright and airy bedrooms and a cosy lounge. Breakfast is served in the cottage-style dining room, and there is a private car park behind the house.

Facilities 9 rms (7 en suite) (2 fmly) (5 GF) ⊗ TVB tea/coffee ✖ Cen ht TVL No coaches **Prices** S £30-£50; D £50-£70✱ **LB** **Parking** 14 **Notes** Closed 21 Dec-3 Jan

FORDINGBRIDGE

MAP 05 SU11

Premier Collection

◆◆◆◆◆

Cottage Crest

Castle Hill, Woodgreen SP6 2AX ☎ 01725 512009
e-mail lupita_cadman@yahoo.co.uk
Dir *3m N of Fordingbridge. Off A338 at Breamore to Woodgreen, right at Post Office/shop, last right*

Located on an elevated position with breathtaking views over the River Avon, on the edge of the New Forest, this charming house stands in a 5-acre garden. The comfortable and spacious bedrooms are equipped with many extra facilities, and there is a garden suite with its own sitting room.

Facilities 3 en suite ⊗ TVB tea/coffee ✖ Cen ht No children 8yrs No coaches **Prices** D £60✱ **Parking** 4 **Notes** ✍

◆◆◆◆ ⌂

Alderholt Mill ◇

Sandleheath Rd SP6 1PU
☎ 01425 653130 ▤ 01425 652868
e-mail alderholt-mill@zetnet.co.uk
web www.alderholtmill.co.uk
Dir *1m W from Fordingbridge, left at x-rds in Sandleheath, 0.5m over bridge on right*

Fresh bread made from home-ground flour can be relished around the communal breakfast table at this delightful working mill. You can also enjoy milling demonstrations, cream teas, barbecues by the river, and private fishing. The bedrooms, lounge and dining room are all well appointed, and dinner is available by arrangement.

Facilities 5 rms (4 en suite) ⊗ TVB tea/coffee Cen ht TVL No children 8yrs No coaches Fishing Dinner Last d 9am **Prices** S £28-£32; D £56-£70 **LB** **Parking** 10

GOSPORT

MAP 05 SZ69

◆◆◆◆

Thirty Three A

33a Anglesey Rd, Alverstoke PO12 2EG
☎ 023 9251 0119 & 07866 400700 ▤ 023 9251 0119
e-mail rob.turnerchina@ntlworld.com
web www.thirtythreea.co.uk
Dir *M27 junct 11. A32 to Gosport. Follow signs for Stokes Bay. Left at rdbt at east end of bay. Pass St Mary's on left, turn right, right again into drive.*

Close to Alverstoke church, the house is tucked away in secluded garden. The friendly proprietors have made the two bedrooms stylish and comfortable, and have flat-screen televisions. Breakfast is a gourmet treat served overlooking the garden, or in the garden in warmer weather.

Facilities 2 en suite (1 fmly) (2 GF) ⊗ FTV TVB tea/coffee ✖ Cen ht No coaches **Prices** D £55-£69✱ **Parking** 2

England

HAYLING ISLAND
MAP 05 SU70

♦♦♦♦
Ravensdale
19 St Catherines Rd PO11 0HF
☎ 023 9246 3203 & 07802 188259 📠 023 9246 3203
e-mail phil.taylor@tayloredprint.co.uk
Dir A3023 at Langstone, cross Hayling Bridge & continue 3m until minirdbt, right onto Manor Rd. After 1m, right by Barley Mow onto Station Rd & 3rd left onto St Catherines Rd

A warm welcome awaits you to this comfortable home, quietly situated near the beach and golf course. Bedrooms are attractive, very comfortable and enhanced with numerous thoughtful extras. Home cooking can be enjoyed at breakfast (and dinner by arrangement) in the dining room, and there is also a lounge area.

Facilities 3 rms (2 en suite) ⊗ TVB tea/coffee 🐾 Cen ht TVL No children 8yrs No coaches Dinner Last d Breakfast **Prices** S £36-£40; D £56-£66✳ **LB** **Parking** 4 **Notes** Closed last 2 wks of Dec 🐾

♦♦♦
Redwalls ◇
66 Staunton Av PO11 0EW ☎ 023 9246 6109
e-mail daphne@redwalls66.freeserve.co.uk
Dir Follow main rd across the island signed 'Beachlands' At funfair turn right along seafront rd. Staunton Ave 4th right. B&B on left.

Facilities 3 en suite ⊗ TVB tea/coffee 🐾 Cen ht TVL No children No coaches **Prices** S £30-£35; D £50✳ **Parking** 4 **Notes** 🐾

♦♦♦
Turanga House ◇
68 West Ln PO11 0JL ☎ 023 9263 7002 & 07770 536053
e-mail rita@turanga-house.co.uk
web www.turanga-house.co.uk
Dir A27, take A3023 for Hayling Island. Roundabout 2nd exit, turn right into Newtown Lane, right again into West Lane. 500yds on right.

Facilities 1 en suite 2 annexe en suite (2 GF) ⊗ TVB tea/coffee 🐾 Cen ht No coaches Dinner Last d 7pm **Prices** S £30-£40; D £50-£60✳ **Parking** 4 **Notes** Closed 1-15 Dec & 15-28 Feb

HIGHCLERE
MAP 05 SU45

♦♦♦♦
The Old Plough B & B
North End RG20 0AY ☎ 01635 254769
e-mail lucydealbuquerque@yahoo.com
Dir Off A343 (N of A34 junct) signed East Woodhay & Ball Hill. Continue 2.5m. After Ball Hill garage, 3rd left signed North End, B&B on right

This family home offers a warm welcome in a peaceful rural retreat. With good access to the A34 and Newbury, it is a perfect location for business and pleasure. The bedrooms have a wealth of thoughtful touches and a hearty breakfast starts your day.

Facilities 2 rms (1 en suite) (1 GF) ⊗ TV1B tea/coffee 🐾 Cen ht No children No coaches **Prices** S £35-£40; D £55-£60✳ **Parking** 2 **Notes** Closed 23 Dec-3 Jan 🐾

HOOK
MAP 05 SU75

♦♦♦
Cherry Lodge
Reading Rd RG27 9DB ☎ 01256 762532 📠 01256 766068
e-mail cherrylodge@btinternet.com
Dir On B3349

This pleasant bungalow is peacefully set back from the Reading road, and is convenient for the M3. Cherry lodge provides extremely friendly hospitality and is popular with business guests. Breakfast is served from 6.30am. A spacious lounge is provided and bedrooms are well equipped.

Facilities 12 en suite (1 fmly) (12 GF) ⊗ in 5 bedrooms ⊗ in dining room ⊗ in lounges STV TVB tea/coffee Direct dial from bedrooms 🐾 Cen ht TVL No coaches **Parking** 20 **Notes** Closed Xmas-New Year

♦♦♦
Oaklea
London Rd RG27 9LA ☎ 01256 762673 📠 01256 762150
e-mail oakleaguesthouse@amserve.net
Dir On A30, 200yds W of Hook centre

You can be sure of a warm welcome at this Victorian house located just a short drive from the M3. Bedrooms are well appointed with modern facilities, there is a comfortable lounge, and the large dining room has a bar.

Facilities 11 en suite (2 fmly) ⊗ in bedrooms ⊗ in dining room TVB tea/coffee Licensed Cen ht TVL No coaches Dinner Last d noon **Prices** S £45-£48; D £55-£60✳ **Parking** 14

HORNDEAN
MAP 05 SU71

♦♦♦
Ship & Bell Hotel
London Rd PO8 0BZ ☎ 023 9259 2107 📠 023 9257 1644
e-mail shipandbell@accommodating-inns.co.uk
web www.accommodating-inns.co.uk
Dir Follow signs for Horndean, B&B attached to Gales Brewery

This popular inn stands in the centre of Horndean next to the George Gale brewery. Bedrooms are well equipped and provide comfort for business or leisure. There is a spacious lounge bar and a casual dining area where a varied selection of dishes are available. Parking is an asset.

Facilities 3 en suite 11 annexe en suite (1 fmly) (4 GF) ⊗ in 5 bedrooms ⊗ in dining room ⊗ in lounges TVB tea/coffee Direct dial from bedrooms 🐾 Cen ht No coaches Pool Table Dinner Last d 8.45pm **Conf** Max 10 Class 10 Board 10 **Parking** 22

ISLE OF WIGHT
See **Wight, Isle of**

LYMINGTON

MAP 05 SZ39

See also **Milford-on-Sea**

Premier Collection

♦♦♦♦♦ 🖺 ☕

The Nurse's Cottage

Station Rd SO41 6BA ☎ 01590 683402

e-mail nurses.cottage@lineone.net

web www.nursescottage.co.uk

For full entry see **Sway**

Premier Collection

♦♦♦♦♦

The Olde Barn

Christchurch Rd, Downton SO41 0LA

☎ 01590 644939 & 07813 679757 📠 01590 644939

e-mail julie@theoldebarn.co.uk

web www.theoldebarn.co.uk

Dir On A337 3m W of Lymington, in Downton

The 17th-century barn and related buildings have been restored to provide stylish accommodation. Bedrooms are smartly furnished, and the spacious bathrooms have power showers. There is a comfortable lounge, and a traditional English breakfast is served around a farmhouse table in the attractive dining room.

Facilities 3 en suite (1 fmly) (3 GF) ⊗ STV TVB tea/coffee ✖ Cen ht TVL No children 10yrs No coaches **Prices** S £45-£60; D £55-£70✱ **Parking** 6

♦♦♦♦ 🖺

Efford Cottage

Everton SO41 0JD ☎ 01590 642315 📠 01590 641030

e-mail effordcottage@aol.com

Dir On A337, 2m W of Lymington

Set in attractive gardens, this charming property offers large comfortable bedrooms which are well furnished and finished with a host of thoughtful extras. There is a spacious and inviting lounge. An extensive breakfast menu, featuring home-made bread, is offered in the smart dining room.

Facilities 3 en suite (1 fmly) ⊗ in bedrooms ⊗ in dining room TVB tea/coffee Direct dial from bedrooms Cen ht No children 14yrs No coaches Dinner Last d 48 hrs in advance **Prices** D £55-£65✱ **LB** **Parking** 4 **Notes** rs Nov-Feb ⊚

♦♦♦♦

1 Honeysuckle Gardens

Everton SO41 0EH ☎ 01590 641282

e-mail mway286978@aol.com

web www.newforest-uk.com/honeysucklebandb

Dir Off A337 Lymington to Christchurch onto Everton Rd, Honeysuckle Gardens 3rd left

Located in a new residential development in the village of Everton, this charming house is a good base for visiting Lymington, New Milton and the New Forest. Bedrooms are well furnished, and useful extra facilities are provided. Full English breakfasts are served around one large table.

Facilities 3 rms (2 en suite) (1 pri facs) (1 fmly) ⊗ TVB tea/coffee Cen ht No children 3yrs No coaches **Prices** S £35-£40; D £60 **LB** **Parking** 3 **Notes** ⊚

♦♦♦♦

Auplands

22 Southampton Rd SO41 9GG ☎ 01590 675944

e-mail sue@auplands.com

web www.auplands.com

Dir On A337 before town centre, opp supermarket

Located just a short walk from High St, this friendly family-run establishment provides neatly decorated and well-equipped bedrooms. Hearty English breakfasts are served at individual tables in the attractive dining room. Off-road parking is available.

Facilities 3 en suite ⊗ TVB tea/coffee ✖ Cen ht No children 5yrs No coaches **Parking** 8 **Notes** ⊚

♦♦♦♦

Elsburn

Pennington SO41 8HF ☎ 01590 676309 & 07817 762455

e-mail shirley.measures@tesco.net

Dir Off A337 Southampton Rd by Tollhouse Inn onto Sway Rd, continue to Wheel Inn, left onto Ramley Rd, Elsburn 50yds past Pennington Garage

Set in a village close to the yachting haven of Lymington and the beautiful New Forest, this friendly guest house has been refurbished to provide a relaxing and comfortable base. The smart bedrooms are filled with thoughtful extras, and a continental breakfast is served in the modern, cafe-style dining room.

Facilities 3 en suite ⊗ TVB tea/coffee ✖ No children 15yrs No coaches **Prices** D £50-£70✱ **LB** **Parking** 3

♦♦♦♦

Harts Lodge

242 Everton Rd, Everton SO41 0HE ☎ 01590 645902

Dir From Lymington 2.5m W to Everton, off A337 onto Everton Rd, 0.5m on left

This attractive bungalow lies in 3 acres of peaceful gardens and paddocks. The bedrooms are furnished to a high standard and feature many thoughtful touches; one room has outside access. Public areas include a lounge and a pleasant breakfast room, with views of the garden and a small wildlife lake.

Facilities 3 en suite (1 fmly) (3 GF) ⊗ TVB tea/coffee Cen ht TVL No coaches **LB** **Parking** 6 **Notes** ⊚

England

LYMINGTON continued

◆◆◆◆

Jevington

47 Waterford Ln SO41 3PT
☎ 01590 672148 📠 01590 672148
e-mail jevingtonbb@lineone.net

Dir *From High St at St Thomas's Church onto Church Ln, left fork onto Waterford Ln*

Situated within walking distance of the town centre and marinas, Jevington offers attractive bedrooms furnished to a high standard with coordinated soft furnishings. An appetising breakfast is served at two tables in the dining room, and the friendly proprietors can suggest local places for dinner.

Facilities 3 en suite (1 fmly) ⊗ FTV TVB tea/coffee Cen ht No children 5yrs No coaches **Prices** D £55-£60✳ **Parking** 3 **Notes** 🐾

◆◆◆◆ 🅰

Glenhurst

86 Wainsford Rd, Everton SO41 0UD
☎ 01590 644256 & 07763 322519 📠 01590 644256
e-mail a.rose@virgin.net
web www.newforest-bedbreakfast.co.uk

Dir *A337 towards Everton. Turn right signed Everton Village. 3rd right into Wainsford Rd. 0.25m to Glenhurst.*

Facilities 2 en suite (2 GF) ⊗ STV FTV TVB tea/coffee Cen ht TVL **Prices** D £50-£60✳ LB **Parking** 4

◆◆◆

Gorse Meadow Country House Hotel

Sway Rd SO41 8LR ☎ 01590 673354 📠 01590 673336
e-mail gorse.meadow.guesthouse@wildmushrooms.co.uk
web www.wildmushrooms.co.uk

Dir *Off A337 from Brockenhurst, right onto Sway Rd before Toll House pub, Gorse Meadow 1.5m on right*

This imposing Edwardian house stands within 14 acres of grounds and most bedrooms have views across the gardens and paddocks. Situated just 1m from Lymington, this is an excellent base to enjoy the New Forest. Meals are also available, and Mrs Tee often uses local wild mushrooms in her dishes.

Facilities 5 en suite (2 fmly) (2 GF) ⊗ in dining room ⊗ in lounges TVB tea/coffee Licensed Cen ht No coaches Dinner Last d 6pm **Prices** D £80-£120✳ **Conf** Max 12 Board 12 **Parking** 20

◆◆◆

Passford Farm

Southampton Rd SO41 8ND ☎ 01590 674103
Dir *Opp Welcome to Lymington sign*

This Grade II listed 17th-century thatched cottage is set in 5 acres with delightful gardens and a pond. With its wealth of beams and fireplaces, Passford Farm is full of character. The proprietors adopt a relaxed and friendly approach, and ensure you enjoy the comfortable facilities.

Facilities 3 en suite (1 fmly) ⊗ in bedrooms ⊗ in dining room TVB tea/coffee 🐕 Cen ht No coaches half size snooker table **Parking** 30 **Notes** 🐾

◆◆◆

Tenneh

Kings Farm Ln, Hordle SO41 0HD ☎ 01425 610169
e-mail roy_sue2000@yahoo.co.uk

Dir *A337 from Lymington. Milford-on-Sea junct on left. Next right onto Everton Rd. Kings Farm Lane 1m on right*

The guest house lies between the villages of Everton and Hordle in a semi-rural area convenient for the coast and the New Forest National Park.

Facilities 3 rms (2 en suite) (1 pri facs) (1 fmly) ⊗ TVB tea/coffee 🐕 Cen ht No children 8yrs No coaches LB **Parking** 6 **Notes** 🐾

◆◆◆

The Thatched House

Hundred Ln, Portmore SO41 5RG
☎ 01590 675211 & 679977
e-mail onesusieb@yahoo.co.uk
web www.thethatchedhouse.co.uk

Dir *Take B3054 signed for Beaulieu. 1m on left is Hundred Ln. B&B 6th on right*

The charming village property has picturesque views and is well placed for exploring the New Forest area. Some of the comfortable bedrooms have fridges and videos. You can enjoy the sunset on the decking or swim in the outdoor pool. Livery stabling is available for those wanting to explore on horseback.

Facilities 2 en suite (1 fmly) (2 GF) ⊗ TVB tea/coffee Cen ht 🐕 **Prices** S £35-£40; D £60-£70 LB **Parking** 6 **Notes** Closed Sep-May 🐾

◆◆

The Victoriana

Victoria Mews, High St SO41 9FT
☎ 01590 688416 📠 01590 688415
Dir *Opp Barclays Bank*

Tucked away in a small mews in the centre of this busy little town, the Victoriana provides comfortable, well-proportioned rooms. Each is well equipped and has a good range of facilities. Breakfast is served at individual tables, and the friendly atmosphere makes this an easy place in which to relax.

Facilities 3 rms (1 en suite) (1 fmly) ⊗ in bedrooms TVB tea/coffee 🐕 Cen ht No coaches **Parking** 3 **Notes** 🐾

LYNDHURST MAP 05 SU30

Premier Collection

♦♦♦♦♦

Rufus House ◇

Southampton Rd SO43 7BQ ☎ 023 8028 2930
e-mail rufushouse@aol.com
web www.rufushouse.com
Dir From Lyndhurst centre onto A35 Southampton Rd, 300yds on left

Located on the edge of town, this delightful family-run Victorian property is well situated for exploring the New Forest. The brightly decorated bedrooms are appointed to a high standard, while the turret lounge and the garden terrace are great spots for relaxing.

Facilities 11 en suite (1 fmly) (2 GF) ⊗ TVB tea/coffee ✱ Cen ht TVL No children 6yrs **Prices** S £30-£45; D £50-£90✱ **LB** **Parking** 16

♦♦♦♦

Clayhill House

SO43 7DE ☎ 023 8028 2304 ▤ 023 8028 2093
e-mail clayhillhouse@tinyworld.co.uk
Dir 1.5m outside village

Set at the edge of this attractive town in the New Forest, the well-appointed house offers friendly service and comfortable accommodation. The bedrooms are particularly well equipped with thoughtful extras. Freshly cooked breakfasts are served in the dining room.

Facilities 3 en suite (1 fmly) ⊗ TVB tea/coffee ✱ Cen ht No children 7yrs No coaches **Prices** S £35-£40✱ **LB** **Parking** 6 **Notes** Closed 22 Dec-4 Jan

♦♦♦♦

Heather House Hotel ◇

Southampton Rd SO43 7BQ
☎ 023 8028 4409 ▤ 023 8028 4431
e-mail enquiries@heatherhouse.co.uk
web www.heatherhouse.co.uk
Dir M27 junct 1, A337 to Lyndhurst. At lights in centre turn left, establishment 800yds on left

This impressive double-fronted Edwardian house stands in attractive gardens on the edge of town with views of the New Forest. Bedrooms are comfortably appointed with some suitable for families. Breakfast is served in the pleasant dining room.

Facilities 10 en suite (1 fmly) (1 GF) ⊗ TVB tea/coffee ✱ Licensed Cen ht TVL No coaches **Prices** S £25-£35; D £50-£80✱ **LB** **Parking** 12 **Notes** Closed 25-26 Dec

♦♦♦♦

Penny Farthing Hotel

Romsey Rd SO43 7AA
☎ 023 8028 4422 ▤ 023 8028 4488
e-mail stay@pennyfarthinghotel.co.uk
web www.pennyfarthinghotel.co.uk
Dir M27 junct 1, A337, on left entering village

This friendly, well-appointed establishment on the edge of town is suitable for business or for exploring the New Forest area. The attractive bedrooms are well-equipped with some located in an adjacent cottage. There is a spacious breakfast room, a comfortable lounge bar and a bicycle store.

Facilities 16 en suite 4 annexe en suite (2 fmly) (3 GF) ⊗ in bedrooms ⊗ in dining room ⊗ in 1 lounge TVB tea/coffee Direct dial from bedrooms ✱ Licensed Cen ht TVL No coaches **Prices** S £49-£78; D £68-£98 **Parking** 23

♦♦♦♦

Whitemoor House Hotel

Southampton Rd SO43 7BU ☎ 023 8028 2186
e-mail whitemoor@aol.com
Dir 0.5m NE of twon centre on A35

A warm welcome is assured at this non-smoking establishment in the New Forest. The comfortable bedrooms are brightly decorated, and you can enjoy drinks in the cosy lounge or the well-maintained garden in fine weather.

Facilities 7 en suite (2 fmly) ⊗ TVB tea/coffee Direct dial from bedrooms ✱ Licensed Cen ht TVL No coaches Dinner Last d 5pm **Parking** 8

England

LYNDHURST continued

◆◆◆◆

The Willows ◇

72 Lyndhurst Rd, Ashurst SO40 7BE
☎ 023 8029 2745 ▤ 023 8029 2745
e-mail the_willows_ashurst@hotmail.com
Dir 3m NE of Lyndhurst on A35 in Ashurst

Located north-east of Lyndhurst, this delightful property has good access to Southampton and the New Forest. Rooms are comfortable and well equipped. A full English breakfast or alternative choices are served at individual tables in the cosy dining room.

Facilities 3 rms (2 en suite) (1 fmly) ⊗ TVB tea/coffee ✖ Cen ht TVL No coaches **Prices** S £25-£35; D £55-£60✳ **LB Parking** 4

MILFORD ON SEA   MAP 05 SZ29

Premier Collection

◆◆◆◆◆

Ha'penny House

16 Whitby Rd SO41 0ND ☎ 01590 641210
e-mail info@hapennyhouse.co.uk
web www.hapennyhouse.co.uk
Dir A337 at Everton onto B3058, through village onto Cliff Rd, right onto Cornwallis Rd, right at T-junct onto Whitby Rd, house 50yds on left

This delightful house is in a peaceful residential area close to the clifftop with stunning views towards the Isle of Wight. Individually styled bedrooms are beautifully appointed, and equipped with a host of thoughtful extras. There is a stylish lounge, and an elegant dining room where superb breakfasts are served.

Facilities 4 en suite ⊗ TVB tea/coffee ✖ Cen ht TVL No children 12yrs No coaches **Prices** S £50-£60; D £62-£75 **LB Parking** 7

◆◆◆◆

Alma Mater

4 Knowland Dr SO41 0RH ☎ 01590 642811
e-mail bandbalmamater@aol.com
web www.newforestalmamater.co.uk
Dir A337 at Everton onto B3058 to Milford on Sea. Pass South Lawn Hotel, right onto Manor Rd, 1st left onto Knowland Dr

Alma Mater is in a quiet residential area within walking distance of the village centre and beaches. The comfortable bedrooms are all well appointed with many extra touches. One room is on the ground floor and another has a small kitchen for longer-staying guests. Dinner is available by arrangement.

Facilities 3 en suite (1 fmly) (1 GF) ⊗ TVB tea/coffee ✖ Cen ht TVL No children 15yrs No coaches **Prices** S fr £40; D £60-£64✳ **LB Parking** 4 **Notes** ⊛

NEW ALRESFORD   MAP 05 SU53

◆◆◆ 🅰

Haygarth ◇

82 Jacklyns Ln SO24 9LJ
☎ 01962 732715 & 07986 372895
Dir B3046 from New Alresford centre for Cheriton, Haygarth 0.5m on right

Facilities 3 rms (2 en suite) (3 GF) ⊗ in dining room TVB tea/coffee ✖ Cen ht TVL No coaches **Prices** S £25-£30; D £50-£60 **LB Parking** 7 **Notes** ⊛

PETERSFIELD   MAP 05 SU72

See also **Rogate (West Sussex)**

◆◆◆◆

Quinhay Farmhouse ◇

Alton Rd, Froxfield GU32 1BZ
☎ 01730 827183 ▤ 01730 827184
e-mail janerothery@hotmail.com
web www.quinhaybandb.co.uk
Dir 4m NW of Petersfield. Off A3 at A272 junct towards Petersfield, at rdbt exit signed Froxfield/Steep, 3.5m on right

Jane Rothery takes great delight in welcoming you to her delightful modern home set in rolling countryside outside Petersfield. The spacious bedrooms are designed with comfort in mind and have a wealth of thoughtful extras, and the large lounge comes with comfy

continued

sofas and a wood-burning stove for cooler months. Jane is a top-twenty finalist for AA Landlady of the Year 2006.

Quinhay Farmhouse

Facilities 2 rms (1 en suite) (1 pri facs) ⊗ TVB tea/coffee ✈ Cen ht TVL No children 12yrs No coaches **Prices** S £30-£35; D £60-£70 **Parking** 10 **Notes** Closed 15 Dec-15 Jan

◆◆◆◆ ⊞

The Good Intent
40-46 College St GU31 4AF
☎ 01730 263838 🖹 01730 302239
e-mail pstuart@goodintent.freeserve.co.uk
Dir *In town centre on one-way system (A2070)*

Named after the ship whose timbers are incorporated into the building, this cosy inn is full of character. Bedrooms are all en suite, comfortable and equipped with thoughtful extras. The restaurant is popular and simple snacks and real ales are also available.

Facilities 2 en suite (1 fmly) ⊗ in bedrooms ⊗ in dining room TVB tea/coffee Cen ht No coaches Dinner Last d 9.30pm **Parking** 10

PORTSMOUTH
MAP 05 SU60

Abbey Lodge
30 Waverley Rd, Southsea PO5 2PW
☎ 023 9282 8285 🖹 023 9287 2943
e-mail linda@abbeylodge.co.uk
web www.abbeylodge.co.uk
Dir *Off A288 South Parade near pier onto B2155 Clarendon Rd & Waverley Rd*

A warm welcome awaits you at this attractive property close to the seafront and within walking distance of the shops. It offers well-equipped bedrooms, and breakfast is served in a small but cosy dining room at individual tables.

Facilities 9 rms (3 en suite) (2 fmly) ⊗ in dining room TVB tea/coffee ✈ Cen ht No coaches **Notes** Closed Xmas & New Year

Sunrise ◇
4 Beach Rd PO5 2JH ☎ 023 9273 0266
e-mail giantsunrise@btinternet.com

Located just a stroll from Southsea seafront, close to shops, restaurants and bars. Bedrooms are well furnished and beautifully coordinated. Although rooms are not en suite, there is much to commend about the quality of this sunny house, and the breakfast will certainly keep you going all day.

Facilities 3 rms (3 pri facs) (1 GF) ⊗ TVB tea/coffee ✈ Cen ht No coaches **Prices** S £30; D £45✳ **Parking** 2 **Notes** Closed 24 Dec-1 Jan ⊠

◆◆◆◆

Hamilton House
95 Victoria Rd North, Southsea PO5 1PS
☎ 023 9282 3502 🖹 023 9282 3502
e-mail sandra@hamiltonhouse.co.uk
web www.hamiltonhouse.co.uk
Dir *M275 junct 12, A3 into Portsmouth, onto A2030, 2nd rdbt right onto A2151 Victoria Rd N*

This spacious Victorian property, carefully renovated by Graham and Sandra Tubb, provides bright, comfortable accommodation with thoughtful facilities. The property is convenient for exploring historic Portsmouth and is close to the university. Breakfast is available from 6am for guests catching the cross-channel ferry. On-road parking is available.

Facilities 9 rms (5 en suite) (3 fmly) ⊗ TVB tea/coffee ✈ Cen ht TVL **Prices** S £35-£55; D £54-£62

◆◆◆◆

St Margarets ◇
3 Craneswater Gate PO4 0NZ
☎ 023 9282 0097 🖹 023 9282 0097
e-mail enquiries@saintmargarethotel.co.uk
web www.saintmargarethotel.co.uk
Dir *From South Parade Pier E along A288 St Helens Parade, 2nd left*

This establishment is in a quiet residential area close to the seafront and town centre. The attractive bedrooms have coordinated soft furnishings and many thoughtful extras. Breakfast is served in the smart dining room and there are two lounges and a cosy bar.

Facilities 14 en suite (1 fmly) ⊗ in 7 bedrooms ⊗ in dining room ⊗ in 1 lounge TVB tea/coffee ✈ Licensed Cen ht TVL No coaches **Prices** S £30-£38; D £52-£70✳ **Parking** 5 **Notes** Closed 21 Dec-2 Jan

England

PORTSMOUTH continued

♦♦♦♦

Upper Mount House Hotel

The Vale, off Clarendon Rd, Southsea PO5 2EQ
☎ 023 9282 0456 ▤ 023 9282 0456
e-mail r.l.moth@uppermount.fsbusiness.co.uk
Dir Off M275 for D-Day Museum, onto road opp museum, over x-rds, right at T-junct, right again

Upper Mount House Hotel is peacefully located in a residential cul-de-sac. This impressive Victorian villa retains many original features and public areas include a comfortable lounge and an attractive dining room with a fine collection of Venetian glassware. The bedrooms are spacious and well equipped and come in a variety of styles.

Facilities 12 en suite (3 fmly) ⊗ in 6 bedrooms ⊗ in dining room STV TVB tea/coffee Direct dial from bedrooms ✱ Cen ht TVL **Prices** S fr £35; D £58-£60✱ **Parking** 12

♦♦♦

The Festing Grove ◇

8 Festing Grove, Southsea PO4 9QA ☎ 023 9273 5239
e-mail thefestinggrove@ntlworld.com
Dir E along seafront to South Parade Pier, after pier sharp left, around lake 3rd left & 2nd right

A well-presented property situated within easy walking distance of the seafront and pier. The rooms offer a high standard of decor and comfort and there is a well-appointed lounge. Breakfast is served in the homely dining room.

Facilities 6 rms (1 en suite) (2 fmly) ⊗ TVB tea/coffee ✱ Cen ht TVL No coaches **Prices** S £28-£42; D £42-£55

♦♦♦

Amberley Court

97 Waverley Rd, Southsea PO5 2PL
☎ 023 9273 7473 ▤ 023 9275 2343
e-mail mail@amberleycourt.co.uk
Dir Off A288 South Parade near pier onto B2155 Clarendon Rd & Waverley Rd

Amberley Court has a convenient location just 0.4m from the seafront and attractions. The comfortable bedrooms have bright modern coordinated fabrics, and come with good facilities. Many rooms and the smart conservatory-dining room are in a second house nearby.

Facilities 9 en suite (4 fmly) ⊗ TVB tea/coffee ✱ Cen ht TVL **Parking** 4

♦♦♦

Bembell Court

69 Festing Rd, Southsea PO4 0NQ
☎ 023 9273 5915 ▤ 023 9275 6497
e-mail keith@bembell.freeserve.co.uk
web www.bembell.co.uk
Dir From South Parade Pier E along A288 St Helens Parade, 4th left

Located a short walk from the seafront, boating lake and the Natural History Museum, this impressive ivy-clad Victorian house provides a good standard of homely accommodation. Comprehensive breakfasts are served in the attractive dining room, and a stunning floral display highlights the exterior in summer.

Facilities 12 rms (11 en suite) (2 fmly) (2 GF) ⊗ in 6 bedrooms ⊗ in dining room ⊗ in lounges TVB tea/coffee ✱ Cen ht TVL **Prices** S £48-£49; D £62-£64✱ **LB Parking** 7

♦♦♦

Norfolk House ◇

25 Granada Rd, Southsea PO4 0RD ☎ 023 9282 4162
e-mail jbpnorfolk@ntlworld.com
web www.thenorfolksouthsea.com
Dir From South Parade Pier E along A288 St Helens Parade, 1st left

Situated within walking distance of Southsea's attractions, Norfolk House is suited for business and leisure. The attractive rooms come with a range of useful extras, and some include a workspace. A lounge is also available.

Facilities 8 en suite (2 fmly) ⊗ TVB tea/coffee ✱ Cen ht **Prices** S fr £28; d fr £40✱ **Parking** 5 **Notes** Closed Xmas

♦♦♦ 🅰

Arden Guest House

14 Herbert Rd PO4 0QA
☎ 023 9282 6409 ▤ 023 9286 2409
Dir At South Parade Pier onto Clarendon Rd to rdbt, 3rd exit onto Waverley Rd, Herbert Rd 3rd right

Facilities 6 rms (4 en suite) (2 fmly) ⊗ TVB tea/coffee ✱ Cen ht TVL No coaches **Parking** 2 **Notes** 🐾

England

◆◆◆

Victoria Court

29 Victoria Rd North, Southsea PO5 1PL
☎ 023 9282 0305
e-mail stay@victoriacourt.co.uk
web www.victoriacourt.co.uk
Dir 1st left at rdbt at the end of motorway, over 3 rdbts for Victoria Rd North

Facilities 6 rms (5 en suite) (2 fmly) (1 GF) ⊗ in bedrooms ⊗ in dining room TV5B tea/coffee ✱ Cen ht No coaches

◆◆

Collingham ◇

89 St Ronans Rd, Southsea PO4 0PR ☎ 023 9282 1549
Dir Signs for Southsea, at seafront E to canoe lake, left fork to Festing Rd, at top turn left, left onto St Ronans Rd

The friendly Collingham is situated a short distance from the shops and the seafront. The bedrooms are neatly decorated and a traditional cooked breakfast is served in the comfortable dining room.

Facilities 6 rms (3 fmly) ⊗ in 4 bedrooms ⊗ in dining room TVB tea/coffee Cen ht TVL No children 4yrs **Prices** S £21-£25; D £42-£50✱ **Notes** Closed 25 Dec 🐾

◆◆

Sherwood Guest House ◇

21 Beach Rd, Southsea PO5 2JH ☎ 023 9273 4108
e-mail kevin.norwood1@ntlworld.com
Dir Off M27 & seafront road to The Pyramids, turn left onto Florence Rd then 2nd right

This friendly house is just a short walk from the seafront. Bedrooms are simply appointed and a hearty breakfast is served in the dining room. A warm welcome is assured.

Facilities 6 rms (1 fmly) ⊗ in dining room TVB tea/coffee ✱ Cen ht No coaches **Prices** S £20-£22; D £38-£45 **Notes** Closed 25-26 Dec 🐾

RINGWOOD   MAP 05 SU10

★★★ Guest Accommodation

Candlesticks Inn

136 Christchurch Rd BH24 3AP
☎ 01425 472587 📠 01425 471600
e-mail info@hotelnewforest.co.uk
web www.hotelnewforest.co.uk
Dir From A31 Ringwood take B3347 to Sopley/Winkton, approx 0.75m & Candlesticks on right

The 18th-century thatched property offers accommodation with a restaurant on the edge of town, and is convenient for Bournemouth and the New Forest National Park. Ample parking.

Facilities 8 annexe en suite (1 fmly) (4 GF) ⊗ in bedrooms ⊗ in dining room TVB tea/coffee Direct dial from bedrooms ✱ Licensed Cen ht No coaches Dinner Last d 9pm **Prices** S £55-£80; D £68-£80✱ LB **Parking** 30 **Notes** Closed 23 Dec-10 Jan

Little Forest Lodge

Poulner Hill BH24 3HS ☎ 01425 478848 📠 01425 473564
Dir 1.5m E of Ringwood on A31

A warm welcome is given to you and your pets at this charming Edwardian house set in 2 acres of woodland. Bedrooms are pleasantly decorated and equipped with thoughtful extras. By arrangement, you can enjoy freshly made meals using local produce. Both the attractive panelled dining room and the delightful lounge, with bar and wood-burning fire, overlook the gardens.

Facilities 6 en suite (3 fmly) (1 GF) ⊗ TVB tea/coffee Licensed Cen ht No coaches ⛳ clock golf, badminton Dinner Last d 7.30pm **Prices** S £45-£50; D £70-£80✱ **Parking** 10

◆◆◆◆

The Old Cottage

Cowpitts Ln, North Poulner BH24 3JX
☎ 01425 477956 📠 01425 477956
e-mail forestgatewines@btinternet.com
Dir A31 E, 0.75m E of Ringwood left to Hangersley, 1st right, 0.5m to x-rds & over, cottage 100yds on right

Set in beautiful gardens with delightful views, this charming 17th-century thatched cottage retains many original characteristics and has good access to the New Forest and Bournemouth. The comfortable bedrooms, one of which has a four-poster bed, are well equipped. A freshly cooked breakfast is served in the elegant lounge-dining room.

Facilities 2 en suite 1 annexe en suite (1 fmly) (1 GF) ⊗ TVB tea/coffee ✱ Cen ht TVL No children 10yrs No coaches **Prices** S £40-£45; D £60-£64✱ **Parking** 3 **Notes** Closed Nov-Dec 🐾

England

♦♦♦♦ 🛏

Picket Hill House

Picket Hill BH24 3HH ☎ 01425 476173 📄 01425 470022
e-mail b+b@pickethill.freeserve.co.uk
Dir *From Burley junct/services 2m E of Ringwood, off A31 to Ringwood, 250yds left to Hightown & Crow*

This is a good choice as a base for exploring the beautiful New Forest, and you will be assured of a warm welcome. The comfortable bedrooms are well furnished and equipped with many extra facilities, and there is a spacious and comfortable first-floor lounge overlooking delightful gardens. Delicious breakfasts are enjoyed at one large table in the dining room.

Facilities 3 en suite ⊗ in bedrooms ⊗ in dining room ⊗ in 1 lounge tea/coffee ✗ Cen ht TVL No children 12yrs No coaches Golf
Prices D £60-£70 **LB** **Parking** 6 **Notes** Closed 23 Dec-2 Jan

♦♦♦♦

Amberwood

3/5 Top Ln BH24 1LF ☎ 01425 476615 📄 01425 476615
e-mail maynsing@aol.com
web www.amberwoodbandb.co.uk
Dir *A31 onto B3347, over rdbt, left onto School Ln, left onto Top Ln*

This delightful Victorian home is situated in a quiet residential area within easy walking distance of the town centre. Bedrooms are attractively furnished and have many thoughtful extras. A substantial breakfast is served around one large table in the conservatory, which overlooks the well-tended garden. A lounge is also available.

Facilities 2 en suite ⊗ in bedrooms ⊗ in dining room ⊗ in 1 lounge TVB tea/coffee Direct dial from bedrooms ✗ Cen ht TVL No children 12yrs No coaches **Parking** 2 **Notes** Closed Xmas & New Year 🍽

♦♦♦♦

Moortown Lodge Hotel

244 Christchurch Rd BH24 3AS
☎ 01425 471404 📄 01425 476527
e-mail enquiries@moortownlodge.co.uk
web www.moortownlodge.co.uk
Dir *1m S of Ringwood. Off A31 at Ringwood onto B3347, signs to Sople, Lodge next to David Lloyds Health Club*

The light and airy accommodation is finished to a high standard, with digital television and broadband available in each room. Two of the

well-equipped bedrooms are on the ground floor and another features a four-poster bed. Breakfast is served in the smart lounge-dining room at separate tables.

Moortown Lodge Hotel

Facilities 7 en suite (3 fmly) (2 GF) ⊗ FTV TVB tea/coffee Direct dial from bedrooms Cen ht No coaches **Prices** D £80-£90✳ **LB** **Parking** 9

♦♦♦♦

Old Stacks

154 Hightown Rd BH24 1NP
☎ 01425 473840 📄 01425 473840
e-mail oldstacksbandb@aol.com
Dir *Off A31 1m E of Ringwood signed Hightown, S onto Eastfield Ln, 0.5m right*

This delightful bungalow lies in charming gardens. Of the two bedrooms, the twin-bed room has an en suite and its own garden entrance, while the double room has an adjoining bathroom. There is a comfortable lounge and a hearty breakfast is served around a large table in the dining room.

Facilities 2 rms (1 en suite) (1 pri facs) (2 GF) ⊗ TVB tea/coffee ✗ Cen ht TVL No children 12yrs No coaches **Prices** D £50-£56✳ **LB** **Parking** 4 **Notes** Closed Xmas & New Year 🍽

♦♦♦♦

Valley View ◇

Cowpits Ln, North Poulner BH24 3JX
☎ 01425 475855 & 07930 463134 📄 01425 472542
e-mail edward_brown@tinyworld.co.uk
Dir *A31 Poulner exit, N onto Gorley Rd, right onto Cowpitts Ln*

This establishment is set in a peaceful location with easy access to the New Forest and the Dorset coast. The bedroom have many considerate extras, and breakfast, featuring home-made preserves, is

continued

continued

served in the family dining room. A home-cooked dinner is available by arrangement.

Facilities 2 rms (2 pri facs) ⊗ in bedrooms TVB tea/coffee ✗ Cen ht No coaches Dinner Last d 4pm **Prices** S £30-£32; D £56-£60✳ LB **Parking** 5 **Notes** ⊕

◆◆◆◆

Zarabanda

Horton Rd, Ashley Heath BH24 2EB ☎ 01425 475566
e-mail stantonborley@waitrose.com
Dir A31 onto Horton Rd, 100yds turn right into cul de sac. Zarabanda on right.

A warm welcome is guaranteed at Zarabanda, set in a residential area close to routes for the Dorset coast and the New Forest. The self-contained annexe is excellently equipped with a kitchen, television lounge and dining room, and overlooks the pretty family garden.

Facilities 1 annexe en suite (1 GF) ⊗ TVB tea/coffee ✗ Cen ht TVL No coaches **Prices** D £56-£70✳ **Parking** 1 **Notes** ⊕

◆◆◆◆

Fraser House

Salisbury Rd, Blashford BH24 3PB
☎ 01425 473958 ▤ 01425 473958
e-mail mail@fraserhouse.net
Dir Off A31 at Ringwood onto A338 Salisbury Rd, house 1m on right

Facilities 6 en suite ⊗ TVB tea/coffee Cen ht TVL No children 12yrs No coaches **Prices** S fr £39; D £58-£62✳ **Parking** 6

◆◆◆

Lochend ◇

Hurst Corner, Salisbury Rd BH24 1AX ☎ 01425 473836
e-mail kenburnsbrown@btinternet.com
Dir A31 onto A338 towards Fordingbridge, 0.25m right onto Hurst Rd

Located on the north side of town with easy access to the shops and the New Forest, this delightful property has both of its spacious and comfortable bedrooms on the ground floor. A charming garden is also available, and cooked English breakfasts are served at one large table.

Facilities 2 rms (1 en suite) (1 fmly) (2 GF) ⊗ TVB tea/coffee Cen ht No coaches **Prices** S £30-£44; D £48✳ LB **Parking** 4 **Notes** Closed Xmas & New Year ⊕

The Lamb Inn ◇

2 Hightown Rd BH24 1NW ☎ 01425 473721
Dir Off A31, 200yds past fire station on left

At the time of going to press the rating for this establishment had not been confirmed. Please check the AA website www.theAA.com for up-to-date information.

Facilities 3 rms (1 en suite) 2 annexe en suite (2 GF) ⊗ in bedrooms ⊗ in dining room TVB tea/coffee ✗ Cen ht No children 14yrs No coaches **Prices** S £30-£35; D £40-£55✳ **Parking** 8

ROMSEY   MAP 05 SU32
See also **East Tytherley**

◆◆◆◆ ✿

Greenvale Farm *(SU278225)*

Melchet Pk, Sherfield English SO51 6FS
☎ 01794 884858 Mrs Brown
web www.greenvalefarm.com
Dir 5m W of Romsey. On S side of A27 through red-brick archway for Melchet Court, Greenvale Farm 150yds on left, left at slatted barn

Located 4m from the New Forest and within easy reach of Salisbury, this self-contained accommodation appeals for its plentiful facilities. With a working farm next door, don't be surprised if you are woken by a cockerel in the morning or hear guinea fowl chattering at night. The hearty breakfast, with freshly laid eggs if you're lucky, will set you up for the day.

Facilities 1 annexe en suite (1 GF) ⊗ TVB tea/coffee ✗ Cen ht No children 14yrs Croquet and bowls facility on Tue/Wed pm 2 acres Poultry **Prices** S £35; D £65 LB **Parking** 10 **Notes** Closed 20 Dec-6 Jan ⊕

◆◆◆◆

Country Accommodation

The Old Post Office, New Rd, Michelmersh SO51 0NL
☎ 01794 368739
Dir 3m N of Romsey, off A3057 onto New Rd into Michelmersh

This attractive guest house is decorated with country memorabilia that reflect the history of this delightful property. The comfortable bedrooms have excellent facilities and many useful extras. This is a good location for business or for touring the beautiful Hampshire countryside.

Facilities 3 annexe en suite (1 fmly) (3 GF) ⊗ in dining room TVB tea/coffee ✗ Cen ht No children 12yrs No coaches **Prices** S fr £33; d fr £55 **Parking** 5

ROWLAND'S CASTLE

MAP 05 SU71

♦♦♦♦ ⌦ ◀

The Fountain Inn ◇

34 The Green PO9 6AB
☎ 023 9241 2291 ▤ 023 9241 2291
e-mail Fountaininn@amserve.com
Dir A3(M) junct 2, B2149 to village centre

This charming coaching inn is set back from the road and overlooks the village green. The well-equipped bedrooms have been carefully refurbished and have many thoughtful touches; one room has a lovely four-poster bed. Public areas consist of a popular local bar and a cosy Thai restaurant.

Facilities 4 en suite (1 fmly) ⊗ TVB tea/coffee Cen ht Golf Dinner Last d 10pm **Prices** S £25-£50; D £50-£75✳ **LB** **Parking** 15

SOUTHAMPTON

MAP 05 SU41

See also **Warsash**

Premier Collection

♦♦♦♦♦

Riverside Bed & Breakfast

4 Tides Reach, 53 Whitworth Rd SO18 1GE
☎ 02380 630315 ▤ 02380 630315
e-mail gordon-funnelle@supanet.com
Dir M27 Junct 5, follow A335 onto Thomas Lewis Way, 1st left to Clocktower, Sharp right Whitworth Crescent leads to Whitworth Rd.

Located in a quiet part of Southampton, a short walk from public transport links and a 10-minute drive from the airport, this small and homely house has wonderful river views. Bedrooms come with thoughtful touches and you have your own comfortable lounge. A wonderful continental breakfast is served in the dining room or on the balcony in warmer weather.

Facilities 2 rms (2 pri facs) ⊗ TVB tea/coffee ✖ Cen ht No children 14yrs No coaches **Prices** S £35-£55; D £50-£60 **Parking** 1 **Notes** ⊛

♦♦♦♦

Alcantara ◇

20 Howard Rd, Shirley SO15 5BN
☎ 023 8033 2966 ▤ 023 8049 6163
e-mail alcantara@btconnect.com
web www.alcantaraguesthouse.co.uk
Dir 0.5m NW of city centre. Off A3057 onto Howard Rd

A warm welcome is assured at this Victorian property, named after the ocean liner to reflect the establishment's shipping connections and close location to the city centre. The comfortable bedrooms are well decorated and have many thoughtful extras. An appetising breakfast is enjoyed in the bright and airy dining room.

Facilities 9 rms (6 en suite) (3 fmly) (2 GF) ⊗ TVB tea/coffee ✖ Cen ht No coaches Limited access to nearby leisure facilities **Prices** S £28-£35; D £55✳ **Parking** 7

♦♦♦♦

Hunters Lodge

25 Landguard Rd, Shirley SO15 5DL
☎ 023 8022 7919 ▤ 023 8023 0913
e-mail hunterslodge.hotel@virgin.net
web www.hunterslodgehotel.net
Dir 500yds NW of Southampton Central station. Off A3057 Shirley Rd onto Languard Rd

Located in a leafy residential area close to the city centre and convenient for the docks, ferry terminal, university and hospital, this double-fronted Victorian house provides business and leisure guests with comfortable, well-equipped bedrooms. A full English breakfast is served at shared tables in the elegant dining room, and there is also a television lounge and a well-stocked bar.

Facilities 14 en suite (1 fmly) (1 GF) ⊗ in bedrooms ⊗ in dining room ⊗ in 1 lounge TVB tea/coffee Direct dial from bedrooms Licensed Cen ht TVL No coaches **Prices** S £40-£55; D £67-£70✳ **Parking** 16

♦♦♦♦

Landguard Lodge

21 Landguard Rd SO15 5DL
☎ 023 8063 6904 ▤ 023 8063 2258
e-mail landguard.lodge@mail.com
web www.landguardlodge.co.uk
Dir 500yds NW of Southampton Central station. Off A3057 Shirley Rd onto Languard Rd

This Victorian house is in a quiet residential area a short walk from the railway station. The bedrooms are bright, comfortable and well

continued

equipped with many thoughtful extras. Smoking is only permitted in the lounge.

Facilities 10 en suite (1 fmly) (1 GF) ⊘ in bedrooms ⊘ in dining room ▮VB tea/coffee ✖ Cen ht No children 5yrs No coaches **Parking** 3

◆◆◆

The Fenland Guest House ◇

79 Hill Ln SO15 5AD ☎ 023 8022 0360 ▤ 023 8048 7575
e-mail fenland@btconnect.com
Dir A33 into Southampton, at rdbt right onto A35 Winchester Rd, left next rdbt, over minirdbt onto Hill Ln, after 2nd lights Fenland on left

Well situated for the city centre, university and ferry terminals, this delightful house provides comfortable rooms with many extra facilities. Two rooms are on the ground floor. Full English or continental breakfasts are served at individual tables.

Facilities 8 rms (5 en suite) (2 fmly) (2 GF) ⊘ TVB tea/coffee ✖ Cen ht No children 2yrs No coaches **Prices** S £28-£40; D £48-£55✳
Parking 6 **Notes** Closed 24 Dec-2 Jan

◆◆◆

Mayview ◇

50 The Polygon SO15 2BN
☎ 023 8022 0907 & 07973 874194 ▤ 07977 017921
e-mail mayviewgh@yahoo.co.uk

Facilities 9 rms (1 en suite) (1 fmly) (1 GF) ⊘ TVB tea/coffee ✖ Cen ht **Prices** S £20-£25; D £40-£55✳ **Notes** Closed 25 Dec

◆◆

The Brimar ◇

10-14 High St, Totton SO40 9HN
☎ 023 8086 2950 ▤ 023 8086 1301
e-mail info@brimar-guesthouse.co.uk
Dir 3m W of city centre, off A35 in Totton High St

This guest house offers practical, comfortable accommodation at reasonable prices. Not all rooms are en suite but the bathrooms are well situated. Breakfast is served in the dining room or as a take-away option. The Brimar is well placed for the M27 and Southampton Docks, and off-road parking is available.

Facilities 21 rms (8 en suite) (2 fmly) (8 GF) ⊘ TVB ✖ Cen ht **Prices** S £27-£35; D £56-£60✳ **Parking** 20

STOCKBRIDGE   MAP 05 SU33

◆◆◆◆ ▮

The White Hart

SO20 6HF ☎ 01264 810663 ▤ 01264 810268
e-mail whitehart@accommodating-inns.co.uk
web www.accommodating-inns.co.uk

The former coaching inn lies on the edge of the village famous for the River Test. Accommodation, split between the main inn and a converted stable block, has modern amenties, and you can enjoy a drink and a meal in the spacious character bar and restaurant.

Facilities 14 en suite (1 fmly) (5 GF) ⊘ in bedrooms ⊘ in area of dining room TVB tea/coffee Direct dial from bedrooms ✖ Cen ht Dinner Last d 9.30pm **Parking** 30

◆◆◆◆

York Lodge

Five Bells Ln, Nether Wallop SO20 8HE ☎ 01264 781313
e-mail bradley@york-lodge.co.uk
web www.york-lodge.co.uk
Dir 3m W of Stockbridge in Nether Wallop

Located in the picturesque village famous for Agatha Christie's Miss Marple series, this charming house has comfortable accommodation in a self-contained wing. Bedrooms are stylish with many thoughtful extra facilities. The dining room overlooks peaceful gardens, and delicious dinners are available by arrangement.

Facilities 2 en suite (2 GF) ⊘ TVB tea/coffee Cen ht No children 8yrs No coaches Dinner Last d 24hrs prior **Prices** S £35-£45; D £60-£70✳ **Parking** 4 **Notes** ⊠

◆◆◆

Carbery

Salisbury Hill SO20 6EZ ☎ 01264 810771 ▤ 01264 811022
Dir On A30 at W end of main street

Situated in extensive landscaped gardens overlooking the River Test, Carbery is within easy walking distance of the village centre. There is a lounge and a games room with pool table, and an outdoor pool is available in warmer months. Dinner is available by arrangement.

Facilities 11 rms (8 en suite) (1 fmly) ⊘ in dining room TVB tea/coffee ✖ Licensed Cen ht No coaches � Pool Table Day membership to nearby leisure centre Dinner Last d 6pm **Prices** S £36-£46; D £58-£65 **Parking** 14 **Notes** Closed 2 wks Xmas

SWAY   MAP 05 SZ29

★★★ Inn

The Forest Heath

Station Rd SO41 6BA ☎ 01590 682287 ▤ 01590 682626
e-mail forestheathhotel@hotmail.co.uk
Dir M27 junct 1, A337 to Brockenhurst, B3055 to Sway, onto Church Ln & Station Rd

Located in a New Forest village, this late Victorian inn is a popular meeting place for the local community. Bedrooms are well equipped and comfortable, and a range of real ales and imaginative meals is offered in the bars and the conservatory-dining room.

Facilities 4 en suite (2 fmly) ⊘ in bedrooms ⊘ in area of dining room TVB tea/coffee Cen ht boules, petanque Dinner Last d 9pm **Prices** S £45; D £65✳ **Parking** 20

England

SWAY continued

Premier Collection

◆◆◆◆◆ 🛏 ⌒

The Nurse's Cottage

Station Rd SO41 6BA ☎ 01590 683402
e-mail nurses.cottage@lineone.net
web www.nursescottage.co.uk
Dir *Off B3055 in village centre, close to shops*

Luxury accommodation, excellent hospitality and service, and carefully prepared food all make for an enjoyable stay at this former district-nurse's cottage. The bedrooms are very comfortable with numerous thoughtful extras, while the bathrooms have lovely toiletries, efficient showers and fluffy towels. The conservatory-restaurant is popular with locals and guests.

Facilities 5 en suite (5 GF) ⊗ TVB tea/coffee Direct dial from bedrooms Licensed Cen ht No children 10yrs No coaches Dinner Last d 8pm
Prices S £80; D £150-£170; (incl. dinner) **LB Parking** 5 **Notes** Closed 3wks Nov

◆◆◆◆

Acorn Shetland Pony Stud

Meadows Cottage, Arnewood Bridge Rd SO41 6DA
☎ 01590 682000
e-mail meadows.cottage@virgin.net
Dir *M27 junct 1, A337 to Brockenhurst, B3055 to Sway, pass Birchy Hill Nursing Home, over x-rds, 2nd entrance left*

Located on the outskirts of Sway, this comfortable establishment stands in over 6 acres of pony paddocks and a water garden. The ground-floor bedrooms are well furnished and have direct access onto patios. The enjoyable, freshly cooked breakfasts use a range of fine produce including delicious home-made bread.

Facilities 3 en suite (1 fmly) (3 GF) ⊗ TVB tea/coffee Cen ht No coaches Carriage driving with Shetland ponies **Prices** D £54-£58✳ **LB Parking** 3 **Notes** ⊛

WARSASH
MAP 05 SU40

◆◆◆◆

Dormy House Hotel

21 Barnes Ln, Sarisbury SO31 7DA
☎ 01489 572626 📠 01489 573370
e-mail dormyhousehotel@warsash.globalnet.co.uk
web www.dormyhousehotel.net
Dir *Off A27 at Sarisbury Green onto Barnes Ln, house 1m on right*

With good access to major routes, this friendly house is popular for leisure and business. The neat bedrooms are well-equipped with many facilities, while the public rooms include a cosy lounge and attractive dining room. Parking is a bonus.

Facilities 12 en suite (1 fmly) (6 GF) ⊗ in 9 bedrooms ⊗ in dining room TVB tea/coffee Direct dial from bedrooms 🐾 Licensed Cen ht TVL No coaches **Prices** S £52-£56; D £64-£75 **Parking** 18

◆◆◆◆

Solent View Hotel

33-35 Newtown Rd SO31 9FY
☎ 01489 572300 📠 01489 572300
Dir *Off A27 at Sarisbury Green onto Barnes Ln & Brook Ln to Warsash, over rdbt, 200yds on left*

This delightful Victorian house, just a short walk from the river, has been extended to provide well-equipped bedrooms. Public areas include an attractive dining room, and a lounge with a well-stocked bar. Dinner is available by arrangement.

Facilities 8 en suite (2 GF) ⊗ in dining room TVB tea/coffee Direct dial from bedrooms Licensed Cen ht TVL No children 8yrs No coaches Dinner Last d 8am **Parking** 8 **Notes** Closed 2 wks Xmas, 1 wk Etr, 2 wks Aug

WINCHESTER
MAP 05 SU42

Premier Collection

★★★★★ Bed & Breakfast

Orchard House

3 Christchurch Gdns, St Cross SO23 9TH
☎ 01962 861544 📠 01962 861988
e-mail hopefamily@hotmail.co.uk

This friendly, family-run property is in a peaceful cul-de-sac, close to Winchester and within easy access of the M3. It offers a relaxed atmosphere, professional service and warm hospitality. The bedroom

continued

is spacious and very well equipped for either business or leisure. Gardens are well tended, and the balcony overlooking the rear garden can be used for breakfast on warm summer mornings. Ample parking is available.

Facilities 1 en suite ⊘ STV TVB tea/coffee ✘ Cen ht TVL No children 6yrs No coaches **Prices** S £50-£55; D £80-£85✳ **Parking** 2 **Notes** ⊛

★★★★ Bed & Breakfast

Kings Worthy Bed & Breakfast

Stoke Charity Rd, Kings Worthy SO23 7LS
☎ 01962 882818 & 07889 131255 📠 01962 882818
e-mail info@kingsworthy.com
Dir M3 junct 9 right fork onto A30 Kings Worthy turning, left onto Lovedon Ln, B&B 1m on left

Kings Worthy is set in a peaceful village near Winchester. The bedroom is in an annexe adjoining the house and has a double bed, lots of useful extras, a shower ensuite and small dining area where an extensive continental breakfast is provided.

Facilities 1 en suite (1 GF) ⊘ TVB tea/coffee ✘ Cen ht No children No coaches **Prices** S £60; D £60 **LB Parking** 6 **Notes** ⊛

★★ Bed & Breakfast

67 St Cross ◇

67 St Cross Rd SO23 9RE ☎ 01962 863002
e-mail bbsaintcross@aol.com

A brick terrace property on the outskirts of Winchester. Two bedrooms, one en-suite and one with private bathroom, provide good levels of comfort, and a full English breakfast is served in the dining room.

Facilities 2 en suite **Prices** S £30-£35; D £35-£55✳

◆◆◆◆

Heybridge

Clifton Rd SO22 5BP ☎ 01962 865007 & 07779 436305
e-mail jacquiekennedy@yahoo.co.uk
Dir Heybridge is between No.13 and No. 14 along the top of Orams Arbour.

Close to the town centre in a quiet suburb, overlooking the park, Heybridge offers very comfortable accommodation. The two bedrooms are both en suite and very smartly appointed. A substantial breakfast is served in the spacious dining room.

Facilities 2 en suite ⊘ TVB tea/coffee ✘ Cen ht No coaches **Prices** S £45-£60; D £60-£70✳ **Parking** 1 **Notes** ⊛

◆◆◆◆ ⊛⊛

The Running Horse

88 Main Rd, Littleton SO22 6QS ☎ 01962 880218
e-mail runninghorse@btconnect.com
Dir From Winchester, 2m on B3049, left to Littleton

Situated in a pretty rural location, with good access to the M3, this is a great location for business and leisure travellers visiting Hampshire. The new accommodation is minimalist in design, providing comfortable beds and a small workstation. A highlight of a stay here is a meal in the smart restaurant or a drink in the bar.

continued

Facilities 9 en suite (1 fmly) (9 GF) ⊘ in bedrooms ⊘ in dining room TVB tea/coffee Direct dial from bedrooms ✘ Licensed Cen ht No children 5yrs No coaches Dinner Last d 9.30pm **Parking** 100

◆◆◆

Casadele

61 Stanmore Ln SO22 4AH ☎ 01962 813412
e-mail adeleradichetti@yahoo.com
Dir M3 junct 11. B3335 to Winchester. Left at T junct, onto A3090. At rdbt take 2nd exit, next rdbt 3rd exit onto B3335. Left at lights onto Lower Stanmore Lane, continue onto Stanmore Lane

This small bed and breakfast is situated in a residential area just outside of the city centre and is easily reached by car or public transport. Both rooms are compact yet comfortable, though the strength of the stay is certainly the warm welcome received from the owner, Adele.

Facilities 2 rms ⊘ TVB tea/coffee ✘ Cen ht TVL No children 15yrs No coaches **Prices** S £35; D £45✳ **Parking** 2 **Notes** ⊛

◆◆◆

31 St Anne's Close ◇

Badgers Farm SO22 4LQ ☎ 01962 622553
e-mail reelhall@yahoo.co.uk
Dir M3 junct 11, onto A3090 Badger Farm Rd, right onto Ridgeway, right onto St Annes Close

This friendly, family-run home is in a quiet residential area. It offers a cosy bedroom with a sitting room with coordinated furnishings, complete with a television and a hospitality tray. A full English breakfast is provided.

Facilities 1 rms (1 pri facs) ⊘ TVB tea/coffee ✘ Cen ht TVL No children No coaches **Prices** S £30; D £42 **Parking** 1 **Notes** Closed 16 Dec-4 Jan ⊛

◆◆◆

24 Clifton Road ◇

SO22 5BU ☎ 01962 851620
e-mail joanne.winchester@virgin.net
Dir B3040 Romsey Rd W from city centre, Clifton Rd 2nd right

This delightful house is in a quiet residential area close to the railway station and High St. It combines town-house elegance with a homey cottage charm, and is handy for good walks. The bedroom is comfortably furnished and the bathroom has a deep claw-foot bath. There is a lounge and a dining room.

Facilities 1 rms (1 pri facs) ⊘ ✘ Cen ht TVL No children No coaches **Prices** S £30; D £50✳ **Parking** 2 **Notes** ⊛

WINCHESTER continued

♦♦♦ ◼

The Westgate Hotel

2 Romsey Rd SO23 8TP ☎ 01962 820222 ▤ 01962 820222
e-mail thewestgatehotel@hotmail.com
Dir *From junct Upper High St & High St onto Romsey Rd, premises beyond Westgate arch*

The Westgate is well placed at the west end of the city near the castle. A popular bar serves good, home-prepared meals and snacks, with an Indian theme in the evening. The attractive bedrooms on two floors have bright modern bathrooms.

Facilities 8 rms (6 en suite) ⊘ in dining room TVB tea/coffee Direct dial from bedrooms ✘ Cen ht No children No coaches Dinner Last d 9.30pm **Conf** Max 12 **Notes** Closed 25-26 Dec

HEREFORDSHIRE

ABBEY DORE

MAP 09 SO33

♦♦♦♦ ▤ ❧

Tan House Farm ◈ *(SO385305)*

HR2 0AA ☎ 01981 240204 ▤ 01981 240204 Mrs G Powell
e-mail jppowell@ereal.net
web www.golden-valley.co.uk/tanhouse
Dir *A465 onto B4347 to Dore Abbey*

This stone farmhouse is close to the 12th-century Cistercian abbey in the beautiful Golden Valley. The traditionally furnished bedrooms have modern facilities. Breakfast is served family-style in the lounge-breakfast room, which has fine antique furnishings. The welcome and hospitality here are second to none.

Facilities 3 en suite ⊘ in bedrooms ⊘ in dining room TVB tea/coffee ✘ Cen ht 350 acres arable cattle sheep horses **Prices** S fr £26; d fr £52✱ **Parking** 3 **Notes** rs Nov-Mar (prior booking only) ⊛

BROCKHAMPTON

MAP 10 SO53

♦♦♦♦ ⬤ ❧

Ladyridge Farm ◈ *(SO592320)*

HR1 4SE ☎ 01989 740220 ▤ 01989 740220 Mrs Grant
e-mail carolgrant@ladyridgefarm.fsworld.co.uk
Dir *Off B4224 signed Brockhampton Church between How Caple & Fownhope. Farm 400yds on right after thatched church*

This working farm in delightful countryside provides a peaceful haven and is also home to rare-breed ducks, poultry and sheep. Bedrooms are spacious, traditional and thoughtfully equipped. Meals are served family-style in the attractive dining room, using local fresh ingredients and home-produced free-range eggs.

Facilities 3 rms (2 pri facs) (1 fmly) ⊘ TVB tea/coffee Cen ht Riding 42 acres alpacas/sheep/poultry/ducks Dinner Last d 24 hrs prior **Prices** S £25; D £40-£44✱ **LB** **Parking** 6 **Notes** ⊛

BROMYARD

MAP 10 SO65

♦♦♦♦

Little Hegdon Farm House

Hegdon Hill, Pencombe HR7 4SL
☎ 01885 400263 & 07779 595445
e-mail howardcolegrave@hotmail.com
Dir *Between Pencombe & Risbury, at top of Hegdon Hill down farm lane for 500yds*

Located in a pretty hamlet, this traditional house has been renovated to provide high standards of comfort. Original features include exposed beams and open fires, and the bedrooms are equipped with lots of thoughtful extras and have stunning views of the surrounding countryside.

Facilities 2 en suite ⊘ in bedrooms ⊘ in dining room ⊘ in 1 lounge TVB tea/coffee ✘ Cen ht No coaches Riding Pool Table ⛳ **Prices** S £35; D £60 **Parking** 4 **Notes** ⊛

continued

England

◆◆◆◆ ✤

Linton Brook Farm *(SO676538)*

Malvern Rd, Bringsty WR6 5TR
☎ 01885 488875 🖹 01885 488875 Mrs Steeds
Dir *Off A44 1.5m E of Bromyard onto B4220 signed Malvern. Farm 0.5m on left*

Dating back some 400 years, this large house has a wealth of character and has been renovated to provide modern comforts. Accommodation is spacious and there is a comfortable sitting room with a welcoming wood-burning stove. The breakfast room has exposed beams, antique furniture and an inglenook fireplace.

Facilities 3 rms (2 en suite) (1 pri facs) ⊗ TVB tea/coffee 🐾 Cen ht TVL 68 acres grassland Dinner **Prices** S £27.50-£35; D £60-£70 LB **Conf** Max 12 **Parking** 12 **Notes** ⊛

BURGHILL

MAP 09 SO44

[U]

Fieldview House

2 Chestnut Ln HR4 7QN ☎ 01432 769101
e-mail amandaamore@hotmail.com
Dir *Approaching Hereford on A4103 continue past Race Course over lights to Tillington, 1st right*

At the time of going to press the rating for this establishment had not been confirmed. Please check the AA website www.theAA.com for up-to-date information.

Facilities 1 rms (1 pri facs) ⊗ TVB tea/coffee 🐾 Cen ht No children No coaches Dinner Last d 4pm **Prices** d fr £50⋇ **Parking** 2 **Notes** Closed 21 Dec-5 Jan ⊛

FOWNHOPE

MAP 10 SO53

◆◆◆◆

Bowens Country House

HR1 4PS ☎ 01432 860430 🖹 01432 860430
e-mail thebowenshotel@aol.com
Dir *6m SE of Hereford on B4224. In Fownhope, opp church*

This 17th-century former farmhouse, set in well-tended grounds, is peaceful and relaxing. The house provides modern and comfortable facilities. Bedrooms are attractively decorated and have many extra touches, and family rooms are available, including a two-bedroom suite. An honesty bar is provided in the lounge, and delicious home-cooked dishes are served at individual tables.

Facilities 6 en suite 4 annexe en suite (3 fmly) (4 GF) ⊗ in bedrooms ⊗ in dining room TVB tea/coffee Direct dial from bedrooms Licensed Cen ht No coaches ⚬ ♨ ⅃ Dinner Last d 8pm **Prices** S £38; d fr £76⋇ LB **Parking** 15

◆◆◆ ◀

Green Man Inn

HR1 4PE ☎ 01432 860243 🖹 01432 860207
e-mail info@thegreenmaninn.co.uk
Dir *M50 junct 3, follow B4224 to Fownhope*

Located in a peaceful village, this welcoming inn has plenty of character with low oak beams and a black and white frontage. An excellent selection of food is available at lunch or dinner in the bar, restaurant or garden. Well suited for business or leisure, bedrooms vary in size and include some in the main building and others around a courtyard.

Facilities 24 en suite (6 fmly) (6 GF) ⊗ in 11 bedrooms ⊗ in dining room STV TVB tea/coffee Direct dial from bedrooms TVL ▣ Fishing Sauna Solarium Gymnasium Pool Table Spa, jacuzzi Dinner Last d 5pm **Conf** Max 30

England

GOODRICH
MAP 10 SO51

★★★★ Bed & Breakfast
Granton House B&B
HR9 6JE ☎ 01600 890277
e-mail info@grantonhouse.co.uk
web www.grantonhouse.co.uk
Dir A40 S from Ross-on-Wye, 2nd Goodrich exit into village, near church

A genuine welcome awaits you at Granton House, set in extensive grounds and gardens on the edge of the village. It dates in part from the late 18th century and was once the home of Victorian artist Joshua Cristall. The house has been carefully renovated to provide high quality and thoughtfully equipped accommodation.

Facilities 3 en suite (1 fmly) ⊗ TVB tea/coffee ✖ Cen ht No children No coaches **Parking** 4 **Notes** Closed 18 Dec-2 Jan ⊛

HEREFORD
MAP 10 SO53
See also **Little Dewchurch & Moccas**

◆◆◆◆ ❦
Holly House (SO456367)
Allensmore HR2 9BH
☎ 01432 277294 & 07889 830223 🖳 01432 261285
Mrs Sinclair
e-mail hollyhousefarm@aol.com
web www.hollyhousefarm.org.uk
Dir A465 S to Allensmore, right signed Cobhall Common, at small x-rds right onto lane, house on right

Surrounded by open countryside, this spacious farmhouse is an utterly peaceful and relaxing base for touring this beautiful area. Homely comforts abound with both bedrooms offering lovely views over fields. Breakfast makes use of local produce along with home-made preserves and marmalade. Pets are very welcome and the proprietor is happy to look after them during the day if required.

Facilities 2 rms (1 en suite) (1 pri facs) ⊗ TVB tea/coffee Cen ht 11 acres Horses **Prices** D £50-£60 **Parking** 32 **Notes** Closed 25-26, 31 Dec & 1 Jan ⊛

◆◆◆◆ ❦
Sink Green Farm ◇ (SO542377)
Rotherwas HR2 6LE
☎ 01432 870223 🖳 01432 870223 Mr Jones
e-mail enquiries@sinkgreenfarm.co.uk
web www.sinkgreenfarm.co.uk
Dir On B4399 2m from junction with A49

This charming 16th-century farmhouse stands in attractive countryside and has many original features, including flagstone floors, exposed beams and open fireplaces. Bedrooms are traditionally furnished and one has a four-poster bed. The pleasant garden has a comfortable summer house, hot tub and barbecue. The friendly and relaxed atmosphere leaves a lasting impression.

Facilities 3 en suite ⊗ TVB tea/coffee Cen ht TVL Jacuzzi & summer house 180 acres beef sheep **Prices** S £28-£40; D £54-£60 LB **Parking** 10 **Notes** Closed Xmas ⊛

◆◆◆◆ ❦
The Vauld House Farm (SO532495)
The Vauld, Marden HR1 3HA
☎ 01568 797347 🖳 01568 797366 Mrs Wells
e-mail wellsthevauld@talk21.com
Dir 6m N of Hereford. Off A49 onto A417, right at Englands Gate Inn, Bodenham. 2m turn right for The Vauld and Litmarsh, at junct farm opp

Judith Wells gives a warm welcome and ensures a relaxing stay at this working farm set in landscaped grounds. The spacious, thoughtfully equipped bedrooms are in converted oast houses, which retain many original features. One is suitable for self-catering and the other is a family suite. Meals are served family style in the main house and dinner can include home-reared Herefordshire beef.

Facilities 2 en suite (1 fmly) (1 GF) ⊗ TVB tea/coffee ✖ Cen ht TVL Golf 18 30 acres mixed Dinner Last d 10am **Parking** 20 **Notes** Closed Dec-Feb ⊛

◆◆◆◆ Ⓐ
Hedley Lodge
Belmont Abbey, Abergavenny Rd HR2 9RZ
☎ 01432 374747 🖳 01432 374754
e-mail hedleylodge@belmontabbey.org.uk
web www.hedleylodge.com
Dir 2m SW of city centre. Off A465 signed Belmont Abbey

Facilities 17 en suite (1 fmly) ⊗ in 13 bedrooms ⊗ in dining room ⊗ in lounges TVB tea/coffee Direct dial from bedrooms ✖ Licensed Cen ht Dinner Last d 8pm **Prices** S £40; D £60✳ **Conf** Max 200 Thtr 200 Class 50 Board 40 Del from £50 ✳ **Parking** 200

England

♦♦♦

Heron House

Canon Pyon Rd, Portway HR4 8NG
☎ 01432 761111 📠 01432 760603
e-mail info@theheronhouse.com
web www.theheronhouse.com
Dir A4103 onto A4110 until Portway x-rds, Heron House 200yds on left

Facilities 2 rms (1 en suite) ⊗ TVB tea/coffee ✖ Cen ht No children 10yrs No coaches **Prices** D £46✳ **Parking** 5 **Notes** ✉

LEDBURY   MAP 10 SO73

★★★ ⊛ Restaurant with Rooms

Seven Ledbury

11 The Homend HR8 1BN
☎ 01531 631317 📠 01531 630168
e-mail jasonkay@btconnect.com
Dir M50 junct 2 onto A417, follow Ledbury for approx 2m

Modern bistro dining hides behind the front of this traditional black and white timber-framed building in the town centre. The refurbished establishment offers friendly and efficient service, and the quality cuisine has more than a hint of the Mediterranean.

Facilities 3 en suite TVB tea/coffee Direct dial from bedrooms ✖ Licensed No coaches Dinner Last d 10pm **Prices** S £65; D £85✳ **Notes** Closed 25 Dec

♦♦♦♦ 🏛

Bodenham Farm

Much Marcle HR8 2NJ ☎ 01531 660222 & 07754 415604
e-mail bodenhamfarm@lineone.net
web www.bodenhamfarm.co.uk
Dir 5m SW of Ledbury. 0.5m S of Much Marcle on A449

Set in well-tended gardens, this impressive and attractive Grade II listed house dates from the 18th century. Full of character, the comfortable accommodation retains many original features including exposed beams and four-poster beds, along with modern facilities. The welcoming proprietors make you feel very much at home.

Facilities 3 en suite ⊗ TVB tea/coffee ✖ Cen ht TVL No children 12yrs No coaches **Prices** S £35; D £60 **Parking** 8 **Notes** ✉

♦♦♦♦

Moor Court Farm ◊ (SO639447)

Stretton, Grandison HR8 2TP
☎ 01531 670408 📠 01531 670408 Mrs Godsall
Dir 1.5m E of A417 at Upper Eggleton

This 15th-century house is situated on a mixed farm with working oast houses where hops are dried. There is a wealth of original features. Bedrooms are thoughtfully equipped and furnished, and one has a four-poster bed. Public areas include a comfortable lounge with an impressive stone fireplace and dining room, where breakfast includes local produce and eggs from the farm.

Facilities 3 en suite ⊗ TVB tea/coffee ✖ Licensed Cen ht No children 8yrs Fishing 200 acres Mixed livestock hops Dinner Last d 6.30pm **Prices** S £30-£40; D £50-£60✳ **Parking** 5 **Notes** ✉

🆄 ❦

Church Farm (SO718426)

Coddington HR8 1JJ ☎ 01531 640271 Mrs West
e-mail jane@dexta.co.uk
web www.dexta.co.uk

At the time of going to press the rating for this establishment had not been confirmed. Please check the AA website www.theAA.com for up-to-date information.

Facilities 3 rms (2 en suite) (1 pri facs) ⊗ in bedrooms ⊗ in dining room ⊗ in 1 lounge TV1B tea/coffee Cen ht TVL 100 acres sheep/arable **Prices** D £56-£70✳ **Conf** Max 12 **Parking** available **Notes** Closed 16 Dec-15 Jan ✉

England

LEOMINSTER MAP 10 SO45

Premier Collection

✦✦✦✦✦ ⬤ ❦

Ford Abbey (SO560579)

Pudleston HR6 0RZ ☎ 01568 760700 🖥 01568 760264
Mr & Mrs O'Donnell
e-mail info@fordabbey.co.uk
web www.fordabbey.co.uk
Dir A44 Leominster towards Worcester, turn left to Pudleston

Attention to detail and a high level of hospitality are the hallmarks of this former property of Benedictine monks, now part of a working farm. Beams, old and new, and original features are everywhere, and there is a choice of lounges. The atmospheric restaurant serves excellent dinners featuring farm produce. Bedrooms are spacious and thoughtfully equipped, and there is also a leisure complex in the grounds.

Facilities 6 en suite (1 GF) ⊘ in bedrooms ⊘ in dining room STV TVB tea/coffee Direct dial from bedrooms Licensed Cen ht TVL 🔲 Solarium Gymnasium 🏑 Clay pigeon shoot on site 320 acres beef Dinner Last d 9.30pm **Prices** D £125-£180✳ **Conf** Max 12 Board 12 **Parking** 20 **Notes** Civ Wed 35

Premier Collection

✦✦✦✦✦ 🖳 ⬤ ❦

Hills Farm (SO564638)

Leysters HR6 0HP ☎ 01568 750205 Mrs Conolly
e-mail conolly@bigwig.net
web www.thehillsfarm.co.uk
Dir Off A4112 Leominster to Tenbury Wells, on edge of Leysters

Set in a peaceful location with views of the surrounding countryside, this property dates in part from the 16th century. The friendly, attentive proprietors provide a relaxing and homely atmosphere. The attractive bedrooms, in the main house and converted barns, are spacious and comfortable. Excellent breakfasts, served in the dining room and conservatory, feature fresh local produce.

Facilities 3 annexe en suite (1 GF) ⊘ FTV TVB tea/coffee ✖ Cen ht No children 12yrs 120 acres arable **Prices** S £32-£45; D £64-£72 **Parking** 8 **Notes** Closed Nov-Feb

✦✦✦✦

Bunns Croft ◈

Moreton Eye HR6 0DP ☎ 01568 615836
Dir 3.5m N of Leominster. Off A49 in Ashton to Moreton Eye, Bunns Croft 1m on right by post box

This timber-framed cottage stands in the small village of Moreton Eye. It has a wealth of charm and has been furnished in a style befitting its character. Bedrooms include a three-room family suite, and all have thoughtful extra touches. There is a spacious lounge, where log fires burn during cold weather. Dinner is available on request and the home-cooked meals feature local produce.

Facilities 4 rms (1 en suite) ⊘ tea/coffee ✖ Cen ht TVL No children 10yrs No coaches Dinner Last d 10am **Prices** S £30; D £60-£68✳ **Parking** 3 **Notes** ⊛

✦✦✦✦ ❦

Lawton Bury Farm Bed & Breakfast
(SO445594)

Lawton HR6 9AX
☎ 01568 709285 & 07947 048943 🖥 01568 709285
Mrs Lyke
e-mail enquiries@visitlawtonbury.co.uk
Dir 3m W of Leominster on B4529 for Eardisland

Dating largely from the 18th century, this charming house is situated on a 180-acre working farm and has been owned by the present family for almost 100 years. Many original features have been successfully combined with stylish additions. Comfort is in abundance, especially the lovely snug sofas in the lounge. Eggs from the resident hens feature in wonderfully tasty and satisfying breakfasts.

Facilities 3 en suite (1 fmly) ⊘ TVB tea/coffee ✖ Cen ht 180 acres mixed **Prices** S £35-£40; D £50-£60✳ **Parking** 6 **Notes** Closed 2wks Xmas ⊛

✦✦✦ ❦

Woonton Court Farm ◈ (SO548613)

Leysters HR6 0HL
☎ 01568 750232 🖥 01568 750232 Mrs Thomas
e-mail thomas.woontoncourt@farmersweekly.net
web www.woontoncourt.co.uk
Dir 3m NE of Leominster. Off A4112 for Woonton (SE of Leysters), farm 0.5m

This attractive 15th-century farmhouse, set in tranquil countryside, has original features such as beams, and displays family mementos. Bedrooms are well equipped, with comfortable furnishings and many facilities. Freshly cooked breakfasts include farm-produced eggs, local sausages and home-made marmalade, served in the comfortable dining room.

Facilities 2 en suite 1 annexe en suite ⊘ FTV TVB tea/coffee ✖ Cen ht TVL 250 acres mixed **Prices** S £30-£35; D £55-£60✳ LB **Parking** 4 **Notes** ⊛

LITTLE DEWCHURCH

MAP 10 SO53

◆◆◆◆ ✔

Cwm Craig Farm ✧ (SO535322)

HR2 6PS ☎ 01432 840250 📠 01432 840250 Mrs Lee

Dir Off A49 into Little Dewchurch, turn right in village, Cwm Craig 1st farm on left

This Georgian farmhouse is situated on the outskirts of the village in glorious countryside and offers spacious accommodation. Bedrooms are carefully furnished with period items. Public areas consist of a comfortable lounge, games room and two dining rooms, one of which is offered for the use of families. A hearty breakfast is supplemented by eggs from the farm's hens.

Facilities 4 en suite (1 fmly) ⊗ TVB tea/coffee ✖ Cen ht TVL Pool Table 190 acres Organic arable **Prices** S £24-£26; D £48✳ **Parking** 6 **Notes** 🐾

MOCCAS

MAP 09 SO34

 Premier Collection

◆◆◆◆◆ 🏠 ➾

Moccas Court

HR2 9LH ☎ 01981 500019 📠 01981 500095
e-mail bencmaster@btconnect.com

Travellers seeking a unique and memorable bed and breakfast need look no further. This Grade I listed Georgian family home is of such historic interest that it is open to the public. Dwell in the lap of luxury, attended to by the most charming and genial hosts. A delicious dinner, served around a large circular table in the splendid dining room, should not be missed.

Facilities 5 rms (4 en suite) (1 pri facs) ⊗ TVB tea/coffee ✖ Licensed Cen ht TVL No coaches Fishing ♨ Dinner Last d 8pm **Prices** S £112-£156; D £140-£195 **LB** **Parking** 35

ROSS-ON-WYE

MAP 10 SO52

See also **Goodrich**

★★★★ 🏵🏵 **Restaurant with Rooms**

Bridge House

Wilton HR9 6AA ☎ 01989 562655 📠 01989 567652
e-mail info@bridge-house-hotel.com
web www.bridge-house-hotel.com
Dir Off junct A40 & A49 into Ross, 300yds on left

Built about 1740, this elegant house is just a stroll across the bridge from the delightful town. Standards are impressive and bedrooms offer ample space, comfort and genuine quality. Period features in the public areas add to the stylish ambience, and the gardens run down to the river. The restaurant serves accomplished cuisine.

Facilities 9 en suite ⊗ TVB tea/coffee Direct dial from bedrooms ✖ Licensed Cen ht No children 14yrs No coaches Fishing Dinner Last d 9pm **Prices** S £65; D £96-£110✳ **LB** **Conf** Max 12 **Parking** 20

 Premier Collection

◆◆◆◆◆ 🏠 ✔

Trecilla Farm (SO533212)

Llangarron HR9 6NQ ☎ 01989 770647 Mrs Dew
e-mail info@trecillafarm.co.uk
web www.trecillafarm.co.uk
Dir A40 onto A4137 to Hereford. 2m x-rds, left signed Llangarron. 1m Llangarron sign, Trecilla Farm 2nd drive on right

Dating from the 16th century, this farmhouse has tremendous character with exposed beams, flagstone floors and an inglenook fireplace. It stands in picturesque gardens with a spring-fed stream, within peaceful countryside. Bedrooms, including a magnificent four poster, offer comfort and quality, and are furnished with fine period pieces. Aga-cooked breakfasts feature local produce and a wonderful selection of home-made preserves. Other facilities include a garden hideaway complete with snooker table. Fishing is available on nearby Garron Brook.

Facilities 3 en suite ⊗ TVB tea/coffee ✖ Cen ht No children 13yrs Fishing Riding Pool Table ♨ 3/4 size snooker table Games room 12 acres Horse livery & Sheep tack **Prices** S £45-£50; D £65-£90✳ **Parking** 7 **Notes** Closed 23 Dec-2 Jan 🐾

◆◆◆◆

Brookfield House

Over Ross St HR9 7AT ☎ 01989 562188
web www.brookfield-house.co.uk
Dir Junct A40 & A449 onto B4234 Ledbury Rd, 0.5m left onto Brookmead & up driveway

Dating from the 18th century, this large detached house lies just north of the town centre. Refurbished to a high standard throughout, the bedrooms are spacious, comfortably appointed and well equipped. Breakfast is served in the light and airy dining room. A relaxing lounge is also available as are the attractive gardens.

Facilities 3 en suite (1 fmly) ⊗ TVB tea/coffee ✖ Cen ht No coaches **Prices** D £54-£64✳ **Parking** 12

ROSS-ON-WYE continued

◆◆◆◆

Brynheulog

Howle Hill HR9 5SP ☎ 01989 562051 📠 01989 562051

Dir *B4234 from Ross-on-Wye take, 1m left signed Howle Hill, 250yds 1st right signed Howle Hill, left at x-rds, 1st house on right past church*

This highly individual guest house has been lovingly designed by the owner to provide a high level of comfort with superb views. The bedrooms are full of character and well equipped, with furniture built by a local craftsman. Two rooms are in a self-contained wing with its own private lounge. Public areas consist of a smart dining room and a relaxing lounge.

Facilities 4 en suite (1 fmly) (2 GF) ⊗ TV3B tea/coffee Cen ht TVL No coaches Dinner **LB Parking** 7 **Notes** 🐾

◆◆◆◆ 🛋

Lea House

Lea HR9 7JZ ☎ 01989 750652 📠 01989 750652
e-mail enquiries@leahouse.co.uk
web www.leahouse.co.uk

Dir *4m SE of Ross on A40, in Lea village*

This former coaching inn near Ross is a good base for exploring the Forest of Dean and the Wye valley. The individually furnished bedrooms are thoughtfully equipped with many extras and toiletries, and the atmosphere is relaxed and homey. Breakfast in the oak-beamed dining room is a tasty choice including freshly squeezed fruit juices, fish and local sausages.

Facilities 3 rms (2 en suite) (1 pri facs) (1 fmly) ⊗ TVB tea/coffee Cen ht TVL No coaches Dinner Last d by prior arrangement **Prices** D £56-£66✱ **LB Parking** 4

◆◆◆◆

Lumleys

Kern Bridge, Bishopswood HR9 5QT
☎ 01600 890040 📠 0870 706 2378
e-mail helen@lumleys.force9.co.uk
web www.lumleys.force9.co.uk/

Dir *Off A40 onto B4229 at Goodrich, over Kern Bridge, right at Inn On The Wye, 400yds opp picnic ground*

This pleasant and friendly guest house overlooks the River Wye and has been a hostelry since Victorian times. It offers the character of a bygone era with modern comforts and facilities. Bedrooms are
continued

individually and carefully furnished and one has a four-poster bed and its own patio. Comfortable public areas include a choice of sitting rooms.

Facilities 3 en suite ⊗ STV FTV TVB tea/coffee Direct dial from bedrooms Cen ht TVL No coaches Dinner Last d 7pm
Prices D £60-£70✱ **Parking** 15 **Notes** 🐾

◆◆◆◆

Sunnymount Hotel

Ryefield Rd HR9 5LS ☎ 01989 563880 📠 01989 566251
e-mail sunnymount@tinyworld.co.uk

Dir *M50 junct 4, A449 for Ross, next rdbt onto A40 Gloucester, B4260 for Ross town centre, 2nd right*

Built in the 1920s, this large house is in a quiet suburb close to to M50 and the A40. Immaculate throughout, the bedrooms are well equipped and the public areas are spacious and comfortable. Diners are offered freshly prepared meals in the pleasant and airy dining room.

Facilities 6 en suite ⊗ in dining room ⊗ in 1 lounge TVB tea/coffee Licensed Cen ht TVL No coaches Dinner Last d 4pm **Parking** 7

◆◆◆◆

Thatch Close

Llangrove HR9 6EL ☎ 01989 770300
e-mail info@thatchclose.co.uk
web www.thatchclose.com

Dir *Off A40 at Symonds Yat West/Whitchurch junct to Llangrove, right at x-rds after Post Office, Thatch Close 0.6m on left*

Standing in 13 acres, this sturdy farmhouse dating from 1760 is full of character. There is a wonderfully warm atmosphere and a genuine welcome from your hosts. The homely bedrooms are equipped for comfort with many thoughtful extras. Breakfast and dinner are served in the elegant dining room, and a lounge is available. The extensive patios and gardens are popular in summer, providing plenty of space to find a quiet corner and relax with a good book.

Facilities 3 en suite ⊗ TVB tea/coffee Cen ht TVL No coaches Dinner Last d 9am **Prices** S £35-£40; D £55-£60✱ **LB Parking** 8 **Notes** 🐾

◆◆◆

Nature's Choice

Raglan House, 17 Broad St HR9 7EA
☎ 01989 763454 📠 01989 763064
e-mail nature@roberts9535.freeserve.co.uk
web www.natures-choice.biz
Dir *Market Place onto Broad St, B&B 100yds left*

This Grade II listed early 18th-century house is located in the town centre. As the name may suggest, the emphasis here is on organic food served with an American influence by the delightfully friendly proprietors. In addition to an excellent choice of Californian style breakfasts, the downstairs cafe serves a range of dishes throughout the day and includes options for vegetarians and vegans.

Facilities 4 en suite ⊗ in 1 bedrooms ⊗ in dining room TVB tea/coffee
✘ Licensed Dinner Last d 9pm

SHOBDON   MAP 09 SO46

◆◆◆◆ 🍴 🍺

The Bateman Arms

HR6 9LX ☎ 01568 708374
e-mail alan@batemanarms.co.uk
web www.batemanarms.co.uk
Dir *On B4362 in Shobdon village*

Located in the village, parts of this refurbished inn date back over four hundred years. Plenty of oak beams and a large log fire add to the ambience. In addition to the friendly welcome, the food is a key feature with carefully prepared, quality local produce in evidence at dinner and breakfast.

Facilities 9 en suite (3 GF) ⊗ in bedrooms ⊗ in dining room
⊗ in 1 lounge TVB tea/coffee Cen ht TVL Pool Table Dinner Last d 9pm
Prices S £55; D £85✳ **LB** **Parking** 40

SYMONDS YAT (EAST)   MAP 10 SO51

◆◆◆◆

Garth Cottage

HR9 6JL ☎ 01600 890364 📠 01600 890364
e-mail val.eden@virgin.net
web www.garthcottage-symondsyat.com
Dir *Off A40 at Little Chef, Whitchurch, signs for Symonds Yat East*

The Eden family's warm hospitality and attention to guest comfort is evident in this attractive and impeccably maintained 18th-century house. The bedrooms are well equipped, and breakfast and dinner are served in the conservatory-dining room overlooking the River Wye. There is also a cosy bar and a choice of lounges, including a sun lounge that also looks over the river.

Facilities 4 en suite ⊗ tea/coffee ✘ Licensed Cen ht TVL No children 12yrs No coaches Fishing Dinner Last d noon **Prices** D £72✳ **Parking** 9
Notes Closed Nov-Mar 🐾

◆◆◆◆ 🍺

Saracens Head Inn

HR9 6JL ☎ 01600 890435 📠 01600 890034
e-mail contact@saracensheadinn.co.uk
web www.saracensheadinn.co.uk
Dir *Off A40 at Little Chef, signed Symonds Yat East*

Dating from the 16th century, the friendly, family-run Saracens Head Inn faces the River Wye and has wonderful views. The well-equipped bedrooms are decorated in a cottage style, and there is a cosy lounge, an attractive dining room, and a popular public bar with a riverside patio.

Facilities 8 en suite 2 annexe en suite (1 fmly) (1 GF) ⊗ in bedrooms
⊗ in dining room ⊗ in 1 lounge FTV TV2B tea/coffee Direct dial from bedrooms ✘ Cen ht TVL No coaches Fishing Pool Table Dinner Last d 9.15pm **Prices** S £48.50; D £70-£130✳ **LB** **Conf** Max 25 Thtr 25 Class 25 Board 25 **Parking** 35

SYMONDS YAT (WEST)   MAP 10 SO51

◆◆◆◆ 🍷 🍴

Norton House

Whitchurch, Symonds Yat HR9 6DJ
☎ 01600 890046 📠 01600 890045
e-mail su@norton.wyenet.co.uk
web www.norton-house.com
Dir 0.5m N of Symonds Yat. Off A40 into Whitchurch village

Built as a farmhouse, Norton House dates back 300 years and retains much character through features such as flagstone floors and beamed ceilings. The bedrooms, including a four-poster room, are individually styled and furnished for maximum comfort. Excellent local produce is used to create an imaginative range of breakfast and dinner options. The charming public areas include a snug lounge with a wood-burning stove. Self-catering cottages are also available.

Facilities 3 en suite ⊗ TVB tea/coffee Cen ht TVL No children 12yrs No coaches Dinner Last d 9am **Prices** S £41-£46; D £74 **Parking** 5 **Notes** Closed 25 Dec 🦮

WEOBLEY   MAP 09 SO45

◆◆◆◆ 🏵 🍽 🍴

The Salutation Inn

Market Pitch HR4 8SJ ☎ 01544 318443 📠 01544 318405
e-mail salutationinn@btinternet.com
Dir Off A44 in village centre

Located in the heart of this village in an Area of Outstanding Natural Beauty, this 500-year-old inn is an integral part of the community. It has a fine reputation for imaginative food, served in the informal dining room or elegant restaurant. Bedrooms are homely and a warm welcome is assured.

Facilities 4 en suite (2 fmly) ⊗ TVB tea/coffee 🎯 Cen ht Dinner Last d 9-9.30pm **Prices** S £53-£56; D £80-£86✳ **LB Conf** Max 40 Class 40 Board 40 **Parking** 14

YARKHILL   MAP 10 SO64

◆◆◆◆ 🐾

Garford Farm ◇ (SO600435)

HR1 3ST ☎ 01432 890226 📠 01432 890707 Mrs Parker
e-mail garfordfarm@lineone.net
Dir Off A417 at Newtown x-rds onto A4103 for Hereford, farm 1.5m on left

The black and white timber-framed farmhouse, set on a large arable holding, dates from the 17th century. Its character is enhanced by period furnishings, and fires burn in the comfortable lounge during cooler weather. The traditionally furnished bedrooms, including a family room, have modern facilities.

Facilities 2 en suite (1 fmly) ⊗ in dining room TVB tea/coffee Cen ht No children 2yrs Fishing 🎣 700 acres arable **Prices** S fr £30; d fr £50✳ **Parking** 6 **Notes** Closed 25-26 Dec 🦮

HERTFORDSHIRE

BISHOP'S STORTFORD   MAP 06 TL42

◆◆◆◆ 🍽 🍴

The Kick & Dicky

Wellpond Gn SG11 1NL ☎ 01920 821424
e-mail kickanddicky@btinternet.com
For full entry see **Standon**

◆◆◆

Broadleaf Guest House ◇

38 Broadleaf Av CM23 4JY ☎ 01279 835467
e-mail b-tcannon@tiscali.co.uk
Dir 1m SW of town centre. Off B1383 onto Whittinton Way & Friedburge Av, Broadleaf Av 6th left

A delightful detached house situated in a peaceful residential area close to the town centre, and within easy reach of the M11 and Stansted Airport. The pleasant bedrooms are carefully furnished and equipped with many thoughtful touches. Breakfast is served in the smart dining room, which overlooks the pretty garden.

Facilities 2 rms (1 fmly) ⊗ TVB tea/coffee Cen ht No coaches **Prices** S £28-£35; D £50-£65✳ **Parking** 2 **Notes** 🦮

continued

♦♦♦

Pearse House

Parsonage Ln CM23 5BQ
☎ 01279 757400 🖷 01279 506591
e-mail pearsehouse@btconnect.com
Dir *M11 junct 8, A120, A1250 into Bishops Stortford. Right at rdbt onto Parsonage Ln, house 1st on left*

An imposing, half-timbered Victorian house situated on the edge of town and just a short drive from Stansted Airport. Bedrooms are smartly appointed and equipped with modern facilities. The spacious public areas include a bar, lounge, dining room and conference facilities.

Facilities 13 en suite 24 annexe en suite (2 fmly) (1 GF) ⊗ in bedrooms ⊗ in dining room ⊗ in lounges TVB tea/coffee Direct dial from bedrooms ✘ Licensed Cen ht TVL Leisure room, Fitness room Dinner Last d 8pm **Prices** S £40-£70; D £50-£80✷ **LB Conf** Max 300 Thtr 150 Class 60 Board 30 Del from £90 ✷ **Parking** 100 **Notes** Closed Xmas & New Year Civ Wed 60

BUNTINGFORD   MAP 12 TL32

♦♦♦♦ ♥

Buckland Bury Farm ◇ *(TL357336)*

Buckland Bury SG9 0PY
☎ 01763 272958 🖷 01763 274722 Mr Hodge
e-mail bucklandbury@shrubbsfarm.demon.co.uk
Dir *3m N of Buntingford on A10, white churn at end of road*

A delightful 300-year-old farmhouse just a short drive from Buntingford. Public rooms retain much of their original character, including exposed beams, and the dining room has a communal table and a large fireplace. The individually furnished bedrooms are well equipped and have a range of thoughtful extras.

Facilities 3 rms (1 en suite) ⊗ in bedrooms ⊗ in dining room TVB tea/coffee ✘ Lift Cen ht TVL 550 acres arable **Prices** S £30-£40; D £50-£60✷ **Parking** 12

♦♦♦♦ ◀

Sword Inn Hand

Westmill SG9 9LQ ☎ 01763 271356
e-mail welcome@theswordinnhand.co.uk
Dir *In village of Westmill, off A10 S of Buntingford*

Set within the peaceful village of Westmill amid rolling countryside, the charming inn offers excellent accommodation and a friendly and relaxed atmosphere within the 16th-century inn. Purpose built ground-floor bedrooms are located just off the rear gardens; well equipped and carefully appointed, they have their own access. Characterful public rooms offer a choice of restaurant and bar dining options, along with draught ales.

Facilities 4 en suite (4 GF) ⊗ in bedrooms ⊗ in dining room STV TVB tea/coffee ✘ Cen ht TVL No children Dinner Last d 9.30pm **Prices** S £60-£70; D £70-£90 **Parking** 25

DATCHWORTH   MAP 06 TL21

[U] ♥

Farmhouse B&B   *(TL271188)*

Hawkins Grange Farm, Hawkins Hall Ln SG3 6TF
☎ 01438 813369 🖷 01438 813369 Mrs Dodson
e-mail farmhousebb@hawkinsgrange.demon.co.uk
web www.farmhousebb.co.uk
Dir *A1(M) junct 7 onto A602 (Hertford). From Bragbury End onto Bragbury Ln, 2m on left after phone box*

At the time of going to press the rating for this establishment had not been confirmed. Please check the AA website www.theAA.com for up-to-date information.

Facilities 4 rms (1 en suite) (1 fmly) ⊗ TVB tea/coffee ✘ Cen ht 48 acres pasture **Prices** S £35-£40; D £60-£70✷ **Parking** 8

HARPENDEN

♦♦♦♦ 🚢 ◀

The Silver Cup

5 St Albans Rd AL5 2JF ☎ 01582 713095 🖷 01582 469713
e-mail info@silvercup.co.uk
web www.silvercup.co.uk
Dir *200yds SW of Harpenden station on A1081 St Albans Rd*

Located south of Harpenden high street opposite the common, this small family-owned inn offers smart modern accommodation. The refurbished public areas and accommodation are well appointed, and the cosy restaurant serves interesting, quality food complemented by real ales and a good wine list. Service is friendly and helpful.

Facilities 4 en suite ⊗ in bedrooms ⊗ in area of dining room ⊗ in 1 lounge TVB tea/coffee Direct dial from bedrooms ✘ Cen ht TVL No coaches Dinner Last d 9.30pm **Parking** 7

HEMEL HEMPSTEAD   MAP 06 TL00

♦♦♦

Alexandra

40/42 Alexandra Rd HP2 5BP
☎ 01442 242897 🖷 01442 211829
e-mail alexhous@aol.com
web www.alexandraguesthouse.co.uk
Dir *Off B487 Queensway in town centre*

This well-managed guest house has a regular business clientele and provides well-equipped bedrooms with practical extras. Breakfast is served in the ground-floor lounge-dining room. A good selection of tourist information is available.

Facilities 16 rms (3 fmly) (3 GF) ⊗ in 10 bedrooms ⊗ in dining room ⊗ in lounges STV TVB tea/coffee ✘ Lift Cen ht TVL No children 2yrs **Parking** 6

HERTFORD

MAP 06 TL31

◆◆◆◆

Mulberry Lodge

Newgate St SG13 8NQ ☎ 01707 879652 ▤ 01707 879653
e-mail bookings@mulberrylodge.org.uk
web www.mulberrylodge.org.uk
Dir M25 junct 25, signs for Paradise Wildlife Park, left at T-junct,
Lodge on left

Mulberry Lodge offers carefully furnished accommodation in a smart
barn conversion in peaceful rural surroundings at Epping Green. The
spacious bedrooms have king-size doubles (or twins) and are very
well equipped for business travellers, providing safes, direct-dial
telephones with modem points, and modern bathrooms. Freshly
cooked breakfasts are served in the open-plan diner, which has a
small lounge area and a 24-hour manned reception desk. Secure
parking is a bonus.

Facilities 12 en suite (12 GF) ⊗ in 10 bedrooms ⊗ in dining room
⊗ in lounges TVB tea/coffee Direct dial from bedrooms Licensed Cen ht
TVL **Prices** S £49.50-£65; D £49.50-£65✱ **Parking** 15 **Notes** Closed
24-26 & 31 Dec & 1 Jan

Ⓤ

Orchard Cottage ◇

East End Green SG14 2PD ☎ 01992 583494
e-mail looadams@btinternet.com
Dir From A414 to Hertingfordbury. At East End Green sign, 5th drive
left on gravel road

At the time of going to press the rating for this establishment had not
been confirmed. Please check the AA website www.theAA.com for up-
to-date information.

Facilities 4 rms (2 en suite) (2 pri facs) (1 fmly) ⊗ STV TVB tea/coffee
✖ Cen ht No coaches **Prices** S £30-£39; D £50-£60✱ **Parking** 6
Notes Closed 21 Dec-3 Jan ⊜

Ⓤ

Two Ways B&B ◇

16a Mangrove Rd SG13 8AJ
☎ 01992 582487 & 07759 186880
e-mail enquiries@two-ways-hertford.co.uk
Dir Exit A414 S of Hertford signed Balls Park, continue to the left.
160mtrs on right in Mangrove Rd

At the time of going to press the rating for this establishment had not

been confirmed. Please check the AA website www.theAA.com for up-
to-date information.

Facilities 3 rms ⊗ TVB tea/coffee ✖ Cen ht No children 9yrs
No coaches **Prices** S £22.50-£25; D £46.80-£52✱ **LB** **Parking** 5
Notes ⊜

HERTFORD HEATH

MAP 06 TL31

Ⓤ

Brides Farm

The Roundings SG13 7PY
☎ 01992 466687 ▤ 01992 478776
Dir Take B1197 to Hertford Heath. Right at Jolly Pinda pub into the
Roundings. Take left fork to Brides Farm

At the time of going to press the rating for this establishment had not
been confirmed. Please check the AA website www.theAA.com for up-
to-date information.

Facilities 3 en suite ⊗ TVB tea/coffee Cen ht No coaches **Prices** S fr
£35; d fr £50✱ **LB** **Parking** 10 **Notes** ⊜

Ⓤ

Rushen ◇

Mount Pleasant SG13 7QY
☎ 01992 581254 ▤ 01992 534737
e-mail wilsonamwell@onetel.com
Dir From A10 exit at Hertford slip road, 1st left onto B1502. 1st right
at top of lane, bear left at village green. Rushen is on left at end

At the time of going to press the rating for this establishment had not
been confirmed. Please check the AA website www.theAA.com for up-
to-date information.

Facilities 3 rms (1 en suite) ⊗ TVB tea/coffee ✖ Cen ht No coaches
Prices S £30-£32; D £50-£55✱ **Parking** 3 **Notes** Closed 22 Dec-3 Jan
⊜

HITCHIN

MAP 12 TL12

◆◆◆◆ ⊚ ⊜ ⊜

Redcoats Farmhouse Hotel

Redcoats Green SG4 7JR
☎ 01438 729500 ▤ 01438 723322
e-mail sales@redcoats.co.uk
web www.redcoats.co.uk

This delightful 15th-century building stands in 4 acres of landscaped
grounds only a short drive from the A1(M). Bedrooms, in the main
house and courtyard annexe, are well appointed and spacious.
Breakfast and dinner are served in the conservatory, which overlooks
the garden, and a series of intimate dining rooms are also available.

Facilities 4 en suite 9 annexe en suite (1 fmly) (9 GF) ⊗ in bedrooms
⊗ in dining room FTV TVB tea/coffee Direct dial from bedrooms
Licensed Cen ht TVL No coaches Dinner Last d 9pm **Prices** S £76-£115;
D £111-£145✱ **LB** **Conf** Max 60 Thtr 60 Class 45 Board 15 Del from
£141 ✱ **Parking** 30 **Notes** Closed 27 Dec-2 Jan & BH Mons Civ Wed 60

continued

♦♦♦ ◧

The Greyhound

London Rd, St Ippollitts SG4 7NL ☎ 01462 440989
e-mail greyhound@freenet.co.uk
Dir On B656 1m S of Hitchin

The popular inn is situated on the outskirts of town amid open farmland. Service is friendly and helpful, and a range of interesting meals is readily available in the bar and dining area. Bedrooms are well equipped and have cheerful colour schemes.

Facilities 5 en suite (1 fmly) ⊗ in bedrooms ⊗ in dining room TVB tea/coffee Cen ht Dinner Last d 9pm **Prices** S £45-£55; D £45-£60✱ LB **Conf** Max 30 **Parking** 25

See advertisement on this page

The Greyhound Inn
An Independent Inn
offering the best British hospitality
London Road, St. Ippolyts, Herts. SG4 7NL
Email greyhound@freenet.co.uk
Prop. Roy Pearce F.B.I.I.   01462 440989

Situated in the beautiful rural countryside of Hertfordshire 2km. south of the historic market town of Hitchin with easy access to the A1(M) and M1 and close to Baldock, Letchworth, Luton, Luton Airport, Welwyn Garden City and Stevenage. This makes us an ideal place to stay for business travellers and visitors. The fast (25mins) train service makes visiting London or Cambridge easy and cheap. We have an excellent reputation for food, hospitality and beer. An Inn existed on this site 300 years ago, it was rebuilt, 1900 and more recently extended by us. We hope it retains its warm welcome and that you enjoy being here in what really is our home. Traditional Sunday roast served every Sunday lunchtime.

♦♦♦

The Lord Lister Hotel

1 Park St SG4 9AH
☎ 01462 432712 & 459451 ▤ 01462 438506
e-mail info@lordlisterhotel.co.uk
web www.lordlisterhotel.co.uk
Dir 200yds S of town centre at minirdbt on B656 (off A602)

The Lord Lister retains many of its original 18th-century features. The well-maintained bedrooms are comfortably appointed, and there is a lounge and a cosy bar. Breakfast is served in the brightly decorated dining room, while helpful advice is available on local eateries.

Facilities 16 en suite 4 annexe en suite (2 fmly) (3 GF) ⊗ in 7 bedrooms ⊗ in dining room ⊗ in lounges FTV TVB tea/coffee Direct dial from bedrooms ✗ Licensed Cen ht TVL **Prices** S £60-£75; D £70-£85✱ **Conf** Max 10 **Parking** 18

NUTHAMPSTEAD   MAP 12 TL43

Ⓤ ◧

The Woodman Inn

SG8 8NB ☎ 01763 848328 ▤ 01763 848328
e-mail woodman.inn@virgin.net
Dir A505 to Royston, take right onto B1368 to Barkway village, 1st left past Tally Ho, 2m turn right, situated on left

At the time of going to press the rating for this establishment had not been confirmed. Please check the AA website www.theAA.com for up-to-date information.

Facilities 2 rms (1 en suite) (1 pri facs) 2 annexe en suite (2 GF) ⊗ TV2B tea/coffee ✗ Cen ht TVL Pool Table Dinner Last d 9pm **Prices** S fr £40; d fr £65✱ **Conf** Max 50 **Parking** 20

England

ST ALBANS
MAP 06 TL10

◆◆◆◆

Ardmore House

54 Lemsford Rd AL1 3PR ☎ 01727 859313 📠 01727 859313
e-mail info@ardmorehousehotel.co.uk
web www.ardmorehousehotel.co.uk
Dir Off Hatfield Rd, near St Albans station

Located in immaculate surroundings close to the town centre and cathedral, this extended Edwardian house has been carefully renovated, providing a range of facilities much appreciated by a loyal commercial clientele. The practically furnished bedrooms offer good facilities and the extensive public areas include a spacious conservatory-dining room.

Facilities 40 en suite (5 fmly) (7 GF) ⊗ in 38 bedrooms ⊗ in dining room ⊗ in 1 lounge STV TVB tea/coffee Direct dial from bedrooms ✖ Licensed Cen ht TVL Dinner Last d 8.30pm **Prices** S £55-£65; D £65-£125 **Conf** Max 50 Thtr 50 Class 40 Board 40 Del from £125 ✳ **Parking** 40 **Notes** Civ Wed 150

◆◆◆◆ 🅰

Fern Cottage

116 Old London Rd AL1 1PU ☎ 01727 834200
e-mail bookinginfo@ferncottage.uk.net
Dir M25 junct 22, A1081 to St Albans, 3rd exit off London Coney rdbt for 1m, under railway bridge, over minirdbt & 2nd left onto Old London Rd. Fern Cottage 400yds on left

Facilities 3 en suite (1 GF) ⊗ STV TVB tea/coffee Cen ht No coaches **Prices** S £38-£45; D £55-£60✳ **Parking** 3 **Notes** ⊜

◆◆◆◆ 🅰

Tresco

76 Clarence Rd AL1 4NG ☎ 01727 864880
e-mail pat_leggatt@hotmail.com
Dir Off A1057 Hatfield Rd onto Clarence Rd at Crown pub, B&B 300yds on right

Facilities 2 rms ⊗ FTV TVB tea/coffee ✖ Cen ht No children 10yrs No coaches **Prices** S £32-£35; D £52-£55 **Parking** 1 **Notes** ⊜

STANDON
MAP 06 TL32

◆◆◆◆ ⊜ 🍴

The Kick & Dicky

Wellpond Green SG11 1NL ☎ 01920 821424
e-mail kickanddicky@btinternet.com
Dir Off A120 signed Wellpond Green, 0.5m down winding road to junct, Kick and Dicky on right

A warm welcome and friendly service is just part of the appeal of this popular inn, situated in the quiet village of Wellpond Green. Modern en suite bedrooms are well appointed and have good showers en suite. The spacious restaurant offers a good range of dishes, as does the bar.

Facilities 6 en suite ⊗ in bedrooms ⊗ in dining room TVB tea/coffee Cen ht No children 12 yrs No coaches Dinner Last d 9.30pm **Prices** S fr £50; d fr £70 **Conf** Thtr 30 Class 40 Board 14 Del from £30 ✳ **Parking** 24 **Notes** Closed 1st wk Jan

WATFORD
MAP 06 TQ19

◆◆◆

Travel Stop Inn

26-28 Upton Rd WD18 0JF
☎ 01923 224298 📠 01923 253553
e-mail info@travelstopinn.com
web www.travelstopinn.com
Dir M1 junct 5, A4008 to Watford centre

Located within easy walking distance of the town centre, this renovation of two Edwardian houses provides a range of bedrooms equipped with lots of homey extras. There is a cocktail bar and restaurant in the White House Hotel opposite, which is under the same ownership and is where registration takes place.

Facilities 26 annexe en suite (1 fmly) (7 GF) ⊗ in 11 bedrooms ⊗ in dining room ⊗ in lounges STV TVB tea/coffee Direct dial from bedrooms ✖ Licensed Cen ht TVL Arrangement with local gym Dinner Last d 9.45pm **Prices** S £54.95; D £59.95; (room only) ✳ **Conf** Max 200 Thtr 200 Class 80 Board 60 Del from £135 ✳ **Parking** 35 **Notes** rs Xmas/New Year Civ Wed 120

WELWYN GARDEN CITY
MAP 06 TL21

🅄

23 Wheatley Close ◈

AL7 3LJ ☎ 01707 884218 & 07836 571578 📠 01707 884218
At the time of going to press the rating for this establishment had not been confirmed. Please check the AA website www.theAA.com for up-to-date information.

Facilities 2rms ⊗ TV2B tea/coffee ✖ Cen ht No coaches **Prices** S £25-£30; D £50-£60✳ **LB Notes** ⊜

WIGGINTON

MAP 06 SP91

◆◆◆◆ 🍴

Rangers Cottage

Tring Park HP23 6EB ☎ 01442 890155 📄 01442 827814
e-mail rangerscottage@aol.com
web www.rangerscottage.com
Dir Off A41 at Tring into Wigginton via Fox Rd, right onto Highfield
Rd, straight ahead into Tring Park

Located in an Area of Outstanding Natural Beauty close to the
Ridgeway, this impressive late 19th-century lodge retains original
features, furnishings and decor. Bedrooms have a wealth of thoughtful
extras, and memorable breakfasts are served in an elegant dining
room overlooking the pretty gardens.

Facilities 3 annexe en suite (1 fmly) (3 GF) ⊗ TVB tea/coffee ✈
Cen ht No coaches **Parking** 5

KENT

ASHFORD

MAP 07 TR04

◆◆◆◆

Bethersden Old Barn

The Old Barn, Bridge Farm, Bethersden TN26 3LE
☎ 0870 740 1180 & 01233 820434 📄 01233 820192
Dir 4m SW of Ashford on A28 S of Bethersden. Avoid entering
Bullbridge Farm

Located near a rural village west of Ashford, this converted 18th-
century barn offers a self-contained guest suite of cosy bedroom,
private lounge and a modern kitchen. You are provided with a
comprehensive breakfast in the main house or by room service.

Facilities 1 rms (1 pri facs) 1 annexe en suite (1 GF) ⊗ TVB tea/coffee
Cen ht No coaches **Parking** 6 **Notes** 🐾

◆◆◆

Croft Hotel

Canterbury Rd, Kennington TN25 4DU
☎ 01233 622140 📄 01233 635271
e-mail info@crofthotel.com
Dir M20 junct 10, 2m on A28 signed Canterbury

An attractive red-brick house situated in 2 acres of landscaped
grounds just a short drive from Ashford railway station. The

generously proportioned bedrooms are in the main house and in
pretty cottages; all are pleasantly decorated and thoughtfully
equipped. Public rooms include a smart Italian restaurant, a bar and a
cosy lounge.

Facilities 27 en suite (6 fmly) (8 GF) ⊗ in 13 bedrooms ⊗ in dining
room ⊗ in 1 lounge TVB tea/coffee Direct dial from bedrooms Licensed
Cen ht TVL No coaches Dinner Last d 9.30pm **Conf** Max 40 Thtr 40
Class 20 Board 22 **Parking** 30 **Notes** Civ Wed 40

◆◆◆ Ⓐ

Ashford Warren Cottage Hotel & Restaurant

136 The Street, Willesborough TN24 0NB
☎ 01233 621905 & 0777 9648882 📄 01233 633587
e-mail booking@warrencottage.co.uk
web www.warrencottage.com
Dir M20 junct 10, B2164 Kennington Rd towards Canterbury. Turn
right onto The Street, house on left

Facilities 6 en suite (1 fmly) ⊗ in bedrooms ⊗ in dining room
⊗ in lounges TVB tea/coffee Licensed Cen ht TVL No coaches Dinner
Last d 7.30pm **Prices** S fr £35; d fr £50; (room only) ✳ **Parking** 20

Ⓤ

The Wife of Bath

4 Upper Bridge St, Wye TN25 5AF
☎ 01233 812540 & 812232 📄 01233 813033
e-mail reservations@wifeofbath.com
Dir M20 junct 9, follow signs for Canterbury, after 4m turn right into
Wye.

At the time of going to press the rating for this establishment had not
been confirmed. Please check the AA website www.theAA.com for up-
to-date information.

Facilities 5 en suite (2 GF) ⊗ in bedrooms ⊗ in dining room TVB
tea/coffee Direct dial from bedrooms ✈ Licensed Cen ht No coaches
Dinner Last d 9.30pm **Prices** S £55; D £75-£95✳ **Parking** 25
Notes Closed 2 wks in Aug, Dec/Jan

AYLESFORD

MAP 06 TQ75

◆◆◆◆ Ⓐ

Wickham Lodge

The Quay, 73 High St ME20 7AY
☎ 01622 717267 📄 01622 792855
e-mail wickhamlodge@aol.com
web www.wickhamlodge.co.uk
Dir M20 junct 5, signs to Aylesford village, The Quay is small road
beside Chequers pub

Facilities 3 rms (2 en suite) (1 pri facs) (1 fmly) (1 GF) ⊗ TVB
tea/coffee Cen ht No coaches **Parking** 4

continued

BIDDENDEN

MAP 07 TQ83

◆◆◆◆

Heron Cottage

TN27 8HH ☎ 01580 291358 🖷 01580 291358

Dir *1m NW of Biddenden. A262 W from Biddenden, 1st right, 0.25m across sharp left bend through stone pillars, left onto unmade road*

Expect a warm welcome at this picturesque extended cottage, set in immaculate gardens in peaceful Kent countryside. The bedrooms are thoughtfully equipped and have coordinated soft furnishings, and breakfast is served in the smart dining room. The cosy sitting has an open fireplace.

Facilities 7 rms (6 en suite) (2 fmly) (1 GF) ⊗ in bedrooms ⊗ in dining room TVB tea/coffee Cen ht TVL No coaches Fishing 🎱 Dinner Last d 9am **Prices** S £40-£45; D £60-£65 **Conf** Max 20 Board 20 **Parking** 8 **Notes** Closed Dec-Feb 🐾

◆◆◆◆

Bishopsdale Oast

TN27 8DR ☎ 01580 291027
e-mail drysdale@bishopsdaleoast.co.uk
web www.bishopsdaleoast.co.uk
Dir *A28 Tenterden to Rolvenden, 1st right after Tenterden onto Cranbrook Rd, 2.5m to B&B sign on left, turn left & signed*

Situated in a peaceful rural location, Bishopsdale Oast has been restored to show much of its original character. Bedrooms are cheerfully decorated with coordinated soft furnishings and have many thoughtful touches. Public areas include a sitting room and a smart dining room, where imaginative dinners feature home-grown produce.

Facilities 5 rms (4 en suite) (1 pri facs) (1 fmly) (2 GF) ⊗ in bedrooms TVB tea/coffee Cen ht TVL No coaches Dinner Last d before noon **Prices** S £56.40; D £80✴ **LB Parking** 6

BROADSTAIRS

MAP 07 TR36

◆◆◆◆

Bay Tree Hotel

12 Eastern Esp CT10 1DR
☎ 01843 862502 🖷 01843 860589
Dir *A255 onto Rectory Rd & Eastern Esplanade*

Expect a warm welcome at this family-run establishment, situated on an elevated position overlooking East Cliff. The attractive bedrooms are well equipped and some have a balcony with a sea view. There is a comfortable lounge bar, and a good breakfast and dinner menu are offered in the dining room.

Facilities 10 en suite (1 GF) ⊗ TVB tea/coffee 🍴 Licensed Cen ht TVL No children 10yrs No coaches Library Dinner Last d breakfast **Prices** S fr £39; D £78-£86 **LB Parking** 11 **Notes** Closed Xmas & New Year

CANTERBURY

MAP 07 TR15

Premier Collection

◆◆◆◆◆

Magnolia House

36 St Dunstan's Ter CT2 8AX
☎ 01227 765121 & 07776 236459 🖷 01227 765121
e-mail info@magnoliahousecanterbury.co.uk
Dir *A2 E onto A2050 for city centre, 1st rdbt left signed University of Kent, St Dunstans Ter 3rd right*

The attractive property offers a warm welcome and superbly appointed bedrooms. The pleasant lounge looks out over the front garden. Evening meals (by arrangement) are delightful, served in the dining room overlooking the stunning walled garden. Breakfast is also of merit, with a wide choice on offer.

Facilities 7 en suite (1 GF) ⊗ TVB tea/coffee 🍴 Cen ht No children 12yrs No coaches Dinner Last d 9am **Prices** S £60; D £100-£135✴ **Parking** 5

Premier Collection

◆◆◆◆◆

Thanington Hotel

140 Wincheap CT1 3RY ☎ 01227 453227 📄 01227 453225
e-mail thanington@lineone.net
web www.thanington-hotel.co.uk
Dir On A28 just outside city walls

This fine Georgian property is close to the city centre and cathedral. The spacious bedrooms are located in the main house or in the smart modern extension, and all have excellent facilities; two rooms in the main house have four-posters. There is a spacious lounge, magnificent dining room and a swimming pool overlooking the elegant courtyard. Secure parking is a bonus.

Facilities 15 en suite (2 fmly) (4 GF) ⊗ in bedrooms ⊗ in dining room TVB tea/coffee Direct dial from bedrooms Licensed Cen ht TVL 🏊 Pool Table Threequarter size snooker table, games room **Conf** Max 16 Board 16 **Parking** 13

◆◆◆◆

Chislet Court Farm

Chislet CT3 4DU ☎ 01227 860309 📄 01227 860444
e-mail chisletcourtfarm@dial.pipex.com
web www.chisletcourtfarm.com
Dir 6m NE of Canterbury. Off A28 in Upstreet to Chislet, farm on right 100yds past church

A warm welcome awaits you at this delightful 18th-century house situated in a pretty village. The house is smartly maintained and set in delightful grounds and gardens. The en suite bedrooms are extremely spacious, well appointed, and have smart modern bathrooms. A hearty breakfast is served in the conservatory-dining room.

Facilities 2 en suite ⊗ TVB tea/coffee ✖ Cen ht No children 12yrs No coaches **Prices** S £45; D £70 **Parking** 4 **Notes** Closed Xmas 📷

◆◆◆◆

Yorke Lodge

50 London Rd CT2 8LF ☎ 01227 451243 📄 01227 462006
e-mail enquiries@yorkelodge.com
web www.yorkelodge.com
Dir 750yds NW of city centre. A2 E onto A2050 to city, 1st rdbt left onto London Rd, premises on left

The charming Victorian property stands in a tree-lined road just a 10-minute walk from the town centre and railway station. The spacious bedrooms are thoughtfully equipped and carefully decorated, and some rooms have four-poster beds. The stylish dining room leads to a conservatory-lounge, which opens onto a superb terrace.

Facilities 8 en suite (1 fmly) ⊗ in bedrooms ⊗ in dining room TVB tea/coffee Cen ht No coaches **Prices** S £45-£55; D £80-£100 **LB** **Parking** 5

◆◆◆◆

Beech Bank

Duckpit Ln, Waltham CT4 5QA
☎ 01227 700302 📄 01227 700302
e-mail beechbank@aol.com
Dir 5.5m S of Canterbury. Off B2068 through Petham, left by telephone onto Duckpit Ln, 2m on left

A 15th-century coach house set in landscaped grounds with magnificent views of the surrounding countryside. Original features include a minstrels' gallery, oak beams and exposed brickwork. Bedrooms are carefully decorated and thoughtfully equipped, and one room has a four-poster bed. Breakfast is served in the elegant Victorian conservatory.

Facilities 3 rms (2 en suite) (1 pri facs) (1 fmly) (2 GF) ⊗ TVB tea/coffee ✖ Cen ht No children 4yrs No coaches ⚬ 🏸 Badminton, Volleyball **Prices** S £40-£47; D £55-£58✱ **Parking** 10 **Notes** Closed 20 Dec-5 Jan 📷

◆◆◆◆

Castle House

28 Castle St CT1 2PT ☎ 01227 761897
e-mail enquiries@castlehousehotel.co.uk
Dir Opp Canterbury Castle ruins, off A28 ring road

Built in the 1730s, this magnificent house takes its name from the castle ruins standing opposite, and is close to the city centre. The bright and spacious bedrooms are well equipped and the decor enhances the character of the property. A hearty breakfast is served in the grand dining room. Ample parking is available.

Facilities 7 en suite (2 fmly) ⊗ in bedrooms ⊗ in dining room ⊗ in 1 lounge TVB tea/coffee ✖ Cen ht TVL No coaches **Prices** S £40-£55; D £65-£70✱ **LB** **Parking** 12 **Notes** 📷

CANTERBURY continued

◆◆◆◆

Clare Ellen

9 Victoria Rd CT1 3SG ☎ 01227 760205 ▤ 01227 784482
e-mail loraine.williams@clareellenguesthouse.co.uk
web www.clareellenguesthouse.co.uk
Dir A2 onto A2050 to Canterbury. Over 1st rdbt, right at 2nd rdbt, right at 3rd rdbt onto A28, 4th left

This attractive, well-maintained guest house is just a stroll from the city walls and Canterbury East railway station. Bedrooms are pleasantly furnished and equipped with useful extras. Breakfast is served at communal tables in the elegant dining room and secure parking is available.

Facilities 6 en suite (2 fmly) ⊗ in dining room STV TVB tea/coffee ✗ Cen ht No coaches **Prices** S £32-£55; D £56-£64 **LB Parking** 9

◆◆◆◆

Ensigne Cottage ◇

1 Ensigne Cottages, Shalmsford St, Chartham CT4 7RF
☎ 01227 738690 & 0770 613381
e-mail margi@margiwalker.wanadoo.co.uk
web http://mysite.wanadoo-members.co.uk/ensigne-cottage
Dir 3m SW of Canterbury. Off A28 for Shalmsford St (ignore Chartham sign), pass pub & Post Office, left after newsagent

This charming cottage, parts of which date back to 1902, is situated on the outskirts of Canterbury and offers a warm welcome, with tea and home-made cakes on arrival. The cosy bedrooms are attractive and well equipped. Breakfast, which includes delicious home-made breads, preserves and local produce, can be enjoyed around the communal table overlooking the courtyard garden.

Facilities 4 rms (1 en suite) (3 pri facs) ⊗ TVB tea/coffee ✗ Cen ht No coaches **Prices** S £25-£30; D £40-£50✳ **Parking** 3 **Notes** Closed 24-27 Dec ⊛

◆◆◆◆

The White House

6 St Peters Ln CT1 2BP ☎ 01227 761836
e-mail whwelcome@aol.com
Dir A290 into city, through Westgate, sharp left onto Pound Ln, 1st right

This attractive Regency house is in a quiet road close to High St and next to the Marlowe Theatre. The attractive bedrooms have modern en suites and a traditional breakfast is served in the smart dining room. This is a non-smoking establishment.

Facilities 8 en suite (1 fmly) ⊗ TVB tea/coffee ✗ Cen ht TVL **Prices** S fr £50; d fr £70 **Notes** ⊛

◆◆◆ ▣

Canterbury Pilgrims Hotel

18 The Friars CT1 2AS ☎ 01227 464531 ▤ 01227 762514
e-mail pilgrimshotel@aol.com
Dir Signs for Marlowe Theatre, establishment opp

Situated in the historic centre opposite the Marlowe Theatre, parts of

continued

the Pilgrims Hotel date back some 350 years. Bedrooms are comfortably appointed and well equipped. The refurbished public rooms include a spacious bar, a smart meeting room and a contemporary restaurant, where a good selection of dishes is available.

Canterbury Pilgrims Hotel

Facilities 15 en suite (1 fmly) ⊗ in 6 bedrooms ⊗ in dining room TVB tea/coffee Direct dial from bedrooms ✗ Cen ht Dinner Last d 9.30pm **Conf** Max 30 Thtr 25 Class 25 Board 20 **Parking** 10

◆◆◆

Cathedral Gate Hotel ◇

36 Burgate CT1 2HA ☎ 01227 464381 ▤ 01227 462800
e-mail cgate@cgate.demon.co.uk
Dir In city centre. Next to main gateway into cathedral close

Dating from 1438, this establishment has an enviable central location next to the cathedral. Old beams and winding corridors are part of the character, and the traditionally furnished bedrooms are equipped to modern standards. Breakfast is served in the cosy breakfast room. Luggage can be unloaded at reception before parking in a local car park.

Facilities 15 rms (4 en suite) 12 annexe rms (10 en suite) (5 fmly) ⊗ in dining room ⊗ in 1 lounge TVB tea/coffee Direct dial from bedrooms Licensed Cen ht Dinner Last d 8pm **Prices** S £30-£65; D £58-£98 **LB**

◆◆◆

Ersham Lodge Hotel

12 New Dover Rd CT1 3AP
☎ 01227 463174 & 768472 ▤ 01227 455482
e-mail ershamlod@aol.com
Dir From Canterbury ring road signs for Dover, premises on right after lights by Blockbuster Videos

The twin-gabled Victorian house is just a short walk from the cathedral

continued

and attractions. Some of the smartly decorated bedrooms are on the ground floor, and there is a cosy lounge-bar and a spacious breakfast room, which looks out onto the well-kept patio and garden.

Ersham Lodge Hotel

Facilities 13 en suite (1 fmly) (5 GF) FTV TVB tea/coffee Direct dial from bedrooms ✖ Cen ht Children's weekend play room with games & videos **Prices** S £39; D £68✳ **LB** **Conf** Max 40 Class 40 **Parking** 15

◆◆◆

St Stephens Guest House ◇

100 St Stephens Rd CT2 7JL
☎ 01227 767644 📠 01227 767644
Dir A290 from city Westgate & sharp right onto North Ln, 2nd rdbt left onto St Stephen's Rd, right onto Market Way, car park on right

The large guest house is situated close to the university and within easy walking distance of the city centre. The pleasant bedrooms are equipped with useful extras and there is a cosy lounge. Breakfast is served at individual tables in the smart dining room.

Facilities 12 rms (11 en suite) (2 fmly) (3 GF) TVB tea/coffee Cen ht TVL No children 5yrs **Prices** S £29-£40; D £58-£60✳ **Parking** 11 **Notes** Closed 18 Dec-mid Jan 😊

CLIFTONVILLE   MAP 07 TR37
See **Margate**

CRANBROOK   MAP 07 TQ73

◆◆◆◆ 🏚 ❦

Hallwood Farm Oast *(TQ755345)*

Hallwood Farm, Hawkhurst Rd TN17 2SP
☎ 01580 712416 & 07814 738212 Mrs Wickham
e-mail hallwoodfm@aol.com
Dir 1m S of Cranbrook. A229 500yds past Hartley Dyke farm shop, farm signed on right

A delightful 17th-century oast house set in beautiful countryside. The property has been converted to retain many original features, and the spacious bedrooms are filled with many thoughtful touches. Imaginative, carefully prepared breakfasts are served in the attractive dining room.

Facilities 2 en suite TVB tea/coffee ✖ No children 12yrs 200 acres apples blackcurrants sheep **Prices** D £65-£70✳ **Parking** 6 **Notes** Closed Xmas & New Year rs Dec/Jan 😊

DARTFORD   MAP 06 TQ57

◆◆◆ 🍽

The Rising Sun Inn

Fawkham Gn DA3 8NL ☎ 01474 872291 📠 01474 872779
Dir M25 junct 3, A20 Brands Hatch. Turn onto Scratchers Ln until sign for Fawkham. Left onto Brandshatch Rd, inn on left

A popular inn situated just a short drive from Brands Hatch. Bedrooms are pleasantly decorated with plain-painted walls and equipped with a good range of useful extras; one room has a superb four-poster bed. There is a busy character bar and restaurant, and a patio for alfresco dining in summer.

Facilities 5 en suite (1 fmly) (2 GF) in bedrooms in dining room in 1 lounge TVB tea/coffee ✖ Cen ht No coaches Dinner Last d 9.30pm **Parking** 20

See advertisement on this page

England

DEAL
MAP 07 TR35

Premier Collection

◆◆◆◆◆ 🍴

Sutherland House Hotel
186 London Rd CT14 9PT
☎ 01304 362853 🖷 01304 381146
e-mail info@sutherlandhouse.fsnet.co.uk
Dir 0.5m W of town centre/seafront on A258

This stylish house has charming bedrooms, and a comfortable lounge extremely well stocked with books and magazines. The elegant dining room is the venue for home-cooked dinners and breakfasts.

Facilities 4 en suite (1 GF) ⊗ in bedrooms ⊗ in area of dining room FTV TVB tea/coffee Direct dial from bedrooms Licensed Cen ht No children 5yrs No coaches Dinner Last d 6.30pm **Prices** S £47-£55; D £55-£65✳ **LB Conf** Max 12 Thtr 12 Class 12 Board 12 Del from £105 ✳ **Parking** 7

◆◆◆◆

Sondes Lodge
14 Sondes Rd CT14 7BW
☎ 01304 368741 🖷 01304 368050
e-mail sondes.lodge@tiscali.co.uk
web www.sondeslodge.co.uk
Dir In town centre

Expect a warm welcome at this smart guest house situated in a side road just off the seafront and a short walk from the town centre. The pleasant bedrooms have coordinated fabrics and many thoughtful touches. Breakfast is served at individual tables in the lower ground-floor dining room.

Facilities 3 en suite (1 fmly) (1 GF) ⊗ in 1 bedrooms ⊗ in dining room ⊗ in lounges TVB tea/coffee ✖ Cen ht No children 10yrs No coaches **Prices** S £35-£38; D £50-£54✳

DOVER
MAP 07 TR34

◆◆◆◆

Beulah House
94 Crabble Hill, London Rd CT17 0SA
☎ 01304 824615 🖷 01304 828850
e-mail owen@beulahhouse94.freeserve.co.uk
web www.beulahguesthouse.co.uk
Dir On A256

This impressive Victorian house is just a stroll from the town centre and close to the ferry port. The spacious bedrooms are pleasantly decorated and thoughtfully equipped. Public rooms include two conservatories and a comfortable lounge. The impressive garden has interesting topiary and a small menagerie.

Facilities 9 rms (6 en suite) (2 fmly) ⊗ TVB tea/coffee ✖ Cen ht TVL 1 acre gardens **LB Parking** 11

◆◆◆◆

Hubert House
9 Castle Hill Rd CT16 1QW
☎ 01304 202253 🖷 01304 210142
e-mail huberthouse@btinternet.com
Dir On A258 by Dover Castle

This charming Georgian house is within walking distance of the ferry port and the town centre. Bedrooms are pleasantly decorated and furnished in a modern style. Breakfast, including full English and healthy options, is served in the smart coffee house, which is open all day. Families are especially welcome.

Facilities 8 en suite (4 fmly) ⊗ TVB tea/coffee Licensed Cen ht Dinner Last d 8.30pm **Prices** S £35-£45; D £45-£50; (room only) ✳ **LB Parking** 6

◆◆◆◆ 🍴

The Park Inn
1-2 Park Pl, Ladywell CT16 1DQ
☎ 01304 203300 🖷 01304 203324
e-mail theparkinn@aol.com
Dir In town centre opp police station

A charming 18th-century inn situated in the heart of the town centre. The open-plan public rooms offer a good level of comfort throughout and include a popular bar and a smart restaurant with an open fireplace. Bedrooms are generally quite spacious; each is carefully decorated with quality soft furnishings and many thoughtful touches.

Facilities 5 en suite (1 fmly) ⊗ in bedrooms ⊗ in dining room STV TVB tea/coffee Direct dial from bedrooms ✖ Cen ht Dinner Last d 9.30pm **Conf** Max 40

◆◆◆ 🍴

The Swingate Inn
Deal Rd CT15 5DP ☎ 01304 204043 🖷 01304 204043
e-mail terry@swingate.com
web www.swingate.com
Dir A2 onto A258 Deal road, 0.25m on right

Pleasantly located on the edge of Dover and very convenient for the ferry, this friendly inn has spacious modern accommodation. The bar offers informal dining while the restaurant carte provides greater choice. The Thursdays jazz evenings are particularly popular and family entertainment is provided on Sunday evenings.

Facilities 11 en suite (2 fmly) ⊗ in 1 bedrooms ⊗ in area of dining room ⊗ in 1 lounge TVB tea/coffee ✖ Cen ht TVL pets corner bird aviary play area Dinner Last d 9.45pm **Prices** S £42; D £50; (room only) ✳ **Conf** Max 100 Thtr 100 Class 100 **Parking** 60 **Notes** Civ Wed 200

◆◆◆

Ardmore Private Hotel
18 Castle Hill Rd CT16 1QW
☎ 01304 205895 🖷 01304 208229
e-mail res@ardmoreph.co.uk
web www.ardmoreph.co.uk
Dir On A258 by Dover Castle

Dating from 1796, this delightful house is situated below Dover Castle. Convenient for the town centre and ferry port, the Ardmore offers

continued

comfortable accommodation and friendly hospitality. The non-smoking bedrooms are well equipped and brightly decorated. Public rooms include a sumptuous lounge and a well-appointed breakfast room.

Facilities 4 en suite (1 fmly) ⊗ TVB tea/coffee ✖ Cen ht
Prices D £45-£60 **Notes** Closed Xmas

◆◆◆

Kernow

189 Folkestone Rd CT17 9SJ ☎ 01304 207797
Dir B2011 W from town centre onto Folkestone Rd

This welcoming guest house is convenient for the ferries and railway station. The neat accommodation is well maintained, and two bathrooms are available. There is adequate parking at the front of the property, and breakfast can be arranged to suit your travel arrangements.

Facilities 3 rms TVB tea/coffee ✖ Cen ht TVL No coaches **Parking** 4
Notes ⊗

◆◆◆

St Martins ◇

17 Castle Hill Rd CT16 1QW
☎ 01304 205938 ▤ 01304 208229
e-mail res@stmartinsgh.co.uk
web www.stmartinsgh.co.uk
Dir On A258 by Dover Castle

Located close to the castle, ferry port and town centre, this smart guest house offers a friendly welcome. The thoughtfully equipped bedrooms have pretty fabrics and decor, and most rooms enjoy a sunny aspect. Breakfast is served in the pine-furnished dining room, and the comfortable lounge has a double aspect.

Facilities 6 en suite (3 fmly) ⊗ TVB tea/coffee ✖ Cen ht
Prices S £30-£35; D £40-£52 **Notes** Closed Xmas

DYMCHURCH
MAP 07 TR12

◆◆◆◆

Waterside

15 Hythe Rd TN29 0LN ☎ 01303 872253 ▤ 01303 872253
e-mail info@watersideguesthouse.co.uk
Dir M20 junct 11 onto A259 follow signs for Hythe then Dymchurch, 0.5m past village sign

Please note that this establishment has recently changed hands. Waterside is an attractive, well-maintained house with picturesque views. It offers brightly decorated, comfortably furnished bedrooms, and a small lounge and bar are available.

Facilities 5 en suite (1 fmly) ⊗ TVB tea/coffee ✖ Licensed Cen ht
TVL No coaches Dinner Last d 7pm LB **Parking** 7

EDENBRIDGE
MAP 06 TQ44

◆◆◆◆ ▣

Ye Old Crown

74-76 The High St TN8 5AR
☎ 01732 867896 ▤ 01732 868316
Dir In town centre

This 15th-century inn, situated in the centre of town, retains much original character. You have the choice of dining in the traditional bar, with its good selection of real ales, or in the beamed restaurant upstairs. Modern, thoughtfully equipped bedrooms are housed in an adjacent converted barn.

Facilities 6 en suite (2 fmly) (2 GF) ⊗ in bedrooms ⊗ in dining room ⊗ in lounges TVB tea/coffee ✖ Cen ht TVL No children 6yrs Golf 18 Dinner Last d 8:50pm **Parking** 30

FARNINGHAM
MAP 06 TQ56

Premier Collection

◆◆◆◆◆ ▾

Beesfield Farm (TQ554660)

Beesfield Ln DA4 0LA ☎ 01322 863900 ▤ 01322 863900
Mr & Mrs Vingoe
e-mail kim.vingoe@btinternet.com
Dir From village centre S onto Beesfield Ln, farm 0.5m on left

Set amid mature gardens and surrounded by open farmland, this attractive house is close to major roads, Brands Hatch and Bluewater Park. The individually decorated bedrooms are beautifully appointed and have many thoughtful touches. Breakfast is served at a large polished table in the elegant dining room, and there is a stylish lounge with plush furnishings.

Facilities 3 en suite ⊗ TVB tea/coffee ✖ Cen ht TVL No children 12yrs 400 acres arable dairy mixed **Prices** S £65-£70; D £75-£90 LB
Parking 10 **Notes** Closed 8 Dec-Jan ⊗

FAVERSHAM

MAP 07 TR06

◆◆◆◆

Yaldings

Staplestreet Rd, Goodnestone ME13 9HT ☎ 01795 538680
e-mail yaldings@btinternet.com
web www.yaldingsguesthouse.com
Dir *M2 junct 7, A299, 0.25m left, on corner on right*

This is a great spot for touring the beautiful Kent countryside. The refurbished home has three bedrooms varying in size, but all are furnished to a high standard with excellent facilities for business and leisure. Aga-cooked breakfasts are served around a communal dining table, and a self-catering cottage is available in the grounds.

Facilities 3 rms (2 en suite) (1 pri facs) (1 fmly) ⊗ TVB tea/coffee ✗ Cen ht No children 15yrs No coaches **Prices** S £45-£55; D £65-£75✱ LB **Parking** 11

FOLKESTONE

MAP 07 TR23

★★★ Inn

The Lighthouse Inn & Restaurant

111 Old Dover Rd, Capel-Le-Ferne CT18 7HT
☎ 01303 223300 ▤ 01303 842270
e-mail sales@thelighthouseinn.co.uk
Dir *2m NE of town centre in Capel-le-Ferne. Off B2011 onto Old Dover Road*

Situated on the clifftop with panoramic views, this charming inn is handy for Eurotunnel and the Dover ferry. The spacious bedrooms are carefully decorated and thoughtfully equipped, and some rooms have lovely sea views. Public rooms include a restaurant and a large open-plan bar.

Facilities 11 rms (9 en suite) (2 pri facs) (3 fmly) (1 GF) ⊗ in bedrooms ⊗ in dining room ⊗ in 1 lounge TVB tea/coffee ✗ Cen ht Dinner Last d 8.45pm **Conf** Max 30 Thtr 30 Class 30 Board 30

◆◆◆◆◆

Hotel Relish

4 Augusta Gdns CT20 2RR
☎ 01303 850952 ▤ 01303 850958
e-mail reservations@hotelrelish.co.uk
web www.hotelrelish.co.uk
Dir *Off A2033 Sandgate Rd*

Expect a warm welcome at this impressive Victorian terrace property, which overlooks Augusta Gardens in the fashionable West End of town. The bedrooms feature contemporary natural-wood furniture, lovely coordinated fabrics, and thoughtful extras like DVD players and free Broadband access. Public rooms include a modern lounge-dining room, and a sun terrace where breakfast is served in the summer.

Facilities 10 en suite (2 fmly) ⊗ TVB tea/coffee Direct dial from bedrooms Cen ht No coaches **Prices** S £55-£115; D £79-£125✱ **Conf** Max 25 Thtr 25 Board 20 **Parking** 2 **Notes** Closed 24 Dec-2 Jan

◆◆◆

Chandos Guest House ◇

77 Cheriton Rd CT20 1DG
☎ 01303 851202 & 07799 886297
e-mail froggydon@aol.com
web www.chandosguesthouse.com
Dir *600yds NW of town centre. M20 junct 12/13, A20 to town centre & onto Cheriton Rd*

Close to the town centre and only a 5-minute drive from Eurotunnel, this pleasant guest house is ideal for continental travellers. Bedrooms are comfortable and well appointed, and hearty breakfasts are served in the ground-floor dining room. Secure parking is available on request.

Facilities 9 rms (6 en suite) (4 fmly) ⊗ TVB tea/coffee ✗ Cen ht No coaches **Prices** S £17.50-£25; D £35-£50 LB **Parking** 5

GOUDHURST

MAP 06 TQ73

◆◆◆◆ ⊜ ◼

The Star & Eagle Hotel

High St TN17 1AL ☎ 01580 211512 ▤ 01580 212444
e-mail starandeagle@btconnect.com
web www.starandeagle.com
Dir *In village on A262 next to church*

A warm welcome is assured at this 15th-century inn located in the
continued

heart of this delightful village. Bedrooms and public areas display original features and character, and delicious home-made dishes are available in the restaurant and bar.

Facilities 10 rms (8 en suite) ⊗ in bedrooms ⊗ in dining room TVB tea/coffee Direct dial from bedrooms ✕ Cen ht Dinner Last d 9.30pm **Prices** D £70-£120 **Conf** Max 30 Thtr 30 Class 15 Board 12 **Parking** 20 **Notes** rs 24-26 Dec Civ Wed 50

HAWKHURST
MAP 07 TQ73

Premier Collection

♦♦♦♦♦

Southgate-Little Fowlers

Rye Rd TN18 5DA ☎ 01580 752526 🖹 01580 752526
e-mail Susan.Woodard@southgate.uk.net
web www.southgate.uk.net
Dir 0.25m E of Hawkhurst on A268

A warm welcome is assured at this wonderful 300-year-old former dower house. Set in immaculate gardens, the renovated property provides attractive accommodation throughout. Spacious bedrooms are carefully decorated and equipped with many thoughtful extras. A hearty breakfast is served at individual tables in the delightful Victorian conservatory.

Facilities 2 en suite (1 fmly) ⊗ TVB tea/coffee ✕ Cen ht TVL No children 8yrs No coaches **Prices** S £55-£65; D £66-£80 **Parking** 5 **Notes** Closed Nov-Feb ⊛

HYTHE
MAP 07 TR13

♦♦♦♦

Seabrook House

81 Seabrook Rd CT21 5QW
☎ 01303 269282 🖹 01303 237822
e-mail info@seabrook-house.co.uk
Dir 0.9m E of Hythe on A259

An imposing Victorian house situated just a few miles from the M20 and Eurotunnel. The property stands in pretty gardens and is within easy walking distance of the beach. The attractive bedrooms are carefully furnished and thoughtfully equipped. Public rooms include an elegant lounge, where tea and coffee are served in the evening, a sunny conservatory and a large dining room.

Facilities 13 en suite (4 fmly) (4 GF) ⊗ in bedrooms ⊗ in dining room ⊗ in 1 lounge TVB tea/coffee ✕ Cen ht TVL **Conf** Max 12 Board 12 **Parking** 13

IVYCHURCH
MAP 07 TR02

Premier Collection

♦♦♦♦♦ 🛖

Olde Moat House

TN29 0AZ ☎ 01797 344700 🖹 01797 343919
e-mail oldemoathouse@hotmail.com
web www.oldemoathouse.co.uk
Dir Off junct A2070 & A259 into Ivychurch, left & 0.75m on left

Tea and home-made cakes are provided on arrival at this charming Grade II listed 16th-century property. The spacious bedrooms are carefully furnished with coordinated fabrics and have many thoughtful touches. Public rooms are full of original character, such as oak beams and open fireplaces; they include an elegant dining room and a cosy lounge with plush furnishings.

Facilities 3 en suite ⊗ TVB tea/coffee ✕ Cen ht TVL No children 16yrs No coaches Dinner Last d 24 hours notice **Parking** 10

LADDINGFORD
MAP 06 TQ64

★★★★ Guest House

The Coach House

Lees Rd ME18 6DB
☎ 01622 873390 & 07958 352507 🖹 020 8850 4747
e-mail susan@thecoachhouseladdingford.co.uk
web www.thecoachhouseladdingford.co.uk

The converted 19th-century coach house stands among orchards and farmland between the villages of Laddingford and Yalding. Laddingford has a good real-ale pub, and the area is ideal for walking and cycling.

Facilities 6 en suite (1 GF) ⊗ TVB tea/coffee ✕ Cen ht

England

England

MAIDSTONE
See also **Marden**

MAP 07 TQ75

Premier Collection

♦♦♦♦♦ ❦

Goldings *(TQ714486)*

Elphicks Farm, Hunton ME15 0SG
☎ 01622 820758 🖷 01622 820754 Mr & Mrs Day
e-mail goldingsoast@btinternet.com
Dir *4m SW of Maidstone. A229 W onto B2163 through Coxheath, 1st left to Hunton, pass church & school, left onto driveway*

Expect a warm welcome at this charming property set amid 180 acres of orchards and farmland. The spacious bedrooms are in converted oast houses, each one having coordinated fabrics and many thoughtful touches. Public areas have a wealth of character with exposed beams and a huge pine staircase. Breakfast is served in the round dining room, and there is a cosy lounge.

Facilities 3 en suite (2 GF) ⊗ STV TVB tea/coffee ✖ Cen ht
No children 14yrs Fishing 180 acres arable, fruit, pasture
Prices D £65-£80✳ **Parking** 8 **Notes** Closed 21 Dec-12 Jan ⊠

Premier Collection

♦♦♦♦♦

Ringlestone House

Ringlestone Hamlet, Harrietsham ME17 1NX
☎ 01622 859911 🖷 01622 859740
e-mail bookings@ringlestone.com
web www.ringlestone.com
Dir *M20 junct 8, A20, at rdbt opp Ramada Hotel left to Hollingbourne, through village, right at x-rds at top of hill*

Dating from 1533 and originally a hospice for monks, it is not surprising that this delightful inn oozes charm and history. Subdued lighting in the public areas enhances the ambience together with oak beams, brick and flint walls and an inglenook fireplace. The bedrooms are in a converted farmhouse opposite and are smartly appointed with lots of useful extras.

Facilities 3 en suite (1 fmly) ⊗ in bedrooms ⊗ in area of dining room
TVB tea/coffee Direct dial from bedrooms ✖ Licensed Cen ht TVL Day membership to local Health Club **Prices** S £95-£130; D £105-£130; (room only) ✳ **LB Conf** Max 50 Thtr 50 Class 30 Board 24 Del from £135 ✳ **Parking** 40 **Notes** Closed 25 Dec

♦♦♦♦ ⬛❚

The Black Horse Inn

Pilgrims Way, Thurnham ME14 3LD
☎ 01622 737185 & 630830 🖷 01622 739170
e-mail info@wellieboot.net
web www.wellieboot.net/home_blackhorse.htm
Dir *M20 junct 7, N onto A249. Right into Detling, opp pub onto Pilgrims Way for 1m*

This charming inn dates from the 17th century, and the public areas have a wealth of oak beams, exposed brickwork and open fireplaces. The stylish bedrooms are in a new building behind the premises, and each one is attractively furnished and thoughtfully equipped.

Facilities 11 annexe en suite (4 fmly) (11 GF) ⊗ in bedrooms ⊗ in area of dining room TVB tea/coffee Cen ht No coaches Dinner Last d 10pm
Prices S £60-£65; D £75-£80✳ **LB Parking** 40
See advertisement on opposite page

♦♦♦♦

Aylesbury Hotel

56-58 London Rd ME16 8QL ☎ 01622 762100 & 664673
e-mail aylesbury@onetel.com
Dir *M20 junct 5, on A20 into Maidstone on left*

Located just a short walk from the town centre, this well-maintained establishment offers a genuine welcome. The carefully decorated bedrooms have coordinated soft fabrics and many thoughtful touches. Breakfast is served in the smart dining room overlooking a walled garden.

Facilities 8 en suite ⊗ in 6 bedrooms ⊗ in dining room TVB tea/coffee ✖ Cen ht No coaches **Prices** S £49; D £65 **LB Parking** 8
Notes Closed 24-26 Dec

◆◆◆◆

Bower Court House

78 Bower Mount Rd ME16 8AT
☎ 01622 752684 ▤ 01622 752684
e-mail mail@bowercourt.co.uk
Dir *0.6m W of the town centre. Off A26 Tonbridge Rd onto Oakwood Rd & right onto Bower Mount Rd*

An imposing Edwardian property situated in a quiet side road just a short walk from the town centre and the railway station. The spacious bedrooms are carefully decorated, thoughtfully equipped and have views over pretty landscaped gardens. Public rooms feature a panelled entrance hall with seating and a smart dining room.

Facilities 10 rms (9 en suite) (1 pri facs) 5 annexe rms (3 en suite) (3 fmly) (4 GF) ⊘ in 3 bedrooms ⊘ in dining room TVB tea/coffee Cen ht **Prices** S £42-£46; D £55-£63✱ **Conf** Max 36 **Parking** 18 **Notes** Closed 25-26 Dec

◆◆◆◆

Conway House ◇

12 Conway Rd ME16 0HD
☎ 01622 688287 ▤ 01622 662589
e-mail conway-house@tiscali.co.uk
Dir *1m NW of town centre off A20 London Rd*

Located in a quiet residential area just a short distance from the M20 and town centre, Conway House offers bedrooms thoughtfully equipped with useful facilities. Breakfast is served around one large table in the pleasant lounge-dining room.

Facilities 3 rms (1 en suite) (1 GF) ⊘ TVB tea/coffee ✖ Cen ht TVL No coaches **Prices** S £25-£35; D £40-£50; (room only) **Parking** 3

◆◆◆◆

Langley Oast

Langley Pk, Langley ME17 3NQ
☎ 01622 863523 ▤ 01622 863523
e-mail margaret@langleyoast.freeserve.co.uk
Dir *2.5m SE of Maidstone off A274. After Parkwood Business Estate lane signed Maidstone Golf Centre*

This traditional Kent oast house is a short drive from the town centre and has views of the surrounding countryside. Bedrooms are spacious and well appointed; two are in the 24-foot diameter towers and one has a jacuzzi. Breakfast is served in an elegant dining room around one large table and there is an attractive garden.

Facilities 3 rms (2 en suite) (1 fmly) ⊘ TVB tea/coffee ✖ Cen ht No coaches Jacuzzi in 1 bedroom **Prices** S £35-£50; D £50-£85✱ **Parking** 5 **Notes** Closed Xmas ⊜

◆◆◆◆

Roslin Villa

11 St Michaels Rd ME16 8BS
☎ 01622 758301 ▤ 01622 761459
e-mail brian.ff@btinternet.com
web www.roslinvillaguesthouse.com
Dir *0.6m W of town centre. Off A26 Tonbridge Rd, brown tourist signs to Roslin Villa*

Expect a warm welcome from the caring hosts at this delightful detached Victorian house, which is within easy walking distance of the town centre and only a short drive from the M20. The smart bedrooms are carefully furnished and equipped with many thoughtful touches. Public rooms include a cosy lounge and an elegant dining room.

Facilities 9 rms (7 en suite) (3 fmly) (1 GF) ⊘ TVB tea/coffee Licensed Cen ht TVL No coaches **Conf** Max 15 Class 15 Board 15 **Parking** 10

England

MAIDSTONE continued

♦♦♦
Rock House Hotel
102 Tonbridge Rd ME16 8SL
☎ 01622 751616 📠 01622 756119
e-mail rock.house@btconnect.com
Dir On A26, 0.5m from town centre

This friendly, family-run guest house is just a short walk from the town centre. Breakfast is served in the conservatory-dining room that overlooks the rear terrace and garden. Bedrooms are brightly decorated and equipped with modern facilities.

Facilities 14 rms (8 en suite) (4 fmly) ⊘ in 4 bedrooms ⊘ in dining room TVB tea/coffee ✘ Cen ht TVL **Parking** 7

♦♦♦ A
The Howard Hotel
22/24 London Rd ME16 8QL
☎ 01622 758778 📠 01622 609984
e-mail howardhotel@btopenworld.com
Dir 400yds W of town centre on A20

Facilities 14 rms (2 GF) ⊘ in dining room ⊘ in lounges TVB tea/coffee ✘ Licensed Cen ht TVL No coaches **Prices** S £32-£38; D £48-£54 **Parking** 15 **Notes** Closed 24 Dec-1 Jan

MARDEN
MAP 06 TQ74

Premier Collection

♦♦♦♦♦
Merzie Meadows
Hunton Rd TN12 9SL ☎ 01622 820500 📠 01622 820500
e-mail pamela.mumford@onetel.net
Dir A229 onto B2079 for Marden, 1st right onto Underlyn Ln, 2.5m Large Chainhurst sign, right onto drive

A detached property set in 20 acres of mature gardens in Kent countryside. The generously proportioned bedrooms are housed in two wings, which overlook a terrace; each room is carefully decorated, thoughtfully equipped and furnished with well-chosen pieces. The attractive breakfast room has an Italian tiled floor and superb views of the garden.

Facilities 2 en suite (1 fmly) (2 GF) ⊘ STV TVB tea/coffee ✘ Cen ht TVL No children 15yrs No coaches **Prices** S £60-£65; D £65-£80✱ **Parking** 4 **Notes** Closed mid Dec-mid Feb ☺

MARGATE
MAP 07 TR37

♦♦♦♦
The Greswolde Hotel ◇
20 Surrey Rd, Cliftonville CT9 2LA
☎ 01843 223956 📠 01843 223956
e-mail jbearl@freeuk.com

An attractive Victorian house set in a peaceful area close to the seafront. The property has a lovely period atmosphere with interesting memorabilia and spacious bedrooms. The pleasant rooms are comfortably appointed and equipped with many useful extras. Breakfast is served in the elegant dining room, and there is a cosy lounge.

Facilities 5 en suite (2 fmly) ⊘ in bedrooms ⊘ in dining room TVB tea/coffee Licensed Cen ht No coaches **Prices** S £30-£35; D £45-£50✱ LB

♦♦♦
Elonville Hotel ◇
70-72 Harold Rd, Cliftonville CT9 2HS
☎ 01843 298635 📠 01843 298635
e-mail bockings@elonvillehotel.com
web www.elonvillehotel.co.uk
Dir From Margate clock tower E onto A2051 coast road, Harold Rd 1m on right

Expect a warm welcome at the Elonville, situated just a short walk from the shops and beach. The pleasant bedrooms vary in size and style, and all are thoughtfully equipped. Public rooms include a lounge bar, and a dining room that overlooks the garden.

Facilities 16 rms (10 en suite) (3 fmly) (1 GF) ⊘ in dining room ⊘ in lounges TVB tea/coffee Licensed Lift TVL Dinner **Prices** S £30; D £60✱ LB

NEW ROMNEY
MAP 07 TR02

♦♦♦♦ ❧
Honeychild Manor Farmhouse ◇
(TR062276)
St Mary In The Marsh TN29 0DB
☎ 01797 366180 & 07951 237821 📠 01797 366925
Mrs Furnival
e-mail honeychild@farming.co.uk
Dir 2m N of New Romney off A259. S of village centre

Expect a warm welcome at this imposing Georgian farmhouse set in landscaped grounds, which is part of a dairy farm on Romney Marsh. A hearty breakfast is served in the elegant dining room and features quality local produce. Bedrooms are pleasantly decorated, well furnished and thoughtfully equipped.

Facilities 3 rms ⊘ TVB tea/coffee ✘ Cen ht ⚬ 1500 acres Arable & dairy **Prices** S £25-£30; D £50-£60✱ **Parking** 10 **Notes** ☺

England

RAMSGATE

MAP 07 TR36

◆◆◆

Belvidere

26 Augusta Rd CT11 8JS
☎ 01843 588809 ▤ 01843 588809
Dir *A299, A255 & Victoria Rd to Ramsgate seafront, right then 2nd right*

A warm welcome is a key feature at this family-run guest house, which is close to the beach, ferry terminal and town centre. A comfortable lounge is available and breakfast is served in the small dining room. Bedrooms, of various sizes, are soundly maintained and suitably appointed. Unrestricted on-road parking is available.

Facilities 7 rms (3 en suite) (2 fmly) ⊗ in dining room ⊗ in lounges STV TVB tea/coffee ✖ Lift Cen ht TVL No children 3yrs **Notes** Closed 24 Dec-2 Jan 🍴

SANDHURST

MAP 07 TQ82

◆◆◆ ❦

Hoads Farm ◇ (TQ805282)

Crouch Ln TN18 5PA
☎ 01580 850296 ▤ 01580 850296 Mrs Nicholas
e-mail ca.nicholas@btinternet.com
Dir *Off A268 0.5m E from Sandhurst onto Crouch Ln*

Situated in peaceful countryside, this 16th-century farmhouse still forms part of a working farm. Public rooms include a spacious beamed lounge with a welcoming open fire. Breakfast is served at a large table in the dining room, which overlooks the garden, and dinner is available by arrangement. Hoads Farm produces award-winning wines.

Facilities 3 rms (1 fmly) ⊗ in dining room tea/coffee ✖ Licensed Cen ht TVL 350 acres Apple Hops Vines Sheep Plums Dinner Last d by arrangment **Prices** S £28; D £48✳ **Parking** 6 **Notes** 🍴

SANDWICH

MAP 07 TR35

◆◆◆ ◪

The New Inn

2 Harnet St CT13 9ES ☎ 01304 612335 ▤ 01304 619133
e-mail new.inn@thorleytaverns.com
Dir *Off A256, one-way system into town centre, inn on right*

A popular inn situated in the heart of this busy historic town. The large open-plan lounge bar offers an extensive range of beers and an

continued

interesting choice of home-made dishes. Bedrooms are furnished in pine and have many useful extras.

Facilities 5 en suite (3 fmly) ⊗ in 3 bedrooms ⊗ in lounges STV TVB tea/coffee Direct dial from bedrooms ✖ Cen ht No coaches Dinner Last d 8pm **Prices** S £49.50; D £79.50✳ **Parking** 17

SEVENOAKS

MAP 06 TQ55

See also **Farningham**

◆◆◆◆

The Studio at Double Dance

Tonbridge Rd, Ightham TN15 9AT
☎ 01732 884198 ▤ 01732 780363
e-mail pennycracknell@doubledance.co.uk
Dir *A227 S from Ightham towards Tonbridge, 1st left onto Mill Ln, driveway 1st right*

A delightful contemporary annexe with peaceful gardens and impressive views of the North Downs, and close to many attractions. Accommodation is self-contained with private access and has a wide range of facilities. An ample continental breakfast is provided for you to prepare at your leisure.

Facilities 1 annexe en suite ⊗ TVB tea/coffee ✖ Cen ht No children No coaches ♨ **Prices** D £50✳ **Parking** 2 **Notes** 🍴

◆◆◆

Barn Cottage ◇

Seven Mile Ln, Borough Gn TN15 8QY ☎ 01732 883384
e-mail suzifilleul@aol.com
Dir *A20 onto B2016 Seven Mile Ln for 1m, over x-rds, Barn Cottage on left*

This pretty, white-boarded cottage is set in a pleasant courtyard with an attractive garden. The bedrooms are neat and comfortably furnished. Breakfast is served in the comfortable, flower-filled conservatory-lounge, which overlooks the garden. Off-road parking is available.

Facilities 3 rms ⊗ tea/coffee ✖ Cen ht No coaches Cycling **Prices** S £28.50; D £57✳ **Parking** 5 **Notes** Closed 25-26 Dec 🍴

SHEERNESS

MAP 07 TQ97

◆ Ⓐ

Sheppey Guest House ◇

214 Queenborough Rd, Halfway ME12 3DF
☎ 01795 665950 ▤ 01795 661200
e-mail sophie@allen3877fsbusiness.co.uk
Dir *M2 onto A249 Sittingbourne/Sheerness, on Isle of Sheppey onto A250, pass The Fields & guest house on left*

Facilities 9 en suite (4 fmly) (2 GF) ⊗ in dining room ⊗ in lounges STV TVB tea/coffee Direct dial from bedrooms Licensed Cen ht TVL No coaches ⊠ Dinner Last d 10pm **Prices** S £20; D £30✳ **Parking** 9 **Notes** 🍴

England

SITTINGBOURNE
MAP 07 TQ96

◆◆◆

Sandhurst Farm Forge ◇

Seed Rd, Newnham ME9 0NE ☎ 01795 886854
e-mail rooms.forge@btinternet.com
Dir 6m SW of Faversham. Off A2 into Newnham, onto Seed Rd by church, establishment 1m on right

A warm welcome is assured at this peaceful location, which also comprises a working forge. The spacious bedrooms are in a converted stable block and are smartly furnished, and breakfast is served in the adjoining dining room. The owner has won an award for green tourism by reducing the impact of the business on the environment.

Facilities 2 en suite (2 GF) ⊗ TVB tea/coffee ✖ Cen ht No children 14yrs No coaches **Prices** S £28-£30; D £56-£58✳ **Parking** 6 **Notes** Closed 23 Dec-1 Jan ⊛

Ⓤ

The Beaumont

74 London Rd ME10 1NS
☎ 01795 472536 ▤ 01795 425921
e-mail info@thebeaumont.co.uk
web www.thebeaumont.co.uk
Dir From M2 or M20 take A249 N. Exit at A2, 1m on left

At the time of going to press the rating for this establishment had not been confirmed. Please check the AA website www.theAA.com for up-to-date information.

Facilities 9 rms (6 en suite) (3 pri facs) (3 GF) ⊗ in bedrooms ⊗ in dining room STV TVB tea/coffee Direct dial from bedrooms Cen ht TVL No coaches **Prices** S £40-£60; D £65-£75✳ **Conf** Max 12 Thtr 12 Class 12 Board 12 **Parking** 9 **Notes** Closed 24 Dec-1 Jan

SMARDEN
MAP 07 TQ84

◆◆◆◆ ▣

The Chequers Inn

The Street TN27 8QA ☎ 01233 770217 ▤ 01233 770623
e-mail jan-mich@supernet.co.uk
web www.thechequerssmarden.com
Dir On main street next to church

Expect a warm welcome at this delightful 16th-century or older inn, which has been renovated by the present owners. Bedrooms are individual in style, including one with a four-poster bed, and all are furnished in keeping with the character of the inn. Public areas have a wealth of charm with original exposed beams and open fireplaces.

Facilities 4 en suite (1 fmly) ⊗ in bedrooms ⊗ in dining room TVB tea/coffee ✖ Cen ht No coaches Dinner Last d 9.30pm **Conf** Max 40 **Parking** 12

SUTTON
MAP 07 TR34

Ⓤ

Sutton Vale Country Club ◇

Vale Rd CT15 5DH
☎ 01304 366233 & 374155 ▤ 01304 381132
e-mail office@sutton-vale.co.uk
Dir A2, left at Whitfield rdbt then immediately right by Archers Pub. 4m on left

At the time of going to press the rating for this establishment had not been confirmed. Please check the AA website www.theAA.com for up-to-date information.

Facilities 4 en suite ⊗ in 1 lounge TVB tea/coffee ✖ Licensed Cen ht TVL ▢ Pool Table Dinner Last d 8pm **Prices** S £30-£40; D £50-£60; (room only) ✳ **LB Conf** Max 100 Thtr 100 Class 60 Board 50 Del from £75 ✳ **Parking** 50

TENTERDEN
MAP 07 TQ83

◆◆◆◆

Collina House Hotel

5 East Hill TN30 6RL
☎ 01580 764852 & 764004 ▤ 01580 762224
e-mail enquiries@collinahousehotel.co.uk
web www.collinahousehotel.co.uk
Dir Off High St E onto B2067 Oaks Rd, property on left opp orchard

This attractive, half-timbered Edwardian house has a peaceful location just a short walk from the town centre. The smart en suite bedrooms are spacious and thoughtfully equipped. Public areas include a formal bar and an elegant restaurant offering imaginative home-made dishes.

Facilities 12 en suite 3 annexe en suite (8 fmly) ⊗ in bedrooms ⊗ in dining room TV14B tea/coffee Direct dial from bedrooms ✖ Licensed Cen ht Dinner Last d 8.30pm **Prices** S £40-£55; D £60-£85✳ **LB Parking** 15 **Notes** Closed 21 Dec-11 Jan

◆◆◆◆ ▣

The White Lion

The High St TN30 6BD ☎ 01580 765077 ▤ 01580 764157
e-mail whitelion@celticinnspubs.co.uk
web www.celticinns.co.uk
Dir In town centre

A delightful 18th-century coaching inn situated on the historic high street. Bedrooms are well appointed, thoughtfully equipped, and some have four-poster beds. Public rooms feature a popular bar, a lounge,

continued

and an oak-panelled restaurant serving an extensive range of dishes. There is also a small function and meeting room.

Facilities 15 en suite (2 fmly) ⊘ in dining room TVB tea/coffee Direct dial from bedrooms Cen ht Dinner Last d 9.30pm LB **Conf** Thtr 50 Class 30 Board 24 **Parking** 35

TUNBRIDGE WELLS (ROYAL)   MAP 06 TQ53

Premier Collection

♦♦♦♦♦

Alconbury

41 Molyneux Park Rd TN4 8DX ☎ 01892 511279

Dir A26 S to town & A264 W, pass hospital, 3rd right onto Molyneux Park Rd

This elegant house, situated in a quiet leafy street, offers pretty floral fabrics, wooden floors and a friendly welcome. Booking is essential for the well-appointed bedroom. Breakfast, using good local produce, can be taken in the bedroom or in the dining room.

Facilities 1 en suite ⊘ TVB tea/coffee ✖ Cen ht TVL No children 12yrs No coaches **Prices** S £45-£60; D £65-£90✳ **Parking** 2 **Notes** 🐾

Premier Collection

♦♦♦♦♦

Danehurst House

41 Lower Green Rd, Rusthall TN4 8TW
☎ 01892 527739 🖷 01892 514804
e-mail info@danehurst.net
web www.danehurst.net

Dir 1.5m W of Tunbridge Wells in Rusthall. Off A264 onto Coach Rd & Lower Green Rd

Situated in pretty gardens in a quiet residential area, this Victorian gabled house is located to the west of the historic spa town. The house retains many original features and is attractively decorated throughout. Public areas include a comfortable lounge with a small bar. The homely bedrooms come with a wealth of thoughtful extras, and excellent breakfasts are served in the conservatory.

Facilities 4 en suite ⊘ TVB tea/coffee ✖ Licensed Cen ht No children 8yrs No coaches **Prices** S £50-£69.50; D £69.50-£95✳ **Parking** 6 **Notes** Closed Xmas

♦♦♦♦ ➾ ◗

The Beacon

Tea Garden Ln, Rusthall TN3 9JH
☎ 01892 524252 🖷 01892 534288
e-mail beaconhotel@btopenworld.com
web www.the-beacon.co.uk

Dir 1.5m W of Tunbridge Wells. Signed left off A264 onto Tea Garden Ln

This charming 18th-century inn is situated on an elevated position amid 16 acres of land and surrounded by open countryside. The open-plan public areas are full of character, and include ornate fireplaces and a superb decorative ceiling. The spacious bedrooms are carefully furnished and have many thoughtful touches.

Facilities 3 en suite ⊘ in bedrooms ⊘ in dining room TV2B tea/coffee Direct dial from bedrooms ✖ Cen ht Fishing Dinner Last d 9.30pm **Prices** S £68.50; D £97✳ **Conf** Thtr 50 Class 40 Board 30 **Parking** 42 **Notes** Civ Wed 100

♦♦♦♦

Bentham Hill Stables

Stockland Green Rd TN3 0TJ ☎ 01892 516602
e-mail derek.waddell1@btopenworld.com

Dir 2m NW of Tunbridge Wells. Off A26 signed Salomons/Speldhurst, 1m right onto Bentham Hill/Stockland Green Rd, sharp right again

The converted stable block is located in peaceful woodlands only a short drive from the town. Bedrooms are light and airy with tiled floors and shuttered windows, and some rooms have small private terraces. A freshly cooked breakfast is served in the delightful dining room.

Facilities 3 en suite (3 GF) ⊘ tea/coffee ✖ Cen ht No children 8yrs No coaches **Prices** S £45-£55; D £65-£75✳ **Parking** 3 **Notes** Closed 23-27 Dec 🐾

WHITSTABLE   MAP 07 TR16

♦♦♦♦

Windy Ridge

Wraik Hill CT5 3BY ☎ 01227 263506
e-mail scott@windyridgewhitstable.co.uk

Dir A299 onto A2990, right at rdbt onto A290, next rdbt 2nd exit, continue 0.5m

Expect a warm welcome at this delightful guest house set in open countryside. The charming public rooms include a smart lounge with a wood-burning stove and comfy sofas. The attractive bedrooms are well equipped and some have stunning views of the north Kent coastline.

Facilities 10 en suite (2 fmly) (3 GF) ⊘ TVB tea/coffee Licensed Cen ht TVL No coaches ◖ Dinner Last d 24hrs **Prices** S £40; D £70-£85✳ LB **Conf** Max 40 Thtr 40 Class 40 Board 40 **Parking** 12 **Notes** Civ Wed 80

LANCASHIRE

ACCRINGTON

MAP 18 SD72

★★★ Guest House

Pilkington's Guest House ◇

135 Blackburn Rd BB5 0AA ☎ 01254 237032

Located close to the railway station, this family-run property comprises of two comfortable bedrooms in the main house and four further bedrooms in the carefully refurbished terrace a short way along the street. Home cooked breakfasts are served in the main house

Facilities 2 rms (2 pri facs) 4 annexe rms (2 fmly) (2 GF) ✪ TVB tea/coffee ✖ Licensed Cen ht No coaches Snooker **Prices** S £25; D £50✳ **Notes** ✪

♦♦♦♦

Maple Lodge Hotel

70 Blackburn Rd, Clayton-Le-Moors BB5 5JH
☎ 01254 301284 ▤ 01254 388152
e-mail maplelod@aol.com
web www.maplelodgehotel.co.uk
Dir *M65 junct 7, signs for Clayton-le-Moors, right at T-junct onto Blackburn Rd*

This welcoming house is convenient for the M65, and provides comfortable, well-equipped bedrooms in the main house and in an adjoining modern bungalow. The inviting lounge has a well-stocked bar, and freshly cooked dinners (by arrangement) and hearty breakfasts are served in the attractive dining room.

Facilities 4 en suite 4 annexe en suite (1 fmly) (4 GF) ✪ TVB tea/coffee Direct dial from bedrooms ✖ Licensed Cen ht TVL No coaches jacuzzi in 1 room, satellite TV in lounge bar Dinner Last d 7.30pm (Mon-Thu) **Prices** S £41.50-£47.50; D £59-£65✳ **LB** **Parking** 7

BLACKBURN

MAP 18 SD62

♦♦♦

Old Dad's Barn

Mellor Ln, Mellor BB2 7EN ☎ 01254 812434
Dir *3m NW of town centre, off A677 into Mellor*

Located between Preston and Blackburn, and part of a riding centre and garden nursery, bedrooms here are thoughtfully furnished and have smart modern shower rooms. Some rooms have country views. Comprehensive breakfasts, using quality local produce, are served in the traditionally furnished dining room, which also has a lounge area.

Facilities 4 en suite ✪ TVB tea/coffee ✖ Cen ht TVL No children 11yrs No coaches Riding **Prices** S £31.95-£34.95; D £51.95-£55.95✳ **LB** **Parking** 6 **Notes** ✪

BLACKPOOL

MAP 18 SD33

★★★ Guest House

The Centenary ◇

338 Queens Prom FY2 9AB ☎ 01253 500040
e-mail vivclayton@centenaryhotel.co.uk

Situated at the quieter northern end of the promenade, you are assured a warm welcome and comfortable accommodation.

continued

Bedrooms are thoughtfully equipped and some have spectacular sea views. Day rooms include a smart lounge-dining room with a small licensed bar.

Facilities 7 rms (6 en suite) (1 pri facs) (3 fmly) ✪ in bedrooms ✪ in dining room ✪ in 1 lounge TVB tea/coffee ✖ Cen ht TVL No coaches Dinner Last d 4pm **Prices** S fr £25; d fr £50✳ **Parking** 4 **Notes** Closed Dec-Feb

★★ Guest House

New Central ◇

64a Reads Av FY1 4DE ☎ 01253 623637 ▤ 01253 620857
e-mail newcentral@hotmail.com

The New Central is just a short walk from the Tower and Promenade. The spacious public areas consist of a well-stocked bar-lounge, a games room, and a large breakfast dining room. Some four-poster beds are available and there is also a night porter.

Facilities 47 rms (46 en suite) (1 pri facs) (10 fmly) ✪ in dining room ✪ in 1 lounge TVB tea/coffee ✖ Licensed Lift Cen ht TVL Pool Table Dinner Last d 3pm **Prices** S £25-£35; (incl. dinner) ✳ **LB** **Parking** 15

♦♦♦♦ 〜

Briar Dene Hotel

56 Kelso Av, Thornton, Cleveleys FY5 3JG
☎ 01253 852312 & 338300 ▤ 01253 338301
e-mail briardene@aol.com
Dir *4m N of Blackpool centre. On A587 in Cleveleys*

This friendly, long-established family-run establishment is near the centre of Cleveleys, one block from the promenade and a short tram ride from Blackpool. The superb new bedrooms have homely extras, and imaginative food is served in the attractive dining room.

Facilities 16 en suite (4 fmly) ✪ in bedrooms ✪ in dining room TVB tea/coffee Direct dial from bedrooms Licensed Cen ht TVL Dinner Last d 9.15pm **Conf** Max 80 Thtr 70 Class 50 Board 50 **Parking** 12 **Notes** Closed 23-30 Dec

◆◆◆◆

Bona Vista Hotel

104-106 Queens Prom FY2 9NX
☎ 01253 351396 🖹 01253 594985
e-mail bona.vista@talk21.com
Dir *0.25m N of Uncle Toms Cabin & Castle Casino*

The Bona Vista has a peaceful seafront location on North Shore within reach of the town's attractions. Its attractive bedrooms are well equipped and some have sea views. There is a spacious dining room and a comfortable bar and lounges.

Facilities 19 rms (17 en suite) (4 fmly) ⊗ in 6 bedrooms ⊗ in dining room ⊗ in 1 lounge TVB tea/coffee Licensed Cen ht TVL Pool Table Dinner **Parking** 18 **Notes** Closed Xmas-Etr

◆◆◆◆

Burlees Hotel ◇

40 Knowle Av FY2 9TQ ☎ 01253 354535 🖹 01253 354535
e-mail marrasimpson@aol.com
web www.burlees-hotel.co.uk
Dir *Off seafront Queen's Promenade at Uncle Tom's Cabin onto Knowle Av*

A genuine welcome awaits you at this well-maintained house, just a stroll from the Promenade. The smartly decorated bedrooms are thoughtfully equipped, and there is a comfortable lounge and a cosy bar. Hearty breakfasts and evening meals by arrangement are served in the pine-furnished dining room.

Facilities 9 en suite (2 fmly) (1 GF) ⊗ in bedrooms ⊗ in dining room ⊗ in lounges TVB tea/coffee Licensed Cen ht TVL No coaches Dinner Last d prev evening **Prices** S £25-£30; D £50-£60 **LB** **Parking** 4 **Notes** Closed 16 Dec-7 Jan

◆◆◆

Beechcliffe Hotel ◇

16 Shaftesbury Av, North Shore FY2 9QQ
☎ 01253 353075
e-mail susan@gregan1988.fslife.co.uk
Dir *0.75m from North Pier, off A584 Promenade*

This smart house has a quiet residential location close to the north promenade and attractions. Bedrooms vary in size and style, but all have been refurbished to ensure a real home from home. Hearty breakfasts are served in the elegant dining room, and a comfortable lounge with a bar is available.

Facilities 8 en suite (2 fmly) ⊗ TVB tea/coffee 🏶 Licensed Cen ht TVL No coaches Dinner Last d breakfast **Prices** S £22.50-£25; D £45-£50✷ **LB** **Parking** 9

◆◆◆

Craigmore Hotel ◇

8 Willshaw Rd, Gynn Sq FY2 9SH
☎ 01253 355098 🖹 01253 355098
e-mail blackpoolhotel@fsbdial.co.uk
Dir *1m N of Tower. A584 N over Gynn rdbt, 1st right*

This well-maintained property is in an attractive location overlooking Gynn Square gardens, with the Promenade and tram stops just yards away. Several of the smart modern bedrooms are suitable for families. There is a comfortable lounge, a sun lounge and patio, and the pretty dining room has a small bar.

Facilities 9 en suite (3 fmly) ⊗ TVB tea/coffee 🏶 Licensed Cen ht TVL Dinner Last d 1pm **Prices** S £27-£31; D £44-£52 **Notes** Closed Dec-Jan rs Feb-Mar

◆◆◆

Hartshead Hotel ◇

17 King Edward Av, North Shore FY2 9TA
☎ 01253 353133 & 357111
e-mail info@hartshead-hotel.co.uk
web www.hartshead-hotel.co.uk
Dir *M55 junct 4, A583 & A584 to North Shore, off Queens Promenade onto King Edward Av*

Popular for its location near the seafront, this enthusiastically run establishment has modern bedrooms of various sizes, equipped with a good range of practical extras. A veranda-sitting room is available, in addition to a comfortable lounge bar, and breakfast and pre-theatre dinners are served in the attractive dining room.

Facilities 10 en suite (3 fmly) ⊗ in bedrooms ⊗ in dining room ⊗ in 1 lounge TVB tea/coffee 🏶 Licensed Cen ht TVL Dinner Last d 2pm **Prices** S £21-£30; D £36-£54✷ **LB** **Parking** 6

◆◆◆

Sunny Cliff ◇

98 Queens Prom, Northshore FY2 9NS ☎ 01253 351155
Dir *On A584 1.5m N of Blackpool Tower, just past Uncle Toms Cabin*

Under the same ownership for four decades, this friendly guest house overlooking the seafront offers a genuine home from home atmosphere. Ther pretty bedrooms, some with sea views, are neatly furnished. There is a cosy bar, a sun lounge, a comfortable lounge, and a smart dining room for good home cooking.

Facilities 9 en suite (3 fmly) ⊗ in dining room TVB tea/coffee 🏶 Licensed Cen ht TVL No coaches Dinner Last d 5pm **Prices** S £27-£29; D £54-£58✷ **LB** **Parking** 6 **Notes** Closed 9 Nov-Etr 🚭

BLACKPOOL continued

◆◆◆

Castlemere Hotel

13 Shaftesbury Av, North Shore FY2 9QQ
☎ 01253 352430 🖷 01253 350116
e-mail sue@hotelcastlemere.co.uk
web www.hotelcastlemere.co.uk

The friendly owners create a relaxing atmosphere at the Castlemere, situated in the residential North Shore area just a short distance from the attractions. The pretty bedrooms are well equipped, and some are suitable for families. There is a cosy bar, and forecourt parking is a bonus.

Facilities 9 en suite (1 fmly) ⊗ in dining room TVB tea/coffee ✖
Licensed Cen ht TVL Dinner Last d noon **LB Parking** 4

◆◆◆

Denely Private Hotel ◇

15 King Edward Av FY2 9TA ☎ 01253 352757
e-mail denely@tesco.net
Dir 1m N of Blackpool Tower

Just a stroll from the Promenade and Gynn Square gardens, the welcoming guest house offers a spacious lounge and a bright dining room along with simply furnished bedrooms. The friendly resident owners provide attentive service, and evening meals are available by arrangement.

Facilities 9 en suite (3 fmly) ⊗ in dining room TVB tea/coffee ✖
Cen ht TVL Dinner Last d 1pm **Prices** S £18-£40; D £35-£45✳ **LB**
Parking 6 **Notes** Closed Dec-Jan

◆◆◆

Funky Towers

297 The Promenade FY1 6AL ☎ 01253 400123
e-mail stay@funkytowers.com
web www.funkytowers.com
Dir On A584 Promenade between Central Pier & South Pier

The friendly, family-run guest house has a prime location facing the sea, between the Pleasure Beach and Central Pier. There is a spacious bar and a modern cafe with direct access to seafront. The bedrooms are equipped with lots of extras; some feature four posters and others have great sea views.

Facilities 14 en suite (5 fmly) (1 GF) ⊗ in 4 bedrooms ⊗ in dining room ⊗ in 1 lounge TVB tea/coffee ✖ Licensed Cen ht TVL Pool Table Dinner Last d noon **Parking** 3 **Notes** Closed Jan-Feb

◆◆◆

Wilmar

42 Osborne Rd FY4 1HQ ☎ 01253 346229
Dir From M55 follow Main Parking Area, right at Waterloo Rd exit, left at lights, left at 2nd lights, bear right at Grand Hotel & right again

This friendly, family-run guest house has a convenient location close to the Pleasure Beach, Sandcastles and the South Promenade attractions. Bedrooms are brightly appointed, well maintained and include a family suite. A cosy lounge and bar are available.

Facilities 7 rms (6 en suite) (1 pri facs) (1 fmly) ⊗ in dining room TVB tea/coffee ✖ Licensed Cen ht TVL No coaches Dinner Last d 10am
Notes Closed 23-27 Dec 🏧

◆◆◆

Windsor Park Hotel

96 Queens Prom FY2 9NS ☎ 01253 357025
e-mail info@windsorparkhotel.net
Dir Queens Promenade, North Shore

Having stunning views, this family-run guest house on the peaceful North Shore is just a tram ride from the attractions. Home-cooked meals and substantial breakfasts are served in the elegant dining room, and there is a pleasant bar area and a sun lounge. The bedrooms have modern amenities.

Facilities 9 en suite (1 fmly) ⊗ in bedrooms ⊗ in dining room ⊗ in 1 lounge TVB tea/coffee Licensed Cen ht TVL No coaches Stair lift Dinner Last d 4pm **LB Parking** 6 **Notes** Closed 8 Nov-Etr (ex Xmas/New Year)

◆◆◆ 🅰

Hotel Pilatus ◇

10 Willshaw Rd, Gynn Sq FY2 9SH
☎ 01253 352470 🖷 01253 352470
e-mail cynthia@pilatushotel.co.uk
Dir From Central Blackpool, head towards Clevelys and Fleetwood on the Queen's promenade.

Facilities 9 en suite (2 fmly) ⊗ in bedrooms ⊗ in dining room ⊗ in 1 lounge TVB tea/coffee ✖ Licensed Cen ht TVL No children 4yrs No coaches Last d 3pm **Prices** S £25-£27; D £40-£44✳ **LB**
Notes Closed 7 Nov-1 Mar

◆◆◆ 🅰

Vidella Hotel ◇

80-82 Dickson Rd FY1 2BU
☎ 01253 621201 🖷 01253 620319
e-mail booking@thevidellahotel.freeserve.co.uk
web www.videllahotel.com
Dir N from North Pier on A584, right onto Cocker St, left at x-rds

Facilities 29 en suite (8 fmly) (4 GF) ⊗ in dining room TVB tea/coffee Licensed Cen ht TVL Pool Table Dinner Last d noon
Prices S £22.50-£42.50; D £45-£85✳ **LB Conf** Max 60 **Parking** 6

continued

◆◆
Briny View Hotel ◇
2 Woodfield Rd FY1 6AX ☎ 01253 346584
e-mail brinyviewhotel@aol.com
Dir *Between Central & South piers, off Promenade,*

Facilities 12 rms (7 en suite) (1 pri facs) (4 fmly) ⊗ in dining room TVB tea/coffee ✖ Licensed Cen ht TVL **Prices** S £18-£25; D £36-£50✳ LB **Notes** Closed Dec 🐾

BOLTON-BY-BOWLAND
MAP 18 SD74

◆◆◆◆
Middle Flass Lodge
Settle Rd BB7 4NY ☎ 01200 447259 📠 01200 447300
e-mail info@middleflasslodge.fsnet.co.uk
web www.middleflasslodge.co.uk
Dir *Off A59 for Sawley. Signs for Bolton-by-Bowland at Copynook, 2nd left signed Middle Flass Lodge, 2m on right*

Set in peaceful countryside within the Forest of Bowland, this smart house provides a warm welcome. Stylishly converted from farm outbuildings, exposed timbers feature throughout, including the attractive restaurant and cosy lounge. The modern bedrooms include family rooms. Thanks to the accomplished chef, the restaurant is also popular with non-residents.

Facilities 5 en suite 2 annexe en suite (1 fmly) ⊗ TVB tea/coffee ✖ Licensed Cen ht TVL No coaches Dinner Last d 6.30pm **Prices** S £36-£45; D £56-£65 LB **Parking** 14

BURNLEY
MAP 18 SD83

◆◆◆◆
Higher Cockden Farm ◇
Todmorden Rd, Briercliffe BB10 3QQ
☎ 01282 831324 📠 01282 831324
e-mail j.hodkinson_bb@tiscali.co.uk
Dir *M65 junct 12, towards Burnley, left at 2nd lights, left at rdbt & right towards Briercliffe, right at x-rds, B&B 400yds on left*

Facilities 3 rms (1 en suite) ⊗ TVB tea/coffee ✖ Cen ht TVL No coaches Fishing Dinner Last d 10am **Prices** S £24; D £48✳ **Parking** 6 **Notes** 🐾

◆◆◆
Ormerod Hotel ◇
121/123 Ormerod Rd BB11 3QW ☎ 01282 423255
Dir *Burnley centre onto A682, 200yds N after rdbt right onto Ormerod Rd, pass Burnley College, 300yds on right*

The welcoming guest house is a short walk from the town centre and is handy for Queens Park, Thompson's Park and Burnley FC. The bright modern bedrooms are well equipped and there is a comfortable lounge. Separate tables are provided in the smart breakfast room.

Facilities 9 en suite (2 fmly) ⊗ in dining room TVB tea/coffee Cen ht TVL **Prices** S £28-£32; D £45✳ **Parking** 8 **Notes** 🐾

CARNFORTH
MAP 18 SD47

◆◆◆
The Silverdale Hotel
Shore Rd, Silverdale LA5 0TP
☎ 01524 701206 📠 01524 702258
Dir *4m NW of Carnforth. In Silverdale village centre*

Facilities 7 en suite (2 fmly) ⊗ in area of dining room TVB tea/coffee Direct dial from bedrooms Licensed Cen ht Pool Table Dinner Last d 9pm **Prices** S fr £42.50; d fr £70✳ **Parking** 38

CHORLEY
MAP 15 SD51
See **Eccleston**

CLITHEROE
MAP 18 SD74

◆◆◆◆
Brooklyn ◇
32 Pimlico Rd BB7 2AH ☎ 01200 428268 & 07971 917664
Dir *M6, A59 to Clitheroe, take Clitheroe North turning, over rdbt, next left, 0.5m on left*

This elegant and welcoming Victorian house is in a peaceful residential area just a stroll from the centre of town. The bedrooms are equipped with lots of thoughtful extras and the attractive dining room has a comfortable lounge area.

Facilities 4 en suite ⊗ TVB tea/coffee ✖ Cen ht No coaches Dinner Last d noon **Prices** S £29-£32; D £50-£55 **Notes** 🐾

England

ECCLESTON
MAP 15 SD51

◆◆◆◆ ❦

Parr Hall Farm (SD522173)
Parr Ln PR7 5SL
☎ 01257 451917 ▤ 01257 453749 Mrs Motley
e-mail parrhall@talk21.com
Dir Off B5250 Towngate in town centre onto Parr Ln

This attractive well-maintained farmhouse, located in a quiet corner of the village, yet close to M6, dates from the 17th century. The majority of bedrooms are located in a barn conversion and include luxury en-suite bathrooms and lots of thoughtful extras. A comprehensive continental breakfast is included in the price.

Facilities 4 en suite 9 annexe en suite (1 fmly) (5 GF) ⊗ TVB tea/coffee ✖ Cen ht ⚘ 15 acres sheep grazing **Prices** S £35-£45; D £60-£80 **Parking** 20

FLEETWOOD
MAP 18 SD34

◆◆◆

Normandy ◇
100 Prom Road FY7 6RF ☎ 01253 872961 ▤ 01253 872961
Dir From A585, Marine Hall on right, left onto Mount Rd & Promenade Rd

This friendly, family-run guest house is close to the town centre, beach and attractions. Bedrooms are carefully decorated and well equipped, and there is also a lounge. Dinner in served by arrangement in the dining room where there is also a small bar.

Facilities 3 en suite (1 fmly) ⊗ in bedrooms ⊗ in dining room TVB tea/coffee ✖ Licensed Cen ht TVL Dinner Last d 10am **Prices** S £21; D £42✶ **LB Notes** Closed 24 Dec-5 Jan ⊠

LANCASTER
MAP 18 SD46

◆◆◆ 🅰

Lancaster Town House ◇
11/12 Newton Ter, Caton Rd LA1 3PB
☎ 01524 65527 ▤ 01524 383148
e-mail hedge-holmes@talk21.com
Dir M6 junct 34, 1m towards Lancaster, house on right

Facilities 8 en suite (1 fmly) ⊗ TVB tea/coffee ✖ Cen ht TVL No coaches **Prices** S £30-£35; D £50✶

LYTHAM ST ANNES
MAP 18 SD32

◆◆◆◆ 🅰

Clifton Park Hotel ◇
299-301 Clifton Dr South, St Annes on Sea FY8 1HN
☎ 01253 725801 & 0845 230 5801 ▤ 01253 721735
e-mail info@cliftonpark.co.uk
Dir On A584 coast road near pier & Pleasure Island

Facilities 42 en suite (4 fmly) (6 GF) ⊗ in bedrooms ⊗ in dining room ⊗ in 1 lounge TVB tea/coffee Direct dial from bedrooms ✖ Licensed Lift Cen ht TVL No children 16yrs ⚐ Gymnasium Jacuzzi Dinner Last d 7pm **Prices** S £29-£59; D £59-£139 **LB Conf** Max 150 Thtr 150 Class 150 Board 50 Del from £59.50 ✶ **Parking** 25

◆◆◆

Endsleigh Private Hotel ◇
315 Clifton Dr South FY8 1HN
☎ 01253 725622 ▤ 01253 720072
Dir On A584 2.5m SE of Blackpool, opp main Post Office

This friendly guest house provides a home from home just a short walk from the promenade. The bedrooms are thoughtfully equipped, well maintained, and include a family suite and ground-floor rooms. Hearty breakfasts are served in the bright dining room, and Aga-cooked dinners are prepared by arrangement.

Facilities 15 en suite (5 fmly) (2 GF) ⊗ in 5 bedrooms ⊗ in dining room ⊗ in lounges TV available tea/coffee ✖ Licensed Cen ht No coaches Dinner Last d 6pm **Prices** S £27-£28; D £54-£56✶ **Parking** 6 **Notes** ⊠

◆◆◆

Strathmore Hotel ◇
305 Clifton Dr South FY8 1HN ☎ 01253 725478
Dir In centre of St Annes opp Post Office

This friendly, family-run property has a central location close to the promenade. The long-established Strathmore offers smartly furnished and well-equipped bedrooms. There is an elegant lounge where you can enjoy a relaxing drink, and a dining room.

Facilities 8 rms (5 en suite) ⊗ in dining room TVB tea/coffee ✖ Cen ht No children 9yrs No coaches **Prices** S £23-£29; D £46-£58 **LB Parking** 10 **Notes** ⊠

MORECAMBE
MAP 18 SD46

◆◆◆

Belle Vue
330 Marine Rd LA4 5AA ☎ 01524 411375 ▤ 01524 411375
Dir On seafront between lifeboat house & bingo hall

Having fine views over the promenade and Morecambe Bay, the Belle Vue provides a range of bedrooms styles on three floors, with most accessible by lift. There are comfortable lounges, and a spacious lounge bar where entertainment is provided when busy. A choice of dishes is available in the large dining room.

Facilities 41 rms (34 pri facs) (3 fmly) ⊗ in bedrooms ⊗ in dining room TVB tea/coffee ✖ Licensed Lift Cen ht TVL No children 14yrs Dinner Last d 5pm **LB Parking** 3 **Notes** Closed Jan-Feb

◆◆◆

The Craigwell ◇
372 Marine Rd East LA4 5AH
☎ 01524 410095 ▤ 01524 409898
e-mail craigwellhotel@tiscali.co.uk
web www.craigwellhotel.co.uk
Dir A589 to seafront, left, Craigwell 400yds

This house is part of a Victorian terrace and looks out over Morecambe Bay to the distant Cumbrian hills. There is a cosy bar lounge with fine views and a spacious breakfast room to the rear. Bedrooms are pleasantly decorated. There is a private car park at the rear, and dinners are available by arrangement.

continued

Facilities 12 en suite (1 fmly) in bedrooms in dining room in 1 lounge TVB tea/coffee Cen ht TVL No coaches Dinner Last d 12pm **Prices** S £23-£27; D £46-£54✱ **LB** **Conf** Thtr 30 Class 15 Board 20 **Parking** 4

◆◆◆

Hotel Prospect ◇

363 Marine Rd East LA4 5AQ
☎ 01524 417819 📠 01524 417819
e-mail peter@hotel-prospect.fsnet.co.uk
Dir On Morecombe promenade near Gala Bingo

Situated on the promenade, this friendly, family-run establishment has panoramic views over the bay to the Cumbrian mountains. Bedrooms are comfortably proportioned and thoughtfully furnished, and the bright dining room extends into a small lounge area, which has a well-stocked bar and overlooks the sea. There is an enclosed car park.

Facilities 13 en suite (4 fmly) (2 GF) in 2 bedrooms in dining room TVB tea/coffee Licensed Cen ht Dinner Last d 3pm
Prices S £19-£20; D £38-£40✱ **LB** **Parking** 14

◆◆◆

The Sea Lynn Guest House ◇

29 West End Rd LA4 4DJ ☎ 01524 411340
e-mail thesealynn@hotmail.com
Dir Signs for West End seafront, turn right, then 3rd right. Hotel 50yds on right

Set just back from the promenade and the attractions, this terrace house with a front patio offers accommodation on four floors, with a comfortable lounge on the first floor and a cosy breakfast room on the ground floor, where the hearty breakfasts are served (evening meal available by arrangement). A hospitable welcome is given and bedrooms are fresh.

Facilities 13 rms (2 en suite) (1 fmly) (3 GF) in dining room TVB tea/coffee TVL No coaches Dinner Last d 5.30pm **Prices** S £20-£22; D £40-£44✱

◆◆◆

The Trevelyan Hotel

27 West End Rd LA4 4DJ ☎ 01524 412013 📠 01524 409381
e-mail david@lawrence8566.fsnet.co.uk
Dir M6 junct 34, signed Morecambe then West End. At seafront right & 3rd right onto West End Rd, 50yds on right

You are assured of a warm welcome at the Trevelyan, a family-run guest house some 50yds from the seafront and well located for the

continued

attractions. Bedrooms are comfortably proportioned and well equipped, and there is an inviting lounge, a cosy bar, and a bright airy dining room where delicious freshly cooked evening meals (by arrangement) and traditional English breakfasts are served at individual tables.

Facilities 10 rms (2 en suite) (3 fmly) (2 GF) in dining room TVB tea/coffee Cen ht TVL No coaches Dinner Last d 5pm **LB**

◆◆◆ 🅰

The Balmoral Hotel ◇

34 Marine Rd West LA3 1BZ
☎ 01524 418526 📠 01524 400502
e-mail info@balmoralhotelmorecambe.co.uk
web www.balmoralhotelmorecambe.co.uk
Dir At SW end of promenade past junct Regent Rd

Facilities 10 rms (8 en suite) (1 fmly) (1 GF) in 2 bedrooms in dining room in lounges TVB tea/coffee ✖ Licensed TVL No coaches Dinner Last d 3pm **Prices** S £19-£24; D £44-£52✱ **LB**
Notes Closed Xmas

🆄

Yacht Bay View ◇

359 Marine Rd East LA4 5AQ ☎ 01524 414481
e-mail yachtbayview@hotmail.com
Dir Junct 34 - follow signposts Morecambe. Straight to Promenade. Turn left at Broadway Hotel. Half mile along promenade

At the time of going to press the rating for this establishment had not been confirmed. Please check the AA website www.theAA.com for up-to-date information.

Facilities 7 en suite (1 fmly) TVB tea/coffee ✖ TVL No coaches Dinner **Prices** S £25-£27.50; D £50-£55✱ **LB** **Notes** 🚭

PRESTON   MAP 18 SD52
See also **Blackburn**

Premier Collection

◆◆◆◆◆ 🏵🏵 🍽

The Park Restaurant Hotel

209 Tulketh Rd, Ashton-On-Ribble PR2 1ES
☎ 01772 726250 & 728096 📠 01772 723743
e-mail parkrestauranthotel@hotmail.com
Dir 1m NW of town centre off A5085 Blackpool Rd

A warm welcome awaits you at this elegant Edwardian house. The fine-dining restaurant serves with flair and creativity, and the caring, attentive service is equally memorable. Accommodation is generally spacious, and there is a stylish lounge bar and plenty of off-road parking.

Facilities 14 en suite (6 GF) TVB tea/coffee Direct dial from bedrooms ✖ Licensed Cen ht No children 10yrs No coaches Dinner Last d 9pm **Prices** S £48-£59; D £75-£85✱ **Conf** Max 40 Board 30 Del £90 ✱ **Parking** 14

WHITEWELL
MAP 18 SD64

Premier Collection

★★★★★ 🏵 **Inn**

The Inn at Whitewell
Forest of Bowland, Clitheroe BB7 3AT
☎ 01200 448222 📄 01200 448298

This long-established culinary destination hides away in countryside just 20 minutes from the M6. The fine-dining restaurant is complemented by two cosy bars with roaring fires, real ales and polished service. Bedrooms are richly furnished with antiques, while many of the bathrooms have Victorian brass showers.

Facilities 13 en suite 4 annexe en suite (1 fmly) (1 GF) STV TVB tea/coffee Direct dial from bedrooms Cen ht No coaches Fishing Dinner Last d 9.30pm **Conf** BC Max 35 Board 35 **Parking** 60 **Notes** Civ Wed 80

YEALAND CONYERS
MAP 18 SD57

Premier Collection

◆◆◆◆◆

The Bower
LA5 9SF ☎ 01524 734585 📄 01524 734585
e-mail info@thebower.co.uk
web www.thebower.co.uk
Dir M6 junct 35, A6 towards Milnthorpe for 0.75m, under narrow bridge, take next left onto Snape Ln & bear left at end

This Georgian house stands in grounds in a charming village. The spacious bedrooms are comfortably furnished, and the homely drawing room is warmed by open fires during cooler months. Dinner can be taken in the stylish dining room or as a light kitchen supper, and breakfast is served around the kitchen table.

Facilities 2 rms (1 en suite) (1 pri facs) (1 fmly) 🚫 TVB tea/coffee 🐾 Cen ht TVL No children 12yrs No coaches 🎵 Bridge games/lessons **Prices** S £44-£54; D £68-£78✳ **Parking** 6

LEICESTERSHIRE

ASHBY-DE-LA-ZOUCH
MAP 11 SK31
See **Coalville**

BARKESTONE-LE-VALE
MAP 11 SK73

◆◆◆◆ 🌱

Woodside Farm (SK797336)
Long Ln NG13 0HQ
☎ 01476 870336 & 07703 299291 Mrs D Hickling
e-mail hickling-woodside@supanet.com
web www.woodsidebandb.co.uk
Dir 1m SE of Barkestone. Off A52 at Bottesford for Harby & Belvoir Castle, after Redmile x-rds, left onto lane, farm 0.5m

A warm welcome awaits you at this friendly working farm, located on the Belvoir Castle estate in the peaceful Vale of Belvoir, within easy reach of Nottingham and Grantham. The smart bedrooms have beautiful views over open countryside, and hearty breakfasts are served in the lounge-dining room. Packed lunches are available on request. Diane Hickling is a top-twenty finalist for AA Landlady of the Year 2006.

Facilities 2 en suite (1 fmly) (1 GF) 🚫 tea/coffee 🐾 Cen ht Golf Fishing Riding Cycle storage Farm visits by arangement 340 acres arable/livestock **Prices** S £35-£45; D £55-£60✳ **LB** **Parking** 4 **Notes** rs mid Sep-mid May 🐾

BARROW UPON SOAR
MAP 11 SK51

◆◆◆◆ ⎚

The Hunting Lodge
38 South St LE12 8LZ ☎ 01509 412337
web www.thehuntinglodgebarrowonsoar.co.uk

The themed bedrooms at this modern inn include a Fagin room, a Chopin room and a Dali room; all are well equipped and have good facilities. There is a popular bar and a good range of interesting food is served in the brasserie.

Facilities 6 en suite (2 fmly) 🚫 in bedrooms 🚫 in dining room TVB tea/coffee Direct dial from bedrooms 🐾 Cen ht Dinner Last d 9.30pm **Prices** D £90-£120 ✳ **Conf** Max 50 Thtr 50 Class 50 Board 30 **Parking** 60

BELTON
MAP 11 SK42

Ⓤ ⎚

The Queen's Head
2 Long St LE12 9TP ☎ 01509 222359 📄 01509 224680
e-mail enquiries@thequeenshead.org
web www.thequeenshead.org
Dir From Loughborough turn left onto B5324, 3m into Belton

At the time of going to press the rating for this establishment had not been confirmed. Please check the AA website www.theAA.com for up-to-date information.

Facilities 6 rms (4 en suite) (2 pri facs) 🚫 in bedrooms 🚫 in dining room TVB tea/coffee Cen ht Dinner Last d 9.30pm **Prices** S £60; D £70-£100✳ **Conf** Max 40 Thtr 40 Class 18 Board 30 Del from £100 ✳ **Parking** 20 **Notes** Civ Wed 50

England

BRUNTINGTHORPE
MAP 11 SP68

◆◆◆◆ ❦

Knaptoft House Farm & The Greenway ◇ (SP619894)

Bruntingthorpe Rd, Lutterworth LE17 6PR
☎ 0116 247 8388 Mrs Hutchinson
e-mail info@knaptofthousefarm.com
web www.knaptoft.com
Dir Off A5199 x-rds for Bruntingthorpe, premises 1m on left after Shearsby Bath Hotel

Set in peaceful landscaped grounds, this family-run farmhouse has wonderful views. The bedrooms, either in the main house or in an adjacent bungalow, are particularly well equipped for business and leisure. Breakfast is served in the farmhouse, and both properties have a lounge and a conservatory.

Facilities 3 rms (2 en suite) 3 annexe en suite (3 GF) ⊗ TVB tea/coffee ✖ Cen ht No children 10yrs Fishing 145 acres sheep **Prices** S fr £30; D £55-£60✳ **LB Parking** 10 **Notes** Closed Xmas & New Year

BUCKMINSTER
MAP 11 SK82

◆◆◆◆

The Tollemache Arms

48 Main St NG33 5SA ☎ 01476 860007
e-mail enquiries@thetollemachearms.com
Dir Off A1 Colsterworth rdbt onto B676 to Buckminster

The revamped village inn has a minimalist decor of neutral colours, and strong shades in the pictures, brown leather chairs and crisp white table linen. Its busy restaurant serves high-quality food.

Facilities 5 en suite (3 fmly) ⊗ in bedrooms ⊗ in dining room TVB tea/coffee Licensed Cen ht No coaches Dinner Last d 9.30pm
Prices S £45; D £60 **LB Conf** Max 20 Class 20 Board 20 **Parking** 21

CASTLE DONINGTON
MAP 11 SK42

See **Nottingham East Midlands Airport**

COALVILLE
MAP 11 SK41

◆◆◆◆

Church Lane Farm House

Ravenstone LE67 2AE ☎ 01530 810536
e-mail annthorne@ravenstone-guesthouse.co.uk
web www.ravenstone-guesthouse.co.uk
Dir Junct A511 & A447 signs for Ibstock, Church Ln 1st right, 2nd house on left

Situated in the heart of Ravenstone village, this early 18th-century house is full of character. The bedrooms are individually decorated and feature period furniture, and local produce is used for dinner and in the extensive breakfast menu. The beamed dining room has an honesty bar and there is also a cosy lounge.

Facilities 3 en suite ⊗ TV available tea/coffee Licensed Cen ht TVL No children 18yrs No coaches Painting tuition Dinner Last d noon
Prices S £32-£37; D £64-£69✳ **LB Parking** 6 **Notes** Closed 23-30 Dec & 1 Jan

CROFT
MAP 11 SP59

◆◆◆◆

Fossebrook

Coventry Rd, LE9 3GP ☎ 01455 283517 01455 283517
Dir 0.6m SE of village centre on B4114

This friendly guest house stands in a quiet rural location with good access to major routes. Bedrooms are spacious, very comfortable and offer an excellent range of facilities including videos in all rooms. Breakfast is served in the bright dining room, which overlooks pleasant gardens and grounds.

Facilities 5 en suite (1 fmly) (4 GF) ⊗ in bedrooms TVB tea/coffee ✖ Cen ht No coaches Riding **Prices** S fr £40; d fr £40✳ **Parking** 16 **Notes** Closed 24 Dec-2 Jan

◆◆◆

Arbor House Bed & Breakfast ◇

44 Arbor Rd LE9 3GD ☎ 01455 283013
e-mail suelooms@tiscali.co.uk
Dir Off B4114 into village centre

This well-furnished house stands in the village with good amenities. The spacious bedrooms are well-equipped, and there is a cosy lounge. Wholesome local farm produce is a feature at breakfast, and honest hospitality is provided by the resident owners.

Facilities 3 rms (1 en suite) (1 fmly) (3 GF) ⊗ TVB tea/coffee Cen ht TVL No coaches Spa bath for use of single room guests **Prices** S £25-£35; D £45-£50✳ **LB Parking** 5 **Notes**

HALLATON
MAP 11 SP79

◆◆◆ ▮

The Bewicke Arms

1 Eastgate LE16 8UB
☎ 01858 555217 & 555784 🖷 01858 555598
web www.bewickearms.co.uk
Dir In village centre

The 400-year-old thatched country inn has a traditional bar featuring open fires and cask ales. Bedrooms are in a converted stable block where original character has been retained. Breakfast is served in the tea room-souvenir shop

Facilities 3 en suite (1 fmly) (2 GF) ⊗ in bedrooms ⊗ in area of dining room ⊗ in 1 lounge TVB tea/coffee ✖ Cen ht No coaches Dinner Last d 9pm **Prices** S fr £40; d fr £55✳ **Parking** 20

England

HUSBANDS BOSWORTH
MAP 11 SP68

Croft Farm B&B ◇ *(SP634860)*
Leicester Rd LE17 6NW ☎ 01858 880679 Mrs Smith
Dir Take A5199 from Husbands Bosworth towards Leicester, 0.25m on left

At the time of going to press the rating for this establishment had not been confirmed. Please check the AA website www.theAA.com for up-to-date information.

Facilities 3 en suite (2 fmly) ⊗ TVB tea/coffee ✖ Cen ht TVL 350 acres Sheep arable beef mixed **Prices** S £30-£35; d fr £60✳ **Parking** 15 **Notes** ✪

KEGWORTH
MAP 11 SK42

See **Nottingham East Midlands Airport & Sutton Bonington (Nottinghamshire)**

KNIPTON
MAP 11 SK83

The Manners Arms
Croxton Ln NG32 1RH ☎ 01476 879222 ▤ 01476 879228
e-mail info@mannersarms.com
web www.mannersarms.com
Dir Off A607 into Knipton

Facilities 10 en suite ⊗ TVB tea/coffee Direct dial from bedrooms Fishing Riding Last d 2.30pm **Prices** S £50-£90; D £80-£120✳ **LB** **Conf** Max 30 Thtr 40 Class 25 Board 20 Del from £75 ✳ **Parking** 40

LEICESTER
MAP 11 SK50

♦♦♦

Stoneycroft
5-7 Elmfield Av, off London Rd LE2 1RB
☎ 0116 270 7605 ▤ 0116 270 6067
e-mail reception@stoneycrofthotel.co.uk
web www.stoneycrofthotel.co.uk
Dir Near city centre on A6 to Market Harborough

Stoneycroft provides comfortable accommodation with helpful service. Public rooms include a foyer-lounge area, a breakfast room and conference facilities. There is also a large restaurant-bar where a good selection of freshly cooked dishes is available. The modern bedrooms come with desks.

Facilities 41 en suite (4 fmly) (6 GF) ⊗ in bedrooms ⊗ in dining room ⊗ in 1 lounge TVB tea/coffee Direct dial from bedrooms Licensed Cen ht TVL Pool Table Dinner Last d 9.30pm **Prices** S £35-£44; D £55-£59✳ **LB** **Conf** Max 150 Thtr 150 Class 20 Board 30 **Parking** 30

♦♦♦

Abinger Guest House ◇
175 Hinckley Rd LE3 0TF
☎ 0116 255 4674 ▤ 0116 241 3956
e-mail bobwel1234@aol.com
Dir 0.5m W of city centre, off A47 or A5460

Facilities 8 rms (2 fmly) (2 GF) ⊗ FTV TVB tea/coffee ✖ Cen ht No coaches **Prices** S £28-£36; D £42-£80✳ **Notes** Closed Xmas

LOUGHBOROUGH
MAP 11 SK51

♦♦♦

Garendon Park Hotel
92 Leicester Rd LE11 2AQ
☎ 01509 236557 ▤ 01509 265559
e-mail info@garendonparkhotel.co.uk
Dir On A6 400yds S of town centre

This late Victorian house is just a short walk from the high street. Bedrooms are individually decorated and feature coordinated fabrics and thoughtful touches. Breakfast and dinner are served at individual tables in the smart dining room and there is a lounge and a cosy bar.

Facilities 9 rms (8 en suite) (1 pri facs) (4 fmly) ⊗ in bedrooms ⊗ in dining room STV TVB tea/coffee Licensed Cen ht TVL Dinner Last d 4pm

♦♦♦

De Montfort Hotel
88 Leicester Rd LE11 2AQ
☎ 01509 216061 ▤ 01509 233667
e-mail thedemontforthotel@amserve.com
Dir On A6 near town centre, opp Southfields Park & Fairfield School

Facilities 10 rms (7 en suite) (3 pri facs) (3 fmly) (1 GF) ⊗ in dining room TVB tea/coffee ✖ Licensed Cen ht TVL No coaches Dinner Last d 5pm

LUTTERWORTH
MAP 11 SP58

No 7 Bennetts Hill
7 Bennetts Hill, Dunton Bassett LE17 5JJ
☎ 07713 681779 & 07704 586455
e-mail no7bennettshill@hotmail.co.uk
Dir M1 junct 20, turn right along A427 to Dunton Bassett. Left at lights to village centre, no7 situated on left

At the time of going to press the rating for this establishment had not been confirmed. Please check the AA website www.theAA.com for up-to-date information.

Facilities 6 en suite ⊗ in bedrooms ⊗ in dining room ⊗ in lounges STV TVB tea/coffee ✖ Licensed Cen ht No children No coaches Last d 10.30pm **Prices** S £55; D £65 ✳ **Parking** 40

England

MARKET HARBOROUGH
MAP 11 SP78

See also **Medbourne**

◆◆◆◆ 🅰

Hunters Lodge

By Foxton Locks, Gumley LE16 7RT
☎ 0116 279 3744 📠 0116 279 3855
e-mail info@hunterslodgefoxton.co.uk
Dir M1 junct 20, A4304 for Market Harborough, after 8m in village of Lubenham take 2nd left signed Foxton. Next left signed Laughton, pass village hall and out of village for 1.5m over hump backed bridge. Next right Gumley in 200yds right, signed Foxton

Facilities 2 en suite (1 fmly) (2 GF) ⊗ STV TVB tea/coffee Cen ht TVL No coaches **Prices** S £35-£38; D £54✶ **Parking** 5

MEDBOURNE
MAP 11 SP89

◆◆◆◆ 🍴

Medbourne Grange ◇ (SP815945)

LE16 8EF
☎ 01858 565249 & 07730 956116 📠 01858 565257
Mrs Beaty
Dir 2m NE of Medbourne. Between Market Harborough & Uppingham off B664

This 150-year-old working farm has unrivalled views of the Welland valley and is well situated for Rutland Water, Uppingham or Market Harborough. Mrs Beaty is a natural host, ensuring that you receive a warm welcome and friendly service. Individually furnished bedrooms are complemented by comfortable day rooms, and freshly prepared breakfasts are served in the smart dining room.

Facilities 3 rms ⊗ TVB tea/coffee 🛏 Cen ht TVL ⚘ 500 acres arable Dinner Last d noon **Prices** S fr £30; d fr £50✶ **Parking** 6 **Notes** ⊠

MELTON MOWBRAY
MAP 11 SK71

See also **Barkestone-le-Vale**

◆◆◆◆

Bryn Barn ◇

38 High St, Waltham-on-the-Wolds LE14 4AH
☎ 01664 464783 & 07791 215614
e-mail glenarowlands@onetel.com
web www.brynbarn.co.uk
Dir 4.5m NE of Melton. Off A607 in Waltham village centre

A warm welcome awaits you at this attractive, peacefully located cottage within easy reach of Grantham, Rutland Water and Belvoir Castle. Bedrooms are smartly appointed and comfortably furnished, while public rooms include an inviting lounge overlooking a wonderful courtyard garden. Meals are available at one of the nearby village pubs.

Facilities 4 rms (3 en suite) (1 pri facs) (2 fmly) (1 GF) ⊗ TVB tea/coffee Cen ht TVL No coaches **Prices** S £30-£38; D £48-£55✶ **LB** **Parking** 4 **Notes** Closed 21 Dec-4 Jan ⊠

◆◆◆ 📧

Noels Arms

31 Burton St LE13 1AE ☎ 01664 562363
Dir On A606 S of town centre at junct Mill St

The traditional inn lies close to the town centre. The bar is the focal point, where breakfast is served and staff and locals generate a relaxed and friendly atmosphere. Bedrooms come in a variety of sizes, each furnished in pine.

Facilities 6 rms (4 en suite) (2 fmly) TVB tea/coffee Cen ht Pool Table **Notes** ⊠

◆◆◆ 🅰

Dairy Farm ◇

8 Burrough End, Great Dalby LE14 2EW ☎ 01664 562783
e-mail dairyfarm@tesco.net
Dir 3m S of Melton Mowbray on B6407. 1st left after Chapel, Dairy Farm on right

Facilities 3 rms (2 en suite) (1 pri facs) ⊗ TVB tea/coffee Cen ht TVL No coaches **Prices** S £20-£25; D £40✶ **Parking** 5 **Notes** ⊠

MOUNTSORREL
MAP 11 SK51

🆄 📧

The Swan Inn

10 Loughborough Rd LE12 7AT
☎ 0116 230 2340 📠 0116 237 6115
e-mail swan@juf.co.uk
Dir A6 onto Mountsorrel main road, in middle of village near turn off to Sileby

At the time of going to press the rating for this establishment had not been confirmed. Please check the AA website www.theAA.com for up-to-date information.

Facilities 1 en suite ⊗ TVB tea/coffee Direct dial from bedrooms 🛏 Cen ht TVL No coaches Dinner Last d 9pm **Prices** S £120; D £120✶ **Parking** 12

England

NOTTINGHAM EAST MIDLANDS AIRPORT

MAP 11 SK42

Premier Collection

◆◆◆◆◆

Kegworth House

42 High St DE74 2DA ☎ 01509 672575 📠 01509 670645
e-mail tony@kegworthhouse.co.uk
web www.kegworthhouse.co.uk
Dir M1 junct 24, A6 to Loughborough. 0.5m 1st right onto
Packington Hill. Left at junct, Kegworth House 50yds on left

Convenient for major routes and East Midlands Airport, this impressive
Georgian house with an immaculate walled garden has been lovingly
restored. The individually styled bedrooms are luxuriously appointed and
equipped with a wealth of thoughtful extras. The elegant dining room is
the setting for memorable dinners by arrangement, and wholesome
breakfasts featuring local produce are served in the attractive kitchen.

Facilities 11 en suite (2 fmly) (2 GF) ⊗ TVB tea/coffee Direct dial from
bedrooms ✖ Licensed Cen ht TVL No coaches 🏋 Arrangement with hotel
to use leisure complex Dinner Last d 7pm **Prices** S £75-£135; D £95-£195✳
LB Conf Max 14 Board 14 **Parking** 20 **Notes** Closed 20 Dec-1 Jan

◆◆◆◆

Donington Park Farmhouse Hotel

Melbourne Rd, Isley Walton DE74 2RN
☎ 01332 862409 📠 01332 862364
e-mail info@parkfarmhouse.co.uk
web www.parkfarmhouse.co.uk
Dir Off A453 at Isley Walton to Melbourne, premises 0.5m on right

Located adjacent to Donington Park and convenient for East Midlands
Airport, this 17th-century former farmhouse has been renovated to a
high standard. The thoughtfully furnished bedrooms, some of which

continued

are in converted outbuildings, are equipped with homey extras.
Imaginative dinners, served in the attractive kitchen-dining room,
make use of home-grown produce.

Facilities 9 en suite 10 annexe en suite (3 fmly) (5 GF) ⊗ in bedrooms
⊗ in dining room TVB tea/coffee Direct dial from bedrooms Licensed
Cen ht Caravan site with play area Deer stalking courses Dinner Last
d 9.30pm **Prices** S £65-£95; D £95-£132✳ **LB Conf** Max 150 Thtr 100
Class 20 Board 30 Del from £105 ✳ **Parking** 60 **Notes** Closed Xmas
Civ Wed 160

SHEPSHED

MAP 11 SK41

Premier Collection

◆◆◆◆◆

The Grange Courtyard

Forest St LE12 9DA ☎ 01509 600189 📠 01509 603834
e-mail linda.lawrence@thegrangecourtyard.co.uk
web www.thegrangecourtyard.co.uk
Dir M1 junct 23, right at lights onto Leicester road, over minirdbt
onto Forest St

Dating from 18th century, this Grade II listed building is set in
attractive mature gardens and grounds, with the bonus of secure
private parking. The accommodation is housed in individually
appointed cottage bedrooms, each immaculately presented and
extensively equipped. You have access to fully equipped kitchens.
Attentive personal service from the charming proprietor and her
helpful team makes a stay here a memorable experience.

Facilities 20 en suite (1 fmly) (12 GF) ⊗ in bedrooms ⊗ in dining
room TVB tea/coffee Direct dial from bedrooms Licensed Cen ht
No children 8yrs No coaches **Prices** S fr £64.63; d fr £76.38✳ **Conf** Max
12 Class 12 Board 12 **Parking** 15

LINCOLNSHIRE

ALFORD

MAP 17 TF47

★★★ Ⓐ Guest House

Half Moon Hotel & Restaurant

25-28 West St LN13 9DG
☎ 01507 463477 📠 01507 462916
e-mail halfmoonalford25@aol.com
Dir A1104 into village centre

Facilities 14 en suite 2 annexe en suite (2 fmly) (4 GF) ⊗ in bedrooms
⊗ in dining room in 1 lounge TVB tea/coffee Direct dial from
bedrooms ✖ Licensed Cen ht Pool Table Dinner Last d 9pm
Prices S £45; D £70✳ **Conf** Max 60 **Parking** 20

ASWARBY

MAP 12 TF03

◆◆◆

The Tally Ho Inn

NG34 8SA

☎ 01529 455205 & 07905 181221 📠 01529 455773

e-mail enquire@tally-ho-aswarby.co.uk

web www.tally-ho-aswarby.co.uk

Dir A15 from Sleaford towards Bourne, Tally Ho 6m on left

Bedrooms at this delightful inn are in an adjacent building, and all are comfortable and well equipped. You can enjoy a wide range of meals at lunch and dinner in the bar or the restaurant, where service is very friendly and attentive.

Facilities 6 en suite (2 fmly) (4 GF) ⊗ TVB tea/coffee Cen ht
No coaches Dinner Last d 9.30pm **Prices** S £40; D £60 **Parking** 40

BARTON-UPON-HUMBER

MAP 17 TA02

◆◆◆

Tobias House

Market Pl, Cross Hill, Barrow-upon-Humber DN19 7BW

☎ 01469 531164 & 07725 640484

e-mail andy-iwona@yahoo.co.uk

Dir Off A15 at Humber Bridge rdbt to Barton, A1077 to Barrow-upon-Humber, right at rdbt on A1077 to bottom of hill, left & 1st right

This neatly presented house stands in the Victorian market square and features comfortable bedrooms and a small dining room. Two ground-floor garden rooms are also available. A substantial breakfast is provided and the hospitality is friendly and genuine. Ample parking is nearby.

Facilities 4 en suite (1 fmly) ⊗ in dining room ⊗ in lounges TVB
tea/coffee ✖ Cen ht No coaches Dinner Last d 8pm **Parking** 2
Notes ⊠

BOSTON

MAP 12 TF34

◆◆◆◆

Palethorpe House

138 Spilsby Rd PE21 9PE

☎ 01205 359000 & 07888 758608 📠 01205 359000

Dir 0.5m from town centre on left, 200yds from Pilgrim Hospital

Friendly and welcoming, this Grade II listed villa, built by John Palethorpe in 1853, stands in a conservation area within easy walking distance of the town centre. The house has been refurbished to a very good standard, offering carefully furnished day rooms that include a lounge with satellite television and a pleasant breakfast room. A continental breakfast only is available during the week, with cooked options at the weekend. Bedrooms are thoughtfully equipped, have quality beds and well-appointed bathrooms.

Facilities 2 en suite (2 fmly) ⊗ STV TVB tea/coffee ✖ Cen ht TVL
No coaches **Prices** S £50-£60; D £70✳ **Parking** 3 **Notes** ⊠

◆◆◆

Boston Lodge

Browns Drove, Swineshead Br PE20 3PX ☎ 01205 820983

e-mail info@bostonlodge.co.uk

Dir 6m W of Boston. Off A1121 by Swineshead railway station

This attractive property lies in open countryside close to Boston. You can enjoy breakfast at individual tables in the lounge-dining room, while evening meals are available at the nearby pub. Bedrooms are pleasantly furnished and thoughtfully equipped. Ample private parking.

Facilities 8 en suite (1 fmly) (3 GF) ⊗ TVB tea/coffee Cen ht TVL
No coaches Dinner Last d 8.pm **Prices** S fr £35; d fr £52✳ LB
Parking 16

BRIGG

MAP 17 TA00

◆◆◆◆

The Queens Head

Station Rd, North Kelsey Moor LN7 6HD

☎ 01652 678055 📠 01652 678954

e-mail info@queens-head.biz

web www.queens-head.biz

Dir At Brigg onto A1084, right onto B1434, left to North Kelsey Moor

A small and friendly family-run inn with purpose-built en suite bedrooms. The rear car park overlooks a small garden. A wide range of ales and wines is available in the friendly bar, and an extensive menu can be enjoyed either in the bar or the popular restaurant.

Facilities 5 en suite (5 GF) ⊗ in bedrooms ⊗ in dining room TVB
tea/coffee ✖ Cen ht Dinner Last d 9pm **Prices** S £35; D £49.50 LB
Conf Max 50 Thtr 50 Class 50 Board 50 **Parking** 50

◆◆◆

Hamsden Garth

Cadney Rd LN7 6LA

☎ 01652 678703 & 07790 200157 📠 01652 678703

e-mail reservations@hamsden.co.uk

Dir A1084 from Brigg, 2m right onto B1434, at Howsham right onto Cadney Rd, 400yds on right

The friendly proprietors welcome you to their home, which offers contemporary bedrooms that share a modern bathroom with separate shower and bath. There is a lounge, and breakfast is served around a large table in the dining room, overlooking an extensive lawned garden.

Facilities 2 rms ⊗ TVB tea/coffee Cen ht TVL No coaches **Parking** 10
Notes Closed 24 Dec-2 Jan ⊠

CAMMERINGHAM
MAP 17 SK98

◆◆◆

Field View

Back Ln LN1 2SH ☎ 01522 730193 🖹 01522 730193
e-mail info@fieldviewbandb.com
web www.fieldviewbandb.com
Dir *Off B1398 in village centre*

A delightful new family home set in open countryside only a short commute from Lincoln or the antiques shops at Hemswell. Very comfortable bedrooms, a hearty breakfast and a very friendly welcome are provided by the Ayrton family.

Facilities 2 rms (1 en suite) (1 pri facs) (1 fmly) ⊗ TVB tea/coffee 🐾 Cen ht No children 3yrs No coaches **Prices** D £50-£55✶ **LB** **Parking** 3 **Notes** ⊛

CLEETHORPES
MAP 17 TA30

★★ Guest House

Mallow View ◇

9-11 Albert Rd DN35 8LX ☎ 01472 691297
e-mail info@mallowviewhotel.co.uk
Dir *Located on the seafront, turn left at Library*

Located a short walk from the seafront, this large terrace house offers comfortable modern bedrooms. A small number of the rooms have en suites, while others share well-equipped bath/shower rooms. Breakfast is served in the pleasant dining room and there is a comfortable lounge-bar area.

Facilities 13 rms (3 en suite) (2 fmly) ⊗ in dining room TVB tea/coffee 🐾 Licensed Cen ht TVL Video library **Prices** S £20-£35; D £45-£55

◆◆◆◆

Adelaide Hotel

41 Isaac's Hill DN35 8JT ☎ 01472 693594 🖹 01472 329717
e-mail robert.callison@ntlworld.com
Dir *Junct A180 & A46, onto A1098 Isaacs Hill, on right at bottom of hill*

This beautifully presented house offers well-equipped bedrooms and comfortable public rooms, and hospitality is a major strength. Good home cooking is provided and there is a small lounge with a bar. Secure parking is available.

Facilities 5 rms (3 en suite) (1 fmly) ⊗ STV TVB tea/coffee 🐾 Licensed Cen ht TVL No children 4yrs No coaches Dinner Last d noon **Parking** available

◆◆◆◆

The Comat ◇

26 Yarra Rd DN35 8LS
☎ 01472 694791 & 591861 🖹 01472 694791
e-mail comat-hotel@ntlworld.com
web www.comat-hotel.co.uk
Dir *Off A1098 Alexandra Rd*

A short walk from the shops and seafront, the welcoming Comat offers cosy, well-equipped bedrooms, one with a four-poster bed.

Tasty English breakfasts are served in the bright dining room, and a quiet sitting room and bar overlook the colourful flower terrace.

Facilities 6 en suite (1 fmly) (2 GF) ⊗ in bedrooms ⊗ in dining room TVB tea/coffee 🐾 Licensed Cen ht TVL No children 3yrs No coaches **Prices** S £30-£40; D £55-£70✶ **LB**

◆◆◆◆

Sherwood Guest House ◇

15 Kingsway DN35 8QU ☎ 01472 692020 🖹 01472 239177
e-mail sherwood.guesthouse@ntlworld.com
Dir *On A1098 seafront road*

The non-smoking Victorian house stands on the seafront overlooking the promenade and the beach, and is a short walk the town centre. Bedrooms are immaculate and the hearty breakfast comes with attentive service. There is a lounge and limited off-road parking is available.

Facilities 6 rms (3 en suite) ⊗ TVB tea/coffee 🐾 Cen ht No children No coaches **Prices** S £22-£35; D £40-£55✶ **LB** **Parking** 2

◆◆◆◆

Tudor Terrace ◇

11 Bradford Av DN35 0BB
☎ 01472 600800 🖹 01472 501395
e-mail tudor.terrace@ntlworld.com
Dir *Off seafront onto Bradford Av*

This guest house offers attractive bedrooms that are thoughtfully designed and furnished to a high standard. You can relax in the lounge, or outside on the patio in the well-maintained garden. Very caring and friendly service is provided, and the house is non-smoking except in the garden. Mobility scooter rental is available.

Facilities 6 en suite (1 GF) ⊗ TVB tea/coffee Cen ht TVL No children No coaches Dinner Last d 2pm **Prices** S £26-£30; D £49.50-£58 **LB** **Parking** 3

◆◆◆

Alpine House

55 Clee Rd DN35 8AD ☎ 01472 690804
e-mail nw.sanderson@ntlworld.com
Dir *On A46 before junct A180 & A1098 Isaacs Hill rdbt*

Carefully run by the resident owners, and convenient for the town centre and attractions, this friendly guest house offers compact, well-equipped bedrooms and a comfortable lounge.

Facilities 5 rms (2 fmly) ⊗ TVB tea/coffee 🐾 Cen ht TVL No children 2yrs **LB** **Parking** 3 **Notes** ⊛

◆◆◆

Brier Park Guest House ◇

27 Clee Rd DN35 8AD ☎ 01472 605591
e-mail graham.sherwood2@ntlworld.com
Dir *Left at bottom of Isaacs Hill, 150yds on left*

Personally managed by the owner, Brier Park offers a friendly atmosphere and comfortable compact bedrooms that are brightly decorated. Breakfast is freshly cooked to order and convenient parking in front is a bonus.

continued

continued

Facilities 5 rms (2 en suite) (1 fmly) (1 GF) ⊗ TVB tea/coffee ✈
Cen ht TVL No children 5yrs No coaches **Prices** S £18-£20; D £35-£45✳
LB **Parking** 2 **Notes** 🐾

♦♦♦

Burlington Guest House ◇

2-4 Albert Rd DN35 8LX ☎ 01472 699071 📄 01472 699071
e-mail burlington2_4@btopenworld.com
Dir *On upper promenade next to library*

This welcoming establishment has a quiet location just off the
seafront, with private rear parking. Bedrooms are neatly presented,
and include some ground-floor rooms. Breakfast is served in the
bright and pleasant dining room.

Facilities 7 rms (2 en suite) (3 fmly) (2 GF) ⊗ in dining room
⊗ in lounges TVB tea/coffee Cen ht No coaches **Prices** S £20; D £40
Parking 8 **Notes** Closed 23 Dec-2 Jan

♦♦♦

Holmhirst Hotel

3 Alexandra Rd DN35 8LQ
☎ 01472 692656 📄 01472 692656

Overlooking the sea and the pier, this Victorian terrace house offers
comfortable well-equipped bedrooms, many with showers en suite.
Tasty English breakfasts and a range of lunchtime and evening meals
are available. There is a well-stocked bar, and the ew resident owners
are fluent in several languages.

Facilities 8 rms (5 en suite) ⊗ TV7B tea/coffee ✈ Licensed Cen ht
TVL No children 4yrs Dinner Last d 8pm

♦♦♦ 🅰

Ginnies

27 Queens Pde DN35 0DF
☎ 01472 694997 📄 01472 593153
e-mail enquiries@ginnies.co.uk
Dir *On A1098 Queens Parade, off seafront Kingsway*

Facilities 7 rms (5 en suite) (2 pri facs) (3 fmly) (1 GF) ⊗ TVB
tea/coffee ✈ Cen ht TVL **Prices** D £40-£60✳ LB **Parking** 4

🅤

White Lion Lodge

12 High St NG33 5NF ☎ 01476 861466 📄 01476 860120
e-mail jim@colsterltd.wanadoo.co.uk

At the time of going to press the rating for this establishment had not
been confirmed. Please check the AA website www.theAA.com for up-
to-date information.

Facilities 4 rms (2 en suite) (1 fmly) (1 GF) ⊗ STV TVB tea/coffee ✈
Licensed Cen ht TVL Pool Table Dinner **Prices** S £37.50-£50;
D £49.50-£80✳ **Conf** Max 60 Class 60 **Parking** 30

♦♦♦♦

The Coachman Inn

2 Bourne Rd NG33 4NS ☎ 01476 550316
e-mail suzi.pearson@virgin.net
Dir *From A1 take Colsterworth rdbt towards Corby Glen 3.5m into
village, Coachman Inn on main rd*

An impressive village inn offering smart en suite bedrooms, some with
direct external access. There is a popular restaurant and a wide
selection of real ales and wines is available in the friendly bar.

Facilities 2 en suite 3 annexe en suite (2 fmly) (3 GF) ⊗ TVB
tea/coffee Cen ht Dinner Last d 9pm

♦♦♦

The Black Horse Inn

Main Rd LN11 9TJ ☎ 01507 343640 📄 01507 343640
e-mail barrett@blackhorse1125.freeserve.co.uk
Dir *In village centre*

An ideal stop for the Viking Way, nearby Cadwell Park, Market Rasen
or the market town of Louth. A wide range of food and beers is
available in this popular inn, and the spacious bedrooms are
comfortable and all en suite.

Facilities 8 en suite (4 GF) ⊗ in bedrooms ⊗ in dining room ⊗ in
1 lounge TVB tea/coffee Cen ht Pool Table Dinner Last d 9pm **Parking** 60

♦♦♦♦

Wesley Guest House ◇

16 Queen St DN9 1HG ☎ 01427 874512 📄 01427 874592
e-mail bookings@wesleyguesthouse.co.uk
web www.wesleyguesthouse.co.uk
Dir *In town centre, 200yds off Market Place*

Situated near the market cross and close to the Old Rectory, this
detached house offers a friendly welcome, modern, non-smoking en
suite rooms, and secure off-road parking. Finningley airport is close by.

Facilities 4 en suite (1 GF) ⊗ TVB tea/coffee ✈ Cen ht No coaches
Snooker Dinner Last d 6pm **Prices** S £30-£50; D £60-£80 LB **Parking** 4

♦♦♦♦

Church Farm B & B

High St DN21 5BS ☎ 01427 668279
e-mail enquiries@churchfarm-fillingham.co.uk
web www.churchfarm-fillingham.co.uk
Dir *Off B1398 into village, 1st house on right*

A traditional stone farmhouse, close to antiques centres and the base
of the Red Arrows. Warm hospitality and very comfortable bedrooms
with modern decor provide a good touring base.

Facilities 3 rms (1 en suite) ⊗ tea/coffee ✈ Cen ht TVL No children
5yrs No coaches **Prices** S fr £35; D £49-£54✳ **Parking** 6 **Notes** Closed
24 Dec-1 Jan 🐾

FOLKINGHAM
MAP 12 TF03

◆◆◆

The White House
25 Market Pl NG34 0SE ☎ 01529 497298
e-mail victoria.strauss@btinternet.com
Dir On A15 in marketplace

This 18th-century house faces the village green in a pretty conservation area. The extensive family home is attractively furnished in period style and retains many original features. Bedrooms, with comfortable beds, are spacious and include many extras. Healthy breakfasts and careful hospitality are assured.

Facilities 3 rms (1 en suite) (2 pri facs) ⊘ tea/coffee ✗ Cen ht TVL No coaches Livery available Dinner Last d previous day **Prices** S £25-£35; D £60-£65✱ LB

GAINSBOROUGH
MAP 17 SK88
See also **Marton**

★★★★ Guest House

Eastbourne House
81 Trinity St DN21 1JF ☎ 01427 679511 ▤ 01427 679511
e-mail info@eastbournehouse.co.uk
Dir On A159 at junct A631 & A156.

Located in a residential area of the town, this impressive Victorian house has been restored to provide high standards of comfort and facilities. Bedrooms are thoughtfully furnished and the comprehensive breakfast uses quality local produce.

Facilities 5 rms (3 en suite) (2 pri facs) (1 fmly) ⊘ TVB tea/coffee ✗ Cen ht No coaches **Prices** S £30; D £40-£60✱

GEDNEY HILL
MAP 12 TF31

◆◆◆◆

Northolme
North Rd PE12 0NX
☎ 01406 330938 & 07810 127961 ▤ 01406 330938
e-mail jonniedep@aol.com
Dir A1073 onto B1166 to Gedney Hill, right at garage, through village, 2nd left after mill, 2m right

Set in peaceful fenland, the smart modern property is ideal for walkers and cyclists. Stables and a cross-country course are available by arrangement to horse riders. Bedrooms are comfortably appointed, the smart bathrooms are well equipped, and helpful service is

continued

---

assured. There is a lounge-diner, and generous tasty breakfasts are served in the breakfast room. Free use of a superb modern gym is also available.

Facilities 3 rms (1 en suite) ⊘ STV TVB tea/coffee ✗ Cen ht TVL No children No coaches Fishing Gymnasium Stabling, sand arena, cross country course **Prices** S £25-£30; D £50✱ LB **Parking** 6 **Notes** ⊛

GRANTHAM
MAP 11 SK93

Premier Collection

◆◆◆◆◆

La Casita
Frith House, Main St NG32 3BH
☎ 01400 250302 & 07836 695282 ▤ 01400 250302
e-mail jackiegonzalez@btinternet.com
web www.lacasitabandb.co.uk
For full entry see **Normanton**

◆◆◆◆

Beechleigh Guest House
55 North Pde NG31 8AT ☎ 01476 572213 ▤ 01476 566058
e-mail info@beechleigh.co.uk
web www.beechleigh.co.uk
Dir A52 onto B1174 by Asda, 200yds on left

The Edwardian house is a short walk from the town centre on the northern approach. Its comfortable bedrooms have many extras, there is a pleasant dining room, and off-road parking is available.

Facilities 3 rms (1 fmly) ⊘ STV TVB tea/coffee Cen ht No children 5yrs No coaches Dinner Last d noon **Prices** S £30-£37.50; D £50-£60✱ **Parking** 5

◆◆◆◆

The Welby Arms
The Green, Allington NG32 2EA
☎ 01400 281361 ▤ 01400 281361
Dir From Grantham take either A1 N, or A52 W. Allington is 1.5m.

Three purpose-built en suites in a converted byre behind the popular village inn, which serves a wide range of real ales and an extensive menu. Just off the busy A1, handy for Grantham, but deep in countryside.

Facilities 3 annexe en suite (3 GF) ⊘ TVB tea/coffee ✗ Licensed Cen ht No coaches Dinner Last d 9.30pm **Parking** 35

HEMSWELL   MAP 17 SK99

◆◆◆◆

Hemswell Court

Lancaster Green, Hemswell Cliff DN21 5TQ
☎ 01427 668508 ⧠ 01427 667335
e-mail function@hemswellcourt.com
Dir *Located on A631 on left as approaching from A15 turn off*

Originally an officers' mess, the Court is now a venue for conferences, weddings or private gatherings. The modern bedrooms and many suites are ideal for families or groups of friends, and all rooms are well equipped. The lounges and dining rooms are enhanced by antique pieces.

Facilities 16 en suite 7 annexe rms (3 en suite) (2 fmly) (7 GF) ⊗ TV4B tea/coffee ✗ Licensed Cen ht TVL ✎ ♨ Dinner Last d 48hrs before **Prices** S £60-£85; D £80-£125✳ **Conf** Max 200 Thtr 200 Class 160 Board 160 Del from £120 ✳ **Parking** 150 **Notes** Closed Xmas & New Year Civ Wed 200

HOLBEACH   MAP 12 TF32

◆◆◆◆

Elloe Lodge

37 Barrington Gate PE12 7LB
☎ 01406 423207 ⧠ 01406 423207
e-mail norman.vasey@btinternet.com
web www.elloelodge.co.uk
Dir *From town centre onto Church St, 2nd left, 1st house on right*

This delightful house is peacefully situated in extensive well-tended grounds and gardens, just a short walk from the town centre. Bedrooms are well appointed and comfortably furnished. Spacious public areas include an inviting lounge and an attractive dining room, where hearty breakfasts are served at individual tables.

Facilities 4 en suite (2 fmly) ⊗ tea/coffee ✗ Cen ht TVL No coaches **Prices** S £32; D £49 LB **Parking** 10 **Notes** Closed Jan

HORNCASTLE   MAP 17 TF26

◆◆◆◆ ❦

Greenfield Farm *(TF175745)*

Mill Ln/Cow Ln, Minting LN9 5PJ
☎ 01507 578457 & 07768 368829 ⧠ 01507 578457
Mrs Bankes Price
e-mail greenfieldfarm@farming.co.uk
Dir *A158 NW from Horncastle. 5m left at The New Midge pub, farm 1m on right*

Located on the outskirts of Minting village, this impressive brick farmhouse has fine views over gardens across the Lincolnshire countryside. The spacious house offers comfortable en suite bedrooms and a cosy lounge. Very kind and attentive hospitality is provided.

Facilities 3 en suite ⊗ TVB tea/coffee ✗ Cen ht TVL No children 10yrs ✎ 307 acres arable **Prices** S £35; D £50-£56✳ LB **Parking** 12 **Notes** Closed Xmas & New Year ⊠

LINCOLN   MAP 17 SK97
See also **Horncastle, Marton & Swinderby**

La Casíta
The ultimate B&B

This converted stable with high beamed ceilings is a spacious guest suite, set independently in the grounds of the owner's home. Private entrance, relaxing interior comprising living area, open log fire, bedroom, bathroom. Private patio with uninterrupted views over the Lincolnshire countryside. Ideally located for Belton, Burghley, Newark Showground, Lincoln, Grantham and RAF Cranwell. Perfect for a business retreat, romantic getaway or family break.

AA ◆◆◆◆◆ approved
Tel/Fax 01400 250302 Mobile 07836 695282
Frith House, Normanton on Cliffe, Grantham,
Lincolnshire NG32 3BH
www.lacasitabandb.co.uk
jackiegonzalez@btinternet.com

Premier Collection

◆◆◆◆◆

Bailhouse & Mews

34 Bailgate LN1 3AP
☎ 01522 520883 & 07976 112233 ⧠ 01522 521829
e-mail info@bailhouse.co.uk
Dir *100yds N of catherdral*

This renovated 18th-century building in the cathedral quarter offers high levels of modern comfort. One room has an exposed cruck beam of a surviving 14th-century hall. A private car park surrounds an old chapel, and customer care is of the highest standard.

Facilities 10 en suite ⊗ TVB tea/coffee Direct dial from bedrooms ✗ Cen ht TVL No coaches ⤳ **Prices** S £64.50-£105.50; D £79-£165; (room only) ✳ LB **Parking** 16

LINCOLN continued

Premier Collection

◆◆◆◆◆

Minster Lodge

3 Church Ln LN2 1QJ ☎ 01522 513220 📠 01522 513220
e-mail info@minsterlodge.co.uk
web www.minsterlodge.co.uk
Dir *N of cathedral*

This delightful non-smoking house has a wonderful location in the old town close to the castle and the cathedral. Bedrooms are comfortable and beautifully furnished, and all have well-appointed, spacious bathrooms. There is an inviting lounge with deep sofas and an attractive dining room where impressive Aga-cooked breakfasts are served. Hospitality and service are warm and attentive.

Facilities 3 en suite ⊘ TVB tea/coffee Direct dial from bedrooms ✸ Cen ht TVL No children 12yrs No coaches **Prices** S £60-£80; D £80-£100 LB **Parking** 6 **Notes** Closed Xmas & New Year rs 24 Dec-14 Jan

◆◆◆◆

6 Lee Road

LN2 4BH ☎ 01522 522577
e-mail carolemann@gmail.com
Dir *A46/B1182 rdbt, right onto B1182 Nettleham Rd. Straight over rdbt, 4th road on left*

A private house within the cathedral quarter of the city offering a high level of comfort and careful hospitality. Off-road parking and landscaped gardens are available, and the delights of the city are close by.

Facilities 1 en suite ⊘ TVB tea/coffee ✸ Cen ht No children No coaches **Prices** D £50-£65 **Parking** 2 **Notes** ⊛

◆◆◆◆

Carholme ◇

175 Carholme Rd LN1 1RU
☎ 01522 531059 📠 01522 511590
e-mail farrelly@talk21.com
Dir *500yds NW of castle. Off B1273 Yarborough Rd onto Carline Rd*

Situated just a short walk from the Marina and university, this small, family-run guest house provides stylish bedrooms, which are attractively decorated, well-maintained and equipped with useful extras. Breakfast is served in the smart dining room and there is a neat lounge and a colourful courtyard garden.

Facilities 5 rms (4 en suite) (1 pri facs) (1 fmly) (1 GF) ⊘ TVB tea/coffee ✸ Cen ht No coaches **Prices** S fr £28; d fr £48✳ LB **Notes** Closed Xmas & New Year ⊛

◆◆◆◆

Carline

1-3 Carline Rd LN1 1HL ☎ 01522 530422 📠 01522 530422
e-mail sales@carlineguesthouse.co.uk
web www.carlineguesthouse.co.uk
Dir *left off A1102, A15 N. Premises 1m from A46 bypass & A57 into city*

This smart double-fronted Edwardian house has a convenient location within easy walking distance of the castle and the cathedral. Bedrooms are particularly smart and have a host of useful extras. Breakfast is served at individual tables in the spacious dining room.

Facilities 9 en suite (1 fmly) (3 GF) ⊘ TVB tea/coffee ✸ Cen ht No children 3yrs No coaches **Prices** D £50-£55✳ LB **Parking** 6 **Notes** Closed Xmas & New Year ⊛

◆◆◆◆

Eagles

552A Newark Rd, North Hykeham LN6 9NG
☎ 01522 686346
e-mail eaglesguesthouse@yahoo.co.uk
Dir *Off A46 onto A1434, 0.5m on right*

This large detached house is very convenient for the bypass and is well furnished and thoughtfully equipped. The bedrooms are bright and fresh, and there is a conservatory. Substantial breakfasts are served in the pleasant dining room.

Facilities 5 rms (4 en suite) (1 pri facs) (2 fmly) (1 GF) ⊘ TVB tea/coffee ✸ Cen ht No children 9yrs No coaches **Parking** 8 **Notes** ⊛

◆◆◆◆

The Loudor Hotel

37 Newark Rd, North Hykeham LN6 8RB
☎ 01522 680333 📠 01522 680403
e-mail info@loudorhotel.co.uk
Dir *3m from city centre. A46 onto A1434 for 2m, on left opp shopping centre*

Opposite the Forum Shopping Centre and a short walk from the sports centre, this friendly house offers well-equipped bedrooms and spacious day rooms. There is ample private parking and easy access to the city's attractions.

Facilities 9 en suite (1 fmly) ⊘ in 4 bedrooms ⊘ in dining room ⊘ in lounges TVB tea/coffee ✸ Cen ht No coaches **Prices** S £37-£48; D £48-£52✳ **Parking** 9 **Notes** Closed 2wks Xmas & New Year

◆◆◆◆

Orchard House

119 Yarborough Rd LN1 1HR ☎ 01522 528795
e-mail orchardhouse50@hotmail.com
Dir *500yds NW of castle on B1273, halfway up hill*

Close to the shopping centre and cathedral, this detached Edwardian house is situated in immaculate gardens complete with an apple orchard and hens that provide fresh eggs for breakfast. Bedrooms are well equipped and homely, and the bright, attractive dining room has wonderful views over the valley.

Facilities 3 en suite (1 fmly) ⊘ TVB tea/coffee ✸ Cen ht No children 10yrs No coaches **Prices** D £50-£55✳ LB **Parking** 6 **Notes** ⊛

England

◆◆◆◆

St Clements Lodge

21 Langworth Gate LN2 4AD
☎ 01522 521532 🖷 01522 521532
e-mail janet@turner2777.fsnet.co.uk
Dir 350yds E of cathedral, down Eastgate onto Langworth Gate

Janet Turner gives a warm welcome to her delightful house. The stylish bedrooms have a host of thoughtful extras, and there is an inviting lounge and an elegant dining room where super breakfasts are served.

Facilities 3 en suite (1 fmly) ⊗ TVB tea/coffee ✖ Cen ht No coaches **Prices** S £45; D £60 **LB** **Parking** 3 **Notes**

◆◆◆◆

The Tennyson

7 South Pk LN5 8EN ☎ 01522 521624 🖷 01522 521355
e-mail tennyson.hotel@virgin.net
web www.tennysonhotel.com
Dir 1m S of city centre on A15 near South Common

This smart house is convenient for the city centre, situated on the ring road overlooking South Common. Bedrooms are attractive and have a host of thoughtful extras. There is a modern lounge and a smart dining room where impressive breakfasts are served.

Facilities 6 en suite ⊗ in dining room ⊗ in lounges TVB tea/coffee ✖ Cen ht No coaches **Prices** S £40; D £50✳ **LB** **Parking** 8 **Notes** Closed 24-31 Dec

◆◆◆◆

Westlyn Guest House ◇

57 Carholme Rd LN1 1RT
☎ 01522 537468 🖷 01522 537468
e-mail westlynbblincoln@hotmail.com
Dir A46 onto A57 to city, Westlyn 1m on left

This friendly guest house is within easy walking distance of the city centre. The smart bedrooms are comfortably furnished, and public areas include a cosy lounge, a conservatory, and a pleasant dining room where hearty breakfasts are served.

Facilities 4 en suite ⊗ TVB tea/coffee ✖ Cen ht No children 12yrs No coaches **Prices** S £25-£30; D £45-£55✳ **Parking** 5 **Notes**

◆◆◆

Elma ◇

14 Albion Crs, Off Long Leys Rd LN1 1EB
☎ 01522 529792 🖷 01522 529792
e-mail ellen.guymer@ntlworld.com
Dir Off A57 onto Long Leys Rd signed St Georges Hospital. 1m left onto Albion Crescent

This friendly, family-run guest house lies in a quiet residential area within walking distance of the city centre. The attractive bedrooms are comfortably furnished and thoughtfully equipped. Breakfast is served around a large table in the dining room and there is a shared lounge.

Facilities 4 rms (1 en suite) ⊗ TVB tea/coffee ✖ Cen ht TVL No children 8yrs No coaches Dinner Last d breakfast **Prices** S £26; D £50✳ **LB** **Parking** 5 **Notes**

◆◆◆

Newport

26-28 Newport Rd LN1 3DF
☎ 01522 528590 🖷 01522 542868
e-mail info@newportguesthouse.co.uk
web www.newportguesthouse.co.uk
Dir On A15 400yds N of cathedral

Situated in the quiet upper part of the city and just a short walk from the cathedral, this double-fronted terrace house offers well-equipped and comfortable bedrooms with broadband Internet access. The public areas include a very comfortable sitting room and a bright and attractive breakfast room.

Facilities 9 en suite (2 GF) ⊗ TVB tea/coffee Cen ht TVL No coaches **Prices** S £35; D £52✳ **Parking** 4

◆◆◆

South Park Guest House ◇

11 South Pk LN5 8EN ☎ 01522 528243 🖷 01522 524603
Dir 1m S of city centre on A15

A Victorian house situated on the inner ring road facing South Common. The staff are friendly and attentive, and bedrooms, though compact, are well equipped. Breakfast is served in a modern dining room overlooking the park.

Facilities 6 en suite 1 annexe en suite (2 fmly) (1 GF) ⊗ in dining room TVB tea/coffee ✖ Cen ht No coaches **Prices** S £30; D £48✳ **LB** **Parking** 7

◆◆◆ 🅰

Wren Guest House

22 St Catherine's LN5 8LY
☎ 01522 537949 🖷 01522 831156
e-mail kateatthewren@aol.com
Dir S of city centre on A15 near A1434 junct

Facilities 3 rms (1 en suite) (1 pri facs) (1 fmly) TVB tea/coffee Cen ht TVL No coaches **Parking** 5 **Notes**

England

LINCOLN continued

♦♦

Jaymar ◇

31 Newland St West LN1 1QQ
☎ 01522 532934 ▤ 01522 820182
e-mail ward.jaymar4@ntlworld.com

Dir A46 onto A57 to city, 1st lights left onto Gresham St, thn 2nd right, 500yds on left

Situated within easy walking distance of the city, this small, friendly guest house has two well-equipped bedrooms. A full English breakfast, with vegetarian options, is served in the cosy dining room, and an early breakfast, from 5 am onwards, is available on request. Children and pets are welcome, and you can be collected from the bus or railway stations if required.

Facilities 2 rms (1 fmly) ⊗ TVB tea/coffee No coaches **Prices** S fr £20; d fr £36 **LB Notes** ⊠

See advertisement on opposite page

LONG BENNINGTON   MAP 11 SK84

♦♦♦♦

Shepherds Bush Farm ◇

Main Rd NG23 5EB ☎ 01400 282163
e-mail culverhay@hotmail.com

Dir A1 S, 4m S of Newark, house driveway opp Fen Ln

Dating from the 19th century, the converted farmhouse and barn lie in arable farmland set back from but with direct access to the A1. The atmosphere is relaxed and informal, and the proprietors offer a friendly welcome. Bedrooms are individually appointed and have nearby private bathrooms.

Facilities 3 rms (3 pri facs) (2 fmly) (1 GF) ⊗ TVB tea/coffee 🐾 Cen ht TVL No coaches **Prices** S £25; D £50 **Parking** 4 **Notes** ⊠

MARKET RASEN   MAP 17 TF18

Premier Collection

♦♦♦♦♦

Blaven

Walesby Hill, Walesby LN8 3UW ☎ 01673 838352
e-mail blavenhouse@hotmail.com

Dir A46 Market Rasen to Grimsby, right at junct with A1103, left at T-junct, Blaven 100yds on right

On the edge of the village of Walesby, this smart house offers warm hospitality and comfortable en suite bedrooms. Freshly prepared breakfasts are served around one table in the dining room, while the large conservatory-lounge overlooks immaculate gardens.

Facilities 3 rms (2 en suite) (1 pri facs) ⊗ TVB tea/coffee 🐾 Cen ht TVL No children 10yrs No coaches **Prices** S £40; D £55✳ **Parking** 4 **Notes** Closed Xmas & New Year ⊠

♦♦♦♦

Chuck Hatch

Kingerby Rd, West Rasen LN8 3NB
☎ 01673 842947 & 07745 288463 ▤ 01673 842947
e-mail info@chuckhatch.co.uk

Dir A631 West Rasen follow signs Osgodby and North Owersby, house 0.5m on left

Built in 1780, Chuck Hatch stands in grounds in peaceful open countryside. The en suite bedrooms are individually styled and well equipped. Public rooms include a lounge and a delightful breakfast room, which looks out over the lake and grounds beyond. Smoking is not permitted in the house.

Facilities 4 en suite ⊗ TVB tea/coffee 🐾 Cen ht TVL No children No coaches Fishing **Prices** S £35-£55; D £55-£70 **LB Parking** 6 **Notes** ⊠

♦♦♦

Wold View House B&B ◇

Bully Hill Top, Tealby LN8 6JA
☎ 01673 838226 ▤ 01673 838226
e-mail irene@woldviewhouse.co.uk

Dir A46 onto B1225 towards Horncastle, after 7m Wold View House at x-rds

Situated at the top of Bully Hill with expansive views across the Wold, this smart tearoom with guest house offers modern bedrooms and warm hospitality. Ideal for walking, riding, or touring the charming nearby villages and coastline, the house is also only a short drive from Lincoln.

Facilities 3 rms (1 en suite) ⊗ TVB tea/coffee 🐾 Licensed Cen ht TVL Riding Dinner Last d 8pm **Prices** S £30-£32; D £45-£50✳ **LB Parking** 15 **Notes** ⊠

MARTON (VILLAGE)
MAP 17 SK88

◆◆◆◆
Black Swan Guest House
21 High St DN21 5AH ☎ 01427 718878 📠 01427 718878
e-mail info@blackswanguesthouse.co.uk
web www.blackswanguesthouse.co.uk
Dir On A156 in village centre

Centrally located in the village, this 18th-century former coaching inn retains many original features, and offers good hospitality and homely bedrooms with modern facilities. Tasty breakfasts are served in the cosy dining room and a comfortable lounge is available. Transport to nearby pubs and restaurants can be provided.

Facilities 6 en suite 4 annexe en suite (3 fmly) (4 GF) TVB tea/coffee Licensed Cen ht TVL No coaches **Prices** S £38-£48; D £60-£70✳ **LB Parking** 10

NORMANTON
MAP 11 SK94

Premier Collection

◆◆◆◆◆
La Casita
Frith House, Main St NG32 3BH
☎ 01400 250302 & 07836 695282 📠 01400 250302
e-mail jackiegonzalez@btinternet.com
web www.lacasitabandb.co.uk
Dir From A1, Normanton on A607 Grantham to Lincoln rd.

A self-contained one-bedroom family suite (can sleep four) built in the gated gardens of the owner's house. Furnished to a high standard with many extras, it offers both comfort and luxury, and the owners give caring service.

Facilities 1 annexe en suite (1 fmly) (1 GF) ⊗ TVB tea/coffee Direct dial from bedrooms ✖ Cen ht TVL No coaches **Prices** S fr £95; d fr £125 **LB Parking** 3 **Notes** ⊛

See advertisement on page 333

SKEGNESS
MAP 17 TF56

◆◆◆
Crawford Hotel
104 South Pde PE25 3HR ☎ 01754 764215 📠 01754 764215
e-mail info@thecrawfordhotel.com
web www.thecrawfordhotel.com
Dir Off main street (Lumley Rd) at clock tower onto South Parade

The Crawford overlooks the putting green to the seafront beyond. There are comfortable lounge areas and a games room, a heated indoor swimming pool with spa bath and sauna, and a bar. The neat bedrooms are well equipped and some are suitable for families.

Facilities 20 en suite (8 fmly) ⊗ in dining room TVB tea/coffee ✖ Licensed Lift Cen ht TVL ⊰ Sauna Pool Table Jacuzzi Dinner Last d noon

◆◆
Manderlay Guest House
49 Grosvenor Rd PE25 2DD
☎ 01754 899029 & 07795 124055 📠 01754 899029
e-mail mikecaroline@fsmail.net
web www.manderlayguesthouse.co.uk

A warm welcome is assured from Caroline and Mike Austin, who ensure your needs are met. Bedrooms are well equipped and come in a variety of sizes. Breakfast is served at individual tables in the dining room, and dinner is available by arrangement.

Facilities 3 en suite (1 fmly) ⊗ TVB tea/coffee Cen ht No coaches Dinner Last d 3pm **Prices** D £36-£45✳ **LB Parking** 2

SLEAFORD MAP 12 TF04
See **Aswarby**

STAMFORD MAP 11 TF00

Premier Collection

◆◆◆◆◆

Rock Lodge

1 Empingham Rd PE9 2RH
☎ 01780 481758 ▤ 01780 481757
e-mail rocklodge@innpro.co.uk
Dir *Off A1 at A606 signed Oakham, into Stamford, Rock Lodge
1.25m on left*

Philip and Jane Sagar have considerable experience in managing
luxury hotels and offer a warm welcome to their imposing 1900 house
near the town centre. The attractive bedrooms are individually
furnished and have a good range of facilities. Character public rooms
include the oak-panelled drawing room with mullion windows.
Breakfast is served in a sunny room overlooking the gardens.

Facilities 6 en suite (1 fmly) (2 GF) ⊘ STV FTV TVB tea/coffee ✖
Cen ht TVL No coaches **Prices** S £66-£88; D £80-£90✳ **Parking** 7

◆◆◆ ▉

The Bull & Swan Inn

24a High St, St Martin's PE9 2LJ
☎ 01780 763558 ▤ 01780 763558
e-mail bullandswan@btconnect.com
Dir *In town centre*

A 17th-century coaching inn on the old Great North Road at the south
approach to the town, The tradition of hospitality is carried on with
real ales, log fires, attentive service and en-suite rooms, and
convenient parking is a bonus.

Facilities 6 rms (5 en suite) (1 pri facs) (3 fmly) ⊘ in bedrooms
⊘ in dining room ⊘ in 1 lounge TVB tea/coffee ✖ Cen ht Dinner Last
d 8.50pm **Prices** S £60-£70; D £70✳ **Conf** Max 30 Class 40 Board 30
Parking 12

SUTTON-ON-SEA MAP 17 TF58

◆◆◆

Athelstone Lodge ◇

25 Trusthorpe Rd LN12 2LR ☎ 01507 441521
web www.athelstonelodge.co.uk
Dir *On A52 N of village*

Situated between Mablethorpe and Skegness and close to the
promenade, Athelstone Lodge has pleasant, soundly maintained
bedrooms equipped with many useful extras. Breakfast is served in
the dining room and there is a bar and a lounge. Enjoyable home-
cooked dinners are available.

Facilities 6 rms (5 en suite) (1 fmly) ⊘ in dining room ⊘ in lounges
TVB tea/coffee Licensed Cen ht TVL No coaches Dinner Last d 4.30pm
Prices S £25-£27; D £50-£54✳ **LB** **Parking** 6 **Notes** Closed Nov-Feb

SWINDERBY MAP 17 SK86

◆◆◆

Halfway Farm Motel & Guest House

Newark Rd (A46) LN6 9HN
☎ 01522 868749 ▤ 01522 868082
e-mail halfwayfarmmotel@hotmail.com
web www.halfway-farm-motel.co.uk
Dir *On A46 opp Swinderby rbt*

This 300-year-old farmhouse is set back from the A46, midway
between Lincoln and Newark. Spacious bedrooms are traditional in
the main house, while motel-style rooms are located around a
courtyard to the rear. There is a bright, airy dining room and a
comfortable lounge. A good base for touring or antique hunters.

Facilities 6 rms (5 en suite) 10 annexe en suite (1 fmly) (13 GF) ⊘ TVB
tea/coffee Direct dial from bedrooms ✖ Cen ht **Conf** Max 30
Parking 25 **Notes** rs Dec-Jan

WOODHALL SPA MAP 17 TF16
See also **Horncastle**

◆◆

Claremont

9/11 Witham Rd LN10 6RW ☎ 01526 352000
web www.woodhall-spa-guesthouse-
bedandbreakfast.co.uk
Dir *On B1191 in centre of Woodhall Spa close to minirdbt*

This large Victorian house is close to the town centre, and has been
owned and run by Mrs Brennan for many years. The bedrooms are
homely, generally quite spacious, traditionally furnished and well
equipped. Breakfast includes home-made preserves.

Facilities 11 rms (5 en suite) (5 fmly) (2 GF) ⊘ TVB tea/coffee
No coaches **Parking** 5 **Notes** ▨

WOOLSTHORPE MAP 11 SK83

◆◆◆◆ ▉

The Chequers Inn

Main St NG32 1LU ☎ 01476 870701 ▤ 01476 870085
e-mail justin@chequers-inn.net
Dir *In village opp Post Office*

A 17th-century coaching inn set in the lee of Belvoir Castle next to the
village cricket pitch, and having its own pétanque pitch (like boules).
Exposed beams, open fireplaces and original stone and brickwork
provide character in the bar along with 24 wines by the glass, a gastro
menu and real ales. Comfortable bedrooms are in a converted stable
block.

Facilities 4 annexe en suite (1 fmly) (3 GF) ⊘ in bedrooms ⊘ in dining
room TVB tea/coffee Cen ht TVL Dinner Last d 9.30pm **Prices** S fr £49;
d fr £59 **Conf** Max 80 Thtr 80 Class 50 Board 25 **Parking** 40

LONDON

E4

♦♦♦

Ridgeway Hotel
Plan 1-G6

115/117 The Ridgeway, North Chingford E4 6QU
☎ 020 8529 1964 📠 020 8524 9130
e-mail bookings@ridgewayhotel.com
web www.ridgewayhotel.co.uk

Dir *In Chingford. Off A110 onto B169, 0.25m on left*

The Ridgeway is within easy reach of the North Circular and the M25
and can cater for meetings and functions. Bedrooms vary in size and
style, including a four-poster room, and public areas include a smart
dining room, lounge bar and an attractive garden.

Facilities 20 en suite (6 fmly) (4 GF) STV TVB tea/coffee Direct dial
from bedrooms Licensed Cen ht TVL Dinner Last d 9pm **Prices** S £52;
D £65✳ **Conf** Max 100 Thtr 40 Class 50 Board 30 **Parking** 9

N1

♦♦♦

Kandara
Plan 1-F4

68 Ockendon Rd N1 3NW
☎ 020 7226 5721 📠 020 7226 3379
e-mail admin@kandara.co.uk
web www.kandara.co.uk

Dir *At Highbury corner rdbt on A1 onto St Pauls Rd for 0.5m, right at
junct onto Essex Rd, Ockendon Rd 5th left*

Facilities 9 rms 2 annexe rms (4 fmly) (2 GF) ⊗ TVB tea/coffee ✸
Cen ht No coaches **Prices** S £42-£49; D £54-£69✳ **Notes** Closed
22-26 Dec

N4

Premier Collection

♦♦♦♦♦

Mount View
Plan 1-F5

31 Mount View Rd N4 4SS ☎ 020 8340 9222
e-mail mountviewbb@aol.com
web www.mountviewguesthouse.com

Dir *Off A1201 Crouch Hill in Crouch End*

This delightful Victorian house is in a quiet, tree-lined residential area
with good transport links to the City and the West End. The bedrooms

continued

and public areas are carefully furnished and facilities include a
washing machine and access to the Internet. Well-prepared breakfasts
are served at a large communal table and the resident owners are
very friendly.

Facilities 3 rms (2 en suite) ⊗ TVB tea/coffee ✸ Cen ht No coaches
Prices S fr £45; D £60-£80

♦♦♦

Majestic Hotel
Plan 1-F5

392/394 Seven Sisters Rd, Finsbury Pk N4 2PQ
☎ 020 8800 2022 📠 020 8802 4131
e-mail Hotelmaj@aol.com
web www.majestic-hotel.sageweb.co.uk

Dir *On A503 near Manor House tube station*

The nearby tube station provides good access to the City and the West
End. Bedrooms vary in size and style with a number of family rooms.
Public areas include an attractive lounge and breakfast room. Free
parking is a bonus.

Facilities 36 rms (20 en suite) (13 fmly) (7 GF) ⊗ in 6 bedrooms
⊗ in dining room TVB tea/coffee ✸ Cen ht TVL Use of local leisure
club **Prices** S £45-£60; D £55-£75✳ **Conf** Max 25 **Parking** 25

♦♦♦

Ossian House
Plan 1-F5

20 Ossian Rd N4 4EA ☎ 020 8340 4331 📠 020 8340 4331
e-mail ann@ossianguesthouse.co.uk
web www.ossianguesthouse.co.uk

Dir *Off A1201 Crouch Hill onto Mount View Rd, 1st right down hill,
1st left*

This pleasant guest house is in a quiet location north of the city.
Bedrooms are stylishly furnished, with a very good range of facilities
and accessories. Breakfast is served round one large table in the
attractive dining room, which doubles as a sitting room.

Facilities 3 en suite ⊗ TVB tea/coffee ✸ Cen ht TVL No coaches
Notes 🚭

England

N6

♦♦♦♦

Winchester Pub Hotel
Plan 1-E5

206 Archway Rd, Highgate N6 5BA
☎ 020 8374 1690 & 0777 037 8818 🖷 020 8374 1690
e-mail valatwinch@aol.com
web www.winchester-hotel.com
Dir *A1 S to City, pass Highgate tube station on left, premises on left*

This delightful traditional pub is close to Highgate tube station and within easy reach of the M1. The smart spacious bedrooms are well equipped and there is a well-stocked bar-lounge. Hearty breakfasts and a good choice of home-cooked meals are served in the elegant dining area.

Facilities 6 en suite (3 fmly) STV TVB tea/coffee ✖ Licensed Cen ht Dinner Last d 9.30pm **Prices** S fr £50; d fr £60✳

N8

♦♦♦

White Lodge Hotel
Plan 1-F5

1 Church Ln, Hornsey N8 7BU
☎ 020 8348 9765 🖷 020 8340 7851
e-mail info@whitelodgehornsey.co.uk
Dir *A406 to Bounds Green, Hornsey High Rd & Church Ln*

This well-maintained, friendly guest house has a quiet yet convenient location close to shops and restaurants. Bedrooms are traditionally appointed and airy public areas include an attractive lounge and spacious breakfast room.

Facilities 16 rms (8 en suite) (5 fmly) (1 GF) ⊗ in 4 bedrooms ⊗ in dining room ⊗ in 1 lounge TVB tea/coffee ✖ Cen ht TVL No coaches **Prices** S £34-£36; D £42-£52

NW1

♦♦♦♦

MIC Hotel & Conference Centre
Plan 2-D5

81-103 Euston St NW1 2EZ
☎ 020 7380 0001 🖷 020 7387 5300
e-mail sales@micentre.com
Dir *Euston Rd left at lights onto Melton St, 1st left onto Euston St, MIC 100yds on left*

Located within walking distance of Euston station, this smart property is convenient for central London. Stylish air-conditioned bedrooms are

continued

thoughtfully equipped for business and leisure, and the airy Atrium Bar and Restaurant offers drinks, light snacks and daily specials. Extensive conference and meeting facilities are available.

Facilities 28 en suite (2 fmly) ⊗ STV TVB tea/coffee Direct dial from bedrooms ✖ Licensed Lift Cen ht TVL Dinner Last d 8.45pm **Prices** S £85-£130; D £85-£130✳ **LB Conf** Thtr 150 Class 50 Board 45

♦♦♦

Euston Square Hotel
Plan 2-C5

152-156 North Gower St NW1 2LU
☎ 020 7388 0099 🖷 020 7383 7165
e-mail reservations@euston-square-hotel.com
web www.euston-square-hotel.com
Dir *On junct Euston Rd, next to Euston Sq tube station*

Situated close to a tube station, this establishment is ideal for business and leisure. The smart compact bedrooms are well equipped, and there are conference facilities and a modern reception area. Breakfast and light snacks are served in Java Joe's on the premises.

Facilities 70 en suite ⊗ STV TVB tea/coffee Direct dial from bedrooms Licensed Lift Cen ht Dinner Last d Breakfast **Conf** Thtr 120 Class 50 Board 50

NW3

♦♦♦♦

Langorf Hotel
Plan 2-E5

20 Frognal, Hampstead NW3 6AG
☎ 020 7794 4483 🖷 020 7435 9055
e-mail info@langorfhotel.com
web www.langorfhotel.com
Dir *Off A41 Finchley Rd, near Finchley Rd tube station*

Located on a leafy and mainly residential avenue within easy walking distance of shops and restaurants, this elegant Edwardian property has been renovated to provide high standards of comfort and facilities. Bedrooms are furnished with flair and a warm welcome is assured.

Facilities 31 en suite (4 fmly) (3 GF) ⊗ in dining room STV TVB tea/coffee Direct dial from bedrooms ✖ Licensed Lift Cen ht TVL No coaches **Prices** S fr £65; D £75-£110✳ **Parking** available

♦♦♦

La Gaffe

Plan 2-E5

107-111 Heath St NW3 6SS
☎ 020 7435 4941 & 7435 8965 🖷 020 7794 7592
e-mail info@lagaffe.co.uk
Dir *On A502, 250yds N of Hampstead tube station*

This guest house, just north of Hampstead High St, offers charm and warm hospitality. The Italian restaurant, which is open most lunchtimes and for dinner, is popular with locals. Bedrooms are compact, but all are en suite.

Facilities 11 en suite 7 annexe en suite (2 fmly) (2 GF) ⊗ in bedrooms TVB tea/coffee Direct dial from bedrooms 🐾 Licensed Cen ht No coaches Dinner Last d 11.30pm

♦♦♦

Quality Hotel Hampstead

Plan 2-E5

5 Frognal, Hampstead NW3 6AL
☎ 020 7794 0101 🖷 020 7794 0100
e-mail quality-h@lth-hotels.com
Dir *Off A41 Finchley Rd, near Finchley Rd tube station*

This modern purpose-built property is only a short walk from the tube station with good access to the West End. The smart bedrooms are well equipped for business and leisure, and the public areas include a bar-lounge and an airy basement breakfast room.

Facilities 57 en suite (10 fmly) (1 GF) ⊗ in 27 bedrooms STV TVB tea/coffee Direct dial from bedrooms Licensed Lift Cen ht TVL **Conf** Max 10 Thtr 10 Class 6 Board 8 **Parking** 20

NW6

♦♦♦♦

Dawson House Hotel

Plan 1-E4

72 Canfield Gdns NW6 3EG
☎ 020 7624 0079 & 7328 4857 🖷 020 7624 6525
e-mail booking@dawsonhousehotel.com
web www.dawsonhouse.com
Dir *From Finchley Rd tube station right onto Canfield Gardens*

A friendly welcome awaits you at Dawson House, situated in a residential area of South Hampstead. Bedrooms are brightly appointed and well equipped for business and leisure, and there are attractive front and rear gardens.

Facilities 15 en suite (2 fmly) (1 GF) ⊗ TVB tea/coffee Direct dial from bedrooms 🐾 Cen ht No children 3yrs No coaches **Prices** S £48; D £75✳

NW8

♦♦♦ 🖃

The New Inn

Plan 1-E4

2 Allitsen Rd, St Johns Wood NW8 6LA
☎ 020 7722 0726 🖷 020 7722 0653
e-mail thenewinn@gmail.com
web www.newinnlondon.co.uk
Dir *Off A41 by St Johns Wood tube station onto Acacia Rd, last right, to end on corner*

Built in 1810, this popular inn is in a leafy suburb only a stroll from the Regent's Park. Bedrooms have been refurbished to a high standard, while Thai cuisine and traditional fare are offered in the atmospheric bar lounge.

Facilities 5 en suite ⊗ in dining room TVB tea/coffee 🐾 Cen ht No coaches Dinner Last d 9.30pm **Prices** S £70; D £70; (room only) ✳

NW9

♦♦♦

Kingsland Hotel

Plan 1-C5

Kingsbury Circle, Kingsbury NW9 9RR
☎ 020 8206 0666 🖷 020 8206 0555
e-mail stay@kingslandhotel.co.uk
web www.kingslandhotel.co.uk
Dir *Junct A4006 & A4140*

Located at the roundabout near Kingsbury station, shops, restaurants and Wembley complex, the Kingsland provides modern bedrooms with smart bathrooms en suite. A continental breakfast is supplied, and a passenger lift and car park are available.

Facilities 28 en suite (5 fmly) (6 GF) ⊗ STV TVB tea/coffee Direct dial from bedrooms 🐾 Lift Cen ht **Prices** S £45-£55; D £55-£65✳ **Parking** 30

England

NW11

♦♦♦

Anchor Hotel
Plan 1-D5

10 West Heath Dr, Golders Green NW11 7QH
☎ 020 8458 8764 📄 020 8455 3204
e-mail reservations@anchor-hotel.co.uk
Dir *Off A598 Finchley Rd near Golders Green tube station*

A friendly atmosphere prevails at this guest house close to a tube station and shops. Bedrooms are comfortably appointed and well equipped for business and leisure, with some rooms suitable for families.

Facilities 11 rms (8 en suite) (3 fmly) (3 GF) ⊗ TVB tea/coffee Direct dial from bedrooms 🐕 Cen ht TVL No coaches **Prices** S £35-£50; D £50-£70✳ **Parking** 5

SE10

♦♦♦ 🍴

The Pilot Inn
Plan 1-G3

68 Riverway, Greenwich SE10 0BE
☎ 020 8858 5910 📄 020 8293 0371
e-mail marron@thepilotinn.fsnet.co.uk
Dir *A102 onto John Harrison Way, left onto West Park Side, 1st right onto Riverway*

There is a friendly atmosphere at this popular inn close to the river and near the Millennium Dome. The practical bedrooms are furnished in a modern style and many have splendid views. An extensive range of British meals are offered, plus a generous breakfast.

Facilities 7 rms (1 fmly) ⊗ TVB tea/coffee 🐕 Cen ht Dinner Last d 9pm **Parking** 20 **Notes** Closed 25 Dec

SE12

♦♦♦♦ 🍴

The Summerfield
Plan 1-G2

60 Baring Rd, Lee SE12 0PS
☎ 020 8857 9247 📄 020 8857 9247
e-mail thesummerfield@aol.com
Dir *A205 onto A2212, 0.25m on right, past school*

A 19th-century tavern offering refurbished, well-equipped en suite accommodation. Just 20 minutes from central London and 10 minutes from the M25, this is a good base for business and leisure. A tasty breakfast is served in the traditionally furnished bar area.

Facilities 4 en suite (3 fmly) ⊗ in bedrooms ⊗ in area of dining room TVB tea/coffee 🐕 Cen ht Pool Table **Prices** S fr £45; d fr £60✳ LB

SE20

♦♦♦♦

Melrose House Hotel
Plan 1-F1

89 Lennard Rd SE20 7LY
☎ 020 8776 8884 📄 020 778 6366
e-mail melrose.hotel@virgin.net
web www.uk-bedandbreakfast.com
Dir *Corner Courtenay Rd & Lennard Rd, off A234 via Kent House Rd*

You are warmly welcomed at this attractive Victorian house in a quiet residential area. The comfortable bedrooms are very well equipped and extra touches include books and luxury toiletries. Breakfast is served in a pleasant dining room around a communal table, while the spacious conservatory overlooks the pretty rear garden.

Facilities 6 rms (5 en suite) (1 pri facs) (1 GF) ⊗ FTV TVB tea/coffee 🐕 Cen ht No children 12yrs No coaches **Prices** S £35-£50; D £55-£70✳ **Parking** 6 **Notes** Closed 23 Dec-2 Jan

SW1

♦♦♦♦

B&B Belgravia
Plan 2-C1

64-66 Ebury St SW1W 9QD
☎ 020 7259 8570 📄 020 7259 8591
e-mail info@bb-belgravia.com
web www.bb-belgravia.com
Dir *Off A3213 Ecclestone St onto Ebury St*

This central Victorian house has been stylishly refurbished. The interior is bright and airy and the bedrooms are minimalist yet comfortable, with flat-screen satellite televisions. You can help yourself to beverages in the lounge and free Internet access is available. A hearty breakfast is served in the contemporary dining room.

continued

Facilities 17 en suite (2 fmly) (1 GF) ⊘ in 13 bedrooms ⊘ in dining room ⊘ in lounges STV TVB Direct dial from bedrooms Cen ht TVL
Prices S fr £94; D £99-£105✱

◆◆◆◆

Best Western Corona Hotel   Plan 2-D1

87-89 Belgrave Rd SW1V 2BQ
☎ 020 7828 9279 📠 020 7931 8576
e-mail info@coronahotel.co.uk

Centrally located, this elegant Victorian property has been refurbished to a high standard. Smartly appointed and well-equipped bedrooms offer modern accommodation. A continental breakfast is served in the basement dining room and room service is also available.

Facilities 51 en suite (8 fmly) (7 GF) ⊘ in 11 bedrooms ⊘ in dining room TVB tea/coffee Direct dial from bedrooms ✖ Licensed Lift
No coaches

◆◆◆◆

Sidney Hotel   Plan 2-C1

68-76 Belgrave Rd SW1V 2BP
☎ 020 7834 2738 📠 020 7630 0973
e-mail reservations@sidneyhotel.com
web www.sidneyhotel.com
Dir *A202 Vauxhall Bridge Rd onto Charlwood St & junct with Belgrave Rd*

This smart property near Pimlico has recently undergone refurbishment to its public areas and many of the bedrooms. The brightly decorated bedrooms are well equipped for business use, while several rooms are suitable for families. Public areas include a bar lounge and an airy breakfast room.

Facilities 82 en suite (13 fmly) (9 GF) ⊘ in 30 bedrooms ⊘ in dining room ⊘ in lounges STV TVB tea/coffee Direct dial from bedrooms ✖ Licensed Lift Cen ht TVL

See advertisement on this page

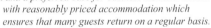
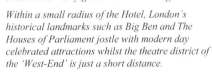

SW1 continued

◆◆◆◆
The Willett
Plan 2-B1

32 Sloane Gdns, Sloane Sq SW1W 8DJ
☎ 020 7824 8415 📄 020 7730 4830
e-mail reservations@eeh.co.uk
web www.eeh.co.uk
Dir Off A3216 Sloane Sq opp tube station

This smart Victorian house is in a tree-lined street just off Sloane Sq and provides comfortable, well-appointed accommodation. Staff are friendly and attentive, and 24-hour room service is available. A full breakfast is served in the lower ground-floor dining room.

Facilities 19 en suite (6 fmly) (3 GF) ⊗ in dining room STV TVB tea/coffee Direct dial from bedrooms ✖ Cen ht No coaches

◆◆◆◆
Windermere Hotel
Plan 2-C1

142/144 Warwick Way, Victoria SW1V 4JE
☎ 020 7834 5163 & 7834 5480 📄 020 7630 8831
e-mail reservations@windermere-hotel.co.uk
web www.windermere-hotel.co.uk
Dir On B324 off Buckingham Palace Rd, at junct Alderney St

This relaxed and informal family-run establishment is within easy reach of Victoria Station and many of the capital's attractions. Bedrooms, while varying in size, are stylish and well equipped. The Pimlico restaurant serves delicious evening meals and hearty breakfasts.

Facilities 20 en suite (3 fmly) (3 GF) ⊗ in 6 bedrooms ⊗ in dining room ⊗ in lounges STV TVB tea/coffee Direct dial from bedrooms ✖ Licensed Cen ht TVL Dinner Last d 10.30pm **Prices** S £89-£99; D £114-£139 **Conf** Max 20

◆◆◆◆
Knightsbridge Green
Plan 2-B2

159 Knightsbridge SW1X 7PD
☎ 020 7584 6274 📄 020 7225 1635
e-mail reservations@thekghotel.com
web www.thekghotel.com
Dir A315 into Knightsbridge, premises opp Knightsbridge Barracks

Facilities 28 en suite (9 fmly) ⊗ STV TVB tea/coffee Direct dial from bedrooms ✖ Licensed Lift Cen ht No coaches **Prices** S £105-£120; D £140-£160; (room only) **Notes** Closed 24-25 Dec

◆◆◆
Elizabeth Hotel
Plan 2-C1

37 Eccleston Sq SW1V 1PB
☎ 020 7828 6812 📄 020 7828 6814
e-mail info@elizabethhotel.com
Dir Exit 1 from Victoria station to end of rd. Turn left onto Belgrave Rd. 1st right onto Eccleston Sq

This friendly, well-run property is just a short walk from Victoria station and within easy reach of central London attractions. The smart, well-equipped bedrooms include some spacious apartments ideal for families. A substantial buffet and cooked breakfast are included.

Facilities 42 rms (39 en suite) (3 pri facs) (24 fmly) (4 GF) ⊗ in dining room TVB tea/coffee Direct dial from bedrooms ✖ Lift Cen ht TVL **Prices** S £79-£82; D £108-£110 **LB**

◆◆◆
Blades Hotel
Plan 2-C1

122 Belgrave Rd, Victoria SW1V 2BL
☎ 020 7976 5552 📄 020 7976 6500
e-mail info@blades-hotel.co.uk

Situated a short walk from Victoria station, this friendly establishment is popular for business and leisure. The comfortably appointed bedrooms include some suitable for families. There is a first-floor conservatory-style lounge, and continental breakfasts are served in the attractive dining room.

Facilities 16 en suite (3 fmly) (3 GF) ⊗ TVB tea/coffee ✖ Cen ht No coaches

◆◆◆
Comfort Inn
Plan 2-C1

8-12 St Georges Dr, Victoria SW1V 4BJ
☎ 020 7834 2988 📠 020 7821 5814
e-mail info@comfortinnbuckinghampalacerd.co.uk
Dir *Off Buckingham Palace Rd onto Elizabeth Bridge & St George's Dr*

Located just a short walk south from Victoria station, this establishment is a good base for visiting the city's attractions. All bedrooms and public areas have been smartly refurbished and offer very good levels of comfort. An extensive continental breakfast is served.

Facilities 51 en suite (4 fmly) (7 GF) ⊗ in 14 bedrooms ⊗ in dining room STV TVB tea/coffee Direct dial from bedrooms ✕ Lift Cen ht TVL No coaches **Prices** S £59-£69; D £69-£89✳ **Conf** Max 20 Thtr 20 Class 20 Board 20

◆◆◆
Comfort Inn Victoria
Plan 2-C1

18-24 Belgrave Rd, Victoria SW1V 1QF
☎ 020 7233 6636 📠 020 7932 0538
e-mail stay@comfortinnvictoria.co.uk

Having a prime location close to Victoria station, this renovated property offers brightly appointed en suite accommodation that is thoughtfully equipped for business and leisure. A continental breakfast is offered in the basement dining room.

Facilities 48 en suite (16 fmly) (9 GF) ⊗ in 26 bedrooms ⊗ in dining room ⊗ in lounges STV TVB tea/coffee Direct dial from bedrooms ✕ Lift Cen ht TVL No coaches

◆◆◆ ▦
The Victoria Inn
Plan 2-C1

65-67 Belgrave Rd, Victoria SW1V 2BG
☎ 020 7834 6721 & 7834 0182 📠 020 7931 0201
e-mail welcome@victoriainn.co.uk
web www.victoriainn.co.uk
Dir *On A3213 0.4m SE of Victoria station, near Pimlico tube station*

A short walk from Victoria station, this Victorian property offers modern, well-equipped accommodation for business and leisure. There is a comfortable reception lounge, and a limited self-service buffet breakfast is available in the basement breakfast room.

Facilities 43 en suite (7 fmly) ⊗ in dining room STV TVB tea/coffee Direct dial from bedrooms ✕ Lift Cen ht No coaches

◆◆◆ 🄰
Hanover Hotel
Plan 2-C1

30 St Georges Dr, Victoria SW1V 4BN
☎ 020 7834 0367 📠 020 7976 5587
e-mail info@hanoverhotel.co.uk
web www.hanoverhotel.co.uk
Dir *Off Buckingham Palace Rd onto Elizabeth Bridge & St George's Dr*

Facilities 41 en suite (8 fmly) (4 GF) ⊗ in 30 bedrooms ⊗ in dining room ⊗ in lounges TVB tea/coffee Direct dial from bedrooms ✕ Cen ht TVL

SW1 continued

♦♦

Central House Hotel

Plan 2-C1

39 Belgrave Rd, Victoria SW1V 2BB
☎ 020 7834 8036 ▤ 020 7834 1854
e-mail info@centralhousehotel.co.uk
Dir Near Victoria station

Located a short walk from Victoria station, the Central House offers sound accommodation. Bedroom sizes vary, and each room has a compact modular shower room. A self-service continental breakfast is offered in the lower ground-floor dining room.

Facilities 54 en suite (4 fmly) TVB tea/coffee Direct dial from bedrooms ✖ Lift Cen ht TVL

See advertisement on page 345

♦♦ 🅰

The Dover - Victoria

Plan 2-C1

42-44 Belgrave Rd, Victoria SW1V 1RG
☎ 020 7821 9085 ▤ 020 7834 6425
e-mail reception@dover-hotel.co.uk
web www.dover-hotel.co.uk
Dir 300yds SE of Victoria station on A3213

Facilities 33 rms (29 en suite) (8 fmly) (5 GF) STV TVB tea/coffee Direct dial from bedrooms ✖ Cen ht No coaches **Prices** S £50-£70; D £55-£80 **LB**

♦♦ 🅰

Stanley House Hotel

Plan 2-C1

19-21 Belgrave Rd, Victoria SW1V 1RB
☎ 020 7834 5042 & 7834 7292 ▤ 020 7834 8439
e-mail cmahotel@aol.com
web www.londonbudgethotels.co.uk
Dir Near Victoria station

Facilities 44 rms (32 en suite) (7 fmly) (8 GF) ⊘ in dining room TVB Direct dial from bedrooms ✖ Cen ht TVL No children 5yrs **Prices** S £35-£45; D £45-£55✳ **LB**

🅤

Hamilton House

Plan 2-C1

60-64 Warwick Way SW1V 1SA
☎ 020 7821 7113 ▤ 020 7630 0806
e-mail info@hamiltonhousehotel.com
web www.hamiltonhousehotel.com

At the time of going to press the rating for this establishment had not been confirmed. Please check the AA website www.theAA.com for up-to-date information.

Facilities 50 en suite (4 fmly) (4 GF) ⊘ in 20 bedrooms ⊘ in dining room ⊘ in lounges STV TVB tea/coffee Direct dial from bedrooms ✖ Lift Cen ht TVL No coaches **Prices** S £59-£69; D £69-£89✳

SW3

Premier Collection

♦♦♦♦♦ 🗎 🖶

L'Hotel

Plan 2-B2

28 Basil St, Knightsbridge SW3 1AS
☎ 020 7589 6286 ▤ 020 7823 7826
e-mail isabel@lhotel.co.uk
Dir W along A4, turn left after Harrods onto Hans Rd, at end turn left onto Basil St

This stylish property offers friendly, attentive service a stone's throw from Harrods in Knightsbridge. Individually styled bedrooms, many with Nina Campbell fabrics on the walls, are crammed with thoughtful extras. The basement bar-restaurant, popular with locals, is the hub of the operation, serving memorable breakfasts and imaginative lunch and dinners.

Facilities 12 en suite (2 fmly) (1 GF) ⊘ in bedrooms STV TVB tea/coffee Direct dial from bedrooms Licensed Lift Cen ht No coaches Preferential rates at nearby gym/spa & pool Dinner Last d 9.30pm

♦♦♦♦

The Claverley Hotel

Plan 2-B3

13-14 Beaufort Gdns, Knightsbridge SW3 1PS
☎ 020 7589 8541 ▤ 020 7584 3410
e-mail reservations@claverleyhotel.co.uk
web www.claverleyhotel.co.uk
Dir Off A4 Brompton Rd, 350yds SW of Knightsbridge tube station

This stylish property is hidden away in a quiet, leafy Knightsbridge cul-de-sac, a short walk from Harrods and the V&A. The bedrooms are individually designed and some have four-poster beds. Public areas include a delightful reading room where you can enjoy tea and coffee, and impressive breakfasts are served in the dining room.

Facilities 29 rms (26 en suite) (3 pri facs) (7 fmly) (2 GF) ⊘ in bedrooms ⊘ in dining room STV TVB Direct dial from bedrooms ✖ Lift Cen ht **Prices** S £84-£99; D £126-£149✳ **LB Conf** Max 40 Thtr 30 Class 14

SW5

★★★★ Guest House

The Mayflower Hotel
Plan 1-D3

26-28 Trebovir Rd SW5 9NJ
☎ 020 7370 0991 📠 020 7370 0994
e-mail info@mayflower-group.co.uk
web www.mayflowerhotel.co.uk
Dir *From Earls Court tube station left onto Trebovir Rd, premises on left*

This smart property is a short walk from Earls Court, and close to Olympia and west London's museums and attractions. The stylish, individually designed bedrooms vary in size, are extremely well equipped and have modern en suites. There is a stylish lounge and breakfast is served in the airy dining room.

Facilities 47 en suite (4 fmly) (5 GF) ⊗ STV TVB tea/coffee Direct dial from bedrooms ✈ Lift Cen ht **Conf** Max 25 Class 25 Board 25 **Parking** 4

See advertisement on this page

♦♦♦♦ 🅰

Kensington International Inn
Plan 1-D3

4 Templeton Pl SW5 9LZ
☎ 020 7370 4333 📠 020 7244 7873
e-mail hotel@kensingtoninternationalinn.com
web www.kensingtoninternationalinn.com
Dir *At Earls Court off A4 onto A3020, 300yds right onto Trebovir Rd & right*

Facilities 58 en suite (3 fmly) (2 GF) ⊗ in 20 bedrooms STV TVB tea/coffee Direct dial from bedrooms Licensed Lift Cen ht TVL **Conf** Max 30 Thtr 20 Class 30 Board 20

♦♦♦

Henley House Hotel
Plan 1-D3

30 Barkston Gdns, Earls Court SW5 0EN
☎ 020 7370 4111 📠 020 7370 0026
e-mail reservations@henleyhousehotel.com
web www.henleyhousehotel.com
Dir *A4 Cromwell Rd S onto A3220 Earls Court Rd, left onto Barkston Gardens after tube station*

Situated close to Earls Court in the relative peace of Barkston Gardens, this Victorian house has been carefully renovated to provide modern comforts. There is a pleasant foyer-lounge and breakfast is served in a conservatory-style dining room. The well-equipped bedrooms have been refurbished with style.

Facilities 21 en suite (1 fmly) (1 GF) ⊗ STV TVB tea/coffee Direct dial from bedrooms ✈ Lift Cen ht No coaches **Prices** S £59-£69; D £65-£89

England

SW5 continued

England

♦♦♦

My Place Hotel

Plan 1-D3

1-3 Trebovir Rd, Earls Court SW5 9LS
☎ 020 7373 0833 🖷 020 7373 9998
e-mail info@myplacehotel.co.uk
web www.myplacehotel.co.uk
Dir A4 West Cromwell Rd onto Earls Court Rd, 3rd right

This Victorian house is in a quiet residential street close to Earls Court station with easy access to the West End. The smart bedrooms vary in size and have an extremely good range of modern facilities. Breakfast is served in the dining room overlooking a spacious garden. Free entry to the on-site nightclub is included.

Facilities 50 en suite (6 fmly) ⊗ in 9 bedrooms ⊗ in dining room STV TVB Direct dial from bedrooms ✗ Licensed Lift Cen ht Night Club **Prices** S £49-£100; D £69-£135 **LB Conf** Max 100 Thtr 100 Class 100 Board 20 Del from £115 ✳

♦♦♦

Rushmore Hotel

Plan 1-D3

11 Trebovir Rd, Earls Court SW5 9LS
☎ 020 7370 3839 & 7370 6505 🖷 020 7370 0274
e-mail rushmore-reservations@london.com
Dir A4 S onto A3220 Earls Court Rd, 4th right

This smart establishment is close to the exhibition halls and just a stroll from the tube station. The stylish bedrooms have individual themes and some are suitable for families, and all have shower rooms en suite. A continental buffet breakfast is served in the modern conservatory.

Facilities 22 en suite (4 fmly) (4 GF) ⊗ in 4 bedrooms ⊗ in dining room ⊗ in lounges STV TVB tea/coffee Direct dial from bedrooms ✗ Cen ht TVL **Prices** S £59-£69; D £79-£89✳ **Conf** Max 24

SW7

♦♦♦♦

The Gallery

Plan 2-A1

8-10 Queensberry Pl, South Kensington SW7 2EA
☎ 020 7915 0000 🖷 020 7915 4400
e-mail reservations@eeh.co.uk
web www.eeh.co.uk
Dir Off A4 Cromwell Rd opp Natural History Museum, near South Kensington tube station

This stylish property, close to Kensington and Knightsbridge, offers friendly hospitality, attentive service and sumptuous bedrooms, some with a private terrace. Public areas include a choice of lounges (one with Internet access) and an elegant bar. There is an option of English or continental breakfast, and 24-hour room service is available.

Facilities 36 en suite ⊗ in dining room ⊗ in 1 lounge STV TVB tea/coffee Direct dial from bedrooms ✗ Licensed Lift Cen ht No coaches **Conf** Max 40 Thtr 40 Board 30

♦♦♦♦

The Gainsborough
Plan 2-A1

7-11 Queensberry Pl, South Kensington SW7 2DL
☎ 020 7957 0000 📠 020 7957 0001
e-mail reservations@eeh.co.uk
web www.eeh.co.uk
Dir *Off A4 Cromwell Rd opp Natural History Museum, near South Kensington tube station*

This smart Georgian house is in a quiet street near the South Kensington museums. Bedrooms are individually designed with fine fabrics, quality furnishings and coordinated colours. A choice of breakfasts is offered in the attractive dining room. There is also a small lounge and 24-hour room service is available.

Facilities 48 en suite (5 fmly) ⊗ in dining room STV TVB tea/coffee Direct dial from bedrooms ✖ Licensed Lift Cen ht No coaches
Conf Max 40 Class 40 Board 30

SW11

♦♦♦ 🅰

The Lavender Guest House
Plan 1-E3

18 Lavender Sweep SW11 1HA
☎ 020 7585 2767 & 7223 1973 📠 020 7924 6274
Facilities 8 en suite (1 fmly) (2 GF) ⊗ TVB tea/coffee Direct dial from bedrooms ✖ Cen ht TVL ♿ **Notes** 🚭

SW14

♦♦♦♦ 🏵🏵 🍴

The Victoria
Plan 1-C3

10 West Temple Sheen SW14 7RT
☎ 020 8876 4238 📠 020 8878 3464
e-mail bookings@thevictoria.net
web www.thevictoria.net
Dir *Off Upper Richmond Rd onto Temple Sheen Rd, left onto West Temple Sheen*

The Victoria is in a quiet residential area close to Sheen high street. Bedrooms are refreshingly simple, stylish and thoughtfully equipped with a host of extras, including PCs with free broadband Internet access. Public areas consist of a small contemporary seating area, a modern bar, and a gastro pub that serves imaginative European food.

Facilities 7 en suite (2 fmly) (3 GF) ⊗ in bedrooms ⊗ in dining room TVB tea/coffee Direct dial from bedrooms ✖ Licensed Cen ht No coaches Dinner Last d 9.45pm **Prices** D £108.50✱ **Parking** 14
Notes rs 4 days over Xmas

SW19

♦♦♦

Trochee Hotel
Plan 1-D2

52 Ridgway Pl, Wimbledon SW19 4SW
☎ 020 8946 9425 📠 020 8946 9400
e-mail reservations@hotelsinwimbledon.com
Dir *From A219, 1.5m along Parkside onto Wimbledon Hill Rd, right onto Worple Rd, 3rd right*

The friendly Trochee is in a quiet residential area within walking distance of the town centre and Wimbledon station. Bedrooms are traditionally furnished and a cooked breakfast is served at individual tables in the breakfast room. Parking is available.

Facilities 18 rms (9 en suite) (2 fmly) (4 GF) ⊗ in 4 bedrooms ⊗ in dining room ⊗ in lounges TVB tea/coffee ✖ Cen ht TVL
Parking 7

W1

◆◆◆◆

Hart House Hotel
Plan 2-B4

51 Gloucester Pl, Portman Sq W1U 8JF
☎ 020 7935 2288 ▤ 020 7935 8516
e-mail reservations@harthouse.co.uk
web www.harthouse.co.uk
Dir *Off Oxford St behind Selfridges, near Baker St or Marble Arch tube stations*

This elegant Georgian house is only a short walk from Oxford St and Madame Tussaud's. Bedrooms and public areas are stylishly furnished and have been carefully restored to retain the house's original character. A cooked English breakfast is served in the stylish dining room.

Facilities 16 en suite (4 fmly) (4 GF) ⊗ TVB tea/coffee Direct dial from bedrooms ✕ Cen ht TVL No coaches **Prices** S £65-£75; D £89-£110
See advertisement on page 349

◆◆◆◆

St George Hotel
Plan 2-B4

49 Gloucester Pl W1U 8JE
☎ 020 7486 8586 & 7486 6567 ▤ 020 7486 6567
e-mail reservations@stgeorge-hotel.net
Dir *Off Marylebone Rd, between Marble Arch & Baker St tube stations*

This attractive, Grade II listed house is in the heart of the West End near Oxford St. Bedrooms are furnished to a high standard and feature excellent facilities, including modem points, safes, hairdryers and minifridges. There is a smart breakfast room and the friendly staff give a very warm welcome.

Facilities 19 en suite (3 fmly) (3 GF) ⊗ in bedrooms ⊗ in dining room ⊗ in 1 lounge STV TVB tea/coffee Direct dial from bedrooms ✕ Cen ht TVL No coaches **Prices** S £60-£90; D £65-£150 LB **Conf** Max 20

◆◆◆

Georgian Hotel
Plan 2-B4

87 Gloucester Pl, Baker St W1U 6JF
☎ 020 7486 3151 ▤ 020 7486 7535
e-mail georgianhotel@btconnect.com
web www.londoncentralhotel.com
Dir *Nr Baker St tube station*

This establishment is a short walk from a tube station and local restaurants, and is well located for London's major attractions.

Bedrooms vary in size, are well equipped for leisure and business, and include some family rooms. A continental buffet breakfast is served in the cosy dinning room.

Facilities 19 rms (11 en suite) (8 pri facs) (4 fmly) (3 GF) ⊗ in 16 bedrooms ⊗ in dining room TVB tea/coffee Direct dial from bedrooms ✕ Lift Cen ht No children 5yrs No coaches **Prices** S £75-£80; D £90-£95✷

◆◆◆

Mermaid Suite Hotel
Plan 2-C4

3-4 Blenheim St W1S 1LA
☎ 020 7629 1875 ▤ 020 7499 9475
e-mail info@mermaidsuite.com
Dir *Off New Bond St near Bond St tube station*

Located just off Oxford St, the Mermaid Suite provides excellent accommodation in one of London's best-known shopping areas. Bedrooms, on several floors, are all smartly presented and well equipped. There is also a popular Italian restaurant, which is open all day.

Facilities 30 rms (29 en suite) (4 fmly) ⊗ in 3 bedrooms STV TVB tea/coffee Direct dial from bedrooms ✕ Licensed Cen ht Dinner Last d 10pm

◆◆◆

The Regency Hotel
Plan 2-C4

19 Nottingham Pl W1U 5LQ
☎ 020 7486 5347 ▤ 020 7224 6057
e-mail enquiries@regencyhotelwestend.co.uk
web www.regencyhotelwestend.co.uk
Dir *A501 Marylebone Rd S onto Baker St, left onto Paddington St, left onto Nottingham Place*

The Regency is a converted mansion close to Baker St tube station, Madame Tussaud's, West End shops and Harley St. Bedrooms are well equipped and some rooms are suitable for families. Breakfast is served in the brightly appointed basement breakfast room.

Facilities 20 en suite (2 fmly) ⊗ in 4 bedrooms ⊗ in dining room ⊗ in lounges STV TVB tea/coffee Direct dial from bedrooms ✕ Lift Cen ht TVL Dinner Last d 7pm **Prices** S £60-£68; D £75-£89 LB

◆◆ 🅰

Bentinck House
Plan 2-C4

20 Bentinck St W1U 2EU
☎ 020 7935 9141 ▤ 020 7224 5903
e-mail reception@bentinck-househotel.co.uk
Dir *From Bond St tube station on Oxford St onto Marylebone Ln, cross Wigmore St, Bentinck St on right*

Facilities 17 rms (12 en suite) (5 fmly) (3 GF) ⊗ in 3 bedrooms ⊗ in dining room STV TVB Direct dial from bedrooms Cen ht

continued

England

♦♦ **A**

Marble Arch Inn

Plan 2-B3

49-50 Upper Berkeley St, Marble Arch W1H 5QR
☎ 020 7723 7888 📠 020 7723 6060
e-mail sales@marblearch-inn.co.uk
web www.marblearch-inn.co.uk
Dir *Near Marble Arch rdbt. A5 N on Edgware Rd, 3rd right*

Facilities 29 rms (23 en suite) (9 fmly) (7 GF) STV TVB tea/coffee
Direct dial from bedrooms ✈ Cen ht No coaches **Prices** S £35-£85;
D £35-£85

W2

★★★★ Bed & Breakfast

Shaftesbury Hyde Park Paddington

Plan 2-A4

78-82 Westbourne Terrace, Paddington W2 6QA ☎ 020
7262 4521 📠 020 7262 7610
e-mail reservations@londonpremierhotels.co.uk
Dir *Off A40 onto Lancaster Ter, at crossing left onto slip road*

This attractive London house has a central location within easy reach
of attractions and high street shops. The en suite bedrooms and
public areas have a smart contemporary feel. While rooms vary in
size, they have useful facilities such as free Internet access, minifridges
and irons.

Facilities 119 en suite (10 fmly) (16 GF) ⊗ in 50 bedrooms ⊗ in area
of dining room STV TVB tea/coffee Direct dial from bedrooms ✈
Licensed Lift Cen ht **Prices** S £89-£199; D £89-£199✳ **Parking** 12

★★★★ Guest House

The New Linden

Plan 1-D4

59 Leinster Sq, Notting Hill W2 4PS
☎ 020 7221 4321 📠 020 7727 3156
e-mail newlindenhotel@mayflower-group.co.uk
Dir *Off A402 Bayswater Rd*

The friendly New Linden has a good location north of Kensington
Gardens. Its stylish en suite bedrooms are richly furnished, and
thoughtfully equipped with CD players and safes; the spacious feature
rooms have seating areas and DVD players. A comprehensive
continental breakfast is served in the attractive dining room.

Facilities 52 en suite ⊗ in 20 bedrooms ⊗ in dining room STV TVB
tea/coffee Direct dial from bedrooms ✈ Lift Cen ht
See advertisement on this page

♦♦♦♦

Best Western Mornington Hotel

Plan 2-A3

12 Lancaster Gate W2 3LG
☎ 020 7262 7361 📠 020 7706 1028
e-mail london@mornington.co.uk
Dir *N of Hyde Park, off A402 Bayswater Rd*

This fine Victorian building is located in a quiet road close to Lancaster
Gate station for easy access to the West End. The bedrooms have
been upgraded to provide stylish accommodation. There is a lounge-
bar and an attractive dining room where an extensive Scandinavian-
style breakfast is served.

Facilities 66 en suite (9 fmly) (2 GF) ⊗ in 33 bedrooms ⊗ in dining
room STV TVB tea/coffee Direct dial from bedrooms Licensed Lift
Cen ht **Conf** Max 14 Thtr 20 Class 14 Board 14

England

W2 continued

◆◆◆◆
Byron Hotel
Plan 2-A3

36-38 Queensborough Ter W2 3SH
☎ 020 7243 0987 ▤ 020 7792 1957
e-mail byron@capricornhotels.co.uk
web www.byronhotel.co.uk
Dir *Off Bayswater Rd near Queensway tube station*

The charming terrace house has been thoughtfully restored to retain original features. Bedrooms are carefully decorated, and thoughtfully equipped with air conditioning, trouser presses and safes. Breakfast is served in the attractive dining room and there is an elegant lounge and a smart conservatory.

Facilities 45 en suite (5 fmly) ⊘ in dining room STV TVB tea/coffee Direct dial from bedrooms ✕ Licensed Lift Cen ht TVL
Prices S £65-£95; D £70-£150✳ LB

◆◆◆◆
The Duke of Leinster
Plan 2-A3

20 Leinster Gdns W2 3AN
☎ 020 7298 3850 ▤ 020 7298 3855
e-mail dukeofleinsterhotel@crystalhotels.co.uk
Dir *Off A402 Bayswater Rd onto Leinster Ter. 350yds NE of Bayswater & Queensway tube stations*

This smart, well-appointed property is close to Kensington Gardens and within easy reach of Paddington station. Decor is stylish throughout and bedrooms have a host of thoughtful extras including minibars and safes. Breakfast is served in the modern, airy basement dining room.

Facilities 36 en suite (10 fmly) (5 GF) ⊘ in bedrooms ⊘ in dining room STV TVB tea/coffee Direct dial from bedrooms Lift Cen ht TVL No coaches **Prices** S £59-£90; D £75-£120; (room only) **Conf** Max 16 Thtr 14 Class 12 Board 10 Del from £119 ✳

◆◆◆◆
Hyde Park Radnor Hotel
Plan 2-A5

7-9 Sussex Pl, Hyde Pk W2 2SX
☎ 020 7723 5969 ▤ 020 7262 8955
e-mail hydeparkradnor@btconnect.com
web www.hydeparkradnor.com
Dir *Off A402 Bayswater Rd onto Lancaster Ter & Sussex Gardens, right onto Sussex Place*

This smart property is within walking distance of Paddington station and close to the central attractions. The smart bedrooms are brightly
continued

appointed, well equipped and have modern en suites. A cooked English breakfast is served in the lower ground-floor dining room.
Facilities 36 en suite (10 fmly) (5 GF) ⊘ in 20 bedrooms ⊘ in dining room ⊘ in lounges STV TVB tea/coffee Direct dial from bedrooms ✕ Lift Cen ht TVL **Parking** 2

◆◆◆◆
Kyriad Princes Square Hotel
Plan 2-A3

23-25 Prince's Sq, off Ilchester Gdns, Bayswater W2 4NJ
☎ 020 7229 9876 ▤ 020 7229 4664
e-mail info@princessquarehotel.co.uk
Dir *From Queensway/Bayswater tube stations N onto Queensway, left onto Portchester Gardens & Princes Sq*

This fine building is in a quiet road close to tube stations for easy access to the West End. The comfortable bedrooms provide stylish accommodation, and there is a small bar and an attractive dining room where a continental breakfast is served.

Facilities 50 en suite (3 fmly) (6 GF) ⊘ in bedrooms ⊘ in dining room STV TVB tea/coffee Direct dial from bedrooms ✕ Licensed Lift Cen ht TVL

◆◆◆◆
Norfolk Plaza Hotel
Plan 2-A4

29/33 Norfolk Sq, Paddington W2 1RX
☎ 020 7723 0792 ▤ 020 7224 8770
e-mail teri@norfolkplazahotel.co.uk
web www.norfolkplazahotel.co.uk
Dir *300yds SE from Paddington station via London St*

This popular establishment is in a quiet residential square in the heart of Paddington, with good access to the West End. The thoughtfully furnished bedrooms are particularly well equipped and include a number of split-level suites. Public areas include a smart bar and lounge, and an attractive restaurant where breakfast is served.

Facilities 87 en suite (6 fmly) (8 GF) ⊘ in 10 bedrooms ⊘ in dining room ⊘ in 1 lounge STV TVB tea/coffee Direct dial from bedrooms ✕ Licensed Lift Cen ht TVL Dinner Last d 11pm **Prices** S £95-£105; D £120-£130 **Conf** Thtr 15 Board 10

◆◆◆◆
Quality Hotel Paddington
Plan 2-A3

8-14 Talbot Sq W2 1TS
☎ 020 7262 6699 ▤ 020 7723 3233
e-mail quality-p@lth-hotels.com
Dir *SE of Paddington station off Sussex Gardens*

The well-presented property is convenient for Hyde Park and Marble Arch. The modern bedrooms are furnished to a good standard and the executive rooms are particularly impressive. Public areas include a compact but stylish bar and lounge, and a basement restaurant where hearty breakfasts are served.

Facilities 75 en suite (8 fmly) (8 GF) ⊘ in 10 bedrooms ⊘ in dining room STV TVB tea/coffee Direct dial from bedrooms ✕ Licensed Lift Cen ht TVL

◆◆◆◆ 🅰

Darlington Hyde Park
Plan 2-A4

111-117 Sussex Gdns, Paddington W2 2RU
☎ 020 7460 8800 📠 020 7460 8828
e-mail darlinghp@aol.com
web www.darlingtonhotel.com
Dir *Situated midway along Sussex Gardens, between Lancaster Gate and Edgeware Rd.*

Facilities 40 en suite (3 fmly) (4 GF) ⊛ TVB tea/coffee ✖ Licensed Lift Cen ht **Conf** Thtr 8 Board 4 **Notes** Closed 24-28 Dec

◆◆◆

Admiral Hotel
Plan 2-A3

143 Sussex Gdns, Hyde Pk W2 2RY
☎ 020 7723 7309 📠 020 7723 8731

The Admiral is a short walk from Paddington station and is convenient for Hyde Park and the West End. The smart bedrooms are enhanced with attractive artworks, and a full English breakfast is provided.

Facilities 21 en suite (12 fmly) (2 GF) ⊛ TVB tea/coffee Direct dial from bedrooms ✖ Cen ht TVL No coaches Dinner Last d 7pm **Prices** S £40-£65; D £55-£85 ✳ **Conf** Max 30 Class 20 Del from £35 ✳ **Parking** available

◆◆◆

Averard Hotel
Plan 2-A3

10 Lancaster Gate W2 3LH
☎ 020 7723 8877 📠 020 7706 0860
e-mail sales@averard.com
Dir *Opp Hyde Park, near Lancaster Gate tube station*

Quietly located close to Kensington Gardens, this Edwardian property retains much original charm. The individually designed bedrooms are well equipped, and many are spacious and suitable for families. There is a comfortable lounge, a bar, and a stylish breakfast room.

Facilities 52 en suite (5 fmly) (2 GF) TVB Direct dial from bedrooms Licensed Lift Cen ht **Prices** S £50-£75; D £70-£100✳ **LB** **Notes** Closed 22-30 Dec

◆◆◆

Camelot House Hotel
Plan 2-A4

18-20 Sussex Gdns, Marble Arch W2 1UL
☎ 020 7723 2219 📠 020 7402 3412
Dir *Off A402 Bayswater Rd onto Lancaster Ter & Sussex Gardens*

Convenient for Oxford St and Paddington, the house has a variety of room types, many en suite. Rooms at the back of the house are more quiet. Helpful and friendly staff are on duty 24 hours a day.

Facilities 26 rms (21 en suite) (3 fmly) (5 GF) ⊛ in 20 bedrooms ⊛ in dining room TVB tea/coffee Direct dial from bedrooms ✖ Cen ht **Parking** 9

◆◆◆

Mitre House Hotel
Plan 2-A4

178-184 Sussex Gdns, Hyde Pk W2 1TU
☎ 020 7723 8040 📠 020 7402 0990
e-mail reservations@mitrehousehotel.com
web www.mitrehousehotel.com
Dir *Off A402 Bayswater Rd onto Lancaster Ter & Sussex Gardens*

This family-run guest house offers a warm welcome and attentive service. It is close to Paddington station and near the West End and major attractions. The well-appointed bedrooms include a number of family suites and there is a lounge bar. A car park is available.

Facilities 70 rms (64 en suite) (3 fmly) (6 GF) ⊛ in 10 bedrooms ⊛ in dining room STV TVB Direct dial from bedrooms ✖ Licensed Lift Cen ht TVL No coaches **Parking** 25

See advertisement under Preliminary Section

◆◆◆

Park Lodge Hotel
Plan 2-A3

73 Queensborough Ter, Bayswater W2 3SU
☎ 020 7229 6424 📠 020 7221 4772
e-mail info@hotelparklodge.com
Dir *Off Bayswater Rd near Queensway tube station*

A short walk from Kensington Gardens and fashionable Queensway, the former house has been converted to provide good, practically equipped bedrooms with bathrooms and power showers. A cooked English breakfast is served in the cosy basement dining room.

Facilities 29 en suite (3 fmly) (3 GF) ⊛ in 5 bedrooms ⊛ in dining room ⊛ in lounges STV TVB tea/coffee Direct dial from bedrooms ✖ Lift Cen ht Last d noon

W2 continued

♦♦♦
Parkwood Hotel
Plan 2-B3

4 Stanhope Pl, Marble Arch W2 2HB
☎ 020 7402 2241 🖷 020 7402 1574
e-mail reception@parkwoodhotel.com
web www.parkwoodhotel.com
Dir *Near Marble Arch tube station*

Located in a quiet residential street next to Marble Arch and Oxford St, the friendly Parkwood provides a central base for budget-conscious shoppers and tourists. Family rooms are available, and a freshly cooked breakfast is served in the attractive basement dining room.

Facilities 16 rms (12 en suite) (1 fmly) (2 GF) 🚫 in bedrooms 🚫 in dining room STV TVB tea/coffee Direct dial from bedrooms ✖ Cen ht TVL No coaches

See advertisement on opposite page

♦♦♦ 🅰
Barry House
Plan 2-A4

12 Sussex Pl, Hyde Pk W2 2TP
☎ 020 7723 7340 & 0845 126 7856 🖷 020 7723 9775
e-mail hotel@barryhouse.co.uk
web www.barryhouse.co.uk
Dir *300yds SE of Paddington station*

Facilities 18 rms (15 en suite) (5 fmly) (2 GF) 🚫 in 6 bedrooms 🚫 in dining room 🚫 in lounges STV TVB tea/coffee Direct dial from bedrooms ✖ Cen ht No coaches **Prices** S £39-£55; D £70-£89✲

♦♦♦ 🅰
Prince William Hotel
Plan 2-A3

42-44 Gloucester Ter W2 3DA
☎ 020 7724 7414 🖷 020 7706 2411
e-mail info@princewilliamhotel.co.uk
web www.princewilliamhotel.co.uk
Facilities 47 rms (43 en suite) (4 GF) 🚫 in 8 bedrooms 🚫 in dining room TVB tea/coffee Direct dial from bedrooms ✖ Lift Cen ht

W6

♦♦
Hotel Orlando
Plan 1-D3

83 Shepherds Bush Rd W6 7LR
☎ 020 7603 4890 🖷 020 7603 4890
e-mail hotelorlando@btconnect.com
web www.hotelorlando.co.uk
Dir *On A219 between Hammersmith & Shepherd's Bush tube stations*

The Orlando is part of a Victorian terrace within easy walking distance of tube stations. Bedrooms, varying in size and style, are soundly furnished and well maintained. Breakfast is served at individual tables in the smart basement dining room.

Facilities 14 en suite (3 fmly) 🚫 TVB tea/coffee Direct dial from bedrooms ✖ Cen ht

W11

♦♦♦
The Gate Hotel
Plan 1-D4

6 Portobello Rd W11 3DG
☎ 020 7221 0707 🖷 020 7221 9128
e-mail bookings@gatehotel.com
web www.gatehotel.com
Dir *From Notting Hill Gate tube station down Pembridge Rd, onto Portobello Rd, premises on right*

The Gate has an enviable position on the famous Portobello Rd, a short walk from South Kensington. Bedrooms vary in size but all have DVD players and minibars. A continental breakfast is served to your room.

Facilities 7 en suite (1 fmly) (1 GF) STV TVB tea/coffee Direct dial from bedrooms ✖ Cen ht No coaches

W14

♦♦♦♦
Avonmore Hotel
Plan 1-D3

66 Avonmore Rd W14 8RS
☎ 020 7603 4296 🖷 020 7603 4035
e-mail reservations@avonmorehotel.co.uk
web www.avonmorehotel.co.uk
Dir *Off Hammersmith Rd opp Olympia Exhibition Centre*

Within walking distance of Olympia and easy reach of central London, this smart guest house offers friendly and attentive service. Bedrooms are attractively coordinated and extremely well equipped. A cooked breakfast is served in the pretty dining room which doubles as a bar area.

continued

Facilities 9 rms (7 en suite) (3 fmly) (2 GF) ⊗ in 2 bedrooms ⊗ in dining room TVB tea/coffee Direct dial from bedrooms ✈ Licensed Cen ht TVL

WC1

◆◆◆

Euro Hotel
Plan 2-D5

51-53 Cartwright Gdns, Russell Sq WC1H 9EL
☎ 020 7387 4321 📠 020 7383 5044
e-mail reception@eurohotel.co.uk
web www.eurohotel.co.uk
Dir Off Euston Rd onto Judd St, right onto Leigh St & Cartwright Gardens. Near Euston tube station

Please note that this establishment has recently changed hands. This friendly guest house is in a leafy Georgian crescent only a short walk from Russell Sq tube station with its direct link to Heathrow. Bedrooms are well equipped and many have bathrooms en suite. Breakfast is served at individual tables in the attractive dining room.

Facilities 31 rms (20 en suite) (3 pri facs) (9 fmly) (4 GF) ⊗ in dining room ⊗ in lounges STV TVB tea/coffee Direct dial from bedrooms ✈ Cen ht ⚲ Prices S £49-£75; D £69-£95✳

◆◆◆

The George Hotel
Plan 2-D5

58-60 Cartwright Gdns WC1H 9EL
☎ 020 7387 8777 📠 020 7387 8666
e-mail ghotel@aol.com
web www.georgehotel.com
Dir From St Pancras 2nd left onto Marchmont St & 1st left onto Cartwright Gardens

The George is within walking distance of Russell Sq and the tube, and convenient for London's central attractions. The brightly appointed bedrooms vary in size, many have en suites, and some rooms are suitable for families. A substantial breakfast is served in the attractive ground-floor dining room.

Facilities 40 rms (14 en suite) (14 fmly) (4 GF) ⊗ in dining room STV TVB tea/coffee Direct dial from bedrooms ✈ Cen ht TVL No coaches ⚲ Free Internet access Prices S £35.50-£70; D £49.50-£89

◆◆◆

Mentone Hotel
Plan 2-D5

54-56 Cartwright Gdns, Bloomsbury WC1H 9EL
☎ 020 7387 3927 & 7388 4671 📠 020 7388 4671
e-mail bookings@mentonehotel.com
web www.mentonehotel.com
Dir Between Euston Rd & Russell Sq

Overlooking pleasant gardens and tennis courts, this Georgian terrace is within easy reach of many central London attractions. Good-value accommodation is provided in thoughtfully equipped rooms. Free Internet access is provided in the reception area, and traditional breakfasts are served in the smart dining room.

Facilities 43 en suite (14 fmly) ⊗ in dining room TVB tea/coffee Direct dial from bedrooms ✈ Lift ⚲ Prices S £49-£60✳ LB

◆◆ 🅰

Guilford House Hotel
Plan 2-D5

6 Guilford St WC1N 1DR
☎ 020 7430 2504 📠 020 7430 0697
e-mail guilford-hotel@lineone.net
Dir A40, pass Marylebone flyover, under Euston underpass. At Kings Cross follow Gray Inn Rd signs. Guilford St at junct with Gray Inn Rd

Facilities 14 en suite (5 fmly) (2 GF) ⊗ in 2 bedrooms ⊗ in dining room TVB tea/coffee Direct dial from bedrooms ✈ Cen ht
Prices S £49-£54; D £64-£69

England

LIVERPOOL
MAP 15 SJ39

◆◆◆

Aachen
91 Mount Pleasant L3 5TB
☎ 0151 709 3477 & 709 3633 🖷 0151 709 1126
e-mail enquiries@aachenhotel.co.uk
web www.aachenhotel.co.uk
Dir Signs for city centre & Mount Pleasant car park

The friendly Aachen is within easy walking distance of the cathedrals, university and the city centre. Its attractive bedrooms are extremely well equipped for business and leisure, and there is a cosy lounge bar.

Facilities 17 rms (11 en suite) (6 fmly) (3 GF) ⊗ in 10 bedrooms ⊗ in dining room STV TVB tea/coffee Direct dial from bedrooms ✖ Licensed Cen ht TVL Dinner Last d 8.30pm **Prices** S £32-£45; D £50-£65 **LB Parking** 2 **Notes** Closed 22 Dec-2 Jan

◆◆◆ **A**

Somersby ◇
100 Green Ln, Allerton L18 2ER
☎ 0151 722 7549 🖷 0151 722 7549
Dir 4m SE of city centre. M62 junct 4 onto A5058, 2m left onto A562, 2nd right onto Green Ln

Facilities 4 rms (2 en suite) (1 fmly) (1 GF) ⊗ in bedrooms TVB tea/coffee Cen ht TVL No coaches **Prices** S £30; D £55 **Parking** 4 **Notes** ⊛

MAGHULL
MAP 15 SD30

◆◆◆◆ **A**

Goose Meadow B&B
Gore House Farm, Acres Ln L31 4EX ☎ 0151 526 0519
e-mail edwards@goosemeadow.co.uk
Dir A5147 onto B5195 to Formby. 1m left onto Acres Ln, B&B 1m on right

Facilities 2 en suite (1 fmly) (1 GF) ⊗ TVB tea/coffee ✖ Cen ht TVL No children 5yrs No coaches Fishing **Prices** S £47; D £60-£66 **LB Parking** 5

SOUTHPORT
MAP 15 SD31

◆◆◆◆◆

Cambridge Town House Hotel
4 Cambridge Rd PR9 9NG
☎ 01704 538372 🖷 01704 547183
e-mail info@cambridgehousehotel.co.uk
Dir A565 N from town centre, over 2 rdbts

Please note that this establishment has recently changed hands. This delightful house is in a peaceful location close to Hesketh Park, a short drive from Lord St. The spacious, individually styled bedrooms, including a luxurious honeymoon suite, are furnished to a very high standard. Stylish public areas include a lounge, a cosy bar and a dining room.

Facilities 16 en suite (2 fmly) ⊗ in bedrooms ⊗ in dining room ⊗ in lounges TVB tea/coffee Direct dial from bedrooms ✖ Licensed Cen ht No coaches Dinner Last d 8pm **LB Conf** Max 40 **Parking** 20

◆◆◆◆ 🍴

Bay Tree House B & B
No1 Irving St, Marine Gate PR9 0HD
☎ 01704 510555 🖷 01704 510551
e-mail baytreehouseuk@aol.com
web www.baytreehousesouthport.co.uk
Dir Off Leicester St

A warm welcome is assured at this immaculate house, located a short walk from the promenade and central attractions. Bedrooms are equipped with a wealth of thoughtful extras, and delicious imaginative breakfasts are served in an attractive dining room overlooking the pretty front patio garden.

Facilities 6 en suite (2 fmly) ⊗ TVB tea/coffee Direct dial from bedrooms Cen ht No coaches Dinner Last d 10am **Prices** S £39.50-£55; D £60-£99 **LB Parking** 2 **Notes** Closed 14 Dec-1 Feb
See advertisement on opposite page

◆◆◆◆

Baytrees Hotel ◇
4 Queens Rd PR9 9HN ☎ 01704 536513 🖷 01704 536513
e-mail stay@baytreeshotel.freeserve.co.uk
Dir From B565 Lord St towards fire station, right at rdbt onto Manchester Rd, left at lights, 200yds on right

Located a short walk from Lord St, this elegant late Victorian house has been refurbished to provide thoughtfully furnished bedrooms with smart
continued

modern bathrooms en suite. Breakfast is served in the attractive dining room overlooking the pretty rear garden, and a lounge is also available.

Facilities 12 en suite (5 fmly) (2 GF) ⊗ TVB tea/coffee ✖ Cen ht TVL **Prices** S £25.29-£29.50; D £45.43-£53✶ **Parking** 11 **Notes** Closed Xmas

◆◆◆◆

Bowden Lodge Hotel

18 Albert Rd PR9 0LE ☎ 01704 543531 ▤ 01704 539112
e-mail stay@bowdenlodge.co.uk
web www.bowdenlodge.co.uk
Dir *A565 N from town centre, over rdbt, 150yds on right*

This stylish house is in a quiet residential area just a stroll from Lord St and the town's attractions. Bedrooms, many suitable for families, are smartly furnished and well equipped. Day rooms include a lounge with deep sofas, and a bright dining room where hearty cooked breakfasts are served. Value for money and a friendly welcome are assured.

Facilities 10 en suite (3 fmly) ⊗ in bedrooms ⊗ in dining room TVB tea/coffee ✖ Licensed Cen ht TVL No coaches Dinner Last d 10am **Parking** 10

◆◆◆◆

Rosedale Hotel ◇

11 Talbot St PR8 1HP ☎ 01704 530604 ▤ 01704 530604
e-mail info@rosedale-hotel.co.uk
Dir *A570 into Southport, left onto Talbot St*

The smart and friendly Rosedale stands in a quiet street only a short walk from the town's attractions. The bright bedrooms are thoughtfully equipped, and there is a comfortable lounge, a cosy bar and a lovely garden.

Facilities 9 rms (8 en suite) (1 pri facs) (2 fmly) ⊗ in dining room ⊗ in lounges TVB tea/coffee ✖ Licensed Cen ht TVL No coaches Dinner **Prices** S £30; D £60 **LB** **Parking** 6 **Notes** Closed 21 Dec-3 Jan

◆◆◆◆

The White Lodge Private Hotel ◇

12 Talbot St PR8 1HP ☎ 01704 536320 ▤ 01704 536320
Dir *In town centre. Off A570 Eastbank St onto Talbot St*

Expect a genuine welcome at this family-run, non-smoking guest house, just a stroll from the town centre. Bedrooms, including one on the ground floor, are thoughtfully equipped, and the public areas feature a comfy lounge and a cosy cellar bar. Evening meals are available by arrangement.

Facilities 8 rms (6 en suite) (2 fmly) (1 GF) ⊗ TVB tea/coffee ✖ Licensed Cen ht Dinner Last d 6pm **Prices** S £30-£45; D £60-£70✶ **LB** **Parking** 6 **Notes** ⊗

◆◆◆◆

Whitworth Falls Hotel ◇

16 Lathom Rd PR9 0JH ☎ 01704 530074
e-mail whitworthfalls@rapid.co.uk
Dir *A565 N from town centre, over rdbt, 2nd left onto Alexandra Rd, 4th right*

Located on a mainly residential avenue within easy walking distance of the seafront and Lord St shops, this Victorian house has been renovated to provide a range of homely bedrooms. Breakfasts and pre-theatre dinners are served in the attractive dining room, and a comfortable sitting room and lounge bar are available.

Facilities 12 en suite (2 fmly) (1 GF) ⊗ in 7 bedrooms ⊗ in dining room ⊗ in lounges TVB tea/coffee Direct dial from bedrooms Licensed Cen ht TVL Dinner Last d noon **Prices** S £22-£28; D £44-£56 **LB** **Parking** 8

England

SOUTHPORT continued

◆◆◆

Edendale House ◇

83 Avondale Rd North PR9 0NE
☎ 01704 530718 📠 01704 547299
e-mail edendalehotel@aol.com
web www.edendalehotel.co.uk
Dir A565 N from town centre, over rdbt, 3rd left onto Leyland Rd, 2nd left

The smart Victorian house is in a peaceful, leafy residential road, a short walk from the promenade and the town centre. Bedrooms are individually styled and have a host of thoughtful facilities. A comfortable bar-lounge is next to the smart dining room where imaginative evening meals (by arrangement) and freshly cooked breakfasts are served.

Facilities 8 en suite (2 fmly) TVB tea/coffee Direct dial from bedrooms Licensed Cen ht Dinner Last d 4pm **Prices** S £25-£40; D £47-£80✳ **LB** **Parking** 8

◆◆

The Berkeley Arms ◇

19 Queens Rd PR9 9HN ☎ 01704 500811
web www.berkeley-arms.com
Dir A565 N from town centre, right at rdbt, 2nd left

A short walk from Lord St, the Berkeley Arms provides a range of practically furnished bedrooms with satellite television and sports channels. The spacious public areas are popular with locals for the real ales and bar meals.

Facilities 12 en suite (1 fmly) in dining room in 1 lounge STV TV11B tea/coffee Direct dial from bedrooms Cen ht Pool Table **Prices** S £25-£35; D £50✳ **Parking** 8

◆◆

Lyndhurst ◇

101 King St PR8 1LQ
☎ 01704 537520 & 07759 526864 📠 01704 537520
Dir Off A570 Eastbank St at McDonalds onto King St

This well maintained, friendly guest house is just a short walk from Lord and the town's main attractions. It offers brightly decorated, comfortable accommodation. Public areas include a cosy lounge that leads onto the breakfast room. Limited off street parking is available.

Facilities 6 rms in dining room in lounges TVB tea/coffee Cen ht TVL No children 12yrs No coaches **Prices** S £20; D £40✳ **LB** **Parking** 2 **Notes** Closed Xmas & New Year

NORFOLK

ALBURGH
MAP 13 TM28

◆◆◆◆◆

The Dove Restaurant with rooms

Holbrook Hill IP20 0EP ☎ 01986 788315 📠 01986 788315
e-mail thedovenorfolk@freeula.com
Dir Between Harleston & Bungay at junct A143 & B1062

Essentially a restaurant with rooms, the bedrooms here are pleasantly decorated, furnished with pine pieces and have modern facilities. Public rooms include a lounge area with a small bar and a smart restaurant with well-spaced tables.

Facilities 2 rms (1 en suite) (1 pri facs) (1 fmly) in bedrooms in dining room in 1 lounge TVB tea/coffee ✖ Licensed Cen ht No coaches Dinner Last d 9pm **Prices** S £32; D £57✳ **Parking** 14

ATTLEBOROUGH
MAP 13 TM09

★★★ Bed & Breakfast

Rylstone B&B

Bell Rd, Rockland St Peter NR17 1UL
☎ 01953 488199 📠 0870 1320816
e-mail margaret@hneale.f9.co.uk
Dir B1077 (Watton) at Attleborough. 4m Rocklands, right at x-rds, Chapel St, Bell Rd

Expect a warm welcome at this delightful detached property situated in a peaceful rural location on the edge of the village. The pleasant bedrooms have coordinated fabrics and many thoughtful touches. Public rooms include a large lounge with a log burner, and breakfast is served in the conservatory with views of the surrounding countryside.

Facilities 3 rms (2 en suite) (1 pri facs) TVB tea/coffee ✖ Cen ht No coaches **Parking** 3 **Notes**

BACTON   MAP 13 TG33

U

Grange Cottage B&B ◇

1 Grange Cottage, Pollard St NR12 0LH ☎ 01692 652219
e-mail grangecottage1@yahoo.co.uk
Dir *North Walsham to Edingthorpe on B1150. Continue to Pollard St, B&B sign on right*

At the time of going to press the rating for this establishment had not been confirmed. Please check the AA website www.theAA.com for up-to-date information.

Facilities 3 rms (1 en suite) ⊗ TVB tea/coffee ✻ Cen ht **Prices** S fr £23; D £46-£50✳ **Parking** 3 **Notes** ⊠

BARNEY   MAP 13 TF93

◆◆◆◆

The Old Brick Kilns ◇

Little Barney Ln NR21 0NL
☎ 01328 878305 ▯ 01328 878948
e-mail enquiries@old-brick-kilns.co.uk
Dir *Off B1354 to Barney, 0.3m left onto Little Barney Ln, B&B 0.75m at end*

This delightful country house, originally three separate cottages, provides attractive accommodation in peaceful grounds. Breakfast is served at a communal table in the lounge-dining room. Due to the narrow access road, no arrivals until after 1pm.

Facilities 3 en suite ⊗ TVB tea/coffee ✻ Licensed Cen ht TVL No children 16yrs No coaches Fishing Pool Table **Prices** S £30; D £58✳ **Parking** 20

BLAKENEY   MAP 13 TG04

Premier Collection

◆◆◆◆◆

Blakeney House

High St NR25 7NX ☎ 01263 740561 ▯ 01263 741750
e-mail blakeneyhouse@aol.com
Dir *In village centre*

Expect a warm welcome at this stunning Victorian manor house set amid 2 acres of attractive landscaped grounds just a short walk from the quay and town centre. The stylish, individually decorated bedrooms have coordinated fabrics and many thoughtful touches.

continued

Breakfast is served at individual tables in the smart dining room, which overlooks the well-stocked front garden.

Facilities 8 rms (7 en suite) (1 pri facs) (1 fmly) ⊗ TVB tea/coffee ✻ Cen ht No children 12yrs No coaches **Prices** S £50-£85; D £60-£130✳ **Parking** 8

BRISTON   MAP 13 TG03

◆◆◆ ▰

John H Stracey ◇

West End NR24 2JA ☎ 01263 860891 ▯ 01263 862984
e-mail johnhstracey@btconnect.com
Dir *On B1354 Norwich Rd, 400yds E of village x-rds*

A friendly, family-run inn, well placed for touring the north Norfolk coast. Bedrooms are pleasantly decorated and equipped with a good range of useful extras. There is a popular bar and a smart restaurant serving interesting dishes.

Facilities 3 rms (1 en suite) ⊗ in bedrooms ⊗ in dining room TVB tea/coffee Cen ht Dinner Last d 9.15pm **Prices** S £26.50-£32.50; D £53-£65✳ **LB Conf** Max 30 **Parking** 30

BROOKE   MAP 13 TM29

◆◆◆◆ ▱

Old Vicarage

48 The Street NR15 1JU ☎ 01508 558329
Dir *Off B1332 in village centre near church*

Set in mature gardens in a peaceful village, this charming house is within easy driving distance of Norwich. The individually decorated bedrooms are thoughtfully furnished and equipped, and one room has a lovely four-poster bed. There is an elegant dining room and a cosy lounge, and dinner is available by arrangement. Service is genuinely helpful, provided in a relaxed and friendly manner.

Facilities 2 en suite ⊗ tea/coffee ✻ Cen ht TVL No children 15yrs No coaches Dinner Last d day before **Prices** D £60 **LB Parking** 4 **Notes** ⊠

If you have to cancel a booking, let the proprietor know immediately

England

BURNHAM MARKET
MAP 13 TF84

See also **Wells-next-the-Sea**

◆◆◆◆

Staffordshire House

Station Rd, Docking PE31 8LS ☎ 01485 518709
e-mail enquiries@staffordshirehouse.com
Dir 5.5m SW of Burnham Market. On B1153 in Docking, 300yds N of
church

Expect a warm welcome at this charming detached property situated
in the centre of a quiet village, well placed for exploring the north
Norfolk coast. The individually decorated bedrooms are thoughtfully
equipped with many useful extras. Public rooms include a smart
dining room and a cosy lounge with plush furnishings.

Facilities 3 rms (1 en suite) (2 pri facs) ⊗ in bedrooms ⊗ in dining
room TVB tea/coffee ✖ Cen ht No coaches **Prices** D £62-£70✳ **LB**
Parking 4

◆◆◆◆ ❦

Whitehall Farm (TF856412)

Burnham Thorpe PE31 8HN
☎ 01328 738416 & 07050 247390 ◨ 01328 730937
Mrs Southerland
e-mail barrysoutherland@aol.com
web www.whitehallfarm-accommodation.com
Dir From Lord Nelson pub in Burnham towards Holkam/Wells, last
building on right leaving village

The large farmhouse forms part of a working arable farm. The
property stands in large landscaped gardens with a menagerie of
animals and offers a relaxing and informal atmosphere. Bedrooms are
spacious, comfortable and equipped with DVDs, televisions and many
extras. Communal hearty breakfasts are served in the cosy dining
room.

Facilities 3 rms (2 en suite) (1 pri facs) (1 fmly) ⊗ in bedrooms
⊗ in dining room ⊗ in lounges TVB tea/coffee ✖ Cen ht TVL Riding
Countryside stewardship access route 560 acres arable **Prices** S £40-£85;
D £65-£85✳ **LB Parking** 7

COLTISHALL
MAP 13 TG21

◆◆◆◆

The Hedges ◇

Tunstead Rd NR12 7AL ☎ 01603 738361 ◨ 01603 738983
e-mail info@hedgesbandb.co.uk
web www.hedgesbandb.co.uk
Dir Off B1354 onto White Lion Rd & right fork

A delightful, family-run guest house situated close to the Norfolk
Broads. Bedrooms have coordinated fabrics and a good range of
useful extras, and most rooms have lovely views of the surrounding
countryside. Breakfast is served at individual tables in the dining room
or the smart conservatory. The comfortably appointed lounge has a
log fire and a fabulous aquarium.

Facilities 5 en suite (2 fmly) (2 GF) ⊗ TVB tea/coffee ✖ Cen ht TVL
Prices S £27.50-£40; D £49-£51 **LB Parking** 10 **Notes** Closed 23-28 Dec

CROMER
MAP 13 TG24

◆◆◆◆ ❦

Shrublands Farm (TG246393)

Church St, Northrepps NR27 0AA
☎ 01263 579297 ◨ 01263 579297 Mrs Youngman
e-mail youngman@farming.co.uk
web www.broadland.com/shrublands
Dir Off A149 to Northrepps, through village, past Foundry Arms,
cream house 50yds on left

Expect a warm welcome from the caring host at this delightful 18th-
century farmhouse, set in landscaped grounds and surrounded by 300
acres of arable farmland. Public areas include a cosy lounge with a
wood-burning stove, and breakfast is served at a communal table in
the elegant dining room.

Facilities 3 rms (1 en suite) (2 pri facs) ⊗ TVB tea/coffee ✖ Cen ht
TVL No children 12yrs 300 acres arable **Prices** S £38-£40; D £56-£60 **LB**
Parking 5

◆◆◆◆

Beachcomber Guest House

17 Macdonald Rd NR27 9AP ☎ 01263 513398
e-mail info@beachcomber-guesthouse.co.uk
Dir Off A149 Runton Rd, 500yds W of pier

A smartly maintained Edwardian house situated in a peaceful side
road close to the seafront and town centre. The pleasant bedrooms
are carefully furnished and equipped with many thoughtful touches.
Breakfast is served in the dining room and the lounge has plush sofas.

Facilities 5 en suite (1 fmly) ⊗ TVB tea/coffee ✖ Cen ht TVL
No children 8yrs **Prices** D £52-£58 **LB Notes** Closed Xmas

◆◆◆◆

Bon Vista

12 Alfred Rd NR27 9AN ☎ 01263 511818 ◨ 01263 512306
e-mail sandra@bonvista777.wanadoo.co.uk
web www.broadland.com/bonvista
Dir From pier onto A148 Copast Rd, 400yds left onto Alfred Rd

Expect a warm welcome at this delightful Victorian terrace house
situated in a quiet side road adjacent to the seafront and just a short
walk from the town centre. The individually decorated bedrooms have
coordinated soft fabrics and many thoughtful touches. Public rooms
include an attractive dining room and a spacious lounge.

continued

Facilities 5 en suite (1 fmly) TVB tea/coffee ✗ Cen ht TVL No children 4yrs No coaches **Prices** D £50-£52✳ LB **Parking** available **Notes** ⊜

◆◆◆◆

Cromer House Bed & Breakfast ◈

10 Alfred Rd NR27 9AN ☎ 01263 510923 🖷 01263 510923 **e-mail** peterscarbrow@tiscali.co.uk

A warm welcome is assured at this friendly guest house situated in a peaceful side road close to the seafront and town centre. Bedrooms are pleasantly decorated and thoughtfully equipped; all rooms have either en suites or private bathrooms. Breakfast is served in the smart dining room and features local produce.

Facilities 6 rms (3 en suite) (3 pri facs) (1 fmly) TVB tea/coffee Cen ht No children 5yrs No coaches **Prices** S £25-£30; D £50-£60✳ LB **Notes** ⊜

◆◆◆◆ ⊜

Morden House

20 Cliff Av NR27 0AN ☎ 01263 513396 🖷 01263 513396 **e-mail** rosevotier@hotmail.co.uk **Dir** Off A149 Norwich Rd onto Overstrand Rd & 1st right

Expect a warm welcome at this impressive Victorian house situated in a peaceful side road yet within easy walking distance of the seafront and town centre. The property stands in mature grounds and has many original features. Bedrooms have coordinated fabrics and many thoughtful touches, and breakfast is served in the smart dining room.

Facilities 6 rms (4 en suite) (1 fmly) TVB tea/coffee ✗ Cen ht TVL No coaches Dinner Last d 6pm **Prices** S £35-£45; D £64-£70✳ LB **Parking** 3 **Notes** Closed Xmas & New Year rs Nov-Mar ⊜

◆◆◆◆

The Stables

Church Farm, Northrepps NR27 0LG ☎ 01263 579790 **Dir** Off A149 2m E of Cromer signed Northrepps, at school turn right & right again

Tea and home-made cake are offered on arrival at this delightful Norfolk flint cottage, which stands in pretty landscaped grounds within open countryside. Public rooms include a cosy lounge and a smart dining room. Bedrooms are simply decorated, have coordinated fabrics and many thoughtful touches.

Facilities 2 rms (1 en suite) (1 pri facs) (1 GF) TVB tea/coffee ✗ Cen ht No children No coaches **Prices** S £39; D £50-£60 **Parking** 4 **Notes** ⊜

◆◆◆◆

Westgate Lodge Private Hotel ◈

10 MacDonald Rd NR27 9AP ☎ 01263 512840 **Dir** Along seafront & left after the Cliftonville Hotel, Westgate Lodge 50yds on right

Situated in a peaceful side road next to the seafront and close to the centre of town, the bedrooms vary in size and style, and each one is pleasantly decorated and has many thoughtful touches. Breakfast and dinner are served in the smart dining room and there is a cosy lounge.

Facilities 11 en suite (3 fmly) TVB tea/coffee ✗ Licensed Cen ht No children 3yrs No coaches Dinner Last d within 24hrs **Prices** S £30-£60; D £50-£64✳ LB **Parking** 11 **Notes** Closed Xmas & New Year

◆◆◆◆

White Cottage

9 Cliff Dr NR27 0AW ☎ 01263 512728 **e-mail** jboocock@whitecottagecromer.freeserve.co.uk **Dir** Off A149 Norwich Rd onto Overstrand Rd, 2nd right

A delightful detached house situated on an elevated position above the beach with panoramic sea views. The immaculate property offers a high degree of comfort: the spacious bedrooms are pleasantly decorated and equipped with many useful extras, and breakfast is served in an elegant lounge-dining room. This is a non-smoking establishment.

Facilities 3 en suite TVB tea/coffee ✗ Cen ht No children 18yrs No coaches **Parking** 3 **Notes** Closed Xmas ⊜

◆◆◆

Glendale ◈

33 Macdonald Rd NR27 9AP ☎ 01263 513278 **e-mail** glendalecromer@aol.com **Dir** A149 coast road from Cromer centre, 4th left

A Victorian property situated in a peaceful side road adjacent to the seafront yet just a short walk from the town centre. Bedrooms are pleasantly decorated, well maintained and equipped with useful extras. Breakfast is served at individual tables in the smart dining room.

Facilities 5 rms (1 en suite) TVB tea/coffee No coaches **Prices** S £20-£29; D £40-£58 LB **Parking** 2 **Notes** Closed 20 Oct-30 Mar

◆◆◆

Sandcliff Private Hotel ◈

Runton Rd NR27 9AS ☎ 01263 512888 🖷 01263 512888 **e-mail** admin@sandcliffhotel.co.uk **Dir** 500yds W of town centre on A149

The family-run Sandcliff stands on the seafront overlooking the promenade and beach, just a short walk from the town centre. The pleasant bedrooms are well maintained and thoughtfully equipped, and some have superb sea views. The spacious public rooms include a large lounge bar and a smart restaurant serving home-cooked food.

Facilities 22 rms (16 en suite) (10 fmly) (3 GF) in dining room TVB tea/coffee Licensed Dinner Last d 6pm **Prices** S £29; D £58-£64✳ LB **Parking** 10 **Notes** Closed 21 Dec-4 Jan ⊜

DEREHAM
MAP 13 TF91

★★★★ Bed & Breakfast

Orchard Cottage
The Drift, Gressenhall NR20 4EH
☎ 01362 860265 📄 01362 860270
e-mail ann@walkers-norfolk.co.uk
web www.walkers-norfolk.co.uk
Dir B1146 Beetley signed Gressenhall@swan right Bittering St. Follow
right at x rd, 2nd right.

An attractive, newly built Norfolk flint cottage situated in the village of
Gressenhall. The comfortable country-style bedrooms are smartly
decorated and situated on the ground floor; one of the rooms has a
superb wet room. Public rooms include a lounge, a dining room and a
study. Dinner is available by arrangement.

Facilities 2 en suite (2 GF) ⊗ FTV TVB tea/coffee ✖ Cen ht TVL
No coaches Dinner Last d 24hrs before **Prices** S £46-£52; D £56-£62 LB
Parking 2 **Notes** 📵

♦♦♦♦ 🍴

Yaxham Mill
Norwich Rd, Yaxham NR19 1RP
☎ 01362 851182 📄 01362 691482
e-mail yaxhammill@btinternet.com
web www.yaxhammill.com
Dir 1.5m S of Dereham. B1135 into Yaxham, at E end of village

A popular inn situated in open countryside just a short drive from
Dereham. The comfortable lounge bar and smart restaurant offer a
good choice of dishes. The bedrooms, in two wings next to the main
building, have attractive pine furnishings and many thoughtful
touches.

Facilities 3 en suite 6 annexe en suite (4 fmly) (4 GF) ⊗ in bedrooms
⊗ in dining room ⊗ in lounges TVB tea/coffee ✖ Cen ht Dinner Last
d 9pm **Prices** S £40-£45; D £55-£65✖ LB **Parking** 60

DOCKING
MAP 13 TF73

♦♦♦

Jubilee Lodge
Station Rd PE31 8LS ☎ 01485
e-mail
web ww
Dir From
school (
Ideally si
Hunstant
Bedroom
suites. Pu
individua

Facilities 3 en suite ⊗ TVB tea/coffee ✖ Cen ht TVL No children
16yrs No coaches **Prices** S £30; D £50✖ LB **Parking** 3 **Notes** 📵

DOWNHAM MARKET
MAP 12 TF60

♦♦♦

The Old Shop ◇
24 London Rd PE38 9AW ☎ 01366 382051
e-mail kcorrall@aol.com
Dir Off A10 at Downham Market exit. Left at lights, house on right
after next minirdbt

The Old Shop was once three separate cottages and has been
refurbished to keep much of the original character. Breakfast is served
at individual tables in the cosy, cottage-style lounge-dining room. The
smart bedrooms are furnished with pine pieces, have coordinated soft
fabrics and many thoughtful touches.

Facilities 3 en suite ⊗ in 1 bedrooms ⊗ in dining room TVB tea/coffee
✖ Cen ht No coaches **Prices** S £30-£35; D £45✖ LB **Notes** 📵

♦♦♦

Crosskeys Riverside House ◇
Bridge St, Hilgay PE38 0LD
☎ 01366 387777 📄 01366 387777
e-mail crosskeyshouse@aol.com
web www.crosskeys.info
Dir S of Downham Market, off A10 into Hilgay. Crosskeys situated on
bridge by river

Located in the small village of Hilgay, just off the A10 on the banks of
the River Wissey, this former coaching inn offers comfortable
accommodation including four-poster bedrooms, and many rooms
with river views. Character public rooms include a dining room with
oak beams and an inglenook fireplace, plus a rustic locals' bar. The
large river frontage has fishing access, while stabling can be provided
for horses. Ample private parking is provided.

Facilities 4 en suite (1 fmly) (1 GF) ⊗ in 2 bedrooms ⊗ in dining
room ⊗ in 1 lounge TVB tea/coffee Cen ht No coaches Fishing Stabling
for guest horses **Prices** S £30-£50; D £50✖ **Parking** 10

FAKENHAM
MAP 13 TF92
See also **Barney**

♦♦♦♦

Holly Tree ◇
40 Sandy Ln NR21 9EZ ☎ 01328 851955 📄 01328 851955
e-mail gartcarving@aol.com
web www.hollytreebandb.co.uk
Dir Off junct A1065 & A148 onto Wells Rd into town centre, 1st right

Expect a warm welcome from the caring hosts at this small family-run
guest house, which is situated in a quiet road on the west edge of
town. The smart bedrooms have coordinated soft furnishings and
many thoughtful touches. Breakfast is served in an attractive dining
room that overlooks the neat gardens.

Facilities 2 en suite (2 GF) ⊗ TVB tea/coffee ✖ Cen ht No children
10yrs No coaches **Prices** S £30-£50; D £50 **Parking** 2 **Notes** 📵

◆◆◆◆

White Horse

Fakenham Rd, East Barsham NR21 0LH
☎ 01328 820645 📠 01328 820645
Dir *A148 onto B1105 towards Walsingham, inn 2m on left just before Barsham Manor*

A delightful inn situated in a rural location just to the north of Fakenham in the small village of East Barsham. The smart bedrooms are carefully furnished and well equipped. An interesting choice of dishes is served in the small dining room and cosy, well-stocked lounge bar.

Facilities 3 en suite (1 fmly) ⊗ in bedrooms ⊗ in dining room TVB tea/coffee 🐾 Cen ht Organised bird watching tours Dinner Last d 9.30pm **Prices** S £40; D £60-£70✱ **Parking** 50

◆◆◆ ♥

Abbott Farm ◇ *(TF975390)*

Walsingham Rd, Binham NR21 0AW
☎ 01328 830519 📠 01328 830519 Mrs Brown
e-mail abbot.farm@btinternet.com
Dir *6m NE of Fakenham. From Binham SW onto Walsingham Rd, farm 0.6m on left*

A detached red-brick house situated in 190 acres of arable farmland. The spacious bedrooms are pleasantly decorated and thoughtfully equipped, and the ground-floor rooms have very spacious showers en suite. Breakfast is served in the attractive conservatory, which has superb views across the countryside.

Facilities 3 en suite (2 GF) ⊗ TVB tea/coffee Cen ht TVL 190 acres arable **Prices** S £24-£26; D £48-£52✱ **Parking** 20 **Notes** 🐾

GORLESTON ON SEA
MAP 13 TG50

◆◆◆◆

Avalon Hotel ◇

54 Clarence Rd NR31 6DR
☎ 01493 662114 📠 01493 668528
e-mail avalonhotel@eurolelonline.com
web www.avalon-gorleston.co.uk
Dir *A12 past James Paget Hospital. Take 2nd exit at rdbt towards Gorleston. Next rdbt 2nd exit, 1st right*

This Edwardian terrace house is just a short walk from the promenade and beach. Breakfast and evening meal are served in a smart dining room and there is a cosy lounge bar; service is helpful and friendly. Bedrooms are thoughtfully equipped and well furnished.

continued

Facilities 11 rms (10 en suite) (6 fmly) (1 GF) ⊗ in bedrooms ⊗ in dining room TVB tea/coffee Licensed Cen ht TVL Dinner Last d 7.15pm **Prices** S £22.50-£30; D £40-£60✱

GREAT ELLINGHAM
MAP 13 TM09

◆◆◆◆

Aldercarr Hall

Attleborough Rd NR17 1LQ
☎ 01953 455766 & 07710 752213 📠 01953 457993
e-mail bedandbreakfast@aldercarr-limited.com
Dir *On B1077 500yds SE of village*

Aldercarr Hall stands in grounds in quiet countryside on the edge of Great Ellingham. Public rooms include a comfortable conservatory and a delightful dining room where breakfast is served around a large table. The excellent facilities include a health, beauty and hairdressing studio, an indoor swimming pool and a jacuzzi.

Facilities 3 annexe en suite (1 fmly) (3 GF) ⊗ in bedrooms ⊗ in dining room TVB tea/coffee 🐾 Cen ht TVL ☐ Golf Fishing Riding Snooker Sauna Pool Table **Conf** Max 125 Board 9 **Parking** 200

GREAT YARMOUTH
MAP 13 TG50

◆◆◆◆

Barnard House

2 Barnard Crescent NR30 4DR
☎ 01493 855139 📠 01493 843143
e-mail enquiries@barnardhouse.com
Dir *0.5m N of town centre. Off A149 onto Barnard Crescent*

Expect a warm welcome at this friendly, family-run guest house, set in mature landscaped gardens in a residential area. The pleasant, carefully furnished bedrooms have many thoughtful touches. Breakfast is served in the smart dining room and there is an elegant lounge.

Facilities 3 rms (2 en suite) (1 pri facs) ⊗ FTV TVB tea/coffee Cen ht TVL No coaches **Prices** S £35; D £50-£60✱ **LB** **Parking** 3
Notes Closed Xmas & New Year

◆◆◆◆

Andover Hotel

28-30 Camperdown NR30 3JB
☎ 01493 843490 📠 01493 843490
e-mail rwadebrown@aol.com
Dir *Opp Wellington Pier onto Waterloo Rd, left onto Wellington Rd, 1st right*

The Andover is located in a peaceful side road just a short walk from the seafront and town centre, and has a wide range of amenities. Breakfast and dinner are served in the basement dining room, and there is a cosy lounge and a smart bar.

Facilities 27 en suite (3 GF) ⊗ in bedrooms ⊗ in dining room ⊗ in lounges TVB tea/coffee 🐾 Licensed Cen ht TVL No children 15yrs Pool Table Dinner Last d 4pm **Prices** S £32-£35; D £64-£70 **Notes** 🐾

England

GREAT YARMOUTH continued

◆◆◆◆

Bonheur ◇

3 Norfolk Sq NR30 1EE ☎ 01493 843042 ▤ 01493 745235
e-mail enq@bonheur-hotel.co.uk
web www.bonheur-hotel.co.uk
Dir *From North Dr on seafront onto Albemarle Rd opp Bowling Greens, 100yds on left.*

The friendly, family-run Victorian house offers spacious and comfortable accommodation close to the beach and attractions. This is a non-smoking establishment.

Facilities 8 en suite (3 fmly) (2 GF) ⊗ TV5B ✘ Licensed Cen ht TVL No coaches Dinner Last d noon **Prices** S £25-£50; D £35-£55✻ LB **Parking** 3

◆◆◆◆

The Classic Lodge

13 Euston Rd NR30 1DY ☎ 01493 852851 ▤ 01493 852851
web www.classiclodge.com
Dir *250yds N of pier, off seafront North Dr*

The impressive Victorian villa is just a stroll from the seafront and town centre. Breakfast is served at individual tables in the large lounge-dining room, and the spacious bedrooms are carefully furnished and equipped with a very good range of facilities.

Facilities 3 en suite ⊗ FTV TVB tea/coffee ✘ Cen ht TVL No children 18yrs No coaches LB **Parking** 3 **Notes** Closed Nov-Apr ⊜

◆◆◆◆

The Elmfield Hotel ◇

38 Wellesley Rd NR30 1EU ☎ 01493 859827
e-mail stay@theelmfield.co.uk
Dir *Off A47 to seafront, last left before seafront*

Please note that this establishment has recently changed hands. The delightful guest house is only a short walk from the seafront and town centre. Breakfast is served in a spacious dining room and there is a cosy lounge bar. The pleasant bedrooms have a good range of useful extras, and some rooms have sea views.

Facilities 9 en suite (3 fmly) ⊗ in dining room ⊗ in 1 lounge TVB tea/coffee ✘ Licensed Cen ht TVL **Prices** S £16-£24; D £32-£48✻ LB **Parking** 4 **Notes** ⊜

◆◆◆◆

The Hamilton

23-24 North Dr NR30 4EW ☎ 01493 844662
e-mail enquiries@hamilton-hotel.co.uk
web www.hamilton-hotel.co.uk
Dir *Off A47 to seafront, left at Britannia Pier, 0.5m N on seafront*

Expect a warm welcome at this friendly, family-run establishment, which is situated at the quiet end of town overlooking the Venetian Waterways and beach. Breakfast and dinner are served in the smart dining room, and there is a cosy bar and a lounge. The pleasant bedrooms are thoughtfully equipped.

Facilities 21 en suite 1 annexe en suite (2 fmly) ⊗ in bedrooms ⊗ in dining room ⊗ in lounges TVB tea/coffee ✘ Licensed Cen ht Dinner Last d 6pm **Parking** 24

◆◆◆◆

Jennis Lodge ◇

63 Avondale Rd, Gorleston-on-Sea NR31 6DJ
☎ 01493 662840 ▤ 01493 662840
e-mail mandy@jennislodge.co.uk
Dir *From A12 signs for seafront, Avondale Rd off Marine Parade*

The friendly, family-run guest house is situated just off the seafront and close to the town centre. Bedrooms are attractive and thoughtfully equipped. Public rooms include a smart dining room and an elegant lounge. Dinner is available by arrangement.

Facilities 7 rms (6 en suite) (3 fmly) ⊗ TVB tea/coffee ✘ Cen ht TVL Dinner Last d noon **Prices** S £21-£30; D £44-£60 LB

◆◆◆◆

Knights Court Hotel ◇

22 North Dr NR30 4EW ☎ 01493 843089 ▤ 01493 850780
e-mail enquiries@knights-court.co.uk
Dir *600yds N of Britannia Pier, opp Waterways and Gardens*

Knights Court stands on the seafront overlooking the Venetian Waterways and the beach. The spacious bedrooms are carefully decorated and equipped with many thoughtful touches, and most rooms have lovely sea views. Breakfast and dinner are served in the smart dining room and there is a cosy lounge bar.

Facilities 14 en suite 6 annexe en suite (5 fmly) (6 GF) ⊗ in 4 bedrooms ⊗ in dining room TVB tea/coffee Direct dial from bedrooms ✘ Licensed Cen ht TVL No coaches Dinner Last d 11am **Prices** S £27-£38; D £52-£64✻ LB **Parking** 21 **Notes** Closed 23 Oct-23 Mar

If you book on bed, breakfast and evening meal terms, you may find that the tariff includes only the set menu

continued

♦♦♦♦
Marine Lodge
19-20 Euston Rd NR30 1DY ☎ 01493 331120
e-mail res@marinelodge.co.uk

The Lodge's enviable seafront position has panoramic views of the bowling greens and beach, and is within easy walking distance of Britannia Pier. Bright modern bedrooms are complemented by smart public areas that include a bar area where light snacks are available during the evening. You also have complimentary use of the indoor swimming pool at the sister Palm Court Hotel.

Facilities 40 en suite (5 fmly) (5 GF) ⊘ in 5 bedrooms ⊘ in dining room FTV TVB tea/coffee ✖ Licensed Lift Cen ht TVL **Prices** S £36-£38; D £47-£57; (room only) ✳ LB **Conf** Thtr 50 Class 35 Board 25 **Parking** 38

♦♦♦♦
Winchester Private Hotel ◇
12 Euston Rd NR30 1DY ☎ 01493 843950
e-mail enquiries@winchesterprivatehotel.com
Dir A12 onto A47, signs for seafront, left at Sainsbury over lights, premises 400yds on right

The friendly hosts a give a warm welcome at their guest house just off the seafront. The pleasant bedrooms vary in size and style and are thoughtfully equipped. Public rooms include a large lower-ground-floor dining room, a small conservatory and a foyer with plush sofas.

Facilities 14 en suite (2 fmly) (5 GF) ⊘ in dining room ⊘ in lounges TVB tea/coffee ✖ Cen ht TVL No children 12yrs No coaches Dinner Last d 10am **Prices** S £20-£30; D £40-£60✳ LB **Parking** 10 **Notes** Closed Dec-Jan rs Oct-Etr ⊠

♦♦♦♦ A
The Corner House ◇
Albert Sq NR30 3JH ☎ 01493 842773
e-mail stay@thecornerhousehotel.co.uk
web www.thecornerhousehotel.co.uk
Dir From A47/A12, Albert Square opposite Wellington Pier

Facilities 8 en suite (2 GF) ⊘ TVB tea/coffee ✖ Licensed Cen ht TVL No children No coaches Dinner Last d 3pm **Prices** S £30-£41; D £60-£82✳ LB **Parking** 8 **Notes** Closed Oct-Apr ⊠

♦♦♦♦ A
Fjaerland Hotel ◇
24-25 Trafalgar Rd NR30 2LD
☎ 01493 856339 ▤ 01493 856339
web www.fjaerland.co.uk
Dir On seafront opp Marina Centre

Facilities 12 en suite (2 fmly) ⊘ in 1 bedrooms ⊘ in dining room ⊘ in 1 lounge TVB tea/coffee ✖ Licensed Cen ht TVL **Prices** S £25-£30; D £45-£50 LB

♦♦♦♦ A
Kensington Hotel
29 North Dr NR30 4EW ☎ 01493 844145
e-mail enquiries@kensington-hotel.co.uk
web www.kensington-hotel.co.uk
Dir On seafront opp Venetian Waterways

Facilities 26 en suite (7 fmly) (3 GF) ⊘ in bedrooms ⊘ in dining room ⊘ in 1 lounge FTV TVB tea/coffee Licensed Lift Cen ht Dinner Last d noon **Prices** S £36-£49; D £57-£69✳ LB **Conf** Thtr 50 Class 50 Board 30 Del from £60 ✳ **Parking** 25

♦♦♦♦ A
Southern Hotel ◇
46 Queens Rd NR30 3JR
☎ 01493 843313 ▤ 01493 843242
e-mail sally@southernhotel.co.uk
web www.southernhotel.co.uk
Dir 500yds S of town centre. Along A1243 S Quay, river on right, left signed Seafront onto Queen's Rd, over lights, premises on left

The well-furnished house offers comfortable bedrooms a short walk from the town centre and the pier.

Facilities 19 en suite (6 fmly) (3 GF) ⊘ in bedrooms ⊘ in dining room TVB tea/coffee ✖ Licensed Cen ht TVL Dinner Last d 4pm **Prices** S £30-£35; D £60-£70✳ LB **Parking** 12

♦♦♦
Spindrift Guest House
36 Wellesley Rd NR30 1EU
☎ 01493 843772 ▤ 01493 850335
e-mail spindrifthotel@btinternet.com
Dir Signs for seafront, along St Nicholas Rd & Euston Rd, 1st left onto Wellesley Rd

Expect a friendly welcome at the Spindrift, which is in a tree-lined avenue just a short walk from the seafront and town centre. The smart bedrooms have coordinated fabrics and many thoughtful touches, and family rooms are available. Breakfast is served at individual tables in the cosy ground-floor breakfast room.

Facilities 7 en suite (2 fmly) ⊘ in dining room ⊘ in lounges FTV TVB tea/coffee ✖ Cen ht No coaches **Prices** D £32-£50✳ LB **Parking** 1

England

◆◆◆

Blenheim Hotel

58 Apsley Rd NR30 2HG
☎ 01493 856469 📠 01493 856469
e-mail densimp@aol.com
Dir Near Britannia Pier

This friendly, family-run property lies on a residential street just a stroll from the Golden Mile beach, theatre and Britannia Pier. Public rooms include a comfortable lounge bar with a large-screen television and a pleasant dining room. Bedrooms vary in style and size, and a number have en suites. Parking is available at the rear.

Facilities 12 rms (8 en suite) (1 fmly) ⊘ in 4 bedrooms ⊘ in dining room TVB tea/coffee ✺ Licensed Cen ht TVL Pool Table Dinner Last d 4pm **LB Notes** ⊛

◆◆◆

Harbour Hotel

20 Pavilion Rd, Gorleston on Sea NR31 6BY
☎ 01493 661031 📠 01493 661031
e-mail jeffchambers@harbourhotel.freeserve.co.uk
Dir A12 into Gorleston on Sea centre & signs to beach, premises near lighthouse

Expect a warm welcome at this guest house near the harbour. The pleasant, well-equipped bedrooms vary in size and style, and some rooms have lovely sea views. Breakfast is served in the spacious dining room, and evening snacks are available in the lounge bar.

Facilities 8 rms (4 en suite) (6 fmly) ⊘ in dining room tea/coffee ✺ Licensed Cen ht TVL No coaches **Prices** S £35-£40; D £50-£54✳ **LB Parking** 3 **Notes** ⊛

◆◆◆

Haydee Hotel ◇

27 Princes Rd NR30 2DG
☎ 01493 844580 📠 01493 844580
e-mail info@haydee.co.uk
Dir Off A47 to seafront, Princes Rd opp Britannia Pier

The Haydee is on a side road just a stroll from the seafront, pier and town centre. The pleasant bedrooms vary in size and style but all are well equipped. Breakfast is served in the smart dining room and there is a cosy lounge bar.

Facilities 8 en suite (2 fmly) ⊘ in 4 bedrooms ⊘ in dining room ⊘ in 1 lounge TVB tea/coffee ✺ Licensed Cen ht TVL No coaches **Prices** S £18-£22.50; D £36-£45 **LB Notes** ⊛

◆◆◆

Amber Lodge ◇

21 Princes Rd NR30 2DG ☎ 01493 843371
e-mail paul@amberlodgehotel.co.uk

Facilities 10 rms (8 en suite) (2 pri facs) (2 fmly) ⊘ in dining room TVB tea/coffee Licensed Cen ht TVL Dinner Last d 10am **Prices** S £12-£25; D £28-£50; (room only) ✳ **LB Notes** rs May-Sep ⊛

◆◆◆

The Chequers ◇

27 Nelson Rd South NR30 3JA ☎ 01493 853091
e-mail chequershotel@greatyarmouth.fsbusiness.co.uk
Dir Off A47 signed Seafront, right onto Marine Parade & Kings Rd, 1st right

Facilities 8 rms (7 en suite) (1 pri facs) (1 fmly) ⊘ in bedrooms ⊘ in dining room TVB tea/coffee ✺ Licensed Cen ht TVL No coaches Dinner Last d Breakfast **Prices** S £22-£26; D £44-£52✳ **LB Parking** 8 **Notes** ⊛

◆◆◆

Swiss Cottage ◇

31 North Dr NR30 4EW ☎ 01493 855742 & 07986 399857
e-mail info@swisscottagebedandbreakfast.co.uk
Dir From A47 or A12 head into Great Yarmouth pass Vauxhall train station and over river Bure bridge. Left at rdbt in Lawn Av. Cont to lights and turn right. Take next immediate left and cont to sea front. Turn right and B&B on right.

Facilities 7 en suite 1 annexe rms (1 fmly) (2 GF) ⊘ FTV TVB tea/coffee Cen ht No children 8yrs No coaches **Prices** S £25-£36; D £45-£66✳ **LB Parking** 9 **Notes** Closed Nov-Feb

◆◆◆

Trevi House ◇

57 Wellesley Rd NR30 1EX ☎ 01493 842821
Dir 400yds N of Britannia Pier.

Facilities 7 rms (5 en suite) (3 fmly) (1 GF) ⊘ TVB tea/coffee ✺ Licensed Cen ht TVL No coaches Dinner Last d At time of booking **Prices** S £20-£25; D £36-£50✳ **LB Notes** Closed Nov-Feb ⊛

◆◆◆

Woods End ◇

49 Wellesley Rd NR30 1EX
☎ 01493 842229 & 07940 099004
Dir Off A12 & A47 for Town Centre & Seafront, pass Sainsbury, over lights & 1st left

Facilities 8 rms (8 pri facs) (3 fmly) (1 GF) ⊘ in bedrooms ⊘ in dining room TVB tea/coffee ✺ Licensed Cen ht TVL No coaches Dinner Last d 3pm **Prices** S £17-£26; D £34-£52✳ **LB Parking** 3 **Notes** ⊛

◆◆

Rhonadean ◇

110-111 Wellesley Rd NR30 2AR ☎ 01493 842004
e-mail barbara@6wheeler0.wanadoo.co.uk
Dir A47 follow sign to Seafront. Fullums Hill, St Nicholas Rd. 3rd right into Wellesley Rd.

Situated on a side road adjacent to the seafront and just a short walk from the town centre, Rhonadean offers a small lounge-bar and a dining room where breakfast and dinner are served at individual tables. Bedrooms vary in size and each one is pleasantly decorated and well equipped.

Facilities 18 rms (17 en suite) (1 pri facs) (7 fmly) (8 GF) ⊘ in bedrooms ⊘ in dining room TVB tea/coffee ✺ Licensed Cen ht TVL Pool Table Dinner Last d 11am **Prices** S £18.50-£26.50; D £37-£53 **Notes** ⊛

HARLESTON

MAP 13 TM28

◆◆◆◆

Heath Farmhouse ◇

Homersfield IP20 0EX ☎ 01986 788417

Dir *A143 onto B1062 towards Flixton, over bridge past Suffolk sign & 2nd farm entrance on left at AA sign*

A charming 16th-century farmhouse set amid attractive landscaped grounds that include a croquet lawn. The property retains original exposed beams, open fireplaces and has wood-burning stoves. The bedrooms are carefully furnished and have many thoughtful touches. Breakfast and dinner are served in the smart dining room overlooking the garden.

Facilities 2 rms (1 fmly) ⊘ in bedrooms ⊘ in dining room ⊘ in 1 lounge tea/coffee ✖ Cen ht TVL No coaches ♨ Table tennis Dinner Last d 10am **Prices** S £30; D £48✳ **Parking** 8 **Notes** ⊠

HEVINGHAM

MAP 13 TG12

◆◆◆◆ A

Marsham Arms Inn

Holt Rd NR10 5NP ☎ 01603 754268
e-mail nigelbradley@marshamarms.co.uk
web www.marshamarms.co.uk

Dir *8.5m N of Norwich. Off A140 near Norwich Airport onto B1149, through Horsford, establishment 2m on right*

Facilities 11 annexe en suite (8 fmly) (11 GF) ⊘ in 8 bedrooms ⊘ in dining room ⊘ in 1 lounge TVB tea/coffee Direct dial from bedrooms ✖ Licensed Cen ht Dinner Last d 9.30pm **Prices** S fr £54.50; d fr £85✳ LB **Conf** Max 50 Thtr 50 Class 30 Board 30 Del from £90 ✳ **Parking** 100

HINDRINGHAM

MAP 13 TF93

◆◆◆◆◆

Field House

Moorgate R
e-mail stay@
Dir *Off A148*
Field House a

A warm welc
hosts at this
location amid

bedrooms have coordinated soft fabrics and many thoughtful touches. Breakfast is served in the lounge-dining room and features quality local produce. Mrs Dalton takes great pride in providing imaginative home-cooked dinners by arrangement.

Field House

Facilities 2 en suite 1 annexe en suite ⊗ FTV TVB tea/coffee ✖ Cen ht No children 10yrs No coaches ♨ Dinner Last d when booking **Prices** D £90-£100 LB **Parking** 3 **Notes** Closed 25-26 Dec ⊠

HOLT

MAP 13 TG03

◆◆◆◆◆

Plantation House

Ashburn, Old Cromer Rd, High Kelling NR25 6AJ
☎ 01263 710121
e-mail info@plantation-house.net
web www.plantation-house.net

Dir *Signs for Kelling Hospital on A148, 1st left & sharp right, 1st house*

Expect a warm welcome at this charming property situated on the outskirts of Holt in the wooded village of High Kelling. The property has been lovingly restored by the current owners and provides smart accommodation throughout. Public rooms feature a colonial-style lounge-dining room with darkwood tables and a leather chesterfield. The stylish bedrooms have a bright and airy feel; each one has attractive solid wood furniture, coordinated fabrics and many thoughtful touches. Marven and Michael are top-twenty finalists for AA Landlady of the Year 2006.

Facilities 4 en suite ⊗ TVB tea/coffee ✖ Cen ht No children 12yrs **Prices** S £60-£70; D £75-£90 LB **Parking** 5 **Notes** ⊠

England

◆◆◆◆

The Old Telephone Exchange

37 New St NR25 6JH ☎ 01263 712992
Dir *Off High St onto New St, establishment 200yds on left*

Expect a warm welcome at this small, family-run guest house, which is situated in a quiet side road close to the town centre. The immaculate bedrooms are carefully decorated and equipped with many thoughtful touches. Public rooms feature a comfortable lounge-dining area with a wide-screen television, books and games.

Facilities 3 en suite (3 GF) ⊗ TVB tea/coffee ✗ Cen ht TVL
No children 10yrs **Prices** S £45-£55; D £50-£60 **LB** **Parking** 2 **Notes** ⊕

Ⓤ

White Cottage B&B

Norwich Rd NR25 6SW ☎ 01263 713353
e-mail whitecottage.holt@fsmail.net
Dir *From A148 from Holt take B1149, 0.5m on left after Police Station*

At the time of going to press the rating for this establishment had not been confirmed. Please check the AA website www.theAA.com for up-to-date information.

Facilities 2 en suite ⊗ TVB tea/coffee ✗ No children 10yrs
No coaches **Prices** D £65-£70✳ **LB** **Notes** Closed 21 Dec-Jan ⊕

HUNSTANTON   MAP 12 TF64

◆◆◆◆

Claremont ◇

35 Greevegate PE36 6AF ☎ 01485 533171
e-mail claremont@amserve.com
Dir *Off A149 onto Greevegate, house before St Edmunds Church*

This Victorian house, close to the shops, beach and gardens, has individually decorated bedrooms with a good range of useful extras. There is also a ground-floor room as well as two feature rooms, one with a four poster, and another has a canopied bed.

Facilities 7 en suite (1 fmly) (1 GF) ⊗ TVB tea/coffee Cen ht TVL
No children 5yrs No coaches **Prices** S £25-£28; D £44-£56✳ **LB**
Parking 4 **Notes** Closed 15 Nov-15 Mar ⊕

◆◆◆◆

The Gables

28 Austin St PE36 6AW ☎ 01485 532514
e-mail bbatthegables@aol.com
web www.thegableshunstanton.co.uk
Dir *A149 onto Austin St to junct with Northgate*

Expect a warm welcome at this friendly, family-run guest house, which is just a short walk from the seafront and town centre. The individually decorated bedrooms have coordinated fabrics and are equipped with many useful extras, including minifridges. Breakfast is served at individual tables in the panelled dining room.

Facilities 6 en suite (4 fmly) ⊗ TVB tea/coffee ✗ Licensed Cen ht
TVL No coaches Dinner Last d 2pm **Prices** S £35-£42; D £50-£64✳ **LB**

◆◆◆◆ ◉ ⊜ ◀

The Neptune Inn & Restaurant

85 Old Hunstanton Rd PE36 6HZ
☎ 01485 532122 & 535314 ▦ 01485 535314
e-mail reservations@theneptune.co.uk
web www.theneptune.co.uk
Dir *On A149*

Expect a warm, friendly welcome from the caring hosts of this charming 19th-century coaching inn, situated on the main coast road in Old Hunstanton. Bedrooms are bright and cheerful with New England style white furniture and coordinated fabrics. Public rooms include a cosy lounge bar and an intimate restaurant.

Facilities 7 en suite ⊗ TVB tea/coffee Direct dial from bedrooms Cen ht
No children 10yrs No coaches Dinner Last d 9.30pm **Prices** S £45-£60;
D £70-£90✳ **Parking** 7

◆◆◆◆

The Priory

2 Lower Lincoln St PE36 6DD ☎ 01485 532737
e-mail mikenal@swootton86.freeserve.co.uk
Dir *A149 onto Greevegate, 2nd right onto Northgate, 2nd right*

The friendly, family-run guest house is situated just a short walk from the seafront and town centre. The well-furnished bedrooms are pleasantly decorated, have coordinated soft fabrics and many thoughtful touches, and some rooms have lovely sea views. Breakfast is served at individual tables in the smart dining room.

Facilities 3 en suite ⊗ TVB tea/coffee ✗ Cen ht No children 2yrs
No coaches **Prices** D £50-£60✳ **LB** **Notes** ⊕

◆◆◆

Sutton House Hotel

24 Northgate PE36 6AP ☎ 01485 532552 ▦ 01485 532552
e-mail benelli@freeuk.com
Dir *Off A149 Cromer Rd onto Greevegate, 2nd right*

The caring hosts provide a warm family welcome at this guest house set in a peaceful residential area close to the seafront and town centre. The pleasant bedrooms are thoughtfully equipped, and some rooms have superb sea views. Breakfast and dinner are served in the smart dining room and there is a cosy lounge bar.

Facilities 8 en suite (2 fmly) ⊗ TVB tea/coffee ✗ Licensed Cen ht
TVL No coaches Dinner Last d breakfast **Prices** S £35-£50; D £49.50-£80✳
LB **Parking** 4

◆◆◆

The White Cottage ◇

19 Wodehouse Rd PE36 6JW ☎ 01485 532380

A charming cottage situated in a quiet side road in Old Hunstanton. The property has been owned and run by Mrs Burton for over 25 years. The spacious bedrooms are attractively decorated, and some have lovely sea views. Dinner is served in the smart dining room and there is a cosy sitting room with a television.

Facilities 3 rms (1 en suite) ⊘ TV1B Cen ht TVL No children 3yrs No coaches Dinner Last d 6.30pm **Prices** S £23-£25✳ **LB** **Parking** 11 **Notes** 🐾

◆◆◆

Richmond House Bed & Breakfast ◇

6-8 Westgate PE36 5AL ☎ 01485 532601

Dir Off A149 onto Westgate

The well-maintained house is well situated for the seafront and town centre. Its pleasant bedrooms vary in size and style, but all are well equipped and some rooms have superb sea views. Public rooms feature a smart restaurant and a cosy lounge bar.

Facilities 14 rms (10 en suite) (5 GF) ⊘ in dining room TVB tea/coffee ✖ Licensed Lift Cen ht No children 18yrs No coaches Dinner Last d 9pm **Prices** S £25-£30; D £45-£50✳ **Notes** Closed Nov-Etr 🐾

◆◆◆ 🅰

Rosamaly ◇

14 Glebe Av PE36 6BS ☎ 01485 534187 & 07775 724484
e-mail vacancies@rosamaly.co.uk

Dir A149 to Hunstanton. At rdbt take 3rd exit staying on A149 towards Cromer. In 1m church on left, Glebe Av is 2nd left, Rosamaly is 50yds on left

Facilities 6 en suite (2 fmly) (1 GF) ⊘ TVB tea/coffee Cen ht TVL No coaches Dinner Last d 1pm **Prices** S £30-£56; D £50-£56✳ **LB** **Notes** Closed 24 Dec-1 Jan 🐾

KING'S LYNN   MAP 12 TF62

◆◆◆◆

Fairlight Lodge ◇

79 Goodwins Rd PE30 5PE
☎ 01553 762234 📠 01553 770280
e-mail enquiries@fairlightlodge-online.co.uk

Dir Off A17/A47 onto A148 into town, over rdbt onto B1144 Vancouver Av, left onto Goodwins Rd

This well-maintained Victorian house stands in attractive gardens on the outskirts of town. The friendly proprietors ensure that good standards are maintained, and the bedrooms are smartly appointed and attractively coordinated. Some delightful ground-floor annexe rooms open onto the garden. A hearty breakfast is served in the bright, cosy dining room.

Facilities 5 rms (2 en suite) 3 annexe en suite (1 fmly) (4 GF) ⊘ TVB tea/coffee ✖ Cen ht No coaches **Prices** S £25-£32; D £41-£49✳ **Parking** 6 **Notes** Closed 24 Dec-2 Jan 🐾

◆◆◆

The Guanock ◇

10-11 Guanock Pl PE30 5QJ
☎ 01553 772959 📠 01553 772959

Dir Signs to town centre, premises on right of South Gates

Located within walking distance of the town centre, this friendly, family-run guest house offers comfortable, practical accommodation. Public areas include a lounge bar, pool room, and a bright dining room where breakfast and evening meals are served. There is also a delightful little roof garden.

Facilities 17 rms (5 fmly) (1 GF) ⊘ in 8 bedrooms ⊘ in dining room STV TVB tea/coffee ✖ Licensed Cen ht Pool Table Dinner Last d on booking **Prices** S £26-£30; D £48-£50 **Parking** 8 **Notes** Closed 24 Dec-3 Jan

◆◆◆

Maranatha Guest House

115/117 Gaywood Rd PE30 2PU
☎ 01553 774596 📠 01553 763747
e-mail maranathaguesthouse@yahoo.co.uk

Dir Signs to College of West Anglia, at junct in front of college onto Gaywood Rd, house opp school

The Victorian house is opposite King Edward School and close to the hospital, and is short walk from the town centre. The attractive bedrooms are practically equipped, and breakfasts is served in the pleasant lounge-dining room, which also has a pool table.

Facilities 10 rms (6 en suite) (2 fmly) ⊘ in 5 bedrooms ⊘ in dining room ⊘ in lounges TVB tea/coffee Cen ht TVL Dinner **Parking** 12

◆◆◆ 🅰

The Victory Inn

Main Rd, Clenchwarton PE34 4AQ ☎ 01553 660682
e-mail trevor.swift2@btinternet.com

Dir A47/A17 rdbt take the exit signed for West Lynn Clenchwarton. Continue for 3m, Victory Inn is on the right

Facilities 2 rms ⊘ in bedrooms ⊘ in dining room ⊘ in 1 lounge TVB tea/coffee Licensed Cen ht Pool Table Dinner Last d 7.30pm **Parking** 50 **Notes** Closed 26 Dec rs 25 Dec 🐾

England

MUNDESLEY
MAP 13 TG33

◆◆◆◆

The Pines
Trunch Rd NR11 8LF ☎ 01263 721019
e-mail thepines123@aol.com
web www.thepines.co.uk
Dir *1m SW of village. From junct A149 & B1436 through Southrepps to Mundesley*

Expect a warm welcome at this delightful property, which is in a peaceful rural location just a short drive from the charming seaside village of Mundesley. The stylish bedrooms have coordinated fabrics and many thoughtful touches. Breakfast is served at individual tables in the smart lounge-dining room.

Facilities 2 rms (1 en suite) (1 pri facs) 1 annexe en suite ⊗ TVB tea/coffee 🐾 Cen ht No children 13yrs No coaches **Prices** D £60-£80✳ **Parking** 5 **Notes** 🖼

NARBOROUGH
MAP 12 TF71

◆◆◆◆ Ⓐ ❦

Little Abbey Farm *(TF727135)*
Low Rd PE32 1JF ☎ 01760 337348 Mrs Howlett
e-mail howlettben@hotmail.com
Dir *Off A47 signed Narborough & Pentney, right at Ship Inn, 0.5m fork left onto Low Rd, 0.5m right bend, farm ahead*

Facilities 3 annexe en suite (3 GF) ⊗ TV1B tea/coffee 🐾 Cen ht TVL 100 acres Arable livestock Dinner Last d noon **Prices** S £35-£40; D £55-£65✳ **LB** **Conf** Max 12 Del from £50 ✳ **Parking** 10 **Notes** 🖼

NEATISHEAD
MAP 13 TG32

◆◆◆◆

R......
Th..)233
e-n.....................................
Dir

Exp...erty,
situ...e
attr...y
tho......................................m and
the

**Fac................................nges
TVB................................ing 6
Notes** 🖼

NORTH WALSHAM
MAP 13 TG23

◆◆◆◆◆ ❦

Whitehouse Farm *(TG302341)*
Knapton NR28 0RX
☎ 01263 721344 & 07879 475220 Mr Moorhouse
e-mail info@whitehousefarmnorfolk.co.uk

Please note that this establishment has recently changed hands. This delightful Grade II listed 18th-century flint cottage is surrounded by open farmland, and has been restored to retain original features. Bedrooms are attractively decorated and equipped with many thoughtful touches. Breakfast is served in the smart dining room and there is a cosy lounge.

Facilities 3 en suite (1 fmly) ⊗ TVB tea/coffee 🐾 Cen ht TVL No children 12yrs arable **Prices** S £40; D £50-£60✳ **Parking** 8

◆◆◆◆

Chimneys
51 Cromer Rd NR28 0HB ☎ 01692 406172 & 07952 117701
e-mail jenny.harmer@ntlworld.com
web www.chimneysbb.co.uk
Dir *0.5m NW of town centre on A149*

Expect a warm family welcome at this delightful Edwardian-style house, set in landscaped grounds close to the town centre. Bedrooms are carefully furnished and thoughtfully equipped; one room has a jacuzzi and wireless Internet access is available. Breakfast is served in the smart dining room and you can relax on the balcony overlooking the garden. Dinner is available by arrangement.

Facilities 3 en suite (1 fmly) ⊗ in bedrooms ⊗ in dining room ⊗ in lounges TVB tea/coffee Cen ht No coaches Pool Table jacuzzi/spa Dinner Last d 4.30pm **Prices** S £35-£40; D £50-£60✳ **Parking** 5 **Notes** 🖼

England

◆◆◆◆
Green Ridges ◇

104 Cromer Rd NR28 0HE
☎ 01692 402448 ▤ 01692 402448
e-mail admin@greenridges.com
web www.greenridges.com
Dir *On A149 from North Walsham to Cromer, at junct of B1145 to Aylsham*

A warm welcome is offered at this attractive detached property, situated on the edge of the busy market town. The bedrooms are pleasantly furnished and equipped with many thoughtful touches. Breakfast is served in the smart dining room, which overlooks mature gardens. Imaginative home-cooked dinners are available by arrangement.

Facilities 3 en suite (1 fmly) (3 GF) ⊗ STV FTV TVB tea/coffee Cen ht No coaches Dinner Last d Previous day **Prices** S £20-£35; D £40-£70✱ **Parking** 6 **Notes** ⊠

◆◆◆
Kings Arms Hotel

Kings Arms St NR28 9JX
☎ 01692 403054 ▤ 01692 500095
Dir *In town centre*

The former coaching inn stands in the heart of the bustling market town. The spacious public areas include a public bar, lounge bar and a popular restaurant. The bedrooms are pleasantly decorated and equipped with a good range of useful extras.

Facilities 7 en suite ⊗ in bedrooms ⊗ in dining room TVB tea/coffee ✖ Cen ht Pool Table Dinner Last d 8.45pm **Conf** Max 100 **Parking** 15

NORWICH   MAP 13 TG20
See also **Stoke Holy Cross**

Premier Collection

◆◆◆◆◆ ⊜
Catton Old Hall

Lodge Ln, Old Catton NR6 7HG
☎ 01603 419379 ▤ 01603 400339
e-mail enquiries@catton-hall.co.uk
web www.catton-hall.co.uk
Dir *2m N of city centre in Old Catton. A1042 N onto B1150, left onto White Woman Ln, left at lights onto Lodge Ln*

Expect a warm welcome from the caring hosts at this superb Jacobean house which dates from 1632. The property is just a short drive from the city centre and airport. Original features include brick and flint walls, oak timbers and reused Caen stone. The stylish bedrooms offer a high degree of comfort; each one carefully furnished. The elegant public areas include a dining room and a cosy lounge with plush furnishings.

Facilities 7 en suite ⊗ STV TVB tea/coffee Direct dial from bedrooms Licensed Cen ht TVL No children 12yrs No coaches Dinner Last d noon **Prices** S £70-£80; D £70-£120✱ **LB** **Parking** 11

◆◆◆◆
Beaufort Lodge

62 Earlham Rd NR2 3DF
☎ 01603 627928 ▤ 01603 440712
e-mail beaufortlodge@aol.com
web www.beaufortlodge.com
Dir *Off A140 onto B1108 Earlham Rd for 0.5m towards city centre*

A warm welcome is offered at this delightful Victorian property, which is only a short walk form the city centre. The attractive bedrooms have coordinated soft fabrics and many thoughtful touches. Breakfast is served at individual tables in the smart dining room. This is a non-smoking establishment.

Facilities 4 en suite ⊗ TVB tea/coffee ✖ Cen ht No children 18yrs No coaches **Prices** S £50-£55; D £60-£65✱ **Parking** 6 **Notes** Closed 28 Dec-2 Jan rs Xmas ⊠

◆◆◆◆
Old Thorn Barn

Corporation Farm, Wymondham Rd, Hethel NR14 8EU
☎ 01953 607785 & 07886 302370 ▤ 01953 601909
e-mail enquires@oldthornbarn.co.uk
Dir *6m SW of Norwich. Follow signs for Lotus Cars from A11 or B1113, on Wymondham Rd*

A delightful Grade II listed barn situated in a peaceful rural location just a short drive from the city centre. The property has stylish, thoughtfully equipped bedrooms with polished wood floors and antique pine furniture. Breakfast is served in the open-plan barn, which also has a wood-burning stove and a cosy lounge area.

Facilities 5 en suite 2 annexe en suite (7 GF) ⊗ FTV TVB tea/coffee ✖ Cen ht TVL No coaches **Prices** S £32-£36; D £50-£56✱ **Parking** 14

England

NORWICH continued

♦♦♦♦

The Arrandale Lodge ◇

431 Earlham Rd NR4 7HL

☎ 01603 250150 ▤ 01603 250150

Expect a friendly welcome at this well-maintained detached property set in neat gardens just a short drive from the city centre. The smartly decorated bedrooms are generally quite spacious and thoughtfully equipped. Breakfast is served at individual tables in the attractive dining room.

Facilities 7 rms (4 en suite) (3 GF) ⊗ TVB tea/coffee ✖ Cen ht No coaches **Prices** S £30-£50; D £50✱ **Parking** 12 **Notes** Closed Xmas

♦♦♦♦

Church Farm

Church St, Horsford NR10 3DB

☎ 01603 898020 ▤ 01603 891649

e-mail churchfarmguesthouse@btopenworld.co.uk

Dir 5m NW of city centre. A140 onto B1149, right at x-rds

A peaceful rural location a short drive from Norwich airport and the city centre. The spacious bedrooms are smartly decorated and have many thoughtful touches. Breakfast is served at individual tables in the conservatory-style lounge-dining room, which overlooks the garden and sun terrace.

Facilities 10 en suite (1 fmly) (3 GF) ⊗ TVB tea/coffee ✖ Cen ht TVL No coaches **Prices** S £35-£40; D £45-£55✱ **Parking** 20

♦♦♦♦

Cringleford Guest House

1 Gurney Ln, Cringleford NR4 7SB

☎ 01603 456456 & 07775 725933

e-mail robandkate@cringlefordguesthouse.co.uk

web www.cringlefordguesthouse.co.uk

Dir From A11/A47 Thickthorn rdbt signs to Norwich, 0.25m slip road to Cringleford, left at junct onto Colney Ln, Gurney Ln 5th on right

This delightful, friendly property is situated just a short drive from the hospital, University of East Anglia and major routes. The well-equipped bedrooms have coordinated fabrics and pine furniture. Breakfast is served at individual tables in the smart dining room.

Facilities 5 en suite (3 fmly) (1 GF) ⊗ TVB tea/coffee ✖ Cen ht No coaches **Prices** S £40-£45; D £60-£65✱ LB **Parking** 5 **Notes** Closed 2 wks Xmas

♦♦♦♦

Earlham Guesthouse ◇

147 Earlham Rd NR2 3RG

☎ 01603 454169 ▤ 01603 454169

e-mail earlhamgh@hotmail.com

Dir A140 onto B1108 Earlham Rd towards city centre, on left after shopping centre

This attractive Victorian property is a short walk from the city centre. The pleasant bedrooms come in a variety of styles, with coordinated fabrics and many thoughtful touches. Freshly cooked breakfasts are served at individual tables in the smart dining room.

Facilities 9 rms (3 en suite) (1 fmly) (1 GF) ⊗ TVB tea/coffee ✖ Cen ht No children 10yrs No coaches **Prices** S £22-£29; D £48-£56✱ LB **Notes** Closed 23-26 Dec

♦♦♦♦

The Gables

527 Earlham Rd NR4 7HN

☎ 01603 456666 ▤ 01603 250320

Dir Off S bypass onto B1108, signs to University of East Anglia, 300yds on left pass Fiveways rdbt, towards city centre

A warm welcome is to be expected at this smartly maintained guest house, which is close to the University of East Anglia and just a short drive from the hospital. The spacious bedrooms are individually decorated and thoughtfully equipped. Public rooms include an attractive conservatory dining room and an elegant lounge.

Facilities 11 en suite (1 fmly) (5 GF) ⊗ TVB tea/coffee Direct dial from bedrooms ✖ Cen ht TVL No coaches **Prices** S £46-£51; D £68-£73✱ **Parking** 11 **Notes** Closed 20 Dec-1 Jan

♦♦♦♦ 🅰

Arbor Linden Lodge

Linden House, 557 Earlham Rd NR4 7HW

☎ 01603 451303 & 250641 ▤ 01603 250641

e-mail info@guesthousenorwich.com

Dir 2m W of city centre. A140 ring road onto B1108 W Earlham Rd

Facilities 6 en suite (2 fmly) (1 GF) ⊗ TVB tea/coffee Direct dial from bedrooms ✖ Cen ht **Prices** S £39-£45; D £53-£60 LB **Parking** 6 **Notes** rs 21-28 Dec

♦♦♦♦ 🅰

Bristol House Hotel

80 Unthank Rd NR2 2RW

☎ 01603 625729 ▤ 01603 625794

Dir From A11 take 2nd exit on left. Unthank Rd located past Welcome to Norwich sign.

Facilities 9 en suite (3 GF) ⊗ in bedrooms ⊗ in dining room TVB tea/coffee ✖ Licensed Cen ht No children No coaches **Parking** 5

continued

◆◆◆
Edmar Lodge

64 Earlham Rd NR2 3DF
☎ 01603 615599 🖨 01603 495599
e-mail mail@edmarlodge.co.uk
web www.edmarlodge.co.uk
Dir *Off A47 S bypass onto B1108 Earlham Rd, follow university and hospital signs*

Located just a 10-minute walk from the city centre, this friendly family-run guest house offers ample private parking. Individually decorated bedrooms are smartly appointed and well equipped. Freshly prepared breakfasts are served in the cosy dining room, and a microwave and a refrigerator are also available. Please note that this establishment is strictly non-smoking.

Facilities 5 en suite (1 fmly) ⊗ FTV TVB tea/coffee Cen ht No coaches **Prices** S £35-£40; D £40-£48✳ **Parking** 6

◆◆◆
The Larches ◇

345 Aylsham Rd NR3 2RU
☎ 01603 415420 🖨 01603 465340
web www.thelarches.com
Dir *On A140 500yds past ring road, on left adjacent to Lloyds Bank*

A modern detached property situated only a short drive from the city centre and airport. The spacious, well-equipped bedrooms are brightly decorated and have coordinated soft fabrics. Breakfast is served at individual tables in the smart lounge-dining room.

Facilities 7 en suite (2 fmly) (1 GF) ⊗ in area of dining room ⊗ in 1 lounge STV TVB tea/coffee Cen ht TVL No coaches **Prices** S fr £30; d fr £45✳ **Parking** 10

◆◆◆
Marlborough House Hotel ◇

22 Stracey Rd, Thorpe Rd NR1 1EZ
☎ 01603 628005 🖨 01603 628005
Dir *Off A1242 0.5m E of city centre*

The personally run establishment is convenient for the railway station and football ground and just a short walk from the city centre. Its pleasant bedrooms have modern facilities, and the public rooms include a cosy lounge bar and a traditionally furnished breakfast room with separate tables.

Facilities 12 rms (7 en suite) (2 fmly) (1 GF) ⊗ TVB tea/coffee ✕ Licensed Cen ht TVL **Prices** S £30-£40; D £54-£58 LB **Parking** 5 **Notes** Closed 25-30 Dec 🐾

RINGSTEAD

MAP 12 TF74

◆◆◆◆ ⊛⊛ ⊜ ◀
The Gin Trap Inn

6 High St PE36 5JU ☎ 01485 525264 🖨 01485 525321
e-mail gintrap@aol.com
Dir *Off A149 into village centre*

The delightful 17th-century inn is in a quiet village near the coast. The public rooms have a relaxed and friendly atmosphere, including the large bar and the cosy restaurant. The accommodation is luxurious: each individually appointed bedroom has been carefully decorated and thoughtfully equipped.

Facilities 3 en suite ⊗ in bedrooms ⊗ in dining room ⊗ in 1 lounge TVB tea/coffee Direct dial from bedrooms Cen ht No coaches Dinner Last d 9pm **Parking** 50

SAXLINGHAM THORPE

MAP 13 TM29

◆◆◆◆ 🐾
Foxhole Farm ◇ *(TM218971)*

Foxhole NR15 1UG ☎ 01508 499226 🖨 01508 499226
Mr & Mrs Spear
e-mail foxholefarm@hotmail.com
Dir *Farm 0.75m E of village. Off A140 at Foxhole sign opp Mill Inn*

Expect a warm welcome at this delightful farmhouse, which is set in pretty landscaped gardens surrounded by open farmland. The attractive bedrooms have coordinated soft fabrics and many thoughtful touches. Breakfast is served at a large communal table in the elegant dining room.

Facilities 2 en suite ⊗ TVB tea/coffee ✕ Cen ht No children 14yrs 5 acres non-working **Prices** S £25-£30; D £45-£50✳ LB **Parking** 8 **Notes** Closed 15 Dec-8 Jan 🐾

SHERINGHAM

MAP 13 TG14

Premier Collection

★★★★★ Guest House
Bench Mark House

32 Morley Rd NR26 8JE ☎ 01263 823551
e-mail benchmark-house@btinternet.com
web www.benchmark-house.co.uk
Dir *0.5m S of town centre. Off A1082 onto Morley Rd*

Tea and home-made scones welcome you to this delightful Edwardian property situated in a peaceful residential road a short walk from the town centre. The spacious bedrooms are carefully appointed with coordinated fabrics and have many thoughtful touches. Public rooms include a cosy lounge-games room, a small lounge bar and an elegant dining room. Breakfast features local organic produce and superb home-cooked dinners are available by arrangement.

Facilities 5 en suite (2 GF) ⊗ TVB tea/coffee ✕ Cen ht No children 10yrs No coaches Dinner Last d 5.30pm **Prices** D £60-£85✳ LB **Parking** 6 **Notes** Closed 3-31 Jan 🐾

England

SHERINGHAM continued

♦♦♦♦
The Eight Acres
Glebe Farm, Holt Rd, Aylmerton NR11 8QA
☎ 01263 838094 ▤ 01263 838094
Dir On A148

A warm welcome is assured at this modern detached farmhouse, set amid open countryside just off the A148 on the outskirts of Cromer. Bedrooms are pleasantly decorated with coordinated soft furnishings and lovely pine furniture. Public rooms feature a large lounge-dining room with plush sofas.

Facilities 2 en suite ⊗ TVB tea/coffee ✖ Cen ht No children No coaches **Parking** 2 **Notes** Closed Oct-Mar ⊠

♦♦♦♦
At Knollside
43 Cliff Rd NR26 8BJ
☎ 01263 823320 & 07771 631 980 ▤ 01263 823320
e-mail millar@knollside.free-online.co.uk
web www.broadland.com/knollsidelodge.html
Dir 250yds E of town centre. A1082 to High St, onto Wyndham St & Cliff Rd

Expect a warm welcome at this delightful Victorian house, which overlooks the beach and sea. Bedrooms are carefully furnished with coordinated soft fabrics and have many thoughtful touches. Breakfast in the elegant dining room features local produce, and there is a comfortable lounge and a cosy bar.

Facilities 3 en suite (1 fmly) ⊗ TVB tea/coffee ✖ Licensed Cen ht No children 2yrs No coaches ♨ Dinner Last d Evening before **Prices** D £60-£70✳ **LB** **Parking** 3 **Notes** ⊠

♦♦♦♦
Amberleigh House
19 Cromer Rd NR26 8AB ☎ 01263 823081
Dir From A148 Holt to Cromer road, turn left to Sheringham. At rdbt turn right, 0.5m on left

A large detached property situated on the outskirts of the town on the A149 coast road. The smartly furnished bedrooms have coordinated fabrics and many thoughtful touches. Breakfast is served in the stylish dining room, which has stripped-wood flooring and individual light oak tables.

Facilities 3 en suite ⊗ TVB tea/coffee Cen ht No coaches Dinner Last d noon **Prices** D £50-£70; (incl. dinner) **LB** **Parking** 7 **Notes** Closed Oct-Mar ⊠

♦♦♦♦
Bay Leaf Guest House
10 St Peters Rd NR26 8QY
☎ 01263 823779 ▤ 01263 820041
e-mail bayleafgh@aol.com
Dir A149 Weybourne Rd onto Church St, 2nd right

This lovely, friendly Victorian house is situated just a short walk from the golf course, steam railway and town centre. There is a smart lounge bar and breakfast is served in the new conservatory-dining room, which overlooks the patio.

Facilities 7 en suite (2 fmly) (2 GF) ⊗ TVB tea/coffee ✖ Licensed Cen ht No children 8yrs No coaches **Prices** S £35-£55; D £52-£65 **LB** **Parking** 4 **Notes** ⊠

♦♦♦♦
Highfield
5 Montague Rd NR26 8LN
☎ 01263 825524 & 07769 628817
e-mail gmcaldwell@aol.com
Dir Off A148, left at minirbt, 1st right. Left at church, left onto South St & Montague Rd

A friendly welcome is offered at this delightful guest house, situated in a peaceful side road within easy walking distance of the shops and beach. The pleasantly furnished house offers smart, thoughtfully equipped bedrooms, and breakfast is served at individual tables in the attractive dining room.

Facilities 7 rms (6 en suite) (2 fmly) ⊗ TVB tea/coffee ✖ Cen ht TVL No children 8yrs **LB** **Conf** Max 20 **Parking** 4 **Notes** Closed 22 Dec-1 Feb ⊠

♦♦♦♦
Homefield Guest House
48 Cromer Rd, West Runton NR27 9AD ☎ 01263 837337
web www.homefieldguesthouse.co.uk
Dir A149 towards Sheringham, B&B on left in West Runton

This imposing detached property, dating from 1890, is on the A149 in the village of West Runton. Bedrooms are cheerfully decorated in pastel shades, with attractive coordinated fabrics and well-chosen furniture, and some rooms have superb sea views. Breakfast is served at individual tables in the smart dining room.

Facilities 6 en suite (1 fmly) ⊗ TVB tea/coffee ✖ Cen ht No children No coaches **Parking** 6 **Notes** ⊠

♦♦♦♦ Ⓐ
The Old Barn
Cromer Rd, West Runton NR27 9QT ☎ 01263 838285
Dir A149 from Cromer to West Runton, B&B 2m opp church

Facilities 3 rms (2 en suite) (1 pri facs) (1 GF) ⊗ TVB tea/coffee Cen ht TVL No children 18yrs No coaches Dinner Last d noon **Prices** S £40-£60; D £60-£65 **Parking** 6 **Notes** ⊠

continued

STOKE HOLY CROSS
MAP 13 TG20

◆◆◆ ❦

Salamanca ◇ (TG235022)
118 Norwich Rd NR14 8QJ ☎ 01508 492322
Mr & Mrs Harrold
Dir At N end of village

A 16th-century farmhouse seet in a peaceful rural location just a short drive from Norwich. Bedrooms are generally quite spacious, pleasantly decorated and have a good range of useful extras. Breakfast is served at individual tables in the dining room and there is a cosy lounge.

Facilities 3 rms (2 en suite) 1 annexe en suite ⊘ TV1B tea/coffee ✗
Cen ht TVL No children 6yrs 165 acres beef **Prices** S £30-£40; D £52-£64
LB **Conf** Max 10 **Parking** 7 **Notes** Closed 15 Dec-15 Jan & Etr 🐾

SWAFFHAM
MAP 13 TF80

◆◆◆◆

Corfield House
Sporle PE32 2EA ☎ 01760 723636
e-mail info@corfieldhouse.co.uk
web www.corfieldhouse.co.uk
Dir 3m E of Swaffham on S edge of village, 0.5m from A47

A delightful 19th-century property set in attractive landscaped gardens on the outskirts of Swaffham. Bedrooms (one of which is on the ground floor) are carefully furnished with coordinated fabrics and have many thoughtful touches. Public rooms include a quiet lounge and a comprehensive breakfast menu is offered in the elegant dining room.

Facilities 4 en suite (1 GF) ⊘ TVB tea/coffee ✗ Cen ht No coaches
Prices D £52✳ **Parking** 5 **Notes** Closed mid Dec-early Jan 🐾

◆◆◆ ▥

Red Lion Motel
87 Market Pl PE37 7AQ ☎ 01760 721022 📇 01760 720664
e-mail gwhoare@aol.com
Dir In town centre next to Woolworths

Located in the market place, the popular inn offers a range of real ales, meals and snacks in the lounge bar. Accommodation is in a motel-style block across the rear courtyard and includes bedrooms with modern facilities and some rooms suitable for families.

Facilities 9 annexe en suite (9 GF) ⊘ in dining room TVB tea/coffee ✗
Cen ht Dinner Last d 9.30pm **Parking** 8

SWANTON ABBOTT
MAP 13 TG22

Premier Collection

◆◆◆◆◆ 🏛

Pheasant Cottage
Long Common Ln NR10 5BH
☎ 01692 538169 📇 01692 538169
e-mail melanie@pheasantcottage.freeserve.co.uk
Dir Off B1150 at x-rds signed Swanton Abbott, turn right over bridge at x rds. Straight across onto Long Common Ln, 1.5m on left

Tea and home-made scones are offered on arrival at this charming 17th-century cottage surrounded by open countryside. The public rooms are full of character, including a cosy lounge with a log-burning stove, and a dining room with an oak-beamed ceiling. The spacious bedrooms have lovely coordinated fabrics and many thoughtful touches.

Facilities 2 en suite ⊘ TVB tea/coffee ✗ Cen ht TVL No coaches
Dinner Last d 6pm **Prices** S £45; D £79-£89✳ LB **Parking** 4 **Notes** 🐾

THOMPSON
MAP 13 TL99

◆◆◆◆ Ⓐ

The Chequers Inn
Griston Rd IP24 1PX ☎ 01953 483360 📇 01953 488092
e-mail richard@chequers-inn.wanadoo.co.uk
Dir 10m NE of Thetford. Off A1075 to Thompson village x-rds

Facilities 3 annexe en suite (1 fmly) (3 GF) ⊘ in bedrooms ⊘ in area of dining room TVB tea/coffee Direct dial from bedrooms Licensed Cen ht Fishing Dinner Last d 9.15pm **Parking** 35

England

THORNHAM

MAP 12 TF74

★★★ ⚫ Inn

The Orange Tree

High St PE36 6LY ☎ 01485 512213 ▤ 01485 512424
e-mail email@theorangetreethornham.co.uk
web www.theorangetreethornham.co.uk
Dir *On A149 in centre of village.*

A smart inn situated on the A149 coast road. Bedrooms are located in an annexe adjacent to the main building, each one pleasantly decorated and thoughtfully equipped. Public areas feature a contemporary bar-restaurant where an interesting choice of freshly prepared dishes is on offer.

Facilities 6 en suite (1 fmly) (6 GF) ⊗ in bedrooms ⊗ in dining room TVB tea/coffee Cen ht Dinner Last d 9pm **Prices** S £40-£50; D £70-£90✳ **Parking** 24

THURNING

MAP 13 TG02

◆◆ ⚘

Rookery Farm ◇ *(TG078307)*

NR24 2JP ☎ 01263 860357 Mrs Fisher
Dir *Off B1354 S through Briston, left at x-rds signed Saxthorpe, farm 0.6m on left*

The delightful 300-year-old brick farmhouse is set amid landscaped grounds in peaceful countryside. The spacious bedrooms are pleasantly decorated and well equipped. Breakfast is served at a large table in the dining room, which doubles as a sitting room.

Facilities 2 rms (1 en suite) (1 fmly) ⊗ tea/coffee ✖ TVL 400 acres arable Dinner Last d By arrangement **Prices** S £23-£25; D £46-£50✳ **Parking** available **Notes** Closed Dec-Jan ⊛

THURSFORD

MAP 13 TF93

★★★★★ Bed & Breakfast

Holly Lodge

The Street NR21 0AS ☎ 01328 878465 ▤ 01328 878465
e-mail info@hollylodgeguesthouse.co.uk
Dir *Off A148 into Thursford village*

Expect a warm welcome at this 18th-century property situated in a picturesque location surrounded by open farmland. The stylish cottage bedrooms are in a converted stable block, each room individually decorated, beautifully furnished and equipped with many useful

continued

extras. The attractive public rooms have a wealth of character, with flagstone floors, oak beams and open fireplaces. There are also superb landscaped grounds to enjoy.

Facilities 3 en suite (3 GF) ⊗ TVB tea/coffee ✖ Cen ht TVL No children 14yrs No coaches Large sundeck overlooking lake and water gardens **LB Parking** 6 **Notes** Closed Jan

WALCOTT

MAP 13 TG33

◆◆◆◆◆ ▤

Holly Tree Cottage

Walcott Gn NR12 0NS ☎ 01692 650721
Dir *1m S of Walcott. B1159 S from Walcott towards Stalham, 2nd left after Lighthouse Inn, then 2nd left again, right at pond, house signed on right*

This charming cottage lies in peaceful countryside within easy driving distance of the Norfolk Broads and the sea. The spacious bedrooms are attractively decorated and thoughtfully equipped. Breakfast is served in the smart dining room and there is also a cosy snug with a wood-burning stove.

Facilities 3 en suite ⊗ TVB tea/coffee ✖ Cen ht No children 18yrs No coaches attractive garden with summer house **Prices** S £40; D £60 **Parking** 4 **Notes** Closed Oct-Apr ⊛

WELLS-NEXT-THE-SEA

MAP 13 TF94

◆◆◆ ⚘

Branthill Farm *(TF900407)*

NR23 1SB ☎ 01328 710246 ▤ 01328 711524 Mrs Maufe
e-mail branthill.farms@macunlimited.net
Dir *1.5m SW of Wells off B1105*

A friendly, family-run farmhouse situated in peaceful countryside just a short drive from the north Norfolk coast. A hearty breakfast is served at the large communal table in the attractive dining room. The one bedroom is equipped with many useful extras and offers a good degree of comfort. A real ales shop is a successful addition to the farm.

Facilities 1 en suite ⊗ TVB tea/coffee ✖ Cen ht No children 12yrs ⚘ Q 1000 acres arable **Prices** D £55-£60; (room only) ✳ **LB Parking** 2 **Notes** ⊛

England

WEST RUNTON
MAP 13 TG14

Corner House

2 Station Rd NR27 9QD
☎ 01263 838540 & 07769 800831 ▤ 01263 838540
e-mail howard@cornerhousenorfolk.com
Dir S off A149, in centre of village, B&B 1st on right.

At the time of going to press the rating for this establishment had not been confirmed. Please check the AA website www.theAA.com for up-to-date information.

Facilities 3 rms (3 pri facs) ⊘ tea/coffee ✖ Cen ht TVL No children No coaches **Prices** D £56✳ **Notes** 🖼

WORSTEAD
MAP 13 TG32

◆◆◆◆

The Ollands

Swanns Yard NR28 9RP ☎ 01692 535150 ▤ 01692 535150
e-mail ollands@worstead.freeserve.co.uk
Dir Off A149 to village x-rds, off Back St

Expect a warm family welcome at this charming detached property in the heart of the picturesque village. The well-equipped bedrooms are carefully furnished, and breakfast served in the elegant dining room features local produce.

Facilities 3 en suite (1 GF) ⊘ in bedrooms ⊘ in dining room TVB tea/coffee Cen ht No coaches Dinner Last d 9am
Prices S £33.50-£36.50; D £52-£57✳ **LB Parking** 8 **Notes** 🖼

WROXHAM
MAP 13 TG31

◆◆◆◆

Bramble House

Cats Com, Norwich Rd, Smallburgh NR12 9NS
☎ 01692 535069 ▤ 01692 535069
e-mail bramblehouse@tesco.net
Dir 4m NE of Wroxham on A1151 Norwich Rd, off lay-by on left

This delightful detached property is situated in a peaceful rural location just a short drive from the busy town. The individually decorated bedrooms are carefully furnished and thoughtfully equipped; one room has a sauna. Breakfast, which includes home-produced free-range eggs and local produce, is served in the smart dining room.

Facilities 3 en suite (1 fmly) ⊘ TVB tea/coffee ✖ Cen ht TVL No children 5yrs No coaches Sauna **Prices** S £38-£40; D £54-£60✳ **LB Parking** 6 **Notes** Closed Xmas & New Year 🖼

◆◆◆◆ Ⓐ

Park Lodge ◇

142 Norwich Rd NR12 8SA ☎ 01603 782991
e-mail parklodge@computer-assist.net
Dir On A1151 in village centre

Facilities 3 en suite ⊘ TVB tea/coffee ✖ Cen ht No children 12yrs No coaches **Prices** S £30-£38; D £48-£54✳ **LB Parking** 4 **Notes** 🖼

◆◆◆

Beech Tree House

Wroxham Rd, Rackheath NR13 6NQ
☎ 01603 781419 & 07889 152063 ▤ 01603 781419
e-mail beechtree@talk21.com
Dir 1.5m SW of Wroxham on A1151 opp Green Man pub

This detached property, set amid pretty landscaped grounds and surrounded by farmland, is only a short drive from Norwich and Wroxham Broads. The spacious bedrooms have coordinated soft furnishings and many useful extras. Breakfast is served in the conservatory-lounge, which overlooks the garden.

Facilities 3 rms (1 en suite) (3 fmly) ⊘ in bedrooms ⊘ in dining room TVB tea/coffee Cen ht TVL No coaches Golf ⚹ **LB Parking** 5 **Notes** Closed 23 Dec-1 Jan 🖼

WYMONDHAM
MAP 13 TG10

◆◆◆◆ Ⓐ

Witch Hazel

55 Church Ln, Wicklewood NR18 9QH
☎ 01953 602247 ▤ 01953 602247
e-mail witchhazel@tiscali.co.uk
web www.witchhazel-norfolk.co.uk
Dir 2m W of Wymondham. Off B1135 to Wicklewood village x-rds, onto Church Ln, 200yds on right

Facilities 3 en suite ⊘ TVB tea/coffee ✖ Cen ht TVL No children 15yrs No coaches Dinner Last d 10.30am **Prices** S £31-£35; D £48-£52 **Parking** 3

NORTHAMPTONSHIRE

CORBY
MAP 11 SP88

◆◆◆◆

Spanhoe Lodge

Harringworth Rd NN17 3AT
☎ 01780 450328 ▤ 01780 450328
e-mail jennie.spanhoe@virgin.net
web www.spanhoelodge.co.uk
For full entry see **Laxton**

◆◆◆◆

Thatches on the Green

School Ln, Weldon NN17 3JN
☎ 01536 266681 ▤ 01536 266659
e-mail tom@thatches-on-the-green.fsnet.co.uk
web www.thatches-on-the-green.fsnet.co.uk
Dir Off A43, opp The Woolpack by village green

Located by the village green, the 16th-century former inn and adjoining cottages have been renovated to provide comfortable accommodation. The friendly proprietors are helpful, and breakfast and imaginative dinners are served in the cosy dining room, which has a small honesty bar. Bedrooms are individually appointed and thoughtfully equipped.

Facilities 10 rms (9 en suite) (1 fmly) (4 GF) ⊘ in bedrooms ⊘ in dining room ⊘ in lounges TVB tea/coffee ✖ Licensed Cen ht No coaches Dinner Last d by arrangement **Parking** 15

England

CORBY continued

♦♦ ◧

Raven Hotel ◇

Rockingham Rd NN17 1AG
☎ 01536 202313 🖷 01536 203159
e-mail info@theravenhotel.com
Dir A6003 towards Rockingham, right onto Rockingham Rd, premises on right after shopping parade

The public areas at the Raven are a haven for music lovers, consisting of Peppers bar, filled with a wealth of Beatles memorabilia, and the spacious and comfortable Piano bar, where a wide range of popular drinks and bar meals are served. Bedrooms are modern in style, and the establishment is popular with contractors and weekend sports groups.

Facilities 17 rms (5 en suite) (3 fmly) ⊗ in 13 bedrooms ⊗ in area of dining room ⊗ in 1 lounge TVB tea/coffee ✖ Cen ht TVL Pool Table Dinner Last d 8.30pm **Prices** S £30-£45; D £44-£55; (room only) **Conf** Max 300 Thtr 250 Board 100 Del from £200 **Parking** 40

KILSBY

MAP 11 SP57

♦♦♦♦ ⊜

Hunt House Quarters

Main Rd CV23 8XR ☎ 01788 823282 🖷 01788 823282
e-mail luluharris@hunthouse.fsbusiness.co.uk
web www.hunthousekilsby.com
Dir On B3048 in village

The thatched 17th-century hunting lodge has been renovated to provide quality bedrooms with smart modern bathrooms in a converted stable block. Comprehensive breakfasts are served in the adjacent L'Olive restaurant, which offers imaginative dinners on four evenings during the week.

Facilities 4 en suite (1 fmly) (4 GF) ⊗ TVB tea/coffee ✖ Licensed Cen ht No coaches Dinner Last d 9pm **Prices** S £59.95-£75; D £75-£85✳ **LB Parking** 8

LAXTON

MAP 11 SP99

♦♦♦♦ 🏠

Spanhoe Lodge

Harringworth Rd NN17 3AT
☎ 01780 450328 🖷 01780 450328
e-mail jennie.spanhoe@virgin.net
web www.spanhoelodge.co.uk
Dir Off A43 to Laxton, through village, Spanhoe Lodge 0.5m on right

This delightful modern house stands in open countryside and has wonderful gardens. You can expect very caring and friendly service, and pleasantly furnished bedrooms. There is a lovely dining room, lounge, and a fine conservatory. Breakfast is very special here and makes use of fresh local produce.

Facilities 4 en suite (3 GF) ⊗ TVB tea/coffee Cen ht TVL Snooker Dinner Last d noon **Prices** S £40-£60; D £65-£90✳ **LB Conf** Max 70 Thtr 70 Class 34 Board 36 **Parking** 50

NORTHAMPTON

MAP 11 SP76

♦♦♦♦

The Poplars Hotel

33 Cross St, Moulton NN3 7RZ
☎ 01604 643983 🖷 01604 790233
e-mail info@thepoplarshotel.com
web www.thepoplarshotel.com
Dir From A43 into Moulton Village. Exit one way system left at Co-op, next right into Cross St.

Located north of the city in the pretty village of Moulton, the ivy-clad house provides warm hospitality. Bedrooms, some of which are located in a quality chalet extension, are filled with a good range of practical extras. The public areas include a comfortable lounge and a

continued

cottage-style dining room where imaginative evening meals are served from Monday to Thursday.

Facilities 17 rms (13 en suite) (1 fmly) (5 GF) ⊗ TVB tea/coffee Direct dial from bedrooms Licensed Cen ht TVL No coaches Dinner Last d 8pm **Prices** S £36-£80; D £62.50-£100✱ **Parking** 16 **Notes** Closed Xmas & New Year rs No dinner available Fri-Sun

OUNDLE
MAP 11 TL08

◆◆◆ ◖▮

The Ship Inn
18-20 West St PE8 4EF ☎ 01832 273918 📠 01832 270232
e-mail enquiries@theshipinn-oundle.co.uk
Dir In town centre

This traditional-style inn is situated in the centre of the historic town. The pleasant bedrooms are split between three converted buildings to the rear of the property; some of the newer rooms have pine furniture and bright coordinated fabrics. Public rooms include a busy taproom, a lounge bar and a separate dining room.

Facilities 14 rms (11 en suite) (1 fmly) (8 GF) ⊗ in dining room TV11B tea/coffee Cen ht TVL Dinner Last d 9pm **Conf** Max 50 Thtr 30 Class 30 Board 30 **Parking** 70

Ⓤ

Bridge Cottage Bed & Breakfast
Oundle Rd, Woodnewton PE8 5EG
☎ 01780 470779 & 07979 644864 📠 01780 470860
e-mail judycolebrook@btinternet.com
web www.bridgecottage.net
Dir Exit A1, take A605 to Northampton and Oundle. Turn right at 1st rdbt to Fotheringhay, 2m to Woodnewton, 1st house on left.

At the time of going to press the rating for this establishment had not been confirmed. Please check the AA website www.theAA.com for up-to-date information.

Facilities 3 rms (2 en suite) (1 pri facs) ⊗ STV TVB tea/coffee ✖ Cen ht TVL No children No coaches **Parking** 3 **Notes** rs 24-26 Dec

SIBBERTOFT
MAP 11 SP68

Ⓤ

Keepers Cottage
NN6 6EZ
☎ 01858 575710 & 07778 526701 📠 01858 575532
e-mail sueniven@hotmail.co.uk
Dir A5119 Welford, towards Naseby. Sulby Grange 1m on left, turn onto concrete road

At the time of going to press the rating for this establishment had not been confirmed. Please check the AA website www.theAA.com for up-to-date information.

Facilities 1 en suite (1 GF) ⊗ STV TVB tea/coffee ✖ Cen ht TVL No coaches 🎱 Snooker Sauna Dinner Last d 8pm **Prices** S £70; D £90✱ **LB Parking** 6 **Notes** Closed 16 Dec-4 Jan 🚭

STANWICK
MAP 11 SP97

Premier Collection

◆◆◆◆◆

The Courtyard
Rutland Lodge, West St NN9 6QY
☎ 01933 622233 📠 01933 622276
e-mail bookings@thecourtyard.me.uk
web www.thecourtyard.me.uk
Dir A45 rdbt to Stanwick, 0.3m right onto drive

Standing in extensive and delightful gardens on the edge of the village, this very well-furnished detached house offers every possible comfort, and the lounge is especially relaxing. Quality breakfasts are served around a large oak table and hospitality is really special.

Facilities 6 en suite (4 GF) ⊗ STV TVB tea/coffee ✖ Cen ht TVL No children No coaches Dinner Last d 9pm **Prices** S £45-£50; D £60-£75✱ **LB Conf** Max 12 **Parking** 12

England

NORTHUMBERLAND

ALNWICK
MAP 21 NU11

◆◆◆◆

Bondgate House
20 Bondgate Without NE66 1PN ☎ 01665 602025
e-mail enquiries@bondgatehouse.co.uk
web www.bondgatehouse.co.uk
Dir *A1 onto B6346 into town centre, 200yds past war memorial on
right*

Originally a doctor's house, this Georgian building stands close to the
historic gateway into the town centre. Friendly service complements
an attractive breakfast room and the cosy lounge. Bedrooms are
furnished in quality pine and include three rooms in converted stables
set in a secluded garden behind the house.

Facilities 3 en suite 3 annexe en suite (2 fmly) (1 GF) ⊗ TVB
tea/coffee ✱ Cen ht TVL No coaches Aromatherapy massage
Prices D £65-£75✳ **Parking** 8 **Notes** Closed Xmas ⊠

◆◆◆ ❦

Rock Farm House B & B *(NU204201)*
Rock NE66 3SE ☎ 01665 579367 Mr & Mrs Corbitt
e-mail stay@rockfarmhouse.co.uk
Dir *Off A1 into village centre*

Do not be misled by the surroundings of this old farmhouse. Inside, a
loving restoration has transformed it into a delightful home. The
spacious and comfortable bedrooms upstairs look out onto walled
gardens, and downstairs there is a cosy lounge with a wood-burning
stove and a charming dining room where breakfast (with healthy
options) is served at a large pine table.

Facilities 3 en suite (1 fmly) ⊗ FTV TVB tea/coffee Cen ht 1 acres
Non-working **Prices** S £39.50; D £49-£59✳ **LB Parking** 10

BARDON MILL
MAP 21 NY76

◆◆◆◆ Ⓐ ❦

Gibbs Hill Farm B&B *(NY749693)*
NE47 7AP ☎ 01434 344030 📠 01434 344030 Mrs Gibson
e-mail val@gibbshillfarm.co.uk
Dir *Off A69 at Bardon Mill, signs to Oncebrewed, over B6318, up hill,
1m right at sign to Gibbs Hill*

Facilities 3 en suite (1 fmly) ⊗ TVB tea/coffee ✱ Cen ht TVL
No children 10yrs Fishing Riding 750 acres Mixed **Prices** S £35-£40;
D £56-£60 **LB Parking** 10 **Notes** Closed Oct-Apr

BELFORD
MAP 21 NU13

◆◆◆◆ 🔔

Market Cross
1 Church St NE70 7LS ☎ 01668 213013
e-mail details@marketcross.net
web www.marketcross.net
Dir *Off A into village, opp church*

Lying in the heart of the village, this Grade II listed building offers
delightful, individually styled and thoughtfully equipped bedrooms.

continued

Breakfast is a real treat, an impressive range of delicious cooked
dishes using local produce.

Facilities 3 en suite (1 fmly) ⊗ FTV TVB tea/coffee Cen ht TVL
No coaches Special rates at local golf courses **Prices** S £45-£70;
D £65-£75✳ **LB Parking** 3

CORBRIDGE
MAP 21 NY96

◆◆◆◆

Riverside
Main St NE45 5LE ☎ 01434 632942 📠 01434 633883
e-mail david@theriversideguesthouse.co.uk
web www.theriversideguesthouse.co.uk
Dir *Off A69/A695 into town centre near bridge*

Occupying a prominent position in the centre of Corbridge, the
historic house has splendid views southwards across the River Tyne.
The original bedrooms are well proportioned, and the ground-floor
wing rooms are bright and modern. There is an inviting lounge and
breakfast is served in a spacious dining room.

Facilities 10 rms (7 en suite) (2 fmly) (4 GF) ⊗ TVB tea/coffee Direct
dial from bedrooms Cen ht No coaches **Prices** S £32-£50; D £52-£70 **LB
Parking** 7 **Notes** Closed Xmas & New Year

CORNHILL-ON-TWEED
MAP 21 NT83

Premier Collection

◆◆◆◆◆ 🔔

Ivy Cottage ◇
1 Croft Gdns, Crookham TD12 4ST
☎ 01890 820667 📠 01890 820667
e-mail ajoh540455@aol.com
Dir *4m E of Cornhill. Off A697 onto B6353 into Crookham village*

Hospitality is second to none at this pristine modern house set in
delightful gardens in a quiet village. One bedroom is furnished in
bright modern style while the upstairs room has antique pine; each
room has a super private bathroom and host of thoughtful touches.
Delicious Aga-cooked breakfasts are served either in the farmhouse-
style kitchen or the cosy dining room. You can enjoy tea in the new
summerhouse.

Facilities 2 rms (2 pri facs) (1 GF) ⊗ TVB tea/coffee Cen ht
No children 5yrs No coaches Dinner Last d am same day
Prices S £39.50; D £60-£69 **LB Parking** 2 **Notes** ⊠

CRASTER
MAP 21 NU21

★★★ Guest Accommodation
The Cottage Inn
Dunstan Village NE66 3SZ ☎ 01665 576658
e-mail enquires@cottageinnhotel.co.uk
Dir Coastal route signs from A1 at Alnwick to Craster

Located in peaceful countryside, families are well catered for here with outdoor play areas and well appointed bedrooms. A wide range of freshly cooked meals is available in the comfortable bar lounge (featuring real ales) or spacious restaurant, with breakfast served in the conservatory.

Facilities 10 en suite (10 GF) ⊗ in bedrooms ⊗ in dining room ⊗ in lounges TVB tea/coffee 🐾 Cen ht Pool Table Dinner Last d 9.30pm **Prices** S £35-£45; D £60-£80✻ **LB** **Parking** 60

FALSTONE
MAP 21 NY78

◆◆◆◆ ◖
The Pheasant Inn
Stannersburn NE48 1DD
☎ 01434 240382 📠 01434 240382
e-mail enquiries@thepheasantinn.com
web www.thepheasantinn.com
Dir A68 onto B6320, signs for Kielder Water

This charming establishment epitomises the traditional country inn: it has character, good food and warm hospitality. Bright modern bedrooms, some with their own entrances, are all contained in stone buildings adjoining the inn. Delicious home-cooked meals are served in the bar with its low-beamed ceilings and exposed stone walls, or in the attractive dining room.

Facilities 8 annexe en suite (1 fmly) (5 GF) ⊗ in bedrooms ⊗ in dining room ⊗ in 1 lounge TVB tea/coffee Cen ht No coaches Dinner Last d 8.50pm **LB** **Parking** 40

◆◆◆ ◖
The Blackcock Inn
NE48 1AA ☎ 01434 240200 📠 01434 240200
e-mail dbdelboy@yahoo.co.uk
Dir A68 onto B6379 to Bellingham & signs for Falstone

The traditional family-run village inn lies close to Kielder Water. A cosy pub, it has a very homey atmosphere, with a welcoming fire in the bar in colder weather. Evening meals are served here and in the non-smoking restaurant, which is reminiscent of a Victorian parlour. The inn is closed during the day on Tuesdays throughout winter.

Facilities 6 rms (4 en suite) (1 fmly) ⊗ in bedrooms ⊗ in dining room TVB tea/coffee Cen ht No coaches Fishing Pool Table Dinner Last d 8.30pm **Prices** S £40; D £60✻ **LB** **Parking** 15

GREENHEAD
MAP 21 NY66

◆◆◆◆
Holmhead
Thirlwall Castle Farm, Hadrians Wall CA8 7HY
☎ 016977 47402 📠 016977 47402
web www.bandbhadrianswall.com
Dir Off B6318 between Ye Olde Forge Tea Rooms & Youth Hostel, over bridge, premises 0.25m along Farm Rd

Built on the course of Hadrian's Wall, the traditional farmhouse offers comfortable, good-value accommodation. The cosy bedrooms are attractively decorated and traditionally furnished. The lounge has an abundance of books, board games and toys, and Pauline Staff's knowledge of local history and archaeology is useful for all. A set dinner is available, and you can chose from possibly the longest breakfast menu in the world.

Facilities 4 en suite 1 annexe en suite (1 fmly) (1 GF) ⊗ tea/coffee 🐾 Licensed Cen ht TVL Badminton Dinner Last d 3pm **Prices** D £60-£66✻ **LB** **Parking** 6 **Notes** Closed 19 Dec-9 Jan rs Nov-Etr

England

HALTWHISTLE
MAP 21 NY76

See also **Brampton (Cumbria)**

◆◆◆◆

Vallum Lodge

Military Rd, Twice Brewed NE47 7AN
☎ 01434 344248 🖺 01434 344488
e-mail stay@vallum-lodge.co.uk
web www.vallum-lodge.co.uk
Dir On B6318, 400yds W of Once Brewed National Park visitors centre

Set in the Northumberland National Park, this well-equipped home from hom provides easy access to Hadrian's Wall. The en suite bedrooms have been refurbished and feature homey extras. Breakfast is served in the smart dining room and there is a cosy lounge. The Lodge is licensed and all accommodation is on the ground floor.

Facilities 6 en suite (1 fmly) (6 GF) ⊗ TVB tea/coffee ✖ Licensed Cen ht TVL No children 3yrs No coaches **Prices** S £46-£56; D £60-£66 **Parking** 15 **Notes** Closed Nov-Feb

HEXHAM
MAP 21 NY96

Premier Collection

◆◆◆◆◆ 🕎

Montcoffer

Bardon Mill NE47 7HZ ☎ 01434 344138 🖺 01434 344730
e-mail john-dehlia@talk21.com
web www.montcoffer.co.uk
Dir Off A69 4m W of Haydon Bridge signed Bardon Mill, 0.25m into village on left

John's passion for period pieces and collectables and Dehlia's design skills have transformed the former stables into a stylish guest house. Dehlia's adjacent studio specialises in fabrics and decorative wall hangings and many of her works adorn the house. The bedrooms have headboards made from reclaimed timber from the chapel at Bagshot House, home of the Earl and Countess of Wessex.

Facilities 2 en suite (1 fmly) (2 GF) ⊗ TVB tea/coffee ✖ Cen ht No coaches Fishing **Prices** S £35-£45; D £66-£75 LB **Parking** 12 **Notes** 😒

◆◆◆◆

Peth Head Cottage ◇

Juniper NE47 0LA ☎ 01434 673286 🖺 01434 673038
e-mail peth_head@btopenworld.com
web www.peth-head-cottage.co.uk
Dir B6306 S from Hexham, 200yds fork right, next left. Continue 3.5m, house 400yds on right after Juniper sign

This lovely sandstone cottage is in the peaceful village of Juniper. Enjoy home-made biscuits on arrival and home-baked bread and preserves at breakfast. The attractive bedrooms are comfortable, and there is a cosy lounge-breakfast room. Self-catering is also available.

Facilities 2 en suite ⊗ TVB tea/coffee ✖ Cen ht TVL No coaches **Prices** S £25; D £50 LB **Parking** 2

◆◆◆◆ 🅰 💘

Rye Hill (NY958580)

Slaley NE47 0AH ☎ 01434 673259 🖺 01434 673259
Mrs Courage
e-mail info@ryehillfarm.co.uk
Dir 5m S of Hexham off B6306, 1st right after Travellers Rest pub then 1st farm road right

Facilities 6 en suite (2 fmly) ⊗ in bedrooms ⊗ in dining room TVB tea/coffee Cen ht Pool Table Games barn, Skittle alley, Table tennis 30 acres sheep Dinner Last d 4pm **Prices** S £35; D £55✳ **Parking** 6

KIRKWHELPINGTON
MAP 21 NY98

◆◆◆ 💘

Horncastle Farm ◇ (NY985846)

NE19 2RA ☎ 01830 540247 Mrs Pittendrigh
e-mail jspitt@horncastle.wanadoo.co.uk
Dir On A696 opp village of Kirkwhelpington

A relaxed atmosphere and a friendly welcome are assured at this upland farmhouse set in sheltered gardens and reached by a farm track across pastureland. It is a family home and offers a ground-floor and an upstairs bedroom, plus a lounge and a dining room where hearty breakfasts are served.

Facilities 2 rms (1 en suite) (1 pri facs) (1 GF) ⊗ tea/coffee ✖ Cen ht TVL 370 acres beef mixed sheep **Prices** S £25-£50; D £50✳ **Parking** 5 **Notes** Closed Apr 😒

LONGFRAMLINGTON
MAP 21 NU10

◆◆◆◆

Dene House Farm

NE65 8EE ☎ 01665 570665 & 570549 🖨 01665 570549
e-mail info@denehousefarm.com
web www.denehousefarm.com

Tucked away in the countryside, this comfortable guest house has many welcome extras including a swimming pool and a gym. One bedroom is in the main house with a feature bath and the others are in the adjoining cottages with easy access shower rooms. Relax in the cosy lounge and enjoy hearty breakfasts in the elegant dining room.

Facilities 4 en suite (4 GF) ⊘ in bedrooms TVB tea/coffee ✖ Cen ht TVL No children 5yrs 🔍 🔍 Sauna Gymnasium 🏌 Pitch & putt, steam room, beauty therapy, archery **Parking** 8 **Notes** 🐾

ROTHBURY
MAP 21 NU00

Premier Collection

◆◆◆◆◆ 🏛

The Orchard House

High St NE65 7TL ☎ 01669 620684
e-mail graham@orchardhouserothbury.com
web www.orchardhouserothbury.com
Dir In village centre

Orchard House stands on a peaceful elevated location within easy walking distance of the village amenities. Bedrooms are luxuriously furnished and have many thoughtful extras. The lounge is stylish and very comfortable with an honesty bar for the evenings. The smart dining room offers interesting breakfasts featuring the best of local and organic produce.

Facilities 4 en suite (1 fmly) ⊘ TVB tea/coffee ✖ Licensed Cen ht No coaches **Prices** D £80-£150 **Notes** Closed Xmas & New Year

See advertisement on this page

WOOLER
MAP 21 NT92

Premier Collection

◆◆◆◆◆ 🏛

The Old Manse ◇

New Rd, Chatton NE66 5PU ☎ 01668 215343
e-mail chattonbb@aol.com
web www.oldmansechatton.co.uk
Dir 4m E of Wooler. On B6348 in Chatton

Built in 1875, this former manse stands in gardens on the edge of the village. There is a four poster upstairs, and a ground-floor room with its own sitting room and patio. Both are thoughtfully equipped with a host of extras including fridge with fruit, CD player, juices and biscuits, and an extensive range of toiletries. Impressive breakfasts are served in the conservatory, but it's Christine Brown's hospitality that makes the greatest impression.

Facilities 3 en suite (1 GF) ⊘ TVB tea/coffee ✖ Cen ht TVL No children 13yrs No coaches **Prices** S £30-£55; D £60-£70✳ **Parking** 4 **Notes** 🐾

WOOLER continued

♦♦♦

Winton House

39 Glendale Rd NE71 6DL ☎ 01668 281362
e-mail enquiries@wintonhousebandb.co.uk
Dir Off A697 into Wooler, off High St

This friendly family home is surrounded by secluded gardens in a quiet residential area just off the village centre. Bedrooms are spacious, as are two of the bathrooms. Breakfasts feature tasty sausages and bacon from a local butcher.

Facilities 3 rms (2 en suite) ⊘ TVB tea/coffee ✖ Cen ht No children 4yrs No coaches **Prices** D £42-£50✳ **Notes** Closed Nov-Feb ⊠

NOTTINGHAMSHIRE

BINGHAM
MAP 11 SK73

♦♦♦♦

Yeung Sing Hotel & Restaurant

15 Market St NG13 8AB
☎ 01949 831831 & 831222 📠 01949 838833
e-mail manager@yeung-sing.co.uk
Dir Off junct A52 & A46

This family-run guest house is in the centre of the market town. The smart ground-floor public rooms include a bar and the highly successful Yeung Sing restaurant, which serves a fine selection of Cantonese and regional Chinese dishes. The bedrooms are well equipped and have modern en suites.

Facilities 15 en suite (2 fmly) ⊘ in dining room ⊘ in 1 lounge TVB tea/coffee Direct dial from bedrooms ✖ Licensed Lift Cen ht TVL Dinner Last d 9.30pm **Conf** Max 100 Thtr 100 Class 30 Board 30 **Parking** 30 **Notes** Closed 25-26 Dec

---

COTGRAVE
MAP 11 SK63

♦♦♦♦

Jerico Farm (SK654307)

Fosse Way NG12 3HG
☎ 01949 81733 📠 01949 81733 Mrs Herrick
e-mail info@jericofarm.co.uk
web www.jericofarm.co.uk
Dir Farm driveway off A46, 1m N of junct A46 & A606

There is a friendly and relaxed atmosphere at this attractive farmhouse, which stands in peaceful extensive grounds just off the A46, close to Nottingham, Melton Mowbray and the Vale of Belvoir. Day rooms include a comfortable lounge and a separate dining room overlooking gardens, in which substantial tasty breakfasts are served. The spacious bedrooms are beautifully appointed and thoughtfully equipped.

Facilities 3 en suite (1 fmly) ⊘ TVB tea/coffee ✖ Cen ht TVL No children 10yrs Fishing 150 acres mixed **Prices** S £38-£42; D £55-£60 **Parking** 4 **Notes** Closed Xmas wk

ELTON
MAP 11 SK73

♦♦♦♦

The Grange

Sutton Ln NG13 9LA
☎ 01949 851561 & 07887 952181 📠 01949 851561
web www.thegrangebedandbreakfastnotts.co.uk
Dir From Grantham A1 onto A52 to Elton x-rds, left 200yds, B&B on right

Parts of this lovely house date from the early 17th century and the rooms command fine views across the gardens and rolling open countryside. Bedrooms contain many thoughtful extras and fine hospitality is assured from the proprietors.

Facilities 3 en suite ⊘ FTV TVB tea/coffee ✖ Cen ht TVL No coaches **Prices** S £38-£45; D £55-£60✳ **Parking** 8 **Notes** ⊠

FARNSFIELD
MAP 16 SK65

♦♦♦

Grange Cottage ◈

Main St NG22 8EA ☎ 01623 882259
e-mail bedandbreakfast@grange-cottage.co.uk
web www.grange-cottage.co.uk
Dir In village opp Plough Inn car park

Grange Cottage is a charming 18th-century property set in 2 acres of delightful gardens and grounds behind security gates. The bedrooms are homely, each individually furnished with lots of family touches. A freshly-cooked breakfast is served at one large table in the elegant dining room.

Facilities 4 rms (1 en suite) (1 pri facs) 1 annexe en suite (1 GF) ⊘ TVB tea/coffee Cen ht No coaches **Prices** S £25-£35✳ **LB Parking** 6 **Notes** ⊠

HOLBECK
MAP 16 SK57

Premier Collection

◆◆◆◆◆

Browns

The Old Orch Cottage S80 3NF
☎ 01909 720659 📠 01909 720659
e-mail browns@holbeck.fsnet.co.uk
Dir *0.5m off A616 Sheffield-Newark road, turn for Holbeck at x-rds*

Set amid beautifully tended gardens with lily ponds and extensive lawns, this mid 18th-century cottage is a tranquil rural hideaway. Breakfasts are served in the Regency-style dining room, and the elegant bedrooms have four-poster beds and many extras. The friendly owners provide attentive service, including courtesy transport to nearby restaurants if required.

Facilities 3 annexe en suite (3 GF) ⊗ in bedrooms ⊗ in dining room TVB tea/coffee ✕ Cen ht No children 18yrs No coaches
Prices S £50-£55; D £65-£75✳ **Parking** 3 **Notes** Closed Xmas wk 🅿

HOLME PIERREPONT
MAP 11 SK63

◆◆◆

Holme Grange Cottage

Adbolton Ln NG12 2LU ☎ 0115 981 0413 📠 0115 981 0174
e-mail jean.colinwightman@talk21.com
Dir *Off A52 SE of Nottingham, opp National Water Sports Centre*

A stone's throw from the National Water Sports Centre, this establishment with an all-weather tennis court is ideal for the active guest. Indeed, when not providing warm hospitality and freshly cooked breakfasts, the proprietor is usually on the golf course.

Facilities 3 rms (1 en suite) (1 fmly) ⊗ TVB tea/coffee Cen ht TVL No coaches ⊙ quarter size snooker table **Prices** S £25-£35; D £45-£60✳ **Parking** 6 **Notes** Closed Xmas 🅿

KEYWORTH
MAP 11 SK63

◆◆◆◆ ♈

Laurel Farm *(SK633305)*

Browns Ln, Stanton On The Wold NG12 5BL
☎ 0115 937 3488 Mrs Moffat
e-mail laurelfarm@yahoo.com
Dir *1m E of Keyworth centre. Off A606 at filling station, 0.5m on right*

Part of this traditional farmhouse is reputedly 300 years old, and all of
continued

the bedrooms are spacious and have many extras. Breakfast, served in the large dining room, is a wide choice of hearty and healthy options, ranging from full English to smoked salmon with scrambled egg. Laurel Farm is not just non-smoking establishment but for non-smokers only.

Facilities 3 rms (1 en suite) (2 pri facs) ⊗ TVB tea/coffee ✕ Cen ht No children 8yrs 4 acres Small holding **Prices** S £37.50-£55; D £55-£70 **Parking** 3

LOWDHAM
MAP 11 SK64

◆◆◆ ▣

The Old Ship Inn

Main St NG14 7BE ☎ 0115 966 3049 📠 0115 966 3426
e-mail robert@oldshipinn.freeserve.co.uk
Dir *Off A6097 at Lowdham Island towards Southwell, 1st left, inn 800yds on right*

A traditional, whitewashed village inn offering accommodation in smartly decorated bedrooms. The beamed lounge and public bar are popular with locals, while the restaurant offers an imaginative choice and an interesting wine list. The inn caters for special occasions, and there are plenty of sporting activities available nearby.

Facilities 6 en suite (1 fmly) ⊗ in bedrooms ⊗ in dining room ⊗ in 1 lounge TVB tea/coffee ✕ Cen ht Pool Table Dinner Last d 9.15pm **Parking** 30

MANSFIELD
MAP 16 SK56

◆◆◆◆

Appleby Guest House

Chesterfield Rd, Pleasley NG19 7PF
☎ 01623 810508 📠 01623 810508
e-mail kay@applebyguesthouse.co.uk
Dir *3.5m NW of Mansfield, on A617 N of Pleasley*

This well-furnished country house stands in well-tended grounds and offers spacious and immaculately presented bedrooms. Public areas include a comfortable lounge and a delightful dining room where substantial breakfasts are served.

Facilities 5 rms (3 en suite) (2 fmly) ⊗ in bedrooms ⊗ in dining room TVB tea/coffee ✕ Cen ht TVL No coaches ⊙ 🅰 **Parking** 8 **Notes** Closed 23 Dec-2 Jan

England

MANSFIELD continued

♦♦♦

Bridleways Holiday Homes & Guest House

Newlands Rd, Forest Town NG19 0HU
☎ 01623 635725 🖹 01623 635725
e-mail bridleways@webnet2000.net
web www.stayatbridleways.co.uk
Dir Off B6030

Beside a quiet bridleway that leads to Vicar Water Country Park and Sherwood Pines Forest Park, this friendly guest house is a good touring base for walkers, cyclists or sightseeing. The new double, twin and family bedrooms are particularly spacious and all rooms are en suite. Lovely breakfasts are served in the cottage-style dining room.

Facilities 9 en suite (1 fmly) (2 GF) ⊗ TVB tea/coffee ✖
Prices S £33; D £62 **Parking** 14 **Notes** ⊜

♦♦♦

Parkhurst ♢

28 Woodhouse Rd NG18 2AF
☎ 01623 627324 🖹 01623 452442
e-mail phil.fletcher@mansfieldhotel.co.uk
web www.parkhurstguesthouse.co.uk
Dir 0.25m N of town centre. Off A60 Woodhouse Rd onto Park Av

This well-furnished Victorian property is only a 10-minute walk from the centre of town. A cosy bar with television is available, and good breakfasts are served in the traditional style dining room. Bedrooms are comfortably appointed.

Facilities 11 rms (6 en suite) (4 fmly) (3 GF) ⊗ in dining room ⊗ in 1 lounge TVB tea/coffee ✖ Licensed Cen ht TVL No coaches
Prices S £25-£30; D £45-£50✹ **Conf** Max 12 Thtr 25 Class 16 Board 20
Parking 9

NEWARK-ON-TRENT   MAP 17 SK75

★★★★ Guest House

Compton House

117 Baldertongate NG24 1RY ☎ 01636 708670
e-mail info@comptonhousenewark.com
web www.comptonhousenewark.com
Dir 500yds SE of town centre. Off B6326 onto Sherwood Av, 1st right onto Baldertongate

Located a short walk from the centre, this elegant period house has been renovated to provide high standards of comfort. Individually themed bedrooms come with a wealth of thoughtful extras and smart modern bathrooms. Comprehensive breakfasts, and wholesome dinners by arrangement, are served in the attractive dining room and a lounge is available.

Facilities 7 rms (6 en suite) (1 pri facs) (1 fmly) (1 GF) ⊗ TVB tea/coffee Cen ht No coaches Dinner Last d 2pm **Conf** Max 10 Thtr 10 Class 10 Board 10 **Parking** 2

♦♦♦ ◀

Willow Tree Inn

Front St, Barnby-in-the-Willows NG24 2SA
☎ 01636 626613 🖹 01636 626060
web www.willowtreeinn.co.uk
Dir Off A1/A17 3.5m to Newark Golf Course, 300yds to Barnby sign, turn right & inn 1m

The Grade II listed Willow Tree dates from the 17th century. Bedrooms of varying styles are in main building and the adjacent annexe; each room is well equipped. The public areas include an attractive lounge bar where real ales and bar food are served. Alternatively, freshly prepared and imaginative meals are offered in the cosy restaurant.

Facilities 2 en suite 5 annexe en suite (4 fmly) (5 GF) ⊗ in bedrooms ⊗ in dining room TVB tea/coffee Direct dial from bedrooms Cen ht Dinner Last d 9pm **Prices** D £49.50✹ **Parking** 50

NOTTINGHAM   MAP 11 SK53
See also **Barkestone-le-Vale (Leics) & Cotgrave**

Premier Collection

♦♦♦♦♦

Greenwood Lodge City Guest House

5 Third Av, Sherwood Rise NG7 6JH
☎ 0115 962 1206 🖹 0115 962 1206
e-mail pdouglas71@aol.com
web www.greenwoodlodgecityguesthouse.co.uk
Dir A60 Mansfield Rd from city, 1st rdbt onto 1st exit to small rdbt, 2nd exit onto A692 Sherwood Rise, 3rd left

A warm welcome is assured at this fine house built in 1834, located in a quiet residential area 1m from the city centre. Day rooms include an elegant drawing room and a conservatory-dining room overlooking the secluded garden. Individually furnished bedrooms, equipped with many thoughtful extras, are decorated in a traditional style, complementing the antique furniture. Off-road parking is a bonus.

Facilities 6 en suite ⊗ TVB tea/coffee ✖ Licensed Cen ht No children 12yrs No coaches **Prices** S £43-£55; D £65-£85 **Parking** 6 **Notes** Closed 24-28 Dec

◆◆◆◆

Beech Lodge

222 Porchester Rd NG3 6HG
☎ 0115 952 3314 ▤ 0115 952 3314
Dir *Off A684 onto Porchester Rd, 8th left, Punchbowl pub on right corner, Beech Lodge on left corner*

A friendly welcome is assured at Beech Lodge and the modern accommodation is well presented. The ground-floor lounge is particularly comfortable, and there is a small conservatory. Breakfast, a good choice of freshly cooked and carefully presented fare, is served in the dining area next to the lounge.

Facilities 4 en suite (1 fmly) ⊗ in bedrooms ⊗ in dining room ⊗ in 1 lounge TVB tea/coffee ✖ Cen ht TVL No children 8yrs No coaches **Prices** S fr £30; d fr £55✳ **LB Parking** 4

◆◆◆◆

The Yellow House

7 Littlegreen Rd, Woodthorpe NG5 4LE ☎ 0115 926 2280
e-mail suzanne.prewsmith1@btinternet.com
Dir *Off A60 Mansfield Rd N from city centre onto A6211, over rdbt, 1st right to x-rds, left, house on left*

A semi-detached private house set in a quiet residential suburb to the north-east of the city. A warm welcome is assured and the family pet dog is also very friendly. The purpose-built bedroom contains many thoughtful extras.

Facilities 1 en suite ⊗ TVB tea/coffee ✖ Cen ht TVL No children No coaches **Prices** S fr £35; d fr £55✳ **Parking** 1 **Notes** ⊛

◆◆◆

Acorn Hotel

4 Radcliffe Rd, West Bridgford NG2 5FW
☎ 0115 981 1297 ▤ 0115 981 7654
e-mail reservations@acorn-hotel.co.uk
Dir *A6011 onto A6520, next to Trent Bridge Cricket Ground*

Located within walking distance of the county cricket ground and football stadia, this property provides a range of bedrooms some with en suites. Breakfast is served in the pine-furnished dining room and parking is available.

Facilities 12 en suite (2 fmly) (1 GF) ⊗ TVB tea/coffee ✖ Licensed Cen ht TVL No coaches **Parking** 12

◆◆◆

Andrews Private Hotel

310 Queens Rd, Beeston NG9 1JA
☎ 0115 925 4902 ▤ 0115 917 8839
e-mail andrews.hotel@ntlworld.com
Dir *A52 onto B6006 to Beeston, right at 4th lights onto Queens Rd, 200yds on right*

This pleasant establishment is close to the shops and park in Beeston, and is popular for business and leisure. There is a comfortable lounge and a dining room. Bedrooms, which vary in size, are well presented.

Facilities 10 rms (3 en suite) (1 fmly) (1 GF) ⊗ in 5 bedrooms ⊗ in dining room TVB tea/coffee ✖ Cen ht TVL No coaches **Prices** S £25-£35; D £50-£60 **Parking** 6 **Notes** ⊛

◆◆◆

Fairhaven Hotel

19 Meadow Rd, Beeston NG9 1JP
☎ 0115 922 7509 ▤ 0870 130 4866
Dir *A52 into B6005 for Beeston station, 200yds after bridge*

This well-established guest house is in the quiet residential suburb of Beeston on the outskirts of Nottingham. There is a stylish reception lounge, and breakfast is served in the cosy dining room. The bedrooms vary in style and size.

Facilities 13 rms (5 en suite) (1 fmly) (1 GF) ⊗ in dining room TVB tea/coffee Licensed Cen ht No coaches **Prices** S £29-£40; D £42-£49✳ **Parking** 13

◆◆◆

Hall Farm House

Gonalston NG14 7JA ☎ 0115 966 3112
Dir *8.5m NE of Nottingham. Off A612 x-rds into Gonalston, 1st right after post box*

The charming 17th-century former farmhouse is tucked away behind trees in the pretty village of Gonalston. Bedrooms are comfortable, and the beamed living rooms are full of character. The extensive grounds include a heated outdoor swimming pool and a tennis court, and there is a good choice of pubs for evening meals nearby.

Facilities 4 rms (2 en suite) (1 fmly) ⊗ TV3B tea/coffee ✖ Cen ht TVL No coaches ⚛ ▱ Large playroom with piano & table tennis **Prices** S £35-£40; D £55-£60✳ **LB Parking** 5 **Notes** Closed 20 Dec-2 Jan ⊛

◆◆◆

Tudor Lodge Hotel

400 Nuthall Rd NG8 5DS
☎ 0115 924 9244 ▤ 0115 924 9243
e-mail tudorlodge@thetudorhotel.com
Dir *M1 junct 26, A610 3m towards Nottingham*

Tudor Lodge is convenient for the M1 and the city centre. Accommodation comes in a variety of sizes and styles, and the ground-floor en suite room has easier access. Breakfast is served in the comfortably furnished dining room.

Facilities 7 rms (5 en suite) (3 fmly) (3 GF) ⊗ TVB tea/coffee ✖ Licensed Cen ht Dinner Last d 8.30pm **Prices** S fr £50; d fr £60✳ **Conf** Max 20 **Parking** 10

England

SOUTHWELL

MAP 17 SK65

◆◆◆

The Old Forge

Burgage Ln NG25 0ER ☎ 01636 812809 🗎 01636 816302
e-mail theoldforgesouthwell@yahoo.co.uk
Dir *Off A612 past Minster, Church St, left onto Newark Rd, 2nd left onto Burgage Ln*

An interesting house packed with pictures and antique furniture. It is central and handy for the Minster, while own parking makes this is a good touring base. Bedrooms are comfortable and a secluded conservatory-lounge and spacious breakfast room are available.

Facilities 3 en suite 1 annexe en suite (1 GF) ⊘ TVB tea/coffee Direct dial from bedrooms Cen ht No coaches **Prices** S £45; D £75✱ **Parking** 4

SUTTON BONINGTON

MAP 11 SK52

◆◆◆ ⬛

Star Inn

Melton Ln LE12 5RQ ☎ 01509 852233
Dir *A6 onto A6006 signed Rempstone, left signed West Leake, Star Inn 400yds on right*

Located on the edge of the village, this small and friendly, characterful inn offers good quality accommodation. Bedrooms have independent access, and each room has a refrigerator complete with a well-stocked continental breakfast tray. Enjoyable home-cooked fare is served in the convivial bar and dining areas.

Facilities 4 rms (2 en suite) (2 pri facs) (2 fmly) ⊘ in bedrooms ⊘ in dining room ⊘ in 1 lounge TVB tea/coffee ✖ Cen ht 🕪 Dinner Last d 8.30pm **Conf** Max 30 **Parking** 70

WELLOW

MAP 17 SK66

◆◆◆ ⬛

Scotts Farm B & B

Wellow Pk Stables, Rufford Ln NG22 0EQ
☎ 01623 861040 & 07860 869378 🗎 01623 835292
e-mail judithcadmam1933@aol.com
web www.wellowpark.co.uk
Dir *A616 SE from New Ollerton, 1m right onto Rufford Ln*

Scotts Farm is a part of Wellow Park Stables, a family equestrian centre located on the quiet outskirts of Wellow in Sherwood Forest. The resident proprietors provide helpful service, and well-proportioned

bedrooms that share a bathroom. Breakfast is served in the kitchen. Stabling, dressage instruction, show jumping and cross-country rides are available by arrangement.

Facilities 3 rms (3 fmly) ⊘ in bedrooms ⊘ in area of dining room TVB tea/coffee ✖ Cen ht No coaches Riding Rufford park golf course adjacent **Parking** 6

WORKSOP

MAP 16 SK57

◆◆◆◆

Acorn Lodge

85 Potter St S80 2HL ☎ 01909 478383 🗎 01909 478383
e-mail denisebiggs@fsmail.net
Dir *A1 onto A57 to Worksop, over two rdbts onto B6040 (town centre) through Manton, Lodge on right*

Originally part of the community house of the priory church, this property is now modernised to offer comfortable, well-appointed accommodation. Good breakfasts are served in the pleasant breakfast room and ample private parking is available at the rear.

Facilities 7 en suite (3 fmly) ⊘ STV TVB tea/coffee ✖ Cen ht TVL **Prices** S £40; D £50✱ **Parking** 20

OXFORDSHIRE

ABINGDON

MAP 05 SU49

◆◆◆◆ 🏛

Rafters

Abingdon Rd OX13 6NU ☎ 01865 391298 🗎 01865 391173
e-mail sigrid@graw.fsnet.co.uk
Dir *A34 onto A415 towards Witney, Rafters on A415 in Marcham by 1st street light on right*

Set amid immaculate gardens, this modern house is built in a half-timbered style and offers spacious accommodation and a warm welcome. Bedrooms are stylishly furnished and equipped with a range of homely extras. Comprehensive breakfasts feature local and organic produce when possible.

Facilities 4 rms (1 en suite) (3 pri facs) ⊘ TVB tea/coffee ✖ Cen ht No coaches **Prices** S £34-£54; D £56-£80 **Parking** 4 **Notes** Closed Xmas & New Year

◆◆◆◆ 🅰

Kingfisher Barn

Rye Farm OX14 3NN
☎ 01235 537538 & 527590 🗎 01235 537538
e-mail info@kingfisherbarn.com
web www.kingfisherbarn.com
Dir *0.5m SE of town centre. A415 S from town centre over River Thames, left into pay & display car park & onto single-track road*

Facilities 10 en suite (4 fmly) (10 GF) ⊘ TVB tea/coffee Cen ht 🔲 **Prices** S £56; D £75 **LB** **Parking** 20

continued

ARDINGTON

MAP 05 SU48

The Boar's Head

Church St OX12 8QA ☎ 01235 833254 ▨ 01235 833254
e-mail info@boarsheadardington.co.uk
Dir *In village next to church*

This characterful inn has been serving the local community for over 150 years and is set in a beautiful and seemingly timeless village. Great care has gone into creating a stylish and welcoming ambience in the comfortable bedrooms and in the bar and restaurant where Bruce Buchan's accomplished cuisine can be enjoyed.

Facilities 3 en suite (1 fmly) ⊗ in bedrooms ⊗ in dining room TVB tea/coffee Direct dial from bedrooms ✖ Cen ht No coaches Dinner Last d 9.30pm **Prices** S £75-£105; D £85-£130✱ **Parking** 20

BANBURY

MAP 11 SP44

The Mill House Country Guest House

North Newington Rd OX15 6AA
☎ 01295 730212 ▨ 01295 730363
e-mail lamadonett@aol.com
web www.themillhousebanbury.com
Dir *M40 junct 11, signs to Banbury Cross, onto B4035 (Shipston-on-Stour), 2m right for Newington*

This 17th-century miller's house belongs to the paper mill first mentioned in Shakespeare's Henry VI. It stands in immaculate peaceful gardens not far from Banbury Cross. There are individually styled bedrooms in the main house or refurbished cottages across the courtyard with lounge-kitchens and en suite bedrooms. There is also a pleasant lounge bar and meeting facilities.

Facilities 3 en suite 4 annexe en suite (2 fmly) ⊗ TVB tea/coffee Direct dial from bedrooms ✖ Licensed Cen ht TVL No coaches **Prices** S £54-£79; D £79-£112 **LB Conf** Max 12 Board 12 **Parking** 20

The Blinking Owl

Main St, North Newington OX15 6AE ☎ 01295 730650
Dir *B4035 from Banbury, 2m sharp bend, right to North Newington, inn opp the green*

An important part of the community in the pretty village of North Newington, this former 17th-century inn retains many original features including impressive open fires. Straightforward food and a range of real ales are served in the beamed bar lounges. The converted barn houses the bedrooms and the restaurant, which is open at weekends.

Facilities 3 en suite ⊗ in 1 bedrooms ⊗ in area of dining room TVB tea/coffee ✖ Cen ht Dinner Last d 9pm **Prices** S £45-£50; D £65 **Parking** 14 **Notes** ⊗

Calthorpe Lodge

4 Calthorpe Rd OX16 5HS ☎ 01295 252325
Dir *S from Banbury Cross on South Bar St, 3rd left onto St Johns Rd, 2nd right*

This terrace house is in a quiet residential area just a short walk from Banbury Cross. Bedrooms are practically furnished, and breakfast is served in the ground-floor lounge-dining room. The property is non-smoking.

Facilities 6 rms (4 en suite) (1 fmly) ⊗ TVB tea/coffee Cen ht No coaches **Parking** 6

Fairlawns

60 Oxford Rd OX16 9AN
☎ 01295 262461 & 07831 330220 ▨ 01295 261296
e-mail fairlawnsgh@aol.com
Dir *M40 junct 11, towards Banbury, left at 2nd island signed town centre. T-junct after 2m, house opp*

This extended Edwardian house retains many original features and has a convenient location. Bedrooms are mixed in size, and all are neatly furnished, some with direct access to the car park. A comprehensive breakfast is served in the traditional dining room and a selection of soft drinks and snacks is also available.

Facilities 12 rms (11 en suite) 6 annexe en suite (5 fmly) (9 GF) ⊗ TVB tea/coffee Direct dial from bedrooms Cen ht **Prices** S £46; D £56✱ **Parking** 18

Lampet Arms

Main St, Tadmarton OX15 5TB
☎ 01295 780070 ▨ 01295 788066
Dir *4m W of Banbury on B4035 in Tadmarton, opp church*

Located between Banbury and Shipston on Stour, this well-proportioned Victorian inn provides warm and inviting open-plan public areas, the setting for home-cooked food and fine wines. The spacious, thoughtfully equipped bedrooms are in a converted coach house.

Facilities 4 annexe en suite (3 fmly) (2 GF) ⊗ TVB tea/coffee Direct dial from bedrooms Cen ht Pool Table Dinner Last d 8.45pm **Conf** Board 20 **Parking** 15

England

BECKLEY
MAP 05 SP51

Premier Collection

◆◆◆◆◆ 🏠 ❦

Lower Farm *(SP565124)*

Otmoor Ln OX3 9TD
☎ 01865 358546 & 07796 693864 Ms Halliday
e-mail lhalliday@tiscali.co.uk
web www.lowerfarmbandb.com
Dir Off B4027 into Beckley

A delightful, restored 18th-century farmhouse in a peaceful location adjoining Otmoor Nature Reserve, only 5m from Oxford. Bedrooms are luxuriously furnished and you are welcome to use the snug television room with log-burning stove. A delicious variety is offered at breakfast around one large table in the pleasant dining room.

Facilities 4 en suite (4 GF) ⊗ tea/coffee ✖ Cen ht TVL 200 acres Arable **Prices** S £60-£80; D £80-£95✳ **Parking** 10 **Notes** Closed 15 Dec-15 Jan

BURFORD
MAP 05 SP21

Premier Collection

◆◆◆◆◆ ◎◎ ◀

Jonathan's at the Angel

14 Witney St OX18 4SN ☎ 01993 822714 📄 01993 822069
e-mail jo@theangel-uk.com
Dir Off A40 at Burford rdbt, down hill, 1st right onto Swan Ln, 1st left to Pytts Ln, left at end onto Witney St

Please note that this establishment has recently changed hands. Peacefully located a short walk from Burford's attractions, this mellow Cotswold-stone, 16th-century one-time coaching inn retains a wealth of original features. Individually themed bedrooms are filled with homely extras and a cosy lounge is available. The rustically furnished ground-floor areas are the setting for imaginative food, which can be served in the secluded walled garden in warmer weather.

Facilities 3 en suite ⊗ in bedrooms ⊗ in dining room TVB tea/coffee Direct dial from bedrooms ✖ Cen ht No children 9yrs No coaches Dinner Last d 9.30pm **Prices** S £77-£82; D £93-£110✳ **Notes** Closed 18 Jan-8 Feb

Premier Collection

◆◆◆◆◆ 🏠

Burford House Hotel

99 High St OX18 4QA ☎ 01993 823151 📄 01993 823240
e-mail stay@burfordhouse.co.uk
web www.burfordhouse.co.uk
Dir Off A40 into town centre

Set in the heart of this famous Cotswold market town, Burford House, marked by a half-timbered and stone exterior, is a haven for travellers. The charming bedrooms come with thoughtful homey extras, and there are two comfortable lounges with roaring log fires. Superb breakfasts and light meals are served in the dining room. The caring hosts ensure that a visit to their home is a memorable one.

Facilities 8 en suite (1 fmly) (1 GF) ⊗ in bedrooms ⊗ in dining room ⊗ in 1 lounge STV TVB Direct dial from bedrooms ✖ Licensed Cen ht No coaches **Prices** D £125-£160✳ LB

◆◆◆◆

Potters Hill Farm

Leafield OX29 9QB ☎ 01993 878018 📄 01993 878018
e-mail potterabout@freenet.co.uk
Dir 4.5m NE of Burford. A361 onto B4437, 1st right, 1st left, 1.5m on left

Located on a working farm in peaceful parkland with diverse wildlife, this converted coach house stands next to the farmhouse. It has been refurbished to offer comfortable bedrooms with many original features. Breakfast features local produce, and undercover parking is available on request.

Facilities 3 annexe en suite (1 fmly) (2 GF) ⊗ TVB tea/coffee ✖ Cen ht **Prices** D £50-£55✳ **Parking** 5 **Notes** ⊛

CHIPPING NORTON
MAP 10 SP32

See also **Long Compton (Warwickshire)**

★★★ Guest House

Nortens

10 New St OX7 5LJ ☎ 01608 645060 📠 01608 645060
e-mail nortens@tiscali.co.uk
Dir On A44 in town centre

The delightful restored guest house lies in the centre of this Cotswold village. It possibly dates from the 17th century and has a 19th-century front. Bedrooms are mostly spacious and original oak beams blend with the contemporary decor. Breakfast is served in the cosy ground floor cafe and there is ample street parking.

Facilities 5 en suite (3 fmly) ⊗ TVB 🐾 Licensed Cen ht No coaches Dinner Last d 6pm

◆◆◆◆

The Forge

Churchill OX7 6NJ ☎ 01608 658173
e-mail enquiries@cotswolds-bedandbreakfast.com
web www.cotswolds-bedandbreakfast.com
Dir B4450 from Chipping Norton to Churchill 2.5m

A warm welcome awaits you at this delightful 200-year-old, honey-coloured house, situated in the delightful village of Churchill, just a short drive from Chipping Norton. Stylish bedrooms are individually designed, some with four-poster beds, and are filled with a host of thoughtful extras. The cottage-style breakfast room leads into a pleasant lounge. Local eateries include the village pub virtually opposite, which has a popular following.

Facilities 5 en suite ⊗ TVB tea/coffee 🐾 Cen ht No children 11yrs No coaches One bedroom with jacuzzi **Prices** S £50-£70; D £65-£85 **Parking** 6

CHISLEHAMPTON
MAP 05 SU59

◆◆◆

Coach & Horses

Watlington Rd OX44 7UX
☎ 01865 890255 📠 01865 891995
e-mail enquiries@coachhorseinn.co.uk
Dir On B480

Located 6m south-east of Oxford, this 16th-century inn retains original exposed beams and open fires, while furniture styles enhance the

continued

character of the building. A wide range of imaginative food is served, and the practically equipped, chalet-style bedrooms have lovely country views.

Facilities 9 en suite ⊗ in bedrooms ⊗ in dining room TVB tea/coffee Direct dial from bedrooms Cen ht Club fishing 200yds Dinner Last d 9.45pm **Prices** S £56; D £65-£75✳ **LB Conf** Max 12 **Parking** 30 **Notes** Closed 25-30 Dec

CHOLSEY
MAP 05 SU58

◆◆◆ 🅰

The Well Cottage ◇

Caps Ln OX10 9HQ
☎ 01491 651959 & 07887 958920 📠 01491 651675
e-mail joanna@thewellcottage.com
Dir Off A329 onto Caps Ln towards village

Facilities 2 annexe en suite (2 fmly) (2 GF) ⊗ TVB tea/coffee Cen ht No coaches Riding **Prices** S £25-£50; D £40-£70✳ **Parking** 5 **Notes** 🈲

DORCHESTER (ON THAMES)
MAP 05 SU59

🆄 ◀

Fleur De Lys

9 High St OX10 7HH ☎ 01865 340502 📠 01865 340502
e-mail mail@fleurdorchester.co.uk
Dir From A4074, exit at Berinsfield rdbt, signed Dorchester

At the time of going to press the rating for this establishment had not been confirmed. Please check the AA website www.theAA.com for up-to-date information.

Facilities 5 en suite ⊗ in bedrooms ⊗ in area of dining room TV3B tea/coffee 🐾 Cen ht No coaches Dinner Last d 9.30pm **Prices** S £55-£75; D £85-£120✳ **Parking** 12

FILKINS
MAP 05 SP20

◆◆◆

The Five Alls Inn

GL7 3JQ ☎ 01367 860306
e-mail info@thefivealls.co.uk
web www.thefivealls.co.uk
Dir Off A361 signed Filkins, inn 400yds

Parts of this inn date from the early 18th century, and it has long fulfilled the varied roles of a village local. A genuine welcome is extended, and traditional hospitality ensures an enjoyable and memorable stay. Bedrooms offer good levels of comfort and quality, including a four-poster room. A choice of dining options is available in the bar and restaurant.

Facilities 4 en suite (1 fmly) ⊗ in bedrooms ⊗ in dining room ⊗ in lounges TVB tea/coffee Licensed Cen ht Dinner Last d 9pm **Prices** S fr £45; D £60-£75✳ **LB Conf** Thtr 60 Class 40 Board 25 **Parking** 20

HENLEY-ON-THAMES — MAP 05 SU78

★★★ Inn

The Catherine Wheel

7-15 Hart St RG9 2AR ☎ 01491 848484 🖹 01491 413409
e-mail henleylodge@jdwetherspoon.co.uk

Situated near to the town centre and river, home of the famous regatta, this popular establishment combines traditional appearances with a smart modern ambience. A comprehensive selection of meals are offered in the extensive and atmospheric bar, while bedrooms are spacious, well presented and filled with useful extras.

Facilities 30 en suite (4 fmly) ⊘ in 22 bedrooms ⊘ in lounges TVB tea/coffee Direct dial from bedrooms ✖ Licensed Lift Cen ht Dinner Last d 10.30-12pm **Prices** S £59; D £65; (room only) ✳ **Conf** Max 40 **Notes** Closed Xmas

Premier Collection

◆◆◆◆◆ 🛢

Thamesmead House Hotel

Remenham Ln RG9 2LR ☎ 01491 574745 🖹 01491 579944
e-mail thamesmead@supanet.com
web www.thamesmeadhousehotel.co.uk
Dir *From town centre E over bridge, 1st left, house signed*

A short walk from the river and the town, this delightful Victorian house has original stained-glass windows and marble fireplaces. You can expect a warm welcome and relaxed atmosphere. Minimalist decor and Scandinavian-style furniture are combined with quality soft furnishings, and superb beds ensure a comfortable rest. Organic produce is a feature at breakfast, which includes a buffet table and home-baked muffins.

Facilities 6 en suite (1 GF) ⊘ STV TVB tea/coffee Direct dial from bedrooms ✖ Licensed Cen ht No children 10yrs No coaches **Prices** S £95-£115; D £130-£145✳ **LB Conf** Max 10 **Parking** 6

Premier Collection

◆◆◆◆◆

Lenwade

3 Western Rd RG9 1JL
☎ 01491 573468 & 0777 941629 🖹 01491 411664
e-mail lenwadeuk@aol.com
web www.w3b-ink.com/lenwade
Dir *A4155 towards Reading, right onto St Andrew's Rd, 2nd left into Western Rd*

The friendly and relaxed Victorian home has attractive, well-equipped bedrooms with free WiFi Internet access in each room. Breakfast is served round one large table.

Facilities 3 rms (2 en suite) (1 pri facs) ⊘ STV TVB tea/coffee ✖ Cen ht TVL No coaches guided walks **Prices** S £45-£50; D £65-£70 **Parking** 2 **Notes** Closed 24-26 Dec 🐾

Premier Collection

◆◆◆◆◆

Milsoms Hotel

20 Market Pl RG9 2AH ☎ 01491 845789 🖹 01491 845781
e-mail henley@milsomshotel.co.uk
web www.milsomshotel.co.uk
Dir *In town centre*

This stylish establishment overlooks the market square of this riverside town. Bedrooms are well proportioned and combine elegance with ease of use. The Loch Fyne fishery company runs the property and the cuisine is centred on their own produce.

Facilities 7 en suite (1 GF) ⊘ TVB tea/coffee ✖ Cen ht No coaches Dinner Last d 10pm **Parking** 7 **Notes** Closed 25 Dec

◆◆◆◆ ➡ ◖▮

The Baskerville

Station Rd, Lower Shiplake RG9 3NY
☎ 0118 940 3332 ▤ 0118 940 4735
e-mail enquiries@thebaskerville.com
Dir 2m S of Henley in Lower Shiplake. Off A4155 onto Station Rd,
B&B signed

Located close to Shiplake station and just a short drive from Henley, this smart accommodation is perfect for business or leisure. It is a good base for exploring the Oxfordshire countryside, and the enjoyable hearty meals served in the cosy restaurant use good local produce.

Facilities 5 rms (4 en suite) (1 fmly) ⊗ in bedrooms ⊗ in dining room TVB tea/coffee Cen ht No coaches Dinner Last d 9.30pm **Prices** S £45; D £75-£95✳ **Conf** Max 15 Thtr 15 Class 15 Board 15 **Parking** 15 **Notes** rs 23 Dec-2 Jan (room only)

◆◆◆◆ ◉ ➡

The Cherry Tree Inn

Stoke Row RG9 5QA ☎ 01491 680430 ▤ 01491 682168
web www.thecherrytreeinn.com
Dir 6m W of Henley. Off B841 into Stoke Row

This stylish Inn is situated in a peaceful rural setting, just 20 minutes away from Reading and motorway connections. Bedrooms are of a modern design, and have spacious bathrooms with luxurious toiletries. Meals are served in the contemporary restaurant, with lunch and dinner being highlights.

Facilities 4 annexe en suite (4 GF) ⊗ TVB tea/coffee ✖ Licensed Cen ht Dinner Last d 10pm **Prices** D £65-£85✳ **Parking** 30 **Notes** Closed 25-26 Dec

◆◆◆◆

Bramley House

7 Gravel Hill RG9 2EF ☎ 01491 577802
e-mail info@bramley-house.net
Dir Town Centre traffic lights, then through Market Place. 150yds
beyond Town Hall on left.

This beautifully restored timber-framed property is situated in the heart of Henley, just a stroll from the shops, bars and restaurants. The three bedrooms are furnished to a high standard and a comfortable lounge is available, where access to the Internet is provided.

Facilities 3rms (1 pri facs) (1 fmly) ⊗ TVB tea/coffee ✖ Cen ht Dinner Last d noon

◆◆◆◆ ▣

Apple Ash

Woodlands Rd, Harpsden Woods RG9 4AB
☎ 01491 574198 ▤ 01491 578183
e-mail appleash@fsmail.net
Dir From Henley exit A4155 towards Caversham, turn right onto
Woodlands Rd, house is 0.5m on right

Facilities 4 rms (3 en suite) (1 pri facs) ⊗ TVB tea/coffee ✖ Cen ht No coaches **Prices** S £50; D £70✳ **Parking** 6 **Notes** ▣

◆◆◆ ▣

Slater's Farm

Peppard Com RG9 5JL ☎ 01491 628675 ▤ 01491 628675
e-mail stay@slatersfarm.co.uk
Dir 3m W of Henley. A4130 onto B481 to Rotherfield Peppard, pass
The Dog pub & fork left to primary school, farm 200yds on right

Facilities 3 rms (1 pri facs) ⊗ TVB ✖ Cen ht No coaches ⊷ Dinner Last d at breakfast **Prices** S £32-£38; D £52-£55✳ **Parking** 5 **Notes** Closed Xmas ▣

HOOK NORTON   MAP 11 SP33

◆◆◆◆ ➡ ◖▮

The Gate Hangs High

OX15 5DF ☎ 01608 737387 ▤ 01608 737870
e-mail gatehangshigh@aol.com
Dir 0.6m N of village on x-rds

This delightful inn located between Banbury and Chipping Norton is convenient for Oxford and the Cotswolds. Stylish, spacious bedrooms are situated around a courtyard in a converted barn. They are comfortably furnished and extremely well equipped. Carefully prepared food is served in the bar or the attractive restaurant.

Facilities 4 en suite (1 fmly) (4 GF) ⊗ in bedrooms ⊗ in dining room FTV TVB tea/coffee Direct dial from bedrooms Cen ht Golf Riding Dinner Last d 10pm **Prices** S £40-£45; D £50-£60 **LB** **Parking** 40

IDBURY **MAP 10 SP21**

◆◆◆◆ ❧

Bould Farm *(SP244209)*

OX7 6RT ☎ 01608 658850 ▤ 01608 658850 Mrs Meyrick
e-mail meyrick@bouldfarm.co.uk
web www.bouldfarm.co.uk
Dir *Off A424 signed Idbury, through village, farm on right*

This delightful 17th-century farmhouse stands amid pretty gardens
between Stow-on-the-Wold and Burford. The spacious bedrooms are
carefully furnished and thoughtfully equipped, and some have
stunning views of the surrounding countryside. Breakfast is served in
the cosy dining room which features a cast-iron stove and flagstone
floors.

Facilities 3 en suite (1 fmly) ⊘ TVB tea/coffee ✖ Cen ht TVL
400 acres arable/sheep **Prices** S £40-£45; D £60-£65✳ **Parking** 6
Notes Closed Dec-Jan ▨

KIDLINGTON **MAP 11 SP41**

◆◆◆

Bowood House Hotel

238 Oxford Rd OX5 1EB ☎ 01865 842288 ▤ 01865 841858
e-mail bowoodhousehotel@aol.com
Dir *4m N of Oxford. On A4260 opp Thames Valley Police HQ*

The comfortable commercial establishment offers spacious, practically
equipped bedrooms, some of which are in a wing surrounding the
patio garden. There is a choice of lounges, and breakfast is served in a
light, spacious room overlooking the garden.

Facilities 10 rms (8 en suite) 12 annexe en suite (4 fmly)
⊘ in 10 bedrooms ⊘ in dining room STV TVB tea/coffee Direct dial
from bedrooms Licensed Cen ht TVL Dinner Last d 8.30pm **Parking** 26
Notes Closed 24 Dec-4 Jan

KINGHAM **MAP 10 SP22**

◆◆◆◆

Moat End

The Moat OX7 6XZ ☎ 01608 658090 & 07765 278399
e-mail moatend@hotmail.com
web www.moatend.co.uk
Dir *Off B4450/A436 into village centre*

The converted barn lies in a peaceful Cotswold village and has
splendid country views. Its well-appointed bedrooms either have a
jacuzzi or large shower cubicles, one with hydro-massage jets, and the
attractive dining room leads to a comfortable beamed sitting room
with a stone fireplace. Quality local ingredients are used in the
wholesome breakfasts. The owner has won an award for green
tourism by reducing the impact of the business on the environment.

Facilities 3 en suite (1 fmly) ⊘ TVB tea/coffee Cen ht No coaches
Prices S £35-£45; D £55-£65 **LB** **Parking** 4 **Notes** Closed Xmas & New
Year ▨

◆◆◆◆ ⊜

The Tollgate Inn & Restaurant

Church St OX7 6YA ☎ 01608 658389
e-mail info@thetollgate.com

Situated in an idyllic Cotswold village, this Grade II listed Georgian
building has been lovingly restored to provide a complete home from
home amid beautiful countryside. Hospitality is warm and welcoming,
ensuring an enjoyable experience. A good choice for lunch and dinner
is available, using fresh local produce. You can also be sure of a hearty
breakfast provided in the modern, well-equipped dining room.

Facilities 5 en suite 4 annexe en suite (1 fmly) (4 GF) ⊘ in bedrooms
⊘ in dining room TVB tea/coffee Licensed Cen ht Dinner Last d 9pm /
9.30pm Fri/Sat **Prices** S fr £60; D £80-£100✳ **Conf** Max 15 **Parking** 12

OXFORD **MAP 05 SP50**

◆◆◆◆◆ ▤

Burlington House

374 Banbury Rd, Summertown OX2 7PP
☎ 01865 513513 ▤ 01865 311785
e-mail stay@burlington-house.co.uk
Dir *Opposite Oxford Conference Centre on A4165 on corner of
Hernes Rd & Banbury Rd*

Please note that this establishment has recently changed hands. This
smart, beautifully maintained Victorian house is within walking
distance of Summertown's fashionable restaurants. Contemporary
bedrooms are filled with a wealth of thoughtful extras, and some open
onto a pretty patio garden. Memorable breakfasts, served in the
delightful dining room, include home-made preserves, fruit breads,
granola and excellent coffee.

Facilities 10 rms (8 en suite) 2 annexe en suite ⊘ TVB tea/coffee Direct
dial from bedrooms ✖ Cen ht No children 12yrs No coaches
Prices S £45-£60; D £80-£90✳ **Parking** 5

◆◆◆◆◆ ▤ ❧

Lower Farm *(SP565124)*

Otmoor Ln OX3 9TD
☎ 01865 358546 & 07796 693864 Ms Halliday
e-mail lhalliday@tiscali.co.uk
web www.lowerfarmbandb.com
For full entry see Beckley

◆◆◆◆

Cotswold House

363 Banbury Rd OX2 7PL
☎ 01865 310558 📠 01865 310558
e-mail d.r.walker@talk21.com
Dir *A40 onto A423 into Oxford city centre, following signs to Summertown, 0.5m on right*

Situated in a leafy avenue close to the northern ring road and Summertown, this well-maintained house offers comfortable, well-equipped bedrooms and a relaxed atmosphere. Enjoy a traditional, hearty breakfast with a vegetarian choice, including home-made muesli and fresh fruit, served in the bright attractive dining room.

Facilities 7 en suite (2 fmly) (1 GF) ⊗ TVB tea/coffee ✖ Cen ht No children 5yrs No coaches **Prices** S £55-£60; D £80-£90 **Parking** 6

◆◆◆◆

Gables

6 Cumnor Hill OX2 9HA ☎ 01865 862153 📠 01865 864054
e-mail stay@gables-oxford.co.uk
web www.oxfordcity.co.uk/accom/gables
Dir *1.5m W of city centre. A34 onto A420 for Oxford/Botley, right at T-junct, 500yds on right*

A warm welcome is assured at this renovated Victorian house located in a residential area a short drive from the city centre. Bedrooms are filled with a wealth of thoughtful extras, and there is a cosy dining room and a conservatory-lounge overlooking the immaculate enclosed rear garden.

Facilities 6 en suite (1 GF) ⊗ STV TVB tea/coffee Direct dial from bedrooms ✖ Cen ht TVL No children 10yrs No coaches Pool Table **Prices** S £46-£50; D £66-£70 **LB** **Parking** 6 **Notes** Closed 24 Dec-1 Jan

◆◆◆◆

All Seasons

63 Windmill Rd, Headington OX3 7BP
☎ 01865 742215 📠 01865 429667
e-mail info@allseasonshouse.com
web www.allseasonshouse.com
Dir *Off ring road onto A 420 towards city centre. 1m left at lights onto Windmill Rd, house 300yds on left*

Within easy walking distance of the suburb of Headington, this double-fronted Victorian house provides homely bedrooms equipped with thoughtful extras. The elegant dining room features an original fireplace, and secure parking is available behind the property.

continued

Facilities 6 rms (4 en suite) ⊗ TVB tea/coffee ✖ Cen ht TVL No children 4yrs **Parking** 6

◆◆◆◆

Brown's

281 Iffley Rd OX4 4AQ ☎ 01865 246822 📠 01865 246822
e-mail brownsgh@hotmail.com
Dir *From city centre onto High St, over Magdalen Bridge, Iffley Rd 3rd exit on rdbt*

Located between the city centre and southern ring road, this Victorian house has been refurbished for leisure and business. Bedrooms have been carefully furnished and some have modern shower rooms en suite. A choice of cosy dining rooms is available for breakfast and an attractive conservatory lounge overlooks the pretty enclosed rear garden.

Facilities 9 rms (4 en suite) ⊗ TVB tea/coffee ✖ Licensed Cen ht TVL No coaches **Parking** 4

◆◆◆◆

Galaxie Private Hotel

180 Banbury Rd OX2 7BT
☎ 01865 515688 📠 01865 556824
e-mail info@galaxie.co.uk
web www.galaxie.co.uk
Dir *1m N of Oxford centre, on right before shops in Summertown*

Situated in the popular Summertown area of the city, the Galaxie has a welcoming atmosphere and very good quality accommodation. The well-equipped bedrooms are all very comfortable and have a good range of facilities. The attractive conservatory-dining room looks over the Oriental garden.

Facilities 32 rms (28 en suite) (3 fmly) ⊗ in bedrooms ⊗ in dining room TV31B tea/coffee Direct dial from bedrooms ✖ Lift Cen ht TVL **Parking** 30

England

OXFORD continued

◆◆◆◆

Pickwicks

15-17 London Rd, Headington OX3 7SP
☎ 01865 750487 📠 01865 742208
e-mail pickwicks@tiscali.co.uk
web www.pickwicksguesthouse.co.uk
Dir Off ring road onto A420 towards city centre, Pickwicks 1.5m on right at junct with Sandfield Rd

Just a short walk from the bustling community of Headington, this double-fronted Edwardian house has been renovated to provide good standards of overall comfort. Bedrooms offer a useful range of facilities, and the attractive breakfast room overlooks pretty gardens.

Facilities 15 rms (13 en suite) (4 fmly) (4 GF) ⊗ in bedrooms ⊗ in dining room FTV TVB tea/coffee Direct dial from bedrooms Licensed Cen ht TVL **Prices** S £30-£50; D £70-£85✳ **Parking** 12 **Notes** Closed 23 Dec-2 Jan

◆◆◆◆

Tilbury Lodge

5 Tilbury Ln OX2 9NB ☎ 01865 862138 📠 01865 863700
e-mail tilburylodge@yahoo.co.uk
Dir A34 at junct A420 (Botley). Right at lights, past shopping centre. Turn right onto Eynsham Rd, 1st right Tilbury Ln

Expect a warm welcome at this well-presented guest house, set in a quiet suburb convenient for major routes. Bedrooms have a modern charm and an impressive range of extras. Breakfast is served in the African-themed dining room overlooking the large, well-kept garden.

Facilities 9 en suite (1 fmly) (2 GF) ⊗ TVB tea/coffee ✖ Cen ht TVL No children 6yrs No coaches Jacuzzi Dinner Last d 9.30am **Prices** S £50-£55; D £70-£80✳ **LB Conf** Max 12 Thtr 12 Class 12 Board 12 **Parking** 9

◆◆◆◆ 🅰

Bath Place Hotel

4-5 Bath Pl, Holywell St OX1 3SU
☎ 01865 791812 📠 01865 791834
e-mail info@bathplace.co.uk
Dir In city centre. Bath Place is cobbled footpath on S side of Holywell St

Facilities 14 en suite (2 fmly) (3 GF) ⊗ in bedrooms ⊗ in dining room TVB tea/coffee Direct dial from bedrooms Licensed Cen ht TVL No coaches **Prices** D £100-£150✳ **Parking** 14

◆◆◆

Conifers Guest House

116 The Slade, Headington OX3 7DX
☎ 01865 763055 📠 01865 742232
e-mail stay@conifersguesthouse.co.uk
Dir Off ring road onto A420 towards city centre. Left onto B4495, house on left past hospital

Located in a residential area close to the hospitals, this impressive Edwardian house has been renovated to provide attractive, pine-furnished bedrooms equipped with thoughtful extras. Breakfast is served in a smart, front-facing dining room.

Facilities 8 en suite (1 fmly) ⊗ TVB tea/coffee ✖ Cen ht No coaches **Prices** S £40-£50; D £60-£75✳ **Parking** 8

◆◆◆

Highfield

91 Rose Hill OX4 4HT ☎ 01865 774083
e-mail highfield.house@tesco.net
Dir Off A4142 Eastern Bypass Rd onto A4158, continue 250yds

This attractive detached house stands in immaculate gardens close to Cowley and provides homely bedrooms with quality pine furniture. The attractive front dining room is the setting for comprehensive breakfasts and there is also a spacious lounge.

Facilities 7 rms (5 en suite) ⊗ FTV TVB tea/coffee ✖ Cen ht TVL **Prices** S £30-£55; D £60-£65✳ **Parking** 6 **Notes** Closed Xmas

◆◆◆

Acorn ◇

260-262 Iffley Rd OX4 1SE ☎ 01865 247998
e-mail acorn@kpattullo.wanadoo.co.uk
Dir Off ring road onto A4158 towards city centre, 1m on left after VW garage

Please note that this establishment has recently changed hands. This double-fronted Victorian house is located between the ring road and the city centre, and offers good-value accommodation. A lift serves one wing of the property. The lounge leads out to a quiet enclosed rear garden.

Facilities 15 rms (6 en suite) (1 pri facs) (1 fmly) ⊗ TVB tea/coffee Lift Cen ht No coaches **Prices** S £30-£35; D £60-£70✳ **Parking** 6

Please mention the AA B&B Guide when booking your stay

◆◆◆
Green Gables

326 Abingdon Rd OX1 4TE
☎ 01865 725870 ▯ 01865 723115
e-mail green.gables@virgin.net
web www.greengables.uk.com
Dir Off ring road onto B4144 towards city centre, Green Gables 0.5m on left

A warm welcome is assured at this Edwardian house, located within easy walking distance of the city centre. Bedrooms are equipped with a range of practical and homey extras and a comprehensive breakfast is served in the cosy dining room. You have free access to the Internet in the smart conservatory-lounge and private parking is available.

Facilities 11 en suite (5 fmly) (4 GF) TVB tea/coffee Direct dial from bedrooms ✖ Cen ht TVL No coaches **Prices** S £48-£52; D £58-£74 **Parking** 9 **Notes** Closed 23-31 Dec

◆◆◆
Heather House

192 Iffley Rd OX4 1SD ☎ 01865 249757 ▯ 01865 249757
e-mail stay@heatherhouseoxford.com
Dir Off A40 at Headington rdbt S onto A4142 to Littlemore rdbt, onto A4158 Iffley Rd, house 1.25m on left after pelican crossing, by Chester St

A short walk from the colleges and city centre, this detached Edwardian house stands in a residential area and offers parking. The en suite bedrooms, lounge and the dining room are bright and comfortable, and one bedroom is on the ground floor. There is a choice of breakfast and lots of tourist information is available.

Facilities 6 rms (5 en suite) (1 pri facs) (2 fmly) (1 GF) TVB tea/coffee Direct dial from bedrooms ✖ Cen ht TVL No coaches **Parking** 4

◆◆◆
Pine Castle Hotel

290-292 Iffley Rd OX4 4AE
☎ 01865 241497 ▯ 01865 727230
e-mail stay@pinecastle.co.uk
Dir Off A4142 Eastern Bypass Rd onto A4158, guest house 1.5m on left after lights

With easy access to the city centre, this Victorian house offers comfortable, well-equipped bedrooms and a light and airy breakfast room. Although close to the main road, the house has a quiet position. Limited parking is available.

Facilities 8 en suite (1 fmly) in bedrooms ⊗ in dining room TVB tea/coffee Direct dial from bedrooms ✖ Licensed Cen ht TVL **Parking** 6

◆◆◆
River Hotel

17 Botley Rd OX2 0AA ☎ 01865 243475 ▯ 01865 724306
e-mail reception@riverhotel.co.uk
web www.riverhotel.co.uk
Dir 500yds W of city centre. On A420 by Osney Bridge

Located beside the Thames, and a short walk from the railway station and centre, this impressive Victorian building has comfortable bedrooms, some of which are in a house opposite. Enjoyable breakfasts are served in the ground-floor dining room, and additional benefits include a lounge bar and parking at the rear.

Facilities 13 rms (11 en suite) (2 pri facs) 7 annexe en suite (5 fmly) in dining room TVB tea/coffee Direct dial from bedrooms ✖ Licensed Cen ht TVL No coaches **Prices** S £70-£75; D £80-£90✱ **Conf** Thtr 30 **Parking** 20 **Notes** Closed Xmas & New Year

◆◆◆ Ⓐ
Beaumont

234 Abingdon Rd OX1 4SP
☎ 01865 241767 ▯ 01865 241767
e-mail info@beaumont.sagehost.co.uk
Dir Off ring road onto A4144 towards city centre, Beaumont 1m on left

Facilities 4 rms (3 en suite) (1 fmly) (1 GF) TVB tea/coffee ✖ Cen ht No coaches

◆◆◆ Ⓐ
Newton House

82-84 Abingdon Rd OX1 4PL
☎ 01865 240561 ▯ 01865 244647
e-mail newton.house@btinternet.com
Dir On A4144 Abingdon Rd

Facilities 13 rms (2 en suite) (11 pri facs) (4 fmly) (4 GF) TVB tea/coffee Direct dial from bedrooms ✖ Cen ht **Prices** S £38-£54; D £50-£72✱ **LB Parking** 8

◆◆
Kings Guest House

363 Iffley Rd OX4 4DP ☎ 01865 205333 ▯ 01865 711544
e-mail KingsGuestHouse@email.com
Dir M40 junct 9, ring road towards A34 turn right on 2nd rdbt

Enthusiastically run by friendly owners, this property is situated on a residential avenue leading to the city centre. Bedrooms are practically equipped, some with shower rooms en suite. Breakfast is served at separate tables in the traditionally furnished dining room.

Facilities 7 rms (4 en suite) (2 fmly) TVB tea/coffee ✖ Cen ht TVL **Parking** 10

continued

England

Ⓤ

Athena Guest House

255 Cowley Rd, Cowley OX4 1XQ
☎ 01865 425700 & 07778 152048 ▤ 01865 240566
e-mail info@athenaguesthouse.com
web www.athenaguesthouse.com
Dir *1.5m SE of city centre on B480*

At the time of going to press the rating for this establishment had not been confirmed. Please check the AA website www.theAA.com for up-to-date information.

Facilities 6 en suite (2 fmly) (1 GF) ⊘ STV TVB tea/coffee ✖ Cen ht TVL Dinner Last d 11.30pm **Prices** S £35-£48; D £55-£68✳ **LB**
Conf Max 15 Del from £40 ✳ **Parking** 4

Ⓤ

Marlborough House

321 Woodstock Rd OX2 7NY
☎ 01865 311321 ▤ 01865 515329
e-mail enquiries@marlbhouse.co.uk
web www.marlbhouse.co.uk
Dir *Junct A34 & A44 N of city, follow city centre signs onto Woodstock Rd, premises on right by lights*

At the time of going to press the rating for this establishment had not been confirmed. Please check the AA website www.theAA.com for up-to-date information.

Facilities 13 en suite 4 annexe en suite (2 fmly) (4 GF) ⊘ in bedrooms STV TVB tea/coffee Direct dial from bedrooms ✖ Licensed Cen ht No coaches **Prices** S £73-£77; D £85-£90✳ **Parking** 6

Ⓤ

Sports View Guest House

106-110 Abingdon Rd OX1 4PX
☎ 01865 244268 ▤ 01865 249270
e-mail stay@sportsviewguesthouse.co.uk
web www.sportsviewguesthouse.co.uk
Dir *Exit Oxford S at Kennington rdbt towards city centre, 1.25m on left*

At the time of going to press the rating for this establishment had not been confirmed. Please check the AA website www.theAA.com for up-to-date information.

Facilities 20 rms (17 en suite) (5 fmly) (6 GF) ⊘ TVB tea/coffee Direct dial from bedrooms ✖ Cen ht No children 2yrs **Prices** S £38-£50; D £60-£72✳ **LB Parking** 10 **Notes** Closed 25-26 Dec

STADHAMPTON · MAP 05 SU69

Premier Collection

★★★★★ ◉◉ **Restaurant with Rooms**

The Crazy Bear

Bear Ln OX44 7UR ☎ 01865 890714 ▤ 01865 400481
e-mail sales@crazybearhotel.co.uk
Dir *M40 junct 7 left at end of slip road, into Stadhampton. Over mini-rdbt at petrol station. Hotel 2nd left*

This popular and attractive venue successfully combines modern chic with old world character. Cuisine is extensive and varied with award-winning Thai and English restaurants under the same roof (both awarded two AA rosettes). Those choosing to make a night of it can enjoy the concept bedrooms, all presented to a very high standard; the new 'infinity suites' have state-of-the-art facilities.

Facilities 5 en suite 12 annexe en suite (3 fmly) (2 GF) ⊘ in area of dining room STV TVB Direct dial from bedrooms ✖ Licensed Cen ht No coaches Beauty salon Treatments Dinner Last d 9.55pm **Prices** S £80-£140; D £120-£375✳ **Conf** Max 40 Thtr 30 Class 30 Board 30 Del from £185 ✳ **Parking** 50 **Notes** Civ Wed 50

TETSWORTH · MAP 05 SP60

♦♦♦♦

Little Acre Bed & Breakfast

4 High St OX9 7AT ☎ 01844 281423 ▤ 01844 281423
e-mail julia@little-acre.co.uk
web www.little-acre.co.uk
Dir *M40 junct 6 or 8a, A40 into Tetsworth*

This impressive, cottage-style house, 2m from the M40, is set in 20 acres of mature grounds that also contain a touring caravan site. The comfortable, individually themed bedrooms are filled with a wealth of thoughtful extras. Separate tables are provided in the cosy breakfast room overlooking the pretty enclosed patio garden.

Facilities 2 en suite (1 fmly) (1 GF) ⊘ in 1 bedrooms ⊘ in dining room TVB tea/coffee Cen ht No coaches **Prices** S fr £40-£4; D £50-£55✳ **LB Parking** 4 **Notes** ⊜

THAME · MAP 05 SP70

♦♦♦♦ Ⓐ

Langsmeade House

Milton Common OX9 2JY
☎ 01844 278727 ▤ 01844 279256
e-mail enquiries@langsmeadehouse.co.uk
Dir *Off A418, B&B on right at end of lane*

Facilities 3 rms (1 en suite) (2 pri facs) ⊘ TVB tea/coffee Cen ht TVL No coaches ₪ Dinner Last d 8pm **Prices** S £40-£45; D £70-£80 **LB Parking** 8

WALLINGFORD

MAP 05 SU68

◆◆◆◆

Little Gables B&B

166 Crowmarsh Hill OX10 8BG
☎ 01491 837834 & 07860 148882 📠 01491 834426
e-mail jill@stayingaway.com
web www.stayingaway.com
Dir 1m E of Wallingford. Off A4130 at Crowmarsh Gifford rdbt onto Crowmarsh Hill & right

Facilities 3 rms (2 en suite) (1 pri facs) (2 fmly) (1 GF) ⊗ TVB
tea/coffee ✗ Cen ht TVL No coaches **Prices** S £40-£55; D £55-£65✳
LB **Parking** 7 **Notes** ✍

WANTAGE

MAP 05 SU38

◆◆◆

Bramley House ◇

Mill Orch, East Hanney OX12 0JH ☎ 01235 868314
Dir Off A338 East Hanney W towards West Hanney, Bramley House 1rd on right on Mill Orchard

This friendly guest house has a village location within easy driving distance of Oxford and Wantage. The bedrooms are filled with thoughtful extras, while the hearty breakfasts are freshly prepared.

Facilities 2 rms (1 en suite) (1 pri facs) (1 fmly) ⊗ TVB tea/coffee ✗ Cen ht No children 10yrs No coaches **Prices** S £25-£30; D £45-£50✳
Parking 2 **Notes** ✍

◆◆◆ ✌

Down Barn Farm ◇ (SU332852)

Sparsholt Down OX12 9XD ☎ 01367 820272 Mrs Reid
e-mail pendomeffect@aol.com
Dir 4m SW of Wantage. Off B4507 S onto Kingston Lisle-Seven Barrows road

Popular with walkers and horse riders (stabling is available), this working farm has glorious views over the Lambourn Downs and is near to the famous Ridgeway. Bedrooms and public areas have a homey aspect while home-produced veal, beef and pork can be anticipated for dinner.

Facilities 3 rms (1 en suite) (3 GF) ⊗ in bedrooms ⊗ in dining room Cen ht TVL Riding 100 acres Organic beef & pig Dinner Last d 1pm
Prices S fr £30✳ LB **Parking** 4 **Notes** ✍

◆◆◆

Greensands Guest House

Reading Rd OX12 8JE ☎ 01235 833338 📠 01235 821632
e-mail sue.bowen@btconnect.com
web www.greensandsguesthouse.co.uk
Dir A4185 to Rowstock rdbt, take A417, 1m on right

This guest house in a peaceful rural setting has good access to local towns, attractions and transport networks. Bedrooms vary in size and are comfortably appointed. Hearty breakfasts are served overlooking the attractive gardens. Ample parking is available.

Facilities 7 rms (6 en suite) (1 pri facs) (2 fmly) (3 GF) ⊗ TVB tea/coffee ✗ Cen ht **Prices** S fr £35; d fr £70✳ LB **Parking** 9

WITNEY

MAP 05 SP31

★★★ Inn

Rose Revived

Newbridge OX29 7QD ☎ 01865 300221
e-mail 5284@greeneking.co.uk
web www.oldenglish.co.uk
Dir On A415 between Abingdon and Witney

Set on the banks of the River Thames, the Rose Revived dates from the 16th century and stands amid attractive countryside. A favorite overnight stopping point for walkers doing the Thames Path, this is an ideal spot to enjoy a drink by the river on a summer's evening. The spacious bar offers a selection of popular dishes.

Facilities 7 rms (3 en suite) (1 fmly) TVB tea/coffee Direct dial from bedrooms Dinner Last d 10pm **Prices** S fr £48; d fr £58✳ **Conf** Max 30 Thtr 30 Class 20 Board 20 **Parking** 50

England

WOODSTOCK
MAP 11 SP41

♦♦♦♦ ◧

Duke Of Marlborough Country Inn
A44, Woodleys OX20 1HT
☎ 01993 811460 ▤ 01993 810165
e-mail sales@dukeofmarlborough.co.uk
web www.dukeofmarlborough.co.uk
Dir 1m N of Woodstock on A44 x-rds

The Duke of Marlborough is just outside the popular town of Woodstock, convenient for local attractions including Blenheim Palace. Bedrooms and bathrooms are in an adjacent lodge-style building and offer high standards of quality and comfort. Dinner includes tempting home-cooked dishes complemented by a good selection of ales and wines.

Facilities 13 annexe en suite (2 fmly) (7 GF) ⊗ TVB tea/coffee Direct dial from bedrooms ✘ Cen ht Dinner Last d 9.30pm **Prices** S £65-£85; D £80-£120✳ **LB** **Conf** Max 20 Thtr 20 Class 16 Board 12 Del from £99.50 ✳ **Parking** 42

See advertisement on opposite page

♦♦♦♦ ⊛ ⊜ ◧

Kings Head Inn & Restaurant
Chapel Hill, Wootton OX20 1DX ☎ 01993 811340
e-mail t.fay@kings-head.co.uk
web www.kings-head.co.uk
Dir 1m N of Woodstock on A44, right signed Wootton. Inn in village centre close to church

Set in the pretty village of Wootton, this mellow-stone inn retains originalexposed beams and open fireplaces, and is decorated in keeping with the style of the building. The homely bedrooms, including one in a barn conversion, are equipped with good practical

continued

extras, and imaginative food is served in the spacious, open-plan public areas.

Facilities 2 en suite 1 annexe en suite (1 fmly) (1 GF) ⊗ TVB tea/coffee ✘ Cen ht No children 12yrs No coaches Dinner Last d 8.30pm **Prices** S £60-£70; D £75-£105✳ **LB** **Parking** 8 **Notes** Closed Xmas

♦♦♦♦

The Laurels
40 Hensington Rd OX20 1JL
☎ 01993 812583 ▤ 01993 810041
e-mail stay@laurelsguesthouse.co.uk
Dir Off A44 onto Hensington Rd by pedestrian lights, 500yds on right opp Catholic church

Located in a peaceful area just a short walk from the historic centre, the Victorian house has been renovated to provide high standards of comfort. Bedrooms come with thoughtful extras, and the elegant period-furnished dining room is the setting for imaginative breakfasts, which feature organic produce whenever possible.

Facilities 2 en suite ⊗ TVB tea/coffee ✘ Cen ht No children 10yrs No coaches **Prices** S £55-£65; D £65-£75 **Parking** 2 **Notes** Closed Xmas & New Year

♦♦♦♦

Town House
15 High St OX20 1TE
☎ 01993 810843 & 07976 315652 ▤ 01993 810864
e-mail info@woodstock-townhouse.com
Dir Off A44 onto High St

Located in the heart of this historic town, close to Blenheim Palace, this 18th-century terrace house provides cosy, attractive bedrooms filled with thoughtful and practical extras, including modern power showers. Breakfasts and afternoon teas are served in the conservatory-kitchen-dining room or on the enclosed patio during summer.

Facilities 5 en suite (1 fmly) ⊗ TVB tea/coffee Direct dial from bedrooms Cen ht **Prices** S £55-£65; D £70-£90

♦♦♦♦

The Blenheim Guest House & Tea Rooms
17 Park St OX20 1SJ ☎ 01993 813814 ▤ 01993 813810
e-mail theblenheim@aol.com
web www.theblenheim.com
Dir Off A44 in Woodstock to County Museum, B&B after museum on left

Facilities 6 rms (5 en suite) (1 pri facs) (2 fmly) ⊗ TVB tea/coffee Direct dial from bedrooms Licensed Cen ht **Prices** S £50-£70; D £60-£70✳

♦♦♦ ◧

The Crown Inn
31 High St OX20 1TE ☎ 01993 811117 ▤ 01993 813339
e-mail thecrowninn@ic24.net
Dir In town centre, off A44 onto High St

The Crown is located in the heart of the historic town. The attractive

continued

England

public areas include a conservatory-style restaurant, La Cucina, which serves Italian food and is popular with locals.

Facilities 6 rms (4 en suite) (1 fmly) ⊘ in bedrooms ⊘ in area of dining room STV TVB tea/coffee 🍴 Cen ht TVL Dinner Last d 9.15pm LB **Conf** Max 40 Class 40 Board 25

◆◆◆

Sturdys Castle

Banbury Rd, Tackley OX5 3EP
☎ 01869 331328 ▤ 01869 331686
e-mail enquiries@sturdyscastle.com
Dir On A4260 Oxford to Banbury Rd

Within easy reach of the historic Woodstock and Blenheim Palace, this well-presented inn is a good touring base. Purpose-built accommodation is located to the rear of the attractive pub where a wide range of traditional fare is on offer. Bedrooms are comfortable and well appointed.

Facilities 20 en suite (4 fmly) (10 GF) ⊘ in bedrooms ⊘ in dining room TVB tea/coffee Direct dial from bedrooms 🍴 Licensed Lift Cen ht Dinner Last d 10pm **Conf** Max 50 **Parking** 40

WOOLSTONE — MAP 05 SU28

★★★ Inn

The White Horse

SN7 7QL ☎ 01367 820726 & 820566 ▤ 01367 820566
Dir Just off B4507 nestling at the foot of Uffington white Horse Hill

Set in Oxfordshire countryside, this 17th-century village inn offers a taste of traditional England. Full of character, the inn has an inviting ambience, with beams, an open fire and a fine collection of malt whiskies. The spacious bedrooms and bathrooms are located in an annexe.

Facilities 5 en suite (5 GF) ⊘ in bedrooms ⊘ in dining room TVB tea/coffee Direct dial from bedrooms 🍴 Cen ht Walking Dinner Last d 9pm **Parking** 40

RUTLAND

OAKHAM — MAP 11 SK80

◆◆◆◆

Kirkee House

35 Welland Way LE15 6SL
☎ 01572 757401 ▤ 01572 757401
e-mail carolbeech@kirkeehouse.demon.co.uk
Dir S of town centre. Off A606 High St onto Mill St, over level crossing, 400yds on left

Located on a leafy avenue a short walk from the town centre, this immaculate modern house provides comfortable bedrooms filled with homely extras. Comprehensive breakfasts, including local sausages and home-made preserves, are served in the elegant conservatory-dining room, which overlooks a pretty garden.

Facilities 2 en suite ⊘ TVB tea/coffee 🍴 Cen ht No children 7yrs No coaches **Prices** D £54-£68✳ **Parking** 2 **Notes** ⊛

UPPINGHAM — MAP 11 SP89

★★★★ Inn

The Marquess of Exeter

52 Main St, Lyddington LE15 9LT
☎ 01572 822477 ▤ 01572 821343
e-mail marquess@btconnect.com
Dir Off A6003 into village centre

The 17th-century thatch and stone inn has been renovated to provide spacious public areas furnished in contemporary style. A wide range of ales and imaginative food is offered, and the smart, modern bedrooms are in a separate building with attractive outdoor seating.

Facilities 19 en suite (1 fmly) (10 GF) ⊘ in bedrooms ⊘ in dining room TVB tea/coffee Direct dial from bedrooms 🍴 Cen ht Dinner Last d 9.30pm **Prices** S fr £55; D £80-£90✳ **Conf** Max 50 Thtr 50 Class 25 Board 25 Del from £100 ✳ **Parking** 50 **Notes** Civ Wed 50

England

WING

MAP 11 SK80

♦♦♦♦ 🛏 🍸

Kings Arms

13 Top St LE15 8SE ☎ 01572 737634 📠 01572 737255
e-mail info@thekingsarms-wing.co.uk
web www.thekingsarms-wing.co.uk
Dir 1.5m off A6003 in village centre

This traditional village inn, with its open fires, flagstone floors and low beams, dates from the 17th century. The refurbished restaurant is more contemporary and offers a wide range of interesting, freshly produced dishes. Service is attentive and friendly. The spacious, well-equipped bedrooms are in The Old Bake House and Granny's Cottage, in the nearby courtyard.

Facilities 8 en suite (4 fmly) (4 GF) ⊗ in bedrooms ⊗ in dining room TVB tea/coffee Direct dial from bedrooms 🐾 Cen ht Dinner Last d 9pm **Prices** S £60-£65; D £70-£75✳ **Conf** Max 20 Thtr 16 Class 16 Board 16 **Parking** 15

BISHOP'S CASTLE

MAP 15 SO38

♦♦♦♦

Norbury Hall

Norbury SY9 5DX ☎ 01588 650517
e-mail holiday@norbury-hall.co.uk
web www.norbury-hall.co.uk
Dir Off A489 near Lydham signed More, Norbury & Wentnor, 2m left for Norbury, Hall on right

A warm welcome awaits you at this carefully modernised 18th-century house. It stands in 35 acres on the edge of the quiet village and has picturesque views. The spotless and impeccably maintained accommodation has two well-equipped double bedrooms. A very pleasant breakfast-sitting room overlooks the garden.

Facilities 2 en suite ⊗ TVB tea/coffee 🐾 Cen ht No children 16yrs No coaches **Prices** S £35-£40; D £52-£58✳ **LB Parking** 3 **Notes** 🚭

♦♦♦♦ 🛏 🍸

The Sun at Norbury

Norbury SY9 5DX ☎ 01588 650680
web www.sunatnorbury.co.uk
Dir 3m NE of Bishops Castle. Off A488/A489 into Norbury village

The delightful stone inn stands in the quiet village of Norbury. Exposed beams and log-burning stoves are enhanced by period furnishings, and the attractive, traditionally furnished bedrooms have modern facilities. Wholesome home-cooked food is available in the elegant dining room or in the popular bar.

Facilities 6 annexe en suite (1 GF) ⊗ in bedrooms ⊗ in dining room ⊗ in 1 lounge TVB tea/coffee 🐾 Cen ht No children 14yrs Dinner Last d 9pm **Prices** D £90-£120✳ **LB Parking** 20

♦♦♦ 🍸

The Boar's Head

Church St SY9 5AE ☎ 01588 638521 📠 01588 630126
e-mail sales@boarsheadhotel.co.uk
Dir In village centre

Located in the heart of the town, the inn retains original flagstone floors, exposed beams and open fireplaces. A wide range of real ales and imaginative food is available in the non-smoking restaurant. The well-equipped bedrooms are situated on the ground floor of a converted outbuilding,

Facilities 4 en suite (1 fmly) (4 GF) ⊗ in dining room ⊗ in 1 lounge TVB tea/coffee Direct dial from bedrooms Cen ht TVL Pool Table Dinner Last d 9pm **Prices** D £60-£70✳ **LB Parking** 20

BRIDGNORTH

MAP 10 SO79

★★★★ 🅰 Guest Accommodation

Churchdown House

14 East Castle St WV16 4AL ☎ 01746 761236
e-mail churchdownhouse@tiscali.co.uk
Dir Off S end High St onto East Castle St

Facilities 3 rms (2 en suite) (1 pri facs) ⊘ TVB tea/coffee ✖ Cen ht No children 12yrs No coaches Dinner 24hrs notice **Prices** S £48-£68; D £72-£85 **Parking** 3 **Notes** 🚭

★★★ Inn

The Halfway House Inn

Cleobury Mortimer Rd WV16 5LS
☎ 01746 762670 📄 01746 768063
e-mail info@halfwayhouseinn.co.uk
web www.halfwayhouseinn.co.uk
Dir 1m from town centre on A4363 to Cleobury Mortimer

Located in a rural area, this 16th-century inn has been renovated to provide good standards of comfort, while retaining original character. The bedrooms, most of which are in converted stables and cottages, are especially suitable for families and groups.

Facilities 10 en suite (10 fmly) (6 GF) ⊘ in 3 bedrooms ⊘ in area of dining room TVB tea/coffee ✖ Cen ht TVL Fishing Pool Table Dinner Last d 9pm **Prices** S £55-£70; D £60-£85✳ LB **Conf** Max 30 Thtr 30 Class 24 Board 20 Del from £75 ✳ **Parking** 30 **Notes** rs Sun eve (ex BHs)

Premier Collection

◆◆◆◆◆

The Albynes ◇

Nordley WV16 4SX ☎ 01746 762261
Dir In Nordley on B4373, 500yds past Nordley village sign

This imposing farmhouse features grand staircases, high ceilings and idyllic views. Cynthia Woolley is a charming and thoughtful hostess, while husband Geoff looks after the crops and sheep. Bedrooms are comfortable, spacious and offer many thoughtful extras. You can enjoy traditional breakfasts cooked on the Aga.

Facilities 3 en suite ⊘ TVB tea/coffee ✖ Cen ht TVL No children 12yrs No coaches **Prices** S £30; D £55-£60✳ **Parking** 10 **Notes** Closed Nov-Mar 🚭

◆◆◆◆

Bearwood Lodge Guest House

10 Kidderminster Rd WV15 6BW ☎ 01746 762159
Dir On A442, 50yds S of Bridgnorth bypass island

This friendly guest house is on the outskirts of Bridgnorth. It provides soundly maintained modern accommodation, including one bedroom on the ground floor. The bright and pleasant breakfast room has an adjacent conservatory, which opens onto the colourful garden. There is also a comfortable lounge.

Facilities 5 en suite (1 GF) ⊘ TVB tea/coffee ✖ Cen ht TVL No coaches **Prices** S £40; D £50✳ LB **Parking** 8 **Notes** 🚭

◆◆◆◆ 🍴

The Fox Inn

46 Hospital St WV15 5AR ☎ 01746 769611 📄 01746 761736
e-mail enquiries@thefoxinnbridgnorth.co.uk
Dir On A442 Kidderminster to Telford road

Please note that this establishment has recently changed hands. Located within Lower Town, this inn has a strong local following for its imaginative food and wines. It has been renovated to provide attractive, rustically furnished public areas, and the thoughtfully furnished bedrooms have modern en suites and free broadband Internet access.

Facilities 5 en suite ⊘ in bedrooms ⊘ in dining room ⊘ in 1 lounge TVB tea/coffee ✖ Cen ht No coaches Dinner Last d 9pm **Prices** S £55-£70; D £60-£80✳ **Parking** 7

◆◆◆◆

The Laurels

Broadoak, Six Ashes WV15 6EQ ☎ 01384 221546
e-mail george@broadoak75.fsnet.co.uk
web www.thelaurelsbandb.co.uk
Dir On right 5m from Bridgnorth travelling towards Stourbridge on the A458

Located in pretty gardens in a hamlet between Bridgnorth and Stourbridge, this immaculate property provides a range of homely bedrooms, some of which are within converted stables. Breakfast is served in an attractive conservatory-dining room, and a lounge and indoor swimming pool are additional attractions.

Facilities 3 rms (2 en suite) (1 pri facs) 3 annexe en suite (1 fmly) (3 GF) ⊘ TVB tea/coffee ✖ Cen ht TVL No coaches ❄ Dinner Last d 7.30pm LB **Parking** 6 **Notes** Closed Xmas & New Year 🚭

◆◆◆◆ 🏛

Oldfield Cottage

Oldfield WV16 6AQ ☎ 01746 789257 📄 01746 789257
e-mail oldfieldcottage@aol.com
Dir B4364 from Bridgnorth, after 3m pass Down Inn, 2nd left signed Oldfield, 0.25m on right

Located in the hamlet of Oldfield and set in mature gardens, this traditional cottage provides homely bedrooms in converted outbuildings. Memorable breakfasts, using quality local or home-made produce, are served in the conservatory.

England

BRIDGNORTH continued

Facilities 2 annexe en suite (2 GF) ⊗ TVB tea/coffee Cen ht TVL No children 10yrs No coaches **Prices** d fr £55✳ **LB Parking** 3 **Notes** Closed Dec-Feb ⊛

◆◆

Wyndene ◇

57 Innage Ln WV16 4HS
☎ 01746 764369 & 0797 794 3074
e-mail wyndene@bridgnorth2000.freeserve.co.uk
Dir 500yds NW of town centre. Off B4373 onto Innage Ln

Situated within walking distance of the centre of Bridgnorth, this small guest house is a home from home. Bedrooms are carefully decorated and one has a four-poster bed. Home-cooked breakfasts are served in an attractive dining room and parking space is available.

Facilities 3 rms (1 en suite) ⊗ TVB tea/coffee ✘ Cen ht No children No coaches Dinner Last d 3pm **Prices** S £27; D £46-£48✳ **Parking** 3 **Notes** ⊛

BURWARTON
MAP 10 SO68

◆◆◆

Peace Haven ◇

The Old School WV16 6QG
☎ 01746 787566 & 07899 844450
e-mail kw.ukla@virgin.net
Dir On B4364 between Bridgnorth & Ludlow. 1st building in Burwarton village.

Located between Bridgnorth and Ludlow, the former Victorian school retains original features and the bedroom accommodation occupies the headmaster's rooms. Owner-managed by a former champion yachtsman, the Haven is also a centre for meditation and yoga. The spacious Gothic beamed classroom is now a comfortable lounge and dining area.

Facilities 3 rms (1 en suite) (1 fmly) ⊗ TVB tea/coffee ✘ Cen ht TVL No coaches ⊾ Yoga/meeting room, meditation room Dinner Last d 6pm **Prices** S £30-£35; D £50-£60✳ **LB Conf** Thtr 50 Class 50 Board 50 Del from £60 ✳ **Parking** 30 **Notes** ⊛

CHURCH STRETTON
MAP 15 SO49

Premier Collection

★★★★★ **Guest House**

Willowfield Guest House

Lower Wood SY6 6LF ☎ 01694 751471

Set in spacious and immaculate gardens, this Edwardian house, parts of which are much older, provides high standards of comfort. The bedrooms are well equipped and have stunning views, while stylish decor and period furnishings add to the charm. A comfortable lounge is available, plus two elegant dining rooms where wholesome home-cooked dinners and hearty breakfasts are served.

Facilities 6 en suite (1 fmly) (1 GF) ⊗ TVB tea/coffee ✘ Cen ht No coaches Dinner Last d 8.30am **Prices** S £45-£50; D £64-£70✳ **LB Parking** 6 **Notes** ⊛

Premier Collection

◆◆◆◆◆ ❧

Rectory Farm (SO452985)

Woolstaston SY6 6NN
☎ 01694 751306 ▤ 01694 751306 Mrs Rodenhurst
e-mail drodenhurst@waitrose.com
Dir 1.5m from A49 Shrewsbury to Ludlow road, turn by Copper Kettle

Located in immaculate grounds within the pretty hamlet of Woolstaston, this early 17th-century half-timbered longhouse retains many original features including a wealth of exposed beams. The spacious bedrooms feature many thoughtful extras, and ground-floor areas include two sitting rooms and an elegant dining room.

Facilities 3 en suite ⊗ TVB tea/coffee ✘ Cen ht TVL No children 12yrs 10 acres non-working **Prices** S £40; D £55-£60✳ **Parking** 6 **Notes** ⊛

◆◆◆◆

The Orchards ◇

Eaton Rd, Ticklerton SY6 7DQ ☎ 01694 722268
e-mail lnutting@btinternet.com
web www.theorchardsticklerton.com
Dir A49 onto B4371, 3m right to Ticklerton, left in village, last house on left

This large new house stands in the quiet hamlet of Ticklerton, 2m south-east of Church Stretton. Surrounded by 4.5 acres of grounds, garden and an orchard, it overlooks picturesque countryside. The comfortable accommodation is thoughtfully equipped and the warm hospitality is a major strength here.

Facilities 3 rms (2 en suite) (1 pri facs) (1 fmly) ⊗ TVB tea/coffee ✘ Cen ht No children 3yrs No coaches **Prices** S £25-£30; D £50-£60 **Parking** 6 **Notes** ⊛

◆◆◆◆

Belvedere

Burway Rd SY6 6DP ☎ 01694 722232 ▤ 01694 722232
e-mail info@belvedereguesthouse.co.uk
Dir Off A49 into town centre, over x-rds onto Burway Rd

Located on the lower slopes of the Long Mynd, this impressive, well-proportioned Edwardian house has a range of homely bedrooms, equipped with practical extras and complemented by modern bathrooms. Ground-floor areas include a cottage-style dining room overlooking the pretty garden and a choice of lounges.

Facilities 7 rms (6 en suite) (2 fmly) ⊗ tea/coffee Cen ht TVL No coaches **Prices** D £54-£60✳ **LB Parking** 9

◆◆◆◆

Brereton's Farm

Woolston SY6 6QD ☎ 01694 781201 📠 01694 781201
e-mail info@breretonsfarm.co.uk
web www.breretonsfarm.co.uk

Dir *A49 N from Craven Arms, at Jewsons turn left A489. Under bridge turn right Wistonstow, top of the village signed left 1.75m to Woolston. Farm on right*

Located among undulating hills within the pretty hamlet of Woolston, this impressive Victorian brick house provides thoughtfully equipped bedrooms with stunning country views. Comprehensive breakfasts are served in an elegant dining room, and the lounge has a wood-burning fireplace.

Facilities 2 en suite ⊘ tea/coffee ✖ Cen ht TVL No coaches
Prices D £52 **Parking** 6 **Notes** Closed 30 Nov-Mar 🚭

◆◆◆◆ ❦

Gilberries Hall Farm (SO514938)

Gilberries Ln SY6 7HZ ☎ 01694 771723 Mrs Hotchkiss
Dir *B4371 E 4m, after Plough Inn left signed Gretton, house 1st on left*

Having stunning views of the surrounding countryside, this well-proportioned house stands in mature gardens and has a large indoor swimming pool. Bedrooms are filled with homey extras and have modern bathrooms. Public areas include an elegant dining room and a lounge.

Facilities 3 en suite (1 fmly) (1 GF) ⊘ TVB tea/coffee ✖ Cen ht TVL
No children 10yrs 🐾 320 acres dairy arable Dinner Last d by 10am on day
Parking 6 **Notes** Closed Dec-Jan 🚭

◆◆◆◆ ❦

North Hill Farm ◈ (SO496942)

Cardington SY6 7LL ☎ 01694 771532
Mr & Mrs Brandon-Lodge
e-mail cbrandon@btinternet.com

Dir *From Cardington village S onto Church Stretton road, right signed Cardington Moor, farm at top of hill on left*

This delightful house has been modernised to provide comfortable accommodation. It is located on a fairly remote 20-acre sheep-rearing holding amid the Shropshire hills. The lounge, with exposed beams, has log fires in cooler weather. You share one large table in the breakfast room.

Facilities 3 rms (2 pri facs) 1 annexe en suite (1 GF) ⊘ TVB tea/coffee
Cen ht No children 10yrs Facilities for guests horses 20 acres
Horses/sheep **Prices** S £27.50; D £48-£60 **LB** **Parking** 6 **Notes** 🚭

◆◆◆ ❦

Malt House Farm (SO459979)

Lower Wood SY6 6LF ☎ 01694 751379 📠 01694 751379
Mr & Mrs Bloor
Dir *A49 N 3m, left signed Lower Wood, 0.5m to farm*

Located on an elevated position north of the town, this house was refashioned in 1772 and retains many original features. Modern bathrooms complement the homely bedrooms. Comprehensive breakfasts, which include free-range eggs, are served in the cosy dining room and a lounge is also available.

continued

Malt House Farm

Facilities 3 en suite ⊘ TVB tea/coffee ✖ Cen ht No children 100 acres
beef sheep Dinner Last d 9am **Prices** D £45-£52✳ **Parking** 3
Notes Closed Nov-Mar 🚭

CLEOBURY MORTIMER   MAP 10 SO67

◆◆◆◆ ◀

The Crown Inn

Hopton Wafers DY14 0NB
☎ 01299 270372 📠 01299 271127
e-mail desk@crownathopton.co.uk
web www.crownathopton.co.uk

Dir *In village on A4117 2m W of Cleobury Mortimer*

Set in extensive gardens with a duck pond, this 16th-century inn retains original exposed beams and has roaring log fires. Bedrooms are individually furnished and have modern facilities. Public areas include an elegant restaurant and spacious bars, where real ales and imaginative food are served.

Facilities 7 en suite ⊘ in bedrooms ⊘ in dining room TVB tea/coffee
Direct dial from bedrooms ✖ Cen ht No children 7yrs No coaches
Dinner Last d 9.15pm **Parking** 40

See advertisement on page 402

◆◆◆◆

Hammonds

10 Lower St DY14 8AA ☎ 01299 270395
e-mail celia@countrybreak.co.uk
web www.countrybreak.co.uk

Dir *On A4117 in village centre*

Hammonds has an excellent location with good access to Birmingham and the West Midlands. The accommodation is located in a nearby annexe and rooms are spacious and well equipped. Imaginative food, using quality local produce, features in the attractive pine-furnished dining room and delicatessen.

Facilities 6 annexe en suite (3 GF) ⊘ TVB tea/coffee Direct dial from
bedrooms ✖ Licensed Cen ht No children 12yrs **Prices** S £55; D £75✳
Conf Max 30 Thtr 30 Class 16 Board 30 **Parking** 10 **Notes** 🚭

England

CLEOBURY MORTIMER continued

♦♦♦♦ 🏛

The Old Bake House ◇

46-47 High St DY14 8DQ ☎ 01299 270193

Dir *On A4117 in village 100yds from church*

A conversion of two 18th-century houses, a village inn and a bakery has resulted in a carefully furnished guest house providing bedrooms filled with a wealth of thoughtful extras. Spacious ground-floor areas include comfortable sitting rooms and a dining section, the setting for memorable breakfasts.

Facilities 3 rms (2 en suite) (1 pri facs) ⊗ in bedrooms ⊗ in dining room ⊗ in 1 lounge tea/coffee Cen ht TVL No coaches Dinner Last d 7pm **Prices** S £25-£28; D £50-£56✶ **Parking** 2 **Notes** 🚭

CLUN

MAP 09 SO38

Premier Collection

♦♦♦♦♦ 🏛

Birches Mill

SY7 8NL ☎ 01588 640409 📠 01588 640224
e-mail gill@birchesmill.fsnet.co.uk
web www.virtual-shropshire.co.uk/birchesmill

Dir *A488 N from Clun for Bishops Castle, 1st left to Bicton, in Bicton 2nd left for Mainstone, pass farm & 1st right*

Set in mature gardens beside a river in an Area of Outstanding Natural Beauty, this 17th-century former mill has original features enhanced by the decor and furnishings. Bedrooms are filled with lots of thoughtful extras, and a comfortable lounge is available in addition to an elegant dining room, which is the setting for imaginative dinners.

Facilities 3 rms (2 en suite) (1 pri facs) ⊗ tea/coffee 🐾 Cen ht TVL No children 12yrs No coaches **Prices** D £72-£80✶ **Parking** 4 **Notes** Closed Nov-Mar

♦♦♦ 🐓

Hurst Mill Farm ◇ *(SO318811)*

SY7 0JA ☎ 01588 640224 📠 01588 640224 Mrs Williams
e-mail hurstmillholidays@tinyworld.co.uk

Dir *0.8m E of Clun, signed off B4368 via driveway*

This farm is quietly located in a picturesque valley about a mile east of the village. Bedrooms are cheerfully decorated. In addition to the comfortable lounge, a conservatory overlooks the garden. There is a shared table in the pleasant dining room. Three self-catering cottages are also available.

Facilities 3 rms (1 en suite) (1 pri facs) (1 fmly) ⊗ in bedrooms ⊗ in dining room ⊗ in 1 lounge TV2B tea/coffee Cen ht TVL Fishing Clay pigeon shooting 100 acres mixed **Prices** S £30; D £50-£54✶ LB **Parking** 6 **Notes** Closed 20-25 Dec 🚭

CRAVEN ARMS

MAP 09 SO48

♦♦♦♦

The Firs

Norton SY7 9LS ☎ 01588 672511 📠 01588 672511
e-mail thefirs@wrb.me.uk

Dir *Off A49 at Craven Arms onto B4368 towards Bridgnorth. 2m right at x-rds & B&B sign to Norton. Pass farm on left to next left, house 100yds on left*

Located in immaculate grounds on an elevated position within the hamlet of Norton, this impressive Victorian house has original features highlighted by period furnishings and quality decor. Bedrooms are filled with thoughtful extras and have stunning views. Breakfast makes use of local produce and is served in an elegant dining room.

Facilities 3 rms (2 en suite) (1 pri facs) ⊗ TVB tea/coffee 🐾 Cen ht TVL No coaches **Parking** 5 **Notes** 🚭

♦♦♦♦ 🐓

Strefford Hall Farm ◇ *(SO444856)*

Strefford SY7 8DE
☎ 01588 672383 📠 0870 132 3818 Mrs Morgan
e-mail strefford@btconnect.com

Dir *A49 2m N, turn right, 0.25m on right*

This well-proportioned Victorian house stands at the foot of Wenlock Edge. The spacious bedrooms, filled with homely extras, have stunning views of the surrounding countryside. Breakfast is served in the elegant dining room and a comfortable lounge is also available.

Facilities 3 en suite ⊗ TVB tea/coffee 🐾 Cen ht TVL 350 acres arable, beef, sheep, pigs, hens **Prices** S £30-£35; D £57-£62✶ LB **Parking** 3 **Notes** Closed Xmas & New Year 🚭

♦♦♦♦

Castle View

Stokesay SY7 9AL ☎ 01588 673712
e-mail joyce@castleviewb-b.fsnet.co.uk

Dir *On A49 south of Craven Arms opp turning to Stokesay Castle*

The Victorian cottage, extended about 20 years ago, stands in delightful gardens on the southern outskirts of Craven Arms, close to Stokesay Castle. Bedrooms are thoughtfully furnished, and breakfasts, featuring local produce, are served in the cosy, traditionally furnished dining room.

Facilities 3 rms (1 en suite) (2 pri facs) ⊗ TVB tea/coffee Cen ht No children 3yrs No coaches **Prices** S £35-£40; D £55-£60✶ LB **Parking** 4 **Notes** 🚭

♦♦♦
London House ◇
Market St SY7 9NW ☎ 01588 672360
e-mail sue@cravenarms.fsbusiness.co.uk
Dir *Off A49, opp supermarket, take 1st right, on left next to St Andrews Church*

This small and pleasant guest house provides modern accommodation and warm hospitality. It is in the town centre and is suitable for leisure and commercial visitors.

Facilities 2 rms (1 en suite) (1 pri facs) ⊗ TVB tea/coffee Cen ht TVL No coaches **Prices** S £25-£28; D £50-£56 **Parking** 1 **Notes** Closed Sun-Thu (except BHs) 🐾

CRESSAGE   MAP 10 SJ50

♦♦♦♦
The Old House B & B
4 Shrewsbury Rd SY5 6AA ☎ 01952 510198
e-mail theoldhouse.bedandbreakfast@virgin.net
Dir *0.3m W of Cressage war memorial on A458*

A warm welcome awaits you at this delightful 17th-century cottage, which has been carefully renovated and extended to provide modern accommodation, including a bedroom on the ground floor. A welcoming wood-burning stove is a feature of the comfortable lounge-breakfast room.

Facilities 2 en suite ⊗ TVB tea/coffee ✖ Cen ht No children 12yrs No coaches **Prices** D £38.50-£46 **Parking** 4

DORRINGTON   MAP 15 SJ40

♦♦♦♦
Ashton Lees ◇
Ashton Lees SY5 7JW ☎ 01743 718378
Dir *On N edge of village on A49. From Shrewsbury, Ashton Lees on right on entering village*

Set in immaculate mature gardens, this well-proportioned mid 20th-century house has been renovated to provide high standards of comfort and facilities. Bedrooms are filled with thoughtful extras, and public areas include a cosy lounge-dining room and a sitting room, both featuring open fires.

Facilities 3 rms (2 en suite) ⊗ TVB tea/coffee ✖ Cen ht TVL No coaches **Prices** S £25-£30; D £50-£60✶ **Parking** 6 **Notes** Closed Dec-Jan 🐾

♦♦♦
Caro's Bed & Breakfast
1 Higher Netley SY5 7JY ☎ 01743 718790 & 07739 285263
e-mail info@carosbandb.co.uk
Dir *Off A49 in Dorrington signed Picklescott, continue 1.3m past bends sign, small hill and narrowed road. Left onto driveway by stone bridge*

Self-contained guest accommodation is provided in this converted barn, south-west of Dorrington. Bedrooms, with smart modern bathrooms, are equipped with thoughtful extras and the open-plan ground-floor area contains a dining area and a comfortable lounge with a wood-burning stove.

Facilities 2 en suite ⊗ TVB tea/coffee ✖ Cen ht No coaches **Parking** 4 **Notes** Closed Xmas 🐾

ELLESMERE   MAP 15 SJ33

Ⓤ
Hordley Hall ◇
Hordley SY12 9BB ☎ 01691 622772
Dir *Leave A5 at Queens Head junct signed Hordley 4m. Take 1st left after village sign, 1st large cream house on right*

At the time of going to press the rating for this establishment had not been confirmed. Please check the AA website www.theAA.com for up-to-date information.

Facilities 4 rms (2 en suite) (2 pri facs) ⊗ TVB tea/coffee ✖ Cen ht TVL No children 10yrs **Prices** S £25-£30; D £50✶ **LB Parking** 4 **Notes** 🐾

HADNALL   MAP 15 SJ52

♦♦♦♦
Hall Farm House
Shrewsbury Rd SY4 4AG ☎ 01939 210269
e-mail hallfarmhouse1@whsmithnet.co.uk
web www.hallfarmhouse.co.uk
Dir *On A49 in centre of Hadnall*

Parts of this elegant former farmhouse, situated within pretty gardens in the village, date from the 16th century. Accommodation is offered in two twin-rooms, and there is a traditionally furnished and spacious breakfast room.

Facilities 2 en suite ⊗ TVB tea/coffee ✖ Cen ht No children 1yr No coaches **LB Parking** 6 **Notes** 🐾

England

HODNET
MAP 15 SJ62

◆◆◆◆

The Grange
Hopton TF9 3LQ ☎ 01630 685579
e-mail beverley@thegrangehopton.freeserve.co.uk
Dir *Off A53 signed West Midland Shooting Grounds, The Grange 0.25m on left*

Set in countryside, this renovated sandstone house has cosy bedrooms furnished in quality pine and complemented by pretty fabrics. Comprehensive breakfasts, using quality fresh produce, are served at one table in the attractive dining room that overlooks the gardens.

Facilities 2 en suite (1 GF) ⊗ TVB tea/coffee ✖ Cen ht No coaches **Prices** S £35-£37.50; D £50-£55 **LB** **Parking** 12 **Notes** ⊛

IRONBRIDGE
MAP 10 SJ60

Premier Collection

◆◆◆◆◆ 🛎

The Library House
11 Severn Bank TF8 7AN
☎ 01952 432299 📠 01952 433967
e-mail info@libraryhouse.com
web www.libraryhouse.com
Dir *50yds from Iron Bridge*

A warm welcome is assured at this renovated Georgian house, once the local library. Bedrooms have a wealth of thoughtful extras and the immaculate gardens and hanging baskets are stunning during spring and summer. Memorable breakfasts are served in the pine- and copper-furnished dining room.

Facilities 3 en suite ⊗ TVB tea/coffee ✖ Licensed Cen ht TVL No children 10yrs No coaches **Prices** S £55-£60; D £70-£80✳ **LB** **Notes** ⊛

◆◆◆◆◆ 🅰

Bridge House
Buildwas Rd TF8 7BN ☎ 01952 432105 📠 01952 432105
Dir *At bottom of Buildwas Bank (A4169) left & next left into car park*

Facilities 4 en suite (1 fmly) ⊗ TVB tea/coffee ✖ Cen ht TVL No coaches Fishing **Prices** S £52-£55; D £70-£75✳ **Parking** 6 **Notes** Closed Xmas-New Year

◆◆◆◆

Broseley House
1 The Square, Broseley TF12 5EW
☎ 01952 882043 📠 01952 882043
e-mail info@broseleyhouse.co.uk
web www.broseleyhouse.co.uk
Dir *1m S of Ironbridge in Broseley town centre*

This impressive Georgian house in the centre of Broseley retains original features alongside many improvements. Bedrooms are well equipped and have thoughtful touches; one room with a kitchen is available for self-catering. Hearty breakfasts are served in the elegant breakfast room.

Facilities 4 en suite (1 fmly) (1 GF) ⊗ TVB tea/coffee ✖ Cen ht No children 5yrs Cycle Hire **Prices** S £35-£40; D £60-£70✳ **Notes** ⊛

◆◆◆◆ 🍴

The Swan
The Wharfage TF8 7NH ☎ 01952 432306 📠 01952 432993
e-mail mcdonald740@msn.com

Reputed to be the oldest inn in Ironbridge, this riverside hostelry has been renovated to provide good standards of comfort and facilities. Rustically furnished bedrooms offer modern facilities including some jacuzzis en suite, and open-plan public areas are the setting for casual dining.

Facilities 8 en suite (3 fmly) ⊗ in bedrooms ⊗ in dining room ⊗ in 1 lounge TVB tea/coffee Direct dial from bedrooms ✖ Cen ht Dinner Last d 9.30pm **Prices** S fr £60; d fr £65✳ **LB** **Conf** Max 50 **Parking** 7

◆◆◆◆

Woodlands Farm Guest House
Beech Rd TF8 7PA ☎ 01952 432741 📠 01952 432741
e-mail woodlandsfarm@ironbridge68.fsnet.co.uk
web www.woodlandsfarmguesthouse.co.uk
Dir *Off B4373 rdbt in Ironbridge onto Church Hill & Beech Rd, house on private lane 0.5m on right*

Located in 4 acres of mature ground with a well-stocked fishing lake, this extended Victorian bungalow provides a range of well-equipped and homey bedrooms, including a family suite with a lounge. A comprehensive breakfast is served in the cosy breakfast room, which overlooks the pretty garden.

Facilities 3 en suite (1 fmly) (3 GF) ⊗ STV FTV TVB tea/coffee Cen ht TVL No coaches **Prices** S £35-£65; D £60-£70 **LB** **Parking** 8 **Notes** Closed 24 Dec-1 Jan

◆◆◆ 🍴

Grove Inn & Fat Frog Restaurant
10 Wellington Rd, Coalbrookdale TF8 7DX
☎ 01952 433269 & 432240 📠 01952 433269
e-mail frog@fat-frog.co.uk
Dir *0.5m N of Ironbridge off A4169*

Located a short walk from the Coalbrookdale Museum, this inn has a continental-style interior with attractive murals. Formal and informal dining rooms provide intimate settings in which to enjoy the imaginative food. Bedrooms are homely and attentive service is assured.

continued

Grove Inn & Fat Frog Restaurant

Facilities 4 en suite (1 fmly) ⊗ in bedrooms ⊗ in dining room ⊗ in 1 lounge TVB tea/coffee Cen ht TVL Dinner Last d 9.30pm **LB** **Parking** 15

KNOCKIN   MAP 15 SJ32

Top Farm House *(SJ334214)*

SY10 8HN
☎ 01691 682582 📠 01691 682070 Mrs Morrissey
e-mail p.a.m@knockin.freeserve.co.uk
web www.topfarmknockin.co.uk
Dir *In Knockin, past Bradford Arms & shop, past turning for Kinnerley*

This impressive half-timbered Tudor house, set amid pretty gardens, retains original exposed beams and open fires. Bedrooms are equipped with many thoughtful extras, and the open-plan ground-floor area includes a comfortable sitting room and elegant dining section, where imaginative and comprehensive breakfasts are served.

Facilities 3 en suite (1 fmly) ⊗ in dining room TVB tea/coffee Cen ht TVL **Prices** S £35-£55; D £60-£70✳ **LB** **Parking** 6

LLANFAIR WATERDINE   MAP 09 SO27

Premier Collection

The Waterdine

LD7 1TU ☎ 01547 528214 📠 01547 529992
e-mail info@waterdine.com
Dir *Off B4355 into village, last property on left before church*

Standing in mature gardens within an Area of Outstanding Natural Beauty, which includes part of Offa's Dyke, this former 16th-century drovers' inn retains much of its original character. Bedrooms are filled

continued

with a wealth of thoughtful extras and have modern bathrooms. Public areas include a cosy lounge bar and an elegant restaurant, the setting for imaginative dinners that use quality, seasonal local produce.

Facilities 3 en suite ⊗ in bedrooms ⊗ in dining room ⊗ in 1 lounge TVB tea/coffee Cen ht No children 12yrs No coaches Dinner Last d 9pm **Prices** d fr £160; (incl. dinner) ✳ **LB** **Parking** 12 **Notes** Closed 1wk Autumn & 1wk Spring rs Sun & Mon (ex BHs)

LUDLOW   MAP 10 SO57

★★★★ Bed & Breakfast

37 Gravel Hill

SY8 1QR ☎ 01584 877524
e-mail dstraker@onetel.com
Dir *In town centre*

This charming old house is within walking distance of the town centre. It provides good quality, thoughtfully equipped accommodation, and there is also a comfortable sitting room. Guests share one large table in the elegant breakfast room.

Facilities 2 rms (1 en suite) (1 pri facs) ⊗ TVB tea/coffee Cen ht TVL No coaches

Premier Collection

Bromley Court B & B

73 Lower Broad St SY8 1PH
☎ 01584 876996 & 0854 065 6192
e-mail phil@ludlowhotels.com
web www.ludlowhotels.com
Dir *Off B4361 at bridge into town centre*

Located close to the river and attractions of the historic town, this renovation of Georgian cottages provides split-level suites. All have comfortable sitting areas and kitchenettes, and the carefully furnished bedrooms are filled with thoughtful extras. A peaceful patio garden is available, and wholesome breakfasts are served in a cottage-style dining room in a separate house.

Facilities 3 en suite ⊗ TVB tea/coffee Direct dial from bedrooms Cen ht TVL No coaches **Prices** S £75-£115; D £95-£120 **LB**

England

LUDLOW continued

Premier Collection

◆◆◆◆◆ ❦

Line Farm (SO494668)

Tunnel Ln, Orleton SY8 4HY
☎ 01568 780400 ▤ 01568 780995 Mrs Lewis
e-mail linefarm@lineone.net
Dir Signed from A49 in Ashton. B&B signs in Tunnel Ln to Line Farm

A warm welcome is assured at this well-maintained, non-smoking farmhouse, which is set in immaculate gardens to the south of Ludlow. Bedrooms, one of which is located in a superb Scandinavian-style chalet that can also be used for self-catering, are filled with a wealth of thoughtful extras and have efficient modern bathrooms. Comprehensive breakfasts are served in an elegant dining room, and a spacious lounge is available.

Facilities 3 en suite ⊘ TVB tea/coffee Direct dial from bedrooms ✻ Cen ht TVL No children 54 acres mixed **Prices** D £60-£65✳ **Parking** 6 **Notes** Closed Nov-Feb ⊜

◆◆◆◆ ⍟⍟ ⌲

The Clive Restaurant with Rooms

Bromfield SY8 2JR
☎ 01584 856565 & 856665 ▤ 01584 856661
e-mail info@theclive.co.uk
web www.theclive.co.uk
Dir 2m N of Ludlow on A49 in village of Bromfield

The Clive is 2m from the busy town of Ludlow and is a convenient base for touring or for business. The bedrooms are spacious and very well equipped, and some are suitable for families. Meals are available in the well-known Clive restaurant or the Cookhouse cafe bar. A small meeting room is also available.

Facilities 15 annexe en suite (9 fmly) (11 GF) ⊘ TVB tea/coffee Direct dial from bedrooms ✻ Licensed Cen ht Dinner **Prices** S £50-£75; D £75-£95✳ **LB Conf** Thtr 40 Class 40 Board 20 Del from £80 ✳ **Parking** 100 **Notes** Closed 25-26 Dec

◆◆◆◆

Angel House

Bitterley SY8 3HT ☎ 01584 891377
e-mail stay@angelhousecleehill.co.uk
web www.angelhousecleehill.co.uk
Dir On A4117 towards Kidderminster

Parts of this former inn date from the 17th century and original features such as timber-framed walls still remain. The bedrooms are spacious, modern and thoughtfully equipped. Facilities include a cosy dining room, and a comfortable lounge with an adjoining conservatory from which there are stunning views towards Ludlow.

Facilities 2 en suite (1 fmly) ⊘ TVB tea/coffee No children 5yrs No coaches Dinner Last d 10.30am **Prices** S £40-£65; D £65 **LB Parking** 10 **Notes** ⊜

◆◆◆◆ ⌦

The Church Inn

The Buttercross SY8 1AW
☎ 01584 872174 ▤ 01584 877146
web www.thechurchinn.com
Dir In town centre at top of Broad St

Set right in the heart of the historic town, this Grade II listed inn has been renovated to provide quality accommodation with smart modern bathrooms, some with spa baths. Other areas include a small lounge, a well-equipped meeting room, and cosy bar areas where imaginative food and real ales are served.

Facilities 9 en suite (3 fmly) ⊘ in area of dining room ⊘ in 1 lounge TVB tea/coffee Direct dial from bedrooms Cen ht TVL No coaches Dinner Last d 9pm **Prices** D £60-£80✳ **Conf** Max 38

◆◆◆◆

The Long House

The Sheet SY8 4JT ☎ 01584 874732
e-mail janice.rose@btopenworld.com
web www.longhouse.org.uk
Dir Off A49 Ludlow bypass W towards Caynham, 400yds on right

Located in the peaceful hamlet of Sheet 1.5m from Ludlow centre, this impressive 400-year-old former farmhouse has comfortable bedrooms equipped with lots of homely extras. Comprehensive breakfasts are served in an attractive hall-dining room and a warm welcome is assured.

Facilities 3 en suite ⊘ TVB tea/coffee ✻ Cen ht No children 12yrs No coaches **Prices** D £50-£60✳ **LB Parking** 4 **Notes** ⊜

◆◆◆◆

The Marcle

Brimfield SY8 4NE ☎ 01584 711459 🖷 01584 711459
e-mail marcle@supanet.com
Dir 4m S of Ludlow, off A49 into village, opp Post Office

This delightful 16th-century house lies in the centre of the pretty village of Brimfield. The elegant lounge and other areas are impeccably maintained. The bedrooms are decorated with pretty wallpapers and equipped with modern facilities. Well-tended lawns and gardens surround the house.

Facilities 3 en suite ⊘ TVB tea/coffee 🐾 Cen ht No children 12yrs No coaches Dinner Last d by arrangement **Parking** 6 **Notes** Closed Jan-Feb

◆◆◆◆

Moor Hall

Cleedownton SY8 3EG ☎ 01584 823209 🖷 08707 492202
e-mail enquiries@moorhall.co.uk
Dir A4117 Ludlow to Kidderminster, left to Brignorth. B4364, follow for 3.5m, Moor Hall on right

This impressive Georgian house, once the home of Lord Boyne, is surrounded by extensive gardens and farmland. Bedrooms are richly decorated, well equipped, and one room has a sitting area. Public areas are spacious and comfortably furnished. There is a choice of sitting rooms and a library bar. Guests dine family-style in the elegant dining room.

Facilities 3 en suite ⊘ in bedrooms ⊘ in dining room TVB tea/coffee Licensed No coaches Fishing Dinner Last d day before **Prices** S £35-£38; D £50-£56✱ **LB Parking** 7 **Notes** Closed 25-26 Dec

See advertisement on this page

◆◆◆◆ 🏠

Number Twenty Eight

28 Lower Broad St SY8 1PQ
☎ 01584 875466 🖷 01584 875466
e-mail enquiries@no28ludlow.co.uk
web www.no28ludlow.co.uk
Dir In town centre. Over Ludford Bridge onto Lower Broad St, 3rd house on right

This 200-year-old property is just a stroll from the centre and has a wealth of character. It provides two double bedrooms, each well-equipped and containing thoughtful extra welcoming touches. There is a cosy lounge-breakfast room and a pleasant small garden.

Facilities 2 en suite ⊘ TVB tea/coffee 🐾 Cen ht No children 16yrs No coaches **Prices** S £60-£80; D £80-£90✱ **Notes** Closed Nov-Mar

◆◆◆◆ ◉◉ 🍽 🍵

The Roebuck Inn

Brimfield SY8 4NE ☎ 01584 711230 🖷 01584 711654
e-mail himleylimes@aol.com
Dir 4m S of Ludlow, off A49 into village

This 15th-century country inn combines a traditional atmosphere with modern style and quality. The attractive bedrooms are comfortable, and relaxing hospitality is provided. Fresh local produce is used to brilliant effect in the dining room, with choices from blackboard specials or the carte.

Facilities 3 en suite ⊘ in bedrooms ⊘ in dining room ⊘ in 1 lounge TVB tea/coffee Direct dial from bedrooms 🐾 Cen ht Dinner Last d 9.30pm **Parking** 25

◆◆◆◆

Southcot

Livesey Rd SY8 1EZ
☎ 01584 879655 & 07787 533718 🖷 01584 878372
e-mail gillandjohn@southcotbandb.co.uk
web www.southcotbandb.co.uk
Dir From lights at Tesco up Station Dr, past station to next lights, left & 1st right, Southcot on left

Located in a residential area just a short walk from the historic centre, this pebble-dashed, semi-detached house has been renovated to provide a range of quality bedrooms with smart modern bathrooms. One ground-floor room has easier access, and a cosy lounge is also available.

Facilities 5 en suite (1 GF) ⊘ TVB tea/coffee 🐾 Cen ht TVL No coaches **Prices** S £50-£80; D £75-£80✱ **Parking** 6

continued

LUDLOW continued

◆◆◆◆

Timberstone Bed & Breakfast ◇

Cleestanton SY8 3EL ☎ 01584 823519 & 07905 967263
e-mail timberstone1@hotmail.com
Dir A4117 Ludlow to Kidderminster, left to Bridgnorth on the B4364, follow for 1.5m, right to Cleestanton, take left fork, follow for 1.5m, 1st left, cottage on left

This historic timber-framed and stone house is located in a rural setting north-east of Ludlow. It has been painstakingly restored without losing any of its considerable charm. There is a choice of lounge areas, one with log fires and a television. Guests share one table at breakfast.

Facilities 3 rms (1 en suite) (1 pri facs) (2 fmly) ⊗ tea/coffee Cen ht TVL No coaches Reflexology Nutritional advice **Prices** S £30-£40; D £50-£70 **Parking** 4 **Notes** 🐾

◆◆◆

Branlea

Brand Ln SY8 1NN ☎ 01584 876093
e-mail sueburshnell@hotmail.com
Dir In centre of town, off Broad St

Located in the heart of the historic centre and within easy walking distance of all attractions. The thoughtfully equipped bedrooms are in a dormer bungalow and breakfast is served in The Smithy, a converted blacksmith's house. Limited secure parking is available.

Facilities 3 annexe en suite (3 GF) ⊗ in 1 bedrooms ⊗ in dining room ⊗ in lounges TVB tea/coffee Cen ht TVL No children 16yrs No coaches **Parking** 3 **Notes** 🐾

◆◆◆ ❦

Haynall Villa ◇ (SO543674)

Little Hereford SY8 4BG
☎ 01584 711589 📠 01584 711589 Mrs Edwards
e-mail rachelmedwards@hotmail.com
web www.haynallvilla.co.uk
Dir A49 onto A456, at Little Hereford right signed Leysters and Middleton on the Hill, 1m on right

Located in immaculate gardens in the pretty hamlet of Little Hereford, this Victorian house retains many original features, which are enhanced by the furnishings and decor. Bedrooms are filled with lots of homely extras and the lounge has an open fire.

Facilities 3 rms (1 en suite) (1 fmly) ⊗ TVB tea/coffee Cen ht TVL No children 6yrs Fishing snooker table 72 acres calves/cattle & sheep Dinner Last d 3pm **Prices** S fr £25; d fr £44✳ **Parking** 3 **Notes** Closed mid Dec-mid Jan 🐾

Ⓤ

De Greys of Ludlow

5-6 Broad St SY8 1NG ☎ 01584 872764 📠 01584 879764
e-mail degreys@btopenworld.com
web www.degreys.co.uk
Dir Off A49, in town centre, 50yds beyond the clock tower

At the time of going to press the rating for this establishment had not been confirmed. Please check the AA website www.theAA.com for up-to-date information.

Facilities 9 en suite (1 GF) ⊗ TVB tea/coffee Licensed Cen ht **Prices** S £50-£100; D £70-£130✳ **LB Notes** Closed 26 Dec & 1 Jan

MARKET DRAYTON   MAP 15 SJ63

◆◆◆◆ ❦

Haywood Farm B & B ◇ (SJ305706)

Haywood Ln, Cheswardine TF9 2LW
☎ 01630 661788 & 07762 139362 📠 01630 661795
Mrs Wilson
e-mail haywoodfarm@hotmail.com
Dir 3m S of Market Drayton. Off A529 for Cheswardine, over canal bridge, 1st left

Located close to Goldstone Common, this 18th-century house has been renovated to provide high standards of comfort and good facilities. The carefully furnished bedrooms are filled with thoughtful extras and breakfast is served in the elegant dining room. A lounge is also available and caring hospitality is assured.

Facilities 5 rms (1 en suite) (1 pri facs) (1 fmly) (1 GF) ⊗ TVB tea/coffee ✖ Cen ht TVL 500 acres arable **Prices** S £30-£45; D £60✳ **Parking** 6 **Notes** 🐾

If you have to cancel a booking, let the proprietor know immediately

England

♦♦♦♦ ◎ ◇
Ternhill Farm House & The Cottage Restaurant
Ternhill TF9 3PX ☎ 01630 638984
e-mail info@ternhillfarm.co.uk
web www.ternhillfarm.co.uk
Dir On junct A53 & A41, archway off A53 to back of property

The elegant Grade II listed Georgian farmhouse stands in a large pleasant garden and has been modernised to provide quality accommodation. There is a choice of comfortable lounges, and the Cottage Restaurant offers imaginative dishes using local produce. Secure parking.

Facilities 5 en suite (2 fmly) ⊘ TVB tea/coffee ✘ Licensed Cen ht Dinner Last d 9pm **Prices** S £35-£50; D £65-£70✳ **LB** **Parking** 13

♦♦♦ ◖◗
The Falcon Inn
Wood Ln, Hinstock TF9 2TA
☎ 01952 550241 ▤ 01952 550765
e-mail info@falcon-inn-hinstock.co.uk
Dir Off A4, on A529 in centre of Hinstock

Located in the village of Hinstock, the inn has been renovated to provide a range of bedrooms equipped with modern facilities. Quality furnishings and decor in the open-plan public areas highlight the original features, and open fires create an inviting atmosphere during the cooler months.

Facilities 6 en suite (1 fmly) ⊘ in bedrooms ⊘ in dining room TVB tea/coffee ✘ Cen ht Dinner Last d 9.30pm **Prices** S fr £45; d fr £70✳ **Parking** 40

♦♦♦ ◖◗
The Four Alls Inn
Woodseaves TF9 2AG ☎ 01630 652995 ▤ 01630 653930
e-mail inn@thefouralls.com
web www.thefouralls.com
Dir On A529 1m S of Market Drayton

This country inn provides spacious open-plan public areas and has a strong local following for the imaginative food and real ales. Bedrooms, which are in a purpose-built chalet block, offer a good balance between practicality and homeliness. Superb beer gardens adorned with attractive floral displays are a feature during the summer.

Facilities 9 annexe en suite (4 fmly) (9 GF) ⊘ in 7 bedrooms ⊘ in area of dining room ⊘ in 1 lounge TVB tea/coffee Direct dial from bedrooms ✘ Cen ht Dinner Last d 2pm **Prices** S fr £40; d fr £59✳ **LB** **Conf** Max 100 Thtr 100 Class 100 Del from £60 ✳ **Parking** 60 **Notes** Closed 24-26 Dec

MINSTERLEY
MAP 15 SJ30

♦♦♦♦
Pool Cottage ◇
Gravels SY5 0JD ☎ 01743 891621
e-mail reservations@poolcottage.com
Dir Off A488, signed Pool Cottage

This small, pleasant and friendly guest house is quietly located amid open countryside 5m south of Minsterley and is set well back from the A488. It provides well-maintained, modern accommodation, as well as a cosy breakfast room with a communal table.

Facilities 3 en suite (1 fmly) (1 GF) ⊘ TVB tea/coffee ✘ Cen ht TVL No coaches Leather workshop **Prices** S £27-£30; D £50✳ **LB** **Parking** 51 **Notes** Closed 24 Dec-2 Jan ⊛

MUCH WENLOCK
MAP 10 SO69

★★★★ 🅰 Bed & Breakfast
Old Quarry Cottage
TF13 6JR ☎ 01746 785596 ▤ 01746 785596
e-mail triciawebb.oldquarrycottage@virgin.net
web www.oldquarrycottage.co.uk
Dir B4378 Much Wenlock to Ludlow, right at x-rds in Brockton towards Easthope. After 200yds, on right

Facilities 2 en suite 1 annexe en suite (1 GF) ⊘ TVB tea/coffee ✘ Cen ht No children 12yrs No coaches **Prices** S £40-£45; D £55-£65 **Parking** 5 **Notes** ⊛

MUCH WENLOCK continued

Yew Tree Farm ◊ (SO543958)

Longville In The Dale TF13 6EB
☎ 01694 771866 🖺 01694 771867 Mr & Mrs Hilbery
e-mail hilbery@tiscali.co.uk
Dir N off B4371 at Longville, left at pub, right at x-rds, farm 1.2m on right

Peacefully located between Much Wenlock and Church Stretton on 10 acres of unspoiled countryside, where rare breed pigs, sheep and chickens are reared and own produce is a feature on the comprehensive breakfast menu. Bedrooms are equipped with thoughtful extras and a warm welcome is assured.

Facilities 2 rms (1 en suite) (1 pri facs) ⊘ TVB tea/coffee Cen ht TVL 10 acres small holding **Prices** S £30-£35; D £50-£60✱ **LB** **Parking** 4 **Notes** 📵

The Plume of Feathers

Harley SY5 6LP ☎ 01952 727360 🖺 01952 728542
e-mail feathersatharley@aol.com
Dir 1m N of Much Wenlock on A458

Located in extensive mature gardens in a rural setting on the town's outskirts, this popular inn provides a range of thoughtfully equipped bedrooms with modern bathrooms en suite. Rustically furnished open-plan public areas are the setting for imaginative food and a good selection of real ales.

Facilities 9 en suite (3 fmly) (2 GF) ⊘ in bedrooms ⊘ in dining room ⊘ in 1 lounge TVB tea/coffee ✖ Cen ht Dinner Last d 9pm **Prices** S £49.95; D £65✱ **Conf** Max 90 Thtr 50 Class 20 Board 20 **Parking** 60

Talbot Inn

High St TF13 6AA ☎ 01952 727077 🖺 01952 728436
e-mail the_talbot_inn@hotmail.com
web www.the-talbot-inn.com
Dir In village centre on A458

Facilities 6 annexe en suite (1 GF) ⊘ in bedrooms ⊘ in dining room TVB tea/coffee Direct dial from bedrooms ✖ Licensed Cen ht TVL Dinner Last d 9.15pm **Parking** 6 **Notes** Closed 25 Dec

MUNSLOW   MAP 10 SO58

Crown Country Inn

SY7 9ET ☎ 01584 841205 🖺 01584 841255
e-mail info@crowncountryinn.co.uk
Dir Off B4368 into village

Located between Much Wenlock and Craven Arms, this impressive pastel-coloured and half-timbered Tudor inn is full of character with stone floors, exposed beams and blazing log fires during winter. Smart pine-furnished bedrooms are in a converted stable block and the spacious public areas include two dining rooms.

continued

Crown Country Inn

Facilities 3 en suite (1 fmly) (1 GF) ⊘ TVB tea/coffee ✖ Cen ht Dinner Last d 8.45pm **Prices** D £65-£70✱ **LB** **Conf** Max 30 Thtr 30 Class 30 Board 20 **Parking** 20 **Notes** Closed 25 Dec

NEWPORT   MAP 15 SJ71

Rosemont House

2 Chetwynd Rd TF10 7JY
☎ 01952 820526 🖺 01952 820526
e-mail owenrigby@btinternet.com
Dir Off N end of High St to B5062 fork in road

This lovely old house dates from the 18th century and has been used for a number of purposes including a private boarding school. The present owners have carefully modernised the property to provide good quality, non-smoking accommodation, including a bedroom on the ground floor and a family room. Warm hospitality and hearty breakfasts are among the memorable qualities here.

Facilities 4 en suite (1 fmly) (1 GF) ⊘ FTV TVB tea/coffee ✖ Cen ht No coaches **Prices** S £38; D £54 **Parking** 4 **Notes** Closed 24 Dec-2 Jan 📵

Norwood House Hotel

Pave Ln TF10 9LQ ☎ 01952 825896 🖺 01952 825896
e-mail info@norwoodhouse.org.uk
Dir Off A41 1m S from Newport, near National Sports Centre

Norwood House has a range of practically furnished bedrooms equipped with thoughtful extras and modern bathrooms. There is a cosy bar on the ground floor, and the attractive spacious restaurant attracts a local following.

Facilities 5 en suite (1 fmly) ⊘ TVB tea/coffee Licensed Cen ht Dinner Last d 9pm **Prices** S £42; D £55✱ **Parking** 30

If you book on bed, breakfast and evening meal terms, you may find that the tariff includes only the set menu

OSWESTRY

MAP 15 SJ22

♦♦♦♦

Navigation Inn & Warehouse Restaurant

Maesbury Marsh SY10 8JB
☎ 01691 672958 📠 01691 672958
e-mail info@thenavigation.co.uk
web www.thenavigation.co.uk

Dir *3m S of Oswestry. Off A483 signed Maesbury, inn 2m near canal bridge*

This inn and canal-side warehouse, dating from 1785, have been restored to provide two well-appointed bedrooms, one of which is a suite. The warehouse is now a spacious restaurant, which has a wealth of character and a well-deserved reputation for its cuisine. There is a choice of bars and an informal bistro.

Facilities 2 en suite (1 fmly) ⊗ in bedrooms ⊗ in dining room ⊗ in 1 lounge TVB tea/coffee Cen ht Dinner Last d 8.45pm
Prices S £45-£55; D £60-£70✱ **LB** **Conf** Board 14 **Parking** 30

♦♦♦♦

Old Vicarage

Llansilin SY10 7PX ☎ 01691 791345
e-mail pam@vicarage-guests.co.uk
For full entry see **Llansilin (Powys)**

♦♦♦♦

Pear Tree Cottage

Crickheath SY10 8BJ ☎ 01691 830766
e-mail mike.bossen@virgin.net
web www.stayatpeartree.co.uk

Dir *A5 onto B4396 through Knockin village, left after Lloyd Animal Feed Mill onto Crickheath Ln, house on right*

This 200-year-old property, reputedly once a pub, is set in quiet gardens alongside a disused section of the Montgomery canal, which is currently being restored. The well-maintained accommodation comprises two thoughtfully equipped bedrooms. Warm hospitality is assured and hearty breakfasts take full advantage of local produce.

Facilities 2 en suite ⊗ TVB tea/coffee 🐾 Cen ht TVL No children 16yrs No coaches **Prices** D £50 **Parking** 3 **Notes** 🐾

♦♦♦♦

The Pentre

Trefonen SY10 9EE ☎ 01691 653952
e-mail helen@thepentre.com
web www.thepentre.com

Dir *4m SW of Oswestry. Off Oswestry-Treflach road onto New Well Ln & signed The Pentre*

This 500-year-old stone farmhouse retains original exposed beams and a superb inglenook fireplace with blazing wood burner during cooler months. Bedrooms are equipped with a range of thoughtful extras, and breakfast and dinner are memorable, with quality produce cooked with flair on an Aga.

Facilities 3 en suite (1 fmly) (1 GF) ⊗ TVB tea/coffee 🐾 Cen ht TVL No coaches Dinner Last d 9pm **LB** **Parking** 10 **Notes** 🐾

♦♦♦♦

Top Farm House (SJ334214)

SY10 8HN
☎ 01691 682582 📠 01691 682070 Mrs Morrissey
e-mail p.a.m@knockin.freeserve.co.uk
web www.topfarmknockin.co.uk
For full entry see **Knockin**

♦♦♦♦

Acorn House

Pen-y-Garreg Ln, Pant SY10 8JS
☎ 01691 831940 & 07969 480632
e-mail enquiries@acornhousepant.co.uk
Dir *Off A483 in Pant onto Pen-y-Garreg Ln opp Co-op shop, B&B 300yds on right*

This deceptively large modern house is quietly located in the village of Pant. It provides friendly hospitality and has two thoughtfully equipped bedrooms. All share one table in the cosy breakfast room, which also doubles as a lounge.

Facilities 2 rms (2 GF) ⊗ TVB tea/coffee 🐾 Cen ht TVL No children 14yrs No coaches **Prices** S £30; D £50✱ **Parking** 2 **Notes** Closed 20 Dec-3 Jan 🐾

♦♦♦♦

Ashfield Farmhouse

Maesbury SY10 8JH
☎ 01691 653589 & 07989 477414 📠 01691 653589
e-mail marg@ashfieldfarmhouse.co.uk
Dir *2.5m S of Oswestry. In Maesbury, farmhouse next to white church*

The farmhouse is located in the hamlet of Maesbury and dates in part from the 16th century. It has been carefully preserved and original features include open fireplaces and a superb polished staircase. Bedrooms, one in a renovated coach house that can also be used for self-catering, are equipped with modern facilities and homely extras. There is a comfortable lounge and a traditionally furnished breakfast room.

Facilities 3 en suite (2 fmly) ⊗ TVB tea/coffee Cen ht TVL No coaches **Prices** S £30-£50; D £50-£68✱ **LB** **Parking** 5

♦♦♦♦

Bradford Arms Hotel

Llanymynech SY22 6EJ ☎ 01691 830582 📠 01691 830728
e-mail info@bradfordarmshotel.com
Dir *5.5m S of Oswestry on A483 in Llanymynech*

Please note that this establishment has recently changed hands. Once a coaching inn on the Earl of Bradford's estate, the Arms provides a range of carefully furnished bedrooms with a wealth of thoughtful extras. The elegant ground-floor areas include lounges, bars, and a choice of formal or conservatory restaurants, the settings for imaginative food and fine wines.

Facilities 5 en suite (1 fmly) (2 GF) ⊗ in bedrooms ⊗ in dining room TVB tea/coffee Direct dial from bedrooms 🐾 Cen ht No coaches Dinner Last d 9-9.30pm **Parking** 20 **Notes** Closed 25-30 Dec rs 24 & 31 Dec

England

OSWESTRY continued

♦♦♦♦

Riseholme

4 Hampton Rd SY11 1SJ ☎ 01691 656394 ▤ 01691 659697
e-mail riseholme.enquiries@tesco.net
Dir 0.5m NW of CAE Glas Park.

This large detached house stands in a large garden in a quiet
residential area, half a mile from the town centre. It has been
renovated to provide good quality, modern accommodation. You have
a choice of comfortable sitting rooms, one of which has access onto
the patio and garden. All guests share one large table at breakfast.

Facilities 3 en suite ⊗ TVB tea/coffee ✖ Cen ht TVL No children
10yrs No coaches **Parking** 5 **Notes** ⊛

♦♦♦ ⬛

The Red Lion ◇

Bailey Head SY11 1PZ ☎ 01691 656077
Dir In town centre. Off Castle St onto Powis Place, 1st left into car
park signed Red Lion Complex

Located in the historic town square, this well-maintained inn provides
spacious, well-furnished open-plan public areas for a wide range of
real ales and bar meals. Bedrooms are well-equipped and have
modern shower rooms en suite.

Facilities 5 en suite (1 fmly) ⊗ in dining room TVB tea/coffee ✖
Cen ht Pool Table **Prices** S £30; D £40✳ **LB** **Parking** 4

PONTESBURY

MAP 15 SJ30

♦♦♦♦

Gatten Lodge

SY5 0SJ ☎ 01743 790038 ▤ 01743 790068
Dir From Pontesbury 1.5m to Habberley, at grass triangle right
signed Westcott & Bridges, 1m right at grass triangle, Lodge 2m on
left over 2 grids

Located on an elevated position with stunning views of the
surrounding countryside, this elegant well-proportioned house is also
the setting for point-to-point racehorse training and game luncheons.
Bedrooms are equipped with thoughtful extras, and a spacious
drawing room with an open log fire is available in addition to a formal
dining room.

Facilities 3 en suite ⊗ in bedrooms TVB tea/coffee ✖ Cen ht
No children 14yrs No coaches Fishing Dinner Last d 9pm **Parking** 6
Notes ⊛

If the freedom to smoke or be in a
non-smoking atmosphere is important
to you, check the rules when you book

RUYTON-XI-TOWNS

MAP 15 SJ32

♦♦♦

Brownhill House ◇

SY4 1LR ☎ 01939 261121 ▤ 01939 260626
e-mail brownhill@eleventowns.co.uk
web www.eleventowns.co.uk
Dir Leave A5 onto B4397, 2m to Ruyton-XI-Towns. Through village.
Brownhill House is a long cream coloured building with blue window
frames on the left of a right-hand bend

A warm welcome is assured at this charming guest house, parts of
which date from the 18th century. The large formal garden has been
painstakingly created on the side of a steep hill above the River Perry,
and you are welcome to explore. Bedrooms have modern facilities
and you share one large table in the cosy kitchen-dining room.

Facilities 3 en suite (1 GF) ⊗ tea/coffee ✖ Cen ht TVL No coaches
Fishing ♨ Last d noon **Prices** S £22.50-£26; D £40-£50✳ **LB** **Parking** 5

SHIFNAL

MAP 10 SJ70

🅤 ⬛

The Hare and Hounds Inn

Crackley Bank TF11 8QT
☎ 01952 460597 ▤ 01952 462254
e-mail hareandhoundsinn@btconnect.com
Dir Situated on main A5 between Red Hill and Weston-Under-Lizard

At the time of going to press the rating for this establishment had not
been confirmed. Please check the AA website www.theAA.com for up-
to-date information.

Facilities 6 en suite (3 GF) ⊗ TVB tea/coffee Direct dial from bedrooms
✖ Cen ht TVL Dinner Last d 9pm **Prices** D £70✳ **Conf** Max 60
Class 40 Board 30 Del from £135 ✳

SHREWSBURY

MAP 15 SJ41

See also **Criggion (Powys), Ruyton-XI-Towns, Wem &
Westbury**

★★★★ Guest House

Abbots Mead

9 St Julian's Friars SY1 1XL
☎ 01743 235281 ▤ 01743 369133
e-mail res@abbotsmeadhotel.co.uk
web www.abbotsmeadhotel.co.uk
Dir Entering town from S 1st left after English Bridge

This nicely maintained Georgian town house is located in a quiet cul-
de-sac near the English Bridge, and close to the River Severn and
town centre. Bedrooms are compact, neatly decorated and well
equipped. The bright dining room overlooks the garden, and a bar
features horseracing pictures.

Facilities 16 en suite (2 fmly) TVB tea/coffee Direct dial from bedrooms
Licensed TVL **Prices** S £50-£60; D £70-£85✳ **LB** **Parking** 10
Notes Closed 24-26 Dec

Premier Collection

◆◆◆◆◆

The Catherine Of Aragon Suite

The Old House, 20 Dogpole SY1 1EN
☎ 01743 271092 🖷 01743 465006
e-mail info@aragonsuite.co.uk

This magnificent timber-framed Tudor mansion is situated in the town centre. It has a wealth of character, and you are given a historical tour of the house and garden. The large, self-contained luxurious suite is carefully furnished and has many thoughtful welcoming touches.

Facilities 1 rms (1 pri facs) (1 fmly) ⊗ FTV TVB ✖ TVL No coaches Dinner Last d previous day **Prices** S £85; D £125✱ **Parking** 1

◆◆◆◆◆

Meole Brace Hall

Meole Brace SY3 9HF ☎ 01743 235566 🖷 01743 236886
e-mail hathaway@meolebracehall.co.uk
web www.meolebracehall.co.uk

Dir 1.5m S of town centre. A5 bypass onto A5112 N to town centre, at large rdbt left onto B4380, left onto Upper Rd & one-way system, 1st left & sharp right onto Church Ln

Facilities 3 en suite ⊗ TVB tea/coffee ✖ Cen ht TVL No children 10yrs No coaches ⚲ ⚲ Dinner **Prices** S £49-£65; D £75-£79✱ **Parking** 10 **Notes** Closed Xmas ⊜

◆◆◆◆

Abbey Court

134 Abbey Foregate SY2 6AU
☎ 01743 364416 🖷 01743 358559
e-mail info@abbeycourt.biz
web www.abbeycourt.biz
Dir N of river off A5112

Located within easy walking distance from the town centre, this Grade II listed house has been refurbished to provide a range of homely bedrooms, some of which are in an attractive extension. Comprehensive breakfasts are served in a cosy dining room and a warm welcome is assured.

Facilities 6 en suite 4 annexe en suite (1 fmly) (4 GF) ⊗ in 6 bedrooms ⊗ in dining room ⊗ in lounges TVB tea/coffee Direct dial from bedrooms ✖ Cen ht **Parking** 10

◆◆◆◆

Fieldside ◇

38 London Rd SY2 6NX ☎ 01743 353143 🖷 01743 354687
e-mail robrookes@btinternet.com
Dir A5 onto A5064, premises 1m on left

Set in a spacious garden and within easy walking distance of the town centre, this immaculately maintained Victorian house provides a range of carefully furnished bedrooms equipped with a wealth of thoughtful extras. Breakfast is served in the elegant, spacious dining room and a warm welcome is assured.

Facilities 4 en suite ⊗ TVB tea/coffee ✖ Cen ht No coaches **Prices** S £30-£40; D £55-£60✱ **Parking** 8 **Notes** ⊜

◆◆◆◆ ▣

The Bull Inn

7 Butcher Row SY1 1UW ☎ 01743 344728
e-mail markglenister@btconnect.com
web www.bull-inn.co.uk
Dir Off main High St right into Butcher Row, next to Prince Rupert Hotel

Originally a slaughter house and situated in the heart of the town's pedestrianised area, this timber-framed hostelry has a wealth of character. Renovated, it provides modern accommodation and spacious bar and restaurant areas, where a wide range of food is served. A pleasant beer garden is also available.

Facilities 6 rms (4 en suite) (2 pri facs) (1 fmly) ⊗ in bedrooms ⊗ in dining room ⊗ in 1 lounge TVB tea/coffee ✖ Cen ht Dinner Last d 9pm **Prices** S fr £40; D £50-£60✱

SHREWSBURY continued

◆◆◆◆ 💜

The Day House (SJ465104)

Nobold SY5 8NL
☎ 01743 860212 📄 01743 860212 Mrs Roberts
e-mail robertsdayhouse@aol.com
Dir A5 onto A5112 N towards Shrewsbury (Meole Brace), signs for
Nuffield Hospital, continue 0.5m past hospital, right onto drive

Set in pretty gardens within a short drive from major routes, this
impressive 18th-century house, extended in Victorian times, retains
many original features. The spacious bedrooms are equipped with
homely extras, and there is a comfortable sitting room and an elegant
dining room.

Facilities 3 en suite (3 fmly) ⊗ in 2 bedrooms ⊗ in dining room TVB
tea/coffee 🛠 Cen ht 400 acres arable dairy **Prices** S £38-£40;
D £56-£60✱ **Parking** 10 **Notes** Closed Xmas & New Year 🖾

◆◆◆◆

Tudor House

2 Fish St SY1 1UR ☎ 01743 351735 & 07870 653040
e-mail enquiry@tudorhouseshrewsbury.co.uk
web www.tudorhouseshrewsbury.co.uk
Dir Enter town over English Bridge, ascend Wyle Cop, 50yds 1st right

Located in the beautiful medieval town centre, this fine 15th-century
house has original beams and fireplaces, enhanced by the decor and
furnishings. Bedrooms are filled with thoughtful extras and breakfast
features local organic produce.

Facilities 3 rms (2 en suite) (1 pri facs) ⊗ TVB tea/coffee 🛠 Cen ht
No children 11yrs No coaches **Notes** 🖾

◆◆◆

Stiperstones ◇

18 Coton Crescent, Coton Hill SY1 2NZ ☎ 01743 246720
e-mail thestiperstones@aol.com
Dir A528 from town centre for Ellesmere, onto B5067 for Baschurch,
next right, house opp x-rds on right

Located in a mainly residential area within easy walking distance from
central attractions, this Edwardian house provides homely, thoughtfully
equipped bedrooms, three of which are in an adjacent separate
property. Comprehensive breakfasts are served in the attractive dining
room and a warm welcome is assured.

Facilities 3 rms (1 en suite) 3 annexe rms (1 fmly) (1 GF) ⊗ TVB
tea/coffee 🛠 Cen ht No coaches **Prices** S £25-£30; D £40-£55✱
Parking 6

◆◆◆

Sydney House Hotel

Coton Crescent, Coton Hill SY1 2LJ
☎ 01743 354681 📄 01743 362122
e-mail info@sydneyhousehotel.co.uk
web www.sydneyhousehotel.co.uk
Dir 500yds N of railway station. Off A528 Coton Hill onto B5067
Berwick Rd, 1st right

Just a short walk from the river and historic centre, this elegant
Edwardian house provides a range of bedrooms with practical and
thoughtful extras. Comprehensive breakfasts are served in the cosy
dining room, and a lounge with bar is available.

Facilities 6 en suite (1 fmly) ⊗ in 4 bedrooms ⊗ in dining room TVB
tea/coffee 🛠 Licensed TVL No coaches **Parking** 7

🇺

The Brooklands Hotel

Mill Rd, Meole Brace SY3 9JT
☎ 01743 344270 📄 01743 369646
e-mail info@thebrooklandshotel.com
Dir 1m S of town centre. A5 bypass onto A5112 N to town centre, at
large rdbt left onto B4380, left onto Mill Rd

At the time of going to press the rating for this establishment had not
been confirmed. Please check the AA website www.theAA.com for up-
to-date information.

Facilities 3 rms (2 fmly) ⊗ TVB tea/coffee Licensed Cen ht TVL Golf
Snooker Pool Table Dinner Last d 9pm **Parking** 60

TELFORD   MAP 10 SJ60

◆◆◆◆ 💜

Avenue Farm ◇ (SJ599099)

Uppington TF6 5HW
☎ 01952 740253 & 07711 219453 📄 01952 740401
Mrs Jones
e-mail jones@avenuefarm.fsnet.co.uk
Dir M54 junct 7, B5061 for Atcham, 2nd left signed Uppington. Right
after sawmill, farm 400yds on right

This impressive, well-proportioned house stands within immaculate
mature gardens in the hamlet of Uppington. Quality furnishings and
decor highlight the many period features, and the bedrooms are
homely. A comfortable sitting room is also available.

Facilities 3 en suite (1 fmly) ⊗ in bedrooms ⊗ in dining room TV2B
tea/coffee 🛠 TVL Riding 430 acres arable **Prices** S £30-£35;
D £50-£55✱ **Parking** 4 **Notes** Closed Xmas 🖾

◆◆◆◆

Church Farm

Wrockwardine village, Wellington TF6 5DG
☎ 01952 244917 📠 01952 244917
e-mail jo@churchfarm.freeserve.co.uk
Dir In village centre opp church

This impressive Grade II listed house stands opposite the village church in the pretty rural community of Wrockwardine. Original features include exposed beams, flagstone floors and open fireplaces. Bedrooms are homely and thoughtfully furnished, a spacious lounge is available, and the elegant dining room is the setting for memorable breakfasts.

Facilities 4 rms (3 en suite) 1 annexe en suite (1 fmly) (2 GF) ⊗ in dining room TVB tea/coffee Cen ht TVL No children 10yrs No coaches **Prices** S £32-£40; D £52-£58✳ **LB Conf** Max 12 **Parking** 10

◆◆◆

Potford House ◇

Little Bolas, Wellington TF6 6PS ☎ 01952 541362
e-mail dsadler@potford.fsnet.co.uk
Dir 7m N of Wellington on A442, turn right signed Little Bolas, 1m om pub. Potford House on left

Located in a peaceful hamlet north of Wellington, this spacious detached house provides a warm welcome and homely bedrooms with thoughtful extras. Wholesome breakfasts using local produce are served in an attractive dining room overlooking the pretty gardens.

Facilities 3 rms (1 fmly) ⊗ TVB tea/coffee ✘ Cen ht TVL No children yrs No coaches **Prices** S fr £22; d fr £44✳ **Parking** 3 **Notes** ✉

WEM   MAP 15 SJ52

◆◆◆ ⊜ ❤

Soulton Hall (SJ543303)

Soulton SY4 5RS
☎ 01939 232786 📠 01939 234097 Mrs Ashton
e-mail enquiries@soultonhall.co.uk
web www.soultonhall.co.uk
Dir 2m NE of Wem off B5065

Located north-east of Wem, this late 17th-century former manor house incorporates part of an even older building. The house stands in 560 acres and provides high levels of comfort. Bedrooms are equipped with homely extras and the ground-floor areas include a spacious hall, sitting room, lounge bar, and an attractive dining room for imaginative dinners.

continued

Facilities 4 en suite 3 annexe en suite (2 fmly) (3 GF) ⊗ TVB tea/coffee Direct dial from bedrooms Licensed Cen ht Fishing 🎣 Birdwatching in 50 acre woodland 560 acres arable Dinner Last d 8.30pm **Prices** S £39-£60; D £78-£120✳ **LB Conf** Max 80 Thtr 80 Board 50 Del from £86 ✳ **Parking** 52

WESTBURY   MAP 15 SJ30

◆◆◆◆

Barley Mow House ◇

Aston Rogers SY5 9HQ ☎ 01743 891234
e-mail colinrigby@astonrogers.fsnet.co.uk
web www.stmem.com/barleymowhouse
Dir 2m S of Westbury. Off B4386 into Aston Rogers, house 400yds opp Aston Hall

Dating in part from the 17th century and extended in the 18th century, this charming property has been restored to provide comfortable accommodation with modern facilities. The house stands in a peaceful village and is surrounded by beautifully maintained gardens.

Facilities 2 en suite (1 fmly) ⊗ TVB tea/coffee ✘ Cen ht TVL No coaches Large flower garden & orchard **Prices** S £26-£32; D £56✳ **LB Parking** 4 **Notes** ✉

WESTON-UNDER-REDCASTLE   MAP 15 SJ52

◆◆◆◆ ☖

Greensboro

SY4 5UX ☎ 01939 200215
e-mail bookings@greensboro.co.uk
web www.greensboro.co.uk
Dir Off A49 into village towards Hawkestone Park Hotel, Greensboro on left

A warm welcome is assured at this immaculate house set amid pretty gardens near Hawkstone Park. The comfortable bedroom has a wealth of thoughtful extras, and memorable breakfasts are served in the elegant dining room overlooking the adjacent golf course practice area.

Facilities 1 en suite ⊗ TVB tea/coffee ✘ Cen ht No children No coaches adjacent to golf club **Prices** S £45-£50; D £65-£70✳ **LB Parking** 1 **Notes** ✉

England

SOMERSET

BATH MAP 04 ST76

For other locations surrounding **Bath** see also **Box (Wiltshire), Bradford on Avon (Wiltshire), Frome** and **Trowbridge (Wiltshire)**

★★★★ Guest House

Oldfields

102 Wells Rd BA2 3AL ☎ 01225 317984 📄 01225 444471
e-mail info@oldfields.co.uk
Dir *Exit A36 onto A367 signed for Radstock. Situated on the corner of Wells Rd.*

This accommodation has been sensitively developed both to maintain some period features and to offer guests luxurious comfort. The attractive, light and airy bedrooms, some of which have four-poster beds and Jacuzzis, are well equipped with considerate extras. The lounge has an open fire during colder days. The elegant dining room, offers a choice of dishes for breakfast.

Facilities 16 en suite (4 fmly) (2 GF) STV TVB tea/coffee Direct dial from bedrooms 🐾 Cen ht No coaches **Prices** S £49-£65; D £59-£150✳ **LB Parking** 12 **Notes** Closed 24-26 Dec

Premier Collection

♦♦♦♦♦

Ayrlington

24/25 Pulteney Rd BA2 4EZ
☎ 01225 425495 📄 01225 469029
e-mail mail@ayrlington.com
web www.ayrlington.com
Dir *A4 onto A36, pass Holburne Museum, premises 200yds on right*

The charm of this impressive Victorian house is evident in the attractive exterior and throughout the rooms, many of which feature Oriental artefacts and pictures. The bedrooms, some with spa baths, four-poster beds and views over Bath cricket ground, are very comfortable. Breakfast is served in the elegant dining room, which shares the enjoyable view.

Facilities 14 en suite (3 fmly) (3 GF) TVB tea/coffee Direct dial from bedrooms 🐾 Licensed Cen ht No children 14 yrs No coaches Unlimited free golf at local golf club **Prices** S £75-£175; D £100-£175✳ **Conf** Max 15 **Parking** 14 **Notes** Closed 22 Dec-5 Jan

See advertisement on opposite page

Premier Collection

♦♦♦♦♦ 🛏

Bradford Old Windmill

4 Masons Ln BA15 1QN ☎ 01225 866842 📄 01225 866648
e-mail aa@bradfordoldwindmill.co.uk
For full entry see **Bradford-on-Avon** (Wiltshire)

Premier Collection

♦♦♦♦♦ 🛏

Haydon House

9 Bloomfield Pk BA2 2BY
☎ 01225 444919 & 427351 📄 01225 444919
e-mail stay@haydonhouse.co.uk
web www.haydonhouse.co.uk
Dir *A36 onto A367 Wells Rd, right onto Bloomfield Rd, 2nd right*

This charming house offers excellent standards of comfort and hospitality. The delightful rooms include four-poster and canopied beds, are decorated with Laura Ashley fabrics, and are provided with many thoughtful extras. Special rates are available November to March. Breakfast is excellent - one option is the Scotch whisky or rum porridge.

Facilities 5 en suite (1 fmly) TVB tea/coffee Direct dial from bedrooms 🐾 Cen ht No coaches **LB Parking** 1

Premier Collection

♦♦♦♦♦ 🛏

Apsley House Hotel

Newbridge Hill BA1 3PT
☎ 01225 336966 📄 01225 425462
e-mail info@apsley-house.co.uk
web www.apsley-house.co.uk
Dir *1.2m W of city centre on A431*

Built in 1830 for the Duke of Wellington, Apsley House is within walking distance of the city centre. The house is extremely elegant, and the spacious bedrooms have pleasant views. There are family rooms and rooms with four-poster beds, while two rooms have direct access to the charming garden. A cosy bar, attractive dining room and a delightful lounge are also available, and light suppers are served by arrangement.

Facilities 11 en suite (2 fmly) (2 GF) STV TVB tea/coffee Direct dial from bedrooms 🐾 Licensed Cen ht **Prices** S £55-£140; D £70-£170 **LB Conf** Max 10 **Parking** 11 **Notes** Closed 1 wk Xmas

Premier Collection

◆◆◆◆◆ 🏛

Athole House

33 Upper Oldfield Pk BA2 3JX
☎ 01225 320000 📠 01225 320009
e-mail info@atholehouse.co.uk
web www.atholehouse.co.uk
Dir A36 onto A367 Wells Rd, 1st right

Refurbished to offer very high standards of comfort, this detached house stands in a quiet location just a 15-minute walk from the city centre. It has modern, well-equipped bedrooms and bathrooms, and the varied breakfast menu includes fresh fruit salad and home-made bread. There is a lovely garden to enjoy in summer, and secure parking with electronic gates.

Facilities 4 en suite (2 fmly) ⊘ STV TVB tea/coffee Direct dial from bedrooms ✗ Cen ht No coaches **Prices** S £48-£58; D £68-£78 LB **Parking** 7

Premier Collection

◆◆◆◆◆

Bamboo Gardens

283 London Rd East, Batheaston BA1 7RL
☎ 01225 859922 📠 01225 859985
e-mail admin@bamboo-gardens.co.uk
web www.bamboo-gardens.co.uk
Dir 2.5m NE of city centre. M4 junct 18, A46 onto A4 E to end of Batheaston dual carriageway, off rdbt signed Batheaston, Bamboo Gardens 200yds on right

A delightful, spacious Edwardian house with far-reaching views across Bathampton Meadow and well located for Bath and the more peaceful Avon valley. The city centre is 2.5m away and can be reached by road or popular river walk. Bedrooms here are luxuriously equipped and immaculately maintained. Breakfast is an extensive choice of dishes, to be enjoyed in the elegant dining room, either around a smart communal table or at separate tables. Dinner is available by arrangement.

Facilities 3 en suite ⊘ TVB tea/coffee ✗ Cen ht No children 8yrs No coaches Pool Table **Parking** 4

The Ayrlington

24/25 Pulteney Road, Bath BA2 4EZ
Tel: 44 (0)1225 425495 • Fax: 44 (0)1225 469029
Email: mail@ayrlington.com • www.ayrlington.com

Built of golden Bath stone, The Ayrlington is a handsome listed Victorian house set in a splendid walled garden with exceptional views of the City and its medieval Abbey. Bath's magnificent historic sites, speciality shops and excellent restaurants are all just a five minute level stroll away. The Hotel's elegant and tranquil interior is a graceful blend of English and Asian antiques, artwork and fine fabrics. All fourteen bedrooms have an individual theme and are beautifully furnished, some with 4 poster beds and spa baths. Privately owned and managed the emphasis is on creating an atmosphere of peace and tranquillity. The Hotel has a residents bar, ample private parking and is entirely non smoking.

PREMIER COLLECTION   AA

England

BATH continued

Premier Collection

♦♦♦♦♦
Cheriton House

9 Upper Oldfield Pk BA2 3JX
☎ 01225 429862 🖷 01225 428403
e-mail info@cheritonhouse.co.uk
web www.cheritonhouse.co.uk
Dir A36 onto A367 Wells Rd, 1st right

Expect a friendly welcome and a relaxed atmosphere at this well-presented Victorian house with panoramic views over Bath. The carefully decorated bedrooms are well equipped and include a two-bedroom suite in a converted coach house. A substantial breakfast is served in the conservatory-breakfast room overlooking the rear garden. There is also a comfortable lounge.

Facilities 11 en suite (2 fmly) (2 GF) ⊘ TVB tea/coffee Direct dial from bedrooms ✸ Cen ht No children 12yrs No coaches **Prices** S £55-£80; D £80-£120 **LB Parking** 11

See advertisement on opposite page

Premier Collection

♦♦♦♦♦ 🛗
Dorian House

1 Upper Oldfield Pk BA2 3JX
☎ 01225 426336 🖷 01225 444699
e-mail info@dorianhouse.co.uk
web www.dorianhouse.co.uk
Dir A36 onto A367 Wells Rd, right onto Upper Oldfield Park, 3rd building on left

This elegant Victorian property has stunning views over the city. The atmosphere is welcoming and the accommodation of high quality.

continued

Several of the rooms have fine period four-poster beds and all offer a range of extra facilities. The attractive lounge has an honesty bar and views of the terraced gardens.

Facilities 11 en suite (1 fmly) (2 GF) ⊘ TVB tea/coffee Direct dial from bedrooms ✸ Licensed Cen ht No coaches **Prices** S £55-£95; D £65-£180 **LB Parking** 11

Premier Collection

♦♦♦♦♦ 🛗
Kennard Hotel

11 Henrietta St BA2 6LL ☎ 01225 310472 🖷 01225 460054
e-mail reception@kennard.co.uk
web www.kennard.co.uk
Dir A4 onto A36 Bathwick St, 2nd right onto Henrietta Rd & Henrietta St

Under new ownership, this attractive Georgian house dates from 1794, and is convenient for the city centre and many places of interest. The stylish bedrooms and public areas are luxuriously appointed. True English breakfasts are served in the dining room where freshly squeezed fruit juice and Kennard chutneys are just two of the many delights.

Facilities 12 rms (10 en suite) (2 GF) ⊘ STV TVB tea/coffee Direct dial from bedrooms ✸ Cen ht No children 14yrs No coaches
Prices S £50-£75; D £90-£125✳

Premier Collection

♦♦♦♦♦
Paradise House Hotel

Holloway BA2 4PX ☎ 01225 317723 🖷 01225 482005
e-mail info@paradise-house.co.uk
web www.paradise-house.co.uk
Dir A36 onto A367 Wells Rd, 3rd left, down hill onto cul-de-sac, house 200yds on left

Set in half an acre of lovely walled gardens, this Georgian house, built of mellow Bath stone, is within walking distance of the city centre. Many bedrooms have fine views over the city, and all are decorated in opulent style. Furnishings are elegant and facilities modern. The lounge is comfortable and relaxing and breakfast is served in the smart dining room. Hospitality and service here are friendly and professional.

Facilities 11 en suite (2 fmly) (4 GF) ⊘ TVB tea/coffee Direct dial from bedrooms ✸ Licensed Cen ht No coaches Boules pitch
Prices S £60-£105; D £89-£175 **LB Parking** 11 **Notes** Closed 3 days Xmas

See advertisement on opposite page

Premier Collection

♦♦♦♦♦
Villa Magdala Hotel

Henrietta Rd BA2 6LX ☎ 01225 466329 🖷 01225 483207
e-mail office@VillaMagdala.co.uk
web www.VillaMagdala.co.uk
Dir A4 onto A36 Bathwick St, 2nd right

This stylish Victorian house is just a short walk from the city's attractions and yet offers a haven of peace and tranquility. There are pleasant views from the attractively furnished and spacious bedrooms, all of which are well equipped. The charming lounge and dining room overlook one of Bath's delightful parks.

continued

Facilities 17 en suite (4 fmly) ⊗ TVB tea/coffee Direct dial from bedrooms ✹ Cen ht No children 7yrs No coaches **Prices** S £70-£110; D £98-£150✳ **LB Parking** 17

Premier Collection

♦♦♦♦♦ ⑩ ⌷

Widbrook Grange

Trowbridge Rd, Widbrook BA15 1UH
☎ 01225 864750 & 863173 🖹 01225 862890
e-mail stay@widbrookgrange.com
web www.widbrookgrange.com
For full entry see **Bradford on Avon (Wiltshire)**

♦♦♦♦♦ 🅰

Carfax Hotel

13-15 Great Pulteney St BA2 4BS
☎ 01225 462089 🖹 01225 443257
e-mail reservations@carfaxhotel.co.uk
web www.carfaxhotel.co.uk
Dir A36 onto Great Pulteney St

Facilities 31 en suite (5 fmly) (4 GF) ⊗ STV TVB tea/coffee Direct dial from bedrooms ✹ Lift Cen ht ch fac Playstations for hire, Internet access Dinner Last d 6.30pm **Prices** S £67-£77; D £94-£142✳ **LB Conf** Max 30 Thtr 25 Class 25 Board 15 Del from £56 ✳ **Parking** 13

♦♦♦♦

Brocks

32 Brock St BA1 2LN ☎ 01225 338374 🖹 01225 334245
e-mail marion@brocksguesthouse.co.uk
web www.brocksguesthouse.co.uk
Dir Off A4 between Circus & Royal Crescent

A warm welcome is extended at this delightful Georgian property, located in the heart of the city just a few hundred yards from Royal Crescent. All rooms reflect the comfortable elegance of the Georgian era. A traditional breakfast is served in the charming dining room.

Facilities 6 en suite (2 fmly) ⊗ TVB tea/coffee ✹ Cen ht No coaches **Parking** 2 **Notes** Closed 24-28 Dec & New Year

♦♦♦♦

Devonshire House

143 Wellsway BA2 4RZ ☎ 01225 312495
e-mail enquiries@devonshire-house.uk.com
web www.devonshire-house.uk.com
Dir 1m S of city centre. A36 onto A367 Wells Rd & Wellsway

Located within walking distance of the City centre and under new ownership, this charming house maintains its Victorian style. Secure parking is available and the friendly proprietors make every effort to ensure your stay is pleasant and memorable. The attractive bedrooms, some refurbished to a high quality standard, have many considerate extras. There is a lounge and freshly cooked breakfasts are served in the pleasant dining room.

Facilities 3 en suite (1 fmly) (1 GF) ⊗ TVB tea/coffee ✹ Cen ht No coaches Games lounge **Prices** S £49-£69; D £69-£89 **LB Parking** 6

BATH continued

◆◆◆◆

The Hollies

Hatfield Rd BA2 2BD ☎ 01225 313366 ▤ 01225 313366
e-mail davcartwright@lineone.net
Dir *A36 onto A367 Wells Rd & Wellsway, 0.7m right opp Devonshire Arms*

This delightful house stands in impressive gardens overlooking a magnificent church, and is within easy reach of the city centre. Individually decorated bedrooms are finished to provide excellent levels of comfort and facilities. Breakfast in the elegant dining room is an enjoyable start to the day.

Facilities 3 rms (2 en suite) (1 pri facs) ⊗ TVB tea/coffee ✖ Cen ht No children 16yrs No coaches **Prices** S £55-£65; D £65-£75 **Parking** 3 **Notes** Closed 15 Dec-20 Jan

◆◆◆◆

Oakleigh House

19 Upper Oldfield Pk BA2 3JX
☎ 01225 315698 ▤ 01225 448223
e-mail oakleigh@which.net
web www.oakleigh-house.co.uk
Dir *A36 onto A367 Wells Rd, 1st right*

This large Victorian house, built of honey-colour Bath stone, offers friendly and spacious accommodation. Bedrooms are well equipped with comfortable pine furnishings and a host of extras. The pleasant lounge has daily papers and plenty of books, games and local information. Freshly cooked breakfasts are served at separate tables in the attractive dining room.

Facilities 3 en suite ⊗ TVB tea/coffee ✖ Cen ht No children 18yrs No coaches **Prices** S £50-£70; D £70-£95 LB **Parking** 4 **Notes** Closed , phone for details

◆◆◆◆

St Leonards

Warminster Rd BA2 6SQ
☎ 01225 465838 ▤ 01225 442800
e-mail stay@stleonardsbath.co.uk
Dir *1m E of city centre. A4 onto A36 Warminster Rd, up hill 200yds on left*

Located in grounds on the eastern side of the city, this impressive Victorian home with its high ceilings has superb views over the town and surrounding countryside. The stylish bedrooms and bathrooms are spacious and very comfortable, and a full English breakfast is served in the attractive dining room.

Facilities 6 en suite (2 fmly) (2 GF) ⊗ TVB tea/coffee ✖ Cen ht No children 6yrs No coaches **Prices** S £45-£85; D £69-£95✳ LB **Parking** 8 **Notes** Closed Xmas

◆◆◆◆

The Town House

7 Bennett St BA1 2QT ☎ 01225 422505 ▤ 01225 422505
e-mail stay@thetownhousebath.co.uk
web www.thetownhousebath.co.uk
Dir *400yds N of city centre. Off A4 Roman Rd at lights onto Lansdown Hill, 2nd on left*

Bath's historical attractions and shops will be on your doorstep if you stay here; Located alongside the Assembly Rooms and just a stones throw away from the Royal Crescent. This stylish Georgian accommodation, which has hints of Africa reflected in some furnishings and decor, offers a good level of comfort. The spacious bedrooms are finished with many thoughtful extras and the friendly hosts are attentive. At breakfast time the atmosphere is relaxed and memorable, with a good choice of freshly prepared dishes to be enjoyed around a communal table.

Facilities 3 en suite ⊗ TVB tea/coffee ✖ Cen ht No children 14yrs No coaches **Prices** S £70-£115; D £85-£115✳ **Parking** 1 **Notes** Closed Jan

◆◆◆◆
Aquae Sulis

174/176 Newbridge Rd BA1 3LE
☎ 01225 420061 & 339064 📠 01225 446077
e-mail enquiries@aquaesulishotel.co.uk
web www.aquaesulishotel.co.uk
Dir *On A4 1.2m W of city centre*

Located within easy reach of the city centre, this attractive Edwardian house offers a genuine welcome. Bedrooms are of a good size and well equipped with many modern facilities such as the Internet and email. There are two inviting lounges, one with a small but well-stocked bar. Breakfast is served in the comfortable dining room and a good selection of meals is available in the evening.

Facilities 13 rms (11 en suite) (2 pri facs) (5 fmly) (2 GF)
⊘ in bedrooms ⊘ in dining room ⊘ in 1 lounge STV TVB tea/coffee
Direct dial from bedrooms Licensed Cen ht TVL Dinner Last d 6pm
Prices S £49-£89; D £55-£95 **LB** **Parking** 12 **Notes** Closed 25-26 Dec

◆◆◆◆
Ashley Villa

26 Newbridge Rd BA1 3JZ
☎ 01225 421683 📠 01225 313604
e-mail reservations@ashleyvilla.co.uk
web www.ashleyvilla.co.uk
Dir *A4 Upper Bristol Rd W from Bath, fork left onto A4 Newbridge Rd, 200yds on right*

Located within walking distance of the city centre, Ashley Villa offers a range of refurbished bedrooms and bathrooms. Facilities include a lounge bar, a patio and an outdoor swimming pool. Breakfast is served in the bright attractive dining room.

Facilities 13 en suite (2 fmly) (4 GF) ⊘ in bedrooms ⊘ in dining room
FTV TVB tea/coffee Direct dial from bedrooms ✖ Licensed Cen ht TVL
⚲ **Prices** D £50-£99✳ **LB** **Parking** 8

◆◆◆◆
Badminton Villa

10 Upper Oldfield Pk BA2 3JZ
☎ 01225 426347 📠 01225 420393
e-mail badmintonvilla@blueyonder.co.uk
Dir *A36 onto A367 Wells Rd, right onto Upper Oldfield Park, premises 300yds on right*

Large comfortable rooms and friendly, welcoming proprietors provide a relaxing base from which to explore the many attractions of Bath. This charming Victorian house is located in a quiet residential area and delightful views over the city can be enjoyed from some of the bedrooms. Breakfast is served in the pleasant dining room and in summer guests can enjoy the conservatory and attractive gardens.

Facilities 5 en suite (1 fmly) ⊘ TVB tea/coffee ✖ Cen ht No children
8yrs No coaches **Prices** S £40-£50; D £65-£75✳ **Parking** 5

◆◆◆◆
Bailbrook Lodge Hotel

35/37 London Rd West BA1 7HZ
☎ 01225 859090 📠 01225 852299
e-mail Hotel@bailbrooklodge.co.uk
Dir *M4 junct 18, A46 S to A4 junct, left signed Batheaston, Lodge on left*

Set in extensive gardens on the east edge of the city, the imposing Georgian building provides smart accommodation. The well-equipped bedrooms include some with four-poster beds and period furniture, and service is professional and efficient. The inviting lounge has a small bar, and light snacks are available from noon until evening. Breakfast is served in the elegant dining room.

Facilities 15 rms (14 en suite) (1 pri facs) (5 fmly) (1 GF) ⊘ STV TVB
tea/coffee ✖ Licensed Cen ht **Prices** S £55-£65; D £70-£135✳ **LB**
Conf Max 20 Thtr 20 Class 10 Board 12 Del from £90 ✳ **Parking** 15
Notes Civ Wed 40

See advertisement on this page

England

BATH continued

♦♦♦♦

Beckfords

59 Upper Oldfield Pk BA2 3LB ☎ 01225 334959
e-mail post@beckford-house.com
web www.beckford-house.com
Dir *Off A36 Lower Bristol Rd onto Lower Oldfield Park at Green Park Tavern opp Renault, 3rd left*

Close to the city's attractions, this Victorian house provides a relaxed and friendly welcome in a quiet location. The spacious bedrooms are carefully furnished and decorated. A varied choice is offered at breakfast including local and organic produce.

Facilities 2 en suite ⊗ FTV TVB tea/coffee ✝ Cen ht No children 11yrs No coaches **Prices** S £48-£65; D £68-£90✻ **LB** **Parking** 2 **Notes** Closed Xmas ⊗

♦♦♦♦

Blairgowrie Guest House

55 Wellsway BA2 4RT ☎ 01225 332266 & 07818 211659
e-mail blairgowrie.bath@ukgateway.net
Dir *A36 onto A367 Wells Rd, house 0.6m up hill past Bear pub*

This elegant Victorian family home offers pleasantly spacious and well-equipped rooms. Convenient for Bath's many attractions, Blairgowrie is also a good base for touring Somerset. A traditional breakfast is served in the lounge-dining room.

Facilities 3 rms (2 en suite) (1 pri facs) (1 fmly) ⊗ TVB tea/coffee ✝ Cen ht No coaches **Prices** S £38-£45; D £58-£65✻ **Parking** 2 **Notes** Closed 24 Dec-1 Jan ⊗

♦♦♦♦

Cranleigh

159 Newbridge Hill BA1 3PX
☎ 01225 310197 🖷 01225 423143
e-mail cranleigh@btinternet.com
web www.cranleighguesthouse.com
Dir *1.2m W of city centre on A431*

This pleasant Victorian house is in a quiet location near the city centre. The well-equipped bedrooms, some on the ground floor, are decorated in the period style and two rooms have four-poster beds. Breakfast is served in the elegant dining room, and there is also an attractive garden.

Facilities 9 en suite (4 fmly) (2 GF) ⊗ TVB tea/coffee Direct dial from bedrooms ✝ Licensed Cen ht No children 5yrs No coaches Spa bath in garden **Prices** S £45-£65; D £60-£95✻ **Parking** 5 **Notes** Closed 25-26 Dec

♦♦♦♦

Dolphin House

8 Northend, Batheaston BA1 7EN ☎ 01225 858915
e-mail georgeandjane@hotmail.com
Dir *2m NE of Bath. Off Batheaston High St to Northend*

This detached Grade II listed Georgian house is convenient for Bath and has a delightful terraced walled garden. Bedrooms, including a suite with lounge, twin bedroom and large bathroom, are very attractive with period decor. Continental breakfasts are served in the bedrooms or on the terrace.

Facilities 2 rms (1 en suite) (1 pri facs) (1 GF) ⊗ TVB tea/coffee ✝ Cen ht No children 12yrs No coaches **Prices** D £55-£75✻ **Parking** 2 **Notes** Closed Xmas rs 24-27 Dec ⊗

♦♦♦♦

Eagle House

Church St, Bathford BA1 7RS
☎ 01225 859946 🖷 01225 859430
e-mail jonap@eagleho.demon.co.uk
web www.eaglehouse.co.uk
Dir *Off A363 onto Church St*

Set in attractive gardens, this delightful Georgian house is pleasantly located on the outskirts of the city. Bedrooms are individually styled, and each has a thoughtful range of extra facilities. The impressive lounge is adorned with attractive pictures, and the dining room has views of the grounds and tennis court.

Facilities 6 en suite 2 annexe en suite (2 fmly) (2 GF) ⊗ in 1 bedrooms ⊗ in dining room TVB tea/coffee Direct dial from bedrooms Cen ht ✎ ♩ Childrens play area & treehouse **Prices** S £48-£68; D £62-£104✻ **LB** **Conf** Max 18 Thtr 18 Class 18 Board 14 Del from £74 ✻ **Parking** 10 **Notes** Closed 12 Dec-8 Jan

♦♦♦♦

Grove Lodge

11 Lambridge BA1 6BJ ☎ 01225 310860
e-mail stay@grovelodgebath.co.uk
Dir *0.6m NE of city centre. Off A4, 400yds W from junct A46*

This fine Georgian house lies within easy reach of the city centre and is reached by a stone path through a neat garden surrounded by *continued*

continued

trees. The spacious bedrooms have period character and all are well equipped. There is an attractive breakfast room and parking is available in nearby side streets.

Grove Lodge

Facilities 5 rms (4 en suite) (1 pri facs) (1 GF) ⊗ TVB tea/coffee ✹ Cen ht No children 6yrs No coaches **Prices** S £40-£45; D £60-£75✳ LB **Notes** Closed Xmas & New Year

◆◆◆◆

Highways House

143 Wells Rd BA2 3AL ☎ 01225 421238 ▤ 01225 481169
e-mail stay@highwayshouse.co.uk
Dir A36 onto A367 Wells Rd, 300yds on left

Please note that this establishment has recently changed hands. This elegant house is just a 10-minute walk from the city centre. The bedrooms are individually styled and well equipped, and one is on the ground floor. An attractive lounge is provided, and breakfast is served at separate tables in the bright dining room, which features artworks by the proprietor.

Facilities 5 en suite (1 GF) ⊗ TVB tea/coffee ✹ Cen ht No children 5yrs No coaches **Parking** 8

◆◆◆◆

Manor Farm Barn Bed & Breakfast

Manor Farm Barn, Englishcombe BA2 9DU
☎ 01225 424195 ▤ 01225 427434
e-mail info@manorfarmbarn.com
Dir 2.5m SW of city centre. Off A367 to Englishcombe village

Located in a quiet lane just 3m from Bath, this converted barn offers comfortable accommodation. Bedrooms, some having views of the pleasant countryside, are well equipped. Breakfast, featuring home-made preserves, is served in the open plan dining area around a large communal table. The hosts are happy to store bicycles during your stay.

Facilities 2 rms (1 en suite) (1 pri facs) ⊗ TVB tea/coffee ✹ Cen ht No coaches **Prices** S £40-£42.50; D £60-£65✳ **Parking** 2

◆◆◆◆

Marlborough House

1 Marlborough Ln BA1 2NQ
☎ 01225 318175 ▤ 01225 466127
e-mail mars@manque.dircon.co.uk
web www.marlborough-house.net
Dir 450yds W of city centre, on junct A4

This elegant house, situated opposite Royal Victoria Park, is convenient for the city centre and close to the Royal Crescent. American hospitality, antique furnishings (including four-poster beds), and globally inspired vegetarian cuisine using organic ingredients make this something out of the ordinary.

Facilities 7 en suite (3 fmly) (1 GF) ⊗ TVB tea/coffee Direct dial from bedrooms Licensed Cen ht No coaches **Prices** S £55-£95; D £65-£115 LB **Parking** 3

◆◆◆◆

Number 30

30 Crescent Gdns BA1 2NB
☎ 01225 337393 ▤ 01225 337393
e-mail david.greenwood12@btinternet.com
web www.numberthirty.com
Dir 0.5m from Queens Sq towards Bristol

The friendly accommodation is just a stroll from the city centre. The hosts ensure a comfortable stay and are happy to provide local information. The freshly prepared breakfast, featuring home-made preserves, is served in the light, pleasant dining room with an original fireplace, which is at the front of the house. Parking available.

Facilities 3 rms (2 en suite) (1 pri facs) ⊗ TVB tea/coffee ✹ Cen ht No children 12yrs No coaches **Prices** S £59-£79; D £82-£109 LB **Parking** 3

continued

Please mention the AA B&B Guide when booking your stay

BATH continued

♦♦♦♦

The Old Red House

37 Newbridge Rd BA1 3HE
☎ 01225 330464 🖷 01225 331661
e-mail oldredhouse@amserve.net
web www.oldredhouse.co.uk

Dir *1m W of city centre along A4 Upper Bristol Rd, house on left after The Weston pub*

This attractive building, a former bakery, stands out among the surrounding honey-colour Bath stone, with its imposing stained-glass windows and period features. It is a friendly home, located just a short, level distance from the centre of town. Bedrooms are pleasantly decorated and many guests return on a regular basis.

Facilities 4 en suite (1 fmly) (2 GF) ⊗ TVB tea/coffee ✖ Cen ht TVL No children 4yrs No coaches **Parking** 4 **Notes** Closed Jan

♦♦♦♦

The Parade Park and Lambrettas Bar

8, 9, 10 North Pde BA2 4AL
☎ 01225 463384 🖷 01225 442322
e-mail info@paradepark.co.uk
web www.paradepark.co.uk

Dir *In city centre. Off A36 Pulteney Rd onto North Parade Rd & North Parade*

This attractive central Georgian property was formerly the home of William Wordsworth. The restored rooms are brightly decorated well equipped with modern facilities. Traditional breakfasts are served in the impressive, panelled first-floor dining room. The modern, Lambretta-theme bar is open to the public.

Facilities 35 rms (29 en suite) (5 fmly) (2 GF) ⊗ in bedrooms ⊗ in dining room ⊗ in 1 lounge TVB tea/coffee ✖ Licensed Cen ht **Prices** S £38-£50; D £55-£90✳ LB **Notes** Closed Xmas

♦♦♦♦

The Plaine

Bell Hill BA2 7LT ☎ 01373 834723 🖷 01373 834101
e-mail theplaine@easynet.co.uk
For full entry see **Norton St Philip**

♦♦♦♦

Roman City

18 Raby Pl, Bathwick Hill BA2 4EH
☎ 01225 463668 & 0789 9777953
e-mail enquire@romancityguesthouse.co.uk

Dir *A4 onto A36 Bathwick St, pass St Mary's Church on left, 2nd rdbt left onto Raby Place*

A warm welcome is assured at this restored 18th-century end of terrace house, located just a stroll from the heart of the historic city. The spacious bedrooms, some with four-poster beds, are comfortable and well equipped with many extra facilities. A pleasant lounge is also available.

Facilities 4 rms (1 fmly) ⊗ TVB tea/coffee ✖ Cen ht TVL **Conf** Board 12

♦♦♦♦

The Firs

2 Newbridge Hill BA1 3PU
☎ 01225 334575 & 07970 602769

Dir *1m W of Bath centre*

Facilities 3 en suite (1 fmly) ⊗ TVB tea/coffee Cen ht TVL No children 3yrs LB **Parking** 4 **Notes** 🐾

♦♦♦

Hermitage

Bath Rd SN13 8DT ☎ 01225 744187 🖷 01225 743447
e-mail hermitage@telecall.co.uk
For full entry see **Box (Wiltshire)**

♦♦♦

Ko Ryu

7 Pulteney Gdns BA2 4HG
☎ 01225 337642 🖷 01225 337642
e-mail japanesekoryu@aol.com

Dir *500yds E of city centre. Off A36 Pulteney Rd onto Pulteney Gardens*

Ko Ryu means 'sunshine' in Japanese and that is exactly the style in this pleasant establishment with bright decor. In keeping with Japanese tradition, you are asked to remove their shoes while in this charming home. Bedrooms are comfortably furnished, and breakfast is served in the sunny dining room around a large communal table.

Facilities 5 en suite (1 fmly) ⊗ TVB tea/coffee ✖ Cen ht No coaches **Prices** S £35-£40; D £55-£60✳ **Parking** 6 **Notes** 🐾

♦♦♦

Lamp Post Villa

3 Crescent Gdns, Upper Bristol Rd BA1 2NA
☎ 01225 331221 🖷 01225 426783

Dir *350yds W of city centre on A4*

Close to the city's attractions, Lamp Post Villa offers comfortable accommodation with good facilities and private parking. There is a lounge and a lower ground-floor dining room, and the freshly cooked breakfasts provide a substantial start to the day.

Facilities 4 en suite (1 fmly) (1 GF) ⊗ in bedrooms ⊗ in dining room TVB tea/coffee Direct dial from bedrooms ✖ Cen ht TVL No children 6yrs No coaches **Prices** D £55-£65 **Parking** 4

Always confirm details with the establishment when booking

England

◆◆◆
Pulteney Hotel
14 Pulteney Rd BA2 4HA
☎ 01225 460991 📄 01225 460991
e-mail pulteney@tinyworld.co.uk
web www.pulteneyhotel.co.uk
Dir *A4 onto A36, pass Holburne Museum, premises 400yds, near railway bridge*

A warm welcome is assured at this large detached property, situated in a colourful garden within walking distance of the city centre. Bedrooms vary in size and are well equipped with useful facilities. Full English breakfasts are served in the dining room at individual tables.

Facilities 12 rms (11 en suite) (1 pri facs) 5 annexe en suite (6 fmly) (2 GF) ⊗ in 5 bedrooms ⊗ in dining room TVB tea/coffee Cen ht TVL **Prices** S £40-£50; D £65-£110✳ **LB** **Parking** 18

◆◆◆
Saint Clair
1 Crescent Gdns, Upper Bristol Rd BA1 2NA
☎ 01225 425543 📄 01225 425543
e-mail hotel-st-clair@ukonline.co.uk
Dir *On A4 350yds W of town centre, near Royal Victoria Park*

There is a relaxed atmosphere at this friendly establishment, situated within walking distance of the city centre. The reception leads to a small comfortable lounge, and breakfast is served in the dining room on the lower-ground floor. Pay and display car park behind property.

Facilities 18 rms (16 en suite) (4 fmly) (3 GF) ⊗ in 8 bedrooms ⊗ in dining room ⊗ in lounges TVB tea/coffee Direct dial from bedrooms ✱ Licensed Cen ht TVL **Prices** S £40-£70; D £50-£80 **LB**

◆◆◆
The White Guest House
23 Pulteney Gdns BA2 4HG
☎ 01225 426075 📄 01225 426075
e-mail thewhiteguesthouse@zoom.co.uk
Dir *A4 onto A36, under railway bridge, 2nd left*

This pleasant house offers cosy accommodation only a short walk from Bath's attractions. The resident proprietors create a friendly and relaxed atmosphere, and a tasty breakfast is served in the country-style dining room. Free permits are available for the residential parking in the area.

Facilities 5 en suite (1 fmly) (2 GF) ⊗ TVB tea/coffee ✱ Cen ht No coaches **Prices** S £35-£45; D £50-£60✳ **LB** **Notes** 🛇

◆◆
Waltons ◇
17-19 Crescent Gdns, Upper Bristol Rd BA1 2NA
☎ 01225 426528 📄 01225 420350
Dir *On A4 350yds W of city centre*

There is a warm welcome at Waltons, situated within strolling distance of the centre of Bath. The cosy bedrooms come with useful extra facilities, and a traditional English breakfast is served at individual tables in the dining room.

Facilities 7 en suite 7 annexe rms (5 en suite) (1 fmly) ⊗ FTV TVB tea/coffee Direct dial from bedrooms ✱ Cen ht **Prices** S £30-£35; D £50-£75✳ **Notes** 🛇

U
Chestnut House
16 Henrietta Rd BA2 6LY ☎ 01225 334279 📄 01225 312236
e-mail reservations@chestnutshouse.co.uk
web www.chestnutshouse.co.uk

At the time of going to press the rating for this establishment had not been confirmed. Please check the AA website www.theAA.com for up-to-date information.

Facilities 5 en suite (1 fmly) (2 GF) ⊗ STV TVB tea/coffee Cen ht TVL No coaches **Prices** S £50-£60; D £60-£80✳ **Parking** 5

BECKINGTON   MAP 04 ST85

◆◆◆◆ ⊜
Pickford House ◇
23 Bath Rd BA11 6SJ ☎ 01373 830329 📄 01373 830329
e-mail ampritchar@aol.com
web www.pickfordhouse.com
Dir *Off A36 (Little Chef rdbt) signed Beckington, follow road for 300yds to 30mph signs by village hall, turn right then sharp left*

This peacefully located Regency-style house is set in secluded walled gardens. The proprietors are welcoming and attentive, and many guests visit this pleasant house on a regular basis. Dinner is an enjoyable experience with a 'pot luck' menu (unless you require vegetarian or special dietary dishes) and, along with the impressive wine list, provides fine dining.

Facilities 2 rms 3 annexe en suite (2 fmly) (1 GF) ⊗ in 2 bedrooms ⊗ in dining room TVB tea/coffee ✱ Licensed Cen ht No coaches ⚲ Dinner Last d 9pm **Prices** S fr £25; D £40-£48 **LB** **Parking** 15 **Notes** Closed Xmas 🛇

BEERCROCOMBE

MAP 04 ST32

Premier Collection

◆◆◆◆◆ ❦

Whittles (ST324194)

TA3 6AH ☎ 01823 480301 🖹 01823 480301 Mr & Mrs Mitchem

e-mail dj.cm.mitchem@themail.co.uk

Dir Off A358 through Hatch Beauchamp to Beercrocombe, 0.75m S of village

For a relaxing break try this 16th-century farmhouse set between the Quantock and Blackdown hills. The friendly and attentive owners have been accommodating guests here for 20 years and all are assured of a caring and genuine welcome. Guests have their own drawing room, dining and sitting room, and the spacious bedrooms are comfortable. Freshly prepared suppers, featuring local produce and farmhouse cheeses, are offered by arrangement.

Facilities 2 en suite ⊗ TVB tea/coffee ✖ Cen ht No children 16yrs 200 acres beef **Prices** S £38-£40; D £60-£64 **Parking** 4 **Notes** Closed Dec & Jan 🐾

BISHOPS LYDEARD

MAP 04 ST12

◆◆◆◆

Warre House

Mount St TA4 3LH ☎ 01823 433682

e-mail gillvlasto@yahoo.co.uk

web www.warre-house.co.uk

Dir A358 towards Minehead. In Bishops Lydeard look for red door in wall marked

This house offers charming hospitality from an attentive host, and spacious, comfortable accommodation. Extensive gardens, with some magnificent specimen trees, and a tranquil village setting provide a super base, close to Taunton yet convenient from which to explore the surrounding countryside. Breakfast, and dinner by arrangement, provides enjoyable dining. Therapy treatments and pampering sessions are also offered here.

Facilities 3 rms (1 fmly) ⊗ tea/coffee ✖ Cen ht TVL No coaches ✎ Dinner Last d Day before **Prices** S fr £45; d fr £65✳ **LB** **Conf** Max 8 Board 8 **Parking** 3 **Notes** 🐾

◆◆◆◆ ➾ ❑

The New Inn

TA4 3AF ☎ 01823 432352 & 07958 636284

e-mail connormuir@yahoo.com

This restored Inn has a contemporary style that has been welcomed by locals and visitors alike. Situated in a 'Chocolate Box' village close to the Somerset Steam Railway, an ideal base for walking, cycling, country pursuits or a simply leisure break. Comfort and quality abound here, beds are comfortable and rooms well appointed. Dining is a feature and menus focus on local produce.

Facilities 5 en suite 2 annexe rms (2 annexe pri facs) (3 fmly) ⊗ in dining room TVB tea/coffee ✖ Cen ht Pool Table Dinner Last d 9pm **LB** **Parking** 25

BLUE ANCHOR

MAP 03 ST04

◆◆◆◆ 🅐

The Langbury

TA24 6LB ☎ 01643 821375

e-mail post@langbury.co.uk

web www.langbury.co.uk

Dir Off A39 at Carhampton signed Blue Anchor

Facilities 5 en suite (1 fmly) (1 GF) ⊗ TVB tea/coffee Licensed Cen ht TVL No children 8yrs No coaches ✎ **Prices** S £37; D £55-£57✳ **Parking** 5

BRIDGWATER

MAP 04 ST23

◆◆◆◆

Model Farm

Perry Gn, Wembdon TA5 2BA ☎ 01278 433999

e-mail info@modelfarm.com

web www.modelfarm.com

Dir 2.5m NW of Bridgwater. Off junct A39 & B3339 to Perry Green, at T-junct follow sign No Through Road, farm 2nd drive on left

This extensive Victorian house has a peaceful rural setting with glorious country views. Guests are assured of a warm welcome and genuine hospitality. Bedrooms are very spacious and include thoughtful touches. By arrangement, the proprietors join you around the large dining room table for a carefully prepared three-course dinner. The converted cider-press barn is now a suite of four conference rooms.

Facilities 3 en suite (1 fmly) ⊗ tea/coffee Licensed Cen ht TVL No children 3yrs No coaches Dinner Last d noon **Prices** S £40; D £70 **Conf** Max 24 Thtr 24 Board 16 **Parking** 6

◆◆◆◆

The Old Vicarage Hotel

45-51 Saint Mary St TA6 3EQ
☎ 01278 458891 🖹 01278 445297

e-mail mail@theoldvicaragehotel.com

web www.theoldvicaragehotel.com

Dir In town centre, next to St Marys Church

This Old Vicarage is a really friendly place to stay, central to the town and a good base for exploring Somerset. Dating from the 14th to the 19th century, its rich past is evident in much of the architecture, and there is a super garden and terrace, a cafe bar, and dining in two rooms. Parking available.

continued

Facilities 8 en suite 7 annexe en suite (2 fmly) (3 GF) ☺ TVB tea/coffee Direct dial from bedrooms ✶ Licensed Cen ht No coaches Dinner Last d 9pm **Prices** S £62.50; D £85-£125✶ **Conf** Max 8 Board 8 **Parking** 8

◆◆◆◆

Rydon Farm Bed & Breakfast

Rydon Farm, North Petherton TA7 0BZ ☎ 01278 663472
e-mail info@rydonfarm.com
Dir M5 junct 24, A38 S, left 1m S of North Petherton, right at T-junct, 1st entrance on right

Facilities 3 rms (1 en suite) (1 pri facs) (1 fmly) ☺ TVB tea/coffee ✶ Cen ht No coaches **Prices** S £35-£38; D £50-£58✶ LB **Parking** 13 **Notes** ✉

◆◆◆ ◧

The Boat & Anchor Inn

Huntworth TA7 0AQ ☎ 01278 662473 ▤ 01278 662542
e-mail boatand.anchorinn@virgin.net
Dir M5 junct 24, 500yds NE to Huntworth, 0.5m N of village across canal bridge

This popular canal-side inn offers easy access to the M5 and is a useful stopover en route for the West Country. Bedrooms vary in size and style and are situated above the busy bars, where an impressive selection is offered from the blackboard menus.

Facilities 11 en suite (3 fmly) ☺ in bedrooms TVB tea/coffee ✶ Cen ht Dinner Last d 9pm **Prices** S £49.50-£55; D £65-£75✶ LB **Conf** Thtr 80 Class 50 Board 45 Del from £79.50 ✶ **Parking** 100

BROMPTON REGIS   MAP 03 SS93

◆◆◆◆ ✙

Holworthy Farm ◈ (SS978308)

TA22 9NY ☎ 01398 371244 ▤ 01398 371244 Mrs G Payne
e-mail holworthyfarm@aol.com
web www.holworthyfarm.co.uk
Dir 2m E of Brompton Regis. Off A396 on E side of Wimbleball Lake

Set in the south-east corner of Exmoor, this working livestock farm has spectacular views over Wimbleball Lake. Bedrooms are traditionally furnished and well equipped. The dining room overlooking the garden is the attractive setting for breakfast (dinner by arrangement).

Holworthy Farm

Facilities 6 rms (4 en suite) (2 pri facs) (2 fmly) (1 GF) ☺ TV5B tea/coffee ✶ Cen ht TVL 200 acres beef/sheep Dinner Last d previous evening **Prices** S fr £30; d fr £60✶ LB **Conf** Max 20 **Parking** 8 **Notes** ✉

◆◆◆

Bruneton House ◈

TA22 9NN ☎ 01398 371224
e-mail brunetonhouse@hotmail.com
Dir Off A396 onto Watchet Rd at Machine Cross, signs for Brompton Regis, establishment 3m at end of churchyard

The warmest of welcomes will be received at this 17th-century family home in the Exmoor National Park. It provides a true taste of the joys of rural life, as one side of the house operates as the village shop. Bedrooms are spacious and comfortable, and a brightly decorated lounge is available. Wonderful views can be enjoyed from the cottage garden.

Facilities 3 rms (1 en suite) (2 pri facs) ☺ in dining room tea/coffee ✶ Cen ht TVL No coaches Dinner Last d 5pm **Prices** S £25-£27.50; D £50-£55 **Parking** 4 **Notes** Closed Xmas & New Year rs Sep-Etr (limited availability) ✉

BUTLEIGH   MAP 04 ST53

◆◆◆

Court Lodge

Sub Rd BA6 8SA ☎ 01458 850575
Dir Off B3151 or B3153 into Butleigh, just N of village x-rds

Situated at the entrance to Butleigh Court and surrounded by pleasant gardens, this charming and attractive house offers comfortable accommodation. Guests are assured of a friendly welcome and made to feel relaxed. Two lounges are available, and at breakfast traditional fare is provided at the single dining table.

Facilities 2 rms ☺ TVB Cen ht TVL No coaches **Parking** available **Notes** ✉

If you have to cancel a booking, let the proprietor know immediately

continued

England

CASTLE CARY

MAP 04 ST63

♦♦♦♦ 🛏 🍴

Clanville Manor ✧ (ST618330)

BA7 7PJ ☎ 01963 350124 & 07966 512732 ▤ 01963 350719
Mrs Snook
e-mail info@clanvillemanor.co.uk
web www.clanvillemanor.co.uk
Dir A371 onto B3153, 0.75m entrance to Clanville Manor via white
gate & cattle grid under bridge

Built in 1743, Clanville Manor is situated on a beef-rearing holding,
and has been owned by the Snook family since 1898. A polished oak
staircase leads up to the individually decorated bedrooms, which
retain a great deal of their original character. Hearty breakfasts are
served in the elegant dining room, which looks out over open
meadows. There is also a spacious and comfortable sitting room.

Facilities 4 en suite ⊗ TVB tea/coffee ✗ Cen ht TVL No children
10yrs ⚲ ♨ 200 acres beef **Prices** S £27.50-£35; D £55-£70✳ **LB**
Parking 6 **Notes** Closed 21 Dec-2 Jan

CATCOTT

MAP 04 ST33

♦♦♦♦

Honeysuckle ✧

King William Rd TA7 9HU ☎ 01278 722890
Dir Off A39 to Catcott, pass King William pub, house 200yds on right

Situated in the village centre, this delightful modern house is a good
base for visiting the many attractions in the area. Bedrooms are
comfortable, and there is a spacious lounge and a charming garden.
Breakfast is served around a communal table in the pleasant dining
room.

Facilities 3 rms (1 en suite) ⊗ TVB tea/coffee ✗ Cen ht No children
7yrs No coaches **Prices** S £20; D £50-£60✳ **Parking** 3 **Notes** Closed
20 Dec-3 Jan 🐾

CHARD

MAP 04 ST30

♦♦♦♦♦ 🍸 🛏 🍽

Bellplot House Hotel & Thomas's Restaurant

High St TA20 1QB ☎ 01460 62600 ▤ 01460 62600
e-mail info@bellplothouse.co.uk
web www.bellplothouse.co.uk
Dir In town centre, 500yds from Guildhall

This grand Georgian property in the centre of town provides stylish
accommodation suitable for business and leisure. There is ample
parking, and the atmosphere is friendly and relaxed. Bedrooms are
well equipped, and the elegant restaurant has an innovative menu.
Wi-Fi Internet access is available.

Facilities 7 en suite (1 fmly) (2 GF) ⊗ in dining room STV TVB
tea/coffee Direct dial from bedrooms ✗ Licensed Cen ht No coaches
Pool Table Use of nearby leisure club & golf course Dinner Last d 9pm
Prices S £69.50; D £79.50; (room only) ✳ **Conf** Max 20 Thtr 20
Class 20 Board 20 **Parking** 12

♦♦♦♦♦ 🍴

Higher Beetham Farm ✧ (ST277120)

Whitestaunton TA20 3PZ
☎ 01460 234460 ▤ 01460 234450 Mrs Cumming
e-mail iandandhilary@higher-beetham.fsnet.co.uk
Dir Off A303 signed Whitestaunton & Cricklease, 0.5m down lane,
2nd gateway on right

This peaceful haven is in a rural setting with sweeping views over
adjacent fields and countryside. Following the warm welcome, every
effort is made to ensure an enjoyable and relaxing stay. The
comfortable, well-furnished accommodation comes with thoughtful
touches and extra facilities.

Facilities 1 en suite ⊗ tea/coffee ✗ Cen ht TVL No children 16yrs
22 acres non-working **Prices** S £30-£35; D £50-£60✳ **LB** **Parking** 3
Notes Closed Xmas & New Year 🐾

♦♦♦♦

Glebelands ✧

1 Forton Rd TA20 2HJ ☎ 01460 62028
e-mail glebelandschard@onetel.com
Dir A358 onto B3162, Glebelands opp church

This attractive former rectory and doctor's surgery is set in pleasant
grounds a stroll form the centre of Chard. The proprietors are
particularly friendly and make you feel most welcome. Bedrooms
come in a range of sizes and all are thoughtfully equipped.

Facilities 3 rms (1 en suite) (2 pri facs) 1 annexe en suite (1 fmly)
(1 GF) ⊗ TV3B tea/coffee ✗ Cen ht TVL **Prices** S £27-£30;
D £48-£60✳ **LB** **Parking** 5 **Notes** 🐾

*Book as early as possible, particularly
in the peak holiday period*

England

♦♦♦

Watermead ◇

83 High St TA20 1QT ☎ 01460 62834 ▤ 01460 67448
e-mail trudy@watermeadguesthouse.co.uk
web www.watermeadguesthouse.co.uk
Dir On A30 in town centre

You will feel at home at this family-run house, a smart
accommodation in a convenient location. Hearty breakfasts are served
in the dining room overlooking the garden. Bedrooms are neat, and
the spacious, self-contained suite is popular with families.

Facilities 9 rms (6 en suite) 1 annexe en suite (1 fmly) ⊗ TVB
tea/coffee Cen ht TVL No coaches **Prices** S £29-£39; D £49-£56 LB
Parking 10

U

Lindens House ◇

Snowden Cottage Ln, High St TA20 1QS
☎ 01460 61137 ▤ 01460 61137
e-mail joan@lindenshouse.fsnet.co.uk
web www.lindenshouse.co.uk
Dir On A30 Wm 0.25m from town centre

At the time of going to press the rating for this establishment had not
been confirmed. Please check the AA website www.theAA.com for up-
to-date information.

Facilities 3 en suite (1 fmly) ⊗ STV TVB tea/coffee Cen ht TVL ⇃
Sauna **Prices** S fr £25; d fr £50✳ LB **Parking** 8 **Notes** ☺

CHEDDAR   MAP 04 ST45
See also **Draycott**

★★★★ A Guest House

Bay Rose House ◇

The Bays BS27 3QN ☎ 01934 741377 ▤ 01934 741377
e-mail enquiries@bayrose.co.uk
web www.bayrose.co.uk
Dir B3135 from Cheddar, start through Gorge, left at Fortes Ice
Cream Parlour, Bay Rose House ahead

Facilities 3 rms (2 en suite) (1 pri facs) (1 fmly) (1 GF) ⊗ TVB
tea/coffee ✖ Licensed Cen ht TVL No coaches Slot car race track
Dinner Last d 9am **Prices** S £25-£45; D £45-£70✳ LB **Parking** 4

Premier Collection

♦♦♦♦♦♦

Batts Farm

Nyland BS27 3UD ☎ 01934 741469
e-mail clare@batts-farm.co.uk
web www.batts-farm.co.uk
Dir A371 from Cheddar towards Wells, 2m right towards Nyland,
Batts Farm 1m on left

Nestled in an idyllic location at the bottom of Nyland Hill, Batts farm is
a 200-year-old property full of character. The peaceful location
overlooks open farmland and the moors at the foot of the Mendips
Hills. The spacious bedrooms are all decorated and furnished to a
high standard and include especially comfortable beds. Guests are

continued

welcome to use the relaxing lounge and the summerhouse in the
delightful garden. Breakfast includes home-made breads and local
jams.

Batts Farm

Facilities 3 en suite ⊗ TVB tea/coffee ✖ Cen ht TVL No children
12yrs No coaches **Prices** S fr £50; D £70-£80✳ LB **Parking** 6
Notes ☺

♦♦♦♦ ❧

Tor Farm *(ST455534)*

Nyland BS27 3UD
☎ 01934 743710 & 07766 026175 ▤ 01934 743710
Mrs Ladd
e-mail info@torfarm.co.uk
web www.torfarm.co.uk
Dir A371 from Cheddar towards Wells, after 2m turn right towards
Nyland. Tor Farm 1.5m on right

Tucked away in the Somerset countryside, this comfortable guest
house has many welcome extras, including its own heated swimming
pool. The smartly furnished bedrooms, including several on the
ground floor, have wonderful views. Guests can relax in the cosy
lounge, or enjoy barbecues in the garden in summer.

Facilities 8 en suite (2 fmly) (5 GF) ⊗ in bedrooms ⊗ in dining room
⊗ in 1 lounge TVB tea/coffee ✖ Licensed Cen ht TVL ⇃ 33 acres
Prices D £65-£90✳ LB **Conf** Class 15 **Parking** 12

Please mention the AA B&B Guide when
booking your stay

CHEDDAR continued

◆◆◆◆

Wassells House ◇

Upper New Rd BS27 3DW
☎ 01934 744317 ▤ 01934 741998
e-mail aflinders@wassells99.freeserve.co.uk
web www.wassellshouse.co.uk
Dir *W of town centre on A371 near reservoir*

You are made to feel like visiting friends at this well-presented guest house on the outskirts of the town and offers a large and well-tended garden. The homely bedrooms are filled with useful extras, while breakfast is invariably a very sociable occasion around one table.

Facilities 4 rms (3 en suite) (1 pri facs) (1 fmly) ⊗ TVB tea/coffee ✖ Cen ht No coaches Dinner Last d 10am **Prices** S £25-£28; D £50-£56✳ **Parking** 4 **Notes** Closed 25 Dec ⊠

◆◆◆ 🅰

Constantine ◇

Lower New Rd BS27 3DY ☎ 01934 741339
Dir *0.5m W of town centre. A371 onto B3151 signed Wedmore, over old railway bridge, Constantine on right opp left turn*

Facilities 4 rms (1 en suite) (1 fmly) ⊗ in bedrooms ⊗ in dining room ⊗ in lounges TVB tea/coffee ✖ Cen ht No coaches Dinner Last d 2pm **Prices** S £20; D £40-£50✳ **Parking** 5 **Notes** Closed Dec ⊠

CLUTTON

MAP 04 ST65

◆◆◆◆ ◧

The Hunters Rest

King Ln, Clutton Hill BS39 5QL
☎ 01761 452303 ▤ 01761 453308
e-mail paul@huntersrest.co.uk
web www.huntersrest.co.uk
Dir *Off A37 onto A368 towards Bath, 100yds right onto lane, left at T-junct, inn 0.25m on left*

The Hunters Rest Inn was originally built around 1750 as a hunting lodge for the Earl of Warwick. Set in delightful countryside, the inn is centrally located among Bath, Bristol and Wells. Bedrooms and bathrooms are furnished and equipped to excellent standards, and the ground floor combines the character of a real country inn with an excellent range of home-cooked meals.

Facilities 5 en suite (1 fmly) ⊗ in bedrooms ⊗ in dining room ⊗ in 1 lounge TVB tea/coffee Direct dial from bedrooms ✖ Cen ht Dinner Last d 9.45pm **Prices** S £62.50-£72.50; D £87.50-£115✳ **LB** **Conf** Max 40 Thtr 40 Class 25 Board 25 Del from £90 ✳ **Parking** 90

If you have to cancel a booking, let the proprietor know immediately

CREWKERNE

MAP 04 ST40

◆◆◆◆

Greenways

Boozer Pit, Merriott TA16 5PW ☎ 01460 72830
e-mail wardill.tim.martine@btinternet.com
Dir *2m N of Crewkerne. Off A356 into Merriott, at N end of village*

Quietly located on the Somerset and Dorset borders, Greenways started life some 300 years ago as a cider house. The one bedroom with its large en suite bathroom is in a self-contained adjoining property with a private entrance. Breakfast is served in the pleasant conservatory where you can also enjoy delicious home-cooked dinners by arrangement.

Facilities 1 en suite (1 GF) ⊗ TVB tea/coffee ✖ Cen ht No coaches Pool Table Dinner Last d 3pm **Prices** S £45; D £60✳ **LB** **Parking** 5 **Notes** ⊠

◆◆◆◆

Kempsters Restaurant

Lower St, West Chinnock TA18 7PT
☎ 01935 881768 ▤ 01935 881768
e-mail debbie@kempsters.fslife.co.uk
Dir *Off A303 towards Crewkerne & 3rd left (signed West Chinnock & Chiselborough)*

This lovingly restored Somerset Longhouse has become well recognised as an award-winning restaurant. Located close to Yeovil in a charming and tranquil village, and convenient for the countryside attractions. Craftsmanship abounds here, not least in the bedrooms, which are most comfortable, particularly well furnished and provided with a host of thoughtful extras. Non-smoking throughout the house, the public areas also have been comfortably appointed. Dining here is a treat; dinner and breakfast offer the best of local produce and skilful cookery.

Facilities 3 rms (1 en suite) ⊗ TVB tea/coffee ✖ Licensed Cen ht No children 14yrs Dinner Last d 8:30-9pm **Prices** S £50-£70; D £80-£110 ✳ **Parking** 14

◆◆◆◆ ❦

Manor Farm ◇ *(ST409071)*

Wayford TA18 8QL
☎ 01460 78865 & 0776 7620031 ▤ 01460 78865
Mr & Mrs Emery
web www.manorfarm.biz
Dir *B3165 from Crewkerne to Lyme Regis, 3m in Clapton right onto Dunsham Ln, Manor Farm 0.5m up hill on right*

Located off the beaten track, this fine Victorian country house has extensive views over Clapton towards the Axe Valley. The comfortably furnished bedrooms are well equipped; front-facing rooms enjoy splendid views. Breakfast is served at separate tables in the dining room, and a spacious lounge is also provided.

Facilities 4 en suite 1 annexe en suite ⊗ STV TV4B tea/coffee ✖ Cen ht TVL Fishing Riding 20 acres breeding beef **Prices** S £30-£45; D £60-£70 **Parking** 14 **Notes** ⊠

♦♦♦ ⌷

The Manor Arms

Middle St, North Perrott TA18 7SG
☎ 01460 72901 ▤ 01460 74055
e-mail bookings@manorarmshotel.co.uk
Dir *In village on A3066*

This Grade II listed building dates from the 16th century and has bars with exposed stone walls and an inglenook fireplace. Bedrooms are in the main building and a converted coach house at the rear of the property. A wide selection of freshly cooked meals is served in the bar or restaurant.

Facilities 8 en suite (1 fmly) (3 GF) ⊗ in bedrooms ⊗ in dining room ⊗ in 1 lounge TVB tea/coffee ✹ Cen ht Dinner Last d 9pm **Conf** Max 18 Thtr 20 Class 15 Board 15 **Parking** 20

♦♦♦ ⌷

The Old Stagecoach Inn

Station Rd TA18 8AL ☎ 01460 72972 ▤ 01460 77023
e-mail info@stagecoach-inn.co.uk
web www.stagecoach-inn.co.uk
Dir *1m from town centre next to station*

Well located for the railway station, and just a short walk to the main town, this relaxing inn provides informal and welcoming accommodation. Rooms are located around a rear courtyard, motel style. The proprietors here are from Belgium and offer a fine selection of beers and cuisine, from their home country.

Facilities 13 annexe en suite (3 fmly) (13 GF) ⊗ in 2 bedrooms ⊗ in dining room TVB tea/coffee Direct dial from bedrooms ✹ Cen ht Dinner Last d 9.30pm **LB Conf** Max 25 **Parking** 25

♦♦♦ Ⓐ

The George Hotel ◇

Market Sq TA18 7LP ☎ 01460 73650 ▤ 01460 72974
e-mail georgecrewkerne@btconnect.com
web www.thegeorgehotelcrewkerne.co.uk
Dir *In town centre*

Facilities 13 rms (10 en suite) (2 fmly) ⊗ in dining room TVB tea/coffee Direct dial from bedrooms Licensed Cen ht TVL Jacuzzi/spa Dinner Last d 9pm **Prices** S £30-£55; D £50-£85 **LB Conf** Max 100 Thtr 100 Class 100 Board 50

CROSCOMBE   MAP 04 ST54

♦♦♦ ⌷

The Bull Terrier ◇

BA5 3QJ ☎ 01749 343658
e-mail barry.vidler@bullterrierpub.co.uk
Dir *On A371 by village cross*

Located in the centre of the village, this attractive country inn has a relaxed and friendly atmosphere. The public areas are particularly enjoyable, as the character of the inn has been retained with the flagstone floors and inglenook fireplace. Bedrooms are brightly decorated and well equipped. Freshly prepared lunches and dinners are available.

Facilities 2 en suite ⊗ in bedrooms ⊗ in area of dining room ⊗ in 1 lounge TVB tea/coffee ✹ Cen ht No children 10yrs Dinner Last d 9pm **Prices** S £30; D £55-£60✱ **Conf** Max 16 **Parking** 3

DINDER   MAP 04 ST54

♦♦♦♦ ⌷

Crapnell Farm *(ST597457)*

BA5 3HG ☎ 01749 342683 ▤ 01749 342683 Mrs Keen
e-mail pamkeen@yahoo.com
Dir *A371 from Shepton Mallet to Wells, after Croscombe right to Dinder, sharp right before village, Crapnell Farm 1.5m*

This charming farmhouse is thought to date from the 17th century. It provides attractive, non-smoking accommodation, including a family bedroom. Separate tables are provided in the breakfast room, which has period furniture. There is also a comfortable lounge, where log fires burn in the inglenook fireplace during cold weather.

Facilities 3 en suite (1 fmly) ⊗ TVB tea/coffee ✹ Cen ht TVL 3/4 size snooker table, Splash pool **Parking** 8 **Notes** Closed 18 Dec-3 Jan ⊗

Always confirm details with the establishment when booking

England

DRAYCOTT
MAP 04 ST45

Oakland House

Wells Rd BS27 3SU ☎ 01934 744195 🖹 01934 744195
e-mail enquiries@oakland-house.co.uk
web www.oakland-house.co.uk
Dir Off A371 at S end of village

Situated a short distance from Cheddar, this friendly home provides comfortable and spacious accommodation. There are splendid views of the Somerset moors and Glastonbury Tor from the sun lounge and the well-appointed and attractive bedrooms. Dinner features fresh fruit and vegetables from the garden.

Facilities 3 en suite (1 fmly) ⊗ in bedrooms ⊗ in dining room STV TVB tea/coffee ✖ Cen ht ch fac No coaches Pool Table Dinner Last d 24 hrs notice **Prices** S fr £42; D £60-£80 LB **Parking** 6 **Notes** 🞨

DULVERTON
MAP 03 SS92
See also **Winsford**

Premier Collection

◆◆◆◆◆ 🞩 🞪 🞫 🞬

Tarr Farm Inn

Tarr Steps, Exmoor National Pk TA22 9PY
☎ 01643 851507 🖹 01643 851111
e-mail enquiries@tarrfarm.co.uk
Dir 4m NW of Dulverton. Off B3223 signed Tarr Steps, signs to Tarr Farm Inn

Tarr Farm, dating from the 16th century, nestles on lower slopes overlooking an old clapper bridge. The new bedrooms provide superb comfort and quality and are equipped with every conceivable extra facility. Tarr Farm is renowned for its cream teas and tasty home-made

continued

snacks. Carefully prepared dinners use the best local ingredients whenever possible.

Facilities 9 en suite (4 GF) ⊗ in bedrooms ⊗ in area of dining room ⊗ in 1 lounge STV TVB tea/coffee Direct dial from bedrooms Cen ht No children 14yrs No coaches Fishing Riding Dinner Last d 9.30pm **Prices** S £80; D £130✳ LB **Conf** Max 18 **Parking** 10

◆◆◆◆

Threadneedle

EX16 9JH ☎ 01398 341598
e-mail info@threadneedlecottage.co.uk
web www.threadneedlecottage.co.uk
Dir On Devon/Somerset border just off B3227 between Oldways End & East Anstey

Situated on the edge of Exmoor near Dulverton, Threadneedle is built in the style of a Devon longhouse. The spacious, well-appointed family home offers comfortable, en suite accommodation. Traditional West Country dishes are served, by arrangement, in the light airy dining room, which overlooks the garden and surrounding countryside.

Facilities 2 en suite (1 fmly) ⊗ in bedrooms TVB tea/coffee Cen ht No coaches Dinner Last d 10am **Prices** D £64-£69 LB **Parking** 12 **Notes** 🞨

◆◆◆◆ 🅰

Town Mills

High St TA22 9HB ☎ 01398 323124
e-mail townmills@onetel.com
web www.townmillsdulverton.co.uk
Dir On B3222 in village centre

Facilities 5 rms (4 en suite) (1 pri facs) (1 GF) ⊗ in 2 bedrooms ⊗ in dining room ⊗ in lounges TVB tea/coffee ✖ Cen ht No children 10yrs No coaches **Prices** S £36-£46; D £54-£62 LB **Parking** 5 **Notes** Closed Xmas

DUNSTER
MAP 03 SS94

★★★★ **Guest Accommodation**

No 7 West Street

7 West St TA24 6SN ☎ 01643 821064
e-mail info@no7weststreet.co.uk
web www.no7weststreet.co.uk
Dir A39 towards Minehead then A396 towards Tiverton. B&B 250yds left after church.

This recently restored 17th cottage, boasts a period features, including a steep, wooden staircase, beams and interesting mullion windows. The comfortable bedrooms are individually furnished and decorated; offering numerous, thoughtful extras. Dinner must not be missed, an imaginative choice using the best of local and organic produce. The rear of the property is a terraced garden, where guests can enjoy views of the surrounding countryside.

Facilities 3 rms (2 en suite) (1 pri facs) (1 fmly) ⊗ tea/coffee Cen ht No children 14yrs No coaches Dinner Last d 8pm **Notes** Closed 22-29 Dec

England

◆◆◆◆◆

Dollons House

10-12 Church St TA24 6SH ☎ 01643 821880
e-mail dollonshouse@btconnect.com
Dir *In village centre*

Situated in the historic village, this charming Grade II listed property, once a pharmacy, now operates as a gift shop as well as offering high-quality accommodation. The attractive, individually furnished bedrooms have lots of character and two overlook the castle. The tasty breakfast includes a complimentary fruit basket for each guest.

Facilities 3 en suite ⊗ TVB tea/coffee 🐾 Cen ht TVL No children 16yrs No coaches **Prices** S £37.50; D £55✱ **Notes** Closed 24-28 Dec

◆◆◆◆

Buttercross ◇

36 St Georges St TA24 6RS ☎ 01643 821413
e-mail robertbuck@onetel.com
Dir *Off A39 into Dunster, right after lights onto St Georges St, pass school and church, last white house on right*

Quietly situated on the edge of the village, this pleasant family home is just a short walk from Dunster Castle and the other interesting sights that the village has to offer. The spacious accommodation is smart, well equipped and has lovely views. A hearty cooked breakfast featuring local produce will set you up for the day.

Facilities 1 en suite (1 fmly) ⊗ FTV TVB tea/coffee 🐾 Cen ht No children 5yrs No coaches **Prices** S £30-£35; D £50-£55✱ LB **Parking** 2 **Notes** Closed 21 Dec-4 Jan 🈂

◆◆◆◆

Higher Orchard ◇

30 St Georges St TA24 6RS ☎ 01643 821915
e-mail lamacraft@higherorchard.fsnet.co.uk
web www.higherorchard.fsnet.co.uk
Dir *In village. Off A396 Church St onto St Georges St*

Set in the fascinating historic village, this charming Victorian house has fine views over the church and castle. You can relax in the gardens surrounding the house or in the lounge. Breakfast is a selection of local produce, home-made marmalade and eggs from the proprietor's own poultry.

Facilities 2 rms (1 en suite) (1 pri facs) ⊗ TVB tea/coffee 🐾 Cen ht No children 10yrs No coaches **Prices** S £30; D £55✱ **Parking** 2 **Notes** Closed Xmas-New Year 🈂

FITZHEAD
MAP 03 ST12

★★★ Guest Accommodation

Fitzhead Inn

TA4 3JP ☎ 01823 400667
web www.fitzheadinn.co.uk
Dir *Off A3065 Taunton to Wiveliscombe road just after Preston Bowyer*

Located in the village of Fitzhead and brimming with character, this delightful inn has a wealth of exposed beams and an inviting log fire. The charming bedrooms are in a converted barn and have modern facilities. Delicious lunches and dinners are served in the cosy bar.

Facilities 6 en suite (1 fmly) (3 GF) ⊗ in bedrooms TVB tea/coffee Cen ht No coaches Dinner Last d 9.15pm **Prices** S £40; D £60✱ LB

FROME
MAP 04 ST74

★★★ 🍴 Inn

Fox & Hounds

Bulls Quarry Rd, Tytherington BA11 5BN ☎ 01373 473902
Dir *From Town Centre, go up Bath Rd to A361, left at rdbt, turn right. B&B on left*

This traditional inn offers friendly hospitality and comfortable accommodation. It is convenient for the countryside and within driving distance of Wells and Glastonbury. Bedrooms are well equipped and good choices can be made at dinner, where Thai and Indonesian specialities are offered along with traditional fare.

Facilities 4 en suite ⊗ in bedrooms ⊗ in dining room ⊗ in lounges TVB tea/coffee Licensed Cen ht Dinner Last d 9pm **Parking** 25 **Notes** Closed 25 Dec

England

FROME continued

◆◆◆◆◆

Lullington House

Lullington BA11 2PG ☎ 01373 831406 🖹 01373 831406
e-mail info@lullingtonhouse.co.uk
web www.lullingtonhouse.co.uk
Dir 2.5m N of Frome. Off A36 into Lullington

Built in 1866 as a rectory, this stone country house stands in extensive grounds and gardens. The spacious, comfortable accommodation comprises two double bedrooms with period furniture and four-poster beds, plus modern facilities. Guests share one table in the very attractive breakfast room.

Facilities 3 en suite ⊗ TVB tea/coffee ✗ Cen ht No children No coaches **Prices** D £80 **Parking** 4 **Notes** Closed Xmas & New Year ⊛

◆◆◆◆◆ 🍴

The Place To Stay

Knoll Hill Farm, Trudoxhill BA11 5DP
☎ 01373 836266 & 07976 226206
e-mail theplacetostaykhf@btinternet.com
web www.theplacetostayuk.com
Dir Off A361 between Frome & Shepton Mallet

Conveniently located for the attractive countryside and within easy distance of Bath, Wells and Glastonbury, this former barn has been tastefully converted to traditional buildings with contemporary design and character by the present owners. Separate to the owner's accommodation the facilities include all ground floor bedrooms which are spacious, comfortable and well equipped. Breakfast is very well cooked and of excellent choice, using quality local and homemade items, served at separate guest tables in the conservatory breakfast room where guests can take in far reaching views to the Longleat estate. Ample secure parking, country walks and a Boules arena are added facilities at this pleasant and friendly guest house.

Facilities 5 en suite (5 GF) ⊗ TVB tea/coffee ✗ Cen ht No children 16yrs No coaches Boules Pit **Prices** D £85-£105✳ **Parking** 10 **Notes** ⊛

◆◆◆◆ 🍺

The Talbot 15th Century Coaching Inn

Mells BA11 3PN ☎ 01373 812254 🖹 01373 813599
e-mail roger@talbotinn.com
web www.talbotinn.com
Dir 3m W of Frome in Mells village

Nestled in the quiet village of Mells, this 15th-century coaching inn has a wealth of character. Bedrooms are all individual in style, comfortable and well equipped. Two have four-poster beds. The restaurant and bar areas retain many original features and offer a good selection of wines and fine ales, along with an interesting selection of freshly prepared food.

Facilities 8 en suite ⊗ in bedrooms ⊗ in dining room TVB tea/coffee Direct dial from bedrooms Garden with Boule court Dinner Last d 9.15pm **Prices** S £75✳ **LB Conf** Max 16 Board 16 **Parking** 10

GLASTONBURY   MAP 04 ST53

See also **Butleigh, Catcott & Somerton**

◆◆◆◆ 🍴

Cradlebridge Farm (ST477385)

BA16 9SD ☎ 01458 831827 Mrs Tinney
Dir A39 S from Glastonbury, after Morlands factory 2nd right, Cradlebridge Farm signed 1m on left

Guests regularly return to Cradlebridge, a 200-acre dairy farm with pleasant views over the Somerset Levels. The relaxing farmhouse has spacious, comfortably furnished bedrooms, and the farm's own sausages feature at breakfast around a communal table.

Facilities 2 annexe en suite (2 fmly) (2 GF) ⊗ TVB tea/coffee ✗ Cen ht No children 3yrs 200 acres dairy **Prices** S £35; D £55✳ **Parking** 6 **Notes** ⊛

◆◆◆◆

Greenacres

Barrow Ln, North Wootton BA4 4HL ☎ 01749 890497
Dir 4m NE of Glastonbury. Off A39 at Browns garden centre, follow campsite signs. Or off A361 at Steanbow, follow campsite signs

Quietly located within sight of Glastonbury Tor, this friendly home offers pleasant accommodation. The bright and comfortable bedrooms share adjacent bath and shower. A separate lounge is provided. Breakfast is served in the conservatory and there is a well-tended garden.

Facilities 2 rms ⊗ TVB tea/coffee ✗ Cen ht TVL No children No coaches **Prices** D £50-£60✳ **Parking** 4 **Notes** ⊛

continued

◆◆◆◆
Parsnips B&B
99 Bere Ln BA6 8BE ☎ 01458 835599
e-mail parsnips.glastonbury@virgin.net
Dir Opp Rural Life Museum at junct Bere Ln & Chilkwell St

Located just a short walk from the town centre and near to the Tor, this accommodation is clean, comfortable and homely. Bedrooms are cosy and well equipped and there is a lounge for guest use. Freshly prepared breakfast is served in the conservatory dining room. There is a pleasant garden with a seating area for relaxing during those warmer months.

Facilities 3 en suite ⊗ TVB tea/coffee 🐾 Cen ht No coaches
Prices S fr £40; d fr £60✳ **Parking** 3 **Notes** 🏵

◆◆◆◆
Wearyall Hill House
78 The Roman Way BA6 8AD ☎ 01458 835510
e-mail enquiries@wearyallhillhouse.co.uk
web www.wearyallhillhouse.co.uk
Dir A39 from Glastonbury to Street. After rdbt (B&Q on right) 1st left onto Roman Way, house 8th on left

Set on an elevated position on the edge of town, and close to places of interest, this delightful late Victorian residence affords sweeping views. Restored to its former glory by the present owners, the property is appropriately decorated and furnished with many extra facilities. The sumptuous breakfasts served in the attractive dining room are a highlight.

Facilities 3 en suite ⊗ STV TVB tea/coffee 🐾 Cen ht No children 10yrs **Parking** 8 **Notes** 🏵

◆◆◆◆
Wood Lane House
Butleigh BA6 8TR ☎ 01458 850354
Dir Off B3151 or B3153 to Butleigh, opp Rose & Portcullis pub

Surrounded by very pleasant gardens and farmland, Wood Lane House offers a relaxing base for visiting the many attractions of the area. The owners provide a warm welcome and many guests return regularly. Breakfast, served at one large table, is an enjoyable start to the day.

Facilities 3 en suite (2 GF) ⊗ TVB tea/coffee 🐾 Cen ht TVL No coaches **Prices** S £40; D £55 **Parking** 3 **Notes** Closed Dec-Jan 🏵

◆◆◆
Apple
25 Norbins Rd BA6 9JF ☎ 01458 834547
e-mail applebnb@ukonline.co.uk
Dir From St Johns Church on High St onto Archers Way, left onto St Edmunds Rd, left onto Norbins Rd, B&B 50yds on right   *continued*

Located in a residential area just a short walk from High St, the atmosphere here is relaxed and the friendly hosts give a warm welcome. Pictures on the walls reflect the proprietors' interest in music. Bedrooms are light and homely, and a continental breakfast is served in the cosy conservatory-dining room, which looks out onto the rear garden.

Facilities 3 rms (1 en suite) (1 GF) ⊗ TVB tea/coffee 🐾 Licensed Cen ht No children 12yrs **Prices** D £50-£55✳ **Parking** 2 **Notes** 🏵

◆◆◆ ❧
Barrow Farm (ST553416)
North Wootton BA4 4HL
☎ 01749 890245 🖳 01749 890245 Mrs White
Dir A361, turn right after Pilton, onto North Wootton, at T-junct in village turn left, house 1.5m on left

This 15th-century working farm is pleasantly located in an attractive setting. Welcoming, well-maintained bedrooms are provided and you are made to feel at home in the relaxed and friendly atmosphere. The lounge and dining room are both comfortable, and fresh, local produce and good cooking all contribute to a memorable stay.

Facilities 3 rms (1 fmly) ⊗ in dining room ⊗ in 1 lounge TVB tea/coffee 🐾 TVL 150 acres working dairy Dinner Last d 9am **Parking** 4 **Notes** Closed Dec-Jan 🏵

◆◆◆
The Priestess House at Pilgrims B & B ◇
12/13 Norbins Rd BA6 9JE ☎ 01458 834722
e-mail pilgrimsbb@hotmail.com
web www.pilgrimsbb.co.uk
Dir From St Johns Church on High St onto Archers Way, left onto St Edmunds Rd, right onto Norbins Rd, B&B opp junct

Just a short walk from the town centre, this comfortable accommodation has two rooms on the ground floor. Breakfast is served around one large table in the kitchen-dining room. There is also a lounge and a small garden to relax in during warm weather. Guests are invited to enjoy the homely environment.

Facilities 4 rms (3 en suite) (1 fmly) (2 GF) ⊗ in bedrooms ⊗ in dining room ⊗ in lounges tea/coffee 🐾 Cen ht TVL No coaches **Prices** S £30-£35; D £55-£60✳ **LB Notes** 🏵

◆◆◆
25 Leg of Mutton Road ◇
BA6 8HH ☎ 01458 831886
e-mail ammonmarie@yahoo.co.uk
Dir At top of High St turn left onto Wells Rd. Take 2nd right, B&B is on the right

Located in a residential area, this refurbished accommodation is well situated for touring Somerset and Wiltshire. The host is friendly and welcoming, the atmosphere is relaxed. A continental breakfast is served in the homely kitchen-dining room around a communal table.

Facilities 2 rms ⊗ tea/coffee 🐾 Cen ht No children 10yrs No coaches **Prices** S £26-£28; D £50-£54✳ **Notes** 🏵

England

GLASTONBURY continued

◆◆

Melrose

17 Bere Ln BA6 8BD ☎ 01458 832016 & 07768 634392
e-mail deeperry@globalnet.co.uk
Dir On A361

A friendly welcome is given at this family home, which is within strolling distance of the town centre. Bedrooms are comfortably furnished and the lounge-dining room looks out over the garden to Glastonbury Abbey.

Facilities 2 en suite (2 fmly) ⊘ TVB tea/coffee ✖ Cen ht TVL No children 8yrs No coaches **Parking** available **Notes** ⊜

U

Bay Tree House

16 Norbins Rd BA6 9JF ☎ 01458 834972 📄 01458 834972
e-mail ssanicho@aol.co.uk
Dir M5 junct 23 onto A39 into Glastonbury, continue along High St. Turn 1st left and 1st left again

At the time of going to press the rating for this establishment had not been confirmed. Please check the AA website www.theAA.com for up-to-date information.

Facilities 2 rms ⊘ STV TVB tea/coffee Cen ht No coaches **Notes** Closed 24 Dec-1 Jan ⊜

U

Hedgehog House B & B ◇

3 Wells Rd BA6 9DN ☎ 01458 833067 & 07835 522582
e-mail alanowarr@hotmail.com
Dir Turn left at top of Glastonbury High St, 1st house on left

At the time of going to press the rating for this establishment had not been confirmed. Please check the AA website www.theAA.com for up-to-date information.

Facilities 4 rms (1 en suite) (1 pri facs) (1 fmly) (1 GF) ⊘ Cen ht TVL No coaches Yoga room Shiatsu Dojo Treatments tuition Dinner Last d am **Prices** S £25-£35; D £55-£70✳ LB **Parking** 2 **Notes** ⊜

U

St Michael's Cottages ◇

30 Hillhead BA6 8AW ☎ 07745 840707
Dir From High St continue to mini-rdbt (A361), left up Fishers Hill then sharp right onto Hillhead.

At the time of going to press the rating for this establishment had not been confirmed. Please check the AA website www.theAA.com for up-to-date information.

Facilities 1 rms (1 pri facs) ⊘ TVB tea/coffee ✖ Cen ht No children **Prices** S £28.50; D £53✳ **Notes** ⊜

HIGHBRIDGE

MAP 04 ST34

◆◆◆◆

Greenwood Lodge

76 Main Rd, West Huntspill TA9 3QU
☎ 01278 795886 📄 01278 795886
e-mail info@greenwood-lodge.co.uk
web www.greenwood-lodge.co.uk
Dir On A38 in West Huntspill village, between Orchard Inn & Sundowner Hotel

Set within 2 acres of land, this 18th-century former farmhouse and family home offers comfortable accommodation in a friendly environment. Breakfast, featuring home-made preserves, is served in the dining room and home-cooked dinners are available by arrangement. There is a lounge for relaxation and the family dog makes all you feel welcome.

Facilities 7 rms (6 en suite) (1 pri facs) (3 fmly) (1 GF) ⊘ in bedrooms ⊘ in dining room TVB tea/coffee Licensed Cen ht TVL No coaches Treatment room for alternative therapies Dinner Last d 6pm **Prices** S £42.50; D £60✳ LB **Conf** Max 30 Thtr 30 Class 20 Board 12 Del from £60 ✳ **Parking** 8

HINTON ST GEORGE

MAP 04 ST41

◆◆◆◆ ▥

The Lord Poulett Arms

High St TA17 8SE ☎ 01460 73149
e-mail steveandmichelle@lordpoulettarms.com
web www.lordpoulettarms.com
Dir Off A303 into village

A quintessential thatched village inn offering comfortable, well-appointed accommodation in the heart of the village. The regularly changing menu offers a range of home-cooked dishes available at

continued

lunch and dinner. Public areas and bedrooms have been refurbished to high standards. A beer garden and private meeting/dining room are available.

Facilities 4 rms (2 en suite) (2 pri facs) (1 fmly) ⊘ in bedrooms ⊘ in area of dining room ⊘ in 1 lounge TVB tea/coffee ✘ Cen ht Boule piste Dinner Last d 9pm **Prices** S £48; D £72✱ **Conf** Max 100 Class 14 Board 14 **Parking** 10

ILCHESTER
MAP 04 ST52

◆◆◆◆

Ilchester Arms Hotel

Church St BA22 8LN ☎ 01935 840220 ▤ 01935 841353

Dir *Ilchester exit from A303, turn left at rdbt to Ilchester. Hotel situated on village square*

Located in the centre of Ilchester, the accommodation combines spacious, very well-equipped bedrooms with friendly hospitality. Downstairs, you can choose from a lively bar or a more-relaxed bistro area where delicious home-cooked meals are freshly prepared.

Facilities 7 en suite (3 fmly) ⊘ in 5 bedrooms ⊘ in dining room ⊘ in 1 lounge TVB tea/coffee Direct dial from bedrooms ✘ Cen ht Dinner Last d 9.30pm **Prices** S £60-£65; D £75-£80✱ **LB** **Conf** Max 35 Thtr 35 Class 30 Board 25 **Parking** 22 **Notes** Closed 26 Dec

ILMINSTER
MAP 04 ST31
See also **Chard**

◆◆◆◆◆ ▤ ⊜

Old Rectory

Cricket Malherbie TA19 0PW
☎ 01460 54364 ▤ 01460 57374
e-mail info@malherbie.co.uk
web www.malherbie.co.uk

Dir *2.5m S of Ilminster. A303 onto A358 S towards Chard, after Donyatt left towards Ilminster, right to Cricket Malherbie, Old Rectory on left*

This stylishly refurbished thatched stone cottage has a peaceful location surrounded by attractive gardens. Unobtrusive yet high levels of hospitality and service are offered, and you are encouraged to enjoy the house-party atmosphere. Bedrooms are individually furnished and provide beautiful views. Dinner is available by arrangement and features only the finest fresh ingredients.

Facilities 5 en suite ⊘ TVB tea/coffee ✘ Licensed Cen ht No children 16yrs No coaches Dinner Last d 10am **Prices** S £65; D £95-£105✱ **LB** **Parking** 5 **Notes** Closed 24-26 Dec Civ Wed 25

KEYNSHAM
MAP 04 ST66

◆◆◆◆

Grasmere Court Hotel

22-24 Bath Rd BS31 1SN
☎ 0117 986 2662 ▤ 0117 986 2762
e-mail grasmerecourt@aol.com
web www.grasmerecourthotel.co.uk
Dir *On B3116 just off A4*

The very friendly, family-run establishment is located between Bath and Bristol. Bedrooms vary in size and one has a four-poster bed. A comfortable lounge and a well-stocked bar are available, and good-value, freshly prepared food is served in the attractive dining room.

Facilities 16 en suite (2 fmly) (4 GF) ⊘ STV TVB tea/coffee Direct dial from bedrooms ✘ Licensed Cen ht TVL No coaches Dinner Last d 7.45pm **Prices** S £52-£65; D £70-£90✱ **LB** **Conf** Max 30 Thtr 30 Class 20 Board 20 **Parking** 18

KILVE
MAP 03 ST14

◆◆◆◆ ◀▮

Hood Arms Hotel

TA5 1EA ☎ 01278 741210 ▤ 01278 741477
e-mail easonhood@aol.com
Dir *12m W of Bridgwater on A39, halfway between Bridgwater & Minehead*

Located in the village of Kilve, this popular 17th-century inn offers well-equipped bedrooms with a good range of facilities. A good range of tasty dishes is available on the blackboard menus in the beamed bars.

Facilities 8 en suite (1 pri facs) 4 annexe en suite (4 fmly) (2 GF) ⊘ TVB tea/coffee Direct dial from bedrooms Cen ht TVL Dinner Last d 9.15pm **Prices** S £45-£65; D £72-£85✱ **LB** **Conf** Max 20 Class 20 Board 16 Del from £75 ✱ **Parking** 12

England

LANGPORT
MAP 04 ST42

◆◆◆ ◖▣

The Old Pound Inn

Aller TA10 0RA ☎ 01458 250469 🖶 01458 250469

Dir On A372 in village centre

Situated in the charming village of Aller, 2m from Langport, this popular inn was once a cider house and now provides comfortable, well-equipped accommodation. With a choice of bars and dining areas, and menus featuring tempting dishes, there is something for everyone. There is also an interesting wine list.

Facilities 6 en suite (1 fmly) ⊗ in bedrooms ⊗ in dining room TVB tea/coffee ✖ Cen ht Pool Table Dinner Last d 9.45pm **Prices** S £40; D £65✱ **Conf** Max 100 Thtr 100 Class 50 Board 50 **Parking** 30

MARTOCK
MAP 04 ST41

◆◆◆◆

Higher Farm

Bladon Hill, Kingsbury Episcopi TA12 6BJ ☎ 01935 823099
e-mail boltonali@aol.com
Dir 2m NW of Martock. Off B3165 to Kingsbury Episcopi, left at Wyndham Arms, farm on right

Located in the scenic village of Kingsbury Episcopi, Higher Farm provides comfortable accommodation with a relaxed and friendly atmosphere. Breakfast is served in the pleasant dining room, which opens onto the rear garden and patio. Two pubs serving evening meals are just a 5-minute walk in either direction.

Facilities 2 en suite (2 fmly) ⊗ TVB tea/coffee ✖ Cen ht No coaches **Prices** S £35; D £50 **Parking** 6 **Notes** ⊚

MINEHEAD
MAP 03 SS94

See also **Dunster**

◆◆◆◆

Glendower House

30-32 Tregonwell Rd TA24 5DU
☎ 01643 707144 🖶 01643 708719
e-mail info@glendower-house.co.uk
web www.glendower-house.co.uk
Dir A39 into Minehead, last exit at minirdbt, 200yds right by school onto Ponsford Rd & Tregonwell Rd

The family-run Glendower House is near the seafront, harbour and town centre. A friendly atmosphere prevails, and there are comfortable bedrooms and smart bathrooms. Public areas are spacious and you can relax in the garden in the summer. Ample parking is a bonus.

Facilities 12 en suite (2 GF) ⊗ TVB tea/coffee ✖ Cen ht No coaches **Prices** S £35-£45; D £60-£75✱ **Parking** 14 **Notes** Closed mid Dec-mid Feb

◆◆◆◆

Kenella House

7 Tregonwell Rd TA24 5DT
☎ 01643 703128 & 07710 889079 🖶 01643 703128
e-mail steveandsandy@kenellahouse.freeserve.co.uk
web www.kenellahouse.co.uk
Dir Off A39 onto Townsend Rd & right onto Ponsford Rd & Tregonwell Rd

A warm welcome and relaxed atmosphere are found at Kenella House. Located close to the town centre, the guest house is also convenient for walkers (heated boot cupboard available) and visitors to the steam railway. The well-maintained bedrooms are very comfortable and have many extras. Home-cooked dinners, available

continued

by arrangement, and hearty breakfasts are served in the smart dining room.

Facilities 6 en suite (1 GF) ⊗ TVB tea/coffee ✈ Cen ht No children 14yrs No coaches Dinner Last d am same day **Prices** D £50-£70✳ LB **Parking** 8 **Notes** Closed 23 Dec-2 Jan ⊛

◆◆◆ ⊟

The Old Ship Aground ◇

Quay St TA24 5UL ☎ 01643 702087 🖥 01643 709066
e-mail enquiries@oldshipaground.co.uk
Dir From town centre along seafront towards harbour

Located at the edge of the harbour and enjoying views of the bay, the Old Ship Aground offers traditional hospitality within a laid-back atmosphere. Bedrooms are spacious and thoughtfully equipped. Bar food is available and breakfast is served in the large dining/ function room.

Facilities 12 en suite (3 fmly) ⊗ in 5 bedrooms ⊗ in area of dining room ⊗ in 1 lounge TV available tea/coffee Cen ht TVL Pool Table Dinner Last d 9.30pm **Prices** S £25-£35; D £50-£55✳ **Conf** Max 60 Thtr 60 Class 60 Board 30 **Parking** 10

NETHER STOWEY   MAP 04 ST13

 Premier Collection

◆◆◆◆◆ ⊜

Castle of Comfort Country House

TA5 1LE ☎ 01278 741264 🖥 01278 741144
e-mail reception@castle-of-comfort.co.uk
web www.castle-of-comfort.co.uk
Dir On A39 1.3m W of Nether Stowey on left

Dating in part from the 16th century, this former inn is situated on the northern slopes of the Quantock Hills in an Area of Outstanding Natural Beauty. Bedrooms and bathrooms are well equipped while the public rooms are smart and comfortable. The delightful gardens and a heated swimming pool are available in summer, and the cuisine involves imaginative dinners.

Facilities 5 en suite 1 annexe en suite (1 fmly) (1 GF) ⊗ TVB tea/coffee Direct dial from bedrooms Licensed Cen ht No coaches ⚲ Stabling with access to bridle paths and hunting Dinner Last d noon **Prices** S £38-£84; D £95-£129✳ **Conf** Max 20 Thtr 20 Class 20 Board 12 Del from £29.50 ✳ **Parking** 10 **Notes** Closed 24 Dec-2 Jan

◆◆◆◆

Trevarrick House

5 The Pavement TA3 6LX ☎ 01823 491319 🖥 01823 491319
e-mail mail@trevarrickhouse.co.uk
Dir Off A361 in village centre

Located in a pleasant village, Trevarrick House is a good base for exploring central Somerset. Both of the friendly proprietors are artists and their impressive work can be seen around the property. A delicious home-cooked dinner is available by arrangement, or you can opt for one of the nearby inns.

Facilities 2 en suite ⊗ TVB tea/coffee ✈ Cen ht No coaches Dinner Last d 10am **Parking** 2 **Notes** Closed 20 Dec-2 Jan ⊛

NORTON ST PHILIP   MAP 04 ST75

◆◆◆◆

The Plaine

Bell Hill BA2 7LT ☎ 01373 834723 🖥 01373 834101
e-mail theplaine@easynet.co.uk
Dir On A366 at village x-rds

Only 15 minutes from Bath, this charming 16th-century home provides comfortable accommodation. All rooms have four-poster beds and have many thoughtful extra touches. Many good inns are within strolling distance and offer good dining options. Breakfast is served around a large table in the charming dining room, which has exposed beams and a stone fireplace.

Facilities 3 en suite (1 GF) ⊗ TVB tea/coffee ✈ Cen ht No coaches **Parking** 5 **Notes** Closed 24 Dec-2 Jan

PORLOCK   MAP 03 SS84

★★★★ ◉◉◉ **Restaurant with Rooms**

Andrews on the Weir

Porlock Weir TA24 8PB ☎ 01643 863300 🖥 01643 863311
e-mail information@andrewsontheweir.co.uk
web www.andrewsontheweir.co.uk
Dir A39 from Minehead to Porlock, through village, 1st right signed Harbour (Porlock Weir) 1.5m

Enjoying a delightful elevated position overlooking Porlock Bay, Andrews on the Weir is furnished and decorated in country house style. Bedrooms are spacious and comfortable; one room boasts a four-poster bed. The sitting room/bar is elegant and a log fire creates a cosy atmosphere. One of the highlights of a stay here is the choice of imaginative and innovative dishes available in the restaurant.

Facilities 5 en suite TVB tea/coffee Licensed No children 12yrs No coaches Dinner Last d 2.30pm **Parking** 6 **Notes** Closed Jan & Mon, Tue

See advertisement on page 445

England

PORLOCK continued

★★★★ Bed & Breakfast

The Cottage ◇

High St TA24 8PU ☎ 01643 862996 📠 01643 862996
e-mail cottageporlock@aol.com
web www.cottageporlock.co.uk
Dir on A39

One of the oldest houses, this cottage is located right in the heart of this ancient village, ideally placed to enjoy village life, exploring Exmoor and walking the South West coastal path. Bedrooms are well equipped and there is a comfortable lounge solely for guest use. Breakfast is served in the pleasant dining room at the front of the house.

Facilities 3 en suite (1 fmly) ⊛ TVB tea/coffee ✈ Cen ht No coaches Dinner Last d 10am **Prices** S £30; D £50-£60✴ **LB Parking** 2 **Notes** ☺

RUDGE   MAP 04 ST85

◆◆◆◆ ◨

Full Moon Hotel

BA11 2QF ☎ 01373 830936 📠 01373 831366
e-mail info@thefullmoon.co.uk
Dir Off A36 into village centre

This quaint village inn is very popular for its extensive range of food. Most of the modern, well-equipped accommodation is on the ground and first floors of two purpose-built annexes; there are some cottage-style suites and two have easier access. Facilities include a fitness centre with swimming pool, a function room and a skittle alley.

Facilities 16 en suite (2 fmly) (4 GF) ⊛ in bedrooms ⊛ in dining room STV TVB tea/coffee Direct dial from bedrooms Cen ht TVL ➘ Gymnasium Dinner Last d 9.30pm **Conf** Thtr 40 Class 20 Board 20 **Parking** 50

SHAPWICK   MAP 04 ST43

★★★★ Bed & Breakfast

Church Cottage

Station Rd TA7 9NH ☎ 01458 210904
e-mail caroline@shapwick.fsnet.co.uk
web www.profileskincare.co.uk/bnb/bnb.html
Dir M5 junct 23, onto A361 into Shapwick, in main street by church.

This four hundred year old cottage has been sensitively restored to offer accommodation with charm and character. Located next to the church

continued

in this tranquil village, there is a pretty rear garden. The room in the main house has a large ensuite bathroom and thoughtful extras, such as a fresh flower and hot water bottle in winter, makes guests feel well cared for. Although there are no beverage facilities within the room, the host is more than happy to prepare and serve a tea or coffee tray. Breakfast, which offers a selection of hot dishes, features local produce (whenever possible) and is served around a large farmhouse style table.

Facilities 1 en suite 1 annexe en suite (1 GF) ⊛ TV1B tea/coffee ✈ Cen ht No children No coaches Dinner **Prices** D £60-£75✴ **LB Notes** ☺

SHEPTON MALLET   MAP 04 ST64

★★★★ Bed & Breakfast

Freedom Cottage

Cumhill BA4 4BG
☎ 01749 890188 & 07729 801130 📠 01749 890188
e-mail bodeefrost@aol.com

This recently developed accommodation is smart, light and airy and located in a tranquil village, ideal for exploring Somerset & Wiltshire. Bedrooms are spacious & are individually styled. There are two lounges, one an open plan mezzanine area, the other a cosy television room. Breakfast, featuring local produce, is served around a family style table, from where the hosts can be seen preparing dishes in the adjoining kitchen. There is a garden to enjoy during warmer weather and a delightful view of the village church from the rear terrace.

Facilities 2 en suite ⊛ TVB tea/coffee ✈ Cen ht TVL No children 12yrs No coaches **Parking** 9 **Notes** Closed End Nov-13 Jan ☺

◆◆◆◆

Cannards Grave Farmhouse

Cannards Grave BA4 4LY ☎ 01749 347091 📠 01749 347091
e-mail sue@cannardsgravefarmhouse.co.uk
web www.cannardsgravefarmhouse.co.uk
Dir On A37 between Shepton Mallet & The Bath & West Showground, 100yds from Highwayman pub towards showground on left

Convenient for the Bath and Wells showground, this 17th-century farmhouse provides thoughtfully equipped en suite bedrooms. There is also a well-furnished lounge. The proprietors offer warm hospitality and breakfast, served in the pleasant conservatory, includes the option of delicious croissants.

Facilities 4 en suite (1 fmly) ⊛ TVB tea/coffee ✈ Cen ht TVL No children 5yrs No coaches **Prices** S £40-£50; D £50-£65✴ **Parking** 6 **Notes** ☺

◆◆◆◆ ⇔ ◨

Thatched Cottage

63-67 Charlton Rd BA4 5QF
☎ 01749 342058 📠 01749 343265
e-mail enquiries@thatchedcottage.info
web www.thatchedcottage.info
Dir 0.6m E of town centre on A361

This delightful Grade II listed 17th-century hostelry has been renovated and upgraded while retaining its original character. The modern accommodation is well equipped and the public areas are very attractively appointed. The inn offers a good choice of food.

continued

Facilities 8 en suite ⊗ in bedrooms ⊗ in dining room STV TVB tea/coffee Direct dial from bedrooms ✖ Cen ht TVL Dinner Last d 9.30pm **Prices** S £72.95-£97.95; D £95-£135✳ **LB** **Conf** Max 45 Thtr 45 Class 35 Board 30 **Parking** 40 **Notes** Closed 1-3 Jan

◆◆◆

The Abbey Barn

Doulting BA4 4QD ☎ 01749 880321
e-mail abbeybarn@btconnect.com
Dir 2m E of Shepton Mallet on A361 in Doulting

Located in the pretty village of Doulting, this 19th-century inn retains many original features. The attractive public areas are enhanced by memorabilia and roaring log fires, which create an inviting atmosphere. Bedrooms have period furniture and modern shower rooms.

Facilities 3 en suite ⊗ in bedrooms ⊗ in dining room TVB tea/coffee ✖ Licensed No children No coaches Skittle Alley **Prices** S £40-£50; D £60-£70✳ **LB** **Parking** 10

◆◆◆

Portman House

Pylle-On-The Fosse BA4 6TA ☎ 01749 830150
e-mail jmooney@portmanarms.freeserve.co.uk
Dir On A37, 2m S of Shepton Mallett

A traditional inn located just a short distance from the Bath and West Showground. The bedrooms and bathrooms are well decorated and have power showers. A good selection of home-made dishes is available including a number of popular blackboard specials.

Facilities 4 en suite (4 GF) ⊗ TVB tea/coffee ✖ Cen ht No children 14yrs No coaches Dinner Last d by arrangement **Prices** D £50✳ **Parking** 10 **Notes** Closed 24-27 Dec

SIMONSBATH   MAP 03 SS73

◆◆◆◆

Barkham

Sandyway EX36 3LU ☎ 01643 831370 ◈ 01643 831370
e-mail adie.exmoor@btinternet.com
web www.exmoor-vacations.co.uk
Dir 4m S of Simonsbath. Off A361 through North Molton, onto moor signed Sandyway, left at x-rds signed Simonsbath, 400yds right

Tucked away in a secret wooded valley at the top of Exmoor, this wonderfully restored Georgian farmhouse is set in 12 acres of pasture with streams and waterfalls. Bedrooms are comfortable and attractively furnished. Traditional breakfasts are served in the impressive oak-panelled dining room. There is also a spacious drawing room. Barkham is the spirtual home of the Two Moors Music Festival.

Facilities 3 rms (2 en suite) (1 pri facs) ⊗ ✖ Licensed Cen ht TVL No children 12yrs No coaches ⚮ Tree house **Prices** S fr £35; D £70-£76✳ **Parking** 6

SOMERTON   MAP 04 ST42

Premier Collection

◆◆◆◆◆

Lydford House

Lydford-on-Fosse TA11 7BU ☎ 01963 240217
e-mail lynn@jamesribbons.demon.co.uk
web www.lydfordhousesomerset.co.uk
Dir At junct A37 & B3153

Built in 1860, this Victorian residence now provides comfortable, elegant accommodation, with part of the house being used as an antique shop. The spacious bedrooms are attractively decorated and have quality furnishings. The sitting-dining area is stylishly furnished and breakfast is served around one large table.

Facilities 4 en suite ⊗ TVB tea/coffee ✖ Cen ht No coaches **Prices** S £50-£60; D £60-£75✳ **Parking** 35

England

SOMERTON continued

◆◆◆◆ 🍃

Lower Farm (ST527309)

Kingweston TA11 6BA
☎ 01458 223237 🖷 01458 223276 Mrs Sedgman
e-mail lowerfarm@btconnect.com
web www.lowerfarm.net
Dir 3m NE of Somerton. On B3153 in Kingweston

Set in the heart of Somerset, this Grade II listed stone farmhouse has been home to the same family for several generations. Furnished in cottage style, the cosy bedrooms combine period charm with modern comforts and have spectacular rural views. Guests are served a hearty breakfast in the Georgian dining room.

Facilities 3 rms (2 en suite) (1 pri facs) (1 fmly) ⊘ FTV TVB tea/coffee ✗ Cen ht 500 acres Arable **Prices** S £45-£60; D £60-£65✱ **Conf** Max 36 Thtr 36 Class 30 Board 20 **Parking** 8 **Notes** Closed Xmas/New Year

◆◆◆◆

Somerton Court Country House

TA11 7AH ☎ 01458 274694 🖷 01458 274693
e-mail owen@newopaul.freeserve.co.uk
web www.somertoncourt.co.uk
Dir B3151 to Somerton & follow B&B signs

Dating back to the 17th century and set in extensive gardens and grounds, Somerton Court Country House is a tranquil haven away from the pressures of modern life. The comfortable bedrooms have lovely views, and breakfast is served in a delightful dining room that overlooks the gardens.

Facilities 6 en suite (2 fmly) ⊘ TVB tea/coffee ✗ Licensed Cen ht Riding **Conf** Max 150 Thtr 200 Class 150 **Parking** 30 **Notes** Closed Xmas & New Year Civ Wed 150

◆◆◆◆

Stowford House

Charlton Adam TA11 7AT
☎ 01458 223717 🖷 01458 223940
e-mail harperr@totalise.co.uk
Dir Off A37 into Charlton Adam, house in village centre

Stowford House is a delightful conversion of a Victorian Methodist chapel and the village school. Centrally situated in peaceful Charlton Adam, it offers charming accommodation and a friendly atmosphere. Bedrooms are cosy and equipped with modern facilities, and the public rooms retain many stunning original features.

Facilities 2 en suite (1 GF) ⊘ in bedrooms TVB tea/coffee Cen ht No children 7yrs No coaches **Prices** S £35; D £60✱ **Parking** 2 **Notes** Closed Xmas ⊛

◆◆◆ ⊜ 📶

The Devonshire Arms

Long Sutton TA10 9LP ☎ 01458 241271 🖷 01458 241037
e-mail mail@thedevonshirearms.com
web www.thedevonshirearms.com
Dir Off A303 onto A372 at Podimore rdbt. After 4m, left onto B3165, signed Martock and Long Sutton

This inn has undergone a dramatic refurbishment to provide stylish public rooms and accommodation. The bedrooms have contemporary furnishings and the spacious public areas are comfortable. A choice of ales, wines and spirits, and interesting cuisine complete the picture in the bar-restaurant.

Facilities 7 rms (6 en suite) (1 pri facs) 2 annexe en suite (1 fmly) (2 GF) ⊘ in bedrooms ⊘ in dining room TVB tea/coffee ✗ Cen ht Dinner Last d 9.30pm **Conf** Thtr 30 Board 20 **Parking** 6

STANTON DREW

MAP 04 ST56

◆◆◆◆

Greenlands

BS39 4ES ☎ 01275 333487 🖷 01275 331211
Dir A37 onto B3130, on right before Stanton Drew Garage

Situated near the ancient village of Stanton Drew in the heart of the Chew Valley, Greenlands is convenient for Bristol Airport and Bath, Bristol and Wells. There are comfortable, well-equipped bedrooms and a downstairs lounge, though breakfast is the highlight of any stay here.

Facilities 4 en suite ⊘ in bedrooms ⊘ in dining room STV TVB tea/coffee Cen ht TVL No children 12yrs No coaches **Parking** 8 **Notes** ⊛

◆◆◆◆ 🍃

Valley Farm (ST595631)

Sandy Ln BS39 4EL
☎ 01275 332723 & 07799 768161 🖷 01275 332723
Mr & Mrs Keel
e-mail highmeade.gardens@virgin.net
Dir Off B3130 into Stanton Drew, right onto Sandy Ln

Located on a quiet country lane, Valley Farm offers relaxing and friendly accommodation. All bedrooms are comfortable and well equipped, and each room has pleasant views over the surrounding countryside. Breakfast is served around a communal table in the dining room, and although dinner is not available the village pub is just a stroll away.

continued

England

Valley Farm

Facilities 3 en suite (1 fmly) (1 GF) ⊗ TVB tea/coffee ✖ Cen ht TVL
No children 8yrs 25 acres **Parking** 6 **Notes** Closed 24-26 Dec ⊛

STAPLE FITZPAINE   MAP 04 ST21

♦♦♦♦ ⊜ ◼

Greyhound Inn

TA3 5SP ☎ 01823 480227 ▤ 01823 481117
e-mail info@the-greyhoundinn.fsbusiness.co.uk
web www.the-greyhoundinn.fsbusiness.co.uk
Dir *Off A358 into village*

Set in an Area of Outstanding Natural Beauty, this picturesque village
inn with its flagstone floors and open fires was formerly a hunting
lodge. An imaginative choice of freshly prepared dishes is offered in
the bars and the more formal restaurant. The delightful bedrooms are
comfortable and well equipped with many extra facilities.

Facilities 4 en suite ⊗ in bedrooms ⊗ in dining room TVB tea/coffee
Direct dial from bedrooms ✖ Cen ht No children 12yrs No coaches Pool
Table Dinner Last d 9pm **Prices** S fr £55; d fr £80✱ **Conf** Max 60
Thtr 60 Class 30 Board 20 **Parking** 60

STOGUMBER   MAP 03 ST03

♦♦♦ ◼

Wick House ◇

Brook St TA4 3SZ ☎ 01984 656422
e-mail sheila@wickhouse.fsbusiness.co.uk
web www.wickhouse.fsbusiness.co.uk
Dir *Off A358 into village, left at x-rds, Wick House 3rd on left*

Facilities 5 en suite (1 GF) ⊗ TVB tea/coffee ✖ Licensed Cen ht TVL
No coaches Stairlift Dinner Last d 2pm **Prices** S £28-£42; D £56-£64 LB
Parking 6

STOKE ST GREGORY   MAP 04 ST32

♦♦♦♦ ◼

Meare Green Farm ◇

Meare Green TA3 6HT
☎ 01823 490759 & 491238 ▤ 01823 490759
e-mail jane.pine@kiteconsulting.com
Dir *M5 junct 25, A358 through Henlade up dual carriageway to
lights and garage, left onto A378, 100yds fork left for North Curry,
1.5m from centre North Curry farm on left opp greystone barn*

Facilities 2 rms (1 en suite) (1 pri facs) (1 fmly) ⊗ TVB tea/coffee Cen ht
TVL No coaches Fishing Riding Dinner Last d Previous day
Prices S £30-£35; D £50-£55✱ LB **Parking** 3 **Notes** Closed 25-28 Dec ⊛

STREET   MAP 04 ST43

♦♦♦♦ ◼

The Birches ◇

13 Housman Rd BA16 0SD
☎ 01458 442902 ▤ 01458 442902
e-mail askins@ukonline.co.uk
Dir *Off B3151 onto Portway at Cider Farm sign. 1st right onto
Housman Rd*

Facilities 2 rms (2 pri facs) (1 fmly) (1 GF) ⊗ TVB tea/coffee ✖
Cen ht No coaches **Prices** S £30-£35; D £52-£60 **Parking** 2 **Notes** ⊛

♦♦♦

Kasuli Bed & Breakfast ◇

71 Somerton Rd BA16 0DN ☎ 01458 442063
Dir *B3151 from Street rdbt for Somerton, house 400yds past Street Inn
on left*

A warm welcome is assured at this charming family home, located
close to Clarke's Shopping Village and with easy access to local places
of historical interest. Bedrooms are comfortable and neat and there is
also a lounge. An enjoyable, traditional breakfast is served at the
family dining table.

Facilities 2 rms ⊗ TVB tea/coffee ✖ Cen ht No children 10yrs
No coaches **Prices** S £21-£22; D £40-£42 **Parking** 2 **Notes** ⊛

TAUNTON   MAP 04 ST22

See also **Bishops Lydeard & Staple Fitzpaine**

♦♦♦♦

Cutsey House

Cutsey, Trull TA3 7NY ☎ 01823 421705 ▤ 01823 421294
e-mail cutseyhouse@btconnect.com
Dir *M5 junct 26, into West Buckland, right at T-junct, 2nd left, next right*

A Victorian house set in over 20 acres of gardens and grounds with
parts of the building dating back to the 15th century. The comfortable
spacious bedrooms have glorious views of the countryside towards
the Blackdown Hills. Dinner is available by arrangement and guests
can enjoy their drinks in the library.

Facilities 3 en suite ⊗ in 1 bedrooms ⊗ in dining room TVB ✖ Cen ht
TVL No coaches Riding Snooker Dinner Last d 5pm **Prices** S £35-£40;
D £60-£70 **Conf** Max 12 **Parking** 11 **Notes** Closed Xmas-Etr ⊛

♦♦♦♦ ⌂ ⊜

The Spinney

Curland TA3 5SE
☎ 01460 234362 & 234193 ▤ 01460 234362
e-mail bartlett.spinney@zetnet.co.uk
web www.somerweb.co.uk/spinney-bb
Dir *2m W off A358 Taunton-Ilminster road*

A warm welcome awaits you at this delightful family home, set in well-
tended gardens and having magnificent views of the Blackdown,
Quantock and Mendip hills. The attractive bedrooms are equipped
with modern comforts and one room has easier access. Using the best
local produce, delicious dinners are available by arrangement and
guests may bring their own wine.

Facilities 3 en suite (2 fmly) (2 GF) ⊗ TVB tea/coffee ✖ Cen ht TVL
No coaches Dinner Last d 4pm **Parking** 6 **Notes** ⊛

England

◆◆◆◆

Blorenge House

57 Staple Grove Rd TA1 1DG
☎ 01823 283005 ▤ 01823 283005
e-mail enquiries@blorengehouse.co.uk
Dir *M5 junct 25, towards cricket ground & Morrisons on left, left at lights, right at 2nd lights, house 150yds on left*

This fine Victorian property offers spacious accommodation within walking distance of the town centre. The individually furnished bedrooms are well equipped and some feature impressive four-poster beds. A lounge, garden and outdoor swimming pool are available. There is also ample parking.

Facilities 25 rms (20 en suite) (4 fmly) (3 GF) ⊗ in 23 bedrooms ⊗ in dining room TVB tea/coffee Cen ht TVL ⬏ **Prices** S fr £38; d fr £58✹ **LB Parking** 25

◆◆◆◆

Brookfield House

16 Wellington Rd TA1 4EQ
☎ 01823 272786 ▤ 01823 272786
e-mail info@brookfieldguesthouse.uk.com
web www.brookfieldguesthouse.uk.com
Dir *From town centre signs to Musgrove Hospital, onto A38 Wellington Rd, on right opp turning to hospital*

This charming Grade II listed Georgian house is just a 5-minute level walk from the town centre. The family take great pride in caring for guests, and the brightly decorated bedrooms are well equipped. Breakfast, featuring local ingredients, is served in the attractive dining room. The property is non-smoking.

Facilities 7 en suite (1 fmly) ⊗ TVB tea/coffee ✖ Cen ht No children 5yrs No coaches Dinner Last d 8.30pm **Prices** S £40-£48; D £65-£75✹ **Parking** 8

◆◆◆◆

Creechbarn Bed & Breakfast

Vicarage Ln, Creech-St-Michael TA3 5PP ☎ 01823 443955
e-mail mick@somersite.co.uk
Dir *M5 junct 25, A358 to Creech St Michael, follow canal boat signs to end Vicarage Ln*

Located next to the canal and on a Sustrans cycle route, this traditional Somerset barn was lovingly converted by the current owners. Bedrooms are comfortable and there is a spacious sitting room with books, a television and table tennis. Breakfast is carefully prepared with free-range eggs and home-made bread.

Facilities 3 rms (1 en suite) ⊗ in bedrooms ⊗ in dining room TV1B tea/coffee Direct dial from bedrooms Cen ht TVL No coaches Bird watching Fishing **Prices** S £33-£44; D £44-£55 **LB Parking** 4
Notes Closed 20 Dec-6 Jan ⊛

◆◆◆◆

Culmhead House

Culmhead TA3 7DU ☎ 01823 421073 & 421074
e-mail enquiries@culmheadhouse.com
web www.culmheadhouse.com
Dir *Off A303 at Eagle x-rds*

Set amid delightful rhododendron and specimen trees, and attractive gardens and fountain, this house has a peaceful location. The rooms are individual suites and are particularly well appointed and comfortable. The proprietors are friendly and attentive hosts and breakfast, served in the large dining room, offers well-cooked and hearty fare.

Facilities 3 en suite (3 fmly) ⊗ TVB tea/coffee Cen ht TVL No coaches ⥀ **Prices** S £40-£45; D £68-£72✹ **LB Parking** 12

◆◆◆◆ ▰

The Hatch Inn

Village Rd, Hatch Beauchamp TA3 6SG
☎ 01823 480245 ▤ 01823 481104
e-mail bagleyjag@aol.com
Dir *6m SE of Taunton. Off A358 into Hatch Beauchamp*

This village inn caters well for locals and leisure or business guests. The majority of bedrooms are particularly spacious and come with a number of useful extras. Relaxed and friendly service continues through dinner and breakfast, which use a good selection of carefully prepared ingredients.

Facilities 7 en suite (1 fmly) ⊗ in bedrooms ⊗ in area of dining room TVB tea/coffee Cen ht No coaches Pool Table Dinner Last d 8.30pm **Parking** 15

◆◆◆◆ ❦

Lower Farm (ST281241)

Thornfalcon TA3 5NR
☎ 01823 443549 ▤ 01823 443549 Mrs Titman
e-mail lowerfarm@talk21.com
web www.somersite.co.uk
Dir *M5 junct 25, 2m SE on A358, left opp Nags Head pub, farm signed 1m on left*

This charming thatched 15th-century farmhouse is set in lovely gardens and is surrounded by open countryside. Hearty breakfasts, served in the farmhouse kitchen, feature home-produced eggs. There is a comfortable sitting room with a log fire. Bedrooms are located in the converted granary, some on the ground floor.

continued

Lower Farm

Facilities 2 rms (1 en suite) (1 pri facs) 9 annexe rms (7 en suite) (2 annexe pri facs) (2 fmly) (7 GF) ⊗ TV9B tea/coffee ✗ Cen ht TVL No children 5yrs 10 acres beef cows poultry **Prices** S £35-£40; D £55-£60✳ **LB Parking** available

◆◆◆◆

Lower Manor Farm

Thornfalcon TA3 5NR ☎ 01823 443634 & 443222
e-mail marion@lowermanorfarm.co.uk
web www.lowermanorfarm.co.uk
Dir M5 junct 25, A358 SE onto dual carriageway, 2nd sign left to Thornfalcon, left by war memorial, farm next right

In a delightful rural setting, Lower Manor Farm provides a high standard of comfortable, well-furnished accommodation. All bedrooms are dual aspect, with views across the surrounding countryside. Tempting breakfasts, featuring home produce when available, are served at individual tables in a cosy dining room.

Facilities 3 rms (2 en suite) (1 fmly) ⊗ TVB tea/coffee ✗ Cen ht No children 10yrs No coaches **Prices** S £30-£35; D £60✳ **LB Parking** 10 **Notes** ⊟

◆◆◆◆ ✿

Lower Marsh Farm ◇ (ST224279)

Kingston St Mary TA2 8AB
☎ 01823 451331 ▤ 01823 451331 Mr & Mrs J Gothard
e-mail b&b@lowermarshfarm.co.uk
Dir From Taunton N towards Kingston St Mary, 0.25m on right

Located at the foot of the Quantock Hills, this delightful family-run farm provides bright comfortable bedrooms complemented by many extra facilities. Evening meals are available by arrangement and, like breakfast, are served at one large table in the attractive dining room. There is also a lounge.

continued

Facilities 3 en suite (1 fmly) ⊗ TVB tea/coffee ✗ Cen ht TVL 300 acres arable/sheep/horses Dinner Last d noon **Prices** S fr £30; d fr £60✳ **Parking** 6 **Notes** ⊟

◆◆◆◆

Meryan House Hotel

Bishop's Hull TA1 5EG ☎ 01823 337445 ▤ 01823 322355
e-mail meryanhousehotel@btclick.com
web www.meryanhouse.co.uk
Dir 1.2m W of town centre. Off A38 onto Bishop's Hull Rd

Located in a pretty village just over 1m from the town centre, this 17th-century property has delightful individually furnished rooms. The comfortable bedrooms feature antiques along with modern facilities. Interesting dishes are available at dinner, and there is also a cosy bar and a spacious lounge.

Facilities 12 en suite (2 fmly) (2 GF) ⊗ in 2 bedrooms ⊗ in dining room ⊗ in 1 lounge STV TVB tea/coffee Direct dial from bedrooms Licensed Cen ht TVL No coaches Dinner Last d 7.30pm **Prices** S £50-£65; D £60-£85✳ **LB Conf** Max 25 Thtr 25 Class 25 Board 18 Del from £100 ✳ **Parking** 17

◆◆◆◆ A

Springfield House

Walford Cross, West Monkton TA2 8QW ☎ 01823 412116
e-mail tina.ridout@btopenworld.com
web www.springfieldhse.co.uk
Dir 3m NE of Taunton. M5 junct 25, A358 towards Taunton, at lights right onto A38 for Bridgwater, 1m onto dual carriageway, 100yds 1st left onto driveway

Facilities 5 annexe en suite (1 fmly) (2 GF) ⊗ TVB tea/coffee ✗ Cen ht No coaches **Prices** S £35-£45; D £55-£65✳ **Parking** 10 **Notes** ⊟

◆◆◆ ✿

Higher Dipford Farm (ST216205)

Trull TA3 7NU ☎ 01823 275770 & 257916 ▤ 01823 257916
Mrs Fewings
e-mail mafewings@tesco.net
Dir A38 S from town centre on Honiton Rd to Trull, right onto Dipford Rd, farm on left

This Grade II listed 17th-century longhouse is part of a working dairy farm. Steeped in character with elm beams and inglenook fireplaces, the house provides well-equipped and homely accommodation. Bedrooms are comfortable and individually decorated, and there is an honesty bar and lounge. Breakfasts and home-cooked dinners, featuring local produce, are served in the spacious dining room.

Facilities 3 en suite ⊗ in bedrooms ⊗ in dining room ⊗ in 1 lounge STV TVB tea/coffee ✗ Licensed Cen ht TVL Pool Table 120 acres beef Dinner Last d 8pm **Prices** S £35-£45; D £54-£70 **LB Parking** 6 **Notes** ⊟

England

TINTINHULL
MAP 04 ST41

◆◆◆◆ ⊜ ◀▮

Crown & Victoria
The Ale House Ltd, Farm St BA22 8PZ
☎ 01935 823341 🖹 01935 825786
e-mail info@crownandvictoriainn.co.uk
web www.crownandvictoriainn.co.uk
Dir Off A303, signs for Tintenhall Gardens

Refurbished to a high standard, the light and airy accommodation has very-well equipped bedrooms. The staff ensure you are cared for, and the contemporary bar and restaurant provide a good selection of carefully prepared dishes.

Facilities 5 en suite ⊘ in bedrooms ⊘ in dining room TVB tea/coffee ✖ Cen ht No children 5yrs No coaches Dinner Last d 9pm **Prices** S fr £65; d fr £85✳ **Parking** 60

WASHFORD
MAP 03 ST04

◆◆◆◆

The Linhay B&B
Williton Rd TA23 0NU ☎ 01984 641252 & 07940 894009
e-mail thelinhay@aol.com
web www.linhay.co.uk
Dir A39 towards Minehead, 2.5m after Williton

Convenient for coastal and country attractions, Linhay offers spacious and friendly accommodation. Hospitality is a feature and you are made to feel at home. The bedrooms are particularly well appointed and well equipped, and a hearty breakfast is served in the dining room. There is an attractive garden and ample parking.

Facilities 2 en suite ⊘ TVB tea/coffee ✖ Cen ht No coaches **Prices** S £40-£45; D £55-£60✳ LB **Parking** 4 **Notes** ⊛

WATCHET
MAP 03 ST04

◆◆◆◆

The Georgian House ◇
28 Swain St TA23 0AD ☎ 01984 639279
e-mail georgianhouse_watchet@virgin.net
Dir A39 over railway bridge onto Watchet main street

This elegant Georgian house is situated in the heart of this increasingly popular coastal resort within a short walk of the impressive new marina. Refurbished with considerable care, the comfortable bedrooms combine quality and individuality. Breakfast (and dinner by

continued

arrangement) is served in the well-appointed dining room. Additional facilities include a lounge and the garden.

Facilities 3 en suite ⊘ in bedrooms TVB ✖ Cen ht No coaches Dinner Last d 9pm **Prices** S £30-£35; D £55-£80✳ LB **Parking** 2

WATERROW
MAP 03 ST02

◆◆◆◆ ◀▮

The Rock Inn
TA4 2AX ☎ 01984 623293 🖹 01984 623293
Dir On B3227

Set in the lush greenery of the Tone valley, this 16th-century inn, as the name suggests, is built against the rock face. There is an abundance of character and the friendly atmosphere draws both locals and visitors. A range of freshly prepared, imaginative meals is available in the bar or restaurant, including Aberdeen Angus steaks from the owner's farm. The bedrooms are comfortable and there is a spacious first-floor lounge.

Facilities 8 en suite (1 fmly) ⊘ in bedrooms ⊘ in dining room ⊘ in 1 lounge FTV TVB tea/coffee Direct dial from bedrooms Cen ht TVL Pool Table Dinner Last d 10pm **Prices** S £40; D £70✳ LB **Parking** 25

WELLINGTON
MAP 03 ST12

◆◆◆◆

Thorne Manor
Thorne St Margaret TA21 0EQ ☎ 01823 672264
e-mail hasell@thornemanor.wanadoo.co.uk
Dir 3m W of Wellington. Off A38 to Thorne St Margaret

This 16th-century manor house stands in a small village near the Blackdown Hills. The accommodation offers character and a good level of comfort, with inglenook fireplaces in the dining room and the lounge. The spacious bedroom is well equipped and you will be well cared for by the hosts. The well-tended garden provides space for relaxation, and breakfast features local produce.

Facilities 1 en suite ⊘ tea/coffee ✖ TVL No children No coaches **Parking** 2 **Notes** Closed mid Dec-mid Jan ⊛

England

✦✦✦✦ ❦
Great Tadbeer Farm (ST034219)
Ashbrittle TA21 0JA ☎ 01398 361594 🖹 01398 361594
Mr & Mrs Marshall
e-mail sue.colinmarshall@btinternet.com
Dir M5 junct 26, A38 bypass Wellington to rdbt. Remain on A38 after
2m, turn right to Greenham. Through Greenham, Tracebridge,
Ashbrittle, turn left in Ashbrittle 1.5m, turn right beside Oakleigh
Bungalow onto track, 0.5m to farm

Hidden away on the Somerset/Devon border, this 16th-century
farmhouse has recently been totally renovated with care and attention
to retain as many original features as possible. Guests are assured of a
warm welcome from the friendly owners. Horse owners may wish to
bring their horses to explore the numerous bridle paths in this area.

Facilities 2 rms (1 en suite) (1 pri facs) ⊘ tea/coffee ✖ Cen ht TVL
No children 14yrs 42 acres Mixed sheep equestrian **Prices** D £44-£50✷
LB Parking 4 **Notes** Closed 16-31 Dec rs midwk 🐾

WELLS
See also **Croscombe**
MAP 04 ST54

MAP 04 ST54

Premier Collection

✦✦✦✦✦ 🏛 ❦
Beaconsfield Farm (ST515475)
Easton BA5 1DU ☎ 01749 870308 Mrs Lloyd
e-mail carol@beaconsfieldfarm.co.uk
web www.beaconsfieldfarm.co.uk
Dir 2.5m from Wells on A371, on right just before village of Easton

Set in pleasant, well-tended gardens on the west side of the Mendip
Hills, Beaconsfield Farm is convenient base for visiting this attractive
area. The welcoming hosts are most friendly and attentive and many
guests return on a regular basis. Bedrooms, which are very
comfortable and equipped with many extra facilities, are delightfully
decorated with coordinated colours and fabrics. A choice of well-
cooked dishes featuring fresh local produce is offered at breakfast.

Facilities 3 en suite ⊘ TVB tea/coffee ✖ Cen ht TVL No children 8yrs
4 acres non-working **Prices** S £57-£62; D £65-£70 **Parking** 10
Notes Closed 22 Dec-3 Jan 🐾

Premier Collection

✦✦✦✦✦
Riverside Grange
Tanyard Ln, North Wootton BA4 4AE ☎ 01749 890761
e-mail riversidegrange@hotmail.com
Dir 2.5m SE of Wells in North Wootton

A delightful restored tannery, built in 1853, the foundations of which
actually sit in the River Redlake, which runs alongside the house. A
warm welcome is guaranteed from the friendly proprietors, who are
most attentive and make every effort to make you feel at home. The
house, furnished throughout with rosewood, is most comfortable.
There are two bedrooms, one en suite and one with a private
bathroom and you can relax in the attractive garden in summer.

Facilities 2 rms (1 en suite) (1 pri facs) ⊘ TVB tea/coffee ✖ Cen ht
No children 10yrs **Prices** S fr £49; d fr £59✷ **Parking** 6 **Notes** Closed
Xmas & New Year 🐾

✦✦✦✦✦ 🅰
Beryl
Hawkers Ln BA5 3JP ☎ 01749 678738 🖹 01749 670508
e-mail stay@beryl-wells.co.uk
Dir Off B3139 Radstock Rd, signed The Horringtons, onto Hawkers Ln
to end

Facilities 9 rms (8 en suite) (1 pri facs) (2 fmly) ⊘ in bedrooms
⊘ in dining room ⊘ in 1 lounge TVB tea/coffee Direct dial from
bedrooms Licensed Lift Cen ht TVL No coaches ⤳ ♨ childrens play
area **Prices** S £55-£75; D £70-£115✷ **LB Parking** 20 **Notes** Closed
25-26 Dec

England

◆◆◆◆ ❦

Double-Gate Farm (ST484424)

Godney BA5 1RX
☎ 01458 832217 ▤ 01458 835612 Mrs Millard
e-mail doublegatefarm@aol.com
web www.doublegatefarm.com
Dir A39 from Wells towards Glastonbury, at Polsham right signed
Godney/Polsham, 2m to x-rds, continue to farmhouse on left after inn

Surrounded by the Somerset Levels and having splendid views of the
Mendips, this farm provides a friendly welcome. The host also gives
comprehensive information on days out in the local areas. Bedrooms
are attractively decorated and are most comfortable, with one room
particularly well suited to the less mobile. Breakfast is served at two
refectory tables where you can choose from an interesting and
extensive menu.

Facilities 3 en suite 3 annexe en suite (1 fmly) (1 GF) ⊛ FTV TVB
tea/coffee ✖ Cen ht TVL Fishing Snooker Table tennis 100 acres mixed
Prices S £45-£50; D £60-£65✱ **Parking** 9 **Notes** Closed Dec-Jan

◆◆◆◆ ⬚ ❦

Hollow Tree Farm ◈ (ST051428)

Launcherley BA5 1QJ
☎ 01749 673715 & 07704 506513 ▤ 01749 673715
Mrs Coombes
Dir A39 from Wells for Glastonbury, 1st left at Brownes Garden
Centre, farm 0.75m on right

Delightfully appointed rooms with bright, cheery colour schemes and
comfortable furnishings are provided at this non-working farm.
Spectacular views of Wells Cathedral and Glastonbury Tor and
delightful flower-filled gardens add to the charm. The friendly hosts
are most welcoming and attentive and home-baked bread, jams and
marmalade are only a part of the delicious breakfast.

Facilities 3 rms (2 en suite) (1 pri facs) (1 fmly) (3 GF) ⊛ TVB
tea/coffee ✖ Cen ht No children 12yrs 27 acres Grazing
Prices S £28-£30; D £44✱ **Parking** 4 **Notes** Closed mid Dec-mid Jan
🐾

◆◆◆◆

Littlewell Farm ◈

Coxley BA5 1QP ☎ 01749 677914
e-mail enquiries@littlewellfarm.co.uk
web www.littlewellfarm.co.uk
Dir A39 from Wells towards Glastonbury, farm 1m on right opp sign
for Coxley

This charming farmhouse stands in spacious gardens at Coxley, on the
outskirts of Wells. It provides well-equipped accommodation and has a
cosy lounge, as well as a very attractive modern breakfast room with
separate tables.

Facilities 5 rms (4 en suite) (1 pri facs) (1 GF) ⊛ TVB tea/coffee ✖
Cen ht TVL No children 10yrs No coaches **Prices** S £25-£30; D £54✱
Parking 10 **Notes** Closed 25 Dec 🐾

◆◆◆◆

Tynings House

Harters Hill Ln, Coxley BA5 1RF
☎ 01749 675368 ▤ 01749 674217
e-mail info@tynings.co.uk
Dir Off A39 between Wells and Glastonbury. At Coxley church, turn
onto Harters Hill Ln, 1st left after houses

Tynings House, dating in part from the 17th century, stands in peaceful
countryside not far from Glastonbury and Wells. It provides well-
equipped modern accommodation and a spacious lounge-dining
room. Hospitality is genuinely friendly and the owners go to great
lengths to ensure you feel welcome. Wholesome home-cooked
dinners are available by arrangement.

Facilities 3 en suite (1 fmly) ⊛ TVB tea/coffee ✖ Cen ht TVL Dinner
Last d 24hrs **Prices** S £36-£50; D £52-£70✱ LB **Parking** 4 **Notes** 🐾

◆◆◆◆

Garden Cottage

60 Southover BA5 1UH ☎ 01749 676348
e-mail wendyandmike@mb2online.net
Dir *500yds SW of cathedral. Off A39 rdbt onto Priory Rd & 1st right*

A warm welcome is assured at this delightful home, well located for the cathedral and the town centre. The pleasant bedrooms are comfortably furnished and include many extra facilities and accessories. Guests are welcome to relax in the large attractive garden. All share one table in the pleasant and spacious lounge-breakfast room.

Facilities 2 en suite ⊗ TVB tea/coffee ✖ Cen ht No coaches
Prices D £52✳ **Parking** 2 **Notes** Closed 16-31 Dec 🐾

◆◆◆◆

Glengarth House

7 Glastonbury Rd BA5 1TW
☎ 01749 674792 📠 01749 674792
Dir *On A39 S, on left past minirdbt*

This pleasant guest house is located on the edge of Wells just a short walk from the central attractions. Bedrooms are brightly decorated and include some welcome extras. A carefully prepared breakfast is provided in the spacious dining room, and there is off-road parking for a couple of cars.

Facilities 4 en suite (1 fmly) ⊗ TVB tea/coffee ✖ Cen ht No coaches
Prices S £30-£40; D £55-£60✳ **LB** **Parking** 5 **Notes** 🐾

◆◆◆◆

Highfield

93 Portway BA5 2BR ☎ 01749 675330
Dir *Enter Wells & signs for A371 Cheddar, Highfield on Portway after last lights at top of hill*

Within walking distance of the city and cathedral, this delightful home maintains its Edwardian style and provides comfortable accommodation. A warm welcome is assured while bedrooms are furnished with attractive coordinated fabrics. Breakfast is served at one large table in the smart dining room, which overlooks the large garden.

Facilities 3 en suite (1 fmly) ⊗ in bedrooms ⊗ in lounges TVB tea/coffee ✖ Cen ht No children 2yrs No coaches **Parking** 7
Notes Closed 23 Dec-1 Jan 🐾

◆◆◆◆

Highgate Cottage

Worth BA5 1LW ☎ 01749 674201 📠 01749 674201
Dir *B3139 into Worth, Pheasant pub on left, Highgate Cottage 200yds on right*

Located in the village of Worth to the west of Wells and set in 2 acres of land, access to this delightful stone cottage is over its own private bridge. The attractive bedrooms are comfortable and quiet. Full English breakfasts are served at individual tables in the lounge-dining room.

Facilities 2 en suite (1 fmly) ⊗ TVB tea/coffee Cen ht No coaches
Parking 6 **Notes** Closed Dec-Jan 🐾

◆◆◆◆

Infield House

36 Portway BA5 2BN ☎ 01749 670989 📠 01749 679093
e-mail infield@talk21.com
web www.infieldhouse.co.uk
Dir *500yds W of city centre on A371 Portway*

This charming Victorian house offers comfortable, spacious rooms of elegance and style. The friendly hosts are very welcoming and provide a relaxing home from home. Guests may bring their pets, by arrangement. Dinners, also by arrangement, are served in the pleasant dining room where good home cooking ensures an enjoyable and varied range of options.

Facilities 3 en suite ⊗ TVB tea/coffee Cen ht TVL No children 12yrs No coaches Dinner Last d 10.30am **Prices** D £52-£56 **Parking** 3

◆◆◆

Amber House

Coxley BA5 1QZ ☎ 01749 679612
e-mail amberhouse@wellscity27.freeserve.co.uk
Dir *On A39 in village, 0.25m S past Pound Inn on right*

Located just 1.5m south from the centre of Wells, this comfortable home is a pleasant place to stay. The friendly proprietors are most welcoming and provide a relaxed atmosphere. Bedrooms are well equipped, and the snug dining room doubles as a lounge. A pleasant garden is available.

Facilities 2 en suite ⊗ TVB tea/coffee ✖ Cen ht TVL No coaches
Prices S £25-£29; D £42-£50 **Parking** 3 **Notes** 🐾

England

WELLS continued

◆◆◆

Birdwood House

Birdwood, Bath Rd BA5 3EW ☎ 01749 679250
e-mail info@birdwood-bandb.co.uk
web www.birdwood-bandb.co.uk
Dir *From town centre follow signs on one-way system to the Horringtons., onto B3139, last house 1.5m on left near double-bend sign*

Set in extensive grounds and gardens just a short drive from the town centre, this imposing detached house dates from the 1850s. The bedrooms are comfortable and equipped with a number of extra facilities. Breakfast is served around a communal table in the pleasant dining room or conservatory, which is also available for guest use and enjoyment throughout the day.

Facilities 4 rms (2 en suite) (1 pri facs) (1 fmly) ⊗ TVB tea/coffee Cen ht TVL No coaches ✿ **Prices** S £25-£30; D £50 **Parking** 12 **Notes** ⊛

◆◆◆

19 St Cuthbert Street

BA5 2AW ☎ 01749 673166
Dir *At bottom of High St opp St Cuthbert's Church*

You are assured of a friendly welcome at this charming terrace house, which is within walking distance of the cathedral and bus station. The accommodation is comfortable and the atmosphere homely. Bedrooms are well appointed, there is a cosy lounge and guests share a table for breakfast, which features home-made marmalade.

Facilities 2 rms ⊗ in lounges TVB tea/coffee Cen ht TVL No children 5yrs No coaches **Prices** S £27.50-£32; D £47-£50✳ **Notes** ⊛

◆◆◆

Number One Portway

1 Portway BA5 2BA ☎ 01749 678864 & 07786 217624
Dir *In town centre, off A39 Strawberry Way onto Tucker St, left onto Portway*

This attractive Victorian house offers comfortable accommodation opposite the Little Theatre. Within walking distance of the cathedral and attractions, it is an excellent base for either a short stay or a longer, relaxing break. Breakfasts feature fresh local produce.

Facilities 2 rms (1 en suite) (1 pri facs) (2 fmly) ⊗ TVB tea/coffee ✖ Cen ht No coaches **Prices** D £45-£50✳ **Notes** ⊛

WESTON-SUPER-MARE   MAP 04 ST36

◆◆◆◆

Beverley Guest House

11 Whitecross Rd BS23 1EP
☎ 01934 622956 ◳ 01934 622956
e-mail beverley11@hushmail.com
web www.beverleyguesthouse.co.uk
Dir *Off A370 Beach Rd onto Ellenborough Park Rd South & 2nd right*

You will be warmly greeted at this Victorian house set in a quiet residential street close to the seafront, the railway station and the town centre. The individually styled bedrooms are thoughtfully equipped and include a family suite. There is a small conservatory-lounge next to the dining room, where hearty breakfasts using local produce are served.

Facilities 5 en suite (3 fmly) (1 GF) ⊗ TVB tea/coffee ✖ Cen ht No coaches **Prices** D £55✳ **LB Parking** 1 **Notes** Closed Xmas

◆◆◆◆

Camellia Lodge

76 Walliscote Rd BS23 1ED
☎ 01934 613534 ◳ 01934 613534
e-mail dachefscamellia@aol.com
Dir *200yds from seafront*

Guests return regularly for the warm welcome they receive at this immaculate Victorian family home, which is just off the seafront and within walking distance of the town centre. Bedrooms have a range of thoughtful touches, and carefully prepared breakfasts are served in the relaxing dining room.

Facilities 5 en suite (2 fmly) ⊗ TVB tea/coffee Cen ht Dinner Last d 10.30am **Prices** S £25-£27.50; D £55-£60

◆◆◆◆

Milton Lodge Hotel

15 Milton Rd BS23 2SH ☎ 01934 623161 ◳ 01934 623210
e-mail info@milton-lodge.co.uk
Dir *M5 junct 21, towards Weston-Super-Mare, onto Locking Rd & Milton Rd*

Located within walking distance of the town centre and the seafront attractions, this comfortable guest house offers spacious, attractive and well-equipped bedrooms, including one on the ground floor. The atmosphere is relaxed and friendly and there is a lounge and attractive dining room. Off-road parking.

Facilities 6 en suite (1 fmly) (1 GF) ⊗ TVB tea/coffee ✖ Cen ht TVL No children 12yrs No coaches Dinner Last d Previous day **Prices** S fr £36; d fr £54✳ **LB Parking** 6 **Notes** ⊛

◆◆◆◆

Oakover Guest House

25 Clevedon Rd BS23 1DA ☎ 01934 620125
e-mail info@oakover.co.uk
web www.oakover.co.uk
Dir *Off A370 Beach Rd near Sea Life Aquarium onto Clevedon Rd*

Oakover is a substantial Victorian property situated a short level walk from the town centre and seafront. Bedrooms and bathrooms have been totally refurbished to offer very good levels of quality and

continued

comfort. A varied breakfast menu is offered in the bright dining room. The friendly resident proprietor maintains an easy-going and welcoming establishment.

Facilities 6 en suite (2 GF) ⊗ in 5 bedrooms ⊗ in dining room STV TVB tea/coffee ✖ Cen ht No children 12yrs **Prices** S £23-£45; D £46-£60✳ **Parking** 7

♦♦♦♦

Rookery Manor

Edingworth Rd, Edingworth BS24 0JB
☎ 01934 750200 ▤ 01934 750014
e-mail enquiries@rookery-manor.co.uk
web www.rookery-manor.co.uk
Dir M5 junct 22, A370 towards Weston, 2m right to Rookery Manor

This 16th-century manor house set in immaculate grounds and gardens is a very popular wedding and function venue. It has been converted to provide well-appointed and comfortable bedrooms, and a smart lounge, bar, and a hard tennis court are available.

Facilities 22 en suite (2 fmly) (10 GF) ⊗ in bedrooms ⊗ in area of dining room ⊗ in 1 lounge TVB tea/coffee Direct dial from bedrooms Licensed Cen ht TVL Golf 9 ✎ Riding Snooker Pool Table ⚐ ⌾ table tennis Dinner Last d 9pm **Prices** S £65; D £85-£105✳ **LB** **Conf** Max 800 Thtr 800 Class 120 Board 120 Del from £124 ✳ **Parking** 460 **Notes** Civ Wed 400

♦♦♦♦ 🅰

The Abbeywood Guest House ◇

148 Milton Rd BS23 2UZ ☎ 01934 627793
Dir from M5 junct 21 follow signs for town centre. Take 3rd exit at 5th rdbt & at 2nd lights right into Milton Rd. Hotel 400yds on right

Facilities 9 en suite (3 fmly) (1 GF) ⊗ TVB tea/coffee ✖ Licensed Cen ht TVL No children 4yrs No coaches ↳ Dinner Last d noon **Prices** S £30-£32; D £50-£52✳ **Parking** 10

♦♦♦♦ 🅰

The Grove

43 Grove Rd, Milton BS22 8HF
☎ 01934 612868 ▤ 01934 429737
e-mail thegrove@weston-super-mare.net
web www.weston-super-mare.net
Dir M5 junct 21 towards Weston-Super-Mare, left onto B3440 for 1.5m, right at rdbt, left at lights & 1st right.

Facilities 4 rms (3 en suite) (1 pri facs) (1 fmly) ⊗ FTV TVB tea/coffee ✖ Cen ht TVL No coaches Dinner Last d noon **LB** **Parking** 20 **Notes** 🐾

♦♦♦

The Weston Bay Hotel

2-4 Clevedon Rd BS23 1DG
☎ 01934 628903 ▤ 01934 417661
e-mail westonbayhotel@btinternet.com
web www.westonbayhotel.co.uk
Dir Opp Sea Life Centre on seafront

Located on the seafront, this family-run property has generally spacious, well-equipped bedrooms with modern en suites. The

comfortable lounge and attractive breakfast room have sea views, and packed lunches are available on request. There is a small private car park.

Facilities 9 en suite (5 fmly) (1 GF) ⊗ in 4 bedrooms ⊗ in dining room TVB tea/coffee ✖ Cen ht TVL No coaches **Prices** S £45-£49; D £59-£65✳ **LB** **Parking** 11 **Notes** Closed mid Nov-mid Mar

♦♦♦

Bella Vista Hotel

19 Upper Church Rd BS23 2DX
☎ 01934 631931 ▤ 01934 620126
Dir A370 to town and seafront, right past Grand Pier. Right after 300yds onto Upper Church Rd & right at x-rds

Situated close to the seafront and town centre, this delightful terrace property has an attractive patio with seating at the front. The bedrooms have televisions and hospitality trays and are well decorated throughout. There is a cosy dining room where full English breakfasts are served, and a large lounge.

Facilities 8 en suite (3 fmly) ⊗ in 2 bedrooms ⊗ in dining room TVB tea/coffee ✖ Cen ht TVL No coaches **Prices** D £44-£50✳ **LB** **Notes** 🐾

♦♦♦

Goodrington Guest House ◇

23 Charlton Rd BS23 4HB ☎ 01934 623229
e-mail vera.bishop@talk21.com
web www.goodrington.info
Dir A370 Beach Rd S onto Uphill Rd, left onto Charlton Rd

The owners make every effort to ensure you enjoy your stay at this charming Victorian house tucked away in a quiet residential area. The spacious bedrooms are comfortably furnished, and there is an attractive lounge. Families are especially welcome and this is a good holiday base.

Facilities 3 rms (2 en suite) (1 pri facs) (1 fmly) (1 GF) ⊗ FTV TVB tea/coffee ✖ Cen ht TVL No coaches Dinner Last d 24hr notice **Prices** S £26-£30; D £48-£52✳ **LB** **Notes** rs Oct-Mar 🐾

🅄

The Beaches ◇

36 Beach Rd BS23 1BG ☎ 01934 629529 ▤ 01934 412614
e-mail info@beacheshotel.co.uk
web www.beacheshotel.co.uk
Dir M5 junct 21 onto A370, follow signs for beach

At the time of going to press the rating for this establishment had not been confirmed. Please check the AA website www.theAA.com for up-to-date information.

Facilities 10 en suite (3 fmly) ⊗ TVB tea/coffee ✖ Cen ht TVL No coaches **Prices** S £25-£30; D £45-£50✳ **LB** **Parking** 8 **Notes** Closed 15 Nov-Mar

continued

England

WESTON-SUPER-MARE continued

U

Church House

27 Kewstoke Rd, Kewstoke BS22 9YD ☎ 01934 633185
e-mail churchhouse@kewstoke.net
web www.churchhousekewstoke.co.uk
Dir From junct 21 M5 follow signs for Kewstoke 2.5m, next to Kewstoke Church

At the time of going to press the rating for this establishment had not been confirmed. Please check the AA website www.theAA.com for up-to-date information.

Facilities 5 en suite ⊗ TVB tea/coffee Cen ht No coaches **Prices** S £50; D £70✱ LB **Parking** 10

U

Edelweiss Guest House ◇

24 Cleveden Rd BS23 1DG
☎ 01934 624705 📠 01934 624705
e-mail edelweissguesthouse@tiscali.co.uk
Dir Turn onto Clevedon Rd off Beach Rd (Seafront) opposite Tropicana. Edelweiss 150yds on right

At the time of going to press the rating for this establishment had not been confirmed. Please check the AA website www.theAA.com for up-to-date information.

Facilities 5 rms (4 en suite) (1 pri facs) (3 fmly) (2 GF) ⊗ TV5B tea/coffee 🐕 Cen ht Dinner **Prices** S £22-£25; D £44-£54✱ LB **Notes** Closed Xmas wk

U

Jamesfield Guest House ◇

1A Ellenborough Park North BS23 1XH
☎ 01934 642898 📠 01934 624933
e-mail jamesfield1@aol.com

At the time of going to press the rating for this establishment had not been confirmed. Please check the AA website www.theAA.com for up-to-date information.

Facilities 7 rms (6 en suite) (1 pri facs) (2 GF) ⊗ TVB tea/coffee 🐕 Cen ht TVL No coaches **Prices** S £24; D £48✱ **Parking** 9

U

Sunfold Inn

39 Beach Rd BS23 1BG ☎ 01934 624700 📠 01934 624700
e-mail enquiries@sunfold-hotel.co.uk

At the time of going to press the rating for this establishment had not been confirmed. Please check the AA website www.theAA.com for up-to-date information.

Facilities 11 en suite (4 fmly) (2 GF) ⊗ in bedrooms ⊗ in dining room ⊗ in 1 lounge TVB tea/coffee Licensed Cen ht TVL Dinner Last d 7.30pm **Prices** D £50-£70✱ LB **Parking** 5

WHEDDON CROSS

MAP 03 SS93

◆◆◆◆ 🍴🛏 🐖

North Wheddon Farm ◇ *(SS923385)*

TA24 7EX ☎ 01643 841791 & 07891 294775 Mrs Abraham
e-mail northwheddonfarm@aol.com
web www.go-exmoor.co.uk
Dir 500yds S of village x-rds on A396. Pass Moorland Hall on left, driveway next right

The farm is a delightfully friendly and comfortable environment with great views. The tranquil grounds include a pleasant garden, and the memorable dinners and breakfasts feature local and the farm's own fresh produce. The bedrooms are thoughtfully equipped and beds are most comfortable. Rachael Abraham is a top-twenty finalist for AA Landlady of the Year 2006.

Facilities 3 rms (2 en suite) (1 pri facs) ⊗ TVB tea/coffee Licensed Cen ht Riding 17 acres Mixed Dinner Last d 10am **Prices** S £27.50; D £55✱ LB **Parking** 5

◆◆◆◆ 🍴

Rest and be Thankful Inn

TA24 7DR ☎ 01643 841222 📠 01643 841813
e-mail enquiries@restandbethankful.co.uk
web www.restandbethankful.co.uk
Dir M5 junct 25, A358 to Minehead, left onto B3224 at sign to Wheddon Cross

The Rest and be Thankful stands in the highest village on Exmoor overlooking Dunkery Beacon. The comfortable bedrooms are extremely well equipped with extras such as fridges and trouser presses. Popular with locals and visitors alike, the convivial bar, complete with log fires, is the place to relax before a wholesome meal in the restaurant.

Facilities 5 en suite (1 fmly) ⊗ in bedrooms ⊗ in dining room TVB tea/coffee Direct dial from bedrooms 🐕 Cen ht Pool Table Skittle alley Dinner Last d 9pm **Prices** S £31-£55; D £60-£68✱ LB **Conf** Max 12 Thtr 12 Class 8 Board 8 Del from £70 ✱ **Parking** 10 **Notes** Closed 24-25 Dec

WINCANTON
MAP 04 ST72

◆◆◆◆

Brookleigh

Holton BA9 8AE ☎ 01963 34685
e-mail theclementss@hotmail.com
Dir *A371 from Wincanton towards Templecombe, at rdbt 1st exit onto A357, B&B signed*

Just a stone's throw from the A303, this well-kept family home is a good stopover or a useful base base for touring Somerset and Wiltshire, with easy access to Stourhead and Longleat. The clean bedrooms are attractively coordinated, and there is also a lounge. Breakfast, served in the conservatory dining room, features eggs from the neighbour's chickens.

Facilities 3 en suite ⊘ TVB tea/coffee ✖ Cen ht TVL No coaches **Prices** S £22.50-£25; D £48✶ **Parking** 6 **Notes** 🈲

WINSFORD
MAP 03 SS93

◆◆◆◆ ⓖ ⊜

Karslake House

Halse Ln TA24 7JE ☎ 01643 851242 📠 01643 851242
e-mail enquiries@karslakehouse.co.uk
Dir *In village centre*

The 16th- or 17th-century Karslake House stands in a peaceful Exmoor village. Its public rooms feature original beams and fireplaces, and an interesting menu of delicious meals is available in the dining room. Bedrooms are thoughtfully furnished and have a number of extra touches.

Facilities 6 rms (5 en suite) (1 pri facs) (1 GF) ⊘ TVB tea/coffee Licensed Cen ht No children 12yrs No coaches Riding, shooting, fishing on request, jeep safari Dinner Last d 8.15pm **Prices** S £55-£70; D £76-£111✶ **Parking** 15 **Notes** Closed Feb & Mar rs Nov-Jan

WITHYPOOL
MAP 03 SS83

★★★★★ Bed & Breakfast

Kings Farm

TA24 7RE ☎ 01643 831381 📠 01643 831381
e-mail info@kingsfarmexmoor.co.uk
Dir *Off B3223 to Withypool, over bridge & sharp left*

This delightful farmhouse, set in an idyllic valley beside the Barle, combines all the character and charm of its 19th century origins with every modern comfort. From the carefully planned bedrooms to the sumptuously furnished sitting room, delicious home-cooked breakfasts and the warmest of welcomes, top quality is most definitely the hallmark of Kings Farm. Over two acres of landscaped gardens beside the river form the backdrop and guests are encouraged to enjoy its unrestrained feeling of freedom and complete peace which is so untypical of today's busy world. Stabling and fishing available.

Facilities 2 rms (1 en suite) (1 pri facs) ⊘ STV TVB tea/coffee ✖ Cen ht No children 14yrs No coaches Fishing **Prices** S £50; D £70-£75✶ **Parking** 3

WIVELISCOMBE
MAP 03 ST02

◆◆◆◆ 🍴 ⊜

The Old Rectory

Huish Champflower TA4 2EF ☎ 01984 623782
e-mail email@huishrectory.co.uk
web www.huishrectory.co.uk
Dir *2.5m W of Wiveliscombe. From Huish Champflower N towards Clatworthy, 300yds left, B&B signed on left*

This impressive, non-smoking, house sits in extensive grounds and has a tranquil location. The proprietors are accomplished hosts and guests are made to feel relaxed and at home here. There is a pleasant lounge, and bedrooms are spacious and comfortable. Dinner, by arrangement, and breakfast, are features not to be missed; carefully sourced local ingredients and skilled cookery make for memorable dining here.

Facilities 3 rms (1 en suite) (2 pri facs) ⊘ tea/coffee Cen ht TVL No coaches Dinner Last d noon **Prices** d fr £56✶ **LB** **Parking** 6 **Notes** 🈲

YEOVIL
MAP 04 ST51

See also **Crewkerne**

Premier Collection

★★★★★ ⊚⊚⊚ **Restaurant with Rooms**

Little Barwick House Ltd

Barwick Village BA22 9TD
☎ 01935 423902 ▤ 01935 420908
e-mail littlebarwick@hotmail.com
Dir *From Yeovil on A37 towards Dorchester, left at 1st rdbt. 1st left, Hotel 0.25m on left*

Situated in a quiet hamlet in 3.5 acres of gardens and grounds, this delightful listed Georgian dower house is an ideal retreat for those seeking peaceful surroundings and good food. Just one of the highlights of a stay here is a meal in the restaurant where, at the helm, Tim Ford cooks from the heart making best use of local ingredients. Each of the bedrooms has its own character, charm and a range of thoughtful extras such as fresh flowers, bottled water and magazines. The informal atmosphere of a private home, coupled with the facilities and comforts of a modern hotel, result in a very special combination.

Facilities 6 en suite TVB tea/coffee Direct dial from bedrooms Licensed No children 5yrs No coaches Dinner Last d 9pm **Prices** S £75-£110; D £126-£140✶ **LB** **Parking** 30

◆◆◆◆ ⊄▤

The Half Moon Inn

Main St, Mudford BA21 5TF
☎ 01935 850289 ▤ 01935 850842
e-mail enquiries@thehalfmooninn.co.uk
Dir *A303 at Sparkford onto A359 to Yeovil, B&B 3.5m on left*

Situated north of Yeovil, this delightful village inn dates from the 17th century. It has a wealth of character, enhanced by exposed beams and flagstone floors. The inn is very popular for its extensive range of wholesome food, and there is a choice of smoking and non-smoking bar and dining areas. Most of the spacious, well-equipped bedrooms are on the ground floor of a separate adjacent building.

Facilities 13 en suite (4 fmly) (9 GF) ⊗ in bedrooms ⊗ in area of dining room STV TVB tea/coffee ✖ Cen ht Dinner Last d 9.45pm **Parking** 48 **Notes** Closed 25-26 Dec

◆◆◆◆ ⊚ ⊜ ⊄▤

The Helyar Arms

Moor Ln, East Coker BA22 9JR
☎ 01935 862332 ▤ 01935 864129
e-mail info@helyar-arms.co.uk
Dir *Off A30 or A37 signed East Coker, pub 100yds from St Michaels Church*

Located in a picture book Somerset village close to Yeovil, this 15th-century inn has a first-rate reputation throughout the area. A wealth of beams and an inglenook fireplace add charm to the bar and restaurant. The menu features local produce, including beef and fish. Bedrooms, some of which are family rooms, are comfortably furnished.

Facilities 6 en suite (3 fmly) ⊗ in bedrooms ⊗ in area of dining room ⊗ in 1 lounge TVB tea/coffee Direct dial from bedrooms Cen ht Dinner Last d 9.30pm **Prices** S £59-£69; D £79✶ **LB** **Conf** Max 40 Thtr 40 Class 20 Board 30 **Parking** 40

◆◆◆ ⊄▤

The Halfway House Inn Country Lodge

Ilchester Rd BA22 8RE ☎ 01935 840350 ▤ 01935 849005
e-mail paul@halfwayhouseinn.com
web www.halfwayhouseinn.com
Dir *A303 onto A37 Yeovil road at Ilchester, inn 2m on left*

This roadside inn offers comfortable accommodation, which consists of bedrooms in the main house and other contemporary style rooms, each having its own front door, in the annexe. All rooms are bright and well equipped. Meals of generous portion are available in the cosy restaurant and bar, where friendly staff ensure a warm welcome.

Facilities 4 en suite 11 annexe en suite (5 fmly) (9 GF) ⊗ in 5 bedrooms ⊗ in dining room STV TVB tea/coffee Cen ht TVL Fishing Pool Table Dinner Last d 9pm **Prices** S £52.50-£57.50; D £67.50-£72.50✶ **LB** **Conf** Max 60 Thtr 30 Class 32 Board 20 **Parking** 49

◆◆◆

Pendomer House

Pendomer BA22 9PB ☎ 01935 862785
e-mail e.armitstead@btinternet.com
web www.pendomerhouse.co.uk
Dir *2.5m S of Yeovil. Off A30 or A37 to East Coker, follow signs to Pendomer village*

This former rectory stands on a hilltop surrounded by beech trees. The bedrooms occupy their own part of the house and some have striking country views. There is a sitting room with a television and refreshment facilities.

Facilities 3 en suite ⊗ tea/coffee ✖ Cen ht TVL No coaches **Prices** S £35-£40; D £55-£65✶ **Parking** available **Notes** ⊗

YEOVILTON
MAP 04 ST52

◆◆◆◆ ⊌

Cary Fitzpaine Farm *(ST549270)*

BA22 8JB
☎ 01458 223250 & 07967 476531 ▤ 01458 223372
Mrs Crang
e-mail acrang@aol.com
web www.caryfitzpaine.com
Dir *A303 at Podimore onto A37 N for 1m, 1st right to farm*

Surrounded by 600 acres of mixed farmland, this charming farmhouse dates from Georgian times. The comfortable bedrooms are well equipped and fitted with modern facilities. Breakfast is served at separate tables, or on sunny mornings can be enjoyed on the veranda.

Facilities 3 en suite (1 fmly) ⊗ TVB tea/coffee Cen ht TVL Fishing 600 acres sheep horses chicken **Prices** S £34-£38; D £54-£60 **LB** **Parking** 6 **Notes** Closed 23-26 Dec

STAFFORDSHIRE

ABBOTS BROMLEY
MAP 10 SK02

◆◆◆ ❦

Marsh Farm ◈ *(SK069261)*

WS15 3EJ ☎ 01283 840323 Mrs Hollins
e-mail marshfarm@meads1967.co.uk
web www.marshfarmstaffs.co.uk
Dir *1m N of Abbots Bromley on B5013*

You are welcome to walk around the fields at this working farm and watch the activities. The farmhouse has been modernised and the bedrooms are carefully furnished and equipped. Comprehensive breakfasts are served in the spacious cottage-style dining room, which operates as a good tea room during the summer.

Facilities 2 rms (1 fmly) ⊗ TVB tea/coffee Cen ht 20 acres mixed
Prices S £24-£28; D £45-£49✶ **Parking** 8 **Notes** Closed Xmas 🐾

ADBASTON
MAP 15 SJ72

◆◆◆◆ 🅰 ❦

Offley Grove Farm *(SJ760270)*

ST20 0QB
☎ 01785 280205 & 07745 170279 🖷 01785 280205
Mrs Hiscoe-James
e-mail accom@offleygrovefarm.freeserve.co.uk
web www.offleygrovefarm.co.uk

Facilities 2 en suite (1 fmly) ⊗ TVB tea/coffee 🐕 Cen ht TVL Fishing ⏚ 45 acres Beef **Parking** available **Notes** Closed 24-31 Dec

ALTON
MAP 10 SK04

◆◆◆

Chained Oak Farm ◈

Farley Ln ST10 4BZ ☎ 01538 702104 🖷 01538 702104
e-mail cross@barn.fslife.co.uk
web www.chainedoak.com
Dir *Between Alton & Farley, opp Alton Towers*

This modern detached house stands in delightful grounds and affords fine all-round views. It is very close to Alton Towers and offers spacious comfortable, ground-floor accommodation, together with attentive service.

Facilities 1 en suite 3 annexe en suite (2 fmly) (4 GF) ⊗ TVB tea/coffee 🐕 Cen ht TVL No coaches **Prices** S £28-£30; D £48✶ **LB** **Parking** 10 **Notes** 🐾

AUDLEY
MAP 15 SJ75

◆◆◆◆ 🍽 ❦

Domvilles Farm *(SJ776516)*

Barthomley Rd ST7 8HT
☎ 01782 720378 🖷 01782 720883 Mrs Oulton
e-mail eileen.oulton@virgin.net
Dir *M6 junct 16, B5078 towards Alsager, 0.5m left to Barthomley, left at White Lion, Domvilles 0.5m on left*

This 260-acre dairy farm is a short drive from major roads is delightfully presented throughout. Quality decor, antiques and

continued

memorabilia highlight the original features of the elegant Georgian property, and bedrooms feature fine Victorian four-poster, half-tester and brass beds. Imaginative food is served and a warm welcome is assured.

Domvilles Farm

Facilities 5 en suite (1 fmly) (3 GF) ⊗ TVB tea/coffee Cen ht TVL 260 acres Dairy/sheep Dinner Last d 7pm **LB** **Conf** Max 40 Board 40 **Parking** 10 **Notes** 🐾

BREWOOD
MAP 10 SJ80

🄄

The Old Vicarage

Vicarage Rd ST19 9HA ☎ 01902 850210
Dir *From A449 to Brewood, right onto The Pavement, then right onto Vicarage Rd, House on left*

At the time of going to press the rating for this establishment had not been confirmed. Please check the AA website www.theAA.com for up-to-date information.

Facilities 3 rms (2 en suite) (1 pri facs) ⊗ TVB tea/coffee 🐕 Cen ht No coaches **Prices** S £35-£38; D £60-£65✶ **Parking** 5 **Notes** Closed Xmas & New Year 🐾

BURTON UPON TRENT
MAP 10 SK22

Premier Collection

◆◆◆◆◆ 🍽

Dovecliff Hall Hotel

Dovecliff Rd, Stretton DE13 0DJ
☎ 01283 531818 🖷 01283 516546
e-mail enquiry@dovecliffhallhotel.co.uk
web www.dovecliffhallhotel.co.uk
Dir *Off A38 at Claymills junct towards Stretton & Rolleston, 0.5m on right*

A fine, spacious Grade II listed Georgian house set in 7 acres of grounds. Bedrooms are all well equipped and delightfully furnished, and service is attentive. Lounges are spacious and comfortable, and a delicious dinner is available in the Orangery restaurant, which overlooks the gardens.

Facilities 16 en suite (5 GF) ⊗ in bedrooms ⊗ in dining room ⊗ in 1 lounge TVB tea/coffee Direct dial from bedrooms 🐕 Licensed Cen ht No children 12yrs Fishing Dinner Last d 9.30pm **LB** **Conf** Max 120 Thtr 100 Board 60 **Parking** 45 **Notes** rs Sun eve, Mon & Sat lunch Civ Wed 50

BURTON UPON TRENT continued

◆◆◆◆

Delter Hotel

5 Derby Rd DE14 1RU ☎ 01283 535115 ▤ 01283 845261
e-mail delterhotel@burtonontrenthotels.co.uk
Dir A511 rdbt onto A5121 Derby Rd, 50yds on left

Please note that this establishment has recently changed hands. This relaxing guest house is on the outskirts of Burton upon Trent, close to the famous Bass Museum. Bedrooms are thoughtfully equipped and carefully decorated, while the public areas consist of the cosy cellar Delter bar and a pleasant breakfast room.

Facilities 7 en suite (2 fmly) (2 GF) ⊗ TVB tea/coffee ✖ Cen ht TVL No coaches **Prices** S £42; D £60 **Parking** 8 **Notes** Closed Xmas

◆◆◆◆

The Edgecote

179 Ashby Rd DE15 0LB ☎ 01283 568966 ▤ 01283 740118
e-mail susanmccabe@hotmail.co.uk
Dir 0.5m E of town centre on A511

Located in a residential area on the outskirts of town, this impressive Edwardian house provides a range of thoughtfully equipped bedrooms, mostly en suite or with private facilities. A comprehensive breakfast is served in the oak-panelled dining room and there is a quiet lounge.

Facilities 11 rms (5 en suite) (2 pri facs) (1 fmly) ⊗ TVB tea/coffee ✖ Cen ht TVL **Prices** S £32-£59; d fr £69✱ **Parking** 6

CHEADLE   MAP 10 SK04
See also **Froghall**

See also **Froghall**

Premier Collection

◆◆◆◆◆

The Grange

Oakamoor Rd ST10 4QR
☎ 01538 754093 ▤ 01538 754093
e-mail the_grange_bb@hotmail.com
Dir On B5417 1m E of Cheadle

Please note that this establishment has recently changed hands. This restored house stands in neat gardens and rolling countryside on the edge of the town. The stylish, well-equipped bedrooms offer flawless levels of comfort and the luxurious bathrooms have multi-jet walk-in power showers. Comprehensive breakfasts are served at an antique oak table, and fine Staffordshire pottery forms an attractive backdrop.

Facilities 3 en suite ⊗ in bedrooms ⊗ in lounges TVB tea/coffee ✖ Cen ht No coaches BBQ area, cycle hire **Parking** 10 **Notes** ⊛

CHEDDLETON   MAP 16 SJ95

Premier Collection

◆◆◆◆◆◆

Choir Cottage and Choir House

Ostlers Ln ST13 7HS ☎ 01538 360561 & 07719 617078
e-mail enquiries@choircottage.co.uk
Dir Off A520 opp Red Lion onto Hollow Ln, pass church & left onto Ostlers Ln, cottage on right at top of hill

Original features complement this carefully decorated 17th-century stone cottage. The bedrooms have lots of thoughtful extras and feature four-poster beds, modern bathrooms and private entrances. Spacious lounge areas are available in an adjacent house, and the attractive dining room is the setting for breakfast.

Facilities 1 en suite 2 annexe en suite (1 fmly) (2 GF) ⊗ TVB tea/coffee Direct dial from bedrooms ✖ Cen ht No children 4yrs No coaches **Prices** S £45-£49; D £60-£75✱ **LB Parking** 5 **Notes** Closed Xmas ⊛

◆◆◆◆ ➾

Prospect House ◇

334 Cheadle Rd ST13 7BW
☎ 01782 550639 ▤ 0870 756 4155
e-mail prospect@talk21.com
web www.prospecthouseleek.co.uk
Dir 4m S of Leek on A520

Prospect House was built from local stone in 1838. It stands on the A520 between Cheddleton and Wetley Rocks. Bedrooms are in a converted coach house behind the house, and facilities include a traditionally furnished dining room together with a cosy lounge, and a pleasant garden with a conservatory.

Facilities 5 en suite (3 fmly) (2 GF) ⊗ in bedrooms ⊗ in dining room ⊗ in 1 lounge TVB tea/coffee Direct dial from bedrooms ✖ Cen ht TVL No coaches Children's play area Dinner Last d 3pm **Prices** S £23-£25; D £46-£50 **LB Parking** 5

CODSALL   MAP 10 SJ80

◆◆◆ ❦

Moors Farm & Country Hotel (SJ859048)

Chillington Ln WV8 1QF
☎ 01902 842330 ▤ 01902 847878 Mrs Moreton
e-mail enquiries@moorsfarm-hotel.co.uk
web www.moorsfarm-hotel.co.uk
Dir Between Codsall & Codsall Wood, onto Chillington Ln to T-junct & turn right

Located to the north of Codsall village and within easy reach of the M54, this working farm provides friendly hospitality and thoughtfully equipped and comfortable accommodation. A self-catering apartment is also available. Wholesome breakfasts are served in the spacious dining room and dinner is available by arrangement.

Facilities 7 rms (4 en suite) (1 fmly) ⊗ TVB tea/coffee ✖ Cen ht No children 4yrs 100 acres mixed Dinner Last d 24hrs prior **Prices** S £40-£45; D £70-£75✱ **LB Parking** 20

DENSTONE
MAP 10 SK04

★★★★ Ⓐ Guest Accommodation

Heywood Hall

College Rd ST14 5HR ☎ 01889 591747
web www.heywoodhall.co.uk
Dir From B5030, 500yds after entering Denstone, turn left onto College Rd

Facilities 6 en suite (4 fmly) (3 GF) ⊛ TVB tea/coffee ✱ Cen ht TVL No coaches Sauna Hot tub Table tennis **Prices** S £39.99; D £60-£75✶ **Parking** 7 **Notes** Closed Nov-16 Mar ⊛

ECCLESHALL
MAP 15 SJ82

◆◆◆◆ ❦

Slindon House Farm ◇ *(SJ826324)*

Slindon ST21 6LX ☎ 01782 791237 Mrs Bonsall
e-mail bonsallslindonhouse@supanet.com
Dir 2m N of Eccleshall on A519

This large, charming, Victorian farmhouse is fronted by a lovely garden and situated on a dairy, arable and sheep farm in the village of Slindon some 2.5m from Eccleshall. It provides no smoking accommodation comprising of one twin and one double bedded room, both of which are thoughtfully equipped. All share one table in the traditionally furnished combined breakfast room and lounge.

Facilities 2 rms (1 en suite) (1 pri facs) ⊛ TVB tea/coffee ✱ Cen ht TVL 175 acres arable dairy sheep beef **Prices** S £30-£35; D £50✶ **Parking** 4 **Notes** Closed 23-27 Dec & 29 Dec-3 Jan ⊛

ELLASTONE
MAP 10 SK14

◆◆◆◆ Ⓐ

Cross Farm ◇

Main Rd DE6 2GZ ☎ 01335 324668
e-mail jane@cross-farm.co.uk
web www.cross-farm.co.uk
Dir On B5032 in village centre

Facilities 2 en suite (1 fmly) ⊛ TVB tea/coffee ✱ Cen ht No coaches **Prices** S £25-£30; D £48-£50✶ **LB** **Parking** 6 **Notes** ⊛

FROGHALL
MAP 10 SK04

◆◆◆ ❦

Hermitage Working Farm *(SK037497)*

ST10 2HQ ☎ 01538 266515 ▤ 01538 266155 Mrs Barlow
e-mail wilma@hermitagefarm.co.uk
Dir A52 onto B5053 in Froghall, farm 0.5m on left at top of hill

Parts of this charming sandstone house date from the 16th century. It is quietly located on an elevated position with panoramic views. There is traditionally furnished accommodation in the main house as well as a converted barn that offers rooms suitable for families. Handy for visiting Alton Towers.

Facilities 3 en suite 6 annexe en suite (3 fmly) (3 GF) ⊛ in bedrooms ⊛ in dining room ⊛ in 1 lounge TVB tea/coffee ✱ Cen ht Riding Shooting 75 acres beef, sheep, poultry **Parking** 12

HINTS
MAP 10 SK10

◆◆◆◆

Great Bangley Barns B & B

Bangley Ln B78 3EA
☎ 0121 308 3023 & 07779 259083 ▤ 0121 308 3023
e-mail sep@rapidial.co.uk
Dir A38 onto A453 towards Tamworth, 2nd left (narrow lane), around sharp bend, enter through 1st arch of 6 arches of barn conversion

Located within The Canwell Estate 4m from Lichfield, this 18th-century former barn has been lovingly restored into a home of real quality. Smart furnishings and subtle decor highlight the many original features, including a wealth of exposed beams. Ground-floor areas include a choice of sitting rooms and a relaxation suite incorporating a sauna.

Facilities 2 en suite (1 fmly) ⊛ TVB tea/coffee ✱ Cen ht TVL No coaches Sauna Pool Table Spa **Parking** 6 **Notes** ⊛

LEEK
MAP 16 SJ95

★★★★ ⊛ Restaurant with Rooms

Number 64

64 Saint Edwards St ST13 5DL
☎ 01538 381900 ▤ 01538 370918
e-mail enquiries@number64.com
web www.number64.com
Dir In town centre near junct A520 & A53

This Grade II listed Georgian house in the centre of the town offers very well furnished bedrooms, one with a four poster. A wide range of eating options are available, including a speciality food shop, a patisserie, and a restaurant for good cooking.

Facilities 3 en suite ⊛ in bedrooms ⊛ in dining room TVB tea/coffee Direct dial from bedrooms ✱ Licensed No coaches Last d 9pm **Conf** Max 14 Board 14 **Prices** S £65-£85; D £75-£95✶ **Notes** Civ Wed 50

LICHFIELD
MAP 10 SK10

◆◆◆◆

Coppers End

Walsall Rd, Muckley Corner WS14 0BG
☎ 01543 372910 ▤ 01543 360423
e-mail info@coppersendguesthouse.co.uk
Dir A5 onto A461 N for 100yds

Formerly the local police station, this family-run guest house provides well-appointed modern accommodation. Two bedrooms are on the ground floor, and most have smart en suites. There is a comfortable lounge, and breakfast is served in a modern conservatory overlooking the pretty rear gardens.

Facilities 6 rms (4 en suite) (2 GF) ⊛ in bedrooms ⊛ in area of dining room TVB tea/coffee ✱ Cen ht TVL No coaches Golf **Prices** D £48-£60✶ **LB** **Parking** 9 **Notes** Closed Xmas & New Year

England

LICHFIELD continued

◆◆◆
8 The Close ◇

8 The Close WS13 7LD ☎ 01543 418483 & 07812 202415
e-mail gill@theclose.fsnet.co.uk
Dir In city centre. Off Beacon St onto The Close (cathedral)

Idyllic location opposite the seventh century cathedral, this late Georgian terrace house offers homely accommodation and a warm welcome is assured. Breakfasts, which are taken at one table in the cosy hall dining room, feature fine local or homemade produce. Free car parking is available within easy walking distance.

Facilities 3 rms (1 en suite) ⊗ TVB tea/coffee ✖ Cen ht No coaches **Prices** S £28-£34; D £48-£54✳ **Notes** ⊠

◆◆◆
Netherstowe House North

Netherstowe Ln WS13 6AY
☎ 01543 473132 & 07803 145438 📄 01543 473132
e-mail ben@uinpromotions.co.uk
Dir Off A5192 Eastern Av onto Netherstowe Ln, sharp left onto Mill Pond, driveway on right

Located in a residential area a few minutes drive from city centre, this elegant Georgian house provides a range of bedrooms, some of which are quite spacious. Comprehensive breakfasts are taken in a cosy dining room and a comfortable guest lounge is also available.

Facilities 4 rms (1 en suite) (1 fmly) ⊗ TVB tea/coffee ✖ Cen ht TVL No coaches **Parking** 15 **Notes** ⊠

◆◆◆
30 Norwich Close ◇

WS13 7SJ ☎ 01543 250151
e-mail bambrushton@hotmail.com
Dir A38 onto A5192 Eastern Ave, 1m to Vauxhall garage, 1st left onto Norwich Close

Located within a residential area on the outskirts of the city, this modern house provides a homely bedroom with separate side entrance to the property and a modern private shower room. Breakfast is taken in an attractive kitchen/dining room overlooking a pretty rear garden.

Facilities 1 rms (1 pri facs) (1 GF) ⊗ TVB tea/coffee ✖ Cen ht No children No coaches **Prices** S £30; D £42✳ **Parking** 2 **Notes** ⊠

Ⓤ
Number Sixty Seven Bed & Breakfast

67 Walsall Rd WS13 8AD
☎ 01543 254816 & 07764 685826
e-mail libbylewis@4net.co.uk
Dir From Lichfield follow signs for Leamonsley.

At the time of going to press the rating for this establishment had not been confirmed. Please check the AA website www.theAA.com for up-to-date information.

Facilities 3 rms (2 en suite) (1 pri facs) ⊗ TVB tea/coffee ✖ Cen ht **Parking** 3 **Notes** Closed 24-26 Dec ⊠

LONGNOR   MAP 16 SK06

★★★★ Restaurant with Rooms
The Crewe and Harpur Arms

Market Sq SK17 0NS ☎ 01298 83205 📄 01298 83689
e-mail enquiries@creweandharpur.co.uk
Dir In village centre

Located in the heart of the Staffordshire moors this Georgian pub has been refurbished with care. Bedrooms are stylish, fully equipped and each has a modern ensuite. Public areas include the oak panelled bar (featuring real ales) and separate dining room - both offering a tempting range of bar meals and frequently changing a la carte menu, using fresh local ingredients.

Facilities 8 en suite 3 annexe rms (3 fmly) ⊗ in bedrooms ⊗ in dining room ⊗ in lounges STV TV8B tea/coffee Direct dial from bedrooms ✖ Cen ht Dinner Last d 9.30pm **Prices** S £35-£65; D £70-£130✳ **LB** **Conf** Max 25 Board 25 **Parking** 100

NEWCASTLE-UNDER-LYME   MAP 10 SJ84

◆◆◆◆
Butterton House

Park Rd, Butterton ST5 4DZ
☎ 01782 619085 & 07977 519497
e-mail buttertonhouse@lineone.net
Dir M6 junct 15, A5182/A53, right onto Park Rd, house 0.5m on right

Set in extensive gardens in a rural location, yet convenient for the town and the M6, this well-furnished house offers comfortable accommodation. Bedrooms are spacious and well equipped, and a hearty breakfast is served around a large table. A comfortable lounge and a tennis court are available.

Facilities 4 en suite (2 fmly) ⊗ TVB tea/coffee ✖ Cen ht TVL No coaches ⊶ ⅃Ⓞ **Conf** Max 10 **Parking** 6 **Notes** ⊠

OAKAMOOR   MAP 10 SK04

◆◆◆◆
The Beehive Guest House ◇

Churnet View Rd ST10 3AE ☎ 01538 702420
e-mail thebeehiveoakamoor@btinternet.com
web www.thebeehiveguesthouse.co.uk
Dir Off B5417 in village N onto Eaves Ln, sharp left onto Churnet View Rd

Standing in the centre of the village and overlooking the river, this spacious detached house offers thoughtfully equipped and
continued

comfortable bedrooms. There is also a comfortable lounge-dining room, where substantial breakfasts are served. This guest house is renowned for its hospitality.

Facilities 5 en suite (1 fmly) (1 GF) ⊗ TVB tea/coffee ✹ Cen ht TVL No coaches Dinner Last d 6pm **Prices** S £30-£50; D £50-£60✳ LB **Parking** 6

◆◆◆◆

Crowtrees Farm

Eaves Ln ST10 3DY ☎ 01538 702260
e-mail dianne@crowtreesfarm.co.uk
web www.crowtreesfarm.co.uk
Dir Off B5417 in village N onto Eaves Ln, 1m on left

This impeccably maintained 200-year-old farmhouse is convenient for the Potteries, the Peak Distinct and Alton Towers. Bedrooms are comfortable and well equipped. It has splendid views and a collection of pets. The friendly owners create a relaxing atmosphere.

Facilities 3 en suite 5 annexe en suite (2 fmly) ⊗ TVB tea/coffee ✹ Cen ht No coaches **Prices** S £35-£40; D £48-£50 LB **Parking** 6 **Notes** Closed 25-26 Dec

◆◆◆◆

Tenement Farm Guest House

Three Lows, Ribden, Oakamoor ST10 3BW
☎ 01538 702333 ▤ 01538 703603
e-mail stanleese@aol.com
web www.tenementfarm.co.uk
Dir Off A52 onto B5417, signed 1st drive on left

Families are particularly welcome at this non-smoking former farmhouse, which has been renovated to provide high standards of comfort throughout. Popular with visitors to Alton Towers, bedrooms are equipped with homely extras. Public areas include a comfortable lounge with honesty bar, an attractive dining room and a children's play room.

Facilities 8 en suite (6 fmly) (2 GF) ⊗ in bedrooms ⊗ in dining room ⊗ in lounges TVB tea/coffee Direct dial from bedrooms ✹ Licensed Cen ht TVL No coaches Dinner Last d 6.30pm **Prices** S £37.50-£40; D £60-£65✳ LB **Parking** 12 **Notes** Closed Nov-Feb

---

PATTINGHAM   MAP 10 SO89

Ⓤ

Beggars Roost Bed & Breakfast

Clive Rd WV6 7EN ☎ 01902 701496 ▤ 01902 701496
e-mail wendybagley@btinternet.com

At the time of going to press the rating for this establishment had not been confirmed. Please check the AA website www.theAA.com for up-to-date information.

Facilities 1 en suite (3 fmly) (1 GF) ⊗ TVB tea/coffee ✹ Cen ht **Prices** S £40; D £60✳ **Parking** 10 **Notes** 🚭

RUGELEY   MAP 10 SK01

◆◆◆◆

Colton House

Colton WS15 3LL ☎ 01889 578580 ▤ 01889 578580
e-mail mail@colton-house.com
web www.colton-house.com
Dir 1.5m N of Rugeley Off B5013 into Colton, B&B 0.25m on right

Set within the pretty village of Colton, this elegant early 18th-century house has been restored to retain original character and provide high standards of comfort and facilities. Bedrooms have a wealth of thoughtful extras, and there is a spacious and comfortable lounge and a panelled bar.

Facilities 3 en suite ⊗ FTV TVB tea/coffee ✹ Cen ht TVL No children 12yrs No coaches Dinner Last d 8pm **Prices** S £39-£65; D £54-£85 **Conf** Max 15 Thtr 15 Class 15 Board 15 **Parking** 15

◆◆◆◆ ⊛ 🖺 🍷

The Plum Pudding Brasserie

Rugeley Rd, Armitage WS15 4AZ
☎ 01543 490330 ▤ 01543 491229
e-mail enquiries@plumpudding.co.uk
web www.theplumpudding.co.uk
Dir 2.5m SE of Rugeley. On A513 at W end of Armitage

Situated on the banks of the Trent and Mersey Canal, Park View Cottage has been restored to offer comfortable, well-equipped accommodation. Meals are served in the adjacent Plum Pudding Brasserie where you can relax beside the canal, enjoy a refreshing drink, and choose from a large selection of tempting, freshly prepared dishes.

Facilities 4 annexe en suite (1 fmly) (2 GF) ⊗ TVB tea/coffee ✹ Cen ht No children 2yrs No coaches Dinner Last d 9.30pm **Parking** 50

England

STAFFORD

MAP 10 SJ92

◆◆◆◆ ❦

Haywood Park Farm (SJ991207)

Shugborough ST17 0XA
☎ 01889 882736 📠 01889 882736 Mr Nichols
e-mail haywood.parkfarm@btopenworld.com
web www.haywoodparkfarm.co.uk
Dir 4m SE of Stafford off A513. Brown signs to Shugborough, B&B on right 400yds past Hall

Part of the Shugborough Estate, this historic house stands on an arable and sheep farm, and provides a livery service for Cannock Chase. Thoughtfully furnished bedrooms have a wealth of thoughtful extras, and breakfast, using local produce, is served in an attractive lounge-dining room.
Facilities 2 en suite (1 fmly) ⊗ STV TVB tea/coffee ✖ Cen ht TVL Fishing Riding Shooting 120 acres sheep/horse livery/friut farm Dinner Last d 11am **Prices** D £65-£70✳ **LB Parking** 4 **Notes** 🐾

◆◆◆◆ 🍴

Yew Tree Inn & Restaurant

Long Compton, Ranton ST18 9JT
☎ 01785 282278 📠 01785 282278
Dir A518 W from Stafford to Haughton, right before Shropshire Inn onto Station Rd, inn 2.5m on right

Quietly set in lovely gardens, this delightful inn started life as a farmhouse in the 17th century and the characterful bars display many original features. Bedrooms are attractively decorated and neatly furnished. As well as a good range of bar food, there is a spacious and attractive restaurant serving a range of international dishes.
Facilities 3 en suite (1 fmly) ⊗ in bedrooms ⊗ in dining room ⊗ in 1 lounge TVB tea/coffee ✖ Cen ht Fishing Dinner Last d 9.15pm **Prices** S £35-£37.50; D £52.50-£55; (room only) ✳ **LB Conf** Max 60 Thtr 60 Class 60 Board 60 Del from £67.50 ✳ **Parking** 60

◆◆◆

Leonards Croft Hotel

80 Lichfield Rd ST17 4LP
☎ 01785 223676 📠 01785 223676
e-mail leonardscroft@hotmail.com
Dir A34 from town centre signed Cannock, 0.5m on left

Located south of the town centre, this well-proportioned late Victorian house has been carefully renovated to provide a range of practically furnished bedrooms, two of which are situated on the ground floor. A range of popular evening dishes is available in addition to comprehensive breakfasts, and a spacious lounge is also available. The gardens are extensive.
Facilities 9 en suite (3 fmly) (2 GF) ⊗ in bedrooms ⊗ in dining room TVB tea/coffee Licensed Cen ht TVL No coaches Dinner Last d 7pm **Prices** S £38-£42; D £50-£55✳ **Parking** 12

◆◆◆

The Old School ◇

Newport Rd, Haughton ST18 9JH
☎ 01785 780358 📠 01785 780358
e-mail info@theoldsc.co.uk
Dir A518 W from Stafford, 3m to Haughton, Old School next to church

Located in the heart of Haughton village, this Grade II listed former Victorian school has been renovated to provide a range of modern bedrooms equipped with thoughtful extras. Breakfast is served at a family table in a cosy lounge-dining room.
Facilities 3 rms (3 GF) ⊗ TVB tea/coffee Cen ht No coaches **Prices** S £22.50; D £45 **Parking** 3 **Notes** 🐾

◆◆

Windsor Hotel ◇

69 Lichfield Rd ST17 4LW
☎ 01785 258531 📠 01785 246875
e-mail info@abbeyhotelstafford.co.uk
Dir 0.6m SE of town centre on A34

The Windsor is popular with contractors and overseas students. It has a range of practically equipped bedrooms, and a large car park. Breakfast is served in the dining room of the adjacent Abbey Hotel, which is under the same ownership.
Facilities 14 rms (3 en suite) ⊗ in dining room ⊗ in 1 lounge STV TVB tea/coffee ✖ Licensed Cen ht TVL No coaches Dinner Last d 8.30pm **Prices** S £25-£45; D £45-£60✳ **Parking** 16 **Notes** Closed 21 Dec-6 Jan

Ⓤ

Bailey Hotel

63 Lichfield Rd ST17 4LL ☎ 01785 214133 📠 01785 227920

At the time of going to press the rating for this establishment had not been confirmed. Please check the AA website www.theAA.com for up-to-date information.
Facilities 10 en suite (1 fmly) (1 GF) ⊗ in bedrooms ⊗ in 1 lounge TV available tea/coffee Cen ht TVL No coaches Dinner Last d 8pm **Parking** 12

England

STONE
MAP 10 SJ93

◆◆◆

Field House

59 Stafford Rd ST15 0HE ☎ 01785 605712 ▤ 01785 605712
e-mail fieldhouse@ntlworld.com
Dir A34 NW into town centre, right onto Stafford Rd, opp Walton
Grange

This family home stands in quiet, pretty gardens close to the town centre. The Georgian house has traditionally furnished bedrooms, some with family pieces. Guests breakfast together in the lounge-dining room, and hospitality is very welcoming.

Facilities 3 rms (1 en suite) (2 fmly) ⊗ in bedrooms ⊗ in dining room ⊗ in 1 lounge TVB tea/coffee ✖ Cen ht TVL No coaches Art tuition on request **Parking** 4 **Notes** ⊚

◆◆ ⊞

The Fitzherbert Arms ◈

Swynnerton ST15 0RA ☎ 01782 796467
Dir Off A51 onto lane signed Swynnerton. B&B 200yds in village on right

A friendly inn located in the centre of the village close to Swynnerton Park. Rooms are attractive and spacious and downstairs there are various bars and lounges where a wide and varied selection of meals are avaiable. There is also a more formal restaurant where substantial breakfasts are served.

Facilities 4 rms ⊗ in bedrooms ⊗ in dining room TVB tea/coffee ✖ Cen ht Dinner Last d 9pm **Prices** S fr £30; d fr £60✳ **Parking** 24

STRETTON
MAP 10 SJ81

◆◆◆

Cottage Garden Roses

Woodlands House ST19 9LG
☎ 01785 840217 ▤ 01902 850193
e-mail teresa@cottagegardenroses.com
Dir M6 junct 12, A5 towards Telford, after 0.5m Gailey Island rdbt, after 2m follow brown tourist signs for cottage

This charming house dates from the mid 18th century. The delightful garden is given over to the commercial production of old roses. At the time of our last inspection there was a traditionally furnished twin bedded room with its own bathroom and sitting-dining room.

Facilities 1 en suite ⊗ tea/coffee Cen ht TVL Dinner Last d day before **Parking** 6 **Notes** Closed Xmas & 2wks annual holiday

TAMWORTH
MAP 10 SK20

Premier Collection

◆◆◆◆◆

Oak Tree Farm

Hints Rd, Hopwas B78 3AA
☎ 01827 56807 ▤ 01827 56807
e-mail oaktreefarm1@aol.com
Dir 2m NW of Tamworth. Off A51 in Hopwas

Chickens, wild fowl and family pets provide an additional welcome at this restored farmhouse, located in peaceful rural surroundings yet only a short drive from the NEC. Spacious bedrooms are filled with homely extras. The elegant dining room, adorned with Oriental artefacts, is the setting for memorable breakfasts. A small conference room is available.

Facilities 2 en suite 5 annexe en suite (2 fmly) (2 GF) ⊗ TVB tea/coffee Direct dial from bedrooms ✖ Cen ht TVL No coaches ⊱ Fishing Sauna **Conf** Max 15 Thtr 15 Class 9 Board 15 **Parking** 20

◆◆◆◆ ⊞

Globe Inn

Lower Gungate B79 7AW ☎ 01827 60455 ▤ 01827 63575
e-mail globe.inn@btinternet.com

Located in the centre of Tamworth, this popular inn provides well-equipped and pleasantly decorated accommodation. The refurbished public areas include a spacious lounge bar and a relaxed dining area where a varied selection of dishes is available. There is also a function room and adjacent parking.

Facilities 18 en suite (2 fmly) ⊗ in 3 bedrooms ⊗ in dining room STV TVB tea/coffee Direct dial from bedrooms ✖ Cen ht Dinner Last d 9pm **Prices** S fr £45✳ **Conf** Class 90 Board 90 **Parking** 30 **Notes** Closed 25 Dec

◆◆◆◆

Harlaston Post Office

Main Rd, Harlaston B79 9JU
☎ 01827 383324 & 383746 ▤ 01827 383746
e-mail info@harlastonpostoffice.co.uk
Dir 4.5m N, off A513 into Harlaston village

Part of the village stores and Post Office, this guest house stands opposite the ancient church. The individually styled bedrooms provide a range of modern facilities in addition to thoughtful extras. Hearty cooked breakfasts can be enjoyed in the attractive dining room and a conservatory lounge overlooks the pretty garden.

Facilities 4 en suite (1 fmly) (1 GF) ⊗ STV TVB tea/coffee Direct dial from bedrooms ✖ Lift Cen ht TVL No coaches **Parking** 5 **Notes** ⊚

England

TAMWORTH continued

◆◆◆◆

The Old Rectory ◇

Churchside, Harlaston B79 9HE
☎ 01827 383583 & 07973 756367 📄 01827 383583
e-mail dandcking@talktalk.net
Dir 4.5m N, off A513 into Harlaston village

This former Victorian rectory stands in the heart of this pretty, award-winning village. A range of bedrooms, furnished in quality pine with pretty co-ordinating fabrics, offer thoughtful extras, and imaginative breakfasts are served in a spacious sunny kitchen-dining room overlooking the immaculate garden.

Facilities 4 rms (3 en suite) (1 fmly) ⊗ TVB tea/coffee Cen ht No coaches ♪ **Prices** S £25; D £45 **Conf** Max 12 Board 12 **Parking** 7 **Notes** 🐾

◆◆◆◆ 🅰

Middleton House Farm

Tamworth Rd, Middleton B78 2BD
☎ 01827 873474 & 872246 📄 01827 872246
e-mail rob.jane@tinyonline.co.uk
Dir 4m S of Tamworth on A4091

Facilities 6 en suite ⊗ TVB tea/coffee ✖ Cen ht TVL No children 12yrs No coaches Woodland Walks **Prices** S £45-£60; D £60-£75✳ **Parking** 8 **Notes** Closed Xmas & New Year

◆◆◆

The Sleepy Owl ◇

20 Church Ln, Edingale B79 9JD
☎ 01827 383436 & 383853
e-mail irene@sleepyowlbb.freeserve.co.uk
Dir 5m N, off A513 into Edingale village

This modern detached house is in a cul-de-sac in the peaceful village of Edingale, not far from Tamworth. Bedrooms are smartly presented and are thoughtfully equipped. There is a spacious lounge, plus a breakfast room overlooking a immaculately maintained gardens.

Facilities 2 rms ⊗ TVB tea/coffee Direct dial from bedrooms ✖ Cen ht TVL No children 5yrs No coaches Dinner Last d 8pm **Prices** S £25; D £45-£50✳ LB **Parking** 3 **Notes** 🐾

UTTOXETER

MAP 10 SK03

◆◆◆◆

High View Cottage ◇

Toothill Rd ST14 8JU ☎ 01889 568183
e-mail chrislewis@publicityservices.freeserve.co.uk
Dir Take Highwood Rd at mini rdbt at Uttoxeter Racecourse. 0.50m at top of hill turn left into Toothill Rd.

Located on the edge Uttoxeter and close to the racecourse, High View Cottage offers comfortable, well equipped accommodation and a friendly atmosphere. Hearty breakfasts are served in the attractive Garden Room which overlooks the court yard.

Facilities 3 en suite (2 fmly) (3 GF) ⊗ TVB tea/coffee ✖ Cen ht No coaches **Prices** S £25-£40; D £50-£60✳ **Conf** Max 8 Board 8 **Parking** 10

◆◆◆

Oldroyd Guest House & Motel ◇

18-22 Bridge St ST14 8AP
☎ 01889 562763 📄 01889 568916
e-mail enquiries@oldroyd-guesthouse.com
Dir On A518 near racecourse

This privately owned and personally run guest house is close to the town centre and 8m from Alton Towers. Bedrooms have modern facilities, and some family and ground-floor rooms are available. Breakfast is served at separate tables in the bright and pleasant breakfast room.

Facilities 12 rms (10 en suite) 3 annexe en suite (7 fmly) (5 GF) ⊗ TVB tea/coffee ✖ Cen ht TVL **Prices** S £27-£35; D £45-£59✳ LB **Parking** 20

WOODSEAVES

MAP 15 SJ72

★★★★ Farm House

Tunstall Hall Farm *(SJ771273)*

ST20 0NH ☎ 01785 280232 📄 01785 280232 Mrs Cooke
e-mail isabel@tunstallha11.fsnet.co.uk
Dir 2m NW of Woodseaves. A41 onto A519, 1st left to Shebdon, right over canal

Located in quiet hamlet, this impressive renovated farmouse dates fron the early 18th century and retains original exposed beams and open fires. The thoughtfully furnished bedrooms have smart modern shower rooms en suite, and breakfast is served in the attractive conservatory.

Facilities 2 en suite (1 fmly) ⊗ TVB tea/coffee ✖ Cen ht TVL 2 acres Mixed dairy **Parking** 6 **Notes** 🐾

England

SUFFOLK

ALDEBURGH

MAP 13 TM45

◆◆◆◆

The Toll House

50 Victoria Rd IP15 5EJ ☎ 01728 453239
e-mail tollhouse@fsmail.net
Dir B1094 into town until rdbt, B&B on right

Expect a warm welcome at this delightful red-brick property situated just a short walk from the seafront and town centre. Bedrooms have coordinated fabrics and many thoughtful touches, while breakfast is served at individual tables in the smart dining room that overlooks the garden.

Facilities 6 en suite (3 GF) ⊘ TVB tea/coffee ✖ Cen ht No coaches
Prices S £60; D £70-£75✱ **Parking** 5

◆◆◆◆ 🅰

The Oak

111 Saxmundham Rd IP15 5JF
☎ 01728 453528 & 453503 📠 01728 452099
e-mail info@ppaskletting.co.uk
web www.ppaskletting.co.uk
Dir 0.5m NW of seafront on A1094

Facilities 2 en suite ⊘ TVB tea/coffee Cen ht No children No coaches
Prices S £45-£50; D £50-£65✱ **LB Parking** 3 **Notes** Closed Dec-30 Jan
🖭

🆄 🔲

The Mill Inn

Market Cross Pl IP15 5BJ
☎ 01728 452563 📠 01728 452563
e-mail peeldennisp@aol.com

At the time of going to press the rating for this establishment had not been confirmed. Please check the AA website www.theAA.com for up-to-date information.

Facilities 4 rms (2 pri facs) TVB tea/coffee Cen ht Dinner Last d 9pm
Prices S £45; D £60✱

BARNINGHAM

MAP 13 TL97

◆◆◆◆

College House Farm

Bardwell Rd, Barningham IP31 1DF
☎ 01359 221512 📠 01359 221512
e-mail jackie.brightwell@talk21.com
Dir Off B1111 to village x-rds & onto Bardwell Rd

Expect a warm welcome at this charming Grade II listed Jacobean property, which stands in a peaceful location close to Bury St Edmunds. Its abundant original character is complemented by fine period furnishings. Bedrooms are generally quite spacious and thoughtfully equipped. Public rooms include an elegant dining room and a cosy lounge.

Facilities 4 rms (1 en suite) 2 annexe en suite (4 fmly) ⊘ TVB tea/coffee ✖ Cen ht No children 5yrs No coaches 🔟 Dinner Last d by arrangement **Conf** Max 10 **Parking** 8 **Notes** 🖭

BEYTON

MAP 13 TL96

Premier Collection

◆◆◆◆◆ 🕯

Manorhouse

The Green IP30 9AF ☎ 01359 270960
e-mail manorhouse@beyton.com
web www.beyton.com
Dir 4m E of Bury St Edmunds. Beyton signed off A14 junct 46

A charming 15th-century Suffolk longhouse set in immaculate gardens in the heart of the village. The restored property retains many original features, such as exposed beams and roaring log fires. Bedrooms, two of which are in an adjacent barn conversion, are very spacious. Each is carefully furnished and filled with lots of thoughtful touches. Breakfast is served in the elegant dining room and there is a relaxing lounge.

Facilities 2 en suite 2 annexe en suite (2 GF) ⊘ TVB tea/coffee ✖ Cen ht TVL No children 12yrs No coaches Dinner Last d by arrangement **Prices** S £45-£55; D £60-£66 **Parking** 6 **Notes** Closed Xmas 🖭

England

BRANDON
MAP 13 TL78

♦♦

Riverside Lodge ◇

78 High St IP27 0AU ☎ 01842 811236 ▤ 01842 811236
e-mail riversidelodge78@tiscali.co.uk
Dir A11 onto A1065 to Brandon, Lodge by river bridge in High St

This 16th-century Grade II listed merchant's house is set in 12 acres of landscaped gardens. Bedrooms are spacious, pleasantly decorated and well equipped. The public rooms feature a bright, cheerful dining room and a comfortably appointed lounge on the first floor. Parking at rear and at entrance.

Facilities 3 en suite (1 fmly) ⊗ in bedrooms ⊗ in dining room ⊗ in 1 lounge TVB tea/coffee Cen ht TVL Fishing **Prices** S fr £30; d fr £50✳ **Parking** 12 **Notes** rs Xmas-New Year

BUNGAY
MAP 13 TM38

♦♦♦♦ ▤ ✿

Earsham Park Farm *(TM304883)*

Old Railway Rd, Earsham NR35 2AQ
☎ 01986 892180 ▤ 01986 894796 Mrs Watchorn
e-mail aa@earsham-parkfarm.co.uk
web www.earsham-parkfarm.co.uk
Dir 3m SW of Bungay on A143

A superb detached Victorian property overlooking open countryside and forming part of a working farm. The property has been restored by the enthusiastic owners and retains many original features. Bedrooms and public areas are attractively furnished, and the excellent breakfasts feature home-made produce including sausages and bacon from the organically reared pigs.

Facilities 3 en suite ⊗ TVB tea/coffee Cen ht 589 acres arable / pigs outdoor **Prices** S £42-£62; D £62-£82✳ **Conf** Max 16 **Parking** 11

BURY ST EDMUNDS
MAP 13 TL86
See also **Kedington**

★★★ Inn

Dog & Partridge, The Old Brewers House

29 Crown St IP33 1QU ☎ 01284 764792
e-mail 1065@greeneking.co.uk
Dir Off A14 signs for Historic Town Centre, 0.25m past Abbey Gates on left of one-way system

Charming inn situated just a short walk from the town centre. Public rooms include a smart conservatory, a lounge bar, a small dining area and a smartly decked terrace to the rear of the property for alfresco dining. Bedrooms are pleasantly decorated, have coordinated fabrics, natural wood furniture and many thoughtful touches.

Facilities 9 en suite (2 fmly) (3 GF) STV TVB tea/coffee Direct dial from bedrooms ✖ Dinner Last d 9pm **Prices** S £49.50-£69.95; D £60-£79.95✳ **LB Parking** 11

Premier Collection

♦♦♦♦♦

Clarice House

Horringer Court, Horringer Rd IP29 5PH
☎ 01284 705550 ▤ 01284 716120
e-mail enquiry@clarice-bury.fsnet.co.uk
web www.clarice.co.uk
Dir 1m SW from town centre on A143 towards Horringer

The large country property stands in pretty landscaped grounds a short drive from the historic town centre. The spacious, well-equipped bedrooms have coordinated fabrics and many thoughtful touches. Public rooms have a wealth of charm and include a smart lounge bar, an intimate restaurant, a further lounge and a conservatory. Superb leisure facilities feature a large swimming pool, gym, a hairdresser and beauty treatment rooms.

Facilities 13 en suite ⊗ STV FTV TVB tea/coffee Direct dial from bedrooms ✖ Licensed Lift Cen ht No children 5yrs No coaches ⊗ Sauna Solarium Gymnasium spa Dinner Last d 8.45pm
Prices S £55-£60; D £85-£100✳ **LB Conf** Thtr 50 Class 50 Board 50 **Parking** 85 **Notes** Closed 24-26 Dec & 31 Dec-1 Jan

♦♦♦♦

Brambles Lodge

Welham Ln, Risby IP28 6QS
☎ 01284 810701 ▤ 01284 811542
e-mail yr.edge@amserve.com
Dir 4m W of Bury. Off A14 junct 41 into Risby

The Lodge stands amid attractive landscaped gardens in the peaceful village of Risby. The individually decorated bedrooms are pleasantly furnished, and breakfast is served at a large table in the smart conservatory that overlooks the gardens.

Facilities 3 rms (1 en suite) 1 annexe en suite (1 fmly) (4 GF) ⊗ TVB tea/coffee ✖ Cen ht No children 6yrs No coaches **Prices** S £35-£40; D £55-£65✳ **Parking** 5 **Notes** ⊗

♦♦♦♦

The Chantry Hotel

8 Sparhawk St IP33 1RY ☎ 01284 767427 ▤ 01284 760946
e-mail chantryhotel1@aol.com
Dir From cathedral S onto Crown St, left onto Sparhawk St

Expect a warm welcome at this attractive Georgian property, just a short walk from the town centre. The individually decorated bedrooms

continued

are furnished with well-chosen pieces and have many thoughtful touches. Dinner and breakfast are served in the smart restaurant, and there is a cosy lounge-bar.

Facilities 12 en suite 3 annexe en suite (1 GF) ⊗ in bedrooms ⊗ in dining room TVB tea/coffee Direct dial from bedrooms Licensed Cen ht No coaches Dinner Last d 7pm **Prices** S £59-£79; D £79-£99✴ **LB** **Parking** 16

 ◆◆◆◆

83 Whiting Street

83 Whiting St IP33 1NX ☎ 01284 704153
e-mail gordon.wagstaff@btinternet.com
Dir In town centre

An attractive three-storey terrace property convenient for exploring this historic town. The spacious, individually decorated bedrooms are furnished with pine and equipped with modern facilities. Breakfast is served in the beamed dining room that features an open fireplace and a wall painting dating from 1530. This is a non-smoking establishment.

Facilities 3 en suite ⊗ TVB tea/coffee ✕ Cen ht No coaches
Prices S £38; D £60✴ **Notes** ⊛

 ◆◆◆◆ ◗

The Fox & Hounds

Felsham Rd, Bradfield St George IP30 0AB
☎ 01284 386379
e-mail bradfieldfox@aol.com
Dir Off A134 Bury onto Sudbury Rd, at Sicklesmere turning to Little Welnetham & Bradfield St George

Delightful inn set in a peaceful rural location surrounded by open countryside. The spacious bedrooms are in a converted barn to the rear of the inn; each one has pine furniture and a good range of useful extras. Public areas include a smart restaurant, a cosy bar and a small conservatory.

Facilities 2 annexe en suite (2 GF) ⊗ in bedrooms ⊗ in dining room TVB tea/coffee Cen ht Petanque pitch Dinner Last d 9pm **Parking** 30 **Notes** Closed 2-9 Jan

 ◆◆◆◆

Nevill's Lodge

Grindle Gdns IP33 2QG ☎ 01284 754168
Dir S of town centre off A134 Cullum Rd onto Beech Rise & Grindle Gardens

Expect a friendly welcome at this charming detached bungalow situated on the outskirts of the historic town. Bedrooms have coordinated fabrics and many thoughtful touches. Breakfast is served in the lounge-dining room around a large table that overlooks the garden.

Facilities 3 rms (1 en suite) ⊗ TVB tea/coffee ✕ No children 5yrs No coaches **Parking** 6 **Notes** ⊛

 ◆◆◆◆ ☒

The Old Cannon Brewery

86 Cannon St IP33 1JR ☎ 01284 768769 🖷 01284 701137
e-mail richardej@cannondsl.clara.co.uk
Dir A14 junct 43, A134 towards town centre. At rdbt after Tesco left then sharp right onto Cadney Ln, left onto Cannon St, B&B on left

This delightful Victorian property was originally a beer house and brewery. The present owner has renovated the building and reopened the brewery, and the finished products can be sampled in the bar. The bar-dining area features a unique mirror-polished stainless-steel mash tun and boiler.

Facilities 5 en suite ⊗ TVB tea/coffee ✕ Licensed Cen ht No children 14yrs Dinner Last d 9.30pm **Prices** S £55-£60; D £65✴ **Parking** 6

 ◆◆◆◆ ☒ ◗

The Six Bells at Bardwell

The Green, Bardwell IP31 1AW
☎ 01359 250820 🖷 01359 250820
e-mail sixbellsbardwell@aol.com
web www.sixbellsbardwell.co.uk
Dir 8m NE, off A143 in village centre

This 16th-century inn lies in the peaceful village of Bardwell. The bedrooms are in a converted stable block next to the main building, and are furnished in a country style and thoughtfully equipped. Public rooms have original character and provide a choice of areas in which to relax.

Facilities 10 en suite (1 fmly) (10 GF) ⊗ in 2 bedrooms ⊗ in dining room ⊗ in 1 lounge TVB tea/coffee Cen ht Dinner Last d 8.45pm **Prices** S £52.50-£59.50; D £65-£75✴ **LB** **Parking** 40 **Notes** Closed 25 Dec-3 Jan

◆◆◆◆ ◗

The Three Kings

Hengrave Rd, Fornham All Saints IP28 6LA
☎ 01284 766979
e-mail thethreekings@keme.co.uk
Dir A14 junct 42, B1106 to Fornham, left onto B1101, establishment on left

An attractive inn situated in the pleasant village of Fornham All Saints. The bedrooms are in a new building adjacent to the main property; each one attractively furnished and equipped with an excellent range of facilities including a minibar. Public rooms feature a smart lounge bar, a conservatory, and a comfortable restaurant.

Facilities 9 annexe en suite (2 fmly) (6 GF) ⊗ in bedrooms ⊗ in 1 lounge TVB tea/coffee Direct dial from bedrooms ✕ Cen ht Pool Table Dinner Last d 9pm **Prices** S fr £57.50; d fr £75✴ **Parking** 28

◆◆◆ ◗

The Black Boy

69 Guildhall St IP33 1QD ☎ 01284 752723
Dir Off A14 to town centre

A popular inn situated in the centre of this historic town. The spacious bedrooms have coordinated fabrics, pine furniture and many thoughtful touches. Public areas feature a large open-plan bar with a good selection of ales and a range of bar snacks are also available.

Facilities 5 en suite ⊗ TV available tea/coffee ✕ Cen ht No coaches Dinner Last d 9pm **Prices** S fr £40; d fr £60✴ **Parking** 6

England

BURY ST EDMUNDS continued

◆◆◆

The Abbey Hotel

35 Southgate St IP33 2AZ
☎ 01284 762020 ▤ 01284 724770
e-mail 01284762020@tel-w.com

Dir A14 junct 44, A1302 to town centre, onto Southgate St, premises 400yds

The Abbey is well placed for visiting the historic town centre. The property is split between several historic buildings, the main core dating fom the 15th century. The public rooms in the Tudor inn section feature a comfortable lounge and an informal dining area. Bedrooms vary in size and style, but all are comfortably furnished and well equipped.

Facilities 9 en suite 3 annexe en suite (1 fmly) (2 GF) ⊘ TVB tea/coffee ✗ Licensed Cen ht No children 3yrs No coaches
Prices S £55-£65; D £75-£85✱ **Parking** 12

◆◆◆

5-6 Orchard Street ◇

IP33 1EH ☎ 01284 750191 & 07946 590265
e-mail mariellascarlett@hotmail.com

Dir In town centre near St John's Church on one-way system

Expect a warm welcome at this terrace property, which is just a short walk from the town centre. The pleasant bedrooms are comfortably appointed and have a good range of useful extras. Breakfast is served at a large communal table in the cosy dining room.

Facilities 3 rms ⊘ TVB tea/coffee ✗ Cen ht No coaches **Prices** S fr £22; d fr £36 **Notes** Closed Aug 🐾

◆◆◆

Hamilton House ◇

4 Nelson Rd IP33 3AG
☎ 01284 703022 & 07787 146553 ▤ 01284 703022
e-mail terrywelsh821@btinternet.co.uk

Dir A14 junct 43, A134, left onto Risbygate St, 1st right

Expect a warm welcome at this relaxing Edwardian villa, which is situated in a quiet side road just a short walk from the town centre. The spacious bedrooms are brightly decorated and have a good range of facilities. Breakfast is served at a communal table in the dining room.

Facilities 4 rms (2 en suite) (1 fmly) ⊘ TVB tea/coffee ✗ Cen ht No coaches **Prices** S £23-£28; D £50 **Notes** 🐾

◆◆◆

St Andrews Lodge

30 Saint Andrews St North IP33 1SZ ☎ 01284 756733
e-mail di.groves@thelodge30.freeserve.co.uk

Dir A14 junct 43, A134 towards town centre, left onto Saint Andrews St North, Lodge on right

This friendly, family-run guest house is convenient for the A14 and the town centre. The well-equipped modern bedrooms are on the ground floor of a separate purpose-built building to the rear of the house.

Breakfast is served at individual tables in the smart dining room, which overlooks the neat courtyard.

Facilities 3 en suite (1 fmly) (3 GF) ⊘ TVB tea/coffee ✗ Cen ht No coaches **Prices** S £37.50; D £60✱ **Parking** 3 **Notes** Closed Xmas & New Year

◆◆◆

St Vincent Guest House ◇

109 Fornham Rd IP32 6AS ☎ 01284 705884
e-mail janetbacchus@aol.com

Dir 0.5m N of town centre on A1101

Expect a warm welcome at this friendly guest house situated close to the railway station and a 15-minute walk from the town centre. Bedrooms are generally quite spacious; each one is pleasantly decorated and thoughtfully equipped. A hearty breakfast is served in the smartly appointed dining room.

Facilities 4 rms (2 en suite) (2 pri facs) (2 fmly) ⊘ TVB tea/coffee ✗ Cen ht No coaches **Prices** S £25-£28; D £55-£60✱ **Parking** 2

◆◆◆ Ⓐ

Dunston Guest House ◇

8 Springfield Rd IP33 3AN
☎ 01284 767981 ▤ 01284 764574

Dir A14 from Cambridge, 1st slip road onto A1302, in 1.5m after pedestrian crossing & Falcon pub left onto Springfield Rd

Facilities 11 rms (7 en suite) (4 pri facs) 6 annexe rms (2 en suite) (5 fmly) (4 GF) ⊘ TVB tea/coffee ✗ Cen ht TVL **Prices** S £25-£40; D £60-£65✱ **Parking** 10 **Notes** 🐾

◆◆

Avery House

2 Newmarket Rd IP33 3SN ☎ 01284 755484

Dir 1m from Bury St Edmunds West, junct off A14 heading to town centre

Large detached, purpose-built property situated on the edge of town within easy walking distance of the shops. The property is well suited to the business traveller and offers value for money accommodation. The practically equipped bedrooms are comfortable and a full English breakfast is provided in the cafeteria style dining room.

Facilities 6 en suite (1 fmly) (3 GF) ⊘ in dining room ⊘ in lounges TVB tea/coffee ✗ Cen ht **Parking** 8 **Notes** 🐾

continued

England

CAMPSEA ASH
MAP 13 TM35

◆◆◆

Dog and Duck
Station Rd IP13 0PT ☎ 01728 748439
Dir *Off A12 for Framlingham, onto B1078, B&B 1.5m on left*

Facilities 5 annexe en suite (2 fmly) (4 GF) ⊗ in bedrooms ⊗ in dining room ⊗ in 1 lounge TVB tea/coffee Licensed Cen ht Dinner Last d 9pm **Prices** S fr £45.50; d fr £64.50✱ **Parking** 20

CLARE
MAP 13 TL74

◆◆◆◆

Ship Stores
22 Callis St CO10 8PX ☎ 01787 277834 ▤ 01787 277183
e-mail shipclare@aol.com
Dir *A1092 to Clare, onto B1063, past church 100yds on right*

A charming property situated in the heart of this historic market town. Bedrooms are split between the main house and a converted stable block; each room is furnished in a country style with bright, coordinated soft furnishings and many thoughtful touches. Public areas include a lounge with comfy sofas, and a contemporary breakfast room with a stripped pine floor.

Facilities 4 en suite 2 annexe en suite (1 fmly) (3 GF) ⊗ in bedrooms ⊗ in dining room TVB tea/coffee ✖ Cen ht No coaches **Prices** S £35-£53; D £53-£58✱ LB **Parking** 3

DEBENHAM
MAP 13 TM16

★★★ ⊛ **Restaurant with Rooms**

The Angel Inn
5 High St IP14 6QL ☎ 01728 860954 ▤ 01728 861854
e-mail d.given@btconnect.com
Dir *On B1077 in village centre*

Expect a warm welcome at this charming inn, set in the heart of this peaceful village. Public rooms include a cosy lounge bar and a comfortable restaurant with pine furniture. Bedrooms are generally quite spacious; each one is simply decorated, tastefully furnished and equipped with modern facilities.

Facilities 3 en suite (1 fmly) TVB tea/coffee ✖ Licensed Dinner Last d 9.30pm **Prices** S fr £50; d fr £70✱ **Conf** Max 50 Thtr 30 Class 30 Board 30 **Parking** 14

ELMSWELL
MAP 13 TL96

◆◆◆

Kiln Farm Guest House
Kiln Ln IP30 9QR ☎ 01359 240442
e-mail davejankilnfarm@btinternet.com
Dir *Exit A14 junct 47, just off A1088*

Please note that this establishment has recently changed hands. Delightful Victorian farmhouse set in a peaceful rural location amid 3 acres of landscaped grounds with lovely views. Bedrooms are housed in a converted barn; each is pleasantly decorated and furnished in country style. Breakfast is served in the bar-dining room and there is a cosy lounge.

continued

Facilities 2 en suite 6 annexe en suite (2 fmly) (6 GF) ⊗ TVB tea/coffee Licensed Cen ht TVL No coaches Dinner Last d 6pm **Prices** D £70-£100✱ **Parking** 20 **Notes** ⊠

EYE
MAP 13 TM17

◆◆◆◆ ⌨

The White Horse inn
Stoke Ash IP23 7ET ☎ 01379 678222 ▤ 01379 678800
e-mail mail@whitehorse-suffolk.co.uk
web www.whitehorse-suffolk.co.uk
Dir *On A140 halfway between Ipswich & Norwich*

A 17th-century coaching inn situated in the village of Stoke Ash. Bedrooms are located in an annexe adjacent to the main building; each is pleasantly decorated in pastel shades, furnished with reproduction pieces and thoughtfully equipped. An interesting choice of dishes is served in the restaurant, which features exposed beams and inglenook fireplaces.

Facilities 11 annexe en suite (1 fmly) (9 GF) ⊗ in 1 bedrooms ⊗ in dining room TVB tea/coffee Direct dial from bedrooms ✖ Cen ht Dinner Last d 9.30pm **Prices** S £50; D £60 LB **Conf** Max 50 Thtr 50 Class 50 **Parking** 60

See advertisement on this page

FRAMLINGHAM

MAP 13 TM26

◆◆◆◆

Woodlands Farm ◇

Brundish IP13 8BP ☎ 01379 384444
e-mail jillatwoodlands@aol.com
Dir *4m N of Framlingham. Off A1120 onto B1116 N, 4th left, 0.5m left onto no-through road*

Quietly located north of the town, this charming house has a wealth of character, including original exposed beams and inglenook fireplaces in the sitting room and the elegant dining room. The pleasant bedrooms are carefully decorated and thoughtfully equipped.

Facilities 3 en suite ⊗ tea/coffee ✱ Cen ht TVL No children 10yrs No coaches **Prices** S £30-£35; D £50-£60 **Parking** 6 **Notes** Closed 24 Dec-2 Jan ⊛

◆◆◆ ❦

Church Farm ◇ *(TM605267)*

Church Rd, Kettleburgh IP13 7LF
☎ 01728 723532 Mrs Bater
e-mail jbater@suffolkonline.net
Dir *Off A12 to Wickham Market, signs to Easton Farm Park & Kettleburgh 1.25m, house behind church*

A charming 300-year-old farmhouse situated close to the village church amid superb grounds with a duck pond, mature shrubs and sweeping lawns. The converted property retains exposed beams and open fireplaces. Bedrooms are pleasantly decorated and equipped with useful extras, and a ground-floor bedroom is available.

Facilities 3 rms (1 en suite) (1 GF) ⊗ tea/coffee ✱ Cen ht TVL Fishing Clay pigeon shooting 70 acres mixed Dinner Last d 7.30pm **Prices** S £26-£28; D £52-£56 **Parking** 10 **Notes** ⊛

If the freedom to smoke or be in a non-smoking atmosphere is important to you, check the rules when you book

FRESSINGFIELD

MAP 13 TM27

◆◆◆◆◆

Chippenhall Hall

IP21 5TD ☎ 01379 588180 🖹 0870 831 5113
e-mail info@chippenhall.co.uk
web www.chippenhall.co.uk
Dir *8m E of Diss: 1.5m outside Fressingfield on B1116 to Framlingham*

This charming country house dates from the 16th and 17th centuries. It stands amid landscaped grounds and open countryside, and has a wealth of original features. The spacious bedrooms are individually decorated, carefully furnished and equipped with many thoughtful touches. Breakfasts and imaginative dinners are served in the elegant dining room. There is also a cosy lounge.

Facilities 3 en suite ⊗ in bedrooms ⊗ in dining room ⊗ in 1 lounge tea/coffee ✱ Licensed Cen ht TVL No children 14yrs No coaches ⚓ ⚐ Clay pigeon shooting Dinner Last d 2.30pm **Conf** Max 80 Class 80 Board 40 **Parking** 20 **Notes** Civ Wed 80

HADLEIGH

MAP 13 TM04

◆◆◆◆◆

Edge Hall

2 High St IP7 5AP ☎ 01473 822458 🖹 01473 827751
e-mail r.rolfe@edgehall-hotel.co.uk
Dir *B1070 into Hadleigh. 1st property in High St on right*

This imposing 16th-century building at the quiet end of High St has been run by the same family for over 25 years. The spacious bedrooms are individually decorated and carefully furnished in period

continued

style - one room has a superb four-poster bed. Breakfast is served in the elegant dining room and there is also a comfortable lounge.

Facilities 6 en suite 4 annexe en suite (2 fmly) (1 GF) ⊘ TVB tea/coffee Cen ht No coaches ↯ **Prices** S £50-£75; D £75-£95✱ LB **Parking** 20 **Notes** ⊚

IPSWICH
MAP 13 TM14

♦♦♦ ◼

The Shipwrights Arms

55-61 Wherestead Rd IP2 8JJ
☎ 01473 602261 ▤ 01473 604255
Dir A14 onto A137 Ipswich Centre, at West Dock, turn left at Audi garage, 50yds on right

Smartly presented inn a 10-minute walk from the town centre. Bedrooms are generally quite spacious; each one is pleasantly decorated with coordinated soft furnishings and many thoughtful touches. Public rooms include a small bar area, two dining rooms and a lovely conservatory.

Facilities 9 en suite (2 GF) ⊘ in bedrooms ⊘ in dining room ⊘ in 1 lounge TVB tea/coffee ✖ Cen ht TVL No coaches Dinner Last d 9pm **Prices** S £45-£55; D £55-£85✱ **Parking** 6 **Notes** rs Sun

KEDINGTON
MAP 12 TL74

Premier Collection

♦♦♦♦♦

The White House

Silver St CB9 7QG ☎ 01440 707731 ▤ 01440 705753
e-mail tobybarclay@nalsparks.co.uk
web www.thewhitehousebandb.co.uk
Dir A143 onto B1061 into Kedington, 3rd left, Kings Hill, house at bottom of hill opp pub

This Grade II listed, timber-framed 17th-century house has a quiet village setting. Extended in the Victorian period, this delightful house has been carefully furnished and restored by enthusiastic proprietors and features exposed beams. The charming, individually furnished bedrooms offer many creature comforts, personal touches and thoughtful extras.

Facilities 3 rms (2 en suite) (1 pri facs) ⊘ TVB tea/coffee ✖ Cen ht No children 12yrs No coaches Shooting tuition **Prices** S £40-£65; D £65✱ **Parking** 5 **Notes** ⊚

LAVENHAM
MAP 13 TL94

Premier Collection

♦♦♦♦♦ ⌂

Lavenham Priory

Water St CO10 9RW ☎ 01787 247404 ▤ 01787 248472
e-mail mail@lavenhampriory.co.uk
web www.lavenhampriory.co.uk
Dir A1141 to Lavenham, turn by side of Swan onto Water St & right after 50yds onto private drive

Expect a warm welcome at this superb Grade I listed building, dating from the 15th century. The property once belonged to Benedictine monks and has been lovingly restored to maintain its original

character. Individually decorated bedrooms are very spacious; each is beautifully furnished and thoughtfully equipped. Breakfast is served in the spectacular Merchants room or in the sheltered courtyard herb garden. Guests also have use of the Great Hall, with inglenook fireplace, and an adjoining lounge.

Lavenham Priory

Facilities 6 en suite ⊘ TVB tea/coffee ✖ Licensed Cen ht TVL No children 10yrs No coaches **Prices** S £75-£85; D £95-£155✱ **Parking** 11 **Notes** Closed 21 Dec-2 Jan

♦♦♦♦ ⊛⊛ ⌂ ⌂

Lavenham Great House Hotel

Market Pl CO10 9QZ ☎ 01787 247431 ▤ 01787 248007
e-mail greathouse@clara.co.uk
web www.greathouse.co.uk
Dir Off A1141 onto Market Ln, behind cross on Market Place

The 18th-century front on Market Place conceals a 15th-century timber-framed building that houses a restaurant with rooms. The restaurant is a pocket of France and offers high-quality rural cuisine served by French staff. The spacious bedrooms are individually decorated and thoughtfully equipped with many useful extras; some rooms have a separate lounge area.

Facilities 5 en suite (2 fmly) ⊘ FTV TVB tea/coffee Direct dial from bedrooms Licensed Cen ht No coaches Dinner Last d 9.30pm **Prices** S £65-£150; D £96-£150; (room only) ✱ LB **Notes** Closed Jan rs Sun nights & Mon

♦♦♦♦

Wood Hall

Little Waldingfield CO10 0SY
☎ 01787 247362 ▤ 01787 248326
e-mail susan@woodhallbnb.fsnet.co.uk
web www.thewoodhall.co.uk
Dir A1141 onto B1115 into Little Waldingfield, Wood Hall 200yds on left past Swan pub

Expect a warm welcome at this delightful 15th-century hall just a short drive from historic Lavenham. The spacious, individually decorated bedrooms are thoughtfully equipped. Breakfast is served in the elegant dining room, which features a superb inglenook fireplace with a wood-burning stove. Parking at rear.

Facilities 2 en suite ⊘ TVB tea/coffee ✖ Cen ht No children 10yrs No coaches ↯ Dinner Last d 48 hrs before **Prices** S fr £40; D £70-£75✱ **Parking** 4 **Notes** Closed 21 Dec-2 Jan ⊚

continued

England

LAVENHAM continued

◆◆◆◆ 🅰

Brett Farm

The Common CO10 9PG ☎ 01787 248533
e-mail brettfarmbandb@aol.com
web www.brettfarm.com
Dir In Lavenham turn by Swan Hotel onto Water St, 4th left & 1st right over white bridge, farm on right

Facilities 3 rms (2 en suite) (3 GF) ⊗ TVB tea/coffee 🐾 Cen ht
No coaches Carriage rides Bike hire **Prices** S £40-£65; D £60-£65✱
Parking 6 **Notes** 🚭

LEISTON   MAP 13 TM46

◆◆◆◆

Field End ◇

1 Kings Rd IP16 4DA ☎ 01728 833527 📠 01728 833527
web www.fieldendbedandbreakfast.co.uk
Dir In town centre off B1122

This Edwardian house has been refurbished to a high standard and is impeccably maintained by the present owners. Bedrooms have coordinated soft furnishings and many thoughtful touches. Breakfast is served in an attractive dining room, which has a large sofa and a range of puzzles and games.

Facilities 5 rms (2 en suite) (1 pri facs) (1 fmly) ⊗ TVB tea/coffee 🐾
Cen ht TVL No children 6mths No coaches **Prices** S £30; D £60✱
Parking 5 **Notes** 🚭

LOWESTOFT   MAP 13 TM59

◆◆◆◆

Abbe Guest House

322 London Rd South NR33 0BG
☎ 01502 581083 & 538133
e-mail info@abbehousehotel.com
web www.abbehousehotel.com
Dir On A12, 1.5m from the Pakefield Water Tower rdbt, 50yds past Rectory Rd

A warm welcome is to be expected from the caring hosts at this charming property, which is situated just a short walk from the seafront and town centre. Bedrooms are pleasantly decorated with coordinated soft furnishings and have many thoughtful extras. Breakfast is served in the elegant dining room and guests have the use of a cosy lounge bar.

Facilities 4 rms (3 en suite) (1 fmly) ⊗ in 2 bedrooms ⊗ in dining room ⊗ in lounges STV TVB tea/coffee 🐾 Licensed Cen ht TVL
No coaches **Parking** 1 **Notes** Closed 21 Dec-6 Jan

◆◆◆◆

Kingsleigh Guest House

44 Marine Pde NR33 0QN ☎ 01502 572513
Dir On A12 S from Lowestoft town centre, house on right, 0.25m from Harbour Bridge

A warm welcome is to be expected on arrival at this well-maintained Victorian property, situated on the south side of town just a short walk from the shops. Bedrooms are attractively decorated in pastel shades

continued

and have coordinated soft furnishings and many thoughtful touches. Most rooms have superb sea views.

Facilities 5 rms (3 en suite) ⊗ TVB tea/coffee Cen ht No coaches
Notes 🚭

◆◆◆◆

Longshore Guest House

7 Wellington Esplanade NR33 0QQ
☎ 01502 565037 📠 01502 582032
e-mail SandraNolan@btconnect.com
Dir On A12 S overlooking sea

A Grade II listed building situated on the south side of town, overlooking the award-winning beach and sea beyond. Bedrooms come in a variety of sizes, all are pleasantly decorated and equipped with modern facilities; some have lovely sea views. Breakfast is served at individual tables in the smart dining room.

Facilities 3 en suite (1 fmly) ⊗ TV6B tea/coffee Cen ht No coaches
Parking 5 **Notes** Closed 20 Dec-1 Jan

◆◆◆◆

Seavilla Hotel ◇

43 Kirkley Cliff Rd NR33 0DF
☎ 01502 574657 📠 01502 574657
Dir A12 into town, right at South Beach, 300yds past Claremont Pier

Expect a warm welcome at the Seavilla, situated on the southern side of town overlooking the beach. The pleasant bedrooms are thoughtfully equipped and many have superb sea views. Breakfast is served in the attractive dining room and there is a cosy lounge bar.

Facilities 9 rms (5 en suite) ⊗ TVB tea/coffee 🐾 Cen ht TVL
No coaches **Prices** S £25-£40; D £50-£65✱ LB

◆◆◆◆

Somerton House

7 Kirkley Cliff NR33 0BY ☎ 01502 565665 📠 01502 501176
e-mail somerton@screaming.net
Dir On A12 S on seafront, 100yds from Claremont Pier

Grade II Victorian terrace situated in a peaceful area of town overlooking the sea. Bedrooms are smartly furnished in a period style and have many thoughtful touches; some rooms have four poster or half-tester beds. Breakfast is served in the smart dining room and guests have the use of a cosy lounge.

Facilities 7 rms (5 en suite) (2 pri facs) (1 fmly) (1 GF) ⊗ STV TVB
tea/coffee Licensed Cen ht TVL No coaches Dinner Last d noon LB
Notes Closed 25-26 Dec

◆◆◆◆

Wavecrest Guest House ◇

31 Marine Pde NR33 0QN
☎ 01502 561268 📠 01502 561268
e-mail sue@wave-crest.freeserve.co.uk
Dir On A12 S just S of Lowestoft Bridge

This Victorian terrace house is situated on the seafront, overlooking the award-winning beach and within easy walking distance of the town centre. The bedrooms are smartly decorated with coordinated soft

continued

furnishings and equipped with modern facilities. Public areas include an elegant dining room where breakfast is served at individual tables.

Facilities 4 en suite (2 fmly) ⊗ TVB tea/coffee ✕ Cen ht No coaches **Prices** S £25-£30; D £43-£55✳ **Notes** Closed 24-31 Dec 🖃

◆◆◆◆

Fishers Hotel & Restaurants

41 London Rd, Pakefield NR33 7AA
☎ 01502 569805 🖹 01502 565383
web www.thefishershotel.co.uk
Dir S of town centre on A12 in Pakefield

Facilities 16 en suite (3 fmly) ⊗ in 10 bedrooms ⊗ in dining room ⊗ in 1 lounge STV TVB tea/coffee Direct dial from bedrooms Licensed Cen ht TVL Dinner Last d 9pm **Parking** 28

◆◆◆

Hotel Katherine

49 Kirkley Cliff Rd NR33 0DF
☎ 01502 567858 🖹 01502 581341
e-mail beauthaicuisine@aol.com
Dir On A1118 seafront road next to Kensington Garden

The large Victorian property lies opposite the beach in the quiet part of town. The spacious public rooms include a smart lounge bar with plush leather sofas and an intimate restaurant serving authentic Thai cuisine. The pleasant bedrooms have coordinated fabrics and many thoughtful touches.

Facilities 10 en suite (5 fmly) ⊗ TVB tea/coffee Direct dial from bedrooms ✕ Licensed Cen ht Dinner Last d 10.30pm **Prices** S £35-£45; D £55-£60✳ **LB** **Parking** 2

◆◆◆

Coventry House ◇

8 Kirkley Cliff NR33 0BY
☎ 01502 573865 🖹 01502 573865
Dir On A12 opp Claremont Pier, 0.25m S from Harbour Bridge

Expect a warm welcome at this impressive Victorian terrace house, which is situated on the seafront opposite the pier. The pleasant bedrooms are thoughtfully equipped and many rooms have lovely sea views. Breakfast is served in the carefully appointed dining room and there is a comfortable lounge.

Facilities 7 rms (5 en suite) (2 pri facs) (3 fmly) (1 GF) ⊗ TVB tea/coffee Cen ht TVL No coaches **Prices** S £22-£30✳ **LB** **Parking** 4 **Notes** Closed 24-27 Dec 🖃

◆◆◆

Edingworth Guest House ◇

395/7 London Rd South NR33 0BJ
☎ 01502 572051 🖹 01502 572051
e-mail enquiries@edingworth.co.uk
web www.edingworth.co.uk
Dir On A12 through Lowestoft towards Great Yarmouth

A friendly, family-run guest house situated within easy walking distance of the town centre and seafront. The spacious bedrooms are

continued

pleasantly decorated and thoughtfully equipped. Breakfast is served in the smart dining room and there is a comfortable television lounge.

Facilities 10 rms (1 en suite) (9 pri facs) (9 fmly) (1 GF) ⊗ in dining room TVB tea/coffee ✕ Cen ht TVL No coaches **Prices** S £28-£30; D £50-£52 **LB** **Parking** 4 **Notes** Closed 24-26 Dec 🖃

◆◆◆

Fairways Guest House ◇

398 London Rd South NR33 0BQ ☎ 01502 572659
e-mail amontali@netmatters.co.uk
Dir S of town centre on A12, 1m from railway and bus station

Expect a friendly welcome at this family-run guest house, which is located at the southern end of the town. Bedrooms come in a variety of sizes and styles; each room is pleasantly decorated and thoughtfully equipped. Breakfast is served in the smart dining room and there is also a cosy lounge.

Facilities 7 rms (4 en suite) (2 fmly) ⊗ TVB tea/coffee Licensed Cen ht TVL **Prices** S £19-£26; d fr £42✳

MENDHAM   MAP 13 TM28

◆◆◆◆ 🐓

Weston House Farm ◇ (TM292828)

IP20 0PB ☎ 01986 782206 Mrs Holden
e-mail holden@farmline.com
Dir Off A143 or B1123 signed Mendham, signs from village centre

This Grade II listed 17th century farmhouse stands in extensive pleasant gardens in the heart of the Waveny valley. The individually decorated bedrooms are generally quite spacious, thoughtfully furnished and well-equipped. Breakfast is served in the dining room overlooking the garden.

Facilities 3 en suite (1 GF) ⊗ TVB tea/coffee ✕ Cen ht TVL No children 10yrs 600 acres Mixed **Prices** S £29-£37; D £48-£60✳ **Parking** 6 **Notes** Closed Dec-Feb 🖃

England

MILDENHALL ◆◆◆◆   MAP 12 TL77

Orchard House

23 North Ter IP28 7AA
☎ 01638 711237 & 07747 655433 ▤ 01638 715403
e-mail orchardhouse23@aol.com
Dir From town centre minirdbt onto A1101 signed Littleport, Orchard House 250yds on left, gates before 2nd school sign

A lovely Victorian house set amid mature gardens near the town centre. The individually decorated rooms have superb beds, natural wood furniture, Italian tiled bathrooms and many thoughtful touches. Breakfast is served at a large table in the elegant dining room and the lounge has plush leather sofas.

Facilities 4 rms (1 en suite) (1 pri facs) ⊗ TVB tea/coffee ✖ Cen ht TVL No children 8yrs No coaches **Prices** S £40-£55; D £65-£75✳ LB **Conf** Max 8 Board 8 **Parking** 7 **Notes** ⊛

NAYLAND   MAP 13 TL93

◆◆◆◆ ⊛⊛ ⊜ ◨

The White Hart Inn

High St CO6 4JF ☎ 01206 263382 ▤ 01206 263638
e-mail nayhart@aol.com
Dir Off A134 into village centre

Relaxation and a warm welcome are guaranteed at this delightful 15th-century inn, in a charming village in the heart of Constable country. The bedrooms are individually decorated and carefully furnished, while the elegant restaurant offers seasonal, local produce.

Facilities 6 en suite ⊗ in bedrooms ⊗ in dining room ⊗ in 1 lounge TVB tea/coffee Direct dial from bedrooms ✖ Cen ht Dinner Last d 9.30pm **Prices** S £69-£87; D £85-£110 **Conf** Max 20 Del from £25 ✳ **Parking** 20 **Notes** Closed 26 Dec-9 Jan Civ Wed 70

◆◆◆◆

Hill House

Gravel Hill CO6 4JB ☎ 01206 262782
e-mail heighamhillhouse@hotmail.com
Dir In village centre. Off B1087 Birch St onto Gravel Hill

Set in secluded grounds in a peaceful village on the edge of Constable Country, this Grade II listed, 16th-century timber-framed building has a wealth of exposed beams, a flagstone hall and inglenooks. The attractive bedrooms are well equipped and overlook the pretty garden. Breakfast is served around a large communal table in the attractive, beamed dining room.

Facilities 2 en suite ⊗ TVB tea/coffee ✖ Cen ht No children 12yrs No coaches ◢◣ **Prices** S £35-£40; D £62-£68 LB **Parking** 4 **Notes** Closed 20 Dec-1 Jan ⊛

◆◆◆◆ **A**

Gladwins Farm

Harper's Hill CO6 4NU ☎ 01206 262261 ▤ 01206 263001
e-mail gladwinsfarm@aol.com
web www.gladwinsfarm.co.uk/b&b.asp
Dir 0.5m NW of Nayland on A134, on top of hill

Facilities 2 en suite ⊗ TVB tea/coffee Direct dial from bedrooms ✖ Licensed Cen ht TVL No children 8yrs No coaches ◢◣ ◥ Fishing Sauna ◢◣ Hot Tub **Prices** S £45; D £65-£70✳ LB **Parking** 17 **Notes** Closed Xmas & New Year

NEWMARKET   MAP 12 TL66
See also **Chippenham & Kirtling (Cambridgeshire)**

◆◆◆◆

Birdcage Walk

2 Birdcage Walk CB8 0NE
☎ 01638 669456 & 07796 013468 ▤ 01638 669456
Dir Off A14 High St onto Birdcage Walk

A warm welcome awaits you at this delightful house located close to the racecourse and only a short walk to the town centre. Bedrooms and bathrooms are smartly appointed and thoughtfully equipped with a host of thoughtful extra touches. A hearty breakfast is served in the elegant dining room, overlooking the well-tended garden.

Facilities 2 en suite ⊗ TVB tea/coffee ✖ Cen ht No children 12yrs No coaches Dinner Last d 10am **Prices** D £60✳ LB **Parking** 5 **Notes** ⊛

◆◆◆◆

The Garden Lodge ◇

11 Vicarage Ln, Woodditton CB8 9SG ☎ 01638 731116
e-mail swedishgardenlodge@hotmail.com
web www.gardenlodge.net
Dir 3m S of Newmarket in Woodditton village

A warm welcome is assured in this home from home, not far from the famous racecourse. The accommodation is carefully decorated and features a number of useful extras. Freshly prepared home-cooked meals are served in the main house.

Facilities 3 en suite (3 GF) ⊗ TVB tea/coffee Cen ht No coaches Dinner Last d noon **Prices** S £30-£35; D £50-£60 **Parking** 6 **Notes** rs Xmas ⊛

SAXMUNDHAM

MAP 13 TM36

 ★★★ Bed & Breakfast

The Red House B&B

11 South Entrance IP17 1DG ☎ 01728 603324

Dir *In village centre on A1121*

Expect a warm welcome at this 19th-century house just a short walk from the village centre and well placed for touring the Suffolk coast. Bedrooms are carefully decorated with well chosen fabrics and have many thoughtful touches. A superb continental breakfast is served in the cosy dining room.

Facilities 3 rms ⊗ TVB tea/coffee ✖ Cen ht No children 3yrs No coaches **Parking** 3 **Notes** ⊛

◆◆◆◆

Sandpit Farm

Bruisyard IP17 2EB ☎ 01728 663445
e-mail susannemarshall@suffolkonline.net
web www.aldevalleybreaks.co.uk

Dir *4m W of Saxmundham. A1120 onto B1120, 1st left for Bruisyard, house 1.5m on left*

A warm welcome awaits you at this delightful Grade II listed farmhouse set in 20 acres of grounds. Bedrooms have many thoughtful touches and lovely country views, and there are two cosy lounges to enjoy. Breakfast features quality local produce and freshly laid free-range eggs.

Facilities 2 en suite ⊗ tea/coffee ✖ Cen ht TVL No coaches ⚘ Riding ↯ **Prices** D £60-£70✳ **LB** **Parking** 4 **Notes** Closed 24-26 Dec ⊛

SOUTHWOLD

MAP 13 TM57

◆◆◆◆

Home @ 21 North Parade

21 North Pde IP18 6LT ☎ 01502 722573
e-mail pauline@lighthouse-view.co.uk
web www.northparade.southwold.info

Dir *On seafront near pier*

Please note that this establishment has recently changed hands. A delightful Victorian property situated on the promenade overlooking the sea. The stylish bedrooms have coordinated soft furnishings and many thoughtful touches, and some rooms have sea views. Breakfast, which includes fresh local produce, is served in the smart dining room and there is a cosy lounge.

Facilities 3 rms (2 en suite) (1 pri facs) ⊗ TVB tea/coffee ✖ Cen ht TVL No children 18yrs No coaches Golf 18 ⚘ **Prices** D £80✳ **Notes** Closed Xmas & New Year ⊛

The Hemsley's

28 Fieldstile Rd IP18 6LD ☎ 01502 723588

Dir *A12 onto A1095. Cross rdbt, 1st left, past church towards seafront. B&B on left with red door & sign.*

At the time of going to press the rating for this establishment had not been confirmed. Please check the AA website www.theAA.com for up-to-date information.

Facilities 3 rms (1 fmly) (1 GF) ⊗ TVB Cen ht No coaches **Notes** Closed Nov-Feb ⊛

STOKE-BY-NAYLAND

MAP 13 TL93

 ◆◆◆◆ ⊛ ⊜ ◀

The Angel Inn

Polstead St CO6 4SA ☎ 01206 263245 ⬚ 01206 263373
e-mail the.angel@tiscali.co.uk

Dir *A12 onto B1068*

This charming inn has welcomed guests since the 16th century; it is popular with the locals and well known for its food. Public areas have a wealth of character and offer a choice of dining rooms that include a smart restaurant with an original well. Bedrooms are pleasantly decorated and thoughtfully equipped.

Facilities 5 en suite 1 annexe en suite ⊗ in bedrooms ⊗ in dining room TVB tea/coffee Direct dial from bedrooms ✖ Cen ht No coaches Dinner Last d 9pm **Parking** 25 **Notes** Closed 25-26 Dec & 1 Jan

STOWMARKET
MAP 13 TM05

Premier Collection

◆◆◆◆◆

Bays Farm

Forward Green IP14 5HU ☎ 01449 711286
e-mail information@baysfarmsuffolk.co.uk
web www.baysfarmsuffolk.co.uk
Dir *A14 junct 50, onto A1120. 1m after Stowupland, turn right at sharp left hand bend signed Broad Green. Bays Farm 1st house on right*

Tea and home-made cake on arrival at this delightful 17th-century former farmhouse, situated amid 4 acres of mature grounds. The property has a wealth of character. Bedrooms are carefully decorated and have coordinated soft furnishings as well as many thoughtful touches. Breakfast, which includes locally sourced produce, is served around a large polished table in the stylish dining room.

Facilities 3 en suite ⊗ TVB tea/coffee Cen ht No children 12yrs No coaches **Prices** S £50-£65; D £60-£75✷ **Parking** 3

WHEPSTEAD
MAP 13 TL85

◆◆◆◆

Folly House Bed & Breakfast

Folly Ln IP29 4TJ
☎ 01284 735207 & 07990 943060 ▤ 01284 735207
e-mail lowerlinda@hotmail.com
Dir *Off B1066 onto Rectory Rd, 1.5m at T-junct right onto Folly Ln*

This former alehouse dates from the 1830s and is set amid landscaped grounds in peaceful countryside. Breakfast is served in the elegant dining room, and there is a conservatory-lounge as well as an indoor swimming pool.

Facilities 3 rms (1 en suite) (1 fmly) ⊗ TVB tea/coffee ✖ Cen ht TVL No coaches ▣ Dinner Last d 9am **Prices** S £35-£50; D £44-£75✷ **Parking** 10 **Notes** ✇

WINGFIELD
MAP 13 TM27

◆◆◆◆

Gables Farm

Earsham St IP21 5RH ☎ 01379 586355
e-mail enquiries@gablesfarm.co.uk
web www.gablesfarm.co.uk
Dir *B1118 left to Wingfield Green, turn right after 1m, B&B 1.7m on right*

A warm welcome is assured at this delightful Grade II listed
continued

farmhouse, set amid 2 acres of moated gardens on the outskirts of the village. The spacious bedrooms are carefully furnished and thoughtfully equipped. Breakfast, which includes locally sourced produce, is served in the smart dining room.

Facilities 3 en suite (1 fmly) ⊗ TVB tea/coffee TVL **Parking** 5
Notes Closed 20-25 Dec ✇

WOODBRIDGE
MAP 13 TM24

Premier Collection

◆◆◆◆◆

Long Springs B&B

Woods Ln, Melton IP12 1LN
☎ 01394 383646 ▤ 01394 383905
e-mail enquiries@longsprings.co.uk
web www.longsprings.co.uk
Dir *0.5m N of town centre. A12 onto A1152 Woods Ln, B&B 500yds on left*

Expect a warm welcome from the caring hosts of this delightful property, situated in 16 acres of landscaped grounds. The stylish bedrooms have an excellent range of facilities (DVDs and players, air conditioning, Sky), and breakfast is served in the superb conservatory that overlooks the garden. Imaginative home-cooked dinners are available, and there is also a log cabin with an indoor swimming pool, a tennis court, croquet lawn and a TV lounge with a plasma screen.

Facilities 4 annexe en suite (2 GF) ⊗ in bedrooms ⊗ in area of dining room ⊗ in 1 lounge STV TVB tea/coffee ✖ Licensed Cen ht TVL No children 18yrs No coaches ▣ ❀ ♨ Dinner Last d 24 hrs previous **Prices** S £65; D £95✷ **Parking** 14

◆◆◆

Grove House

39 Grove Rd IP12 4LG ☎ 01394 382202 & 07795 094234
e-mail thereception@grovehousehotel.co.uk
Dir *W of town centre on A12*

A warm welcome is assured at this owner-managed establishment on the west side of town. It provides a range of thoughtfully furnished bedrooms with efficient en suite shower rooms, and comprehensive breakfasts are served in the attractive dining room.

Facilities 9 en suite (1 fmly) (6 GF) ⊗ TVB tea/coffee ✖ Cen ht TVL **Prices** S £50; D £65✷ **LB Parking** 12

England

YAXLEY
MAP 13 TM17

Premier Collection

♦♦♦♦♦ ◉◉ ≘ ⌂

The Bull Auberge

Ipswich Rd IP23 8BZ ☎ 01379 783604 ▤ 01379 788486
e-mail deestenhouse@fsmail.net
Dir *On the A140 between Norwich & Ipswich at B1117 x-rds Eye/Stadbloke*

Charming 15th-century inn, which has been lovingly converted by the present owners into a smart restaurant with rooms. The public areas have a wealth of character, such as exposed brickwork and beams. The spacious bedrooms are carefully furnished and thoughtfully equipped.

Facilities 4 en suite (2 GF) ⊗ TVB tea/coffee Direct dial from bedrooms ✗ Licensed Cen ht No coaches Dinner Last d 9pm **Parking** 40

SURREY

ALBURY
MAP 06 TQ04

♦♦♦ ◾

Drummond Arms

The Street GU5 9AG ☎ 01483 202039 ▤ 01483 205361
e-mail drummondarms@btconnect.com
Dir *Off A25 between Guildford & Dorking onto A248 signed Albury, establishment 1m on right*

The inn stands in the centre of this picturesque village, with attractive gardens running down to a small river at the rear of the property. The well-appointed en suite bedrooms are a highlight, while the separate restaurant offers an extensive menu. A good selection of traditional pub food is available in the popular bar.

Facilities 7 en suite 4 annexe en suite (1 fmly) (1 GF) ⊗ in area of dining room TVB tea/coffee Direct dial from bedrooms ✗ Cen ht No children 14yrs No coaches Fishing Sauna in one room Dinner Last d 9.30pm **Conf** Max 40 Thtr 40 Class 40 **Parking** 50
See advertisement on this page

CHARLWOOD
MAP 06 TQ24
For accommodation details see under **Gatwick Airport (London), (Sussex, West)**

CHIDDINGFOLD
MAP 06 SU93

★★★★ ⊜ **Restaurant with Rooms**

The Swan Inn

Petworth Rd GU8 4TY ☎ 01428 682073 ▤ 01428 683259
e-mail the-swan-inn@btconnect.com

The 14th-century village inn offers home-cooked food, real ales, and a good choice of wines. There are terraced gardens and parking is available. The dining area has a friendly atmosphere.

Facilities 11 rms (10 en suite) (1 fmly) TVB tea/coffee Direct dial from bedrooms ✗ No children No coaches Dinner Last d 10pm **Parking** 40

CHOBHAM
MAP 06 SU96

♦♦♦♦

Pembroke House

Valley End Rd GU24 8TB
☎ 01276 857654 ▤ 01276 858445
e-mail pembrokehouse@macunlimited.net
Dir *A30 onto B383 signed Chobham, 3m right onto Valley End Rd, B&B 1m on left*

Proprietor Julia Holland takes obvious pleasure in treating you as a friend at her beautifully appointed and spacious home. The elegantly proportioned public areas include an imposing entrance hall and dining room with views over the surrounding countryside. Bedrooms are restful and filled with thoughtful extras.

Facilities 5 rms (2 en suite) (1 pri facs) (1 fmly) ⊗ STV TVB tea/coffee Cen ht No children 6yrs No coaches ⚲ **Prices** S £40-£50; D £80-£120✳ **Parking** 10 **Notes** ⊠

COLDHARBOUR
MAP 06 TQ14

♦♦♦♦ 🛏 🍴

The Plough Inn
RH5 6HD ☎ 01306 711793 🖹 01306 710055
e-mail theploughinn@btinternet.com
web www.ploughinn.com
Dir 3.5m SW of Dorking in village. Coldharbour signed from A2003 in Dorking

Originally a 17th-century coaching inn, this establishment is the highest free house above sea level in South East England. The refurbished accommodation offers high levels of quality and a wealth of facilities. Hearty home-cooked cuisine can be enjoyed in the restaurant. Traditional ales are brewed on the premises.

Facilities 6 en suite ⊗ in bedrooms ⊗ in dining room TVB tea/coffee ✖ Cen ht No children 14yrs Dinner Last d 9.30pm
Prices S £59.50-£69.50; D £69.50-£95✳ **Parking** 6 **Notes** rs 26 Dec evening & 1 Jan evening

EWELL
MAP 06 TQ26

♦♦♦

Nonsuch Park Hotel
355/357 London Rd KT17 2DE
☎ 020 8393 0771 🖹 020 8393 1415
e-mail manager@nonsuchpark.com
Dir A240 onto A24 London Rd for 0.75m

This comfortable accommodation stands opposite Nonsuch Park. The attractive bedrooms have good facilities, and the public areas include a small bar area and a lounge-dining room overlooking the rear patio. Evening meals and parking are available.

Facilities 11 rms (9 en suite) (2 pri facs) (2 fmly) (4 GF) ⊗ in bedrooms ⊗ in dining room in lounges FTV TVB tea/coffee Direct dial from bedrooms ✖ Licensed Cen ht TVL Dinner Last d 8.30pm
Prices S £59.50-£85; D £89.50-£99.50 **Parking** 11 **Notes** Closed 2-3 wks Xmas

FARNHAM
MAP 05 SU84

★★★ Inn

Exchange Hotel
Station Hill GU9 8AD ☎ 01252 726673
e-mail info@exchangehotel.co.uk
Located close the centre of town and the railway station this establishment offers comfortable, well-equipped accommodation. A wide variety of meals are available in the Seafood and Steak restaurant, plus there is a bar and a large beer garden.

Facilities 9 en suite (6 fmly) ⊗ TVB tea/coffee ✖ Cen ht TVL Dinner Last d 9.30pm **Prices** S £49.95; D £69.95✳ **LB Conf** Max 30 Thtr 30 Class 30 Board 30 **Parking** 14

♦♦♦♦♦

Bentley Mill
Bentley GU10 5JD
☎ 01420 23301 & 07768 842729 🖹 01420 22538
e-mail ann.bentleymill@supanet.com
Dir Off A31 Farnham-Alton road, opp Bull Inn, turn left onto Gravel Hill Rd

This delightful former corn mill, sitting beside the river Wey in beautifully tended gardens, has been expertly converted to provide two bedroom suites of the highest standard. Luxurious beds, antique furnishings and a host of thoughtful extra touches compliment the original features and maximise the immense character and charm of this Georgian property. Ann and David Hallett's hospitality knows no bounds: they do everything to ensure you enjoy your wonderful country home.

Facilities 2 rms (2 pri facs) 2 annexe en suite (3 fmly) (1 GF) ⊗ STV TVB tea/coffee Direct dial from bedrooms ✖ Cen ht TVL No children 8yrs No coaches Fishing ⚑ Dinner Last d 8pm **Prices** S £70-£95; D £95-£120✳ **Conf** Board 8 **Parking** 6

♦♦♦♦

Rosebarton ◇
Cherry Tree Walk, Rowledge GU10 4AD
☎ 01252 793580 🖹 01252 790486
e-mail rosebarton@btinternet.com
Dir Off A325 near Birdworld to Rowledge, right onto Lickfolds Rd, 2nd right onto Cherry Tree Walk

Dating in part from the 18th century, this delightful guest house provides a real home from home atmosphere. Bedrooms vary in size but all are decorated in a traditional English style, featuring a number of useful extras. The landscaped gardens enhance the peaceful surroundings. Easily accessible from the A31.

Facilities 5 rms (2 en suite) (1 pri facs) ⊗ TVB tea/coffee Cen ht TVL No coaches ✕ **Prices** S £30-£35; D £60-£65✳ **Parking** 10 **Notes** ⊛

♦♦♦♦

Dares Farm House
Farnham Rd, Ewshot GU10 5BB
☎ 01252 851631 🖹 01252 852367
e-mail daresfarm@tiscali.co.uk
Dir 3m NW of Farnham. M3 junct 5, A287 towards Farnham for 5m, up hill past Dares Ln, 1st left

This attractive Grade II listed, 17th-century timber-framed cottage property is within easy reach of the M3 and A31. You can expect a warm welcome and a comfortable sleep in the cosy, individually decorated bedrooms. The hearty breakfast in the farmhouse kitchen sets you up for the day.

Facilities 3 en suite ⊗ TV available tea/coffee ✖ Cen ht TVL No children 14yrs No coaches **Prices** S fr £40; D £70-£80✳ **Parking** 3 **Notes** ⊛

◆◆◆◆
Sandiway ◇
24 Shortheath Rd GU9 8SR
☎ 01252 710721 ▤ 01252 710721
e-mail john@shortheath.freeserve.co.uk
Dir *Onto A287 Hindhead, at lights at top of hill right onto Ridgway Rd, past green on left, Sandiway 300yds on right*

Guests are warmly greeted at this delightful house, set in attractive gardens in a quiet residential area. Smart bedrooms have a thoughtful range of facilities and share a spacious, well-appointed bathroom. Guests have use of a comfortable lounge during the day and evening, which doubles as the dining room at breakfast.

Facilities 3 rms ⊘ tea/coffee 🐾 Cen ht TVL No coaches
Prices S £25-£30; D £45-£50✱ **Parking** 3 **Notes** Closed 21-31 Dec

GUILDFORD MAP 06 SU94

★★★★ Guest Accommodation
Asperion
73 Farnham Rd GU2 7PF
☎ 01483 579299 ▤ 01483 457977
e-mail enquiries@asperion.co.uk

The stylish and luxurious Asperion provides contemporary rooms, a healthy organic breakfast, and caring service.

Facilities 15 rms (14 en suite) (1 pri facs) (1 fmly) (9 GF) ⊘ STV TVB tea/coffee Direct dial from bedrooms 🐾 Cen ht TVL No children 12yrs No coaches **Prices** S £50-£65; D £75-£120✱ **Parking** 11 **Notes** Closed 22-31 Dec

◆◆◆
Blanes Court Hotel
Albury Rd GU1 2BT ☎ 01483 573171 ▤ 01483 532780
e-mail reservations@blanes.demon.co.uk
web www.blanes.demon.co.uk
Dir *0.7m E of town centre, off A246 Epsom Rd*

This large Edwardian house stands in a quiet residential area close to the town centre and has ample private parking. Public areas include a small seating area with a bar, and a conservatory overlooking the attractive rear garden. Bedrooms vary in size, but each is individually decorated and all offer a useful range of facilities.

Facilities 17 rms (16 en suite) (1 pri facs) (3 fmly) (6 GF) ⊘ in bedrooms ⊘ in dining room ⊘ in 1 lounge TVB tea/coffee 🐾 Licensed Cen ht No coaches Small heated outdoor pool
Prices S £50-£64; D £84-£88✱ LB **Parking** 22 **Notes** Closed 1wk Xmas

◆◆ 🅐
Three Gates
26 Worplesdon Rd GU2 9RS
☎ 01483 578961 & 07879 482185 ▤ 01483 578961
e-mail rhthresher@aol.com
Dir *A3 onto A322, Three Gates at junct Ardmore Way & Wendy Crescent*

Facilities 3 rms ⊘ in bedrooms ⊘ in dining room TVB tea/coffee 🐾 Cen ht TVL No coaches **Parking** 4 **Notes**

HASLEMERE MAP 06 SU93

◆◆◆ ❦
Ashleigh ◇ *(SU949313)*
Fisherstreet Farm GU28 9EJ ☎ 01428 707229
Mr & Mrs Thomas
e-mail gu284sx@yahoo.co.uk
Dir *3.5m E of Haslemere. B2131 onto A283 S*

Stephen and Madeleine Thomas make you feel like friends at their charming farmhouse. A homely ambience is evident throughout the spacious lounge and the elegant dining room. Breakfast, served family style, uses farm produce whenever possible.

Facilities 3 rms (1 pri facs) (1 fmly) ⊘ STV TVB tea/coffee 🐾 Cen ht TVL 450 acres Beef/Arable Last d noon **Prices** S £25-£30; D £50-£60✱ **Parking** 6 **Notes**

◆◆◆ ➡ 🍴
The Wheatsheaf Inn
Grayswood Rd, Grayswood GU27 2DE
☎ 01428 644440 ▤ 01428 641285
e-mail thewheatsheef@aol.com
Dir *1m N of Haslemere on A286 in Grayswood*

Situated in a small village just outside Haslemere, this well-presented inn has a friendly atmosphere. The smart conservatory restaurant is a new addition, which complements the attractive dining area and popular bar. Bedrooms are furnished to a good standard, all but one on the ground floor.

Facilities 7 en suite (6 GF) ⊘ in bedrooms ⊘ in dining room TVB tea/coffee Direct dial from bedrooms Cen ht No coaches Dinner Last d 9.45pm **Prices** S £55-£65; D £75-£85✱ **Parking** 21

HORLEY MAP 06 TQ24
For accommodation details see under **Gatwick Airport (London), (Sussex, West)**

If you book on bed, breakfast and evening meal terms, you may find that the tariff includes only the set menu

England

England

LINGFIELD

MAP 06 TQ34

◆◆◆◆

The Blacksmiths Head

Newchapel Rd RH7 6LE ☎ 01342 833697
e-mail alexduarteuk@aol.com
Dir A22 onto B2028 towards Lingfield, Blacksmiths Head 200yds on left

A warm welcome is guaranteed at this award winning traditional inn, located within easy driving distance of the M25, Gatwick airport and local attractions such as Hever castle and Chartwell; home of Winston Churchill. Bedrooms are decorated to a high standard and provide good levels of comfort. Delicious freshly prepared food is available in the bar or restaurant, popular with both locals and residents.

Facilities 5 rms (4 en suite) (1 pri facs) ⊗ TVB ✹ Cen ht Dinner Last d 9.15pm **Prices** S fr £55; d fr £75✳ **Parking** 25

OCKLEY

MAP 06 TQ14

◆◆◆◆ ◪

The Kings Arms Inn

Stane St RH5 5TS ☎ 01306 711224 ▤ 01306 711224
e-mail enquiries@thekingsarmsockley.co.uk
Dir On A29 in village centre

This charming 500-year-old inn provides individually styled and well-equipped bedrooms. It is located midway between Horsham and Dorking, just 20 minutes from Gatwick airport. Enjoyable, well-prepared meals are served in the beamed bar, or in the attractive restaurant. A roaring log fire welcomes visitors in winter and the colourful garden is a haven in summer.

Facilities 6 en suite ⊗ in 1 bedrooms ⊗ in dining room ⊗ in 1 lounge TVB tea/coffee Direct dial from bedrooms ✹ Cen ht No children 14yrs Dinner Last d 9pm **Prices** S £50-£75; D £70-£75✳ **Parking** 40

REDHILL

MAP 06 TQ25

◆◆◆◆

Stop Over For Gatwick

87A-89A Brighton Rd RH1 6PS ☎ 01737 772452
e-mail slawrence@sweethavenuk.com
Dir A23 out of Redhill, under railway arch on right, entrance at side of Lawrence House Antique Centre

As the name suggests this venue is specifically for guests flying to and from Gatwick, which is only a 15-minute drive away. The room price includes transfers to and from the airport and secure parking. The bedrooms are comfortable and well appointed. A comprehensive continental breakfast is available before flying off.

Facilities 2 rms (2 pri facs) ⊗ FTV TVB tea/coffee 🐾 Cen ht TVL No coaches Dinner Last d 48hrs prior **Parking** 10 **Notes** 🚭

◆◆◆

Lynwood Guest House ◇

50 London Rd RH1 1LN
☎ 01737 766894 & 762804 ▤ 01737 778253
e-mail lynwoodguesthouse@yahoo.co.uk
Dir 0.25m from railway station, next to Memorial Park

A large, friendly Victorian house located close to the town centre and railway station, and within easy reach of the M25. The spacious bedrooms provide comfortable accommodation, either en suite or with in-room showers. Breakfast is served in the attractive dining room.

Facilities 9 rms (3 en suite) (4 fmly) (1 GF) ⊗ in 4 bedrooms ⊗ in dining room ⊗ in lounges TVB tea/coffee ✹ Cen ht TVL **Prices** S £30-£35; D £50-£55✳ **Parking** 8

SUSSEX, EAST

BATTLE

MAP 06 TQ71

Premier Collection

◆◆◆◆◆ ▨ ❦

Farthings Farm (TQ734149)

Catsfield TN33 9BA ☎ 01424 773107 Mr & Mrs Rodgers
e-mail Penny.Rodgers@btopenworld.com
web www.farthingsfarm.co.uk
Dir A271 W from Battle, left onto B2204 towards Catsfield, farm 1m on left of sharp S-bend & farmhouse 0.5m down lane

Superbly located in 70 acres of unspoiled countryside, this refurbished farmhouse is a stylish mix of traditional and modern. Bedrooms have been renovated to an excellent standard and ensure a high level of comfort. Breakfast and dinner, served around a communal dining table, feature organic and local produce and are real delights.

Facilities 2 en suite ⊗ TVB tea/coffee ✹ Cen ht No children 70 acres beef, pigs **Prices** D £60✳ **Parking** 2 **Notes** Closed Dec-Jan rs Closed Sun-Tue 🚭

England

◆◆◆◆

Fox Hole Farm *(TQ694166)*

Kane Hythe Rd TN33 9QU
☎ 01424 772053 ▤ 01424 772053 Mr & Mrs Collins
e-mail foxholefarm@amserve.com
Dir *Off A271 onto B2096 farm 0.75m from junct on right*

A delightful 18th-century woodcutter's cottage set in 40 acres of
grounds a short drive from historic Battle. The spacious bedrooms are
individually decorated and thoughtfully equipped. Breakfast is served
in the charming dining room and the cosy sitting room has exposed
beams and an inglenook fireplace.

Facilities 3 en suite (1 GF) ⊗ TVB tea/coffee Cen ht 40 acres ducks
sheep chickens **Prices** S £37-£45; D £55-£65 **Parking** 6 **Notes** Closed
Dec-Jan

◆◆◆ ▣

The Chequers Inn

Lower Lake TN33 0AT ☎ 01424 772088
e-mail thechequersinnbattle.co.uk
web www.thechequersinnbattle.co.uk
Dir *Off S end of High St onto Upper Lake & Lower Lake*

Expect a warm welcome at this charming inn, which is situated in the
heart of the historic town of Battle, just a short walk from the
Monastery. Bedrooms are cheerfully decorated and have coordinated
fabrics. Public rooms include a beamed restaurant and a spacious
lounge bar with an open fireplace.

Facilities 3 en suite (2 fmly) ⊗ in bedrooms ⊗ in dining room TVB
tea/coffee ✖ Cen ht Pool Table Dinner Last d 9pm **Parking** 20
Notes ⊛

BEXHILL   MAP 06 TQ70

◆◆◆◆

The Arosa Hotel ◇

5 Albert Rd TN40 1DG ☎ 01424 212574 ▤ 01424 212574
e-mail info@arosahotel.co.uk
Dir *From seafront N onto Devonshire Rd, 1st left, next left onto Albert
Rd*

The attractive property is in a conservation area close to town centre and
within easy walking distance of the seafront. Its pleasant bedrooms are
thoughtfully equipped, and public rooms include a comfortable lounge
and a smart dining room where you can enjoy a hearty breakfast.

Facilities 9 rms (6 en suite) (2 fmly) (1 GF) ⊗ in 2 bedrooms
⊗ in dining room ⊗ in lounges TVB tea/coffee Direct dial from
bedrooms ✖ Cen ht No coaches **Prices** S £25-£30; D £45-£55✱ LB
Notes ⊛

BRIGHTON & HOVE   MAP 06 TQ30

◆◆◆◆

Adelaide Hotel

51 Regency Sq BN1 2FF ☎ 01273 205286 ▤ 01273 220904
e-mail adelaide@pavilion.co.uk
Dir *On seafront square opp West Pier*

This attractive, well-kept Grade II listed Regency house is located in a
quiet garden square just off the seafront and close to the town centre.

continued

Each individual bedroom features a variety of useful extras, and public
areas include an elegant period-style lounge and a cheerful downstairs
dining room.

Facilities 12 en suite (1 fmly) (1 GF) ⊗ TVB tea/coffee Direct dial from
bedrooms ✖ Cen ht No children 12yrs No coaches **Prices** S £35-£55;
D £68-£96✱ LB **Notes** Closed 25-26 Dec

◆◆◆◆

Alvia Hotel ◇

36 Upper Rock Gdns BN2 1QF
☎ 01273 682939 ▤ 01273 626287
e-mail enquiries@alviahotel.co.uk
web www.alviahotel.co.uk
Dir *A23 to Brighton Pier, left onto Marine Parade, 500yds left at
lights onto Lower Rock Gdns & Upper Rock Gdns*

This fine Victorian house is just a short walk from the seafront and
town centre, and offers a choice of comfortable and well-equipped
bedrooms. Full English and vegetarian breakfasts are offered, served in
the bright dining room. Some parking is available, which should be
booked in advance.

Facilities 10 rms (9 en suite) (1 fmly) ⊗ TVB tea/coffee ✖ Cen ht
Prices S £25-£38; D £85-£150✱ LB **Parking** 4

◆◆◆◆

Ambassador Hotel

22-23 New Steine, Marine Pde BN2 1PD
☎ 01273 676869 ▤ 01273 689988
e-mail info@ambassadorbrighton.co.uk
web www.ambassadorbrighton.co.uk
Dir *A23 to Brighton Pier, left onto A259, 9th left, onto Garden Sq, 1st
left*

At the heart of bustling Kemp Town, overlooking the attractive garden
square adjacent the seaside, this well established property has a
friendly and relaxing atmosphere. Bedrooms are well equipped and
vary in size with the largest having the best views. A small lounge with
a separate bar is available.

Facilities 24 en suite (9 fmly) (3 GF) ⊗ in 12 bedrooms ⊗ in dining
room ⊗ in 1 lounge TVB tea/coffee Direct dial from bedrooms Licensed
Cen ht **Prices** S £36-£65; D £55-£115✱ **Conf** Max 20 Thtr 20 Board 14

◆◆◆◆

Brighton House Hotel

52 Regency Sq BN1 2FF ☎ 01273 323282
e-mail enquiries@brightonhousehotel.co.uk
Dir *Opp West Pier*

This charming property is situated close to the seafront. The smartly
appointed bedrooms and bathrooms come in a variety of sizes and
are located on four floors while a substantial continental breakfast is
provided and served in the spacious elegant dining room. The
establishment has arrangements for parking with the nearby
underground car park.

Facilities 14 en suite (2 fmly) ⊗ TVB tea/coffee ✖ Licensed Cen ht
No children 12yrs No coaches **Prices** S £35-£55; D £50-£140

England

BRIGHTON & HOVE continued

♦♦♦♦

Brighton Pavilions

7 Charlotte St BN2 1AG ☎ 01273 621750 ▤ 01273 622477
e-mail sanchez-crespo@lineone.net
web www.brightonpavilions.com
Dir *A23 to Brighton Pier, left onto A259 Marine Parade, Charlotte St 15th left*

This well-run operation is in one of Brighton's Regency streets, a short walk from the seafront and town centre. Bedrooms have style themes such as Titanic or Pompeii, and are very smartly presented. The cosy dining room has a nautical theme and there is a small seating area and patio.

Facilities 10 rms (7 en suite) (1 fmly) (1 GF) ⊗ TVB tea/coffee Direct dial from bedrooms Cen ht No coaches **Prices** S £40-£100; D £90-£150✶

♦♦♦♦

George IV

34 Regency Sq BN1 2FJ ☎ 01273 321196 & 07940 808753
e-mail georgeiv@stevesue.plus.com
Dir *Opp West Pier, at top of square*

Situated at the top of this prominent Regency square, overlooking the gardens and sea, the restored property provides smartly furnished bedrooms with modern bathrooms and good facilities. There is a lift to all floors, and a continental breakfast is served in your bedroom.

Facilities 8 en suite (1 fmly) ⊗ TVB tea/coffee ✻ Lift Cen ht No coaches **Prices** S £40-£50; D £60-£120; (room only) **Notes** Closed Xmas-mid Jan

♦♦♦♦

Gullivers Hotel

10 New Steine BN2 1PB ☎ 01273 695415 ▤ 01273 622663
e-mail reservation@gulivershotel.com
Dir *A23 to Brighton Pier, left onto Marine Parade, New Steine on left after Wentworth St*

This guest house is close to the seafront in one of Brighton's Regency squares. The spacious bedrooms are well equipped and some have sea views. There is a cosy lounge, where a wide choice of English, vegetarian, vegan or continental breakfasts is served. There is street parking in front of the property.

Facilities 11 rms (8 en suite) (4 fmly) (1 GF) ⊗ in dining room TVB tea/coffee Direct dial from bedrooms ✻ Cen ht TVL No children 5yrs Dinner Last d 9.30pm **Conf** Max 25 Thtr 20 Class 15 Board 15

♦♦♦♦

New Steine Hotel

12a New Steine, Marine Pde BN2 1PB
☎ 01273 681546 ▤ 01273 679118
e-mail reservation@newsteinehotel.com
web www.newsteinehotel.com
Dir *A23 to Brighton Pier, left onto Marine Parade, premises 300yds on left*

Situated in an impressive Regency square close to the town and seafront, the New Steine has much to offer. Compact rooms use

clever design and contemporary colours to ensure comfort, and some have quality shower rooms en suite. The lounge, decorated with fine art, and brasserie are super areas in which to relax and dine.

New Steine Hotel

Facilities 11 rms (7 en suite) (1 GF) ⊗ in dining room TVB tea/coffee Direct dial from bedrooms ✻ Licensed Cen ht TVL No children 8yrs No coaches Dinner **Conf** Max 30 Thtr 30 Class 15 Board 15

♦♦♦♦

Nineteen

19 Broad St BN2 1TJ ☎ 01273 675529 ▤ 01273 675531
e-mail info@hotelnineteen.co.uk
web www.hotelnineteen.co.uk
Dir *A23 to Brighton Pier, left onto, Broad St 3rd on left*

The contemporary establishment lies at the heart of this popular resort, only minutes from Brighton Pier. Bedrooms are freshly decorated with white walls, wooden floors and stylish artworks. The continental breakfast (served with champagne at the weekend) is superb, providing a fine start to the day.

Facilities 8 en suite (2 GF) ⊗ TVB ✻ Cen ht No children 10yrs No coaches DVD/CD library **Prices** S £60-£90; D £90-£250✶

♦♦♦♦ 🛏

Paskins Town House ◇

18/19 Charlotte St BN2 1AG
☎ 01273 601203 ▤ 01273 621973
e-mail welcome@paskins.co.uk
web www.paskins.co.uk
Dir *A23 to pier, turn left, Charlotte St 11th left*

This environmentally friendly Victorian house is in a quiet street within walking distance of the seafront and town centre. Bedrooms are a comfortable mix of Victorian and art nouveau styles. The Art Deco

continued

continued

breakfast room offers a variety of vegetarian and vegan dishes and traditional English breakfasts, featuring home-made vegetarian sausages and much organic produce. Room service is available.

Facilities 19 rms (16 en suite) (2 fmly) ⊗ in area of dining room FTV TVB tea/coffee Direct dial from bedrooms Cen ht **Prices** S £30-£55; D £60-£155✷ LB

◆◆◆◆

Penny Lanes

11 Charlotte St BN2 1AG ☎ 01273 603197
e-mail welcome@pennylanes.co.uk
Dir A23 to Brighton Pier, left onto Marine Parade, after 2nd lights 4th left

This small, friendly guest house is in a quiet road not far from the seafront and the centre. Bedrooms are smart and well equipped. Breakfast offers a good selection in the wood-panelled dining room, including vegetarian options. There is a smart bar-lounge.

Facilities 12 rms (7 en suite) (1 GF) ⊗ in 5 bedrooms ⊗ in dining room TVB tea/coffee Licensed Cen ht TVL No coaches

◆◆◆◆

Topps Hotel

17 Regency Sq BN1 2FG
☎ 01273 729334 ▤ 01273 203679
e-mail toppshotel@aol.com
Dir Opp West Pier

An attractive Regency house located in one of the seafront squares. Most bedrooms are particularly spacious with comfortable sofas, fireplaces, minibars and many extra touches; some even have four-poster beds. The dining room, where full English breakfasts are served, has a warm atmosphere with large tables.

Facilities 15 en suite (3 fmly) (4 GF) ⊗ in 3 bedrooms ⊗ in dining room TVB tea/coffee Direct dial from bedrooms ✖ Licensed Lift No coaches Dinner Last d 4pm **Notes** Closed Last 2wks Dec

◆◆◆◆

Trouville Hotel

11 New Steine, Marine Pde BN2 1PB ☎ 01273 697384
Dir A23 to Brighton Pier, left onto A259, 300yds on left

This attractive Grade II listed building is part of a Regency seafront square. The bedrooms are individually decorated and designed with contemporary colours and fabrics. Well-cooked breakfasts are served in the bright lounge-dining room.

Facilities 8 rms (6 en suite) (2 fmly) ⊗ TVB tea/coffee ✖ Cen ht TVL No coaches **Prices** S £35-£59; D £65-£85 **Notes** Closed Xmas & Jan

◆◆◆◆

The Twenty One Guest House

21 Charlotte St, Marine Pde BN2 1AG
☎ 01273 686450 ▤ 01273 695560
e-mail the21@pavilion.co.uk
Dir Off A23 onto A259 towards Newhaven, 0.5m Charlotte St on left

This well-established guest house is convenient for the town centre and the seafront. Bedrooms are all individually decorated, and the good facilities include phones and refrigerators. Enjoyable traditional breakfasts, including vegetarian options, are served in the attractive dining room.

Facilities 8 en suite (1 fmly) ⊗ in dining room TVB tea/coffee Direct dial from bedrooms ✖ Cen ht No children 12yrs Sauna Pool Table Jacuzzi **Prices** S £39-£50; D £65-£115✷ LB

◆◆◆◆ Ⓐ

Cavalaire House

34 Upper Rock Gdns BN2 1QF
☎ 01273 696899 ▤ 01273 600504
e-mail welcome@cavalaire.co.uk
web www.cavalaire.co.uk
Dir A23 to seafront, left onto A259, left at 1st lights onto Lower Rock Gardens & over next lights

Facilities 10 en suite (2 fmly) ⊗ TVB tea/coffee ✖ Licensed Cen ht No children 9yrs No coaches **Prices** D £65-£99✷ LB **Parking** 3

◆◆◆◆ Ⓐ

The Dove Hotel ◇

18 Regency Sq BN1 2FG ☎ 01273 779222 ▤ 01273 746912
e-mail enquiries@thedovehotel.co.uk
web www.thedovehotel.co.uk
Dir Along seafront to West Pier, onto Regency Sq, Dove on left

Facilities 9 en suite (2 fmly) (2 GF) ⊗ in dining room ⊗ in lounges TVB tea/coffee ✖ Licensed Cen ht TVL No coaches **Prices** S £25-£45; D £60-£115✷

◆◆◆◆ Ⓐ

Esteban Lodge ◇

35 Upper Rock Gdns BN2 1QF
☎ 01273 681161 ▤ 01273 676945
e-mail reservations@estebanhotel.co.uk
web www.estebanhotel.co.uk
Dir A23 to Brighton Pier, left onto Marine Parade, 2nd lights left onto Lower Rock, over lights

Facilities 12 rms (11 en suite) (3 fmly) ⊗ TVB tea/coffee ✖ Cen ht **Prices** S £25-£35; D £65-£95 LB **Parking** 5 **Notes** ⊛

BRIGHTON & HOVE continued

♦♦♦♦

Genevieve Hotel

18 Madeira Pl BN2 1TN ☎ 01273 681653 🖃 01273 681653
e-mail infoaa@genevievehotel.co.uk
web www.genevievehotel.co.uk
Dir A23 to Brighton Pier, left onto A259, 5th left

Facilities 13 en suite (2 GF) ⊗ TVB tea/coffee ✱ Cen ht No children
12yrs No coaches **Prices** S £40-£60; D £70-£120 **LB**

♦♦♦

Adastral Hotel

8 Westbourne Villas BN3 4GQ
☎ 01273 888800 🖃 01273 883839
e-mail info@adastralhotel.co.uk
Dir Off A259, 2m W of Brighton Pier

Located just off the Hove seafront, this double-fronted Victorian villa
offers a variety of well-equipped bedrooms, many of which are
suitable for families. Public areas include a small lounge and bar area,
and a restaurant serving breakfast and evening meals.

Facilities 19 en suite (11 fmly) (2 GF) ⊗ in dining room ⊗ in lounges
TVB tea/coffee Direct dial from bedrooms Licensed Cen ht No coaches
Dinner Last d 5pm **Prices** S £50-£58; D £95-£105 **Parking** 2

♦♦♦

Aquarium Guest House

13 Madeira Pl BN2 1TN ☎ 01273 605761
e-mail info@aquarium-guesthouse.co.uk
web www.aquarium-guesthouse.co.uk
Dir A23 to Brighton Pier, left onto A259, 5th left

Located close to Brighton Pier and the town centre, Aquarium Guest
House offers comfortable accommodation and a friendly atmosphere.
Bedrooms are attractively decorated and equipped with a number of
thoughtful extras. An appetising breakfast is available in the bright
basement dining room.

Facilities 7 rms (6 en suite) (1 pri facs) (1 GF) ⊗ FTV TVB tea/coffee
✱ Cen ht No children 9yrs **Prices** S £45-£84; D £58-£84✶ **LB**

♦♦♦

Avalon ◇

7 Upper Rock Gdns BN2 1QE
☎ 01273 692344 🖃 01273 692344
e-mail info@avalonbrighton.co.uk
Dir A23 to Brighton Pier, left onto Marine Parade, 400yds at lights
left onto Lower Rock Gardens, over lights Avalon on left

A warm welcome is assured at this guest house just a short walk from
the seafront and The Lanes. Bedrooms, some redecorated, vary in size
and style. Parking is restricted but vouchers are available for purchase
from the proprietor.

Facilities 7 en suite (1 fmly) (1 GF) ⊗ FTV TVB tea/coffee Cen ht
No coaches **Prices** S £25-£35; D £65-£125✶

♦♦♦

Court Craven Hotel ◇

2 Atlingworth St BN2 1PL
☎ 01273 607710 🖃 01273 695430
e-mail info@courtcravenhotel.co.uk
Dir Facing pier, turn left and follow Marine Parade for 0.25m.
Atlingworth St on left after lights

This terrace guest house is in a quiet street close to the seafront and
Brighton Pier. Bedrooms are sited on three floors and enjoy a
comprehensive range of guest extras. There is also the facility of a
licenced bar and a hearty breakfast can be enjoyed in the bright and
airy dining room.

Facilities 12 rms (9 en suite) (2 fmly) (1 GF) ⊗ in 3 bedrooms
⊗ in dining room TVB tea/coffee ✱ Licensed Cen ht TVL No children
10yrs **Prices** S £28-£35; D £50-£65✶ **Notes** Closed 21-29 Dec

♦♦♦

The Heathers

4 & 5 Lower Rock Gdns BN2 1PG
☎ 01273 626545 🖃 01273 608350
e-mail angelique@lincarhotels.co.uk
web www.lincarhotels.co.uk

Close to the beaches, this friendly guest house has bright bedrooms
refurbished in a modern style, and a few rooms are designed for
families. Bathrooms have good showers and are well lit.

Facilities 19 rms (18 en suite) (1 pri facs) (5 fmly) (5 GF)
⊗ in 5 bedrooms ⊗ in dining room ⊗ in lounges STV TVB tea/coffee
Cen ht **Parking** 3

♦♦♦

Marina West Hotel ◇

26 Oriental Pl BN1 2LL ☎ 01273 323087 🖃 01273 206888
e-mail info@marinawest.co.uk
Dir A23 to Brighton Pier, right along seafront past West Pier, 3rd
right onto Oriental Place

Located just a stroll from the seafront or the town centre, this popular
accommodation has undergone refurbishment to provide well-
decorated bedrooms and a comfortable lounge. Rooms on the upper
floors share a bathroom but others are en suite.

continued

England

Facilities 11 rms (3 en suite) (1 fmly) (1 GF) ⊗ in bedrooms ⊗ in dining room ⊗ in 1 lounge STV TVB tea/coffee Direct dial from bedrooms ✻ Licensed Cen ht TVL **Prices** S £25-£35; D £70-£90 LB **Conf** Thtr 22 Class 22 Board 22

♦♦♦

The Market Inn

1 Market St BN1 1HH ☎ 01273 329483 📠 01273 777227
e-mail marketinn@reallondonpubs.com
web www.reallondonpubs.com/market.html
Dir *In city centre, on pedestrian road 50yds from junct North St & East St*

This lively period inn is within walking distance of the seafront and is at the centre of The Lanes. Bedrooms are attractively decorated and feature a range of extra facilities. Popular bar food is served all day in the bars, which retain original character.

Facilities 2 en suite ⊗ in bedrooms TVB tea/coffee ✻ Cen ht No children No coaches **Prices** D £60-£75✳

♦♦♦

Millards

23 Broad St BN2 1TJ ☎ 01273 694314 📠 01273 676826
e-mail info@millards-hotel-brighton.com
Dir *A23 to Brighton Pier, left onto Marine Parade, left onto Manchester St, right onto St James St & 2nd right*

This refurbished establishment is near to the seafront and town centre. Bedrooms are comfortable and finished with considerate extras, including a safe. Breakfast, which is part self-service, is served in the dining area next to the reception.

Facilities 8 en suite (2 GF) ⊗ in 4 bedrooms ⊗ in dining room TVB tea/coffee Direct dial from bedrooms ✻ Licensed Cen ht

♦♦♦

Prince Regent Hotel

29 Regency Sq BN1 2FH
☎ 01273 329962 📠 01273 748162
web www.princeregent.com
Dir *A23 to Brighton Pier, right onto A259, at West Pier onto Regency Sq*

Located close to the seafront and the town centre attractions, the Prince Regent offers a warm welcome. Bedrooms are individually and imaginatively decorated and a number have four-poster beds. Full English breakfasts are an excellent start to the day, and are served at individual tables in the cosy dining room.

continued

Prince Regent Hotel

Facilities 20 en suite ⊗ in dining room TVB tea/coffee Direct dial from bedrooms ✻ Cen ht No children 16yrs No coaches

♦♦♦

Westbourne Hotel ◇

46 Upper Rock Gdns BN2 1QF
☎ 01273 686920 📠 01273 686920
e-mail welcome@westbournehotel.net
Dir *A23 to Brighton Pier, left onto Marine Parade, 100yds left at lights, premises on right*

Please note that this establishment has recently changed hands. Just a short walk from the seafront, this Victorian house is run by friendly owners. Public rooms include a lounge with huge sofas, and a breakfast room with a small bar. The attractive bedrooms are well furnished.

Facilities 11 rms (7 en suite) (1 fmly) (2 GF) ⊗ in 8 bedrooms ⊗ in dining room ⊗ in lounges TVB tea/coffee ✻ Licensed TVL No coaches **Prices** S £25-£45; D £50-£85✳ **Parking** 1 **Notes** Closed 23-31 Dec

♦♦♦ 🅰

Sandpiper Guest House ◇

11 Russell Sq BN1 2EE ☎ 01273 328202 📠 01273 329974
e-mail sandpiper@brighton.co.uk
Dir *After conference centre on King's Rd, right onto Cannon Place. Russel Sq at end of street*

Facilities 6 rms (1 fmly) ⊗ in 3 bedrooms ⊗ in dining room ⊗ in lounges TVB tea/coffee ✻ Cen ht No coaches **Prices** S £15-£39; D £30-£70 LB

♦♦

Regency Landsdowne Guest House ◇

45 Landsdowne Pl BN3 1HF
☎ 01273 321830 📠 01273 777067
e-mail regencylansdowne@aol.com
web www.regencylansdowne.co.uk
Dir *A23 to Brighton Pier, right onto A259, 1m right onto Lansdowne Place, house on left before Western Rd*

A warm welcome is guaranteed at this Regency house, located only minutes from the seafront. Comfortable bedrooms are functionally equipped with a good range of facilities. An extensive continental breakfast is served at a communal table overlooking attractive gardens. On-road parking a short walk away.

Facilities 7 rms (5 en suite) ⊗ TVB tea/coffee ✻ Lift Cen ht **Prices** S £25-£75; D £80✳

BRIGHTON & HOVE continued

♦♦

Chatsworth Hotel ◇

9 Salisbury Rd BN3 3AB ☎ 01273 737360 🖹 01273 737360

Dir A23 to Brighton Pier, right onto A259 into Hove, right onto First
Av, right onto Church Rd, left onto Salisbury Rd, Chatsworth on left

Facilities 8 rms (4 en suite) (2 fmly) (1 GF) ⊗ in dining room
⊗ in lounges FTV TVB tea/coffee Cen ht TVL No coaches
Prices S £30-£40; D £70-£80✳ LB

BURWASH   MAP 06 TQ62

♦♦♦♦

Judins

Heathfield Rd TN19 7LA ☎ 01435 882455 🖹 01435 883775
e-mail sjudins@aol.co.uk

Dir A265 to Burwash, through village, past BP station on right, house
0.5m on left

A warm welcome is offered at this charming 300-year-old country
house, set amid pretty landscaped grounds, which also include a
swimming pool open during the warmer months. Bedrooms are
equipped with a wealth of thoughtful extras and day rooms include a
sunny conservatory, a lounge and an elegant dining room. Evening
meals are available by arrangement.

Facilities 3 en suite ⊗ STV TVB tea/coffee ✖ Cen ht TVL No coaches
⁔ Dinner Last d 9pm LB **Parking** 8

CROWBOROUGH   MAP 06 TQ53

♦♦♦♦

Yew House Bed & Breakfast

Crowborough Hill TN6 2EA
☎ 01892 610522 🖹 07789 993982
e-mail yewhouse@yewhouse.com
web www.yewhouse.com

Dir From High St over minirdbt, pass police station on left, Yew
House on left

A warm welcome is guaranteed at this brand new Eco friendly house.
The property is just minutes from local transport links and within easy
reach of many tourist attractions. The bright and spacious bedrooms
have been finished to a high standard with many thoughtful extras. A
hearty breakfast and home-cooked evening meals, by arrangement,
can be enjoyed in the pleasant dining room overlooking the garden.

continued

Facilities 4 rms (2 en suite) ⊗ FTV TVB tea/coffee Direct dial from
bedrooms ✖ Cen ht TVL No coaches Dinner Last d Previous evening
Prices S £35-£60; D £55-£60; (incl. dinner) ✳ **Parking** 3 **Notes** Closed
25 Dec 🐾

♦♦♦ 🐷

Plough & Horses Inn

Walshes Rd TN6 3RE ☎ 01892 652614 🖹 01892 652614

Dir A26 onto B2100, under railway bridge, right onto Western Rd,
over railway to Walshes Rd

This pleasant inn has been welcoming guests for many years, and
over the last two decades the present owners have made this an
attractive and popular place. The spacious bedrooms feature well-
chosen pine furniture, and public rooms include a traditional bar, a
restaurant, and a further lounge bar.

Facilities 15 en suite (3 fmly) ⊗ in bedrooms ⊗ in area of dining room
TVB tea/coffee Cen ht TVL Dinner Last d 10pm **Parking** 40
Notes Closed 24-25 Dec

EASTBOURNE   MAP 06 TV69

★★★★ Guest Accommodation

The Berkeley

3 Lascelles Ter BN21 4BJ ☎ 01323 645055
e-mail info@theberkely.net

Dir Follow signs to seafront, Lascelles Terrace opposite the Wish
Tower

The Berkeleys central location is convenient for seafront, theatre and
the town centre, and the smart bedrooms and public areas ensure
you have an enjoyable stay.

Facilities 13 en suite (4 fmly) (1 GF) ⊗ in 5 bedrooms ⊗ in dining
room STV TVB tea/coffee Cen ht No coaches **Prices** S £31-£35;
D £62-£70✳ LB

Premier Collection

♦♦♦♦♦

Ocklynge Manor

Mill Rd BN21 2PG ☎ 01323 734121 & 07979 627172
e-mail ocklyngemanor@hotmail.com
web www.ocklyngemanor.co.uk

Dir From Eastbourne Hospital follow town centre/seafront sign, 1st
right onto Kings Av, Ocklynge Manor at top of road

The charming home of Wendy and David Dugdill dates mainly from
the early 19th century. An air of peace and relaxation is evident in the
delightful public rooms and well-tended gardens or the spacious and
homely bedrooms filled with useful extras.

Facilities 3 rms (2 en suite) (1 pri facs) (1 fmly) ⊗ STV FTV TVB
tea/coffee ✖ Cen ht No coaches **Prices** D £60-£70✳ **Parking** 3
Notes 🐾

Premier Collection

◆◆◆◆◆
The Manse B & B

7 Dittons Rd BN21 1DW ☎ 01323 737851
e-mail anne@themansebandb.co.uk
web www.themansebandb.co.uk
Dir *A22 to town centre railway station, onto Old Orchard Rd, right onto Arlington Rd*

This delightful home is in a quiet residential area only a 5-minute walk from the town centre. It was built as a Presbyterian manse at the end of the 19th century and much original character remains. The beautifully decorated bedrooms are very comfortable and have a wide range of useful extras. Breakfast is served in the elegant dining room with stripped wooden floors and an outlook onto a pretty courtyard. Annie Walker is a top-twenty finalist for AA Landlady of the Year 2006.

Facilities 3 en suite ⊗ TVB tea/coffee ✖ Cen ht No coaches
Prices S £40-£45; D £64-£72✳ **LB Parking** 2 **Notes** ⊛

◆◆◆◆
Beachy Rise Guest House ◇

5 Beachy Head Rd BN20 7QN
☎ 01323 639171 ▤ 01323 645006
Dir *A22 into Eastbourne, right just before signpost to Beachy Head*

This friendly family-run guest house has a quiet residential location close to Meads Village. Bedrooms are individually styled with coordinated soft furnishings and feature many useful extras. Breakfast is served in the light and airy dining room overlooking the garden, which you are welcome to use.

Facilities 4 en suite (2 fmly) ⊗ in 2 bedrooms ⊗ in dining room TVB tea/coffee ✖ Cen ht No children 12yrs No coaches **Prices** S £22-£45; D £45-£75✳ **Notes** ⊛

◆◆◆◆
Bella Vista

30 Redoubt Rd BN22 7DH ☎ 01323 724222
e-mail enquiries@hotelbellavista.co.uk
Dir *A22 onto A2021 to seafront & Redoubt Fortress, onto Redoubt Rd, Bella Vista on left*

Situated on the east side of town, just off the seafront, this is a friendly and attractive flint house. Bedrooms are generally spacious and neatly appointed with modern facilities. There is a lounge and parking is a bonus.

Facilities 12 en suite (1 pri facs) (1 fmly) (3 GF) ⊗ TVB tea/coffee ✖ Licensed Cen ht TVL No coaches Dinner Last d 24hrs before
Prices S £36-£45; D £52-£60 **LB Parking** 10

◆◆◆◆
Cromwell Private Hotel ◇

23 Cavendish Pl BN21 3EJ
☎ 01323 725288 ▤ 01323 725288
e-mail info@cromwellhotel.co.uk
web www.cromwellhotel.co.uk
Dir *Cavendish Pl opp pier, premises 50yds on right before lights*

A warm welcome is assured at this delightful guest house near the seafront and town centre. Bedrooms vary in size and have a variety of thoughtful extras. Public areas include a cosy lounge and dining room, where freshly prepared meals are served.

Facilities 8 en suite (2 GF) ⊗ TVB tea/coffee ✖ Licensed Cen ht TVL No children 14yrs No coaches Dinner Last d 3pm **Prices** S £27-£29; D £54-£58✳ **LB Notes** Closed Nov-Etr

◆◆◆◆
The Gladwyn Hotel ◇

16 Blackwater Rd BN21 4JD ☎ 01323 733142
e-mail gladwynhotel@aol.com
Dir *A259 into town centre, off South St onto Hardwick Rd & Blackwater Rd. Hotel overlooks Devonshire Park*

A warm welcome is guaranteed at this delightful guest house located opposite the famous tennis courts. Bedrooms each feature an individual theme and character, and all provide good levels of comfort. Freshly prepared breakfasts are served in the cosy dining room overlooking the garden, which is available during the summer.

Facilities 10 en suite (1 fmly) (2 GF) ⊗ TVB tea/coffee Licensed TVL
Prices S £30-£32; D £60-£64✳

If you have to cancel a booking, let the proprietor know immediately

England

EASTBOURNE continued

◆◆◆◆

Ivydene Hotel

5-6 Hampden Ter, Latimer Rd BN22 7BL
☎ 01323 720547 ▤ 01323 411247
e-mail carolyn@ivydene-eastbourne.wanadoo.co.uk
web www.ivydenehotel-eastbourne.co.uk
Dir From town centre/pier NE along seafront, past Redoubt Fortress, onto St Aubyns Rd, 1st right onto Hampden Ter

Located within walking distance of the seafront, the Ivydene is a true home from home. The spacious bedrooms are decorated to a high standard, and freshly prepared home-cooked dinners are served in the cosy dining room. There is also a lounge bar.

Facilities 14 en suite (2 fmly) (1 GF) ⊘ in bedrooms ⊘ in dining room ⊘ in 1 lounge TVB tea/coffee ✖ Licensed Cen ht No children 5yrs Dinner Last d 4pm **Prices** S £25-£30; D £50-£60 **LB** **Notes** Closed Jan-Feb 🐾

◆◆◆◆

The Mowbray

2 Lascelles Ter BN21 4BJ ☎ 01323 720012
e-mail mowbrayhotel@btconnect.com
Dir SW of pier off seafront Parade

Just a stroll from the seafront and the Devonshire Theatre, the Victorian property has good practical bedrooms, reached by a lift. Breakfast (and dinner by arrangement) is served in the attractive lower-ground-floor dining room and a smart lounge is available.

Facilities 13 en suite (4 fmly) (1 GF) ⊘ in dining room TVB tea/coffee Licensed Lift Cen ht Dinner Last d 4pm **Prices** S £29-£33; D £58-£66✱ **LB**

◆◆◆◆

Rosedale

13 Bourne St BN21 3ES ☎ 01323 720215 ▤ 01323 738477
e-mail rosedalehotel@aol.com
Dir A22 to town centre, train station on left, 3rd right, bottom of hill on left

Convenient for the seafront and the many attractions of the town centre, the Rosedale offers a warm welcome and smart, individually styled bedrooms. Dinner is available on request, and well-cooked breakfasts are served in the dining room. A small lounge, with a well-stocked bar, is available.

Facilities 5 en suite (1 fmly) ⊘ in dining room TVB tea/coffee ✖ Cen ht No children 4yrs No coaches **Prices** S £25-£34; D £50-£56✱

◆◆◆◆

St Omer Hotel

13 Royal Pde BN22 7AR ☎ 01323 722152 ▤ 01323 723400
e-mail stomerhotel@hotmail.com
web www.st-omer.co.uk
Dir On seafront, 0.25m from pier & town centre

A warm welcome is assured at this seafront establishment. The smartly decorated bedrooms vary in size but all are thoughtfully equipped. Breakfast and dinner are served at individual tables in the large oak-panelled dining room. Public areas include a comfortable lounge bar and small conservatory.

Facilities 11 en suite (1 fmly) (1 GF) ⊘ TVB tea/coffee ✖ Licensed Cen ht TVL No coaches Dinner Last d 5pm **Prices** S £30-£33; D £60-£66✱ **LB**

◆◆◆

Beach Haven

61 Pevensey Rd BN21 3HS ☎ 01323 726195
e-mail enquiries@beach-haven.co.uk
web www.beach-haven.co.uk
Dir Off A259

The attractive terrace property is just a short walk from the seafront and attractions. Bedrooms are located on three floors, some offer ensuite facilities and all have a thoughtful range of guest extras. There is also a comfortable dining room, a cosy lounge and a basement chapel.

Facilities 7 rms (3 en suite) (1 GF) ⊘ TVB tea/coffee ✖ Cen ht No children 1yr No coaches Dinner Last d 10am **Prices** S £25-£35✱ **LB**

◆◆◆

Camelot Lodge Hotel

35 Lewes Rd BN21 2BU ☎ 01323 725207 ▤ 01323 722799
e-mail info@camelotlodgehotel.com
web www.camelotlodgehotel.com
Dir A22 onto A2021, premises 0.5m after hospital

This delightful Edwardian property is within walking distance of the seafront and local amenities. The attractive bedrooms feature a range of facilities, and there is a spacious lounge-bar area. Meals are served in the conservatory dining room, and dinner is available by arrangement.

Facilities 7 en suite (3 fmly) (1 GF) ⊘ in bedrooms ⊘ in dining room ⊘ in 1 lounge TVB tea/coffee ✖ Licensed Cen ht TVL No coaches Dinner **Prices** S £30-£40; D £60-£70✱ **LB** **Parking** 11

♦♦♦

The Bay Lodge

61-62 Royal Pde BN22 7AQ
☎ 01323 732515 📠 01323 735009
e-mail baylodgehotel@fsmail.net
Dir NE of town centre. Off A259 onto Redoubt Rd & Royal Parade

This family-run guest house offers a warm welcome in comfortable surrounds opposite the Redoubt and Pavilion gardens. Many of the attractive bedrooms have superb sea views, and there is a sun lounge and a cosy bar.

Facilities 11 rms (10 en suite) (1 pri facs) (1 fmly) (2 GF) ⊗ TVB tea/coffee ✖ Licensed Cen ht TVL No coaches Dinner Last d 10am
Prices S £25; D £50-£70✳ **LB** **Parking** 3

♦♦♦

Birling Gap Hotel

Seven Sisters Cliffs, Birling Gap, East Dean BN20 0AB
☎ 01323 423197 📠 01323 423030
e-mail reception@birlinggaphotel.co.uk
web www.birlinggaphotel.co.uk
Dir 4m W of Eastbourne. Off A259 at Eastdean onto Gilberts Dr, Birling Gap 1.5m

The friendly, family-run establishment has a superb clifftop location and many of the bedrooms have lovely sea views. Public rooms include a spacious lounge bar, a coffee shop, and a restaurant offering a wide range of popular dishes.

Facilities 9 en suite (3 fmly) (9 GF) ⊗ in area of dining room STV TVB tea/coffee Direct dial from bedrooms ✖ Licensed Cen ht Pool Table Dinner Last d 9pm **Prices** S fr £30; d fr £60✳ **LB** **Conf** Max 150 Thtr 150 Class 100 Board 80 **Parking** 100

♦♦♦

Far End Private Hotel

139 Royal Pde BN22 7LH ☎ 01323 725666
e-mail wal@camp61.fsnet.co.uk
Dir 0.5m NE of pier. A259 onto Channel View Rd & Royal Parade, next to Princess Park

Located north-east of the town centre, next to the popular Princess Park and the marina, this family-run guest house offers a warm welcome. Bedrooms vary in size but are comfortably appointed, some having sea views. Breakfast (dinner by arrangement) is served in the bright ground-floor dining room.

Facilities 10 rms (6 en suite) ⊗ TVB tea/coffee Licensed Cen ht No children 6yrs No coaches Dinner Last d 2pm **Prices** S £32-£42; D £64-£77✳ **LB** **Parking** 8

♦♦♦

The Halcyon Hotel

8 South Cliff BN20 7AF ☎ 01323 723710 📠 01323 411743
e-mail james-finch@btconnect.com
Dir A22 to Eastbourne & W end of seafront, premises just past Grand Hotel opp Wish Tower Gardens

The Halcyon is on the quiet South Cliff end of town, within easy walking distance of Beachy Head and the pier, and has stunning views. Bedrooms are mainly large, and meals (dinner by arrangement) are served in the attractive ground-floor dining room.

Facilities 15 en suite (3 fmly) (2 GF) ⊗ TVB tea/coffee ✖ Licensed Cen ht TVL No coaches Dinner Last d 4pm **LB**

♦♦♦

Loriston Guest House

17 St Aubyns Rd BN22 7AS ☎ 01323 726193
e-mail loriston@tiscali.co.uk
Dir Directly off Seafront, east of pier. With 'York House Hotel' on corner of Rd.

This friendly guest house is the home of Harry and Pam Pope who clearly enjoy making their guests feel welcome. Bedrooms are bright and airy and come in a variety of sizes while a walk along the nearby seafront can be taken after a freshly cooked and hearty breakfast.

Facilities 6 en suite (1 fmly) ⊗ TVB tea/coffee Cen ht No coaches
Prices S £25-£35; D £50-£70✳ **LB**

♦♦♦

Meridale Guest House

91 Royal Pde BN22 7AE
☎ 01323 729686 & 639180 📠 01323 639180
Dir On seafront opp Treasure Island

Located on the seafront and within easy walking distance of the town centre and the pier, this cosy guest house provides charming bedrooms that are well decorated and presented. In the mornings, a freshly cooked full English breakfast is served at individual tables.

Facilities 6 en suite (2 fmly) ⊗ in 4 bedrooms ⊗ in dining room ⊗ in lounges TVB tea/coffee Cen ht No coaches

♦♦♦

Savoy Court

11-15 Cavendish Pl BN21 3EJ
☎ 01323 723132 📠 01323 737902
e-mail info@savoycourthotel.co.uk
Dir 100yds N of pier

Please note that this establishment has recently changed hands. With an impressive restored façade, this attractive Regency house is just a stroll from the beach. Bedrooms vary in size and are all pleasantly decorated. A comfortable lounge and bar are available as well as a cosy dining room where dinner and breakfast are served.

Facilities 29 en suite (4 fmly) (6 GF) ⊗ in bedrooms ⊗ in dining room ⊗ in 1 lounge TVB tea/coffee ✖ Licensed Lift Cen ht TVL Dinner Last d 4.30pm **Prices** S £23-£30; D £46-£60✳ **LB** **Conf** Class 12 Board 12 Del from £40 ✳

England

EASTBOURNE continued

♦♦♦

Sheldon Hotel ◈

9-11 Burlington Pl BN21 4AS
☎ 01323 724120 🖹 01323 430406
e-mail sheldonhotel@tiscali.co.uk
web www.thesheldonhotel.co.uk
Dir 500yds SE of pier off seafront Parade

This impressive Victorian house is convenient for the town centre and only a short walk from the seafront. Bedrooms vary in size but are cheerfully decorated. Traditional home-cooked food is served in the smart dining room.

Facilities 28 en suite (5 fmly) (2 GF) ⊗ in bedrooms ⊗ in dining room TVB tea/coffee Direct dial from bedrooms ✘ Licensed Lift Cen ht TVL Dinner Last d 4pm **Prices** S £28-£36; D £56-£72✱ LB **Parking** 20

EAST HOATHLY   MAP 06 TQ51

♦♦♦♦ 🅰

Aberdeen House Bed & Breakfast

5 High St BN8 6DR ☎ 01825 840219
e-mail jo@aberdeenhouse.freeserve.co.uk
Dir Off A22 into village centre

Facilities 3 rms (1 en suite) (1 fmly) ⊗ TVB tea/coffee ✘ Cen ht TVL No coaches **Prices** S £35-£50; D £50-£65 ✱ LB **Parking** 4 **Notes** 🐾

FOREST ROW   MAP 06 TQ43

♦♦♦ 🍺

Brambletye Hotel

The Square RH18 5EZ ☎ 01342 824144 🖹 01342 824833
e-mail brambletyehotel@accommodating-inns.co.uk
web www.accommodating-inns.co.uk
Dir On A22, 2m S of East Grinstead

Located in the centre of the village, The Brambletye has provided accommodation since 1866. The refurbished public areas include a smart, spacious bar-restaurant, and the neat bedrooms are well coordinated and equipped. Parking available.

Facilities 22 en suite (1 fmly) (4 GF) ⊗ in 16 bedrooms ⊗ in dining room TVB tea/coffee Direct dial from bedrooms Cen ht Dinner Last d 9.30pm **Conf** Max 30 **Parking** 45

HALLAND   MAP 06 TQ41

♦♦♦♦♦

Tamberry Hall

Eastbourne Rd BN8 6PS
☎ 01825 880090 🖹 01825 880090
e-mail bedandbreakfast@tamberryhall.fsbusiness.co.uk
web www.tamberryhall.co.uk
Dir In Halland on A22, 200yds N of junct with B2192 at Black Lion Inn

A warm welcome is assured at this attractive house sitting in three acres of wonderful landscaped gardens. Individually decorated bedrooms vary in size and are all equipped with a variety of thoughtful extras. An inglenook fireplace and exposed beams are a character of this establishment. Hearty breakfasts are served in a delightful dining room or on the terrace, weather permitting.

Facilities 3 en suite (1 fmly) ⊗ TVB tea/coffee ✘ Cen ht TVL No coaches **Prices** S £45-£60; D £60-£75 LB **Parking** 3

♦♦♦♦

Shortgate Manor Farm

BN8 6PJ ☎ 01825 840320 🖹 01825 840320
e-mail david@shortgate.co.uk
web www.shortgate.co.uk
Dir A22 onto B2192 signed Lewes, farm 0.75m on left

Situated in an idyllic spot on the South Downs and yet only minutes away from the historic town of Lewes, this attractive guest house offers a warm welcome. The attractive bedrooms are well equipped, have pleasant views and contain a range of thoughtful extras. Breakfast is served around a communal table in the smart sitting-dining room.

Facilities 3 en suite ⊗ TVB tea/coffee ✘ Cen ht TVL No children 10yrs No coaches **Prices** S £40-£45; D £70-£80✱ LB **Parking** 6 **Notes** 🐾

HARTFIELD   MAP 06 TQ43

♦♦♦♦

Bolebroke Watermill

Perry Hill, Edenbridge Rd TN7 4JP
☎ 01892 770061 🖹 01892 770425
Dir A264 S onto B2026 signed Hartfield. 1m past Perryhill Nurseries left onto unsurfaced farm road 400yds

This charming converted 18th-century watermill originates from the 11th century and stands in a peaceful location. The bedrooms are in

continued

the adjacent barn and are full of character. A shared lounge is on the ground floor. Breakfast is served nearby in Bolebroke Castle. The nearby Winnie the Pooh walk takes in the sites of AA Milne's famous books.

Facilities 3 en suite (1 GF) ⊗ TVB tea/coffee ✖ Cen ht No coaches **Prices** D £79-£99✳ **Parking** 10

HASTINGS & ST LEONARDS   MAP 07 TQ80

★★★ Bed & Breakfast
Filsham Farmhouse ◇ (TQ784096)
111 Harley Shute Rd TN38 8BY
☎ 01424 433109 Mrs Yorke
e-mail filshamfarmhouse@talk21.com
Dir Off A21 turn left onto Old Harrow Rd, house on right after railway bridge.

Guests can expect a warm welcome at this charming 17th-century house. Public rooms are elegantly appointed with fine period furniture and memorabilia. The individually decorated bedrooms are attractively furnished and thoughtfully equipped; some have superb sea views. Breakfast is served in the delightful dining room, which features a magnificent inglenook fireplace.

Facilities 3 rms (2 en suite) (1 pri facs) (1 fmly) ⊗ TVB tea/coffee Cen ht TVL No children 7yrs **Prices** S £30-£35; D £50-£70✳ LB **Parking** 4 **Notes** Closed 23-28 Dec

◆◆◆◆◆
Parkside House ◇
59 Lower Park Rd TN34 2LD
☎ 01424 433096 ▤ 01424 421431
e-mail bkent.parksidehouse@talk21.com
Dir A2101 to town centre, right at rdbt, 1st right

You can expect a friendly welcome at this attractive Victorian house overlooking Alexandra Park, just a 10-minute walk from the town centre and seafront. The bedrooms are carefully furnished and have many thoughtful touches, and the cosy lounge has plush furniture. Breakfast is served at individual tables in the elegant dining room.

Facilities 5 rms (4 en suite) (1 fmly) ⊗ TVB tea/coffee ✖ Cen ht TVL No coaches **Prices** S £30-£45; D £60-£65 LB

◆◆◆◆◆
Stream House
Pett Level Rd, Fairlight TN35 4ED
☎ 01424 814916 & 07794 191 1379
e-mail info@stream-house.co.uk
web www.stream-house.co.uk
Dir 4m NE of Hastings. Off A259 on unclassified road between Fairlight & Cliff End

Lovingly converted from three cottages, the house stands in 3 acres of tranquil grounds 1m from Winchelsea beach. The well-appointed bedrooms vary in size and are individually decorated. Delicious breakfasts are served in the lounge-dining room with an original inglenook fireplace, and during warmer months you can enjoy the garden and its Koi pond.

Facilities 2 rms (1 en suite) (1 pri facs) ⊗ TVB tea/coffee ✖ Cen ht TVL No children 10yrs No coaches Table tennis **Prices** D £65-£80✳ **Parking** 4 **Notes** Closed Dec-Feb 🌐

◆◆◆◆
Tower House Hotel
26-28 Tower Rd West TN38 0RG
☎ 01424 427217 & 421217 ▤ 01424 430165
e-mail enquiries@Towerhousehotel.com
web www.towerhousehotel.com
Dir 1m NW of Hastings centre. Off A21 London Rd onto A2102 London Rd, 250yds right onto Tower Rd West

An elegant double-fronted Victorian property situated on an elevated position in a peaceful residential area. Bedrooms are carefully furnished and equipped with a wealth of thoughtful extras. Ground-floor areas include a sumptuous lounge, a formal bar, and a superb conservatory-dining room with access to immaculate gardens.

Facilities 10 en suite (1 fmly) (5 GF) ⊗ in bedrooms ⊗ in dining room ⊗ in lounges STV TVB tea/coffee ✖ Licensed Cen ht TVL No coaches Dinner Last d 4pm **Prices** S £49.50-£55; D £65-£75✳ LB

◆◆◆◆
Hotel Lindum ◇
1A Carlisle Pde TN34 1JG
☎ 01424 434070 ▤ 01424 718833
e-mail Hotellindum@aol.com
web www.hotellindum.co.uk
Dir On seafront 350yds E of pier

The Hotel Lindum is just a short walk from the pier and town centre. The converted house offers stylish contemporary accommodation and bathrooms, some rooms boast balconies with great sea views. A continental breakfast is served to the room, ideal for early starters.

Facilities 12 en suite (1 GF) ⊗ STV FTV TVB tea/coffee Direct dial from bedrooms ✖ Cen ht **Prices** S £25-£45; D £40-£85✳ LB **Notes** Closed 1wk Xmas

England

HASTINGS & ST LEONARDS continued

◆◆◆◆

The Old School House

57 All Saints St, Old Town TN34 3BN
☎ 01424 457750 ▤ 01424 433133
e-mail oldschoolyard@aol.com
web www.oldschool-house.co.uk
Dir follow A21 to Hastings at seafront, turn left to old town

Situated in the heart of the Old Town, the seafront, shops and restaurants are just a stroll away. The two bedrooms are spacious and comfortable and a small lounge dining room is available. On street parking is available after 6pm or all day at the local pay and display car park.

Facilities 2 rms (1 en suite) (1 pri facs) (1 fmly) ⊗ TVB tea/coffee ✖ Cen ht

◆◆◆◆

White Cottage

Battery Hill, Fairlight TN35 4AP
☎ 01424 812528 ▤ 01424 812285
e-mail JuneandJohn@whitecottagebb.fsnet.co.uk
Dir 3m E off A259 Hastings-Rye, signed Fairlight

This modern house is set among mature gardens on the outskirts of the peaceful village of Fairlight, between Hastings and Rye. White Cottage offers pleasantly decorated, thoughtfully furnished and well-equipped bedrooms throughout. Breakfast is served at a large communal table in the lounge-dining area, which overlooks the beautiful garden.

Facilities 3 en suite (1 GF) ⊗ TVB tea/coffee ✖ Cen ht No children 12yrs No coaches **Prices** D £60-£70✳ **LB** **Parking** 4 **Notes** Closed Dec ⊛

See advertisement on opposite page

◆◆◆◆ Ⓐ

Seaspray Guest House ◇

54 Eversfield Pl TN37 6DB ☎ 01424 436583
e-mail jo@seaspray.freeserve.co.uk
web www.seaspraybb.co.uk
Dir A21 to town centre & seafront, Seaspray 100yds W of pier

Facilities 10 rms (8 en suite) (3 fmly) (1 GF) ⊗ TVB tea/coffee ✖ Cen ht No coaches **Prices** S £25-£35; D £50-£65 **LB** **Notes** ⊛

◆◆◆

Eagle House

Pevensey Rd TN38 0JZ
☎ 01424 430535 & 441273 ▤ 01424 437771
e-mail info@eaglehousehotel.co.uk
Dir Off seafront onto London Rd, premises next to St Leonards Shopping Centre

Victorian property situated in a peaceful residential area within easy walking distance of the shops, college and seafront. The spacious bedrooms are traditionally decorated and simply furnished. An interesting breakfast can be enjoyed in the dining room, which overlooks the gardens.

Facilities 20 en suite (2 fmly) ⊗ in 10 bedrooms ⊗ in dining room TVB tea/coffee Direct dial from bedrooms ✖ Licensed Cen ht No coaches **Prices** S £42; D £61 **Parking** 13

HEATHFIELD
MAP 06 TQ52

◆◆◆◆ Ⓐ

Iwood Bed & Breakfast ◇

Mutton Hall Ln TN21 8NR ☎ 01435 863918
e-mail iwoodbb@aol.com
web www.iwoodbb.com
Dir A265 through Heathfield High St towards Burwash. At top of hill sharp left at lights onto Mutton Hall Ln, last house on left

Facilities 4 rms (3 en suite) (1 pri facs) (1 fmly) (1 GF) ⊗ TVB tea/coffee ✖ Cen ht TVL No coaches **Prices** S £25-£40; D £50-£70✳ **Parking** 2 **Notes** Closed Xmas & New Year

◆◆◆◆ Ⓐ

Spicers Bed & Breakfast ◇

21 Spicers Cottage, Cade St TN21 9BS
☎ 01435 866363 ▤ 01435 866363
e-mail spicersbb@surfree.co.uk
Dir On B2096, 1m from junct with A265, opp Half Moon

Facilities 3 rms (2 en suite) (1 pri facs) (1 GF) ⊗ FTV TVB tea/coffee Lift Cen ht TVL No coaches Dinner **Prices** S £25-£35; D £48-£60 **Parking** 3

HERSTMONCEUX
MAP 06 TQ61

Premier Collection

◆◆◆◆◆

Wartling Place

Wartling Pl, Wartling BN27 1RY
☎ 01323 832590 📠 01323 831558
e-mail accom@wartlingplace.prestel.co.uk
Dir *Off A271 signed Wartling, Wartling Place on right opp St Mary Magdelan Church*

Located in a sleepy village, this beautiful Grade II listed country home is set in 2 acres of well-tended gardens. The individually decorated bedrooms, two featuring four-poster beds, are luxurious and have a host of thoughtful extras. Delicious breakfasts are served in the elegant dining room. This is an ideal base for exploring the castles, gardens and National Trust houses of Sussex and Kent, or enjoying the many local golf courses.

Facilities 4 en suite (1 fmly) ⊗ TVB tea/coffee ✗ Cen ht No coaches Dinner Last d 24hrs in advance **Prices** S £70-£90; D £95-£145 **LB**
Conf Max 12 **Parking** 10

LEWES
MAP 06 TQ41

★★★★ Inn

The Blacksmiths Arms ◇

London Rd, Offham BN7 3QD ☎ 01273 472971
e-mail blacksmithsarms@tiscali.co.uk
web www.theblacksmithsarms-offham.co.uk
Dir *A27 onto A277, left at Lewes Prison. A275 N to Chailey, 2m on left*

Situated just outside Lewes, this is a great location for touring the south coast, offering high quality accommodation in comfortable bedrooms. Enjoyable meals are available in the cosy bar downstairs and this is where the hearty cooked breakfast is also served.

Facilities 4 en suite ⊗ TVB tea/coffee ✗ Cen ht No children 5yrs No coaches Dinner Last d 9pm **Prices** S £30-£45; D £60-£75✳ **Parking** 22

◆◆◆◆

Number 6

6 Gundreda Rd BN7 1PX ☎ 01273 472106
e-mail jacquelinelucas@yahoo.co.uk
Dir *50yds NW of town centre. Off A275 Nevill Rd onto Prince Edwards Rd & 3rd left*

This attractive house is located in a quiet residential area not far from the centre of Lewes. The stylish bedrooms and bathrooms are smartly

presented and have many thoughtful extra facilities. Breakfast is served in the conservatory, which looks over the garden.

Facilities 3 rms (2 en suite) (1 pri facs) (1 fmly) ⊗ TVB tea/coffee ✗ Cen ht **Prices** d fr £60✳ **Notes** Closed Xmas

NEWHAVEN
MAP 06 TQ40

◆◆◆

The Harbourside

Fort Rd BN9 9EL ☎ 01273 513340 📠 01273 512372
Dir *A259 into Newhaven, follow signs to Fort. Turn left onto South Rd, leads onto Fort Rd*

This smartly refurbished inn is, as the name suggests, conveniently situated for the ferry terminals and harbour attractions. Bedrooms are spacious and some enjoy views of the marina. Hearty meals can be enjoyed in the attractive bar and dining area and there is also a useful car park to the rear.

Facilities 10 rms (3 en suite) (5 fmly) ⊗ in bedrooms ⊗ in dining room TVB tea/coffee ✗ Cen ht Pool Table Dinner Last d 8.50pm **Conf** Max 50 **Parking** 25

◆◆◆ 🅰

Newhaven Lodge ◇

12 Brighton Rd BN9 9NB ☎ 01273 513736
e-mail newhavenlodge@aol.com
Dir *250yds W of town centre on A259*

Facilities 6 rms (3 en suite) (4 fmly) (2 GF) ⊗ TVB tea/coffee Cen ht No coaches **Prices** S £25-£30; D £45-£60✳ **LB** **Parking** 5

continued

NORTHIAM
MAP 07 TQ82

◆◆◆◆

Wellington House

Dixter Rd TN31 6LB ☎ 01797 253449
e-mail fanny@frances14.freeserve.co.uk
Dir Into Northiam from S, turn left after Post Office signed Great Dixter Gardens. B&B 50yds up Dixter Rd on left

This charming Victorian house sits in the peaceful village of Northiam, a short walk away from Great Dixter House. The traditional spacious bedrooms offer a high level of comfort with thoughtful added extras such as remote-control televisions and radios, home-made biscuits and hot water bottles disguised as teddy bears. Guests can enjoy afternoon tea by the open fire in the lounge and a hearty, locally sourced breakfast at the communal table in the dining room.

Facilities 2 en suite ⊗ in bedrooms ⊗ in dining room TVB tea/coffee Cen ht TVL No children 7yrs No coaches Dinner Last d Day before **Parking** 1 **Notes** Closed 15 Dec-15 Jan ⊛

RYE
MAP 07 TQ92

See also **Hastings & St Leonards**

Premier Collection

◆◆◆◆◆

Little Orchard House

West St TN31 7ES ☎ 01797 223831 🖺 01797 223831
e-mail info@littleorchardhouse.com
Dir A259 into town via Landgate Arch & High St, 3rd left

This delightful 18th-century property is right in the heart of the historic town. The house has been renovated to retain much of its original character, and the attractive bedrooms are individually decorated and thoughtfully equipped. Breakfast is served in the elegant dining room, and there is also a lounge with an open fire and a wood-panelled reading room.

Facilities 2 en suite ⊗ TVB tea/coffee 🕱 Cen ht No children 12yrs No coaches **Prices** S £50-£70; D £80-£110✳ LB **Parking** 2

Premier Collection

◆◆◆◆◆ ⊜

Manor Farm Oast

Windmill Ln TN36 4WL ☎ 01424 813787 🖺 01424 813787
e-mail manor.farm.oast@lineone.net
web www.manorfarmoast.co.uk
Dir 4m SW of Rye. A259 W past Icklesham church, left at x-rds onto Windmill Ln, after sharp left bend left into orchards

The charming 19th-century oast house stands amid peaceful orchards in open countryside. The spacious bedrooms are individually styled and include numerous thoughtful extras for your comfort. A choice of lounges is available, one heated by a roaring log fire in winter, and home-produced dinners are a feature of any stay. Kate Mylrea is a runner-up for AA Landlady of the Year 2006.

Facilities 3 rms (2 en suite) (1 pri facs) (1 fmly) ⊗ TVB tea/coffee 🕱 Licensed Cen ht No children 11yrs No coaches 🏊 Garden quoits Dinner Last d 7.30pm **Prices** S £54-£64; D £74-£84✳ LB **Conf** Max 20 **Parking** 8 **Notes** Closed 28 Dec-15 Jan Civ Wed 40

Premier Collection

◆◆◆◆◆ 🖺

Olde Moat House

TN29 0AZ ☎ 01797 344700 🖺 01797 343919
e-mail oldemoathouse@hotmail.com
web www.oldemoathouse.co.uk
For full entry see **Ivychurch (Kent)**

Premier Collection

◆◆◆◆◆ 🖺

The Old Vicarage Guesthouse

66 Church Sq TN31 7HF ☎ 01797 222119 🖺 01797 227466
e-mail info@oldvicaragerye.co.uk
web www.oldvicaragerye.co.uk
Dir A259 into town via Landgate Arch & High St, 3rd left onto West St, footpath by church to Vicarage

Expect a warm welcome at this delightful detached Georgian property next to the church. The individually decorated bedrooms have attractive soft furnishings, and extras such as home-made biscuits and fudge. Breakfast, served in the attractive dining room overlooking the walled garden, includes home-made preserves, breads and scones.

Facilities 4 en suite (1 fmly) ⊗ TVB tea/coffee 🕱 Cen ht TVL No children 8yrs No coaches **Prices** D £90-£100 LB **Parking** 4 **Notes** Closed 24-26 Dec ⊛

Premier Collection

◆◆◆◆◆

The Benson

15 East St TN31 7JY ☎ 01797 225131 🖹 01797 225512
e-mail info@thebenson.co.uk
web www.thebenson.co.uk
Dir *A268, through Landgate arch onto East Cliff & High St, East St 1st left*

Situated in a quiet side road just off the bustling high street, The Benson offers spacious, individually decorated bedrooms, carefully furnished and equipped with modern facilities. Breakfast is served in the attractive dining room at individual tables, and there is a lounge as well as a conservatory, which overlooks the terraced garden and River Rother beyond.

Facilities 3 en suite (2 fmly) ⊗ TVB tea/coffee Direct dial from bedrooms 🐾 Licensed Cen ht No coaches **Prices** D £84-£104✳ **LB**

Premier Collection

◆◆◆◆◆

Jeake's House

Mermaid St TN31 7ET ☎ 01797 222828 🖹 01797 222623
e-mail stay@jeakeshouse.com
web www.jeakeshouse.com
Dir *Approach from High St or The Strand*

Previously a 17th-century wool store and then a 19th-century Baptist school, this delightful house stands on a cobbled street in one of the most beautiful parts of this small, bustling town. The individually decorated bedrooms combine elegance and comfort with modern facilities. Breakfast is served at separate tables in the galleried dining room, and there is an oak-beamed lounge as well as a stylish book-lined bar with old pews.

Facilities 11 en suite (2 fmly) ⊗ in dining room ⊗ in 1 lounge TVB tea/coffee Direct dial from bedrooms Licensed Cen ht No children 8yrs No coaches **Prices** S £50-£75; D £88-£120 **Parking** 21

See advertisement on this page

◆◆◆◆

The Strand House

Tanyards Ln, Winchelsea TN36 4JT
☎ 01797 226276 🖹 01797 224806
e-mail info@thestrandhouse.co.uk
Dir *2m SW of Rye on A259, 1st on left after Winchelsea town sign*

Dating from the 15th century, this fine riverside house retains original inglenook fireplaces and exposed beams. The bedrooms are full of quality furnishings and thoughtful extras, and the ground-floor areas include a comfortable lounge, cosy dining room and an honesty bar.

Facilities 10 en suite (1 fmly) (1 GF) ⊗ TVB tea/coffee 🐾 Licensed Cen ht No children 5yrs No coaches **Prices** S £50; D £60-£85✳ **LB** **Parking** 12

England

RYE continued

♦♦♦♦
Little Saltcote

22 Military Rd TN31 7NY ☎ 01797 223210 📠 01797 224474
e-mail info@littlesaltcote.co.uk
Dir Off A268 onto Military Rd signed Appledore, house 300yds on left

This refurbished, family-run guest house stands in quiet surroundings within walking distance of the charming town centre. The pleasant en suite bedrooms are equipped with modern facilities, and you can enjoy afternoon tea in the conservatory. A hearty breakfast is served at individual tables in the dining room.

Facilities 5 en suite (3 fmly) (1 GF) ⊗ TVB tea/coffee Cen ht
Prices S £36-£56; D £63-£73✱ LB **Parking** 5

♦♦♦♦
Old Borough Arms Hotel

The Strand TN31 7DB ☎ 01797 222128 📠 01797 222128
e-mail info@oldborougharms.co.uk
web www.oldborougharms.co.uk
Dir A259 onto The Strand. Hotel at foot of Mermaid St overlooking Strand Quay

Expect a warm welcome at this former sailors' inn, which has a peaceful, elevated setting close to the centre. Bedrooms come in a variety of sizes and styles; each one is pleasantly decorated and thoughtfully equipped. Breakfast is served in the charming dining room and there is a cosy lounge bar.

Facilities 9 en suite (2 fmly) (4 GF) ⊗ TVB tea/coffee 🐾 Licensed Cen ht TVL **Prices** S £40-£55; D £70-£110✱

♦♦♦♦
Simmons of the Mint

68/69 The Mint TN31 7EW ☎ 01797 226862
e-mail simmonsofthemint@aol.com
web
www.rye.org.uk/establishments/simmons/simmons.html
Located on one of the town's oldest streets, this house is full of character. Bedrooms are individually decorated and vary in size. Hearty breakfasts are served in the ground-floor dining room, which has its original fireplace. There are a number of dining options within easy walking distance.

Facilities 4 rms (3 en suite) (1 pri facs) (1 fmly) ⊗ TVB tea/coffee 🐾 Licensed Cen ht No children 5yrs No coaches Dinner **Prices** S £40-£60; D £60-£90✱ LB

♦♦♦ ❦
Cliff Farm (TQ933237)

Military Rd, Iden Lock TN31 7QD
☎ 01797 280331 📠 01797 280331 Mrs Sullivin
e-mail info@cliff-farm.com
Dir 2m along Military Rd to Appledore, turn left at hanging milk churn

Expect a warm welcome at this farmhouse situated in a peaceful rural location just a short drive from Rye and Hastings. Bedrooms are pleasantly decorated and comfortably furnished. Breakfast is served at individual tables in the dining room and there is also a cosy sitting room with a wood-burning stove and television.

Facilities 3 rms (1 fmly) ⊗ tea/coffee Cen ht TVL 6 acres smallholding
Prices D £44-£50✱ LB **Parking** 6 **Notes** Closed Nov-Feb ⓦ

SEAFORD
MAP 06 TV49

♦♦♦♦
The Gallery

Cliff Rd BN25 1BB ☎ 01323 491755
e-mail jackie@wrightplace.info
web www.wrightplace.info
Dir Off A259 onto Marine Parade, E along Esplanade to tower, left & 1st right

A warm welcome is guaranteed at this refurbished house near Seaford Head cliffs. Wonderful sea views, coastal walks, and easy access to the town centre are benefits here. Bedrooms, themed after the French impressionists, are spacious and well appointed, and local artworks adorn the public areas.

Facilities 3 en suite ⊗ TVB tea/coffee 🐾 Cen ht No coaches
Prices D £55-£80✱ LB **Parking** 3 **Notes** ⓦ

♦♦♦♦
Avondale Hotel ◇

Avondale Rd BN25 1RJ ☎ 01323 890008 📠 01323 490598
e-mail avondalehotel@btconnect.com
Dir In town centre, off A259 behind war memorial

Please note that this establishment has recently changed hands. The friendly, family-run Avondale is convenient for the Newhaven to Dieppe ferry service. The bedrooms are pleasantly furnished and thoughtfully equipped, there is a cosy lounge, and breakfast and dinner are served in the attractive dining room. The caring owners provide a warm welcome.

Facilities 16 rms (10 en suite) (4 fmly) ⊗ TVB tea/coffee 🐾 Lift Cen ht TVL No coaches **Prices** S £25-£35; D £45-£60✱ LB **Conf** Max 15 Class 15 Board 15

####◆◆◆◆
The Silverdale

21 Sutton Park Rd BN25 1RH
☎ 01323 491849 ▤ 01323 890854
e-mail silverdale@mistral.co.uk
web www.silverdale.mistral.co.uk
Dir *On A259 in the centre of Seaford, close to memorial*

A warm welcome is assured at this family-run establishment, which is well situated for the town centre and the seafront. The pleasant bedrooms have many useful extras, and breakfast and dinner are served in the dining room. The cosy well-stocked lounge bar specialises in English wines and malt whiskies.

Facilities 7 en suite (2 fmly) (1 GF) ⊘ in 4 bedrooms ⊘ in dining room TVB tea/coffee Direct dial from bedrooms Licensed Cen ht No coaches Dinner Last d 2pm **Prices** D £60-£75 **LB** **Parking** 5

WADHURST   MAP 06 TQ63

◆◆◆◆
Best Beech Inn

Mayfield Ln TN5 6JH ☎ 01892 782046 ▤ 01892 785092
e-mail roger_felstead@hotmail.com
Dir *From Wadhurst onto B2100 signed Mark Cross, inn 1m on left*

Facilities 7 rms (4 en suite) (3 pri facs) (1 fmly) ⊘ in bedrooms ⊘ in dining room TVB tea/coffee Cen ht No coaches horseriding by arrangement Dinner Last d 9pm **Prices** S £49.90-£54.90; D £59.90-£64.90✳ **LB** **Conf** Thtr 24 Class 20 Board 20 Del from £120 ✳ **Parking** 30

◆◆◆ A
Spring Cottage

Best Beech Hill TN5 6JH
☎ 01892 783896 & 785752 ▤ 01892 784866
e-mail penny@southerncrosstravel.co.uk
Dir *A267 from Tunbridge Wells to Mark Cross, left onto B2100, cottage 2m up hill on left*

Facilities 2 rms (1 en suite) (1 fmly) ⊘ TVB tea/coffee ✱ Cen ht No coaches **Parking** 4 **Notes** Closed 24-27 Dec 🐾

WILMINGTON   MAP 06 TQ50

★★★★ ⚜⚜ **Restaurant with Rooms**
Crossways

Lewes Rd BN26 5SG ☎ 01323 482455 ▤ 01323 487811
e-mail stay@crosswayshotel.co.uk
web www.crosswayshotel.co.uk
Dir *On A27 between Lewes and Polegate, 2m E of Alfriston rdbt*

A well-established restaurant with a good local reputation is the focus of this attractive property. Bedrooms are also provided, and all are individually decorated with taste and style and superior rooms are available. Guest comfort is paramount and there are excellent facilities and the kind of hospitality that ensures guests return often.

Crossways

Facilities 7 en suite TVB tea/coffee Direct dial from bedrooms ✱ Licensed No children 12yrs No coaches Dinner Last d 8.30pm **Prices** S £62; D £85-£110✳ **LB** **Parking** 30 **Notes** Closed 24 Dec-23 Jan

SUSSEX, WEST

AMBERLEY   MAP 06 TQ01

◆◆◆◆
Stream Cottage

The Square BN18 9SR ☎ 01798 831266 ▤ 01798 831266
e-mail enquiries@streamcottage.co.uk
web www.streamcottage.co.uk
Dir *Off B2139 into village centre*

Located on the edge of the South Downs and within easy reach of Arundel, Goodwood and Chichester, this picturesque thatched cottage has a wealth of beams and brick floors, and was reputedly built in 1587. The comfortable, well-equipped bedroom comes with a private sitting room. Breakfast is a wealth of imaginative ideas.

Facilities 1 rms (1 pri facs) (1 fmly) ⊘ TVB tea/coffee ✱ Cen ht TVL No coaches **Prices** S £50; D £70✳ **LB** **Parking** 1 **Notes** Closed Xmas & New Year 🐾

◆◆◆◆
Woody Banks Cottage

Crossgates BN18 9NR ☎ 01798 831295 & 07719 916703
e-mail woodybanks@btinternet.com
web www.woodybanks.co.uk
Dir *Off B2139 into village, right at Black Horse pub, Woody Banks 0.5m on left past Sportsman pub*

Located 4m from Arundel on an elevated position with stunning views over the Wildbrooks, this immaculately maintained house and gardens is very popular with walkers. It provides comfortable, homely bedrooms filled with thoughtful extras. Imaginative breakfasts are served in the panoramic lounge-dining room.

Facilities 2 rms (1 pri facs) (1 fmly) ⊘ TVB tea/coffee ✱ Cen ht TVL No children 6yrs No coaches **Prices** D £55-£65✳ **LB** **Parking** 3 **Notes** Closed 24-27 Dec 🐾

continued

England

ARUNDEL
MAP 06 TQ00

Premier Collection

♦♦♦♦♦ 😊

Arundel House Restaurant and Rooms

11 High St BN18 9AD ☎ 01903 882136
e-mail mail@arundelhouseonline.co.uk
web www.arundelhouseonline.co.uk
Dir In town centre opp Post Office

With its High St setting, handsome Georgian exterior and smart modern interior, Arundel House has much to offer. Dining too is an event and a popular restaurant occupies the ground floor providing freshly prepared and appetising cuisine. The well-appointed bedrooms are situated on two floors and parking can be arranged.

Facilities 5 en suite ⊘ FTV TVB Direct dial from bedrooms ✖
Licensed Cen ht No children 12yrs Dinner Last d 9.30pm
Prices D £60-£160 **Notes** Closed 2 wks mid Feb rs Sun

♦♦♦♦ ❦

Blakehurst Farm (TQ046066)

BN18 9QG ☎ 01903 889562 📠 01903 889562
Mr & Mrs Lock
web www.blakehurstfarm.co.uk
Dir 3m E of Arundel. N off A27 dual carriageway signed Blakehurst

This fine Georgian property is situated on a working farm and has good country views. Bedrooms are spacious and cheerfully decorated, and there is a comfortable lounge. Breakfast is served around a single table. Mountain bikes can be hired.

Facilities 3 rms (2 en suite) (1 pri facs) ⊘ TVB tea/coffee Cen ht
1000 acres arable **Prices** D £60-£80✳ **Parking** 3 **Notes** rs Nov-Mar

♦♦♦♦ 😊 🍷

Swan Hotel

27-29 High St BN18 9AG
☎ 01903 882314 📠 01903 883759
e-mail swanhotel@accommodating-inns.co.uk
web www.accommodating-inns.co.uk
Dir In town centre

The Swan overlooks the river at the lower end of High St and has comfortable bedrooms with quality facilities like telephones, flat-screen

continued

televisions and tea trays. Blackboards show the daily dishes, and wines are displayed above the bar.

Facilities 15 en suite (1 fmly) ⊘ in bedrooms ⊘ in dining room
⊘ in lounges TVB tea/coffee Direct dial from bedrooms ✖ Cen ht
Dinner Last d 9pm **Prices** S £65; D £69-£105

♦♦♦

Arden Guest House

4 Queens Ln BN18 9JN ☎ 01903 882544

This well-maintained, non-smoking Victorian guest house is situated by the River Arun and is only a short walk from the town centre. The practical bedrooms show excellent standards of housekeeping. Comprehensive breakfasts are served in the bright and attractive dining room.

Facilities 8 rms (3 en suite) (2 GF) ⊘ TVB tea/coffee ✖ Cen ht
No children 5yrs No coaches **Prices** S £32-£38; D £53-£58✳ **Parking** 4
Notes 😊

🅄

The Old Parsonage

Burpham BN18 9RJ ☎ 01903 882160 📠 01903 884627
e-mail www.burphamchh@ukonline.co.uk
Dir 3m NE off A27 turn by Arundel Railway Station signed to Hotel, Warringcamp and Burpham. Continue for 2.5m along lane, located on right

At the time of going to press the rating for this establishment had not been confirmed. Please check the AA website www.theAA.com for up-to-date information.

Facilities 10 en suite (1 GF) ⊘ TVB tea/coffee Direct dial from
bedrooms ✖ Licensed Cen ht TVL No children 12yrs No coaches
Prices S £40-£45; D £65-£120✳ **LB** **Conf** Board 20 **Parking** 10

BOGNOR REGIS
MAP 06 SZ99

♦♦♦♦

The Old Priory

80 North Bersted St PO22 9AQ
☎ 01243 863580 📠 01243 826597
e-mail old.priory@btinternet.com
web www.old-priory.com
Dir 1.6m NW of Bognor. Off A259 Chichester Rd to North Bersted, Old Priory sign on left

Located in the mainly residential area of North Bersted, this 400-year-old property retains many original features. Bedrooms are well

continued

equipped and homely and one has a four-poster waterbed and a double air bath. There is an outdoor pool and attractive grounds, perfect for the summer.

Facilities 2 en suite 3 annexe en suite (3 GF) ⊘ in dining room ⊘ in lounges STV TVB tea/coffee ✖ Cen ht No coaches ⤳
Prices S £40; D £60-£90✳ **Parking** 6

◆◆◆

Jubilee Guest House

5 Gloucester Rd PO21 1NU
☎ 01243 863016 & 07702 275967 ▤ 01243 868017
e-mail JubileeGuestHouse@breathemail.net
web www.jubileeguesthouse.com
Dir A259 to seafront, house opp Day Entrance to Butlins Family Entertainment Resort

This property is close to Butlin's, the seafront and the town centre. The brightly decorated and well-equipped bedrooms vary in size, and all have clock radios and hairdryers. A generous and freshly cooked breakfast, including provision for vegetarians, is served in the attractive dining room.

Facilities 6 rms (2 en suite) (2 fmly) ⊘ in dining room TVB tea/coffee ✖ Cen ht No coaches **Parking** 4 **Notes** Closed Xmas, Jan & Feb

◆◆◆

The Regis Lodge ◇

3 Gloucester Rd PO21 1NU
☎ 01243 827110 ▤ 01243 827110
e-mail frank@regislodge.co.uk
web www.regislodge.co.uk
Dir A259 to Bogner, signs for Southcoast World. Regis Lodge opp entrance to Southcoast World

Located within easy walking distance of the seafront and attractions, this family-run guest house offers a high standard of hospitality. Bedrooms vary in size and are well presented and suitably equipped. The brightly decorated dining room has separate tables and a good choice is offered at breakfast.

Facilities 6 en suite (5 fmly) ⊘ TVB tea/coffee ✖ Cen ht No children 5yrs No coaches **Prices** S £30-£35; D £50-£60✳ **LB** **Parking** 4 **Notes** Closed Oct-Mar ⊛

BOSHAM MAP 05 SU80

◆◆◆◆

White Barn Guest House

Crede Ln PO18 8NX ☎ 01243 573113 ▤ 01243 573113
e-mail chrissie@whitebarn.biz
web www.whitebarn.biz
Dir A259 Bosham rdbt, turn S signed Bosham Quay, 0.5m to T-junct, left signed White Barn, 0.25m turn left signed White Barn, 50yds turn right

This delightful single storey property is close to Bosham Harbour, Goodwood Race Circuit, Chichester and Portsmouth, and has cosy bedrooms with colour coordinated soft furnishings and many thoughtful extras. The open-plan dining room overlooks an attractive garden.

Facilities 2 en suite 1 annexe en suite (3 GF) ⊘ TVB tea/coffee ✖ Cen ht No children 12yrs No coaches **Prices** S £45-£85; D £65-£90✳ **Parking** 3

Ⓤ

Charters B&B

Bosham Ln PO18 8HS ☎ 01243 572644
e-mail louise@chartersbandb.co.uk
Dir From A27 onto A259, after 3m turn left at rdbt. At T-junct turn right, B&B 100mtrs on right

At the time of going to press the rating for this establishment had not been confirmed. Please check the AA website www.theAA.com for up-to-date information.

Facilities 4 en suite ⊘ TVB tea/coffee ✖ Cen ht No children 5yrs **Prices** S £50; D £80-£110✳ **Parking** 4 **Notes** Closed Xmas & New Year

BRACKLESHAM MAP 05 SZ89

★★★ **Guest Accommodation**

Romany

East Bracklesham Dr, Bracklesham Bay PO20 8JH
☎ 01243 673914 & 07761 683998

Situated in Bracklesham Bay, within easy reach of Chichester, this family home has an enviable seafront location. The comfortable bedroom benefits from it's own entrance and a small kitchen area. Breakfast is delivered to you in the morning and guests can choose from a traditional cooked breakfast or continental option.

Facilities 1 annexe en suite (1 fmly) (1 GF) ⊘ TVB tea/coffee ✖ Cen ht No coaches Dinner Last d 5pm **Parking** 2 **Notes** ⊛

England

BURGESS HILL
MAP 06 TQ31

◆◆◆◆ 🏚

The Homestead
Homestead Ln, Valebridge Rd RH15 0RQ
☎ 01444 246899 & 0800 064 0015 📠 0870 165 6035
e-mail homestead@burgess-hill.co.uk
web www.burgess-hill.co.uk
Dir 0.5m N of Burgess Hill. From Wivelsfield station onto Valebridge
Rd, 0.5m right to end of Homestead Ln

The Homestead has a country setting surrounded by 7 acres of garden
and woodland just a short distance from the town centre. Bedrooms
vary in size but all are well equipped and include generous extras. A
good choice of breakfast includes vegetarian options. The attractive
dining room overlooks the garden and there is a comfortable
conservatory-lounge.

Facilities 3 en suite (2 GF) ⊗ STV FTV TVB tea/coffee Direct dial from
bedrooms 🐾 Cen ht No children 12yrs No coaches 🎿 Gymnasium
Jacuzzi, mini gym **Prices** S £35-£40; D £70-£75 **Parking** 50

◆◆◆◆

Abbey House ◇
2 The Holt RH15 0RF ☎ 01444 233299
e-mail info@abbey-house.biz
Dir 0.5m E of town centre. Off A2113 Folders Ln onto Kings Way, 3rd
left onto The Holt

This renovated accommodation is set within a comfortable family
home. It is in a pleasant residential area and just a short walk from the
town centre and main line station. The modern bedrooms are well
equipped and include hair dryers, televisions, video recorders and cd
players. A well-cooked breakfast is served around a large communal
dining table.

Facilities 3 rms (2 en suite) (1 pri facs) (2 fmly) ⊗ FTV TVB tea/coffee
Direct dial from bedrooms 🐾 Cen ht No children 10yrs
Prices S £25-£35; D £55-£70✳ **Notes** Closed 24 Dec-2 Jan

If the freedom to smoke or be in a
non-smoking atmosphere is important
to you, check the rules when you book

CHARLTON
MAP 06 SU81

◆◆◆◆

Woodstock House Hotel
PO18 0HU ☎ 01243 811666 📠 01243 811666
e-mail info@woodstockhousehotel.co.uk
web www.woodstockhousehotel.co.uk
Dir Off A286 at Singleton, 1m to Charlton, premises on left

Woodstock House is in the quiet village of Charlton, close to a range
of good inns and restaurants and convenient for Chichester and
Goodwood. The bedrooms are individually decorated and come with
many useful extras. Several rooms overlook the pleasant rear garden,
and one is on the ground floor of a separate building in the garden.
The proprietors offer an especially friendly welcome.

Facilities 12 en suite 1 annexe en suite (2 GF) ⊗ in bedrooms
⊗ in dining room ⊗ in 1 lounge TVB tea/coffee Direct dial from bedrooms
Licensed Cen ht No coaches **Prices** S £55-£66; D £82-£110 **Parking** 13

CHICHESTER
MAP 05 SU80
See also **Bosham & Chilgrove**

Premier Collection

★★★★★ ◉◉ **Restaurant with Rooms**

West Stoke House
Downs Rd, West Stoke PO18 9BN
☎ 01243 575226 📠 01243 574655
e-mail info@weststokehouse.co.uk
Dir Turn off B286 1.5m just beyond West Stoke village next to St
Andrews Church

The large 18th-century house lies on the edge of the South Downs.
The large bedrooms have contemporary bathrooms and great country
views, and a terrace leads to over 5 acres of lawns and gardens. The
restaurant, open to non-residents, offers a relaxed atmosphere.

Facilities 6 en suite (1 fmly) TVB tea/coffee Direct dial from bedrooms
Licensed No coaches ♨ Dinner Last d 9pm **Prices** S £85-£150;
D £130-£150✳ **LB Conf** Max 30 **Parking** 20 **Notes** Closed 24-28 Dec
Civ Wed 140

★★★★ Bed & Breakfast

Old Chapel Forge ◇
Lower Bognor Rd, Lagness PO20 1LR ☎ 01243 264380
e-mail info@oldchapelforge.co.uk
web www.oldchapelforge.co.uk
Dir 4m SE of Chichester. Off A27 Chichester bypass at Bognor rdbt
signed Pagham/Runcton, onto B2166 Pagham Rd & Lower Bognor
Rd, Old Chapel Forge on right

Great local produce features in the hearty breakfasts at this
comfortable property, an idyllic 17th-century house and chapel set in
mature gardens with panoramic views of the South Downs. Old
Chapel Forge is a short drive from Chichester, Goodwood, Pagham
Harbour nature reserve and the beach. Bedrooms, including suites in
the chapel, are luxurious, and all have Internet access. The owner has
won an award for green tourism by reducing the impact of the
business on the environment.

Facilities 4 annexe en suite (2 fmly) (4 GF) ⊗ TVB tea/coffee Cen ht
No coaches Dinner Last d Breakfast **Prices** S £25-£65; D £55-£110✳ **LB**
Parking 6

★★★ Bed & Breakfast

Tamarisk

East Ashling PO18 9AS ☎ 01243 574669
e-mail pamelaquilter@hotmail.com
Dir *Approaching village from Chichester on Funtington Rd. On first bend, on left.*

A detached bungalow, which is within easy reach of Chichester and the South Coast. The bedroom is spacious and comfortable, breakfast is served in the cosy lounge dining room and as the accommodation is all on the ground floor access is easier for people with mobility problems.

Facilities 1 rms (1 pri facs) (1 GF) ⊗ in bedrooms tea/coffee ✖ Cen ht No children 16yrs No coaches **Parking** 3 **Notes** ⊠

★★ Guest Accommodation

The Suffolk House & Restaurant

3 East Row PO19 1PD ☎ 01243 778899 ▤ 01243 787282
e-mail admin@suffolkhousehotel.co.uk
Dir *In city centre, 500yds E of cathedral. Off A286 onto East St, onto Little London & East Row*

This Georgian residence is in a quiet side street a short walk from the city centre. Bedrooms vary in size and offer a good level of comfort and facilities. There is a small bar area, a pleasant patio and a peaceful breakfast room. Phone for advice on parking.

Facilities 11 en suite (2 fmly) (4 GF) TVB tea/coffee Direct dial from bedrooms ✖ Licensed TVL No coaches Dinner Last d 1pm **Conf** Max 30 Thtr 25 Class 12 Board 16

Premier Collection

◆◆◆◆◆ ⊛ 🍵 ☕ ◼

Royal Oak Inn

Pock Ln PO18 0AX ☎ 01243 527434 ▤ 01243 775062
e-mail ro@thesussexpub.co.uk
Dir *2m N of Chichester. Off A286 into East Lavant village centre*

Located close to the Goodwood Estate and Rolls Royce headquarters, this delightful inn is full of character, with beamed ceilings, timber floors and open fires in the public areas. Bedrooms are finished to a very high standard, with comfortable beds and state-of-the-art electronic equipment. Award-winning meals are served in the popular restaurant.

Facilities 3 en suite 3 annexe en suite (1 fmly) ⊗ in bedrooms ⊗ in dining room ⊗ in 1 lounge STV TVB tea/coffee Direct dial from bedrooms ✖ Cen ht No coaches Riding Dinner Last d 9.30pm **Prices** S £60-£70; D £90-£130✱ **Parking** 25

◆◆◆◆

Abelands Barn

Bognor Rd, Merston PO20 1DY
☎ 01243 533826 & 783576 ▤ 01243 783576
e-mail snooze@abelandsbarn.co.uk
Dir *A259(S) 250yds S of Drayton/Oving rdbt on the left.*

Located between Chichester and Bognor Regis, this beautifully restored barn offers an elegant and tranquil retreat. Public areas include a characterful upstairs lounge and an open plan dining room while the homely bedrooms are located on two floors. A substantial breakfast en famille complete with country views rounds off the stay.

Facilities 4 rms (2 en suite) (2 pri facs) (1 fmly) (2 GF) ⊗ TVB tea/coffee ✖ Cen ht TVL Dinner Last d 10pm **Prices** S £35-£80; D £40-£110✱ **Parking** 5

◆◆◆◆

Downfields

Level Mare Ln, Eastergate PO20 3SB
☎ 01243 542012 & 542306
Dir *A27 W from Fontwell rdbt 2nd left, Downfields on right*

Downfields is set in a quiet rural location and provides comfortable and homely accommodation. The bedroom is spacious and well equipped. A full English breakfast is served in the bright and comfortable dining room overlooking the delightful rear garden.

Facilities 2 rms (1 en suite) ⊗ in bedrooms TV1B tea/coffee ✖ Cen ht No children 10yrs No coaches ◖◗ **Prices** S £30-£35; D £60✱ LB **Parking** 6 **Notes** Closed 21-31 Dec ⊠

◆◆◆◆

Wilbury House Bed & Breakfast

Main Rd, Fishbourne PO18 8AT
☎ 01243 572953 ▤ 01243 572953
e-mail jackiepenfold@onetel.com
Dir *Off A27 Chichester bypass onto A259 W to Fishbourne and Bosham, 1m on left from Tesco rdbt*

This modern and well-appointed house is located on the edge of the village surrounded by countryside. Personally supervised by the charming owner, the atmosphere is friendly. Bedrooms are individually decorated, nicely furnished and include two ground-floor garden rooms. A generous English breakfast is served in the kitchen, overlooking the rear garden or in the dining room.

Facilities 3 rms (1 en suite) 2 annexe en suite (1 fmly) (2 GF) ⊗ TVB tea/coffee ✖ Cen ht No children 6yrs No coaches **Prices** S £35-£45; D £60-£70 **Parking** 7 **Notes** Closed mid Dec-mid Jan ⊠

England

CHICHESTER continued

♦♦♦♦ 🅰

The Bruford's

66 The Street, Boxgrove PO18 0EE
☎ 01243 774085 & 775146 📠 01243 781235
e-mail room4me@brufords.org
web www.brufords.org
Dir *3m NE of Chichester. Off A27 into Boxgrove, signed on right*

Facilities 2 en suite 3 annexe en suite (4 GF) ⊗ TVB tea/coffee ✖
Cen ht No children 12yrs No coaches Snooker **Prices** S £35-£45;
D £60-£75✱ **Parking** 4

♦♦♦ 🍵

The Woolpack Inn

71 Fishbourne Rd West, Fishbourne PO19 3JJ
☎ 01243 785707 & 782792
e-mail oflanaganpubco@aol.com
Dir *A27 onto A259 at Fishbourne, Woolpack Inn 0.75m on left*

This former 1930s hostelry offers a convenient location and has a
popular local following. The modern accommodation, situated in a
separate annexe, includes a bedroom with easier access. The
restaurant adjoins the bar where dinner can be selected from freshly
prepared dishes or lighter bar snacks.

Facilities 10 en suite (1 fmly) (10 GF) ⊗ in bedrooms ⊗ in dining
room ⊗ in 1 lounge TVB tea/coffee ✖ Cen ht TVL No coaches Bar
Billiards Dinner Last d 9.30pm **Conf** Max 200 Thtr 60 Class 60 Board 60
Parking 40

CHILGROVE   MAP 05 SU81

♦♦♦♦ 🌀🌀 🍵 🍵

The White Horse Chilgrove

PO18 9HX ☎ 01243 535219 📠 01243 535301
e-mail info@whitehorsechilgrove.co.uk
web www.whitehorsechilgrove.co.uk
Dir *Off A286 onto B2141 to village*

Dating in part from the 17th century, this homely inn retains much
original charm with its beams and stone floors. Food and service
however are completely up to date and memorable, while the smart
bedrooms are situated in a nearby annexe and are well equipped and
furnished.

Facilities 8 en suite (5 GF) ⊗ TVB tea/coffee Direct dial from bedrooms
Cen ht No coaches Massage can be arranged with prior notice Dinner
Last d 9pm **Prices** S £50-£95; D £75-£120 **LB** **Parking** 60 **Notes** Closed
Sun evening & all day Mon

CRAWLEY   MAP 06 TQ23

For accommodation details see **Gatwick Airport
(London)**

GATWICK AIRPORT (LONDON)   MAP 06 TQ24

See also **Redhill (Surrey)**

♦♦♦♦

Acorn Lodge Gatwick

79 Massetts Rd RH6 7EB ☎ 01293 774550
e-mail info@acornlodgegatwick.co.uk
web www.acornlodgegatwick.co.uk
Dir *M23 junct 9, A23 into Horley, off A23 Brighton Rd*

This upgraded and refurbished accommodation provides a 24-hour
transfer service to the airport and has on-site parking. Bedrooms are
comfortably furnished, and come with a practical desk area and useful
touches. The breakfast is a good start to your travels and is served in a
comfortable dining room.

Facilities 13 en suite (4 fmly) (6 GF) ⊗ TVB tea/coffee ✖ Cen ht TVL
Dinner Last d 10pm **Prices** S £49; D £64 **Parking** 20

♦♦♦♦

April Cottage

10 Langley Ln, Ifield Green RH11 0NA
☎ 01293 546222 📠 01293 518712
e-mail info@aprilcottageguesthouse.co.uk
Dir *M23 junct 10, signs to Crawley, 1st rdbt signed Horsham, 3rd
rdbt right to Ifield, over 2 minirdbts & left (Ifield Green), left after pub,
cottage 4th on right*

This attractive cottage is located on the edge of town and offers a cosy
atmosphere in a strictly non-smoking environment.Thoughtful extras
help you feel at home in the comfortable bedrooms, and breakfast,
served around one large table with friendly hosts, is served with home-
made preserves.

Facilities 3 rms (1 en suite) 1 annexe en suite (1 fmly) (1 GF) ⊗ TVB
tea/coffee ✖ Cen ht No coaches **Prices** D £48-£53✱ **Parking** 8

♦♦♦♦

Corner House Hotel

72 Massetts Rd RH6 7ED
☎ 01293 784574 📠 01293 784620
e-mail info@thecornerhouse.co.uk
web www.thecornerhouse.co.uk
Dir *M23 junct 9, A23 into Horley, off A23 Brighton Rd*

Well located for Gatwick Airport with a 24-hour courtesy transfer
service, the Corner House provides a range of thoughtfully furnished

continued

bedrooms, some in a separate house. Ground-floor areas include an attractive dining room and a comfortable lounge bar.

Facilities 13 en suite 12 annexe en suite (6 fmly) (4 GF) ⊘ in bedrooms ⊘ in dining room ⊘ in 1 lounge TVB tea/coffee Direct dial from bedrooms 🐾 Licensed Cen ht TVL Membership to local sports centre Dinner Last d 10pm **Conf** Max 15 Class 15 Board 15 **Parking** 40

◆◆◆◆

Jordans

70 Smallfield Rd RH6 9AT ☎ 01293 783057
e-mail jordansbb@hotmail.com
web www.jordansbb.co.uk
Dir *E of town centre. A23 onto B2036 Balcombe Rd, left at lights, over minirdbt, 100yds on right*

This 15th-century farmhouse, just a short drive from Gatwick Airport, offers parking and airport transfers. The accommodation features traditional oak beams and inglenook fireplaces, and the spacious en suite bedrooms have good facilities. A hearty breakfast is served around a communal dining table.

Facilities 3 en suite (1 fmly) (1 GF) ⊘ TVB tea/coffee 🐾 Cen ht No coaches **Prices** S £40-£45; D £50-£60✳ **Parking** 10 **Notes** 🐕

◆◆◆◆

The Lawn Guest House

30 Massetts Rd RH6 7DF
☎ 01293 775751 📠 01293 821803
e-mail info@lawnguesthouse.co.uk
web www.lawnguesthouse.co.uk
Dir *M23 junct 9, signs to A23 (Redhill), 3rd exit at rdbt by Esso station, 300yds right at lights*

Convenient for Gatwick Airport, this fine detached Victorian house offers comfortable bedrooms, equipped with many thoughtful extras. The atmosphere is relaxed, the welcome friendly, and an Internet facility is available. A choice of breakfast is served in an attractive dining room. Holiday parking is a real bonus.

Facilities 12 en suite (4 fmly) ⊘ TVB tea/coffee Direct dial from bedrooms Cen ht No coaches **Prices** S £40-£45; D £58-£60✳ **Parking** 15

◆◆◆◆

Rosemead Guest House

19 Church Rd RH6 7EY ☎ 01293 784965 📠 01293 430547
e-mail info@rosemeadguesthouse.co.uk
web www.rosemeadguesthouse.co.uk
Dir *M23 junct 9, A23 into Horley, off A23 Brighton Rd*

This large Edwardian guest house is ideally located for Gatwick Airport and is within walking distance of the town centre, with a wealth of local amenities. All bedrooms are en suite, and are individually furnished with coordinated decor. Secure parking is provided.

Facilities 6 en suite (2 fmly) ⊘ STV TVB tea/coffee Cen ht No coaches **Prices** S £36-£42; D £58✳ **Parking** 30

◆◆◆◆

Springwood Guest House

58 Massetts Rd RH6 7DS
☎ 01293 775998 📠 01293 823103
e-mail pauline@springwoodguesthouse.co.uk
Dir *2m NE of airport off A23 Brighton Rd*

This large Victorian house is close to the airport and services are well suited to travellers. The comfortable bedrooms vary in size and include two with ground-floor access. All rooms have good facilities, and breakfasts are served at separate tables in the bright dining room.

Facilities 11 rms (10 en suite) (4 fmly) (2 GF) ⊘ TVB tea/coffee Direct dial from bedrooms 🐾 Cen ht TVL No coaches **Conf** Max 10 **Parking** 13

GATWICK AIRPORT (LONDON) continued

◆◆◆◆

Trumbles

Stan Hill RH6 0EP ☎ 01293 863418 🖷 01293 862925
e-mail trumbles-gatwick@fsmail.net
web www.trumbles.co.uk
Dir 0.5m N of Charlwood. From village centre onto Norwoodhill Rd, 1st left onto Stan Hill

This attractive house, within easy reach of Gatwick, enjoys a quiet and secluded setting in this charming village. Bedrooms are spacious with a good range of facilities. The conservatory offers an ideal environment for guests to relax and enjoy either continental or full English breakfast. Parking is available, along with airport transfers.
Facilities 6 en suite (2 fmly) (1 GF) ⊗ TVB tea/coffee ✖ Cen ht
No coaches **Prices** S fr £50; D £60-£70✳ **Parking** 20 **Notes** Closed
24-26 Dec

◆◆◆◆

Vulcan Lodge Guest House

27 Massetts Rd RH6 7DQ
☎ 01293 771522 🖷 01293 775376
e-mail reservations@vulcan-lodge.com
Dir M23 junct 9, A23 into Horley, off A23 Brighton Rd

A particularly warm and friendly welcome is offered by the hosts of this charming period house, which sits back from the main road and is convenient for Gatwick Airport. Bedrooms are all individually decorated, well equipped and feature many thoughtful extras. A choice of breakfast is offered, including vegetarian, and is served in a delightful dining room.
Facilities 4 rms (3 en suite) (1 pri facs) (1 fmly) ⊗ FTV TVB tea/coffee
Cen ht TVL No coaches **Prices** S £36-£40; D £55✳ **Parking** 13

◆◆◆

Gainsborough Lodge

39 Massetts Rd RH6 7DT
☎ 01293 783982 🖷 01293 785365
e-mail enquiries@gainsborough-lodge.co.uk
Dir 2m NE of airport off A23 Brighton Rd

Please note that this establishment has recently changed hands. Close to Gatwick, this fine Edwardian house offers bright bedrooms that are comfortably appointed, and a varied breakfast served in the conservatory-dining room. There is also an attractive lounge.
Facilities 16 rms (14 en suite) 14 annexe en suite (5 fmly) (12 GF)
⊗ in 8 bedrooms ⊗ in dining room TVB tea/coffee Direct dial from bedrooms ✖ Cen ht TVL No coaches Free membership of local Gym
Prices S £31-£42; D £47-£56✳ **Parking** 30

◆◆◆

Gatwick White House Hotel

50-52 Church Rd RH6 7EX
☎ 01293 402777 & 784322 🖷 01293 424135
e-mail hotel@gwhh.com
web www.gwhh.com
Dir In Horley centre off A23 Brighton Rd

Convenient for the airport and major routes, this establishment offers smart, well-equipped accommodation. There is a bar, restaurant and good parking, and a 24-hour transfer service to Gatwick is available on request.
Facilities 27 rms (22 en suite) (2 fmly) (10 GF) ⊗ in bedrooms
⊗ in dining room ⊗ in 1 lounge TVB tea/coffee Direct dial from bedrooms ✖ Licensed Cen ht TVL Dinner Last d 6pm **Parking** 30

Ⓤ

Latchetts Cottage ◈

Norwood Hill RH6 0ET ☎ 01293 862831 🖷 01293 862832
e-mail davidjlees@tiscali.co.uk
Dir On A217, 2m S of Reigate turn right onto Ironsbottom, then 2nd right onto Collendean Ln, 0.9m straight over x-rds, 200yds on left

At the time of going to press the rating for this establishment had not been confirmed. Please check the AA website www.theAA.com for up-to-date information.
Facilities 3 rms ⊗ TVB tea/coffee ✖ Cen ht No children 5yrs
No coaches **Prices** S fr £30; D £50-£55✳ **Parking** 10 **Notes** Closed
25-26 Dec ⊜

HENFIELD   MAP 06 TQ21

◆◆◆◆ ⅋

Frylands ◈ (TQ231197)

Wineham BN5 9BP
☎ 01403 710214 🖷 01403 711449 Mrs Fowler
e-mail b&b@frylands.co.uk
Dir 2m NE of Henfield. Off B2116 towards Wineham, 1.5m left onto Fryland Ln, Frylands 0.3m on left

The friendly hosts offer comfortable accommodation at this delightful 16th-century timber-framed farmhouse, set in peaceful countryside. Day rooms and bedrooms are full of character and the well-appointed

continued

England

dining room is the setting for freshly cooked breakfasts. Ample off-road parking and free car storage for travellers using Gatwick Airport is available.

Facilities 3 rms (1 pri facs) (1 fmly) ⊗ TVB tea/coffee ✻ Cen ht 🔍 ⫟ Fishing Coarse fishing 250 acres Mixed **Prices** S £30-£35; D £50-£55✳ **Parking** 6 **Notes** Closed 20 Dec-1 Jan

◆◆◆◆

Lyndhurst

38 Broomfield Rd BN5 9UA
☎ 01273 494054 & 07788 988414 📠 01273 494054
e-mail linda.slingsby@ukgateway.net
Dir *A281 Henfield high St onto Church St (opp White Hart Inn), 3rd left onto Broomfield Rd*

Located on a residential avenue within this pretty village, quality furnishing and décor schemes highlight the many retained features of this elegant period house. Bedrooms are equipped with a wealth of thoughtful extras and wholesome Aga cooked breakfasts are taken in an attractive dining room, overlooking the well maintained gardens.

Facilities 4 rms (2 en suite) (2 pri facs) (1 fmly) ⊗ TVB tea/coffee Cen ht TVL No coaches **Prices** S £35-£45; D £45-£60✳ **Parking** 5 **Notes** Closed annual hol

HORSHAM   MAP 06 TQ13

Premier Collection

◆◆◆◆◆

Random Hall

Stane St, Slinfold RH13 0QX
☎ 01403 790558 📠 01403 791046
e-mail nigelrandomhall@btconnect.com
web www.randomhall.co.uk
Dir *4m W of Horsham. On A29 W of Slinfold*

This 16th-century farmhouse combines character with good quality accommodation and service from the resident proprietors. The comfortable bedrooms are equipped with useful extras. Beams, flagstone floors and quality fabrics add style to the bar and public areas, and an enjoyable dinner is served Monday to Thursday.

Facilities 13 en suite (5 GF) ⊗ STV TVB tea/coffee Direct dial from bedrooms ✻ Licensed Cen ht No coaches Golf 18 Dinner Last d 9pm **Prices** S £69-£80; D £99✳ **Conf** Max 16 Thtr 20 Class 16 Board 16 Del from £125 ✳ **Parking** 50 **Notes** Closed 1wk Aug BH rs 24 Dec-2 Jan

◆◆◆

Birchwood ◇

Broadwater ln, Cospsale RH13 6QW ☎ 01403 731313
e-mail wendy@copsale.fsnet.co.uk
Dir *3.5m S of Horsham. Off A24 signed Copsale, 1st left onto Broadwater Ln, 0.5m on right before postbox on left*

This pleasant country home stands in quiet woodlands. The delightful hosts offer a warm welcome and a true home from home, and the spacious bedrooms are well equipped.

Facilities 2 rms (1 fmly) (2 GF) ⊗ TVB tea/coffee ✻ Cen ht No children 12yrs No coaches **Prices** S £30-£35; D £50-£55✳ **Parking** 6 **Notes** Closed 20 Dec-4 Jan

◆◆◆

Broadbridge Farmhouse

Old Wickhurst Ln, Broadbridge Heath RH12 3NA
☎ 01403 252805 & 0771 0325828
e-mail genevieve@brunwin.com
Dir *2m SW of town centre. A24 W onto A264, left at 1st rdbt, farmhouse on left*

Please note that this establishment has recently changed hands. The 14th-century farmhouse stands in beautiful countryside convenient for Gatwick airport and many Sussex attractions. The spacious bedrooms are full of character, and breakfast is served at a communal table in the beamed dining room or in the sunny garden on warmer days.

Facilities 2 rms (1 en suite) (1 fmly) ⊗ ✻ Cen ht TVL No coaches **Parking** 6 **Notes**

LITTLEHAMPTON   MAP 06 TQ00

◆◆◆◆

Racing Greens

70 South Ter BN17 5LQ ☎ 01903 732972 📠 01903 719389
e-mail racinggreens@aol.com
web www.littlehampton-racing-greens.co.uk
Dir *A259 onto B2187 for Littlehampton seafront, brown signs to seafront, B&B faces the Greens and sea near Harbour Park Entertainment Centre*

This Victorian seafront home offers comfortable, light and airy accommodation. Breakfast, featuring interesting dishes and a variety of breads, is served around one large table in the pleasant dining room, which overlooks the Greens.

Facilities 2 rms (1 en suite) (1 pri facs) ⊗ FTV TVB tea/coffee ✻ Cen ht No children No coaches **Prices** S £35-£55; D £60-£80✳ LB

MIDHURST   MAP 06 SU82
See also **Rogate**

Premier Collection

★★★★★ **Bed & Breakfast**

Rivermead House

Hollist Ln GU29 9RS ☎ 01730 810907 & 07885 699479
e-mail mail@bridgetadler.com
Dir *0.5 m from A286. 1m from centre of Midhurst.*

Situated in a semi-rural area on the outskirts of Midhurst, in a quiet location, offering friendly and relaxed bed & breakfast accommodation. The bedroom is on the front of the house and enjoys wonderful south facing views over the garden and farmland with distant views of the South Downs. It is spacious and comfortable and breakfast is served in the farmhouse style kitchen.

Facilities 1 en suite (1 fmly) ⊗ TVB tea/coffee Cen ht Golf Dinner Last d 6pm **Parking** 2 **Notes** Closed 24-26 Dec

England

MIDHURST continued

♦♦♦♦♦

Park House Hotel

Bepton GU29 0JB ☎ 01730 819000 ▤ 01730 819099
e-mail reservations@parkhousehotel.com
Dir *3m SW of Midhurst off A286*

This delightful, family-run guest house stands in landscaped gardens
in the peaceful village of Bepton. The attractive, spacious bedrooms
are thoughtfully equipped, and there is an elegant drawing room and
an honesty bar. Breakfast and dinner are served in the dining room.

Facilities 12 en suite 2 annexe en suite (2 fmly) (1 GF) ⊗ in bedrooms
⊗ in dining room STV TVB tea/coffee Direct dial from bedrooms
Licensed Cen ht No coaches ⤳ ⚲ ♨ ♿ Dinner Last d 8.45pm
Prices S £85-£290; D £120-£350✳ **LB** **Conf** Max 50 Thtr 50 Class 50
Board 25 **Parking** 30 **Notes** Civ Wed 54

♦♦♦♦♦

York House Rooms

Easebourne St, Easebourne GU29 0AL
☎ 01730 814090 ▤ 01730 814090
e-mail felicity@yorkhouserooms.co.uk
web www.yorkhouserooms.co.uk
Dir *0.6m NE of Midhurst. Off A272 in Easebourne onto Easebourne
St, 150yds on left*

A warm welcome awaits guests at this delightful house in a quiet
village. The two high-quality contemporary suites are in a separate
cottage, each having a sitting room and a bedroom with bathroom en
suite. Modern facilities blend with the many thoughtful touches.
Guests share one table in the cosy breakfast room, or breakfast can be
served in the pretty garden when the weather permits.

Facilities 2 annexe en suite ⊗ tea/coffee ✖ Cen ht TVL No children
No coaches Golf 18 Dinner Last d by arrangement only
Prices D £90-£180 **LB** **Parking** 2 **Notes** Closed Xmas

♦♦♦♦

Amberfold

Amberfold, Heyshott GU29 0DA
☎ 01730 812385 ▤ 01730 813559
e-mail erlingamberfold@aol.com
Dir *Off A286 signed Graffham/Heyshott, after 1.5m pass pond,
Amberfold on left*

Please note that this establishment has recently changed hands. A
delightful Grade II listed 17th-century cottage, set in attractive gardens
in peaceful countryside. The accommodation is provided in two very
different self-contained units, a cottage annexe and a modern open-
plan lodge. Each has its own dining area, where you help yourself to a
continental breakfast, and each bedroom has thoughtful extras.

Facilities 1 en suite 2 annexe en suite (2 GF) ⊗ TVB tea/coffee ✖
Cen ht No children 14yrs No coaches **Prices** S £50-£75; D £65-£95✳
Parking 2 **Notes** Closed Nov-Feb

♦♦♦♦

Cowdray Park Golf Club

GU29 0BB ☎ 01730 813599 ▤ 01730 815900
e-mail enquiries@cowdraygolf.co.uk
Dir *1m E on A272*

This renovated lodge provides contemporary bedrooms, with some
rooms overlooking the internationally famous polo grounds. The
immaculate golf course itself provides a challenge to members and
visitors. Refreshments and meals are taken in the new clubhouse with
modern facilities.

Facilities 8 en suite (5 GF) ⊗ STV TVB tea/coffee ✖ Licensed Cen ht
TVL No children 10yrs No coaches Golf 18 ♨ Dinner Last d 8pm
Prices S £60; D £100✳ **LB** **Conf** Max 60 Thtr 60 Class 60 Board 20
Parking 10

♦♦♦♦

Holly Tree Lodge

Easebourne St GU29 0BE
☎ 01730 813729 & 07746 523094 ▤ 01730 813729
e-mail eabhamilton@yahoo.co.uk
Dir *N from A272 at Easebourne Church into Easebourne St. Holly
Tree Lodge on left.*

A warm welcome is guaranteed at this family home, set in lovely
gardens, just 1m from the centre of Midhurst. The large, bright en
suite bedroom can accommodate a family, and a cosy double room is
available. Breakfast is served in the sunny dining room or conservatory
overlooking pretty gardens.

Facilities 2 rms (1 en suite) (2 GF) ⊗ TV available tea/coffee ✖
Cen ht No coaches **Prices** D £50-£80✳ **Parking** 5 **Notes**

♦♦♦♦ ❦

Loves Farm *(SU912235)*

Easebourne St GU29 0BG
☎ 01730 813212 & 07789 228400 Mr Renwick
e-mail renwick@lovesl.fsnet.co.uk
Dir *A272 Midhurst to Petworth. Turn left opposite St Marys Church
into Easebourne St. Follow signs for Loves Farm.*

This 17th century farmhouse is set on a 300-acre farm with wonderful
views of the Southdowns from the windows. The two comfortable
rooms have their own entrance and both benefit from king size beds
and ensuite or private shower rooms. A great location for access to
Midhurst, Cowdray Park and Goodwood.

Facilities 2 rms (1 en suite) (1 pri facs) ⊗ TVB tea/coffee ✖ Cen ht
No children 300 acres Arable/Sheep/Horses **Prices** D £60-£65✳
Parking 2 **Notes** 🐾

*Book as early as possible, particularly
in the peak holiday period*

◆◆◆◆
Redford Cottage

Redford GU29 0QF ☎ 01428 741242

Dir *Off A272 1m W of Midhurst signed Redford, Redford Cottage 400yds past Redford village sign on left*

This delightful farmhouse stands in an Area of Outstanding Natural Beauty. Bedroom styles vary, with a traditional cottage room in the main house and a garden suite of stylish Swedish design; each room has access to a private sitting room. The new timber-framed lounge opens onto the attractive mature gardens, and breakfasts are served family-style in a separate dining room.

Facilities 1 en suite 2 annexe en suite (1 GF) ⊗ TVB tea/coffee 🏵 Cen ht TVL No coaches **Prices** S £55-£60; D £85-£95✱ **Parking** 10 **Notes** Closed Xmas & New Year 🖾

◆◆◆
Fairoak Cottage B&B ◇

Severals Rd, Bepton GU29 0LT ☎ 01730 812770
e-mail fairoakcotts.bepton@virgin.net

Dir *S on A286, right to Bepton, and right at Country Inn. Fairoak on right*

Set on the outskirts of Midhurst in a quiet hamlet, Fairoak Cottage offers a warm welcome from proprietors Georgina and Tom Harris and a comfortable stay in the form of well-appointed accommodation. A hearty breakfast can be enjoyed in the cosy dining room before making the most of the extensive local walks.

Facilities 2 rms ⊗ TVB tea/coffee 🏵 Cen ht No children 10yrs No coaches **Prices** S £30-£45; D £60-£90 **LB Parking** 2 **Notes** 🖾

PETWORTH
MAP 06 SU92

◆◆◆ 🍴
Stonemasons Inn

North St GU28 9NL ☎ 01798 342510 ▤ 01798 342515
e-mail stonemasons@onetel.com
web www.thestonemasonsinn.co.uk

Dir *On A283 N of Petworth, 100yds from A272 junct*

A row of 15th-century cottages has been restored to create this historic inn, located opposite Petworth House and Park. The intimate public areas retain many original features including a wealth of exposed beams and open log fires for the cooler months. Wholesome food is complimented by an imaginative wine list.

Facilities 5 en suite (2 fmly) (1 GF) ⊗ in bedrooms ⊗ in dining room FTV TVB tea/coffee 🏵 Cen ht Dinner Last d 9.30pm **Prices** S £65-£90; D £75-£100✱ **Conf** Max 20 Thtr 20 Class 10 Board 12 Del from £110 ✱ **Parking** 24

PULBOROUGH
MAP 06 TQ01

◆◆◆◆ 🍷 🍱
Orchard Mead

Toat Ln RH20 1BZ ☎ 01798 872640
e-mail siggy.rutherford@ukonline.co.uk

Dir *Off A29 1m N of Pulborough onto Blackgate Ln, left onto Pickhurst Ln & right onto Toat Ln, Orchard Mead at end*

This detached home is set in a peaceful rural location but is within easy reach of the local train station. Bedrooms are comfortably furnished with thoughtful touches. A delicious light supper or full dinner can be provided on request.

Facilities 2 en suite (2 GF) ⊗ TVB tea/coffee 🏵 Cen ht TVL No children 12yrs No coaches Dinner Last d 10am **Parking** 2 **Notes** Closed Xmas & Etr 🖾

◆◆◆
Arun House ◇

Bury RH20 1NT ☎ 01798 831736
e-mail arunway@hotmail.com
web www.arunhousesussex.co.uk

Dir *5m S of Pulborough. On A29, signed near Carringdales & Turners garages*

Located on the A29 and convenient for Arundel, Amberley Castle and the South Downs Way, this friendly family home is popular with ramblers and cyclists and offers comfortable accommodation. Guests may sit in the conservatory or on the terrace and enjoy the views across 2 acres of garden, with its pond, ducks and free-range chickens.

Facilities 3 rms (1 fmly) ⊗ TVB tea/coffee 🏵 Licensed Cen ht No coaches Dinner Last d 24hrs prior **Prices** S £30; D £48✱ **Conf** Max 40 Class 40 Board 40 **Parking** 6 **Notes** 🖾

◆◆◆
Harkaway

8 Houghton Ln, Bury RH20 1PD ☎ 01798 831843
e-mail carol@harkaway.org.uk
web www.harkaway.org.uk

Dir *5m S of Pulborough. Off A29 into Bury, at x-rds onto Houghton Ln, on left past Coombe Crescent*

Located north of Arundel in the pretty village of Bury, this property was once the home of John Galsworthy. The homely bedrooms include one on the ground floor and all areas of the house are non-smoking. Breakfast is served in the attractive dining room overlooking the well-maintained garden.

Facilities 4 rms (1 en suite) (1 GF) ⊗ 🏵 Cen ht TVL No children 6yrs No coaches **Parking** 2 **Notes** 🖾

England

ROGATE MAP 05 SU82

Premier Collection

◆◆◆◆◆ ❦

Mizzards *(SU803228)*

GU31 5HS ☎ 01730 821656 📠 01730 821655 Mrs Francis
e-mail francis@mizzards.co.uk

Dir *0.6m S from Rogate x-rds, over river & signed right*

This charming 16th-century house stands near the River Rother in 2 acres of landscaped gardens complete with a lake and the proprietor's own sculptures. Relax in either the conservatory or the split-level drawing room, and the airy, well-appointed bedrooms look over the grounds. There is a dining room, and a swimming pool is available in summer.

Facilities 3 en suite ⊛ TVB tea/coffee ✕ Cen ht No children 9yrs ⚞ ⚙ outdoor chess 13 acres sheep non-working **Prices** D £70-£80✳
Parking 12 **Notes** Closed Xmas ⊛

RUSTINGTON MAP 06 TQ00

◆◆◆◆

Kenmore Guest House ◇

Claigmar Rd BN16 2NL ☎ 01903 784634 📠 01903 784634
e-mail thekenmore@amserve.net

Dir *A259 follow signs for Rustington, turn for Claigmar Rd between war memorial & Alldays. Kenmore on right as Claigmar Rd bends*

A warm welcome is assured at this Edwardian house, located close to the sea and convenient for touring West Sussex. Spacious bedrooms, all individually decorated, are provided with many useful extras. There is a comfortable lounge in which to relax and a bright dining room where a good choice of breakfast is served.

Facilities 7 rms (6 en suite) (2 fmly) (2 GF) ⊛ TVB tea/coffee Cen ht No coaches **Prices** S £28-£32; D £56-£60✳ **Parking** 7

SELSEY MAP 05 SZ89

◆◆◆◆

St Andrews Lodge Hotel

Chichester Rd PO20 0LX
☎ 01243 606899 📠 01243 607826
e-mail info@standrewslodge.co.uk
web www.standrewslodge.co.uk

Dir *B2145 into Selsey, on right just before the church*

This friendly establishment is close to restaurants and pubs and 0.5m

from the seafront. The refurbished bedrooms are bright and spacious, and have useful extras. Five ground-floor rooms, one with easier access, overlook the large south-facing garden, which is ideal for a drink on a summer evening.

Facilities 5 en suite 5 annexe en suite (3 fmly) (5 GF) ⊛ in bedrooms ⊛ in dining room ⊛ in 1 lounge TVB tea/coffee Direct dial from bedrooms Licensed Cen ht TVL No coaches **Conf** Max 15 **Parking** 14 **Notes** Closed 18 Dec-7 Jan

◆◆◆◆ 🅰

Greenacre Bed & Breakfast

5 Manor Farm Court PO20 0LY ☎ 01243 602912
e-mail greenacre@zoom.co.uk

Dir *B2145 to Selsey, over a small rdbt, next left (Manor Farm Court), bear left & Greenacre on left*

Facilities 4 rms (3 en suite) (1 fmly) (1 GF) ⊛ in bedrooms ⊛ in dining room STV TVB tea/coffee Cen ht TVL No coaches **Parking** 7

See advertisement on opposite page

SLINFOLD MAP 06 TQ13

◆◆◆ ⊜ ◗

The Red Lyon

The Street RH13 0RR ☎ 01403 790339 📠 01403 791863
e-mail enquiries@theredlyon.co.uk
web www.theredlyon.co.uk

Dir *Off A29*

Located in the village centre, this delightful 18th-century inn, with parts dating from the 14th century, has a wealth of beams. Tasty meals at lunch and dinner are offered in the timber-panelled dining room. The bedrooms and bathrooms are bright, spacious and well equipped. A pleasant beer garden and ample parking are also available.

Facilities 4 rms (3 en suite) (1 pri facs) (1 fmly) ⊛ in bedrooms ⊛ in dining room TVB tea/coffee ✕ Cen ht TVL Dinner Last d 9.30pm **Prices** D £45-£60; (room only) ✳ **Parking** 30

SOUTH HARTING MAP 05 SU71

◆◆◆◆

Torberry Cottage

Hurst GU31 5RG ☎ 01730 826883 📠 01730 826883
e-mail torberry.cottage@virgin.net

Dir *1m W of South Harting on B2146*

Located in a rural setting north of the South Downs, this pleasantly furnished house offers well-equipped bedrooms and fine hospitality. Breakfasts, using fresh produce and served around a large table, are a feature. The house stands in very pleasant gardens.

Facilities 2 en suite ⊛ TVB tea/coffee ✕ Cen ht No children 10yrs No coaches **Prices** S £35; D £60✳ **Parking** 4 **Notes** Closed Xmas ⊛

continued

STEYNING

MAP 06 TQ11

★★★★ Guest House

The Penfold Gallery Guest House

30 High St BN44 3GG ☎ 01903 815595
e-mail johnturner57@aol.com
Dir *Leave A27 between Brighton and Worthing and follow signs to Steyning on A283.*

The Grade II listed house at the east end of High Street dates in part from the 15th century. Original beams and wattle and daub walls survive, and the large en suite bedrooms have satellite television.

Facilities 3 en suite ⊘ STV TVB Direct dial from bedrooms ✝
Licensed Cen ht TVL No children 12yrs No coaches Dinner Last d By arrangement

◆◆◆◆

Springwells Hotel

9 High St BN44 3GG
☎ 01903 812446 & 812043 ▤ 01903 879823
e-mail contact@springwells.co.uk
Dir *Off A283 bypass into town centre, House opp Methodist Church*

Located in the heart of Steyning, this former Georgian merchant's house retains many original features. The comfortable bedrooms have many thoughtful extras. Ground floor areas include an elegant dining room and an attractive conservatory-lounge bar overlooking the immaculate mature gardens. An outdoor heated swimming pool is also available to in the warmer months.

Facilities 10 rms (8 en suite) (1 fmly) ⊘ in 1 lounge TVB tea/coffee
Direct dial from bedrooms Licensed Cen ht TVL No coaches ⸖ Sauna
Prices S £41-£62; D £69-£117✳ **LB** **Conf** Max 25 Thtr 25 Class 12
Board 12 **Parking** 6 **Notes** Closed 24 Dec-1 Jan

WORTHING

MAP 06 TQ10

◆◆◆◆

The Beacons

18 Shelley Rd BN11 1TU ☎ 01903 230948
e-mail beaconshotel@amserve.net
Dir *500yds W of town centre. Off A259 onto Crescent Rd & 3rd left, signed*

Convenient for the shopping centre, marine garden, pier and promenade, the Beacons has a comfortable lounge and bedrooms with useful facilities. It is a good location for touring the Sussex coast

Facilities 8 en suite (1 fmly) (3 GF) ⊘ TV available tea/coffee Licensed
Cen ht No coaches **Prices** S £36-£40; D £60-£76✳ **Parking** 8

◆◆◆◆

The Burlington

Marine Pde BN11 3QL ☎ 01903 211222 ▤ 01903 209561
e-mail info@theburlingtonworthing.co.uk
Dir *On seafront 0.5m W of Worthing Pier, Wordsworth Rd junct*

Modern and vibrant accommodation on the seafront that appeals mainly to a younger crowd. The popular and lively bar extends to a nightclub on certain nights of the week. The refurbished bedrooms

are spacious and very well equipped. A good selection of food is available and there is also a comfortable lounge.

Facilities 26 en suite (6 fmly) ⊘ in bedrooms TVB tea/coffee Direct
dial from bedrooms ✝ Licensed Cen ht No coaches Dinner Last
d 8.45pm **Prices** S £60; D £80-£85✳ **Conf** Max 100 Thtr 50 Class 35
Board 40

◆◆◆◆

The Conifers Guest Accommodation

43 Parkfield Rd BN13 1EP
☎ 01903 265066 & 07947 321096
e-mail conifers@hews.org.uk
Dir *A24 or A27 onto A2031 at Offington rdbt, over lights, Parkfield Rd 5th right*

Located in a quiet residential area within easy reach of the town centre, this immaculately kept home from home with attractive gardens offers a warm welcome. Individually decorated rooms are comfortable and equipped with a variety of thoughtful extras. Hearty breakfasts and home-cooked dinners are served in the oak panelled dining room.

Facilities 2 rms ⊘ TVB tea/coffee ✝ Cen ht No children 12yrs
No coaches Dinner Last d 24hrs notice **Prices** S £32.50-£40; D £70-£80
Parking 2 **Notes** ⊛

continued

England

WORTHING continued

◆◆◆◆
John Henry's At Marigold Cottage

The Forge, Nepcote Ln, Findon Village BN14 0SE
☎ 01903 877277 & 07850 661230 🖷 01903 877178
e-mail enquiries@john-henrys.com
Dir *Off A24 rdbt into Findon village, over x-rds at bottom of hill,
300yds on left*

Located in a quiet village, this delightful converted cottage provides
accommodation of outstanding quality. Bedrooms, which vary in size,
offer comfortable beds and superb facilities. Dinner and breakfast are
served in the bar-brasserie just opposite. Parking available.

Facilities 5 en suite (3 fmly) (2 GF) ⊗ in bedrooms ⊗ in dining room
⊗ in 1 lounge TVB tea/coffee Licensed Cen ht No coaches Pool Table
Dinner Last d 9pm **Parking** 12

◆◆◆◆
Manor Guest House ◇

100 Broadwater Rd BN14 8AN
☎ 01903 236028 & 07713 633168
e-mail stay@manorworthing.com
Dir *A27 onto A24 to town centre. House 175yds on left after St Marys
Church*

This attractive guest house is 0.5m from Worthing town centre.
Bedrooms are smartly presented and include thoughtful extras as
standard. Well-cooked breakfasts and dinner are served at separate
tables in the bright dining room. Limited parking available.

Facilities 6 rms (3 en suite) (2 fmly) (1 GF) ⊗ FTV TVB tea/coffee
Licensed Cen ht No children 8yrs Dinner Last d 7pm **Prices** S £30-£35;
D £80-£100✳ **LB Conf** Max 15 Thtr 15 Class 15 Board 15 **Parking** 6

◆◆◆◆
Marina Guest House ◇

191 Brighton Rd BN11 2EX
☎ 01903 207844 🖷 01903 207844
e-mail marinaworthing@ntlworld.com
Dir *A27 onto A24 to seafront. Left, pass swimming pool, guest house
500yds*

Having a superb location on the seafront, this attractive guest house
provides a warm welcome. Bedrooms vary in size but are all
individually decorated and a number share bathroom facilities. Well-
cooked breakfasts are served in the bright and cheerful dining room.

Facilities 5 rms (2 en suite) (2 fmly) (1 GF) ⊗ TVB tea/coffee ✈
Cen ht **Prices** S £27-£30; D £58-£70✳ **LB Notes** ⊛

◆◆◆◆
Moorings ◇

4 Selden Rd BN11 2LL
☎ 01903 208882 & 07818 433112 🖷 01903 236878
e-mail annette@mooringshotel.fsnet.co.uk
Dir *0.5m E of pier off A259 towards Brighton*

Please note that this establishment has recently changed hands. The
well-presented Victorian house is in a quiet residential area near the
seafront and town centre. Bedrooms are coordinated in bright colours,
and there is a smart dining room and a small lounge with magazines
and games.

Facilities 6 en suite (2 fmly) ⊗ TVB tea/coffee Direct dial from
bedrooms ✈ Cen ht No coaches **Prices** S £30; D £60✳

◆◆◆◆
Olinda Guest House ◇

199 Brighton Rd BN11 2EX ☎ 01903 206114
e-mail info@olindaguesthouse.co.uk
web www.olindaguesthouse.co.uk
Dir *Off A27 follow signs for Town Centre, head for A259 Coast Rd.
Close to pier*

Guests are assured a warm welcome at this establishment, which is
located on the seafront just a walk away from the town centre. The
bedrooms are cosy and comfortable and breakfast is taken in the
pleasantly appointed dining room/ lounge.

Facilities 6 rms (3 en suite) ⊗ TVB tea/coffee ✈ Cen ht No children
14yrs **Prices** S £25-£30; D £54-£60

◆◆◆◆
The Park House Hotel

4 St Georges Rd BN11 2DS
☎ 01903 207939 🖷 01902 207939
e-mail theparkhouse@aol.com

Within a few minutes walk from seafront and town centre, a warm
welcome is assured at this well maintained, elegant property.
Bedrooms are equipped with lots of thoughtful extras and
comprehensive breakfasts are taken in an attractive and comfortable
dining room, which is furnished with an oriental theme.

Facilities 7 en suite (2 fmly) ⊗ TVB tea/coffee Cen ht No coaches
Parking 4

◆◆◆◆
Tudor Guest House ◇

5 Windsor Rd BN11 2LU ☎ 01903 210265 🖷 01903 210265
e-mail info@tudor-worthing.co.uk
Dir *Off A259 seafront road*

The Tudor Guest House is a friendly and attractive establishment
situated just off the seafront on the east side of town. Bedrooms are
generally spacious and neatly appointed with modern facilities. There
is a bright breakfast room and parking is a bonus.

Facilities 8 en suite (2 GF) ⊗ TVB tea/coffee ✈ Cen ht No children
8yrs No coaches **Prices** S £30-£32; D £60-£65✳ **Parking** 5
Notes Closed 24 Dec-3 Jan

◆◆◆

Avalon Guest House

8 Windsor Rd BN11 2LX ☎ 01903 233808 🖨 01903 215201
e-mail avalon.worthing@ntlworld.com
Dir 0.75m E from town centre off A259 seafront road

This family-run guest house provides a warm welcome and is only a
stroll from the beach. Bedrooms vary in size but all are well
appointed, suiting a variety of travellers. Hearty breakfasts are served
in the bright and cheerful ground-floor dining room.

Facilities 7 rms (2 en suite) (1 fmly) (1 GF) ⊗ TVB tea/coffee ✖
Cen ht No children 5yrs No coaches **Prices** S £20-£25; D £40-£50✷
Parking 3 **Notes** 🐾

◆◆◆

Beechwood Hall

Wykeham Rd BN11 4JD ☎ 01903 205049 🖨 01903 238165
e-mail reception@beechwoodhall.co.uk
Dir 500yds W of town centre on A259

This lively, family-run establishment is within walking distance of the
seafront and the town centre. The attractive bedrooms have a range of
facilities, and popular dishes are served in the restaurant. The well-
kept gardens are an attractive feature.

Facilities 8 en suite (2 fmly) ⊗ in bedrooms ⊗ in area of dining room
TVB tea/coffee Licensed Cen ht Dinner Last d 9.15pm **Prices** S £30-£55;
D £65-£120✷ **LB Parking** 40

TYNE & WEAR

SOUTH SHIELDS   MAP 21 NZ36

★★★★ Guest House

Ocean Breeze

11 Urfa Ter NE33 2ES ☎ 0191 456 7442
e-mail info@oceanbreezeguesthouse.co.uk
Dir A183 towards town centre, onto Lawe Rd, 3rd left

Situated within a short walk of the seafront and town centre, this
smartly appointed terrace house offers modern, fully equipped
bedrooms, most with ensuite shower rooms. Guests are given a
genuine warm welcome and hearty breakfasts, made using fresh local
ingredients are served in the pleasant dining room.

Facilities 5 rms (3 en suite) (1 fmly) ⊗ STV TVB tea/coffee ✖ Cen ht
No children 5yrs No coaches **Prices** D £45-£50✷ **Notes** Closed
16 Dec-6 Jan 🐾

◆◆◆

The Magpie's Nest

75 Ocean Rd NE33 2JJ
☎ 0191 455 2361 & 07703 161047 🖨 0191 455 1709
e-mail christine.taylor3@btinternet.com
web www.magpies-nest.co.uk
Dir On A183 towards town centre

Set in a terrace convenient for the town centre, the Magpie's Nest has
been smartly refurbished in a minimalist style. Choose your own table

continued

in the cosy breakfast room or share a communal table in the attractive
bay-windowed dining room.

Facilities 7 en suite (2 fmly) (1 GF) ⊗ in dining room ⊗ in lounges
STV TVB tea/coffee Cen ht Dinner **Prices** S £26-£30; D £44-£60✷

SUNDERLAND   MAP 19 NZ35

◆◆◆

Mowbray Guest House

6 Mowbray Rd SR2 8HU ☎ 0191 510 9611
Dir 0.5m S of city centre off A1018 Ryhope Rd

This substantial and long established family house stands in a leafy
residential area south of the centre. Bedrooms are mainly well-
proportioned, furnished in pine, and have modern bathrooms en
suite. There is a spacious lounge-dining room.

Facilities 7 en suite (2 fmly) ⊗ in dining room TVB tea/coffee ✖
Cen ht TVL No coaches Dinner Last d 7pm **LB Parking** 6 **Notes** 🐾

WHITLEY BAY   MAP 21 NZ37

◆◆◆◆

Lindsay Guest House

50 Victoria Av NE26 2BA
☎ 0191 252 7341 🖨 0191 252 7505
e-mail info@lindsayguesthouse.co.uk
Dir Off Promenade by tennis courts and bowling green

The Lindsay forms part of a terrace close to the seafront. Behind the
unassuming façade is a stylish and immaculately maintained guest
house, with contemporary, eye-catching furniture in the lounge and
dining room. Modern bathrooms complement smart bedrooms.

Facilities 4 en suite (4 fmly) ⊗ in dining room STV TVB tea/coffee
Cen ht TVL No coaches **Prices** S £39-£49; D £60-£70✷ **Parking** 3

◆◆◆◆ 🅰

Marlborough Hotel

20-21 East Pde, Central Prom NE26 1AP
☎ 0191 251 3628 🖨 0191 252 5033
e-mail reception@marlborough-hotel.com
Dir In town centre. Off A193 onto Promenade

Facilities 16 rms (15 en suite) (4 fmly) (2 GF) ⊗ in 10 bedrooms
⊗ in dining room TVB tea/coffee Direct dial from bedrooms Licensed
TVL **Parking** 7 **Notes** Closed Xmas & New Year

◆◆◆

Cherrytree House

35 Brook St NE26 1AF ☎ 0191 251 4306 🖨 0191 251 4306
e-mail johncoleman@blueyonder.co.uk
Dir Off Promenade onto Brook St

This double-fronted Edwardian house in a quiet residential area close
to the seafront, yet away from the busy nightlife. The traditionally
furnished bedrooms are comfortable, and there is also a homely
lounge. Hearty breakfasts are cheerfully served at individual tables in
the pleasant dining room.

Facilities 5 rms (3 en suite) (1 GF) ⊗ TVB tea/coffee Cen ht TVL
No coaches **Prices** S £24-£40; D £36-£55✷ **LB Parking** 1

England

WARWICKSHIRE

ALCESTER MAP 10 SP05

◆◆◆◆

Globe Hotel

54 Birmingham Rd B49 5EG
☎ 01789 763287 ▤ 01789 763287
Dir N from town centre, next to Italian restaurant

Located within easy walking distance of the historic centre, this impressive detached house provides a range of practically furnished bedrooms with smart modern shower rooms. Ground floor areas include conference facilities, an attractive lounge bar and a spacious dining room, the setting for comprehensive breakfasts and a range of imaginative dinner options.

Facilities 10 rms (9 en suite) (1 fmly) ⊗ in bedrooms ⊗ in dining room ⊗ in 1 lounge TVB tea/coffee Direct dial from bedrooms ✖ Licensed Cen ht TVL No coaches Dinner Last d 8.30pm **Conf** Max 35 Thtr 35 Class 20 Board 20 **Parking** 11

◆◆◆◆

The Throckmorton Arms

B49 5HX ☎ 01789 766366 ▤ 01789 762654
e-mail info@thethrockmortonarms.co.uk
Dir On A435 between Studley and Alcester, 200yds from Coughton Court

Located north of town opposite the National Trust estate of Coughton Hall, this very well-maintained inn offers thoughtfully furnished bedrooms with lots of extras and rural views. Spacious and comfortable open-plan public areas provide the setting for imaginative food and a range of real ales.

Facilities 10 en suite (2 fmly) ⊗ in bedrooms ⊗ in dining room ⊗ in 1 lounge TVB tea/coffee Direct dial from bedrooms ✖ Cen ht TVL Dinner Last d 8.45pm **Prices** S £55-£65; D £65-£75✳ **LB Conf** Max 10 Board 10 **Parking** 45

◆◆◆

The Green Dragon Inn

The Green, Sambourne B96 6NU
☎ 01527 892465 & 07759 288890 ▤ 01527 893255
e-mail info@thegreendragon.demon.co.uk
Dir Hotel located 0.5m from A435, between Studley and Coughton.

Located on the village green in pretty Sambourne, the early 18th-century inn is a focal point of the community and hosts meetings of

continued

vintage car enthusiasts. The cosy, traditionally furnished areas are the setting for imaginative food and a good range of real ales. The chalet style bedrooms are next to the colourful beer garden.

Facilities 6 en suite (6 GF) ⊗ TVB tea/coffee Direct dial from bedrooms ✖ Cen ht Dinner Last d 9pm **Prices** S £50; D £50 **Parking** 30

ALDERMINSTER MAP 10 SP24

◆◆◆◆

The Bell

Shipston Rd CV37 8NY ☎ 01789 450414 ▤ 01789 450998
e-mail info@thebellald.co.uk
web www.thebellald.co.uk
Dir On A3400 3m S of Stratford-upon-Avon on Shipston-Oxford road

A focal part of the local community, this former coaching house has original features enhanced by quality decor in the public areas. The late 18th-century inn specialises in gastronomic festivals throughout the year and the thoughtfully furnished bedrooms are in a renovated separate house or a converted coach house, reached via immaculate gardens.

Facilities 7 annexe rms (3 en suite) (2 annexe pri facs) (2 fmly) (3 GF) ⊗ TV available tea/coffee Cen ht Dinner Last d 9.30pm **Conf** Max 12 Thtr 12 Class 12 Board 12 **Parking** available

BAGINTON MAP 11 SP37

★★★★ **Inn**

Old Mill

Mill Hill CV8 3AH ☎ 024 7630 2241 ▤ 024 7630 7070
e-mail oldmillhotel@thespiritgroup.com
Dir In village 0.25m from junct A45 & A46

Enjoying a peaceful riverside location, yet within easy reach of the motorway networks, the Old Mill has been furnished to a high standard. Public areas include the popular Chef & Brewer bar and restaurant, with a pleasant patio for summer evenings. Spacious bedrooms are smartly appointed and well equipped.

Facilities 28 en suite (6 fmly) TVB tea/coffee Direct dial from bedrooms ✖ Dinner Last d 9.30pm **Prices** S £49-£80; D £49-£80; (room only) ✳ **LB Conf** Max 18 Thtr 30 Class 16 Board 20 **Parking** 200

BARNACLE MAP 11 SP38

◆◆◆◆

Park Farm House (SP384848)

Spring Rd CV7 9LG
☎ 024 7661 2628 ▤ 024 7661 6010 Mrs Grindal
Dir M6 junct 2 onto B4065 to Shilton. Left at lights, left again over M69, right into Barnacle

Excellent accommodation and hospitality is provided at this delightful farmhouse which dates from 1655 and also has a peaceful location. The spacious bedrooms are well equipped and there is a cosy lounge. Good breakfasts are provided around a large table and dinner is available by arrangement.

England

Park Farm House

bathrooms. Ground-floor areas include a lounge-dining room and a games room with pool table.

Facilities 9 en suite (1 fmly) ⊗ TVB tea/coffee Cen ht TVL Pool Table **Prices** S £45; D £65 **Parking** 16

ETTINGTON
MAP 10 SP24

Premier Collection

◆◆◆◆◆

Fulready Manor

Fulready CV37 7PE ☎ 01789 740152 ▤ 01789 740247
e-mail stay@fulreadymanor.co.uk
web www.fulreadymanor.co.uk
Dir *2.5m SE of Ettington. 0.5m S off A422 at Pillerton Priors*

Located in 120 acres of arable farmland, this impressive, new Cotswold-stone house provides very high levels of comfort. The spacious ground-floor areas are furnished with quality and flair, and feature fine furniture and art. The individually themed bedrooms have a wealth of thoughtful extras, and memorable breakfasts are served in the elegant dining room overlooking immaculate gardens. AA Guest Accommodation of the Year for England 2006.

Facilities 3 en suite ⊗ ✖ Cen ht No children 15yrs No coaches **Prices** D £105-£135 **Parking** 6 **Notes** ⊗

Facilities 3 en suite ⊗ TVB tea/coffee ✖ Cen ht No children 12yrs Golf 18 Riding 200 acres Beef & Arable Dinner Last d 12hrs notice **Prices** S fr £39; d fr £70 **Conf** Max 8 Board 8 Del from £76 **Parking** 6 **Notes** ⊗

COLESHILL
MAP 10 SP28

◆◆◆◆

The Old Vicarage

Shawbury Ln, Shustoke B46 2LA
☎ 01675 481331 ▤ 01675 481331
e-mail jbhawk@doctors.org.uk
Dir *A446 onto B4114 for Coleshill, B4114 Coleshill-Nuneaton road for Shustoke, 0.5m after village right at sharp left bend (Griffin Inn) & sharp left towards church*

Standing opposite the magnificent church of St Cuthbert, at the edge of Shustoke, this impressive guest house is set in pretty mature gardens. The house is stylishly decorated and furnished throughout, and retains many original features. Bedrooms are filled with a wealth of thoughtful extras, and superb breakfasts are served in the elegant dining room.

Facilities 3 rms (2 en suite) ⊗ TVB tea/coffee ✖ Cen ht No coaches **Prices** S £35-£40; D £50-£60✳ **Parking** 6 **Notes** Closed Xmas

◆◆◆

Ye Olde Station Guest House

Church Rd, Shustoke B46 2AX
☎ 01675 481736 ▤ 01675 481736
web www.yeoldestationguesthouse.co.uk
Dir *2.5m NE, on B4114 300yds past Griffin pub*

This converted Victorian railway station has been modernised to provide a range of practically furnished bedrooms with efficient

continued

England

ETTINGTON continued

◆◆◆ **A**

The Houndshill

Banbury Rd CV37 7NS ☎ 01789 740267 ▤ 01789 740075
Dir *4m S of Stratford-upon-Avon. 1m N of Ettington village on A422*

Facilities 8 en suite (2 fmly) TVB tea/coffee Direct dial from bedrooms
Licensed Cen ht Dinner Last d 9.30 pm **Prices** S fr £45; d fr £70✳
Conf Thtr 30 Board 18 **Parking** 50 **Notes** Closed 25-28 Dec

See advertisement on page 515

GREAT WOLFORD   MAP 10 SP23

Premier Collection

◆◆◆◆◆

The Old Coach House

CV36 5NQ ☎ 01608 674152
e-mail theoldcoachhouse2@tiscali.co.uk
Dir *Off A44 signed Great Wolford, B&B 1.25m, 1st on right*

Located in a historic Cotswold village next to a fine country inn, this
former coach house has been restored to provide high levels of
comfort and facilities. Bedrooms are equipped with a wealth of
thoughtful extras, and quality decor and furnishings enhance the
intrinsic charm of the property.

Facilities 2 en suite ⊘ TVB tea/coffee ✕ Cen ht TVL No children 8yrs
No coaches **Prices** S £50; D £80 LB **Parking** 2 **Notes** ⊗

◆◆◆◆ **⬛**

The Fox & Hounds Inn

CV36 5NQ ☎ 01608 674220 ▤ 01608 674953
e-mail info@thefoxandhoundsinn.com
Dir *Off A3400, 1.5m to Great Wolford*

Please note that this establishment has recently changed hands. Very
much a focal point of the local community, this 16th-century inn
retains many original features, which are enhanced by rustic furniture
and memorabilia. The thoughtfully furnished bedrooms are in
converted outbuildings, and a warm welcome is assured.

Facilities 3 annexe en suite ⊘ in bedrooms ⊘ in area of dining room
TVB tea/coffee Cen ht No children 12yrs No coaches Dinner Last d 9pm
Prices S £50; D £80 **Parking** 10 **Notes** Closed 1st wk in Jan rs Mon

GRENDON   MAP 10 SP29

◆◆◆◆ **A**

The Chestnuts Country Guest House

Watling St CV9 2PZ ☎ 01827 331355 ▤ 01827 896951
e-mail cclltd@aol.com
web www.thechestnutshotel.com
Dir *500yds NW of Grendon rdbt on A5*

Facilities 4 en suite (1 fmly) ⊗ TVB tea/coffee ✕ Licensed Cen ht
TVL No coaches Dinner Last d 5pm **Conf** Max 10 **Parking** 6
Notes Closed Xmas & New Year

KENILWORTH   MAP 10 SP27

★★★★ Guest House

Stoneleigh Park Lodge

Stoneleigh Pk CV8 2LZ
☎ 024 7669 0123 ▤ 024 7669 0789
e-mail info@stoneleighparklodge.com
web www.stoneleighparklodge.com
Dir *2m E of Kenilworth in National Agricultural Centre*

The guest house lies within the National Agricultural Centre grounds
and provides modern, well-equipped accommodation. Meals, using
local produce, are served in the Park View Restaurant overlooking the
showground. Various conference and meeting facilities are available.

Facilities 58 en suite (4 fmly) (26 GF) ⊗ FTV TVB tea/coffee Direct
dial from bedrooms ✕ Licensed Cen ht TVL No coaches Fishing Dinner
Last d 9.30pm **Parking** 60 **Notes** Closed Xmas

★★★★ **A** Guest House

Ferndale House

45 Priory Rd CV8 1LL ☎ 01926 853214 ▤ 01926 858336
e-mail ferndalehouse@tiscali.co.uk
web www.kenilworth-guesthouse-accommodation.com
Dir *Off A46 onto Warwick road, 1st right after Texaco service station
onto Waverley Rd, continue on to Priory Rd*

Facilities 8 en suite (2 fmly) (1 GF) ⊗ TVB tea/coffee ✕ Cen ht TVL
No coaches **Prices** S £34-£35; D £57-£58✳ **Parking** 6

◆◆◆◆

Victoria Lodge Hotel

180 Warwick Rd CV8 1HU
☎ 01926 512020 ▤ 01926 858703
e-mail info@victorialodgehotel.co.uk
Dir *On A452 opp St Johns Church*

Please note that this establishment has recently changed hands. This
Victorian property is on the fringe of the historic town, within easy
walking distance of the castle and restaurants. It has been extended to
provide thoughtfully furnished bedrooms with homely extras. There is
a beautiful walled garden, and off-road parking is available. The
Victoria Lodge is convenient for the National Exhibition Centre.

continued

Victoria Lodge Hotel

Facilities 10 en suite (1 fmly) (2 GF) ⊘ TVB tea/coffee Direct dial from bedrooms ✖ Licensed Cen ht No coaches **Prices** S £47; D £70-£80✱ **Parking** 9 **Notes** Closed 24 Dec-1 Jan

◆◆◆

Hollyhurst Guest House ◇

47 Priory Rd CV8 1LL ☎ 01926 853882 🖹 01926 853882
e-mail admin@hollyhurstguesthouse.co.uk
Dir On A452 in town centre

Located on a mainly residential avenue within easy walking distance of the castle and town centre, this constantly improving establishment offers a range of bedrooms, some of which have the benefit of modern shower rooms. Ground-floor areas include a comfortable lounge in addition to an attractive dining room.

Facilities 7 rms (3 en suite) (1 pri facs) (1 fmly) ⊘ TVB tea/coffee ✖ Cen ht TVL No coaches **Prices** S £29-£37; D £48-£55 **Parking** 7 **Notes** Closed Xmas/New Year ⊠

LEAMINGTON SPA (ROYAL)   MAP 10 SP36

◆◆◆◆

Adams Hotel

22 Avenue Rd CV31 3PQ ☎ 01926 450742 🖹 01926 313110
e-mail bookings@adams-hotel.co.uk
Dir 500yds W of town centre. Off A452 Adelaide Rd onto Avenue Rd

Please note that this establishment has recently changed hands. Just a short walk from town centre, this elegant 1827 Regency house offers a relaxing setting and quality accommodation. Public areas include a lounge bar with leather armchairs, and a pretty garden. The attractive bedrooms are very well appointed, and have modem points and bathrobes.

Facilities 10 en suite (1 fmly) (2 GF) ⊘ TVB tea/coffee Direct dial from bedrooms Licensed Cen ht **Prices** S £50-£66; D £72-£84✱ **Conf** Thtr 20 Class 20 Board 15 **Parking** 14

◆◆◆◆

Bubbenhall House

Paget's Ln CV8 3BJ
☎ 024 7630 2409 & 07746 282541 🖹 024 7630 2409
e-mail wharrison@bubbenhallhouse.freeserve.co.uk
Dir 5m NE of Leamington. Off A445 at Bubbenhall S onto Pagets Ln, 1m on single-track lane (over 4 speed humps)

Located between Leamington Spa and Coventry in extensive mature grounds with an abundance of wildlife, this impressive late Edwardian house, once the home of the Mini's designer, contains many interesting features including a Jacobean-style staircase. Thoughtful extras are provided in the bedrooms and public areas include an elegant dining room and choice of sumptuous lounges.

Facilities 3 en suite ⊘ in bedrooms ⊘ in dining room TVB tea/coffee Cen ht TVL No coaches ⚲ ♫ Petanque, spa hot tub Dinner Last d 7.30pm **Prices** S £50-£55; D £65-£75✱ **LB** **Parking** 12 **Notes** ⊠

◆◆◆◆ ❤

Hill Farm ◇ (SP343637)

Lewis Rd, Radford Semele CV31 1UX
☎ 01926 337571 Mrs Gibbs
e-mail rebecca@hillfarm3000.fsnet.co.uk
web www.hillfarm.info
Dir 2m SE on A425, in Radford Semele right onto Lewis Rd to bottom

Peacefully located within the village of Radford Semele, this Victorian house provides thoughtfully equipped bedrooms complemented by modern, efficient bathrooms. Ground-floor areas include an attractive dining room and a lounge, while the immaculate mature garden is ablaze with colour during the summer.

Facilities 4 en suite ⊘ TVB tea/coffee ✖ Cen ht TVL No children 12yrs 350 acres arable mixed sheep **Prices** S £25-£35; D £50-£60 **Parking** 6 **Notes** Closed Xmas & New Year ⊠

continued

England

LIGHTHORNE
MAP 10 SP35

◆◆◆◆ ♥

Redlands Farm ◇ (SP334570)

Banbury Rd CV35 0AH
☎ 01926 651241 ▤ 01926 651241 Mrs Stanton
Dir Off B4100, 5m S of Warwick

A unique collection of railway memorabilia adorns the interior of this peacefully located house, situated in extensive gardens with an outdoor swimming pool. Bedrooms are comfortable and homely, and smart modern bathrooms include power showers. There is a cosy dining room and comfortable lounge featuring an open fire during the cooler months.

Facilities 3 rms (1 en suite) (1 fmly) ⊗ TVB tea/coffee ✖ Cen ht TVL
⚘ **Prices** S £27.50-£35; D £55-£60✱ **Parking** 7 **Notes** Closed Xmas ⊗

LONG COMPTON
MAP 10 SP23

◆◆◆◆ ♥

Tallet Barn B & B (SP289328)

Yerdley Farm CV36 5LH
☎ 01608 684248 ▤ 01608 684248 Mrs Richardson
e-mail talletbarn@btinternet.com
Dir Off A3400 in village onto Vicarage Ln opp Post Office/stores

A converted barn and grain store in the heart of this unspoiled Cotswold village provide comfortable bedrooms with thoughtful extras. Comprehensive breakfasts are served in the elegant beamed dining room in the main house, which also has a comfortable lounge.

Facilities 2 annexe en suite (1 fmly) (1 GF) ⊗ TVB tea/coffee ✖
Cen ht No children 6yrs 420 acres arable **Prices** S £35; D £55-£60
Parking 3 **Notes** ⊗

NEWBOLD ON STOUR
MAP 10 SP24

◆◆◆ 🅰 ♥

The Poplars ◇ (SP246459)

Mansell Farm CV37 8BZ
☎ 01789 450540 & 07989 662864 ▤ 01789 450540
Ms Spencer
e-mail judith@poplarsfarmhouse.co.uk
Dir A3400 S into Newbold village, right at church, farm 200yds right

Facilities 3 en suite ⊗ TVB tea/coffee Cen ht TVL Riding 190 acres
Mixed/arable/beef/sheep Dinner Last d day before **Prices** S £30-£40;
D £50-£60✱ **Notes** Closed Xmas

NUNEATON
MAP 11 SP39

◆◆◆◆◆ ⊜

Leathermill Grange Country Guest House

Leathermill Ln, Caldecote CV10 0RX
☎ 01827 714637 ▤ 01827 716422
e-mail davidcodd@leathermillgrange.co.uk
web www.leathermillgrange.co.uk
Dir B4114/B4111 2.5m NW from Nuneaton, Leathermill Ln on right before railway bridge

Located in stunning rural surroundings close to major roads and historic attractions, this impressive Victorian house has been renovated to provide high standards of accommodation. Quality furnishings and decor enhance the many original features. Imaginative dinners are served in an elegant dining room, and a spacious lounge with a conservatory is available. There are 5 acres of mature grounds with a well-stocked carp lake. Excellent hospitality is assured.

Facilities 3 en suite ⊗ TVB tea/coffee ✖ Licensed Cen ht No children 16yrs No coaches Fishing Pool Table ⚐ Exercise machine - golf practice lawn Dinner Last d 24hr prior **Prices** S £60-£70; D £80-£90 **Conf** Board 12 **Parking** 20

OXHILL
MAP 10 SP34

◆◆◆◆ ♥

Nolands Farm ◇ (SP312470)

CV35 0RJ ☎ 01926 640309 ▤ 01926 641662 Mrs Hutsby
e-mail inthecountry@nolandsfarm.co.uk
web www.nolandsfarm.co.uk
Dir 1m E of Pillarton Priors on A422

The farmhouse stands in peaceful countryside and the bedrooms are in converted stables and milking sheds. Comprehensive breakfasts and imaginative dinners are served in the former granary. Balloon flights, clay pigeon shooting and cycle rides can be arranged and there is also a fishing lake.

Facilities 6 annexe en suite (6 GF) ⊗ in bedrooms ⊗ in dining room FTV TVB tea/coffee ✖ Licensed Cen ht No children 7yrs Fishing Clay shooting, bike hire, Hot air ballooning 200 acres arable **Prices** S fr £30; D £50-£75✱ **LB Conf** Max 10 **Parking** 12 **Notes** Closed Xmas & New Year

England

RUGBY
MAP 11 SP57

◆◆◆ ▣
The White Lion Inn ◇

Coventry Rd, Pailton CV23 0QD
☎ 01788 832359 🖹 01788 832359

Dir 4.5m NW of Rugby. A426 onto B4112 to Pailton village, fork left, inn 200yds

Facilities 9 rms (5 en suite) (2 fmly) (3 GF) ⊛ in 6 bedrooms ⊛ in area of dining room ⊛ in 1 lounge TVB tea/coffee Direct dial from bedrooms Licensed Cen ht TVL Dinner Last d 10pm **Prices** S £26-£36; D £46-£56✳ **Conf** Max 20 **Parking** 60

SHIPSTON ON STOUR
MAP 10 SP24

◆◆◆◆ ◼
The Falcon

Church St CV36 4AS ☎ 01608 664414 🖹 01608 664414
e-mail the.falcon@btconnect.com

Dir M40 junct 15, take A429 towards Chippenham & Stow. Follow until A3400, turn left towards Oxford & Shipston on Stour. The Falcon 2.5m on right

This friendly inn stands in the centre of the village and offers very well-furnished and comfortable bedrooms together with a popular and busy bar where quality food is also available. Staff are very attentative and a range of real ales is available. Parking beside the inn.

Facilities 5 en suite ⊛ in bedrooms ⊛ in dining room TVB tea/coffee Direct dial from bedrooms ✻ Cen ht No coaches Dinner Last d 9.30pm **Parking** 6

◆◆◆◆ ❦
Highfield Farm *(SP270424)*

Honington CV36 5DP ☎ 01608 662101 Mrs Newbery
e-mail highfieldsbandb@gmail.com

Dir From A3400 take turn towards Honington. Highfield Farm is 500yds from Honington on Whatcote Rd.

On the outskirts of the pretty hamlet of Honington within an Area of Outstanding Natural Beauty, this carefully extended farmhouse provides thoughtfully furnished bedrooms with smart modern shower rooms. Hearty breakfasts are served in the attractive lounge-dining room.

Facilities 2 en suite ⊛ TVB tea/coffee ✻ Cen ht TVL No children 12yrs 300 acres Arable & Sheep **Prices** S £32; D £55✳ **LB** **Parking** 4 **Notes** ☖

◆◆◆◆
Holly End Bed & Breakfast

London Rd CV36 4EP ☎ 01608 664064
e-mail enquiries@holly-end.co.uk
web www.holly-end.co.uk

Dir 0.5m S of Shipston on Stour on A3400

Located between Oxford & Stratford-upon-Avon and a short walk from town centre, this immaculate detached house offers bedrooms with lots of thoughtful extras. Comprehensive breakfasts use the best of local produce.

Facilities 3 rms (2 en suite) (1 fmly) ⊛ TVB tea/coffee ✻ Cen ht No children 9yrs No coaches **Prices** S £45-£65; D £65-£90✳ **LB** **Parking** 6 **Notes** ☖

◆◆◆◆ ◼
The Red Lion

Main St, Long Compton CV36 5JS
☎ 01608 684221 🖹 01608 684968
e-mail red@redlion3.wanadoo.co.uk
Dir 5m S of Shipston on Stour on A3400

Located in the pretty rural village of Long Compton, this mid-18th-century posting house retains many original features, highlighted by rustic furniture in the warm and inviting public areas. Bedrooms are furnished with a good range of practical facilities, and menus use quality local produce.

Facilities 5 en suite (1 fmly) ⊛ in bedrooms TVB tea/coffee Cen ht TVL Pool Table Dinner Last d 9pm **Prices** D £70-£80 **Parking** 60

STRATFORD-UPON-AVON
MAP 10 SP25
See also **Alderminster & Oxhill**

★★★★ Guest House
Moonraker House

40 Alcester Rd CV37 9DB
☎ 01789 268774 🖹 01789 268774
e-mail moonrakerhouse@btinternet.com
Dir 200yds from railway station on A422 Alcester Rd

Just a short walk from the railway station and the central attractions, this establishment provides a range of stylish bedrooms. The sitting area during the day is the setting for the freshly cooked breakfasts. The attractive exterior is enhanced by a magnificent floral display during the warmer months.

Facilities 7 en suite (1 fmly) (2 GF) ⊛ TVB tea/coffee ✻ Cen ht No children 6yrs **Prices** S £40-£55; D £65-£75✳ **LB** **Parking** 8

England

STRATFORD-UPON-AVON continued

★★★ Farm House

Whitchurch Farm ◇ (SP222485)

Whitchurch CV37 8PD
☎ 01789 450359 ▤ 01789 450359 Mrs E James
e-mail jweeah@aol.com
Dir *A3400 S from Stratford-upon-Avon. After 4m, turn right for Wimpstone, then left at telephone box, 0.5m through village*

Dating in part from the 17th century, this characterful farmhouse enjoys a peaceful rural setting and yet is only a short drive away from the attractions of Stratford on Avon. The spacious bedrooms offer country views while Mrs James' award winning cuisine utilises locally sourced produce wherever possible.

Facilities 3 en suite (2 fmly) ⊗ TVB tea/coffee ✱ Cen ht TVL 400 acres sheep/arable/beef Dinner Last d Breakfast **Prices** S £25-£30; D £50-£60✳ **Parking** 5 **Notes** Closed Dec-Jan

Premier Collection

◆◆◆◆◆

Cherry Trees

Swans Nest Ln CV37 7LS ☎ 01789 292989
e-mail gotocherrytrees@aol.com
web www.cherrytrees-stratford.co.uk
Dir *250yds SE of town centre over bridge. Off A422, next to Butterfly Farm*

Comfortably located close to the theatre and the centre of town Cherry Trees offer spacious, luxurious, well - equipped rooms. Guests have a separate entrance and hearty breakfasts are served in the attractive upstairs dining room.

Facilities 3 en suite (3 GF) ⊗ FTV TVB tea/coffee ✱ Cen ht No children 10yrs No coaches **Prices** S £45-£55; D £80-£95✳ **LB** **Parking** 11

◆◆◆◆

Ambleside Guest House ◇

41 Grove Rd CV37 6PB ☎ 01789 297239 ▤ 01789 295670
e-mail ruth@amblesideguesthouse.com
Dir *On A4390 opp Firs Park*

This attractive, spotlessly clean and friendly house is situated close to the market square and town centre. The bedrooms are carefully decorated, well appointed and some have smart modern shower rooms. Breakfast is served in the light airy dining room overlooking the pretty front garden.

continued

Ambleside

Facilities 7 rms (5 en suite) (4 fmly) (2 GF) ⊗ TVB tea/coffee ✱ Cen ht No children 4yrs **Prices** S £25-£35; D £56-£80 **Parking** 7

◆◆◆◆ ✿

Loxley Farm (SP273553)

Loxley CV35 9JN ☎ 01789 840265 ▤ 01789 840645
Mr & Mrs Horton
e-mail loxleyfarm@hotmail.com
web www.loxleyfarm.co.uk
Dir *4m SE off A422 to village T-junct, left, 3rd house on right*

This thatched former farmhouse stands in attractive cottage gardens in the peaceful village of Loxley. The thoughtfully equipped bedrooms are in a converted 17th-century shieling or cart barn, and each room has an adjacent sitting area. Tasty breakfasts are served around a family table in the main house.

Facilities 2 en suite (2 GF) ⊗ TVB tea/coffee Cen ht TVL 6 acres **Prices** S fr £50; d fr £75 **Parking** 10 **Notes** Closed Xmas & New Year ⊠

◆◆◆◆ ✿

Cadle Pool Farm (SP173563)

The Ridgeway CV37 9RE ☎ 01789 292494 Mrs Turney
Dir *2m W of Stratford. A422 Alcester Rd W from Stratford, right onto Ridgeway Rd, bridge over A46, farm 800yds on right*

Located on large, immaculately maintained grounds which include a duck pond, this impressive detached house provides good standards of comfort and facilities. Bedrooms are spacious and ground-floor areas include an elegant dining room and a very comfortable lounge.

Facilities 2 en suite (1 fmly) ⊗ TVB tea/coffee ✱ Cen ht TVL No children 10yrs Reflexology, Aromatherapy and massage treatments 450 acres Arable **Prices** d fr £64✳ **LB** **Parking** 6 **Notes** Closed mid Dec-Jan ⊠

England

◆◆◆◆

Clopton Orchard Farm *(SP165455)*

Lower Clopton, Upper Quinton CV37 8LH
☎ 01386 438669 & 07765 414636 ▤ 01386 438669
Mrs Coldicott
e-mail mail@clopton-orchard.fsnet.co.uk
Dir *6m S of Stratford on B4632. S through Lower Clopton, farm opp clock tower, signed*

A warm welcome is assured at this attractive modern farmhouse located between Broadway and Stratford-upon-Avon. The spacious bedrooms come with practical and thoughtful extras, and comprehensive breakfasts are served around a family table in the cosy pine-furnished first-floor dining room.

Facilities 2 en suite (1 fmly) ⊗ TVB tea/coffee ✱ Cen ht 300 acres arable sheep **Prices** S £35-£40; D £55-£60✱ LB **Parking** 5 **Notes** ⊠

◆◆◆◆ ✿

Cross o'th' Hill Farm *(SP202534)*

Broadway Rd CV37 8HP ☎ 01789 204738
Mr & Mrs Noble
e-mail decimanoble@hotmail.com
web www.crossothhillfarm.com
Dir *0.5m S of Stratford. A3400 S from Stratford for Shipston, 0.75m onto B4632, farm signed 0.25m on right, farmhouse 200yds*

This large farmhouse, dating from 1860, stands among pasture and a small orchard a short walk from the centre of Stratford. Original architectural details have been lovingly preserved, and relaxed, understated elegance marks the bedrooms and public areas.

Facilities 3 rms (2 en suite) (1 pri facs) ⊗ TVB tea/coffee ✱ Cen ht TVL No children 5yrs ♨ 150 acres arable beef **Prices** S fr £57; d fr £74 **Conf** Max 10 **Parking** 22 **Notes** Closed 25 Dec-Feb ⊠

◆◆◆◆

Eastnor House Hotel

33 Shipston Rd CV37 7LN ☎ 01789 268115
e-mail eastnorhouse@ntlworld.com
Dir *On A3400 at junct with A422*

This Victorian house is convenient for the town centre and local attractions. Bedrooms are equipped with a wide range of homely extras. Comprehensive buffet breakfasts are served in the cosy dining room and a lounge bar is also available.

Facilities 10 en suite (4 fmly) (3 GF) ⊗ in bedrooms ⊗ in dining room ⊗ in 1 lounge STV TVB tea/coffee Direct dial from bedrooms Cen ht No coaches **Parking** 10

◆◆◆◆

Emsley Guest House

4 Arden St CV37 6PA ☎ 01789 299557 ▤ 01789 299557
e-mail val@theemsley.co.uk
web www.theemsley.co.uk
Dir *A46 onto A3400 into Stratford, right at lights onto A4390 Arden St*

Emsley Guest House is just a short walk from Stratford centre and the railway station, and is a good base for visiting the many local attractions. Bedrooms are carefully decorated and well equipped. Substantial breakfasts, including vegetarian options, are served in the attractive dining room. There is also a comfortable lounge, and parking nearby is arranged by the owners.

Facilities 5 en suite (3 fmly) ⊗ TVB tea/coffee ✱ Cen ht TVL No coaches **Prices** S £55-£70; D £60-£70 **Parking** 19 **Notes** Closed 24 Dec-1 Jan

◆◆◆◆ ⊛ ⊜

The Fox & Goose Inn

Armscote CV37 8DD ☎ 01608 682293 ▤ 01608 682293
e-mail mail@foxandgoose.co.uk
web www.foxandgoose.co.uk
Dir *7m S of Stratford. Off A3400 near church in Newbold on Stour signed Armscote 1m, bear right in village*

A conversion of two cottages and a blacksmith's forge, this inn retains many original features that are enhanced by the quality furnishings and decor. The Cluedo-themed bedrooms are designed with individual flair, and imaginative and hearty food is served in the candlelit dining room.

Facilities 4 en suite ⊗ in bedrooms ⊗ in area of dining room ⊗ in 1 lounge TVB tea/coffee ✱ Cen ht No coaches Dinner Last d 9.30pm **Conf** Max 20 Thtr 20 Class 20 Board 20 **Parking** 20

Always confirm details with the establishment when booking

England

STRATFORD-UPON-AVON continued

◆◆◆◆

Hardwick House

1 Avenue Rd CV37 6UY ☎ 01789 204307
e-mail hardwick@waverider.co.uk
web www.hardwickstratford.co.uk
Dir Off A439 at St Gregorys Church onto St Gregorys Rd, house 200yds on right

Located in a leafy residential area a short walk from the central attractions, this impressive red-brick Victorian house provides a range of thoughtfully furnished bedrooms complemented by modern bathrooms. Comprehensive breakfasts are served in the attractive dining room, and the cricket memorabilia adorning the public areas depicts the proprietor's former professional career.

Facilities 8 en suite (1 GF) ⊗ TVB tea/coffee ✖ Cen ht No children 12yrs No coaches **Prices** S £35-£42; D £60-£80 LB **Parking** 6

◆◆◆◆

The Melita

37 Shipston Rd CV37 7LN
☎ 01789 292432 📠 01789 204867
e-mail info@melitaguesthouse.co.uk
web www.melitaguesthouse.co.uk
Dir 200yds SE from Clopton Bridge on A3400

Located within easy walking distance of the central attractions, this spacious Victorian house offers pleasant accommodation with friendly service. Bedrooms vary in style and all have thoughtful extras. The breakfast room overlooks a pretty garden and the lounge has a feature fireplace and an honesty bar.

Facilities 12 rms (10 en suite) (2 pri facs) (2 fmly) (3 GF) ⊗ TVB tea/coffee Direct dial from bedrooms Cen ht TVL **Prices** S £39-£55; D £60-£95✳ LB **Parking** 12 **Notes** Closed 20 Dec-2 Jan

◆◆◆◆

Monk's Barn Farm ◇ (SP206516)

Shipston Rd CV37 8NA
☎ 01789 293714 📠 01789 205886 Mrs Meadows
e-mail ritameadows@btconnet.com
Dir 2m S of Stratford on A3400, on right after bungalows on left

With stunning views of the surrounding countryside, a warm welcome is assured at this impressive renovated house. Bedrooms, some of which are located in former outbuildings, are filled with a wealth of thoughtful extras and memorable breakfasts are served in the spacious and cosy lounge-dining room.

Facilities 4 rms (3 en suite) 3 annexe en suite (4 GF) ⊗ TVB tea/coffee ✖ Cen ht TVL 75 acres mixed **Prices** S £24-£30; D £48-£53 **Parking** 7 **Notes** Closed 25-26 Dec

◆◆◆◆

Twelfth Night ◇

13 Evesham Pl CV37 6HT
☎ 01789 414595 & 07899 974461 📠 01789 414595
e-mail reservations@twelfthnight.co.uk
web www.twelfthnight.co.uk
Dir In town centre off A4390 Grove Rd

This delightful Victorian villa is within easy walking distance of the town centre. Quality decor and furnishings enhance the charming original features, and the elegant dining room is the setting for imaginative English breakfasts.

Facilities 6 en suite ⊗ TVB tea/coffee ✖ Cen ht No children 12yrs **Prices** S £30-£50; D £55-£70 LB **Parking** 7

◆◆◆◆

Victoria Spa Lodge

Bishopton Ln, Bishopton CV37 9QY
☎ 01789 267985 📠 01789 204728
e-mail ptozer@victoriaspalodge.demon.co.uk
web www.stratford-upon-avon.co.uk/victoriaspa.htm
Dir A3400 1.5m N to junct A46, 1st left onto Bishopton Ln, 1st house on right

Located within immaculate mature gardens beside the canal on the outskirts of town, this impressive Victorian house retains many original features enhanced by the furnishings and decor. Bedrooms are filled with thoughtful extras and the spacious dining room, furnished with quality antiques and ornaments, also contains a cosy lounge area.

Facilities 7 en suite (3 fmly) ⊗ TVB tea/coffee ✖ Cen ht No coaches
Prices S £50 **Parking** 12

See advertisement on this page

◆◆◆

Arden Way Guest House ◇

22 Shipston Rd CV37 7LP
☎ 01789 205646 📠 01789 205646
e-mail info@ardenwayguesthouse.co.uk
Dir On A3400 S of River Avon on left

A warm welcome is assured at this constantly improving no-smoking house, located within easy walking distance of the Butterfly Farm and cricket ground. The homely bedrooms are filled with lots of thoughtful extras and an attractive dining room, overlooking the pretty rear garden, is the setting for comprehensive breakfasts.

Facilities 6 rms (5 en suite) (1 pri facs) (2 fmly) (2 GF) ⊗ TVB tea/coffee ✖ Cen ht No coaches **Prices** S £27-£55; D £52-£64✱ **Parking** 6

◆◆◆

Clomendy Guest House

10 Broad Walk CV37 6HS ☎ 01789 266957
e-mail clomendy@amserve.com
web www.clomendy.co.uk
Dir In town centre off A4390 Evesham Place

Located on a peaceful avenue within easy walking distance of central attractions, this immaculately maintained house offers homely, thoughtfully equipped bedrooms with modern bathrooms. Breakfast is served at a family table in the elegant dining room, which opens to the pretty rear patio garden.

Facilities 2 rms (1 en suite) (1 pri facs) ⊗ TVB tea/coffee ✖ Cen ht No children 5yrs No coaches **Prices** S £40; D £40-£55 **LB** **Parking** 1
Notes 🐾

◆◆◆

Forget-me-Not

18 Evesham Pl CV37 6HT
☎ 01789 204907 📠 01789 204907
e-mail kate@forgetmenotguesthouse.co.uk
Dir On B439 in the town centre, on the pedestrain crossing near junct of Evesham Place and Chestnut Walk.

This guest house is receiving lots of care and attention from new owners. Bedrooms offer super comfortable beds and shower rooms. Breakfast is offered in a pretty. bright dining room

Facilities 5 en suite (1 fmly) ⊗ TVB tea/coffee Cen ht Dinner
Parking 2

◆◆◆

Avon Lodge

Ryon Hill, Warwick Rd CV37 0NZ ☎ 01789 295196

Located in immaculate mature gardens on the outskirts of town, this former Victorian cottage has been carefully modernised and extended to provide cosy bedrooms. Imaginative breakfasts are served in the attractive cottage-style dining room.

Facilities 6 en suite (1 fmly) ⊗ TV5B tea/coffee Cen ht TVL No coaches Golf **Parking** 7 **Notes**

England

STRATFORD-UPON-AVON continued

◆◆◆

Hunters Moon ◇

150 Alcester Rd CV37 9DR
☎ 01789 292888 📠 01789 204101
e-mail thehuntersmoon@ntlworld.com
web www.huntersmoonguesthouse.com
Dir 0.6m W of town centre on A422 Alcester Rd

Hunters Moon is close to Anne Hathaway's Cottage and other tourist attractions on the northern side of Stratford. Accommodation is comfortable, well equipped and some bedrooms have views over the well-tended garden.

Facilities 6 en suite 1 annexe en suite (3 fmly) (2 GF) ⊗ TVB tea/coffee ✘ Cen ht No children 5yrs **Prices** S £30-£38; D £56-£72 LB **Parking** 6 **Notes** Closed 25 Dec

◆◆◆

Parkfield Guest House ◇

3 Broad Walk CV37 6HS ☎ 01789 293313 📠 01789 293313
e-mail parkfield@btinternet.com
web www.ParkfieldBandB.co.uk
Dir B439 from Stratford, Parkfield just off road on left before 1st rdbt

This attractive Victorian house stands in a quiet road close to the town centre. Much of its original character has been maintained and bedrooms offer comfortable accommodation. Attractive theatrical themed paintings adorn the walls of the cottage style dining room, the setting for comprehensive breakfasts.

Facilities 7 rms (6 en suite) (1 pri facs) (1 fmly) ⊗ TVB tea/coffee ✘ Cen ht No children 5yrs No coaches **Prices** S £30; D £55 LB **Parking** 7

◆◆◆

Stretton House ◇

38 Grove Rd CV37 6PB ☎ 01789 268647 📠 01789 268647
e-mail shortpbshort@aol.com
web www.strettonhouse.co.uk
Dir On A439 in town centre road behind police station

This attractive Edwardian terrace house is within easy walking distance of the railway station and Shakespeare's birthplace. Bedrooms are carefully decorated, well equipped, and many have modern shower rooms en suite. The pretty front garden is a very welcoming feature.

Facilities 7 rms (4 en suite) (2 fmly) (1 GF) ⊗ TVB tea/coffee Cen ht **Prices** S £20-£25; D £50-£60✳ **Parking** 7 **Notes** 📵

◆◆◆

Travellers Rest ◇

146 Alcester Rd CV37 9DR ☎ 01789 266589
e-mail enquiries@travellersrest.biz
web www.travellersrest.biz
Dir 0.5m W from town centre on A422, past railway station

Located on the Alcester Road with easy access to town centre, this attractive semi-detached house provides cosy bedrooms, each with a modern shower room, and filled with thoughtful extras. Breakfast is taken in an attractive front-facing dining room and a warm welcome is assured.

Facilities 3 en suite (1 fmly) ⊗ TVB tea/coffee Cen ht No coaches **Prices** S £25-£45; D £45-£70✳ LB **Parking** 5 **Notes** Closed 24-26 Dec 📵

◆◆◆

Salamander Guest House ◇

40 Grove Rd CV37 6PB ☎ 01789 205728 📠 01789 205728
e-mail p.delin@btinternet.com
web www.salamanderguesthouse.co.uk
Dir On A439 Stratford-Evesham road, opp Firs Garden

Facilities 7 rms (6 en suite) (1 pri facs) (5 fmly) (1 GF) ⊗ TVB tea/coffee ✘ Cen ht Dinner Last d 2wks prior **Prices** S £20-£37.50; D £40-£65 LB **Parking** 12

WARWICK   MAP 10 SP26
See also **Lighthorne**

★★★ Ⓐ Guest House

Austin House ◇

96 Emscote Rd CV34 5QJ
☎ 01926 493583 📠 01926 493679
e-mail mike.austinhouse96@ntlworld.com
Dir 0.75m NE of town centre on A445

Facilities 7 rms (5 en suite) (2 fmly) (1 GF) ⊗ in 5 bedrooms ⊗ in dining room ⊗ in lounges TVB tea/coffee ✘ Cen ht No coaches **Prices** S £25-£28; D £42-£50 **Parking** 6 **Notes** Closed Xmas

If you have to cancel a booking, let the proprietor know immediately

◆◆◆◆
Croft Guesthouse ◇

Haseley Knob CV35 7NL
☎ 01926 484447 📠 01926 484447
e-mail david@croftguesthouse.co.uk
web www.croftguesthouse.co.uk
Dir *4.5m NW of Warwick. Off A4177 into Haseley Knob, signed*

The friendly proprietors provide homely accommodation at this modern detached house, set in peaceful countryside and convenient for Warwick and the NEC, Birmingham. The conservatory-dining room overlooks large well-kept gardens where fresh eggs from home-reared chickens are used for memorable English breakfasts.

Facilities 7 rms (5 en suite) (2 pri facs) 2 annexe rms (1 en suite) (1 annexe pri facs) (2 fmly) (4 GF) ✆ TVB tea/coffee Cen ht TVL No coaches **Prices** S £35-£45; D £55-£65✳ **Parking** 9 **Notes** Closed Xmas wk

◆◆◆◆
Dockers Barn Farm

Oxhill Bridle Rd, Pillerton Hersey CV35 0QB
☎ 01926 640475 📠 01926 641747
e-mail jwhoward@onetel.com
web www.dockersbarnfarm.co.uk
Dir *A422 Stratford-upon-Avon to Banbury, left in Pillerton Priors to Pillerton Hersey, 1st right Oxhill Bridle Rd for 0.75m. Or M40 junct 12 onto B4451 to Pillerton Hersey, after 6m left by village seat onto Oxhill Bridle Rd*

Superbly located in an Area of Outstanding Natural Beauty, this former 18th-century threshing barn retains many original features including a wealth of exposed beams and flagstone floors. The bedrooms, one of which is in a converted a granary, are equipped with lots of thoughtful extras and the open-plan ground-floor areas are furnished with style and quality.

Facilities 2 en suite (1 fmly) (1 GF) ✆ TVB tea/coffee Cen ht No children 8yrs No coaches Garden hot-tub with hydrotherapy jets **Prices** S £38-£40; D £54-£59✳ **Parking** 9 **Notes** Closed Xmas 🈯

◆◆◆◆ 🈐
The Hare on the Hill

37 Coventry Rd CV34 5HN ☎ 01926 491366
e-mail prue@thehareonthehill.co.uk
web www.thehareonthehill.co.uk
Dir *On A429 Coventry Rd near Warwick station*

This well-furnished Victorian house is very convenient for the town and provides well-equipped and characterful bedrooms and a delightful lounge. The use of organic produce is of great importance here and excellent breakfasts are served around a large table in the hall, which retains its original mosaic floor. You can be sure of friendly and attentive service at all times.

Facilities 7 en suite (1 fmly) (1 GF) ✆ TVB tea/coffee Cen ht TVL No children 8yrs No coaches 🕪 Dinner Last d 9.30pm **Prices** S £65; D £80-£95✳ **Conf** Max 12 Del from £80 ✳ **Parking** 12 **Notes** Closed 24 Dec-3 Jan

WEST MIDLANDS

BALSALL COMMON MAP 10 SP27

◆◆◆ 🍺
Brickmakers Arms

307 Station Rd, Berkswell CV7 7EG ☎ 01676 533890
e-mail vix@thebrickmakers.net
Dir *Off A452 rdbt onto Station Rd, 1st pub on left*

This attractive old inn offers a good range of well-prepared food in the comfortably furnished bars and service is friendly and attentive. The bedrooms, next to the inn, are well furnished, and a continental breakfast is provided to the rooms.

Facilities 4 rms (2 GF) ✆ TVB tea/coffee 🐾 Cen ht No coaches Pool Table Dinner Last d 8.45pm **Prices** S fr £35; D fr £50✳ **Parking** 25

England

BIRMINGHAM
MAP 10 SP08

Premier Collection

◆◆◆◆◆

Westbourne Lodge

25-31 Fountain Rd, Edgbaston B17 8NJ
☎ 0121 429 1003 ▤ 0121 429 7436
e-mail info@westbournelodge.co.uk
web www.westbournelodge.co.uk
Dir 100yds from A456

Located on a quiet residential avenue close to the Hagley Rd, this well-maintained property provides a range of non-smoking, thoughtfully furnished bedrooms, some of which are on the ground floor. Breakfast, and dinner by arrangement, are served in the attractive dining room overlooking a pretty patio garden. A comfortable sitting room and lounge bar are also available.

Facilities 24 en suite (7 fmly) (3 GF) ⊗ in bedrooms ⊗ in dining room TVB tea/coffee Direct dial from bedrooms Licensed Cen ht TVL Dinner Last d 8pm **Prices** S £45-£55; D £65-£85✱ **Parking** 12 **Notes** Closed 24 Dec-1 Jan

◆◆◆◆

Black Firs

113 Coleshill Rd, Marston Green B37 7HT
☎ 0121 779 2727 ▤ 0121 779 2727
e-mail julie@b-firs.co.uk
web www.b-firs.co.uk
Dir M42 junct 6, A45 W, onto B4438, signs for Marston Green

This elegant house is set in immaculate gardens in a mainly residential area close to the NEC. Thoughtfully equipped bedrooms are complemented by smart shower rooms. Memorable breakfasts are served in an attractive dining room and a lounge is also available.

Facilities 6 en suite ⊗ TVB tea/coffee ✖ Cen ht TVL No coaches **Prices** S £59-£89; D £69-£89✱ **Conf** Max 14 **Parking** 6 **Notes** ⊗

◆◆◆◆

Olton Cottage Guest House ◇

School Ln, Old Yardley Village, Yardley B33 8PD
☎ 0121 783 9249 ▤ 0121 789 6545
e-mail olton.cottage@virgin.net
Dir 3.5m E of city centre. Off A45 onto A4040 to Yardley, 1m right onto Vicarage Rd, right onto Church Rd, left onto School Ln

A warm welcome is assured at this carefully renovated Victorian house, located in a peaceful residential area close to city centre. The cosy bedrooms contain a wealth of thoughtful extras and ground-floor areas include a cottage-style dining room and comfortable lounge overlooking the pretty enclosed garden.

Facilities 6 rms (2 en suite) (1 fmly) ⊗ TVB tea/coffee ✖ Cen ht TVL **Prices** S £24-£30; D £48-£50 **Parking** 2 **Notes** ⊗

◆◆◆

Tri-Star Hotel

Coventry Rd, Elmdon B26 3QR
☎ 0121 782 1010 & 782 6131 ▤ 0121 782 6131
Dir On A45

Located a short drive from airport, international station and the NEC, this owner-managed property provides a range of thoughtfully furnished bedrooms with modern bathrooms. The open-plan ground-floor area includes a bright, attractive dining room, a comfortable lounge bar and a separate conference room.

Facilities 15 en suite (3 fmly) (6 GF) ⊗ in 10 bedrooms ⊗ in dining room TVB tea/coffee ✖ Licensed Cen ht TVL Pool Table Games room Dinner Last d 8pm **Prices** S £49-£80; D £59-£90✱ **Conf** Max 20 Thtr 20 Class 10 Board 20 **Parking** 25

◆◆◆

Awentsbury Hotel

21 Serpentine Rd, Selly Pk B29 7HU
☎ 0121 472 1258 ▤ 0121 472 1258
e-mail ian@awentsbury.com
Dir A38 2m SW from city centre, left onto Bournbrook Rd, left & 1st right

This large Victorian house is in a quiet residential area within easy walking distance of the university and local restaurants. Bedrooms are simply furnished and many have showers en suite. Breakfast is served in the lounge-dining room, which overlooks the garden.

Facilities 16 rms (7 en suite) (1 fmly) (4 GF) ⊗ TVB tea/coffee Direct dial from bedrooms Cen ht Dinner Last d 7pm **Prices** S £42-£52; D £56-£64✱ **Parking** 12

◆◆◆

Cape Race

929 Chester Rd, Erdington B24 0HJ
☎ 0121 373 3085 ▤ 0121 373 3085
e-mail philjones@caperacehotel.co.uk
Dir On A452 between A38 & A5127, 2m from M6 junct 5

Located on a tree-lined avenue close to major roads and the city centre, this attractive detached house provides a range of homely bedrooms with modern bathrooms. Breakfast is served in a cosy, cottage-style dining room, and there is a lounge and bar.

Facilities 9 rms (8 en suite) ⊗ TVB tea/coffee Direct dial from bedrooms ✖ Licensed Cen ht TVL No coaches Dinner Last d 8pm **Prices** d fr £48 **Parking** 9

◆◆◆

La Caverna Restaurant & Hotel

2327-2329 Coventry Rd, Sheldon B26 3PG
☎ 0121 743 7917 & 07956 230020 ▤ 0121 722 3307
Dir M42 junct 6, A45 W, 2m to Texaco station

Please note that this establishment has recently changed hands. Well located for the city centre and airport, La Caverna provides modern bedrooms with practical facilities. Authentic Italian dishes, including a wide selection of fresh seafood, are served in the spacious restaurant. Two cosy bar-lounges are also available.

continued

Facilities 19 en suite (2 fmly) ⊗ in dining room STV TVB tea/coffee Direct dial from bedrooms ✖ Licensed Cen ht TVL Dinner Last d 10.30pm **Prices** S £45; D £65✳ **Conf** Max 40 **Parking** 19

◆◆◆

Central Guest House

1637 Coventry Rd, South Yardley B26 1DD
☎ 0121 706 7757 ▤ 0121 706 7757
e-mail mmou826384@aol.com
web www.centralguesthouse.com
Dir M42 junct 6, A45 W, past McDonalds & shops, on left

Located between the airport and city centre, this comfortable house is made a real home from home by the friendly and attentive proprietors. Bedrooms are equipped with plenty of thoughtful extras. Breakfast is served in an attractive dining room and you can relax in the attractive garden.

Facilities 5 en suite (1 fmly) ⊗ in dining room TVB tea/coffee Cen ht No coaches **Parking** 4 **Notes** ⊛

◆◆◆

The Old Barn Guest House

Birmingham Rd, Coleshill B46 1DP
☎ 01675 463692 ▤ 01675 466275
Dir M6 junct 4, A446 towards Coleshill, over 1st rdbt, left next rdbt onto B4114, house 0.5m on left

The friendly, family-run guest house offers en suite bedrooms and a self-contained chalet for families or larger groups. There is a licensed bar, a seasonal indoor heated swimming pool (April to September), and a large car park.

Facilities 9 en suite 2 annexe en suite (3 fmly) (6 GF) ⊗ in bedrooms ⊗ in dining room TVB tea/coffee ✖ Licensed Cen ht TVL ▷ Pool Table **Prices** S £40; D £68.50-£80✳ **Parking** 25 **Notes** Closed Xmas & New Year

◆◆

Rollason Wood Hotel ◇

130 Wood End Rd, Erdington B24 8BJ
☎ 0121 373 1230 ▤ 0121 382 2578
e-mail rollwood@globalnet.co.uk
Dir M6 junct 6, A5127 to Erdington, right onto A4040, 0.25m on left

Well situated for routes and the city centre, this owner-managed establishment is popular with contractors. The choice of three different bedroom styles suits most budgets, and rates include full English

breakfasts. Ground-floor areas include a popular bar, cosy television lounge and a dining room.

Facilities 35 rms (11 en suite) (5 fmly) ⊗ in 14 bedrooms ⊗ in dining room ⊗ in 1 lounge TVB tea/coffee Licensed Cen ht TVL Pool Table Dinner Last d 8.30pm **Prices** S £21.95-£39.95; D £36-£49.50✳ **Parking** 35

BIRMINGHAM   MAP 10 SP08
(NATIONAL EXHIBITION CENTRE)
See **Hampton-in-Arden & Solihull**

COVENTRY   MAP 10 SP37

◆◆◆◆

Acacia Guest House

11 Park Rd, Cheyles More CV1 2LE
☎ 024 7663 3622 ▤ 024 7663 3622
e-mail acaciaguesthouse@hotmail.com
Dir Off city ring road junct 6 to railway station & left

Located within easy walking distance of the train station and city centre, the Acacia provides a range of carefully furnished bedrooms, many of which are on the ground floor. A range of popular dishes is served in the attractive dining room and a cosy lounge bar is available.

Facilities 11 en suite (4 fmly) (6 GF) ⊗ in 6 bedrooms TVB tea/coffee ✖ Licensed Cen ht TVL Dinner Last d 8.30pm **Parking** 12 **Notes** ⊛

◆◆◆◆

Toffs Hotel

Wall Hill Road, Corley CV7 8AD
☎ 024 7633 2030 ▤ 024 7633 2255
e-mail stay@toffs-hotel.co.uk
web www.toffs-hotel.co.uk
Dir 4m NW of city centre. Off A45 onto Oak Ln signed Corley, along Bridle Brook Ln, right at T-junct right, Toffs 100yds on left

Toffs is set in an attractive rural setting close to road links to the city. Bedrooms have country views, and there are digital televisions in all rooms. There is a choice of lounges, a bar and also a games room.

Facilities 10 en suite (1 GF) ⊗ FTV TVB tea/coffee Cen ht No coaches ⚲ Pool Table ♬ **Prices** S £49.50-£59.50; D £65-£75✳ **Parking** 14

continued

England

COVENTRY continued

♦♦♦

Ashleigh House

17 Park Rd CV1 2LH ☎ 024 7622 3804 🖹 024 7622 3804

Dir *Off city ring road junct 6 to railway station & left*

A few minutes' walk from the mainline railway station and convenient for the city centre, this attractive, well-maintained house has the benefit of secure parking. Efficient and friendly service is provided and guests have the use of a bar and lounge

Facilities 10 en suite (5 fmly) TVB tea/coffee ✖ Licensed Cen ht TVL No coaches Dinner Last d 8.45pm **Parking** 12 **Notes** Closed 23 Dec-1 Jan 🐾

♦♦♦

Croft on the Green ◇

23 Stoke Green CV3 1FP
☎ 024 7645 7846 🖹 024 7645 7846
e-mail croftonthegreen@aol.com
web www.croftonthegreen.co.uk
Dir *1m E of city centre off A428 Binley Rd*

An impressive Victorian villa located within a conservation area close to city centre. A range of practically furnished bedrooms is provided and ground floor areas include a spacious attractive dining room, overlooking the pretty garden and a comfortable lounge bar.

Facilities 12 rms (9 en suite) (2 fmly) ⊘ TVB tea/coffee ✖ Licensed Cen ht TVL **Prices** S £26-£35; D £45-£55✱ **Parking** 12

♦♦♦ Ⓐ

Ashdowns Guest House ◇

12 Regent St CV1 3EP ☎ 024 7622 9280
Dir *A429 to city centre, over rdbt before ring road, 1st left onto Grosvenor Rd, right onto Westminster Rd, right onto Regent St*

Facilities 8 rms (7 en suite) (3 fmly) (1 GF) ⊘ TVB tea/coffee ✖ Cen ht TVL No children 13yrs **Prices** S £30-£35; D £50-£55 LB **Parking** 8 **Notes** Closed 22 Dec-1 Jan 🐾

HAMPTON-IN-ARDEN   MAP 10 SP28

♦♦♦♦

The Cottage Guest House

Kenilworth Rd B92 0LW ☎ 01675 442323 🖹 01675 443323
e-mail roger@cottage88.wanadoo.co.uk
Dir *2m SE of Hampton on A452*

A fine collection of antique memorabilia adorns the public areas of this delightful cottage, which is convenient for visiting the NEC, Birmingham, or exploring the area. Many guests return for the friendly and relaxing atmosphere and the attentive service. Freshly cooked traditional breakfasts, served in the cottage dining room, provide a good start to the day.

Facilities 9 en suite (2 GF) ⊘ in 5 bedrooms ⊘ in dining room TVB tea/coffee Cen ht TVL **Prices** S £35-£45; D £50-£65✱ **Parking** 14 **Notes** Closed Xmas 🐾

SOLIHULL   MAP 10 SP17

♦♦♦

The Gate House ◇

Barston Ln, Barston B92 0JN ☎ 01675 443274
e-mail enquiries@gatehousesolihull.co.uk
web www.enquiriesgatehousesolihull.co.uk
Dir *4m E of Solihull. Off B4101 or B4102 to Barston, on W side of village*

This elegant Victorian building stands in landscaped grounds with secure parking, and is within easy driving distance of the NEC, Birmingham. The resident proprietor is most welcoming and provides spacious comfortable accommodation. Breakfast is served in an elegant dining room overlooking the pretty gardens.

Facilities 4 rms (2 en suite) ⊘ TVB tea/coffee ✖ Cen ht TVL No children 5yrs No coaches **Prices** S £30-£45; D £60-£75✱ **Parking** 20 **Notes** 🐾

STOURBRIDGE   MAP 10 SO88

Ⓤ

The Willows B&B ◇

4 Brook Rd DY8 1NH ☎ 01384 396964 & 07967 557830
e-mail trickard@blueyonder.co.uk

At the time of going to press the rating for this establishment had not been confirmed. Please check the AA website www.theAA.com for up-to-date information.

Facilities 3 rms (2 en suite) (1 pri facs) (1 fmly) ⊘ TVB tea/coffee ✖ Cen ht TVL **Prices** D £25-£45✱ **Parking** 4 **Notes** 🐾

SUTTON COLDFIELD   MAP 10 SP19

♦♦♦♦

Windrush ◇

337 Birmingham Rd, Wylde Green B72 1DL
☎ 0121 384 7534 🖹 0121 384 7534
e-mail windrush59@hotmail.com
Dir *M6 junct 6, on A5127 to Sutton Coldfield, house before surgery*

A warm welcome is assured at this elegant Victorian house, located between the city centre and Sutton Coldfield. Bedrooms are filled with a wealth of thoughtful extras and the bathroom contains a modern shower. Memorable breakfasts are served in an elegant dining room.

Facilities 3 rms (1 en suite) ⊘ STV TVB tea/coffee ✖ Cen ht No children 16yrs No coaches **Prices** S £30-£35; D £50-£60✱ **Parking** 5 **Notes** Closed 19 Dec-3 Jan 🐾

continued

WIGHT, ISLE OF

ARRETON
MAP 05 SZ58

♦♦♦♦

Blandings
Horringford PO30 3AP
☎ 01983 865720 & 865331 📠 01983 862099
e-mail robin.oulton@horringford.com
web www.horringford.com/bedandbreakfast.htm
Dir S through Arreton (B3056), pass Stickworth Hall on your right, 300yds on left farm entrance signed Horringford Gardens. Take U turn to left, drive to end of poplar trees, turn right. Blandings on left

This recently built detached home stands in the grounds of Horringford Gardens. The bedroom has private access and has a decking area for warm summer evenings. Breakfast is a highlight with local island produce gracing the table.

Facilities 1 en suite (1 GF) ⊗ TVB tea/coffee Cen ht No coaches LB **Parking** 3 **Notes** ⊠

BEMBRIDGE
MAP 05 SZ68

♦♦♦♦ 🅰

Sea Change
22 Beachfield Rd PO35 5TN
☎ 01983 875558 📠 01983 875667
e-mail enquiries@seachangewight.co.uk
Dir From town centre (past harbour) onto Foreland Rd, left onto Lane End Rd, right onto Egerton Rd, left & right onto Beachfield Rd

Facilities 3 en suite ⊗ STV FTV TVB tea/coffee ✖ Cen ht No children 5yrs No coaches Riding stables nearby **Prices** S £32.50-£37.50; D £55-£65 **Parking** 4 **Notes** Closed Nov-Feb ⊠

BONCHURCH
MAP 05 SZ57

Premier Collection

♦♦♦♦♦

Winterbourne Country House
Bonchurch Village Rd PO38 1RQ ☎ 01983 852535
e-mail info@winterbournehouse.co.uk
Dir 1m E of Ventnor. Off A3055 into Bonchurch village

Please note that this establishment has recently changed hands. During his stay in 1849, Charles Dickens described Winterbourne as 'the prettiest place I ever saw in my life, at home or abroad'. Today, the comfortable bedrooms are all well equipped and differ in size, and include luxurious rooms with sea views. There are two lounges and a secluded terrace.

Facilities 7 rms (6 en suite) (1 pri facs) ⊗ in bedrooms ⊗ in dining room ⊗ in 1 lounge TVB tea/coffee Direct dial from bedrooms Licensed Cen ht TVL No children 6yrs No coaches ⚲ **Prices** S £50-£60; D £90-£160✶ **Parking** 8 **Notes** Closed Xmas

BRIGHSTONE
MAP 05 SZ48

🆄

Teapots
9 St Mary's Court, Main Rd PO30 4AH ☎ 01983 740998
At the time of going to press the rating for this establishment had not been confirmed. Please check the AA website www.theAA.com for up-to-date information.

Facilities 3 rms (1 pri facs) (1 fmly) ⊗ TVB tea/coffee ✖ Cen ht TVL No coaches **Parking** 2 **Notes** Closed Xmas wk ⊠

CHALE
MAP 05 SZ47

Premier Collection

♦♦♦♦♦♦

Chale Bay Farm
Military Rd PO38 2JF ☎ 01983 730950 📠 01983 730395
e-mail info@chalebayfarm.co.uk
Dir By A3055 Military Rd in Chale, near St Andrew's Church

Guests are assured of a warm welcome at Chale Bay Farm, situated on the National Trust Heritage Coastline, with spectacular coastal and rural views of The Needles and Tennyson Downs. All of the spacious bedrooms, many with their own private patios, are located on the ground floor. Hearty, home-cooked breakfasts are served at individual tables.

Facilities 8 en suite (2 fmly) (8 GF) ⊗ in 2 bedrooms ⊗ in area of dining room TVB tea/coffee ✖ Licensed Cen ht No coaches **Conf** Max 20 Class 20 **Parking** 50

♦♦♦♦ 🍴

The Old House
Gotten Manor, Gotten Ln PO38 2HQ
☎ 01983 551368 & 07746 453398
e-mail aa@gottenmanor.co.uk
web www.gottenmanor.co.uk
Dir 1m N of Chale. Off B3399 onto Gotten Ln (opp chapel), house at end

Located in countryside close to the coast, this 17th-century house has 18th- and 19th-century additions. Restoration has created comfortable, rustic bedrooms with antique bathtubs within the rooms. Comprehensive breakfasts using the finest ingredients are served in the cosy dining room, and there is a spacious lounge with an open fire.

Facilities 2 en suite ⊗ STV TVB tea/coffee ✖ Cen ht No children 12yrs No coaches ⚲ **Prices** D £70-£90 LB **Parking** 4 **Notes** ⊠

England

COWES

MAP 05 SZ49

◆◆◆◆

1 Lammas Close ◇

PO31 8DT ☎ 01983 282541 🖹 01983 282541

Dir 0.5m W of town centre. Off The Parade onto Castle Hill & Baring Rd, 3rd right onto Lammas Cl, 1st house on left

Yachts people will find kindred spirits in the very friendly Mr and Mrs Rising. Their modern accommodation looks across the Solent and is packed with useful extras, and an enjoyable hearty breakfast is served in the elegant dining room.

Facilities 1 rms (1 pri facs) FTV TVB tea/coffee Cen ht No children 12yrs No coaches Golf 9 **Prices** S £35-£40; D £60-£80✳ **Parking** 2 **Notes** 🄴

◆◆◆

Busigny Guest House

16 Castle Rd PO31 7QZ ☎ 01983 291919
e-mail sally@busignyhouse.co.uk

This comfortable family home has been extended to provide a wide rage of accommodation, and is a good base for touring the island, yachting fanatics and business travellers alike. Just a 5-minute walk from the harbour side, the establishment has bedrooms that are practical, bright and airy.

Facilities 3 en suite ⊘ TVB 🏋 Cen ht TVL No coaches **Parking** 1 **Notes** 🄴

◆◆◆

Windward House ◇

69 Mill Hill Rd PO31 7EQ
☎ 01983 280940 & 07771 573580 🖹 01983 280940
e-mail sueogston1@tiscali.co.uk

Dir A320 Cowes-Newport, halfway up Mill Hill Rd on right from floating bridge from E Cowes (Red Funnel Ferries)

A friendly atmosphere prevails at this comfortable Victorian house, located close to the centre of Cowes. Bedrooms are bright and neat, and downstairs there is a spacious lounge equipped with satellite television, video and music systems. Breakfast is served in a separate dining room around a shared table.

Facilities 6 rms (3 en suite) (2 fmly) (1 GF) ⊘ TVB tea/coffee Cen ht TVL No coaches ⚡ **Prices** S £20-£25; D £40-£60✳ **Parking** 4 **Notes** 🄴

EAST COWES

MAP 05 SZ59

◆◆◆◆

The Moorings Bed & Breakfast

3 Cambridge Rd PO32 6AE ☎ 01983 292779
e-mail themooringsbandb@hotmail.com

Dir By East Cowes Esplanade opp harbour breakwater

The bedrooms at this elegant Victorian terrace house all look over the Solent, providing a great view of the yachts and many events. Situated just off the Esplanade with ample free on-road parking, The Moorings is a 5-minute walk from the ferry and only a short drive from historic Osborne House.

continued

Facilities 4 rms (1 GF) ⊘ 🏋 TVL No children 14yrs No coaches
Prices S £33-£43; D £66-£86 **LB** **Notes** Closed Sep-May rs Jun-3 Sep 🄴

FRESHWATER

MAP 05 SZ38

◆◆◆◆

Seagulls Rest ◇

Colwell Chine Rd PO40 9NP ☎ 01983 754037 & 754929
e-mail selena.flint@btinternet.com
web www.seagullsrest.com

Dir A3054 W from Yarmouth, 2.5m at Colwell Bay Inn right for beach, 300yds on left

Situated just a stroll from the beach, this smart modern detached house has bright and spacious bedrooms, and there is a comfortable lounge. Breakfast and evening meals (by arrangement) are served in the cheery dining room.

Facilities 4 en suite (2 fmly) (1 GF) ⊘ TVB tea/coffee 🏋 Cen ht No coaches Dinner Last d 10am **Prices** S £27-£37; D £54✳ **LB** **Parking** 9 **Notes** 🄴

◆◆◆

Buttercup House

Camp Rd PO40 9HL ☎ 01983 752772
e-mail enquiries@buttercuphouse.co.uk

Situated on the quieter, western side of the island, this attractive stone house dates back in part to 1836. The atmosphere is relaxed and welcoming. Bedrooms are comfy and spacious and have a number of extra facilities. Breakfast is served around the dining room table, providing a tasty and satisfying start to the day, perhaps before setting off to explore on foot or bicycle.

Facilities 3 en suite (1 fmly) ⊘ FTV TVB tea/coffee Cen ht No children 8yrs No coaches **Prices** D £50-£60✳ **Parking** 3 **Notes** 🄴

GODSHILL

MAP 05 SZ58

Premier Collection

◆◆◆◆◆ 🏠 💝

Godshill Park Farm House (SZ537814)

Shanklin Rd PO38 3JF ☎ 01983 840781 Mrs Domaille
e-mail info@godshillparkfarm.co.uk
web www.godshillparkfarm.uk.com

Dir From ferry teminal towards Newport, onto A3020 & signs to Sandown, at Blackwater Corner right to Godshill, farm on right after Griffin pub

This delightful 200-year-old stone farmhouse is set in 270 acres of organic farmland with lakes and woodlands. Bedrooms, one with a four-poster bed and the other overlooking the millpond, are comfortably furnished with many extra facilities. Delicious full English breakfasts are served at one large table in the oak panelled Great Hall.

Facilities 2 en suite (1 fmly) ⊘ TVB Direct dial from bedrooms 🏋 Cen ht No children 8yrs Fishing 270 acres Mixed Dinner Last d 9am **Prices** S fr £50; D £80-£99✳ **Conf** Board 12 **Parking** 4 **Notes** 🄴

U

Arndale

High St PO38 3HH ☎ 01983 842003
Dir *On A3020, High Street*

At the time of going to press the rating for this establishment had not been confirmed. Please check the AA website www.theAA.com for up-to-date information.

Facilities 2 rms (2 pri facs) (2 fmly) (1 GF) ⊗ TVB ✖ Cen ht TVL No coaches Riding Dinner Last d 7pm **Prices** S £45-£50; D £55-£60✱ **Parking** 4 **Notes** ⊛

U

Koala Cottage

Church Hollow PO38 3DR ☎ 01983 842031

At the time of going to press the rating for this establishment had not been confirmed. Please check the AA website www.theAA.com for up-to-date information.

Facilities 3 en suite (3 pri facs) (3 GF) ⊗ STV TVB tea/coffee ✖ Cen ht TVL No children No coaches Sauna Spa **Parking** 6 **Notes** ⊛

NEWPORT   MAP 05 SZ58

◆◆◆◆ ⊜

Braunstone House Hotel

33 Lugley St PO30 5ET ☎ 01983 822994 ▤ 01983 526300
e-mail lugleys@isleofwight.com

Occupying a central location in Newport, this Georgian house has lots of charm. Bedrooms retain elegant proportions and ambience and are well provided with extras. The popular brasserie restaurant has a modern aspect and well-prepared and appealing cuisine.

Facilities 5 rms (4 en suite) (1 pri facs) ⊗ in bedrooms ⊗ in dining room ⊗ in 1 lounge TVB tea/coffee ✖ Licensed Cen ht Dinner Last d 9.30pm **Prices** S £65-£80; D £85-£95✱ **LB**

If the freedom to smoke or be in a non-smoking atmosphere is important to you, check the rules when you book

◆◆◆◆

Castle Lodge ◇

54 Castle Rd PO30 1DP
☎ 01983 527862 & 07854 742353 ▤ 01983 559030
e-mail castlelodge@hotmail.co.uk
Dir *Newport High St for 0.25m towards Monument on Green, Castle Rd on left.*

This well-presented establishment is located in a quiet residential area within close walking distance of the famous Carisbrooke Castle. A comfortable stay is assured with attractive and restful bedrooms together with a bright and airy dining room where a substantial breakfast can be enjoyed.

Facilities 3 rms (1 en suite) 5 annexe rms (2 en suite) (1 fmly) (5 GF) ⊗ TVB tea/coffee ✖ Cen ht No coaches **Prices** S £23-£26; D £50-£60✱ **Parking** 8 **Notes** ⊛

RYDE   MAP 05 SZ59

◆◆◆◆ ❧

Grange Farm B&B *(SZ528905)*

Grange Farm, Staplers Rd, Wootton PO33 4RW
☎ 01983 882147 Mrs Horne
e-mail grange@wightfarmholiday.co.uk
Dir *4m W of Ryde next to Butterfly World, Wootton Common*

The homely, family-run property is in a quiet rural setting between Newport and Ryde. The comfortable bedrooms and bathrooms are equipped with a large range of extra facilities, and there is also a cosy lounge. Substantial English breakfasts are served house-party style around one large table.

Facilities 2 en suite ⊗ TVB tea/coffee Cen ht TVL No children 4yrs 5 acres arable **LB Parking** 6

◆◆◆

Abingdon Lodge Hotel ◇

20 West St PO33 2QQ ☎ 01983 564537 ▤ 01983 566722
e-mail abingdonlodge@aol.com
Dir *0.4m SW of pier. Off A3054 onto West St*

Abingdon Lodge has a loyal clientele who return for the friendly hospitality. The en suite bedrooms come with useful extras, there is a conservatory bistro and bar, and you can enjoy the terrace in warmer months.

Facilities 15 en suite (2 fmly) (3 GF) ⊗ in 1 bedrooms ⊗ in dining room TVB tea/coffee Licensed Cen ht table tennis Dinner Last d 8.30pm **Prices** S £30-£35; D £50-£75✱ **LB Parking** 8

ST HELENS   MAP 05 SZ68

◆◆◆◆

Sheepstor Cottage ◇

West Green PO33 1XA ☎ 01983 873132
Dir *A3055 onto B3330 to the Green, left onto Field Ln, 3rd house on right*

A friendly welcome awaits you from the proprietor and her family of cats at this cosy cottage-style guest house. The attractive bedrooms are en suite, and freshly prepared breakfasts are served in the pleasant dining room, which looks over the surrounding countryside.

Facilities 2 en suite (1 fmly) ⊗ TVB tea/coffee ✖ Cen ht No coaches **Prices** S £30; D £60 **Notes** ⊛

SANDOWN MAP 05 SZ58

★★ Guest House

Culver Lodge

17 Albert Rd PO36 8AW ☎ 01983 403819 📄 01983 403819

Dir *In town centre off High St*

Culver Lodge is in a quiet residential area a short walk from the seafront and town centre. Bedrooms are well equipped and the public areas are spacious, including an attractive lounge, bar and games room. Outside, you can enjoy the sun in the pool and on the terrace.

Facilities 22 en suite (6 fmly) (4 GF) ⊗ in bedrooms ⊗ in dining room ⊗ in 1 lounge TVB tea/coffee 🇽 Licensed Cen ht TVL ⟋ Pool Table Bike Hire,Table Football/tennis Dinner Last d 7pm **Conf** Thtr 40 Class 40 Board 40 **Parking** 22

◆◆◆◆

Montague House Hotel ◇

109 Station Av PO36 8HD
☎ 01983 404295 📄 01983 403322
e-mail enquiries@montaguehousehotel.fsnet.co.uk

Dir *A3055 from Ryde to Sandown, onto Station Av following signs for beach*

This large, detached, late Victorian house is just a short walk from the town centre and seafront. The friendly hosts have recently renovated the property extensively to provide good quality, well-equipped modern accommodation. Separate tables are provided in the very attractive dining room and you can relax in either the comfortable lounge or the pleasant conservatory.

Facilities 11 rms (9 en suite) (2 fmly) (3 GF) ⊗ in bedrooms ⊗ in dining room TVB tea/coffee 🇽 Cen ht TVL No children 5yrs No coaches Dinner Last d 1pm **Prices** S £21-£26; D £50-£60✳ LB

◆◆◆◆

Carisbrooke House Hotel ◇

11 Beachfield Rd PO36 8NA
☎ 01983 402257 📄 01983 402257
e-mail carisbrookehotel@aol.com
Dir *Off High St onto Beachfield Rd, 200yds past Post Office on right*

Please note that this establishment has recently changed hands. Located within walking distance of the town centre and seafront, this delightful guest house provides a warm welcome and comfortable bedrooms. A full English breakfast is served at individual tables in the large dining room, and the bar leads to a cosy television lounge.

continued

Facilities 11 rms (9 en suite) (2 pri facs) (4 fmly) (3 GF) ⊗ in bedrooms ⊗ in dining room TVB tea/coffee Licensed Cen ht TVL **Prices** S £23-£28; D £50-£60 LB

◆◆◆◆

The Lawns ◇

72 Broadway PO36 9AA ☎ 01983 402549
e-mail lawnshotel@aol.com
web www.lawnshotelisleofwight.co.uk
Dir *On A3055 N of town centre*

This Lawns stands in grounds just a short walk from the beach, public transport and town centre. There is a comfortable lounge and bar, and evening meals (by arrangement) and breakfast are served in the bright dining room. Service is friendly and attentive, and the bedrooms are well equipped.

Facilities 16 rms (10 en suite) (5 fmly) (3 GF) ⊗ TVB tea/coffee 🇽 Licensed Cen ht TVL Dinner Last d noon **Prices** S £22-£32; D £44-£64✳ LB **Parking** 15

See advertisement on opposite page

◆◆◆

The Regent Hotel ◇

48 High St PO36 8AE ☎ 01983 403219 📄 01983 408135
Dir *In town centre*

You can expect a warm welcome at this seafront establishment. The lively cafe-bar overlooking the sea is open throughout the day; it offers an appetising menu (children eat free) and drinks can be enjoyed on the terrace. The non-smoking bedrooms are well equipped, and some have a sea view.

Facilities 12 en suite (2 fmly) (1 GF) ⊗ TVB tea/coffee Licensed Cen ht TVL ch fac Dinner Last d 9pm **Prices** S £25-£35; D £50-£70✳ **Conf** Max 25 **Parking** 2 **Notes** Closed Nov-Feb

◆◆◆

Chester Lodge Hotel

7 Beachfield Rd PO36 8NA ☎ 01983 402773
Dir *On B3395 S from seafront/High St*

This family-run property is within walking distance of the seafront and shops. The neat bedrooms include some on the ground floor with easier access, and there is a comfortable bar and lounge. Breakfast is served in the bright dining room.

Facilities 13 en suite (3 fmly) (4 GF) ⊗ in bedrooms ⊗ in dining room ⊗ in 1 lounge TVB tea/coffee 🇽 Licensed TVL Dinner Last d tbc **Parking** 14

England

◆◆◆
Corner House Hotel

1-5 Fitzroy St PO36 8HY ☎ 01983 403176

A warm welcome awaits you at this central, family-run property close to the shops, beach and pavilion. There is a choice of well-equipped bedrooms, and the licenced bar provides a relaxing atmosphere in the evening. Enjoyable meals are served in the dining room.

Facilities 24 en suite (9 fmly) (3 GF) ⊘ in dining room ⊘ in lounges TVB tea/coffee ✗ Licensed Cen ht No coaches Dinner Last d Breakfast **Parking** 3

◆◆◆
Fernside Hotel ◇

30 Station Av PO36 9BW
☎ 01983 402356 🖷 01983 403647
e-mail enquiries@fernsidehotel.co.uk
web www.fernsidehotel.co.uk
Dir Off Broadway opp Londis shop onto Station Av, Hotel on left

Located within walking distance of the town centre and sandy beaches, the family-run Fernside provides comfortable bedrooms with useful facilities. Some rooms are on the ground floor, as are the lounge and the bar, and a full English breakfast is served at individual tables.

Facilities 12 rms (11 en suite) (2 fmly) (3 GF) ⊘ TVB tea/coffee ✗ Cen ht TVL No coaches **Prices** S £22-£26; D £44-£52✳ LB **Parking** 6 **Notes** Closed Xmas & New Year

◆◆◆
The Philomel ◇

21 Carter St PO36 8BL ☎ 01983 406413 🖷 0870 094 0601
e-mail enquiries@philomel-hotel.co.uk
Dir A3055 into Sandown, 1st rdbt onto B3329 Avenue Rd, right onto Carter St

Please note that this establishment has recently changed hands. This charming establishment is close to the town centre and seafront. Bedrooms are well presented and there is a delightful garden, a television lounge, bar, and a pleasant dining room where hearty breakfasts are served. Evening meals are available by arrangement.

Facilities 9 rms (6 en suite) (1 fmly) ⊘ in bedrooms ⊘ in dining room TV2B tea/coffee ✗ Licensed TVL No coaches Dinner Last d 9am **Prices** S £19-£23; D £42-£50✳ **Parking** 5

◆◆◆ A
The Montpelier ◇

Pier St PO36 8JR ☎ 01983 403964 🖷 07092 212734
e-mail info@themontpelier.co.uk
web www.themontpelier.co.uk
Dir A3055 onto Melville St, over junct onto Pier St

Facilities 8 en suite (2 fmly) TVB tea/coffee ✗ No coaches **Prices** S £20-£26; D £40-£52✳ LB

◆◆
Lorron Hotel

90 Sandown Rd, Lake PO36 9JX
☎ 01983 403666 🖷 01983 403666
e-mail lorron-hotel@hotmail.com
Dir S of town centre on A3055, pass Lake working mens club, Lorron on left

The Lorron is within easy reach of Sandown, Shanklin and sandy beaches. You will receive a warm welcome, and there is a large bar/function room and a cosy lounge. Breakfast is served at individual tables in the spacious dining room.

Facilities 15 en suite (4 fmly) (6 GF) ⊘ TVB tea/coffee ✗ Licensed Cen ht TVL **Conf** Max 30 Thtr 30 Board 30 **Parking** 12 **Notes** Closed Dec-Jan rs 19 Apr-16 Jul

Lawns Hotel◆◆◆◆

72 Broadway, Sandown
Isle of Wight PO36 9AA

Tel: 01983 402549
Email: lawnshotel@aol.com
www.lawnshotelisleofwight.co.uk

Nick & Stella offer you a warm welcome to The Lawns Hotel, a fully licensed family run hotel, which is completely **non-smoking**, in the popular resort of Sandown, Isle of Wight. We have ample parking for 15 cars which is CCTV protected. The Hotel is situated in a pleasant area of Sandown, with all the amenities in walking distance including the Railway Station and bus stops to enable you to explore the rest of the Island during your stay. The award winning blue flag beach is just a 5 minutes stroll away.

SHANKLIN   MAP 05 SZ58

Premier Collection

◆◆◆◆◆

Foxhills

30 Victoria Av PO37 6LS
☎ 01983 862329 📠 01983 866666
e-mail info@foxhillshotel.co.uk
web www.foxhillshotel.co.uk
Dir *A3020 from Shanklin centre towards Newport, Foxhills 450yds on left*

An idyllic getaway for the weary business traveller and leisure guest alike, Foxhills offers something a little bit special. Individually styled rooms offer high levels of comfort and many thoughtful extras, and any stay here isn't complete without using the spa or having a treatment in the beauty salon.

Facilities 8 en suite (1 GF) ⊘ TVB tea/coffee Direct dial from bedrooms 🐾 Licensed Cen ht No children 16yrs No coaches Solarium Jacuzzi Health & beauty treatments **Prices** D £78-£98✳ **LB** **Conf** Max 25 Class 20 Board 12 **Parking** 13 **Notes** Closed 3-31 Jan

◆◆◆◆

Aqua Hotel ◇

17 The Esplanade PO37 6BN
☎ 01983 863024 📠 01983 864841
e-mail aa@aquahotel.co.uk
web www.aquahotel.co.uk
Dir *Off A3055 North Rd onto Hope Rd & seafront Esplanade*

This friendly, family-run establishment has been in the same hands since 1980. The bright and airy public areas include a spacious lounge bar, where live entertainment is available on most evenings, and the attractive Boaters Restaurant, which serves a selection of freshly made dishes. Many of the well-equipped bedrooms have sea views and some have a balcony.

Facilities 22 en suite (4 fmly) ⊘ in bedrooms ⊘ in dining room TVB tea/coffee 🐾 Licensed Cen ht Dinner Last d 4pm **Prices** S £30-£40; D £60-£86✳ **LB** **Notes** Closed 21 Dec-Jan

◆◆◆◆

Avenue Hotel

6 Avenue Rd PO37 7BG ☎ 01983 862746
e-mail info@avenuehotelshanklin.co.uk
Dir *A3055 from Sandown, through Lake, right onto Avenue Rd before x-rds lights*

This friendly, family-run guest house is in a quiet location just a 5-minute walk from the town centre and beaches. The well-equipped bedrooms are generally spacious, and there is a bar-lounge, a conservatory and a comfortable breakfast room. An attractive terraced courtyard lies to the rear.

Facilities 10 en suite (2 fmly) (2 GF) ⊘ in bedrooms ⊘ in dining room ⊘ in 1 lounge TVB tea/coffee 🐾 Licensed Cen ht No coaches **Prices** D £50-£60✳ **LB** **Parking** 6 **Notes** Closed Nov-Feb

◆◆◆◆

Bedford Lodge Hotel

4 Chine Av PO37 6AQ ☎ 01983 862416 📠 01983 868704
e-mail aa@bedfordlodge.co.uk
Dir *A3055 onto Chine Av, Lodge opp Tower Cottage Gardens*

A warm welcome is assured at this delightful property set in grounds close to the beach and town centre. Bedrooms are well equipped, and a full English breakfast is served at individual tables in the charming dining room. There is also a lounge and a bar.

Facilities 12 en suite (4 fmly) (3 GF) ⊘ in 9 bedrooms ⊘ in dining room ⊘ in lounges TVB tea/coffee 🐾 Licensed Cen ht TVL No children 3yrs No coaches **Prices** D £54-£80✳ **LB** **Parking** 8 **Notes** Closed Jan

◆◆◆◆

Belmont ◇

8 Queens Rd PO37 6AN ☎ 01983 867875 & 862864
e-mail enquiries@belmont-iow.co.uk
web www.belmont-iow.co.uk
Dir *Off High St onto Chine Av & Queens Rd, opp St Saviour's Church*

This Victorian residence stands in well-tended grounds a short walk from the picturesque old village and Shanklin Chine. Bedrooms are comfortable and some have distant sea views. There is also a spacious and well-proportioned lounge, a cosy bar and an elegant breakfast room overlooking the swimming pool.

continued

Belmont

Facilities 13 en suite (4 fmly) (2 GF) ⊗ in bedrooms ⊗ in dining room ⊗ in 1 lounge TVB tea/coffee Direct dial from bedrooms ✖ Licensed Cen ht No children 3yrs No coaches ⚡ Swimmimg pool heated late May-early Sep **Prices** S £27-£61; D £50-£82✳ **LB Parking** 9 **Notes** Closed Nov-Feb

Clifton Hotel ◇

1 Queens Rd PO37 6AN ☎ 01983 863015 ▤ 01983 865911 **e-mail** grahamsitton@hotmail.com
Dir *Off A3055 at lights, signed to the beach. Bear left signed Ventnor onto Queens Rd*

A warm welcome is assured at this delightful property, located on the clifftop with sweeping sea views. It is just a short walk from the cliff lift, beaches and Shanklin old village. Guests can enjoy the delightful flower-filled gardens, and there is a bar and two lounges. Evening meals are available.

Facilities 17 rms (14 en suite) (3 pri facs) (2 fmly) (1 GF) ⊗ TVB tea/coffee ✖ Licensed Cen ht No children 5yrs Lawn Dinner Last d at breakfast **Prices** S £25-£37.50; D £50-£80 **LB Parking** 16 **Notes** Closed Nov-Jan rs Feb & Oct

The Grange

9 Eastcliff Rd PO37 6AA ☎ 01983 867644 ▤ 01983 865537 **e-mail** hotel@thegrangebythesea.com
web www.thegrangebythesea.com
Dir *A3055 to Shanklin. The Grange is on right just before old village.*

This delightful house specialises in holistic breaks and enjoys a tranquil yet convenient setting in manicured grounds close to the seafront and village centre. Extensive refurbishment has resulted in

continued

beautifully presented bedrooms and spacious public areas. Breakfast is taken en famille (outside in fine weather).

Facilities 17 rms (14 en suite) (3 pri facs) (1 fmly) (6 GF) ⊗ TVB tea/coffee ✖ Licensed Cen ht TVL No coaches Sauna Treatment room **Prices** S £63; D £76-£90✳ **Parking** 8 **Notes** Civ Wed 100

See advertisement on this page

◆◆◆◆

Rowborough Hotel

32 Arthurs Hill PO37 6EX
☎ 01983 866072 & 863070 ▤ 01983 867703
Dir *1m S of Lake at junct of A3055 & A3056*

Located on the main road into town, this charming, family-run establishment provides comfortable bedrooms with many extra facilities. The non-smoking conservatory overlooks the garden, along with a lounge and a bar. Dinner is available by arrangement.

Facilities 9 en suite (2 fmly) (1 GF) ⊗ in bedrooms ⊗ in dining room ⊗ in 1 lounge TVB tea/coffee Licensed Cen ht TVL No coaches Dinner Last d 6.30pm **Parking** 5

England

SHANKLIN continued

♦♦♦♦

St Brelades Hotel

15 Hope Rd PO37 6EA ☎ 01983 862967
e-mail info@st-brelades-hotel.co.uk
Dir A3055 into Shanklin, left onto Hope Rd signed Esplanade

Please note that this establishment has recently changed hands. A warm welcome is assured at this delightful establishment, located within easy walking distance of the beach and town centre. The cosy bedrooms are brightly decorated and equipped with many useful extras. There is also a lounge and bar, and tasty evening meals are available by arrangement.

Facilities 15 en suite (4 fmly) ⊗ in 4 bedrooms ⊗ in dining room TVB tea/coffee Licensed Cen ht TVL Dinner Last d by prior notice **Parking** 10 **Notes** rs Nov-Feb

♦♦♦♦

The White House Hotel

Eastcliff Prom PO37 6AY
☎ 01983 862776 & 867904 ▤ 01983 865980
e-mail white_house@netguides.co.uk
web www.whitehouseshanklin.co.uk
Dir A3055 from Sandown, onto B3328 at lights, 2nd left, right at top of hill onto Park Rd

A warm welcome is assured at this delightful, family-run establishment on a clifftop location. Many of the well-equipped bedrooms have wonderful views of Shanklin Bay. Public areas include a sun lounge, bar, television lounge and a garden. Delicious home-cooked evening meals are available by arrangement.

Facilities 11 en suite (3 fmly) ⊗ in dining room TVB tea/coffee Direct dial from bedrooms ✘ Licensed Cen ht TVL No coaches Dinner Last d 5pm **LB Parking** 12 **Notes** Closed Nov

♦♦♦♦ A

The Richmond Hotel ◇

23 Palmerston Rd PO37 6AS ☎ 01983 862874
e-mail info@richmondhotel-shanklin.co.uk
Dir Off Shanklin High St at Conservative Club

Facilities 9 en suite (3 fmly) ⊗ TVB tea/coffee ✘ Licensed Cen ht TVL No coaches Dinner Last d 1pm **Prices** S £26-£28; D £52-£56✳ **LB Parking** 5

♦♦♦

Hayes Barton

7 Highfield Rd PO37 6PP
☎ 01983 867747 ▤ 01983 862104
e-mail williams.2000@virgin.net
Dir A3055 onto A3020 Victoria Av, 3rd left

Hayes Barton has the relaxed atmosphere of a family home and provides well-equipped bedrooms and a range of comfortable public areas. Dinner is available from a short selection of home-cooked dishes and there is a cosy bar lounge. The old village, beach and promenade are all within walking distance.

Facilities 9 en suite (4 fmly) (2 GF) ⊗ in bedrooms ⊗ in dining room ⊗ in lounges TVB tea/coffee Licensed Cen ht TVL No coaches Dinner Last d noon **Prices** S £50-£55; D £100-£110; (incl. dinner) ✳ **LB Parking** 10 **Notes** Closed Nov-Mar

♦♦♦

Mount House Hotel ◇

20 Arthurs Hill PO37 6EE
☎ 01983 862556 ▤ 01983 867551
e-mail graham.mounthouse@openworld.com
web www.netguides.co.uk/wight/mount.html
Dir A3055 towards Sandown, on outskirts of town on corner Clarence Rd

A warm welcome awaits you to this family-run property with a homely atmosphere. The bright bedrooms have modern facilities and neat bathrooms en suite, and home-cooked dinners and breakfast are served in the spacious dining room. The town centre, cliffs and beach are all within easy walking distance.

Facilities 9 en suite (2 fmly) (1 GF) ⊗ in dining room TVB tea/coffee Cen ht TVL No children 2yrs No coaches **Prices** S £22-£24; D £42-£46✳ **Parking** 5 **Notes** Closed 22 Dec-Jan

♦♦♦

Norfolk House ◇

19 Esp PO37 6BN ☎ 01983 863023
e-mail norfolkhouseiow@aol.com
Dir A3055 Sandown to Shanklin, at Arthur's Hill lights left onto Hope Rd, signed Esplanade

A warm welcome is assured at this friendly, family-run establishment, located on the seafront with the beach just across the road. Bedrooms are comfortable and have many extras. There is a bar, lounge and a garden, and the proprietors here set a convivial atmosphere.

Facilities 8 en suite (1 fmly) ⊗ TVB tea/coffee ✘ Licensed Cen ht Dinner Last d at breakfast **Prices** S £20-£33; D £40-£66✳ **LB**

If you book on bed, breakfast and evening meal terms, you may find that the tariff includes only the set menu

♦♦♦

Courtlands Hotel

15 Paddock Rd PO37 6PA
☎ 01983 862167 🖷 01983 863308
e-mail enquiries@courtlandshotel.co.uk
web www.courtlandshotel.co.uk
Dir *In town centre. Off A3020 Victoria Av onto Highfield Rd, 1st left*

Located just a short walk from High St and the old village, this welcoming establishment offers comfortable accommodation, a spacious bar area and a comfortable lounge. Breakfast is served in the dining room and dinner is available by arrangement.

Facilities 19 rms (18 en suite) (4 fmly) (6 GF) ⊘ in bedrooms ⊘ in dining room ⊘ in 1 lounge TVB tea/coffee ✖ Licensed Cen ht TVL ➤ Pool Table Dinner Last d 2pm **Prices** S £25-£29; D £50-£58✳ **LB Parking** 12 **Notes** Closed Jan-Feb

♦♦♦

Glendene Guest House

7 Carter Av PO37 7LQ ☎ 01983 862924
e-mail janderek@glendene48.freeserve.co.uk
Dir *A3020 into Shanklin, left onto St John's Rd & Brook Rd to Carter Av x-rds*

Located in the heart of Shanklin and within walking distance of the sandy beach, The Glendene offers comfortable accommodation within a friendly environment. Breakfast is served in the attractive dining room and a delicious home-cooked dinner is available by arrangement.

Facilities 7 rms (4 en suite) (2 fmly) ⊘ TVB tea/coffee TVL No coaches Dinner Last d at breakfast **Prices** S £19-£21; D £42-£46✳ **LB Parking** 5

♦♦♦

Perran Lodge

2 Crescent Rd PO37 6DH
☎ 01983 862816 🖷 01983 862816
e-mail bookings@bethnabas.co.uk
web www.bethnabas.co.uk
Dir *Off A3055 onto Queens Rd, up hill onto Crescent Rd, Lodge on left*

Expect a warm welcome at this friendly, family-run guest house, which is just a short walk from the beach and town centre. The pleasant bedrooms have a good range of extra facilities, and the public areas include a dining room and a smart lounge bar with a dance floor.

Facilities 23 en suite (7 fmly) (5 GF) ⊘ TVB tea/coffee ✖ Licensed Cen ht Dinner Last d previous day **Prices** S £18-£35; D £36-£70✳ **Parking** 8

♦♦♦

Shoreside Hotel

39 The Esplanade PO37 6BG ☎ 01983 863169
e-mail info@shoresidehotel.co.uk
Dir *Off A3055 onto Hope Rd to seafront Esplanade*

You are assured of a warm welcome at this family-run seafront establishment, just a 10-minute walk from the town centre via the cliff lift. Ground-floor areas are open to the public, and include a bar and cafe-style restaurant where meals are available all day.

Facilities 16 en suite (5 fmly) ⊘ in bedrooms ⊘ in dining room ⊘ in 1 lounge TVB tea/coffee ✖ Licensed Cen ht Dinner Last d 9.30pm **LB Parking** 12 **Notes** Closed Nov-Mar

♦♦♦

The Triton Hotel

23 Atherley Rd PO37 7AU
☎ 01983 862494 🖷 01983 861281
e-mail jackie@tritonhotel.freeserve.co.uk

Located within easy walking distance of the town centre, Shanklin old village and the seafront, this charming and friendly guest house provides well-appointed rooms, a lounge and a bar. Tasty home-cooked dinners are available by arrangement.

Facilities 17 rms (9 en suite) (4 fmly) ⊘ in 2 bedrooms ⊘ in dining room ⊘ in 1 lounge TVB tea/coffee Licensed Cen ht TVL Dinner Last d 1pm **Prices** S £25-£30; D £50-£60✳ **LB**

TOTLAND BAY   MAP 05 SZ38

♦♦♦♦

The Hoo

Colwell Rd PO39 0AB ☎ 01983 753592 🖷 01983 753592
e-mail jerjohnston@btinternet.com
Dir *From Yarmouth ferry right onto A3054, 2.25m enter Colwell Common, The Hoo on corner Colwell & Warden Rd*

Located close to the port and beaches, this friendly family home provides a peaceful setting. The house has many Japanese features and guests are asked to wear slippers. The spacious bedrooms are impressively equipped and comfortably furnished. English breakfast is most enjoyable and is served overlooking the attractive gardens.

Facilities 3 rms (1 en suite) (2 fmly) ⊘ in bedrooms ⊘ in dining room TVB tea/coffee Cen ht No children 5yrs No coaches **Prices** S £25-£44; D £40-£77✳ **Parking** 1 **Notes** Closed 25-26 Dec & 2 Jan-3-Mar

♦♦♦ 🅰

Highdown Inn

Highdown Ln PO39 0HY
☎ 01983 752450 🖷 01983 752450
e-mail highdowninn@hotmail.com
web www.highdowninn.com
Dir *B3322 to Alum Bay new road, 1m left, doubling back onto Alum Bay old road, follow to Highdown Inn*

Facilities 3 en suite ⊘ in bedrooms ⊘ in dining room ⊘ in 1 lounge TVB tea/coffee Licensed Cen ht Childrens play area Dinner Last d 8.30pm **Parking** 30

🅄

The Golf House

Alum Bay New Rd PO39 0JA ☎ 01983 753293
e-mail sue_blakemore@btinternet.com
Dir *Totland B3322, at War Memorial rdbt take 2nd exit onto Church Hill 1m*

At the time of going to press the rating for this establishment had not been confirmed. Please check the AA website www.theAA.com for up-to-date information.

Facilities 2 rms (2 pri facs) ⊘ TV1B tea/coffee ✖ Cen ht TVL No children 8yrs No coaches **Prices** S £30-£35; D £60-£65✳ **LB Parking** 3

England

VENTNOR MAP 05 SZ57

★★★★ Guest Accommodation

St Maur

Castle Rd PO38 1LG
☎ 01983 852570 & 853645 ▤ 01983 852306
e-mail sales@stmaur.co.uk
Dir *Exit A3055 at the end of Park Ave onto Castle Rd, premises 150 yards on the left*

Guests will find a warm welcome awaits them at this Victorian villa, which is pleasantly and quietly located in an elevated position overlooking the bay. The well-equipped bedrooms are traditionally decorated whilst public areas include a spacious lounge and cosy residents' bar. The gardens here are a delight.

Facilities 11 en suite (2 fmly) ⊗ STV TVB tea/coffee ✗ Licensed Cen ht No children 5yrs No coaches Dinner Last d 7pm
Prices D £76-£110 **LB Parking** 11 **Notes** Closed Dec

★★★ 🅰 Farm House

Little Span Farm

Rew Ln, Wroxall PO38 3AU
☎ 01983 852419 ▤ 01983 852419
e-mail info@spanfarm.co.uk
web www.spanfarm.co.uk
Dir *2m N of Ventnor. B3327 to Wroxall, at Post Office onto West St & Rew Ln, up hill round sharp bend, farm 300yds on right from bend*

Facilities 4 en suite ⊗ STV TVB tea/coffee Cen ht No coaches **LB Parking** 4 **Notes** 🚭

See advertisement on opposite page

Premier Collection

♦♦♦♦♦

Winterbourne Country House

Bonchurch Village Rd PO38 1RQ ☎ 01983 852535
e-mail info@winterbournehouse.co.uk
For full entry see **Bonchurch**

♦♦♦♦

Lake Hotel

Shore Rd, Bonchurch PO38 1RF ☎ 01983 852613
e-mail enquiries@lakehotel.co.uk
Dir *Opp Bonchurch village pond*

A warm welcome is assured at this friendly, family-run property set in 2 acres of well-tended gardens close to the sea. Bedrooms are equipped with modern facilities and the elegant public rooms offer a high standard of comfort. A choice of menus is offered at dinner and breakfast.

Facilities 11 en suite 9 annexe en suite (7 fmly) (4 GF) ⊗ in bedrooms ⊗ in dining room ⊗ in 1 lounge TVB tea/coffee Licensed Cen ht TVL No children 3yrs No coaches Dinner Last d 6.30pm **Prices** S £40-£55; D £70-£85 **LB Parking** 20 **Notes** rs Nov-Feb 🚭

♦♦♦♦

The Old Rectory

Ashknowle Ln, Whitwell PO38 2PP ☎ 01983 731242
e-mail rectory@ukonline.co.uk
Dir *Next to church at S end of Whitwell*

Located in the centre of the village of Whitwell, this fine stone Victorian country house stands in grounds and was built nearly 150 years ago as the rectory to the neighbouring church. Now fully restored and refurbished this delightful property provides spacious bedrooms, which are equipped with numerous extra facilities.

Facilities 3 en suite ⊗ TVB tea/coffee Direct dial from bedrooms ✗ Cen ht TVL No children 14yrs No coaches **Prices** S £40-£50; D £60-£72✳ **LB Parking** 12

♦♦♦♦

Burwynns Guest House

9 Steephill Rd PO38 1UF ☎ 01983 854172 ▤ 01983 854172
e-mail burwynns@amserve.com
Dir *A3055 from Ventnor towards St Lawrence, house 0.25m on the right beyond Ventnor Park*

Burwynns Guest House, located 0.5m from the centre of Ventnor, provides comfortable accommodation within a homely and friendly environment. Breakfast is served in the pleasantly appointed dining room, which overlooks the rear garden and swimming pool, and delicious home-cooked dinners are available by arrangement. There is also a quiet lounge for relaxation.

Facilities 3 en suite (1 fmly) ⊗ TVB tea/coffee ✗ Cen ht TVL No children 10yrs No coaches ⚲ Dinner Last d 3pm **Prices** S £35-£37; D £50-£64✳ **LB Parking** 3 **Notes** 🚭

♦♦♦♦

Cornerways Hotel ◇

39 Madeira Rd PO38 1QS
☎ 01983 852323 ▤ 01983 852323
e-mail cornerwayshotel@aol.com
Dir *Off Trinity Rd (south coast road) near Trinity Church onto Madeira Rd, house on left*

This guest house is quietly located between Bonchurch and the town centre, yet is only a stroll from the beach, shops and many places of interest. Bedrooms are comfortable and well equipped and there is a lounge and cosy bar. Full English breakfasts are served at individual tables.

Facilities 9 en suite (3 fmly) (1 GF) ⊗ in bedrooms ⊗ in dining room TVB tea/coffee ✗ Licensed Cen ht TVL No children 5yrs No coaches Dinner Last d 10.30am **Prices** S £26-£33; D £52-£66 **LB Parking** 6 **Notes** 🚭

◆◆◆◆
Gothic View
Town Ln, Chale Gn PO38 2JS ☎ 01983 551120
e-mail info@gothicview.co.uk

A warm welcome is guaranteed at this charming converted Victorian chapel. Situated in a village, this property has picturesque views, and is only a short drive from many beaches and tourist attractions. Bedrooms offer a high level of comfort and quality with many thoughtful extras. An appetising breakfast can be enjoyed overlooking the attractive garden and expertly cooked evening meals are available by arrangement.

Facilities 3 rms (1 en suite) (2 pri facs) (3 GF) ⊗ TVB tea/coffee ✻ Cen ht No coaches Dinner Last d 8.30pm **Parking** 1 **Notes** ⊛

◆◆◆◆
The Harbour View Hotel
Esp PO38 1TA ☎ 01983 852285 ▤ 01983 856630
e-mail enquiries@harbourviewhotel.co.uk
web www.harbourviewhotel.co.uk
Dir Opp harbour

Located on an elevated position with spectacular sea views, this delightful Victorian property next to the Winter Gardens provides well-equipped and comfortable bedrooms. Public areas include a conservatory dining room, lounge, cosy bar, small garden and patio area, all with sea views.

Facilities 10 en suite ⊗ STV TVB tea/coffee Direct dial from bedrooms ✻ Licensed Cen ht TVL No children No coaches ⚲ **Prices** S £48; D £72-£94✳ **Conf** Class 30 **Parking** 8 **Notes** Closed 5 Jan-1 Feb

◆◆◆◆
Horseshoe Bay House
Shore Rd PO38 1RN ☎ 01983 856800
e-mail howard@horseshoebayhouse.com
web www.horseshoebayhouse.co.uk
Dir Turn off A3055 to Bonchurch, B&B opposite pond.

Set at the very edge of the beach in the pretty village of Bonchurch, this super place offers spacious accommodation in a memorable location. Hospitality is friendly and the proprietors here are attentive hosts. Bedrooms are smartly styled in tranquil colours and comfortably appointed, most rooms enjoy the spectacular views. Breakfast offers a good range of choice and provides and excellent start to the day.

Facilities 5 rms (4 en suite) (1 pri facs) (1 GF) ⊗ TVB tea/coffee Licensed Cen ht TVL No children 8yrs No coaches **Prices** S £35-£50; D £55-£75✳ **LB** **Parking** 6

If you have to cancel a booking, let the proprietor know immediately

◆◆◆
Brunswick House
Victoria St PO38 1ET ☎ 01983 852656 ▤ 01983 852656
e-mail brunswickhousehotel@btinternet.com
Dir On A3055 one-way system round the town, before Leslie's Garage on left

Located in the centre of town yet only a short walk from the beach and various local attractions, this property offers comfortable rooms with coordinated decor. A small outdoor sitting area is available. Guests can choose from a selection of evening meals, served, as are the hearty English breakfasts, at individual tables.

Facilities 7 en suite (1 fmly) ⊗ in bedrooms ⊗ in area of dining room ⊗ in 1 lounge TVB tea/coffee ✻ Licensed Cen ht Dinner Last d 9.30pm **Conf** Thtr 20 Class 20 Board 16

◆◆◆
Flat 1 'Fawlty Towers'
1 Marine Pde PO38 1JN ☎ 01983 852115
e-mail looney_june@hotmail.com
Dir From Ventnor seafront take foot path up by Hongshoremans Museum. End property at top of steps

This friendly guest house enjoys fine sea views from its hillside location and is located within a short walk of the seafront and restaurants. The accommodation is cosy and thoughtfully equipped and a hearty breakfast can be enjoyed on the patio in fine weather.

Facilities 1 en suite (2 fmly) (1 GF) ⊗ TVB tea/coffee Cen ht No children 12yrs **Prices** d fr £50✳ **Notes** ⊛

England

VENTNOR continued

♦♦♦

Llynfi Hotel ◇

23 Spring Hill PO38 1PF
☎ 01983 852202 ▤ 01983 852202
e-mail info@llynfihotel.co.uk
Dir A3055 from Shanklin, right before sharp S-bend onto St Boniface
Rd, left onto Spring Hill

You are assured of a warm welcome at this family-run property,
located just a short way up the hill from the main street. Bedrooms
are bright and comfortably appointed, and the extensive public areas
include a conservatory with an adjoining terrace, and a cosy bar and a
dining room. Dinner is available by arrangement.

Facilities 9 rms (8 en suite) (1 pri facs) (5 fmly) ⊘ in 3 bedrooms
⊘ in dining room ⊘ in lounges TVB tea/coffee ✖ Licensed Dinner
Last d 4pm **Prices** S £28-£30; D £56-£60✳ **LB Parking** 7

♦♦♦

Picardie Hotel

Esp PO38 1JX ☎ 01983 852647 ▤ 01983 852647
e-mail postmaster@picardie.f9.co.uk
web www.picardie.f9.co.uk

Superbly situated on the beachfront, this early-Victorian villa is
furnished with an abundance of memorabilia, which gives the
property a homely atmosphere full of character. Guests can enjoy tasty
English breakfasts in the pleasant dining room, with dinners available
by arrangement. There is also a sitting room with sea views.

Facilities 20 rms (10 en suite) (10 pri facs) (2 fmly) ⊘ TV10B tea/coffee
✖ Licensed Lift Cen ht TVL ⚲ Dinner Last d 7pm **Prices** S £35-£55;
D £65-£95✳ **LB Conf** Max 30 Class 15 Board 15 Del from £85 ✳
Notes rs Nov/Dec, Feb ⊜

[U]

Will-O-Wisp Bed & Breakfast

Castle Rd, Wroxall PO38 3DU
☎ 01983 854241 & 07890 137512
e-mail hazeandkeith@wisp.wanadoo.co.uk
web www.will-o-wisp.co.uk
Dir B3323 towards Ventnor leads to Wroxall, left at St John's Church
onto Castle Rd

At the time of going to press the rating for this establishment had not
been confirmed. Please check the AA website www.theAA.com for up-
to-date information.

continued

Facilities 1 en suite (3 GF) ⊘ TVB tea/coffee ✖ Cen ht No children
Prices d fr £44✳ **Parking** 3 **Notes** ⊜

WOOTTON
MAP 05 SZ59

♦♦

Island Charters ◇

Sea Urchin, 26 Barge Ln PO33 4LB
☎ 01983 882315 ▤ 01983 882315

The accommodation here is in two adjacent converted static barges.
Cabins vary in size, and some have limited facilities. There is a saloon
area with a television and a large well-equipped galley with sun deck
where guests can enjoy refreshments. Breakfast is served in the galley
on board one of the boats.

Facilities 5 rms (1 fmly) ⊘ TV2B ✖ Cen ht TVL No coaches lake
fishing, canoeing **Prices** S £20; D £40✳ **LB Parking** 10 **Notes** Closed
Nov-Mar ⊜

WILTSHIRE

AMESBURY
MAP 05 SU14

♦♦♦♦

Mandalay

15 Stonehenge Rd SP4 7BA
☎ 01980 623733 ▤ 01980 626642
Dir 500yds W of town centre, off High St onto Church St &
Stonehenge Rd

Quietly located on the edge of the town, yet within easy reach of
Stonehenge, the cathedral, and this delightful property provides
individually decorated rooms. Freshly cooked breakfasts are served in
the pleasant breakfast room, which overlooks the landscaped gardens.

Facilities 5 en suite (2 fmly) ⊘ TVB tea/coffee ✖ Cen ht TVL
No coaches **Prices** S £40-£50; D £55-£65 **Parking** 5

♦♦♦♦

Park House Motel

SP4 0EG ☎ 01980 629256 ▤ 01980 629256
Dir Junct A303 & A338

This family-run establishment offers a warm welcome and is extremely
convenient for the A303. Bedrooms are practically equipped with
modern facilities and come in a variety of sizes. There is a large dining
room where dinner is served during the week, and a cosy bar in
which to relax.

continued

Facilities 30 rms (27 en suite) (1 pri facs) (9 fmly) (25 GF) ⊗ in 5 bedrooms ⊗ in dining room ⊗ in lounges STV TVB tea/coffee Licensed Cen ht TVL Dinner Last d 8.30pm **Prices** S £35-£52; D £66✶ **Parking** 40

See advertisement on this page

♦♦♦

Catkin Lodge

93 Countess Rd SP4 7AT
☎ 01980 624810 & 622139 🖹 01980 622139
e-mail info@catkinlodge.fsnet.co.uk
web www.catkinlodge.fsnet.co.uk
Dir *A303 at Amesbury onto A345 Marlborough road, 400yds on left*

Popular for business and leisure, Catkin Lodge is close to Stonehenge and offers off-road parking. The three bedrooms, including two on the ground floor, offer good levels of comfort and can accommodate children if required. The artwork of the talented proprietor is displayed around the property, adding further interest.

Facilities 3 rms (2 en suite) (1 fmly) (2 GF) ⊗ TVB tea/coffee ✻ Cen ht No children 5yrs No coaches **Parking** 7 **Notes** ⊠

ASHTON KEYNES   MAP 05 SU09

♦♦♦♦

Wheatleys Farm *(SU049934)*

High Rd SN6 6NX
☎ 01285 861310 🖹 01285 861310 Ms Freeth
e-mail gill@wheatleysfarm.co.uk
web www.wheatleysfarm.co.uk
Dir *In village centre*

Wheatleys Farm is a modern house surrounded by attractive gardens, part of a working farm within the Cotswold Water Park. The friendly owners milk 200 cows and rear the offspring. The bedrooms have numerous thoughtful extras, and the good farmhouse breakfast certainly prepares you for the day ahead.

Facilities 2 en suite (1 fmly) ⊗ TVB tea/coffee ✻ Cen ht TVL 500 acres Dairy **Prices** S £35-£40; D £50-£60✶ **Parking** 6 **Notes** ⊠

♦♦♦

The Firs ◇

High Rd SN6 6NX ☎ 01285 860169 & 07989 857435
e-mail thefirsbb@yahoo.co.uk
Dir *Off A419 towards Ashton Keynes, turn left after 3m at junct, after 300yds then take left fork*

Situated in a charming village, close to the Thames walkway, this friendly home offers comfortable accommodation. There is a pleasant lounge and an attractive garden. The house is adjacent to a pleasant country pub where evening meals are available. Breakfast is served at the kitchen table, fresh from the stove.

Facilities 4 rms (1 en suite) (1 GF) ⊗ in 1 bedrooms TVB tea/coffee Cen ht TVL No coaches **Prices** S £30-£32; D £45-£55✶ **Parking** 4 **Notes** rs Nov-Mar ⊠

AVEBURY   MAP 05 SU16

★★ Inn

Red Lion

High St SN8 1RF ☎ 01672 539266
e-mail 7928@greeneking.co.uk
Dir *From A4 head towards Avebury, located in centre of Avebury Stone Circle*

The 16th-century thatched inn stands inside the villages famous prehistoric stone circle

Facilities 3 rms (2 en suite) (1 pri facs) (1 fmly) TVB tea/coffee ✻ Dinner Last d 5pm **Prices** S £40; D £80✶ **Parking** 25

BERWICK ST JAMES   MAP 05 SU03

♦♦♦♦

Mill House

SP3 4TS ☎ 01722 790331 🖹 01722 790753
Dir *From A303 or A36 onto B3083 signed Berwick St James, through village, past Boot Inn, just before sharp bend.*

Set in peaceful grounds within a pretty village, Mill House is a good base for touring Wiltshire, Somerset and Dorset. Stonehenge is just a 3m hike over pleasant countryside. The hosts are keen to share their home and offer spacious public areas and delightful gardens. A traditional English breakfast is served in the smart dining room, which is adorned with family photographs.

Facilities 6 rms (4 en suite) (1 pri facs) (1 fmly) ⊗ TVB tea/coffee ✻ Cen ht TVL No children 5yrs No coaches Fishing **Prices** S £35-£50; D £70✶ **Parking** 6 **Notes** ⊠

England

BOSCOMBE

MAP 05 SU23

◆◆◆◆ 🏛

The Close

Tidworth Rd SP4 0AB ☎ 01980 611989
e-mail theclose@moocowco.com
web www.moocowco.com/theclose
Dir Off A338 towards Boscombe Church. The Close is next to church

This 17th-century Grade II listed former farmhouse and family home, offers charm, style and comfort. Suited to both business and leisure, the spacious bedrooms are carefully furnished and the many thoughtful extras make your stay memorable. There is a relaxing drawing room, where a log fire burns in the inglenook fireplace, creating an inviting atmosphere for those cooler evenings and during warmer weather, French doors open onto the pretty cottage garden. The breakfast menu offers a varied and interesting choice of freshly prepared dishes, featuring local produce and is served around a communal table in the smart dining room.

Facilities 2 en suite (1 fmly) ⊛ TVB tea/coffee ✖ No coaches
Parking 2 **Notes** Closed 24-26 Dec 🈯

BOX

MAP 04 ST86

Premier Collection

◆◆◆◆◆ 🏛

Spinney Cross

Lower Kingsdown Rd, Kingsdown SN13 8BA
☎ 01225 742019 & 461518
e-mail dotcom@spinneycross.co.uk
Dir from Bath A4 towards Chippenham, at Bathford take A353 to Bradford on Avon. Under railway bridge, left at Crown PH uphill to Kingsdown, left at Swan PH bear right at bottom of hill, Spinney Cross 500yds on left

A warm welcome is assured at this delightful home set in a wonderful location in the quiet village of Kingsdown. The views are a pleasure to behold. Bedrooms are spacious and attractively styled; all have their own private access to the patio and garden. A varied range of tasty options is available at breakfast.

Facilities 3 rms (2 en suite) (1 fmly) (3 GF) ⊛ in bedrooms
⊛ in dining room ⊛ in lounges TVB tea/coffee ✖ Cen ht No coaches
Parking 6

Premier Collection

◆◆◆◆◆

White Smocks

Ashley SN13 8AJ ☎ 01225 742154 📄 01225 742212
e-mail whitesmocksashley@hotmail.com
Dir A4 1m W of Box turn opp The Northy, at T-junct White Smocks right of thatched cottage

Quietly located in the pleasant village of Ashley, and just a short drive from Bath with its many attractions, White Smocks offers a relaxing escape where guests are encouraged to enjoy the pleasant garden in the summer, real fires in the winter and the jacuzzi all year round. The two bedrooms and bathrooms are immaculately presented and comfortably furnished. Guests are also welcome to use the lounge.

Facilities 2 en suite (1 fmly) ⊛ TVB tea/coffee ✖ Cen ht TVL
No coaches **Parking** 3

◆◆◆◆

Lorne House

London Rd SN13 8NA ☎ 01225 742597
e-mail lornehouse2003@yahoo.co.uk
Dir On A4 in village, E of High St

This attractive house was once the home of Reverend Audry, author of the Thomas the Tank Engine stories. The rooms are comfortable and well-equipped, and decorated with bright and pleasant colours and fabrics. The attentive proprietors offer a good choice of freshly prepared dishes at breakfast.

Facilities 4 en suite (1 fmly) ⊛ TVB tea/coffee ✖ Cen ht TVL
No coaches Hot tub **Prices** S £35-£45; D £55-£65✳ **Parking** 6

◆◆◆

The Hermitage

Bath Rd SN13 8DT ☎ 01225 744187 📄 01225 743447
e-mail hermitage@telecall.co.uk
Dir On A4 at W end of village

This 16th-century house is located in a pleasant village 5m from Bath. The spacious bedrooms are comfortably furnished, with two rooms in a small adjacent cottage. Breakfast is served in the dining room. There is also a lounge area, and delightful gardens with a heated swimming pool.

continued

Hermitage

Facilities 3 en suite 2 annexe en suite (2 fmly) (1 GF) ⊘ in 3 bedrooms ⊘ in dining room ⊘ in lounges TVB tea/coffee ✖ Cen ht No coaches ⛏ **Prices** S £35-£45; D £55-£65✳ **Parking** 6 **Notes** Closed 22 Dec-6 Jan 🐾

BRADFORD-ON-AVON

MAP 04 ST86

Premier Collection

◆◆◆◆◆ 🏠

Bradford Old Windmill
4 Masons Ln BA15 1QN
☎ 01225 866842 📄 01225 866648
e-mail aa@bradfordoldwindmill.co.uk
Dir *Off A363 300yds N of town centre. Driveway on E side of Masons Ln, no sign or number*

This unique property has been restored to retain many of the original features. Bedrooms are individually decorated and include a number of interesting options such as a round room, a waterbed or a suite with minstrels' gallery. An extensive breakfast menu, featuring local and organic products whenever possible, offers a range of alternatives from devilled mushrooms or passion fruit pancakes to the more traditional choices. A comfortable lounge is also available.

Facilities 3 en suite ⊘ TVB tea/coffee ✖ Cen ht No children 6yrs Dinner Last d previous day **Prices** S £59-£99; D £79-£109 **Parking** 3 **Notes** Closed Nov-Feb rs Mar-Oct

Premier Collection

◆◆◆◆◆ ◉ ⊜

Widbrook Grange
Trowbridge Rd, Widbrook BA15 1UH
☎ 01225 864750 & 863173 📄 01225 862890
e-mail stay@widbrookgrange.com
web www.widbrookgrange.com
Dir *1m SE of Bradford. On A363 diagonally opp Bradford Marina & Arabian Stud*

This former farmhouse, built as a model farm in the 18th century, has been carefully renovated to provide modern comforts. Some bedrooms are in the main house, but most are in adjacent converted buildings and many are on the ground floor, each with their own courtyard entrance. All rooms offer an abundance of comfort and considerate extras and service is attentive. Enjoy an aperitif in one of two elegant drawing rooms prior to dinner, or in the pretty gardens. Other attractions include a large indoor heated swimming pool and a spacious conference suite.

Facilities 5 en suite 15 annexe en suite (4 fmly) (13 GF) ⊘ in 18 bedrooms ⊘ in dining room ⊘ in 1 lounge TVB tea/coffee

---

Direct dial from bedrooms ✖ Licensed Cen ht TVL ▦ Gymnasium Children 's weekend play room Dinner Last d 8.45pm **Prices** S £85-£95; D £110-£130 **Conf** Max 50 Thtr 50 Class 20 Board 24 Del from £130 ✳ **Parking** 50 **Notes** Closed 24-30 Dec rs Sun Civ Wed 50

◆◆◆◆ ◉◉ ⊜ ◀

The Tollgate Inn
Ham Green, Holt BA14 6PX
☎ 01225 782326 📄 01225 782805
e-mail alison@tollgateholt.co.uk
web www.tollgateholt.co.uk
Dir *2m E on B3107, at W end of Holt village*

The Tollgate Inn combines the comforts of a traditional inn with excellent quality food served in delightful surroundings. It stands near the village green at Holt, and is only a short drive from Bath. Bedrooms, varying in size, are well decorated and thoughtfully equipped with welcome extras.

Facilities 4 en suite ⊘ in bedrooms ⊘ in dining room TVB tea/coffee Direct dial from bedrooms ✖ Cen ht No children 16yrs No coaches Dinner Last d 9.30pm **Prices** S £50-£95; D £75-£95✳ **Conf** Max 30 Thtr 36 Board 30 Del from £110 ✳ **Parking** 40

◆◆◆◆

Home Farm
Farleigh Rd, Wingfield BA14 9LG
☎ 01225 764492 📄 01225 764492
e-mail info@homefarm-guesthouse.co.uk
Dir *2m S in Wingfield village on A366*

This delightful former farmhouse offers comfortable, well-equipped accommodation. Guests are assured of a warm welcome, and are free to use of the charming gardens, which have wonderful views over farmland. A full English breakfast is served at individual tables.

Facilities 3 en suite (1 fmly) (1 GF) ⊘ TVB tea/coffee ✖ Cen ht TVL No coaches **Prices** d fr £60✳ **Parking** 30

England

BRADFORD-ON-AVON continued

◆◆◆◆

Midway Cottage

Farleigh Wick BA15 2PU
☎ 01225 863932 🖃 01225 863932
e-mail midwaycottage@btinternet.com
web www.midwaycottage.co.uk
Dir 2m NW of Bradford on A363, next to Fox & Hounds pub

Under new ownership, a warm welcome is assured at this delightful Victorian cottage, located near Bradford-on-Avon and Bath. The comfortable bedrooms are equipped with a variety of thoughtful extras, and there is a pleasant garden. Breakfast is served around a communal table in the lounge-dining room.

Facilities 3 en suite (1 GF) ⊗ TVB tea/coffee ✗ Cen ht TVL No children 5yrs No coaches **Prices** S £35-£40; D £55-£60✶ **Parking** 3 **Notes** Closed Xmas-5 Jan

◆◆◆◆

Serendipity

19f Bradford Rd, Winsley BA15 2HW ☎ 01225 722380
e-mail vanda.shepherd@tesco.net
Dir A36 onto B3108, 1.5m right into Winsley, establishment on right on main road

Set in a quiet residential area, Serendipity is convenient for visiting the town and nearby Bath. The proprietors are friendly and welcoming, and bedrooms are brightly decorated and equipped with a range of extras. Two are on the ground floor. Guests can watch badgers and local wildlife in the gardens during the evening. Breakfast is served in the conservatory overlooking the garden.

Facilities 3 en suite (1 fmly) (2 GF) ⊗ TVB tea/coffee ✗ Cen ht No coaches ♨ **Prices** S £40-£55; D £45-£55✶ **LB Parking** 5 **Notes** ✉

◆◆◆

The Coppers Bed & Breakfast

21b Leigh Rd, Holt BA14 6PW ☎ 01225 783174
e-mail jbradbury1@toucansurf.com
Dir B3107 from Bradford into Holt, 1st left opp Toll Gate Inn onto Leigh Rd, signed 1st left

This pleasant guest house is in a quiet location just a stroll from the pleasant village of Holt with its choice of inns. Hospitality is relaxed and friendly, and you can enjoy the views of the surrounding countryside. There are two neatly furnished bedrooms, one en suite and one with private facilities.

Facilities 2 rms (1 en suite) (1 pri facs) (1 fmly) (2 GF) ⊗ TVB tea/coffee Cen ht No coaches Dinner Last d breakfast **Prices** S £40-£50; D £50-£60✶ **LB Parking** 8 **Notes** ✉

◆◆ 🅰

Conifers ◇

4 King Alfred Way, Winsley BA15 2NG ☎ 01225 722482
Dir A363 onto B3108, after 2m 2nd left onto Dane Rise, 2nd right

Facilities 2 rms ⊗ TV1B tea/coffee Cen ht TVL No coaches
Prices S £30-£35; D £47-£50✶ **Parking** 4 **Notes** ✉

CALNE

MAP 04 ST97

Premier Collection

◆◆◆◆◆

Chilvester Hill House

SN11 0LP
☎ 01249 813981 & 815785 🖃 01249 814217/813747
e-mail gill.dilley@talk21.com
web www.chilvesterhillhouse.co.uk
Dir A4 from Calne towards Chippenham, after 0.5m take right turn marked Bremhill, driveway on right

The owners extend a very warm welcome at this elegant Victorian house set in well-kept gardens and grounds. Bedrooms are spacious, comfortable and well equipped, with many thoughtful extras. A set dinner is available by arrangement and is served at one large table. Dishes are freshly prepared from the best local produce and many of the fruit and vegetables used are home grown.

Facilities 3 en suite ⊗ in dining room ⊗ in 1 lounge TVB tea/coffee ✗ Licensed Cen ht TVL No children 12yrs No coaches Golf 18 Stables and golf course avaliable locally Dinner Last d 11am **Prices** S £55-£65; D £85-£95✶ **Parking** 8

CHIPPENHAM

MAP 04 ST97

◆◆◆

Diana Lodge Bed & Breakfast

Grathie Cottage, 72 Marshfield Rd SN15 1JR
☎ 01249 650306
e-mail apple@onetel.net
Dir 500yds NW of town centre on A420 Marshfield Rd, into West End Club car park

A cheerful welcome awaits guests at this late 19th-century cottage, within walking distance of the town centre and the railway station. Well-equipped bedrooms and adjacent parking.

Facilities 4 rms (2 en suite) (4 fmly) (1 GF) ⊗ in dining room TVB tea/coffee ✗ Cen ht TVL No coaches **Parking** available

CORSHAM

MAP 04 ST87

★★★★ **Farm House**

Pickwick Lodge Farm (ST857708)

Guyers Ln SN13 0PS
☎ 01249 712207 🖃 01249 701904 Mrs G Stafford
e-mail b&b@pickwickfarm.co.uk
web www.pickwickfarm.co.uk
Dir Off A4, Bath side of Corsham, onto Guyers Ln, farmhouse at end on right

This Grade II listed 17th-century farmhouse is peacefully located on a 300-acre beef and arable farm, within easy reach of Bath. The spacious bedrooms are well-equipped with modern facilities and many thoughtful extras. A hearty breakfast using the best local produce is served at a communal table in the dining room.

continued

Pickwick Lodge Farm

Facilities 3 rms (2 en suite) (1 pri facs) ⊗ TVB tea/coffee ✖ Cen ht TVL No children 12yrs Fishing 300 acres arable beef **Prices** S £35-£50; D £60-£65 **LB** **Parking** 6 **Notes** Closed Xmas & New Year ⊛

◆◆◆◆

Thurlestone Lodge

13 Prospect SN13 9AD ☎ 01249 713397 & 07815 731131
e-mail v_ogilvie_robb@hotmail.com
Dir 0.25m from Corsham Centre on B3353. 150yds on right after Great Western pub

This charming Victorian house is delightfully located in the attractive town of Corsham, convenient for the countryside and attractions of the Cotswolds and Bath areas. Bedrooms are comfortable, spacious and well appointed. Hospitality is friendly; the proprietors here are attentive hosts. Breakfast is served in the spacious dining room and provides a hearty start to the day.

Facilities 2 en suite (1 fmly) ⊗ TVB tea/coffee ✖ Cen ht No coaches **Prices** D £54-£60✱ **Parking** 5 **Notes** ⊛

CRICKLADE　　　　　　　　　MAP 05 SU09

◆◆◆◆ ✔

Leighfield Lodge Farm (SU058911)

Malmesbury Rd, Leigh SN6 6RH
☎ 01666 860241 ▤ 01666 860241 Mrs Read
e-mail claireread@leighfieldlodge.fsnet.co.uk
web www.leighfieldlodge.com
Dir B4040 from Cricklade to Malmesbury, 3m left after Foresters Arms pub

Located at the end of a half-mile drive, this working farm is peaceful and secluded. Guests enjoy the relaxed and friendly atmosphere. The very comfortable bedrooms feature numerous thoughtful extra

continued

facilities. A hearty breakfast is served around one large table, with several locally produced items available.

Facilities 2 en suite ⊗ TVB tea/coffee ✖ Cen ht TVL No children 100 acres Beef & Sheep Dinner Last d 24hrs notice **Prices** S £35-£45; D £60-£70 **Parking** 4 **Notes** ⊛

◆◆◆

Upper Chelworth Farm ◇

Upper Chelworth SN6 6HD ☎ 01793 750440
Dir B4040 W from Crickdale, 1.5m left at x-rds for Chelworth Upper Green

Close to the M4 and Swindon, Upper Chelworth Farm offers a genuinely friendly welcome in addition to comfortable bedrooms of varying sizes. There is a spacious lounge with a wood-burning stove, games room with a pool table and a lovely garden. Breakfast is served in the farmhouse-style dining room.

Facilities 7 rms (6 en suite) (1 fmly) ⊗ in 2 bedrooms ⊗ in dining room TV6B tea/coffee ✖ Cen ht TVL No children 5yrs No coaches Pool Table **Prices** S £25-£30; D £45-£50✱ **Parking** 10 **Notes** Closed mid Dec-mid Jan ⊛

DEVIZES　　　　　　　　　MAP 04 SU06

Premier Collection

◆◆◆◆◆ �🛏 ✔

Blounts Court Farm (SU996583)

Coxhill Ln, Potterne SN10 5PH ☎ 01380 727180
Mr & Mrs Cary
e-mail carys@blountscourtfarm.co.uk
Dir A360 to Potterne, turn onto Coxhill Ln opp George & Dragon, at fork turn left and follow drive to farmhouse

A warm welcome is assured at this delightful arable farm, overlooking the village cricket field. The barn and cider press have been converted to provide three attractive bedrooms on the ground floor, one of which has a four-poster bed. The elegant decor is in keeping with the exposed beams and character of the house. Breakfast, which features home-made and local produce, is served in the farmhouse dining room.

Facilities 3 en suite (3 GF) ⊗ TVB tea/coffee ✖ Cen ht TVL No children 8yrs 200 acres arable **Prices** S £34-£40; D £56-£60✱ **Parking** 20

England

◆◆◆◆

Littleton Lodge

Littleton Panell (A360), West Lavington SN10 4ES
☎ 01380 813131 ▤ 01380 816969
e-mail stay@littletonlodge.co.uk
web www.littletonlodge.co.uk
Dir On A360 in Littleton Panell

Convenient for Stonehenge and for touring the many attractions of this pleasant area, Littleton Lodge offers spacious and comfortable accommodation and a relaxed friendly atmosphere. Breakfast is served in the stylish dining room and freshly cooked dishes provide a pleasant start to the day.

Facilities 3 en suite ⊘ TVB tea/coffee ✖ Cen ht No coaches Golf
Prices S £40-£45; D £60-£65✳ **LB** **Parking** 4

◆◆◆◆ 🅰

Glebe House

Chittoe SN15 2EL ☎ 01380 850864 ▤ 01380 850189
e-mail gscrope@aol.com
web www.glebehouse-chittoe.co.uk
Dir Off A342 to Chittoe & Spye Park, over x-rds, 2nd house on left

Facilities 3 rms (1 GF) ⊘ in bedrooms tea/coffee ✖ Cen ht TVL
No children 8yrs No coaches Fishing Riding Dinner Last d 9pm
Parking 4 **Notes** Closed Xmas & New Year 🐾

◆◆◆

Eastcott Manor ◇

Easterton SN10 4PH ☎ 01380 813313
e-mail janetlnfirth@aol.com
Dir 6m S of Devizes. On B3098 in Easterton

This 16th-century farmhouse offers comfortable accommodation in a rural setting. Bedrooms vary in size and are suitably furnished and equipped. Breakfast and evening meals are served in the delightful dining room around one large table. A pleasant lounge and a conservatory are also available.

Facilities 4 rms (2 en suite) (2 pri facs) ⊘ TVB tea/coffee TVL
No coaches Stabling Chair lift Dinner Last d 24hrs in advance
Prices S £30-£32; D £65-£68 **Parking** 6 **Notes** Closed 23 Dec-1 Jan 🐾

★★★★ 🅰 Bed & Breakfast

Marshwood Farm B&B

SP3 5ET ☎ 01722 716334
e-mail marshwood1@btconnect.com
Dir A30 onto B3089 into Dinton, turn right to Wylye, B&B 0.5m on left

Facilities 2 en suite (1 fmly) ⊘ TVB tea/coffee ✖ Cen ht No coaches
❧ **Prices** S £35-£60; D £50-£60 **LB** **Parking** 4 **Notes** 🐾

◆◆◆◆ 🌐 🍽 ◧

Forester Inn

Lower St SP7 9EE ☎ 01747 828038 ▤ 01747 828050
e-mail enquiries@foresterinndonheadstandrew.co.uk
web www.foresterinndonheadstandrew.co.uk
Dir In village centre

This thatched village inn, 4m from Shaftesbury, is a good base for touring Wiltshire and Dorset. Carefully refurbished, its character has been retained, yet quality and modern comforts abound. The atmosphere of the bar-restaurant, where freshly prepared lunch and dinner are available, is relaxed and service is attentive. Bedrooms are equipped with considerate extras and are suited to business and leisure. A continental breakfast is available.

Facilities 2 en suite (1 fmly) ⊘ in bedrooms ⊘ in dining room
⊘ in lounges TVB tea/coffee ✖ Cen ht No coaches Dinner Last d 9pm
Prices S £57.50-£95; D £65-£110✳ **LB** **Conf** Max 30 Thtr 30 Class 30
Board 20 **Parking** 30

◆◆◆

Barnfield

Salisbury Rd SP5 3HZ
☎ 01725 513386 & 07905 514917 ▤ 01725 513386
e-mail joanbrennanlewis@hotmail.com
Dir 5m S of Salisbury on A338

Barnfield is set back from the main road on the west edge of the village of Downton. Expect friendly hospitality and a relaxed atmosphere, and a selection of inns is available just a stroll away in the village.

Facilities 2 en suite ⊘ in bedrooms ⊘ in dining room ⊘ in 1 lounge
TVB tea/coffee ✖ Cen ht No coaches **Prices** S £35-£39; D £45-£49✳
LB **Parking** 6 **Notes** 🐾

FIRSDOWN

MAP 05 SU23

◆◆◆◆

Junipers

3 Juniper Rd SP5 1SS ☎ 01980 862330
e-mail junipersbedandbreakfast@btinternet.com
web www.junipersbedandbreakfast.co.uk
Dir *5m from Sailisbury on A30, A343 to London follow Junipers brown signs into Firsdown*

Located in a quiet residential area, just five miles from the City, this homely accommodation is located at ground floor level. Bedrooms are well equipped with thoughtful extras. The hosts, who have craft skills, are happy to show guests their interesting items constructed in medieval style. Breakfast, featuring local produce, is served in the cosy dining room/ lounge.

Facilities 3 en suite (3 GF) ⊗ TVB tea/coffee ✖ Cen ht No children No coaches **Prices** D £55-£60 LB **Parking** 6 **Notes** ⊛

GRITTLETON

MAP 04 ST88

★★ Bed & Breakfast

Staddlestones

SN14 6AW ☎ 01249 782458 ◰ 01249 782458
e-mail staddlestonesbb@btinternet.com
Dir *50yds from village hall between stone pillars up drive on left.*

The large modern bungalow lies at the east end of the small village, and is convenient for the M4. The local pub is just a stroll away and ample parking is available.

Facilities 3 rms (3 GF) ⊗ TVB tea/coffee ✖ Cen ht TVL No coaches **Prices** S £35-£65; D £50-£80 **Parking** 5 **Notes** ⊛

HINDON

MAP 04 ST93

◆◆◆◆ ⊜ ◖

The Lamb Inn

SP3 6DP ☎ 01747 820573 ◰ 01747 820605
e-mail nick@boisdale.co.uk
Dir *Off B3089 in village centre*

The 17th-century coaching inn is in a pretty village within easy reach of the Salisbury and Bath. It has been refurbished in an eclectic style, and some of the well-equipped bedrooms have four-poster beds. Enjoyable, freshly prepared dishes are available at lunch and dinner in the restaurant or bar, where log fires provide a welcoming atmosphere on colder days.

continued

Facilities 14 en suite (1 fmly) ⊗ in area of dining room ⊗ in 1 lounge STV TVB tea/coffee Direct dial from bedrooms Cen ht Dinner Last d 9.30pm **Conf** Max 40 Thtr 40 Class 16 Board 24 **Parking** 16

LACOCK

MAP 04 ST96

Premier Collection

◆◆◆◆◆ ◰ ⊜

At the Sign of the Angel

6 Church St SN15 2LB ☎ 01249 730230 ◰ 01249 730527
e-mail angel@lacock.co.uk
web www.lacock.co.uk
Dir *Off A350 into Lacock, follow Local Traffic sign*

You cannot fail to be impressed by the character of this 15th-century former wool merchant's house, set in the National Trust village of Lacock. Bedrooms range in size and style from the atmospheric rooms in the main house to others in an adjacent new building. Excellent dinners and breakfasts are served in the beamed dining rooms, and there is also a first-floor lounge and a pleasant rear garden.

Facilities 6 en suite 5 annexe en suite (1 fmly) (4 GF) ⊗ in bedrooms ⊗ in dining room TVB tea/coffee Direct dial from bedrooms Licensed Cen ht No coaches Dinner Last d 9pm **Prices** S £72-£85; D £105-£155✱ **Conf** Max 14 Board 14 **Parking** 7 **Notes** Closed 23-30 Dec rs Mon (ex BHs) Civ Wed 25

◆◆◆◆

The Old Rectory

Cantax Hill SN15 2JZ ☎ 01249 730335 ◰ 01249 730166
e-mail sexton@oldrectorylacock.co.uk
web www.oldrectorylacock.co.uk
Dir *A350 S from Chippenham, left at lights into Lacock, 1st on right*

Located on the edge of the medieval village of Lacock, this imposing Grade II listed Victorian property is situated in delightful gardens with its own croquet lawn and tennis court. Bedrooms and bathrooms are comfortably furnished and equipped with a wide range of useful extra facilities. Full English breakfasts are served in the spacious dining room.

Facilities 6 rms (4 en suite) (2 pri facs) (2 fmly) (1 GF) ⊗ TVB tea/coffee Cen ht TVL ✎ ♨ **Prices** S £35-£50; D £60-£75✱ LB **Conf** Max 20 Board 14 Del from £40 ✱ **Parking** 8 **Notes** Closed 24-26 Dec ⊛

England

U

New Forest Lodge

Southampton Rd SP5 2ED
☎ 01794 390999 🖷 01794 390066
e-mail info@newforestlodge.co.uk

At the time of going to press the rating for this establishment had not been confirmed. Please check the AA website www.theAA.com for up-to-date information.

Facilities 14 en suite (6 fmly) (6 GF) ⊘ in bedrooms ⊘ in dining room TVB tea/coffee Direct dial from bedrooms Cen ht TVL Dinner Last d 11pm **Prices** S £57-£65; D £69.50-£74.50✱ **Parking** 35

♦♦♦♦ ⊛ ➾ ◀

Compasses Inn

SP3 6NB ☎ 01722 714318 🖷 01722 714318
e-mail thecompasses@aol.com
web www.thecompassesinn.com
Dir Off A30 signed Lower Chicksgrove, 1st left onto Lagpond Ln, single-track lane to village

This charming 17th-century inn, within easy reach of the Bath, Salisbury, Glastonbury and the Dorset coast, offers comfortable accommodation in a peaceful setting. Carefully prepared dinners are enjoyed in the warm atmosphere of the bar-restaurant, while breakfast is served in a separate dining room.

Facilities 4 en suite (1 fmly) ⊘ in bedrooms ⊘ in area of dining room ⊘ in lounges TVB tea/coffee Cen ht Dinner Last d 9.30pm **Prices** S £55-£65; D £75-£85 **LB** **Conf** Max 14 **Parking** 40 **Notes** Closed 25 & 26 Dec rs Mon (ex BH) & Tue after BH

★★★★ 🅰 Farm House

Lovett Farm ◇

Little Somerford SN15 5BP
☎ 01666 823268 & 07808 858612 🖷 01666 823268
e-mail lovettfarm@btinternet.com
Dir 3m from Malmesbury on B4042 opp 2nd turning to the Somerfords

Facilities 2 en suite ⊘ TVB tea/coffee ✖ Cen ht No children 2yrs No coaches **Prices** S £30-£40; D £50-£60 **Parking** 4

♦♦♦♦ 🅰

Monks Rest Lodge

Salisbury Rd SN8 4AE ☎ 01672 512169
e-mail stay@monksrest.co.uk
Dir A346 Salisbury Rd, after rdbts at junct with A4, take 1st left into Savernake Court

Facilities 3 en suite (2 fmly) (3 GF) ⊘ TVB tea/coffee ✖ Licensed Cen ht No coaches **Parking** 6

★★★ Inn

The George Inn ◇

The Square BA12 6DR ☎ 01747 860427
e-mail rob.binstead@btconnect.com
web www.thegeorgeinnmere.co.uk
Dir A303 junct signed Mere. Centre of town, opposite clock tower

This charming Inn has historical character; with a log fire burning in the bar during cold winter months, creating a welcoming atmosphere. Equally welcoming are the friendly hosts, who ensure guests feel at home. Breakfast is served in the cosy dining room; the inn is open for lunch and an extensive choice of dishes are available for dinner, which can be enjoyed in the bar/ restaurant.

Facilities 7 en suite (3 fmly) ⊘ in bedrooms ⊘ in 1 lounge TVB tea/coffee ✖ Cen ht Dinner Last d 8.45pm **Prices** S £30-£45; D £55-£60✱ **Conf** Max 30 Class 30 Board 30 **Parking** 15

♦♦♦♦

Chetcombe House

Chetcombe Rd BA12 6AZ ☎ 01747 860219 🖷 01747 860111
e-mail mary.butchers@lineone.net
Dir Off A303

Chetcombe House has wonderful views across 1 acre of well-tended gardens towards Gillingham and the Blackmore Vale. The house, built in 1937, provides elegance and charm, and is pleasantly spacious and comfortable. The bedrooms are well equipped and are provided with many extra facilities. Breakfast is served in the attractive dining room.

Facilities 5 en suite (1 fmly) ⊘ TVB tea/coffee ✖ Cen ht TVL No coaches **Prices** S £36-£45; D £55 **Parking** 10 **Notes** ⊛

England

NETTLETON
MAP 04 ST87

◆◆◆◆

Fosse Farmhouse
Nettleton Shrub SN14 7NJ
☎ 01249 782286 📠 01249 783066
e-mail caroncooper@compuserve.com
web www.fossefarmhouse.com
Dir *1.5m N from Castle Combe on B4039, left at Gib, farm 1m on right*

Set in quiet Wiltshire countryside close to Castle Combe, the guest house has well-equipped bedrooms decorated in keeping with its 18th-century origins. Excellent dinners are served in the farmhouse, and cream teas can be enjoyed in the old stables or the delightful garden.

Facilities 3 en suite (1 fmly) ⊗ in bedrooms ⊗ in dining room TVB tea/coffee Licensed Cen ht Golf 18 Dinner Last d 8.30pm
Prices S £55-£68; D £85-£135 **LB Conf** Max 15 Thtr 10 Class 10 Board 10 Del from £65 ✳ **Parking** 12

PURTON
MAP 05 SU08

Premier Collection

◆◆◆◆◆ 🛏

The Old Farmhouse
Bagbury Ln, Restrop SN5 4LX ☎ 01793 770130
e-mail stay@theoldfarmhouse.net
Dir *M4 junct 16, signs for Purton, right at 1st x-rds, Bagbury Ln 1st left*

The Old Farmhouse has a tranquil location in the countryside yet is easily reached from the motorway and is only a short distance from Swindon centre. Each bedroom is individually styled, all are very comfortable and are provided with a host of facilities and thoughtful nick-knacks. The proprietors are most friendly and attentive. An impressive continental breakfast is served in each room. There is a private, nine-hole golf course here for guests.

Facilities 6 annexe en suite (4 GF) ⊗ TVB tea/coffee Direct dial from bedrooms ✖ Cen ht No children No coaches Golf 9 ⚐ Boules Court,Helipad landing facility **Prices** D £109-£150✳ **LB Parking** 20

SALISBURY
MAP 05 SU12

See also **Amesbury, Boscombe, Sixpenny Handley (Dorset), Stoford & Winterbourne Stoke**

★★★★ Guest House

Cricket Field House
1 Cricket Field Cottages, Wilton Rd SP2 9NS
☎ 01722 322595 📠 01722 322595
e-mail cricketfieldcottage@btinternet.com
web www.cricketfieldhousehotel.co.uk
Dir *A36 W of Salisbury*

The friendly, family-run 19th-century gamekeepers cottage is within walking distance of the city centre and railway station. It stands in large gardens and looks over the picturesque South Wiltshire Cricket Ground.

Facilities 4 en suite 10 annexe en suite (1 fmly) (10 GF) ⊗ TVB tea/coffee ✖ Licensed Cen ht No children 14yrs **Prices** S £55-£65; D £65-£95✳ **Conf** Thtr 20 Class 14 Board 16 **Parking** 25

◆◆◆◆

Avonlea House ◇
231 Castle Rd SP1 3RY ☎ 01722 338351 📠 01722 338351
e-mail guests@avonleahouse.co.uk
web www.avonleahouse.co.uk
Dir *On A345 Salisbury/Amesbury Rd. Near old Sarum.*

The Avonlea has most comfortable and well equipped bedrooms and a well cooked breakfast is offered with a choice of fresh local items. The property is located close to the Old Sarum and within walking distance to Salisbury City centre for the Cathedral and riverside walks. There is leisure facilities close by in a swimming pool and gym, and there is easy access to Stonehenge, the New Forest and the South coast. A good base from which to tour.

Facilities 2 en suite ⊗ TVB tea/coffee ✖ Cen ht No children 12yrs No coaches **Prices** S £30-£45; D £50-£55✳ **Parking** 2 **Notes** Closed Xmas & New Year

If the freedom to smoke or be in a non-smoking atmosphere is important to you, check the rules when you book

England

SALISBURY continued

◆◆◆◆
Clovelly Hotel

17-19 Mill Rd SP2 7RT ☎ 01722 322055 📠 01722 327677
e-mail clovelly.hotel@virgin.net
web www.clovellyhotel.co.uk
Dir *500yds W of market square*

The Clovelly provides quality accommodation and service within easy reach of the railway station and city centre. The proprietor is a Blue Badge Guide and offers personalised driving tours around Wessex. All bedrooms are neatly decorated with coordinated furnishings. Public areas include a delightful lounge and a light and airy breakfast room.

Facilities 14 en suite (3 fmly) ⊗ TVB tea/coffee ✖ Cen ht No children **Prices** S £50-£60; D £70-£80✳ LB **Conf** Thtr 20 Class 20 Board 20 **Parking** 15

◆◆◆◆
Salisbury Old Mill House

Warminster Rd, South Newton SP2 0QD
☎ 01722 742458 📠 01722 742458
e-mail salisburymill@yahoo.com
Dir *4m NW on A36 by 30mph sign in South Newton*

This restored watermill exudes character, and the mill machinery is still on view. Friendly and welcoming, the property offers comfortable, well-appointed bedrooms, a lounge with wood-burning stove, and a dining area where delicious dinners are available by arrangement. The garden features the original millpond.

Facilities 4 en suite (1 fmly) ⊗ TVB tea/coffee ✖ Licensed Cen ht No coaches Dinner Last d 24hr prior **Parking** 10 **Notes** Closed 25 Dec & 1 Jan ⊜

◆◆◆◆
Briden House

West St, Barford St Martin SP3 4AH ☎ 01722 743471
e-mail bridenhouse@hotmail.com
Dir *5.5m W of Salisbury. A30 onto B3089 to Barford St Martin, near village church*

This charming Grade II listed property, situated not far from Salisbury, has been restored to its former glory. Bedrooms are pleasantly furnished and well equipped. There is also a ground-floor garden bedroom with its own sitting room. Breakfast is served in the delightful beamed dining room.

Facilities 3 en suite (1 fmly) (1 GF) ⊗ TVB tea/coffee Cen ht No coaches **Prices** S £55-£60; D £65-£70✳ **Parking** 6

◆◆◆◆
Cathedral View

83 Exeter St SP1 2SE ☎ 01722 502254
e-mail wenda.rampton@btopenworld.com
Dir *200yds E of cathedral. Off A338 ring road onto Exeter St, signs for Old George Mall*

The friendly home has views of the cathedral, which is just a 2-minute walk away, and provides attractive refurbished bedrooms with numerous thoughtful extras. Breakfast is a good selection served around one large table in the dining room.

Facilities 4 en suite (1 fmly) ⊗ TVB tea/coffee ✖ Cen ht No children 10yrs No coaches **Prices** D £60-£65✳ **Notes** ⊜

◆◆◆◆
The Edwardian Lodge

59 Castle Rd SP1 3RH ☎ 01722 413329 📠 01722 503105
e-mail richard.white59@ntlworld.com
web www.edwardianlodge.co.uk
Dir *0.5m N of city centre on A345. Turn onto Victoria Rd to car park*

Located close to the city centre, this fine Edwardian home is convenient for the many nearby places of interest. It has spacious, comfortably furnished and well-equipped bedrooms, some located on the ground floor. Breakfast is served in the conservatory.

Facilities 8 en suite (1 fmly) (3 GF) ⊗ TVB tea/coffee ✖ Cen ht No children 6mths **Prices** D £56-£62✳ **Parking** 7 **Notes** Closed 20-28 Dec

◆◆◆◆
Glen Lyn House

6 Bellamy Ln, Milford Hill SP1 2SP
☎ 01722 327880 📠 01722 327880
e-mail glen.lyn@btinternet.com
web www.glenlynbandbatsalisbury.co.uk
Dir *A36 Southampton Rd onto Tollgate Rd & Rampart Rd, at lights right onto Milford Hill, left onto Bellamy Ln*

This Victorian house is in a quiet cul-de-sac close to the town and Salisbury College. The proprietors have a well-deserved reputation for exceptional hospitality. Their traditionally furnished bedrooms are comfortable and some are en suite. The spacious lounge contains books, maps and tourist information.

continued

continued

Facilities 7 rms (4 en suite) (1 fmly) ⊗ TVB tea/coffee Licensed Cen ht No coaches **Prices** S £38-£65; D £51.50-£74.70✳ **Parking** 5 **Notes** Closed 22 Dec-2 Jan

◆◆◆◆

Newton Farmhouse

Southampton Rd SP5 2QL ☎ 01794 884416
e-mail newtonfarmhouse1@aol.com
For full entry see **Whiteparish**

◆◆◆◆

The Old House

161 Wilton Rd SP2 7JQ ☎ 01722 333433 ▤ 01722 335551
Dir On A36 1m W from city centre

Located close to the city centre, this non-smoking property dates from the 17th century. Bedrooms have modern facilities and one room has a four-poster bed. There is a spacious lounge, cosy cellar bar, and large gardens to enjoy - weather permitting.

Facilities 7 en suite (1 fmly) ⊗ TVB tea/coffee ✖ Cen ht TVL No children 7yrs No coaches Games room, Table tennis **Prices** S £40-£55; D £50-£55✳ LB **Parking** 10 **Notes** ⊛

◆◆◆◆

Stratford Lodge

4 Park Ln Rd SP1 3NP ☎ 01722 325177 ▤ 01722 325177
e-mail enquiries@stratfordlodge.co.uk
web www.stratfordlodge.co.uk
Dir 0.6m N of city centre. Off A345 Castle Rd onto Park Ln, an unadopted road between Victoria Park & Co-op shop

Close to the city centre, Stratford Lodge has a peaceful setting, tucked away in a lane overlooking Victoria Park. Bedrooms are spacious and pretty; one features a four-poster bed. Breakfast is served in the conservatory and a cosy lounge is available.

Facilities 8 en suite (2 fmly) (1 GF) ⊗ TVB tea/coffee ✖ Licensed Cen ht TVL No children 5yrs Dinner Last d 6.30pm **Prices** S £59.75-£62; D £79.75-£85 LB **Parking** 12

◆◆◆◆

Websters

11 Hartington Rd SP2 7LG
☎ 01722 339779 ▤ 01722 339779
e-mail enquiries@websters-bed-breakfast.com
Dir From city centre onto A360 Devizes Rd, 0.25m left

Please note that this establishment has recently changed hands. This delightful property is located in a quiet cul-de-sac close to the city centre. The charming, well-presented bedrooms are equipped with numerous extras and one ground-floor room has easier access. The Internet is available in the cosy lounge.

Facilities 5 en suite (1 GF) ⊗ TVB tea/coffee ✖ Cen ht No children 12yrs No coaches **Prices** S £40-£50; D £50-£60 LB **Parking** 5 **Notes** rs Xmas & New Year

◆◆◆◆

Wyndham Park Lodge

51 Wyndham Rd SP1 3AB
☎ 01722 416517 & 07771 560552 ▤ 01722 328851
e-mail enquiries@wyndhamparklodge.co.uk
web www.wyndhamparklodge.co.uk
Dir Off A36 S onto Castle St towards city centre, 2nd left

This friendly, family home is close to the city centre, with good access to the cathedral and local tourist attractions. The coordinated furnishings are in keeping with its Victorian origins, and the comfortable bedrooms brim with thoughtful extras. A full English breakfast is served at individual tables - homemade marmalade is a speciality.

Facilities 3 en suite 1 annexe en suite (1 fmly) ⊗ FTV TVB tea/coffee ✖ Cen ht No coaches **Prices** S £38-£42; D £50-£55✳ **Parking** 3

◆◆◆

Byways Guest House

31 Fowlers Rd SP1 2QP ☎ 01722 328364 ▤ 01722 322146
e-mail info@bywayshouse.co.uk
Dir A30 onto A36 signed Southampton, follow Youth Hostel signs to hostel, Fowlers Rd opp

Located in a quiet street with off-road parking, Byways is within walking distance of the town centre. Several bedrooms have been decorated in a Victorian style and another two have four-poster beds. All rooms offer good levels of comfort, with one adapted for easier access.

Facilities 23 en suite (6 fmly) (13 GF) ⊗ in 15 bedrooms ⊗ in dining room ⊗ in lounges TVB tea/coffee Licensed Cen ht **Prices** S £39-£60; D £50-£75✳ **Parking** 15 **Notes** Closed Xmas & New Year

◆◆◆

Hayburn Wyke Guest House

72 Castle Rd SP1 3RL ☎ 01722 412627 ▤ 01722 412627
e-mail hayburn.wyke@tinyonline.co.uk
Dir 0.5m N from city centre on A345, on left

Located close to the city centre and Victoria Park, this homely guest house provides a friendly and comfortable base from which to explore the area. The bright and airy bedrooms are equipped with many useful extras, and one bedroom is on the ground floor allowing easy access.

Facilities 7 rms (4 en suite) (3 fmly) (1 GF) ⊗ in 4 bedrooms ⊗ in dining room ⊗ in lounges TVB tea/coffee ✖ Cen ht TVL **Prices** D £48-£70 **Parking** 7

England

SALISBURY continued

♦♦

Holmhurst

Downton Rd SP2 8AR ☎ 01722 410407 📠 01722 323164
e-mail holmhurst@talk21.com
Dir *Off ring road onto A338 S, Holmhurst on left near Shell station*

Holmhurst lies on the outskirts of the city within walking distance of the cathedral and centre. This family-run property provides comfortable, well-equipped bedrooms and a traditional breakfast is served at individual tables in the bright dining room.

Facilities 5 rms (4 en suite) (2 fmly) ⊘ TVB tea/coffee 🐾 Cen ht Table tennis **Prices** S £35-£45; D £50-£60 **Parking** 9

STAPLEFORD
MAP 05 SU03

🔲

Oak Bluffs

4 Church Furlong SP3 4QE
☎ 01722 790663 📠 01722 790663
Dir *In village centre off B3083*

At the time of going to press the rating for this establishment had not been confirmed. Please check the AA website www.theAA.com for up-to-date information.

Facilities 1 en suite (1 GF) ⊘ TVB tea/coffee 🐾 Cen ht No coaches **Parking** 1 **Notes** ⊛

STOFORD
MAP 05 SU03

♦♦♦

The Swan Inn

SP2 0PR ☎ 01722 790236 📠 01722 790115
e-mail info@theswanatstoford.co.uk
Dir *On A36 in village centre*

This family-run establishment is well located for touring the region. Attractively furnished bedrooms are available and extra facilities include a skittle alley and fishing on a private stretch of river. Tasty home-cooked meals are available at lunch and dinner in either the popular pub bar or in the restaurant.

Facilities 9 en suite (2 fmly) ⊘ in bedrooms ⊘ in dining room TVB tea/coffee 🐾 Cen ht Fishing Pool Table Skittle alley Dinner Last d 9.15pm **Prices** S £45-£65; D £55-£85 **Conf** Max 40 Thtr 30 Class 30 Board 20 Del from £59.95 ✳ **Parking** 70

If you book on bed, breakfast and evening meal terms, you may find that the tariff includes only the set menu

SWINDON
MAP 05 SU18
See also **Ashton Keynes**

★★★ Guest House

Fairview Guest House

52 Swindon Rd, Wootton Bassett SN4 8EU
☎ 01793 852283 📠 01793 848076
e-mail fairview@woottonb.wanadoo.co.uk
web fairviewguesthouse.mysite.wanadoo-members.co.uk
Dir *On A3102 to Wootton Bassett, 1.25m from M4 junct 16 & 5m from Swindon centre.*

Family-run property with easy access to the M4 and the town of Swindon. Bedrooms are between the main house and the bungalow annexe and breakfast is served in an open plan dining come sitting room with an open fire on cooler mornings.

Facilities 8 rms (3 en suite) 4 annexe rms (3 en suite) (1 annexe pri facs) (2 fmly) (4 GF) ⊘ TVB tea/coffee 🐾 Cen ht TVL No coaches **Parking** 14

Premier Collection

♦♦♦♦♦ 🛏

The Old Farmhouse

Bagbury Ln, Restrop SN5 4LX ☎ 01793 770130
e-mail stay@theoldfarmhouse.net
For full entry see **Purton**

♦♦♦♦ 🍴

Tawny Owl

Queen Elizabeth Dr, Taw Hill SN25 1WP
☎ 01793 706770 📠 01793 706785
e-mail tawnyowl@arkells.com
Dir *2.5m NW of town centre, signed from A419*

Expect a genuinely friendly welcome from the staff at this modern inn on the north-west outskirts of Swindon. It has comfortable, well-equipped bedrooms and bathrooms. A varied selection of enjoyable home-cooked meals is on offer at dinner, and a range of Arkells ales and wines. A private function room is available.

Facilities 5 en suite (1 fmly) ⊘ in bedrooms ⊘ in dining room ⊘ in 1 lounge TVB tea/coffee Direct dial from bedrooms 🐾 Cen ht TVL Stairlift Dinner Last d 9pm **Prices** S £39-£45; D £65-£75✳ **Conf** Max 55 Thtr 55 Class 55 Board 55 **Parking** 75 **Notes** rs Xmas/New Year Civ Wed 50

♦♦♦♦

Ardecca

Fieldrise Farm, Kingsdown Ln, Blunsdon SN25 5DL
☎ 01793 721238 & 07791 120826
e-mail chris-graham.ardecca@fsmail.net
web www.ardecca-bedandbreakfast.co.uk
Dir Off A419 at Turnpike rdbt for filling station, left onto Turnpike Rd, 1st right

Quietly located in 16 acres of pastureland with easy access to Swindon and the Cotswolds. All rooms are on the ground floor and are well furnished and equipped. An especially friendly welcome is provided and freshly cooked home-made dinners are available by arrangement.

Facilities 4 rms (4 pri facs) (1 fmly) (4 GF) ⊗ TVB tea/coffee ✖
Cen ht No children 10yrs No coaches Dinner Last d prior notice needed
Parking 5 **Notes** ⊛

♦♦♦♦

Crown Inn

Ermin St SN3 4NL ☎ 01793 827530 🖷 01793 831683
e-mail thecrownstratton@aricells.com
Dir A419 onto B4006 Stratton St Margaret, left onto Ermin St

This popular inn, dating back to 1868, is situated in Stratton St Margaret near to Swindon centre and the M4. Public areas are furnished in traditional style with crackling log fires adding to the character. Bedrooms are located within the main building and in a newer adjacent block, and all offer high standards of comfort and quality.

Facilities 21 en suite (7 GF) ⊗ in area of dining room STV TVB
tea/coffee Direct dial from bedrooms ✖ Cen ht No coaches Dinner Last
d 9.15pm **Parking** 60

♦♦♦♦

Parklands Hotel & Bentleys Restaurant

High St, Ogbourne St George SN8 1SL
☎ 01672 841555 🖷 01672 841533
e-mail enquiries@parklandshoteluk.co.uk
web www.parklandshoteluk.co.uk
Dir 7.5m S of Swindon in Ogbourne St George

Originating from the 17th century, Parklands is a peaceful spot for business or pleasure. The dining room has plenty of character and there is a pleasant bar-lounge area. A selection of freshly prepared dishes is available in the restaurant, and the less formal bar offers

lighter snacks. The well-furnished bedrooms have a number of extra facilities.

Facilities 12 en suite (2 GF) ⊗ in bedrooms ⊗ in dining room
⊗ in 1 lounge TVB tea/coffee Direct dial from bedrooms Licensed
Cen ht Dinner Last d 8.45pm **Conf** Max 16 Thtr 16 Class 16 Board 16
Parking 12

♦♦♦

The Check Inn

Woodland View, North Wroughton SN4 9AA
☎ 01793 845584 🖷 01793 814640
e-mail information@checkinn.co.uk
web www.checkinn.co.uk
Dir A361 (Swindon to Devizes), after dual carriageway bridge over M4 take the 1st right onto Woodland View

Located close to the M4, The Check Inn combines a traditional freehouse inn offering eight continually changing real ales with more modern, well-decorated and furnished bedrooms and bathrooms. A large car park is provided at the rear. A good selection of generously portioned, home-cooked meals is available.

Facilities 3 en suite (1 fmly) ⊗ in bedrooms ⊗ in dining room
⊗ in 1 lounge TVB tea/coffee Cen ht Petanque/boules terrain Dinner
Last d 9pm **Prices** S fr £38.50; D fr £42.50✶ (room only) **LB Parking** 5
Notes rs Xmas & New Year

Parking 48

♦♦♦

Heart in Hand

43 High St, Blunsdon SN26 7AG
☎ 01793 721314 🖷 01793 727026
e-mail leppardsteve@aol.com
Dir Off A419 at High St, 200yds on right

Located in the village centre, this family-run inn offers a relaxed and friendly welcome together with a wide selection of home-cooked food. Bedrooms are spacious, well equipped and offer a number of useful extras including writing desks. A pleasant rear garden with seating is also available.

Facilities 4 en suite (1 fmly) ⊗ in bedrooms ⊗ in dining room
⊗ in lounges TVB tea/coffee ✖ Cen ht Dinner Last d 9pm **Parking** 17

♦♦♦

Internos B&B ◇

3 Turnpike Rd, Blunsdon SN26 7EA
☎ 01793 721496 🖷 01793 721496
web www.internos-bedandbreakfast.co.uk
Dir 4m N of Swindon. Alongside A419 between Little Chef & Cold Habour pub

Situated just off the A419 towards Cirencester, this establishment offers comfortable accommodation and a relaxed and friendly atmosphere. The gardens open onto a field, which is a haven for wildlife. Guests enjoy a freshly cooked breakfast served in the dining room, and a cosy lounge is also available.

Facilities 3 rms (1 fmly) ⊗ in dining room FTV TVB ✖ Cen ht TVL
No coaches **Prices** S £25-£28; D £42✶ **Parking** 6 **Notes** ⊛

continued

SWINDON continued

◆◆◆

Leftwich Manor Guest House ◇

79 Cheney Manor Rd SN2 2NX
☎ 01793 610560 & 07884 445430 📠 01793 610560
e-mail lorna.leftwich@ntlworld.com
Dir *Signs for Cheney Manor on Great Western Way ring road, B&B next to Manor pub*

Many guests return to this friendly and very popular house close to the city's amenities. The proprietors ensure are most welcoming, and the bedrooms have many thoughtful extras. Dinner is available by arrangement.

Facilities 4 en suite (2 fmly) ⊗ in dining room TVB tea/coffee ✗ Cen ht No coaches Dinner Last d 24hrs in advance **Prices** S £30-£35; D £40-£45✳ **Notes** rs 25-27 Dec & 1 Jan ⊛

◆◆◆

Portquin Guest House

Broadbush, Broad Blunsdon SN26 7DH ☎ 01793 721261
e-mail portquin@msn.com
Dir *A419 onto B4019 at Blunsdon signed Highworth, continue 0.5m*

This friendly guest house near Swindon provides a warm welcome and views of the Lambourn Downs. The rooms vary in shape and size, with six in the main house and three in an adjacent annexe. Full English breakfasts are served at two large tables in the kitchen-dining area.

Facilities 6 en suite 3 annexe en suite (2 fmly) (4 GF) ⊗ TVB tea/coffee Direct dial from bedrooms Cen ht No coaches **Prices** S £35-£45; D £50-£70✳ **Conf** Max 16 Thtr 12 Class 16 Board 16 **Parking** 12

◆◆◆ 🅰

Fir Tree Lodge

17 Highworth Rd, Stratton St Margaret SN3 4QL
☎ 01793 822372 📠 01793 822372
e-mail info@firtreelodge.com
Dir *A419 onto B4006 signed Stratton/Town Centre. B&B 500yds opposite Rat Trap pub.*

Facilities 12 en suite 2 annexe en suite (5 GF) ⊗ in dining room ⊗ in lounges TVB tea/coffee Cen ht **Prices** S £32.32-£40; D £52.88-£60✳ **Parking** 14

◆◆ ▥

Saracens Head

High St, Highworth SN6 7AG
☎ 01793 762284 📠 01793 767869
e-mail arkells@arkells.com

The Saracens Head stands on the main street of this pleasant market town, 6 miles north-west of Swindon. It offers plenty of character, including a popular bar dating from 1828. A fine selection of real ales and home-cooked food are highlights. Bedrooms are generally compact and bathrooms feature good quality showers. A rear car park and outdoor seating are available.

Facilities 13 en suite (2 fmly) TVB tea/coffee Direct dial from bedrooms ✗ Cen ht **Conf** Max 10 Thtr 10 Class 10 Board 10 **Parking** 30

TROWBRIDGE
MAP 04 ST85

◆◆◆◆

Biss Barn B & B

Chiswood, West Ashton BA14 6DG
☎ 01225 710372 📠 01225 710372
e-mail derek.dee@bissbarn.com
web www.bissbarn.com
Dir *On A350, turn for Trowbridge at x-rds in West Ashton. B&B is 900yds on the right*

This spacious modern guest house is, as the name would suggest, a barn conversion. It stands in extensive gardens on the outskirts of Trowbridge. The modern accommodation is thoughtfully equipped and contains many extra welcoming touches. Breakfast is served in the large farmhouse-style kitchen, with its low-beamed ceiling. There is also a spacious, comfortable lounge.

Facilities 3 en suite (1 fmly) ⊗ TVB tea/coffee ✗ Cen ht TVL No children 12yrs No coaches **Prices** S fr £40; D £60 **Parking** 6 **Notes** Closed Xmas

◆◆◆◆

Eastbrook Cottage ◇

Hoopers Pool, Southwick BA14 9NG ☎ 01225 764403
e-mail enquiries@eastbrookcottage.co.uk
web www.eastbrookcottage.co.uk
Dir *A36 onto A361 to Trowbridge. After Rode take 2nd right into Hoopers Pool.*

This cottage, situated just of the main Frome road, has been renovated to provide fresh, smart accommodation. Although the bedrooms are not the most spacious, they are finished to a high level of quality and equipped with many thoughtful extras. To add to this, the host offers genuine hospitality and friendliness. Guests may not want to move from the wood-burning stove in the snug lounge. Breakfast, featuring local produce wherever possible, is enjoyed around a large oak table.

Facilities 3 rms (2 en suite) (1 pri facs) ⊗ TVB tea/coffee ✗ Cen ht No children 10yrs No coaches **Prices** S £30-£45; D £60-£70✳ **Parking** 5 **Notes** ⊛

◆◆◆◆ 🅰

Paxcroft Cottage ◇

62B Paxcroft Cottages, Devizes Rd, Hilperton BA14 6JB
☎ 01225 765838
e-mail paxcroftcottages@hotmail.com
web www.paxcroftcottages.pwp.blueyonder.co.uk
Dir *2m NE of Trowbridge. On A361 near Paxcroft Farm, 0.5m from the Paxcroft Mead Estate*

Facilities 3 en suite (1 fmly) ⊗ TVB tea/coffee ✗ Cen ht TVL No coaches **Prices** S £28-£30; D £50-£55✳ **LB** **Parking** 6 **Notes** ⊛

Please mention the AA B&B Guide when booking your stay

♦♦♦
The Old Police House B&B

51 Rutland Crescent BA14 0NY ☎ 0774 365 6617

Dir *Off A350 opp supermarket, B&B 100yds on right*

Located within a high-density residential area, just a few miles from Bradford on Avon and within easy reach of Bath, Salisbury and Glastonbury, this establishment offers comfortable and homely accommodation. Breakfast is served in the pleasant dining room and there is also a cosy lounge.

Facilities 4 rms (1 en suite) (1 fmly) ⊗ in bedrooms ⊗ in dining room TVB tea/coffee ✖ Cen ht TVL No coaches Dinner Last d 9pm **Conf** Max 20 **Parking** 10

♦♦♦
Watergardens

131 Yarnbrook Rd, West Ashton BA14 6AF
☎ 01225 752045 📋 01225 719427
e-mail lucy@heard28.freeserve.co.uk

Dir *On A350, 200yds from junct A350 & A363*

Well located for touring, this house offers comfortable and modern accommodation. The friendly proprietors ensure you are made to feel at home and the well-equipped rooms are spacious and attractive. Freshly cooked breakfast is served in either the dining room or the conservatory, which overlooks the water gardens.

Facilities 2 en suite (1 fmly) (2 GF) ⊗ TVB tea/coffee ✖ Cen ht No coaches **Parking** 4 **Notes** Closed 21 Dec-2 Jan 🚭

♦♦♦ 🅰
Bridge House Bed & Breakfast ◇

Canal Bridge, Semington BA14 6JT
☎ 01225 703281 & 706101 📋 01225 790892
e-mail jeanpaynDHPS@aol.com

Dir *Off A361 into Semington village, over bridge, B&B on right*

Facilities 4 rms ⊗ TVB tea/coffee ✖ Cen ht No coaches **Prices** S £22-£25; D £44-£50✻ **Parking** 6 **Notes** Closed Xmas & New Year 🚭

Book as early as possible, particularly in the peak holiday period

WARMINSTER   MAP 04 ST84

♦♦♦♦ ◼
The George Inn

Longbridge Deverill BA12 7DG
☎ 01985 840396 📋 01985 841333

Dir *3m S on the A350*

Located in the village of Longbridge Deverill, the George Inn combines a friendly village pub atmosphere with modern well-equipped bedrooms, one of which has a four-poster bed. In addition to the pleasant bar and restaurant, there is a lounge and the delightful river garden.

Facilities 1 en suite (1 fmly) ⊗ in 9 bedrooms ⊗ in dining room TVB tea/coffee Direct dial from bedrooms ✖ Cen ht· Dinner Last d 9.30pm **Prices** S £55; D £75✻ **Conf** Max 100 Thtr 100 Class 40 Board 30 **Parking** 70

♦♦♦♦
Deverill End

Sutton Veny BA12 7BY ☎ 01985 840356
e-mail riversgreathead@amserve.net

Dir *2.5m SE of Warminster. Off A36 at Heytesbury rdbt to Sutton Veny, over x-rds, 200yds on left*

This guest house is located midway between Bath and Salisbury, and is within easy reach of Stonehenge, Longleat and Stourhead. The comfortable well-equipped bedrooms have spectacular southern views, and in summer you can relax in the flower-filled garden.

Facilities 3 en suite (3 GF) ⊗ TVB tea/coffee ✖ Cen ht TVL No children 10yrs No coaches **Prices** D £55-£60 **Parking** 4 **Notes** Closed 20 Dec-Jan 🚭

♦♦♦♦ ☁ ◼
The Dove Inn

Corton BA12 0SZ ☎ 01985 850109 📋 01985 851041
e-mail info@thedove.co.uk

Dir *5m SE of Warminster. Off A36 to Corton village*

The relaxing inn stands in the heart of the peaceful village. There are carefully furnished courtyard rooms and a non-smoking conservatory, and in cooler months a roaring log fire accompanies the imaginative bar menu.

Facilities 5 annexe en suite (1 fmly) (4 GF) ⊗ in bedrooms ⊗ in dining room TVB tea/coffee Cen ht Dinner Last d 9pm **Prices** S £55; D £75-£95✻ **LB** **Parking** 24

♦♦♦♦
The Granary Bed & Breakfast

Manor Farm, Upton Scudamore BA12 0AG
☎ 01985 214835 📋 01985 214835

Dir *2m NW of Warminster. Off A350 into Upton Scudamore*

The Granary is located in the peaceful village of Upton Scudamore and has delightful country views. It offers ground-floor bedrooms, each with a private terrace, stylishly decorated with coordinated fabrics and comfortable furnishings. The many thoughtful extras include a fridge, and breakfast is served in your room.

Facilities 2 annexe en suite (2 GF) ⊗ TVB tea/coffee ✖ Cen ht No children 8yrs No coaches Golf **Prices** S fr £50; d fr £60✻ **LB** **Parking** 3 **Notes** 🚭

WARMINSTER continued

◆◆◆◆
White Lodge
22 Westbury Rd BA12 0AW
☎ 01985 212378 🖶 01985 212378
e-mail carol@lioncountry.co.uk
Dir 0.5m N of town centre. Off High St onto Portway signed Westbury, White Lodge 0.75m on left

Situated on the outskirts of Warminster, this attractive house, with art deco features, is well placed for touring Wiltshire and Somerset. Individually styled bedrooms, which overlook well-tended grounds, are comfortable and well-appointed.

Facilities 3 rms (1 en suite) (2 pri facs) (1 fmly) ⊗ TVB tea/coffee ✗ Cen ht No children 5yrs No coaches **Prices** S £40-£50; D £60-£65✳
Parking 8 **Notes** Closed Xmas rs Jan 🖀

WHITEPARISH   MAP 05 SU22

◆◆◆◆
Brayford ◇
Newton Ln SP5 2QQ ☎ 01794 884216
e-mail reservations@brayford.org.uk
Dir Off A36 at Newton x-rds onto Newton Ln towards Whiteparish, Brayford 150yds on right

A genuine welcome awaits guests at this comfortable family home. Peacefully located with views over neighbouring farmland, the house is just a short drive off the A36. Suitable for business and leisure travellers, bedrooms are well equipped with many thoughtful extras. Guests are invited to relax in the lounge dining room, where a tasty breakfast is served.

Facilities 3 rms (2 pri facs) (1 fmly) (2 GF) ⊗ TVB tea/coffee ✗ Cen ht TVL No coaches Gymnasium **Prices** S £30-£40; D £55-£60
Parking 2 **Notes** Closed Xmas & New Year 🖀

◆◆◆◆
Newton Farmhouse
Southampton Rd SP5 2QL ☎ 01794 884416
e-mail newtonfarmhouse1@aol.com
Dir 7m SE of Salisbury on A36 1m S of A27 junct

Dating back to the 16th century, this delightful farmhouse was gifted to Lord Nelson's family as part of the Trafalgar estate. The house has been thoughtfully restored and bedrooms, most with four-poster beds, have been adorned with personal touches. Carefully prepared breakfasts are available in the relaxing conservatory. The pleasant gardens include an outdoor swimming pool.

Facilities 6 en suite 3 annexe en suite (3 fmly) (5 GF) ⊗ TVB tea/coffee ✗ Cen ht TVL No coaches ⸚ ⅏ Trampoline, table tennis **Prices** S £50-£80; D £65-£90✳ **LB Parking** 9 **Notes** Closed 24-27 Dec 🖀

WHITLEY   MAP 04 ST86

★★★★★ ◉◉ **Restaurant with Rooms**

The Pear Tree Inn
Top Ln SN12 8QX ☎ 01225 709131 🖶 01225 702276
e-mail enquiries@thepeartreeinn.com

This inn provides luxurious bedrooms, some in an adjoining annexe at ground floor level, some in the main building. The restaurant draws visitors from a wide area to experience the interesting menu, the rustic atmosphere and the friendliness of the hosts.

Facilities 4 en suite 4 annexe en suite (2 fmly) (4 gf) ⊗ in bedrooms ⊗ in dining room TVB FTV tea/coffee ✗ Cen ht Dinner 9.30pm
Prices S £75; D £105✳ **Parking** 45

WINTERBOURNE STOKE   MAP 05 SU04

◆◆◆◆
Scotland Lodge Farm
SP3 4TF ☎ 01980 621199 🖶 01980 621188
e-mail william.lockwood@bigwig.net
Dir 0.25m W of village on A303, near B3083 junct & Scotland Lodge

Set in 46 acres of paddocks and grassland, this farm provides comfortable, well-appointed rooms featuring numerous thoughtful extra touches. Full English breakfasts are served at the large farmhouse table in the conservatory/lounge overlooking the paddocks. The proprietors are keen equestrians and are happy to offer stabling. Dogs are welcome by arrangement.

Facilities 3 en suite (1 fmly) (2 GF) ⊗ TVB tea/coffee Cen ht No coaches **Parking** 5 **Notes** Closed 24-26 Dec

WOODFALLS

MAP 05 SU12

◆◆◆◆ ◀▌

The Woodfalls Inn

The Ridge SP5 2LN ☎ 01725 513222 ▤ 01725 513220
e-mail woodfallsi@aol.com
web www.woodfallsinn.co.uk
Dir *M27 junct 1, onto B3079, then B3078 towards Fordingbridge, onto B3080*

Located in the quiet village centre, within easy reach of Salisbury and the New Forest, this attractive inn provides comfortable, well-furnished bedrooms, two with four-poster beds. There are public and lounge bars, and a cosy restaurant area. Breakfast is served in the conservatory.

Facilities 10 en suite (1 fmly) ⊗ in bedrooms ⊗ in dining room ⊗ in 1 lounge TVB tea/coffee Direct dial from bedrooms Cen ht Dinner Last d 9.30pm **Prices** S £49.95-£55; D £77.90-£85; (room only) LB **Conf** Max 100 Thtr 100 Class 70 Board 50 Del from £95 ✳ **Parking** 30

WOOTTON BASSETT

MAP 05 SU08

◆◆◆◆ ❦

Little Cotmarsh Farm ◇ (SU090797)

Broad Town SN4 7RA ☎ 01793 731322 Mrs Richards
e-mail maryrichards@btinternet.com
Dir *2.5m SE on Broad Hinton road, left into Cotmarsh, left at T-junct*

This lovely Grade II listed farmhouse is just a short drive from Wootton Bassett and is convenient for Swindon. Bedrooms are comfortable and character is apparent in the dining room with its fireplace and wood-burning stove. Breakfast is cooked to order and served around a communal dining table.

Facilities 3 rms (2 en suite) (1 fmly) ⊗ TVB tea/coffee ✱ Cen ht 108 acres organic beef **Prices** S £28-£33; D £50-£60✳ **Parking** 6 **Notes** Closed Dec-Jan 🐾

ABBERLEY

MAP 10 SO76

◆◆◆◆ ❦

Orleton Court B & B ◇ (SO702670)

WR6 6SU ☎ 01584 881248 ▤ 01584 881159
Mr & Mrs Spilsbury
e-mail pmspilsbury@aol.com
Dir *4m W of Abberley. A443 onto B4203 through Stanford Bridge, 1st right, 1m right into Orleton Court*

This Georgian farmhouse situated by the River Teme is part of a working hop farm. There are two comfortable ensuite bedrooms. Hearty breakfasts are served in the parlour and a comfortable lounge is available. Coarse fishing, golf and shooting are available by arrangement.

Facilities 3 rms (2 en suite) (2 fmly) ⊗ in bedrooms ⊗ in dining room TV2B tea/coffee ✱ Cen ht TVL Fishing ♨ 550 acres mixed/fruit/hop/sheep **Prices** S fr £30; d fr £55✳ **Parking** 20

◆◆◆◆

Whoppets Wood

WR6 6BU ☎ 01299 896545
Dir *A443 onto A451, 2m 1st left, 1.3m from Shavers End*

A warm welcome is assured at this former farmhouse, superbly located in pretty, mature gardens with stunning country views. Bedrooms are filled with thoughtful extras and a sunny hall-lounge is available. Memorable breakfasts are served in the cosy dining room.

Facilities 3 rms (2 en suite) (1 fmly) ⊗ TV2B tea/coffee ✱ Cen ht No children 4yrs No coaches **Parking** 3 **Notes** Closed Dec-1 Jan 🐾

England

England

ALVECHURCH
MAP 10 SP07

◆◆◆◆

Amberley ◇
Aqueduct Ln B48 7BS ☎ 0121 445 6526 & 07854 496006
e-mail a.patterson@ftel.co.uk
web www.alvechurchguesthouse.co.uk
Dir M42 junct 2 towards Birmingham, 1st left at next rdbt, 1st right at next rdbt, immediately left into Aqueduct Lane, 5th house on left after bridge.

Peacefully located on two acres of immaculate mature gardens within a peaceful residential area close to major road links, this impressive detached house provides a range of thoughtfully furnished bedrooms, some with modern en-suite facilities. Comprehensive breakfasts are taken in an attractive dining room and a spacious lounge is also available.

Facilities 4 rms (3 en suite) (1 pri facs) (1 fmly) ⊗ TVB tea/coffee ✖ Cen ht No children 3yrs Outdoor hot tub **Prices** S £30-£40; D £50-£60✱ **Parking** 10 **Notes** ⊛

◆◆◆ 🅰

Alcott Farm
Icknield St, Weatheroak B48 7EH
☎ 01564 824051 📄 01564 829799
Dir 2m NE of Alvechurch. M42 junct 3, A435 for Birmingham, left signed Weatheroak, left at x-rds down steep hill, left past pub, farm 0.5m on right up long driveway

Facilities 4 en suite ⊗ in bedrooms ⊗ in dining room TVB tea/coffee Cen ht TVL No children 10yrs No coaches **Prices** S £35; D £55✱ **Parking** 6 **Notes** ⊛

BECKFORD
MAP 10 SO93

★★★ Inn

The Beckford
Cheltenham Rd GL20 7AN
☎ 01386 881532 📄 01386 882021
e-mail norman@thebeckford.com
Dir A46 Cheltenham Rd. 6m from Evesham or junct 9 M5 A46 to Evesham.

Looking more like a country mansion than a typical Inn, The Beckford is a superb Cotswold stone building with it's origins in the 18th century. Comfortable accommodation is provided in the eight bedrooms and a good selection and range of choices for dinner and breakfast is offered. A splendid venue for parties, weddings or conferences with The Garden Restaurant being well appointed with 84

continued

covers and non-smoking. A snug is available with a wall mounted widescreen television, where you can watch your favourite sports or other programmes. There is ample parking surrounding this established property with disabled access.

Facilities 8 rms (7 en suite) (1 fmly) ⊗ in bedrooms ⊗ in dining room ⊗ in 1 lounge TVB tea/coffee Direct dial from bedrooms ✖ Cen ht TVL Dinner Last d 9.40pm **Conf** Max 100 Thtr 100 Board 100 **Parking** 70

BEWDLEY
MAP 10 SO77

Premier Collection

◆◆◆◆◆ 🔔

Number Thirty
30 Gardners Meadow DY12 2DG
☎ 01299 402404 📄 01299 402404
e-mail info@numberthirty.net
Dir Off Load St/Bewdley bridge onto Severnside South, 2nd right

This smart modern house is close to the town centre and cricket ground. Bedrooms are luxuriously furnished and have lots of thoughtful extras. There is a lounge and hearty breakfasts are served in the attractive dining room overlooking the sun deck.

Facilities 4 rms (3 en suite) (1 pri facs) ⊗ TVB tea/coffee ✖ Cen ht TVL No children 10yrs No coaches **Prices** S £50-£70; D £70-£90✱ **Parking** 6 **Notes** ⊛

◆◆◆◆ 🍽 🍺

The Mug House Inn
12 Severnside North DY12 2EE ☎ 01299 402543
e-mail drew@mughousebewdley.co.uk
Dir A456 onto B4190 into Bewdley. Turn right after bridge. B&B on the Riverfront.

Located on the opposite side of the River Severn to Bewdley Rowing Club, the 18th-century inn has been renovated to combine high standards of comfort and facilities with the original features. Bedrooms are thoughtfully furnished, there is a separate breakfast rooom, and imaginative dinners are served in the restaurant.

Facilities 4 en suite 3 annexe en suite (2 fmly) (1 GF) ⊗ in dining room TVB tea/coffee ✖ Cen ht No coaches Dinner Last d 9pm **Prices** S £60-£75; D £75-£95✱

◆◆◆

Bank House

14 Lower Park DY12 2DP ☎ 01299 402652
e-mail fleur.nightingale@virgin.net
web www.bewdley-accommodation.co.uk
Dir *In town centre. From junct High St & Lax Ln, Bank House after junct on left*

Once a private bank, this Victorian house retains many original features and offers comfortable accommodation. The cosy dining room is the setting for tasty English breakfasts served at one family table. Owner Mrs Nightingale has a comprehensive knowledge of the town and its history.

Facilities 4 rms (1 fmly) ⊗ TVB tea/coffee ✖ Cen ht No coaches
Prices S £28-£30; D £52-£54 **Parking** 2 **Notes** Closed 24-26 Dec rs 27-31 Dec 🚭

◆◆◆

Pewterers' House

Pewterers' Alley DY12 1AE ☎ 01299 401956
e-mail pewterershouse@tiscali.co.uk
web www.pewterershouse.co.uk
Dir *B4190 into Bewdley, under railway bridge, B&B opp Black Boy Hotel*

A short walk from the River Severn and historic centre, this traditional cottage has been renovated to offer good standards of comfort and facilities. Bedrooms are equipped with lots of thoughtful extras and efficient modern shower rooms. Comprehensive breakfasts feature local produce.

Facilities 3 rms (2 en suite) ⊗ TVB tea/coffee Cen ht No coaches
Prices S £40-£45; D £50-£55✳ **Parking** 2 **Notes** 🚭

BROADWAY   MAP 10 SP03

Premier Collection

★★★★★ ◉◉ **Restaurant with Rooms**

Russell's

20 High St WR12 7DT ☎ 01386 853555 📠 01386 853555
e-mail info@russellsofbroadway.com
Dir *Opp village green*

Situated in the centre of the picturesque village, Russell's is a great base for exploring the Cotswolds. The superb bedrooms, each with their own character, have air conditioning and a wide range of extras. Cuisine is a real draw, with fresh local produce prepared with skill.

Facilities 4 en suite (4 fmly) STV TVB tea/coffee Licensed No coaches
Parking 16

Premier Collection

◆◆◆◆◆

Mill Hay House

Snowshill Rd WR12 7JS ☎ 01386 852498 📠 01386 858038
e-mail millhayhouse@aol.com
web www.millhay.co.uk
Dir *0.7m S of Broadway towards Snowshill, house on right*

Set in 3 acres of immaculate grounds beside a medieval watermill, this impressive early 18th-century stone house has many original features complemented by quality decor, period furniture and works of art. The spacious bedrooms are filled with thoughtful extras and one has a balcony. Imaginative breakfasts are served in the elegant dining room and there is a spacious drawing room.

Facilities 3 en suite ⊗ in bedrooms ⊗ in dining room ⊗ in 1 lounge FTV TVB tea/coffee Direct dial from bedrooms ✖ Cen ht TVL No children 12yrs No coaches 3 acre garden with medieval pond & moat
Prices S £126-£162; D £140-£180✳ **LB** **Parking** 15

◆◆◆◆ 🐾

Bowers Hill Farm *(SP086420)*

Bowers Hill, Willersey WR11 7HG
☎ 01386 834585 & 07966 171861 📠 01386 830234
Mr & Mrs Bent
e-mail sarah@bowershillfarm.com
web www.bowershillfarm.com
Dir *3m NW of Broadway. A44 onto B4632 to Willersey, at minirdbt signs to Badsey/industrial estate, farm 2m on right by postbox*

An impressive Victorian house set in immaculate gardens on a diverse farm, where point-to-point horses are also bred. The house has been renovated to provide very comfortable bedrooms with modern bathrooms. Breakfast is served in the elegant dining room or the magnificent conservatory, and a lounge with open fire is also available.

Facilities 3 en suite (1 fmly) ⊗ TVB tea/coffee ✖ Cen ht TVL 30 acres horse breeding **Prices** S £35-£45; D £55-£65✳ **LB** **Conf** Max 8 Class 8 Board 8 **Parking** 5

◆◆◆◆

Leasow House

Laverton Meadows WR12 7NA
☎ 01386 584526 📠 01386 584596
e-mail leasow@clara.net
web www.leasow.co.uk
For full entry see **Laverton (Gloucestershire)**

BROADWAY continued

◆◆◆◆ ⊜ ◼

Horse & Hound

54 High St WR12 7DT ☎ 01386 852287 🖷 01386 853784
e-mail k2mtk@aol.com
Dir Off A46 to Evesham

In the heart of this beautiful Cotswold village this delightful inn can be found. A warm welcome is guaranteed whether dining in the inviting pub or staying overnight in the attractive and well-appointed bedrooms. Breakfast and dinner is a feature not to be missed, with carefully prepared local produce.

Facilities 5 en suite (1 fmly) ⊛ in bedrooms ⊛ in dining room TVB tea/coffee Cen ht Dinner Last d 9pm **Prices** S £50-£80; D £70-£90⋇ LB **Parking** 15

◆◆◆◆ ⋎

Mount Pleasant Farm (SP056392)

Childswickham WR12 7HZ
☎ 01386 853424 🖷 01386 853424 Mrs Perry
e-mail helen@mount-pleasant.fslife.co.uk
Dir Onto B4632 for Winchcombe, 50yds right to Childswickham (3m). Farm 1.5m W on left

Located in immaculate, mature grounds in a pretty hamlet, this impressive Victorian house provides spacious, traditionally furnished bedrooms with smart modern bathrooms. Comprehensive breakfasts are served in an elegant dining room, and a comfortable lounge is available.

Facilities 3 en suite (1 fmly) ⊛ in bedrooms ⊛ in dining room ⊛ in lounges TVB tea/coffee ✖ Cen ht No children 5yrs 950 acres Arable **Prices** S £40; D £55-£60⋇ **Parking** 10

◆◆◆◆

Southwold House

Station Rd WR12 7DE
☎ 01386 853681 & 07747 625726 🖷 01386 854610
e-mail elvira@cotswolds-broadway-southwold.co.uk
web www.cotswolds-broadway-southwold.co.uk
Dir In village from W end of High St

A warm welcome is guaranteed at this delightful Edwardian property that is only a short distance from the centre of this well-known village. The renovated house has a comfortable, homely feel. Public areas include a spacious lounge and a cosy breakfast room. Ample off-road parking is available.

continued

Facilities 8 en suite (1 fmly) ⊛ TVB tea/coffee ✖ Cen ht TVL
Prices S £40-£42; D £65-£85⋇ LB **Conf** Max 10 **Parking** 8

BROMSGROVE   MAP 10 SO97

◆◆◆◆ 🅰

Overwood B & B ◇

Woodcote Ln, Woodcote B61 9EE
☎ 01562 777193 & 07941 188652
e-mail info@overwood.net
Dir A448 from Bromsgrove, 2.5m right onto Woodcote Ln, 100yds on left

Facilities 3 rms (2 en suite) (1 pri facs) ⊛ TVB tea/coffee ✖ Cen ht No children 14yrs No coaches **Prices** S £30-£42; D £45-£57⋇ LB **Parking** 5

◆◆◆ ⋎

Lower Bentley Farm ◇ (SO962679)

Lower Bentley B60 4JB ☎ 01527 821286
Mr & Mrs Gibbs
e-mail anthony@lowerbentleyfarm.force9.co.uk
web www.lowerbentleyfarm.co.uk
Dir B4091 S past Navigation pub, left signed Woodgate, 1st right onto Woodgate Rd, 3rd left onto Lower Bentley Ln

Located a short drive from major roads, this impressive red brick Victorian house is full of original features and stylishly decorated and furnished throughout. Bedrooms are filled with lots of thoughtful extras and a comfortable lounge is provided in addition to an elegant dining room, the setting for memorable breakfasts.

Facilities 2 en suite ⊛ TVB tea/coffee ✖ Cen ht TVL 346 acres dairy **Prices** S £30-£33; D £50⋇ **Parking** 5 **Notes** ⊛

FLYFORD FLAVELL   MAP 10 SO95

◆◆◆◆ ◼

The Boot Inn

Radford Rd WR7 4BS ☎ 01386 462658 🖷 01386 462547
e-mail enquiries@thebootinn.com
Dir In village centre, signed from A422

Please note that this establishment has recently changed hands. An inn has occupied this site since the 13th century, though The Boot itself dates from the Georgian period. Modernisation has retained its character, while the bedrooms, furnished in antique pine, are equipped with practical extras and have modern bathrooms. A range

continued

England

of ales, wines and imaginative food is offered in the cosy public areas, which include an attractive conservatory and patio.

Facilities 5 en suite (2 GF) ⊗ in bedrooms ⊗ in dining room TVB tea/coffee Direct dial from bedrooms ✖ Cen ht Golf Pool Table Arrangement with Vale Golf Club Dinner Last d 9.50pm **Parking** 31

KEMPSEY
MAP 10 SO84

◆◆◆ ⚔

Walter de Cantelupe Inn

Main Rd (A38) WR5 3NA ☎ 01905 820572
e-mail walter.depub@fsbdial.co.uk
web www.walterdecantelupeinn.com
Dir On A38 in village centre

This inn provides cosy bedrooms with smart bathrooms, and is convenient for the M5 and Worcester. The intimate, open-plan public areas are the setting for a range of real ales, and imaginative food featuring local produce and a fine selection of British cheeses.

Facilities 3 rms (2 en suite) (1 pri facs) ⊗ in bedrooms ⊗ in area of dining room TVB tea/coffee Cen ht No coaches Dinner Last d 9pm (Fri/Sat 10pm) **Parking** 24

KIDDERMINSTER
MAP 10 SO87

◆◆◆◆

Bewdley Hill House

8 Bewdley Hill DY11 6BS
☎ 01562 60473 ▤ 0871 236 1608
e-mail info@bewdleyhillhouse.co.uk
web www.bewdleyhillhouse.co.uk
Dir A456 W from town centre, on left before filling station

Located on the edge of Kidderminster, Bewdley Hill offers comfortable accommodation in a friendly family atmosphere and makes a good business or leisure base for the surrounding areas. Rooms are freshly decorated and well equipped and breakfast is served in the attractive dining room.

Facilities 6 en suite (2 fmly) (1 GF) ⊗ TVB tea/coffee ✖ Cen ht No coaches Last d day before **Prices** S £35; D £55 **Parking** 6
Notes Closed 22 Dec-5 Jan

◆◆◆

Victoria House ◇

15 Comberton Rd DY10 1UA ☎ 01562 67240
e-mail victoriakidderminster@yahoo.co.uk
Dir On A448, 0.5m from town centre, 200yds from Kidderminster station

Located a short walk from the Severn Valley Railway, this impressive Victorian house has been renovated to provide homely bedrooms. Breakfast is served in a spacious and attractive dining room. There is a private car park.

Facilities 7 rms (5 en suite) (1 fmly) ⊗ TVB tea/coffee ✖ Cen ht No children 5yrs No coaches **Prices** S £27-£30; D £49 **Parking** 5

MALVERN
MAP 10 SO74

★★★ Inn

The Anchor Inn

Drake St, Welland WR13 6LN
☎ 01684 592317 ▤ 01684 592317
e-mail theanchor13@hotmail.com
web www.upton.uk.net
Dir A4104, 2.5m from Upton on Severn.

This well appointed Inn is set in the Malvern's in a very quiet location where the owners offer a warm welcome to all their guests. The food is of a high standard with a very good selection taken from the Inn blackboard. Bedrooms are comfortable and well appointed with many added extras. Ideal base for walking the Malvern Hills or visiting the Three Counties Showground which is 5 minutes away, Malvern Theatre and Eastnor Castle are other local attractions within easy distance. Parking is ample to the front and side of the property.

Facilities 2 rms (1 en suite) (1 pri facs) ⊗ TVB tea/coffee ✖ Cen ht Golf 18 Dinner Last d 8.45pm **Prices** S £45; D £60-£70✳ **Parking** 62

★★★ Inn

Wyche Inn

74 Wyche Rd WR14 4EQ
☎ 01684 575396 ▤ 01684 575396
e-mail reservations@thewycheinn.co.uk
Dir On B4102 towards Malvern and Colwall.

Located in an elevated position on the outskirts and with stunning views over the surrounding countryside, this inn is popular with both locals and visiting walkers. Thoughtfully furnished bedrooms provide good levels of comfort and a good range of ales and food is offered with some value 'specials' nights.

Facilities 4 en suite ⊗ in 1 bedrooms ⊗ in dining room TVB tea/coffee ✖ Cen ht No coaches Pool Table Dinner Last d 8.30pm **Parking** 4

Please mention the AA B&B Guide when booking your stay

England

MALVERN continued

◆◆◆◆
The Dell House

Green Ln, Malvern Wells WR14 4HU
☎ 01684 564448 🖶 01684 893974
e-mail burrage@dellhouse.co.uk
web www.dellhouse.co.uk
Dir *2m S of Great Malvern on A449. Turn left off A449 onto Green Ln. House at top of road on right*

This impressive, well-proportioned Victorian house retains many unique features, several of which were introduced by the resident scholar and vicar during its period as a rectory. Spacious bedrooms are filled with thoughtful extras and a comprehensive breakfast is served in an elegant dining room with superb views of the surrounding countryside and mature grounds in which the house sits.

Facilities 3 en suite ⊗ TVB tea/coffee 🛏 Cen ht TVL No children 10yrs No coaches **Prices** S £33-£42; D £56-£64✱ **Parking** 6 **Notes** ⊜

◆◆◆◆
Bredon House Hotel

34 Worcester Rd WR14 4AA
☎ 01684 566990 🖶 01684 577530
e-mail ragella@bredonhouse.co.uk
Dir *200yds N of Great Malvern centre on A449, large fir tree in front car park*

Please note that this establishment has recently changed hands. Superbly located on the east side of the Malvern Hills, with stunning views of the Vale of Evesham and the Severn valley, this elegant Regency house still has many original features. The spacious bedrooms offer many practical extras, and a comfortable lounge is available.

Facilities 10 en suite (2 fmly) (1 GF) ⊗ in bedrooms ⊗ in dining room TVB tea/coffee Direct dial from bedrooms Licensed Cen ht TVL No children **Prices** S £45-£65; D £75-£90✱ **Parking** 7

◆◆◆◆
Cowleigh Park Farm

Cowleigh Rd WR13 5HJ ☎ 01684 566750
e-mail cowleighpark@ukonline.co.uk
Dir *From Great Malvern (A449) take B4219 towards Bromyard. Farmhouse 0.50m on right, just before de-restriction sign.*

This attractive black and white timber framed former farmhouse, within close proximity to the famous Malvern Hills dates back in parts to the early 13th century. Bedrooms retain a period charm but still cater well for the modern guest. Breakfast is taken in the elegant dining room.

Facilities 3 en suite ⊗ TVB tea/coffee Cen ht No children 7yrs **Prices** S £40-£60; D £65-£70✱ **Parking** 8 **Notes** Closed Xmas

◆◆◆◆
Pembridge Hotel

114 Graham Rd WR14 2HX
☎ 01684 574813 🖶 01684 566885
Dir *A449 onto Church St, 1st left*

Located on a leafy residential road close to the town centre, this large Victorian house retains many original features, including a superb staircase. Bedrooms, which include a ground-floor room, are well equipped. Other areas include a comfortable sitting room with a small bar and an elegant dining room.

Facilities 8 en suite (1 fmly) (1 GF) ⊗ in bedrooms ⊗ in dining room TVB tea/coffee Direct dial from bedrooms 🛏 Licensed Cen ht TVL No children 7yrs No coaches **Conf** Max 12 **Parking** 10

◆◆◆◆
St Just

169 Worcester Rd WR14 1EU ☎ 01684 562023
e-mail tricia@stjust.clara.co.uk
Dir *N of Great Malvern on A449, 350yds W of Malvern Link Shopping Centre. Car park via Albert Park Rd*

Located in pretty, mature gardens close to Malvern Link, this impressive Victorian house retains many original features and is stylishly decorated and furnished. Bedrooms have a wealth of thoughtful extras and comprehensive breakfasts are served in an elegant dining room. Secure private parking.

Facilities 3 rms (2 en suite) (1 pri facs) ⊗ TVB tea/coffee 🛏 Cen ht No children 12yrs No coaches **Prices** D £50-£70✱ **LB Parking** 8 **Notes** Closed Xmas ⊜

◆◆◆◆
Woodpeckers

66 Peachfield Rd, Malvern Wells WR14 4AL
☎ 01684 562827 ▤ 01684 562827
e-mail woodpeckers@cmail.co.uk
Dir 1m s of town centre. Off B4208 onto Peachfield Rd, left onto private road after railway bridge

Set in an unspoiled wooded hollow close to the Three Counties Showground, this attractive bungalow provides homely accommodation with quality modern bathrooms. Breakfast is served in the cosy dining room, which has a glass wall overlooking the pretty, mature garden. The interior is enhanced by the proprietor's fine original art and sculpture.

Facilities 2 en suite (2 GF) ⊗ TVB tea/coffee ✖ Cen ht No children 12yrs No coaches Dinner Last d 5pm **Prices** S £30-£38; D £56-£64✱ LB **Parking** 2 **Notes** 🐾

◆◆◆
Four Hedges

The Rhydd, Hanley Castle WR8 0AD ☎ 01684 310405
e-mail fredgies@aol.com
Dir 4m E from Malvern at junct of B4211 & B4424

Situated in a rural location, this detached house stands in mature grounds with wild birds in abundance. The bedrooms are equipped with thoughtful extras. Tasty English breakfasts, using free-range eggs, are served in a cosy dining room at a table made from a 300-year-old elm tree.

Facilities 4 rms (2 en suite) ⊗ TV1B tea/coffee Cen ht TVL No coaches Fishing ⚘ **Prices** S fr £20✱ **Parking** 5 **Notes** Closed Xmas 🐾

◆◆◆
Sidney House Hotel

40 Worcester Rd WR14 4AA
☎ 01684 574994 ▤ 01684 574994
e-mail info@sidneyhouse.co.uk
web www.sidneyhouse.co.uk
Dir On A449 200yds N from town centre

This impressive Grade II Georgian house is close to the central attractions and has stunning views. Bedrooms are filled with thoughtful extras, and some have small shower rooms en suite. The spacious dining room looks towards the Cotswolds and there is a comfortable lounge.

Facilities 8 rms (5 en suite) (1 fmly) ⊗ in bedrooms ⊗ in dining room ⊗ in 1 lounge TVB tea/coffee Licensed Cen ht TVL No coaches **Prices** S £25-£55; D £59-£75✱ **Parking** 9 **Notes** Closed 24 Dec-3 Jan

Ⓤ
Portocks End House

Portocks Ln, Clevelode WR13 6PE ☎ 01684 310276
e-mail mpa-cameron@countyside-inter.net
Dir On B4424, 4m N of Upton-On-Severn, opposite Riverside Caravan Park

At the time of going to press the rating for this establishment had not been confirmed. Please check the AA website www.theAA.com for up-to-date information.

Facilities 2 rms (2 pri facs) (1 fmly) ⊗ tea/coffee No coaches **Prices** S £22.50; D £45✱ **Parking** 4 **Notes** Closed Dec-Feb 🐾

MARTLEY   MAP 10 SO76

◆◆◆◆ ☕
Admiral Rodney Inn

Berrow Green WR6 6PL ☎ 01886 821375 ▤ 01886 822048
e-mail rodney@admiral.fslife.co.uk
web www.admiral-rodney.co.uk
Dir A44 onto B4197 at Knightwick, 2m on left

Located in the pretty village of Berrow Green, this 16th-century inn has been renovated to provide high standards of comfort and facilities. Spacious, carefully furnished bedrooms are complemented by luxurious modern bathrooms. Ground floor areas include quality bars with log fires and a unique tiered and beamed restaurant, where imaginative dishes are served.

Facilities 3 en suite ⊗ in area of dining room ⊗ in 1 lounge TVB tea/coffee Direct dial from bedrooms Cen ht Pool Table Skittle alley Dinner Last d 9.30pm **Prices** D £55-£65✱ **Conf** Max 30 Class 30 **Parking** 40

STOURPORT-ON-SEVERN   MAP 10 SO87

◆◆◆◆
Garden Cottages

Stoney Ln, Crossway Gn DY13 9SL
☎ 01299 250626 ▤ 01299 250626
e-mail accommodation@gardencottages.co.uk
web www.gardencottages.co.uk
Dir 3m SE of Stourport off A449 rdbt

Convenient for Worcester and the surrounding area, these carefully converted cottages have modern, well-equipped bedrooms and a comfortable lounge with beams and a log burner. There is also a large conservatory overlooking the attractive garden. Evening meals are available by arrangement using fresh produce from the nearby farm.

Facilities 4 rms (3 en suite) (1 pri facs) (1 fmly) (1 GF) ⊗ TVB tea/coffee Cen ht TVL No coaches Dinner Last d previous day **Prices** S £35-£40; D £45-£70✱ LB **Conf** Max 12 Board 12 **Parking** 5 **Notes** Closed Xmas 🐾

If you book on bed, breakfast and evening meal terms, you may find that the tariff includes only the set menu

England

TENBURY WELLS · MAP 10 SO56

★★★★ Restaurant with Rooms

The Peacock Inn

Worcester Rd WR15 8LL ☎ 01584 810506 📄 01584 811236
e-mail peacockinn001@aol.com
Dir A456 from Worcester take A443 to Tenbury Wells. Inn 1.25m E of
Tenbury Wells

A warm welcome can be expected from resident proprietors at this
14th-century roadside inn, which has a wealth of original features such
as wood panelling, beams and low ceilings. The atmospheric bar and
restaurant are popular locally, and bedrooms are not only spacious
and comfortable but are also usefully and thoughtfully equipped.

Facilities 6 en suite (1 fmly) (1 GF) TVB tea/coffee Direct dial from
bedrooms ✖ Licensed Dinner Last d 9pm **Prices** S £55; D £75-£85✱
LB Conf Max 30 Thtr 20 Class 30 Board 20 **Parking** 30

WORCESTER · MAP 10 SO85

◆◆◆◆ ◀▮

Bants

Worcester Rd WR7 4NN ☎ 01905 381282 📄 01905 381173
e-mail info@bants.co.uk
web www.bants.co.uk
Dir 5m E of Worcester. On A422 at Upton Snodsbury

A family-run 16th-century pub with a modern atmosphere. Bedrooms
are carefully decorated and well equipped, with some rooms separate
from the inn. A wide range of freshly cooked meals is available in the
free-house bar or served in the large conservatory.

Facilities 9 rms (7 en suite) (2 pri facs) (3 GF) ⊘ in bedrooms
⊘ in dining room ⊘ in 1 lounge TVB tea/coffee ✖ Cen ht Dinner Last
d 9.30pm **Parking** 40

◆◆◆◆

Burgage House ◇

4 College Precincts WR1 2LG
☎ 01905 25396 📄 01905 25396
e-mail contact@burgagehouse.co.uk
Dir M5 junct 7, A44 into city centre, left onto Edgar St, College
Precincts is pedestrian only on right

Located next to the cathedral and the historic centre, this impressive
Georgian house has original features, including a fine stone staircase,
enhanced by the decor and furnishings. Bedrooms, including the

ground-floor Cromwell Room, are spacious and homely. An elegant
dining room is the setting for comprehensive English breakfasts.

Facilities 4 en suite (1 fmly) (1 GF) ⊘ TVB tea/coffee ✖ Cen ht
Prices S £30-£35; D £55-£60✱ **Notes** Closed 23-30 Dec 🐾

◆◆◆◆ ▲

Oaklands B&B

Claines WR3 7RS ☎ 01905 458871 📄 01905 759362
e-mail barbara.gadd@zoom.co.uk

Facilities 4 en suite (2 fmly) ⊘ in bedrooms ⊘ in dining room
⊘ in lounges TVB tea/coffee Cen ht Snooker Complimentary golf
available **Prices** S fr £40; d fr £65 **LB Parking** 6 **Notes** Closed
Xmas & New Year 🐾

◆◆◆

Croft Guest House

WR6 5JD ☎ 01886 832227 📄 01886 830037
e-mail brb@crofthousewr6.fsnet.co.uk
Dir 4m SW of Worcester. On A4103 Leigh exit at Bransford rdbt,
driveway on left

This cottage-style property, dating in parts from the 16th century, is
convenient for the city centre and the Malverns. Bedrooms are homely
and the pretty gardens have a water feature. Dogs are welcome with a
current vaccination certificate.

Facilities 5 rms (3 en suite) (1 fmly) ⊘ TVB tea/coffee Licensed Cen ht
TVL No coaches Arrangement with golf course opposite. Dinner
Parking 5

◆◆◆

Park House Guest Accommodation ◇

12 Droitwich Rd WR3 7LJ ☎ 01905 21816 📄 01905 22578
Dir 1m N of city centre at junct A38 & A449

Located 1m from the city centre and having a spacious car park, this
Victorian house provides a range of thoughtfully furnished bedrooms.
Breakfast is served in a cosy dining room, and there is also a lounge.

Facilities 4 rms (3 en suite) ⊘ STV TVB tea/coffee Cen ht TVL
No coaches **Prices** S £25-£35; D £50-£55 **Parking** 8 **Notes** 🐾

◆◆◆

Wyatt Guesthouse ◇

40 Barbourne Rd WR1 1HU
☎ 01905 26311 📄 01905 26311
e-mail wyatt.guest@virgin.net
Dir On A38 0.5m N from city centre

Located within easy walking distance from shops, restaurants and
central attractions, this Victorian house provides a range of
thoughtfully furnished bedrooms. Breakfast is served in the cosy
dining room and a lounge is available.

Facilities 8 rms (7 en suite) (3 fmly) (1 GF) ⊘ in 3 bedrooms
⊘ in dining room ⊘ in lounges STV TVB tea/coffee Cen ht No coaches
Prices S £28-£35; D £48-£50✱

continued

YORKSHIRE, EAST RIDING OF

BEVERLEY MAP 17 TA03

See also **Leven**

Premier Collection

♦♦♦♦♦

Burton Mount Country House

Malton Rd, Cherry Burton HU17 7RA

☎ 01964 550541 🖷 01964 551955

e-mail pg@burtonmount.co.uk

web www.burtonmount.co.uk

Dir 3m NW of Beverley. B1248 for Malton, 2m right at x-rds, house on left

A charming country house 3m from Beverley, set in delightful gardens and offering luxurious accommodation. Bedrooms are well equipped and have thoughtful extra touches. The spacious drawing room has a blazing fire in the cooler months, and an excellent, Aga-cooked Yorkshire breakfast is served in the morning room. Pauline Greenwood is renowned locally for her customer care, culinary skills and warm hospitality.

Facilities 3 en suite ⊗ STV TVB tea/coffee ✖ Licensed Cen ht TVL No children 8yrs No coaches ⚙ ⚖ Dinner Last d 4.30pm **Prices** S £51; D £40-£79.50✴ **LB** **Conf** Max 30 Thtr 30 Class 20 Board 20 **Parking** 20

BRIDLINGTON MAP 17 TA16

★★★ **Guest Accommodation**

The Langdon ◇

13-16 Pembroke Ter YO15 3BX

☎ 01262 400124 🖷 01262 605377

e-mail cruxon@fsmail.net

Dir Off A165 onto Shaftesbury Rd, pass Spa Theatre, Pembroke Ter on left opp gardens.

Located on the seafront, the Langdon has a cosy bar and lounge where regular evening entertainment is held, and the reception rooms extend to a small garden porch. Home-cooked meals are served in the cheerful dining room or the stylish new restaurant.

Facilities 30 en suite (7 fmly) ⊗ in dining room STV TVB tea/coffee ✖ Licensed Lift Cen ht TVL Pool Table Dinner Last d noon **Prices** S £30-£45; D £60-£90; (incl. dinner) ✴ **LB** **Conf** Max 50 Board 50

Premier Collection

♦♦♦♦♦

Marton Grange

Flamborough Rd, Marton cum Sewerby YO15 1DU

☎ 01262 602034 🖷 01262 602034

e-mail martongrange@talk21.com

web www.marton-grange.co.uk

Dir 2m NE of Bridlington. On B1255, 600yds W of Links golf club

There is a welcoming atmosphere at this country guest house and the bedrooms are all of high quality, with a range of extra facilities; ground-floor rooms are available. There are attractive lounges with views over the immaculate gardens while substantial breakfasts are served in the delightful dining room.

continued

Marton Grange

Facilities 11 en suite (3 GF) ⊗ TVB tea/coffee Licensed Lift Cen ht No children 12yrs No coaches **Prices** S £40-£48; D £64-£76✴ **Parking** 11 **Notes** Closed Dec-Feb

♦♦♦♦

Burlington Quays ◇

20 Meadowfield Rd YO15 3LD

☎ 01262 676052 🖷 01262 676052

e-mail burlingtonquays@axis-connect.com

Dir Off South Marine Dr going S, 3rd on right after Spa Theatre & Royal Hall

A few streets from The Spa and close to the beach, this personally run guest house offers light spacious bedrooms and very attentive hospitality, truly a home from home. A comfortable lounge and excellent cooking are special features.

Facilities 5 en suite (3 fmly) ⊗ TVB tea/coffee ✖ Licensed Cen ht TVL No coaches Dinner Last d 1pm **Prices** S £25-£35; D £50-£54✴ **LB** **Conf** Max 10 Board 10 **Parking** 2 **Notes** ⊛

♦♦♦♦

The Mount ◇

2 Roundhay Rd YO15 3JY

☎ 01262 672306 🖷 01262 672306

Dir A165 N to Bridlington (Kingsgate), right onto Shaftesbury Rd, 3rd left onto Roundhay Rd

Friendly and attentive service is provided at this substantial Victorian building. Bedrooms are prettily furnished, and home-cooked five-course meals are served in the bright dining room. Afterwards you can relax in the lounge or enjoy a drink at the bar.

Facilities 8 en suite (2 fmly) ⊗ in dining room TVB tea/coffee ✖ Licensed Cen ht TVL No coaches Dinner Last d 2pm **Prices** S £25-£27; D £50-£54✴ **LB** **Parking** 2 **Notes** Closed 28 Nov-mid Feb ⊛

Book as early as possible, particularly in the peak holiday period

England

BRIDLINGTON continued

◆◆◆◆

Royal Hotel

1 Shaftesbury Rd YO15 3NP
☎ 01262 672433 📄 01262 672433
e-mail info@royalhotelbrid.co.uk
Dir A615 N to Bridlington (Kingsgate), right onto Shaftesbury Rd

Located next to the promenade, this immaculate property has a range of thoughtfully furnished bedrooms with smart modern bathrooms. Spacious public areas include a large dining room, conservatory-sitting room, and a cosy television lounge. Imaginative dinners are a feature and a warm welcome is assured.

Facilities 14 rms (13 en suite) (1 pri facs) 3 annexe en suite (7 fmly) (3 GF) ⊘ in bedrooms ⊘ in dining room ⊘ in 1 lounge TVB tea/coffee Licensed Cen ht TVL Dinner Last d 5.30pm **Prices** S fr £32; d fr £64✳ **LB Conf** Max 85 Thtr 85 Class 20 Board 40 **Parking** 7

◆◆◆◆

Shearwater

22 Vernon Rd YO15 2HE ☎ 01262 679883
e-mail shearwaterhotel@amserve.com
Dir In town centre, off B1254 Promenade onto Trinity Rd & Vernon Rd

Please note that this establishment has recently changed hands. This well-furnished house is in a residential area near the seafront. Bedrooms are very comfortably furnished and equipped. There is a cosy lounge and meals are provided in the modern dining room.

Facilities 6 en suite (3 fmly) ⊘ TVB tea/coffee Licensed Cen ht No coaches Dinner Last d 4pm **Prices** D £50 **LB**

◆◆◆

Bay Ridge Hotel

11/13 Summerfield Rd YO15 3LF
☎ 01262 673425 📄 01262 673425 & 674589
e-mail bayridgehotel@aol.com
Dir Off A614/A165 towards seafront South Marine Dr, onto Summerfield Rd

This friendly guest house, located in a side road just off the seafront, is family run and offers value for money accommodation. Public areas are comfortable and consist of a spacious bar lounge, separate sitting room, and a well-appointed dining room. The modern bedrooms are generously equipped.

Facilities 14 rms (12 en suite) (5 fmly) (1 GF) ⊘ in bedrooms ⊘ in dining room ⊘ in 1 lounge TVB tea/coffee Licensed Cen ht TVL ch fac Bar billiards Stairlift Dinner Last d 10am **Prices** S £32-£35; D £64-£70; (incl. dinner) **LB Parking** 6 **Notes** 🐾

◆◆◆

Edelweiss Guest House ◇

86-88 Windsor Crescent YO15 3JA ☎ 01262 673822
e-mail edelweiss1st@aol.com
Dir Follow signs for Bridlington Harbour, off A1038

Situated in a quiet side road just off the seafront, this friendly guest house offers comfortably furnished bedrooms. There is also a separate bar, a comfortable first-floor television lounge, and a pleasant dining room where a hearty breakfast is provided.

Facilities 11 en suite (2 fmly) ⊘ in bedrooms ⊘ in dining room ⊘ in 1 lounge TVB tea/coffee Licensed Cen ht TVL **Prices** S £29; D £48✳ **LB Notes** Closed Dec-Jan

◆◆◆

Lansdowne House ◇

33 Lansdowne Rd YO15 2QT ☎ 01262 604184
e-mail david@french4383.fsnet.co.uk
Dir Signs for Leisure World, turn opp onto Lansdowne Rd, last house on left

Located in a residential area, not far from the town centre, Lansdowne House is a small and friendly well-maintained guest house. The cosy bedrooms are and neatly decorated and single rooms are available. Meals are served in a bright dining room.

Facilities 9 rms (7 en suite) (4 fmly) ⊘ in bedrooms ⊘ in dining room TVB tea/coffee Licensed Cen ht TVL Dinner Last d 9am **Prices** S £20-£22; D £40-£44✳ **LB Notes** 🐾

◆◆◆

Richmond Guest House

9 The Crescent YO15 2NX
☎ 01262 674366 & 07773 100387
Dir From town centre along promenade, left at Cliff St towards harbour, left onto The Crescent

Located a short walk from the seafront and the central attractions, this Victorian terrace property is adorned with pretty hanging baskets during the summer. There is a range of homely bedrooms and comprehensive breakfasts are served in an attractive dining room.

Facilities 9 rms (2 en suite) (1 pri facs) (2 fmly) (1 GF) ⊘ TVB tea/coffee Stairlift **LB Parking** 2 **Notes** 🐾

◆◆◆

Sandra's Guest House ◇

6 Summerfield Rd, South Marine Dr YO15 3LF
☎ 01262 677791
Dir From town centre 2nd right off South Marine Dr past Royal Hall

Close to the south beach and the Spa Theatre, this friendly guest house offers very homely and comfortable accommodation with good home cooking. There is a comfortable lounge and the dining room has a bar.

Facilities 7 rms (6 en suite) (1 pri facs) ⊘ in dining room TVB tea/coffee Licensed Cen ht TVL No children 12yrs No coaches Dinner Last d 4pm **Prices** S £27; D £44-£47 **LB Notes** rs Xmas (3 day package) 🐾

♦♦♦

The Tennyson ◇

19 Tennyson Av YO15 2EU
☎ 01262 604382 & 07729 149729
e-mail tennysonhotel@daisybroadband.co.uk
Dir B1255 towards Flamborough. Right at rdbt towards town centre. Take next right after Trinity Church. B&B 100yds on right.

Situated in a quiet side road close to the town centre and attractions, this friendly guest house offers attentive service, comfortable bedrooms and a cosy bar.

Facilities 7 rms (6 en suite) (1 pri facs) (1 fmly) ⊗ TVB tea/coffee Licensed Cen ht TVL No coaches **Prices** S £22; D £48-£55✳ **LB Notes** ☺

♦♦♦

Thiswilldo ◇

31 St Hilda St YO15 3EE ☎ 01262 678270
Dir A165, A1038 to town centre, right onto Windsor Crescent & Saint Hilda St

Pam Smith and Don Bashforth offer a warm welcome to their traditional guest house, which offers excellent value for money in a residential area close to the shops. Bedrooms sizes vary but all are comfortable. Substantial evening meals and breakfasts are served in the pleasant dining room next to the cosy lounge.

Facilities 6 rms (2 fmly) ⊗ in 6 bedrooms ⊗ in dining room ⊗ in lounges TVB tea/coffee ✻ Cen ht TVL No coaches Dinner Last d 9am **Prices** S £18-£23; D £36-£46; (incl. dinner) ✳ **LB Notes** ☺

♦♦♦

Ivanhoe Guesthouse

63 Cardigan Rd YO15 3JS ☎ 01262 675983
Dir Follow main roads towards Town Centre. Turn right at lights after B&Q store.

Facilities 8 en suite (4 fmly) ⊗ in bedrooms ⊗ in dining room ⊗ in lounges TVB tea/coffee ✻ Licensed Cen ht TVL No coaches Dinner Last d noon **Parking** 9

♦♦

Pembroke Seafront Hotel

6 Pembroke Ter YO15 3BX
☎ 01262 675643 🖳 01262 678181
Dir Off A1038 at harbour onto South Cliff Rd, on seafront on left

This seaside guest house offers traditional accommodation in a prime position between the harbour and the Spa Theatre. A variety of bedrooms are available, and many rooms and the lounge have spectacular sea views. Meals are served in the basement dining room, which also has a bar.

Facilities 10 rms (3 en suite) (5 pri facs) (2 fmly) (2 GF) ⊗ in dining room TVB tea/coffee ✻ TVL **LB**

♦♦

Westward-Ho Guest House

8 West St YO15 3DX ☎ 01262 670110
e-mail westward.ho@homecall.co.uk
Dir A165 follow signs for South Beach or Spa Theatre

Situated in a side road and close to the Spa centre, this family owned guest house offers good hospitality together with pleasant bedrooms and a cosy dining room where hearty breakfasts are served.

Facilities 4 rms (2 fmly) ⊗ in bedrooms ⊗ in area of dining room TVB tea/coffee ✻ Licensed Cen ht TVL No coaches **Notes** ☺

ⓤ

The Chimes Guest House ◇

9 Wellington Rd YO15 2BA ☎ 01262 401659
e-mail sandisbb@aol.com
Dir A165 into town centre, Quay Rd, take 3rd left after level crossing at Christchurch

At the time of going to press the rating for this establishment had not been confirmed. Please check the AA website www.theAA.com for up-to-date information.

Facilities 8 rms (1 en suite) (2 fmly) ⊗ in dining room ⊗ in lounges TVB tea/coffee Cen ht TVL Dinner Last d Lunctime **Prices** S £18-£20; D £35-£40✳ **Parking** 3

HUGGATE   MAP 19 SE85

♦♦♦

The Wolds Inn

Driffield Rd YO42 1YH ☎ 01377 288217
e-mail huggate@woldsinn.freeserve.co.uk
Dir Huggate signed off A166 & brown signs to Wold Inn

Nestling at the end of the highest village in the Yorkshire Wolds, midway between York and the coast, this ancient inn is a rural haven beside the Wolds Way walk. Substantial meals are served in the dining room and a good range of well-kept beers is available in the bar. Bedrooms, varying in size, are well equipped and comfortable.

Facilities 3 en suite ⊗ in bedrooms ⊗ in dining room TVB tea/coffee ✻ Cen ht Pool Table Dinner Last d 9pm **Prices** S fr £35; d fr £45; (room only) **Parking** 50

KINGSTON UPON HULL   MAP 17 TA02

♦♦♦

Earlsmere Hotel ◇

76/78 Sunnybank, Spring Bank West HU3 1LQ
☎ 01482 341977 🖳 01482 473714
e-mail su@earlsmerehotel.karoo.co.uk
Dir From town centre N onto A1079, left onto Spring Bank, 0.5m left onto Spring Bank West, 1st left onto Hymers Av & 1st right

This friendly establishment is in a quiet location overlooking a college sports fields. Bedrooms are well appointed and most have en suites. There is a comfortable lounge and an attractive breakfast room. Ample street parking outside.

Facilities 10 rms (7 en suite) (6 fmly) (2 GF) ⊗ in dining room ⊗ in lounges TVB tea/coffee Licensed Cen ht TVL **Prices** S £23.50-£35.25; D £35.50-£45✳ **LB**

England

♦♦♦ ▥

The New Inn ◇

44 South St HU17 5NZ ☎ 01964 542223 🖷 01964 545828
Dir Off A1035, in village centre

This central red-brick inn was built in the early 19th century. The modern bedrooms are brightly decorated and all rooms have showers en suite. There is an attractive breakfast room and a friendly atmosphere in the bars where traditional ales are served. The property has ample parking.

Facilities 10 en suite (1 fmly) ⊘ in 1 bedrooms ⊘ in dining room ⊘ in 1 lounge TVB tea/coffee Cen ht TVL Golf 18 Pool Table Dinner Last d 9pm **Prices** S £25-£30; D £35-£40✱ **Parking** 55

♦♦♦

Robeanne House ◇

Driffield Ln, Shiptonthorpe YO43 3PW
☎ 01430 873312 🖷 01430 873312
e-mail robert@robeanne.freeserve.com
Dir 1.5m NW on A614

Set back off the A614 in a quiet location, this delightful modern family home was built as a farmhouse. York, the coast, and the Yorkshire Moors and Dales are within easy driving distance. All bedrooms have country views and include a large family room. A charming wooden chalet is available in the garden.

Facilities 2 en suite 3 annexe en suite (2 fmly) (2 GF) ⊘ in 2 bedrooms ⊘ in dining room TVB tea/coffee Cen ht No coaches Outdoor hot-tub Dinner Last d 24hrs prior **Prices** S £30-£35; D £50-£55✱ **LB** **Parking** 10

If you have to cancel a booking, let the proprietor know immediately

♦♦♦♦

Rudstone Walk Country Accommodation

HU15 2AH ☎ 01430 422230 🖷 01430 424552
e-mail office@rudstone-walk.co.uk
web www.rudstone-walk.co.uk
Dir M62 junct 38, onto B1230, over A1034, Rudstone Walk 200yds on left

A delightful farm conversion that offers a very comfortable lounge, a charming little bar and a beautiful dining room. Dinner is available by arrangement. The former stables are now comfortable bedrooms overlooking a courtyard garden.

Facilities 14 en suite (2 fmly) (10 GF) ⊘ in 11 bedrooms ⊘ in dining room ⊘ in lounges TVB tea/coffee Direct dial from bedrooms Licensed Cen ht Dinner Last d 7pm **Conf** Max 120 Thtr 50 Class 30 Board 26 **Parking** 50 **Notes** rs 24-28 Dec & 31 Dec-2 Jan Civ Wed 50

YORKSHIRE, NORTH

♦♦♦

Lucy Cross ◇

DL11 7AD ☎ 01325 374319 & 07931 545985
e-mail sally@lucycross.co.uk
Dir A1 onto B6275 at Barton, white house 3m from Barton rdbt on left

Located close to major roads, a relaxed atmosphere and friendly welcome is assured. The traditionally furnished bedrooms are comfortable, and one is on the ground floor. A lounge is available and

continued

hearty breakfasts are served around one big table. Evening meals are available by arrangement, and internet access is available.

Facilities 6 rms (3 en suite) (2 pri facs) (1 fmly) (1 GF) ⊗ TVB tea/coffee ✖ Cen ht TVL Riding Stabling available Dinner Last d 6pm **Prices** S £25-£30; D £50-£55 **LB Conf** Max 12 Board 12 Del from £50 **Parking** 10

AMPLEFORTH
MAP 19 SE57

Premier Collection

◆◆◆◆◆

Shallowdale House

West End YO62 4DY ☎ 01439 788325 🖹 01439 788885
e-mail stay@shallowdalehouse.co.uk
web www.shallowdalehouse.co.uk
Dir Off A170 at W end of village

An outstanding example of an architect-designed 1960s house, Shallowdale lies in 2 acres of hillside gardens. There are stunning views from every room, and the elegant public rooms include a choice of lounges. Spacious bedrooms blend traditional and 60s style with many home comforts. Expect excellent service and genuine hospitality from Anton and Phillip. The very imaginative, freshly cooked dinners are not to be missed.

Facilities 3 rms (2 en suite) (1 pri facs) ⊗ TVB tea/coffee ✖ Licensed Cen ht No children 12yrs No coaches Dinner Last d 48hrs **Prices** S £67.50-£77.50; D £85-£105 **Parking** 3 **Notes** Closed Xmas & New Year

ASKRIGG
MAP 18 SD99

◆◆◆◆

Whitfield

Helm DL8 3JF ☎ 01969 650565 🖹 01969 650565
e-mail empsall@askrigg-cottages.co.uk
web www.askrigg-cottages.co.uk
Dir Off A684 at Bainbridge signed Askrigg, right at T-junct, 150yds to No Through Rd sign, left up hill 0.5m

Set high in the fells, this smart accommodation is in a carefully converted barn, built of Yorkshire limestone. Both bedrooms are homely, and have stunning views of the Wensleydale countryside. Hearty breakfasts are served around a communal table in the inviting lounge-dining room.

Facilities 2 en suite ⊗ TVB tea/coffee Cen ht TVL No coaches **Prices** S £39; D £50-£58✱ **LB Parking** 1 **Notes** Closed 23 Dec-2 Jan

AYSGARTH
MAP 19 SE08

◆◆◆◆ ⊜

Stow House

DL8 3SR ☎ 01969 663635
e-mail info@stowhouse.co.uk
web www.stowhouse.co.uk
Dir 0.6m E of Aysgarth on A684

Nestling in grounds set back from the road, this former Victorian vicarage is delightfully furnished and decorated throughout. Bedrooms, most offering panoramic views over the Dales, are bright and homely. The smart dining room is the venue for hearty, carefully prepared breakfasts. Creative dinners are a highlight of any stay.

Facilities 9 en suite (1 GF) ⊗ in bedrooms ⊗ in dining room TVB tea/coffee Licensed Cen ht No coaches ⚲ ♫ Dinner Last d 2pm **Prices** S £44-£53; D £72-£90✱ **LB Parking** 10 **Notes** Closed 24-26 Dec

BEDALE
MAP 19 SE28

Premier Collection

◆◆◆◆◆ 📖 💐

Mill Close Farm (SE232922)

Patrick Brompton DL8 1JY
☎ 01677 450257 🖹 01748 813612 Mrs Knox
e-mail pat@millclose.co.uk
Dir 3m NW of Beale. A684 to Patrick Brompton & brown tourist signs to farm

A real home from home atmosphere prevails at this working farm. Bedrooms are furnished with quality and style; one has a four-poster and two have spa baths, but all rooms feature homely extras including fridges. Well-prepared breakfasts are one of the highlights of a stay and feature home-made produce cooked in the Aga of the farm kitchen.

Facilities 3 en suite ⊗ TVB tea/coffee ✖ Cen ht No children 10yrs 240 acres Mixed **Prices** S £50-£70; D £70-£80✱ **LB Parking** 6 **Notes** Closed Dec-Feb

England

England

BEDALE continued

◆◆◆◆

Elmfield House

Arrathorne DL8 1NE ☎ 01677 450558
e-mail stay@elmfieldhouse.co.uk
web www.elmfieldhouse.co.uk
Dir *4m NW of Bedale. A684 from Bedale for Leyburn, right after Patrick Brompton towards Richmond, B&B 1.5m on right*

Originally a gamekeeper's cottage, and now carefully extended, Elmfield has uninterrupted views of the surrounding countryside. The comfortable bedrooms are generally spacious and very well equipped. The attractive public rooms are also well proportioned and offer a comfortable lounge with a small bar, as well as a conservatory-lounge and games room.

Facilities 4 en suite 3 annexe en suite (2 fmly) (2 GF) ⊗ FTV TVB tea/coffee ✗ Licensed Cen ht No coaches Fishing Dinner Last d at booking **Prices** S £45-£49; D £70-£78✳ **LB** **Conf** Max 16 Class 10 Board 16 **Parking** 7

◆◆◆◆ ◧

The Castle Arms Inn

Snape DL8 2TB ☎ 01677 470270 🖨 01677 470837
e-mail castlearms@aol.com
Dir *2m S of Bedale. Off B6268 into Snape*

Nestled in the quiet village of Snape, this former coaching inn is full of character. Bedrooms are in a converted barn, and each room is very comfortable and carefully furnished. The restaurant and public bar offer a good selection of fine ales, along with an interesting selection of freshly prepared dishes.

Facilities 9 annexe en suite (8 GF) ⊗ in bedrooms ⊗ in dining room TVB tea/coffee Cen ht No coaches Dinner Last d 8.30pm **Prices** S £45-£55; D £60-£70✳ **LB** **Parking** 15

◆◆◆

Southfield ◇

96 Southend DL8 2DS ☎ 01677 423510
Dir *On B6285 SE of Bedale centre, fronted by white stones*

Located in a residential area on the edge of town, this family-run guest house extends a friendly welcome. Bedrooms are traditionally furnished and decorated, and are equipped with many thoughtful touches. Guests are free to enjoy the delightful lounge and neatly tended garden. This is a non-smoking house.

Facilities 4 rms (2 en suite) ⊗ tea/coffee ✗ Cen ht TVL No coaches **Prices** S £30-£40; D £48✳ **Parking** 4 **Notes** Closed Xmas and New Year ⊛

BOLTON ABBEY   MAP 19 SE05

◆◆◆◆

Howgill Lodge

Barden BD23 6DJ ☎ 01756 720655
e-mail info@howgill-lodge.co.uk
Dir *B6160 from Bolton Abbey signed Burnsall, 3m right at Barden Tower signed Appletreewick, Howgill Lodge 1.25m on right at phone box*

Having an idyllic position high above the valley, this converted stone granary provides a quality get-away-from-it-all experience. The uniquely styled bedrooms provide a host of thoughtful touches and are dsigned to feature original stonewalls, flagstone floors and timber beams. All of the rooms boast spectacular, memorable views. Breakfasts make excellent use of fresh local ingredients.

Facilities 4 en suite (4 GF) ⊗ TVB tea/coffee ✗ Cen ht No coaches **Prices** S £42-£45; D £66-£70 **Parking** 6 **Notes** Closed 2 Nov-5 Dec

BUCKDEN   MAP 18 SD97

◆◆◆◆

Hartrigg House

BD23 5JA ☎ 01756 760443 & 761014 🖨 01756 760843
e-mail hartrigg@aol.com
Dir *On B6160 from Grassington. 1st property on left on entering Buckden*

A warm welcome awaits you at this delightful Victorian house, located in the quiet village. The smart bedrooms are nicely furnished and well equipped and both have private bathrooms. The cosy guest lounge has a real fire in the cooler months and overlooks the fells; hearty breakfasts are served in the attractive dining room. The house is totally non-smoking.

Facilities 3 rms (1 en suite) (2 pri facs) (3 fmly) ⊗ TVB tea/coffee ✗ Cen ht TVL No children 6yrs No coaches **Prices** D £60✳ **LB** **Parking** 3 **Notes** ⊛

BURNSALL
MAP 19 SE06

◆◆◆

Burnsall Manor House Hotel ◇

Main St BD23 6BW ☎ 01756 720231 ▤ 01756 720231
e-mail joe@manorhouseuk.co.uk
Dir On B6160 in village centre

A warm welcome awaits you at this 19th-century house, situated on the River Wharfe. Bedrooms are traditionally furnished and have delightful views. Freshly prepared meals can be enjoyed in the spacious dining room. There is also a cosy bar, television lounge, and in the warmer months, the large garden provides a peaceful setting in which to relax.

Facilities 8 rms (7 en suite) ⊘ tea/coffee Licensed Cen ht TVL Fishing ♨ **Prices** S £26.50-£42.50; D £53-£61 LB **Parking** 11

CARPERBY
MAP 19 SE08

◆◆◆ 🅰

The Wheatsheaf

DL8 4DF ☎ 01969 663216 ▤ 01969 663019
e-mail wheatsheaf@paulmit.globalnet.co.uk
Dir Off A684 signed Aysgarth Falls to village centre

Facilities 8 en suite 5 annexe en suite (1 fmly) (1 GF) ⊘ in 1 bedrooms ⊘ in dining room TVB tea/coffee Licensed Cen ht Fishing Dinner Last d 9pm **Prices** S £33; D £64-£85✳ LB **Conf** Max 20 Board 20 **Parking** 40

CASTLETON
MAP 19 NZ60

◆◆◆◆ 🍴

The Downe Arms Inn

3 High St YO21 2EE ☎ 01287 660223 ▤ 01287 660223
e-mail info@thedowneams.co.uk
Dir 4m S off A171 in village centre

Located in the heart of the village and very much a focal point for the local community, renovation of this historic inn has resulted in thoughtfully furnished bedrooms with smart modern bathrooms en suite. Imaginative menus using fresh local produce are a feature and a warm welcome is assured.

Facilities 5 en suite (2 fmly) TVB tea/coffee ✖ Cen ht No coaches Pool Table Dinner Last d 9pm **Prices** S £35-£40; D £60-£70✳ LB **Parking** 6

CATTERICK
MAP 19 SE29

◆◆◆

Rose Cottage Guest House ◇

26 High St DL10 7LJ ☎ 01748 811164
Dir Off A1 in village centre, opp newsagents

Convenient for exploring the Dales and Moors, this well-maintained guest house lies in the middle of Catterick. Bedrooms are nicely presented and comfortable. The cosy public rooms include a cottage-style dining room adorned with Mrs Archer's paintings. Dinner is available by arrangement during the summer.

Facilities 4 rms (2 en suite) (1 fmly) ⊘ in dining room ⊘ in lounges TVB tea/coffee Cen ht No coaches Dinner Last d 9.30am **Prices** S £28-£34; D £44-£50 **Parking** 4 **Notes** Closed 24-26 Dec 🐾

CLAPHAM
MAP 18 SD76

◆◆◆

Brookhouse Guest House ◇

Station Rd LA2 8ER ☎ 015242 51580
e-mail admin@brookhouseclapham.co.uk
Dir Off A65 into village

Located in the pretty conservation village of Clapham beside the river, this well maintained and friendly guest house provides thoughtfully furnished bedrooms and a popular ground floor café, serving a selection of meals and snacks throught the day

Facilities 3 rms ⊘ TVB tea/coffee ✖ Cen ht No coaches Dinner Last d 9pm **Prices** S fr £28; d fr £45✳ LB **Notes** 🐾

CLOUGHTON
MAP 19 TA09

◆◆◆ 🍴

Blacksmiths Arms

High St YO13 0AE ☎ 01723 870244
Dir On A171 in village centre

Located 6m north of Scarborough, this inn features smartly furnished bedrooms. Four are in converted stone buildings and all have private entrances. A good range of dishes is served in the bar and dining room, which have the ambience of a country inn, including open fires and traditional furniture.

Facilities 7 en suite 4 annexe en suite (1 fmly) (4 GF) ⊘ in bedrooms ⊘ in dining room ⊘ in lounges TVB tea/coffee ✖ Cen ht No coaches Dinner Last d 9.45pm **Prices** S £39-£46; D £65-£75 LB **Parking** 35

Ⓤ

Rockhaven ◇

Newlands Rd YO13 0AR ☎ 01723 871971
e-mail newboup@tiscali.co.uk
Dir 6m N of Scarborough on A171. At junct of Staintondale Rd & Hood l n

At the time of going to press the rating for this establishment had not been confirmed. Please check the AA website www.theAA.com for up-to-date information.

Facilities 3 en suite ⊘ TVB tea/coffee ✖ Cen ht No children No coaches badminton lawn Dinner Last d noon **Prices** S £25-£32.50; D £50-£65✳ LB **Parking** 6 **Notes** Closed Dec-Jan rs Feb-Mar, Oct-Nov

England

ESCRICK

MAP 16 SE64

♦♦♦♦

Black Bull Inn

Main St YO19 6JP ☎ 01904 728245 ▤ 01904 728154
e-mail blackbullhotel@btconnect.com
web www.yorkblackbullinn.co.uk
Dir Off A19 into village centre

Set in a picturesque village just 6m south from York, the Black Bull is popular with locals and visitors. Freshly cooked meals are offered in the main bar area, and breakfast is served in the adjacent dining room. All bedrooms are well equipped; one has a sunken bath and another has a superb four-poster bed.

Facilities 10 en suite (2 fmly) ⊗ in bedrooms ⊗ in dining room ⊗ in 1 lounge TVB tea/coffee ✄ Cen ht TVL Dinner Last d 9.30pm **Parking** 15 **Notes** Closed 24-26 Dec

FILEY

MAP 17 TA18

♦♦♦♦

Gables Guest House

2A Rutland St YO14 9JB ☎ 01723 514750
e-mail thegablesfiley@aol.com
Dir Off A165 signs for town centre, right onto West Av, 2nd left onto Rutland St, the Gables opp church

Located in a quiet residential area, just a stroll from the centre and promenade, this smart Edwardian house extends a warm welcome. Bedrooms are brightly decorated and well equipped and some are suitable for families. Breakfasts are substantial and a varied evening menu is available.

Facilities 5 en suite (3 fmly) ⊗ TVB tea/coffee Cen ht No coaches Golf 18 ⚲ Dinner Last d noon **Prices** d fr £56 **LB Parking** 2

FLIXTON

MAP 17 TA07

♦♦♦♦

Orchard Lodge

North St YO11 3UA
☎ 01723 890202 & 892172 ▤ 01723 890202
web www.orchard-lodge.com
Dir Off A1039 in village centre

Located 6m south of Scarborough, just off the main road, this establishment offers spacious and comfortable bedrooms. It is a good base for touring the coast, the North York Moors or the Wolds. Hearty breakfasts feature home-made preserves. This is a non-smoking house.

Facilities 6 en suite ⊗ TVB tea/coffee ✄ Cen ht No children 3yrs No coaches **Prices** S £40-£45; D £60-£70 **LB Parking** 8 **Notes** Closed Jan-Feb

FYLINGTHORPE

MAP 19 NZ90

Ⓤ

Thorpe Green House

3 Sledgates YO22 4TY ☎ 01947 880339 ▤ 01947 880339
e-mail janet.tgh@btinternet.com
Dir From A171 onto B1447 to Robin Hoods Bay, turn right onto Thorpe Ln & continue to Fylingthorpe.

At the time of going to press the rating for this establishment had not been confirmed. Please check the AA website www.theAA.com for up-to-date information.

Facilities 2 en suite (1 fmly) ⊗ TVB tea/coffee ✄ Cen ht **Prices** D £55-£60✳ **LB Notes** Closed 24-26 Dec

GANTON

MAP 17 SE97

Ⓤ ◗

Ganton Greyhound

Main St YO12 4NX ☎ 01944 710116 ▤ 01944 712705
e-mail gantongreyhound@yahoo.co.uk
Dir On A64 between Sherburn and Straxton

At the time of going to press the rating for this establishment had not been confirmed. Please check the AA website www.theAA.com for up-to-date information.

Facilities 18 rms (17 en suite) (1 pri facs) (4 fmly) (5 GF) ⊗ in bedrooms ⊗ in dining room ⊗ in lounges TVB Direct dial from bedrooms ✄ Cen ht TVL Dinner Last d 9pm **Prices** S £35-£50; D £70-£100✳ **LB Conf** Max 70 Thtr 70 Class 70 Board 70 **Parking** 29

GIGGLESWICK

MAP 18 SD86

♦♦♦♦ 🅰

Harts Head Hotel

Belle Hill BD24 0BA
☎ 01729 822086 & 824995 ▤ 01729 824992
e-mail hartshead@hotel52.freeserve.co.uk
web www.hartsheadhotel.co.uk
Dir On B6480, 1m from A65

Facilities 7 en suite 3 annexe en suite (1 fmly) ⊗ in bedrooms ⊗ in dining room STV TVB tea/coffee ✄ Licensed Cen ht Snooker Pool Table Dinner Last d 9pm **LB Conf** Max 30 Class 30 Board 20 **Parking** 25

GILLING EAST

MAP 19 SE67

◆◆◆◆

The Fairfax Arms

Main St YO62 4JH ☎ 01439 788212 ▤ 01439 788819
e-mail doyle145@aol.com

A friendly welcome awaits you at this attractive inn in this quiet village. Food is the focus of the pub, where a choice of rustic eating areas makes for atmospheric dining. The well-equipped bedrooms blend contemporary and traditional styles.

Facilities 24 rms (16 en suite) (8 pri facs) 6 annexe rms (4 en suite) (2 annexe pri facs) (2 fmly) ⊗ TVB tea/coffee ✗ Cen ht No coaches Golf 9 Dinner Last d 9pm **Parking** 10

GOATHLAND

MAP 19 NZ80

◆◆◆◆

Whitfield House Hotel

Darnholm YO22 5LA ☎ 01947 896215 ▤ 01947 896043
e-mail adriancaulder@btconnect.com
web www.whhotel.com
Dir Off A169 into village centre, opp shops follow brown signs for 0.5m

Located in the peaceful hamlet of Darnholm, parts of this property date from the 17th century and good standards of comfort and facilities are provided. Bedrooms are equipped with thoughtful extras and ground-floor areas include an attractive dining room and cosy lounge.

Facilities 9 en suite (1 fmly) ⊗ TVB tea/coffee ✗ Cen ht No children 5yrs No coaches Dinner Last d 24hrs prior **Prices** S £36; D £72✳ LB **Parking** 9

GRASSINGTON

MAP 19 SE06

◆◆◆◆◆

Ashfield House Hotel

Summers Fold BD23 5AE
☎ 01756 752584 ▤ 07092 376562
e-mail info@ashfieldhouse.co.uk
web www.ashfieldhouse.co.uk
Dir B6265 to village centre Main St, left onto Summers Fold

Guests are greeted like old friends at this beautifully maintained 17th-century house, peacefully tucked away a few yards from the village

continued

square. The smart lounges offer a high level of comfort and an honesty bar. The freshly prepared three-course dinner (by arrangement) is a highlight of any stay. The attractive bedrooms are well furnished and thoughtfully equipped.

Facilities 8 rms (7 en suite) (1 pri facs) ⊗ TVB tea/coffee ✗ Licensed Cen ht No children 5yrs No coaches Dinner Last d 24hrs in advance **Prices** S £61-£115; D £85-£120✳ LB **Conf** Max 8 Board 8 Del from £160 ✳ **Parking** 8

◆◆◆◆◆

Grassington Lodge

8 Wood Ln BD23 5LU ☎ 01756 752518 ▤ 01756 752518
e-mail relax@grassingtonlodge.co.uk
web www.grassingtonlodge.co.uk
Dir B6265 into village centre

This impressive house, built in 1898, is thoughtfully furnished and welcoming home. The attractive bedrooms are equipped with homely extras, and on chilly days a log fire blazes in the lounge. Breakfasts using local produce are served in the stylish breakfast room.

Facilities 10 rms (9 en suite) (1 pri facs) (1 GF) ⊗ TVB tea/coffee ✗ Licensed Cen ht TVL No children 12yrs No coaches **Prices** D £70-£90✳ LB **Parking** 8 **Notes** ⊛

GREAT AYTON

MAP 19 NZ51

◆◆◆ ◙

Royal Oak Hotel

123 High St TS9 6BW
☎ 01642 722361 & 723270 ▤ 01642 724047
e-mail info@royaloak-hotel.co.uk

This 18th-century former coaching inn is very popular with locals and visitors to the village. Bedrooms are all comfortably equipped. The restaurant and public bar retain many original features and offer a good selection of fine ales; an extensive range of food is available all day and is served in the bar or the dining room.

Facilities 5 en suite ⊗ in bedrooms ⊗ in dining room TVB tea/coffee Direct dial from bedrooms Cen ht Dinner Last d 9.30pm **Prices** S £35-£45; D £70✳ **Conf** Max 30

GUISBOROUGH

MAP 19 NZ61

★★★★ ⊛ Restaurant with Rooms

Pinchinthorpe Hall

Pinchinthorpe TS14 8HG
☎ 01287 630200 ▤ 01287 632000
e-mail nybrewery@pinchinthorpe.wanadoo.co.uk
Dir Between Guisborough & Great Ayton on A173

An elegant 17th-century country manor house that has stylish bedrooms, each very individually and tastefully decorated and with many thoughtful extras. The Brewhouse Bistro serves interesting dishes using home grown and local produce, and offers caring and attentive service.

Facilities 6 en suite TVB tea/coffee Direct dial from bedrooms ✗ Licensed Dinner Last d 9.30pm **Conf** Max 50 Thtr 50 Class 20 Board 24 **Parking** 110 **Notes** Civ Wed 80

England

GUISBOROUGH continued

◆◆◆◆

The Kings Head Hotel & Restaurant

The Green TS9 6QR ☎ 01642 722318 ▤ 01642 724750
e-mail info@kingsheadhotel.co.uk
web www.kingsheadhotel.co.uk
Dir *A171 towards Guisborough, at rdbt onto A173 to Newton under Roseberry, under Roseberry Topping landmark*

Converted from a row of traditional cottages, the friendly, family-owned Kings Head offers modern accommodation with original features. The stylish modern bedrooms are thoughtfully equipped, and the adjacent restaurant offers a choice of wines, beers and a very good range of dishes.

Facilities 8 en suite (1 fmly) (2 GF) ◎ FTV TVB tea/coffee Direct dial from bedrooms ✖ Licensed Cen ht TVL Mountain biking Dinner Last d 9.30pm **Prices** S £55-£95; D £69.50-£99.50✱ **Conf** Max 20 Class 20 **Parking** 96 **Notes** Closed 25 Dec

HACKNESS   MAP 19 SE99

◆◆◆◆

Troutsdale Lodge

Troutsdale YO13 0BS ☎ 01723 882209
e-mail clive@troutsdalelodge.fsnet.co.uk
web www.troutsdalelodge.com
Dir *Off A170 at Snainton signed Troutsdale*

Reminiscent of an Indian hill station this Edwardian house overlooks a peaceful valley with the forest beyond. The house retains the Edwardian style throughout and offers good all-round comforts. Guests can expect fine hospitality from the resident owners.

Facilities 4 en suite (1 fmly) (4 GF) ◎ TVB tea/coffee Licensed Cen ht TVL No coaches ᴊᴑ Dinner Last d 8pm **Parking** 8 **Notes** 😺

HARROGATE   MAP 19 SE35

★★★ ◎ Restaurant with Rooms

Harrogate Brasserie with Rooms

28-30 Cheltenham Pde HG1 1DB
☎ 01423 505041 ▤ 01423 722300
e-mail info@brasserie.co.uk
web www.brasserie.co.uk
Dir *On A61 town centre behind theatre*

This town-centre establishment has a distinctly continental style. The brasserie covers three cosy and richly decorated dining areas, and live jazz features on Wednesday, Friday and Sunday nights. The individual bedrooms have period collectibles, lots to read, and many rooms have DVD players.

Facilities 17 en suite (3 fmly) TVB tea/coffee Direct dial from bedrooms Licensed ch fac No coaches Dinner **Prices** S fr £55; d fr £85✱ LB **Parking** 12 **Notes** Closed 26 Dec-2 Jan

Premier Collection

◆◆◆◆◆

Ruskin Hotel

1 Swan Rd HG1 2SS ☎ 01423 502045 ▤ 01423 506131
e-mail ruskin.hotel@virgin.net
web www.ruskinhotel.co.uk
Dir *Off A61 Ripon road, left opp The Majestic Hotel*

The mid 19th-century house stands in secluded tree-studded gardens, only a 5-minute walk from the town centre. It retains many original features and has a relaxing lounge. Excellent, freshly prepared breakfasts are served in the elegant dining room, and the thoughtfully equipped bedrooms range from compact to spacious, all furnished in Victorian pine.

Facilities 7 en suite (2 fmly) (1 GF) ◎ in bedrooms ◎ in dining room TVB tea/coffee Direct dial from bedrooms ✖ Licensed Cen ht No coaches Free use of local leisure club **Prices** S £65-£85; D £85-£140 LB **Parking** 7

◆◆◆◆◆ 🅰

Cold Cotes

Cold Cotes Rd, Felliscliffe HG3 2LW
☎ 01423 770937 ▤ 01423 779284
e-mail coldcotes@btopenworld.com
web www.coldcotes.com
Dir *7m W of Harrogate. Off A59 after Black Bull, 3rd entrance on right*

Facilities 3 en suite ◎ TVB tea/coffee ✖ Cen ht No children 12yrs No coaches **Prices** S £50; D £65✱ **Parking** 10 **Notes** Closed Xmas-Jan

◆◆◆◆
Alexa House & Stable Cottages

26 Ripon Rd HG1 2JJ ☎ 01423 501988 🗎 01423 504086
e-mail alexahouse@msn.com
web www.alexa-house.co.uk
Dir On A61 0.25m from junct A59

This popular establishment has stylish, well-equipped bedrooms split between the main house and cottage rooms. All rooms come with homely extras. Light meals are available and dinners are available for groups by arrangement. The opulent day rooms include an elegant lounge with honesty bar, and a bright dining room. The hands-on proprietors ensure high levels of customer care.

Facilities 9 en suite 4 annexe en suite (2 fmly) (4 GF) ⊗ in bedrooms ⊗ in dining room TVB tea/coffee Direct dial from bedrooms Licensed Cen ht No coaches Dinner Last d 10am **Prices** S £35-£52.50; D £70-£85✳ **LB Conf** Max 20 Thtr 20 Class 20 Board 20 Del from £85 ✳ **Parking** 10

◆◆◆◆
April House

3 Studley Rd HG1 5JU ☎ 01423 561879
e-mail info@aprilhouse.com
Dir Off A59/A61 onto Kings Rd signed Harrogate International Centre, opp Moat House Hotel

Located in a quiet residential area just a short walk from the conference centre, this impeccable Victorian house retains many original features. The comfortable bedrooms come with an array of homely touches, and breakfast is served in an attractive dining room.

Facilities 5 rms (4 en suite) (1 pri facs) (1 fmly) ⊗ TVB tea/coffee ✈ TVL No coaches **Prices** S £35-£45; D £65-£80✳ LB

◆◆◆◆
Ashwood House Guest House

7 Spring Grove HG1 2HS
☎ 01423 560081 🗎 01423 527928
e-mail ashwoodhouse@aol.com
web www.ashwoodhouse.co.uk
Dir A61 Ripon Rd onto Springfield Av, 3rd left

This delightfully decorated and furnished Edwardian house is situated in a quiet area of town. The spacious bedrooms are individually styled and thoughtfully equipped, and one has a four-poster bed. There is a cosy lounge and an elegant dining room where full English breakfasts are served.

Facilities 5 en suite (1 fmly) ⊗ TVB tea/coffee ✈ Cen ht TVL No children 7yrs No coaches **Prices** S £40-£45; D £65-£75✳ LB **Parking** 3 **Notes** Closed Xmas/New Year 🐾

◆◆◆◆
The Camberley Hotel

52-54 Kings Rd HG1 5JR ☎ 01423 561618 🗎 01423 536360
e-mail camberleyhotelharrogate@yahoo.co.uk
Dir Opp conference centre

Located directly opposite the convention centre and with the benefit of private car parking, this constantly improving owner managed guest house provides comfortable accommodation and a warm welcome is assured. A spacious guest lounge is available in addition to a period themed basement dining room, the setting for comprehensive breakfasts utilising local produce.

Facilities 11 rms (9 en suite) (2 pri facs) (2 fmly) (1 GF) ⊗ TVB tea/coffee Direct dial from bedrooms ✈ Cen ht No coaches **Prices** S £30-£50; D £50-£90✳ LB **Parking** 8 **Notes** Closed 24-25 Dec

◆◆◆◆
The Cavendish

3 Valley Dr HG2 0JJ ☎ 01423 509637 🗎 01423 504434
Dir In town centre beside The Valley Gardens

The welcoming Cavendish is only a short walk from the conference centre and the town centre. The well-equipped bedrooms have homely extras, and there is a very comfortable lounge. The resident proprietors provide friendly service.

Facilities 9 en suite ⊗ in bedrooms ⊗ in dining room TVB tea/coffee Direct dial from bedrooms ✈ Cen ht No coaches **Prices** S £38-£45; D £60-£75✳

England

HARROGATE continued

◆◆◆◆
The Dales
101 Valley Dr HG2 0JP ☎ 01423 507248
e-mail reservations@dales-hotel.co.uk
Dir A61 N into Harrogate, left before Bettys on Parliament St, to rdbt
& 2nd exit, left onto Valley Dr

Set in a peaceful residential area overlooking Valley Gardens, the cosy
property has well-equipped bedrooms with either en suite or private
facilities. The stylish sunny lounge has an honesty bar. Quality
breakfasts are served in the dining room, and service is friendly and
attentive.

Facilities 8 rms (6 en suite) (2 pri facs) ⊗ FTV TVB tea/coffee ✕
Licensed Cen ht TVL No coaches **Prices** S £36-£40; D £58.50-£65 LB

◆◆◆◆
Fountains B & B
27 Kings Rd HG1 5JY ☎ 01423 530483 ▤ 01423 705312
e-mail dave@fountains.fsworld.co.uk
Dir 500yds N of town centre. Off A59 Skipton Rd onto Kings Rd,
0.75m on right

This delightful guest house offers comfortable accommodation close
to the conference centre. Carefully decorated throughout, the
bedrooms have coordinated soft fabrics and an elegant lounge is
available. Substantial breakfasts are served in the neat dining room.

Facilities 10 en suite (2 fmly) (2 GF) ⊗ TVB tea/coffee ✕ Cen ht TVL
No children 6yrs No coaches **Prices** S £38-£55; D £65✳ **Parking** 8
Notes Closed 24 Dec-2 Jan

◆◆◆◆
Grafton Hotel
1-3 Franklin Mount HG1 5EJ
☎ 01423 508491 ▤ 01423 523168
e-mail enquiries@graftonhotel.co.uk
web www.graftonhotel.co.uk
Dir Signs to International Centre, onto Kings Rd with Centre on left,
Franklin Mount 450yds on right

The delightful family-run Grafton is in a quiet location just a short walk
from the conference centre and town. Bedrooms are well appointed
and comfortably furnished, and there are lounges with a small cosy
bar. Breakfast is served in the light and spacious dining room, which
overlooks the garden.

Facilities 17 en suite (3 fmly) ⊗ in bedrooms ⊗ in dining room TVB
tea/coffee Direct dial from bedrooms ✕ Licensed Cen ht TVL
Prices S £45-£50 LB **Parking** 3 **Notes** Closed 15-28 Dec

◆◆◆◆
Wynnstay House
60 Franklin Rd HG1 5EE ☎ 01423 560476 ▤ 01423 562539
e-mail wynnstayhouse@tiscali.co.uk
web www.wynnstayhouse.com
Dir Off A61 in town centre onto Kings Rd, right onto Strawberry Dale,
2nd left

Located in a residential area a short distance from the conference
centre, shops and attractions, this friendly, family-run guest house is
ideal for business or leisure. There is a passion for ruined castles at
Wynnstay House: the attractive, well-equipped bedrooms are each
named after a spectacular fortress.

Facilities 6 en suite ⊗ TVB tea/coffee ✕ Cen ht No children 14yrs
No coaches **Prices** S £45-£70; D £60-£75✳ LB

◆◆◆
Pigeon Olde Farm Lodge
Bilton Hall Dr HG1 4DW ☎ 01423 868853
e-mail maureen@tatemd.fsnet.co.uk
web www.pigeonoldefarm.co.uk
Dir 2.5m NE of Harrogate. Off A59 Forest Ln Head opp golf club
onto Bilton Hall Dr

A warm welcome awaits you at this delightful guest house converted
from farm buildings and barns. It has a peaceful location opposite
Harrogate Golf Club, and Knaresborough and Harrogate town centres
are within easy reach. The smart bedrooms are attractively furnished
in pine, and a continental breakfast is served in the cosy breakfast
room.

Facilities 2 en suite 4 annexe en suite (6 GF) ⊗ TVB tea/coffee ✕
Cen ht No coaches **Prices** S fr £42; d fr £54✳ **Parking** 10 **Notes** ⊠

◆◆◆
The Courtyard ◇
12 Franklin Mount HG1 5EJ ☎ 01423 569930
e-mail roger.morris@ntlworld.com
web www.courtyardguesthouse.co.uk
Dir Signs to International Centre, onto Kings Rd with Centre on left,
Franklin Mount 450yds on right

In summer the front garden of this small friendly guest house makes a
colourful greeting. The house is in a quiet residential area close to the
town and the conference centre. The two bedrooms are stylish and
well equipped, and breakfasts are served in the cosy lounge-dining
room. This is a non-smoking establishment.

Facilities 3 rms (2 en suite) (1 pri facs) (2 fmly) ⊗ TVB tea/coffee ✕
Cen ht TVL No children 3yrs **Prices** S £28-£35; D £55-£70✳
Notes Closed Xmas & New Year

Princes Hotel ◇

7 Granby Rd HG1 4ST ☎ 01423 883469 📠 01423 881417
e-mail info@princeshotel.co.uk
Dir *Off A59 at Empress rdbt*

A tranquil and relaxing atmosphere is found at this Victorian house set on the edge of the town and convenient for the Yorkshire showground and General Hospital. The bedrooms are traditionally furnished and breakfast is served in the spacious dining room overlooking the gardens.

Facilities 6 rms (4 en suite) (2 pri facs) (2 fmly) ⊘ in 1 bedrooms ⊘ in dining room ⊘ in lounges TVB tea/coffee Direct dial from bedrooms Cen ht No children 3yrs No coaches **Prices** S £24-£38; D £48-£59✳ **Parking** 1 **Notes** ⊛

Shelbourne Guest House

78 Kings Rd HG1 5JX ☎ 01423 504390 📠 01423 504390
e-mail sue@shelbourne house.co.uk
web www.shelbournehouse.co.uk
Dir *Signs to International Centre, over lights by Moat House Hotel, premises on right*

Situated opposite the conference centre and near to the town centre, this elegant Victorian house provides bright, cheerful bedrooms of varying size and has a friendly atmosphere. There is a lounge and an attractive breakfast room.

Facilities 8 en suite (2 fmly) ⊘ TVB tea/coffee Licensed Cen ht TVL No coaches **Prices** S £35-£40; D £65-£75✳ **LB** **Parking** 1

HAWES
MAP 18 SD88

Premier Collection

Rookhurst Country House

West End, Gayle DL8 3RT ☎ 01969 667454
e-mail enquiries@rookhurst.co.uk
Dir *A684 into Hawes, turn S onto Gayle Ln (signed Creamery & Kettlewell). In 600yds at the sharp left bend, do not cross bridge, turn sharp right, 300yds to Rookhurst Country House*

A warm welcome awaits you at this elegant 17th-century property, extended in the Victorian period. Quality furnishing and decor highlight the many original features. Bedrooms are furnished with fine period pieces and a wealth of thoughtful extras. Ground-floor areas include a sumptuous sitting room and an elegant dining room, the setting for imaginative dinners.

Facilities 5 en suite ⊘ TVB tea/coffee 🐾 Licensed Cen ht No children 12yrs No coaches Dinner Last d 10.30am **Prices** S £55-£120; D £90-£120✳ **LB** **Parking** 5 **Notes** Closed 22 Dec-4 Jan Civ Wed 20

Steppe Haugh ◇

Town Head DL8 3RH ☎ 01969 667645
e-mail info@steppehaugh.co.uk
Dir *On A684, W side of Hawes, next to filling station*

Over 350 years old, the stone house retains much original charm. The thoughtfully furnished bedrooms are cosy, and the spacious
continued

lounge has a welcoming log fire in the cooler seasons. Private parking is available.

Facilities 5 rms (4 en suite) ⊘ TVB tea/coffee Cen ht TVL No children 7yrs No coaches **Prices** S £30-£35; D £60-£65 **Parking** 5 **Notes** Closed Xmas ⊛

HAWNBY
MAP 19 SE58

◆◆◆◆ ⚑ ❦

Laskill Grange *(SE562007)*

Hawnby YO62 5NB
☎ 01439 798268 📠 01439 798498 Mrs Smith
e-mail suesmith@laskillfarm.fsnet.co.uk
web www.laskillgrange.co.uk
Dir *6m N of Helmsley on B1257*

Country lovers will enjoy this charming 19th-century farmhouse. Guests can take a walk in the surrounding countryside, fish the River Seph which runs through the grounds, or visit nearby Rievaulx. Comfortable bedrooms are in the main house or in converted farm buildings and are well furnished and supplied with many thoughtful extras.

Facilities 4 annexe en suite (4 GF) ⊘ TVB tea/coffee Licensed Cen ht TVL Fishing Riding 1000 acres beef & sheep **Parking** 20

HELLIFIELD
MAP 18 SD85

Premier Collection

◆◆◆◆◆

Ribblecote Manor

Swinden BD23 4LS ☎ 01729 850446 📠 01729 850446
e-mail harrison.ribblecote@virgin.net
Dir *A59 onto A682, 4m on right*

This impressive stone house stands on pretty landscaped grounds. The carefully furnished bedrooms are equipped with thoughtful extras and one has a spa bath. Additional facilities include an indoor swimming pool and a games room with a full-size snooker table. Breakfasts, using quality local produce, are served in an attractive dining room, and a spacious lounge is available.

Facilities 3 en suite (1 fmly) ⊘ TVB tea/coffee 🐾 Cen ht TVL No children 2yrs No coaches ▧ Snooker Dinner Last d 24hrs **Prices** D £60-£90 **LB** **Parking** 4 **Notes** ⊛

HELMSLEY
MAP 19 SE68
See also **Hawnby**

Premier Collection

◆◆◆◆◆ ⚑ ⊜

Shallowdale House

West End YO62 4DY ☎ 01439 788325 📠 01439 788885
e-mail stay@shallowdalehouse.co.uk
web www.shallowdalehouse.co.uk
For full entry see **Ampleforth**

England

England

HELMSLEY continued

◆◆◆◆

Plumpton Court

High St, Nawton YO62 7TT ☎ 01439 771223
e-mail mail@plumptoncourt.com
Dir A170 from Helmsley into Beadlam & Nawton, 3rd left (Plumpton Court signed), 60yds on left

Located in the village of Nawton, in the foothills of the North Yorkshire Moors, this characteristic 17th-century stone-built house offers a warm welcome. The cosy lounge bar has an open fire. Bedrooms are comfortable, modern and well equipped, one with a four-poster bed.

Facilities 9 en suite (1 fmly) (1 GF) ⊘ TVB tea/coffee ✖ Licensed Cen ht No children 12yrs No coaches **Prices** S fr £40; D £53-£56 **Parking** 9 **Notes** Closed Dec-Jan

◆◆◆◆

The Carlton Lodge

Bondgate YO62 5EY ☎ 01439 770557 📄 01439 770623
e-mail aaenquiries@carlton-lodge.com
Dir 400yds E of Market Sq on A170

Facilities 8 rms (7 en suite) (1 pri facs) (2 GF) ⊘ FTV TVB tea/coffee Direct dial from bedrooms Licensed Cen ht No coaches Last d 8pm **Prices** S £37.50-£40; D £75-£85 **LB Parking** 10

HOVINGHAM
MAP 19 SE67

◆◆◆

Hovingham Country Guest House ◇

Park St YO62 4JZ ☎ 01653 628740
e-mail enquiries@hovinghamguesthouse.fsnet.co.uk
Dir B1257 into Hovingham, off Main St onto Park St

Situated in the heart of the attractive village, this friendly family-run guest house offers well-equipped bedrooms, which are all ensuite. There is lounge dining room where substantial breakfasts are served.

Facilities 3 en suite (1 fmly) ⊘ STV FTV TVB tea/coffee Direct dial from bedrooms ✖ Cen ht No coaches **Prices** S £25-£35; D £50-£70 **LB Parking** 5 **Notes**

HUBY
MAP 19 SE56

◆◆◆

The New Inn Motel

Main St YO61 1HQ ☎ 01347 810219 📄 01347 810219
e-mail enquiries@newinnmotel.freeserve.co.uk
Dir Off A19 E into village centre, motel on left

Nestling behind the New Inn, this modern motel style accommodation has a quiet location in the village of Huby, 9m north of York. Comfortable bedrooms are spacious and neatly furnished, and breakfast is served in the cosy dining room. The reception area hosts an array of tourist information and the resident owners provide a friendly and helpful service.

The New Inn Motel

Facilities 8 en suite (3 fmly) (8 GF) ⊘ TVB tea/coffee Cen ht No coaches **Prices** S £35-£45; D £55-£60✳ **LB Parking** 8 **Notes** Closed Nov-Dec & Jan

HUNTON
MAP 19 SE19

◆◆◆◆ ◀

The Countryman's Inn

Hunton, Bedale DL8 1PY ☎ 01677 450554
e-mail countrymans.inn@virgin.net
Dir Off A684 into village centre

Set in the heart of this quiet village, the inn is popular with visitors and locals and serves good home-made food. The resident owners provide warm hospitality, and the bedrooms are smartly furnished and comfortably equipped.

Facilities 3 en suite ⊘ in bedrooms ⊘ in dining room TVB tea/coffee ✖ Cen ht No children 7yrs No coaches Dinner Last d 9pm **Prices** S fr £35; D £48-£55✳ **LB Parking** 10

INGLETON
MAP 18 SD67

◆◆◆◆

Gale Green Cottage

Westhouse LA6 3NJ ☎ 015242 41245 & 077867 82088
e-mail rooms@galegreen.com
Dir Just off A65 at Masongill x-rds between Ingleton & Kirkby Lonsdale

Peacefully located in a rural hamlet, this 300-year-old house has been lovingly renovated to provide modern facilities without compromising original charm and character. Thoughtfully furnished bedrooms feature smart modern en-suite shower rooms and a guest lounge is also available.

Facilities 3 en suite (1 fmly) ⊘ TVB tea/coffee ✖ Cen ht TVL No coaches **Prices** S £37-£39; D £54-£58✳ **Parking** 6 **Notes** Closed Xmas & New Year

◆◆◆◆

Inglenook Guest House

20 Main St LA6 3HJ ☎ 01524 241270
e-mail inglenook20@hotmail.com
web www.inglenookguesthouse.com
Dir Off A65 New Rd onto Main St

Close to the River Greta with lovely views of Ingleborough peak, this comfortable Victorian house extends a warm welcome. Bedrooms are

continued

continued

freshly decorated and have a host of comforts. Home-cooked four-course dinners are available by arrangement, served in the spacious dining room. A lounge is also available.

Facilities 4 rms (3 en suite) (1 pri facs) 1 annexe en suite (1 GF) ⊗ TVB tea/coffee ✖ Cen ht TVL No children 5yrs No coaches Dinner Last d Time of booking **Prices** D £50-£54✳ **LB** **Notes** Closed Xmas

◆◆◆

Seed Hill Guest House

LA6 3AB ☎ 01524 241799 ◻ 01524 241799
e-mail adrianseedhill@hotmail.com
web www.come2ingleton.com
Dir In village centre, parking at rear

At this cottage-style guest house, which exudes charm, no two walls are alike. The garden can be a riot of colour from the many potted plants that are on display and for sale. The cosy bedrooms are carefully furnished. Freshly cooked breakfasts are served in the characterful dining room, and genuine hospitality is assured.

Facilities 2 en suite ⊗ TVB tea/coffee Cen ht **Parking** 4

KETTLEWELL   MAP 18 SD97

◆◆◆◆

Littlebeck

The Green BD23 5RD ☎ 01756 760378
e-mail stay@little-beck.co.uk
web www.little-beck.co.uk
Dir B6160 from Skipton into Kettlewell, right at Old Smithy shop, onto the Maypole, Littlebeck on left

A real home from home atmosphere prevails at this establishment, nestling in the quiet village close to major walks and attractions. Bedrooms are very comfortable, featuring homely extras. Breakfast is served family style in the smart dining room. There is also a lounge and parking.

Facilities 3 en suite ⊗ TVB tea/coffee ✖ Cen ht No children No coaches **Parking** 4 **Notes** Closed Xmas

KILBURN   MAP 19 SE57

◆◆◆

Forresters Arms Hotel

YO61 4AH ☎ 01347 868386 & 868550 ◻ 01347 868386
e-mail paulcussons@forrestersarms.fsnet.co.uk
web www.forrestersarms.fsnet.co.uk
Dir S off A170, 3m into village

Situated beneath the famous White Horse, and next to the renowned Mouseman furniture showroom, this traditional inn originates from the Middle Ages. Bedrooms are well equipped and comfortable, and a wide range of popular food is served either in the dining room or one of the cosy, characterful bars.

Facilities 10 en suite (1 fmly) (1 GF) ⊗ in dining room TVB tea/coffee Direct dial from bedrooms Cen ht Pool Table Dinner Last d 9pm **Prices** S £40; D £52-£62✳ **LB** **Parking** 40 **Notes** Closed 25 Dec

KIRKBYMOORSIDE   MAP 19 SE68

◆◆◆◆

Brickfields Farm

Kirby Mills YO62 6NS ☎ 01751 433074
e-mail janet@brickfieldsfarm.co.uk
web www.brickfieldsfarm.co.uk
Dir A170 E from Kirkbymoorside, 0.5m right into Kirby Mills (signed), farm 1st right

Standing in open countryside close to the village, this converted farmhouse offers very individual, carefully furnished bedrooms and comfortable public rooms Breakfast is served in the conservatory overlooking fields and excellent hospitality is provided. Well-produced dinners are available by arrangement. The house is non-smoking.

Facilities 3 en suite (2 GF) ⊗ TVB tea/coffee ✖ Cen ht No children No coaches Golf Dinner Last d by arrangement **Prices** D £68-£76✳ **LB** **Parking** 6 **Notes** 🔄

◆◆◆◆

Appletree Court

9 High Market Pl YO62 6AT
☎ 01751 431536 ◻ 01751 431536
e-mail appletreecourt@hotmail.com
Dir Off A170 at rdbt into village, Appletree Court 500yds on left after Kings Head

Dating from around 1750, this delightful stone house was once a working farm and retains many original features. Today the friendly guest house offers individually decorated, well-equipped bedrooms, all of which are named after different types of apple. This is a good base for touring the Ryedale area.

Facilities 5 en suite (1 fmly) ⊗ TVB tea/coffee ✖ Cen ht No children 8yrs No coaches **Prices** S £35-£56; D £50-£60 **LB**

Book as early as possible, particularly
in the peak holiday period

England

KNARESBOROUGH
MAP 19 SE35

♦♦♦♦

Gallon House
47 Kirkgate HG5 8BZ ☎ 01423 862102
e-mail gallon-house@ntlworld.com
web www.gallon-house.co.uk
Dir Next to railway station

This delightful Tudor-style building has spectacular views over the River Nidd, and offers very stylish accommodation and a homely atmosphere. The bedrooms are all individual with many homely extras. Rick's culinary delights are not too be missed: dinner (by arrangement) features quality local and home-made produce.

Facilities 3 en suite ⊗ in bedrooms ⊗ in dining room ⊗ in lounges TVB tea/coffee Licensed Cen ht No coaches Dinner Last d noon **Prices** S £75; D £99✱ **LB** **Conf** Max 12 Thtr 12 Class 12 Board 12 **Notes** ⊛

See advertisement on opposite page

♦♦♦♦

Newton House
5-7 York Pl HG5 0AD ☎ 01423 863539 📄 01423 869748
e-mail newtonhouse@btinternet.com
web www.newtonhouseyorkshire.com
Dir On A59 in Knaresborough, 500yds from town centre

The delightful 18th-century former coaching inn is only a short walk from the river, castle and market square. The property is entered by an archway into a courtyard. The attractive, very well-equipped bedrooms include some four-posters and also king-size doubles. There is a comfortable lounge, and memorable breakfasts are served in the attractive dining room.

Facilities 9 rms (8 en suite) (1 pri facs) 2 annexe en suite (3 fmly) (3 GF) ⊗ in bedrooms ⊗ in dining room TVB tea/coffee Direct dial from bedrooms Licensed Cen ht TVL No coaches **Prices** S fr £50; D £85-£95✱ **LB** **Parking** 10 **Notes** Closed 1 wk Xmas

See advertisement on page 575

LEYBURN
MAP 19 SE19

★★★★ **Bed & Breakfast**

Thorney Hall
Spennithorne DL8 5PW ☎ 01969 622120 & 07836 269453

This beautiful, lovingly restored country house offers period features, open fireplaces and elegant furnishings. Bedrooms are well appointed

continued

and each has either a modern ensuite or private bathroom. Guests receive a warm welcome and have use of an attractive lounge. Well cooked evening meals and hearty breakfasts are served at a traditional table in the grand dining room.

Facilities 3 rms (2 en suite) (1 pri facs) ⊗ TVB tea/coffee ✖ Cen ht No children No coaches 🔊 **Parking** 10 **Notes** ⊛

♦♦♦♦

The Old Town Hall Guest House ◇
The Old Town Hall, Redmire DL8 4ED
☎ 01969 625641 📄 01969 624982
e-mail enquiries@theoldtownhall.co.uk
Dir In village centre, signs for tea room & guest house

Originally built in 1862 as a drill hall then used by the community as the town hall until its conversion in the 1960's. The extended old town hall now offers very welcoming well-equipped accommodation. Bedrooms vary in style and all offer many thoughtful extras. A hearty breakfast is served in the bright airy dining room, which transforms into a tearoom throughout the day.

Facilities 3 rms (1 en suite) (2 pri facs) (1 fmly) ⊗ STV FTV TVB tea/coffee ✖ Cen ht No coaches Holistic therapies/nail treatments **Prices** S £30-£55; D £55-£90 **LB** **Parking** 3

♦♦♦

The Old Horn Inn
Spennithorne DL8 5PR ☎ 01969 622370
e-mail desmond@furlong1706.fsbusiness.co.uk
Dir 1.5m from Leyburn on A684 towards Bedale, right at The Pheasant pub into Harmby and follow road to end, turn right at x-rds. Inn on outskirts of village on right

Nestling in the quiet village of Spennithorne, the inn is full of character and the resident owners offer a friendly welcome. The two bedrooms are comfortable and well equipped. The restaurant and public bar offer a good selection of wines and fine ales, along with an interesting selection of freshly prepared dishes.

Facilities 2 en suite ⊗ in bedrooms ⊗ in dining room TVB tea/coffee Cen ht No children 10yrs Dinner Last d 9pm **Prices** D £52-£55✱ **Parking** available **Notes** ⊛

LONG PRESTON
MAP 18 SD85

♦♦♦♦

Jubilee Croft B&B ◇
5 Jubilee Croft BD23 4QZ ☎ 01729 840806
e-mail gailcater@8salters.freeserve.co.uk
Dir Off A65 in Long Preston, opp The Boars Head

Located within a quiet cul-de-sac I the village of Long Preston, this honey stone, new detached house provides modern thoughtfully furnished bedrooms equipped with lots of thoughtful extras. Comprehensive breakfasts are served in the attractive dining room overlooking the surrounding countryside.

Facilities 2 rms (1 en suite) (1 pri facs) ⊗ TVB tea/coffee ✖ Cen ht No children 6 yrs No coaches **Prices** S £30-£40; D £55-£65 **LB** **Parking** 2 **Notes** ⊛

Boars Head Hotel

9 Main St BD23 4ND ☎ 01729 840217 ▤ 01729 840217
e-mail ivan-linda@huff.fslife.co.uk
web www.boarsheadyorkshiredales.com
Dir On A65 between Skipton and Settle

Located in the heart of the village, this inn has been completely
transformed in recent years to provide comfortable bedrooms with
modern bathrooms en suite. Imaginative food and a wide selection of
real ales are served in the spacious open-plan ground-floor area. A
warm welcome is assured.

Facilities 5 en suite (2 fmly) ⊗ in bedrooms ⊗ in dining room TVB
tea/coffee ✱ Cen ht Golf 18 ⚲ Fishing Snooker Pool Table Dinner Last
d 8.45pm **Prices** S £35; D £50✳ **Parking** 50

MALHAM   MAP 18 SD96

River House Hotel

BD23 4DA ☎ 01729 830315
e-mail info@riverhousehotel.co.uk
web www.riverhousehotel.co.uk
Dir Off A65, 7m N to Malham

A warm welcome awaits you at this attractive house, which dates from
1664. The bedrooms are bright and comfortable, with one on the
ground floor. Public areas include a cosy lounge and a large, well-
appointed dining room, the setting for imaginative breakfasts featuring
local produce.

Facilities 8 en suite (1 GF) ⊗ TVB tea/coffee Licensed Cen ht
No children 8yrs No coaches Dinner Last d 8pm **Prices** S £45-£65;
D £60-£65✳ **LB** **Parking** 5

Beck Hall ◇

Cove Rd BD23 4DJ ☎ 01729 830332
e-mail alice@beckhallmalham.com
web www.beckhallmalham.com
Dir A65 to Gargrave, turn right to Malham. B&B 100yds on right after
minirdbt

You have to negotiate a small stone footbridge over a bubbling stream
to get to this delightful property. Dating from 1710, the house has true
character, with bedrooms carefully furnished with four-poster beds.
Delicious afternoon teas are available in the colourful garden in
warmer months, while roaring log fires welcome you in the winter.

continued

Facilities 11 rms (10 en suite) (1 pri facs) (1 fmly) ⊗ STV TV8B
tea/coffee Licensed Cen ht ch fac Fishing Riding Dinner Last d 5.30pm
Prices S £25-£60; D £50-£64✳ **LB** **Conf** Max 35 Thtr 30 Class 30
Board 30 Del from £50 ✳ **Parking** 40

MALTON   MAP 19 SE77

Walgate House ◇

Main St, Burythorpe YO17 9LJ
☎ 01653 658101 ▤ 01653 658101
e-mail walgatehouse@aol.com
web www.walgatehouse.co.uk
Dir 4.5m S of Malton. Off A64/A166 to Burythorpe village

Standing near the village pub where good food is served, this stone
house offers excellent home from home accommodation. The
bedrooms are very well furnished, and the resident owners provide a
substantial breakfast and fine hospitality.

Facilities 2 rms (1 en suite) (1 pri facs) ⊗ TVB tea/coffee ✱ Cen ht
No children 10yrs No coaches **Prices** S £30-£40; D £50-£70 **Parking** 2
Notes ⊗

England

MASHAM

MAP 19 SE28

◆◆◆◆

Bank Villa Guest House

HG4 4DB ☎ 01765 689605
e-mail bankvilla@btopenworld.com
web www.bankvilla.com
Dir Enter on A6108 from Ripon, property on right

An elegant Georgian house set in a pretty walled garden. Individually decorated bedrooms feature stripped pine, period furniture and crisp white linen. Imaginative home-cooked meals are served in the attractive dining room. Character public rooms include a choice of lounges, or relax in the garden in summer.

Facilities 6 rms (4 en suite) (2 pri facs) (2 fmly) ⊗ tea/coffee ✖ Licensed Cen ht TVL No children 5yrs No coaches Dinner Last d breakfast **Prices** S £45-£65; D £50-£85✳ **LB Parking** 6

MIDDLEHAM

MAP 19 SE18

◆◆◆◆

The Old Estate Yard

Jervaulx HG4 4PH ☎ 01677 460360
e-mail theoldestateyard@supanet.com
Dir From Middleham towards Masham, Old Estate Yard 3m on left before Jervaulx Abbey

Located on the Jervaulx Estate, these outbuildings have been converted to a modern property while retaining original features. Bedrooms are equipped with lots of thoughtful extras and breakfast uses quality local produce. Dinner is available by arrangement.

Facilities 2 en suite (2 fmly) (2 GF) ⊗ TVB tea/coffee Cen ht No coaches Dinner Last d noon **Prices** S £35-£40; D £55-£60✳ **LB Parking** 5 **Notes** Closed 25-30 Dec 🐾

MIDDLESBROUGH

MAP 19 NZ41

◆◆◆◆

The Grey House Hotel

79 Cambridge Rd, Linthorpe TS5 5NL
☎ 01642 817485 📄 01642 817485
e-mail dwattis@fsmail.net
Dir A19 N onto A1130 & A1032 Acklam Rd, right at lights

This Edwardian mansion stands in mature gardens in a quiet residential area, and is lovingly maintained to provide a relaxing retreat. The master bedrooms are well sized, and the upper rooms,

though smaller, also offer good comfort. Downstairs there is an attractive lounge and the breakfast room.

Facilities 9 en suite (1 fmly) ⊗ in bedrooms ⊗ in dining room ⊗ in 1 lounge TVB tea/coffee Direct dial from bedrooms Cen ht No coaches **Prices** S £45-£50; D £60✳ **Parking** 10

MUKER

MAP 18 SD99

◆◆◆◆ ♥

Oxnop Hall (SD931973)

Low Oxnop, Gunnerside DL11 6JJ
☎ 01748 886253 📄 01748 886253 Mrs Porter
Dir Off B6270 between Muker and Gunnerside

Nestling in beautiful Swaledale scenery, this smartly presented 17th-century farmhouse has been furnished with thought and care. The attractive bedrooms are well equipped and some boast original exposed beams and mullion windows. Hearty farmhouse breakfasts are served, using local and home-made produce where possible. A cosy lounge is also available.

Facilities 4 en suite 1 annexe en suite (1 GF) ⊗ TVB tea/coffee ✖ Cen ht No children 10yrs 1000 acres beef sheep hill farming **Prices** S £31-£45; D £60-£70✳ **Parking** 10 **Notes** Closed Dec-15 Feb 🐾

NORTHALLERTON

MAP 19 SE39

★★★★ Restaurant with Rooms

Three Tuns

9 South End, Osmotherley DL6 3BN
☎ 01609 883301 📄 01609 883988
e-mail enquiries@threetunsrestaurant.co.uk
Dir Turn of A19 signed Northallerton/Osmotherley. Turn at junct signed Osmotherley at Kings Head Hotel. Into village, Inn straight ahead

Situated in the popular village of Osmotherley, this restaurant-with-rooms is full of character. Bedrooms, set above the bar and also in an adjoining building, vary in size but are stylishly furnished in pine and equipped to meet the needs of tourists and business travellers alike. The restaurant offers an imaginative menu of wholesome, modern British dishes.

Facilities 3 en suite 4 annexe en suite (1 fmly) (1 GF) ⊗ TVB tea/coffee Direct dial from bedrooms ✖ Licensed TVL Dinner Last d 9.30pm **Prices** S fr £55; d fr £75✳ **Parking** 2

continued

◆◆◆◆
Windsor Guest House

56 South Pde DL7 8SL ☎ 01609 774100 🖨 01609 774100
Dir *On A684 at S end of High St*

The Victorian terrace house is convenient for the town centre. Spotlessly maintained accommodation consists of bright, cheerful, and thoughtfully equipped bedrooms. The attractive dining room overlooks the landscaped garden and dinner is available by arrangement.

Facilities 6 rms (5 en suite) ⊗ TVB tea/coffee ✖ Licensed Cen ht TVL No coaches Dinner Last d am

OSMOTHERLEY   MAP 19 SE49

◆◆ 🗲
Queen Catherine Hotel ◇

7 West End DL6 3AG ☎ 01609 883209
e-mail info@queencatherinehotel.co.uk
Dir *Off A19 into village centre*

This traditional inn nestles in the heart of the picturesque village. Bedrooms are compact yet comfortably equipped and decorated. The cosy bar offers imaginative menus and the hearty breakfasts make good use of fresh local produce.

Facilities 5 en suite ⊗ in bedrooms ⊗ in dining room TVB tea/coffee ✖ Cen ht TVL Dinner Last d 8.45pm **Prices** S £25-£35; D £50-£70

PICKERING   MAP 19 SE78

Premier Collection

◆◆◆◆◆
The Moorlands Country House Hotel

Levisham YO18 7NL ☎ 01751 460229 🖨 01751 460470
e-mail ronaldoleonardo@aol.com
Dir *A169 N from Pickering 6m, left to Lockton & Levisham*

The Moorlands stands on the edge of the peaceful village of Levisham, with stunning views of the North York Moors National Park and Heartbeat country. Stylish throughout, this country house offers luxury accommodation and genuine hospitality. Bedrooms are very thoughtfully equipped and there is also a comfortable lounge. A hearty breakfast is served in the elegant dining room and dinner is available by arrangement.

Facilities 7 en suite (1 GF) ⊗ TVB tea/coffee ✖ Licensed Cen ht TVL No children 15yrs Stabling available Dinner Last d 8pm **Parking** 10 **Notes** Closed Dec-Feb 🐾

◆◆◆◆ 🗲
The New Inn

Maltongate, Thornton Le Dale YO18 7LF ☎ 01751 474226
e-mail terryandjo1@btconnect.com
Dir *on A177 in centre of Thornton le Dale*

Originally a coaching inn standing in the centre of the village overlooking the village green. There is a friendly atmosphere in the locals' bar and a popular restaurant serves interesting local dishes. Bedrooms are comfortable and offer many extras.

Facilities 6 en suite ⊗ in bedrooms ⊗ in dining room TVB tea/coffee ✖ Cen ht Dinner Last d 8:45pm **Prices** S £43-£48; D £66-£76✳ **Parking** 15

POTTO   MAP 19 NZ40

◆◆◆ 🗲
Dog and Gun Country Inn

Cooper Ln DL6 3HQ ☎ 01642 700232 🖨 01642 700232
e-mail enquiries@dogandguncountryinn.co.uk
Dir *A19 onto A172 to Stokesley, 1m left to Potto, continue 1m*

Please note that this establishment has recently changed hands. This refurbished village inn is full of character. Bedrooms vary in size and a family room is also available. Public areas include a choice of dining options including the new conservatory restaurant. Interesting dishes are offered including an all day carvery on a Sunday.

Facilities 5 en suite (1 fmly) ⊗ in bedrooms ⊗ in dining room ⊗ in lounges TVB tea/coffee ✖ Cen ht Pool Table Dinner Last d 9.30pm **LB** **Conf** Max 80 Thtr 80 Class 80 Board 36 **Parking** 50

RAINTON   MAP 19 SE37

🆄 🗲
The Bay Horse Inn

YO7 3PX ☎ 01845 578697 & 07816 896628
e-mail nigel.bayhorse@btinternet.com
Dir *0.75m off A1(M) junct 49*

At the time of going to press the rating for this establishment had not been confirmed. Please check the AA website www.theAA.com for up-to-date information.

Facilities 7 en suite ⊗ in bedrooms ⊗ in dining room TVB tea/coffee Cen ht TVL Dinner Last d 9pm **Prices** S £35-£50; D £70-£100✳ **LB** **Conf** Max 40 Board 40 Del from £32.50 ✳ **Parking** 20

England

RAMSGILL
MAP 19 SE17

Premier Collection
★★★★★ ◎◎◎ **Restaurant with Rooms**

Yorke Arms
HG3 5RL ☎ 01423 755243 📄 01423 755330
e-mail enquiries@yorke-arms.co.uk
web www.yorke-arms.co.uk
Dir Off B6265 at Pateley at Nidderdale filling station onto Low Wath Rd, signed to Ramsgill 4.5m

A welcoming atmosphere pervades this ivy-clad former hunting lodge overlooking the village green in picturesque Nidderdale. Flagstone floors lead to the cosy bar, and beams and open fires grace the delightful dining rooms where excellent cuisine is matched by caring service. The bedrooms have been refurbished to a high standard.

Facilities 14 en suite (2 fmly) (5 GF) TVB tea/coffee Direct dial from bedrooms 🐾 Licensed No coaches Shooting Mountain biking Dinner Last d 8.45pm **Prices** S £100-£150; D £150-£340✳ **LB Conf** Max 10 Class 20 Board 10 **Parking** 20

RAVENSCAR
MAP 19 NZ90

◆◆◆◆ 🅰

Smugglers Rock Country House
YO13 0ER ☎ 01723 870044
e-mail info@smugglersrock.co.uk
Dir Off A171 towards Ravenscar. House 0.5m before Ravenscar, opp stone windmill

Facilities 8 en suite (3 fmly) ⊗ TVB tea/coffee 🐾 Cen ht TVL No coaches **Prices** S £32-£34; D £54-£58✳ **LB Parking** 12 **Notes** Closed Nov-Mar

REDCAR
MAP 19 NZ62

◆◆◆

Claxton Hotel ◇
196 High St TS10 3AW ☎ 01642 486745 📄 01642 486522
e-mail enquiries@claxtonhotel.co.uk
web www.claxtonhotel.co.uk
Dir Off A174 at double rdbt signed Redcar, over railway crossing, right at lights by St Peters Church, rear car park on left

This friendly, family-owned commercial establishment overlooks the sea and is popular for local functions. Bedrooms are comfortable and the public areas are spacious. Hearty breakfasts are served in the attractive dining room and dinner is also available.

Facilities 27 rms (26 en suite) (2 fmly) (5 GF) ⊗ in 4 bedrooms ⊗ in dining room ⊗ in 1 lounge TVB tea/coffee Licensed Cen ht TVL Dinner Last d 9pm **Prices** S £23.50-£30.55; D £41.13-£43.48✳ **Parking** 10 **Notes** Closed 23-27 Dec rs 28 Dec-2 Jan

REETH
MAP 19 SE09

◆◆◆◆ ⌷ ◀

Charles Bathurst Inn
Arkengarthdale DL11 6EN
☎ 01748 884567 📄 01748 884599
e-mail info@cbinn.co.uk
web www.cbinn.co.uk
Dir B6270 to Reeth, at Buck Hotel turn N to Langthwaite, pass church on right, inn 0.5m on right

The CB Inn, as it is known, is surrounded by magnificent scenery high in the Dales. Food is the focus of the pub, where a choice of rustic eating areas makes for atmospheric dining. The well-equipped bedrooms blend contemporary and traditional styles and cosy lounge areas are available. A well-equipped function suite is also available.

Facilities 19 en suite (2 fmly) (5 GF) ⊗ in bedrooms ⊗ in dining room FTV TVB tea/coffee Direct dial from bedrooms Cen ht Fishing Pool Table Dinner Last d 9pm **Prices** D £72.50-£110✳ **LB Conf** Max 70 Thtr 70 Class 30 Board 30 Del from £85.50 ✳ **Parking** 35 **Notes** Closed Xmas Day

RICCALL
MAP 16 SE63

◆◆◆◆ 🅰

Dairymans of Riccall ◇
14 Kelfield Rd YO19 6PG
☎ 01759 248532 📄 0871 2513863
e-mail bookings@dairymansriccall.co.uk
Dir Off A19 into village, off Main St onto Silver St & Kelfield Rd

Facilities 4 en suite (1 fmly) ⊗ TVB tea/coffee 🐾 Cen ht TVL **Prices** S £30; D £60-£75✳

◆◆◆

Park View Hotel
20 Main St YO19 6PX ☎ 01757 248458 📄 01757 249211
e-mail geoffandsue@hotel-park-view.co.uk
Dir A19 from Selby, left for Riccall by water tower, 100yds on right

The well-furnished and comfortable Park View stands in grounds and offers well-equipped bedrooms. There is a cosy lounge plus a small bar, while breakfasts are served in the dining room. Dinner is available each evening.

Facilities 7 en suite (1 fmly) ⊗ in bedrooms ⊗ in dining room ⊗ in 1 lounge TVB tea/coffee Direct dial from bedrooms Licensed Cen ht No coaches Dinner Last d When Booking **Parking** 10

If you have to cancel a booking, let the proprietor know immediately

If the freedom to smoke or be in a non-smoking atmosphere is important to you, check the rules when you book

RICHMOND MAP 19 NZ10

See also **Reeth**

♦♦♦♦ ❤

Whashton Springs Farm (NZ149046)

DL11 7JS ☎ 01748 822884 📄 01748 826285 Mrs Turnbull
e-mail whashtonsprings@btconnect.com
web www.whashtonsprings.co.uk
Dir *In Richmond N at lights towards Ravensworth, 3m down steep hill, farm at bottom on left*

A friendly welcome awaits you at this farmhouse accommodation, situated in the heart of the countryside yet convenient for major routes. Bedrooms are split between the courtyard rooms and the main farmhouse. Hearty breakfasts are served in the spacious dining room overlooking the gardens. A stylish lounge is also available.

Facilities 3 en suite 5 annexe en suite (2 fmly) (5 GF) ⊗ TVB tea/coffee ✖ Licensed Cen ht No children 5yrs 600 acres arable beef mixed sheep **Prices** S fr £35; D £56-£60✳ LB **Conf** Max 16 Board 16 **Parking** 10 **Notes** Closed late Dec-Jan 🌐

♦♦♦ 🅰

Pottergate Guest House ◇

4 Pottergate DL10 4AB ☎ 01748 823826
Dir *A1608 to Richmond, over 1st rdbt & lights, 50yds on left*

Facilities 6 rms (1 en suite) (2 pri facs) (1 fmly) ⊗ TV1B tea/coffee ✖ Cen ht No children 3yrs No coaches **Prices** S £23-£35; D £50-£57 **Parking** 2 **Notes** 🌐

RIPON MAP 19 SE37

★★ Bed & Breakfast

Blue Pots

24 Glovers Crescent HG4 2TB ☎ 01765 604380
Dir *A61 to Ripon. Glovers Crescent 0.5m on left immediately after bridge.*

Pleasant modern townhouse over three floors located in quiet residential area of Ripon and within a short walk of the Market Square. Accommodation consists of one spacious and comfortable bedroom with smart ensuite bathroom at the top of the house. Breakfast is served in the family lounge/dining room, which guests are also welcome to use during their stay.

Facilities 1 en suite ⊗ TVB tea/coffee ✖ Cen ht No children No coaches **Parking** 1 **Notes** 🌐

♦♦♦♦♦ ❤

Mallard Grange (SE270704)

Aldfield HG4 3BE
☎ 01765 620242 📄 01765 620242 Mrs Johnson
e-mail maggie@mallardgrange.co.uk
web www.mallardgrange.co.uk
Dir *B6265 W fom Ripon, Mallard Grange 2.5m on right*

Located near Fountains Abbey, the original features of this early 17th-century farmhouse are highlighted by quality furnishings and decor. Bedrooms, two of which are in a converted smithy, are filled with a wealth of thoughtful extras, and comprehensive breakfasts feature home-reared or local produce.

Facilities 2 en suite 2 annexe en suite (2 GF) ⊗ TVB tea/coffee ✖ Cen ht No children 12yrs 500 acres Mixed, beef, sheep, arable **Prices** D £70-£85✳ LB **Parking** 6 **Notes** Closed Xmas & New Year

♦♦♦♦ ❤

Bay Tree Farm (SE263685)

Aldfield HG4 3BE
☎ 01765 620394 📄 01765 620394 Mrs Leeming
e-mail val@btfarm.entadsl.com
web www.baytreefarm.co.uk
Dir *4m W of Ripon. S off B6265*

A warm welcome awaits you at this farmhouse set in the countryside close to Fountains Abbey and Studley Park. Bedrooms are suitably equipped, there is a cosy lounge with a log-burning stove, and breakfast is traditional home-cooked fare. Dinner is available for groups of 8 or more by arrangement.

Facilities 6 en suite (1 fmly) (3 GF) ⊗ TVB tea/coffee Cen ht 400 acres beef arable Last d 10am **Prices** D £70-£80 **Parking** 10

England

RIPON continued

◆◆◆◆ 🛏 🍴

St George's Court (SE237697)

Old Home Farm, Grantley HG4 3PJ
☎ 01765 620618 🖷 01765 620618 Mrs Hitchen
e-mail stgeorgescourt@bronco.co.uk
web www.stgeorges-court.co.uk
Dir B6265 W from Ripon, right signed Grantley & Winksley, up hill 1m past Risplith sign & next right

This renovated farmhouse is a great location to get away from it all, in the delightful countryside close to Fountains Abbey. Attractive, well-equipped ground-floor bedrooms are located around a central courtyard. Imaginative breakfasts are served in the conservatory-dining room, which has splendid views of the surrounding countryside.

Facilities 5 en suite (1 fmly) (5 GF) ⊗ TVB tea/coffee 🐾 Cen ht Fishing 20 acres beef /sheep **Prices** S £35-£45; D £60-£75✳ LB **Conf** Max 12 **Parking** 12

ROBIN HOOD'S BAY   MAP 19 NZ90

◆◆◆◆ 🍷

The Flask Inn ◇

Robin Hoods Bay, Fylingdales YO22 4QH
☎ 01947 880305
e-mail flaskinn@aol.com
web www.flaskinn.com
Dir On A171, 7m S from Whitby

The Flask, originally a 16th-century hostel, is now a comfortable inn offering a good range of real ales and food. Thoughtfully equipped bedrooms are furnished in attractive pine and have modern shower rooms en suite. The spacious bar has a friendly atmosphere.

Facilities 6 en suite (2 fmly) ⊗ TVB tea/coffee 🐾 Cen ht No coaches Pool Table Dinner Last d 9pm **Prices** S £27.50-£30; D £55✳ LB **Conf** Max 80 Del from £15 ✳ **Parking** 20

[U]

Bramblewick

2 King St YO22 4SH
☎ 01947 880960 & 880339 🖷 01947 880960
e-mail bramblewick@btinternet.com
Dir A171 onto B1447 to rdbt, straight over & down steep hill into 'Old Village'. Situated at bottom on the left

At the time of going to press the rating for this establishment had not

continued

been confirmed. Please check the AA website www.theAA.com for up-to-date information.

Bramblewick

Facilities 3 en suite ⊗ TVB tea/coffee 🐾 Licensed Cen ht No coaches Dinner Last d 8.30pm **Prices** D £65-£70✳ LB **Notes** Closed 24-26 Dec

ROSEDALE ABBEY   MAP 19 SE79

◆◆◆◆

Sevenford House

YO18 8SE ☎ 01751 417283
e-mail sevenford@aol.com
web www.sevenford.com
Dir Off A170 at sign for Rosedale Abbey, in village turn sharp left at Coach & House Restaurant & right at White Horse

Nestling in the heart of the national park, this elegant Victorian house stands in a peaceful garden within walking distance of the village. The well-proportioned bedrooms are comfortable, well equipped and have stunning panoramic views. There is also an inviting lounge and a spacious breakfast room with grand piano.

Facilities 3 en suite (1 fmly) ⊗ TVB tea/coffee 🐾 Cen ht No coaches **Prices** S £40-£45; D £55-£60 LB **Parking** 6 **Notes** 🚭

SCARBOROUGH   MAP 17 TA08

★★★★ Bed & Breakfast

Foulsyke Farm House B&B ◇

Barmoor Ln, Scalby YO13 0PG ☎ 01723 507423
e-mail info@foulsykefarmhouse.co.uk
Dir A171into Scalby village. Follow North St to duck pond, turn left then 1st right

In the pretty village of Scalby this delightful house is situated on a working farm. Recently renovated, the house offers elegantly furnished

continued

...edrooms, with thoughtful accessories and well equipped bathrooms. ...warm welcome is assured and a hearty breakfast is served in the ...right, attractive dining room.

...acilities 3 rms (2 en suite) (1 pri facs) ⊗ TVB tea/coffee ✱ Cen ht ...o children 10yrs No coaches Prices S £30; D £50✳ Parking 6 ...otes ⊛

★★★ Guest Accommodation

Geldenhuis ◇

43-147 Queens Pde YO12 7HU ☎ 01723 361677
e-mail geldenhuis1@yahoo.co.uk

Overlooking the North Bay, a warm welcome is assured and guests ...ave use of a comfortable lounge, fully licensed bar and spacious ...estaurant. Bedrooms are well equipped, most benefiting from ...ompact ensuites and some with stunning sea views.

...acilities 24 rms (23 en suite) (1 pri facs) (4 fmly) ⊗ in 6 bedrooms ...⊗ in dining room TVB tea/coffee Licensed Cen ht TVL Dinner Last d ...oon Prices S £25-£35; D £50-£60✳ LB Parking 23

◆◆◆◆

Croft Hotel ◇

7 Queens Pde YO12 7HT
☎ 01723 373904 ▤ 01723 350490
e-mail information@crofthotel.co.uk
web www.crofthotel.co.uk
Dir Tourist signs for North Bay seafront, along front towards castle ...eadland, right turn up cliff, right at top, premises on left

...flexible approach to your needs is a key feature of this friendly ...stablishment. It overlooks the bay, and you can enjoy the view from ...e comfortable lounge or from the patio in fine weather. Meals are ...erved in the very pleasant bar or in the well-appointed dining room.

...acilities 6 rms (5 en suite) (1 pri facs) (4 fmly) ⊗ TVB tea/coffee ✱ ...censed Cen ht TVL No coaches Golf arranged at local courses Dinner ...ast d 6.30pm Prices S £23-£25; D £46-£50✳ LB Parking 4 ...otes Closed Nov-mid Feb

◆◆◆◆

Hotel Columbus

24 Columbus Ravine YO12 7QZ
☎ 01723 374634 & 07930 545964
e-mail hotel.columbus@lineone.net
Dir On A165 towards North Bay, near Peasholm Park

Yorkshire hospitality at its best is offered here, and Bonnie Purchon is ...welcoming hostess. The establishment is well located for the beach ...nd attractions. Bedrooms are compact, well equipped and homely. A ...ery comfortable lounge is provided. In the dining room a good ...reakfast is served, as are evening meals during the main season.

...acilities 11 en suite (2 fmly) ⊗ TVB tea/coffee ✱ Licensed Cen ht ...VL No children 2yrs Dinner Last d am Prices S £32.50-£37.50; ...£65-£75✳ LB Parking 8 Notes Closed Jan-Feb

◆◆◆◆

Hotel Danielle ◇

9 Esp Road, South Cliff YO11 2AS ☎ 01723 366206
e-mail hoteldanielle@yahoo.co.uk
Dir S of town centre. Off A165 Filey Rd onto Victoria Av, left onto Esplanade, left onto Esplanade Rd

A warm welcome is assured at this elegant Victorian house situated a short walk from the Spa Cliff Lift. Bedrooms are equipped with thoughtful extras and day rooms include an attractive dining room and a lounge.

Facilities 9 rms (7 en suite) (3 fmly) ⊗ in bedrooms ⊗ in dining room TVB tea/coffee ✱ Licensed Cen ht TVL No children 2yrs
Prices S £24-£26; D £52-£60✳ LB Notes Closed Dec-mid Feb

◆◆◆◆

North End Farm Country Guesthouse ◇

88 Main St, Seamer YO12 4RF ☎ 01723 862965
e-mail northendfarm@tiscali.co.uk
Dir A64 N onto B1261 through Seamer, farmhouse next to rdbt

Located in Seamer, a village inland from Scarborough, this 18th-century farmhouse contains comfortable, well-equipped en suite bedrooms. Breakfast is served at individual tables in the smart dining room, and the cosy lounge has a large-screen television.

Facilities 3 en suite ⊗ TVB tea/coffee ✱ Cen ht TVL No coaches
Prices S £25-£35; D £42-£50✳ Parking 6 Notes ⊛

◆◆◆◆

Paragon Hotel ◇

123 Queens Pde YO12 7HU
☎ 01723 372676 ▤ 01723 372676
e-mail enquiries@paragon-hotel.fsnet.co.uk
web www.paragonhotel.com
Dir On A64, follow signs for North Bay. Hotel on clifftop

This welcoming Victorian terrace house has been carefully renovated to provide stylish, thoughtfully equipped, non-smoking accommodation. Hearty English breakfasts are served in the attractive dining room and there is also a lounge bar with a fabulous sea view.

Facilities 14 en suite (1 fmly) ⊗ TVB tea/coffee Direct dial from bedrooms ✱ Licensed Cen ht No children 3yrs No coaches Dinner Last d 1pm Prices S £30-£35; D £49-£54✳ LB Parking 6 Notes Closed 20 Nov-24 Jan

England

SCARBOROUGH continued

◆◆◆◆

Raincliffe Hotel

21 Valley Rd YO11 2LY ☎ 01723 373541 ▤ 01723 373541
e-mail enquiries@raincliffehotel.co.uk
Dir Off A64/A170 towards South Bay/spa complex

Located a short walk from South Bay, this elegant Victorian house offers a range of thoughtfully furnished bedrooms with homely extras. Day rooms, which feature original decorative features, include an attractive dining room and a lounge.

Facilities 11 rms (9 en suite) (2 pri facs) (3 fmly) ⊗ TVB tea/coffee ✖ Licensed Cen ht TVL No children 5yrs No coaches Dinner Last d 9pm
Conf Max 22

◆◆◆◆

The Ramleh ◇

135 Queens Pde YO12 7HY
☎ 01723 365745 ▤ 01723 365745
e-mail Johncramlehhotel@aol.com
Dir A64, A165 to North Bay & Peasholm Park, right onto Peasholm Rd, 1st left

Overlooking North Bay, this welcoming terrace house has a friendly atmosphere. The modern bedrooms are bright and comfortable, and delicious home-cooked meals are served in the spacious dining room, which also has a well-stocked bar. A pleasant lounge is also available.

Facilities 8 annexe en suite (3 fmly) ⊗ in bedrooms ⊗ in dining room TVB tea/coffee ✖ Licensed Cen ht TVL No coaches Dinner Last d 1pm
Prices S £20-£24; D £40-£48✶ LB **Parking** 6 **Notes** Closed 24-26 Dec rs Oct-Mar

◆◆◆◆

The Whiteley Hotel ◇

99/101 Queens Pde YO12 7HY
☎ 01723 373514 ▤ 01723 373007
e-mail whiteleyhotel@bigfoot.com
Dir A64, A165 to North Bay & Peasholm Park, right onto Peasholm Rd, 1st left

The Whiteley is an immaculately run, sea-facing home from home. Bedrooms, if compact, are carefully decorated and have many thoughtful extras. There's a small garden at the rear, a choice of lounges, and a bar. The establishment has some superb views, and the owners provide personal attention and good home cooking.

Facilities 10 en suite (3 fmly) (1 GF) ⊗ TVB tea/coffee ✖ Licensed Cen ht TVL No children 3yrs No coaches **Prices** S £30; D £48-£52 LB **Parking** 8 **Notes** Closed 30 Nov-Jan

◆◆◆◆

The Windmill Bed & Breakfast

Mill St, Off Victoria Rd YO11 1SZ
☎ 01723 372735 ▤ 01723 377190
e-mail info@windmill-hotel.co.uk
web www.windmill-hotel.co.uk
Dir A64 into Scarborough. Pass Sainsbury, left onto Victoria Rd, 3rd left onto Mill St

Situated in the centre of town but having its own car park, this unique establishment has modern bedrooms situated around a courtyard next to a windmill dating from 1784. The base of the mill includes a spacious breakfast room and a toy museum which is only viewable by guests.

Facilities 11 en suite (3 fmly) (6 GF) ⊗ TVB tea/coffee ✖ Cen ht No coaches **Prices** S £35-£60; D £54-£90✶ **Parking** 7

◆◆◆◆

Wharncliffe Hotel

26 Blenheim Ter YO12 7HD ☎ 01723 374635
e-mail info@thewharncliffehotel.co.uk
web www.thewharncliffehotel.co.uk
Dir In Scarborough signs to the Castle, left at Albion pub, Wharncliffe 200yds on left

Facilities 12 en suite (1 fmly) ⊗ TVB tea/coffee ✖ Licensed Cen ht TVL No children 16yrs No coaches **Prices** S £36-£60; D £52-£60 LB

◆◆◆

Plane Tree Cottage Farm *(SE999984)*

Staintondale YO13 0EY ☎ 01723 870796 Mrs Edmondson
Dir A171 N from Scarborough. At Cloughton onto Staintondale road, farm 2m N of Cloughton

The Edmondson family are welcoming hosts, and their animals include unusual breeds of sheep and hens. This is an interesting and pleasant venue, either for its tranquil, secluded setting, or as a base for walking. There is good home cooking, comfortable bedrooms, and a cosy lounge and dining room.

Facilities 3 rms (2 en suite) (1 GF) ⊗ tea/coffee ✖ Cen ht TVL No children 60 acres sheep hens Dinner Last d 10am **Prices** d fr £50✶ **Parking** 3 **Notes** Closed Nov-Feb ⊠

◆◆◆

Argo Hotel ◇

134 North Marine Rd YO12 7HZ ☎ 01723 375745
Dir Near Scarborough Cricket Club main entrance

A haven for cricket fans, the pleasant Argo offers a warm welcome and comfortable bedrooms, with some overlooking the championship ground. The attractive dining room has a small, well-stocked bar.

Facilities 8 rms (5 en suite) (2 fmly) ⊗ in 2 bedrooms ⊗ in dining room TVB tea/coffee ✖ Cen ht TVL No children 3yrs No coaches Dinner Last d 3pm **Prices** S £18-£19; D £42-£44 LB **Notes** Closed Dec ⊠

England

Chessington Hotel ◇

The Crescent YO11 2PP ☎ 01723 365207 📠 01723 375206
e-mail chessingtonhotel@onetel.net
web www.chessingtonhotel.co.uk
Dir *A64 to town centre lights, right, left at next lights & right at next lights, Chessington on left*

This Grade II listed building occupies a fine position overlooking the Crescent and is close to the town centre. The bedrooms are well equipped, and the spacious dining room is the setting for comprehensive breakfasts. A sitting room and lounge bar are available.

Facilities 10 en suite (2 fmly) ⊗ in bedrooms ⊗ in dining room ⊗ in 1 lounge TVB tea/coffee ✗ Licensed Cen ht TVL No coaches **Prices** S £29; D £58 **LB Conf** Max 10 **Notes** Closed Jan

Jalna House Hotel

Facilities 10 rms (6 en suite) (6 fmly) (2 GF) ⊗ in bedrooms ⊗ in dining room TVB tea/coffee Cen ht TVL Dinner Last d noon **Prices** S fr £21; d fr £42✳ **LB Notes** Closed 21 Dec-7 Jan 🐾

Grosvenor Hotel ◇

51 Grosvenor Rd YO11 2LZ
☎ 01723 363801 📠 01723 363801
e-mail grosvenorhotelscarborough@msn.com
Dir *Signs for South Bay along Valley Rd, Grosvenor Rd on left*

You can expect good hospitality from all the family at the Grosvenor, situated a short walk from the town and the seafront. The friendly guest house offers comfortable accommodation and a spacious lounge.

Facilities 14 en suite (3 fmly) (3 GF) ⊗ in bedrooms ⊗ in dining room TVB tea/coffee ✗ Licensed Cen ht TVL No coaches **Prices** S £23.50-£28; D £47-£56✳ **LB Notes** Closed 10 Dec-10 Jan

Jalna House Hotel ◇

168 North Marine Rd YO12 7HZ
☎ 01723 360668 📠 01723 360668
e-mail jalna@btconnect.com
Dir *A165 to Peasholm Park, onto Peasholm Rd & North Marine Rd, near cricket ground*

A well-furnished house close to Peasholm Park and within walking distance of the North Beach and the town centre. Compact bedrooms are comfortable, there is a cosy lounge and a dining room serving tasty home-cooked meals.

Parmelia Hotel

17 West St YO11 2QN ☎ 01723 361914
e-mail info@parmeliahotel.co.uk
web www.parmeliahotel.co.uk
Dir *Off A64 at The Mere onto Queen Margarets Rd, left at next rdbt (A165) onto Ramshill Rd, right for Esplanade Gdns Rd*

Only a short walk from the Esplanade on the south cliff, this large guest house provides modern coordinated bedrooms. Cheerful hospitality makes you feel at home. There is an attractive lounge to relax in and a spacious lounge bar.

Facilities 15 rms (12 en suite) (1 pri facs) (4 fmly) (2 GF) ⊗ in bedrooms ⊗ in dining room ⊗ in 1 lounge TVB tea/coffee ✗ Cen ht TVL No children 4yrs No coaches **LB Notes** Closed Dec-Feb 🐾

Peasholm Park Hotel ◇

21-23 Victoria Park YO12 7TS ☎ 01723 500954
e-mail peasholmparkhotel@btconnect.com

A warm welcome awaits you at this family-run guest house, which is within easy walking distance of the town centre. Bedrooms are comfortable, and feature homely extras. Evening meals are available by arrangement.

Facilities 12 en suite (3 fmly) ⊗ TVB tea/coffee ✗ Licensed Cen ht TVL No children 4yrs No coaches Dinner Last d Noon **Prices** S £24.90-£29; D £49.80-£58 **LB Parking** 2 **Notes** rs 22 Dec-2 Jan

continued

England

SCARBOROUGH continued

♦♦♦

Warwick House Hotel

70 Westborough YO11 1TS
☎ 01723 374343 ▤ 01723 374343
e-mail warwick@onetel.net
Dir *On outskirts of town centre, just before railway station on left*

Close to the Stephen Joseph Theatre, station and shops, this friendly guest house has a comfortable rooms, a smart bright lounge and a pleasant basement dining room. Private parking is available.

Facilities 6 rms (2 en suite) (4 fmly) ⊗ in dining room ⊗ in lounges TVB tea/coffee Licensed Cen ht TVL No coaches **LB Parking** 5 **Notes** ⊛

♦♦♦ Ⓐ

Hotel Phoenix ◇

8/9 Rutland Ter YO12 7JB
☎ 01723 501150 ▤ 01723 500762
e-mail info@hotel-phoenix.co.uk
web www.hotel-phoenix.co.uk
Dir *From railway station follow brown signs to Castle.*

Facilities 15 en suite (5 fmly) (1 GF) ⊗ TVB tea/coffee ✖ Licensed Cen ht TVL Holistic treatments Dinner Last d 10am **Prices** S £30-£40; D £50-£60✳ **LB Parking** 15

Ⓤ

The Hillcrest ◇

2 Peasholm Av YO12 7NE ☎ 01723 361981
e-mail enquiries@hillcresthotel.co.uk
web www.hillcresthotel.co.uk
Dir *A165 to North Bay/leisure parks, onto Peasholm Dr & Peasholm Crescent*

At the time of going to press the rating for this establishment had not been confirmed. Please check the AA website www.theAA.com for up-to-date information.

Facilities 7 en suite (1 fmly) ⊗ TVB tea/coffee ✖ Licensed Cen ht TVL Dinner Last d 10am **Prices** S £23-£30; D £46-£55✳ **LB Parking** 3 **Notes** Closed 22-29 Dec

Ⓤ

Olivers

34 West St YO11 2QP ☎ 01723 368717
e-mail olivershotel@scarborough.co.uk

At the time of going to press the rating for this establishment had not been confirmed. Please check the AA website www.theAA.com for up-to-date information.

Facilities 6 en suite (2 fmly) (1 GF) ⊗ TVB tea/coffee ✖ Cen ht Dinner Last d breakfast **Notes** Closed 20-28 Dec

SCOTCH CORNER

MAP 19 NZ20

♦♦♦ Ⓐ

The Vintage Inn ◇

DL10 6NP ☎ 01748 824424 & 822961 ▤ 01748 826272
e-mail thevintagescotchcorner@btinternet.com
Dir *A1 at Scotch Corner onto A66 towards Penrith, premises 200yds on left*

Facilities 8 rms (5 en suite) ⊗ in dining room ⊗ in 1 lounge TVB tea/coffee Direct dial from bedrooms ✖ Licensed Cen ht TVL Dinner Last d 9pm **Prices** S £23.50-£39.50; D £35.50-£49.50; (room only) ✳ **LB Conf** Max 48 Thtr 40 Class 30 Board 20 **Parking** 40

SETTLE

MAP 18 SD86

See also **Clapham, Hellifield & Long Preston**

♦♦♦♦ ◖▮

Golden Lion

5 Duke St BD24 9DU ☎ 01729 822203 ▤ 01729 824103
e-mail goldenlion@yorks.net
Dir *In town centre opp Barclays Bank*

This traditional former coaching inn is in the town centre, just a short walk from the railway station. The Golden Lion provides a wide range of freshly prepared meals, served in the spacious bar or the stylish restaurant. Most of the bedrooms have been refurbished to complement the modern bathrooms.

Facilities 12 rms (10 en suite) (2 fmly) ⊗ in dining room TVB tea/coffee ✖ Cen ht Pool Table Dinner Last d 9pm **Prices** S £34-£41; D £60-£81✳ **LB Conf** Max 12 **Parking** 11

♦♦♦♦

Jubilee Croft B&B

5 Jubilee Croft BD23 4QZ ☎ 01729 840806
e-mail gailcater@8salters.freeserve.co.uk
For full entry see **Long Preston**

♦♦♦♦

Whitefriars Country Guesthouse

Church St BD24 9JD ☎ 01729 823753
e-mail info@whitefriars-settle.co.uk
Dir *Off A65 through Settle market place, premises signed 50yds on left*

This friendly, family-run house stands in peaceful gardens just a stroll from the town centre and railway station. Bedrooms, some quite spacious, are attractively furnished and thoughtfully equipped. A hearty breakfast is served in the traditional, beamed dining room, and a cosy lounge is available.

Facilities 9 rms (5 en suite) (1 pri facs) (2 fmly) ⊗ TVB tea/coffee ✖ Cen ht TVL No coaches **Prices** D £44-£55✳ **Parking** 9 **Notes** Closed 25 Dec ⊛

SKIPTON

MAP 18 SD95

◆◆◆◆

Clay Hall

Broughton Rd BD23 3AA ☎ 01756 794391
Dir On A59 1m from Skipton towards Broughton

A warm welcome is assured here on the outskirts of the town next to the Leeds and Liverpool canal. The house has been restored to provide carefully furnished bedrooms with smart modern shower rooms en suite and a wealth of thoughtful extras. Comprehensive breakfasts are served in an attractive dining room.

Facilities 2 en suite ⊗ TVB tea/coffee ✖ Cen ht No children 12yrs No coaches LB **Parking** 4 **Notes** ⊠

◆◆◆◆ ✤

Low Skibeden Farmhouse *(SD013526)*

Marrogate Rd BD23 6AB
☎ 01756 793849 & 07050 207787 Mrs Simpson
web
www.yorkshirenet.co.uk/accgde/lowskibeden/index.html
Dir At E end of Skipton bypass off A65/A59, 1m on right

A genuine welcome awaits you at this 16th-century stone farmhouse, set in lovingly tended gardens on the outskirts of town. Heather Simpson is a perfect hostess and offers afternoon tea, suppertime drinks and hearty breakfasts. A range of accommodation is available including spacious family rooms.

Facilities 5 rms (4 en suite) (2 fmly) ⊗ tea/coffee ✖ Cen ht TVL No children 40 acres sheep **Prices** S £36-£48; D £48-£60✳ LB **Parking** 6

◆◆◆◆

Westfield House

50 Keighley Rd BD23 2NB ☎ 01756 790849
Dir 500yds S of town centre on A6131, S of canal bridge

Just a stroll from the town centre, this friendly, non-smoking guest house provides smart accommodation. Bedrooms are well presented and most have large beds and many accessories including bathrobes. A hearty breakfast is served in the cosy dining room, and permission to use nearby parking is a bonus. Hospitality here is warm and nothing is too much trouble.

Facilities 4 en suite ⊗ TVB tea/coffee ✖ Cen ht No children No coaches **Prices** D £50-£52 **Notes** ⊠

◆◆◆

Craven House

56 Keighley Rd BD23 2NB
☎ 01756 794657 📠 01756 794657
e-mail info@craven-house.co.uk
web www.craven-house.co.uk
Dir 500yds S of town centre on A6131, S of canal bridge

A warm welcome awaits you at this centrally located guest house. The Victorian house has been renovated to provide comfortable accommodation. Bedrooms vary in size, and feature homely extras.

Facilities 5 rms (3 en suite) (2 pri facs) ⊗ TVB tea/coffee Cen ht No coaches **Prices** S £32-£34; D £48-£50✳

◆◆◆

Rockwood House ◇

14 Main St, Embsay BD23 6RE
☎ 01756 799755 & 07976 314980 📠 01756 799755
e-mail jstead@v21.me.uk
web www.stayinyorkshire.co.uk
Dir 2m NE of Skipton. Off A59 into Embsay village centre

This Victorian terrace house has a peaceful location in the village of Embsay. Bedrooms are thoughtfully furnished, individually styled and reassuringly comfortable. The traditionally styled dining room sets the venue for hearty breakfasts. Hospitality is a feature here with a genuine and friendly welcome.

Facilities 3 en suite (1 fmly) (1 GF) ⊗ TVB tea/coffee ✖ Cen ht TVL No coaches **Prices** S £30-£50; D £50-£60✳ LB **Parking** 3

England

SNAINTON

MAP 17 SE98

Coachman Inn

Pickering Rd West YO13 9PL
☎ 01723 859231 📠 01723 850008
e-mail enquiries@coachmaninn.co.uk
web www.coachmaninn.co.uk
Dir *On W edge of Snainton, just off A170 on B1258*

Located between Scarborough and Pickering, this Grade II Georgian coaching inn has been renovated to provide an elegant dining room, the setting for imaginative food, using local produce. Bedrooms include some for families, and a warm welcome and attentive service are assured.

Facilities 5 en suite (1 fmly) ⊗ in bedrooms ⊗ in dining room ⊗ in lounges TVB tea/coffee ✗ Cen ht No coaches Dinner Last d 9pm **Parking** 20

SUTTON-ON-THE-FOREST

MAP 19 SE56

◆◆◆◆ ◉ ◠ ◀

The Blackwell Ox Inn

Huby Rd YO61 1DT
☎ 01347 810328 & 690758 📠 01904 691529
e-mail enquiries@blackwelloxinns
web www.blackwelloxinn.co.uk
Dir *Off A1237, onto B1363 to Sutton-on-the-Forest. Left at T-junct, 50yds on right*

Standing in the lovely village, this refurbished inn and restaurant offers very good bedrooms and pleasing public rooms. Cooking is well worth seeking out and staff are very keen and friendly.

Facilities 5 en suite ⊗ TVB tea/coffee Direct dial from bedrooms ✗ Lift Cen ht TVL No coaches Dinner Last d 9.30pm **Prices** S £90; D £90✻ **Parking** 18

See advertisement on opposite page

TADCASTER

MAP 16 SE44

★★★ Bed & Breakfast

The Old Presbytery Guest House

London Rd, Saxton LS24 9PU
☎ 01937 557708 & 557392 📠 01937 557392
e-mail guest@presbytery.plus.com
web www.presbyteryguesthouse.co.uk
Dir *4m S of Tadcaster on A162. 100yds N of Barkston Ash on E side of road*

Dating from the 18th century, this former dower house has been modernised to provide comfortable accommodation with original features. The hall lounge features a wood-burning stove, and extensive breakfasts are served at an old oak dining table in a cosy breakfast room.

Facilities 4 rms (3 en suite) (1 pri facs) (1 fmly) ⊗ TVB tea/coffee ✗ Cen ht TVL No coaches Golf 18 **Prices** S fr £35; d fr £66✻ **Conf** Max 8 **Parking** 6

◆◆

Little House

Kirkby Wharfe LS24 9DD
☎ 01937 833402 📠 01937 833402
e-mail suzybeeneat@aol.com
web www.stayatlittlehouse.co.uk
Dir *2.5m SE of Tadcaster. Signed off B1223 W of Ulleskelf*

A spacious family home located in the hamlet of Kirkby Wharfe within the open countryside of the Wharfe valley. Convenient for the A64 and the M1, this is a good touring base with a friendly atmosphere and sincere hospitality.

Facilities 2 rms ⊗ in bedrooms ⊗ in area of dining room ⊗ in lounges TV1B tea/coffee ✗ Cen ht TVL No coaches Dinner Last d 6pm **Parking** 1 **Notes** ⊗

THIRSK

MAP 19 SE48

Premier Collection

◆◆◆◆◆ 🏠 ◠

Spital Hill

York Rd YO7 3AE ☎ 01845 522273 📠 01845 524970
e-mail spitalhill@amserve.net
Dir *1.5m SE of town, set back 200yds from A19, driveway marked by 2 white posts*

Set in gardens, this substantial Victorian country house is delightfully furnished. The spacious bedrooms are thoughtfully equipped with

continued

many extras, one even has a piano, but no televisions or kettles; the proprietor prefers to offer tea as a service. Delicious meals feature local and home-grown produce and are served house-party style around one table in the interesting dining room.

Facilities 3 rms (2 en suite) (1 pri facs) 2 annexe en suite (1 GF) ⊘ Direct dial from bedrooms ✘ Licensed Cen ht TVL No children 12yrs No coaches ♫ Dinner Last d 2pm **Prices** S £56-£61; D £84-£95✳ LB **Parking** 6

WESTOW
MAP 19 SE76

◆◆◆◆ ✔

Woodhouse Farm ◇ (SE749637)

YO60 7LL

☎ 01653 618378 & 07904 293422 🖹 01653 618378

Mrs Wardle

e-mail stay@wood-house-farm.co.uk

web www.wood-house-farm.co.uk

Dir Off A64 to Kirkham Priory & Westow. Right at T-junct, farm drive 0.5m out of village on right

The owners of this guest house are a young farming family who open their home and offer caring hospitality. Home-made bread, preserves and farm produce turn breakfast into a feast, and the views from the house across open fields are splendid.

Facilities 3 en suite (1 fmly) ⊘ TVB tea/coffee ✘ Cen ht TVL Fishing 550 acres arable/beef/sheep **Prices** S £30-£40; D £55-£70✳ LB **Parking** 12 **Notes** Closed Xmas, New Year & Mar-mid Apr 🚭

◆◆◆ ✔

Clifton Farm (SE776463)

YO60 7LS

☎ 01653 658557 & 07776 112530 🖹 01653 658557

Ms Laughton

e-mail lynn@cliftonfarm.co.uk

web www.cliftonfarm.co.uk

Dir 2m SE of Westow. Off A64 signed Harton then Howsham, pass Howsham towards Leavening, over x-rds & Clifton Farm 1m on right

Situated in countryside on the edge of Leavening village, this comfortable, well-furnished farmhouse offers outstanding hospitality and service. Bedrooms are well equipped, breakfasts are hearty, and a lounge is available. Lynn Laughton is a top-twenty finalist for AA Landlady of the Year 2006.

Facilities 3 rms (2 en suite) (1 pri facs) (1 fmly) ⊘ TVB tea/coffee ✘ Cen ht TVL No children 10yrs 120 acres Mixed **Prices** S £35-£40; D £55-£70✳ LB **Parking** 6

WHITBY
MAP 19 NZ81

See also **Robin Hood's Bay**

★★★★ Guest House

Chiltern Guest House ◇

13 Normanby Ter, West Cliff YO21 3ES ☎ 01947 604981

e-mail tjchiltern@aol.com

Dir Whalebones next to Harbour, sea on right. Royal Hotel on left, 200yds. Royal Gardens turn left, 2nd road on left 6th House on right

The Victorian terrace house offers a warm welcome and comfortable accommodation within walking distance of the town centre and seafront. Public areas include a smartly decorated lounge and a bright, attractive dining room. Bedrooms are thoughtfully equipped and many have small, modern en suites.

Facilities 9 rms (5 en suite) (1 pri facs) (3 fmly) ⊘ in 4 bedrooms ⊘ in dining room ⊘ in lounges TVB tea/coffee Cen ht TVL Golf 9 **Prices** S £23-£25; D £50-£60✳ **Notes** 🚭

WHITBY continued

★★★★ **Restaurant with Rooms**

Estbek House

East Row, Sandsend YO21 3SU
☎ 01947 893424 📠 01947 893625
e-mail reservations@estbekhouse.co.uk
Dir On Cleveland Way, within Sandsend, next to East Beck

A speciality seafood restaurant on the first floor is the focus of this listed building in a small coastal village north west of Whitby. Below is a small bar and breakfast room, while up above are four individually presented en-suite bedrooms offering luxury and comfort, that vary in size.

Facilities 4 rms (3 en suite) ⊗ TVB tea/coffee Licensed Cen ht No children 14yrs No coaches Jacuzzi Dinner Last d 9pm **Prices** S £50; D £80-£100✳ **LB Parking** 6

♦♦♦♦

Netherby House Hotel

90 Coach Rd, Sleights YO22 5EQ
☎ 01947 810211 📠 01947 810211
e-mail info@netherby-house.co.uk
web www.netherby-house.co.uk
Dir In village of Sleights, off A169 Whitby-Pickering road

This fine Victorian house has been lovingly refurbished and now offers thoughtfully furnished, individually styled bedrooms together with delightful day rooms. There is a fine conservatory and the grounds are extensive with exceptional views from the summerhouse at the bottom of the garden. Imaginative dinners feature produce from the extensive kitchen garden.

Facilities 6 en suite 5 annexe en suite (1 fmly) (5 GF) ⊗ TVB tea/coffee ✖ Licensed Cen ht TVL No coaches Pool Table ♫ Dinner Last d 8pm **Prices** S £34-£38.50; D £68-£77✳ **LB Parking** 17 **Notes** Closed 21-26 Dec

♦♦♦♦

Corra Lynn ◇

28 Crescent Av YO21 3EW
☎ 01947 602214 📠 01947 602214
Dir Corner A174 & Crescent Av

Occupying a prominent corner position, this property mixes traditional values with a trendy and artistic style. Bedrooms are thoughtfully equipped, individually furnished and have bright colours schemes, but it is the delightful dining room with corner bar and a wall adorned with clocks that takes the eye.

Facilities 5 en suite (1 fmly) STV TVB tea/coffee Direct dial from bedrooms ✖ Licensed Cen ht No coaches **Prices** S fr £24; d fr £52✳ **Parking** 5 **Notes** Closed 21 Dec-5 Jan

See advertisement on opposite page

♦♦♦♦

The Europa

20 Hudson St YO21 3EP ☎ 01947 602251 📠 01947 606678
e-mail europahotel-whitby@btconnect.com
Dir Signs to West Cliff, A174 onto Royal Crescent, 2nd right

A friendly atmosphere prevails at the Europa, which lies in a quiet terrace near the seafront. There is an attractive dining room and a cosy lounge with bar. Bedrooms vary in size, but all are bright and cheerful.

Facilities 7 en suite ⊗ TVB tea/coffee Cen ht No coaches **Prices** S £49-£60; D £60✳

♦♦♦♦

Kimberley House ◇

7 Havelock Pl YO21 3ER ☎ 01947 604125
e-mail enquiries@kimberleyhouse.com
web www.kimberleyhouse.com
Dir Signs to West Cliff, A174 onto Crescent Av, right onto Hudson St, next junct

This 19th-century house was built for a local seafaring family. It stands in a quiet residential area within walking distance of the West Cliff promenades and the historic town centre. Bedrooms are well equipped and comfortable, and a wide choice of breakfasts is available. Julie and Stephen are friendly hosts.

Facilities 8 rms (7 en suite) (1 pri facs) (2 fmly) (1 GF) ⊗ TVB tea/coffee ✖ Cen ht **Prices** S £23-£32; D £54✳ **LB Notes** Closed Dec-Jan

♦♦♦♦

Whitehaven

29 Crescent Av YO21 3EW ☎ 01947 601569
e-mail simon@whitehavenguesthouse.co.uk
Dir Signs to West Cliff, A174 onto Cresent Av

Occupying a corner position close to the sports complex and indoor swimming pool, this house provides colourful bedrooms in contrasting styles. All rooms have minifridges and most have DVD facilities. Vegetarian options are available at breakfast served in the attractive dining room.

Facilities 4 rms (3 en suite) (1 pri facs) ⊗ TVB tea/coffee ✖ Cen ht No coaches **Prices** D £54-£56 **LB Notes** Closed 18-27 Dec 📷

The Haven Guest House ◇

4 East Crescent YO21 3HD
☎ 01947 603842 ▤ 0870 094 1103
e-mail info@thehavenwhitby.co.uk
web www.thehavenwhitby.co.uk
Dir A171 onto A174 in Whitby. At rdbt left onto Chubb Hill, next rdbt 4th exit onto St Hilda's Ter, left onto Cliff St, left onto East Crescent

Facilities 8 en suite ⊗ TVB tea/coffee ✖ Cen ht No coaches
Prices S £30; D £55-£65✳ **Notes** ⊛

◆◆◆

Lansbury Guesthouse

29 Hudson St YO21 3EP ☎ 01947 604821
e-mail jill@lansbury44.fsnet.co.uk
Dir In town centre, off A174 Upgang Ln onto Crescent Av, 2nd right

A short walk from the historic harbour, a warm welcome is assured at this elegant Victorian terrace house which has been renovated to provide good standards of comfort and facilities. Bedrooms are equipped with thoughtful extras, and comprehensive breakfasts using local produce are served in an attractive dining room.

Facilities 8 rms (7 en suite) (1 pri facs) (1 fmly) (1 GF)
⊗ in 5 bedrooms ⊗ in dining room TVB tea/coffee ✖ Cen ht
Prices D £46-£58✳ **LB**

◆◆◆

The Middleham ◇

3 Church Sq YO21 3EG ☎ 01947 603423
e-mail myra@themiddleham.co.uk

Standing in a quiet square opposite the church, this friendly family-run guest house offers well equipped bedrooms and spacious public rooms. The hearty breakfast is a good start to the day.

Facilities 9 rms (8 en suite) (1 pri facs) (3 fmly) ⊗ TVB tea/coffee ✖ Cen ht TVL **Prices** S £22-£30; D £50✳

◆◆◆

The Sandbeck Private Hotel

1 & 2 Crescent Ter, West Cliff YO21 3EL
☎ 01947 604012 & 603349 ▤ 01947 606402
e-mail dysonsandbeck@tesco.net
Dir On West Cliff opp theatre

Commanding a prominent corner position on the seafront, Sandbeck is being progressively upgraded. Bedrooms are generally well proportioned and front rooms have fine sea views. Public rooms comprise a bar, quiet lounge, and a spacious dining room offering various breakfast options.

Facilities 23 en suite (4 fmly) ⊗ in bedrooms ⊗ in dining room ⊗ in 1 lounge TVB tea/coffee ✖ Licensed Lift Cen ht No coaches Last d 9pm **Prices** S £35.50-£37.50; D £58-£90✳ **Notes** Closed Dec-Jan

◆◆◆ ◉ ⬭

The White Horse & Griffin

Church St YO22 4BH
☎ 01947 825026 & 604857 ▤ 01947 604857
e-mail info@whitehorseandgriffin.co.uk
Dir From town centre E across Bridge St bridge, 2nd left

This historic inn, now more a restaurant with rooms, is as quaint as the cobbled side street in which it lies. Cooking is good with the emphasis on fresh fish. The bedrooms, some reached by steep staircases, retain a rustic charm but are well equipped and include CD players.

Facilities 10 en suite (1 fmly) ⊗ in bedrooms ⊗ in dining room ⊗ in lounges TVB tea/coffee ✖ Licensed Cen ht No coaches Dinner Last d 9pm **Conf** Max 30 Thtr 30

YORK

MAP 16 SE65

Premier Collection

♦♦♦♦♦

Alexander House

94 Bishopthorpe Rd YO23 1JS ☎ 01904 625016
e-mail info@alexanderhouseyork.co.uk
web www.alexanderhouseyork.co.uk
Dir *600yds S of city centre. A64 E onto A1036 York West into city centre, right onto A59 Scarcroft Rd, right at end, Alexander House 100yds on left*

You will feel very much at home at this Victorian terrace house, which is just a short walk from the city centre. Stylishly decorated and furnished throughout, the owners take delight in sharing their beautiful home and have created superbly equipped and comfortable rooms. Delicious breakfasts featuring quality local produce are served in the well-appointed dining room.

Facilities 4 en suite ⊗ TVB tea/coffee ✖ Cen ht No children 12yrs No coaches **Prices** S £55-£75; D £65-£85 **LB** **Parking** 3 **Notes** Closed Xmas-New Year

♦♦♦♦

Ascot House ◇

80 East Pde YO31 7YH ☎ 01904 426826 ▤ 01904 431077
e-mail admin@ascothouseyork.com
web www.ascothouseyork.com
Dir *0.5m NE of city centre. Off A1036 Heworth Green onto Mill Ln, 2nd left*

June and Keith Wood provide friendly service at the 1869 Ascot House, a 15-minute walk from the town centre. Bedrooms are thoughtfully equipped, many with four-poster or canopy beds and other period furniture. Reception rooms, including a cosy lounge, also retain original features.

Facilities 15 rms (12 en suite) (3 fmly) (2 GF) ⊗ in bedrooms ⊗ in dining room TVB tea/coffee Licensed Cen ht TVL Sauna **Prices** S £30-£65; D £60-£75✱ **LB** **Parking** 14 **Notes** Closed 21-28 Dec

♦♦♦♦

Ashbourne House

139 Fulford Rd YO10 4HG
☎ 01904 639912 ▤ 01904 631332
e-mail ashbourneh@aol.com
Dir *On A19 to York city centre. Through Fulford, after two lights establishment on right*

Aileen and David Minns extend a very friendly welcome. The bedrooms at Ashbourne House are comfortable and thoughtfully equipped. Public areas include a spacious lounge with an honesty bar.

Facilities 7 rms (6 en suite) (1 pri facs) (2 fmly) ⊗ TVB tea/coffee Direct dial from bedrooms ✖ Licensed Cen ht No coaches **Parking** 7 **Notes** Closed 24 Dec-1 Jan

♦♦♦♦

Barbican House

20 Barbican Rd YO10 5AA
☎ 01904 627617 ▤ 01904 647140
e-mail info@barbicanhouse.com
web www.barbicanhouse.com
Dir *Signs to city centre, premises 100yds from Barbican Leisure Centre near junct A19 & A1079*

This Victorian residence is very well furnished throughout and provides attractive and well-equipped bedrooms with a host of homely extras. A hearty Yorkshire breakfast is served in the cosy dining room and you can expect friendly and attentive service.

Facilities 7 en suite 1 annexe en suite (1 fmly) (2 GF) ⊗ FTV TVB tea/coffee ✖ Cen ht No children 10yrs No coaches **Prices** S £62-£80; D £74-£85 **LB** **Parking** 6

See advertisement on opposite page

England

◆◆◆◆
Church View B & B ◇

87 The Village, Stockton-On-The-Forest YO32 9UP
☎ 01904 400403 & 07752 273371 📠 01904 400325
e-mail manners@87churchview.fsnet.co.uk
web www.churchviewyork.co.uk
Dir 4.5m NE of York. Off A64 to Stockton on the Forest, Church View opp church

Set in the centre of the village, this 200-year-old house offers three very well-equipped bedrooms, one on the ground floor and two reached by a spiral staircase. CD and video players are provided. There is a very cosy lounge and dining room and hospitality is very good as is the service provided. Dinner is available by arrangement.

Facilities 3 en suite (3 fmly) (1 GF) ⊗ TVB tea/coffee 🐾 Cen ht TVL No coaches Golf 18 Dinner Last d 10am **Prices** S £30-£65; D £50-£65✳ LB **Parking** 3 **Notes** Closed 20 Dec-1 Jan

◆◆◆◆
City Guest House

68 Monkgate YO31 7PF ☎ 01904 622483
e-mail info@cityguesthouse.co.uk
Dir NE of city centre on B1036

Just a stroll from the historic Monk Bar, this guest house is well located for business, shopping and sightseeing. Carefully furnished bedrooms boast stylish interior design and come equipped with a host of thoughtful touches. The smart dining room is the venue for a good breakfast.

Facilities 7 en suite (1 fmly) (1 GF) ⊗ TVB tea/coffee 🐾 Cen ht No children 8yrs No coaches **Parking** 6 **Notes** Closed 20 Dec-1 Feb

◆◆◆◆
Curzon Lodge and Stable Cottages

23 Tadcaster Rd, Dringhouses YO24 1QG
☎ 01904 703157 📠 01904 703157
Dir A64 onto A1036 N towards city centre, 2m on right between Holiday Inn & Marriott Hotel

Close to York's famous Knavesmire Racecourse, this charming 17th-century Grade II listed house sits in gardens on the grand royal route into the city. Comfortable, pine-furnished bedrooms are located either in the main house or in the converted coach house and stables. Breakfast is served in the cottage-style dining room.

Facilities 5 en suite 5 annexe en suite (1 fmly) (4 GF) ⊗ TVB tea/coffee 🐾 Cen ht No children 10yrs No coaches
Prices S £47.50-£54.50; D £65-£82✳ LB **Parking** 16 **Notes** Closed 24 Dec-1 Jan

England

YORK continued

◆◆◆◆

The Hazelwood

24-25 Portland St YO31 7EH
☎ 01904 626548 📠 01904 628032
e-mail reservations@thehazelwoodyork.com
web www.thehazelwoodyork.com
Dir 400yds N from York Minster off Gillygate/inner ring road

A renovation of two elegant Victorian houses in residential side street near the Minster. Bedrooms are equipped with thoughtful extras, and comprehensive breakfasts are served in an attractive dining room. There is a cosy garden-level lounge and a private car park.

Facilities 13 en suite (2 fmly) (2 GF) ⊗ TVB tea/coffee ✖ Licensed Cen ht No children 8yrs **Prices** S £50-£105; D £80-£110✱ **LB Parking** 8

◆◆◆◆

The Heathers Guest House

54 Shipton Rd, Clifton - Without YO30 5RQ
☎ 01904 640989 📠 01904 640989
web www.heathers-guest-house.co.uk
Dir N of York on A19, halfway between A1237 ring road & York city centre

Lying back off the main road just north of the city, this friendly family-run guest house extends a warm welcome. The modern bedrooms, some of which are on the ground floor, are neatly decorated and furnished. Hearty breakfasts are served in the pleasant breakfast room, which looks out onto the gardens.

Facilities 6 rms (4 en suite) (2 pri facs) (2 fmly) ⊗ TVB tea/coffee ✖ Cen ht TVL No children 10yrs No coaches **Prices** S £48-£126; D £52-£130 **Parking** 9 **Notes** Closed Xmas

◆◆◆◆

Holly Lodge

204-206 Fulford Rd YO10 4DD ☎ 01904 646005
e-mail geoff@thehollylodge.co.uk
web www.thehollylodge.co.uk
Dir On A19 south side, 1.5m on left from A64/A19 junct, or follow A19 Selby signs from city centre to Fulford Rd

Located just a short walk from the historic centre, this pleasant Georgian property has coordinated, well-equipped bedrooms. The spacious lounge houses a grand piano, and hearty breakfasts are served in the cosy dining room. You can also use the delightful walled garden.

Facilities 5 en suite (1 fmly) (1 GF) ⊗ TVB tea/coffee ✖ Cen ht No children 7yrs No coaches **Prices** S £58-£88; D £68-£98 **Parking** 6 **Notes** Closed 24-27 Dec

◆◆◆◆

Holmwood House Hotel

112/114 Holgate Rd YO24 4BB
☎ 01904 626183 📠 01904 670899
e-mail holmwood.house@dial.pipex.com
Dir On A59 York to Harrogate, on left 300yds past The Fox pub

With ample parking, a 15-minute walk from this delightful Victorian house takes you into the centre of York. Elegantly individually styled bedrooms are richly decorated and smartly furnished with many antiques. There is a delightful lounge and a substantial breakfast is served in the pleasant basement dining room.

Facilities 14 en suite (1 fmly) (4 GF) ⊗ TVB tea/coffee Direct dial from bedrooms ✖ Licensed Cen ht TVL **Prices** D £60-£120✱ **LB Parking** 8

♦♦♦♦

Carlton House Hotel

134 The Mount YO24 1AS
☎ 01904 622265 🖃 01904 637157
e-mail enquiries@carltonhouse.co.uk
Dir A64 E onto A1036 signed York West, 1m pass racecourse on right & up hill to lights, 100yds on left

Facilities 13 en suite (6 fmly) ⊗ TVB tea/coffee ✈ Cen ht **Parking** 7

♦♦♦♦

Midway House

145 Fulford Rd YO10 4HG ☎ 01904 659272
e-mail midway.house@virgin.net
Dir A64 to York, 3rd exit A19 to York city centre, over 2nd lights & house 50yds on right

Facilities 12 rms (10 en suite) (3 fmly) (1 GF) ⊗ TVB tea/coffee ✈ Cen ht TVL No children 5yrs No coaches **Prices** S £34-£42; D £52-£72✴ **LB Parking** 14 **Notes** Closed 23-28 Dec

♦♦♦

Adam's House ◇

5 Main St, Fulford YO10 4HJ
☎ 01904 655413 🖃 01904 643203
e-mail adams.house2@virgin.net
Dir A64 onto A19, 200yds on right after lights

Adam's House offers comfortable accommodation 1.5m from York centre in the suburb of Fulford, close to the university. It has many fine period features, pleasant, well-proportioned bedrooms and an attractive dining room. The resident owners are friendly and attentive, and collect various military memorabilia.

Facilities 8 rms (7 en suite) (4 fmly) (2 GF) ⊗ TVB tea/coffee ✈ Cen ht No coaches Dinner Last d By arrangement **Prices** S £28-£35; D £62-£68✴ **Parking** 8

♦♦♦

Cavalier Hotel

39 Monkgate YO31 7PB ☎ 01904 636615 🖃 01904 636615
e-mail julia@cavalierhotel.fsnet.co.uk
Dir On A1036 to Malton, 250yds from York inner ring road & city wall

Only a stroll from Monk Bar, a medieval city gateway with a working portcullis, this early Georgian house is an ideal base for sightseeing in York. The cosy bedrooms are comfortable and well equipped, and an English breakfast is served in the elegant dining room. Parking available.

Facilities 10 rms (7 en suite) (4 fmly) ⊗ TVB tea/coffee ✈ Cen ht TVL No coaches Sauna **Parking** 7
See advertisement on this page

England

YORK continued

♦♦♦
Cumbria House

2 Vyner St, Haxby Rd YO31 8HS ☎ 01904 636817
e-mail candj@cumbriahouse.freeserve.co.uk
web www.cumbriahouse.com
Dir *A1237 onto B1363 S towards city centre, pass hospital, left at lights, 400yds on left*

Expect a warm welcome at this family-run guest house, which is located 0.6m north from of the Minster. The attractive bedrooms are well furnished and equipped with many useful extras. Freshly cooked breakfasts are served in the smart dining room at individual tables. This is a non-smoking establishment.

Facilities 6 rms (2 en suite) (2 fmly) ⊗ TVB tea/coffee ✖ Cen ht No coaches **Prices** S £26-£30; D £50-£60✶ LB **Parking** 5 **Notes** Closed 24-28 Dec

♦♦♦
Greenside

124 Clifton YO30 6BQ ☎ 01904 623631 ▤ 01904 623631
e-mail greenside@amserve.com
web www.greensideguesthouse.co.uk
Dir *A19 N towards city centre, over lights for Greenside, on left opp Clifton Green*

Overlooking Clifton Green, this detached house is just within walking distance of the city centre. Accommodation consists of simply furnished bedrooms and there is a cosy lounge and a dining room, where dinners by arrangement and traditional breakfasts are served. It is a family home, and other families are welcome.

Facilities 6 rms (3 en suite) (2 fmly) (3 GF) ⊗ in 3 bedrooms ⊗ in dining room TVB tea/coffee Cen ht TVL Dinner Last d 6pm **Prices** S fr £25; d fr £46✶ LB **Parking** 6 **Notes** Closed Xmas & New Year ⊜

♦♦♦
Hillcrest Guest House

110 Bishopthorpe Rd YO23 1JX
☎ 01904 653160 ▤ 01904 656168
e-mail hillcrest@accommodation.gbr.fm
Dir *A64 onto A1036 N to city centre. 1st right after Marriott Hotel, left at T-junct, Hillcrest 0.33m on right*

A warm welcome awaits you at this central guest house with private parking. The Victorian house has been renovated to provide
continued

comfortable accommodation. Bedrooms vary in size, there is a comfortable lounge, and breakfast is served in the small, bright dining room.

Facilities 13 rms (7 en suite) (4 fmly) (1 GF) ⊗ TVB tea/coffee ✖ Cen ht TVL No children 2yrs No coaches **Prices** S £26-£30; D £46-£56 LB **Parking** 7

♦♦♦
Moat Bed & Breakfast

Nunnery Ln YO23 1AA ☎ 01904 652926
Dir *Signs to city centre, on A19 adjacent to city walls*

Aptly named, the delightful, family-run guest house stands beside the city walls, only a short walk from the main attractions. The bedrooms have splendid antique furniture, and some rooms have half-tester beds. Breakfast is served in the elegant dining room and ample private parking is a bonus.

Facilities 8 en suite ⊗ TVB tea/coffee ✖ Licensed Cen ht No children 7yrs No coaches **Parking** 10 **Notes** Closed Xmas/New Year
See advertisement on page 599

♦♦♦
The Priory Hotel

126-128 Fulford Rd YO10 4BE
☎ 01904 625280 ▤ 01904 637330
e-mail reservations@priory-hotelyork.co.uk
web www.priory-hotelyork.co.uk
Dir *500yds S of city centre on A19*

The same family has run this well-established establishment for four generations. Reception rooms include a dining room, comfortable foyer, lounge and cosy bar, all decorated in keeping with the large Victorian house. Bedrooms are modern in style and provide a high standard of comfort. Gothic arches lead to the landscaped gardens and the large car park.
continued

England

Facilities 16 en suite (5 fmly) (1 GF) FTV TVB tea/coffee Direct dial from bedrooms Licensed Cen ht TVL **Prices** S £45-£70; D £60-£85✳ LB **Parking** 25 **Notes** Closed Xmas

◆◆◆

St Denys Hotel

St Denys Rd YO1 9QD
☎ 01904 622207 & 646776 📠 01904 624800
e-mail info@stdenyshotel.co.uk
web www.stdenyshotel.co.uk
Dir A1079 to inner ring road, through Walmgate Bar, 500yds left, premises opp St Denys Church

This former vicarage is located in the heart of the city centre. Its en suite bedrooms are comfortably furnished and equipped with homely extras, and the neat dining room leads to a conservatory-lounge with a well-stocked bar.

Facilities 13 en suite (4 fmly) (3 GF) ⊗ in bedrooms ⊗ in dining room TVB tea/coffee Direct dial from bedrooms ✖ Licensed Cen ht TVL No coaches Dinner Last d 9pm **Prices** S £40-£65; D £49-£85 LB **Parking** 9

◆◆◆

St Georges

6 St Georges Pl, Tadcaster Rd YO24 1DR
☎ 01904 625056 📠 01904 625009
e-mail sixstgeorg@aol.com
web www.members.aol.com/sixstgeorg
Dir A64 onto A1036 N to city centre, as racecourse ends, St Georges Place on left

Located near the racecourse, this family-run establishment is within walking distance of the city. The attractive bedrooms are equipped with modern facilities, and some rooms have four-poster beds and others can accommodate families. A cosy lounge is available and hearty breakfasts are served in the delightful dining room.

Facilities 10 en suite (5 fmly) (1 GF) ⊗ TVB tea/coffee Cen ht No coaches Dinner Last d 11am **Prices** S £40-£50; D £55-£65 LB **Parking** 7 **Notes** Closed 20 Dec-2 Jan

◆◆◆

Bishopgarth ◇

3 Southlands Rd YO23 1NP ☎ 01904 635220
e-mail megspreckley@aol.com
Dir Off A64 E onto A1036 (city centre), pass York racecourse, right onto Scarcroft Rd, 3rd right onto Millfield Rd & Southlands Rd

Facilities 5 en suite (2 fmly) ⊗ TVB tea/coffee ✖ Cen ht No coaches **Prices** S £30-£60; D £50-£60 LB **Notes** Closed mid Dec-mid Jan

YORKSHIRE, SOUTH

BARNSLEY   MAP 16 SE30

◆◆◆

Churchills Hotel

1 High St, Wombwell S73 0DA
☎ 01226 340099 📠 01226 211126
e-mail churchillshotel@btconnect.com
web www.churchillshotel-wombwell.co.uk

Churchills offers good accommodation and a friendly welcome. There is an informal atmosphere in the bar areas, where a good range of meals and snacks is available, and entertainment is provided on some evenings during the week. Bedrooms are of good comfortable proportions and are well equipped.

Facilities 14 en suite (2 fmly) ⊗ in area of dining room ⊗ in 1 lounge TVB tea/coffee ✖ Cen ht No coaches Pool Table Dinner Last d 9pm **Prices** S £39.50; D £45✳ **Conf** Max 20 Board 20 **Parking** 20

DONCASTER   MAP 16 SE50

◆◆◆◆

Canda Lodge

Hampole Balk Ln, Skellow DN6 8LF
☎ 01302 724028 📠 01302 727999
Dir 6m NW of Doncaster. Off A1 onto B1220 into Skellow

Well located for the A1, this stone house has well-tended gardens and spacious parking. Garden bedrooms are attractively decorated, well-equipped and delightfully furnished. The public areas consist of a pleasant breakfast room with individual tables and a small lounge area. Service is friendly and caring.

Facilities 2 rms 4 annexe en suite (1 fmly) (6 GF) ⊗ TVB tea/coffee Direct dial from bedrooms ✖ Cen ht TVL No children 13yrs No coaches **Prices** S £32-£36; D £42-£45✳ **Parking** 20

◆◆◆◆

East Farm

Owston Ln, Owston, Bentley DN5 0LP
☎ 01302 338300 & 726224 📠 01302 726224
e-mail frank@eastfarm.co.uk
Dir A19 from Doncaster towards Selby, left onto B1220, 1st right, farm 200yds on right

These former farm buildings have been converted into well-appointed, comfortable bedrooms, and a spacious luxurious lounge and sunroom. The owners provide a friendly atmosphere and excellent breakfasts. Three golf courses are close-by, the A1 is about five minutes, and Doncaster centre about fifteen minutes' drive.

Facilities 15 en suite (2 fmly) (14 GF) ⊗ in bedrooms ⊗ in dining room ⊗ in 1 lounge TVB tea/coffee ✖ Cen ht TVL No coaches **Prices** S fr £34; d fr £50✳ **Parking** 12

HOOTON PAGNELL
MAP 16 SE40

U ❦

Rock Farm ◇ (SE484081)
DN5 7BT ☎ 01977 642200 🖷 01977 642200 Ms Harrison
e-mail info@rockfarm.info
web www.rockfarm.info

At the time of going to press the rating for this establishment had not been confirmed. Please check the AA website www.theAA.com for up-to-date information.

Facilities 3 rms (1 en suite) (1 fmly) ⊘ TVB tea/coffee ✖ Cen ht TVL 200 acres Horses/arable/beef **Prices** S £22-£25; D £50-£52✳ **Parking** 15 **Notes** 🐾

ROTHERHAM
MAP 16 SK49

◆◆◆

Stonecroft Hotel
138 Main St, Bramley S66 2SF
☎ 01709 540922 🖷 01709 540922
e-mail stonecrofthotel@btconnect.com
web www.stonecrofthotel.com
Dir 3m E of Rotherham. Off A631 into Bramley village centre

The converted stone cottages in the centre of Bramley provide a good base for visiting Rotherham or Sheffield. Some bedrooms are around a landscaped courtyard with private parking, and there is a lounge with an honesty bar. Imaginative home-cooked meals are available.

Facilities 3 en suite 4 annexe en suite (1 fmly) (4 GF) ⊘ TVB tea/coffee ✖ Licensed Cen ht TVL No coaches Dinner Last d 8pm **Prices** S £49.50-£59; D £69-£75✳ **LB** **Parking** 7 **Notes** Closed 25-26 Dec

SHEFFIELD
MAP 16 SK38

Premier Collection

◆◆◆◆◆

Westbourne House Hotel
25 Westbourne Rd, Broomhill S10 2QQ
☎ 0114 266 0109 🖷 0114 266 7778
e-mail guests@westbournehousehotel.com
web www.westbournehousehotel.com
Dir A61 onto B6069 Glossop Rd, past university, after Hallamshire Hospital over lights, next left

A Victorian residence situated in beautiful gardens close to the university and hospitals. There is an attractive licensed restaurant where carefully prepared imaginative meals are served by arrangement. The modern bedrooms are individually furnished and decorated, and extremely well equipped. A comfortable lounge overlooks the terrace and garden.

Facilities 10 rms (9 en suite) (2 fmly) ⊘ TVB tea/coffee Direct dial from bedrooms ✖ Licensed Cen ht No coaches **Prices** S £50-£75; D £85-£95✳ **Conf** Max 15 Thtr 15 Class 15 Board 15 **Parking** 12

◆◆◆◆ 🏠

Quarry House
Rivelin Glen Quarry, Rivelin Valley Rd S6 5SE
☎ 0114 234 0382 🖷 0114 234 0382
e-mail penelopeslack@aol.com
web www.quarryhouse.org.uk
Dir 2.5m W of Sheffield. Off A6101 Rivelin Valley Rd at sharp bend, uphill to car park, signed

A warm welcome is given at this delightful former quarry master's house in the picturesque Rivelin valley. Well-appointed bedrooms include many thoughtful extras. The tasty evening meals and comprehensive breakfasts have a strong organic influence, and there is a cosy lounge and a smart dining room.

Facilities 3 rms (2 en suite) (1 pri facs) (1 fmly) (1 GF) ⊘ TVB tea/coffee Cen ht TVL No coaches Dinner Last d 10pm **Prices** S fr £40; d fr £80✳ **Parking** 8 **Notes** Closed 24 Dec-1 Jan 🐾

◆◆◆◆

Padley Farm B & B ◇
Dungworth Green S6 6HE
☎ 0114 285 1427 🖷 0114 285 1427
e-mail aandlmbestall@btinternet.com
web www.padleyfarm.co.uk
Dir M1 onto A61 to Loxley, B6077 to Bradfield & B6076 to Dungworth

The barn conversion offers high quality en suite rooms with spectacular views of open countryside. An allergy free environment and warm hospitality ensure a pleasant stay.

Facilities 7 en suite (4 fmly) (2 GF) ⊘ TVB tea/coffee ✖ Cen ht Snooker Table Tennis **Prices** S £27-£37; D £54-£60✳ **LB** **Conf** Max 20 Class 20 **Parking** 8 **Notes** 🐾

◆◆◆

Parklands ◇
113 Rustlings Rd S11 7AB ☎ 0114 267 0692
Dir A625 SW from city centre, over rdbt, 1st right

Situated near the Hunter's Bar area of the city and convenient for the university and hospitals, this Edwardian villa looks out over parkland at front and rear. Friendly hospitality is provided in a home from home atmosphere, and a choice of breakfasts is available.

Facilities 3 rms (2 en suite) (2 fmly) ⊘ TVB tea/coffee Cen ht TVL No coaches **Prices** S fr £25; d fr £50✳ **LB** **Notes** 🐾

The Cross Scythes

Baslow Rd, Totley S17 4AE ☎ 0114 236 0204
Dir On A621

At the time of going to press the rating for this establishment had not been confirmed. Please check the AA website www.theAA.com for up-to-date information.

Facilities 4 en suite (1 fmly) ⊗ in bedrooms ⊗ in dining room ⊗ in 1 lounge TVB tea/coffee Direct dial from bedrooms ✖ Licensed Cen ht No coaches Dinner Last d 9pm **Prices** S £59.95; D £59.95✷
Parking 50

YORKSHIRE, WEST

BINGLEY
MAP 19 SE13

Five Rise Locks

Beck Ln BD16 4DD ☎ 01274 565296 📠 01274 568828
e-mail info@five-rise-locks.co.uk
Dir Off Main St onto Park Rd, 0.25m left onto Beck Ln

A warm welcome and comfortable accommodation await you at this impressive Victorian building. Bedrooms are of a good size and feature homely extras. The restaurant offers imaginative dishes and the bright breakfast room overlooks the countryside.

Facilities 9 en suite (2 fmly) (2 GF) ⊗ in bedrooms ⊗ in dining room TVB tea/coffee Direct dial from bedrooms Licensed Cen ht No coaches Dinner Last d 9pm **Prices** S £50-£60; D £72✷ **Conf** Max 25 Thtr 25 Class 25 Board 20 Del from £75 ✷ **Parking** 20

GUISELEY
MAP 19 SE14

◆◆◆

Moor Valley Leisure Ltd

Moor Valley Park, Mill Ln, Hawksworth LS20 8PG
☎ 01943 876083 📠 01943 870335
Dir Off A6038 W through Hawksworth village, left onto Mill Ln

The thoughtfully equipped bedrooms are housed in a chalet opposite an attractive lounge bar complex, set within a landscaped holiday park in the countryside west of Guiseley. A continental breakfast is taken within your room.

Facilities 3 en suite (1 fmly) (3 GF) ⊗ TV available tea/coffee Licensed Cen ht TVL No coaches Pool Table **Prices** S £39.50; D £42.50
Parking 30

HALIFAX
MAP 19 SE02

◆◆◆◆ ⊛⊛ ⊜ ◼

Shibden Mill

Shibden Mill Fold, Shibden HX3 7UL
☎ 01422 365840 📠 01422 362971
e-mail shibdenmillinn@zoom.co.uk
Dir 3m NE of Halifax off A58

Nestling in a fold of Shibden Dale, this 17th-century inn features exposed beams and open fires. Guests can dine well in the two lounge-style bars, the restaurant, or outside in summer. The stylish bedrooms come in a variety of sizes, and all are thoughtfully equipped and have access to a free video library. Service is friendly and obliging.

Facilities 11 en suite ⊗ in 2 bedrooms ⊗ in dining room ⊗ in lounges STV TVB tea/coffee Direct dial from bedrooms Cen ht Free use of gym and leisure facilities nearby Dinner Last d 9.30pm **Prices** S £68-£110; D £85-£130✷ **Conf** Max 50 Thtr 50 Class 21 Board 24 **Parking** 100

◆◆◆◆

Pinfold

Dewsbury Rd, Upper Edge, Elland HX5 9JU
☎ 01422 372645 📠 01422 327616
e-mail steve@pinfoldguesthouse.co.uk
web www.pinfoldguesthouse.co.uk
Dir M62 junct 24, A643 towards Brighouse, 1m left at lights, 0.75m on left

This genuinely friendly guest house stands on an elevated position and has panoramic views from the front-facing rooms. Bedrooms are thoughtfully equipped and provide good all-round comforts. Healthy, carefully prepared breakfasts are served in the bright dining room and there is an inviting lounge.

Facilities 8 en suite (1 fmly) (1 GF) ⊗ STV TVB tea/coffee Cen ht TVL No coaches Library **Parking** 10 **Notes** ⊛

HAWORTH

MAP 19 SE03

★★★★ Guest House

Ashmount Guest House

Mytholmes Ln BD22 8EZ
☎ 01535 645726 ▤ 01535 645726
e-mail ashmounthaworth@aol.com
web www.ashmounthaworth.com

Built in 1870, this impressive Victorian House offers spectacular views and is a short distance from local attractions. With many period features retained, accommodation consists of large, thoughtfully equipped bedrooms, with hearty breakfasts served in the pleasant dining room.

Facilities 7 rms (6 en suite) (1 pri facs) (2 fmly) (2 GF) ⊗ TVB tea/coffee Cen ht No coaches ▥ **Prices** S £35-£40; D £50-£60✳ **Parking** 12

★★★ ⑧ Restaurant with Rooms

Weavers Restaurant with Rooms

13/17 West Ln BD22 8DU
☎ 01535 643822 ▤ 01535 644832
e-mail weaversinnhaworth@aol.com
Dir A629/B6142 towards Haworth/Stanbury & Colne. At top of village pass Brontë Weaving Shed on right. Left after 100yds to Parsonage car park

Centrally located on the cobbled main street, this family-owned restaurant provides well-equipped, stylish and comfortable accommodation. Each of the three rooms is en suite and have many thoughtful extras. The kitchen serves both modern and traditional dishes with flair and creativity.

Facilities 3 en suite TVB tea/coffee Direct dial from bedrooms Licensed Dinner Last d 9pm **Prices** S £55; D £90✳

HEBDEN BRIDGE

MAP 19 SD92

U

The Dusty Miller & Coiners Restaurant

Burnley Rd, Mytholmroyd HX7 5LH
☎ 01422 885959 & 07748 113181
e-mail philwebs51@hotmail.com
web www.dustymiller.co.uk

At the time of going to press the rating for this establishment had not been confirmed. Please check the AA website www.theAA.com for up-to-date information.

Facilities 5 en suite (1 fmly) ⊗ TVB tea/coffee Cen ht Dinner Last d 9pm **Prices** S £40-£60; D £60✳ **LB Parking** 25

HOLMFIRTH

MAP 16 SE10

◆◆◆◆ A

Uppergate Farm

Hepworth HD9 1TG ☎ 01484 681369 ▤ 01484 687343
e-mail info@uppergatefarm.co.uk
Dir 0.5m off A616

Facilities 2 en suite (1 fmly) ⊗ TVB tea/coffee Cen ht TVL ch fac No coaches ▥ Sauna **Prices** S £40; D £60✳ **LB Parking** 6

HUDDERSFIELD

MAP 16 SE11

◆◆◆◆ ⑧⑧ ⌑

Weavers Shed Restaurant with Rooms

Knowl Rd, Golcar HD7 4AN
☎ 01484 654284 ▤ 01484 650980
e-mail info@weaversshed.co.uk
web www.weaversshed.co.uk

Dir 3m W of Huddersfield. A62 onto B6111 to Milnsbridge & Scar Ln to Golcar, right onto Knowl Rd, signed Colne Valley Museum

This converted house has spacious bedrooms named after local textile mills; all are extremely well equipped. An inviting bar-lounge leads into the well-established restaurant where fresh produce, much from the establishment's own gardens, forms the basis of excellent meals.

Facilities 5 en suite (2 GF) ⊗ in bedrooms ⊗ in dining room TVB tea/coffee Direct dial from bedrooms Licensed Cen ht No coaches Dinner Last d 9pm **Prices** S fr £70; d fr £90✳ **LB Conf** Max 16 Board 16 **Parking** 20 **Notes** Closed Xmas/New Year

◆◆◆◆

The Huddersfield Central Lodge

11/15 Beast Market HD1 1QF
☎ 01484 515551 ▤ 01484 435269
e-mail enquiries@centrallodge.com
web www.centrallodge.com
Dir In town centre off Lord St. Signs for Beast Market from ring road

This friendly, family-run operation offers smart spacious bedrooms with modern en suites. Some rooms are in the main building, while new rooms with kitchenettes are situated across a courtyard. Public rooms include a bar and a conservatory, and there are arrangements for local restaurants to charge meals to guests' accounts. Secure complimentary parking.

Facilities 9 en suite 13 annexe en suite (2 fmly) ⊗ in dining room ⊗ in 1 lounge STV TVB tea/coffee Direct dial from bedrooms Licensed Cen ht TVL **Parking** 40

◆◆◆◆ ⬛

The Woodman Inn

Thunderbridge Ln HD8 0PX
☎ 01484 605778 ▤ 01484 604110
e-mail thewoodman@connectfree.co.uk
web www.woodman-inn.co.uk
For full entry see **Kirkburton**

KEIGHLEY MAP 19 SE04

◆◆◆

Bankfield ◇

1 Station Rd, Cross Hills BD20 7EH ☎ 01535 632971
Dir *Off A650/A629 Aire Valley Rd at Kildwick rdbt, onto weight-limit road towards Cross Hills, 0.5m on right*

A real home from home atmosphere prevails at this guest house, which is close to major roads and attractions. Bedrooms are comfortable and spacious, and all feature homely extras. Breakfast is served family-style in the smart dining room. There is a cosy sitting room and private parking.

Facilities 3 rms (2 en suite) (1 fmly) ⊗ in bedrooms ⊗ in dining room TVB tea/coffee Cen ht TVL ch fac No coaches **Prices** S £30-£35; D £50-£55 **Parking** 5 **Notes** ⊠

KIRKBURTON MAP 16 SE11

◆◆◆◆ ◐

The Woodman Inn

Thunderbridge Ln HD8 0PX
☎ 01484 605778 ◫ 01484 604110
e-mail thewoodman@connectfree.co.uk
web www.woodman-inn.co.uk
Dir *1m SW of Kirkburton. Off A629 in Thunder Bridge*

The Woodman offers traditional innkeeping and is extremely popular with locals. The air-conditioned restaurant holds an extensive range of wines, while the popular bar offers a wide selection of ales and lagers. Bedrooms are comfortable and comprehensively furnished, making this an ideal base for walking, visiting the National Mining Museum, or simply escaping to the country.

Facilities 12 en suite (3 GF) ⊗ in bedrooms ⊗ in dining room TVB tea/coffee Direct dial from bedrooms ✈ Cen ht Pool Table Dinner Last d 9pm **Conf** Max 60 Thtr 50 Class 60 Board 30 **Parking** 50

LEEDS MAP 19 SE33

◆◆◆◆

Ash Mount Hotel

22 Wetherby Rd, Oakwood LS8 2QD
☎ 0113 265 8164 & 265 4263 ◫ 0113 265 8164
e-mail bookings@ashmounthotel.co.uk
web www.ashmounthotel.co.uk
Dir *3m NE of city centre. Off A58 at McDonalds rdbt onto Oakwood Ln, 0.5m right onto Wetherby Rd, premises on left*

This delightful Victorian house is close to Roundhay Park and the Canal Gardens, and within easy access of Leeds city centre and the motorway. Bedrooms are carefully decorated and thoughtfully equipped. Public areas include a beautifully appointed lounge with a well-stocked bar, and a stylish dining room that looks out to the landscaped leafy garden.

Facilities 12 rms (9 en suite) (2 fmly) (1 GF) ⊗ TVB tea/coffee Direct dial from bedrooms ✈ Licensed Cen ht TVL No coaches **Prices** S £33-£43; D £64-£67✱ **Parking** 10 **Notes** Closed 25 Dec-3 Jan

◆◆◆

Trafford House & Budapest Hotel ◇

18 Cardigan Rd, Headingley LS6 3AG
☎ 0113 275 2034 & 275 6637 ◫ 0113 274 2422
e-mail traffordhouse@hotmail.com
Dir *A65 from city centre for airport/Ickley, 1m right for Headingley, 1m on left*

A haven for cricket enthusiasts, this large property next to Headingley cricket ground has super views of the action from many of the bedrooms and a purpose-built gallery. The three adjacent Victorian villas offer a variety of bedrooms, and breakfast is served at individual tables in the bright dining room. Dinner is available by arrangement.

Facilities 8 rms (4 en suite) 19 annexe rms (16 en suite) (4 fmly) (6 GF) ⊗ in 10 bedrooms ⊗ in dining room TVB tea/coffee Direct dial from bedrooms ✈ Licensed Cen ht TVL **Prices** S £30-£45; D £46-£62✱ **Parking** 30 **Notes** Closed 24-26 Dec

◆◆◆ 🅰

The Boundary Hotel Express

Cardigan Rd, Headingley LS6 3AG
☎ 0113 275 7700 ◫ 0113 275 7700
e-mail info@boundaryhotel.co.uk
web www.boundaryhotel.co.uk
Dir *Follow signs for Headlingley Stadium*

Facilities 18 rms (7 en suite) (2 fmly) ⊗ in bedrooms ⊗ in dining room STV TVB tea/coffee Licensed Cen ht TVL Dinner Last d 8pm **Parking** 11

MARSDEN MAP 16 SE01

◆◆◆◆ ◉ ⌣

Olive Branch

Manchester Rd HD7 6LU ☎ 01484 844487
e-mail mail@olivebranch.uk.com
web www.olivebranch.uk.com
Dir *On A62 between Slaithwaite & Marsden. 6m SW of Huddersfield.*

A roadside inn now developed into a popular restaurant with three comfortable bedrooms. The menu features the best of seasonal produce cooked with flair and enthusiasm. The surrounding countryside has many historic attractions and pleasant walking.

Facilities 3 en suite ⊗ TVB tea/coffee Direct dial from bedrooms ✈ Licensed Cen ht No coaches **Prices** S £55; D £70; (room only) **Parking** 25 **Notes** Closed 2-17 Jan

OSSETT
MAP 16 SE22

◆◆◆◆ ▣

Mews Hotel
Dale St WF5 9HN
☎ 01924 273982 & 07973 137547 📄 01924 279389
e-mail enquiries@mews-hotel.co.uk
Dir M1 junct 40, A638 towards Dewsbury, onto B6129 Ossett & Dale St

This friendly family guest house provides comfortable public rooms and well-furnished bedrooms. Hand-pulled ales and a good variety of meals are served in the bar, which is popular with the locals.

Facilities 14 en suite (1 fmly) (5 GF) ⊗ in bedrooms ⊗ in dining room TVB tea/coffee Direct dial from bedrooms Cen ht Dinner Last d 9.30pm **Prices** S £44.50-£49.50; D £62.50-£68✱ **Conf** Max 30 Thtr 30 Class 25 Board 16 **Parking** 40

◆◆◆

Heath House
Chancery Rd WF5 9RZ ☎ 01924 260654 📄 01924 263131
e-mail jo.holland@amserve.net
web www.heath-house.co.uk
Dir M1 junct 40, A638 towards Dewsbury, at end dual carriageway exit rdbt 2nd left, house 20yds on right

The spacious Victorian family home stands in 4 acres of tranquil gardens 1.5m from the M1. It has elegant en suite bedrooms, and the courteous and friendly owners provide healthy, freshly cooked breakfasts.

Facilities 2 en suite 2 annexe en suite (1 fmly) (2 GF) ⊗ TVB tea/coffee Cen ht No coaches Fishing small farm, sheep, hens, rabbits & ferrets **Parking** 16

PONTEFRACT
MAP 16 SE42

◆◆◆◆

Wentvale
Great North Rd, Knottingley WF11 8PF ☎ 01977 676714
e-mail wentvale1@btconnect.com
Dir 1.5m NE of Pontefract. Off A1 S for A645, sharp right

Original features at this welcoming Victorian house include the stained-glass front door and a panelled hall. Double-glazing in the attractive bedrooms provides effective sound insulation. There is a comfortable lounge, a separate dining room and also a lounge bar.

Facilities 8 en suite 3 annexe en suite (4 GF) ⊗ TVB tea/coffee ✖ Cen ht TVL No children 12yrs Dinner Last d 7.30pm **Prices** S £37; D £55 **Parking** 15 **Notes** Closed Xmas & New Year

◆◆◆

Rolands Croft Guest House ◇
Featherstone WF7 6ED ☎ 01977 790802 & 07776 336953
e-mail audl15@dsl.pipex.com
web www.rolandscroftguesthouse.co.uk
Dir Off M62 junct 32 towards Pontefract & B6134 to Featherstone x-rds

Four ground floor en-suite bedrooms formed within a barn conversion that opens directly onto a garden and parking area. Breakfast is served in the main house across the garden, and this makes an ideal touring location for both the immediate attractions and the surrounding area.

Facilities 4 en suite (1 fmly) (4 GF) ⊗ TVB tea/coffee Cen ht TVL Golf **Prices** S fr £27; d fr £39 **Parking** 8

TODMORDEN
MAP 18 SD92

◆◆◆ ▣

Staff of Life
550 Burnley Rd, Knotts Grove OL14 8JF ☎ 01706 812929
e-mail staffoflife@btconnect.com
Dir 1.5m NW of Todmorden on A646

Situated out of town on the Burnley road, this stone-built inn offers value-for-money accommodation in a friendly ambience. The comfortable bedrooms are pleasingly decorated and the bar, serving real ales, is full of character. Comprehensive breakfasts are served in a cosy first floor panelled dining room.

Facilities 3 en suite TVB tea/coffee Cen ht No coaches Dinner Last d 9.00pm **Prices** S £40; D £45✱ **Parking** 26 **Notes** Closed 25, 26, 31 Dec, 1 Jan

WAKEFIELD
MAP 16 SE32

◆◆◆◆ ▣

Midgley Lodge Motel
Barr Ln, Midgley WF4 4JJ
☎ 01924 830069 📄 01924 830087
e-mail midgleylodgemotel@tiscali.co.uk
Dir 6m SW of Wakefield. M1 junct 38, A637 Huddersfield road to Midgeley

Facilities 25 en suite (10 fmly) (13 GF) ⊗ in 12 bedrooms ⊗ in lounges STV TVB tea/coffee Direct dial from bedrooms ✖ Licensed Cen ht TVL Golf 9 **Prices** S £39.95; D £48; (room only) **Parking** 55 **Notes** Closed 25 Dec-1 Jan

◆◆◆

Stanley View Guest House ◇
226-230 Stanley Rd WF1 4AE
☎ 01924 376803 📄 01924 369123
e-mail enquiries@stanleyviewguesthouse.co.uk
Dir M62 junct 30, on A642 N of city centre

Part of an attractive terrace, this well-established guest house is just 0.5m from the city centre and has private parking at the rear. The well-equipped bedrooms are brightly decorated, and there is a licensed bar and comfortable lounge. Hearty home-cooked meals are served in the attractive dining room.

Facilities 17 rms (12 en suite) (6 fmly) ⊗ in bedrooms ⊗ in dining room STV TVB tea/coffee Direct dial from bedrooms Licensed Cen ht TVL Dinner Last d 8pm **Prices** S £25-£45; D £45✱ **Parking** 10

England

WETHERBY
MAP 16 SE44

◆◆

Prospect House ◇
8 Caxton St LS22 6RU ☎ 01937 582428
Dir In town centre off A661 West Gate

A friendly welcome awaits at this centrally located guest house. Clean and comfortable bedrooms are provided and a traditional breakfast served. Mrs Watkin's hand worked tapestries are quite a talking point in the dining room.

Facilities 6 rms (4 en suite) tea/coffee Cen ht TVL No coaches
Prices S £27-£28; D £54-£56✳ **Parking** 6 **Notes** 🐾

CHANNEL ISLANDS
GUERNSEY

FOREST
MAP 24

★★★★ Guest House

Maison Bel Air Guest House
La Chene GY8 0AL ☎ 01481 238503 ▤ 01481 239403

The Maison Bel Air stands amid peaceful landscaped gardens just a short drive from the airport and well placed for touring the island. Its attractive bedrooms are thoughtfully equipped, and breakfast is served at individual tables in the smart dining room. There is also a cosy lounge.

Facilities 6 en suite (1 fmly) ⊗ TVB tea/coffee ✗ Cen ht No children 3yrs **Parking** 8

JERSEY

LA GREVE DE LECQ
MAP 24

◆◆◆

Hotel Des Pierres ◇
JE3 2DT ☎ 01534 481858 ▤ 01534 485273
e-mail despierres@jerseyhols.com
Dir E from airport, left at rdbt, along A12 St Ouen's Rd for 0.25m, at fork right to Mont de La Greve Lecq

A fantastic location in the north of the island, just a stroll from the picturesque Greve de Lecq Bay, where the friendly proprietors have been welcoming guests for over 25 years. Bedrooms and bathrooms are neatly furnished, some enjoying views over the bay. A regularly changing menu provides many options both at dinner and breakfast.

Facilities 16 en suite (4 fmly) (5 GF) ⊗ TVB tea/coffee ✗ Licensed Cen ht Cycling Dinner Last d 7pm **Prices** S £26.50-£39; D £53-£64✳ LB **Parking** 13 **Notes** Closed 15 Nov-15 Jan

GROUVILLE
MAP 24

◆◆◆◆

Lavender Villa Hotel ◇
La Rue A Don JE3 9DX ☎ 01534 854937 ▤ 01534 856147
e-mail lavendervilla@jerseymail.co.uk
web www.lavendervilla.co.uk
Dir On right side of road to Gorey village past Esso station

Set in a peaceful location overlooking the Royal Jersey golf course, this comfortable establishment offers a warm welcome and spacious bedrooms, with some on the ground floor. Freshly cooked dinners are available in the beamed dining room, and there is also a cosy bar and a lounge.

Facilities 21 en suite (2 fmly) (6 GF) ⊗ in bedrooms ⊗ in dining room ⊗ in lounges TVB tea/coffee ✗ Licensed Cen ht TVL No coaches ⚞ Table tennis Trampoline Dinner Last d 6.15pm **Prices** S £22-£36; D £44-£72✳ LB **Parking** 21 **Notes** Closed Dec-Feb rs Mar-Nov

ST AUBIN
MAP 24

◆◆◆◆

The Panorama
La Rue du Crocquet JE3 8BZ
☎ 01534 742429 ▤ 01534 745940
e-mail info@panoramajersey.com
web www.panoramajersey.com
Dir In village centre

Having spectacular views across St Aubin's Bay, the Panorama is a long-established favourite with visitors. The welcome is genuine and many of the well-equipped bedrooms have wonderful views. Public areas also look seaward and have attractive antique fireplaces. Breakfast is excellent.

Facilities 14 en suite (3 GF) ⊗ STV TVB tea/coffee ✗ Cen ht No children No coaches **Prices** S £36-£61; D £72-£122 **Notes** Closed mid Oct-mid Apr

England

ST AUBIN continued

◆◆◆

Peterborough House

La Rue Du Croquet JE3 8BZ
☎ 01534 741568 ▤ 01534 746787
e-mail fernando@localdial.com

Dir From St Helier right signed Red Houses, 400yds left before St Aubin, continue until cobbles, house on left

Situated on the old St Aubin high street, this well-presented guest house dates from 1690. The bedrooms are comfortably appointed and the sea-facing rooms are always in high demand. One of the two lounge areas has a bar, or you enjoy the view with a drink on the outdoor terrace. Breakfast is a choice of traditonal and continental options.

Facilities 14 rms (12 en suite) (1 fmly) (2 GF) ⊗ in bedrooms ⊗ in dining room ⊗ in 1 lounge TVB tea/coffee 🎝 Licensed Cen ht TVL No children 12yrs No coaches **Prices** S £27-£37.75; D £44-£70.50✳ LB **Notes** Closed Nov-Feb

ST HELIER   MAP 24

★★★★ Guest Accommodation

Bay View Guest House

12 Havre des Pas JE2 4UQ
☎ 01534 720950 & 07797 720100 ▤ 01532 720950
e-mail bayview.guesthouse@jerseymail.co.uk

Dir Through tunnel, right at rdbt, down Green St and turn left, B&B 100yds on left.

Located across the road from the Havre des Pas Lido and beach and a ten-minute walk to the centre of St Helier. Bedrooms are well equipped and extra facilities include a bar and a television lounge with free wireless Internet access. There is a small garden terrace to the front of the establishment.

Facilities 13 rms (11 pri facs) (3 fmly) ⊗ in bedrooms ⊗ in dining room TVB tea/coffee 🎝 Licensed Cen ht TVL

◆◆◆◆

Millbrook House Hotel

Rue De Trachy, Millbrook JE2 3JN
☎ 01534 733036 ▤ 01534 724317
e-mail millbrook.house@jerseymail.co.uk
web www.millbrookhousehotel.com

Dir 1.5m W of town off A1

The pleasant Georgian mansion, set in 10 acres of well-tended grounds, is just a short drive from St Helier. Most of the spacious bedrooms have delightful views of the gardens, and some have more distant sea views. Dinner is an interesting range of home-cooked dishes accompanied by an impressive choice of wines.

Facilities 27 en suite (2 fmly) (6 GF) ⊗ in bedrooms ⊗ in dining room ⊗ in 1 lounge TVB tea/coffee Direct dial from bedrooms 🎝 Licensed Lift TVL No coaches Golf 5 Dinner Last d 7pm **Prices** S £39-£43; D £78-£86✳ LB **Parking** 20 **Notes** Closed Oct-early May

◆◆◆◆

Sarum Hotel

19-21 New St John's Rd JE2 3LD
☎ 01534 758163 ▤ 01534 731340
e-mail sarum@jerseyweb.demon.co.uk
web www.jersey.co.uk/hotels/sarum

Dir NW edge of St Helier, 0.5m from town centre & close to seafront

The Sarum offers self-catering bedrooms and a few suites just 400yds from the beach. The friendly staff provide a warm welcome, and there is a spacious recreational lounge with a pool table, plasma screen television and Internet access. A garden and outdoor pool are also available.

Facilities 47 en suite 5 annexe en suite (6 fmly) (3 GF) ⊗ in dining room ⊗ in lounges STV TVB tea/coffee Direct dial from bedrooms 🎝 Licensed Lift Cen ht TVL ⚲ Pool Table **Prices** S £30-£47; D £40-£73; (room only) ✳ LB **Parking** 10

England

SARK

SARK MAP 24

◆◆◆◆ ◎ 🔆 ⌷

Hotel Petit Champ

GY9 0SF ☎ 01481 832046 🗎 01481 832469
e-mail info@hotelpetitchamp.co.uk
web www.hotelpetitchamp.co.uk
Dir Signs from the Methodist Chapel

Guests can expect a very warm welcome from the caring hosts at this delightful property. Most of the bedrooms, the gardens and lounges have wonderful views of the sea and neighbouring islands. A five-course dinner is included in the half-board terms, and a well-stocked wine cellar and bar add to the pleasure.

Facilities 10 en suite (2 fmly) ⊘ in dining room ⊘ in 1 lounge ✗
Licensed Cen ht TVL No children 7yrs ↖ ⬡ ⬡ Dinner Last d 8.30pm
Prices S £59.75-£69.25; D £115.50-£134.50; (incl. dinner) ✳ LB
Notes Closed Nov-Etr

MAN, ISLE OF

DOUGLAS MAP 24 SC37

◆◆◆◆ ⌷

Dreem Ard

Ballanard Rd IM2 5PR ☎ 01624 621491 🗎 01624 621491
Dir From St Ninians Church along Ballanard Rd for 1m, over Johnny Watterson Ln x-rds, past farm on left, Dreem Ard on left

Dreem Ard is a relaxing sanctuary, with superb views over the glens just to the north of Douglas. Bedrooms are spacious and well equipped, and the caring hosts are genuinely hospitable and attentive. Breakfast and dinner are served around a large table, where good food and good company go hand-in-hand.

Facilities 3 en suite (1 fmly) (2 GF) ⊘ STV TVB tea/coffee ✗ Cen ht
No children 8yrs No coaches Large garden & sun terrace Dinner Last d breakfast **Prices** D £50-£65 LB **Parking** 6 **Notes** ⊜

◆◆◆◆

Rosslyn Guest House ◇

3 Empire Ter, Central Prom IM2 4LE
☎ 01624 676056 🗎 01624 674122
e-mail rosslynhotel@manx.net
web www.rosslynhotelisleofman.co.uk
Dir From ferry along Promenade 1m, left onto Mona Dr & right

This friendly guest house is a super base for exploring the island. The bedrooms are neatly decorated and thoughtfully equipped, and you can enjoy an extra cup of morning coffee on the sofas in the attractive breakfast room. Children are welcome with prior notice.

Facilities 12 rms (10 en suite) (1 pri facs) (3 fmly) ⊘ in bedrooms ⊘ in dining room ⊘ in 1 lounge TVB tea/coffee Direct dial from bedrooms ✗ Licensed Cen ht TVL **Prices** S £27-£42; D £50-£70✳ LB

◆◆◆ 🅰

All Seasons ◇

11 Clifton Ter, Broadway IM2 3HX
☎ 0871 855 0603 🗎 0871 855 0603
e-mail hansonsales@pilogene.co.uk
Dir Off Central Promenade at Villa Marina, premises in 1st row of hotels on left

Facilities 6 rms (4 en suite) (2 pri facs) (6 fmly) ⊘ TVB tea/coffee ✗
Licensed Cen ht TVL No children 12yrs No coaches ↺ Dinner Last d 5pm **Prices** S £27-£49; D £49-£98✳ LB

PORT ST MARY MAP 24 SC26

Premier Collection

◆◆◆◆◆ 🔆

Aaron House

The Promenade IM9 5DE ☎ 01624 835702
web www.aaronhouse.co.uk
Dir Signs for South & Port St Mary, left at Post Office, house in centre of Promenade overlooking harbour

Aaron House is truly individual. From the parlour down to the detail of the cast-iron baths, the house has been restored to its Victorian origins. The family work hard to offer the best quality, whether its providing luxury and comfort in the bedrooms, or even to offering home-made cakes on arrival.

Facilities 4 rms (2 en suite) (2 pri facs) ⊘ tea/coffee ✗ Cen ht TVL
No children 16yrs No coaches **Prices** D £70-£118✳ **Notes** Closed 21 Dec-3 Jan ⊜

RAMSEY MAP 24 SC49

Premier Collection

◆◆◆◆◆ 🔆

River House

IM8 3DA ☎ 01624 816412 🗎 01624 816412

A beautiful Georgian house, standing in extensive mature gardens beside the River Sulby. The accommodation is comfortable and spacious with luxurious facilities and the bedrooms overlook the river. The breakfast room also overlooks the river, and hospitality is spontaneous and friendly.

Facilities 3 en suite (1 GF) ⊘ in dining room STV TVB tea/coffee ✗
Cen ht No coaches **Prices** D £75-£95✳ **Parking** 12 **Notes** Closed Feb/Mar ⊜

Scotland

University of St Andrews, Fife

ABERDEEN CITY

ABERDEEN   MAP 23 NJ90

he Jays Guest House

22 King St AB24 3BR ☎ 01224 638295 🖹 01224 638360
mail alice@jaysguesthouse.co.uk
eb www.jaysguesthouse.co.uk
ir A90 from S onto Main St & Union St & A92 to King St N

uests are warmly welcomed to this attractive granite house on the
orth side of the city. Maintained in first-class order throughout, it
fers attractive bedrooms, smartly furnished to appeal to business
ests and tourists. Freshly prepared breakfasts are enjoyed in the
refully appointed dining room.

acilities 10 rms (8 en suite) (2 pri facs) (1 GF) ⊗ STV TVB tea/coffee
ℋ Cen ht No children 12yrs No coaches Prices S £40-£50; D £70-£90
arking 9 Notes Closed mid Dec-mid Jan

trathisla Guest House ◇

08 Gt Western Rd AB10 6NR ☎ 01224 321026
mail elza@strathisla-guesthouse.co.uk
r A90 over Dee Bridge, over rdbt, on dual-carriageway, over 2nd
bt to lights, right onto Great Western Rd

comfortable granite-built terrace house on the west side of the city,
rathisla has attractive bedrooms, all individual and inviting, with
lded touches such as alarm clocks and a complimentary slice of cake
th the beverage facilities. Vegetarian options are available at
eakfast.

cilities 5 en suite (1 fmly) ⊗ TVB tea/coffee Cen ht No coaches
rices S £26-£34; D £42-£50✳ Parking 1

◆◆

rkaig Guest House ◇

3 Powis Ter AB25 3PP ☎ 01224 638872 🖹 01224 622189
mail info@arkaig.co.uk
r On A96 at junct with Bedford Rd

friendly welcome and relaxed atmosphere is assured at this well-
esented guest house, situated on the north side of the city close to
e university and city centre. Bedrooms vary in size, are attractively
ecorated and are all thoughtfully equipped to appeal to business and
isure guests. There is a cosy sun lounge with magazines, and an
tractive breakfast room where delicious freshly cooked breakfasts are
erved. Parking is also available.

cilities 8 rms (6 en suite) (1 fmly) (5 GF) ⊗ TVB tea/coffee Direct
al from bedrooms Cen ht TVL Prices S £26-£36; d fr £55✳
arking 10

◆◆◆

Bimini Guest House

69 Constitution St AB24 5ET
☎ 01224 646912 🖹 01224 647006
e-mail info@bimini.co.uk
Dir In town centre, off A96 East N St onto Park St, 1st right

This friendly, smartly presented guest house is located just to the
north of the city centre and is convenient for the beach and
attractions. Bedrooms vary in size, are thoughtfully equipped and have
modern en suites. There is a stylish basement dining room and
parking is available behind the building.

Facilities 8 en suite ⊗ TVB tea/coffee ℋ Cen ht TVL No coaches
Prices S £37-£45; D £55-£60 Parking 7

◆◆◆

Kildonan Guest House ◇

410 Great Western Rd AB10 6NR ☎ 01224 316115
e-mail jim@kildonan-guesthouse.com
Dir On A93, 100 metres from junct of A90

This well-presented Victorian end of terrace house is in a residential
area close to the city centre. The brightly decorated bedrooms, some
suitable for families, come in various sizes. Many original features
have been retained and the dining room has an ornate ceiling.

Facilities 8 rms (7 en suite) (2 fmly) (3 GF) ⊗ TVB tea/coffee ℋ
Cen ht No coaches Prices S £27; D £46-£48✳ Parking 3

PETERCULTER   MAP 23 NJ80

Furain Guest House

92 North Deeside Rd AB14 0QN
☎ 01224 732189 🖹 01224 739070
e-mail furain@btinternet.com
Dir 7m W of city centre on A93

Facilities 8 en suite (2 fmly) (3 GF) ⊗ TVB tea/coffee Licensed Cen ht
No coaches Dinner Last d 8.15pm Prices S £36-£40; D £47-£58✳
Parking 7 Notes ★★★ Closed Xmas & New Year

Scotland

Scotland

ABERDEENSHIRE

BRAEMAR

MAP 23 NO19

◆◆◆◆

Callater Lodge Guest House ◇

9 Glenshee Rd AB35 5YQ
☎ 013397 41275 📠 013397 41345
e-mail hampsons@hotel-braemar.co.uk
web www.hotel-braemar.co.uk
Dir Next to A93, 300yds S of Braemar centre

Callater Lodge is an impressive Victorian villa set in well-tended grounds. There is a comfortable lounge, a cosy library incorporating a small licensed bar and a bright dining room where breakfast is served. A snack menu is also available. The attractive, individually styled bedrooms vary in size and have homely extras.

Facilities 6 en suite (2 fmly) ⊗ TVB tea/coffee ✖ Licensed Cen ht TVL No coaches **Prices** S £30-£32; D £56-£60✳ **Parking** 6 **Notes** Closed Xmas & New Year

OLDMELDRUM

MAP 23 NJ82

🅰

Cromlet Hill Guest House ◇

South Rd AB51 0AB ☎ 01651 872315 📠 01651 872164
e-mail johnpage@cromlethill.co.uk
Dir From Aberdeen turn off A947 onto A920 signed Inverurie/town centre, Cromlet Hill is 200yds on the right. From Inverurie through town square on Aberdeen Rd, Cromlet Hill is 200yds on left

Facilities 3 en suite (1 fmly) ⊗ TVB tea/coffee ✖ Cen ht TVL No coaches **Prices** S £30-£42.50; D £48-£60✳ **Parking** 4 **Notes** ★★★★ 🍴

STONEHAVEN

MAP 23 NO88

◆◆◆◆

Woodside Of Glasslaw

AB39 3XQ ☎ 01569 763799 📠 01569 763799
e-mail aileenpaton@hotmail.com
Dir A90 N, 1st sign for Stonehaven, at end bend turn right, next left

Set amid farmland and gardens, yet close to major roads, this guest house is popular for business and leisure. The comfortable bedrooms are spacious and attractively decorated, and hearty breakfasts are served at individual tables lounge-dining room.

Facilities 6 en suite (1 fmly) (4 GF) ⊗ TVB tea/coffee Cen ht TVL No coaches **Prices** S fr £28; D fr £48✳ **Parking** 5 **Notes** 🍴

ANGUS

BRIDGEND OF LINTRATHEN

MAP 23 NO25

★★★★ 🏵🏵 **Restaurant with Rooms**

Lochside Lodge & Roundhouse Restaurant

DD8 5JJ ☎ 01575 560340 📠 01575 560251
e-mail enquiries@lochsidelodge.com
Dir B951 from Kirriemuir towards Glenisla for 7m & take left turn to Lintrathen. Follow road over top of loch & into village. Located on left

This converted farmstead enjoys a rural location in the heart of Angus. The comfortable bedrooms that offer private facilities are in a former hayloft & the original windows have been retained. Accomplished modern cuisine is served in the Roundhouse Restaurant. A spacious bar featuring agricultural implements & church pews, has a wide range of drinks including local beers.

Facilities 6 en suite (1 fmly) (2 GF) FTV TVB tea/coffee Licensed Dinner Last d 8.30pm **Prices** S £77-£115; D £135-£175; (incl. dinner) ✳ **LB** **Conf** Class 20 Board 25 **Parking** 40 **Notes** Closed 25-26 Dec & 1-24 Jan rs Sun & Mon

CARNOUSTIE

MAP 21 NO53

◆◆◆◆

Park House

12 Park Av DD7 7JA ☎ 01241 852101 📠 01241 852101
e-mail parkhouse@bbcarnoustie.fsnet.co.uk
web www.bbcarnoustie.fsnet.co.uk
Dir In town centre off A930 High St

A warm welcome is assured at this delightful Victorian villa, set in well-tended gardens just short walk from the town centre and golf course. Most bedrooms, which vary in size, overlook the garden, as do the dining room and the comfortable lounge.

Facilities 3 en suite ⊗ TVB tea/coffee ✖ Cen ht TVL No coaches BBQ area, Table Tennis, Badminton **Parking** 5 **Notes** Closed Xmas & New Year 🍴

ORFAR   MAP 23 NO45

Finavon Hotel

Finavon DD8 3QE ☎ 01307 850234 🖩 01307 850435
e-mail mail@finavonhotel.co.uk
Dir 6m N of Forfar on junct A90 & B957

Facilities 8 en suite (3 fmly) ⊗ TVB tea/coffee ✗ Licensed Cen ht
Dinner Last d 9pm **Conf** Max 150 Thtr 150 Class 100 Board 100
Parking 40 **Notes** ★★★ Closed 26 Dec & 1 Jan Civ Wed 120

INVERKEILOR   MAP 23 NO64

Gordon's

Main St DD11 5RN ☎ 01241 830364 🖩 01241 830364
e-mail gordonsrest@aol.com
Dir Off A92, follow signs for Inverkeilor

Gordon's is a family-run restaurant with rooms that has earned two
AA Rosettes for dinner, though the excellent breakfast is also
memorable. A huge fire dominates the restaurant on cooler evenings.
The attractive bedrooms are thoughtfully equipped and two are
furnished in pine.

Facilities 3 rms (2 en suite) (1 pri facs) ⊗ TVB ✗ Licensed Cen ht
No children 12yrs No coaches Dinner Last d 9pm **Prices** S fr £60; d fr
£90✱ **Parking** 6 **Notes** Closed Jan

MONTROSE   MAP 23 NO75

◆◆◆

Oaklands Guest House ◇

10 Rossie Island Rd DD10 9NN
☎ 01674 672018 🖩 01674 672018
e-mail oaklands1@btopenworld.com
Dir On A92 at S end of town

A genuine welcome and attentive service is assured at this smart
detached house, situated at the south side of the town. Comfortable
bedrooms come in a variety of sizes and are well equipped. There is a
lounge on the ground floor next to the attractive dining room, where
hearty breakfasts are served. Motorcycle guided tours can be arranged
with tourists travelling with their own motorbikes.

Facilities 7 en suite (1 fmly) (1 GF) ⊗ TVB tea/coffee Cen ht TVL
No coaches **Prices** S £27-£32; D £44-£49✱ **Parking** 8

ARGYLL & BUTE

APPIN   MAP 20 NM94

U

Bealach Country House

Duror PA38 4BW ☎ 01631 740298
e-mail info@bealach-house.co.uk
Dir Off A828, 2m S of Duror. 1.5m into the Glen

At the time of going to press the rating for this establishment had not
been confirmed. Please check the AA website www.theAA.com for up-
to-date information.

Facilities 3 en suite ⊗ tea/coffee ✗ Cen ht TVL No children 14yrs
Dinner Last d 6pm **Prices** S £67.50-£72.50; D £105-£115; (incl. dinner) ✱
Parking 6 **Notes** Closed 19 Dec-Jan

BARCALDINE   MAP 20 NM94

U

Barcaldine House

PA37 1SG ☎ 01631 720219
e-mail enquiries@barcaldinehouse.co.uk
web www.barcaldinehouse.co.uk
Dir Turn off A828 Oban to Fort William Rd as it passes through
village of Barcaldine

At the time of going to press the rating for this establishment had not
been confirmed. Please check the AA website www.theAA.com for up-
to-date information.

Facilities 8 en suite (1 fmly) ⊗ TVB tea/coffee ✗ Licensed Cen ht
No coaches Snooker **Prices** S £70-£85; D £96-£115✱ **Conf** Max 24
Thtr 24 Board 24 **Parking** 12 **Notes** Civ Wed 36

BENDERLOCH   MAP 20 NM93

A

Hawthorn

PA37 1QS ☎ 01631 720452
e-mail junecurrie@hawthorncottages.com
web www.hawthorncottages.co.uk
Dir A85 onto A828 Fort William road for 3m past church, 1st left,
house 3rd on right

Facilities 3 en suite (2 fmly) (3 GF) ⊗ STV TVB tea/coffee ✗ Cen ht
TVL No children 3yrs No coaches Fishing Dinner Last d 6pm
Prices S £40-£45; D £50-£60✱ **LB Parking** 4 **Notes** ★★★★

Scotland

Scotland

CARDROSS
MAP 20 NS37

Premier Collection

◆◆◆◆◆

Kirkton House

Darleith Rd G82 5EZ ☎ 01389 841951 📠 01389 841868
e-mail aa@kirktonhouse.co.uk
web www.kirktonhouse.co.uk
Dir 0.5m N of village. Turn N off A814 onto Darleith Rd at W end of village. Kirkton House 0.5m on right

Dating from the 18th century, this converted farmstead around an attractive courtyard has stunning views over the Clyde estuary from its elevated location. The individually styled bedrooms are well equipped and generally spacious, with two on the ground floor. Stone walls and large fireplaces feature in public areas, and home-cooked meals using fresh produce are served in the delightful dining room.

Facilities 6 en suite (4 fmly) (2 GF) ⊘ TVB tea/coffee Direct dial from bedrooms Cen ht TVL No coaches Riding **Prices** S £38-£41; D £54-£60 **LB Parking** 12 **Notes** Closed Dec-Jan

CONNEL
MAP 20 NM93

◆◆◆◆ 🏠

Ards House

PA37 1PT ☎ 01631 710255 📠 01631 710857
e-mail info@ardshouse.com
web www.ardshouse.com
Dir On A85, 4m N of Oban

This delightful Victorian villa on the approaches to Loch Etive has stunning views over the Firth of Lorne and the Morven Hills beyond. The stylish bedrooms come with added touches such as home-made shortbread and mineral water. There is an inviting drawing room complete with piano, games and books, plus a fire on cooler evenings. The attractive dining room is the setting for delicious breakfasts.

Facilities 4 en suite ⊘ TVB tea/coffee ✖ Cen ht TVL No children 10yrs No coaches **Prices** S £45-£65; D £70-£90✳ **LB Parking** 12 **Notes** Closed Dec-Jan

◆◆◆◆

Ronebhal Guest House ◇

PA37 1PJ ☎ 01631 710310 📠 01631 710310
e-mail ronebhal@btinternet.com
Dir A85 W from village centre, 4th house after turning for Fort William

The Strachan family extends a friendly welcome to their lovely detached home, which has stunning views of Loch Etive. The bedrooms are well equipped and comfortably furnished in modern styles. There is a sitting room, and an attractive dining room where hearty traditional breakfasts are served at individual tables.

Facilities 5 rms (4 en suite) (1 fmly) (1 GF) ⊘ TVB tea/coffee ✖ Cen ht TVL No children 7yrs No coaches **Prices** S £25-£28; D £50-£70✳ **LB Parking** 6 **Notes** Closed Nov-Feb

DUNOON
MAP 20 NS17

◆◆◆◆ 🏠 🍵

Dhailling Lodge

155 Alexandra Pde PA23 8AW ☎ 01369 701253
e-mail fraser@dhaillinglodge.com
Dir On A815 between the ferry terminals at Dunoon & Hunters Quay

Having a seafront location overlooking the Forth of Clyde, this elegant Victorian villa is a haven of comfort, hospitality, delicious food and fine wines. Bedrooms are equipped with many thoughtful extra touches; one bedroom has been adapted for better access and a lift is available. There is a cosy lounge, and an intimate dining room where a daily changing menu features the best of local produce.

Facilities 7 en suite ⊘ TVB tea/coffee ✖ Licensed Lift Cen ht No coaches Dinner Last d 6pm **Prices** S £32-£36; D £62-£68✳ **LB Parking** 8 **Notes** Closed Nov

◆◆◆◆

Coylet Inn

Loch Eck PA23 8SG ☎ 01369 840426 📠 01369 840426
e-mail coylet@btinternet.com
web www.coylet-locheck.co.uk
Dir 9m N of Dunoon on A815

This charming 17th-century coaching inn stands on the shore of Loch Eck. Local outdoor pursuits include hill walking, golf, water sports and pony trekking, and boats are available for fishing on the loch. Bedrooms vary in size, and all are comfortably furnished. Agile guests can take the original spiral staircase. The cosy, well-stocked bar comes

continued

complete with a log fire, and delicious, imaginative food is served in the spacious dining room.

Facilities 4 en suite (1 fmly) ⊗ tea/coffee ✘ Cen ht No coaches Dinner Last d 8.45pm **Prices** S £37.50-£40; D £65-£75✳ LB **Conf** Max 28 Thtr 28 Board 28 **Parking** 35 **Notes** Closed 25 Dec rs Closed Mon-Tue in Nov-Apr Civ Wed 30

HELENSBURGH
MAP 20 NS28

See also **Cardross**

◆◆◆◆◆

Lethamhill

West Dhuhill Dr G84 9AW
☎ 01436 676016 & 07974 798593 📄 01436 676016
e-mail Lethamhill@talk21.com
Dir 1m N of pier/town centre. Off A818 onto West Dhuhill Dr

From the red phone box in the garden to the old typewriters and slot machines inside, this fine house is an Aladdin's cave of unusual collectibles and memorabilia. The house itself offers spacious and comfortable bedrooms with superb bathrooms. The home-cooked breakfasts and delicious baking earn much praise.

Facilities 3 en suite ⊗ TVB tea/coffee ✘ Cen ht TVL No coaches LB **Parking** 6

OBAN
MAP 20 NM82

◆◆◆◆◆

Blarcreen House

Ardchattan, Connel PA37 1RG
☎ 01631 750272 📄 01631 750132
e-mail info@blarcreenhouse.com
web www.blarcreenhouse.com
Dir NE of Oban. N over Connel Bridge, 1st right for 7m, pass church and Ardchattan Priory Gardens, Blarcreen House 1m

Built in 1886 this elegant Victorian farmhouse stands on the shores of Loch Etive and has lovely views of the surrounding mountains. Bedrooms are beautifully furnished and very well equipped. There is a comfortable drawing room with deep sofas, a plentiful supply of books and videos, and a log burning fire. Delicious home-cooked fare featuring the very best of local produce is served in the nearby dining room. Hospitality is strong and the atmosphere relaxed in this charming house.

continued

Blarcreen House

Facilities 3 en suite ⊗ FTV TVB tea/coffee ✘ Licensed Cen ht TVL No children 16yrs No coaches Dinner Last d 24 hours prior **Prices** S £59.50-£69.50; D £85-£99✳ LB **Parking** 5

◆◆◆◆

Glenburnie House

The Esplanade PA34 5AQ
☎ 01631 562089 📄 01631 562089
e-mail graeme.strachan@btinternet.com
Dir On Oban seafront. Follow signs for Ganavan

This impressive seafront Victorian house has been lovingly restored to a high standard. Bedrooms (including a four-poster room and a minisuite) are beautifully decorated and very well equipped. There is a cosy ground-floor lounge and an elegant dining room, where hearty traditional breakfasts are served at individual tables.

Facilities 12 en suite (2 GF) ⊗ TVB tea/coffee ✘ Cen ht No children 12yrs No coaches **Prices** S £40-£50; D £80-£100 LB **Parking** 12 **Notes** Closed Nov-Mar

◆◆◆◆

Alltavona House

Corran Esplanade PA34 5AQ
☎ 01631 565067 & 07771 708301 📄 01631 565067
e-mail carol@alltavona.co.uk
Dir From Oban centre along seafront past cathedral, 5th house from the end of Esplanade

Alltavona is an elegant Victorian villa with a delightful location on the Corran Esplanade with stunning views over Oban bay to the islands of Lismore and Kererra. The attractive bedrooms are individually styled and feature quality furnishings. Delicious breakfasts featuring the best of local produce are served in the charming dining room.

Facilities 6 en suite (3 fmly) ⊗ TVB tea/coffee ✘ Cen ht No children 12yrs No coaches **Prices** S £35-£70; D £60-£80✳ LB **Parking** 6 **Notes** Closed 12-30 Dec

Scotland

Scotland

OBAN continued

◆◆◆◆

Braeside

Kilmore PA34 4QR ☎ 01631 770243 ◳ 01631 770343
e-mail braeside.guesthouse@virgin.net
Dir *On A816 5m from Oban*

The family-run bungalow stands in gardens overlooking the spectacular Loch Feochan. Bedrooms, all en suite, are bright and airy, well equipped and have easy access. The lounge-dining room has a loch view, a bar with a range of single malts and wines, and offers a varied choice of tasty home-cooked evening meals and breakfasts.

Facilities 5 en suite (1 fmly) (5 GF) ⊗ TVB tea/coffee Direct dial from bedrooms ✗ Licensed Cen ht No children 8yrs No coaches Dinner Last d noon **Prices** D £50-£54 **LB** **Parking** 6

◆◆◆◆

Corriemar House

Corran Esplanade PA34 5AQ
☎ 01631 562476 ◳ 01631 564339
e-mail corriemar@tinyworld.co.uk
web www.corriemarhouse.co.uk
Dir *A85 to Oban. Down hill in right lane & follow sign for Gamavan at minirdbt onto Esplanade*

Billy and Sandra Russell have created a stylish haven of tranquillity at this detached Victorian house close to the town centre. Bedrooms are furnished with panache, range from massive to cosy and even include a suite. Those to the front of the house have stunning views across Oban Bay to the Isle of Mull. Expect a substantial breakfast and friendly attentive service.

Facilities 9 en suite 4 annexe en suite (3 fmly) (1 GF) ⊗ TVB tea/coffee ✗ Cen ht **Parking** 9

◆◆◆◆

Greencourt

Benvoullin Rd PA34 5EF ☎ 01631 563987
e-mail relax@greencourt-oban.co.uk
Dir *At Oban, left at Kings Knoll Hotel, over x-rds & follow Dalriach Rd. Pass leisure centre and bowling green on left then turn left. Left again and sharp left onto lane, Greencourt 2nd house on left*

This welcoming family home stands on an elevated location overlooking the bowling green and leisure centre. The delightful detached house has attractive, comfortable bedrooms of varying sizes,

and all are well equipped. Freshly prepared breakfasts are served in the bright airy dining room, which has lovely views.

Facilities 6 rms (5 en suite) (1 pri facs) (6 GF) ⊗ TVB tea/coffee ✗ Cen ht No coaches **Parking** 6 **Notes** Closed Dec-Jan

◆◆◆◆

Thornloe Guest House ◇

Albert Rd PA34 5JD ☎ 01631 562879 ◳ 01631 562879
e-mail thornloeoban@aol.com
web www.thornloeoban.co.uk
Dir *From A85 left at Kings Knoll Hotel and pass swimming pool, last house on right*

Thornloe is an impressive Victorian house with stunning views from an elevated position overlooking Oban Bay. The house has been refurbished by attentive new owners and the bedrooms are comfortable with attractive furnishings. The public areas comprise a bright dining room where hearty breakfasts are served, and a comfortable conservatory lounge.

Facilities 7 en suite (1 fmly) ⊗ TVB tea/coffee ✗ Cen ht TVL No coaches **Prices** S £27-£32; D £54-£74✱ **Parking** 5

◆◆◆

Wellpark House

Esplanade PA34 5AQ ☎ 01631 562948 ◳ 01631 565808
e-mail enquiries@wellparkhouse.co.uk
web www.wellparkhouse.co.uk
Dir *A85 to Oban seafront, right 200yds to Wellpark*

This welcoming family-run guest house on the Esplanade has a lovely outlook over the bay to the Isle of Mull beyond. Bedrooms are well equipped and furnished in a modern style. There are excellent views from the lounge and hearty breakfasts are served at individual tables in the dining room.

Facilities 19 en suite (4 GF) ⊗ in bedrooms ⊗ in dining room TVB tea/coffee Direct dial from bedrooms ✗ Cen ht No coaches **Parking** 16 **Notes** Closed Nov-Feb rs Etr

◆◆

Lancaster Hotel ◇

Corran Esplanade PA34 5AD
☎ 01631 562587 ◳ 01631 562587
e-mail john@lancasteroban.com
Dir *On seafront next to Columba's Cathedral*

There are lovely views over the bay towards the Isle of Mull from this welcoming, family-run establishment on the Esplanade. Public areas include a choice of lounges and bars.

Facilities 27 rms (24 en suite) (3 fmly) ⊗ TVB tea/coffee Licensed Cen ht TVL ⛲ Sauna Pool Table Steam Room,Spa **Prices** S £30-£35; D £64-£74✱ **LB** **Conf** Max 30 Thtr 30 Class 20 Board 12 **Parking** 20

continued

Scotland

T CATHERINES
MAP 20 NN10

★★★★ Guest House

Thistle House Guest House

A25 8AZ ☎ 01499 302209 📠 01499 302531
e-mail info@thistlehouseguesthouse.com
web www.thistlehouseguesthouse.com
Dir A83 to Inveraray onto A815 to Dunoon, B&B 3m on left

Overlooking the majestic shores of world famous Loch Fyne this recently refurbished house boasts well-appointed bedrooms many of which benefit from the picture post card views. Many extras provided as standard will make your stay as warm as the open fire in the cosy lounge. Breakfast will really set you up for the day regardless of your activities.

Facilities 7 en suite (2 fmly) ⊗ TVB tea/coffee ✖ Cen ht TVL No children 12yrs No coaches Dinner Last d 9pm **Parking** 12

CITY OF EDINBURGH

EDINBURGH
MAP 21 NT27
See also **East Calder (West Lothian)**

Premier Collection

★★★★★ 🏵 Restaurant with Rooms

The Witchery by the Castle

52 Castlehill, The Royal Mile EH1 2NF
☎ 0131 225 5613 📠 0131 220 4392
e-mail mail@thewitchery.com
web www.thewitchery.com
Dir At the top of the Royal Mile at the gates of Edinburgh Castle

Originally built in 1595, the Witchery by the Castle is situated in a historic building at the gates of Edinburgh Castle. The two luxurious and theatrically decorated suites, known as the Inner Sanctum and the Old Rectory are located above the restaurant and are reached via a winding stone staircase. Filled with antiques, opulently draped beds, large roll-top baths and a plethora of memorabilia, this ancient and exciting establishment is often described as one of the world's most romantic destinations.

Facilities 2 en suite 5 annexe en suite (1 GF) STV TVB tea/coffee Direct dial from bedrooms ✖ Licensed No children 12yrs No coaches Dinner Last d 11.30pm **Prices** S £295; D £295⋇ **Notes** Closed 25-26 Dec

★★★★ Guest House

Aonach Mor Guest House ◇

4 Kilmaurs Ter EH16 5DR ☎ 0131 667 8694
e-mail info@aonachmor.com
web www.aonachmor.com
Dir A7 to Cameron Toll rdbt. Follow city centre signs. Dalkeith Rd 5th entrance on right.

Situated in a residential area within easy reach of the city centre and major attractions, Aonach Mor offers stylish, well-equipped accommodation. Internet access is available in the comfortable lounge-dining room, and for choice and quality, the breakfast puts many hotels to shame.

Facilities 7 rms (5 en suite) (2 fmly) ⊗ FTV TVB tea/coffee ✖ Cen ht No children 3yrs **Prices** S £27-£45; D £54-£130⋇

★★★ Guest House

Ardblair Guest House ◇

1 Duddington Crescent EH15 3AS ☎ 0131 620 3081
e-mail ardblairhouse@yahoo.co.uk
web www.ardblair.com
Dir From A1 turn, exit at Newcraighall junct. Continue for 1.5m.

Located on the edge of Edinburgh, benefiting from off road car parking with good public transportation into the city. Bedrooms are comfortable & well presented & cater well for the needs of the modern traveller. The hearty breakfast will give a good start to the day regardless of your activities for the day.

Facilities 5 rms (1 en suite) (3 pri facs) (2 fmly) (1 GF) ⊗ TVB tea/coffee ✖ Cen ht TVL **Prices** S £30-£35; D £60-£90⋇ **Parking** 6 **Notes** 🈂

NEAR EDINBURGH
ASHCROFT FARMHOUSE
East Calder
½ mile from East Calder on B7015

Runner up Top 20 AA Landlady Award, 2005.
Enjoy true Scottish hospitality in our ranch-style farmhouse on our small farm, only 10m City Centre, 5m Airport, Ingliston, A720, M8/M9, Livingston. Regular bus/train nearby to City Centre, therefore no parking problems. Choice of delicious breakfasts using local produce. Credit Cards accepted. No smoking – No pets indoor.
STB ★★★★   AA ♦♦♦♦♦   RAC ♦♦♦♦♦
Telephone: 01506 881810
Fax: 01506 884327
www.ashcroftfarmhouse.com
E-mail: scottashcroft7@aol.com

EDINBURGH continued

★★★ Guest House

Arden Guest House

126 Old Dalkeith Rd EH16 4SD
☎ 0131 664 3985 📠 0131 621 0866
e-mail linda.arden@ntlworld.com
Dir *On A7 200yds W of hospital. Nr Craigmillar Castle*

Colourful flowering baskets adorn the front of this welcoming, personally run guest house situated on the south side of the city, convenient for leisure and business travellers. The modern bedrooms offer good overall freedom of space. Traditional Scottish breakfasts are served at individual tables in the conservatory-dining room. Off-road car parking is a bonus.

Facilities 11 en suite (3 fmly) (6 GF) ⊗ STV TVB tea/coffee 🛏 Cen ht Golf **Prices** S £40-£80; D £55-£90 LB **Parking** 12

★★★ 🅰 Bed & Breakfast

Corner House

1 Greenbank Pl EH10 6EW ☎ 0131 447 1077
e-mail keith_t@lineone.net
Dir *Off A720 Lothianburn junct onto A702 towards city centre, pass filling station on right, right at lights & 1st left onto Greenbank Pl*
Facilities 3 rms (2 fmly) ⊗ TVB tea/coffee 🛏 Cen ht **Notes** ⊛

Premier Collection

◆◆◆◆◆ 🍷

Elmview

15 Glengyle Ter EH3 9LN ☎ 0131 228 1973
e-mail nici@elmview.co.uk
web www.elmview.co.uk
Dir *0.5m S of city centre. Off A702 Leven St onto ValleyField St, one-way to Glengyle Ter*

Elmview offers stylish accommodation on the lower ground level of a fine Victorian terrace house The bedrooms and smart bathrooms are comfortable and extremely well equipped, with thoughtful extras such as safes, and fridges with fresh milk and water. Breakfasts are excellent and are served at a large, elegantly appointed table in the charming dining room.

Facilities 3 en suite (3 GF) ⊗ TVB tea/coffee Direct dial from bedrooms 🛏 Cen ht No children 15yrs No coaches Free pitch & putt adjacent **Prices** D £80-£110✳ **Parking** 2 **Notes** Closed Dec-Feb

Premier Collection

◆◆◆◆◆ ☕

Dunstane House Hotel

4 West Coates, Haymarket EH12 5JQ
☎ 0131 337 6169 & 337 5320 📠 0131 337 6060
e-mail reservations@dunstanehousehotel.co.uk
web www.dunstane-hotel-edinburgh.co.uk
Dir *On A8 between Murrayfield Stadium and Haymarket railway station. 5 mins from city centre 15 mins from airport*

This splendid Victorian villa combines architectural grandeur (crow step gables, ornate fireplaces and other original features) with an intimate country-house atmosphere. The bedrooms are comfortable, stylish and well equipped. Fish from the proprietors' native Orkney Islands features in the restaurant, and lighter meals and a wide selection of malt whiskies are offered in the bar.

Facilities 16 en suite (4 fmly) ⊗ TVB tea/coffee Direct dial from bedrooms 🛏 Licensed Cen ht TVL Dinner Last d 9.30pm **Prices** S £59-£95; D £98-£190 LB **Conf** Max 35 Thtr 35 Class 18 Board 20 **Parking** 12 **Notes** Civ Wed 42
See advertisement on opposite page

Premier Collection

◆◆◆◆◆

Kew House

1 Kew Ter, Murrayfield EH12 5JE
☎ 0131 313 0700 📠 0131 313 0747
e-mail info@kewhouse.com
web www.kewhouse.com
Dir *On A8 Glasgow road, 1m W of city centre, close to Murrayfield Rugby Stadium*

Forming part of a listed Victorian terrace, Kew House lies within walking distance of the city centre, and is convenient for Murrayfield
continued

ugby stadium and tourist attractions. Meticulously maintained
hroughout, it offers attractive bedrooms in a variety of sizes, all
houghtfully equipped to suit business and leisure guests. There is a
:omfortable lounge offering a supper and snack menu. Internet access
s also available.

Facilities 6 en suite (1 fmly) (2 GF) ⊗ FTV TVB tea/coffee Direct dial
from bedrooms Licensed Cen ht No coaches Last d 8pm
Prices S £70-£75; D £85-£150 **LB** **Parking** 6

◆◆◆◆◆ ➾

Kildonan Lodge Hotel

27 Craigmillar Park EH16 5PE
☎ 0131 667 2793 📠 0131 667 9777
e-mail info@kildonanlodgehotel.co.uk
web www.kildonanlodgehotel.co.uk
Dir From city by pass (A720), exit A701 city centre, continue 2.75m
to large rdbt straight on, located 6 buildings on right

Lying on the south side of the city, this delightful Victorian house has
been carefully and lovingly restored. Bedrooms are beautifully
decorated and very well appointed, some have splendid four-poster
beds. Super hospitality is provided and nothing is too much trouble.
The splendid residents lounge provides a tranquil haven to relax by an
open fire while enjoying a dram from the honesty bar. Delicious full
Scottish breakfast is served in the elegant dining room.

Facilities 12 en suite (1 fmly) ⊗ TVB tea/coffee Direct dial from
bedrooms ✘ Licensed Cen ht TVL **Parking** 16 **Notes** Closed Xmas

◆◆◆◆◆

The Lodge Hotel

6 Hampton Ter, West Coates EH12 5JD
☎ 0131 337 3682 📠 0131 313 1700
Dir On A8, 0.75m W of Princess S, 6m east of airport

Please note that this establishment has recently changed hands. Set in
Edinburgh's West End, this fine Georgian house is within walking
distance of the city centre and also on the main bus route. The
comfortable bedrooms are carefully decorated and well-equipped for
leisure and business travellers. There is an elegant ground-floor
lounge and an attractive dining room for the hearty breakfasts.

Facilities 12 en suite (2 fmly) (4 GF) ⊗ TVB tea/coffee Direct dial from
bedrooms ✘ Licensed Cen ht TVL **Conf** Max 30 **Parking** 8

◆◆◆◆◆ 🛏

Violet Bank House

167 Lanark Rd West, Currie EH14 5NZ ☎ 0131 451 5103
e-mail reta@violetbankhouse.co.uk
web www.violetbankhouse.co.uk
Dir On A70 in village centre, corner Lanark Rd West & Kirkgate

Lying to the south of the City within easy reach of the bypass, the
Airport and Heriot Watt University, Violet Bank House offers smart,
very well equipped bedrooms and stylish bathrooms. There is an
inviting lounge, which overlooks the beautiful rear garden, and a
charming dining room where delicious breakfasts feature the best of
Scottish produce.

Facilities 3 rms (2 en suite) (1 pri facs) (1 GF) ⊗ STV TVB tea/coffee
✘ Cen ht TVL No children 14yrs No coaches Fishing Free use of
bicycles **Prices** S fr £45; d fr £80 **LB** **Parking** 3

EDINBURGH continued

♦♦♦♦♦

The Knight Residence

12 Lauriston St EH3 9DJ
☎ 0131 622 8120 ▤ 0131 622 7363
e-mail info@theknightresidence.co.uk
web www.theknightresidence.co.uk
Dir *A702 to Lauriston Place, 2nd left to Lady Lawson St, left to West Port, left to Lauriston St*
Facilities 19 en suite (19 fmly) (3 GF) ⊘ STV FTV TVB tea/coffee Direct dial from bedrooms ✈ Lift Cen ht No coaches **Prices** S £95-£180; D £115-£180; (room only) **LB** **Parking** 19 **Notes** ★★★★★

♦♦♦♦

Bonnington Guest House

202 Ferry Rd EH6 4NW ☎ 0131 554 7610 ▤ 0131 554 7610
e-mail booking@thebonningtonguesthouse.com
web www.thebonningtonguesthouse.com
Dir *On A902*

This delightful Georgian house offers individually furnished bedrooms, on two floors, that retain many of their original features. Family rooms are also available. A substantial freshly prepared breakfast is served in the newly refurbished dining room. Off street parking is an added bonus.
Facilities 7 rms (5 en suite) (2 pri facs) (4 fmly) (1 GF) ⊘ FTV TVB tea/coffee ✈ Cen ht **Prices** S fr £45; D £60-£90✳ **Parking** 9

♦♦♦♦

Priory Lodge

The Loan EH30 9NS ☎ 0131 331 4345 ▤ 0131 331 4345
e-mail calmyn@aol.com
web www.queensferry.com
For full entry see **South Queensferry**

♦♦♦♦

Aarajura

14 Granville Ter EH10 4PQ
☎ 0131 229 6565 ▤ 0131 229 0447
e-mail info@aarajura.co.uk
web www.aarajura.co.uk

Situated in a terrace just south-west of the city centre, this restored Victorian house offers bedrooms in mixed sizes but all are thoughtfully presented and most have smart modern en suites. There is a bright, attractive breakfast room, but why not treat yourself to a continental breakfast in bed?
Facilities 9 rms (5 en suite) (3 fmly) (1 GF) ⊘ TVB tea/coffee Cen ht **Parking** 2

♦♦♦♦

Abcorn Guest House ◇

4 Mayfield Gdns EH9 2BU
☎ 0131 667 6548 ▤ 0131 667 9969
e-mail sales@abcorn.com
Dir *1.5m S from city centre*

This well-presented guest house is situated to the south of the city. Bedrooms are carefully decorated and, with the exception of one small single, are thoughtfully laid out and comfortably proportioned. Hearty Scottish breakfasts are served at well-spaced tables in the attractive dining room.
Facilities 7 en suite (1 fmly) (2 GF) ⊘ TVB tea/coffee ✈ Cen ht **Prices** S £30-£42; D £60-£84✳ **LB** **Parking** 7 **Notes** Closed 20-26 Dec

♦♦♦♦

Allison House Hotel

17 Mayfield Gdns EH9 2AX
☎ 0131 667 8049 ▤ 0131 667 5001
e-mail info@allisonhousehotel.com
web www.allisonhousehotel.com

Part of a Victorian terrace, Allison House offers modern comforts in a splendid building. It's convenient for the city centre, theatres, tourist attractions and is on the main bus route. The attractive bedrooms are generally spacious and very well equipped. Breakfast is served at individual tables in the ground-floor dining room. Off-road parking is available.
Facilities 11 rms (10 en suite) (1 pri facs) (1 fmly) (2 GF) ⊘ in 3 bedrooms ⊘ in dining room ⊘ in lounges TVB tea/coffee Direct dial from bedrooms Cen ht No coaches **Prices** S £45-£60; D £65-£115✳ **LB** **Parking** 6

♦♦♦♦

Ashgrove House

12 Osborne Ter EH12 5HG
☎ 0131 337 5014 ▤ 0131 313 5043
e-mail info@theashgrovehouse.com
web www.theashgrovehouse.com
Dir *On A8 between Murrayfield & Haymarket opp Donaldsons College for Deaf, under 1m to Princes St*

This detached, well-proportioned Victorian house lies just west of the city centre. Bedrooms are comfortably furnished in modern style and

continued

Scotland

equipped with many extras including trouser press and radio. There is a lounge and a bright attractive dining room.

Facilities 7 rms (5 en suite) (2 fmly) (1 GF) ⊗ TVB tea/coffee Direct dial from bedrooms ✗ Licensed Cen ht TVL No coaches **Prices** S £32-£45; D £65-£90 **Parking** 10 **Notes** Closed 24-26 Dec

See advertisement on this page

♦♦♦♦

Ben Craig House

3 Craigmillar Park, Newington EH16 5PG
☎ 0131 667 2593 ▤ 0131 667 1109
e-mail bencraighouse@hotmail.com
Dir A720 onto A201 (city centre), over junct, Craigmillar Park opp Royal Blind School

Ben Craig is an attractive detached Victorian villa on the south side of the city. Bedrooms are well presented, thoughtfully equipped and come with smart en suites. Breakfast is mainly continental and is served in the attractive conservatory overlooking the garden.

Facilities 7 en suite (1 fmly) (3 GF) ⊗ TVB tea/coffee ✗ Cen ht **Conf** Max 14 **Parking** 6

♦♦♦♦

Corstorphine Lodge Hotel ◇

186-188 St Johns Rd, Corstorphine EH12 8SG
☎ 0131 539 4237 & 476 7116 ▤ 0131 539 4945
e-mail corsthouse@aol.com
web www.corstorphinehotels.co.uk
Dir From M8 take city bypass N towards city centre for 1m along A8. Hotel on left

Occupying two large detached Victorian villas, Corstorphine is convenient for the airport and the city centre. Bedrooms, which vary in size, are carefully decorated and well equipped. There is a spacious conservatory-dining room where traditional, continental or vegetarian breakfasts can be enjoyed at individual tables. Ample off-road parking is available.

Facilities 12 en suite 5 annexe en suite (8 fmly) (5 GF) ⊗ STV TVB tea/coffee ✗ Cen ht TVL ch fac **Prices** S £29-£69; D £49-£119 LB **Parking** 14

♦♦♦♦

Dorstan Private Hotel

7 Priestfield Rd EH16 5HJ
☎ 0131 667 6721 & 667 5138 ▤ 0131 668 4644
e-mail reservations@dorstan-hotel.demon.co.uk
Dir Off A7 near Commonwealth Pool onto Priestfield Rd

Set in a quiet residential area on the south side of the city, this delightful Victorian villa offers comfortable, stylish accommodation. Bedrooms, which differ in size, are thoughtfully equipped and enhanced by quality fabrics. On the ground floor there is a comfortable lounge adjacent to the cosy dining room where hearty breakfasts are served.

Facilities 14 rms (12 en suite) (2 fmly) (3 GF) ⊗ TVB tea/coffee Direct dial from bedrooms ✗ Cen ht No coaches Dinner Last d 10am **Parking** 8

♦♦♦♦

Ellesmere House

11 Glengyle Ter EH3 9LN ☎ 0131 229 4823
e-mail celia@edinburghbandb.co.uk
web www.edinburghbandb.co.uk
Dir S of city centre off A702

This delightful terrace house overlooks Bruntsfield Links and is convenient for the city centre. The attractive bedrooms vary in size and have many thoughtful touches. Breakfast, featuring the best of local produce, is enjoyed in the elegant lounge-dining room.

Facilities 4 en suite (1 fmly) ⊗ TVB tea/coffee ✗ Cen ht TVL No children 14yrs No coaches **Prices** S £35-£48; D £70-£96 **Notes** ⊛

EDINBURGH continued

♦♦♦♦

Heriott Park

256 Ferry Rd, Goldenacre EH5 3AN ☎ 0131 552 3456
e-mail reservations@heriottpark.co.uk
web www.heriottpark.co.uk
Dir *M8, turn off signs for Leith, along Ferry Rd, Heriott Park on left 300yds after Goldenacre lights*

A conversion of two adjoining properties, which retain many original features. The guest house is on the north side of the city and has lovely panoramic views of the Edinburgh skyline including Edinburgh Castle and Arthur's Seat. The attractive bedrooms are well equipped and have excellent bathrooms en suite.

Facilities 15 rms (14 en suite) (7 fmly) (1 GF) ⊗ TVB tea/coffee ✖ Cen ht

See advertisement on opposite page

♦♦♦♦

The International Guest House ◇

37 Mayfield Gdns EH9 2BX
☎ 0131 667 2511 ▤ 0131 667 1112
e-mail intergh1@yahoo.co.uk
web www.accomodation-edinburgh.com
Dir *On A701 1.5m S of Princes St*

Guests are assured of a warm and friendly welcome at this attractive Victorian terrace house situated to the south of the city centre. The smartly presented bedrooms are thoughtfully decorated, comfortably furnished and well equipped. Hearty Scottish breakfasts are served at individual tables in the traditionally styled dining room, which boasts a beautiful ornate ceiling.

Facilities 9 en suite (3 fmly) (1 GF) ⊗ STV TVB tea/coffee Direct dial from bedrooms ✖ Cen ht **Prices** S £30-£65; D £50-£120✷ LB **Parking** 3
See advertisement on opposite page

♦♦♦♦

The Lairg

11 Coates Gdns EH12 5LG
☎ 0131 337 1050 ▤ 0131 346 2167
e-mail lairgmarie@aol.com
Dir *From A8 under rail bridge, stately home 150yds on left, Coates Gardens next 2nd left*

Please note that this establishment has recently changed hands. Situated in a residential area close to the Haymarket at the west end of

continued

the city, the Lairg is well located for the train station, Murrayfield, and the city centre. It offers attractive, generally spacious, well-equipped accommodation. Breakfast is served at individual tables in the elegant ground-floor dining room.

Facilities 9 en suite (2 fmly) (1 GF) ⊗ TVB tea/coffee Direct dial from bedrooms ✖ Cen ht No coaches

♦♦♦♦

Sherwood Guest House ◇

42 Minto St EH9 2BR ☎ 0131 667 1200 ▤ 0131 667 2344
e-mail enquiries@sherwood-edinburgh.com
web www.sherwood-edinburgh.com
Dir *On A701 S of the city centre*

Lying on the south side of the city, this guest house is immaculately maintained and attractively presented throughout. Bedrooms vary in size, the smaller ones being thoughtfully appointed to make the best use of space. All include iron/board and several come with a fridge and microwave. Comprehensive breakfasts are served in an elegant dining room.

Facilities 6 rms (5 en suite) (1 pri facs) (2 fmly) (1 GF) ⊗ FTV TVB tea/coffee ✖ Cen ht **Prices** S £30-£60; D £45-£75✷ LB **Parking** 3 **Notes** Closed 20-29 Dec

♦♦♦♦

Six Mary's Place Guest House

6 Mary's Pl, Raeburn Pl, Stockbridge EH4 1JH
☎ 0131 332 8965 ▤ 0131 624 7060
e-mail info@sixmarysplace.co.uk
web www.sixmarysplace.co.uk
Dir *From Waverley station W onto Princes St, right onto Fredrick St & Howe St, left onto Circus Place, house 0.5m on left before rugby grounds*

A relaxed and friendly atmosphere is assured at this Georgian terrace property, located in a popular suburb. In contrast to the original facade, the public areas and bedrooms are bright and contemporary. There is an inviting lounge with Internet access, and a conservatory dining room where tasty vegetarian breakfasts can be enjoyed overlooking the pretty, enclosed garden.

Facilities 8 rms (7 en suite) (1 pri facs) (1 fmly) ⊗ TVB tea/coffee Direct dial from bedrooms ✖ Cen ht TVL No coaches Internet access **Prices** S £40-£50; D £70-£90 **Conf** Thtr 12 Board 8 **Notes** Closed 24-26 Dec

Scotland

◆◆◆◆
Southside Guest House

8 Newington Rd EH9 1QS
☎ 0131 668 4422 📠 0131 667 7771
e-mail info@southsideguesthouse.co.uk
web www.southsideguesthouse.co.uk
Dir E end of Princes St take North Bridge to the Royal Mile, continue
S 0.5m, house on right

Situated within easy reach of the city centre and convenient for the
major attractions, Southside is an elegant sandstone house. Bedrooms
are individually styled, comfortable and thoughtfully equipped.
Traditional, freshly cooked Scottish breakfasts are served at individual
tables in the smart ground-floor dining room.

Facilities 8 en suite (2 fmly) (1 GF) ⊗ TVB tea/coffee Direct dial from
bedrooms ✹ Licensed Cen ht **Prices** S £42-£70; D £64-£140✳ LB

◆◆◆◆
The Walton Hotel

79 Dundas St EH3 6SD ☎ 0131 556 1137 📠 0131 557 8367
e-mail enquiries@waltonhotel.com
web www.waltonhotel.com

Set in a Georgian terrace just north of the city centre, The Walton
provides a friendly atmosphere. Smartly decorated and well-furnished
in pine, the comfortable bedrooms are well-equipped to include
telephones with modem points, radios and hair dryers. Hearty Scottish
breakfasts are served at individual tables in the bright cheerful dining
room.

Facilities 10 en suite (4 fmly) (4 GF) ⊗ TVB tea/coffee Direct dial from
bedrooms ✹ Cen ht **Prices** S £35-£75; D £65-£139✳ **Parking** 8

EDINBURGH continued

The Ben Doran

11 Mayfield Gdns EH9 2AX
☎ 0131 667 8488 📠 0131 667 0076
e-mail info@ben-doran.com
web www.ben-doran.com

Dir *From E side of Princes Street, take A701, Ben Doran on left, approx 1m.*

Facilities 11 rms (7 en suite) ⊗ TVB tea/coffee Direct dial from bedrooms ✕ Cen ht No children 12yrs No coaches Dinner Last d 11.30am **Prices** S £45-£99; D £60-£199✱ **LB Conf** Max 20 Del £175 ✱ **Parking** 10 **Notes** ★★★★

Gildun ◇

9 Spence St EH16 5AG ☎ 0131 667 1368 📠 0131 668 4989
e-mail gildun.edin@btinternet.com

Dir *A720 city bypass to Sheriffhall rdbt onto A7 for 4m to Cameron Toll rdbt go under railway bridge follow A7 sign onto Dalkeith Rd, Spence St is 4th on left opp church*

Facilities 8 rms (6 en suite) (5 fmly) (2 GF) ⊗ TVB tea/coffee ✕ Cen ht No coaches **Prices** S £28-£45; D £56-£90✱ **LB Parking** 4 **Notes** ★★★★

◆◆◆

Abbotsford Guest House ◇

36 Pilrig St EH6 5AL ☎ 0131 554 2706 📠 0131 555 4550
e-mail info@abbotsfordguesthouse.co.uk

Situated just off Leith Walk and within easy walking distance of the city centre, this charming and friendly guest house offers individually decorated, pleasantly furnished and thoughtfully equipped bedrooms. There is an elegant ground-floor dining room where hearty breakfasts are served at individual tables.

Facilities 8 rms (5 en suite) ⊗ STV TVB tea/coffee ✕ Cen ht **Prices** S £30-£50; D £60-£120

◆◆◆

Parklands Guest House ◇

20 Mayfield Gdns EH9 2BZ
☎ 0131 667 7184 📠 0131 667 2011
e-mail reservations@parklands-guesthouse.co.uk

Dir *1.5m S of Princes St on A7/A701*

This friendly, long-established, family-run guest house lies on the south side of the city, on the main bus route and convenient for Edinburgh's centre and many tourist attractions. The comfortable bedrooms are attractively decorated and well equipped. Hearty traditional breakfasts are served at individual tables in the elegant ground-floor dining room.

continued

Parklands

Facilities 6 rms (5 en suite) (1 fmly) (2 GF) ⊗ TVB tea/coffee ✕ Cen ht No coaches **Prices** S £30-£50; D £46-£80 **LB Parking** 1 **Notes** 🐾

◆◆◆

Averon City Centre Guest House ◇

44 Gilmore Pl EH3 9NQ ☎ 0131 229 9932
e-mail info@averon.co.uk
web www.averon.co.uk

Dir *From W end of Princes St onto A702, right at Kings Theatre*

Situated within walking distance of the west end of the city and close to the Kings Theatre, this guest house offers comfortable good value accommodation, with a small, secure car park to the rear.

Facilities 10 rms (6 en suite) (3 fmly) ⊗ TVB tea/coffee ✕ Cen ht **Prices** S £26-£32; D £48-£84✱ **Parking** 19
See advertisement on opposite page

◆◆◆

Ecosse International

15 McDonald Rd EH7 4LX
☎ 0131 556 4967 📠 0131 556 7394
e-mail erlinda@ecosseguesthouse.fsnet.co.uk

Dir *Off A900 NE of city centre*

Situated just off Leith Walk to the north, and within easy walking distance of the city centre, this well-maintained guest house offers comfortable and cheerful accommodation. The cosy lounge area and the adjacent dining room, where hearty breakfasts are served at individual tables, are situated on the lower-ground floor.

Facilities 5 en suite (3 fmly) ⊗ TVB tea/coffee ✕ Cen ht TVL No coaches

◆◆◆

Elder York Guest House

38 Elder St EH1 3DX ☎ 0131 556 1926 📠 0131 624 7140
e-mail morag@elderyork.co.uk
web www.elderyork.co.uk

Dir *From Princes St onto Queen St, then York Place*

Occupying the third and fourth floors of a terrace building, this guest house offers comfortable accommodation and is well situated for Princes St and the city's attractions. Refurbishment has resulted in smartly appointed bedrooms. A freshly prepared breakfast is served in the spacious dining room.

Facilities 13 rms (8 en suite) (1 fmly) ⊗ TVB tea/coffee ✕ Cen ht

◆◆◆

Fraoch House

66 Pilrig St EH6 5AS ☎ 0131 554 1353
e-mail info@fraochhouse.com
Dir 1m from Princes St

Situated within walking distance of the city centre and convenient for many attractions, Fraoch House, which dates from the 1900s, has been carefully refurbished to offer well-equipped and thoughtfully furnished bedrooms. Delicious, freshly cooked breakfasts are served in the charming dining room on the ground floor.

Facilities 6 rms (4 en suite) (2 pri facs) (1 fmly) ⊗ TVB tea/coffee ✕ Cen ht Free use of DVDs and CDs, and internet access.

◆◆◆

Galloway ◇

22 Dean Park Crescent EH4 1PH
☎ 0131 332 3672 📠 0131 332 3672
e-mail galloway_theclarks@hotmail.com
Dir Off A90, 0.5m from W end of Princes St

Located in a peaceful residential area, conveniently situated for both the shops and bistros north of the city centre, this guest house provides smart, thoughtfully equipped bedrooms. Breakfasts featuring a comprehensive selection of starters and hot dishes are served in the ground floor dining room.

Facilities 10 rms (6 en suite) (1 pri facs) (6 fmly) (1 GF) ⊗ in 3 bedrooms TVB tea/coffee Cen ht **Prices** S £30-£45; D £45-£70 LB

◆◆◆

Hermitage Guest House ◇

16 East Hermitage Pl, Leith Links EH6 8AB
☎ 0131 555 4868
e-mail info@hermitageguesthouse.com
Dir Bottom of Leith Walk right to rdbt, turn left, 0.75m on right opp Leith Links

Set in a terrace overlooking Leith Links, this friendly family-run guest house offers bright, cheerfully decorated bedrooms. There is a spacious ground-floor dining room where traditional breakfasts are served at individual tables

Facilities 6 rms (5 en suite) (1 pri facs) (3 fmly) ⊗ TVB tea/coffee ✕ Cen ht **Prices** S £25-£40; D £50-£80✳ LB

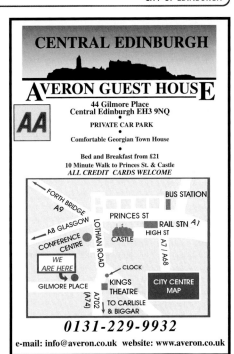

EDINBURGH continued

◆◆◆

Kariba Guest House

10 Granville Ter EH10 4PQ
☎ 0131 229 3773 📠 0131 229 4968
e-mail karibaguesthouse@hotmail.com
web www.karibaguesthouse.co.uk

Recognised by its colourful flower displays in summer, this guest house lies to the south-west of the city centre. The pine-furnished bedrooms include some with spacious accommodation for families, and there is a bright and attractive breakfast room.

Facilities 9 rms (8 en suite) (1 pri facs) (3 fmly) ⊘ TVB tea/coffee Cen ht TVL No coaches **Prices** S £35-£75; D £60-£90✳ **Parking** 7

◆◆◆

Relax Guest House ◇

11 Eyre Pl EH3 5ES ☎ 0131 556 1433 📠 0131 466 8281
e-mail info@relaxguesthouse.co.uk
web www.relaxguesthouse.co.uk
Dir Off B901 N of city centre

Relax Guest House offers comfortable well-equipped accommodation within walking distance of the city centre and major attractions. Bedrooms are bright and airy, and are en suite. Delicious traditional breakfasts are served at individual tables in the spacious lounge-dining room. A stair lift goes up to the first floor.

Facilities 10 en suite (3 fmly) ⊘ STV FTV TVB tea/coffee Direct dial from bedrooms ✱ Licensed Lift Cen ht TVL Dinner Last d 5pm **Prices** S £30-£60; D £60-£120✳ **LB Conf** Max 20 **Parking** 1

◆◆◆

Rowan Guest House ◇

13 Glenorchy Ter EH9 2DQ
☎ 0131 667 2463 📠 0131 667 2463
e-mail angela@rowan-house.co.uk
web www.rowan-house.co.uk
Dir Off A701, left at Bright's Crescent

A friendly welcome is assured at this family-run guest house, situated in a peaceful residential area on the city's south side. Two styles of accommodation are available with the en suite rooms offering the higher standard. Hearty breakfasts, which include delicious homemade scones, are served at individual tables in the dining room.

Facilities 7 rms (3 en suite) (2 fmly) ⊘ TVB tea/coffee Cen ht No coaches **Prices** S £30-£50; D £54-£80 **Parking** 2 **Notes** Closed Xmas

◆◆◆

Terrace Hotel

37 Royal Ter EH7 5AH ☎ 0131 556 3423 📠 0131 556 2520
e-mail Terracehotel@btinternet.com
web www.terracehotel.co.uk
Dir From Waverley station/Princes St, E along Regent Rd, left onto Regent Ter & Royal Ter

Forming part of an impressive Georgian terrace on the eastern side of the city, this spacious B&B offers comfortably furnished, well-proportioned bedrooms. There is an elegant lounge and a bright airy breakfast room.

Facilities 14 rms (11 en suite) (7 fmly) ⊘ TVB tea/coffee ✱ Cen ht No coaches

◆◆◆

Western Manor House Hotel

92 Corstophine Rd, Murrayfield EH12 6JG
☎ 0131 538 7490 📠 0131 538 7490
e-mail info@westernmanorhousehotel.co.uk
Dir On A8 1.5m W of city centre. Follow signs for zoo.

Situated at the western edge of the city and convenient for the airport, motorway and Murrayfield Stadium, Western Manor House offers comfortable accommodation in a friendly relaxed environment. Bedrooms are well equipped, some with easier access, and there is an inviting bar-lounge. Delicious breakfasts are served at individual tables in the bright dining room, and self-catering is also available.

Facilities 11 rms (7 en suite) (4 fmly) (3 GF) ⊘ STV TVB tea/coffee ✱ Licensed Cen ht TVL Dinner Last d 6pm **Prices** S £45-£55; D £70-£95✳ **LB Conf** Max 50 **Parking** 10

Ⓐ

Charleston House ◇

38 Minto St EH9 2BS
☎ 0131 667 6589 & 07904 022205 📠 0131 668 3800
e-mail joan_wightman@hotmail.com
web www.charleston-house.co.uk
Dir 1.5m SE of city centre on A701 at corner Duncan St

Facilities 5 rms (2 en suite) (2 fmly) (1 GF) ⊘ TVB tea/coffee Cen ht TVL **Prices** S £30-£60; D £40-£85✳ **LB Notes** ★★★ Closed 24-27 Dec

Ⓐ

The St Valery

36 Coates Gdns, Haymarket EH12 5LE
☎ 0131 337 1893 📠 0131 346 8529
e-mail info@stvalery.co.uk
web www.stvalery.com
Dir A8 towards city centre, pass Donaldson school on left, two streets before Haymarket station on left

Facilities 11 en suite (3 fmly) (1 GF) ⊘ STV TVB tea/coffee Direct dial from bedrooms Cen ht **Prices** S £35-£55; D £60-£104✳ **Notes** ★★★

♦♦

The Osbourne Hotel

51-59 York Pl EH1 3JD ☎ 0131 556 5577 📠 0131 556 1012
e-mail reservations@osbourne-hotel.com

The friendly Osbourne offers budget accommodation close to the city
centre. Its well-equipped bedrooms vary in size, and there is a lounge
on the ground floor. Traditional breakfasts are served at individual
tables in the spacious dining room.

Facilities 49 rms (46 en suite) (10 fmly) TVB tea/coffee Direct dial from
bedrooms ✖ Lift Cen ht TVL

Garfield Guest House ◇

264 Ferry Rd EH5 3AN ☎ 0131 552 2369
e-mail enquiries@garfieldguesthouse.co.uk

At the time of going to press the rating for this establishment had not
been confirmed. Please check the AA website www.theAA.com for up-
to-date information.

Facilities 7 rms (6 en suite) (1 pri facs) (1 GF) ⊘ TVB tea/coffee
Cen ht **Prices** S £22.50-£50; D £45-£100✳ LB

SOUTH QUEENSFERRY   MAP 21 NT17

♦♦♦♦

Priory Lodge ◇

The Loan EH30 9NS ☎ 0131 331 4345 📠 0131 331 4345
e-mail calmyn@aol.com
web www.queensferry.com

Dir Off W end of High St

This charming, purpose-built guest house has a dramatic location
between the two Forth bridges. The attractive bedrooms are superbly
equipped, comfortably furnished in antique pine and adorned with
many thoughtful extras. There is a small lounge with Internet access, a
modern kitchen facility and a lovely conservatory-dining room.

Facilities 5 en suite (3 fmly) (2 GF) ⊘ TVB tea/coffee ✖ Cen ht TVL
No children 5yrs No coaches **Prices** S £30-£60; D £60-£70✳ **Parking** 5
Notes Closed 22-28 Dec

CITY OF GLASGOW

GLASGOW   MAP 20 NS56

♦♦♦♦

Kelvingrove Hotel

944 Sauchiehall St G3 7TH
☎ 0141 339 5011 📠 0141 339 6566
e-mail kelvingrove.hotel@business.ntl.com
web www.kelvingrove-hotel.co.uk

Dir M8 junct 18, 0.5m along road signed Kelvingrove Museum, on left

This friendly, well-maintained establishment is in a terrace just west of
the city centre, and easily spotted in summer with its colourful floral
displays. Bedrooms, including several rooms suitable for families, are
well equipped and have smart, fully tiled bathrooms en suite. There is
a bright breakfast room, and the reception lounge is open 24 hours.

continued

Facilities 22 en suite (5 fmly) (3 GF) ⊘ TVB tea/coffee Direct dial from
bedrooms Cen ht No coaches **Prices** S £40-£65; D £50-£80✳ LB

♦♦♦

Clifton Hotel

26-27 Buckingham Ter, Great Western Rd G12 8ED
☎ 0141 334 8080 📠 0141 337 3468
e-mail kalam@cliftonhotelglasgow.co.uk

Dir 1.25m NW of city centre off A82 Inverquhomery Rd

Located north-west of the city centre, the Clifton forms part of an
elegant terrace and is ideal for business and leisure. The attractive
bedrooms are spacious, and there is an elegant lounge. Hearty
breakfasts are served at individual tables in the dining room.

Facilities 23 rms (14 en suite) (6 fmly) (3 GF) ⊘ STV TVB tea/coffee
Direct dial from bedrooms ✖ Cen ht TVL **Parking** 8

♦♦♦

Kelvin Private Hotel ◇

15 Buckingham Ter, Great Western Rd, Hillhead G12 8EB
☎ 0141 339 7143 📠 0141 339 5215
e-mail enquiries@kelvinhotel.com
web www.kelvinhotel.com

Dir M8 junct 17, A82 Kelvinside/Dumbarton, 1m on right before
Botanic Gardens

Two substantial Victorian terrace houses on the west side of the city
have been combined to create this friendly establishment close to the
Botanical Gardens. The attractive bedrooms are comfortably
proportioned and well equipped. The dining room on the first floor is
the setting for hearty traditional breakfasts served at individual tables.

Facilities 21 rms (9 en suite) (5 fmly) (2 GF) ⊘ TVB tea/coffee Cen ht
Prices S £25-£45; D £48-£62 **Parking** 5

♦♦♦

Lomond Hotel ◇

6 Buckingham Ter, Great Western Rd, Hillhead G12 8EB
☎ 0141 339 2339 📠 0141 339 0477
e-mail info@lomondhotel.co.uk
web www.lomondhotel.co.uk

Dir M8 junct 17, A82 Dumbarton, 1m on right before Botanic
Gardens

Situated in the west end of the city in a tree-lined Victorian terrace, the
Lomond Hotel offers well maintained, good value accommodation in
a friendly environment. Bedrooms are brightly appointed and suitably
equipped for business or leisure. Hearty breakfasts are served at
individual tables in the bright ground-floor dining room.

Facilities 17 rms (6 en suite) (5 fmly) (3 GF) ⊘ TVB tea/coffee Direct
dial from bedrooms Cen ht **Prices** S £25-£45; D £50-£80 LB

Scotland

Scotland

GLASGOW continued

♦♦♦

McLays

264/276 Renfrew St, Charing Cross G3 6TT
☎ 0141 332 4796 📠 0141 353 0422
e-mail info@mclays.com
Dir *In city centre, parallel street N of Sauchiehall St*

This large friendly guest house, close to the city centre, is popular with the budget tourist and commercial travellers. Bedrooms, several of which have been smartly refurbished, are well equipped. There is a smart lounge and two dining rooms where traditional breakfasts are served.

Facilities 62 rms (39 en suite) (14 fmly) ⊗ STV TVB tea/coffee Direct dial from bedrooms ✖ Lift Cen ht TVL

♦♦♦

The Merchant Lodge

52 Virginia St G1 1TY ☎ 0141 552 2424 📠 0141 552 4747
e-mail themerchant@ukonline.co.uk
web www.merchantlodgehotel.com
Dir *Off George Sq onto North Hanover St, towards Ingram St, onto Virginia Place & Virginia St*

Set within The Merchant City and close to Argyle St, this former home of a tobacco lord features a cobbled courtyard and stone turnpike stair. The house, on five floors, has been fully modernised with pine floors, pine furniture and pleasant and understated decor. Breakfast is fully self-service in a bright and cheerful lower level room.

Facilities 34 en suite 6 annexe en suite (8 fmly) (6 GF) ⊗ TVB tea/coffee Direct dial from bedrooms Cen ht

♦♦♦

Victorian House

212 Renfrew St G3 6TX ☎ 0141 332 0129 📠 0141 353 3155
e-mail info@thevictorian.co.uk
web www.thevictorian.co.uk
Dir *In city centre, parallel street N of Sauchiehall St*

Close to the Art School and Sauchiehall St, this raised terrace house has been extended to offer a range of well-equipped bedrooms. Some rooms have polished floors and bright modern decor, while others are more traditional. A comfortable lounge area leads into the breakfast room, where buffet-style meals are served.

Facilities 58 rms (54 en suite) (12 fmly) (8 GF) ⊗ STV TVB tea/coffee Direct dial from bedrooms ✖ Cen ht **Prices** S £32-£39; D £46-£60

♦♦

Georgian House

29 Buckingham Ter, Great Western Rd, Kelvinside G12 8ED
☎ 0141 339 0008 & 07973 971563
e-mail thegeorgianhouse@yahoo.com
web www.thegeorgianhousehotel.com
Dir *1.25m NW of city centre off A82 Inverquhomery Rd*

The friendly guest house offers good value accommodation at the west end of the city in a peaceful tree-lined Victorian terrace near the Botanic Gardens. Bedrooms vary in size and are furnished in modern style, and breakfast is served in the first-floor lounge-dining room.

Facilities 11 rms (10 en suite) (1 pri facs) (4 fmly) (3 GF) ⊗ TVB tea/coffee ✖ Cen ht TVL **LB Conf** Max 20 **Parking** 7

A

Adelaides Guest House ◇

209 Bath St G2 4HZ ☎ 0141 248 4970 📠 0141 226 4247
e-mail info@adelaides.freeserve.co.uk
web www.adelaides.co.uk
Dir *In city centre at corner Bath St & Pitt St*

Facilities (2 fmly) ⊗ TV available tea/coffee Direct dial from bedrooms ✖ Cen ht No coaches **Prices** S £25-£43; D £40-£50; (room only) ✳ **LB Conf** Thtr 400 Class 400 Board 60 **Notes** ★★ Closed Xmas & New Year

A

Craigielea House B&B ◇

35 Westercraigs G31 2HY ☎ 0141 554 3446
e-mail craigielea.b-b@amserve.net
Dir *M8 junct 15, left at filter light onto Cathedral St, at lights turn right onto Castle St. Through next lights, left at next lights onto Duke St, pass Tennents Brewery and turn left at lights into Westercraigs*

Facilities 4 rms (2 GF) ⊗ TVB tea/coffee ✖ Cen ht No children 3yrs No coaches **Prices** S £25-£30; D £38-£44✳ **Parking** 3 **Notes** ★★ 🐾

continued

CLACKMANNANSHIRE

TILLICOULTRY
MAP 21 NS99

◆◆◆◆

Westbourne House

10 Dollar Rd FK13 6PA ☎ 01259 750314
e-mail info@westbournehouse.co.uk
Dir A91 to St Andrews. Establishment on left just past minirdbt

This former mill-owner's home, set in wooded gardens on the edge of the village, is adorned with memorabilia gathered by the owners during their travels abroad. They offer a friendly welcome and an excellent choice is offered at breakfast.

Facilities 3 rms (2 en suite) (1 pri facs) (1 fmly) (1 GF) ⊗ TVB tea/coffee Cen ht TVL No coaches ♬ **Prices** S £35-£40; D £50-£54 **Parking** 3 **Notes** Closed Xmas-New Year

DUMFRIES & GALLOWAY

CASTLE DOUGLAS
MAP 21 NX76

◆◆◆◆◆ 🍷 ☕ ✲

Craigadam (NX797728)

Craigadam DG7 3HU
☎ 01556 650233 & 650100 📠 01556 650233 Ms Pickup
e-mail enquiry@craigadam.com
web www.craigadam.com
Dir From Castle Douglas E on A75 to Crocketford. In Crocketford turn left on A712 for 2m. House on hill

Set on a working farm, this elegant country house offers gracious living in a relaxed environment. The large bedrooms, most set around a courtyard, are strikingly individual in style. Public areas include a billiard room with comprehensive honesty bar and the panelled dining room features a magnificent 15-seater table, the setting for Celia Pickup's delightful meals.

Facilities 10 en suite (2 fmly) (7 GF) ⊗ TVB tea/coffee Licensed Cen ht Fishing Snooker ♬ Shooting 700 acres Organic sheep Dinner Last d 8am **Conf** Max 22 **Parking** 12 **Notes** Closed Xmas & New Year Civ Wed

◆◆◆◆◆ 🍷

Smithy House

The Buchan DG7 1TH ☎ 01556 503841 & 07743 331949
e-mail enquiries@smithyhouse.co.uk
web www.smithyhouse.co.uk
Dir A75 onto B736 at W end Castle Douglas bypass, B&B 50yds on left

Situated not far from the centre of Castle Douglas, Smithy House is a peaceful haven with well-equipped and carefully furnished bedrooms, two of which enjoy lovely views across Carlingwark Loch. There is a cosy sitting room, which is well stocked with books and games, and a charming dining room where delicious breakfasts featuring the best of locally sourced produce are served.

Facilities 3 rms (2 en suite) (1 pri facs) ⊗ TVB tea/coffee ✻ Cen ht TVL No children 16yrs No coaches **Parking** 4 **Notes** Closed Xmas & New Year

◆◆◆◆

Douglas House ◇

63 Queen St DG7 1HS ☎ 01556 503262 📠 01556 503262
e-mail steve@douglas-house.com
web www.douglas-house.com
Dir A75 W, left at rdbt signed Castle Douglas, 2nd left next rdbt, B&B 500yds on left

Located near the town centre, this immaculately restored house offers quality accommodation and high levels of personal attention. Bedrooms are individual in style and range from the cosy single to the spacious ground-floor double/twin with a magnificent bathroom. The lounge-breakfast room is comfortable and a substantial breakfast is served around the elegant communal table.

Facilities 4 en suite (2 GF) ⊗ TVB tea/coffee ✻ Cen ht No children 12yrs No coaches Dinner Last d 10am **Prices** S £27-£35; D £60-£90✱

Scotland

Scotland

DUMFRIES MAP 21 NX97

Premier Collection

♦♦♦♦♦
Wallamhill House

Kirkton DG1 1SL ☎ 01387 248249
e-mail wallamhill@aol.com
Dir *Off A701 signed Kirkton, 1.5m on right*

Wallamhill House is set in well-tended gardens, in a delightful rural area 3m from Dumfries. Bedrooms are spacious and extremely well equipped. There is a peaceful drawing room, and a mini health club with sauna, steam shower and gym equipment. Evening meals (by arrangement) are served in the charming dining room around one large table, and you are invited to bring your own wine.

Facilities 3 en suite (1 fmly) ⊗ TVB tea/coffee ✖ Cen ht TVL No coaches Sauna Gymnasium ♨ Steam room Dinner **Parking** 6

♦♦♦♦
Rivendell ◇

105 Edinburgh Rd DG1 1JX
☎ 01387 252251 🖷 01387 263084
e-mail info@rivendellbnb.co.uk
web www.rivendellbnb.co.uk
Dir *On A701 Edinburgh Rd, 400yds S of A75 junct*

Situated just north of the town and close to the bypass, this lovely 1920s house, standing in extensive landscaped gardens, has been restored to reflect the period style of the property. Bedrooms are thoughtfully equipped, many are spacious and offer modern facilities. Traditional breakfasts are served in the elegant dining room.

Facilities 5 en suite (2 fmly) ⊗ TVB ✖ Cen ht No coaches **Prices** S £24-£54; D £48-£54✶ **LB** **Parking** 12

♦♦♦♦
Southpark Country House ◇

Quarry Rd, Locharbriggs DG1 1QG
☎ 01387 711188 & 0800 9701588 🖷 01387 711155
e-mail info@southparkhouse.co.uk
web www.southparkhouse.co.uk
Dir *3.5m NE of Dumfries. Off A701 in Locharbriggs onto Quarry Rd, last house on left*

Having a peaceful location with stunning views, this well-maintained guest house offers comfortable, attractive and well-equipped bedrooms. The peaceful lounge has a log fire on colder evenings, and
continued

fax and e-mail facilities are available. Friendly proprietor Ewan Maxwell personally oversees the hearty Scottish breakfasts served in the bright, open-plan dining room.

Southpark Country House

Facilities 4 en suite (1 fmly) ⊗ TVB STV tea/coffee ✖ Cen ht TVL No coaches 2 acres of garden **Prices** S £28-£35; D £45-£57.50 **LB** **Parking** 10

ESKDALEMUIR MAP 21 NY29

Premier Collection

♦♦♦♦♦ ⊛ 🖺 ⊜
Hart Manor

DG13 0QQ ☎ 013873 73217
e-mail visit@hartmanor.co.uk
web www.hartmanor.co.uk
Dir *1m S of village on B709 Langholm road*

Far from the madding crowd, this immaculate property lies in a peaceful hamlet only 20 minutes from the M74. John and Kath Leadbeater's hospitality is second to none. Bedrooms are as bright and cheerful as the service and there is a choice of cosy lounges. Kath's superb breakfasts and excellent dinners are memorable.

Facilities 5 en suite ⊗ TVB tea/coffee ✖ Licensed Cen ht No children 10yrs No coaches Fishing Dinner Last d 7.30pm **Prices** S £82.50-£85.50; D £145-£151; (incl. dinner) ✶ **LB** **Parking** 10 **Notes** Closed Xmas & New Year

GRETNA (WITH GRETNA GREEN)

MAP 21 NY36

◆◆◆

Surrone House

Annan Rd DG16 5DL ☎ 01461 338341 📠 01461 338341
e-mail enquiries@surronehouse.co.uk
web www.surronehouse.co.uk
Dir *In town centre on B721*

You are assured of a warm welcome at this well-maintained guest house set in attractive gardens well back from the road. Bedrooms are sensibly furnished and including a delightful honeymoon suite. Dinner, drinks and light refreshments are available.

Facilities 7 rms (6 en suite) (1 pri facs) (4 fmly) (2 GF) ⊘ TVB tea/coffee 🏋 Licensed Cen ht TVL No coaches Dinner Last d 8pm
Prices S £45; D £60 **Parking** 10

◆◆◆

Barrasgate

Millhill DG16 5HU
☎ 01461 337577 & 07711 661938 📠 01461 337577
e-mail info@barrasgate.co.uk
web www.barrasgate.co.uk
Dir *M74 junct with A6071 signed Longtown. From S follow A6071 1m take 2nd left signed Gretna Green establishment on left. From N follow signs for Longtown, Barrasgate House on right 1m from motorway*

This detached house lies in attractive gardens in a rural setting yet is convenient for the motorway. Bedrooms are well presented and there is a cosy lounge where breakfasts and light suppers are served around the one table.

Facilities 4 en suite (1 fmly) (1 GF) ⊘ TV3B tea/coffee Cen ht TVL No coaches **Parking** 8 **Notes** 🐾

KIRKCUDBRIGHT

MAP 20 NX65

Premier Collection

◆◆◆◆◆◆

Baytree House

110 High St DG6 4JQ ☎ 01557 330824 📠 01557 330824
e-mail jackie@baytreehouse.net
web www.baytreehouse.net
Dir *Off A711 main street onto St Cuthbert's St & Castle St*

Baytree House is a beautifully restored Georgian house just off the town centre. The attractive bedrooms are thoughtfully equipped and
continued

furnished in keeping with style of the house, and the bright airy ground-floor dining room overlooks the secluded garden. Jackie Callander's fine hospitality, breakfasts and magnificent upstairs drawing room make a lasting impression.

Facilities 3 en suite (1 GF) ⊘ TVB tea/coffee Cen ht No children 12yrs No coaches **Notes** 🐾

LOCKERBIE

MAP 21 NY18

◆◆◆◆

Rosehill Guest House

Carlisle Rd DG11 2DR ☎ 01576 202378 📠 01576 202378
Dir *0.5m S of town centre on B723*

This immaculately maintained detached Victorian house lies in attractive gardens on the south side of town. Bedrooms are thoughtfully furnished and boast attractive soft furnishings and good levels of comfort. Day rooms include an inviting lounge and elegant dining room where hearty breakfasts are served.

Facilities 5 rms (3 en suite) (2 pri facs) (1 fmly) ⊘ TVB tea/coffee Cen ht TVL No coaches Garden quoits **Parking** 5 **Notes** 🐾

MOFFAT

MAP 21 NT00

◆◆◆◆

Queensberry House ◇

12 Beechgrove DG10 9RS ☎ 01683 220538
e-mail queensberryhouse@amserve.net
Dir *Off A701 Edinburgh Rd onto Beechgrove, house opp tennis courts*

A warm welcome is assured at this well-maintained house, peacefully located opposite tennis courts a short walk from the town centre. Accommodation includes an attractive pine-furnished dining room, a cosy lounge, and thoughtfully furnished bedrooms equipped with lots of homely extras.

Facilities 3 en suite ⊘ TVB tea/coffee 🏋 Cen ht TVL No children 5yrs No coaches **Prices** S £30-£35; D £50✶ **LB Notes** Closed 24-26 Dec 🐾

MOFFAT continued

◆◆◆◆

Bridge Guest House

Bridge House, Well Rd DG10 9JT ☎ 01683 220558
e-mail info@bridgehousemoffat.co.uk
Dir Off A708 The Holm onto Burnside & Well Rd, house 0.5m on left

A fine Victorian property, Bridge House lies in attractive gardens in a quiet residential area on the fringe of the town. Family-run, the atmosphere is friendly and relaxed. The chef-proprietor provides excellent dinners for guests and non-residents.

Facilities 7 en suite (1 fmly) ⊘ TVB tea/coffee ✗ Licensed Cen ht No coaches Dinner Last d 8.30pm **Prices** S £35-£40; D £56-£75 LB **Parking** 7 **Notes** Closed Xmas & New Year

◆◆◆◆

Hartfell House

Hartfell Crescent DG10 9AL
☎ 01683 220153 ▤ 01683 220153
e-mail enquiries@hartfellhouse.co.uk
Dir Off High St at war memorial onto Well St & Old Well Rd, Hartfell Crescent on right

Set in attractive gardens in a conservation area above the town, this impressive Grade B listed Victorian house has lovely views of the Moffat Hills. Family run, its beautifully maintained bedrooms offer high quality and there is an inviting first-floor lounge. Delicious breakfasts and evening meals are served in the dining room. Moffat centre is only a short walk away.

Facilities 9 rms (7 en suite) (1 pri facs) (2 fmly) (2 GF) ⊘ TVB tea/coffee Licensed Cen ht No coaches **Prices** S £35; D £60 LB **Parking** 6 **Notes** Closed 2 Jan-Feb

◆◆◆◆

Limetree House

Eastgate DG10 9AE ☎ 01683 220001
e-mail info@limetreehouse.co.uk
web www.limetreehouse.co.uk
Dir Off High St onto Well St, left onto Eastgate, house 100yds

A warm welcome is assured at this well-maintained guest house, quietly situated behind the main high street. Recognisable by its colourful flower baskets in season, it provides an inviting lounge and bright cheerful breakfast room. Bedrooms are smartly furnished in pine and include a large family room.

Facilities 6 en suite (1 fmly) (1 GF) ⊘ TVB tea/coffee Cen ht No children 5yrs No coaches Dinner Last d 5pm LB **Parking** 3

◆◆◆

Barnhill Springs Country Guest House ◇

DG10 9QS ☎ 01683 220580
Dir A74(M) junct 15, A701 towards Moffat, Barnhill Rd 50yds on right

This former farmhouse has a quiet rural location south of the town and within easy reach of the M74. Bedrooms are well proportioned; none have bathrooms en suite, though one room on the ground floor has a private shower room. There is a comfortable lounge and separate dining room.

Facilities 5 rms (1 en suite) (1 fmly) (1 GF) ⊘ tea/coffee Cen ht TVL No coaches Dinner Last d 9am **Prices** S £27-£28; D £54-£56 **Parking** 10 **Notes** ⌘

STRANRAER MAP 20 NX06

◆◆◆

Fernlea Guest House

Lewis St DG9 7AQ ☎ 01776 703037 ▤ 01776 703037
e-mail fernleaguesthouse@msn.com
web www.fernleaguesthouse.co.uk
Dir In town centre on A718, next to leisure centre

Set in gardens, this Victorian house is handy for the town centre and the ferry terminal. Bright and attractive throughout, it has well-proportioned bedrooms and a lounge-breakfast room that provides space and comfort.

Facilities 3 en suite ⊘ TVB tea/coffee ✗ Cen ht TVL No coaches **Prices** S £35-£45; D £45-£50✳ **Parking** 5 **Notes** Closed 24-27 Dec & 31 Dec-2 Jan ⌘

THORNHILL MAP 21 NX89

Premier Collection

◆◆◆◆◆

Gillbank House

8 East Morton St DG3 5LZ
☎ 01848 330597 ▤ 01848 331713
e-mail hanne@gillbank.co.uk
web www.gillbank.co.uk
Dir *In town centre off A76*

Gillbank House was originally built for a wealthy Edinburgh merchant. Convenient for the many outdoor pursuits in this area, such as fishing and golfing, this delightful house offers comfortable and spacious bedrooms and smart shower rooms en suite. Breakfast is served at individual tables in the bright, airy dining room, which is next to the comfortable lounge.

Facilities 6 en suite (2 GF) ⊗ TVB tea/coffee ✘ Cen ht No children 8yrs No coaches **Prices** S £40; D £60✶ **Parking** 8

EAST AYRSHIRE

DALRYMPLE MAP 20 NS31

◆◆◆ ▥

The Kirkton Inn Hotel

1 Main St KA6 6DF ☎ 01292 560241 ▤ 01292 560835
e-mail kirkton@cqm.co.uk
web www.kirktoninn.co.uk
Dir *In village centre*

Dating from the 19th century, this friendly village inn has a reputation for enjoyable meals, served in the various dining areas. The cosy Malt Room offers an impressive range of malt whiskies, while a magnificent mural of the River Doon graces the public bar. Accommodation comprises three comfortable bedrooms, and self-catering units are available.

Facilities 3 en suite ⊗ in dining room TVB tea/coffee Cen ht Pool Table Dinner Last d 8.45pm **Conf** Max 30 Class 30 Board 15 **Parking** 40

KILMARNOCK MAP 20 NS43

▲ ✤

Aulton Farm (NS386422)

Kilmaurs KA3 2PQ
☎ 01563 538208 & 01294 211584 Mrs Hawkshaw
Dir *1m W of Kilmaurs. A769 N, 1st right after Cunninghamhead x-rds, 1st farm on left*

Facilities 4 rms (1 en suite) (1 pri facs) (1 fmly) (2 GF) ⊗ TVB tea/coffee ✘ Cen ht TVL Riding 22 acres beef **Parking** 8 **Notes** ★★★ ⊛

SORN MAP 20 NS52

★★★★ ◉◉ **Restaurant with Rooms**

The Sorn Inn

35 Main St KA5 6HU ☎ 01290 551305 ▤ 01290 553470
e-mail craig@sorninn.com
Dir *A70 from S or A76 from N onto B743 to Sorn*

Centrally situated in this rural village, which is convenient for many of Ayrshire's attractions, this renovated inn is now a fine dining restaurant with a cosy lounge area. There is also a popular chop house with a pub-like environment. The freshly decorated bedrooms have comfortable beds and good facilities.

Facilities 4 en suite (1 fmly) ⊗ TVB tea/coffee Direct dial from bedrooms ✘ Licensed Cen ht Fishing Dinner Last d 9pm **Prices** S £35-£50; D £70-£90✶ **LB** **Parking** 9 **Notes** Closed 2wks Jan

EAST LOTHIAN

EAST LINTON MAP 21 NT57

Premier Collection

◆◆◆◆◆ ▤ ⌂

Kippielaw Farmhouse

EH41 4PY ☎ 01620 860368 ▤ 01620 860368
e-mail info@kippielawfarmhouse.co.uk
Dir *From East Linton follow Traprain sign 0.75m, after farm turn right onto lane, 0.5m on left*

Set on an elevated position sheltered by well-tended gardens and a small courtyard, Kippielaw has stunning views of the Tyne valley. The pretty cottage-style bedrooms are thoughtfully equipped and overlook the gardens. The welcoming lounge has a log fire, and breakfast is served house-party style around one table in the attractive dining room.

Facilities 2 rms (1 en suite) (1 pri facs) ⊗ TVB tea/coffee ✘ Cen ht No children 13yrs No coaches **Prices** S £42; D £64 **LB** **Parking** 4

HADDINGTON MAP 21 NT57

▲

Eaglescairnie Mains

By Gifford EH41 4HN ☎ 01620 810491 ▤ 01620 810491
e-mail williams.eagles@btinternet.com
Dir *3.5m S of Haddington. B6368 from Haddington signed Humbie & Bolton. Through Bolton, at top of hill fork left signed Eaglescairnie & Gifford, 0.5m on left*

Facilities 3 en suite ⊗ tea/coffee Cen ht TVL No coaches ⌕ **Prices** S £35-£45; D £60-£70✶ **Parking** 10 **Notes** ★★★★ Closed Xmas

Scotland

FIFE

ANSTRUTHER
MAP 21 NO50

★★★★ Guest Accommodation

The Spindrift
Pittenweem Rd KY10 3DT
☎ 01333 310573 ▤ 01333 310573
e-mail info@thespindrift.co.uk
web www.thespindrift.co.uk
Dir *Entering town from W on A917, 1st building on left*

This immaculate Victorian villa stands on the western edge of the village. The attractive bedrooms offer a wide range of extra touches; the Captain's Room, a replica of a wood-panelled cabin, is a particular feature. The inviting lounge has an honesty bar, while imaginative breakfasts, and enjoyable home-cooked meals by arrangement, are served in the cheerful dining room.

Facilities 8 rms (7 en suite) (1 pri facs) (2 fmly) ⊗ TVB tea/coffee Direct dial from bedrooms Licensed Cen ht No children 10yrs No coaches Dinner Last d noon **Prices** S £38.50-£48; D £55-£76 **LB Parking** 12
Notes Closed Xmas-late Jan

♦♦♦♦

The Waterfront ◇
18-20 Shore St KY10 3EA
☎ 01333 312200 ▤ 01333 312288
e-mail chris@anstruther-waterfront.co.uk
web www.anstruther-waterfront.co.uk
Dir *From the roundabout at St Andrews Rd towards the harbour, B&B opposite the marina on the left.*

Situated overlooking the harbour the Waterfront offers spacious, stylish, contemporary accommodation with the bedrooms located in the lovingly restored buildings situated in a courtyard behind the restaurant. There is a comfortable lounge with a smartly fitted kitchen and dining room, and laundry facilities are available in the granary. Dinner and breakfast are served in the attractive restaurant that offers a comprehensive menu featuring the best of local produce.

Facilities 8 annexe en suite (3 fmly) (1 GF) ⊗ STV TVB tea/coffee ✠ Licensed Cen ht TVL Dinner Last d 10pm **Prices** S £22.50-£38; D £45-£76✱ **LB**

DUNFERMLINE
MAP 21 NT08

♦♦♦♦

Hillview House ◇
9 Aberdour Rd KY11 4PB
☎ 01383 726278 ▤ 01383 726278
e-mail info@hillviewhousedunfermline.co.uk
web www.hillviewhousedunfermline.co.uk
Dir *M90 junct 2, A823 to Dunfermline, after 3rd rdbt right at lights onto Aberdour Rd, Hillview House 200yds on right*

Located south of the town centre and convenient for the motorway, this welcoming guest house offers comfortable, well-equipped bedrooms that include televisions with VCR and access to a large video library. Freshly prepared breakfasts are served at individual tables in the attractive, bright dining room.

Facilities 3 en suite ⊗ TVB tea/coffee Direct dial from bedrooms ✠ Cen ht No children 12yrs No coaches Video library **Prices** S £30-£35; D £46-£50✱ **Parking** 4

♦♦♦♦

Hopetoun Lodge ◇
141 Halbeath Rd KY11 4LA ☎ 01383 620906
e-mail hopetounlodge@aol.com
web www.hopetounlodge.co.uk
Dir *M90 junct 3, A907 to Dunfermline, pass Halbeath Retail Park, over rdbt & 2 lights, Lodge on left after Kwik-Fit*

The attractive, well-proportioned ground-floor bedrooms at Hopetoun Lodge are features. Two rooms have modern en suites and one has a splendid art-deco bathroom. The guest house is on the eastern side of town, handy for the motorway.

Facilities 3 rms (2 en suite) (1 fmly) (3 GF) ⊗ TVB tea/coffee ✠ Cen ht No coaches **Prices** S £27-£30; D £48-£52✱ **Parking** 4
Notes Closed 25-26 Dec & 1-2 Jan 🐾

INVERKEITHING
MAP 21 NT18

♦♦♦♦

The Roods ◇
16 Bannerman Av KY11 1NG
☎ 01383 415049 ▤ 01383 415049
e-mail isobelmarley@hotmail.com
web www.theroods.com
Dir *N of town centre off B981 Church St-Chapel Pl*

This charming house stands in secluded, well-tended gardens close to
continued

the station. Bedrooms are individually styled and have new state-of-the-art bathrooms. There is an inviting lounge, and breakfast is served at individual tables in an attractive conservatory.

Facilities 2 en suite (2 GF) ⊗ TVB tea/coffee Direct dial from bedrooms ✖ Cen ht TVL No coaches Dinner Last d 9am **Prices** S £26-£30; D £50-£60✳ **LB** **Parking** 4 **Notes** ⊠

LEUCHARS
MAP 21 NO42

◆◆◆◆

Hillpark House

96 Main St KY16 0HF ☎ 01334 839280 📠 01334 839051
e-mail enquiries@hillparkhouse.com
web www.hillparkhouse.com
Dir Leaving Leuchars for St Michaels, house last on right

Lying peacefully on the edge of the village, Hillpark House an impressive Edwardian home offers comfortable, well-appointed and equipped bedrooms. There is an inviting lounge, a conservatory and a peaceful dining room.

Facilities 5 rms (3 en suite) (1 pri facs) (1 fmly) ⊗ TVB tea/coffee ✖ Cen ht TVL No coaches **Parking** 6

LEVEN
MAP 21 NO30

◆◆◆◆

Dunclutha Guest House ◇

16 Victoria Rd KY8 4EX ☎ 01333 425515 📠 01333 422311
e-mail pam.leven@blueyonder.co.uk
web www.dunclutha.myby.co.uk
Dir A915, B933 Glenlyon Rd into Leven, rdbt left onto Commercial Rd & Victoria Rd, Dunclutha opp church on right

Set in a quiet street close to the town centre, Dunclutha House is an inviting Victorian property that was formerly the rectory for the nearby Episcopalian church. Lovingly restored and refurbished to its original splendour it offers comfortable, well-equipped accommodation. A splendid lounge adjoins the dining room where hearty breakfasts are served at individual tables.

Facilities 4 rms (3 en suite) (1 pri facs) (2 fmly) ⊗ TVB tea/coffee ✖ Cen ht TVL No coaches Piano **Prices** S £28-£35; D £54-£60✳ **Parking** 3 **Notes** rs 2 wks Jan

Sandilands ◇

20 Leven Rd, Lundin Links KY8 6AH
☎ 01333 329881 📠 01333 329881
e-mail sandilands@lundinlinks.wanadoo.co.uk
Dir 2m NE of Leven. On A915 in village centre

Facilities 3 en suite ⊗ FTV TVB tea/coffee ✖ Cen ht No children 5yrs No coaches **Prices** S £30-£35; D £46-£56✳ **Parking** 3 **Notes** ★★★★

MARKINCH
MAP 21 NO20

◆◆◆◆

Town House Hotel

1 High St KY7 6DQ ☎ 01592 758459 📠 01592 755039
e-mail townhousehotel@aol.com
web www.townhousehotel-fife.co.uk
Dir In town centre opp railway station

This friendly establishment offers bedrooms with pleasant colour schemes, modern furnishings, and a good range of facilities. The attractive bar-restaurant is popular with locals and serves a choice of good-value dishes.

Facilities 4 rms (3 en suite) (1 fmly) ⊗ TVB tea/coffee ✖ Cen ht No coaches Dinner Last d 9pm **Prices** S £35-£45; D £70-£80✳ **Conf** Max 20 Thtr 20 Class 15 Board 15 **Notes** Closed 25-26 Dec & 1-2 Jan

NEWBURGH
MAP 21 NO21

◆◆

The Abbey Inn ◇

East Port KY14 6EZ ☎ 01337 840761 📠 01337 842220
e-mail drew@lindoresabbey.co.uk
Dir On A913 High St

Situated at the east end of the village, the Abbey Inn offers comfortable good value accommodation. The bright, well-appointed bedrooms are on the first floor and are all en suite. There is a popular public bar and home-made meals are served in the lounge bar.

Facilities 3 en suite ⊗ TVB tea/coffee ✖ Licensed Cen ht No coaches Pool Table Dinner Last d 9pm **Prices** S £25-£30; D £50-£60 **LB**

Scotland

ST ANDREWS

MAP 21 NO51

 ★★★★ ◉◉ **Inn**

The Inn at Lathones

Largoward KY9 1JE ☎ 01334 840494 📠 01334 840694
e-mail lathones@theinn.co.uk
web www.theinn.co.uk
Dir *5m S of St Andrews on A915, 0.5m before village of Largoward on left just after hidden dip*

A lovely country inn, full of character and individuality, that is 400 years old in part. The friendly staff helps to create a relaxed atmosphere. Smart, contemporary bedrooms are situated in two separate wings, both accessed from the outside. The colourful, cosy restaurant is the main focus - the menu offers modern interpretations to Scottish and European dishes.

Facilities 13 annexe en suite (1 fmly) (11 GF) ⊗ STV TVB tea/coffee Direct dial from bedrooms Cen ht TVL Dinner Last d 9.30pm **Prices** S £95-£110; D £130-£160; (incl. dinner) ✳ **LB Conf** BC Max 40 Thtr 40 Class 10 Board 20 Del from £125 ✳ **Parking** 35 **Notes** Closed 26 Dec & 3-23 Jan rs 24 Dec Civ Wed 45

Premier Collection

 ♦♦♦♦♦ 🗼

The Paddock

Sunnyside, Strathkinness KY16 9XP
☎ 01334 850888 📠 01334 850870
e-mail thepaddock@btinternet.com
web www.thepadd.co.uk
Dir *3m W from St Andrews off B939. The Paddock signed from village centre*

Situated in a peaceful village overlooking rolling countryside, this friendly, family-run guest house offers stylish and very well-equipped bedrooms. Superb fish tanks, one freshwater, the other salt, line the entrance hall and contain beautiful and unusual fish. The lounge-dining room in the conservatory is a lovely setting for the delicious breakfasts.

Facilities 4 en suite (1 fmly) (2 GF) ⊗ TVB tea/coffee ✖ Cen ht No coaches **Parking** 8

 ♦♦♦♦

Annandale Guest House

23 Murray Park KY16 9AW
☎ 01334 475310 📠 01334 475310
e-mail info@annandale-standrews.com
Dir *A91 to St Andrews. Onto one-way system, right again, 1st guest house on left*

Forming part of a Victorian row, this welcoming B&B is convenient for the seafront and central amenities. The comfortable bedrooms are bright, modern and well equipped. Hearty breakfasts are served in the lounge-dining room. Internet access is available.

Facilities 6 en suite (2 fmly) ⊗ TVB tea/coffee ✖ Cen ht No children 12yrs **Prices** S £48-£65; D £60-£84✳

 ♦♦♦♦

Craigmore Guest House

3 Murray Park KY16 9AW
☎ 01334 472142 📠 01334 477963
e-mail enquiries@standrewscraigmore.com
web www.standrewscraigmore.com
Dir *A91 from Cupar, over 2 mini rdbts, 1st left onto Golf Place, 1st right & 1st right again to top of street*

Lying between the town centre and the seafront, this immaculately maintained guest house forms part of a Victorian row. Close to the Old Course, it is adorned with lots of amusing golfing touches. The stylish bedrooms are attractively decorated and well equipped. Breakfasts are served at individual tables in the elegant lounge-dining room.

Facilities 7 en suite (4 fmly) (1 GF) ⊗ FTV TVB tea/coffee ✖ Cen ht TVL No coaches **Prices** D £64-£90 **LB**

 ♦♦♦♦

Glenderran Guest House ◇

9 Murray Park KY16 9AW
☎ 01334 477951 📠 01334 477908
e-mail info@glenderran.com
web www.glenderran.com
Dir *A91 into St Andrews, over 2 rdbts, 2nd left onto Murray Place, right onto Murray Park*

This smart terrace house has a super location just minutes from the town centre, seafront, West Sands beach and the Old Course. Aviation-theme pictures and memorabilia decorate the public rooms. Well-equipped bedrooms come in a variety of sizes, and carefully prepared breakfasts are enjoyed in the ground-floor dining room.

Facilities 5 rms (4 en suite) (1 pri facs) ⊗ FTV TVB tea/coffee ✖ Cen ht TVL No children 12yrs No coaches **Prices** S £30-£45; D £60-£90✳ **LB**

 ♦♦♦♦

Hazelbank

28 The Scores KY16 9AS
☎ 01334 472466 📠 01334 472466
e-mail michael@hazelbank.com
web www.hazelbank.com
Dir *Right at Royal & Ancient Clubhouse, 150yds on right*

There is a friendly atmosphere at the personally run Hazelbank, which overlooks the bay and is close to the famous Old Course. The well-equipped bedrooms are smartly furnished and have good bathrooms. Freshly prepared breakfasts are served at individual tables in the attractive bright dining room.

Facilities 10 en suite (4 fmly) (1 GF) ⊗ FTV TVB tea/coffee Direct dial from bedrooms ✖ Licensed Cen ht TVL No coaches **Prices** S £60-£120; D £80-£140✳ **LB Notes** Closed 20 Dec-16 Jan

◆◆◆◆

Lorimer House

19 Murray Park KY16 9AW
☎ 01334 476599 🖷 01334 478463
e-mail info@lorimerhouse.com
web www.lorimerhouse.com
Dir *A91 to St Andrews, turn left onto Golf Place, turn right onto The Scores, turn right into Murray Park*

A warm and friendly welcome is assured at this delightful Victorian terrace house, situated within easy reach of the famous Old Course, the seafront and town centre. Bedrooms are attractive, comfortably furnished and well equipped. Freshly prepared Scottish breakfasts are served in the stylish dining room, which also has a lounge area and offers free Broadband Internet access.

Facilities 5 en suite (1 GF) ⊘ STV TVB tea/coffee ✖ Cen ht TVL
No children 12yrs No coaches **Prices** D £60-£86

◆◆◆◆

Spinkstown Farmhouse ◇ *(NO541144)*

KY16 8PN ☎ 01334 473475 🖷 01334 473475 Mrs Duncan
e-mail anne@spinkstown.com
Dir *2m E on A917 to Crail, 3rd farmhouse on right*

This immaculately maintained modern farmhouse is surrounded by gently rolling countryside. Bedrooms are stylish, spacious and well-equipped. The comfortable lounge, complete with baby grand piano, overlooks the well-tended rear garden. Breakfast is served around a communal table in the dining room.

Facilities 3 en suite ⊘ TVB tea/coffee ✖ Cen ht TVL 250 acres
arable/cattle/sheep **Prices** S £30-£35; D £54-£56✳ **Parking** 3

◆◆◆

Edenside House

Edenside KY16 9SQ ☎ 01334 838108 🖷 01334 838493
e-mail admin@edenside-house.co.uk
web www.edenside-house.co.uk
Dir *2m W of St Andrews on estuary shore, visible from A91*

Overlooking the Eden estuary and nature reserve, this modernised 18th-century house is family run and offers a friendly home from home atmosphere. Bedrooms are comfortable, bright and cheerful, and are mostly accessed externally. There is a cosy lounge and a pretty dining room where hearty breakfasts are served.

Facilities 2 en suite 6 annexe en suite (1 fmly) (6 GF) ⊘ TVB tea/coffee
✖ Cen ht No coaches **Prices** S £36-£60; D £50-£64✳ **Parking** 10

HIGHLAND

ARDELVE   MAP 22 NG82

◆◆◆

Caberfeidh House ◇

IV40 8DY ☎ 01599 555293
e-mail info@caberfeidh.plus.com
web www.caberfeidh.plus.com
Dir *A87 over Dornie Bridge into Ardelve, 1st left, 100yds on right*

Set in a peaceful location overlooking Lochs Alsh and Duich, Caberfeidh House offers good value, comfortable accommodation in relaxed and friendly surroundings. Bedrooms are traditionally furnished and thoughtfully equipped, and there is a cosy lounge with a wide selection of books, games and magazines. Hearty breakfasts are served at individual tables the dining room.

Facilities 6 rms (3 en suite) (2 fmly) ⊘ TVB tea/coffee ✖ Cen ht TVL
No coaches **Prices** S fr £23; D £40-£50✳ **Parking** 4

ARDGOUR   MAP 22 NN06

🅰

The Inn at Ardgour

PH33 7AA ☎ 01855 841225 🖷 01855 841214
e-mail theinn@ardgour.biz
web www.ardgour.biz
Dir *On A861 in village. Ferry from Corran on A82*

Facilities 12 en suite (2 fmly) (5 GF) ⊘ TVB tea/coffee Licensed
Cen ht No coaches Dinner Last d 9pm **Parking** 28 **Notes** ★★★

Scotland

AULTBEA

MAP 22 NG88

◆◆◆◆ ⌂

Mellondale

47 Mellon Charles IV22 2JL
☎ 01445 731326 🖺 01445 731326
e-mail mellondale@lineone.net
web www.mellondale.co.uk
Dir A832 to Aultbea & Mellon Charles

Set in 1 acre of well-tended gardens on an elevated location, Mellondale offers spectacular views of Loch Ewe. Bedrooms are attractively decorated, well presented and have many thoughtful extra touches. There is a spacious lounge where a friendly relaxed atmosphere prevails, and a homely dining room where delicious home-cooked meals are served at individual tables.

Facilities 4 en suite (2 GF) ⊘ TVB tea/coffee 🐾 Cen ht TVL No coaches Dinner **Parking** 6 **Notes** Closed Nov-Mar

AVIEMORE

MAP 23 NH81

Premier Collection

◆◆◆◆◆

The Old Minister's House

Rothiemurchus PH22 1QH
☎ 01479 812181 🖺 01479 812181
e-mail theoldministershouse@btinternet.com
Dir B970 from Aviemore signed Glenmore & Coylumbridge, establishment 0.75m at Inverdruie

Built originally as a manse in 1906, The Old Minister's House stands in well-tended grounds close to Aviemore. The house is beautifully furnished and immaculately maintained. Bedrooms are spacious, attractively decorated and thoughtfully equipped. There is an inviting lounge and a dining room where hearty breakfasts are served.

Facilities 4 en suite (1 fmly) ⊘ TVB tea/coffee 🐾 Cen ht No children 12yrs No coaches **Prices** S £42; D £65-£70✲ **Parking** 4

◆◆◆◆

Ravenscraig Guest House ◇

Grampian Rd PH22 1RP ☎ 01479 810278 🖺 01479 810210
e-mail info@aviemoreonline.com
web www.aviemoreonline.com
Dir N end of main street, 250yds N of police station

This friendly, family-run guest house is on the north side of the village, a short walk from local amenities. Bedrooms vary between the traditionally styled rooms in the main house and modern spacious rooms in a brand new chalet style annexe. There is a relaxing lounge and separate dining room, where freshly prepared breakfasts are served at individual tables.

Facilities 6 en suite 6 annexe en suite (6 fmly) (6 GF) ⊘ TVB tea/coffee 🐾 Cen ht TVL **Prices** S £25-£35; D £50-£70✲ **Parking** 15

◆◆◆

Cairngorm

Grampian Rd PH22 1RP ☎ 01479 810630
e-mail conns@lineone.net
Dir Off A9 at Aviemore junct, then left at B9152. On N side of Main Rd, opp war memorial

The Cairngorm is an extended detached house within easy walking distance of the village centre and amenities. All of the bedrooms are bright, well equipped and comfortable. There is a relaxing lounge with a log fire and a selection of games. Breakfast is served at individual tables in the conservatory dining room.

Facilities 12 en suite (2 fmly) (5 GF) ⊘ TVB tea/coffee 🐾 Cen ht TVL No coaches Corporate member of Dalfaber country leisure club. **Prices** D £50-£80✲ LB **Parking** 12

Dell Druie Guest House ◇

Inverdruie, Rothiemurchus PH22 1QH ☎ 01479 810934
e-mail delldruiebandb@btinternet.com
Dir *From Aviemore take B970 to Cairngorms, take sharp left after Rothiemurchus Vistor Centre. Dell Drurie is last house in cul-de-sac.*

At the time of going to press the rating for this establishment had not been confirmed. Please check the AA website www.theAA.com for up-to-date information.

Facilities 3 rms (2 en suite) (1 GF) ⊗ STV TVB tea/coffee ✖ Cen ht TVL No children 14yrs No coaches Fishing **Prices** S £28-£35; D £60-£70✱ **Parking** 6 **Notes** Closed 12-19 Jun 🐾

BONAR BRIDGE   MAP 23 NH69

◆◆◆

Kyle House ◇

Dornoch Rd IV24 3EB ☎ 01863 766360 📄 01863 766360
e-mail kylehouse360@msn.com
Dir *On A949 N from village centre*

A spacious house with splendid views of the Kyle of Sutherland and the hills beyond. Bedrooms are comfortably furnished in traditional style and equipped with all the expected facilities. There is a lounge and hearty breakfasts are enjoyed in the dining room.

Facilities 5 rms (3 en suite) (2 fmly) ⊗ TVB tea/coffee ✖ Cen ht TVL No children 5yrs No coaches **Prices** S £23-£26; D £46-£52 **Parking** 5 **Notes** Closed Dec-Jan rs Oct & Apr 🐾

BRORA   MAP 23 NC90

Premier Collection

◆◆◆◆◆ 🏠

Glenaveron

Golf Rd KW9 6QS ☎ 01408 621601
e-mail glenaveron@hotmail.com
web www.glenaveron.co.uk
Dir *A9 NE into Brora, right onto Golf Rd, 2nd house on right*

Glenaveron stands in lovely landscaped gardens a short distance from the beach and golf course. This delightful family home offers a friendly and relaxing atmosphere. The comfortabe bedrooms are spacious and well equipped, with a ground-floor bedroom for easier access. There is an inviting lounge, and excellent breakfasts are served house-party style in the elegant dining room.

continued

Facilities 3 en suite (1 GF) ⊗ TVB tea/coffee ✖ Cen ht No coaches **Prices** S £35-£50; D £60-£64✱ **Parking** 6

CARRBRIDGE   MAP 23 NH92

◆◆◆◆ 🏠 ☕

Carrmoor Guest House ◇

Carr Rd PH23 3AD ☎ 01479 841244 📄 01479 841244
e-mail christine@carrmoorguesthouse.co.uk
web www.carrmoorguesthouse.co.uk
Dir *Carr Rd opp church & village hall, Carrmoor on left*

A welcoming atmosphere prevails at this immaculately maintained guest house. Bedrooms feature attractive colour schemes, are well-equipped and comfortably modern in appointment. There is a cosy lounge for peaceful relaxation and an inviting dining room where delicious cuisine using quality fresh ingredients is served. Vegetarian and children's options are available.

Facilities 6 en suite (1 fmly) (1 GF) ⊗ TV1B tea/coffee Licensed Cen ht TVL No coaches Dinner Last d 8pm **Prices** S £30; D £52 **Parking** 6

◆◆◆

Pines Country House ◇

Duthil PH23 3ND ☎ 01479 841220 📄 01479 841220 *51
e-mail Lynn@thepines-duthil.fsnet.co.uk
Dir *2m E of Carrbridge in Duthil on A938*

A warm welcome is assured at this comfortable home in the Cairngorms National Park. The bright bedrooms are traditionally furnished and offer the good amenities. Enjoyable home-cooked fare is served around a communal table. You can relax watching squirrels feed in the nearby wood from the conservatory-lounge.

Facilities 4 en suite (1 fmly) (1 GF) ⊗ STV TVB tea/coffee Cen ht No coaches Dinner Last d 4pm **Prices** S £30; D £45-£46✱ LB **Parking** 5

Ⓐ

The Cairn Hotel ◇

Main Rd PH23 3AS ☎ 01479 841212 📄 01479 841362
e-mail info@cairnhotel.co.uk
web www.cairnhotel.co.uk
Dir *In village centre*

Facilities 7 rms (5 en suite) (2 fmly) ⊗ STV TVB tea/coffee Direct dial from bedrooms ✖ Licensed Pool Table Dinner Last d 8.30pm **Prices** S £24-£32; D £52 **Parking** 20 **Notes** ★★★ Closed 25 Dec

DALCROSS

MAP 23 NH74

◆◆◆◆

Easter Dalziel Farmhouse

Easter Dalziel Farm IV2 7JL
☎ 01667 462213 🖶 01667 462213
e-mail aa@easterdalzielfarm.co.uk
Dir From Inverness A96 5m NE, left onto B9039 signed Castle Stuart, farm 2m on right, farmhouse 300yds

Expect a friendly welcome at this Victorian farmhouse, which stands amid wooded countryside near Inverness Airport. Bedrooms are furnished in traditional styles. The lounge has a piano, stereo and a television, and breakfasts are served at a communal table in the adjacent dining room. Self catering is also available.

Facilities 3 rms ⊗ in dining room tea/coffee TVL Dinner Last d 24hrs
Parking 10 **Notes** Closed 20 Dec-6 Jan rs 1-19 Dec & 7 Jan-Feb

DORNOCH

MAP 23 NH78

Premier Collection

◆◆◆◆◆ ⊛⊛ 🔒 ⬡

2 Quail Restaurant and Rooms

Castle St IV25 3SN ☎ 01862 811811
e-mail theAA@2quail.com
Dir On main street, 200yds from cathedral

This delightful restaurant with rooms is close to the town centre and historic cathedral. The stylish, individual bedrooms are all thoughtfully equipped. Food is a real feature, with local produce featuring extensively on the creative menu.

Facilities 3 en suite (1 fmly) ⊗ TVB tea/coffee Direct dial from bedrooms ✘ Licensed Cen ht No children 8yrs No coaches Dinner **Prices** S £70-£90; D £80-£100✹ **LB Notes** Closed Xmas & 2 wks Feb/Mar rs Nov-Mar

◆◆◆

Achandean

The Meadows IV25 3SF ☎ 01862 810413 🖶 01862 810413
e-mail basilhellier@amserve.net
Dir A9 onto A949 to Dornoch, right opp Eagle Hotel, 1st left & house on left opp fire station

This modern bungalow stands in well-tended gardens just behind the main street and is an excellent base for exploring the northern Highlands. The friendly proprietors warmly welcome guests old and new. The spacious bedrooms are well equipped and comfortable, two being particularly spacious.

Facilities 3 en suite (3 GF) ⊗ TVB tea/coffee Cen ht TVL No children No coaches **Parking** 3 **Notes** Closed mid Oct-Feb rs Mar ⊜

DRUMNADROCHIT

MAP 23 NH53

◆◆◆◆

Ferness Cottage

Lewiston IV63 6UW ☎ 01456 450564 🖶 01456 459055
e-mail glenferness@btopenworld.com
web www.lochnessaccommodation.co.uk
Dir A82, from Inverness turn right after Esso service station, from Fort William left before Esso service station, 0.25m telephone box Ferness is opp 4th house on left

This rose-covered cottage dating from the 1840s has a peaceful location within easy walking distance of the village centre. The two charming bedrooms are well equipped, with many thoughtful extra touches. Traditional breakfasts in the cosy lounge-dining room feature the best of local produce. Guests can use the patio and garden, and self-catering apartments are available.

Facilities 2 rms (1 en suite) (1 pri facs) ⊗ TVB tea/coffee Cen ht No coaches Fishing **Prices** S £35-£60; D £44-£60✹ **LB Parking** 6

◆◆◆◆

Clunebeg Lodge

Clunebeg Estate IV63 6US
☎ 01456 450387 🖶 01456 450152
e-mail info@clunebeg.com
web www.clunebeg.com
Dir Off A82 S of Drumnadrochit signed Bunloit. 100yds next right up private track to Clunebeg Estate

A warm welcome awaits you here in the unspoiled Glen Urquhart. It is ideal for walkers and cyclists as the Great Glen Way passes the doorstep. The attractive ground-floor bedrooms are very well equipped, and there is a spacious lounge-dining room with Internet access, a wide-screen television, a DVD and a video. A luxury apartment in the main house is beautifully furnished and equipped. A

continued

full breakfast, snacks and packed lunches are available, and there are two patios.

Facilities 6 en suite (6 GF) ⊘ TVB tea/coffee Licensed Cen ht TVL No children 15yrs No coaches Fishing **Prices** S £41-£54; D £55-£72✳ LB **Parking** 6

◆◆◆◆
Glen Rowan Guest House ◇
West Lewiston IV63 6UW ☎ 01456 450235
e-mail info@glenrowan.co.uk
Dir *From Inverness A82 to Drumnadrochit & Lewiston, right after Esso station, Glen Rowan 600yds on left*

Please note that this establishment has recently changed hands. Set in a peaceful village, Glen Rowan offers smartly furnished and well-equipped accommodation. Neat gardens surround the house and rooms at the rear overlook the River Coiltie. There is a choice of comfortable lounges, and a smart dining room where delicious home-cooked fare is served at individual tables. Bicycle storage and drying facilities are available.

Facilities 3 en suite (2 fmly) (3 GF) ⊘ TVB tea/coffee ✻ Cen ht No coaches Fishing **Prices** S £22-£37.50; D £44-£55✳ LB **Parking** 3

Ⓐ
Elmbank Bed & Breakfast ◇
Lewston IV63 6UW ☎ 01456 450372
e-mail info@elmbank-lochness.co.uk
web www.elmbank-lochness.co.uk
Dir *A28 Drumnadrochit, 600yds off main road at West Lewston Rd*
Facilities 2 annexe en suite (2 GF) ⊘ tea/coffee ✻ Cen ht No coaches
Prices S £20-£34; D £40-£48✳ LB **Parking** 3 **Notes** ★★★

FORT WILLIAM
MAP 22 NN17
See also **Spean Bridge**

◆◆◆◆◆
Ashburn House
8 Achintore Rd PH33 6RQ
☎ 01397 706000 ▤ 01397 702024
e-mail christine@no-1.fsworld.co.uk
web www.highland5star.co.uk
Dir *500yds S of town centre on A82*

Having spectacular views of Loch Linnhe and the Ardgour Hills, this

elegant Victorian villa is within easy walking distance of the town centre. It has been lovingly restored to its former glory and offers spacious, individually decorated and well-equipped bedrooms. There is a sunny conservatory lounge and an attractive dining room, which is an appropriate setting for the delicious breakfasts.

Ashburn House

Facilities 7 en suite (1 fmly) (2 GF) ⊘ TVB tea/coffee ✻ Cen ht No coaches phone line for internet access **Prices** S £40-£50; D £80-£100✳ LB **Parking** 8

◆◆◆◆◆
The Grange
Grange Rd PH33 6JF ☎ 01397 705516 ▤ 01397 701595
e-mail info@thegrange-scotland.co.uk
web www.thegrange-scotland.co.uk
Dir *A82 S from Fort William, 300yds from rdbt left onto Ashburn Ln, at top on left*

This lovely Victorian villa stands in immaculate gardens on an elevated position with beautiful views of Loch Linnhe. Attractive decor and pretty fabrics have been used to good effect in the charming bedrooms, two of which have loch views. There is ample provision of books and fresh flowers in the carefully furnished lounge, and the elegant dining room is a lovely setting for hearty breakfasts.

Facilities 4 en suite ⊘ TVB tea/coffee ✻ Cen ht No children 13yrs **Prices** D £95-£110✳ LB **Parking** 4 **Notes** Closed Nov-Mar

continued

Scotland

FORT WILLIAM continued

◆◆◆◆◆ 🏛

Distillery House ◇

Nevis Bridge, North Rd PH33 6LR
☎ 01397 700103 📄 01397 702980
e-mail disthouse@aol.com
Dir A82 from Fort William towards Inverness, on left after Glen Nevis rdbt

Situated in the grounds of the former Glenlochy Distillery, this friendly guest house was once the distillery manager's home. Bedrooms are attractively decorated, comfortably furnished and very well equipped. There is a relaxing lounge, which features a superb range of games, and a bright airy dining room where traditional Scottish breakfasts are served at individual tables.

Facilities 10 en suite (1 fmly) (1 GF) ⊗ TVB tea/coffee ✈ Cen ht
No coaches **Prices** S £28-£40; D £56-£90✳ **LB Parking** 21

◆◆◆◆

Lochan Cottage Guest House

Lochyside PH33 7NX ☎ 01397 702695
e-mail lochanco@btopenworld.com
web www.fortwilliam-guesthouse.co.uk
Dir A82 N from Fort William signed Inverness, left onto A830, left onto B8006 by Farm Foods to Lochyside

A friendly welcome is extended at this charming house, situated in 1 acre of beautiful well-tended gardens with stunning panoramic views over Ben Nevis and Aonach Mor. Bedrooms are comfortable, attractive and well equipped. There is a spacious lounge and a charming conservatory style dining room where delicious breakfasts are served.

Facilities 6 en suite (6 GF) ⊗ TVB tea/coffee ✈ Cen ht No children 16yrs No coaches **Prices** D £48-£66✳ **LB Parking** 10 **Notes** Closed Xmas

◆◆◆◆

Mansefield Guest House ◇

Corpach PH33 7LT ☎ 01397 772262 & 0845 6449432
e-mail mansefield@btinternet.com
web www.fortwilliamaccommodation.com
Dir 2m N of Fort William A82 onto A830, house 2m on A830 in Corpach

Peacefully set in its own well-tended garden this friendly, family-run guest house provides comfortable, attractively decorated and well-equipped accommodation. There is a cosy lounge, where a roaring coal fire burns on cold evenings, and an attractive dining room where delicious, home-cooked evening meals and breakfasts are served at individual tables.

Facilities 6 en suite (1 fmly) (1 GF) ⊗ TVB tea/coffee ✈ Cen ht TVL No children 12yrs No coaches Dinner Last d noon **Prices** S £22-£32; D £44-£56✳ **LB Parking** 7

◆◆◆◆

Seangan Croft

Seangan Bridge, Banavie PH33 7PB
☎ 01397 773114 & 772228
e-mail seangan-chalets@fortwilliam59.freeserve.co.uk
Dir A82 onto A830, 1m right onto B8004 Gairlochy, house 2m opp An Crann Restaurant

This modern bungalow on the north side of the Caledonian Canal has stunning views of Ben Nevis and the ski slopes of Aonach Mor. The well-equipped bedrooms are contemporary in style and there is a spacious comfortable lounge. Full breakfasts are served in the neat dining room. If dinner is required guests can eat at the An Crann (The Plough) Restaurant across the road, also run by Sinè Ross.

Facilities 3 en suite ⊗ TVB tea/coffee Licensed Cen ht TVL No coaches Dinner Last d 9pm **Parking** 6 **Notes** Closed Dec-Feb

◆◆◆

Glenlochy Guest House ◇

Nevis Bridge PH33 6LP ☎ 01397 702909
e-mail glenlochy1@aol.com
Dir A82 from Inverness, guest house on left after 2nd lights

The well-tended garden of this friendly, family-run guest house marks the end of the famous West Highland Way. Bedrooms are pleasantly decorated and well equipped. There is a comfortable first-floor lounge and a bright, airy ground-floor dining room, where hearty breakfasts are served at individual tables.

Facilities 10 rms (9 en suite) (1 pri facs) 2 annexe en suite (2 fmly) (7 GF) ⊗ TVB tea/coffee ✈ Cen ht TVL No coaches **Prices** S £25-£65; D £50-£76 **LB Parking** 13

See advertisement on opposite page

◆◆◆
Benview Guest House ◇

Belford Rd PH33 6ER ☎ 01397 702966
e-mail benview@gowanbrae.co.uk
Dir *Near town centre on A82 Inverness-Glasgow road*

There is a friendly welcome at this popular guest house, which stands at the northern end of town. Bedrooms are well equipped and have smart decor, and there is a choice of lounges. Traditional breakfasts are served at individual tables the bright airy dining room.

Facilities 11 rms (9 en suite) (2 pri facs) ⊗ TVB tea/coffee ✖ Cen ht TVL **Prices** S £20-£34; D £43-£62✳ **LB** **Parking** 20 **Notes** Closed Nov-Feb ⊛

◆◆◆
Stobhan B & B ◇

Fassifern Rd PH33 6BD ☎ 01397 702790 📄 01397 702790
e-mail boggi@supanet.com
Dir *A82 onto Victoria Rd beside St Mary's Church, right onto Fassifern Rd, 1st house on right*

Stobhan Bed and Breakfast occupies an elevated location overlooking Loch Linnhe and offers comfortable, good-value accommodation. Bedrooms, one of which is on the ground floor, are traditionally furnished and have en suite facilities. Breakfast is served in the ground-floor dining room, which is adjacent to the lounge.

Facilities 4 en suite (1 GF) ⊗ TVB tea/coffee Cen ht Dinner Last d 6pm **Prices** S £22-£28; D £40-£56

Berkeley House ◇

Belford Rd PH33 6BT ☎ 01397 701185
e-mail berkeleyhouse67@hotmail.com
Dir *On A82 at N end of town adjacent to St Mary's Church*

Facilities 7 en suite (1 fmly) (1 GF) ⊗ TVB tea/coffee ✖ Cen ht TVL No coaches **Prices** S £22-£32; D £44-£60✳ **Parking** 7 **Notes** ★★★ Closed 23-27 Dec

🅰
Lochview

Heathercroft, Argyll Rd PH33 6RE ☎ 01397 703149
e-mail info@lochview.co.uk
Dir *Off A82 rdbt at S end of town centre onto Lundavra Rd, left onto Argyll Ter, 1st right onto Heathercroft to top*

Facilities 6 en suite ⊗ TVB tea/coffee ✖ Cen ht No coaches **Prices** S £32-£40; D £54-£64 **Parking** 6 **Notes** ★★★ Closed Oct-Apr

FOYERS
MAP 23 NH42

◆◆◆◆ ⊜
Foyers Bay House

Lochness IV2 6YB ☎ 01456 486624 📄 01456 486337
e-mail carol@foyersbay.co.uk
web www.foyersbay.co.uk
Dir *Off B852 into Lower Foyers*

Situated in sloping grounds with pines and abundant colourful rhododendrons, this delightful Victorian villa has stunning views of Loch Ness. The attractive bedrooms vary in size and are well equipped. There is a comfortable lounge next to the plant-filled conservatory-cafe, where delicious evening meals and traditional breakfasts are served. Self-catering accommodation is also available.

Facilities 6 en suite (1 GF) ⊗ TVB tea/coffee Direct dial from bedrooms ✖ Licensed Cen ht TVL No coaches Dinner Last d 8pm **Prices** S £33-£48; D £56-£66✳ **LB** **Parking** 6

Scotland

GAIRLOCH

MAP 22 NG87

◆◆◆◆

The Old Inn

Flowerdale Glen IV21 2BD
☎ 01445 712006 📠 01445 712445
e-mail info@theoldinn.net
web www.theoldinn.co.uk
Dir A832 into Gairloch, establishment on right opp Gairloch harbour

Situated close to the harbour, this well-established and lively inn has an idyllic location overlooking the burn and the old bridge. A good range of meals, many featuring seafood, are served in the bars and dining areas, and outside at picnic tables on finer days. Live music is a feature several evenings a week. Bedrooms are well equipped and attractively decorated.

Facilities 14 en suite (3 fmly) (2 GF) ⊘ STV TVB tea/coffee Direct dial from bedrooms Cen ht No coaches Pool Table Dinner Last d 9.30pm
Conf Max 20 Thtr 35 Class 15 Board 20 **Parking** 40 **Notes** Civ Wed 40

GLENCOE

MAP 22 NN15

◆◆◆◆

Fern Villa

Loanfern PH49 4JE ☎ 01855 811393 📠 01855 811727
e-mail fernctg@aol.com
web www.fernvilla.com
For full entry see **South Ballachulish**

◆◆◆◆

Lyn-Leven Guest House

West Laroch PH49 4JP ☎ 01855 811392 📠 01855 811600
e-mail macleodcilla@aol.com
For full entry see **South Ballachulish**

◆◆◆

Scorrybreac Guest House ◇

PH49 4HT ☎ 01855 811354 📠 01855 811024
e-mail info@scorrybreac.co.uk
Dir Off A82 just outside village, 500yds from Bridge of Coe

Having a stunning location above the village and overlooking the loch, this charming family-run guest house offers guests a warm welcome. Bedrooms are attractive, well equipped and comfortably furnished. There is a cosy lounge where books, board games and maps abound, and a bright airy dining room where delicious breakfasts and evening meals (by arrangement) are served at individual tables.

Facilities 6 en suite (6 GF) ⊘ TVB tea/coffee ✖ Cen ht No coaches Permits available for fishing 0.25m from house Dinner Last d 3pm
Prices S £28-£34; D £42-£52 **LB Parking** 8

GRANTOWN-ON-SPEY

MAP 23 NJ02

Premier Collection

◆◆◆◆◆

An Cala Guest House

Woodlands Ter PH26 3JU
☎ 01479 873293 📠 01479 873293
e-mail ancala@globalnet.co.uk
web www.ancala.info
Dir From Aviemore on the A95 bear left on the B9102 at the rdbt outside Grantown. After 400yds, 1st left & An Cala opp

An Cala is an impressive Victorian house on an elevated location within easy walking distance of the town centre. Bedrooms are beautifully furnished, attractively decorated and well equipped. There is a comfortable lounge complete with log burning stove and an elegant dining room, where delicious evening meals and hearty breakfasts are served.

continued

Facilities 4 en suite (1 fmly) ⊘ TVB tea/coffee ✗ Cen ht TVL
No children 3yrs No coaches Dinner Last d 24hrs notice
Prices S £47-£55; D £56-£60 **LB** **Parking** 6 **Notes** Closed Xmas

◆◆◆◆ 🏛

Rossmor Guest House ◇

Woodlands Ter PH26 3JU
☎ 01479 872201 📄 01479 872201
e-mail RossmorGrantown@yahoo.com
web www.rossmor.co.uk
Dir 500yds SW of village centre on B9102

Built in 1887, this delightful house has an elevated position in
landscaped gardens, close to the town centre. Bedrooms, including
one with a beautifully crafted four-poster bed, are well proportioned.
The lounge and dining room have fine views over the surrounding
hills. Dinners are available, in winter only, by arrangement.

Facilities 6 en suite (2 fmly) ⊘ TVB tea/coffee ✗ Cen ht No children
16yrs No coaches Dinner Last d prior day **Prices** S £28-£40; D £54-£76✳
LB **Parking** 6

◆◆◆◆

Holmhill House ◇

Woodside Av PH26 3JR ☎ 01479 873977
e-mail enquiries@holmhillhouse
Dir S of town centre off A939 Spey Av

Built in 1895, and situated in a large well-tended garden within
walking distance of the town centre, Holmhill House combines
Victorian character with modern comforts. The attractive bedrooms are
well equipped, and all but two are en suite. There is a games room
suitable for all ages, and a ramp and lift is available for easier access
plus a specially equipped bathroom. Children are also well catered for
with games, toys, crayons and videos available.

Facilities 6 rms (4 en suite) (2 pri facs) (2 fmly) ⊘ TVB tea/coffee ✗
Lift Cen ht No coaches Childrens indoor playroom **Prices** S £25-£30;
D £60-£70✳ **Parking** 8 **Notes** Closed Nov-Mar 🐾

INVERGARRY
MAP 22 NH30

Forest Lodge Guest House

South Laggan PH34 4EA
☎ 01809 501219 & 07790 907477 📄 01809 501476
e-mail info@flgh.co.uk
Dir 0.5m on left past sign for South Laggan.

Facilities 7 rms (6 en suite) (1 pri facs) (3 fmly) (3 GF) ⊘ tea/coffee
Licensed Cen ht TVL No coaches Dinner Last d 5pm **Prices** S £33; d fr
£50✳ **LB** **Parking** 11

◆◆◆◆

Craigard Guest House ◇

PH35 4HG ☎ 01809 501258
e-mail bob@craigard.saltire.org
Dir A82 onto A87, house on right, 0.5m beyond village towards Skye

A warm welcome awaits you at this delightful family-run guest house,
which stands in a well-tended garden at the edge of the village.
Bedrooms are spacious and well equipped, and several have original
fireplaces. The comfortable lounge has a wide selection of reading
material. Breakfast is served at individual tables in the attractive
ground-floor dining room.

Facilities 7 rms (5 en suite) ⊘ STV TVB tea/coffee ✗ Licensed TVL
No children 12yrs No coaches **Prices** S £28.50-£30; d fr £55✳
Parking 10

INVERNESS
MAP 23 NH64
See also **Dalcross**

Premier Collection

◆◆◆◆◆ 🏛 🍽

The Lodge-Daviot Mains

Daviot Mains IV2 5ER ☎ 01463 772215 📄 01463 772099
e-mail info@thelodge-daviotmains.co.uk
web www.thelodge-daviotmains.co.uk
Dir Off A9 5m S of Inverness onto B851 signed Croy. B&B 1m on left

Standing in 80 acres of peaceful pasture land, this impressive
establishment offers attractive, well-appointed and equipped
bedrooms. The master bedroom is furnished with a four-poster bed.
There is a tranquil lounge with deep sofas and a real fire, and a
peaceful dining room where delicious evening meals (by
arrangement) and hearty breakfasts featuring the best of local produce
are served.

Facilities 7 en suite (1 GF) ⊘ FTV TVB tea/coffee Direct dial from
bedrooms Licensed Cen ht TVL No children 5yrs No coaches Dinner
Last d 10am **Prices** S £40-£45; D £75-£95✳ **LB** **Parking** 10
Notes Closed telephone for dates

See advertisement on page 647

Scotland

Scotland

INVERNESS continued

Premier Collection

◆◆◆◆◆
Trafford Bank

96 Fairfield Rd IV3 5LL ☎ 01463 241414 📠 01463 241421
e-mail info@traffordbankhotel.co.uk
Dir *Off A82 at Kenneth St, Fairfield Rd 2nd left, 600yds on right*

This impressive Victorian house lies in a quiet residential area within easy walking distance of the canal and city centre. Stylish modern bedrooms come with thoughtful extra touches. There is also a choice of homely lounges. Carefully prepared breakfasts are served in the new conservatory breakfast room, which features interesting wrought-iron chairs.

Facilities 5 en suite (2 fmly) ⊗ TVB tea/coffee ✖ Cen ht TVL **Parking** 8
See advertisement on opposite page

Premier Collection

◆◆◆◆◆ 🛏
Ballifeary Guest House

10 Ballifeary Rd IV3 5PJ ☎ 01463 235572 📠 01463 717583
e-mail william.gilbert@btconnect.com
web www.ballifearyhousehotel.co.uk
Dir *Off A82, 0.5m from town centre, turn left onto Bishops Rd & sharp right onto Ballifeary Rd*

This charming detached house has a peaceful residential location within easy walking distance of the town centre and Eden Court Theatre. The attractive bedrooms are carefully appointed and well equipped. There is an elegant ground-floor drawing room and a comfortable dining room, where delicious breakfasts, featuring the best of local produce, are served at individual tables.

Facilities 6 en suite (1 GF) ⊗ TVB tea/coffee ✖ Cen ht No children 15yrs No coaches **Prices** S £35-£65; D £60-£76 **LB Parking** 6
Notes Closed 25-28 Dec

◆◆◆◆◆
Moyness House

6 Bruce Gdns IV3 5EN ☎ 01463 233836 📠 01463 233836
e-mail stay@moyness.co.uk
web www.moyness.co.uk
Dir *Off A82 Fort William road, almost opp Highland Regional Council headquarters*

Situated in a quiet residential area just a short distance from the city centre, this elegant Victorian villa dates from 1880 and offers beautifully decorated, comfortable bedrooms and well-appointed bathrooms. There is an attractive sitting room and an inviting dining room, where traditional Scottish breakfasts are served. Guests are welcome to use the secluded and well-maintained back garden.

Facilities 7 en suite (1 fmly) (2 GF) ⊗ TVB tea/coffee Cen ht
No coaches **Prices** S £32-£40; D £64-£80 **LB Parking** 10

◆◆◆◆
Westbourne

50 Huntly St IV3 5HS ☎ 01463 220700 📠 01463 220700
e-mail richard@westbourne.org.uk
Dir *A9 onto A82 at football stadium, over 3 rdbts & Friars Bridge, 1st left onto Wells St & Huntly St*

The immaculately maintained Westbourne Guest House looks across the River Ness to the city centre. This friendly, family-run house has bright modern bedrooms of varying size, all attractively furnished in pine and very well equipped. The ground-floor bedroom has been specially furnished for easier access. A relaxing lounge with Internet access, books, games and puzzles is available. Richard Paxton is a top-twenty finalist for AA Landlady of the Year 2006.

Facilities 10 en suite (3 fmly) (1 GF) ⊗ TVB tea/coffee Cen ht
No coaches **Prices** S £42; D £60-£70 **LB Parking** 6 **Notes** Closed Xmas & New Year

♦♦♦♦

Acorn House

2A Bruce Gdns IV3 5EN
☎ 01463 717021 & 240000 📠 01463 714236
e-mail enquiries@acorn-house.freeserve.co.uk
web www.acorn-house.freeserve.co.uk
Dir *From town centre onto A82, on W side of river, right onto Bruce Gardens*

A warm welcome awaits you at this attractive detached house, just a 5-minute walk from the town centre. Bedrooms are attractive and well equipped. Breakfast and dinner are served at individual tables in the bright spacious dining room, followed by coffee in the comfortable lounge.

Facilities 6 en suite (3 fmly) ⊘ STV TVB tea/coffee Cen ht TVL Sauna Dinner Last d 4.30pm **Prices** S £40-£49.95; D £59-£65✳ **LB Parking** 7

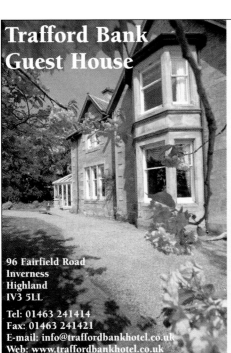

Scotland

INVERNESS continued

◆◆◆◆

The Ghillies Lodge

16 Island Bank Rd IV2 4QS
☎ 01463 232137 ▤ 01463 713744
e-mail info@ghillieslodge.com
Dir *1m SW from town centre on B862, pink house facing the river*

Situated on the banks of the River Ness not far from the city centre, Ghillies Lodge offers comfortable accommodation in a relaxed, peaceful environment. The attractive bedrooms, one of which is on the ground floor, are all en suite, and are individually styled and well equipped. There is a comfortable lounge-dining room, and a conservatory that overlooks the river.

Facilities 3 en suite (1 GF) ⊗ STV TVB tea/coffee Cen ht TVL
No coaches **Prices** S £35-£50; D £50-£60✳ **Parking** 4

◆◆◆◆ ❦

Taransay *(NH707436)*

Lower Muckovie Farm, Inshes IV2 5BB
☎ 01463 231880 ▤ 01463 231880 Mrs Munro
e-mail aileen@munro2.freeserve.co.uk
web www.scotland-info.co.uk/taransay
Dir *A9 onto B9177, past Drumossie Hotel, down hill, B&B signed at farm road on right*

This comfortable modern home is adjacent to the family farm on the outskirts of town, and has stunning views of the Moray Firth. The attractive bedrooms are designed to make good use of space, and are well equipped. There is a comfortable lounge, and substantial breakfasts are served around a large communal table in the adjacent dining room.

Facilities 2 rms (1 en suite) (1 pri facs) (1 fmly) (2 GF) ⊗ TVB
tea/coffee ✖ Cen ht TVL 170 acres beef **Prices** D £42-£44 **Parking** 3
Notes ⊛

◆◆◆

Fraser House ◇

49 Huntly St IV3 5HS ☎ 01463 716488 ▤ 01463 716488
e-mail fraserlea@btopenworld.com
web www.fraserhouse.co.uk
Dir *A82 W over bridge, left onto Huntly St, house 100yds*

Situated on the west bank of the River Ness, Fraser House has a commanding position overlooking the city, and is within easy walking

distance of the central amenities. Bedrooms, all en suite, vary in size and are comfortably furnished and well equipped. The ground-floor dining room is the setting for freshly cooked Scottish breakfasts.

Facilities 5 en suite (2 fmly) ⊗ TVB tea/coffee Cen ht
Prices S £30-£35; D £50-£60 **Notes** ⊛

◆◆◆

Park Guest House

51 Glenurquhart Rd IV3 5PB ☎ 01463 231858
e-mail hendry.robertson@connectfree.co.uk
Dir *From town centre onto A82, on W side of river*

The substantial, ivy-clad Victorian villa has a neat front garden, the attractive bedrooms are comfortable and well equipped. There is a peaceful ground-floor lounge, and a cheerful breakfast room where traditional breakfasts are served at individual tables.

Facilities 6 rms (3 en suite) (3 fmly) ⊗ TVB tea/coffee Cen ht TVL
No coaches **Parking** 6

◆◆◆

St Ann's House

37 Harrowden Rd IV3 5QN
☎ 01463 236157 ▤ 01463 236157
e-mail stannshous@aol.com
Dir *Off rdbt junct A82 & A862 on W side of bridge*

Located only a 10-minute walk from the city centre, this family-run guest house offers a warm welcome. The attractive bedrooms are well equipped, and refreshments can be enjoyed in the inviting lounge. Tasty breakfasts are served at individual tables in the bright airy dining room, which overlooks the delightful rear garden.

Facilities 6 rms (5 en suite) (1 pri facs) (2 fmly) (1 GF) ⊗ TVB
tea/coffee ✖ Licensed Cen ht TVL No coaches **Prices** D £50-£72 **LB**
Parking 4 **Notes** ⊛

continued

♦♦♦
Sunnyholm ◇
12 Mayfield Rd IV2 4AE ☎ 01463 231336 📠 01463 715788
e-mail sunnyholm@aol.com
web www.invernessguesthouse.com
Dir *500yds SE of town centre. Off B861 Culduthel Rd onto Mayfield Rd*

Situated in a peaceful residential area within easy walking distance of the city centre, Sunnyholm offers comfortably proportioned and well-equipped bedrooms. A spacious conservatory-lounge overlooks the rear garden, and there is a another lounge next to the bright, airy dining room.

Facilities 4 en suite (4 GF) ⊗ TVB tea/coffee ✖ Cen ht No children 3yrs No coaches **Prices** S £30-£35; D £45-£50✳ **Parking** 6 **Notes** ✿

🅰
Cedar Villa ◇
33 Kenneth St IV3 5DH ☎ 01463 230477
e-mail cedarvilla@guesthouseinverness.co.uk
web www.guesthouseinverness.co.uk
Dir *A9 onto A82 across Friars Bridge, left at rdbt onto Kenneth St*

Facilities 6 rms (3 en suite) (1 pri facs) (3 fmly) ⊗ TVB tea/coffee ✖ Cen ht **Prices** S £25-£30; D £40-£60✳ LB **Notes** ★★★ Closed 19-29 Dec

JOHN O' GROATS
MAP 23 ND37

♦♦♦♦ 🏰🍴
Creag-Na-Mara ◇
KW14 8XL ☎ 01847 851850 📠 01847 851713
e-mail helen@suttonh.fsworld.co.uk
web www.creagnamara.co.uk
Dir *On A836, 5m W of John O'Groats*

Lying some 5m west of John O'Groats and just over 1m from the Castle of Mey, Creag-Na-Mara has stunning views towards the Pentland Firth, Dunnet Head and the Orkney Islands beyond. Bedrooms, one of which is suitable for families are well equipped, attractive and comfortably proportioned. There is a peaceful lounge complete with a fire for the cooler days, and a spacious conservatory-lounge and restaurant where delicious fare featuring the best of local produce is served at individual tables.

Facilities 4 en suite (1 fmly) (1 GF) ⊗ TVB tea/coffee ✖ Licensed Cen ht TVL No children 3yrs No coaches Dinner Last d 8.30pm **Prices** S £23-£35; D £46-£60✳ **Parking** 4

KINGUSSIE
MAP 23 NH70

Premier Collection

★★★★★ ◉◉◉ 🏰🍴 **Restaurant with Rooms**
The Cross at Kingussie
Tweed Mill Brae, Ardbroilach Rd PH21 1LB
☎ 01540 661166 📠 01540 661080
e-mail relax@thecross.co.uk
Dir *From lights in Kingussie centre, along Ardbroilach Rd for 300mtrs, left into Tweed Mill Brae*

Situated in the valley above the town of Kingussie, the old tweed mill lies next to a river, with wild-flower gardens and a sunny terrace. Hospitality and food are clearly strengths at this special restaurant with rooms. Bedrooms are spacious and airy, fluffy towels and handmade toiletries provide extra luxury

Facilities 8 en suite (1 fmly) TVB Direct dial from bedrooms ✖ Licensed No children 8yrs No coaches Petanque Dinner Last d 8.30pm **Prices** S £120-£210; D £180-£250; (incl. dinner) ✳ LB **Conf** Max 20 Thtr 20 Class 20 Board 20 Del from £105 ✳ **Parking** 12 **Notes** Closed Xmas & Jan (ex New Year) rs Sun & Mon

Premier Collection

♦♦♦♦♦ 🏰🍴
Osprey Hotel ◇
Ruthven Rd PH21 1EN ☎ 01540 661510 📠 01540 661510
e-mail jmbseil@aol.com
web www.ospreyhotel.co.uk
Dir *At S end of the main street*

This smart, family-run house in the village centre has a well-deserved reputation for fine food and hospitality. Dinner is a lavish affair emphasising local produce, while hearty breakfasts include home-baked breads and preserves. The comfortable bedrooms vary in size and style, and 20 varieties of malt whisky are available in the bar. Kingussie is in the Spey valley and is overlooked by the Monadhliath and Grampian ranges

Facilities 8 en suite (2 GF) ⊗ TVB tea/coffee Licensed Cen ht TVL No coaches Library Wireless Broadband Dinner Last d 6.30pm **Prices** S £25-£32.50; D £55-£65✳ LB

Scotland

LOCHINVER
MAP 22 NC02

Premier Collection

★★★★★ ⑥⑥ **Restaurant with Rooms**

The Albannach

Badidarrach IV27 4LP ☎ 01571 844407 📠 01571 844285
e-mail info@thealbannach.co.uk
web www.thealbannach.co.uk

Dir *0.75m NW of village centre. Off A837 signed Baddidarrach & Highland Stoneware Potter, 0.5m over cattle grid & left*

Enjoying a fine reputation for its cooking and stylish accommodation, the Albannach is a must on any gastronomic tour of Scotland. Dinner, a theatrical indulgence of fresh produce, and the outstanding breakfasts showcase the seasons of the local larder. The bedrooms are furnished with flair and have stunning loch and mountain views, while the professional and caring staff greet you like old friends.

Facilities 5 en suite 1 annexe en suite (1 GF) ⊗ STV TVB tea/coffee Direct dial from bedrooms Licensed No children 12yrs No coaches Dinner **Prices** S £125-£145; D £220-£290; (incl. dinner)✱ **Parking** 8 **Notes** Closed mid Nov-mid Mar rs mid Mar-mid Nov, excl Mon

MELVICH
MAP 23 NC86

Premier Collection

◆◆◆◆◆

The Sheiling Guest House

KW14 7YJ ☎ 01641 531256 📠 01641 531256
e-mail thesheiling@btinternet.com
web www.thesheiling.co.uk

Dir *In village on A836*

The long drive through glorious highland scenery to this delightful guest house is well worthwhile. The house stands on an elevated position to the east of the village and has glorious sea views. The attractive bedrooms are comfortable, well equipped and superbly maintained, and there is a comfortable lounge. The excellent hosts Joan and Hugh Campbell serve outstanding breakfasts around a communal table, showcasing the region's natural produce.

Facilities 3 en suite ⊗ tea/coffee ✶ Cen ht TVL No children 12yrs No coaches **Prices** D £64-£70✱ **Parking** 5 **Notes** Closed Oct-Apr

NAIRN
MAP 23 NH85

U

North End ◇

18 Waverley Rd IV12 4RQ ☎ 01667 456338
e-mail reservations@northendnairn.co.uk
Dir *On corner of A96 (Academy St) and Waverley Rd*

At the time of going to press the rating for this establishment had not been confirmed. Please check the AA website www.theAA.com for up-to-date information.

Facilities 3 rms (2 en suite) (1 pri facs) ⊗ TVB tea/coffee ✶ Cen ht TVL No coaches **Prices** S £20-£25; D £40-£50✱ **LB Parking** 4 **Notes** Closed Dec-Jan

NEWTONMORE
MAP 23 NN79

◆◆◆◆

Crubenbeg House ◇

Falls of Truim PH20 1BE ☎ 01540 673300
e-mail enquiries@crubenbeghouse.com
web www.crubenbeghouse.com

Dir *4m S of Newtonmore. Off A9 for Crubenmore, over railway bridge & right, signed*

Set in peaceful rural location, Crubenbeg House has stunning country views and is well located for touring the the Highlands. The attractive bedrooms are individually styled and well equipped, while the ground-floor bedroom provides easier access. You can enjoy a dram in front of the fire in the inviting lounge, while breakfast features the best of local produce in the adjacent dining room. Irene England is a top-twenty finalist for AA Landlady of the Year 2006.

Facilities 4 rms (3 en suite) (1 pri facs) (1 GF) ⊗ TVB tea/coffee Licensed Cen ht No children No coaches Dinner **Prices** S £30-£36; D £50-£75 **LB Parking** 10

SOUTH BALLACHULISH
MAP 22 NN05

Premier Collection

◆◆◆◆◆ ⑥⑥

Ballachulish House

Ballachulish House PH49 4JX
☎ 01855 811266 📠 01855 811498
e-mail McLaughlins@btconnect.com
web www.ballachulishhouse.com

Dir *A82 onto A825 Oban road, establishment 0.25m on left after Ballachullish Hotel*

Adjacent to the interestingly named Dragons Tooth golf course, this 17th-century house has a rich history. In 1752 the 'Red Fox' was murdered here, providing the inspiration for Robert Louis Stevenson to write Kidnapped. The well-appointed bedrooms are spacious and elegant. Dinner is a highlight of any visit; inventive five-course menus feature skilfully prepared local ingredients.

Facilities 8 en suite (2 fmly) ⊗ tea/coffee Direct dial from bedrooms ✶ Licensed TVL No children 10yrs Golf 9 Fishing ▞ ⚐ Badminton Dinner Last d 7pm **Conf** Max 25 Board 12 **Parking** 6

Premier Collection

♦♦♦♦♦ 🛎 🍽

Craiglinnhe House

Lettermore PH49 4JD ☎ 01855 811270
e-mail info@craiglinnhe.co.uk
web www.craiglinnhe.co.uk
Dir From village A82 onto A828, Craiglinnhe 1.5m on left

Built during the reign of Queen Victoria, Craiglinnhe House enjoys an elevated position with stunning views across Loch Linnhe to the village of Onich, and up to the Ballachulish Bridge and the Pap of Glencoe. The attractive bedrooms vary in size, are stylishly furnished, and are well equipped. There is a ground-floor lounge and a charming dining room where delicious breakfasts, and evening meals by arrangement, are served at individual tables.

Facilities 5 en suite 🚫 TVB tea/coffee 🐾 Licensed Cen ht No children 12yrs No coaches Dinner Last d 10am **Prices** S £40-£65; D £56-£80✱ **LB Parking** 5 **Notes** Closed Jan

♦♦♦♦

Fern Villa

Loanfern PH49 4JE ☎ 01855 811393 🖷 01855 811727
e-mail fernctg@aol.com
web www.fernvilla.com
Dir Off A82 into village, off Albert Rd onto Loanfern

A warm welcome is assured at this elegant Victorian house. The bedrooms are well equipped and maintained, with those at the front of the house providing breathtaking views of the stunning scenery. There is a comfortable lounge with a selection of board games, and an attractive dining room where the proprietor's delicious home cooking can be enjoyed. Self catering cottages situated nearby are also available.

Facilities 5 en suite (1 GF) 🚫 TVB tea/coffee 🐾 Licensed Cen ht TVL No children 10yrs No coaches Golf 9 Dinner Last d 4pm **Prices** D £50-£54✱ **LB Parking** 5

♦♦♦♦

Lyn-Leven Guest House

West Laroch PH49 4JP ☎ 01855 811392 🖷 01855 811600
e-mail macleodcilla@aol.com
Dir Off A82 signed on left West Laroch

Genuine Highland hospitality and high standards are part of the appeal of this comfortable guest house. The attractive bedrooms vary in size, are well equipped, offering many thoughtful extra touches.
continued

There is a spacious lounge and a smart dining room where delicious home-cooked evening meals and breakfasts are served at individual tables.

Facilities 8 en suite 4 annexe en suite (3 fmly) (12 GF) 🚫 TVB tea/coffee Licensed Cen ht TVL Dinner Last d 7pm **LB Parking** 12 **Notes** Closed Xmas

SPEAN BRIDGE MAP 22 NN28

♦♦♦♦ 🍽

Corriechoille Lodge

PH34 4EY ☎ 01397 712002
web www.corriechoille.com
Dir Off A82 signed Corriechoille, continue 2.25m, left at road fork (10mph sign). At end of tarmac, turn right up hill & left

This fine country house stands above the River Spean. There are magnificent views of the Nevis range and surrounding mountains from the comfortable first-floor lounge and some of the spacious, well-appointed bedrooms. Friendly and attentive service is provided, as are traditional breakfasts and delicious evening meals by arrangement.

Facilities 4 en suite (2 fmly) (1 GF) 🚫 TVB tea/coffee 🐾 Licensed Cen ht No children 7yrs No coaches Dinner Last d previous day **Prices** S £31-£37; D £52-£70✱ **Parking** 7 **Notes** Closed Nov-Mar rs Mon & Tue

♦♦♦♦ 🎮 🛎 🍽

Smiddy House

Roy Bridge Rd PH34 4EU
☎ 01397 712335 🖷 01397 712043
e-mail enquiry@smiddyhouse.co.uk
web www.smiddyhouse.co.uk
Dir In village centre, A82 onto A86

Once the village smithy, Smiddy House is now a friendly guest house. The attractive bedrooms, which are named after Scottish places and whiskies, are comfortably furnished and well equipped. Delicious evening meals are served in Russell's Bistro, where the best of local produce is used to good effect.

Facilities 4 en suite (1 fmly) 🚫 TVB tea/coffee Licensed Dinner Last d 9.30pm **Prices** S £45-£70; D £60-£75✱ **Parking** 15 **Notes** Closed Nov

Scotland

SPEAN BRIDGE continued

♦♦♦♦

Distant Hills

PH34 4EU
☎ 01397 712452 & 07748 296287 🖷 01397 712452
e-mail enquiry@distanthills.com
Dir A82 onto A86 at Spean Bridge, establishment 0.5m on right

Please note that this establishment has recently changed hands. Distant Hills stands in a large, well-tended garden, and the bedrooms are maintained to a high standard with modern appointments. There is a spacious split-level lounge, with access to the garden. Home-cooked evening meals (by arrangement) and Scottish breakfasts are served at individual tables in the peaceful dining room.

Facilities 7 en suite (7 GF) ⊗ TVB tea/coffee Cen ht TVL No coaches Dinner Last d 2pm **Prices** S £45-£55; D £50-£70 **Parking** 10 **Notes** Closed Xmas rs Nov-Jan

♦♦♦ ❦

Achnabobane Farmhouse ◈ *(NN195811)*

PH34 4EX ☎ 01397 712919 Mr and Mrs Ockenden
e-mail enquiries@achnabobane.co.uk
web www.achnabobane.co.uk
Dir 2m S of Spean Bridge on A82

Having breathtaking views of Ben Nevis, Aonach Mhor and the Grey Corries, the farmhouse offers comfortable, good-value accommodation in a friendly family environment. Bedrooms are traditional in style and well equipped. Breakfast and evening meals are served in the conservatory-dining room. Pets welcome.

Facilities 3 rms (1 en suite) (1 fmly) (1 GF) ⊗ STV TVB tea/coffee Cen ht TVL Dinner Last d 1pm **Prices** S £25-£27; D £50-£54✱ **Parking** 5 **Notes** Closed Xmas

Ⓐ

The Braes Guest House ◈

PH34 4EU ☎ 01397 712437
e-mail enquiry@thebraes.co.uk
web www.thebraes.co.uk
Dir On A86, eastern outskirts of Spean Bridge.

Facilities 7 rms (6 en suite) (1 pri facs) (1 GF) ⊗ tea/coffee ✖ Cen ht TVL No children 7yrs Dinner Last d noon **Prices** S £25-£35; D £50-£66✱ LB **Parking** 10 **Notes** ★★★

STRATHPEFFER   MAP 23 NH45

♦♦♦

Inver Lodge ◈

IV14 9DL ☎ 01997 421392
e-mail derbyshire@inverlg.fsnet.co.uk
Dir A834 through Strathpeffer centre, turn beside Spa Pavilion signed Bowling Green, Inver Lodge on right

You are assured of a warm welcome at this Victorian lodge, situated within easy walking distance of the town centre. Bedrooms are comfortable and well equipped. Imaginative breakfasts, and by arrangement enjoyable home-cooked evening meals, are served at a communal table.

Facilities 2 rms (1 fmly) ⊗ TVB tea/coffee ✖ Cen ht No coaches Fishing and riding can be arranged Dinner Last d 4pm **Prices** S £25-£27; D £36✱ LB **Parking** 2 **Notes** Closed mid Dec-Feb

STRATHY POINT   MAP 23 NC86

♦♦♦♦

Catalina

Aultivullin KW14 7RY ☎ 01641 541395 🖷 0870 124 7960
e-mail catalina.bandb@virgin.net
Dir A836 at Strathy onto Strathy Point Rd, 1.5m then left & 1m to end

Having a tranquil setting close to the sea, this former croft house provides a getaway location for those seeking relaxation. The self-contained bedroom is in a wing that includes a dining room and a cosy lounge. Cuisine is home-cooked and meal times are flexible.

Facilities 1 en suite (1 GF) ⊗ TVB tea/coffee ✖ Cen ht TVL No children No coaches Bird watching Dinner Last d 7.15pm **Prices** S £35; D £48 **Parking** 2 **Notes** 🐾

TOMATIN   MAP 23 NH82

♦♦♦

Glenan Lodge Guest House ◈

IV13 7YT
☎ 01808 511217 & 08456 445793 🖷 08456 445794
e-mail glenanlodgecouk@hotmail.com
web www.glenanlodge.co.uk
Dir Off A9 at Little Chef to Tomatin, signed to Lodge

Peacefully located on the edge of the village, this relaxed and homely guest house offers a warm welcome. The comfortable bedrooms are traditionally furnished and suitably equipped. An inviting lounge is available, and delicious home-cooked evening meals and breakfasts are served in the dining room. A 2m stretch of the River Findhorn is available for fly-fishing, and golfers, walkers and bird watchers are also well provided for locally.

Facilities 7 en suite (2 fmly) ⊗ TVB tea/coffee Licensed Cen ht TVL No coaches Fishing Dinner Last d 6pm **Prices** S fr £26; d fr £52✱ LB **Parking** 7

ULLAPOOL   MAP 22 NH19

Dromnan Guest House

Garve Rd IV26 2SX ☎ 01854 612333 🖹 01854 613364
e-mail info@dromnan.com
web www.dromnan.com
Dir *A835 S into town, left at 30mph sign*

Facilities 7 en suite (2 fmly) ⊗ TVB tea/coffee ✖ Cen ht TVL
No coaches free entry to Lochbroom Leisure Centre **Prices** D £50-£62✴
Parking 7 **Notes** ★★★★

WICK   MAP 23 ND35

◆◆◆◆

The Clachan ◇

13 Randolph Pl, South Rd KW1 5NJ ☎ 01955 605384
e-mail enquiry@theclachan.co.uk
Dir *Off A99 0.5m S of town centre*

A warm welcome is assured at this immaculate detached home, by
the main road on the south edge of the town. The bright, airy
bedrooms (all on the ground floor) are compact, carefully decorated
and offer lots of thoughtful touches. Breakfast is served at individual
tables in the attractive lounge-dining room.

Facilities 3 en suite (3 GF) ⊗ TVB tea/coffee ✖ Cen ht TVL
No children 12yrs **Prices** S £30-£35; D £44-£48✴ **Parking** 3
Notes Closed Xmas & New Year 🐾

◆◆◆

Bilbster House ◇

KW1 5TB ☎ 01955 621212 🖹 01955 621212
e-mail ianstewart@bilbster.freeserve.co.uk
Dir *From Wick on A882, after 5m Bilbster House signed. Turn right
down lane past cottage*

Set in 5 acres of well-tended gardens and woodland, this attractive
17th-century country house offers traditionally furnished and
individually styled bedrooms. There is a comfortable ground-floor
lounge and a peaceful dining room where hearty breakfasts are
served at individual tables.

Facilities 3 rms (2 en suite) (3 fmly) ⊗ tea/coffee Cen ht TVL
No coaches **Prices** S £20-£22.50; D £40-£45✴ **Parking** 7 **Notes** Closed
Xmas & New Year rs Oct-Etr 🐾

MIDLOTHIAN

ROSLIN   MAP 21 NT26

◆◆◆ ⬛

The Original Roslin Hotel

4 Main St EH25 9LE ☎ 0131 440 2384 🖹 0131 440 2514
e-mail enquiries@theoriginalhotel.co.uk
Dir *Off city bypass at Straiton for A703, Inn is close to Roslin Chapel*

The delightful village inn offers well-equipped bedrooms with
upgraded en suites. Four of of the rooms have four-poster beds. In

continued

addition to the attractive Victorian restaurant, the lounge and
conservatory offer a comprehensive selection of bar meals.

The Original Roslin Hotel

Facilities 6 en suite (2 fmly) ⊗ STV TVB tea/coffee Cen ht Dinner
Last d 9.30pm **Prices** S £50-£65; D £70-£85✴ **LB** **Conf** Max 100
Thtr 130 Class 80 Board 60 Del from £100 ✴ **Parking** 8
Notes Civ Wed 180

MORAY

ELGIN   MAP 23 NJ26

🅰

The Pines

East Rd IV30 1XG ☎ 01343 552495 🖹 01343 552495
e-mail thepines@dsl.pipex.com
Dir *E end of town on A96*

Facilities 6 en suite (1 fmly) ⊗ TVB tea/coffee ✖ Cen ht No coaches
Prices S £40-£45; D £50-£58✴ **LB** **Conf** Max 15 Board 15 **Parking** 8
Notes ★★★★

FOCHABERS   MAP 23 NJ35

◆◆◆◆ 🍃

Castlehill Farm *(NJ310600)*

Blackdam IV32 7LJ
☎ 01343 820351 🖹 01343 821856 Mrs Shand
web www.accommodation-fochabers.co.uk
Dir *3m W of Fochabers on A96*

Castlehill Farm is a working family farm situated in gently rolling
countryside close to the River Spey. It is convenient for a number of
golf courses, distilleries and castles. The attractive bedrooms are
smartly furnished and well equipped. There is a cosy lounge-dining
room with a roaring coal fire, where delicious home-cooked breakfasts
are served.

Facilities 2 rms (1 en suite) (2 GF) ⊗ tea/coffee ✖ Cen ht TVL
No children 224 acres mixed **Prices** D £40-£50✴ **LB** **Parking** 4
Notes Closed Nov-Feb 🐾

Scotland

HOPEMAN MAP 23 NJ16

◆◆◆◆

Ardent House

43 Forsyth St IV30 5SY ☎ 01343 830694 📠 01343 830694
e-mail ardenthouse@freeuk.com
Dir *A9 to Inverness, A96 to Elgin, B9012 to Hopeman. Ardent House on main road opp Bowling Green*

Ardent House in the picturesque fishing village of Hopeman has a relaxed and friendly atmosphere. A carefully tended walled rose garden leads up to the conservatory lounge, and the bedrooms are well equipped and furnished in a bright modern style. Breakfast, which includes home-smoked fish, fresh garden produce and delicious home baking, is an excellent start to the day and is served in the attractive dining room.

Facilities 3 rms (2 en suite) (1 GF) ⊗ TVB tea/coffee ✖ Cen ht TVL No coaches **Parking** 5 **Notes** Closed 13 Dec-3 Jan 🐾

KEITH MAP 23 NJ45

◆◆◆◆

The Haughs Farm ◇

AB55 6QN ☎ 01542 882238 📠 01542 882238
e-mail jiwjackson@aol.com
web www.haughsfarmbedandbreakfast.net
Dir *0.5m NW of Keith off A96, signed Inverness*

Expect a friendly welcome at this comfortable farmhouse on the outskirts of town. The spacious bedrooms are inviting and have a comprehensive range of accessories. Public areas include a relaxing lounge, and meals are served in the sun room overlooking the garden.

Facilities 3 en suite (1 fmly) (3 GF) ⊗ TVB tea/coffee ✖ Cen ht TVL No coaches Dinner Last d 3pm **Prices** S £30-£33; D £44-£48 **Parking** 11 **Notes** Closed Oct/Easter 🐾

LOSSIEMOUTH MAP 23 NJ27

◆◆◆

Lossiemouth House ◇

33 Clifton Rd IV31 6DP ☎ 01343 813397 📠 01343 813397
e-mail frances@lossiehouse.com
Dir *On A941, on right before police station by East Beach*

There's a friendly atmosphere at this 16th-century dower house, which stands in a beautifully tended walled garden close to the beach. The

comfortable bedrooms are individual in style and traditionally furnished. There is a lounge with a wide range of tourist information, and breakfast is served at separate tables in the smart dining room.

Facilities 5 rms (3 en suite) (2 pri facs) (2 fmly) ⊗ TVB tea/coffee ✖ Cen ht No coaches **Prices** S £20-£25; D £40-£45✱ **Parking** 6 **Notes** 🐾

URQUHART MAP 23 NJ26

🅰

The Old Church of Urquhart

Parrandier, Meft Rd IV30 8NH
☎ 01343 843063 📠 01343 843063
e-mail parrandier@freeuk.com
web www.oldkirk.co.uk
Dir *Off A96 E of Elgin into Lhanbryde, brown tourist signs to B&B*

Facilities 3 rms (2 en suite) (1 pri facs) (1 fmly) (2 GF) ⊗ tea/coffee Licensed Cen ht TVL No coaches Bicycle hire Dinner Last d 10am **Prices** S £34-£36; D £48-£52✱ **Parking** 5 **Notes** ★★★★ Civ Wed 12

NORTH AYRSHIRE

LARGS MAP 20 NS25

◆◆◆◆

Whin Park

16 Douglas St KA30 8PS ☎ 01475 673437 📠 01475 687291
e-mail enquiries@whinpark.co.uk
web www.whinpark.co.uk
Dir *N of Largs off A78 signed Brisbane Glen*

Situated just a stroll from the seafront, this comfortable bungalow takes its name from the gorse bushes that grow in profusion on the surrounding hillsides. Bedrooms, one of which is on the ground floor, are attractively decorated and well equipped. There is an elegant lounge and a lovely dining room. Resident proprietors provide excellent levels of customer care.

Facilities 5 en suite (1 fmly) (1 GF) ⊗ TVB tea/coffee ✖ No coaches **Prices** S £34-£36; D £60-£64✱ **Parking** 4 **Notes** Closed Feb

◆◆◆◆ 🍴 🌱

South Whittlieburn Farm ◇ *(NS218632)*

Brisbane Glen KA30 8SN
☎ 01475 675881 📠 01475 675080 Mrs Watson
e-mail largsbandb@southwhittlieburnfarm.freeserve.co.uk
Dir *2m NE of Largs off A78 signed Brisbane Glen, after Vikingar centre*

This comfortable and welcoming farmhouse is on a working sheep farm surrounded by gently rolling countryside. The attractive bedrooms are well equipped with all having DVD and Video players. There is a spacious ground-floor lounge and a bright airy dining room where delicious breakfasts are served.

Facilities 3 en suite (1 fmly) ⊗ TVB tea/coffee ✖ Cen ht TVL 155 acres sheep/horses **Prices** S £30-£35; D £55-£60 **LB Parking** 10 **Notes** rs Xmas 🐾

continued

SALTCOATS
MAP 20 NS24

Lochwood Farm Steading (NS265450)
KA21 6NG ☎ 01294 552529 Mrs Murdoch
e-mail info@lochwoodfarm.co.uk
Dir 1m off Saltcoats-Dalry road

Built in the 18th century and set in 200 acres of glorious rolling countryside, this immaculately maintained dairy and arable farm offers warm hospitality with delicious food. The attractive bedrooms, in a converted traditional stone byre, are comfortably furnished and well equipped. There is a choice of lounges, and a spacious dining room where hearty farmhouse fare is served at a large communal table. There is also an outdoor jacuzzi hot tub to relax in.

Facilities 4 en suite (4 GF) ⊗ TVB tea/coffee ✹ Cen ht TVL Outdoor hot tub 200 acres Beef & Dairy **Prices** S £35-£45; D £50-£60✳ **Parking** 8 **Notes** Closed Dec-Jan

---

NORTH LANARKSHIRE

AIRDRIE
MAP 21 NS76

◆◆◆◆

Shawlee Cottage ◇
108 Lauchope St, Chapelhall ML6 8SW
☎ 01236 753774 📄 01236 749300
e-mail shawleecottage@tiscali.co.uk
web www.csaitken.fsbusiness.co.uk/index.htm
Dir M8 junct 6, A73 to Chapelhall, left onto B799, Shawlee 600yds on right

Shawlee Cottage is close to motorway and rail networks, and within easy reach of Edinburgh and Glasgow. This delightful cottage dates from the 19th century and has comfortable, well-equipped bedrooms with wide doors and a ramp at the entrance. Scottish breakfasts (and dinner by arrangement) are served in the attractive dining room.

Facilities 5 en suite (5 GF) ⊗ TVB tea/coffee Direct dial from bedrooms ✹ Cen ht No coaches Dinner **Prices** S £30-£40; D £50-£60 **Parking** 6

🅰

Calder Guest House
13 Main St, Calderbank ML6 9SG
☎ 01236 769077 📄 01236 750506
e-mail calderhouse13@aol.com
Dir 2m S of Airdrie, next to primary school on A802 in Calderbank

Facilities 4 rms (1 en suite) (3 pri facs) (1 fmly) ⊗ TVB tea/coffee Cen ht TVL No coaches Pool Table **Parking** 6 **Notes** ★★★ 🈵

COATBRIDGE
MAP 20 NS76

◆◆◆

Auchenlea ◇
153 Langmuir Rd, Bargeddie G69 7RT
☎ 0141 771 6870 & 07775 791381 📄 0141 771 6870
e-mail helenbarr153@hotmail.com
Dir N off A8 onto A752 for 0.4m

Backing onto farmland, yet only a short distance from the motorway, this detached house is well placed for Glasgow and Edinburgh. Satisfying, well-cooked breakfasts are served at a communal table in the bright dining room, and there is an attractive conservatory and adjoining lounge. The bedrooms, all on the ground floor, are modern in style with one designed for easier access.

Facilities 6 en suite (1 fmly) (6 GF) ⊗ TVB tea/coffee ✹ Cen ht TVL **Prices** S £25-£35; D £45-£55✳ **Parking** 10 **Notes** 🈵

PERTH & KINROSS

ALYTH
MAP 23 NO24

Premier Collection

◆◆◆◆◆

Tigh Na Leigh Guesthouse
22-24 Airlie St PH11 8AJ
☎ 01828 632372 📄 01828 632279
e-mail bandcblack@yahoo.co.uk
web www.tighnaleigh.co.uk
Dir In town centre on B952

Situated in the heart of the town in glorious Perthshire countryside, Tigh Na Leigh (Gaelic for the house of the Doctor or Physician) has been lovingly restored to its Victorian glory. The smart bedrooms are spacious and well equipped, while the en suites have super showers and spa baths. There is a choice of stylish lounges, and delicious evening meals and breakfasts are served in the spacious conservatory-dining room overlooking the lovely garden. AA Guest Accommodation of the Year for Scotland 2006.

Facilities 5 en suite (1 GF) ⊗ FTV TVB tea/coffee Licensed Cen ht TVL No children 12yrs No coaches Dinner Last d 9pm **Prices** S £35; D £80-£100✳ **Parking** 5 **Notes** Closed Nov-Feb

Scotland

BLAIR ATHOLL
MAP 23 NN86

◆◆◆◆

Dalgreine Guest House
PH18 5SX ☎ 01796 481276 🖹 01796 481276
Dir *Off A9 to Blair Atholl. Turn off main street at garage, next left & follow signs for Dalgreine*

The friendly, family-run Dalgreine offers beautifully furnished and well-equipped accommodation in a peaceful village location near Blair Castle. Its inviting lounge has deep sofas and a real fire, and enjoyable home-cooked fare is served in the dining room.

Facilities 6 rms (2 en suite) (1 pri facs) ⊗ TVB tea/coffee ✻ Cen ht TVL No children 15yrs No coaches **Parking** 9 **Notes** 🐾

BLAIRGOWRIE
MAP 21 NO14

◆◆◆◆

Gilmore House
Perth Rd PH10 6EJ ☎ 01250 872791 🖹 01250 872791
e-mail jill@gilmorehouse.co.uk
Dir *On A93 S*

This attractive detached house stands in a well-tended garden on the south side of town. The pretty bedrooms are comfortably furnished in antique pine, and are well equipped. There are two lounges, one of which has lovely views of the surrounding countryside. Hearty traditional breakfasts are served in the attractive ground-floor dining room.

Facilities 3 en suite ⊗ FTV TVB tea/coffee Cen ht TVL No coaches **Prices** D £45-£50 **Parking** 3 **Notes** Closed Xmas 🐾

CRIEFF
MAP 21 NN82

◆◆◆◆

Merlindale
Perth Rd PH7 3EQ ☎ 01764 655205 🖹 01764 655205
e-mail merlin.dale@virgin.net
web www.merlindale.co.uk
Dir *On A85 350yds from E end of High St*

Situated in a quiet residential area within walking distance of the town centre, this delightful detached house stands in well-tended grounds and offers a warm welcome. The pretty bedrooms are comfortably furnished and well equipped. There is a spacious lounge, an impressive library, and an elegant dining room where delicious evening meals and traditional breakfasts are served.

Facilities 3 en suite (1 fmly) ⊗ STV TVB tea/coffee ✻ Cen ht TVL No coaches Dinner Last d 24hrs in advance **Prices** S £45-£65; D £60-£75✶ **Parking** 3 **Notes** Closed 9 Dec-10 Feb 🐾

◆◆◆◆

Comely Bank Guest House ◇
32 Burrell St PH7 4DT ☎ 01764 653409 🖹 01764 654309
e-mail marion@comelybank.demon.co.uk
web www.comelybank.demon.co.uk
Dir *On A822 near Meadow Inn*

Centrally located, Comely Bank offers comfortable, bright airy bedrooms with attractive soft furnishings. There is a ground-floor

bedroom with easier access, which is next to the inviting lounge. Breakfasts and by arrangement evening meals are served at individual tables in the peaceful dining room.

Facilities 5 rms (3 en suite) (2 fmly) (1 GF) ⊗ TVB tea/coffee Cen ht TVL No coaches Dinner Last d noon **Prices** S £20-£25; D £40-£48✶ **LB Notes** 🐾

DUNKELD
MAP 21 NO04

🅰

Birnam Guest House
4 Murthly Ter, Birnam PH8 0BG
☎ 01350 727201 🖹 01350 727201
e-mail birnamguesthouse@hotmail.com
Dir *Off A9 signed Birnam & Dunkeld. Into Birnam village, house 50yds past church*

Facilities 5 en suite (1 fmly) ⊗ TVB tea/coffee ✻ Licensed Cen ht No coaches **Parking** 5 **Notes** ★★★

GLENSHEE (SPITTAL OF),
MAP 21 NO17

◆◆◆◆

Dalhenzean Lodge
PH10 7QD ☎ 01250 885217 🖹 0871 7335419
e-mail mikepurdie@onetel.com
Dir *On A93 2m S of Spittal of Glenshee*

Dalhenzean Lodge was built in 1715, and is situated in the shadow of Meall Uaine, overlooking Shee Water. Some 7m from the ski slopes at The Cairnwell, it is well located for fishing, hill walking and climbing, with the Cateran Trail nearby. Bedrooms are beautifully decorated and have many thoughtful extras. Hearty breakfasts featuring the best of local produce are served in the ground-floor dining room.

Facilities 2 rms (1 en suite) (1 pri facs) ⊗ STV TVB tea/coffee ✻ Cen ht No coaches **Prices** D £45-£50✶ **LB Parking** 2 **Notes** 🐾

KIRKMICHAEL
MAP 23 NO05

◆◆◆ ▥

Kirkmichael Hotel
Main St PH10 7NT ☎ 01250 881769 🖹 01250 881779
e-mail info@kirkmichaelhotel.co.uk
Dir *In village centre on A924*

This friendly establishment is the hub of the village. Hearty, well-prepared meals are served in the restaurant or in the bar with its cosy snug, and the spacious bedrooms are well equipped and smartly furnished.

Facilities 5 en suite (1 fmly) ⊗ TVB tea/coffee Direct dial from bedrooms Cen ht No coaches Dinner Last d 9pm **Parking** 8

continued

PERTH   MAP 21 NO12

◆◆◆◆

Cherrybank Bed & Breakfast

217-219 Glasgow Rd PH2 0NB
☎ 01738 451982 & 561336 ▤ 01738 561336
e-mail m.r.cherrybank@blueyonder.co.uk
Dir 1m SW of town centre on A93

Convenient for the town and motorway, Cherrybank has been
extended and carefully refurbished to offer well equipped and
beautifully presented bedrooms, one of which is on the ground floor.
There is a relaxing lounge and delicious breakfasts are served at
individual tables in the bright airy dining room.

Facilities 4 rms (3 en suite) (1 pri facs) (2 fmly) (1 GF) ⊗ TVB
tea/coffee ✖ Cen ht No coaches **Prices** S £35-£40; D £50✻ LB
Parking 4

◆◆◆◆

Adam Guest House ◇

6 Pitcullen Crescent PH2 7HT
☎ 01738 627179 ▤ 01738 627179
e-mail enquiresadam@aol.com
Dir From town centre over bridge onto A94 Coupar road, house on
left

This friendly family-run guest house offers comfortable, well-equipped
accommodation. Bedrooms are attractively furnished in pine and well
maintained. There is a relaxing ground-floor lounge and a cosy dining
room where freshly cooked breakfasts are served at good-sized
individual tables.

Facilities 4 en suite (1 fmly) (1 GF) ⊗ TVB tea/coffee Cen ht TVL
Prices S £30-£40; D £50-£60 LB **Parking** 6

◆◆◆◆

Almond Villa Guest House ◇

51 Dunkeld Rd PH1 5RP ☎ 01738 629356
e-mail enquiries@perth-guesthouse.co.uk
web www.perth-guesthouse.co.uk
Dir N from town centre onto A912 Dunkeld Rd, house 150yds on left

Guests are assured of a warm welcome at Almond Villa, situated 0.5m
north of the town centre. The attractive bedrooms are well appointed
and equipped. There is a comfortable lounge with a video library, and
a peaceful dining room where delicious breakfasts are served.

Facilities 5 en suite (1 fmly) (1 GF) ⊗ TVB tea/coffee ✖ Cen ht
No coaches **Prices** S £30-£45; D £50-£60 **Parking** 4

◆◆◆◆

Westview

49 Dunkeld Rd PH1 5RP ☎ 01738 627787 ▤ 01738 447790
e-mail angiewestview@aol.com
Dir On A912 0.5m NW from town centre opp Royal Bank of Scotland

Expect a warm welcome from enthusiastic owner Angie Livingstone.
She is a fan of Victoriana, and her house captures that period, one
feature being the teddies on the stairs. Best use is made of available
space in the bedrooms, which are full of character. Public areas
include an inviting lounge and a dining room.

Facilities 5 rms (3 en suite) (1 fmly) (1 GF) ⊗ STV TVB tea/coffee
Cen ht TVL No coaches Dinner Last d 12.30pm **Parking** 4 **Notes** ⊠

◆◆◆

Anglers Inn ◇

Main Rd, Guildtown PH2 6BS
☎ 01821 640329 ▤ 01821 640329
web www.anglersinn.co.uk
Dir 5m N of Perth on A93

This friendly establishment in the village of Guildtown is part of the
local community. The spacious dining area offers freshly prepared
meals and a well-stocked bar. The comfortable, modern
accommodation is thoughtfully equipped and includes some recently
added bedrooms.

Facilities 6 en suite (2 fmly) ⊗ TVB tea/coffee Licensed Cen ht TVL
Pool Table Dinner Last d 9pm **Prices** S £25-£30; D £50-£60✻ LB
Conf Max 70 **Parking** 30

◆◆◆

Clunie Guest House ◇

12 Pitcullen Crescent PH2 7HT
☎ 01738 623625 ▤ 01738 623238
e-mail ann@clunieguesthouse.co.uk
Dir On A94 on E side of river

Lying on the east side of town, this family-run guest house offers a
friendly welcome. The comfortable bedrooms, which vary in size, are
attractively decorated and well equipped. Breakfast is served at
individual tables in the elegant ground-floor dining room.

Facilities 7 en suite (1 fmly) ⊗ TVB tea/coffee Cen ht No coaches
Prices S £28-£35; D £50-£60✻ LB **Parking** 8

Scotland

Scotland

PERTH continued

Comely Bank Cottage ◇

19 Pitcullen Crescent PH2 7HT
☎ 01738 631118 📠 01738 571245
e-mail comelybankcott@hotmail.com
Dir M90 junct 11, A85 to 3rd lights, right onto A94, 250yds on right

Facilities 3 en suite (1 fmly) (1 GF) ⊗ TVB tea/coffee Cen ht TVL
No coaches **Prices** S £26-£35; D £45-£50✶ **LB** **Parking** 3 **Notes** ★★★
Closed 15 Dec-5 Jan

PITLOCHRY   MAP 23 NN95

Premier Collection

Easter Dunfallandy House

Logierait Rd PH16 5NA ☎ 01796 474128 📠 01796 474446
e-mail sue@dunfallandy.co.uk
Dir 1m S of Pitlochry. Off A924 Perth Rd in town onto Bridge Rd, fork left, house 1m on right

This establishment is situated on an elevated location close to the historic Dunfallandy Pictish stone, and has stunning views over Ben-y-Vrackie Mountain and the Tummel valley beyond. Bedrooms, all of which are en suite, are beautifully decorated, well equipped and comfortable. There is a stylish lounge and a charming dining room with original woodwork from the early 20th century, a fine environment in which to enjoy Scottish gourmet breakfasts.

Facilities 3 en suite (1 GF) ⊗ STV TVB tea/coffee ✖ Cen ht TVL
No coaches **LB** **Parking** 10 **Notes** Closed Xmas

◆◆◆◆

Craigroyston House

2 Lower Oakfield PH16 5HQ
☎ 01796 472053 📠 01796 472053
e-mail reservations@craigroyston.co.uk
web www.craigroyston.co.uk
Dir In town centre near information centre car park

The Maxwell family delight in welcoming you to their home, an impressive detached Victorian villa set in a colourful garden. The bedrooms have pretty colour schemes and are comfortably furnished in period style. There is an inviting sitting room, complete with deep sofas for those wishing to relax and enjoy the tranquillity. Scottish breakfasts are served at individual tables in the attractive dining room.

Facilities 8 en suite (1 fmly) (1 GF) ⊗ TVB tea/coffee ✖ Cen ht
No coaches **Prices** D £50-£66✶ **LB** **Parking** 9 **Notes** 🐾

◆◆◆◆

Dundarave House ◇

Strathview Ter PH16 5AT ☎ 01796 473109 📠 01796 473109
e-mail dundarave.guesthouse@virgin.net
Dir From Pitlochry main street onto West Moulin Rd, 2nd left

Set in it own terraced gardens this house sits high above the town and offers a stunning vista of the Tummel valley. The comfortable lounge and attractive dining room enjoy the views, as do most of the bedrooms.

Facilities 7 rms (5 en suite) (1 fmly) (1 GF) ⊗ TVB tea/coffee ✖
Cen ht No coaches Dinner Last d noon **Prices** S £24-£30; D £48-£60 **LB**
Parking 7

Torrdarach House ◇

Golf Course Rd PH16 5AU
☎ 01796 472136 📠 01796 472136
e-mail torrdarach@msn.com
Dir In town centre. Off A924 Atholl Rd onto Larchwood Rd to top of hill, left, red house on right

From its elevated location overlooking the Tummel Valley, this impressive, detached Victorian villa stands in a delightful secluded garden, home to a family of red squirrels. The attractive bedrooms are comfortably furnished and well equipped. Delicious, freshly cooked breakfasts are served at individual tables in the ground-floor dining room.

Facilities 7 rms (6 en suite) (1 pri facs) (1 GF) ⊗ TVB tea/coffee ✖
Licensed Cen ht No coaches **Prices** S £24-£32; D £48-£64 **LB**
Parking 7

♦♦♦♦

Wellwood House

13 West Moulin Rd PH16 5EA
☎ 01796 474288 📠 01796 474299
e-mail wellwoodhouse@aol.com
web www.wellwoodhouse.com
Dir *In town centre opp town hall*

Set in lovely grounds on an elevated position overlooking the town, Wellwood House has stunning views of the Vale of Atholl and the surrounding countryside. The comfortably proportioned bedrooms are attractively decorated and well equipped. The elegant lounge has an honesty bar and a fire on cooler evenings, and the spacious dining room is the setting for hearty breakfasts served at individual tables.

Facilities 10 rms (7 en suite) (1 fmly) ⊗ TVB tea/coffee ✶ Licensed Cen ht TVL No coaches **Parking** 20 **Notes** Closed 22-29 Dec

RENFREWSHIRE

GLASGOW AIRPORT   MAP 20 NS46

Premier Collection

♦♦♦♦♦

East Lochhead

Largs Rd PA12 4DX
☎ 01505 842610 & 07785 565131 📠 01505 842610
e-mail admin@eastlochhead.co.uk
web www.eastlochhead.co.uk
For full entry see Lochwinnoch

LOCHWINNOCH   MAP 20 NS35

Premier Collection

♦♦♦♦♦ 🏠

East Lochhead

Largs Rd PA12 4DX
☎ 01505 842610 & 07785 565131 📠 01505 842610
e-mail admin@eastlochhead.co.uk
web www.eastlochhead.co.uk
Dir *A737 onto A760, premises 2m on left, brown tourist sign*

A relaxed country-house atmosphere prevails at this former farmhouse, which dates from the 19th century. Standing in colourful and immaculate grounds, the house has magnificent views over Barr Loch. The stylishly furnished bedrooms are superbly equipped. Delicious breakfasts are served in the lounge-dining room. A converted barn has five self-contained units with their own private entrances, and a separate barn has a function room.

Facilities 3 en suite (1 fmly) (1 GF) ⊗ TVB tea/coffee Licensed Cen ht TVL No coaches Cycle hire **Prices** S £45-£50; D £80-£90✳ **LB**
Parking 24

SCOTTISH BORDERS

AUCHENCROW   MAP 21 NT86

♦♦♦ 🍽 ◀

The Craw Inn

TD14 5LS ☎ 018907 61253
e-mail info@thecrawinn.co.uk
web www.thecrawinn.co.uk
Dir *Tourist sign off A1*

Built in the 18th century, this atmospheric country inn has been refurbished to offer modern comforts with character. Bedrooms are traditionally furnished and a family room is available. Relax in the bar, with its low beams, exposed brickwork and a log-burning stove, before enjoying delicious home-cooked fare in the intimate dining room.

Facilities 3 en suite (1 fmly) ⊗ TVB tea/coffee ✶ Cen ht No coaches Dinner Last d 9pm **LB Conf** Max 14 **Parking** available

BROUGHTON   MAP 21 NT13

♦♦♦♦

The Glenholm Centre

ML12 6JF ☎ 01899 830408 📠 01899 830408
e-mail info@glenholm.co.uk
Dir *2m S of Broughton. Off A701 to Glenholm, on right before cattle grid*

Surrounded by peaceful farmland, this former schoolhouse has a distinct African theme. The home-cooked meals and baking have received much praise and are served in the spacious lounge-dining room. The bright airy bedrooms are thoughtfully equipped, and the service is friendly and attentive. Computer courses are available.

Facilities 4 en suite (1 fmly) (1 GF) ⊗ TVB tea/coffee Direct dial from bedrooms Licensed Cen ht TVL No coaches Dinner Last d 6pm
Conf Max 20 Class 20 **Parking** 14 **Notes** Closed Jan

Scotland

Scotland

COLDSTREAM
MAP 21 NT83

Premier Collection

◆◆◆◆◆

Ruthven House

TD12 4JU ☎ 01890 840771 ▤ 01890 840680
e-mail gradidge@worldonline.co.uk
web www.bordersovernight.co.uk
Dir From Coldstream turn at Mercedes garage N onto Guards Rd,
after 3m Ruthven signed on right

Set in beautiful Borders countryside, this impressive Victorian family
home stands in 7 acres of well-tended gardens and grounds and has
stunning views of the Cheviot Hills. The spacious bedrooms are
beautifully furnished and very well equipped, and the bathrooms have
extraordinary bathtubs. There is a comfortable drawing room, and
hearty breakfasts are served in the dining room (delicious evening
meals by arrangement).
Facilities 4 rms (3 pri facs) 2 annexe rms (2 annexe pri facs) ⊛ TV4B
tea/coffee ✖ Cen ht No coaches Dinner Last d previous day
Prices S £40-£50; D £65-£75✶ **Parking** 7 **Notes** ⊛

CRAILING
MAP 21 NT62

◆◆◆◆ ▤ ⬭

Crailing Old School B & B ◇

TD8 6TL ☎ 01835 850382 ▤ 01835 850382
e-mail jean.player@virgin.net
web www.crailingoldschool.co.uk
Dir A698 onto B6400 signed Nisbet, Crailing Old School also signed

This delightful rural retreat, built in 1887 as the village school, has
been imaginatively renovated to combine Victorian features with
modern comforts. The spacious bedrooms are beautifully maintained

continued

and decorated, and filled with homely extras. The lodge annexe suite
located 10yds from the house offers easier ground-floor access. The
best of local produce produces tasty breakfasts, served in the stylish
lounge-dining room (evening meals by arrangement).
Facilities 3 rms (1 en suite) 1 annexe en suite (1 GF) ⊛ TVB tea/coffee
✖ Cen ht TVL No children 9yrs Dinner Last d 7.30pm
Prices S £27.50-£30; D £53-£64✶ **LB Parking** 7 **Notes** Closed
24-27 Dec & 2 wks Feb and Nov

GALASHIELS
MAP 21 NT43

◆◆◆ ⬗

Over Langshaw (NT524400)

Langshaw TD1 2PE
☎ 01896 860244 ▤ 01896 860668 Mrs Bergius
e-mail bergius@overlangshaw.fsnet.co.uk
Dir 3m N of Galashiels. A7 N from Galashiels, 1m right signed
Langshaw, right at T-junct into Langshaw, left signed Earlston, Over
Langshaw 1m, signed

There are fine panoramic views from this organic hillside farm. It offers
two comfortable and spacious bedrooms, one en suite on the ground
floor, and one upstairs with a private bathroom. Hearty breakfasts are
provided at individual tables in the lounge.
Facilities 2 en suite (1 fmly) (1 GF) ⊛ tea/coffee Cen ht TVL 500 acres
dairy/sheep/organic Dinner Last d at breakfast **Parking** 4 **Notes** ⊛

INNERLEITHEN
MAP 21 NT33

★★★★ Guest House

Caddon View

14 Pirn Rd EH44 6HH ☎ 01896 830208
e-mail contact_us@caddonview.co.uk
web www.caddonview.co.uk
Dir Just off A72

This Victorian former doctor's house stands in beautiful gardens just
off the village centre, and offers delightful, individually styled
bedrooms and super bathrooms. Relax and feel at home beside the
the log fire in the sumptuous drawing room.
Facilities 8 rms (7 en suite) (1 pri facs) (3 fmly) (2 GF) ⊛ TVB
tea/coffee ✖ Licensed Cen ht No coaches **Prices** S £45-£55;
D £85-£110 **Parking** 7

★★★ Inn

Corner House ◇

1 Chapel St EH44 6HN ☎ 01896 831181 ▤ 01896 831182
e-mail cornerhousehotel@hotmail.com

Behind its corner street frontage lies a friendly family-run inn.
Accommodation includes three family bedrooms, but it is the good
value home-cooked food served all day that is the main attraction. The
cosy and characterful restaurant is the venue for hearty breakfasts,
morning coffees, lunches, afternoon teas and dinners. There is also a
small bar.
Facilities 7 en suite (3 fmly) ⊛ TVB tea/coffee Cen ht Dinner Last
d 9pm **Prices** S fr £30; d fr £60✶ **LB Parking** 8

JEDBURGH MAP 21 NT62

Premier Collection

◆◆◆◆◆

The Spinney

Langlee TD8 6PB ☎ 01835 863525
e-mail thespinney@btinternet.com
web www.thespinney-jedburgh.co.uk
Dir 2m S of Jedburgh on A68

Set in countryside south of the town, two roadside cottages have been transformed into an attractive modern home with delightful landscaped gardens, which are well screened from the road. The bright and airy bedrooms are adorned with thoughtful touches that ensure a restful stay. Breakfast is served at individual tables in the dining room and there is a comfortable lounge. Three self-catering lodges are also available.

Facilities 3 rms (2 en suite) (1 pri facs) ⊗ TVB tea/coffee ✖ Cen ht TVL No coaches **Prices** D £52-£54 **Parking** 8 **Notes** Closed Dec-Feb

◆◆◆◆

Allerton House

Oxnam Rd TD8 6QQ ☎ 01835 869633 ▤ 01835 869885
e-mail info@allertonhouse.co.uk
Dir Off A65 bypass onto Oxwam Rd at Waterside Fitness Centre

Set in gardens within a quiet residential area a short walk from the town centre, this fine Georgian house has been refurbished in a bright contemporary style. Smart bedrooms include DVD players and Internet access. An attractive lounge-dining room provides daily papers and enjoyable breakfasts, and service is truly friendly.

Facilities 6 en suite (1 fmly) (2 GF) ⊗ STV TVB tea/coffee ✖ Licensed Cen ht ch fac Complementary use of local swimming pool Dinner Last d 9pm **Prices** S £35-£40; D £60-£75✳ **Conf** Max 20 **Parking** 7

◆◆◆◆

Glenfriars House ◇

The Friars TD8 6BN ☎ 01835 862000 ▤ 01835 862112
e-mail glenfriars@edenroad.demon.co.uk
Dir In town centre, off High St W onto Exchange St & 1st right

A substantial and interesting house, Glenfriars stands in secluded gardens overlooking the town, yet only a short walk from the centre. The comfortable bedrooms are mostly well proportioned, and the house is being restored to its former glory.

Facilities 6 en suite (3 fmly) ⊗ TVB tea/coffee Cen ht TVL No coaches Country sports can be arranged **Conf** Max 10 Thtr 10 Class 10 **Prices** S £30; d £60✳ LB **Parking** 6 **Notes** Closed 22 Dec-7 Jan

◆◆◆ ▱

Ferniehirst Mill Lodge ◇

TD8 6PQ ☎ 01835 863279 ▤ 01835 863279
e-mail ferniehirstmill@aol.com
web www.ferniehirstmill.co.uk
Dir 2.5m S on A68, onto private track to end

Reached by a narrow farm track and a rustic wooden bridge, this chalet-style house has a secluded setting by the River Jed where

continued

wildlife abounds. Bedrooms are small and functional but there is a comfortable lounge in which to relax. Excellent home-cooked dinners and hearty breakfasts are served in the cosy dining room.

Facilities 7 en suite (1 GF) ⊗ tea/coffee Direct dial from bedrooms Licensed Cen ht TVL No coaches Fishing Riding Dinner Last d 5pm **Prices** S £20-£25; D £40-£50✳ **Parking** 10

KELSO MAP 21 NT73

◆◆◆◆ ▱

Queens Head Hotel

Bridge St TD5 7JD
☎ 0870 2424453 & 01573 228868 ▤ 01573 224459
e-mail info@garymoorerestaurants.co.uk
Dir In town centre

The former coaching inn has been offering comfortable, well-appointed accommodation in a relaxed and friendly environment for almost 300 years. The attractive bedrooms are generally spacious and well equipped. The Queens Bistro, which is operated separately by chef-patron Gary Moore, is the setting for hearty breakfasts, and evening meals by arrangement.

Facilities 13 en suite (7 fmly) ⊗ TVB tea/coffee Licensed Cen ht TVL Fishing Dinner Last d 9pm **Prices** S £50-£70; D £65-£110✳ **Conf** Max 30 Thtr 30 Class 15 Board 16

LAUDER MAP 21 NT54

◆◆◆◆ ▤ ▱ ◧

Black Bull

Market Pl TD2 6SR ☎ 01578 722208 ▤ 01578 722419
e-mail enquiries@blackbull-lauder.com
web www.blackbull-lauder.com
Dir On A68 in village centre

This 18th-century coaching inn has been completely transformed. The lovely bedrooms are furnished in the period character and thoughtfully equipped with modern amenities. All with wooden floors, the cosy bar and four dining areas are charming, the main dining room being a former chapel. A tremendous range of food makes this a destination gastro pub.

Facilities 8 en suite (2 fmly) ⊗ TVB tea/coffee Direct dial from bedrooms Cen ht Dinner Last d 9pm **Prices** S £50-£72.50; D £80-£90✳ LB **Conf** Max 40 **Parking** 8 **Notes** Closed 1st 2 wks of Feb Civ Wed 40

Scotland

MELROSE
MAP 21 NT53

Premier Collection

◆◆◆◆◆ ⬠

Fauhope House
Gattonside TD6 9LU
☎ 01896 823184 & 822245 📄 01896 822245
e-mail fauhope@bordernet.co.uk
Dir *0.7m N of Melrose over River Tweed. N off B6360 at Gattonside 30mph sign (E) up long driveway*

It's hard to imagine a more complete experience than a stay at Fauhope, set high on a hillside on the north-east edge of the village. Hospitality is first class, breakfasts are excellent, and the delightful country house has a splendid interior. Bedrooms are luxurious, each individual and superbly equipped. Public areas are elegantly decorated and furnished, and enhanced by beautiful floral arrangements; the dining room is particularly stunning.

Facilities 3 en suite ⊗ TVB tea/coffee 🛏 Cen ht No coaches ✎ Riding Dinner Last d 7.30pm **Prices** S £55-£65; D £80-£90✳ LB **Parking** 10

SWINTON
MAP 21 NT84

★★★★ ◎◎ Restaurant with Rooms

Wheatsheaf at Swinton
TD11 3JJ ☎ 01890 860257 📄 01890 860688
e-mail reception@wheatsheaf-swinton.co.uk
Dir *From Edinburgh turn off A697 onto B6461. From East Lothian, turn off A1 onto B6461*

Overlooking the village green, the Wheatsheaf has built its reputation on food. Bedrooms are stylishly furnished, all having smart en suites,

and the largest ones feature a bath and separate shower cubicle. The recently added executive bedrooms are of a very high standard.

Facilities 10 en suite (2 fmly) (1 GF) FTV TVB tea/coffee Direct dial from bedrooms 🛏 No coaches Dinner Last d 9pm **Prices** S £67-£94; D £102-£132✳ LB **Conf** Max 18 Thtr 18 Class 18 Board 12 **Parking** 7 **Notes** Closed 25-27 Dec rs Dec-3 Jan Civ Wed 50

SOUTH AYRSHIRE

AYR
MAP 20 NS32
See also **Dalrymple (East Ayrshire) & Dunure**

◆◆◆◆

Craggallan ◇
8 Queens Ter KA7 1DU ☎ 01292 264998
e-mail margot@craggallan.com
web www.craggallan.com
Dir *Off A719 onto Wellington Sq & Bath Place, turn right*

This immaculately maintained and comfortable guest house, with excellent gardens, lies in a quiet residential street just off the seafront and within easy walking distance of the town centre. The attractive bedrooms are mostly spacious and are comfortably furnished. Overseas golfing visitors are especially welcome as the owner provides some useful local services for this sport.

Facilities 5 rms (4 en suite) (1 pri facs) ⊗ TVB tea/coffee 🛏 Cen ht No coaches Pool Table Dinner Last d 7pm **Prices** S £30-£40; D £56-£70✳ LB **Parking** 4

◆◆◆◆

Daviot House ◇
12 Queens Ter KA7 1DU
☎ 01292 269678 📄 01292 880567
e-mail annthedaviot@aol.com
web www.daviothouse.com
Dir *Off A719 onto Wellington Sq & Bath Place, turn right*

This well-maintained Victorian house stands in a peaceful location close to the beach and town centre. Bedrooms are modern in style and well equipped. Public areas include a comfortable lounge and dining room, where enjoyable home-cooked evening meals and hearty breakfasts are served. A member of Golf South Ayrshire Hoteliers golf booking service for local municipal courses.

Facilities 5 en suite (3 fmly) ⊗ TVB tea/coffee Cen ht No coaches Last d 5pm **Prices** S £30-£35; D £54-£60✳ LB **Parking** 2 **Notes** 🍽

continued

◆◆◆◆

Glenmore Guesthouse

35 Bellevue Crescent KA7 2DP
☎ 01292 269830 ▤ 01292 269830
Dir S of town centre, off A719 Racecourse Rd onto Bellevue Crescent

Marie Mitchell's fine Victorian house lies in a peaceful tree-lined terrace within easy reach of the town centre and the beach. The stylish bedrooms have quality period furniture. There is a comfortable lounge and a neat dining room where a hearty traditional breakfast is served.

Facilities 5 en suite (2 fmly) ⊗ TVB tea/coffee ✹ Cen ht TVL
No coaches **Notes** ⊛

◆◆◆◆

Greenan Lodge

39 Dunure, Doonfoot KA7 4HR ☎ 01292 443939
e-mail helen@greenanlodge.com
Dir 2m south of town centre on A719 coastal road

Guests are made to feel truly welcome at this modern bungalow in a quiet residential area, convenient for the coast and attractions around Ayr. The bright, well-furnished bedrooms offer numerous extras and there is a spacious lounge. Expect a generous Scottish breakfasts.

Facilities 3 en suite (3 GF) ⊗ TVB tea/coffee ✹ Cen ht TVL
No children 7yrs No coaches **Prices** S £40-£45; D £56-£60✱ **Parking** 10
Notes ⊛

◆◆◆

Belmont Guest House ◇

15 Park Circus KA7 2DJ ☎ 01292 265588 ▤ 01292 290303
e-mail belmontguesthouse@btinternet.com
web www.belmontguesthouse.co.uk
Dir S of town centre, off A719 Racecourse Rd onto Park Circus

This traditionally run terrace house is in a quiet tree-lined area close to the town centre. Spacious bedrooms come with thoughtful extras. Public areas include a lounge with a vast array of books and a comfortable dining room. The host has a genuine concern for conservation and the environment.

Facilities 5 en suite (3 fmly) (2 GF) ⊗ FTV TVB tea/coffee Cen ht TVL
No coaches **Prices** S £28-£30; D £52-£54✱ LB **Parking** 5 **Notes** Closed Xmas & New Year

Ⓤ

The Crescent

26 Bellevue Crescent KA7 2DR
☎ 01292 287329 ▤ 01292 286779
e-mail carrie@26crescent.freeserve.co.uk
Dir S of town centre, off A719 Racecourse Rd onto Bellevue Crescent

At the time of going to press the rating for this establishment had not been confirmed. Please check the AA website www.theAA.com for up-to-date information.

Facilities 5 en suite ⊗ TVB tea/coffee ✹ Cen ht No children 5yrs
Prices S £40-£45; D £60-£70✱ **Notes** rs Dec-Mar

BALLANTRAE MAP 20 NX08

◆◆◆◆ ▤ ⌁

Balkissock Lodge

Balkissock KA26 0LP ☎ 01465 831537
e-mail info@balkissocklodge.co.uk
web www.balkissocklodge.co.uk
Dir Off A77 1st left S of river, 3m to T-junct. Turn right, Lodge signed 1m ahead

Originally built as a shooting lodge to serve the Laggan Estate, this charming Georgian house is set in 1 acre of gardens and woodland and is well situated for walking, cycling, golf and fishing. Bedrooms have been refurbished to a high standard, and there is a comfortable lounge with a log fire and a cosy dining room where delicious home-cooked meals feature fresh local produce.

Facilities 4 rms (3 en suite) (2 GF) ⊗ TVB tea/coffee ✹ Cen ht
No children No coaches Dinner Last d 5pm **Parking** 6

COYLTON MAP 20 NN50

◆◆◆ ⌁ ◧

The Finlayson Arms Hotel

24 Hillhead KA6 6JT ☎ 01292 570298 ▤ 01292 571545
Dir On A70 in village opp parish church

The friendly, family-owned Finlayson Arms is some 200 years old. Lying in the heart of Ayrshire, it is convenient for the coast, many golf courses and the famous landmarks of Burns country. Several of the well-equipped bedrooms are on the ground floor, and there is a cosy bar, an inviting lounge and a spacious dining room where delicious home-cooked fare is served at individual tables.

Facilities 8 en suite (1 fmly) (5 GF) ⊗ TVB tea/coffee ✹ Cen ht
No coaches Pool Table Dinner Last d 8.30pm **Prices** S £35; D £49✱
Parking 12

DUNURE

MAP 20 NS21

Premier Collection

♦♦♦♦♦

Dunduff Farm

Dunure KA7 4LH ☎ 01292 500225 📄 01292 500222
e-mail gemmelldunduff@aol.com
Dir *On A719 400yds past village school*

Parts of this working farm date from the 15th and 17th centuries. It stands on an elevated position with stunning views across the River Clyde towards Arran and the Mull Of Kintyre. The stylish bedrooms are modern in design and well-equipped. The comfortable lounge is the scene for genuine Scottish hospitality, and breakfast specialities include locally smoked kippers.

Facilities 3 rms (2 en suite) (1 pri facs) (2 fmly) ⊗ TVB tea/coffee ✖ Cen ht TVL No coaches Fishing **Parking** 10 **Notes** Closed Nov-Feb

PRESTWICK

MAP 20 NS32

♦♦♦♦

Golf View

17-19 Links Rd KA9 1QG
☎ 01292 671234 & 470396 📄 01292 671244
e-mail welcome@golfviewhotel.com
web www.golfviewhotel.com
Dir *From Prestwick Airport A79 to town centre signed Prestwick Cross. Take outside lane at 1st lights, turn right, proceed under railway bridge, 200yds on left*

Occupying adjoining properties, this guest house is situated close to the esplanade and overlooks the Old Prestwick Golf Club where the first Open Championship was played in 1860. Bedrooms are stylishly decorated, smartly furnished and well equipped. Upstairs lounges offer fine views and traditional Scottish breakfasts are served in the comfortable dining room.

Facilities 11 rms (10 en suite) (1 pri facs) (1 fmly) (1 GF) ⊗ TVB tea/coffee ✖ Licensed Cen ht TVL No coaches **Prices** S £45; D £78-£86✱ **Parking** 11

SOUTH LANARKSHIRE

BIGGAR

MAP 21 N103

🅰

Lindsaylands

ML12 6NR ☎ 01899 220033 📄 01899 221009
e-mail elspeth@lindsaylands.co.uk
Dir *0.6m SW of town centre. Off A702 Coulter Rd onto Lindsaylands Rd*

Facilities 3 rms (2 en suite) (1 pri facs) (1 fmly) ⊗ tea/coffee ✖ Cen ht TVL No coaches ✎ ⏰ Dinner Last d 10am same day **Prices** S £35-£38; D £58-£62✱ **Conf** Max 12 **Parking** 8 **Notes** ★★★★ Closed Dec-Feb 📖

KIRKMUIRHILL

MAP 21 NS74

♦♦♦ ❦

Dykecroft Farm ◇ *(NS776419)*

ML11 0JQ ☎ 01555 892226 📄 01555 892226 Mrs McInally
e-mail dykecroft.bandb@ tiscali.co.uk
Dir *M74 junct 9/10, B7086 W for 1.5m, 1st bungalow on left past Boghead*

A friendly welcome is assured at this modern bungalow, situated in an open rural location on the road to Strathaven. The comfortable bedrooms are traditionally furnished, and there is a bright airy lounge-dining room with lovely country views.

Facilities 3 rms (3 GF) ⊗ tea/coffee Cen ht TVL 60 acres sheep **Prices** S £24-£25; D £44-£45✱ **Parking** 4 **Notes** 📖

STRATHAVEN

MAP 20 NS74

♦♦♦ ⊛ ⏾

Springvale Hotel and Rissons Restaurant

18 Lethame Rd ML10 6AD
☎ 01357 521131 & 520234 📄 01357 521131
e-mail rissons@msn.com
Dir *A71 into Strathaven, W of town centre off Townhead St*

You are assured of a warm welcome at this charming establishment close to the town centre. The bedrooms vary in size and style, and are usefully equipped. Food, though, is the main feature, and a range of interesting, well-prepared dishes is served in Rissons Restaurant.

Facilities 11 en suite (1 fmly) (2 GF) ⊗ TVB tea/coffee ✖ Licensed Cen ht No coaches Dinner Last d 9.30pm **Prices** D £60-£70✱ **Parking** 10 **Notes** Closed 1st wk Jan

STIRLING

ABERFOYLE
MAP 20 NN50

◆◆◆◆

Balavulin

Lochard Rd FK8 3TD ☎ 01877 382771 ▤ 01877 382771
e-mail info@balavulin.co.uk
web www.balavulin.co.uk
Dir Off A821 Main St onto B829, B&B 1.1m on right

Balavulin is a peaceful haven in the heart of the scenic Queen Elizabeth Forest Park. Bedrooms are well equipped and attractively furnished. There is a charming lounge and a conservatory-dining room where delicious breakfasts are served at individual tables. Fishing and free corporate membership to nearby Hotel leisure facilities are available.

Facilities 3 en suite (3 GF) ⊗ tea/coffee ✖ Cen ht TVL No coaches
Parking 6 **Notes** ⊗

BALMAHA
MAP 20 NS49

◆◆◆ ⬛

Oak Tree Inn

G63 0JQ ☎ 01360 870357 ▤ 01360 870350
e-mail info@oak-tree-inn.co.uk
Dir Junct A811 & A809, follow A811 into Drymen. Follow signs for Balmaha 4m. Oak Tree Inn is on left opp car park

Standing in the shade of a magnificent 500-year-old oak tree on the quiet eastern shore of Loch Lomond, this friendly family-run inn is a great base for exploring the surrounding countryside. The attractive bedrooms have been refurbished to a high standard and are individually styled and well equipped. The rustic bar is complete with beams, a roaring log fire and local memorabilia, while the dining room serves delicious home-cooked fare.

Facilities 8 en suite (1 fmly) ⊗ TVB tea/coffee ✖ Cen ht No coaches
Dinner Last d 9pm **Prices** D £70✳ **Parking** 6 **Notes** Closed 25 Dec,
1 Jan, 26 Feb

CALLANDER
MAP 20 NN60

◆◆◆◆

Arden House

Bracklinn Rd FK17 8EQ ☎ 01877 330235 ▤ 01877 330235
e-mail ardenhouse@onetel.com
Dir Off A84 Main St onto Bracklinn Rd, house 200yds on left

This impressive Victorian villa lies in beautiful mature grounds in a
continued

peaceful area of the town. It featured in the 1960s hit television series Dr Finlay's Casebook and is a friendly, welcoming house. The comfortable bedrooms are thoughtfully furnished and equipped. There is a stylish lounge in addition to the attractive breakfast room where delicious breakfasts are served at individual tables.

Facilities 6 en suite (2 GF) ⊗ TVB tea/coffee ✖ Cen ht No children
14yrs No coaches ⚴ **Prices** S £32.50-£35; D £60-£72✳ **Parking** 10
Notes Closed Nov-Mar

◆◆◆◆

Lubnaig House

Leny Feus FK17 8AS ☎ 01877 330376
e-mail info@lubnaighouse.co.uk
web www.lubnaighouse.co.uk
Dir From centre A84 W, right onto Leny Feus

Lubnaig House is set in a delightful tree-lined secluded garden just a 5-minute walk from the town centre. The house, built in 1864, has been modernised to provide comfortable well-appointed bedrooms, including some ground-floor rooms. There are two cosy lounges, and an impressive dining room where hearty traditional breakfasts are served at individual tables.

Facilities 6 en suite 2 annexe en suite ⊗ TVB tea/coffee ✖ Cen ht
No children 7yrs No coaches **Prices** S £40-£54; D £60-£78✳ LB
Parking 10 **Notes** Closed Nov-Apr

◆◆◆◆

Annfield Guest House ◇

18 North Church St FK17 8EG
☎ 01877 330204 ▤ 01877 330674
e-mail reservations@annfieldguesthouse.co.uk
Dir Off A84 Main St onto North Church St, at top on right

Situated within easy reach of the town centre, this welcoming family-run guest house offers comfortable, good value accommodation. The spacious bedrooms are attractively decorated and well equipped. An elegant first-floor lounge invites peaceful relaxation, and hearty breakfasts are served at individual tables in the pretty dining room. Self-catering accommodation is also available.

Facilities 7 rms (5 en suite) (1 pri facs) (1 fmly) ⊗ FTV TVB tea/coffee
✖ Cen ht TVL No children 5yrs No coaches **Prices** S £25-£35;
D £48-£60✳ **Parking** 9 **Notes** Closed 19 Dec-5 Jan ⊗

Scotland

CALLANDER continued

♦♦♦

The Crags Hotel

101 Main St FK17 8BQ ☎ 01877 330257 📠 01877 339997
e-mail nieto@btinternet.com
web www.cragshotel.co.uk
Dir *In town centre*

Set in the main street, this guest house provides hearty breakfasts and also has a bar. The well-equipped bedrooms range from the compact to spacious rooms on the ground floor, including one with easier access.

Facilities 7 en suite (1 fmly) (3 GF) ⊗ TVB tea/coffee Licensed Cen ht TVL No coaches **Parking** 7

CRIANLARICH   MAP 20 NN32

♦♦♦♦

The Lodge House

FK20 8RU ☎ 01838 300276 📠 01838 300276
e-mail admin@lodgehouse.co.uk
Dir *On A82 NW, 0.5m from of village on right*

This guest house has a superb location. The well-proportioned bedrooms are comfortable, and the adjacent Scandinavian-style chalet is ideal for a family. A cosy well-stocked bar adjoins the stylish lounge, and both have open fires in the winter. Set meals are served in the attractive dining room, which has stunning views of the surrounding mountains.

Facilities 5 en suite 1 annexe en suite (1 fmly) ⊗ TVB tea/coffee ✖ Licensed Cen ht No coaches Dinner Last d 2pm **Parking** 12

KILLIN   MAP 20 NN53

♦♦♦♦

Fairview House ◇

Main St FK21 8UT ☎ 01567 820667
e-mail info@fairview-killin.co.uk
web www.fairview-killin.co.uk
Dir *On A827 in village centre*

From its elevated location in the heart of the village, Fairview House has lovely views of the surrounding countryside and hills. The attractive bedrooms are comfortably furnished and well equipped, and breakfast is served at individual tables in the dining room. Enjoyable

home-made evening meals are available by arrangement with after-dinner coffee served in the quiet lounge.

Facilities 6 en suite (1 fmly) ⊗ TV2B tea/coffee ✖ Cen ht TVL No coaches Dinner Last d 11am **Prices** S £26-£35; D £26-£52✳ **Parking** 7 **Notes** ⊛

LOCHEARNHEAD   MAP 20 NN52

♦♦♦♦

Mansewood Country House

FK19 8NS ☎ 01567 830213 & 830485 📠 01567 830485
e-mail stay@mansewoodcountryhouse.co.uk
Dir *A84 N to Lochearnhead, 1st building on left*

This spacious former manse dates from the 18th century and lies in a well-tended garden to the south of the village. Bedrooms are well appointed and equipped and offer high standards of comfort. Refreshments can be enjoyed in the cosy bar or the elegant lounge, and meals prepared with flair are served in the attractive restaurant.

Facilities 5 en suite ⊗ TVB tea/coffee Licensed Cen ht No coaches Dinner Last d 5pm **Prices** D £50-£60✳ **LB** **Parking** 10 **Notes** Closed Dec-Jan

STIRLING   MAP 21 NS79

♦♦♦♦

Linden Guest House

22 Linden Av FK7 7PQ
☎ 01786 448850 & 07974 116573 📠 01786 448850
e-mail fay@lindenguesthouse.co.uk
Dir *0.5m SE of city centre off A9*

Situated within walking distance of the town centre, this friendly guest house offers attractive and very well-equipped bedrooms, including a family room. There is a bright dining room where delicious breakfasts are served at individual tables.

Facilities 4 rms (3 en suite) (1 pri facs) (2 fmly) (1 GF) ⊗ STV TVB tea/coffee Cen ht No coaches **Prices** D £50-£60 **LB** **Parking** 2

continued

STRATHYRE
MAP 20 NN51

★★★★★ ◉◉ **Restaurant with Rooms**

Creagan House

FK18 8ND ☎ 01877 384638 ▤ 01877 384319
e-mail eatndstay@creaganhouse.co.uk
web www.creaganhouse.co.uk
Dir 0.25m N of Strathyre on A84

Originally a farmhouse dating from the 17th century, this restored little gem has operated as a restaurant with rooms for many years. The baronial-style dining room provides a wonderful setting for sympathetic cooking providing superbly flavoursome dishes. Warm hospitality and attentive service are the highlight of any stay.

Facilities 5 en suite (1 fmly) (1 GF) tea/coffee Licensed Dinner Last d 8.30pm **Prices** S £65; D £110✳ **LB** **Conf** Thtr 35 Class 12 Board 35 **Parking** 26 **Notes** Closed 21 Jan-9 Mar & 4-23 Nov rs 24 Nov-20 Dec

WEST DUNBARTONSHIRE

BALLOCH
MAP 20 NS38

◆◆◆

Sunnyside ◇

35 Main St G83 9JX ☎ 01389 750282 & 07717 397548
e-mail enquiries@sunnysidebb.co.uk
Dir On A813, 1m S of junct A811

Set in its own grounds well back from the road by Loch Lomond, Sunnyside is an attractive, traditional detached house, parts of which date back to the 1830s. Bedrooms are attractively decorated and provide comfortable modern accommodation. The dining room is located on the ground floor, and is an appropriate setting for hearty Scottish breakfasts.

Facilities 6 en suite (2 fmly) (1 GF) ⊗ TVB tea/coffee Cen ht No coaches **Prices** S £25-£35; D £40-£53✳ **Parking** 8

Anchorage Guest House

31 Balloch Rd G83 8SS ☎ 01389 753336
e-mail anchorage_gh@hotmail.com
Dir In town centre, off A811 Lomond Rd onto Balloch Rd, house next to tourist information

Facilities 5 en suite (1 fmly) (5 GF) ⊗ FTV TVB tea/coffee Cen ht No coaches **Prices** D £50-£60✳ **LB** **Parking** 6 **Notes** ★★

DUMBARTON
See Cardross (Argyll & Bute)

WEST LOTHIAN

BLACKBURN
MAP 21 NS96

◆◆◆

Cruachan B & B ◇

78 East Main St EH47 7QS
☎ 01506 655221 ▤ 01506 652395
e-mail cruachan.bb@virgin.net
Dir On A705 in Blackburn

Ideally located for both the leisure and business traveller to central Scotland, with Edinburgh's city centre only some 30 minutes away by train from nearby Bathgate and Glasgow only 35 minutes away by car. Cruachan is the comfortable, friendly home of the Harkins family. Bedrooms are bright, attractive and very well equipped. Breakfast, featuring the best of local produce is served at individual tables in the ground floor dining room.

Facilities 4 rms (3 en suite) (1 pri facs) (1 fmly) ⊗ TVB tea/coffee ✖ Cen ht **Prices** S £30-£35; D £50-£60 **Parking** 5

Scotland

EAST CALDER   MAP 21 NT06

Premier Collection

◆◆◆◆◆ ❦

Ashcroft Farmhouse (NT095682)

EH53 0ET ☎ 01506 881810 📠 01506 884327
Mr & Mrs Scott
e-mail scottashcroft7@aol.com
web www.ashcroftfarmhouse.com
Dir On B7015, off A71, 0.5m E of East Calder, near to Almondell
Country Park

With over 40 years' experience in caring for guests, Derek and
Elizabeth Scott ensure a stay at Ashcroft will be memorable. Their
modern home sits in lovely award-winning landscaped gardens and
provides attractive and well-equipped ground-floor bedrooms. The
comfortable lounge includes a video library. Breakfast, featuring
home-made sausages and the best of local produce, is served at
individual tables in the stylish dining room.

Facilities 6 en suite (2 fmly) (6 GF) ⊗ TVB tea/coffee ✱ Cen ht TVL
No children 12yrs 5 acres Arable **Prices** S £45-£60; D £64-£70✳
Parking 8

See advertisement on page 617

◆◆◆◆

Whitecroft Bed & Breakfast ◇

7 Raw Holdings EH53 0ET
☎ 01506 882494 📠 01506 882598
e-mail lornascot@aol.com
Dir A71 onto B7015, establishment on right

A relaxed and friendly atmosphere prevails at this charming modern
guest house. The bedrooms, all of which are on the ground floor, are

continued

attractively colour coordinated, well-equipped and contain many
thoughtful extra touches. Breakfast is served at individual tables in the
smart dining room.

Facilities 3 en suite ⊗ TVB tea/coffee ✱ Cen ht No children 12yrs
No coaches **Prices** S £30-£50; D £56-£70✳ **Parking** 5

◆◆◆ ❦

Overshiel Farm (NT099689)

EH53 0HT ☎ 01506 880469 & 07888 754999 Mrs Dick
e-mail enquiries@overshielfarm.com
Dir 1m NW of East Calder. A71 onto B7015, 2nd right, 0.5m on right

This large Victorian farmhouse is set in sheltered gardens next to the
farm and is a convenient base for visiting Edinburgh. Two of the
relaxing rooms have external access, while the room in the main
house is particularly spacious. Breakfast is served around one large
table and there is a comfortable lounge.

Facilities 1 rms 2 annexe en suite (2 GF) ⊗ TVB tea/coffee ✱ Cen ht
340 acres mixed **Parking** 6 **Notes** 🐾

See advertisement on page 625

LINLITHGOW   MAP 21 NS97

Premier Collection

◆◆◆◆◆

Arden Country House

Belsyde EH49 6QE ☎ 01506 670172 📠 01506 670172
e-mail info@ardenhouse-scotland.co.uk
web www.ardencountryhouse.com
Dir 1.5m SW of Linlithgow. A706 over Union Canal, entrance 200yds
on left at Lodge Cottage

Situated in the picturesque grounds of the Belsyde Country Estate and
close to the Royal Burgh of Linlithgow, Arden House offers

continued

Scotland

immaculate, stylishly furnished and spacious bedrooms. There is a cosy ground-floor lounge and a charming dining room where delicious breakfasts feature the best of local produce. Beth Cruickshank is the runner-up for AA Landlady of the Year 2006.

Facilities 3 en suite (1 GF) ⊗ TVB tea/coffee ✖ Cen ht No children 12yrs No coaches **Prices** S £42-£80; D £64-£80✶ **LB Parking** 4 **Notes** Closed 25-26 Dec

◆◆◆◆ ✤

Bomains Farm *(NS990791)*

Bo'Ness EH49 7RQ
☎ 01506 822188 & 822861 📠 01506 824433 & 822188
Mrs Kirk
e-mail buntykirk@tiscali.co.uk
web www.bomains.co.uk
Dir A706 1.5m N towards Bo Ness, left at golf course x-rds, 1st farm on right

From its elevated location this friendly farmhouse has stunning views of the Firth of Forth. The bedrooms which vary in size are beautifully decorated, well equipped and enhanced by quality fabrics, with many thoughtful extra touches. Delicious home-cooked fare featuring the best of local produce is served a stylish lounge-dining room.

Facilities 5 rms (4 en suite) (1 pri facs) ⊗ STV TVB tea/coffee Cen ht TVL 180 acres Arable Dinner Last d 5.30pm **Parking** 8 **Notes** ⊜

◆◆◆◆

Belsyde House ◇

Lanark Rd EH49 6QE ☎ 01506 842098 📠 01506 842098
e-mail hay@belsydehouse.co.uk
Dir 1.5m SW on A706, 1st left over Union Canal

Reached by a tree-lined driveway, this welcoming farmhouse is peacefully situated in attractive grounds close to the Union Canal.

There are well-proportioned double, twin and family rooms, and a cosy single. All are nicely furnished and well equipped. Breakfast, including a vegetarian menu, is served at good-size tables in the dining room, next to the lounge.

Facilities 3 rms (1 en suite) (1 fmly) ⊗ TVB tea/coffee ✖ Cen ht TVL Golf **Prices** S fr £25; d fr £50✶ **Parking** 10 **Notes** Closed Xmas

◆◆◆◆

Thornton

Edinburgh Rd EH49 6AA ☎ 01506 844693
e-mail inglisthornton@hotmail.com
web www.thornton-scotland.co.uk
Dir 0.3m E of town centre on B9080. Pass disused garage on left, right after high stone wall house

This delightful Victorian house is situated within easy reach of the centre of historic Linlithgow and is convenient for both Edinburgh and Glasgow. A welcoming home-from-home, bedrooms are thoughtfully equipped and more often than not guests are free to use house's sitting room. The memorable breakfasts are a feature, and were a former winner of our Best Scottish Breakfast award.

Facilities 2 en suite (2 GF) ⊗ TVB tea/coffee ✖ Cen ht TVL No children 12yrs No coaches **Prices** S £35-£45; D £60-£65 **Parking** 2 **Notes** Closed Dec-Feb

LIVINGSTON   MAP 21 NT06

◆◆◆◆

Redcraig Bed & Breakfast ◇

Redcraig, Midcalder EH53 0JT
☎ 01506 884249 📠 01506 884249
e-mail jcampbelljack@aol.com
web www.redcraigbedandbreakfast.co.uk
Dir 3m S of Livingston. Off A71 at Morton sign at Oakbank

Enjoying a peaceful location within easy reach of central Scotland's major motorway and rail network, and situated half way between Edinburgh and Glasgow this friendly family home offers spotless, comfortable and stylish accommodation in a relaxed environment. Bedrooms are attractive and well equipped with two situated on the ground floor. Hearty breakfasts are served in the smart dining room.

Facilities 3 en suite (2 GF) ⊗ TVB tea/coffee ✖ Cen ht No coaches **Prices** S £30-£35; D £50-£56 **Parking** 6 **Notes** ⊜

continued

Scotland

Scotland

LIVINGSTON continued

♦♦♦♦

Whitecroft

7 Raw Holdings EH53 0ET
☎ 01506 882494 🖹 01506 882598
e-mail lornascot@aol.com
For full entry see **East Calder**

SCOTTISH ISLANDS
ARRAN, ISLE OF

BRODICK　　　　　　　　　MAP 20 NS03

★★★★ Guest House
Allandale

KA27 8BJ ☎ 01770 302278 🖹 01770 302278
e-mail info@allandalehouse.co.uk
Dir 2 mins from Brodick Pier, turn left at junct & follow sign to
Lamlash, up hill take 2nd left at Corriegills sign. Guest House on
corner of main road

Under enthusiastic ownership, this comfortable guest house is set in
delightful gardens. Guests can relax with a drink in the lounge before
enjoying wholesome home-cooked fare in the dining room. Bedrooms
vary in size and have pleasing colour schemes and mixed modern
furnishings along with the thoughtful amenities.

Facilities 4 rms (3 en suite) (1 pri facs) 2 annexe en suite (3 fmly)
(2 GF) ⊗ TVB tea/coffee ✖ Licensed Cen ht Dinner Last d 24hrs
notice **Prices** D £62-£66 **LB** **Parking** 6 **Notes** Closed Nov-Jan

♦♦♦♦

Dunvegan House

Dunvegan Shore Rd KA27 8AJ
☎ 01770 302811 🖹 01770 302811
e-mail dunveganhouse1@hotmail.com
Dir Turn right from ferry terminal, 500yds along Shore Rd

Dunvegan is a delightful detached home overlooking the bay towards
Brodick Castle with Goat Fell beyond. The comfortable lounge and
attractive dining room, as well as the pine-furnished bedrooms, enjoy
the views. A daily-changing dinner menu and an interesting wine list
encourage guests to dine in.

Dunvegan House

Facilities 9 en suite (1 fmly) (3 GF) ⊗ TVB tea/coffee ✖ Licensed
Cen ht No coaches Dinner Last d 4pm **Parking** 10 **Notes** Closed
Xmas & New Year 🐾

HARRIS, ISLE OF

LEVERBURGH　　　　　　　　MAP 22 NG08

★★★★ Guest House
Grimsdale Guest House

HS5 3TS ☎ 01859 520460
e-mail farky@grimsdale.co.uk
web www.grimsdale.co.uk
Dir 1m along A859 heading N from Leverburgh Ferry Terminal

Grimsdale Guest House stands on a peninsula overlooking a
freshwater salmon and trout loch, surrounded by the natural
tranquillity of South Harris. This modern, purpose-built house has
spacious comfortable rooms all with wonderful views and the first-
floor lounge overlooking Loch Steisevat is ideal for relaxing or
enjoying the selection of DVDs available.

Facilities 3 en suite (1 fmly) (3 GF) ⊗ TVB tea/coffee Cen ht TVL
No coaches Fishing Dinner Last d 24hrs notice **Prices** S £50; D £70✳
Parking 6 **Notes** Closed Nov-Mar

SCARISTA　　　　　　　　　MAP 22 NG09

★★★★ ⊛⊛ Restaurant with Rooms
Scarista House

HS3 3HX ☎ 01859 550238 🖹 01859 550277
e-mail timandpatricia@scaristahouse.com
Dir On A859, 15m S of Tarbert

A former manse, Scarista House is now a haven for food lovers who
seek to explore the magnificent island of Harris. The house enjoys
breathtaking views of the Atlantic and is just a short stroll from miles
of golden sandy beaches. The house is run in a relaxed country-house
manner by the friendly hosts. Expect wellies in the hall and masses of
books and CDs in one of two lounges. Bedrooms are cosy, and
delicious set dinners and memorable breakfasts are provided.

Facilities 3 en suite 2 annexe en suite (2 GF) tea/coffee Direct dial from
bedrooms Licensed No coaches Dinner Last d 8pm **Prices** S £120-£140;
D £165-£190✳ **LB** **Parking** 12 **Notes** Closed Xmas rs Nov-Mar
Civ Wed 40

continued

ISLAY, ISLE OF

BOWMORE　　　　　　　　　　MAP 20 NR35

Premier Collection

 ♦♦♦♦♦ ⍟⍟ ≙ ⌣ ◧

The Harbour Inn and Restaurant

PA43 7JR ☎ 01496 810330 ▤ 01496 810990
e-mail info@harbour.inn.com
Dir *Next to harbour*

No trip to Islay would be complete without experiencing a night or two at the Harbour Inn. The humble whitewashed exterior conceals a sophisticated, quality environment that draws discerning travellers from all over the world. Spacious bedrooms have been refurbished to a high standard and a new conservatory-lounge has stunning views over Loch Indaal to the peaks of Jura. The cosy bar is popular with locals, while the smart dining room showcases some of the finest seafood in British waters. Welcome peat fires burn in cooler months.

Facilities 7 en suite (1 GF) ⊗ TVB tea/coffee Direct dial from bedrooms ✘ No children 10yrs No coaches Complimentary use of local leisure centre Dinner Last d 9pm **Prices** S £65-£135; D £105-£135✳ LB

SHETLAND

LERWICK　　　　　　　　　　MAP 24 HU44

♦♦♦♦

Glen Orchy House

20 Knab Rd ZE1 0AX ☎ 01595 692031 ▤ 01595 692031
e-mail glenorchy.house@virgin.net
Dir *Next to coastguard station*

This welcoming and well-presented guest house lies above the town with views over the Knab, and is within easy walking distance of the centre. Bedrooms are modern in design and there is a choice of lounges with books and board games, one with an honesty bar. Breakfasts are as substantial as dinner, chosen from the daily-changing menu.

Facilities 24 en suite (4 fmly) (4 GF) ⊗ STV FTV TVB tea/coffee Licensed Cen ht No coaches Dinner Last d 2pm **Prices** S fr £47; d fr £74✳ **Parking** 10

SKYE, ISLE OF

COLBOST　　　　　　　　　　MAP 22 NG24

Premier Collection

★★★★★ ⍟⍟⍟ **Restaurant with Rooms**

The Three Chimneys & The House Over-By

IV55 8ZT ☎ 01470 511258 ▤ 01470 511358
e-mail eatandstay@threechimneys.co.uk
web www.threechimneys.co.uk
Dir *4m W of Dunvegan village on B884 signed Glendale*

A visit to this delightful property and restaurant will make a trip to Skye memorable. Shirley Spear's stunning food is the result of a deft approach using quality local ingredients. Breakfast is an impressive array of local fish, meats and cheeses, served with fresh home baking and home-made preserves. The stylish, thoughtfully equipped bedrooms in the House Over-By have spacious en suites and wonderful views across Loch Dunvegan.

Facilities 6 en suite (1 fmly) ⊗ STV TVB tea/coffee Direct dial from bedrooms ✘ Cen ht Dinner Last d 9.30pm **Prices** D £250✳ **Parking** available

EDINBANE
MAP 22 NG35

◆◆◆◆

Shorefield House

Edinbane IV51 9PW ☎ 01470 582444 📄 01470 582414
e-mail shorefieldhouse@aol.com
web www.shorefield.com

Dir *12m from Portree & 8m from Dunvegan, off A850 into Edinbane, 1st on right*

Shorefield stands in the village of Edinbane and looks out to Loch Greshornish. Bedrooms range from single to family, while a ground-floor room has easier access. All rooms are thoughtfully equipped and have CD players. Breakfast is an impressive choice and there is also a child-friendly garden.

Facilities 5 en suite (2 fmly) (4 GF) ⊘ tea/coffee ✖ Cen ht TVL
No coaches **Prices** S £30-£45; D £60-£80 **Parking** 10 **Notes** Closed Nov-mid Mar

PORTREE
MAP 22 NG44

◆◆◆◆

Quiraing House

Viewfield Rd IV51 9ES ☎ 01478 612870 📄 01478 612870
e-mail quirainghouse@hotmail.com

Dir *On A87 from S, Bridge End, pass BP filling station & guest house 400yds on right*

This stylishly furnished bungalow stands in a well-tended garden on the southern approach to the town, which is only a short walk away. Bedrooms are bright, airy and immaculately maintained. All are well equipped to include fridges. There is a comfortable lounge and an attractive dining room where hearty breakfasts are served at individual tables.

Facilities 6 en suite (6 GF) ⊘ TVB tea/coffee ✖ Cen ht TVL
No coaches **Prices** S £40; D £60 **Parking** 8

UIG
MAP 22 NG36

◆◆◆

Woodbine House

IV51 9XP ☎ 01470 542243 📄 01470 542243
e-mail shona_mcclure@hotmail.com

Dir *From Portree into Uig Bay, pass Ferry Inn & right onto A855 Staffing Rd, house 300yds on right*

Built in the late 19th century, Woodbine House occupies an elevated location overlooking Uig bay and the surrounding countryside and is well situated for walking and birdwatching. Bedrooms are attractive, well equipped and comfortable. The ground-floor lounge and dining room have lovely views, delightful settings for relaxation or delicious evening meals and hearty breakfasts.

Facilities 4 en suite (1 fmly) ⊘ TVB tea/coffee Cen ht TVL No children 10yrs No coaches Dinner **Prices** S £40-£55; D £40-£55✳ **Parking** 4

Scotland

Wales

Tintern Abbey,
Monmouthshire

ANGLESEY, ISLE OF

Wales

CEMAES BAY
MAP 14 SH39

◆◆◆◆

Hafod Country House

LL67 0DS ☎ 01407 711645
e-mail hbr1946@aol.com
Dir A5025 to Cemaes Bay rdbt, take rd signposted Llanfechell. Hafod is 500yds on left.

Guests are assured of a warm welcome at this large and spacious Edwardian house, which stands in extensive gardens and is quietly located on the outskirts of the village. It provides well equipped accommodation, as well as a comfortable lounge and a pleasant breakfast room, where separate tables are provided.

Facilities 3 en suite ⊗ TVB tea/coffee ✱ Cen ht No children 7yrs No coaches **Prices** S fr £35; d fr £55✳ **Parking** 3 **Notes** Closed Oct-Mar

HOLYHEAD
MAP 14 SH28

◆◆◆◆

Yr Hendre

Porth-y-Felin Rd LL65 1AH
☎ 01407 762929 📄 01407 762929
e-mail rita@yr-hendre.freeserve.co.uk
web www.yr-hendre.co.uk
Dir From A5 in town centre left at war memorial. Next left, up steep hill, over x-rds, house on right

A short walk from the promenade, this delightful house is convenient for the nearby Ireland ferry terminal. Bedrooms are attractively decorated with rich fabrics and wallpapers, and all are thoughtfully equipped. The reception rooms offer similar stylish comfort, and the freshly prepared breakfast is strong on local produce.

Facilities 3 en suite ⊗ TVB tea/coffee ✱ Cen ht TVL No coaches **Parking** 7 **Notes**

◆◆◆

Wavecrest ◇

93 Newry St LL65 1HU ☎ 01407 763637 📄 01407 764862
e-mail cwavecrest@aol.com
web www.holyheadhotels.com
Dir Left at end A55, 600yds turn by railings, premises 100yds up hill on right

Well located for the Irish ferry terminals and within easy walking distance of the town centre, the Wavecrest is proving to be a popular overnight stop-off. Pretty bedrooms are equipped with satellite television and other modern facilities. There is a comfortable lounge and evening meals may be booked in advance.

Facilities 4 rms (2 en suite) (3 fmly) ⊗ STV TVB tea/coffee Cen ht TVL No coaches Dinner Last d 3pm **Prices** S £22-£25; D £40-£50✳ **Parking** 1 **Notes** Closed 24-31 Dec 🐾

LLANERCHYMEDD
MAP 14 SH48

◆◆◆◆ 🐾

Tre-Wyn *(SH454851)*

Maenaddwyn LL71 8AE ☎ 01248 470875 Mrs Bown
e-mail nia@trewyn.fsnet.co.uk
Dir A5025 to Benllech Bay, B5108 to Brynteg x-rds, take Llannerchymedd road 3m to Maenaddwyn. Right after 6 houses, 0.5m to farm

An extremely friendly welcome is extended at this spacious farmhouse. Rooms are well equipped and attractively furnished. The dining room and the relaxing lounge with its log fire have wonderful views across the gardens and countryside to Bodafon Mountain.

Facilities 3 en suite (1 fmly) ⊗ TVB tea/coffee ✱ Cen ht TVL 240 acres arable beef sheep **Parking** 5

MENAI BRIDGE
MAP 14 SH57

Premier Collection

◆◆◆◆◆ 🍽️ 🐾

Wern Farm *(SH550740)*

Pentraeth Rd LL59 5RR ☎ 01248 712421 📄 01248 715421
Mr & Mrs P Brayshaw
e-mail wernfarmanglesey@onetel.com
web www.angleseyfarms.com/wern.htm
Dir A55 junct 8 over Britannia Bridge onto A5025, over rdbt & pass large garage, farm on right

A warm welcome is assured at this immaculate farm guest house, located on superb grounds, which include an ornamental pond and all-weather tennis court. Spacious bedrooms are furnished with style and a wealth of thoughtful extras enhance guest comfort. Memorable breakfasts are served in the attractive conservatory-dining room, and a sumptuous lounge and games room, featuring an antique three-quarter size billiard table, are also features of this home from home.

Facilities 3 rms (2 en suite) (2 fmly) ⊗ TVB tea/coffee ✱ Cen ht TVL No children 12yrs ⚬ Snooker ⛳ Boules Whirlpool Baths 150 acres mixed **Prices** S £42-£70; D £64-£75✳ **Parking** 10 **Notes** Closed Nov-Feb

BRIDGEND

BRIDGEND   MAP 09 SS97

Ewenny Farm Guest House

Ewenny Cross, Ewenny CF35 5AB
☎ 01656 658438 🖹 01656 655565
web www.ewennyfarmguesthouse.co.uk
Dir M4 junct 35, follow A473 for 2.5m to Bridgend, then A48 W for
0.5m. Pick up Ewenny Rd for Southern Down and Ewenny

Facilities 7 en suite (2 fmly) (6 GF) ⊘ in 4 bedrooms ⊘ in dining
room ⊘ in lounges TVB tea/coffee Direct dial from bedrooms ✖
Cen ht Fishing Riding Gymnasium **Parking** 20 **Notes** ★★★

Hunters Gate ◈

Maudlam CF33 4PL ☎ 01656 740735
e-mail janehampton@maudlam.fsnet.co.uk
Dir M4 junct 37, take road to Porthcawl. Right at 1st rdbt into North
Cornelly. Through village pass Green Acres Motel and left at x-rds
towards Maudlam. Left after the Angel Inn and follow road to village.
Hunters Gate on right

Facilities 3 rms (2 en suite) (1 pri facs) ⊘ TVB tea/coffee ✖ Cen ht
TVL No children 9yrs No coaches Dinner Last d 5pm **Prices** S fr £25; d
fr £45✷ **Parking** 6 **Notes** ★★★ 🐾

CAERPHILLY

CAERPHILLY   MAP 09 ST18

◆◆◆

The Cottage Guest House

Mountain View, Pwllypant CF83 3HW
☎ 029 2086 9160 🖹 029 2086 9160
Dir M4 junct 32, A470 Merthyr Tydfil, 2nd exit A468 Caerphilly,
cottage on rdbt junct A468 & A469

Enthusiastic proprietor Carole Beacham is always on hand to welcome
you to her 300-year-old home, which occupies a convenient roadside
location near to the town centre. Bedrooms are well and thoughtfully
appointed, and there is a spacious and comfortable lounge. Breakfast
is served in the attractive dining room.

Facilities 3 en suite ⊘ TVB tea/coffee ✖ Cen ht TVL No coaches
Parking 8 **Notes** 🐾

CARDIFF

CARDIFF   MAP 09 ST17

★★★★ ◉◉ **Restaurant with Rooms**

The Old Post Office

Greenwood Ln, St Fagans CF5 6EL
☎ 029 2056 5400 🖹 029 2056 3400
e-mail heiditheoldpost@aol.com
Dir M4 Junct 33 onto A4323. Take Culverhouse Cross exit then 1st
exit then left onto Michaelston Rd. Over rdbt and level crossing, left at
Castle Hill, right past church.

Located just five miles from Cardiff in the historic village of St Fagans,
this establishment offers contemporary style based on New England
design. Bedrooms, like the dining room, feature striking white walls
with spotlights offering a fresh, clean feel. Delicious meals include a
carefully prepared selection of local produce.

Facilities 6 en suite (2 fmly) (6 GF) TVB tea/coffee Direct dial from
bedrooms ✖ Licensed No coaches Last d 9pm **Prices** S £70; D £100 ✷
LB **Parking** 40

◆◆◆◆

Annedd Lon Guest House

157 Cathedral Rd, Pontcanna CF11 9PL
☎ 029 2022 3349 🖹 029 2064 0885
Dir From Cardiff Castle, W across the river Taff. 1st right is Cathedral
Rd. On left hand just after 4th side street

Just a leisurely stroll from Sophia Gardens and the Millennium
Stadium, this impressive Victorian house is centrally located. The
house retains many original features and is attractively furnished.
Elegant public areas include a comfortable lounge as well as a cosy
dining room.

Facilities 6 rms (5 en suite) (2 fmly) ⊘ TVB tea/coffee ✖ Cen ht TVL
No coaches **Prices** S fr £35; d fr £55✷ **Parking** 7 **Notes** Closed
24-29 Dec

Wales

CARDIFF continued

◆◆◆◆

The Big Sleep Hotel

Bute Ter CF10 2FE ☎ 029 2063 6363 📠 029 2063 6364
e-mail bookings.cardiff@thebigsleephotel.com
Dir *Opp Cardiff International Arena*

Part of the Cardiff skyline, this city-centre establishment offers well-equipped bedrooms ranging from standard to penthouse, with spectacular views over the city towards the bay. There is a bar on the ground floor and secure parking. Choose between a continental breakfast or Breakfast to Go, an alternative for travellers making an early start.

Facilities 81 en suite (6 fmly) ⊗ in 60 bedrooms ⊗ in dining room ⊗ in 1 lounge STV TVB tea/coffee Direct dial from bedrooms Licensed Lift Cen ht **Prices** D £45-£150✱ **LB** **Conf** Max 60 Thtr 60 Class 20 Board 20 **Parking** 20

◆◆◆◆

Marlborough Guest House

98 Newport Rd CF24 1DG
☎ 029 2049 2385 📠 029 2046 5982

This friendly, family-run guest house is just 500yds from the city centre. Bedrooms are mostly spacious and all are well furnished and equipped. Bathrooms are particularly well fitted. A comfortable lounge is available and hearty breakfasts are served in the pleasant breakfast room.

Facilities 8 rms (6 en suite) (2 fmly) ⊗ STV TVB tea/coffee ✖ Cen ht TVL **Parking** 8

◆◆◆◆

Tanglewood

4 Tygwyn Rd, Penylan CF23 5JE
☎ 029 2047 3447 & 07971 546812 📠 0870 706 1808
e-mail reservations@tanglewoodguesthouse.com
web www.tanglewoodguesthouse.com
Dir *Towards Cardiff E & Docks. 3rd exit at rdbt. Next rdbt 1st exit. Left at lights. Right just past next lights. Establishment 120yds on right*

An elegant, well-kept Edwardian house, Tanglewood is in a quiet residential district and has attractive gardens. The pleasant bedrooms are thoughtfully equipped and there is a comfortable lounge overlooking the gardens.

Tanglewood

Facilities 4 rms (1 en suite) ⊗ TVB tea/coffee ✖ Cen ht TVL No coaches **Parking** 8 **Notes** Closed 15 Dec-10 Jan ⊛

CARMARTHENSHIRE

AMMANFORD   MAP 08 SN61

🅰

Bryncoch Farm

Llandyfan SA18 2TY ☎ 01269 850480 📠 01236 850480
e-mail robrich@bryncochfarm.co.uk
Dir *M4 junct 29, A483 to Ammanford, onto A474, 0.75m left signed Trap, farm 3m*

Facilities 3 en suite (1 fmly) ⊗ in dining room ⊗ in lounges TVB tea/coffee Cen ht TVL **Parking** 10 **Notes** ★★

BRECHFA   MAP 08 SN53

◆◆◆◆

Dan y Coed

Nant y Ffin SA32 7RE ☎ 01267 202795 📠 01267 202794
e-mail stella@danycoed.co.uk
web www.danycoed.co.uk
Dir *2m NE of Brechfa on B4310 on left*

A warm welcome awaits guests at this well-maintained modern bungalow. The two bedrooms are thoughtfully equipped and contain many extra welcoming touches. Set in extensive grounds and gardens and surrounded by hills and forests, the guest house is located in the peaceful Cothi valley.

Facilities 2 rms (1 en suite) (1 pri facs) (2 GF) ⊗ TVB tea/coffee ✖ Cen ht TVL No children 12yrs No coaches **Prices** D £70 **Parking** 4

continued

Wales

CARMARTHEN

MAP 08 SN42

See also **Brechfa & Cwmduad**

◆◆◆◆

Capel Dewi Uchaf Country House

Capel Dewi SA32 8AY ☎ 01267 290799 📠 01267 290003
e-mail uchaffarm@aol.com
Dir On B4300 between Capel Dewi & junct B4310

Located in 30 acres of grounds with stunning views and private fishing on the River Towy, this Grade II listed 16th-century house retains many magnificent features and has a wealth of character. It is convenient for the National Botanic Garden, 2m south-east. Generous Welsh breakfasts are a feature here.

Facilities 3 en suite ⊗ TVB tea/coffee ✖ Cen ht TVL No coaches Fishing Riding Dinner Last d 10am **Prices** S £47; D £70 LB **Conf** Max 8 Board 8 **Parking** 10 **Notes** Closed Xmas

◆◆◆◆

Sarnau Mansion

Llysonnen Rd SA33 5DZ ☎ 01267 211404 📠 01267 211404
e-mail fernihough@so1405.force9.co.uk
web www.sarnaumansion.co.uk
Dir 5m W of Carmarthen. Off A40 onto B4298 & Bancyfelin road, Sarnau on right

Located west of Carmarthen in 16 acres of grounds and gardens, including a tennis court, this large Grade II listed late-Georgian house retains much original character and is stylishly decorated. There is a lounge with a log fire, an elegant dining room, and spacious bedrooms with stunning rural views.

Facilities 3 en suite ⊗ TVB tea/coffee ✖ Cen ht TVL No children 5yrs No coaches ⚲ Dinner Last d 24hrs **Prices** S £40-£45; D £55-£65 **Parking** 10

◆◆◆◆

Shakeshafts ◇

Lower Penddaulwyn, Capel Dewi SA32 8AY
☎ 01267 290627
e-mail elaine@shakeshafts.com
Dir On B4300 3m E of Carmarthen

Peacefully located in the beautiful Towy Valley with three acres of grounds to the rear, Shakeshafts offers a friendly and relaxing style of accommodation. The modern bedrooms and bathrooms are newly furnished and comfortable. Guests are welcome to enjoy the surrounding gardens or on colder days may prefer the latest addition of a conservatory.

Facilities 3 en suite (1 GF) ⊗ TVB tea/coffee ✖ Cen ht No children 8yrs No coaches ♫ **Prices** S £27.50-£40; D £45-£60 LB **Parking** 10 **Notes** ⊗

CWMDUAD

MAP 08 SN33

◆◆◆◆

Neuadd-Wen Guest House ◇

SA33 6XJ ☎ 01267 281438 📠 01267 281438
e-mail goodbourn@neuaddwen.plus.com
Dir On A484, 9m N of Carmarthen, towards Cardigan

Excellent customer care is assured at this combined Post Office and house situated in pretty gardens in an unspoiled village. Bedrooms are filled with thoughtful extras and there is a choice of lounges. One bedroom is in a carefully renovated Victorian toll cottage across the road. There is an attractive dining room that serves imaginative dinners using fresh local produce.

Facilities 8 rms (6 en suite) 1 annexe en suite (2 fmly) (2 GF) ⊗ TV8B tea/coffee Direct dial from bedrooms Licensed Cen ht TVL No coaches Dinner Last d 5pm **Prices** S £21-£25; D £42-£50 LB **Parking** 12

DREFACH-FELINDRE

MAP 08 SN33

◆◆◆

Cilwendeg House B & B

Waungilwen SA44 5YH ☎ 01559 370685 📠 01559 370685
e-mail info@cilwendeghouse.co.uk
Dir A484 from Carmarthen towards Cardigan, left at Pentrecagal signed Drefach-Felindre, B&B 1m on left

Delightfully located being surrounded by over 5 acres of mature gardens, Cilwendeg lives up to its meaning of 'place to escape and seek refuge'. Bedrooms are extremely spacious and the whole house exudes a pleasant ambience. Guests are welcome to wander the grounds and in summer may enjoy freshly cooked breakfast on the patio.

Facilities 2 rms ⊗ in bedrooms ⊗ in dining room TVB tea/coffee ✖ Cen ht No coaches **Prices** d fr £50✴ LB **Parking** 6 **Notes** ⊗

Wales

LLANDEILO
MAP 08 SN62

♦♦♦♦

Brynteilo Guest House

Manordeilo SA19 7BG ☎ 01550 777040 ▤ 01550 777884
e-mail enquiries@brynteilo.com
web www.brynteilo.com
Dir On A40, 4m NE of Llandeilo & 8m SW of Llandovery

This personally run, no smoking, friendly guest house is situated just
north-east of Llandeilo. In the heart of the Towy Valley and
surrounded by lovely countryside this establishment offers smart,
modern and well-equipped accommodation including a family room
and several ground-floor bedrooms. A self-catering flat is also
available. Separate tables are provided in the attractive dining room.

Facilities 11 en suite (1 fmly) (6 GF) ⊛ TVB tea/coffee Direct dial from
bedrooms ⚞ Cen ht No coaches **Prices** S £45; D £60✳ **Parking** 15

LLANDYBIE
MAP 08 SN61

♦♦♦ ❧

Glynhir Mansion (SN635152)

Glynhir Rd SA18 2TD
☎ 01269 850438 ▤ 01269 851275 Mrs Jenkins
e-mail enquiries@theglynhirestate.com
web www.theglynhirestate.com
Dir 1m N of Ammanford on A483

Nestling at the foot of the Black Mountains in an Area of Outstanding
Natural Beauty, Glynhir Mansion dates from the end of the 17th
century. The dining room and lounge have open fires and attractive
period furnishings. The 200 acres of grounds include some lovely
walks alongside the River Loughor, where a 30ft waterfall is a
spectacle not to be missed.

Facilities 4 en suite (1 fmly) ⊛ ⚞ Licensed Cen ht TVL Pool Table
Table tennis 200 acres sheep/horses Dinner Last d 10.30am
Prices S £32-£36; D £64✳ **LB** **Conf** Max 40 Class 40 Board 30
Parking 12 **Notes** Closed mid Dec-mid Jan rs mid Jan-Mar Civ Wed 45

LLANELLI
MAP 08 SN50

♦♦

Awel Y Mor ◇

86 Queen Victoria Rd SA15 2TH
☎ 01554 755357 ▤ 01554 755357`
e-mail office@awelymor.fsnet.co.uk
Dir A484 town centre signs to Asda on the right, half circle around
Asda, over lights, over minirdbt, establishment 300yds on right

This friendly and relaxed guest house is situated close to the town
centre and offers bright accommodation, including some family
rooms. Public areas include a lounge-dining room, and there is an
enclosed rear car park.

Facilities 11 rms (7 en suite) (3 fmly) (1 GF) ⊛ in bedrooms
⊛ in dining room ⊛ in 1 lounge TVB tea/coffee ⚞ Licensed Cen ht
TVL Dinner Last d 5pm **Prices** S £25-£30; D £40-£45✳ **LB** **Parking** 10

NANTGAREDIG
MAP 08 SN42

♦♦♦♦

Dolau Guest House ◇

Felingwm Isaf SA32 7PB ☎ 01267 290464
e-mail brightdolau@aol.com
Dir 1.5m NE of Nantgaredig. A40 onto B4310 to Felingwm Isaf, right
in village, over bridge on left

Quietly situated in 5 acres of delightful gardens alongside the Cloidach
Brook, this much-extended and modernised house stands on the site
of a former woollen mill. The bedrooms vary in size, but all are well
equipped. There is a cosy lounge, and separate tables are provided in
the conservatory-breakfast room.

Facilities 3 rms (2 en suite) (1 pri facs) ⊛ TV2B tea/coffee ⚞ Cen ht
TVL No coaches Gardens Dinner Last d 6pm **Prices** S £27-£30;
D £48-£52✳ **LB** **Parking** 6 **Notes** ⊠

RHANDIRMWYN
MAP 09 SN74

♦♦♦ ◧

The Royal Oak Inn

SA20 0NY ☎ 01550 760201 ▤ 01550 760332
e-mail royaloak@rhandirmwyn.com
web www.rhandirmwyn.com
Dir From A40 at Llandovery signs to Rhandirmwyn

Located north of Llandovery in an Area of Outstanding Natural Beauty,
this 17th-century former hunting lodge for the Cawdor Estate offers a
wealth of character within its public areas. There is a wide range of
real ales and imaginative food served. Comfortable bedrooms are
equipped with both practical and homely extras.

Facilities 5 rms (3 en suite) (1 fmly) TV3B tea/coffee Pool table Clay
pigeon wknds Last d 9.30pm **Parking** 20

If you have to cancel a booking, let the
proprietor know immediately

ST CLEARS
MAP 08 SN21

Premier Collection

◆◆◆◆◆

Coedllys Country House

Llangynin SA33 4JY ☎ 01994 231455 🖨 01994 231441
e-mail keith@harber.fsworld.co.uk
web www.coedllyscountryhouse.co.uk

Set in a peaceful valley within rolling countryside, Coedllys is the beautiful home of Keith and Val Harber, who are adept at making visitors feel like honoured guests. Bedrooms are lavishly furnished, and the thoughtful and useful extras make a stay memorable. There is a cosy lounge and meals are taken with the family.

Facilities 3 en suite ⊗ TVB tea/coffee Cen ht No children 8yrs
No coaches 🦶 Sauna Gymnasium Hydro-Therapy facility Dinner Last
d 24 hours prior **Parking** 6 **Notes** Closed Xmas

See advertisement on this page

CEREDIGION

ABERAERON
MAP 08 SN46

Premier Collection

◆◆◆◆◆

Harbourmaster Hotel

Pen Cei SA46 0BA ☎ 01545 570755
e-mail info@harbour-master.com
web www.harbour-master.com
Dir In town centre beside tourist office and harbour

Located right on the harbour, this Grade II listed building was previously the harbourmaster's house. The bedrooms are delightfully furnished and have excellent showers, and the proprietors and staff are very friendly and professional. Dinner and breakfast are a real treat too, a varied range of carefully prepared dishes using much local produce.

Facilities 7 en suite 2 annexe en suite ⊗ in bedrooms ⊗ in dining room
⊗ in lounges STV TVB tea/coffee Direct dial from bedrooms 🦶
Licensed Cen ht No children 5yrs No coaches Dinner Last d 9pm
Prices S £55; D £110-£140 **LB** **Parking** 5 **Notes** Closed 24 Dec-10 Jan rs
Sun eve & Mon lunch

◆◆◆◆

Arosfa Harbourside Guesthouse

Cardigan Bay SA46 0BU ☎ 01545 570120
e-mail arosfabandb@btinternet.com
web www.arosfaguesthouse.co.uk
Dir A487 in town centre onto Market St towards sea, 150yds to
Arosfa car park

A warm welcome is assured at this renovated Georgian house, located by the harbour in this historic town. Bedrooms are filled with thoughtful extras and have modern bathrooms. Other areas include a cosy lounge, stairways enhanced by quality art and memorabilia, and a bright attractive dining room, the setting for imaginative Welsh breakfasts.

Facilities 3 en suite 1 annexe en suite (1 fmly) (1 GF) ⊗ TVB
tea/coffee 🦶 Cen ht No coaches **Prices** S £35-£45; D £56-£70 **LB**
Notes ⊗

Wales

ABERPORTH
MAP 08 SN25

◆◆◆◆

Ffynonwen

SA43 2HT ☎ 01239 810312 🖹 01239 814910
e-mail ffynon.wen@tesco.net
web
www.cardiganshirecoastandcountry.com/ffynonwen.htm
Dir A487 N from Cardigan, 2nd left signed Aberporth B4333.
Continue 0.5m & Ffynonwen signed to the left. Follow lane 0.5m &
Ffynonwen on right

Quietly located in 20 acres of grounds 1m from the sea, this 17th-
century former farmhouse provides comfortable, traditionally
furnished accommodation. The homely bedrooms include a two-
bedroom family suite. The spacious public areas include a dining
room and a separate bar, where welcoming log fires burn in cold
weather. Other facilities include fishing lakes and a clay pigeon shoot.

Facilities 4 en suite (1 fmly) ⊗ in bedrooms ⊗ in dining room TVB
tea/coffee Licensed Cen ht No coaches Fishing Private Clay Pigeon
Shoot/Air Rifle Range Dinner Last d 8.30pm **Parking** 11

ABERYSTWYTH
MAP 08 SN58

Premier Collection

◆◆◆◆◆

Awel-Deg

Capel Bangor SY23 3LR ☎ 01970 880681
e-mail awel-deg@tiscali.co.uk
web www.awel-deg.co.uk
Dir 5m E of Aberystwyth. On A44 in village of Capel Bangor

Located 5m from the historic university town, this attractive bungalow,
set in pretty gardens, provides high standards of hospitality, comfort

and facilities. Immaculately maintained throughout, spacious
bedrooms are equipped with a wealth of thoughtful extras and smart,
modern en suite shower rooms. Comprehensive breakfasts are served
at one table in the elegant dining room and a choice of lounges is
available.

Facilities 2 en suite (2 GF) ⊗ TVB tea/coffee 🗶 Cen ht TVL
No children 11yrs No coaches **Prices** S £40; D £56✱ **LB** **Parking** 8
Notes Closed 20-30 Dec 🖾

◆◆◆◆

Bodalwyn Guest House

Queen's Av SY23 2EG ☎ 01970 612578 🖹 01970 639261
e-mail hilary.d@lineone.net
web www.bodalwyn.co.uk
Dir N along promenade towards Cliff railway. 1st right after Marine
Hotel & over x-rds, guest house opp North Rd Clinic

Located a short walk from the promenade, this imposing Edwardian
house, built for a college professor, has been totally refurbished to
provide high standards of comfort and good facilities. Smart modern
bathrooms complement the spacious bedrooms, which are equipped
with a wealth of thoughtful extras. Family rooms are available.
Comprehensive Welsh breakfasts are served in the elegant
conservatory-dining room.

Facilities 8 en suite (2 fmly) ⊗ TVB tea/coffee 🗶 Cen ht No coaches
Prices S £35-£40; D £55-£65✱ **Notes** Closed 24 Dec-1 Jan 🖾

◆◆◆◆

Glyn-Garth ◈

South Rd SY23 1JS ☎ 01970 615050 🖹 01970 636835
e-mail glyngarth@aol.com
Dir A487 onto South Rd, Glyn-Garth on right near south promenade

Privately owned and personally run by the same family, for nearly 50
years, this immaculately maintained guest house provides a range of
thoughtfully furnished bedrooms with smart modern bathrooms.
Breakfast is served in the attractive dining room and a lounge is also
available.

Facilities 10 rms (6 en suite) (2 fmly) ⊗ STV TVB tea/coffee 🗶 Cen h
TVL No coaches **Prices** S £25-£26; D £58-£66✱ **Parking** 2
Notes Closed 2 wks Xmas & New Year 🖾

continued

Wales

◆◆◆◆
Llety Ceiro Country House ◇

Peggy Ln, Bow St, Llandre SY24 5AB
☎ 01970 821900 📠 01970 820966
e-mail marinehotel1@btconnect.com

Located north of Aberystwyth, this house is immaculately maintained throughout. Bedrooms are equipped with a range of thoughtful extras in addition to smart modern bathrooms. A spacious conservatory lounge is available in addition to an attractive dining room, and bicycle hire is also available.

Facilities 10 en suite (2 fmly) (3 GF) 🚭 in bedrooms 🚭 in dining room 🚭 in 1 lounge TV8B tea/coffee Direct dial from bedrooms Licensed Cen ht TVL Free use of facilities at sister hotel Dinner Last d 9.30pm **Prices** S £30-£60; D £50-£90✳ LB **Conf** Max 55 Thtr 60 Class 40 Board 40 Del from £79 ✳ **Parking** 21 **Notes** Civ Wed 65

◆◆◆◆
Yr Hafod ◇

1 South Marine Ter SY23 1JX
☎ 01970 617579 📠 01970 636835
e-mail johnyrhafod@aol.com
Dir On south promenade between harbour & castle

An immaculately maintained, end of terrace Victorian house in a commanding location overlooking the South Bay. The spacious bedrooms are comfortable and some have smart modern shower rooms. Breakfast is served in the attractive front-facing dining room.

Facilities 7 rms (2 en suite) 🚭 TVB tea/coffee 🐾 Cen ht TVL No coaches **Prices** S £26-£27; D £52-£70 **Parking** 1 **Notes** Closed Xmas & New Year 🚭

◆◆◆
Nanteos Mansion

Rhydyfelin SY23 4LU ☎ 01970 624363
e-mail info@nanteos.co.uk
Dir 3m SE of Aberystwyth off B4340, small sign onto private lane

This Grade I listed Georgian mansion stands in extensive grounds on the outskirts of Aberystwyth. For well over 200 years it was the home of the Powell family, who were reputed to be custodians of the Holy Grail. The present owners are restoring the property and offer a selection of function and conference rooms, and the magnificent music room is licensed for civil weddings. Pets welcome by arrangement.

Facilities 5 en suite (1 fmly) 🚭 FTV TVB tea/coffee Licensed Cen ht No coaches Dinner Last d 6pm **Prices** D £80-£100✳ **Conf** Max 150 Thtr 150 Class 80 **Parking** 40 **Notes** Civ Wed 100

◆◆◆
Queensbridge Hotel

Promenade, Victoria Ter SY23 2DH
☎ 01970 612343 📠 01970 617452
Dir 500yds N of town centre near Constitution Hill

The friendly Queensbridge is on the promenade at the north end of the town. The bedrooms, some suitable for families, have modern facilities and many have fine sea views. There is a comfortable lounge, and a bar where snacks are available. A lift serves all floors.

Facilities 15 en suite (2 fmly) 🚭 in 6 bedrooms 🚭 in dining room 🚭 in 1 lounge TVB tea/coffee Direct dial from bedrooms Licensed Lift Cen ht TVL Golf LB **Conf** Max 50 Thtr 50 Class 30 Board 25 **Parking** 6

◆◆◆
Y Gelli

Dolau, Lovesgrove SY23 3HP ☎ 01970 617834
e-mail pat.twigg@virgin.net
Dir Off A44 2.75m E of town centre

Located in spacious grounds on the town's outskirts, this modern detached house contains a range of practically furnished bedrooms and three further rooms are available in an adjacent Victorian property. Comprehensive breakfasts are served in the attractive dining room and a lounge is also available.

Facilities 6 rms (2 en suite) 3 annexe rms (1 en suite) (3 fmly) (1 GF) 🚭 TVB tea/coffee 🐾 Cen ht TVL No coaches Snooker Pool Table Table tennis, Stabling can be provided Dinner Last d early morning **Conf** Thtr 30 Class 30 Board 20 Del from £30 ✳ **Parking** 20 **Notes** 🚭

LAMPETER   MAP 08 SN54

◆◆◆
Haulfan ◇

6 Station Ter SA48 7HH ☎ 01570 422718
e-mail haulfanguesthouse@lampeter.freeserve.co.uk
Dir From S, A485 through town centre, right by fountain, next right

Very popular for visitors to the nearby university, this Victorian house provides modern furnished and equipped bedrooms. Facilities here include a homely, comfortable lounge and generous breakfasts are served in the cosy dining room, where separate tables are provided. A warm welcome is assured from proprietors, who have an excellent knowledge of the area.

Facilities 3 rms (2 en suite) (1 fmly) 🚭 STV TVB tea/coffee 🐾 Cen ht TVL No coaches **Prices** S £25-£30; D £46-£50 LB **Parking** 1 **Notes** Closed 20 Dec-mid Jan 🚭

Wales

LLANDYSUL

MAP 08 SN44

◆◆◆◆

Plas Cerdin ◇

Ffostrasol SA44 4TA ☎ 01239 851329
web www.plascerdin.co.uk
Dir 4.5m NW of Llandysul. Off A486 N, right onto private road

The very well-maintained modern house stands in lovely gardens north of the town on an elevated position with stunning views of the Cerdin Valley and the Cambrian Mountains. One of homely bedrooms is ideal for a family, and a lounge is also available.

Facilities 3 en suite (1 fmly) (1 GF) ⊗ TVB tea/coffee Cen ht TVL No children 3yrs No coaches **Prices** S £26-£30; D £46-£50✻ **LB** **Parking** 4 **Notes** Closed Dec & Jan ⊠

NEW QUAY

MAP 08 SN35

◆◆◆

Brynarfor Hotel

New Rd SA45 9SB ☎ 01545 560358 ▤ 01545 561204
e-mail enquiries@brynarfor.co.uk
web www.brynarfor.co.uk
Dir A487 Llanina junct onto B4342 towards New Quay, premises 2m on left

The Brynarfor stands in sloping landscaped gardens close to the harbour and attractions and has impressive sea views. It provides a range of homely bedrooms, and there is an extensive choice of dishes at dinner, served at separate tables in the dining room. There is a lounge bar, a second lounge and also a games room.

Facilities 7 en suite (3 fmly) (2 GF) ⊗ in bedrooms ⊗ in dining room ⊗ in 1 lounge TVB tea/coffee 🍴 Licensed Cen ht TVL No coaches Pool Table Dinner Last d 6pm **Parking** 10 **Notes** Closed Nov-Jan

CONWY

BETWS-Y-COED

MAP 14 SH75

Premier Collection

★★★★★ ⑨⑨⑨ **Guest House**

Tan-y-Foel Country House

Capel Garmon LL26 0RE ☎ 01690 710507 ▤ 01690 710681
e-mail enquiries@tyfhotel.co.uk
web www.tyfhotel.co.uk
Dir Exit A5 at Betws-y-Coed onto A470, then 2m at Capel Garmon sign on right, turn towards Capel Garmon 1.5m, hotel sign on left

Situated high above the Conwy Valley and set in six acres of woodland with attractive gardens and rural walks within the grounds, this delightful country house offers superb views in all directions. The accommodation comprises six main house rooms and two in converted outbuildings; these are individually decorated and include four-poster, canopied and king-size beds along with every modern facility. There are two elegant sitting rooms where log fires burn in winter, and a swimming pool is available for the summer. Fresh local produce features on the small but interesting menu.

Facilities 4 en suite 2 annexe en suite (1 GF) ⊗ TVB tea/coffee Direct dial from bedrooms 🍴 Licensed No children 7yrs No coaches Dinner Last d 8.15pm **Prices** S £99-£120; D £141-£155 **LB** **Parking** 16 **Notes** Closed Dec rs Jan

★★★★ **Guest House**

The Ferns Guest House

Holyhead Rd LL24 0AN ☎ 01690 710587
e-mail ferns@betws-y-coed.co.uk
Dir On A5 near Waterloo Bridge

Situated near the centre of the village, this guest house offers friendly hospitality. The bedrooms are neatly decorated, all are equipped with modern facilities, and some of the beds have attractive canopies. Breakfast is served in a spacious, attractive dining room, which overlooks the pretty garden and valley.

Facilities 9 en suite (2 fmly) ⊗ TVB tea/coffee 🍴 Cen ht TVL No children 7yrs No coaches **Prices** D £50-£60 **LB** **Parking** 9

★★★★ **Guest House**

Park Hill

Llanrwst Rd LL24 0HD ☎ 01690 710540 ▤ 01690 710540
e-mail welcome@park-hill.co.uk
web www.park-hill.co.uk
Dir 0.5m N of Betws-y-Coed on A470 Llanrwst road

This friendly guest house benefits from a peaceful location overlooking the village. Comfortable bedrooms come in a wide range of sizes and are well equipped; a room with a four-poster bed and also family rooms are available. There is a choice of lounges, a heated swimming pool, sauna and whirlpool bath for guests' use.

Facilities 9 en suite ⊗ in dining room TVB tea/coffee 🍴 Licensed Cen ht TVL No children 8yrs No coaches ⩗ Sauna Jacuzzi Dinner Last d 6pm **Prices** S £50-£74; D £56-£74✻ **LB** **Parking** 11

If you book on bed, breakfast and evening meal terms, you may find that the tariff includes only the set menu

continued

Wales

◆◆◆◆

Afon View Non Smokers Guest House ◇

Holyhead Rd LL24 0AN ☎ 01690 710726 ▤ 01690 710726
e-mail welcome@afon-view.co.uk
web www.afon-view.co.uk
Dir On A5 150yds E of HSBC bank

A warm welcome is assured at this impressive Victorian house, built from local stone and standing in the heart of this renowned village. Bedrooms are carefully furnished and equipped with thoughtful extras. Wholesome breakfasts are served in an attractive cottage-style dining room, and a lounge is also available.

Facilities 7 en suite (1 fmly) ⊗ TVB tea/coffee ✖ Cen ht No children 4yrs **Prices** S £30-£32; D £60-£65 **LB** **Parking** 7

◆◆◆◆

Bryn Bella Guest House

Lon Muriau, Llanrwst Rd LL24 0HD ☎ 01690 710627
e-mail welcome@bryn-bella.co.uk
web www.bryn-bella.co.uk
Dir A5 onto A470, 0.5m right onto driveway signed Bryn Bella

Located on an elevated position on the town's outskirts and having stunning views of the surrounding countryside, this elegant Victorian house provides a range of thoughtfully equipped bedrooms with smart modern bathrooms. A fine collection of memorabilia adorns the public areas, which include an attractive dining room and a comfortable lounge. A warm welcome is assured and guest services include a daily weather forecast.

Facilities 5 en suite (1 GF) ⊗ TVB tea/coffee ✖ Cen ht TVL No coaches **Prices** D £55-£80 **LB** **Parking** 7

◆◆◆◆

The Courthouse (Henllys)

Old Church Rd LL24 0AL
☎ 01690 710534 ▤ 01690 710884
e-mail henllys@betws-y-coed.co.uk
Dir Off A5 in village centre onto Old Church Rd towards golf club

Superbly located in immaculate gardens beside the river, the Victorian former police station and magistrates' court have been renovated to provide accommodation of immense charm; one bedroom is a former cell, and memorable breakfasts are served in the original courtroom. A warm welcome is assured.

Facilities 9 en suite (1 fmly) (3 GF) ⊗ TVB tea/coffee ✖ Cen ht No children 4yrs No coaches **Prices** D £50-£80✳ **LB** **Parking** 10 **Notes** Closed Jan

◆◆◆◆

Penmachno Hall Country House

LL24 0PU ☎ 01690 760410 ▤ 01690 760410
e-mail stay@penmachnohall.co.uk
web www.penmachnohall.co.uk
Dir 5m S of Betws-y-Coed. A5 onto B4406 to Penmachno, over bridge, at Eagles pub signed Ty Mawr

Set in over 2 acres of mature grounds including a mountain stream and woodland, this impressive Victorian rectory has been lovingly restored to provide high standards of comfort and facilities. Stylish decor and quality furnishings highlight the many original features throughout the ground-floor areas, and the bedrooms have a wealth of thoughtful extras. Lauraine Awdry is a top-twenty finalist for AA Landlady of the Year 2006.

Facilities 3 en suite ⊗ TVB tea/coffee ✖ Licensed Cen ht No coaches Boules Badminton Dinner Last d 24hrs before **Prices** D £70-£90 **Parking** 3 **Notes** Closed Xmas & New Year

Wales

BETWS-Y-COED continued

◆◆◆◆
Aberconwy House

Lon Muriau LL24 0HD ☎ 01690 710202
e-mail welcome@aberconwy-house.co.uk
web www.aberconwy-house.co.uk
Dir On A470, 0.5m N from A5 junct

Please note that this establishment has recently changed hands. This large Victorian house has stunning views over the Llugwy and Conwy valleys from many of the rooms. The spacious, attractive bedrooms are comfortably furnished and equipped with a wealth of thoughtful extras. Breakfast is served in an attractive dining room and a lounge is also provided.

Facilities 8 en suite (1 fmly) (1 GF) ⊗ TVB tea/coffee ✗ Cen ht TVL No coaches **Prices** S £49-£55; D £54-£70✱ **LB Parking** 10

◆◆◆◆
The Fairhaven ◇

Holyhead Rd LL24 0AY ☎ 01690 710307
e-mail stay@fairhaven-snowdonia.co.uk
Dir Located on M5 in centre of village, next to Craft Cymru shop.

Located in the main street close to the centre of town The Fairhaven offers comfortable well-equipped accommodation and a friendly atmosphere. Breakfast is served in the attractive tearoom which overlooks the River Conwy.

Facilities 6 en suite ⊗ TVB tea/coffee ✗ Cen ht No children No coaches **Prices** S £25-£30; D £50-£60 **Notes** Closed 20 Dec-3 Jan

◆◆◆◆ ⊜ ◼
Ty Gwyn Inn ◇

LL24 0SG ☎ 01690 710383 ▤ 01690 710383
e-mail mratcl1050@aol.com
Dir Junct of A5 & A470, by Waterloo Bridge

Situated on the edge of the village, close to the Waterloo Bridge, this historic coaching inn retains many original features. Quality furnishing styles and memorabilia throughout enhance its intrinsic charm. Bedrooms, some of which feature antique beds, are equipped with thoughtful extras and imaginative food is provided within the cosy bars or restaurant.

Facilities 13 rms (10 en suite) (2 fmly) (1 GF) ⊗ in 1 bedrooms ⊗ in dining room TVB tea/coffee Cen ht TVL Dinner Last d 9pm **Prices** S £30-£60; D £44-£100✱ **LB Parking** 14 **Notes** Closed Mon-Wed in Jan

◆◆◆ ❤
Cwmanog Isaf Farm ◇ (SH799546)

Fairy Glen LL24 0SL ☎ 01690 710225 Mrs Hughes
e-mail h.m.hughes@amserve.net
Dir 1m S of Betws-y-Coed off A470 by Fairy Glen Hotel, 500yds on farm lane

Peacefully located on 30 acres of undulating land, which also contains the renowned Fairy Glen, this 200-year-old house on a working livestock farm has been restored to provide comfortable, thoughtfully furnished bedrooms. Breakfast and dinners use home-reared or organic produce, and the raised position of the property provides stunning views of the surrounding countryside.

Facilities 3 rms (2 en suite) (1 pri facs) (1 GF) ⊗ TVB tea/coffee ✗ Cen ht No children 15yrs 30 acres Mixed Dinner Last d 10am **Prices** S fr £30; D £48-£52✱ **Parking** 4 **Notes** 🐾

◆◆◆
Bryn Llewelyn Guest House ◇

Holyhead Rd LL24 0BN ☎ 01690 710601 ▤ 01690 710601
e-mail stay@bryn-llewelyn.co.uk
Dir On A5 W, 300yds past village green on left

This friendly and popular guest house offers a warm welcome and good-value accommodation. The pretty bedrooms are equipped with modern facilities and some are suitable for families. There is a cosy lounge and a separate breakfast room, where a wide choice is offered at breakfast.

Facilities 7 rms (5 en suite) (2 pri facs) (2 fmly) ⊗ TVB tea/coffee ✗ Cen ht TVL No children 4yrs No coaches **Prices** S £30-£32; D £45-£56 **LB Parking** 8

◆◆◆ ◼
The White Horse Inn

Capel Garmon LL26 0RW
☎ 01690 710271 ▤ 01690 710721
Dir A470 Llanwrst to Betws road, left at Snowdonia and Capel Garmon sign

This 16th-century inn has a wealth of character, enhanced by original exposed timbers, stone walls and log fires. The bars feature an impressive collection of pottery and china. A good selection of home-cooked food is available, served in either the bars or in the cottage-style restaurant. The non-smoking bedrooms are compact and thoughtfully furnished with modern facilities.

Facilities 5 en suite ⊗ in bedrooms ⊗ in dining room ⊗ in lounges TVB tea/coffee ✗ Cen ht No children Pool Table Dinner Last d 9pm **Parking** 20

Ⓐ
Gorphwysfa House ◇

Holyhead Rd, Pentre-du LL24 0BY ☎ 01690 710401
e-mail gorphwysfa@amserve.net
Dir From village on A5 towards Swallow Falls, past Cross Keys Inn, 0.25m further and Gorphwysfa is on corner

Facilities 3 en suite ⊗ TVB tea/coffee ✗ Cen ht TVL No children 12yrs No coaches Dinner Last d day before **Prices** S £24-£27 **LB Parking** 4 **Notes** ★★★ 🐾

Wales

BYLCHAU
MAP 14 SH96

◆◆◆◆ 🏠 ❤

Hafod Elwy Hall 💠 (SH938562)

LL16 5SP ☎ 01690 770345 Mrs Charles-Warner
e-mail enquiries@hafodelwyhall.co.uk
web www.hafodelwyhall.co.uk
Dir A5 onto A543, 5.5m right onto track signed Hafod Elwy Hall

A warm welcome awaits you at this charming house, which originates from the 14th century. The peraceful property overlooks the surrounding countryside and is located on a 60 acre sheep and pig-rearing holding. Rooms are well equipped and have many thoughtful extras.

Facilities 3 rms (2 en suite) (1 pri facs) (1 GF) ⊗ STV TV1B tea/coffee
✗ Cen ht TVL No children 10yrs Fishing Shooting 60 acres Mixed small holding Dinner Last d 7pm **Prices** S £30-£70; D £55-£90 **LB** **Parking** 4

COLWYN BAY
MAP 14 SH87

◆◆◆◆

Whitehall Hotel 💠

51 Cayley Promenade, Rhos-On-Sea LL28 4EP
☎ 01492 547296
e-mail mossd.cymru@virgin.net
web www.whitehall-hotel.co.uk
Dir A55 onto B5115 Brompton Av, right at rdbt onto Whitehall Rd to seafront

Overlooking the promenade, this popular, family-run establishment is convenient for Rhos-on-Sea's shops and amenities. The pretty bedrooms include family rooms, and video and CD players are among the excellent facilities. There is bar and a separate lounge for guests, and hearty, home-cooked meals and bar snacks are available.

Facilities 12 rms (10 en suite) (2 pri facs) (4 fmly) ⊗ STV TVB tea/coffee Direct dial from bedrooms Licensed Cen ht TVL Dinner Last d 4.30pm **Prices** S £29.50-£45; D £59-£70✷ **LB** **Parking** 5

◆◆◆

The Northwood 💠

47 Rhos Rd, Rhos-on-Sea LL28 4RS ☎ 01492 549931
e-mail welcome@thenorthwood.co.uk
web www.thenorthwood.co.uk
Dir A55 onto B5115 Brompton Av, over rdbt, 2nd right

The Northwood's friendly atmosphere brings back many regular guests. It's a short walk from the seafront and shops,. And the
continued

bedrooms are furnished in modern style . Freshly prepared meals can be enjoyed in the spacious dining room-bar, and light refreshments are offered in the lounge.

Facilities 12 rms (10 en suite) (1 pri facs) (3 fmly) (2 GF) ⊗ TVB tea/coffee Licensed TVL No coaches Dinner Last d 7pm **Prices** S £28-£30; D £56-£62✷ **LB** **Conf** Max 20 **Parking** 12

See advertisement on page 690

◆◆◆

Cabin Hill Private Hotel 💠

College Av, Rhos-on-Sea LL28 4NT ☎ 01492 544568
Dir 1.5m NW of Colwyn Bay in Rhos-on-Sea. Off seafront Marine Dr onto College Av

Cabin Hill lies in a quiet residential area within walking distance of the seafront and local shops. Bedrooms are neatly decorated and thoughtfully furnished and equipped. Ground floor areas include an attractive spacious dining room and a lounge.

Facilities 9 rms (7 en suite) (2 fmly) ⊗ in dining room TVB tea/coffee Cen ht TVL Dinner Last d 4.30pm **Prices** S £22; D £44 **LB** **Parking** 2 **Notes** ⊛

CONWY
MAP 14 SH77

Premier Collection

★★★★★ ⊛⊛⊛ **Guest Accommodation**

The Old Rectory Country House

Llanrwst Rd, Llansanffraid Glan Conwy LL28 5LF
☎ 01492 580611 📠 01492 584555
e-mail info@oldrectorycountryhouse.co.uk
web www.oldrectorycountryhouse.co.uk
Dir 0.5m S from A470/A55 junct on left, by 30mph sign

This very welcoming accommodation has fine views over the Conwy estuary and towards Snowdonia. The elegant day rooms are luxurious and home-baked afternoon teas are available in the lounge. Bedrooms share the delightful views and are thoughtfully furnished, and the genuine hospitality creates a real home from home. Dinner is only available until December 10 2006.

Facilities 4 en suite 2 annexe en suite TVB tea/coffee Direct dial from bedrooms Licensed No children 5yrs No coaches Dinner Last d 8pm **Prices** S £79-£129; D £99-£159✷ **LB** **Parking** 10 **Notes** Closed 14 Dec-15 Jan rs Sun (ex BHs)

Wales

CONWY continued

Premier Collection

◆◆◆◆◆ 🍽

Sychnant Pass House

Sychnant Pass Rd LL32 8BJ
☎ 01492 596868 📠 01492 585486
e-mail bre@sychnant-pass-house.co.uk
web www.sychnant-pass-house.co.uk
Dir 1.75m W of Conwy. Off A547 Bangor Rd in town onto Mount
Pleasant & Sychnant Pass Rd, 1.75m on right near top of hill

Fine views are to be had from this Edwardian house set in landscaped
grounds. Bedrooms, including suites and four poster rooms, are
individually furnished and equipped with a range of thoughtful extras.
Lounges, warmed by open fires in the chillier months, are comfortable
and inviting, and imaginative dinners and suppers are served in the
attractive dining room.

Facilities 10 en suite (3 fmly) (2 GF) ⊗ in bedrooms ⊗ in dining room
⊗ in 1 lounge TVB tea/coffee Licensed Cen ht No coaches 🔲 Sauna
Gymnasium ♫ Dinner Last d 8.30pm **Prices** S £70-£150; D £90-£170✳
LB **Parking** 30 **Notes** Civ Wed 100

See advertisement on opposite page

◆◆◆◆

Glan Heulog Guest House ◇

Llanrwst Rd, Woodlands LL32 8LT ☎ 01492 593845
e-mail glanheulog@no1guesthouse.freeserve.co.uk
web www.walesbandb.co.uk
Dir From Conwy Castle take B5106, house 0.25m on left

This late 19th-century house lies in an elevated location, with fine
views over the town and castle from many rooms. Bedrooms are
decorated with pretty wallpapers, are well equipped and one has a
four-poster bed. A pleasant breakfast room and conservatory are
provided and hospitality from the proprietors is very friendly.

Facilities 6 en suite (1 fmly) ⊗ TVB tea/coffee Cen ht TVL No coaches
Prices S £30-£35; D £48-£55✳ **Parking** 7

◆◆◆◆

Gwern Borter Country Manor

Barkers Ln LL32 8YL ☎ 01492 650360 📠 01492 650360
e-mail mail@snowdoniaholidays.co.uk
web www.snowdoniaholidays.co.uk
Dir From Conwy B5106 for 2.25m, right towards Rowen for 0.5m
then right, left as road forks, Gwern Borter 0.5m on left

This delightful mansion has walls covered in climbing plants and is set
in several acres of lawns and gardens. Children are very welcome and
there is a rustic play area, games room and many farmyard pets.
Bedrooms are furnished with antiques and modern facilities, and one
room has an Edwardian four-poster bed. There is an elegant lounge
and Victorian-style dining room, where freshly cooked breakfasts are
served.

Facilities 3 en suite (1 fmly) ⊗ in bedrooms ⊗ in dining room TVB
tea/coffee ✗ Cen ht TVL No children 3yrs No coaches Riding Sauna
Gymnasium LB **Parking** 16

LLANDUDNO
MAP 14 SH78

★★★★ Guest Accommodation

Oak Alyn ◇

2 Deganwy Av LL30 2YB ☎ 01492 860320

A warm and friendly welcome is assured at Oak Alyn, which is situated
close to the town centre, the promenade and other amenities.
Bedrooms vary in size, but all are thoughtfully equipped, modern and
soundly maintained. A private car park is available.

Facilities 12 en suite (2 fmly) ⊗ in 3 bedrooms ⊗ in dining room TVB
tea/coffee ✗ Licensed Cen ht Dinner Last d 7pm **Prices** S £28-£32;
D £56-£64✳ LB **Parking** 16 **Notes** Closed 22-31 Dec 🐾

Premier Collection

◆◆◆◆◆

Abbey Lodge

14 Abbey Rd LL30 2EA ☎ 01492 878042 📠 01492 878042
e-mail enquiries@abbeylodgeuk.com
Dir A546 to N end of town, onto Clement Av, right onto Abbey Rd

This impressive Victorian villa is on a leafy avenue within easy walking
distance of the promenade. It has been lovingly restored, and stylish
decor and furniture add to its charm. Bedrooms come with a wealth
of thoughtful extras, and there is a choice of sumptuous lounges and
an elegant dining room.

continued

Facilities 4 en suite ⊗ TVB tea/coffee ✱ Cen ht TVL No children 12yrs No coaches **Prices** S £50; D £75✳ **Parking** 4 **Notes** Closed 21 Dec-9 Jan ⊜

◆◆◆◆◆

Bryn Derwen

34 Abbey Rd LL30 2EE ☎ 01492 876804 🖷 01492 876804
e-mail brynderwen@fsmail.net
web www.bryn-derwen.co.uk
Dir *A470 into Llandudno, left at The Parade promenade to cenotaph, left, over rdbt, 4th right onto York Rd, Bryn Derwen at top*

A warm welcome is assured at this impressive Victorian house, which retains original tiled floors and some fine stained-glass windows.

continued

Quality decor and furnishings highlight the historic charm of the property, which is apparent in the sumptuous lounges and attractive dining room, the setting for imaginative dinners and breakfasts. Bedrooms are equipped with a wealth of thoughtful extras, and the establishment also has a fully equipped beauty salon.

Facilities 9 en suite (1 fmly) ⊗ TVB tea/coffee ✱ Licensed Cen ht TVL No children 7yrs No coaches Solarium Dinner Last d 4pm **Prices** S £46-£50; D £72-£82✳ LB **Parking** 9 **Notes** Closed Dec-Jan

◆◆◆◆

Brigstock House ◈

1 St David's Pl LL30 2UG ☎ 01492 876416
e-mail mtajmemory@brigstock58.fsnet.co.uk
web www.brigstockhouse.co.uk
Dir *A470 into Llandudno, left onto The Parade promenade, left onto Lloyd St, left onto St Davids Rd & left onto St Davids Place*

This impressive Edwardian property is in a quiet residential cul-de-sac within easy walking distance of the seafront and central shopping area. The attractive bedrooms are very well equipped, and a comfortable lounge is available. Substantial breakfasts and dinners (by arrangement) are served in the elegant dining room.

Facilities 9 rms (8 en suite) (1 pri facs) ⊗ TVB tea/coffee ✱ Licensed Cen ht TVL No children 12yrs No coaches Dinner Last d 10am **Prices** S £27-£31; D £54-£62✳ **Parking** 6

Wales

LLANDUDNO continued

◆◆◆◆
Britannia Hotel
15 Craig-y-Don Pde LL30 1BG ☎ 01492 877185
Dir On seafront close to Llandudno Conference Centre

Please note that this establishment has recently changed hands. The Britannia offers comfortably furnished bedrooms towards the Little Orme end of the promenade. Breakfast and dinner are served in the attractive dining room overlooking the colourful front garden and the seafront.

Facilities 10 rms (8 en suite) (2 pri facs) (4 fmly) (2 GF) ⊗ TVB tea/coffee ✖ Cen ht No coaches Dinner Last d noon **Prices** D £40-£60✻ **LB Notes** Closed Nov-Feb 🐾

◆◆◆◆
Carmel Private Hotel
17 Craig-y-Don Pde LL30 1BG
☎ 01492 877643 📄 01492 877643
e-mail bookingenquiries@carmelhotel.co.uk
Dir A470 to Llandudno & The Parade promenade, right, Carmel 200yds on right

Located on the Craig-y-Don section of the promenade between the Great and Little Ormes, this well-maintained non-smoking Victorian house offers a warm welcome and high standard of hospitality. Bedrooms, some of which have stunning sea views, are equipped with homely extras, and the comfortable hall-lounge features Eygptian artefacts.

Facilities 9 rms (8 en suite) (1 pri facs) (2 fmly) (1 GF) ⊗ TVB tea/coffee ✖ Licensed Cen ht TVL No children 5yrs No coaches Dinner Last d noon **LB Parking** 6 **Notes** Closed Dec-Jan rs early Feb 🐾

◆◆◆◆
Lynton House Hotel
80 Church Walks LL30 2HD
☎ 01492 875057 & 875009 📄 01492 875057
e-mail info@lyntonhousehotel.co.uk
Dir A546 The Parade towards pier, right at T-junct by cenotaph, left at rdbt after pier, premises on right

This immaculate property lies just off the seafront below Great Orme. Bedrooms are smart and modern, with well-chosen decor, and two have four-poster beds. There is a comfortable lounge and hospitality is welcoming.

Facilities 14 en suite (5 fmly) (1 GF) ⊗ FTV TVB tea/coffee Direct dial from bedrooms ✖ Licensed Cen ht TVL No coaches **Prices** S £35; D £58-£68✻ **LB Parking** 5 **Notes** Closed 17-30 Dec

◆◆◆◆
Sefton Court ◇
49 Church Walks LL30 2HL ☎ 01492 875235
e-mail seftoncourt@aol.com
web www.seftoncourt-hotel.co.uk
Dir A546 N towards pier, left onto Church Walks

An impressive Grade II listed Victorian house that retains many original features, especially within the public areas. Many of the spacious bedrooms have stunning views, and there is a comfortable lounge with honesty bar, an elegant split-level dining room, and a car park.

Facilities 11 en suite (3 fmly) ⊗ TVB tea/coffee ✖ Cen ht **Prices** S £28-£30; D £56-£60✻ **LB Parking** 11 **Notes** Closed Nov-Feb

◆◆◆◆
Stratford Hotel ◇
8 Craig-y-Don Pde LL30 1BG
☎ 01492 877962 📄 01492 877962
e-mail stratfordhtl@aol.com
Dir A55 onto A470 to Llandudno, at rdbt 4th exit signed Craig Y Don, right at Promenade

This friendly holiday guest house stands on the Craig-y-Don promenade near the conference centre and theatre, and a short walk from the shops. Ground-floor bedrooms are available and some rooms have sea views, as does the pleasant breakfast room.

Facilities 10 en suite (3 fmly) (2 GF) ⊗ TVB tea/coffee Cen ht No coaches **Prices** S £30-£35; D £46-£55✻ **LB**

◆◆◆◆ Ⓐ
St Hilary Hotel ◇
16 Craig-Y-Don Pde LL30 1BG
☎ 01492 875551 📄 01492 877538
e-mail info@sthilaryhotel.co.uk
web www.sthilaryhotel.co.uk
Dir 0.5m E of town centre. On B5115 seafront road near North Wales Theatre

Facilities 11 rms (9 en suite) (3 fmly) (3 GF) ⊗ TV11B tea/coffee ✖ Cen ht No coaches **Prices** S £22-£40.50; D £40-£58 **LB Notes** ★★★★ Closed mid Nov-Jan

♦♦♦

Beach Cove

8 Church Walks LL30 2HD ☎ 01492 879638
e-mail david@beachcove.freeserve.co.uk
Dir From promenade towards pier, at rdbt left onto Church Walks, 100yds on left

Located a short walk from the pier and town centre, this Victorian terrace house provides a range of homely and thoughtfully furnished bedrooms, and public areas adorned with Japanese memorabilia. Comprehensive breakfasts, featuring local produce, are served in an attractive front-facing dining room.

Facilities 7 rms (5 en suite) in dining room TVB tea/coffee ✈
Cen ht No coaches **Parking** 3

♦♦♦

The Kestrel Hotel ◇

25 Deganwy Av LL30 2YB
☎ 01492 875108 ▤ 01492 874875
e-mail kestrelllandudno@msn.com
web www.kestrelllandudno.co.uk
Dir A55 onto A546 for 4m, right onto Gloddaeth Av, Deganwy Av 4th on right

A warm welcome is assured at this Victorian terrace house close to the main shopping centre and leisure facilities. Bedrooms feature some family accommodation and ground-floor areas include an attractive dining room with adjacent lounge bar.

Facilities 10 en suite (3 fmly) in 7 bedrooms in dining room TVB tea/coffee Licensed Cen ht TVL No coaches Dinner Last d before lunch
Prices S £26; D £48-£58✳ LB **Parking** 4 **Notes** Closed Nov-Etr ▦

♦♦♦

Minion ◇

21-23 Carmen Sylva Rd, Craig-y-Don LL30 1EQ
☎ 01492 877740
Dir A470 to The Parade promenade, right & 3rd right

Situated at the western end of the promenade, the Minion has been owned by the same family for over 50 years and continues to extend a warm welcome. Bedrooms are smart and comfortable, and two are on the ground floor. There is a cosy bar and a colourful garden.

Facilities 10 en suite (1 fmly) (2 GF) tea/coffee Licensed TVL
No children 2yrs No coaches Dinner Last d 4pm **Prices** S £20-£22.50;
D £40-£45✳ **Parking** 8 **Notes** Closed Oct-Mar ▦

♦♦♦

The Quinton Bed & Breakfast

36 Church Walks LL30 2HN
☎ 01492 876879 ▤ 01492 876879
Dir A546 N towards pier, left onto Church Walks

The Quinton is convenient for the town centre and both beaches. Personally run by the same owners for over 25 years, it provides friendly hospitality and value for money. Bedrooms are well equipped and include one on the ground floor.

Facilities 9 en suite (3 fmly) (1 GF) ⊘ in dining room TVB tea/coffee Direct dial from bedrooms Licensed Cen ht TVL No children 12yrs Pool Table Dinner Last d 7pm **Parking** 12 **Notes** ▦

♦♦♦

Sunnyside Private Hotel

Llewelyn Av LL30 2ER ☎ 01492 877150

The Sunnyside with its pretty front garden is in a quiet location within easy walking distance of shops, restaurants and the promenade. The attractive bedrooms have very comfortable beds, and the bar, lounge, and dining room are all popular. Entertainment is available on several evenings during the week.

Facilities 25 en suite (4 fmly) in 1 bedrooms in dining room TVB tea/coffee Licensed Cen ht TVL Last d 6.30pm **Notes** Closed mid Oct-Etr ▦

♦♦♦

The Victoria Town House

5 Church Walks LL30 2HD ☎ 01492 876144
Dir A546 N towards pier, left onto Church Walks

Located a short walk from the pier and main shops, this Victorian terrace house has been renovated to provide comfortable bedrooms with modern facilities. Rooms have a homely feel, and there is a cottage-style lower ground-floor dining room and a comfortable lounge.

Facilities 6 en suite (1 fmly) in dining room TVB tea/coffee ✈
Cen ht TVL No coaches **Notes** ▦

♦♦♦

Vine House ◇

23 Church Walks LL30 2HG
☎ 01492 876493 & 07977 059220
e-mail gavin.jacob@tesco.net
Dir By Great Orme tram station

Vine House is a friendly family-run house located a short walk from the seafront and pier, opposite the historic tram station. Bedrooms vary in size and style and include some spacious, stylish refurbished rooms with separate sitting areas and modern bathrooms. All rooms have views of the sea or the Orme.

Facilities 4 rms (2 en suite) (2 pri facs) (1 fmly) TVB tea/coffee No coaches **Prices** S £23-£25; D £40-£44 **Notes** ▦

♦♦♦

Wedgwood Guest House

6 Deganwy Av LL30 2YB ☎ 01492 878016 ▤ 01492 870014
e-mail yvonne@wedgwoodguest.fsnet.co.uk
Dir A470 into Llandudno. From High St left at HSBC onto Lloyd St then 2nd left onto Deganwy Av

Located on a wide avenue close to central amenities, this impressive Victorian house provides a range of homely bedrooms, some suitable for families. A cosy dining room is the setting for breakfast or dinner, and a separate bar and comfortable lounge areas are also available.

Facilities 10 en suite (2 fmly) TVB tea/coffee Licensed Cen ht TVL Dinner Last d 3pm **Parking** 7 **Notes** Closed Nov-Mar ▦

Wales

LLANDUDNO continued

[U]

All Seasons ◇

7-8 Hill Ter LL30 2LS ☎ 01492 876277 🖷 01492 876277
e-mail all.seasons@virgin.net

At the time of going to press the rating for this establishment had not been confirmed. Please check the AA website www.theAA.com for up-to-date information.

Facilities 24 en suite (4 fmly) (2 GF) ⊗ in bedrooms ⊗ in dining room ⊗ in 1 lounge TVB tea/coffee ✖ Licensed TVL Dinner Last d 5pm **Prices** S £30-£43; D £60-£86; (incl. dinner) ✳ **LB** **Parking** 5 **Notes** Closed Jan

RHOS-ON-SEA   MAP 14 SH88
See also **Colwyn Bay**

The Northwood

RHOS-ON-SEA, CONWY, WALES   Tel: 01492 549931
Email: welcome@thenorthwood.co.uk

The Northwood is a family run guesthouse situated in the heart of lovely Rhos-on-Sea, some 175 yards from the high class shops and Promenade. Mid Week and "Mini-Break" bookings are accepted and special rates offered. There is adequate PRIVATE car parking. Our excellent chef can cater for most special dietary needs; he has vast experience with gluten and dairy free meals. Vegetarians and diabetics also have a nice choice as we only use fresh local Welsh produce.

◆◆◆◆◆ 🏠

Plas Rhos

Cayley Promenade LL28 4EP
☎ 01492 543698 🖷 01492 540088
e-mail info@plasrhos.co.uk
web www.plasrhos.co.uk
Dir A55 junct 20 for Rhos-on-Sea, follow Promenade signs, at seafront fourth building on left

Stunning sea views are a feature of this renovated Victorian house, which provides high standards of comfort and hospitality. Cosy bedrooms are filled with a wealth of thoughtful extras and public areas include a choice of sumptuous lounges featuring smart decor, quality soft furnishings and memorabilia. Breakfast is served in the attractive dining room, overlooking the pretty patio garden. This is a non-smoking property.

Facilities 8 en suite ⊗ FTV TVB tea/coffee ✖ Licensed Cen ht TVL No children 12yrs No coaches **Prices** S £40-£55; D £60-£90✳ **LB** **Parking** 4 **Notes** Closed 21 Dec-Jan

TREFRIW   MAP 14 SH76

[U]

Hafod Country House

LL27 0RQ ☎ 01492 640029 🖷 01492 641351
e-mail hafod@breathemail.net
Dir On B5106, 2nd entrance on right on entering Trefriw from S

At the time of going to press the rating for this establishment had not been confirmed. Please check the AA website www.theAA.com for up-to-date information.

Facilities 6 en suite ⊗ TVB tea/coffee Direct dial from bedrooms Licensed Cen ht No children 11yrs No coaches Dinner Last d 9pm **Prices** S £35-£43; D £60-£75✳ **LB** **Parking** 14 **Notes** Closed early Jan-mid Feb

DENBIGHSHIRE

CORWEN   MAP 15 SJ04

Premier Collection

Bron-y-Graig

LL21 0DR ☎ 01490 413007 📠 01490 413007
e-mail business@north-wales-hotel.co.uk
web www.north-wales-hotel.co.uk
Dir *On A5 on E edge of Corwen*

A short walk from the town centre, this impressive Victorian house retains many original features including fireplaces, stained glass and a tiled floor in the entrance hall. Bedrooms, complemented by luxurious bathrooms, are thoughtfully furnished, and two are in a renovated coach house. Ground-floor areas include a traditionally furnished dining room and a comfortable lounge. A warm welcome, attentive service and imaginative food is assured.

Facilities 8 en suite 2 annexe en suite (3 fmly) ⊗ in bedrooms ⊗ in dining room ⊗ in 1 lounge STV TVB tea/coffee Direct dial from bedrooms Licensed Cen ht Fishing Dinner Last d 9.30pm **Prices** S £39-£49; D £59✳ LB **Conf** Max 20 Class 20 Board 15 **Parking** 15

◆◆◆◆

Plas Derwen Country House

London Rd LL21 0DR ☎ 01490 412742
e-mail bandb@plasderwen.supanet.com
Dir *On A5 0.5m E of Corwen*

Located on the outskirts on an elevated position with superb rural views, this elegant late 19th-century house has been restored to provide high levels of comfort and facilities. Quality furnishings and decor highlight the many original features and a warm welcome is assured.

Facilities 3 rms (2 en suite) (1 pri facs) (2 fmly) ⊗ TVB tea/coffee ✱ Cen ht TVL No coaches **Prices** S fr £34; D £48-£60 LB **Parking** 6 **Notes** Closed Dec-Jan ⊠

◆◆◆◆

Powys Country House

Holyhead Rd, Bonwm LL21 9EG ☎ 01490 412367
e-mail info@powyscountryhouse.co.uk
Dir *On A5 1m E from Corwen, on left*

This delightful country house stands in 3 acres of peaceful gardens and woodland. The impressive entrance hall is wood-panelled, and

continued

the spacious dining room is the setting for imaginative breakfasts. Bedrooms are equipped with modern facilities and include one with a four-poster bed. Hospitality is warm, and self-catering cottages are also available.

Facilities 4 en suite (1 fmly) (1 GF) ⊗ in bedrooms ⊗ in dining room TVB tea/coffee Licensed Cen ht **Parking** 10

DENBIGH   MAP 15 SJ06
See also **Bylchau (Conwy)**

◆◆◆

Cayo Guest House ◇

74 Vale St LL16 3BW ☎ 01745 812686
e-mail stay@cayo.co.uk
Dir *Off A525 into town, at lights turn up hill, supermarket on right. Guest house up hill on left*

A warm welcome is assured at this Victorian house, which is situated on the main street, just a short walk from the town centre. Bedrooms are comfortably and thoughtfully furnished with lots of homely extras. Good home cooking is provided in a Victorian-themed dining room, and a cosy basement lounge is also available.

Facilities 5 rms (4 en suite) ⊗ TVB tea/coffee Cen ht TVL No coaches **Prices** S £25; D £50✳ **Notes** Closed Xmas-New Year

LLANDRILLO   MAP 15 SJ03

★★★★ ◎◎ Restaurant with Rooms

Tyddyn Llan

LL21 0ST ☎ 01490 440264 📠 01490 440414
e-mail tyddynllan@compuserve.com
web www.tyddynllan.co.uk
Dir *Take B4401 from Corwen to Llandrillo. Tyddyn Llan on the right leaving the village.*

An elegant Georgian house set within grounds in a peaceful and relaxing location. Bedrooms vary in size but all are comfortably furnished and include welcome extras. The restaurant and lounges are quite delightful and look over the surrounding gardens. Local produce is carefully prepared by the chef-proprietor and his team.

Facilities 13 en suite (1 GF) ⊗ TVB Direct dial from bedrooms Licensed ch fac No coaches 🕪 Dinner **Prices** S £65-£95; D £110-£180✳ LB **Conf** Max 30 Thtr 30 Class 10 Board 20 **Parking** 20 **Notes** Closed 2 wks Jan rs Nov-Mar Civ Wed 40

Ⓐ

Y Llwyn Guest House

LL21 0ST ☎ 01490 440455 📠 01490 440455
e-mail info@yllwyn.co.uk
web www.yllwyn.co.uk
Dir *On B4401 250yds W of village bridge*

Facilities 2 en suite (1 fmly) ⊗ TVB tea/coffee ✱ Cen ht TVL No coaches Dinner Last d before noon **Prices** D £55-£65✳ LB **Parking** 3 **Notes** ★★★★ Closed 3 Jan-3 Mar ⊠

Wales

LLANGOLLEN

MAP 15 SJ24

See also **Corwen**

♦♦♦♦

Oakmere

Regent St LL20 8HS ☎ 01978 861126
e-mail oakmeregh@aol.com
web www.oakmere.llangollen.co.uk
Dir A5 from lights in Llangollen towards Oswestry, 300yds on right

A well-proportioned Victorian house standing on pretty grounds. Furnishings and decor highlight the many retained original features and bedrooms are spacious and comfortable. Ground-floor areas include a large dining room with a Gothic-style conservatory and a lounge.
Facilities 6 rms (4 en suite) (2 pri facs) (1 fmly) ⊗ TVB tea/coffee ✖ Cen ht No children 10yrs No coaches **Prices** S £40-£50; D £55-£60 **Parking** 10 **Notes** ⊠

♦♦♦♦ ❥

Tyn Celyn Farmhouse *(SJ218412)*

Tyndwr LL20 8AR
☎ 01978 861117 ▤ 01978 861771 Mrs Bather
e-mail j.m.bather-tyncelyn@talk21.com
Dir A5 to Llangollen, pass golf club on right, next left signed Youth Hostel, 0.5m sharp left onto Tyndwr Rd, left past youth hostel

This 300-year-old timber-framed farmhouse has stunning views over the Vale of Llangollen. Bedrooms, one of which is located on the ground floor, provide a range of thoughtful extras in addition to fine period furniture. Breakfast is served at a magnificent carved table in a spacious sitting-dining room.
Facilities 3 en suite (1 fmly) (1 GF) ⊗ TVB tea/coffee ✖ Cen ht TVL **Prices** D £52-£56✱ **LB Parking** 5 **Notes** ⊠

♦♦♦♦

Whitegate

Grange Rd LL20 8AP ☎ 01978 860960 ▤ 01978 861699
e-mail veda@whitegate-llangollen.co.uk
Dir No car access on Grange Rd. Up Hill St (behind Grapes Hotel on A5) & past Plas Newydd on left. Whitegate on right after short narrow road

This impressive Edwardian family house is a short walk from the town centre, and stands in pretty gardens. The comfortable, traditionally furnished bedrooms have thoughtful extras in addition to modern showers en suite; two rooms have fine views over the Vale of Llangollen. There is a comfortable lounge-dining room and at breakfast the emphasis is on fresh local produce.
Facilities 3 en suite ⊗ tea/coffee ✖ Cen ht TVL No coaches **Parking** 8 **Notes** ⊠

RHYL

MAP 14 SJ08

♦♦♦♦ ⊛ ⬚ ⬚

Barratt's Restaurant at Ty'N Rhyl

Ty'N Rhyl, 167 Vale Rd LL18 2PH
☎ 01745 344138 & 0773 095 4994 ▤ 01745 344138
e-mail EBarratt5@aol.com
Dir A55 onto A525 to Rhyl, pass Sainsburys & B&Q, garden centre on left, Barratts 400yds on right

This delightful 16th-century house lies in a secluded location surrounded by attractive gardens. It is really a restaurant with rooms and the quality of food reflects the skill of the owner-chef. Public areas are smartly furnished and include a panelled lounge and separate bar with attractive conservatory. Bedrooms are comfortable and equipped with lots of thoughtful extras.
Facilities 3 en suite ⊗ in bedrooms ⊗ in dining room TVB tea/coffee ✖ Licensed Cen ht TVL ⏰ Dinner Last d 9pm **Parking** 20

RUTHIN

MAP 15 SJ15

♦♦♦♦

Eyarth Station

Llanfair Dyffryn Clwyd LL15 2EE
☎ 01824 703643 ▤ 01824 707464
e-mail stay@eyarthstation.com
Dir Off A525 1m S of Ruthin onto lane, 600yds to Eyarth Station

Until 1964 and the Beeching cuts, this was a sleepy country station. A comfortable lounge and outdoor swimming pool occupy the space

continued

Wales

once taken up by the railway and platforms. Bedrooms are carefully decorated and full of thoughtful extras. Family rooms are available, and one room is in the former stationmaster's house adjoining the main building.

Facilities 4 en suite 2 annexe en suite (2 fmly) (4 GF) ⊗ in bedrooms ⊗ in dining room ⊗ in 1 lounge TV1B tea/coffee Licensed Cen ht TVL No coaches ⃗ Dinner Last d 7pm **Prices** S £45; D £62 **LB Parking** 6 **Notes** Closed 2 wks Nov

◆◆◆◆

Firgrove Country House B & B

Firgrove, Llanfwrog LL15 2LL
☎ 01824 702677 ▤ 01824 702677
e-mail meadway@firgrovecountryhouse.co.uk
web www.firgrovecountryhouse.co.uk
Dir Exit Ruthin on A494 to Bala, at minirdbt take B5105 to Cerrig-y-Drudion. Pass church on right & Cross Key Inn on left. Firgrove is 0.25m on right

Standing in immaculate mature gardens in a peaceful rural location, this well-proportioned house retains many original features, highlighted by the quality decor and furnishings. Bedrooms are equipped with a wealth of thoughtful extras and memorable breakfasts, using home-made or local produce, are served in the elegant dining room.

Facilities 3 en suite (1 GF) ⊗ TVB tea/coffee ✹ Cen ht No children No coaches Dinner Last d 24hrs **Prices** D £60-£80✳ **Parking** 4 **Notes** Closed Dec-Jan

◆◆◆◆ ✿

Tyddyn Chambers ◇ (SJ102543)

Pwllglas LL15 2LS ☎ 01824 750683 Mrs Williams
e-mail williams@tyddynchambers.fsnet.co.uk
web www.tyddynchambers.co.uk
Dir A494 from Ruthin for Bala, 3m to Pwllglas, right after the Fox & Hounds pub, signed

This charming little farmhouse has been extended to provide carefully appointed, modern accommodation, which includes a family room. The pleasant, traditionally furnished breakfast room has separate tables and a lounge is also available. The house stands on an elevated position with panoramic views.

Facilities 3 en suite (1 fmly) ⊗ TVB tea/coffee ✹ Cen ht TVL 180 acres Beef, dairy, sheep **Prices** S £28-£32; D £48-£56✳ **LB Parking** 3 **Notes** Closed Xmas & New Year ▨

◆◆◆◆ ◉ ◣

The Wynnstay Arms

Well St LL15 1AN ☎ 01824 703147
e-mail resevations@wynnstayarms.wanadoo.co.uk
web www.wynnstayarms.com
Dir In town centre

This former town centre pub has been renovated by new owners to provide good quality accommodation and a smart cafe-bar. The Fusions restaurant is earning a high reputation for its modern cuisine.

Facilities 6 en suite (1 fmly) ⊗ TVB tea/coffee Cen ht Dinner Last d 9.30pm **Prices** S £45-£55; D £65-£75 **LB Conf** Max 30 Thtr 30 Class 20 Board 16 Del from £79 ✳ **Parking** 14

ST ASAPH   MAP 15 SJ07

◆◆◆◆ ✿

Bach-Y-Graig (SJ075713)

Tremeirchion LL17 0UH
☎ 01745 730627 ▤ 01745 730971 Mrs Roberts
e-mail anwen@bachygraig.co.uk
web www.bachygraig.co.uk
Dir A55 onto A525 to Trefnant, left at lights onto A541 to x-rds with white railings, left down hill, over river bridge, right

Dating from the 16th century, this Grade II listed building was the first brick-built house in Wales and retains many original features including a wealth of exposed beams and inglenook fireplaces. Bedrooms are furnished with fine period pieces and quality soft fabrics. Ground floor areas include a quiet lounge and a sitting-dining room, featuring a superb Jacobean oak table.

Facilities 3 en suite (1 fmly) ⊗ TVB tea/coffee ✹ Cen ht TVL Fishing 200 acres dairy viewing gallery **Prices** S £40-£50; D £68-£74 **LB Parking** 3 **Notes** Closed Xmas & New Year ▨

Ⓤ

Tan-Yr-Onnen Guest House

Waen LL17 0DU ☎ 01745 583821 ▤ 01745 583821
e-mail tanyronnenvisit@aol.com
Dir W on A55 junct 28, turn left in 300yds

At the time of going to press the rating for this establishment had not been confirmed. Please check the AA website www.theAA.com for up-to-date information.

Facilities 3 en suite (1 fmly) (2 GF) ⊗ TVB tea/coffee Cen ht No coaches **Prices** S £50-£80; D £70-£100✳ **Parking** 8

Wales

Wales

FLINTSHIRE

HOLYWELL
MAP 15 SJ17

🅰 ❦

Greenhill Farm ◇ (SJ186776)

CH8 7QF ☎ 01352 713270 Mrs Jones
e-mail mary@greenhillfarm.fsnet.co.uk
web www.greenhillfarm.co.uk

Dir *From Holywell signs to St Winfred's Well, left opposite Royal Oak pub & follow lane to end.*

Facilities 4 rms (2 en suite) (2 pri facs) (2 fmly) ⊗ TVB tea/coffee ✖ Cen ht TVL Childrens play area 120 acres dairy mixed Dinner Last d 9am
Prices S £26✳ **LB Conf** Max 12 Board 12 **Parking** 6 **Notes** ★★★ rs Dec-Jan

MOLD
MAP 15 SJ26

See also **Nannerch**

◆◆◆

Heulwen ◇

Maes Bodlonfa CH7 1DR
☎ 01352 758785 ▤ 01352 758785

Dir *In town centre off A5119 New St*

This soundly maintained guest house is in a quiet residential area next to a park and bowling greens, a short walk from the town centre. It provides modern furnished and equipped accommodation, including a family room. Guests share one table in the pleasant breakfast room.

Facilities 2 rms (1 fmly) ⊗ TVB tea/coffee ✖ Cen ht No coaches
Prices S £22.50-£28; D £45 **Parking** 3 **Notes** ⊗

NANNERCH
MAP 15 SJ16

◆◆◆◆

The Old Mill

Melin-Y-Wern, Denbigh Rd CH7 5RH ☎ 01352 741542
e-mail mail@old-mill.co.uk
web www.old-mill.co.uk

Dir *A541 NW from Mold, 7m enter Melin-Y-Wern, Old Mill on right*

This converted stone stable block was once part of a Victorian watermill complex. The site also includes a craft and art gallery, and a restaurant and wine bar. The non-smoking guest house offers modern, well-equipped bedrooms with private bathrooms, suitable for leisure and business.

Facilities 6 en suite (2 GF) ⊗ FTV TVB tea/coffee Direct dial from bedrooms ✖ Cen ht No coaches Dinner Last d 24hrs notice
Prices S £50; D £72-£77✳ **LB Parking** 12

GWYNEDD

ABERDYFI
MAP 14 SN69

◆◆◆◆

Cartref Guest House

LL35 0NR ☎ 01654 767273 ▤ 01654 767000
e-mail enquiries@cartref-guesthouse.com

Dir *On A493 at W end of village opp road to railway station*

Situated on the edge of the village, close to a golf course and bowling green, this detached Edwardian-style villa is an easy walk from the sandy beach. Bedrooms are quite spacious and well-equipped, and family accommodation is available. There is a comfortable lounge.

Facilities 4 rms (3 en suite) (1 pri facs) (1 fmly) ⊗ TVB tea/coffee Cen ht TVL No coaches **Parking** 4 **Notes** Closed Dec-Jan

🅰

Awel Y Mor ◇

4 Bodfor Ter LL35 0EA ☎ 01654 767058
e-mail awelymor@lineone.net
web www.awelymor-aberdovey.co.uk

Dir *200yds W of village centre on A493*

Facilities 7 rms (6 en suite) (1 pri facs) (3 fmly) (2 GF) ⊗ TVB tea/coffee Cen ht No coaches **Prices** S £30; D £54-£64✳ **LB Notes** ★★★

ABERSOCH
MAP 14 SH32

◆◆◆◆

Riverside Hotel

LL53 7HW ☎ 01758 712419 ▤ 01758 712671
e-mail info@riversideabersoch.co.uk
web www.riversideabersoch.co.uk

Dir *On A499 before Abersoch*

Set close to harbour and town centre, the aptly named Riverside has a river-bank garden that is ideal for watching wildlife. The bedrooms are thoughtfully equipped, and some have good family facilities and direct access to the gardens. There is a Mediterranean theme restaurant and smart modern cocktail bar.

Facilities 12 en suite (5 fmly) (3 GF) ⊗ in bedrooms ⊗ in dining room ⊗ in 1 lounge TVB tea/coffee ✖ Licensed Cen ht Fishing Pool Table Dinner Last d 9.30pm **Prices** S £45-£68; D £60-£110✳ **LB Parking** 20

BALA
MAP 14 SH93

◆◆◆◆

Erw Feurig Guest House

Cefnddwysarn LL23 7LL
☎ 01678 530262 & 07786 168399 ▤ 01678 530262
e-mail erwfeurig@yahoo.com
web www.erwfeurig.com

Dir *3m NE of Bala off A494. 2nd left after telephone box, B&B signed*

A warm welcome is assured at this delightful and peaceful farm cottage situated on a hillside with panoramic views of the Berwyn Mountains. The individually styled bedrooms have a range of additional extras, and a cosy lounge and a cheerful ground-floor breakfast room are available.

continued

Erw Feurig

Facilities 4 rms (2 en suite) (2 pri facs) (1 GF) ⊗ TVB tea/coffee ✼ Cen ht TVL No children No coaches Fishing **Parking** 6 **Notes** 📧

◆◆◆◆ ❦

Pen-Y-Bryn Farmhouse ◇ (SH967394)

Sarnau LL23 7LH
☎ 01678 530389 🖹 01678 530389 Mrs Jones
e-mail jonespenbryn@lineone.net
web www.bala-wales.com/penbryn/
Dir *3m NE of Bala off A494. Pass telephone box at Cefnddwysarn, 2nd left, B&B signed, 2nd farm*

A genuine welcome is assured at this stone Victorian house, located on an elevated position overlooking Sarnau and the surrounding mountains. Bedrooms are thoughtfully furnished and have modern en suites. Hearty breakfasts are served in the attractive conservatory with stunning views.

Facilities 3 en suite (1 GF) ⊗ tea/coffee ✼ Cen ht TVL Bird watching, walking, cycling 90 acres mixed **Prices** S £28-£30; D £48-£50✳ LB **Parking** 6 **Notes** Closed 25-26 Dec 📧

BARMOUTH   MAP 14 SH61
See also **Dyffryn Ardudwy**

◆◆◆◆

Richmond House

High St LL42 1DW ☎ 01341 281366 & 07976 833069
e-mail info@barmouthbedandbreakfast.co.uk
web www.barmouthbedandbreakfast.co.uk
Dir *In town centre. Car park at rear on Jubilee Rd*

A warm welcome awaits you at this lovely Victorian house, which has been modernised to provide good quality and thoughtfully equipped

continued

accommodation. Two of the bedrooms have sea views, as do the lounge and dining room, where there are separate tables. There is also a pleasant garden.

Facilities 3 en suite (1 fmly) ⊗ TVB tea/coffee ✼ Cen ht No coaches **Prices** D £60-£80✳ LB **Parking** 5

◆◆◆◆ ➣ ❦

Llwyndu Farmhouse (SH599185)

Llanaber LL42 1RR ☎ 01341 280144 Mrs Thompson
e-mail Intouch@llwyndu-farmhouse.co.uk
web www.llwyndu-farmhouse.co.uk
Dir *A496 towards Harlech where street lights end, on outskirts of Barmouth, take next right*

This converted 16th-century farmhouse retains many original features including inglenook fireplaces, exposed beams and timbers. There is a cosy lounge and meals are enjoyed at individual tables in the character dining room. Bedrooms are modern and well equipped, and some have four-poster beds. Four rooms are in nearby buildings.

Facilities 3 en suite 4 annexe en suite (2 fmly) ⊗ TVB tea/coffee Licensed Cen ht TVL 4 acres non-working Dinner Last d 6.30pm **Prices** D £76-£80✳ LB **Parking** 10 **Notes** Closed 25-26 Dec rs Sun

◆◆◆◆ ◧

Tal-y-Don Inn

High St LL42 1DL ☎ 01341 280508 🖹 01341 280885
e-mail david@tal-y-don.co.uk
web www.tal-y-don.co.uk
Dir *A496 one-way system, right onto Beach Rd, right at end*

This very friendly and popular town centre hostelry provides attractive, good-quality accommodation. Public areas include lounge and public bar areas and a beer garden. A good range of freshly prepared food is available, served in either the pleasant restaurant or in the bar.

Facilities 5 en suite ⊗ in bedrooms ⊗ in dining room TVB tea/coffee Direct dial from bedrooms ✼ Cen ht No coaches Dinner Last d 8.45pm

BEDDGELERT
MAP 14 SH54

◆◆◆◆

Sygun Fawr Country House
LL55 4NE ☎ 01766 890258 📠 01766 890258
e-mail sygunfawr@aol.com
web www.sygunfawr.co.uk
Dir A498 N, turn right over river at brown sign onto lane

Sygun Fawr is set in a spectacular location within the Snowdonia National Park. The surrounding countryside and immaculate gardens are a mass of colour in the spring. Bedrooms are neat and pretty and many have superb views. Stone walls and exposed timbers abound, and a cosy bar and several comfortable sitting rooms are provided.

Facilities 12 en suite (1 GF) ⊗ in bedrooms ⊗ in dining room ⊗ in 1 lounge tea/coffee Licensed Cen ht TVL Dinner Last d 8pm **Prices** S fr £51; D £72-£95✱ **LB** **Conf** Thtr 10 Board 10 **Parking** 20 **Notes** Closed Jan

BETWS GARMON
MAP 14 SH55

◆◆◆◆

Betws Inn
LL54 7YY ☎ 01286 650324
e-mail stay@betws-inn.co.uk
web www.betws-inn.co.uk
Dir On A4085 Caernarfon to Beddgelert, opp Bryn Gloch Caravan Park

Set in the western foothills of the Snowdonia, this 17th-century former inn has been restored to provide an establishment of immense charm. A warm welcome and caring service are assured. Bedrooms have a wealth of homely extras, and imaginative dinners feature local produce. Breakfast includes home-made bread and preserves.

Facilities 3 en suite ⊗ tea/coffee ✖ Cen ht TVL No coaches Dinner Last d 2pm **Prices** S £40-£50; D £60-£70✱ **Parking** 3

If you have to cancel a booking, let the proprietor know immediately

BLAENAU FFESTINIOG
MAP 14 SH74

🅰

Cae Du ◇
Manod LL41 4BB ☎ 01766 830847 📠 01766 830847
e-mail caedu@tinyworld.co.uk
web www.caedu.co.uk
Dir 0.33m off A470, between Llau Festiniog and Blaenau Ffestiniog

Facilities 3 en suite ⊗ TVB tea/coffee ✖ Cen ht TVL No children 11yrs No coaches Dinner Last d breakfast **Prices** S £25-£35; d fr £50✱ **Parking** 6 **Notes** ★★★

CAERNARFON
MAP 14 SH46
See also Clynnog Fawr & Penygroes

◆◆◆◆ ❦

Pengwern (SH459587)
Saron LL54 5UH ☎ 01286 831500 📠 01286 830741
Mr & Mrs Rowlands
e-mail janepengwern@aol.com
Dir A487 S from Caernarfon, pass supermarket on right, right after bridge, 2m to Saron, over x-rds, 1st driveway on right

A beautifully maintained farmhouse surrounded by 130 acres of farmland running down to Foryd Bay, which is noted for its birdlife. Spacious bedrooms are equipped with modern, efficient bathrooms in addition to a wealth of thoughtful extras. Imaginative breakfasts are served in an elegant dining room and a lounge is also available.

Facilities 3 en suite ⊗ TVB tea/coffee ✖ Cen ht Car hire 130 acres beef sheep Dinner Last d noon **Prices** S £45; D £60-£70✱ **LB** **Parking** 3 **Notes** Closed Nov-Mar

◆◆◆◆

Caer Menai
15 Church St LL55 1SW ☎ 01286 672612
e-mail caer.menai@btopenworld.com
web www.caermenai.co.uk
Dir follow signs to the Castle & Old Town Walls, Caer Menai is 250yds from the castle within the walled town

This friendly guest house, originally the late 19th-century county school, is within the walled town, 250yds from the castle. The medieval town wall forms the boundary of the back garden. There is an attractive breakfast room and a lounge, and the cheerful bedrooms are equipped with modern facilities.

Facilities 7 en suite (2 fmly) ⊗ TVB tea/coffee ✖ Cen ht TVL No coaches pets corner **Prices** S £35; D £55-£60✱ **LB** **Notes**

◆◆◆◆

Country Manor Guest House
Griffiths Crossing LL55 1TS
☎ 01248 671030 📠 01248 671030
Dir A55 junct 10, A487, 1st rdbt 1st left, 2nd rdbt 1st left, 3rd rdbt 3rd left. Country Manor on left

Close to Caernarfon and overlooking the Menai Strait, this guest house has been extensively renovated and offers comfortable, well-equipped accommodation and friendly service. There is a popular tea

continued

Wales

room where a wide selection of home-made meals and snacks is available, as also a comfortable lounge and an extensive garden that looks on to the Strait.

Facilities 6 en suite (1 fmly) ⊗ TVB tea/coffee Licensed Cen ht No coaches Dinner Last d 8.30pm **Prices** S fr £35; d fr £55✱ **Parking** 12 **Notes** Closed 15 Dec-15 Jan

A

Plas Tirion Farm

Llanrug LL55 4PY ☎ 01286 673190 📠 01286 671883
e-mail cerid@plastirion.plus.com
web www.plas-tirion.co.uk
Dir *4m E of Caernarfon. Off A4806 Llanrug village square towards Ffordd Glanmoelyn, over x-rds, farm 1m (2nd on right)*

Facilities 3 en suite ⊗ in bedrooms ⊗ in dining room ⊗ in 1 lounge TVB tea/coffee 🐾 Cen ht TVL Dinner **Parking** 6 **Notes** ★★★★ Closed Nov-Mar ⊛

CLYNNOG FAWR   MAP 14 SH44

◆◆◆◆

Bryn Eisteddfod Country House Hotel

LL54 5DA ☎ 01286 660431
e-mail bryn.eisteddfod@virgin.net
web www.bryneisteddfod.com
Dir *Off A499 at village*

This Victorian house, near the Lleyn Peninsula and Snowdonia, offers comfortable accommodation and is especially popular with golfers. The traditionally furnished bedrooms are well equipped. There is a comfortable lounge and a large attractive conservatory bar-dining room, where evening meals can be served.

Facilities 8 rms (7 en suite) (1 pri facs) (3 fmly) ⊗ TVB tea/coffee 🐾 Licensed Cen ht No coaches Dinner Last d by arrangement **Prices** S £35-£45; D £55-£70✱ LB **Parking** 25

CRICCIETH   MAP 14 SH43

◆◆◆◆

Abereistedd Hotel ◇

West Pde LL52 0EN ☎ 01766 522710 📠 01766 523526
e-mail info@abereistedd.co.uk
web www.abereistedd.co.uk
Dir *A487 through Criccieth towards Pwllheli, left 400yds after filling station following signs for beach, on left at seafront*

An extremely warm welcome is asssured at this Victorian property with

continued

uninterrupted mountain and coastal views. The attractive bedrooms are very well equipped with thoughtful extras, the ground-floor lounge has a bar extension, and the bright dining room overlooks the seafront.

Facilities 12 en suite (3 fmly) ⊗ TVB tea/coffee Direct dial from bedrooms Licensed Cen ht No coaches Dinner Last d 2pm **Prices** S £28-£32; D £56-£64✱ LB **Parking** 9 **Notes** Closed Nov-Mar

◆◆◆◆

Glyn-Y-Coed Hotel

Porthmadog Rd LL52 0HP
☎ 01766 522870 📠 01766 523341
e-mail julie@glyn-y-coed.co.uk
web www.glynycoedhotel.co.uk
Dir *500yds from castle on main street in village*

A warm welcome is assured at this impressive refurbished Victorian house with views of Tremadog Bay and the surrounding mountains, and only a short walk from the beach. The en suite bedrooms include four-poster, king-size, family, and ground-floor options, and there is a sitting room and a south-facing patio for relaxing. Wholesome breakfasts are served in the spacious dining room, and private parking is available.

Facilities 9 en suite 1 annexe en suite (1 fmly) (1 GF) ⊗ TVB tea/coffee Direct dial from bedrooms 🐾 Licensed Cen ht **Prices** S £45-£59; D £59-£71✱ LB **Parking** 14

◆◆◆◆ ⊜

Bron Rhiw Hotel

Caernarfon Rd LL52 0AP ☎ 01766 522257
e-mail clairecriccieth@yahoo.co.uk
Dir *Off High St onto B4411*

A warm welcome and high standards of comfort and facilities are assured at this renovated, non-smoking Victorian property just a short walk from the seafront. The ground-floor areas include a sumptuous lounge, a cosy bar, and an elegant dining room where imaginative dinners and memorable breakfasts are served.

Facilities 9 en suite (2 fmly) ⊗ TVB tea/coffee 🐾 Licensed Cen ht No children 5yrs **Prices** S £37.50-£68; D £60-£68✱ LB **Parking** 3 **Notes** Closed Nov-Feb

Wales

CRICCIETH continued

◆◆◆◆

Cefn Uchaf Farm Guest House

Garndolbenmaen LL51 9PJ ☎ 01766 530239
e-mail cefnuchaf@tiscali.co.uk
Dir 3m N of Criccieth. Off A487 between Dolbenmaen & Bryncir signed Cefn Uchaf

The large, pleasant farmhouse stands in a remote location amid stunning scenery. Some of the thoughtfully furnished modern bedrooms are ideal for families, and a spacious lounge is available. Breakfast is served in the bright dining room.

Facilities 8 rms (7 en suite) (1 pri facs) (3 fmly) ⊗ TVB tea/coffee ✖ Licensed Cen ht TVL Dinner Last d noon **Prices** S £40-£50; D £54-£60✳ **Parking** 12

◆◆◆◆

Min y Gaer Hotel ◇

Porthmadog Rd LL52 0HP
☎ 01766 522151 📄 01766 523540
e-mail info@minygaer.co.uk
web www.minygaer.co.uk
Dir On A497 200yds E of junct with B4411

The friendly, family-run Min y Gaer has superb views from many of the rooms. The smart, modern bedrooms are furnished in pine, and the welcoming proprietors also provide a bar and a traditionally furnished lounge.

Facilities 10 en suite (2 fmly) ⊗ TVB tea/coffee Licensed Cen ht TVL No coaches **Prices** S £27; D £54✳ **Parking** 12 **Notes** Closed Nov-Feb

DOLGELLAU   MAP 14 SH71

★★★★ Bed & Breakfast

Coed Cae

Taicynhaeaf LL40 2TU ☎ 01341 430628 & 07909 996983
e-mail info@coedcae.co.uk
Dir Just off A496, opposite the toll bridge.

A warm welcome awaits at this charming old house, which is set in its own extensive wooded grounds, overlooking spectacular views of the Mawddach Estuary. The thoughtfully equipped accommodation includes a bedroom on ground floor level. All share one table in the spacious combined dining room and lounge, where guests can enjoy skilfully prepared, imaginative food.

Facilities 3 rms (2 en suite) (1 pri facs) (1 fmly) (1 GF) ⊗ TVB tea/coffee ✖ Cen ht No coaches Dinner Last d 4pm **Conf** Max 8 Board 8 **Parking** 8

Premier Collection

◆◆◆◆◆ ❦

Tyddynmawr Farmhouse *(SH704159)*

Cader Rd, Islawrdref LL40 1TL ☎ 01341 422331 Mrs Evans
Dir From town centre left at top of square, left at garage onto Cader Rd for 3m, 1st farm on left after Gwernan Lake

A warm welcome is assured at this 18th-century farmhouse which lies at the foot of Cader Idris amid breathtaking scenery. Bedrooms are spacious, with Welsh Oak furniture; the upper one has a balcony and the ground-floor room has a patio area. Bathrooms are large and luxurious. Superb breakfasts are a feast of home-made items; bread, preserves, muesli or smoked fish - the choice is excellent. Self-catering cottages are also available.

Facilities 3 en suite (1 GF) ⊗ TVB tea/coffee ✖ Cen ht TVL No children Fishing 800 acres beef sheep **Prices** S fr £45; d fr £60✳ **Parking** 8 **Notes** Closed Jan

◆◆◆◆

The Clifton ◇

Smithfield Sq LL40 1ES ☎ 01341 422554 📄 07092 197785
e-mail info@clifton-house-hotel.co.uk
web www.clifton-house-hotel.co.uk
Dir On one-way system in town

This impressive early 19th-century detached house, built of local stone, stands on the site of the former Merionydd county gaol. The restaurant has been created from the original cellar, providing a room with plenty of character in which to enjoy imaginative food. Bedrooms are furnished with thoughtful extras and a warm welcome is assured.

Facilities 7 rms (4 en suite) (1 GF) ⊗ TVB tea/coffee ✘ Licensed
Cen ht No coaches Dinner Last d 6.30pm **Prices** S £30; D £58-£66✱ LB
Notes Closed Xmas/New Year

◆◆◆◆

Dolgun Uchaf Guesthouse

Dolgun Uchaf LL40 2AB ☎ 01341 422269
e-mail dolgunuchaf@guesthousessnowdonia.com
web www.guesthousessnowdonia.com
Dir Off A470 at Little Chef just S of Dolgellau, Dolgun Uchaf 1st
property on right

Located in a peaceful area with stunning views of the surrounding
countryside, this 500-year-old late medieval hall house retains many
original features, including exposed beams and open fireplaces.
Bedrooms are equipped with thoughtful extras and a lounge is also
available.

Facilities 3 en suite 1 annexe en suite (1 GF) ⊗ TVB tea/coffee Cen ht
TVL No children 5yrs Dinner Last d 24hrs prior **Parking** 6

◆◆◆

Ivy House

Finsbury Sq LL40 1RF ☎ 01341 422535 ▤ 01341 422689
e-mail marg.bamford@btconnect.com
Dir From top of main square, house on left after bend

Friendly hospitality is offered at this house, situated in the centre of
Dolgellau at the foot of Cader Idris. Bedrooms are brightly decorated
and thoughtfully equipped. Ground floor rooms include a comfortable
lounge and a spacious dining room where dinner is available by
arrangement.

Facilities 6 rms (4 en suite) (1 fmly) ⊗ TVB tea/coffee Cen ht TVL
No coaches Dinner Last d 5pm **Notes** Closed 24-26 Dec

Ⓤ

Plas Dolmelynllyn

Ganllwyd LL40 2HP ☎ 01341 440273 ▤ 01341 440640
e-mail info@dolly-hotel.co.uk
web www.dolly-hotel.co.uk
Dir 5m N of Dolgellau on A470

At the time of going to press the rating for this establishment had not
been confirmed. Please check the AA website www.theAA.com for up-
to-date information.

Facilities 10 en suite (2 fmly) ⊗ STV TVB tea/coffee Direct dial from
bedrooms ✘ Licensed Cen ht No coaches Fishing Mountain bike riding
Dinner Last d 8pm **Conf** Max 15 Class 15 Board 15 **Parking** 16
Notes Closed Jan

DYFFRYN ARDUDWY   MAP 14 SH52

◆◆◆◆ ☏

Cadwgan Inn

LL44 2HA ☎ 01341 247240
e-mail cadwgan.hotel@virgin.net
Dir In Dyffryn Ardudwy onto Station Rd, over railway crossing

This very pleasant, privately owned pub stands in grounds close to
Dyffryn Ardudwy station, between Barmouth and Harlech. The beach
is a short walk away. The good quality, well-equipped modern
accommodation includes family rooms and a room with a four-poster
bed. Public areas include smoking and non smoking rooms, a family
room with games, a meeting room and a beer garden

Facilities 6 en suite (3 fmly) ⊗ in bedrooms ⊗ in dining room TVB
tea/coffee ✘ Cen ht TVL No coaches Dinner Last d 9.30pm
Prices S £50; D £70 LB **Parking** available

◆◆◆◆

The Old Farmhouse ◇

Tyddyn Du LL44 2DW ☎ 01341 242711 ▤ 01341 242711
e-mail metcalfe.oldfarmhouse@virgin.net
Dir Signed on A496 between Harlech & Barmouth, 0.5m from road

Located in well-maintained grounds including a swimming pool and
hot tub, this renovated former farmhouse provides a range of
thoughtfully furnished bedrooms, two of which are in a separate
garden cottage. The comfortable sitting-dining room has stunning
views of the surrounding coastline.

Facilities 3 en suite 2 annexe en suite (2 fmly) (5 GF) ⊗ STV TVB
tea/coffee ✘ Cen ht TVL No children 5yrs No coaches ⚓ Hot spa
Prices S £27.50-£32.50; D £55-£65 LB **Parking** 10 **Notes** Closed
24-31 Dec ⊛

FFESTINIOG

MAP 14 SH74

◆◆◆◆
Ty Clwb

The Square LL41 4LS ☎ 01766 762658 🖷 01766 762658
e-mail tyclwb@talk21.com
web www.tyclwb.co.uk
Dir On B4391 in of Ffestiniog, opp church

Located opposite the historic church, this elegant house has been carefully modernised and is immaculately maintained throughout. Bedrooms are thoughtfully furnished and in addition to an attractive dining room, a spacious lounge with sun patio provides stunning views of the surrounding mountain range.

Facilities 3 en suite ⊗ tea/coffee Cen ht TVL No coaches
Prices D £46-£52

◆◆◆
Morannedd

Blaenau Rd LL41 4LG ☎ 01766 762734
e-mail morannedd@talk21.com
Dir At edge of village on A470 towards Blaenau Ffestiniog

This guest house is set in the Snowdonia National Park and is well located for touring north Wales. A friendly welcome is offered and the atmosphere is relaxed and informal. Bedrooms are smart and modern and a cosy lounge is available. Hearty home cooking can be enjoyed here.

Facilities 4 en suite ⊗ TVB tea/coffee Cen ht No coaches
Notes Closed Xmas 📷

HARLECH

MAP 14 SH53

◆◆◆◆
Gwrach Ynys Country Guest House ◇

Talsarnau LL47 6TS ☎ 01766 780742 🖷 01766 781199
e-mail aa@gwrachynys.co.uk
web www.gwrachynys.co.uk
Dir 2m N of Harlech on A496

This delightful Edwardian house nestles in idyllic lawns and gardens with dramatic views of the surrounding mountains. Bedrooms are thoughtfully equipped with modern facilities. Two comfortably furnished lounges promote a home from home feel and hospitality is welcoming. Hearty meals can be enjoyed at separate tables in the dining room.

Facilities 7 rms (6 en suite) (3 fmly) ⊗ TVB tea/coffee ✖ Cen ht TVL
Prices S £28-£30; D £56-£70✳ **LB Parking** 10 **Notes** Closed Dec-Jan
📷

◆◆◆◆
Pensarn Hall Country Guest House

Pensarn LL45 2HS ☎ 01341 241236
e-mail welcome@pensarn-hall.co.uk
Dir S on A496 past Harlech. After 1.75m, Pensarn Hall on left

This lovely Victorian country house stands in spacious gardens overlooking the Artro Estuary and Shell Island. The house has an interesting history, including connections with David Lloyd-George. It

continued

provides friendly hospitality as well as thoughtfully equipped accommodation, including a room with a four-poster bed.

Facilities 7 en suite (1 fmly) ⊗ TVB tea/coffee Cen ht TVL No children 2yrs No coaches **Prices** S £45-£50; D £65-£85✳ **LB Parking** 8

LLANBEDR

MAP 14 SH52

◆◆◆◆
Bryn Artro Country House

LL45 2LE ☎ 01341 241619 & 07775 585729
e-mail julie@llanbedr-brynartro.com
Dir On A496 3m S of Harlech, opp Maes Artro Centre

Located in mature grounds with a water garden, this Victorian house, faced in local slate, has original tiled floors and stained-glass windows. Bedrooms are thoughtfully equipped with homely extras, and comprehensive Welsh breakfasts are provided in a spacious dining room that overlooks the pretty rear gardens.

Facilities 7 en suite (4 fmly) ⊗ TVB tea/coffee ✖ Licensed Cen ht TVL Bike hire Dinner Last d 8pm **Prices** S £35-£40; D £60-£70✳ **LB Conf** Max 16 **Parking** 20

◆◆◆◆ ▣
Victoria Inn

LL45 2LD ☎ 01341 241213 🖷 01341 241644
e-mail junevicinn@aol.com
Dir In village centre

This former coaching inn lies beside the River Artro in a very pretty village. Many original features remain, including the Settle bar with its flagstone floor, black polished fireplace and unusual circular wooden settle. The menu is extensive and is supplemented by blackboard specials. Bedrooms are spacious and thoughtfully furnished.

Facilities 5 en suite ⊗ in bedrooms ⊗ in dining room TVB tea/coffee ✖ Cen ht Dinner Last d 9pm **LB Conf** Max 30 **Parking** 75

LLANBERIS

MAP 14 SH56

★★★★ ▲ Bed & Breakfast
Plas Coch Guest House

High St LL55 4HB ☎ 01286 872122 🖷 01286 872648
e-mail reservations@plas-coch.co.uk
web www.plas-coch.co.uk
Dir A4086 into Llanberis, on W side of High St 500yds N of Snowdon railway

Facilities 8 en suite (3 fmly) (1 GF) ⊗ TVB tea/coffee ✖ Licensed Cen ht TVL No coaches **Parking** 8 **Notes** 📷

MAENTWROG

MAP 14 SH64

♦♦♦

Bryn Maen ◇

LL41 4HN ☎ 01766 590417
e-mail welcome@brynmaen.com
Dir *On A496 in village centre*

The former shop frontage of this 19th-century stone property gives little indication of the character and hospitality that await within. The bedrooms are furnished in the period style of the house and have modern facilities. There is a spacious breakfast room, a comfortable lounge, and picturesque views towards Tan-y-Bwlch.

Facilities 3 rms (1 en suite) (1 fmly) ⊗ TVB tea/coffee ✖ Cen ht TVL No coaches **Prices** S £30-£40; D £60-£70✱ LB

MALLWYD

MAP 14 SH81

♦♦♦♦

Brigand's Inn

SY20 9HJ ☎ 01650 511999 ▤ 01650 531208
e-mail info@brigandsinn.co.uk
Dir *In village at junct A458 & A470*

This 15th-century inn has extensive shooting and fishing rights, and has been renovated to provide high standards of comfort and facilities. Quality furnishing and decor highlight the many original features, and comfortable bedrooms have luxurious bathrooms with power showers.

Facilities 10 en suite (1 fmly) ⊗ in bedrooms ⊗ in dining room ⊗ in 1 lounge TVB tea/coffee Direct dial from bedrooms ✖ Cen ht Fishing Dinner Last d 9pm **Prices** S fr £50; D £80-£95✱ LB **Conf** Thtr 30 Class 20 Board 20 Del £86 ✱ **Parking** 50

PENYGROES

MAP 14 SH45

♦♦♦ ❧

Llwyndu Mawr Farmhouse ◇ *(SH475536)*

Carmel Rd LL54 6PU
☎ 01286 880419 ▤ 01286 880845 Mrs Williams
Dir *From village onto B4418, 500yds left for Carmel, 500yds up hill after cemetery, 1st left*

This hillside farmhouse dates from the 19th century. Home from home hospitality is provided and you are welcome to take part in the life of this working sheep farm. Pretty bedrooms look over the Menai Strait toward Snowdonia. A choice of smoking and non-smoking lounges is available.

continued

Facilities 4 rms (2 en suite) (1 fmly) (1 GF) ⊗ in bedrooms ⊗ in dining room ⊗ in 1 lounge TVB tea/coffee Cen ht TVL 98 acres sheep Dinner Last d 4pm **Prices** S £20-£22; D £40-£44✱ LB **Parking** 7 **Notes** Closed 20 Dec-6 Jan ▨

PORTHMADOG

MAP 14 SH53

Premier Collection

♦♦♦♦♦ ❧

Tyddyn-Du Farm Holiday Suites

(SH691398)

Gellilydan, Ffestiniog LL41 4RB
☎ 01766 590281 ▤ 01766 590281 Mrs Williams
e-mail theaa@snowdoniafarm.com
web www.snowdonia-farm-holidays-wales.co.uk
Dir *1st farmhouse on left after junct A487 & A470, near Gellilydan*

Superbly located on an elevated position with stunning views of the surrounding countryside, this 400-year-old stone property provides a range of spacious, beautifully furnished and equipped bedrooms, converted from former stables and barns. Superb breakfasts are served in a cosy pine-furnished dining room in the main house, and a lounge with log fire is available. Families and pets are especially welcome.

Facilities 4 en suite (4 fmly) (4 GF) ⊗ TVB tea/coffee Cen ht TVL ⚬ Ponies & chickens 150 acres organic/sheep Dinner Last d 5pm **Prices** S £45-£95; D £65-£105✱ LB **Parking** 10 **Notes** rs Xmas ▨

TYWYN

MAP 14 SH50

♦♦♦♦ ❧

Eisteddfa *(SH651055)*

Eisteddfa, Abergynolwyn LL36 9UP
☎ 01654 782385 ▤ 01654 782228 Mrs Pugh
Dir *On B4405 between Abergynolwyn & Dolgoch Falls*

Eisteddfa is a modern stone bungalow situated less than a mile from Abergynolwyn, in a spot ideal for walking or for visiting the local railway. Rooms are well equipped, and the lounge and dining room look over the valley.

Facilities 3 rms (2 en suite) (3 GF) STV TVB tea/coffee Cen ht TVL 1200 acres mixed **Notes** Closed Dec-Feb ▨

Y FELINHELI

MAP 14 SH56

♦♦♦♦ Ⓐ

Hotel Plas Dinorwic

Ffordd Siabod LL56 4XA
☎ 01248 670559 & 671122 ▤ 01248 670300
e-mail plasdinorwic@btconnect.com
web www.hotelplasdinorwic.com
Dir *A55 junct 10, signs for Y Felinheli/Menai Marina*

Facilities 32 en suite (5 fmly) (16 GF) ⊗ in bedrooms ⊗ in dining room ⊗ in lounges FTV TVB tea/coffee ✖ Licensed Cen ht TVL ▣ Sauna Dinner Last d 9.30pm **Prices** S £50; D £60-£145; (room only) ✱ **Conf** Max 80 Thtr 80 **Parking** 64 **Notes** ★★★★

MERTHYR TYDFIL

MERTHYR TYDFIL MAP 09 SO00

◆◆◆◆

Penrhadw Farm

Pontsticill CF48 2TU
☎ 01685 723481 & 722461 ▤ 01685 722461
e-mail info@penrhadwfarm.co.uk
web www.penrhadwfarm.co.uk
Dir 5m N of Merthyr Tydfil, map on website

A warm welcome can be expected at this former Victorian farmhouse in the glorious Brecon Beacons National Park. The house has been totally refurbished to provide quality modern accommodation. The well-equipped, spacious, non-smoking bedrooms include two new large suites in cottages adjacent to the main building. There is also a comfortable lounge. Separate tables are provided in the cosy breakfast room.

Facilities 5 en suite (2 fmly) (1 GF) ⊗ STV TVB tea/coffee ✘ Cen ht TVL Dinner Last d by arrangement **Prices** S £46-£50; D £60-£80✳ LB **Conf** Max 10 Thtr 10 Class 10 **Parking** 22

◆◆◆◆

Llwyn Onn Guest House

Cwmtaf CF48 2HT ☎ 01685 384384 ▤ 01685 359310
e-mail reception@llwynonn.co.uk
Dir Off A470 2m N of Cefn Coed, overlooking Llwyn-on Reservoir

Fronted by a large pleasant garden, this delightful house overlooks Llwyn-on Reservoir. Bedrooms are spacious and carefully appointed, and the lounge opens onto the terrace and garden, as does the bright breakfast room. The friendly proprietors are attentive hosts and a stay here will be a memorable experience.

Facilities 11 en suite (3 GF) ⊗ in bedrooms ⊗ in dining room STV TVB tea/coffee Direct dial from bedrooms ✘ Cen ht TVL No coaches **Prices** S £45-£85; D £70-£85✳ LB **Parking** 9

MONMOUTHSHIRE

ABERGAVENNY MAP 09 SO21

◆◆◆◆ ❤

Hardwick Farm (SO306115)

NP7 9BT
☎ 01873 853513 & 854238 ▤ 01873 854238 Mrs Jones
e-mail carol.hardwickfarm@virgin.net
Dir 1m from Abergavenny, off A4042, farm sign on right

Quietly located in the Usk valley with wonderful views, this large family-run farmhouse provides warm hospitality. The spacious bedrooms are comfortably furnished, well equipped, and include one suitable for a family. Farmhouse breakfasts are served at separate tables, in the traditionally furnished dining room.

Hardwick Farm

Facilities 2 en suite (1 fmly) ⊗ TVB tea/coffee Cen ht 230 acres dairy mixed **Prices** S £40; D £58 LB **Parking** 2 **Notes** Closed Xmas 🚭

◆◆◆ ❤

Penyclawdd Farm ◇ (SO291173)

Llanvihangel Crucorney NP7 7LB
☎ 01873 890591 Mrs Davies
e-mail info@penyclawdd.co.uk
web www.penyclawdd.co.uk
Dir 5m N of Abergavenny. Off A465 signed Pantygelli

This attractive modern house is located in immaculate gardens off the Abergavenny to Hereford road. It offers homely bedrooms filled with many thoughtful extras. A traditionally furnished dining room is the setting for imaginative breakfasts, and a lounge with a wood burner is available.

Facilities 2 en suite (2 fmly) ⊗ TVB tea/coffee ✘ Cen ht TVL 160 acres sheep beef, working farm **Prices** S £30; D £55 **Parking** 6 **Notes** 🚭

A

The Wenallt

Gilwern NP7 0HP ☎ 01873 830694 ▤ 01873 830694
Dir A465 from Abergavenny for Merthyr Tydfil 3m, over rdbt, 1st left 0.25m, The Wenallt at top of lane

Facilities 4 rms (1 en suite) 5 annexe en suite (1 fmly) ⊗ in bedrooms ⊗ in dining room ⊗ in 1 lounge STV TV available tea/coffee Licensed Cen ht TVL No coaches Dinner Last d 6pm **Conf** Max 20 **Parking** 20 **Notes** ★★★ 🚭

A

Pentre Court Country House

Llanwenarth Citra NP7 7EW
☎ 01873 853545 ▤ 01873 851354
e-mail judith@pentrecourt.com
web www.pentrecourt.com
Dir On A40 opp Lamb and Flag Inn

Facilities 3 en suite (1 fmly) ⊗ in bedrooms ⊗ in dining room TVB tea/coffee Cen ht TVL No coaches ⛷ ♘ Dinner Last d Day before **Parking** 6 **Notes** ★★ Closed 23 Dec-1 Jan 🚭

CHEPSTOW MAP 04 ST59
See **Tintern Parva**

continued

LLANDOGO
MAP 04 SO50

◆◆◆

The Sloop Inn

NP25 4TW ☎ 01594 530291
e-mail thesloopinn@btconnect.co.uk
Dir On A466 in village centre

This welcoming Inn is centrally located close to the River Wye in a valley of outstanding natural beauty. The inn offers a selection of traditional food, as well as friendly hospitality. The refurbished dining room has delightful views over the valley, and the spacious bedrooms are equipped for business and leisure.

Facilities 4 en suite (1 fmly) ⊗ in bedrooms ⊗ in dining room TVB tea/coffee ✖ Cen ht Pool Table Dinner Last d 9pm **Parking** 50

MONMOUTH
MAP 10 SO51

Premier Collection

◆◆◆◆◆ ➲ ❦

Hendre Farm House (SO457124)

Hendre, Wonastow NP25 4DJ
☎ 01600 740484 📄 01600 740177 Mrs P J Baker
e-mail thehendrefarmhouse@hotmail.com
web www.pam-baker.org
Dir B4233 from Monmouth to Rockfield & onto Hendre, Roels Golf Course on left, sharp left, farm 1.5m on right

A warm welcome is assured at this relaxing farmhouse overlooking meadows and hills, where the present family has lived since 1885. The bedrooms and lounge combine traditional charm with modern comforts. Delicious home-cooked meals are a highlight and are available by arrangement.

Facilities 3 en suite (1 fmly) ⊗ STV TVB tea/coffee ✖ Cen ht TVL Fishing 73 acres Mixed Dinner Last d 24hrs before **Prices** S fr £40; d fr £66✱ **Conf** Max 12 **Parking** 20 **Notes** ⊛

◆◆◆◆ ❦

Penylan Farm ◇ (SO445162)

The Hendre NP25 5NL ☎ 01600 716435 📄 01600 719391
Mr & Mrs Bowen
e-mail penylan@fsmail.net
Dir 5m NW of Monmouth. Off B4233 towards Newcastle, 1.5m 1st left, next left, farm 0.5m on right

This converted barn was originally part of the Hendre Estate, once owned by the Rolls family. The bedrooms are housed in a former
continued

granary, and are equipped with many thoughtful extras. Breakfasts focus on local produce, and a lounge is available.

Facilities 3 rms (2 en suite) (1 pri facs) ⊗ TVB tea/coffee ✖ Cen ht TVL ♨ 90 acres Beef/Arable Dinner Last d 24hrs prior **Prices** S £30-£35; D £46-£55✱ LB **Parking** 4 **Notes** Closed Xmas & New Year

◆◆◆

Church Farm Guest House ◇

Mitchel Troy NP25 4HZ ☎ 01600 712176
Dir 2m S of Monmouth. A40 onto B4293, left into Mitchel Troy

Located in the village of Mitchel Troy, this 16th-century former farmhouse retains many original features including exposed beams and open fireplaces. There is a range of bedrooms and a spacious lounge, and breakfast is served the traditionally furnished dining room.

Facilities 9 rms (7 en suite) (2 pri facs) (3 fmly) ⊗ TV2B tea/coffee Cen ht TVL No coaches Dinner Last d noon **Prices** S £27-£28; D £48-£56 LB **Parking** 12 **Notes** ⊛

SKENFRITH
MAP 09 SO42

Premier Collection

★★★★★ ⊛⊛ **Restaurant with Rooms**

The Bell at Skenfrith

NP7 8UH ☎ 01600 750235 📄 01600 750525
e-mail enquiries@skenfrith.co.uk
web www.skenfrith.co.uk
Dir A40/A466 N towards Hereford 4m, turn left onto B4521 signed Abergavenny, Hotel 2m on left

The Bell is a beautifully restored, 17th-century former coaching inn which still retains much of its original charm and character. It is peacefully situated on the banks of The Monnow, a tributary of the River Wye, and is ideally placed for exploring the numerous delights of the counties of Herefordshire and Monmouthshire. Natural materials have been used to create a relaxing atmosphere, while the bedrooms, which include full suites and rooms with four-poster beds, are stylish, luxurious and equipped with DVD players.

Facilities 8 en suite TVB tea/coffee Direct dial from bedrooms Licensed No coaches Dinner Last d 9.30pm **Prices** S £75-£120; D £100-£180✱ **Conf** Max 20 Thtr 20 Board 16 Del £185 ✱ **Parking** 36 **Notes** Closed last wk Jan-1st wk Feb rs 6 Oct-Mar

TINTERN PARVA
MAP 04 SO50

◆◆◆

The Cherry Tree Inn

Forge Rd NP16 6TH ☎ 01291 689292 📄 01291 689787
e-mail steve@thecherry.co.uk
Dir A466 from Chepstow, 1st left after Tintern Abbey

Located on a quiet road, yet just a short walk from Tintern Abbey, this friendly hostelry offers all the comforts and welcome of a real inn. No televisions or games machines here, but a fine selection of real ales, delicious home cooking served in very generously sized portions and cosy, individually furnished bedrooms. Outdoor patio seating is available in fine weather.

Facilities 4 en suite ⊗ tea/coffee Direct dial from bedrooms ✖ Cen ht No children 16yrs Dinner Last d 9pm **Prices** D £60 **Parking** 4

TINTERN PARVA continued

♦♦♦ ◼

Fountain Inn

Trellech Grange NP16 6QW
☎ 01291 689303 🖨 01291 689303
e-mail thefountaininn04@aol.com
web www.fountaininn-tintern.com
Dir *Off A466 signed Raglan before Royal George Hotel, continue 2m bearing right, Fountain Inn at top of hill on left*

Located in a peaceful valley north of Tintern, this 17th-century inn retains many original features highlighted by rustic-style furniture. The cosy bedrooms are compact, with thoughtful extras. A range of dishes is available in the various bars.

Facilities 4 rms (3 en suite) ⊗ in bedrooms ⊗ in dining room TVB tea/coffee ✗ Cen ht Dinner Last d 9.30pm **Conf** Max 30 Board 20 **Parking** 30

TRELLECK
MAP 04 SO50

🅰

Heather Dean ◇

Mary Land NP25 4QN ☎ 01600 860566 🖨 01600 860566
e-mail val@heatherdean.co.uk

Facilities 3 en suite (1 fmly) ⊗ TVB tea/coffee ✗ Cen ht TVL No children 10yrs No coaches Dinner Last d 24hrs prior **Prices** S £30; D £50✳ **Parking** 10 **Notes** ★★★ Closed Nov-Etr 🐾

USK
MAP 09 SO30

★★★★ ◉◉ **Restaurant with Rooms**

The Newbridge

Tredunnock NP15 1LY ☎ 01633 451000 🖨 01633 451001
e-mail thenewbridge@tinyonline.co.uk
web www.thenewbridge.co.uk

This 200-year-old inn stands alongside the River Usk at Tredunnock, just four miles south of Usk. It has been renovated and converted into a spacious, traditionally furnished restaurant occupying the ground and first-floor levels. Six smart, modern and well-equipped bedrooms are located in a stone-clad, purpose-built unit adjacent to the restaurant.

Facilities 6 en suite ⊗ in bedrooms ⊗ in dining room ⊗ in 1 lounge FTV TV available tea/coffee Direct dial from bedrooms Licensed Cen ht No coaches Fishing Dinner Last d 9.30pm **Prices** S £95-£105; D £140-£160✳ **Conf** Max 20 Thtr 20 **Parking** 60 **Notes** Closed 1 wk Jan Civ Wed 80

WHITEBROOK
MAP 04 SO50

Premier Collection

★★★★★ ◉◉ **Restaurant with Rooms**

The Crown at Whitebrook

NP25 4TX ☎ 01600 860254 🖨 01600 860607
e-mail crown@whitebrook.demon.co.uk
Dir *0.5m W of village, off A449*

The 17th-century former drover's cottage lies in a secluded wooded valley that falls to the River Wye. Its refurbished bedrooms have a contemporary feel with modern facilities, and the restaurant and lounge combine original features with a bright fresh look to create a very comfortable and appealing environment. The memorable cuisine features local ingredients, skilfully prepared.

Facilities 8 en suite ⊗ FTV TVB tea/coffee Direct dial from bedrooms ✗ Licensed Cen ht No children 12yrs No coaches Fishing Shooting Dinner Last d 9.15pm **Prices** S £70-£85; D £85-£120✳ LB **Conf** Max 10 Thtr 16 Board 10 Del from £105 ✳ **Parking** 20 **Notes** Closed 26 Dec-12 Jan rs Sun-Mon

See advertisement on opposite page

NEATH PORT TALBOT

NEATH
MAP 09 SS79

♦♦♦♦ ◒ ◼

Dulais Rock

Main Rd, Aberdulais SA10 8EY
☎ 01639 644611 🖨 01639 646611
e-mail stay@dulaisrock.co.uk
Dir *M4 junct 43, follow signs for Aberdulais Falls for 3m*

The Dulais Rock is some 350 years old and has been refurbished to offer high levels of quality and comfort. The well-equipped bedrooms are located above the modern Mediterranean style restaurant. Dinner is a highlight, using carefully chosen ingredients with a varied selection of wines.

Facilities 3 en suite ⊗ in bedrooms ⊗ in dining room ⊗ in 1 lounge TVB tea/coffee ✗ Cen ht Fishing Dinner Last d 9.30pm **Conf** Thtr 30 Class 20 Board 14 **Parking** 20

Wales

♦♦♦♦
Cwmbach Cottages
Cwmbach Rd, Cadoxton SA10 8AH
☎ 01639 639825 & 641436
e-mail l.morgan5@btinternet.com
web www.cwmbachcottages.co.uk
Dir 1.5m NE of Neath. A465 onto A474 & A4230 towards Aberdulais, left opp Cadoxton church, guest house signed

A terrace of former miners' cottages has been restored to provide a range of thoughtfully furnished bedrooms, with one on the ground floor for easier access. Spacious public areas include a comfortable lounge and a pleasant breakfast room with separate tables. A superb decked patio overlooks a wooded hillside rich with wildlife.

Facilities 5 en suite (1 fmly) (1 GF) ⊗ TVB tea/coffee ✖ Cen ht TVL
No children 12yrs No coaches Golf 18 **Prices** S £32-£38; D £52-£58✳ LB
Parking 7 **Notes** 🐾

NEWPORT
CAERLEON MAP 09 ST39

Premier Collection
★★★★★ Bed & Breakfast
Radford House
Broadway NP18 1AY ☎ 01633 430101
e-mail radfordhouse@btconnect.com
web www.radfordhouse.co.uk
Dir In village centre opp museum & church

Located in the heart of the historic town of Caerleon, refurbished Radford House more than meets its brochure description of providing rooms of distinction for the discerning traveller. The spacious bedrooms and bathrooms have been beautifully designed and sumptuously furnished, and include fresh flowers, bottles of water, an extensive selection of teas, chocolates, fresh fruit, and flat-screen televisions. A comfortable drawing room, impressive staircase and smart breakfast room add to the air of luxury and relaxation. AA Guest Accommodation of the Year for Wales 2006.

Facilities 3 en suite (2 fmly) ⊗ FTV TVB tea/coffee ✖ Cen ht
No children 12yrs No coaches **Prices** S £55-£65; D £75-£85✳

NEWPORT MAP 09 ST38

♦♦♦♦
Crescent Guest House
11 Caerau Crescent NP20 4HG
☎ 01633 776677 🖷 01633 761279
e-mail lex4172@aol.com
web www.crescentguesthouse.com
Dir M4 junct 27, to town centre, over lights with Handpost pub on right, Caerau Crescent 50yds on left

Located on a quiet residential avenue within easy walking distance of the centre, this elegant Victorian house retains many original features, including a fine tiled hall and stained-glass windows. The comfortable bedrooms are filled with thoughtful extras and have modern bathrooms. Breakfasts, using quality local produce, are served in an attractive dining room.

Facilities 9 en suite (2 fmly) (2 GF) ⊗ TVB tea/coffee ✖ Cen ht
No coaches Solarium **Parking** 5

The Crown at Whitebrook
near Monmouthshire NP25 4TX

The Crown at Whitebrook is set in 3 acres of gardens surrounded by forest views in the heart of the breathtakingly beautiful Wye Valley. Eight luxurious bedrooms have been lovingly refurbished to the highest standard with attention to detail throughout. Individual themes and character define each room. All boast modern en-suite bathrooms with under-floor heating, high-speed Internet access and flat screen televisions. The restaurant has a warm, relaxed ambience and a superb Modern British fine dining menu draws from the best of local ingredients.

Tel: 01600 860254   Fax: 01600 860607
Email: info@crownatwhitebrook.co.uk
Website: www.crownatwhitebrook.co.uk

Wales

NEWPORT continued

◆◆◆◆

Kepe Lodge Guest House

46A Caerau Rd NP20 4HH
☎ 01633 262351 📄 01633 262351
e-mail kepelodge@hotmail.com
Dir M4 junct 27, town centre signs, 2nd lights left, premises on right

This attractive guest house in a quiet residential area is set back from the road in pleasant gardens. Guests can expect attentive service and comfortable homely bedrooms. Breakfast is served at individual tables in the well-appointed dining room. A comfortable lounge is also available.

Facilities 8 rms (3 en suite) ⊗ TVB tea/coffee ✻ Cen ht No children 10yrs No coaches Dinner Last d before noon **Prices** S £31-£41; d fr £62✳ **Parking** 12 **Notes** ⊗

◆◆◆◆ ◁

The Rising Sun

1 Cefn Rd, Rogerstone NP10 9AQ
☎ 01633 895126 📄 01633 891020
Dir M4 junct 27, B4591 signed Highcross, establishment 0.5m on left

Located a short drive from M4 in the community of Rogerstone, this Edwardian inn provides high levels of comfort and facilities. Bedrooms are equipped with quality furnishings and lots of thoughtful extras. Spacious public rooms include a magnificent split-level conservatory, and the grounds feature a children's play area.

Facilities 6 rms (5 en suite) (1 pri facs) (1 fmly) ⊗ in dining room ⊗ in lounges TVB tea/coffee ✻ Cen ht Pool Table Dinner Last d 9pm **Prices** S £42-£50; D £60-£70✳ **Parking** 100

◆◆◆

The Knoll Guest House

145 Stow Hill NP20 4FZ ☎ 01633 263557 📄 01633 212168
e-mail jacqueline_griffiths@hotmail.com
Dir M4 junct 27, B4591 to Newport, 1m on right, corner Stow Hill & Stow Park Av

This former Victorian residence has been converted into an elegant guest house, located on the main road into town. Bedrooms are attractively decorated, of varying size and offer a good range of facilities. Breakfast is served in the cosy dining room and there is also a lounge.

Facilities 12 en suite (4 fmly) (3 GF) ⊗ in 2 bedrooms ⊗ in dining room TVB tea/coffee ✻ Licensed Cen ht Dinner Last d 9pm **Prices** S £41.12-£56.40; D £56.40-£82.25✳

REDWICK   MAP 09 ST48

Premier Collection

◆◆◆◆◆ ⊜

Brickhouse Country Guest House

North Row NP26 3DX ☎ 01633 880230 📄 01633 882441
e-mail brickhouse@compuserve.com
Dir M4 junct 23A, follow steelworks road for 1.5m. Left after sign for Redwick, Brickhouse 1.5m on left

This impressive country house is in a peaceful location with attractive, well-tended gardens. The friendly hosts are most attentive and provide a relaxing atmosphere. Bedrooms are spacious and well furnished, and there is a choice of lounges. Delightful dinners feature local and home-grown produce.

Facilities 7 rms (5 en suite) (1 fmly) ⊗ TVB ✻ Licensed Cen ht TVL No children 10yrs No coaches Dinner Last d noon **Prices** S £45; D £60 **Parking** 7

ST BRIDES WENTLOOGE   MAP 09 ST28

Premier Collection

◆◆◆◆◆ ⊛ ⊜ ◀

The Inn at the Elm Tree

NP10 8SQ ☎ 01633 680225 📄 01633 681035
e-mail inn@the-elm-tree.co.uk
Dir 4m SW of Newport. On B4239 in St Brides village

A stylish barn conversion on the tranquil Wentlooge Levels. Individually decorated bedrooms combine the traditional and the contemporary:- hand-made brass beds, beamed ceilings and sumptuous fabrics blend with minimalist bathrooms (some with a jacuzzi), ISDN lines and business services. The restaurant offers an extensive choice including seafood and game in season, with the emphasis on quality ingredients.

Facilities 10 en suite (1 fmly) (2 GF) ⊗ in bedrooms ⊗ in dining room ⊗ in 1 lounge TVB tea/coffee Direct dial from bedrooms Cen ht 🔟 Dinner Last d 9.30pm **Prices** S £64.50-£80; D £80-£130 **LB** **Conf** Max 20 Board 20

PEMBROKESHIRE

DALE   MAP 08 SM80

◆◆◆◆

Richmond House

SA62 3RB ☎ 07974 925009 & 01646 692132
e-mail cilla@richmond-house.com

This charming old house on the seafront has been renovated and modernised to provide bright and thoughtfully equipped accommodation, which includes a bedroom on the ground floor with easier access, and a bunkhouse attic room. There is an attractive lounge-breakfast room with separate table, and the establishment is popular with walkers and water-sport enthusiasts.

Facilities 4 rms (3 en suite) (1 fmly) (1 GF) ⊗ TV3B tea/coffee ✻ Cen ht TVL **Prices** S fr £35; d fr £60✳ **LB** **Parking** 4

FISHGUARD MAP 08 SM93

◆◆◆◆ 💜

Erw-Lon (SN028325)

Pontfaen SA65 9TS ☎ 01348 881297 Mrs McAllister

Dir 5.5m SE of Fishguard on B4313

Located in the Pembrokeshire Coast National Park, with stunning views of the Gwaun Valley, this attractive farmhouse has been converted to provide modern well-equipped bedrooms with a wealth of homely extras. The McAllisters give the warmest of welcomes, and their memorable dinners feature the finest local produce. **Lilwen McAllister is AA Landlady of the Year 2006.**

Facilities 3 rms (2 en suite) (1 pri facs) ⊗ TVB tea/coffee ✗ Cen ht TVL No children 10yrs 128 acres beef sheep Dinner Last d 24hrs in advance **Prices** S £35; D £54-£60✳ **LB** **Parking** 5 **Notes** Closed Dec-Mar ⊗

HAVERFORDWEST MAP 08 SM91

See also **Dale & Narberth**

◆◆◆◆

College Guest House

93 Hill St, St Thomas Green SA61 1QL

☎ 01437 763710 📠 01437 763710

e-mail colinlarby@aol.com

Dir In town centre, signs for St Thomas Green car park

Located in a mainly residential area within easy walking distance of the attractions, this impressive Georgian house has been upgraded to offer good levels of comfort and facilities. There is range of practically equipped bedrooms, and public areas include a spacious lounge (with internet access) and an attractive pine-furnished dining room, the setting for comprehensive breakfasts.

Facilities 8 en suite (4 fmly) ⊗ TVB tea/coffee Cen ht TVL **Prices** S £38-£45; D £55-£60 **Parking** 2

◆◆◆◆ 💜

Lower Haythog Farm (SM996214)

Spittal SA62 5QL

☎ 01437 731279 📠 01437 731279 Mrs Thomas

e-mail nesta@lowerhaythogfarm.co.uk

web www.lowerhaythogfarm.co.uk

Dir 5m N on B4329 to railway bridge, farmhouse entrance on right

Located in 250 acres of unspoiled countryside, this 14th-century farmhouse with adjacent cottage provides high standards of comfort and good facilities. Bedrooms, including a two-bedroom family suite, are modern and well equipped. The elegant oak-beamed dining room is the setting for imaginative home-cooked dinners. Welcoming real fires burn during cold weather in the comfortable lounge, and a second conservatory-lounge overlooks the large, attractive garden.

Facilities 6 en suite (2 fmly) (1 GF) ⊗ TVB tea/coffee Cen ht TVL Fishing 250 acres dairy Dinner **Prices** S £35-£45; D £65-£75✳ **LB** **Parking** 5 **Notes** ⊗

KILGETTY MAP 08 SN10

◆◆◆◆

Manian Lodge

Begelly SA68 0XE ☎ 01834 813273 📠 01834 811591

e-mail information@manianlodge.com

web www.manianlodge.com

Dir A447 N onto A478, 0.5m on right in Begelly

The family-run Lodge is convenient for Tenby and the South Pembrokeshire Heritage Coast, as also the Pembroke Dock ferry terminal. The owners provide well-equipped modern bedrooms, including some on the ground floor. There is a comfortable lounge bar, a lounge, and a very attractive restaurant where a good choice of meals is offered. Self-catering accommodation is also available.

Facilities 6 en suite 8 annexe en suite (8 fmly) (3 GF) ⊗ in 1 bedrooms ⊗ in dining room ⊗ in 1 lounge TVB tea/coffee ✗ Licensed Cen ht Dinner Last d 9.30pm **Prices** D £50-£70✳ **LB** **Conf** Max 40 Thtr 40 Class 10 Board 18 Del from £40 ✳ **Parking** 19

MILFORD HAVEN

See **Dale**

NARBERTH MAP 08 SN11

◆◆◆

Highland Grange Farm

Robeston Wathen SA67 8EP

☎ 01834 860952 📠 01834 860952

e-mail info@highlandgrange.co.uk

web www.highlandgrange.co.uk

Dir 2m NW of Narberth on A40 Robeston Wathen, near Bush Inn

This modern bungalow is popular with people travelling to and from Ireland via the ferry terminal at Fishguard. The spacious bedrooms are on the ground floor. Separate tables are provided in the dining room and evening meals are available by arrangement. There is also a spacious and comfortable lounge where a real fire is lit in cold weather.

Facilities 3 rms (2 en suite) (1 fmly) (3 GF) ⊗ TVB tea/coffee ✗ Licensed Cen ht TVL No coaches Dinner Last d 5pm **Parking** 6 **Notes** ⊗

See advertisement on page 709

Wales

PEMBROKE

MAP 08 SM90

See also **Narberth**

◆◆◆◆ ❧

Poyerston Farm *(SM027025)*

Cosheston SA72 4SJ

☎ 01646 651347 ▤ 01646 651347 Mrs Lewis

e-mail poyerstonfarm@btinternet.com

web www.poyerstonfarm.co.uk

Dir *A477 towards Pembroke Dock, continue through Milton village, 0.75m on left opp Vauxhall garage*

This carefully modernised and impeccably maintained Victorian farmhouse stands on a family-run, 350-acre dairy farm. Bedrooms are well-equipped and some are in the adjacent former dairy. Ground-floor bedrooms and family rooms are available. There is a cosy lounge and an elegant dining room, which extends into a conservatory with direct access to the gardens.

Facilities 6 en suite (3 fmly) (3 GF) ⊛ TVB tea/coffee ✖ Cen ht TVL 350 acres Working-arable beef dairy **Prices** S £35-£40; D £56-£70 LB **Parking** 10 **Notes** Closed Xmas 🐾

ST DAVID'S

MAP 08 SM72

See also **Solva**

◆◆◆◆

Alandale Guest House ◇

43 Nun St SA62 6NU ☎ 01437 720404

e-mail alandale@tinyworld.co.uk

web www.stdavids.co.uk/guesthouse/alandale.htm

Dir *From centre of St Davids onto Nun St signed Fishguard, Alandale on left*

This charming, non-smoking guest house is the end property of Grade II listed terrace, a short walk from the city centre, cathedral and other attractions. Privately owned and personally run, it provides warm hospitality and well-equipped modern bedrooms. There is a cosy lounge and separate tables are provided in the breakfast room.

Facilities 5 en suite (2 fmly) ⊛ TVB tea/coffee ✖ Cen ht No children 5yrs No coaches **Prices** S £30-£32.50; D £60-£65 **Notes** 🐾

◆◆◆◆

Ramsey House

Lower Moor SA62 6RP ☎ 01437 720321

e-mail info@ramseyhouse.co.uk

web www.ramseyhouse.co.uk

Dir *From Cross Sq in St Davids towards Porthclais, house 0.5m on left*

This pleasant guest house is surrounded by countryside just south-west of St David's. The modern, well-equipped bedrooms come with plenty of welcome extras in advance, and carefully prepared dinners featuring quality local produce are available by arrangement.

Facilities 5 en suite (2 GF) ⊛ TVB tea/coffee ✖ Licensed Cen ht No children 14yrs No coaches **Prices** S £40; D £70✳ **Parking** 6 **Notes** Closed Nov-Feb 🐾

◆◆◆◆

The Waterings

Anchor Dr, High St SA62 6QH

☎ 01437 720876 ▤ 01437 720876

e-mail waterings@supanet.com

web www.waterings.co.uk

Dir *On A487 on E edge of St Davids*

Situated a short walk from the centre of St David's, The Waterings offers spacious bedrooms that are accessed from a courtyard garden. Most rooms have their own separate seating area. Breakfast, from a good selection of local produce, is served in a smart dining room in the main house.

Facilities 5 annexe en suite (4 fmly) (5 GF) ⊛ in bedrooms ⊛ in dining room ⊛ in lounges FTV TVB tea/coffee ✖ Licensed Cen ht No children 5yrs No coaches ♨ ↕ **Prices** S £50-£80; D £70-£80✳ **Conf** Max 15 Board 15 **Parking** 20 **Notes** 🐾

◆◆◆◆

Y-Gorlan Guest House

77 Nun St SA62 6NU

☎ 01437 720837 & 07974 108029 ▤ 01437 721148

e-mail mikebohlen@aol.com

Dir *In centre of St Davids*

This personally run guest house is just a stroll from the city's attractions. The well-maintained accommodation includes a family room and a room with a four-poster bed. The comfortable first-floor lounge has excellent views towards the coast across the surrounding countryside, and home-cooked dinners are available by arrangement.

Facilities 5 en suite (1 fmly) ⊛ STV TVB tea/coffee ✖ Cen ht TVL No children 5yrs No coaches Last d 6pm **Prices** S £32-£36; D £62-£70✳ **Parking** 2

If the freedom to smoke or be in a non-smoking atmosphere is important to you, check the rules when you book

Wales

SAUNDERSFOOT   MAP 08 SN10   **A**

Vine Cottage ◇

The Ridgeway SA69 9LA ☎ 01834 814422
e-mail enquiries@vinecottageguesthouse.co.uk
web www.vinecottageguesthouse.co.uk
Dir A477 S onto A478, left onto B4316, after railway bridge right
signed Saundersfoot, cottage 100yds on left

This 200-year-old former farmhouse has a convenient location on the
outskirts of the village, and is set in extensive mature gardens.
Bedrooms, which include a ground-floor room, are modern and well
equipped, and some are suitable for families. There is a comfortable,
airy lounge, and breakfast and dinner are served in the dining room.

Facilities 5 en suite (2 fmly) (1 GF) ⊗ TVB tea/coffee Cen ht
No children 6yrs No coaches Dinner Last d 10am **Prices** S £30-£60;
D £50-£70 **LB Parking** 10 **Notes** ⌼

Woodlands Hotel

St Brides Hill SA69 9NP ☎ 01834 813338
e-mail mail@hotelwoodlands.co.uk
web www.hotelwoodlands.co.uk
Dir From village centre towards Tenby, 500yds up hill on right

Located on an elevated position within easy walking distance of the
harbour, the house provides a range of thoughtfully equipped
bedrooms, some of which have sea views. A lounge is available, and a
bar with access to the pleasant garden and patio. Evening meals by
arrangement.

Facilities 10 en suite (3 fmly) ⊗ in bedrooms ⊗ in dining room
⊗ in 1 lounge TVB tea/coffee ✗ Licensed Cen ht TVL No children 5yrs
Ch fac No coaches Dinner Last d 3pm **Prices** S £35-£45; D £49-£66✱
LB **Parking** 10 **Notes** Closed Nov-Mar ex New Year

*If you book on bed, breakfast and evening
meal terms, you may find that the tariff
includes only the set menu*

Moreton House

Moreton Ln SA69 9EA ☎ 01834 814266 ▤ 01834 813386
e-mail roger.woods@tesco.net
web www.moretonhouse.co.uk
Dir A478 at Pentlepoir onto Valley Rd, under railway bridge, onto
coach park bridleway. Right at T-junct, 1st house on left

Facilities 3 en suite (1 fmly) ⊗ TVB tea/coffee Cen ht No children
10yrs No coaches Dinner Last d 5pm **Prices** D £55 **LB Parking** 10
Notes ★★★ ⌼

*Book as early as possible, particularly
in the peak holiday period*

Wales

SOLVA

MAP 08 SM82

Premier Collection

◆◆◆◆◆ ❧

Lochmeyler Farm Guest House ◇

(SM855275)

Llandeloy SA62 6LL
☎ 01348 837724 🗎 01348 837622 Mrs Jones
e-mail stay@lochmeyler.co.uk
web www.lochmeyler.co.uk

Dir From Haverfordwest A487 St Davids Rd to Penycwm, right to Llandeloy

Located on a 220-acre dairy farm in an Area of Outstanding Natural Beauty, this farmhouse provides high levels of comfort and excellent facilities. The spacious bedrooms, some in converted outbuildings, are equipped with a wealth of thoughtful extras and four have private sitting rooms. Comprehensive breakfasts are served in the dining room and two sumptuous lounges are also available.

Facilities 11 en suite (11 fmly) (5 GF) ⊗ TVB tea/coffee Direct dial from bedrooms Licensed Cen ht TVL 220 acres dairy Dinner Last d 2pm **Prices** S £27.50-£55; D £55-£80 **LB** **Parking** 11 **Notes** Closed Xmas & New Year

TENBY

MAP 08 SN10

★★★ Guest Accommodation

Clarence House ◇

Esplanade SA70 7DU ☎ 01834 844371 🗎 01834 844372
e-mail clarencehotel@freeuk.com
web www.clarencehotel-tenby.co.uk

Dir Off South Parade by town walls onto St Florence Parade & Esplanade

Owned by the same family for over 50 years, Clarence House has superb views from its elevated position. Many of the bedrooms have sea views and all are comfortably furnished. The bar leads to a sheltered rose garden or else there are a number of lounges. Entertainment is provided in high season, and the place is particularly popular with coach tour parties.

Facilities 68 en suite (6 fmly) ⊗ in bedrooms ⊗ in dining room ⊗ in 1 lounge TVB tea/coffee Licensed Lift Cen ht TVL Pool Table In house entertainment, live music Dinner Last d 7.30pm **Prices** S £19-£53; D £38-£102✳ **LB** **Notes** Closed 18-28 Dec

See advertisement on opposite page

◆◆◆◆

Esplanade Hotel

The Esplanade SA70 7DU
☎ 01834 842760 & 843333 🗎 01834 845633
e-mail esplanade.tenby@virgin.net

Dir Signs to South Beach, premises on seafront next to town walls

Superbly located beside the historic town walls and with stunning views over the sea to Caldey Island, the Esplanade provides a range of standard and luxury bedrooms, some ideal for families. Breakfast is offered in the elegant front-facing dining room, which contains a comfortable lounge-bar area.

Facilities 14 en suite (3 fmly) (1 GF) ⊗ in bedrooms ⊗ in dining room ⊗ in 1 lounge TVB tea/coffee Direct dial from bedrooms Licensed Cen ht **Prices** S £55-£90; D £70-£130 **LB**

◆◆◆◆

Giltar Grove Country House ◇

Penally SA70 7RY ☎ 01834 871568
e-mail giltarbnb@aol.com

Dir 2m SW of Tenby. Off A4139, 2nd right after railway bridge

continued

continued

Just a short walk from the spectacular Pembrokeshire Coast Path, this impressive Victorian farmhouse retains many original features. The non-smoking bedrooms include rooms with four-poster beds and rooms on the ground floor. All are filled with homely extras. There is a cosy sitting room, an elegant dining room, and spacious conservatory that is used for breakfast.

Facilities 6 en suite (2 GF) ⊘ TVB tea/coffee ✗ Cen ht No children 12yrs No coaches **Prices** S £25-£35; D £50-£60✶ **Parking** 10 **Notes** Closed Dec-Feb ⊛

♦♦♦♦

Rosendale

Lydstep SA70 7SQ ☎ 01834 870040
e-mail rosendalewales@yahoo.com
web www.rosendalepembrokeshire.co.uk
Dir *3m SW of Tenby. A4139 W towards Pembroke, Rosendale on the right after Lydstep village*

Located on the outskirts of the pretty village of Lydstep, this house provides modern, well-equipped bedrooms, some with coast or country views. Three rooms are on the ground floor of a separate building to the rear of the main house and some of the modern bathrooms contain a separate shower. The attractive dining room is the setting for comprehensive breakfasts, and there is also a large, comfortable lounge.

Facilities 7 en suite (3 GF) ⊘ TVB tea/coffee Cen ht No coaches **Parking** 7 **Notes** Closed Dec-Jan

♦♦♦

Brambles Lodge Guest House ◇

Penally SA70 7QE ☎ 01834 842393
e-mail sparksemail@tiscali.co.uk
Dir *A4139 from Tenby signed Penally & Pembroke, 2nd turning into Penally, 200yds after Penally train station*

Please note that this establishment has recently changed hands. This quietly located property is just a short drive from Tenby. A number of pleasant walks are available from here or you can relax in the garden or lounge. Bedrooms vary in size but all feature welcome extras. A good choice is available at breakfast including an American-style option with crispy bacon and maple syrup.

Facilities 7 rms (6 en suite) (1 pri facs) (1 fmly) ⊘ TVB tea/coffee ✗ Licensed Cen ht TVL No coaches Dinner Last d 9am **Prices** S £25-£30; D £50-£54✶ **LB** **Parking** 7 **Notes** ⊛

♦♦♦

Gumfreston Private Hotel ◇

15 Culver Park SA70 7ED
☎ 01834 842871 ▤ 01834 842871
e-mail gumf@supanet.com
Dir *50yds from Rectory car park, 150yds from South Beach*

A short walk from South Beach and the town centre, this friendly house offers homely bedrooms, some with family facilities. Ground-floor areas include a cosy lounge, intimate basement bar, and an attractive dining room where generous Welsh breakfasts are served. Dinner is available by arrangement.

Facilities 9 en suite (2 fmly) ⊘ in bedrooms ⊘ in dining room ⊘ in lounges TVB tea/coffee ✗ Licensed Cen ht TVL Dinner Last d Lunchtime **Prices** S £26-£30; D £52-£65✶ **LB** **Notes** ⊛

Clarence House

Esplanade, Tenby, Pembrokeshire SA70 7DU
Tel: 01834 844371 & Fax: 01834 844372
E-mail: clarencehotel@freeuk.com
www.clarencehotel-tenby.co.uk
South seafront near old walled town.
Superb coastal views to Caldey Island.
Bar-patio rose garden. Seaview
restaurant, excellent cuisine. Auto-
safety Otis lift to all floors. All bedrooms
WC/Shower, Col. TV, T/C inc. Groups
welcome, Free brochure/Tariff.

Wales

TREFIN   MAP 08 SM83

Premier Collection

♦♦♦♦♦

Awel-Mor Bed & Breakfast

Penparc SA62 5AG ☎ 01348 837865 ▤ 01348 837865
e-mail robin.jill@awel-mor.freeserve.co.uk
Dir *A487 from Fishguard, 300yds past Square and Compass pub right signed Trefin, 100yds 2nd left & Awel Mor on left*

This modern house has stunning coastal views. It provides high standards of comfort and facilities, as well as friendly hospitality. Bedrooms, which include a two-room family suite and a room on the ground floor, have many thoughtful extras. Hearty breakfasts are served at separate tables in the dining room. There is a spacious and comfortable lounge and a pleasant conservatory overlooking the immaculate gardens.

Facilities 3 rms (2 en suite) (1 GF) ⊘ TVB tea/coffee ✗ Licensed Cen ht TVL No children 6yrs No coaches **Prices** S £35-£70; D £60-£70✶ **LB** **Parking** 6 **Notes** Closed Nov-Mar

Always confirm details with the
establishment when booking

POWYS

BRECON
MAP 09 SO02

See also **Sennybridge**

Premier Collection

★★★★★ Bed & Breakfast

Canal Bank

Ty Gardd LD3 7HG ☎ 01874 623464 & 625844
e-mail enquiries@accommodation-breconbeacons.co.uk
web www.accommodation-breconbeacons.co.uk
Dir *Take B4601 signed for Brecon, turn left over bridge before petrol station and continue on to end of rd.*

A very warm welcome awaits at this delightful property, which was developed from a row of five 18th century former cottages. It provides very high quality, comfortable and well-equipped accommodation and stands alongside the canal in a semi-rural area on the outskirts of Brecon, yet within walking distance of the town centre. Facilities here include a comfortable lounge, a very attractive breakfast room and a lovely garden.

Facilities 3 en suite ⊘ TVB tea/coffee ✱ Cen ht No children
No coaches **Parking** 5 **Notes** ⊜

★★★★ ⊛ Inn

The Usk Inn

Station Rd, Talybont-On-Usk LD3 7JE
☎ 01874 676251 📠 01874 676392
e-mail stay@uskinn.co.uk
Dir *Off A40 6m E of Brecon*

This delightful inn is located in the village of Talybont-on-Usk. It is personally run in a friendly manner and has been renovated to a very high standard. Thoughtfully equipped and appointed bedrooms include a room with a four-poster bed and a family room. Public areas have a wealth of charm and the inn has a well-deserved reputation for its food.

The Usk Inn

Facilities 11 en suite (1 fmly) ⊘ in bedrooms ⊘ in dining room
⊘ in 1 lounge TVB tea/coffee Direct dial from bedrooms ✱ Cen ht TVL
Dinner Last d please give notice **LB Conf** Max 10 Board 10 **Parking** 30
Notes Closed 25-27 Dec

♦♦♦♦

The Beacons

16 Bridge St LD3 8AH ☎ 01874 623339 📠 01874 623339
e-mail beacons@brecon.co.uk
web www.beacons.brecon.co.uk
Dir *On B4601 opp Christ College*

Located west of the historic town centre over the bridge, this 17th-century former farmhouse by the river has been renovated to provide a range of homely bedrooms, some in converted barns and outbuildings. Dinner is available by arrangement and there is a cosy bar. This is a non-smoking establishment.

Facilities 11 rms (9 en suite) 3 annexe en suite (3 fmly) (3 GF) ⊘ TVB
tea/coffee ✱ Licensed Cen ht Dinner Last d 8.30pm **Prices** S £40-£65;
D £54-£72 **Parking** 21

♦♦♦♦

The Coach House

Orchard St LD3 8AN ☎ 07050 691216 📠 07050 691217
e-mail info@coachhousebrecon.co.uk
web www.coachhousebrecon.co.uk
Dir *From town centre W over bridge onto B4601, Coach House 200yds on right*

This former coach house with cottage dates from the early 19th century. It now provides good quality, modern accommodation, including family rooms. The attractive dining room has separate tables and a room is available for private dinner parties or meetings. There is also a pleasant garden. This is a non-smoking establishment.

Facilities 7 en suite (3 fmly) (1 GF) ⊘ TVB tea/coffee Direct dial from
bedrooms ✱ Licensed Cen ht No coaches Resident holistic therapist
Dinner Last d 8pm **Prices** S £35-£50; D £50-£70✱ **Conf** Max 24 Thtr 24
Board 20 Del from £55 ✱ **Parking** 8

See advertisement on opposite page

♦♦♦♦ ⊜ ◨

The Felin Fach Griffin

Felin Fach LD3 0UB ☎ 01874 620111 📠 01874 620120
e-mail enquiries@eatdrinksleep.ltd.uk
web www.eatdrinksleep.ltd.uk
Dir *4m NE of Brecon on A470*

This delightful inn stands in an extensive garden at the northern end of Felin Fach village. The public areas have a wealth of rustic charm and provide the setting for the excellent food. Service and hospitality are commendable. The bedrooms are carefully appointed and have modern equipment and facilities.

Facilities 7 en suite (1 fmly) ⊘ in bedrooms ⊘ in dining room
tea/coffee Direct dial from bedrooms Cen ht No coaches ℔ Dinner Last
d 9.30pm **Prices** S fr £67.50; D £97.50-£125✱ **LB Conf** Max 15 Board 15
Parking 61 **Notes** Closed 25-26 Dec rs Mon (ex BH's)

♦♦♦ ❦
Llanddetty Hall *(SO124205)*

Talybont-on-Usk LD3 7YR
☎ 01874 676415 📠 01874 676415 Mrs Atkins
Dir *7m SE off B4558*

This impressive Grade II listed 17th-century farmhouse in the beautiful Usk valley has much character. The friendly proprietors ensure a comfortable stay. Bedrooms are very pleasant and feature traditional furnishings, exposed timbers and polished floorboards. Welcoming log fires are lit during cold weather in the comfortable lounge, and guests dine around one table in the dining room.

Facilities 3 rms (2 en suite) (1 pri facs) 1 annexe en suite (1 GF) ⊗ TV1B tea/coffee ✖ Cen ht TVL No children 12yrs 48 acres sheep **Prices** S £33; D £54-£56 **Parking** 6 **Notes** Closed 16 Dec-14 Jan rs Feb-Apr 🚭

♦♦♦
Cherrypicker House ◇

Orchard St, Llanfaes LD3 8AN ☎ 01874 624665
e-mail info@cherrypickerhouse.com
web www.cherrypickerhouse.com
Dir *From town centre W over bridge onto B4601, house 200yds on right*

A warm welcome is assured at Cherrypicker House, which is just a short walk from the town centre. The bedrooms are comfortably furnished and many thoughtful extras are provided. This hospitable guest house is convenient for the Brecon Beacons National Park and major routes into central Wales.

Facilities 3 rms (1 en suite) ⊗ TVB tea/coffee ✖ Cen ht TVL No coaches **Prices** S £30-£40; D £45-£50✳ **Parking** 1 **Notes** 🚭

♦♦♦
Borderers Guesthouse ◇

47 The Watton LD3 7EG ☎ 01874 623559
e-mail ian@borderers.com
web www.borderers.com
Dir *200yds SE from town centre on B4601, opp church*

This guest house was originally a 17th-century drovers' inn. The courtyard, now a car park, is surrounded by many of the bedrooms, and pretty hanging baskets are seen everywhere. The non-smoking bedrooms are attractively decorated with rich floral fabrics. A room suitable for easier access is available.

Facilities 4 rms (3 en suite) (1 pri facs) 5 annexe en suite (2 fmly) (4 GF) ⊗ TVB tea/coffee Cen ht No coaches **Prices** S £30-£40; D £50-£50✳ **Parking** 6

♦♦♦
Cyfronnydd ◇

Old Glanrhyd, Libanus LD3 8NF ☎ 01874 625633
e-mail jean@cyfronnydd.com
web www.cyfronnydd.co.uk
Dir *Off A470 5m from Brecon. Lane opp A4215, 1st house on right*

This charming house, set in a spacious, pleasant garden, is quietly situated amid the spectacular scenery of the Brecon Beacons National Park, near the village of Libanus, south-west of Brecon. It provides modern accommodation and friendly hospitality.

Facilities 3 rms (1 en suite) ⊗ STV TVB tea/coffee Cen ht No coaches Badminton Bikes for children **Prices** S £25-£32; D £50-£56✳ **Parking** 8 **Notes** 🚭

♦♦♦ ▪
The Old Ford Inn

Llanhamlach LD3 7YB ☎ 01874 665391 & 665220
Dir *On A40 3m SE from Brecon*

Parts of this former drovers' inn date from the Middle Ages. The non-smoking bedrooms, which include family rooms, have modern facilities and most look out towards the Brecon Beacons. Public areas have a wealth of character and include a choice of bars and a cottage-style dining room.

Facilities 5 rms (5 pri facs) (1 fmly) ⊗ in bedrooms ⊗ in dining room ⊗ in lounges TVB tea/coffee ✖ Cen ht Dinner Last d 8.45pm **Parking** 20

Wales

A

The Flag and Castle

11 Orchard St, Llanfaes LD3 8AN ☎ 01874 625860
e-mail flagandcastle@btinternet.com
web www.flagandcastlehouse.co.uk
Dir W side of Brecon on the B4601 opp Christ College

Facilities 3 en suite ⊗ TVB tea/coffee ✗ Cen ht TVL No coaches
Prices D £50-£60✳ **Parking** 2 **Notes** ★★★ Closed 14 Dec-14 Jan 🅿

BUILTH WELLS   MAP 09 SO05

Premier Collection

★★★★★ ◉◉ **Restaurant with Rooms**

The Drawing Room

Cwmbach, Newbridge-on-Wye LD2 3RT ☎ 01982 552493
e-mail post@the-drawing-room.co.uk
Dir A470 towards Rhayader, 3m on left

This delightful Georgian country house has been extensively and tastefully renovated by the present owners, to provide three comfortable and very well equipped bedrooms, all with luxurious en-suite facilities. Public rooms include two comfortable lounges with welcoming log fires, a room for private dining and a very elegant and intimate dining room, which provides the ideal setting to appreciate the high quality cuisine and excellent cooking skills of Colin Dawson.

Facilities 3 en suite ⊗ TVB ✗ Licensed Cen ht No children 12yrs
No coaches Dinner Last d 9pm **Prices** S £120; D £190-£220; (incl. dinner) ✳ **Parking** 14 **Notes** Closed Sun & Mon, 2wks Jan & end of summer

CAERSWS   MAP 15 SO09

Premier Collection

◆◆◆◆◆ ◉ 🏆 ⊜ ◗█

The Talkhouse

Pontdolgoch SY17 5JE ☎ 01686 688919 📄 01686 689134
e-mail info@talkhouse.co.uk
Dir 1.5m NW of Caersws on A470

A highlight of this delightful 19th-century inn is the food, home-made dishes making good use of local produce. Bedrooms offer luxury in every area and the cosy lounge, filled with sofas, is the place to while away a glass of wine or a pot of tea. The bar features a large fireplace.

Facilities 3 en suite ⊗ in bedrooms ⊗ in dining room ⊗ in lounges
TVB ✗ Cen ht No children 14yrs No coaches Dinner Last d 8.45pm
Prices S £70; D £95✳ **LB** **Parking** 50 **Notes** Closed 1st 2 wks Jan rs
Sun eve & Mon

CARNO   MAP 14 SN99

◆◆◆◆

Tremallt B&B

Tremallt SY17 5LT ☎ 01686 420411
e-mail tremalltbb@hotmail.com

Built as a manse for the local Methodist chapel in 1826, Tremallt stands in very pleasant gardens with attractive views, and has a play area for children. The thoughtfully equipped accommodation comes with warm hospitality.

Facilities 3 en suite (1 GF) ⊗ TVB tea/coffee ✗ Cen ht IVL
No coaches Dinner Last d noon **Parking** 3 **Notes** Closed Xmas 🅿

CHURCHSTOKE   MAP 15 SO29

◆◆◆◆ 🏠 ❦

The Drewin Farm (SO261905)

SY15 6TW ☎ 01588 620325 📄 01588 620325 Mrs Richards
e-mail drewinfarm@hotmail.com
Dir 3m SE of Churchstoke. A489 from Churchstoke towards Newtown, left onto B4385, 1m 2nd right Cwm/Pantglas, next right & next left, left fork to Mainstone, 1st on left

This impressive 17th-century stone farmhouse stands on a working farm with superb views, and lies next to Offa's Dyke. Original features include an abundance of exposed timbers and inglenook fireplaces. Two sitting rooms are provided and bedrooms are well-equipped and comfortable. Memorable Welsh breakfasts and imaginative dinners are provided.

Facilities 3 rms (2 en suite) (1 pri facs) (1 fmly) ⊗ TVB tea/coffee ✗
Cen ht TVL 102 acres mixed Dinner Last d 5pm **Parking** 6
Notes Closed Nov-Feb 🅿

CRICKHOWELL   MAP 09 SO21

Premier Collection

◆◆◆◆◆

Glangrwyney Court

NP8 1ES ☎ 01873 811288 📄 01873 810317
e-mail info@glancourt.co.uk
web www.glancourt.co.uk
Dir 2m SE of Crickhowell on A40 near county boundary

Located in extensive mature grounds, this impressive Georgian house has been renovated to provide high standards of comfort and facilities. The spacious bedrooms are equipped with a range of homely extras, and bathrooms include a jacuzzi or steam shower. The interior has been decorated with style. Comprehensive breakfasts are taken at one table in the elegant dining room and a luxurious lounge is also provided.

Facilities 5 rms (4 en suite) (1 pri facs) (1 fmly) (1 GF) ⊗ STV TVB
tea/coffee ✗ Licensed Cen ht TVL No coaches ᕼ ♨ Boules Dinner
Last d 72hrs notice **Prices** S £50-£75; D £65-£85✳ **LB** **Parking** 12
Notes Civ Wed 23

See advertisement on opposite page

continued

Wales

CRIGGION
MAP 15 SJ21

◆◆◆◆ ✿

Brimford House ◇ (SJ310150)

SY5 9AU ☎ 01938 570235 🖷 01938 570235 Mrs Dawson
e-mail info@brimford.co.uk
Dir Off B4393 W of Crew Green, on left after pub

This elegant Georgian house stands in lovely open countryside and is a good base for touring central Wales and the Marches. Bedrooms are spacious, and thoughtful extras enhance guest comfort. A cheery log fire burns in the lounge during colder weather and the hospitality is equally warm, providing a relaxing atmosphere throughout.

Facilities 3 en suite ⊘ TVB tea/coffee Cen ht TVL Fishing 250 acres arable, beef **Prices** S £25-£35; D £50-£70✳ **LB Parking** 4 **Notes** ⊜

DYLIFE
MAP 14 SN89

◆◆◆ ▟

Star Inn ◇

SY19 7BW ☎ 01650 521345
Dir 1.5m off B4518 between Llanidloes & Machynlleth

This friendly historic inn is a popular watering hole amid beautiful countryside. It's a good base for active walking, cycling, birdwatching, or just relaxing. The menu offers a wide choice and the comfortable bedrooms are practically furnished.

Facilities 6 rms (2 en suite) (1 fmly) ⊘ in dining room ⊘ in 1 lounge TV2B tea/coffee Cen ht TVL Pool Table Dinner Last d 10pm
Prices S £25-£37; D £44-£50✳ **LB Parking** 30

ERWOOD
MAP 09 SO04

◆◆◆◆

Hafod-y-Garreg

LD2 3TQ ☎ 01982 560400
e-mail john-annie@hafod-y.wanadoo.co.uk
web www.hafodygarreg.co.uk
Dir 1m S of Erwood. Off A470 at Trericket Mill, sharp right, up track past cream farmhouse towards pine forest, through gate

This remote Grade II listed farmhouse dates in part from 1401 and is the oldest surviving traditional house in Wales. It has tremendous character and has been furnished and decorated to befit its age, while the bedrooms have modern facilities. There is an impressive dining room and a lounge with an open fireplace. Warm hospitality from John and Annie McKay is another major strength here.

continued

Facilities 2 en suite (1 fmly) ⊘ in dining room TVB tea/coffee Cen ht Dinner Last d Day before **Prices** D £50-£55.50 **LB Parking** 6
Notes Closed Xmas ⊜

GARTH
MAP 09 SN94

◆◆◆◆

Garth Mill

LD4 4AS ☎ 01591 620572
e-mail dave@pigsfolly.fsnet.co.uk
Dir On A483 in village

This former brickworks has been renovated to provide quality accommodation, plus a farm shop and pets' corner complete with llamas, pigs, ducks, chickens and ponies. The spacious bedrooms are homely, and the dining room is the setting for wholesome food using home-reared or local produce. In addition to the lounge there is also a large lounge bar where bar meals are available.

Facilities 8 rms (4 en suite) (1 fmly) ⊘ in bedrooms ⊘ in dining room ⊘ in 1 lounge TVB tea/coffee ✗ Licensed Cen ht Dinner Last d 9pm
Prices S £45-£65; D £45-£65✳ **LB Conf** Max 60 Class 60 Board 40
Parking 40

HAY-ON-WYE
MAP 09 SO24
See **Erwood**

Wales

LLANDRINDOD WELLS   MAP 09 SO06

◆◆◆◆ 🏛 🛥

Guidfa House

Crossgates LD1 6RF ☎ 01597 851241 📠 01597 851875
e-mail guidfa@globalnet.co.uk
web www.guidfa-house.co.uk
Dir *3m N of Llandrindod Wells, at junct of A483 & A44*

Expect a relaxed and pampered stay at this elegant Georgian house just outside the town. Comfort is the keynote here, whether in the attractive and well-equipped bedrooms or in the homely lounge, where a real fire burns in cold weather. Food is also a strength, due to the proprietor's skilful touch.

Facilities 6 rms (5 en suite) (1 pri facs) (1 GF) ⊗ TVB tea/coffee ✖ Licensed Cen ht No children 10yrs No coaches Dinner Last d previous day **Prices** S £40-£48; D £62-£70✳ **LB Parking** 10

Dolberthog Farm *(SO048602)*

LD1 5ED ☎ 01597 822255 Mrs Evans
Dir *A483 S, on leaving town garage on left, 500yds right, over railway bridge, farmhouse 0.5m*

This sturdy Victorian stone farmhouse is set in beautiful open countryside and yet is only a short drive from the town. Bedrooms are comfortable and relaxing and there is also a homely lounge. Meals are served in a traditional dining room complete with antique Welsh dresser. The house is non-smoking.

Facilities 3 rms (2 en suite) (1 pri facs) (1 fmly) ⊗ TVB tea/coffee ✖ Cen ht TVL Fishing 250 acres mixed Dinner Last d noon **Prices** D £48-£50✳ **LB Parking** 4 **Notes** 🐾

Holly Farm ◇ *(SO045593)*

Holly Farm, Howey LD1 5PP
☎ 01597 822402 📠 01597 822402 Mrs Jones
e-mail hollyfarm@ukworld.net
Dir *2m S on A483 near Howey*

This working farm dates from Tudor times and is surrounded by its own fields. Bedrooms are homely and full of character, and the comfortable lounge has a log fire in cooler months. Traditional home cooking using local produce can be sampled in the dining room.

Facilities 3 en suite (1 fmly) ⊗ TVB tea/coffee ✖ Cen ht TVL 70 acres beef sheep Dinner Last d 5pm **Prices** S £30-£35; D £48-£60✳ **LB Parking** 4

◆◆◆

Kincoed Hotel

Temple St LD1 5HF ☎ 01597 822656 📠 01597 824660
Dir *On A483 50yds beyond hospital*

Located close to the town centre, this friendly guest house offers well-equipped bedrooms. There is a snug bar, and freshly prepared breakfasts and evening meals are served in the bay-fronted dining room.

Facilities 10 rms (5 en suite) (3 fmly) ⊗ in 2 bedrooms TVB tea/coffee Direct dial from bedrooms Licensed Cen ht TVL No coaches **Parking** 10

🅰

Brynllys Guest House

High St LD1 6AG ☎ 01597 823190
Dir *In town centre*

Facilities 3 en suite ⊗ TVB tea/coffee ✖ Licensed Cen ht TVL No coaches Dinner Last d 9pm **Notes** ★★

LLANDRINIO   MAP 15 SJ21

🅰

Orchard Holidays ◇

Unity House SY22 6SG ☎ 01691 831976 📠 01691 831976
e-mail info@orchard-holidays.com
Dir *A483 onto B4393 signed Llandrinio, through village, right before church, large white house ahead*

Facilities 3 en suite (3 GF) ⊗ TVB tea/coffee ✖ Cen ht TVL No coaches Fishing **Prices** S £30; D £50 **LB Parking** 20 **Notes** ★★★ Closed 31 Oct-1 Mar

LLANGAMMARCH WELLS   MAP 09 SN94

◆◆◆◆

Cammarch Hotel

LD4 4BY ☎ 01591 610802 📠 01591 610807
e-mail mail@cammarch.com
Dir *Off A483 at Garth signed Llangammarch Wells*

The stone property dates from the 1850s and was built as a hotel by the railway company. It now provides modern, well-equipped accommodation, including suites and some self-catering accommodation. A comfortable lounge overlooks the attractive garden and extensive grounds.

Facilities 10 en suite (3 fmly) ⊗ TVB tea/coffee Licensed Cen ht TVL Fishing 🎱 Dinner Last d 24hrs in advance **LB Conf** Max 10 **Parking** 15

LLANGEDWYN
MAP 15 SJ12

U

Plas Uchaf
SY10 9LD ☎ 01691 780588 ▤ 0845 2802188
e-mail maureenwise@hotmail.com

At the time of going to press the rating for this establishment had not been confirmed. Please check the AA website www.theAA.com for up-to-date information.

Facilities (2 pri facs) ⊘ TV available tea/coffee Licensed ⚲ Pool Table Dinner Last d 11am **Prices** S fr £30; D fr £60 **LB** **Conf** Max 12 **Parking** 20

LLANGURIG
MAP 09 SN97

♦♦♦♦

Old Vicarage ◇
SY18 6RN ☎ 01686 440280 ▤ 01686 440280
e-mail theoldvicarage@llangurig.fslife.co.uk
web www.theoldvicaragellangurig.co.uk
Dir A44 into Llangurig, 1st right, 100yds on left

Set in the heart of this quiet village, the Old Vicarage offers attractively furnished, well-equipped bedrooms. A small bar serves the dining room and two lounges, where there are collections of porcelain and antiques. Evening meals and afternoon teas make good use of local produce.

Facilities 4 en suite (1 fmly) ⊘ in bedrooms ⊘ in dining room ⊘ in 1 lounge TVB tea/coffee Licensed Cen ht TVL No coaches Dinner Last d 5pm **Prices** S £30-£40; D £46-£50✳ **LB** **Parking** 5 **Notes** Closed Xmas & New Year ⊠

LLANIDLOES
MAP 09 SN98

♦♦♦♦ ◨

Mount Inn ◇
China St SY18 6AB ☎ 01686 412247 ▤ 01686 412247
e-mail mountllani@aol.com
Dir In town centre

This establishment is believed to occupy part of the site of a motte and bailey castle and started life as a coaching inn. The traditional bars are full of character, with exposed beams and timbers as well as cobbled flooring and log fires. Bedrooms, which include some in a new separate building, are carefully furnished and equipped with practical and thoughtful extras.

Facilities 3 en suite 6 annexe en suite (3 fmly) (3 GF) ⊘ in bedrooms ⊘ in dining room ⊘ in lounges TVB tea/coffee ✻ Cen ht TVL Pool Table Outdoor play area for children Dinner Last d 9pm **Prices** S fr £37; d fr £55✳ **Conf** Max 12 Class 12 **Parking** 12

LLANSILIN
MAP 15 SJ22

♦♦♦♦ 🏛

The Old Vicarage
SY10 7PX ☎ 01691 791345
e-mail pam@vicarage-guests.co.uk
Dir B4580 from Oswestry, entrance near phone box by Give Way sign

Set in well-tended, secluded gardens and having splendid country views, this former vicarage dates from 1792. The attentive hosts provide a friendly welcome. The comfortable bedrooms are spacious and attractively decorated. Traditional, freshly cooked breakfasts are served in the dining room and feature home-made preserves.

Facilities 3 rms (2 en suite) (1 pri facs) ⊘ tea/coffee ✻ Cen ht TVL No children 12yrs No coaches **Prices** S £35-£40; D £59-£65✳ **LB** **Parking** 4 **Notes** Closed Dec-Jan

LLANWRTYD WELLS
MAP 09 SN84

★★★ ◉◉◉ **Restaurant with Rooms**

Carlton House
Dolycoed Rd LD5 4RA ☎ 01591 610248
e-mail info@carltonrestaurant.co.uk
Dir Centre of town

Guests are made to feel like one of the family at this character property, set amidst stunning countryside in what is reputedly the smallest rural town in Britain. Carlton House offers award-winning cuisine for which Mary Ann Gilchrist relies on the very best of local ingredients. The menu is complemented by a well-chosen wine list and dinner is served in an atmospheric restaurant. The themed bedrooms, like the public areas, have period furniture and are decorated in warm colours.

Facilities 6 rms (5 en suite) (2 fmly) TVB tea/coffee Licensed No coaches Dinner Last d 8.30pm **Prices** S £40-£45; D £60-£90✳ **LB** **Notes** Closed 15-30 Dec rs All year

LLANYMYNECH
MAP 15 SJ22

♦♦♦♦ ◉ ◪

Bradford Arms Hotel
Llanymynech SY22 6EJ ☎ 01691 830582 ▤ 01691 830728
e-mail info@bradfordarmshotel.com
For full entry see **Oswestry (Shropshire)**

♦♦♦

Ty-Coch Bungalow ◇
Four Crosses SY22 6QZ ☎ 01691 830361
e-mail bill_lee@talk21.com
Dir 1m S of Llanymynech on A483

Built in 1984, this large bungalow provides friendly hospitality, modern accommodation and a comfortable lounge. Guests share one large breakfast table in the kitchen-dining room.

Facilities 2 en suite (2 GF) ⊘ TVB tea/coffee ✻ Cen ht TVL ch fac No coaches Dinner Last d 24hrs notice **Prices** S £28; D £50✳ **LB** **Parking** 6 **Notes** ⊠

Wales

MACHYNLLETH
MAP 14 SH70

◆◆◆◆
Penmaendyfi
Cwrt, Pennal SY20 9LD ☎ 01654 791246 🖹 01654 791616
e-mail shana@penmaendyfi.co.uk
Dir On A493 between Machynlleth & Aberdyfi

Delightfully located within sweeping grounds, Penmaendyfi offers a wealth of history in addition to stunning views over the Dyfi estuary to the mountains beyond. Bedrooms and bathrooms are particularly spacious and include one on the ground floor. Guests are welcome to use the comfortable lounge with honesty bar and the large outdoor swimming pool.

Facilities 7 en suite (2 fmly) (1 GF) ⊗ TVB tea/coffee Direct dial from bedrooms ✖ Cen ht No coaches ✦ ✎ Fishing **Prices** S £50; D £70-£90✳ **LB** **Parking** 10

◆◆◆◆
Maenllwyd
Newtown Rd SY20 8EY ☎ 01654 702928 🖹 01654 702928
e-mail maenllwyd@btinternet.com
web www.cyber-space.co.uk/maenllwyd.htm
Dir On A489 opp hospital

This Victorian house lies on the outskirts of this historic town, a short walk from local amenities. A warm welcome has been offered to guests here for many years and friendly hospitality can be enjoyed. Bedrooms are attractively decorated with modern facilities provided. There is a comfortable lounge and a separate dining room.

Facilities 8 en suite (1 fmly) ⊗ in bedrooms ⊗ in dining room TVB tea/coffee Cen ht TVL No coaches **Prices** S fr £35; d fr £54✳ **Parking** 11 **Notes** Closed 25-26 Dec

◆◆◆◆
Yr Hen Felin (The Old Mill)
Abercegir SY20 8NR ☎ 01650 511818
e-mail yrhenfelin@tiscali.co.uk
Dir 4m E of Machynlleth. Off A489 into Abercegir, right onto unmade road after telephone kiosk, over bridge

This converted water mill on the River Gwydol has exposed beams and superb polished timber floors. Two bedrooms overlook the river where trout and herons are often seen. There is a very comfortable lounge, and the bedrooms, in a variety of sizes, come with a wealth of thoughtful extras.

Facilities 3 en suite ⊗ tea/coffee ✖ Licensed Cen ht TVL No coaches Dinner Last d 4.30pm **Prices** S £32-£34; D £50-£54✳ **LB** **Parking** 5 **Notes** 🐾

🅰
Dolgelynen Farm B & B ◇
Dolgelynen SY20 9JR ☎ 01654 702026 🖹 01654 702026
e-mail elinordyfi@tiscali.co.uk
web www.dolgelynenfarmhouse.co.uk
Dir 1.5m NW of Machynlleth. A487 onto A493, 1st left onto Farm Ln, follow river 1m to farm

Facilities 3 rms (2 en suite) (1 pri facs) ⊗ TVB tea/coffee ✖ Cen ht No children 12yrs No coaches **Prices** S £30; D £50✳ **Parking** 4 **Notes** ★★★ Closed Nov-Etr 🐾

NEWTOWN
MAP 15 SO19

◆◆◆◆
Yesterdays ◇
Severn Sq SY16 2AG ☎ 01686 622644 🖹 01686 622644
e-mail info@yesterdayshotel.com
web www.yesterdayshotel.com
Dir Off junct High St & Broad St onto Severn St to Severn Sq

Dating from the 17th century, this attractive guest house has spacious rooms equipped with many thoughtful extras. The friendly hosts provide a genuine welcome and attentive service in the centre of this fine market town, which lies on the Severn Way long-distance path.

Facilities 5 en suite 1 annexe en suite (2 fmly) (2 GF) ⊗ TVB tea/coffee ✖ Licensed Cen ht No coaches Dinner **Prices** S £30-£35; D £50-£60

SENNYBRIDGE
MAP 09 SN92

◆◆◆ 🌿
Maeswalter (SN932237)
Heol Senni LD3 8SU ☎ 01874 636629 Mrs Mayo
e-mail joy@maeswalter.fsnet.co.uk
web www.maeswalter.co.uk
Dir A470 onto A4215, 2.5m left for Heol Senni, farm 1.5m on right over cattle grid

Set in a peaceful country location with splendid views of the Senni Valley, this 17th-century farmhouse offers a friendly and relaxing place to stay. The accommodation is well maintained and includes a suite on the ground floor of an adjacent building. A lounge-dining room is provided, and freshly cooked farmhouse breakfasts can be enjoyed.

continued

Maeswalter

Facilities 4 rms (3 en suite) (1 pri facs) (1 fmly) (1 GF) ⊗ STV TVB tea/coffee ✹ Cen ht TVL No children 5yrs 2 acres Non-working Dinner Last d noon **Parking** 11

WELSHPOOL　　　　　　　　MAP 15 SJ20

See also **Criggion**

★★★★★ Farm House

Moors Farm B & B *(SJ243092)*

Oswestry Rd SY21 9JR ☎ 01938 553395 & 07957 882967
Mr & Mrs M Slack
e-mail moorsfarm@tiscali.co.uk
web www.moors-farm.com
Dir 1.5m NE of Welshpool off A483

A very warm welcome awaits you at this impressive house, parts of which date from the early 18th century. It has a wealth of character, including exposed beams and log-burning fires, and has been carefully renovated to provide very good quality spacious accommodation. Skilfully prepared dinners are available by arrangement.

Facilities 6 en suite (2 fmly) ⊗ TVB tea/coffee ✹ Cen ht TVL Shooting 100 acres Sheep / Beef Dinner Last d Breakfast

◆◆◆◆ ⌂ ❦

Heath Cottage ◇ *(SJ239023)*

Kingswood, Forden SY21 8LX
☎ 01938 580453 ▤ 01938 580453 Mr & Mrs Payne
e-mail heathcot@bushinternet.com
Dir 4m S of Welshpool. Off A490 behind Forden Old Post Office, opp Parrys Garage

Furnishings and decor highlight the original features of this early 18th-century farmhouse. Bedrooms have stunning country views, and a choice of lounges, one with a log fire, is available. Memorable breakfasts feature free-range eggs and home-made preserves.

Facilities 3 en suite (1 fmly) ⊗ tea/coffee ✹ Cen ht TVL 6 acres Poultry/sheep **Prices** S £25; D £50 **Parking** 4 **Notes** Closed Nov-Etr ⊛

◆◆◆◆ ❦

Tynllwyn Farm *(SJ215085)*

SY21 9BW ☎ 01938 553175 Ms Emberton
e-mail caroline@tynllwyn.fsnet.co.uk
web www.tynllwynfarm.co.uk
Dir A490 N towards Llanfyllin, 1m on left

A warm welcome is assured at this impressive Victorian house, located on an elevated position with stunning views of the surrounding countryside. The spacious bedrooms, some in separate cottages (available for self-catering), are filled with thoughtful extras, and there is a cosy lounge and an attractive dining room, the setting for comprehensive breakfasts.

Facilities 5 en suite (4 fmly) ⊗ in bedrooms ⊗ in dining room ⊗ in lounges TVB tea/coffee Licensed Cen ht TVL 52 acres Non-working **Parking** 12 **Notes** ⊛

YNYSYBWL　　　　　　　　MAP 09 ST09

◆◆◆

Tyn-Y-Wern Country House ◇

CF37 3LY ☎ 01443 790551 ▤ 01443 790551
e-mail tynywern2002@yahoo.com
Dir B4273 from Pontypridd, war memorial on left. 1st right after terrace on right

This large Victorian house, once a mine manager's residence, is in a quietly location 3m from Pontypridd, and its elevated position has good views. It has been extensively restored and provides modern yet traditionally furnished accommodation, plus an attractive dining room and a lounge. There is an extensive garden with self-catering cottages, a games room and a laundry room.

Facilities 3 rms (1 en suite) ⊗ TVB tea/coffee Cen ht No coaches Pool Table Games room, Table Tennis **Prices** S £28-£30; D £50-£55✳ LB **Parking** 10 **Notes** Closed 20 Dec-6 Jan ⊛

Wales

SWANSEA

MUMBLES   MAP 08 SS68

◆◆◆◆
Little Langland Hotel
2 Rotherslade Rd, Langland SA3 4QN
☎ 01792 369696 ▤ 01792 366995
e-mail enquiries@littlelangland.co.uk
Dir Off A4067 in Mumbles onto Newton Rd, 4th left onto Langland Rd, 2nd left onto Rotherslade Rd

This friendly establishment stands near the beaches and coastal walks of this popular area. The non-smoking bedrooms are furnished to a high standard and are well equipped, including family rooms, and there is a bar and a lounge.

Facilities 6 en suite ⊗ TVB tea/coffee Direct dial from bedrooms ✕ Licensed Cen ht No children 8yrs No coaches **Prices** S fr £65; d fr £100✳ **Parking** 6

🅰
Alexandra House
366 Mumbles Rd SA3 5TN
☎ 01792 406406 ▤ 01792 405605
Dir 500yds N of Oystermouth on A4067

Facilities 6 en suite (1 fmly) (1 GF) ⊗ TVB tea/coffee ✕ Cen ht No children 5yrs No coaches **LB Parking** 6 **Notes** ★★★★ Closed 23 Dec-2 Jan 🐾

🅰
The Coast House ◇
708 Mumbles Rd SA3 4EH ☎ 01792 368702
e-mail thecoasthouse@aol.com
web www.thecoasthouse.co.uk
Dir From A483 onto A4067 to Mumbles. At shopping area in Mumbles, continue straight over mini-rdbt. 0.5m along on right

Facilities 6 rms (5 en suite) (2 fmly) ⊗ TVB tea/coffee Cen ht No coaches **Prices** S £30-£45; D £50-£65✳ **Notes** ★★★ Closed Nov-Dec

🅰
Glenview Guest House
140 Langland Rd SA3 4LU
☎ 01792 367933 ▤ 01792 363514
e-mail glenview@btinternet.com
web www.mumblesglenview.com
Dir M4 junct 42, signs for Swansea and Mumbles. Turn right at the White Rose pub, 4th road on left, Langland Rd

Facilities 5 en suite (2 fmly) (2 GF) ⊗ TVB tea/coffee Cen ht TVL No coaches **Parking** 5 **Notes** ★★★

OXWICH   MAP 08 SS48

◆◆◆◆
Little Haven Guest House
SA3 1LS ☎ 01792 390940
Dir Off A4118 signed Oxwich/Slade, 1.5m right at x-rds, after 700yds in village, house on left

This friendly little guest house is just a short walk from the beach. The modern bedrooms are all on the ground floor and each has direct access to the pleasant garden with its heated swimming pool. One bedroom has been adapted for easier access. Breakfast is served at separate tables in the pleasant conservatory.

Facilities 5 en suite (1 fmly) (5 GF) ⊗ TVB tea/coffee ✕ Cen ht No coaches ⌇ Heated outdoor spa (summer only) **Prices** S £35; D £50-£60✳ **LB Parking** 7 **Notes** Closed Dec 🐾

PARKMILL (NEAR SWANSEA)   MAP 08 SS58

◆◆◆◆ 🐾
Parc-le-Breos House (SS529896)
SA3 2HA ☎ 01792 371636 ▤ 01792 371287 Mrs Edwards
Dir On A4118, right 300yds after Shepherds shop, next left, signed

This imposing early 19th-century house is at the end of a forest drive and set in 70 acres of delightful grounds. Many charming original features have been retained in the public rooms, which include a lounge and a games room. The bedrooms have comfortable furnishings, and many are suitable for families.

Facilities 10 en suite (7 fmly) (1 GF) ⊗ in bedrooms ⊗ in lounges TVB tea/coffee ✕ Cen ht TVL Riding Pool Table Games room, Table tennis 65 acres arable horses pigs chickens Dinner Last d 3pm **Conf** Max 30 Thtr 30 **Parking** 12 **Notes** Closed 25-26 Dec 🐾

SWANSEA   MAP 09 SS69

★★★ Guest Accommodation
The White House
4 Nyanza Ter SA1 4QQ ☎ 01792 473856 ▤ 01792 455300
e-mail reception@thewhitehousehotel.co.uk
Dir On A4118, 1m W of city centre

Part of a short early Victorian terrace within fashionable Uplands, this house retains many original features. It has been restored to provide thoughtfully furnished and equipped quality accommodation. Bedrooms are filled with many extras, and the memorable Welsh breakfasts include cockles and laverbread.

continued

Wales

Facilities 9 en suite (4 fmly) ⊘ in dining room STV TVB tea/coffee Direct dial from bedrooms ✗ Licensed Cen ht TVL No coaches Dinner Last d 8.15pm **Prices** S £42-£54; D £72✶ **LB Conf** Max 16 Thtr 16 Class 16 Board 10 Del from £95 ✶ **Parking** 8

◆◆◆◆

Crescent Guest House

132 Eaton Crescent, Uplands SA1 4QR
☎ 01792 466814 🖷 01792 466814
e-mail crescentguesthouse@hotmail.co.uk
Dir Off A4118 W from centre, 1st left after St James's Church

This friendly guest house is on a leafy avenue close to the restaurants, bars and shops of Swansea's Uplands area. The Edwardian house has been refurbished to provide well-equipped bedrooms with modern en suites, Internet connections and flat-screen televisions, and family rooms are also available. Breakfast is served in a cosy dining room, and the spacious lounge has impressive views of Swansea Bay.

Facilities 6 en suite (1 fmly) ⊘ FTV TVB tea/coffee ✗ Cen ht TVL No coaches **Prices** S £36-£39; D £56-£59✶ **Parking** 6

◆◆◆◆

The Grosvenor House

Mirador Crescent - 1A, Uplands SA2 0QX
☎ 01792 461522 🖷 01792 461522
e-mail enquires@grosvenor-guesthouse.co.uk
web www.grosvenor-guesthouse.co.uk
Dir Off A4118 onto Mirador Crescent, guest house 75yds on left

This immaculately maintained, non-smoking guest house is located in the fashionable Uplands district and is convenient for touring the Gower Peninsular and the Mumbles. Under new ownership, comfortable and thoughtfully furnished accommodation, as well as a friendly welcome, are assured. Secure parking, a comfortable lounge and an attractive breakfast room complement the facilities of this attractive home.

Facilities 7 en suite (2 fmly) ⊘ TVB tea/coffee ✗ Cen ht TVL No coaches **Prices** S £37-£42; D £60-£66 **Parking** 1 **Notes** Closed 30 Dec-15 Jan

◆◆◆

Alexander Hotel

3 Sketty Rd, Uplands SA2 0EU
☎ 01792 470045 🖷 01792 476012
e-mail reception@alexander-hotel.co.uk
web www.alexander-hotel.co.uk
Dir On A4118, 1m from city centre on road to Gower

Located in fashionable Uplands between Gower and the city centre, this Victorian house has been modernised to provide good levels of comfort and facilities. Bedrooms are filled with practical extras and other areas include a cosy dining room and a comfortably furnished lounge with guest bar.

continued

Alexander Hotel

Facilities 7 rms (6 en suite) (3 fmly) ⊘ TVB tea/coffee Direct dial from bedrooms Licensed Cen ht No coaches Pool Table

🅰

Hurst Dene Guest House ◇

10 Sketty Rd, Uplands SA2 0LJ
☎ 01792 280920 🖷 01792 280920
e-mail hurstdenehotel@yahoo.co.uk
Dir 1m W of city centre. A4118 through Uplands shopping area onto Sketty Rd, Hurst Dene on right

Facilities 10 rms (8 en suite) (3 fmly) (1 GF) ⊘ in 2 bedrooms ⊘ in dining room TVB tea/coffee ✗ Cen ht TVL **Prices** S £30-£35; D £55✶ **Parking** 7 **Notes** ★★★

See advertisement on this page

Wales

TORFAEN

PONTYPOOL

MAP 09 SO20

♦♦♦♦ ❤

Ty-Cooke Farm (SO310052)

Mamhilad NP4 8QZ

☎ 01873 880382 🖹 01873 880382 Mrs Price

e-mail tycookefarm@hotmail.com

Dir *Off A4042 to Mamhilad, in 2m 1st farm on left past Horseshoe Inn*

This working farm is quietly located in an attractive setting with lovely views. It is reputed to date from 1700 and has a wealth of character. The traditionally furnished accommodation is comfortable and well equipped. Breakfasts are served at one table by a magnificent, ornate marble fireplace, and there is also a spacious lounge.

Facilities 3 en suite (1 fmly) (1 GF) ⊗ TVB tea/coffee ✘ Cen ht TVL 135 acres beef sheep **Parking** 6

VALE OF GLAMORGAN

COWBRIDGE

MAP 09 SS97

🄰

Greenlands

CF62 4QL ☎ 01446 751390

e-mail gailatgreenlands@aol.com

web www.greenlandshouse.co.uk

Dir *3m SE of Cowbridge. S through St Mary Church onto St Athan Rd, pass Newbarn sign, 3rd house on right*

Facilities 3 rms (1 en suite) ⊗ TVB tea/coffee Licensed Cen ht No coaches Dinner **Parking** 3 **Notes** ★★★

ST GEORGE'S

MAP 09 ST17

🄰

Greendown Inn Hotel

Drope Rd CF5 6EP ☎ 01446 760310 🖹 01446 760937

e-mail enquiries@greendownhotel.co.uk

web www.greendownhotel.co.uk

Dir *0.6m SE of St Georges. M4 junct 33, A4232, left onto A48 & sharp left onto Michaelstone Rd, left at school onto Drope Rd, hotel 1.5m on left*

Facilities 5 en suite 10 annexe en suite (3 fmly) (10 GF) ⊗ in 10 bedrooms ⊗ in dining room ⊗ in 1 lounge TVB tea/coffee Direct dial from bedrooms Licensed Cen ht Dinner Last d 10pm **Prices** S £39.95-£60; D £60-£100; (incl. dinner) ✳ LB **Conf** Max 60 Thtr 60 Class 60 Board 60 Del from £70 ✳ **Parking** 90 **Notes** ★★★ Civ Wed 90

Wales

Ireland

Ha'penny Bridge in Dublin

NORTHERN IRELAND
CO ANTRIM

BUSHMILLS MAP 01 C6

◆◆◆◆

GH Whitepark House

150 Whitepark Rd BT54 6NH ☎ 028 2073 1482
e-mail bob@whiteparkhouse.com
Dir *On A2 at Whitepark Bay, 6m E of Bushmills*

Whitepark House nestles above a sandy beach and has super views of
the ocean and Scotland's Western Isles. The house features bijouterie
gathered from Far Eastern travels, while the traditional bedrooms are
homely. Breakfasts are served around a central table in the open-plan
hallway, and hospitality is warm and memorable.

Facilities 3 rms ⊗ in bedrooms ⊗ in dining room tea/coffee 🐾
Cen ht No children 10yrs No coaches **Prices** S £40; D £70 **Parking** 6

CUSHENDUN MAP 01 D6

◆◆◆◆ 🏠

GH Drumkeerin ◇

201A Torr Rd BT44 0PU
☎ 028 2176 1554 📠 028 2176 1556
e-mail drumkeerin@zoom.co.uk
web www.drumkeerinbedandbreakfast.co.uk
Dir *Cushendun to Ballycastle via Torr Rd, 50yds on left on bend turn
onto lane, house 0.25m*

Mary and Joe McFadden continue to provide the very highest
standards of personal care and service. Their house nestles high above
the village in rolling countryside, and this peaceful haven has
unrivalled views of the Antrim coast and Irish Sea towards Scotland.
The bedrooms are attractively decorated, and there is a comfortable
lounge whose focus is a bay window overlooking the glen and
harbour. Breakfasts are substantial and make excellent use of organic
produce and delicious home-baked delicacies.

Facilities 3 en suite (3 GF) ⊗ STV TVB tea/coffee 🐾 Cen ht TVL
Painting tuition **Prices** S £30-£35; D £50-£55✱ **LB** **Parking** 4 **Notes** ⊛

◆◆◆◆

GH *The Villa Farm House*

185 Torr Rd BT44 0PU ☎ 028 2176 1252 📠 028 2176 1252
e-mail maggiescally@amserve.net
Dir *From Cushendun on B92 right onto Torr Rd, 0.5m right at T-junct,
farmhouse 3rd left, black & white sign*

This delightful Tudor-style two-storey farmhouse sits in well-kept
gardens and provides stunning views of the Bay of Cushendun and
the village, which houses the smallest pub in Ireland. The well-
equipped bedrooms are traditionally styled and some are suitable for
families. Friendly service and freshly cooked meals are assured.

GH The Villa Farm House

Facilities 3 en suite (2 fmly) ⊗ TVB tea/coffee 🐾 Cen ht TVL Riding
Stairlift Dinner Last d noon **Conf** Max 20 Board 20 **Parking** 25
Notes ⊛

LARNE MAP 01 D5

◆◆◆◆

GH Manor Guest House ◇

23 Older Fleet Rd, Harbour Highway BT40 1AS
☎ 028 2827 3305 📠 028 2826 0505
e-mail welcome@themanorguesthouse.com
web www.themanorguesthouse.com
Dir *Near Larne ferry terminal & harbour train station*

This grand Victorian house continues to prove popular with travellers
thanks to its convenient location next to the ferry terminal. There is an
elegant sitting room and a separate cosy breakfast room. The well-
equipped bedrooms vary in size and are furnished in modern or
period style. Hospitality is especially good to ensure a real home from
home experience.

Facilities 8 en suite (2 fmly) ⊗ TVB tea/coffee 🐾 Cen ht
Prices S £25-£27; D £45-£48 **LB** **Parking** 6 **Notes** Closed 25-26 Dec

◆◆◆

GH *Derrin House*

2 Princes Gdns BT40 1RQ
☎ 028 2827 3269 📠 028 2827 3269
e-mail info@derrinhouse.co.uk
Dir *Off A8 Harbour Highway onto A2 coast route, 1st left after lights
at Main St*

Just a short walk from the town centre, and a short drive from the
harbour, this comfortable Victorian house offers a very friendly
welcome. The bedrooms are gradually being refurbished to offer
smartly presented modern facilities. Public areas are light and inviting,
hearty breakfasts are offered in the stylish dining room.

Facilities 7 rms (3 en suite) (1 pri facs) (2 fmly) (2 GF) ⊗ TVB
tea/coffee Cen ht TVL No coaches **Parking** 7

Please mention the AA B&B Guide when
booking your stay

continued

Ireland

PORTRUSH
MAP 01 C6

◆◆◆◆ **A**

GH Albany Lodge

2 Eglington St BT56 8DX
☎ 028 7082 3492 ▤ 028 7082 1227
e-mail info@albanylodgeni.co.uk
Facilities 10 en suite ⊘ STV TVB tea/coffee Direct dial from bedrooms
★ Cen ht TVL Dinner Last d noon **Prices** S £60-£100; D £80-£130✴
LB

◆◆◆

GH Beulah Guest House ◇

16 Causeway St BT56 8AB
☎ 028 7082 2413 ▤ 028 7082 5900
e-mail stay@beulahguesthouse.com
Dir *Approach Portrush & signs for Bushmills/East Strand car park onto Causeway St, house 300yds on left*

Situated just a stroll from the East Strand and the town's attractions, this guest house offers a friendly welcome. Bright and attractive throughout, the comfortable bedrooms are well equipped. There is a also a first-floor lounge and secure parking behind the house.

Facilities 9 en suite (3 fmly) (1 GF) ⊘ TVB tea/coffee **★** Cen ht TVL
No coaches Dinner Last d noon **Prices** S £30-£50; D £50-£60✴ **LB**
Parking 10 **Notes** Closed 25-26 Dec

BELFAST

BELFAST
MAP 01 D5

◆◆◆◆

GH Tara Lodge

36 Cromwell Rd BT7 1JW
☎ 028 9059 0900 ▤ 028 9059 0901
e-mail info@taralodge.com
web www.taralodge.com

Friendly staff and comfortable bedrooms make this new establishment popular for tourism and business. The stylish dining room is the scene for memorable breakfasts, while secure off-road parking is a bonus so close to the city centre.

Facilities 19 en suite (12 fmly) ⊘ in 6 bedrooms ⊘ in dining room
⊘ in lounges STV TVB tea/coffee Direct dial from bedrooms **★** Lift
Cen ht TVL **Prices** S fr £65; d fr £75✴ **LB** **Parking** 19 **Notes** Closed
24-28 Dec & 11-13 Jul

CO DOWN

BANGOR
MAP 01 D5

◆◆◆◆

GH Hebron House

68 Princetown Rd BT20 3TD
☎ 028 9146 3126 ▤ 028 9146 3126
e-mail reception@hebron-house.com
web www.hebron-house.com
Dir *A20 onto B20 for 3m, 1st rdbt onto Princetown Rd*

Hebron House stands in a peaceful elevated location within easy walking distance of the town amenities. Bedrooms are luxuriously furnished and have many thoughtful extras. The elegant lounge is richly styled and very comfortable. Breakfast offers home-made and local produce around a communal table in the smart dining room. Dinners are available by arrangement Monday to Thursday.

Facilities 3 en suite (1 GF) ⊘ TVB tea/coffee **★** Cen ht TVL No coaches
Dinner **Prices** S £45-£70; D £65-£70 **Notes** Closed 22 Dec-1 Jan

◆◆ **A**

GH Tara Guest House ◇

49/51 Princetown Rd BT20 3TA
☎ 028 9145 8820 ▤ 028 9146 8924
e-mail taraguesthouse@lineone.net
Dir *A2 to Bangor, down Main St, left onto Queens Parade to minirdbt (Gray Hill) right onto Princetown Rd*

Facilities 13 en suite (3 fmly) ⊘ in dining room ⊘ in 1 lounge TVB
tea/coffee Direct dial from bedrooms Cen ht TVL **Prices** S £30; D £46
Parking 8 **Notes** Closed 25-30 Dec

See advertisement on page 727

COMBER
MAP 01 D5

◆◆◆◆ ⬭

GH The Old Schoolhouse Inn

Castle Espie BT23 6EA ☎ 028 9754 1182 ▤ 028 9754 2583
e-mail info@theoldschoolhouseinn.com
Dir *A22 to Comber, right at end of road. 0.5m past Castle Espie*

This privately owned and personally run establishment originated as a school built in 1929. The school itself is now a charming restaurant, while the modern bedrooms are spacious and well equipped.

Facilities 12 en suite (12 GF) ⊘ in dining room ⊘ in 1 lounge STV TVB
tea/coffee Direct dial from bedrooms **★** Licensed Cen ht TVL Golf 9
Dinner Last d 9.30pm **Prices** S £45; D £65 **LB** **Conf** Max 60 Thtr 60
Class 30 Board 30 **Parking** 100

If you book on bed, breakfast and evening meal terms, you may find that the tariff includes only the set menu

DOWNPATRICK

MAP 01 D5

Premier Collection

◆◆◆◆◆ 🏠 🌱

Pheasants' Hill Country House

(J4493483)

37 Killyleagh Rd BT30 9BL
☎ 028 4483 8707 & 4461 7246 📠 028 4461 7246
Mrs Bailey
e-mail info@pheasantshill.com
web www.pheasantshill.com
Dir On A22, 3m N of Downpatrick

This modern farmhouse has a rural setting on the border of The Quoile Pondage, just north of the town. Surrounded by fields, this working farm has pigs and horses and grows organic crops, and the farm shop sells a wide range of organic goods. The stylish bedrooms feature country-style furniture and there is a comfortable lounge.

Facilities 5 en suite (1 fmly) (1 GF) ⊗ STV TVB tea/coffee ✗ Cen ht TVL 12 acres rare breeds **Parking** 10 **Notes** Closed Nov-Feb

NEWTOWNARDS

MAP 01 D5

Premier Collection

◆◆◆◆◆ 🏠

GH Edenvale House

130 Portaferry Rd BT22 2AH
☎ 028 9181 4881 📠 028 9182 6192
e-mail edenvalehouse@hotmail.com
web www.edenvalehouse.com
Dir 2m S of Newtownards on A20

A genuine warm welcome is provided at this beautifully restored

continued

Georgian house, set in grounds and furnished with antiques. Bedrooms are decorated in period style and feature many thoughtful extras, and one of the elegant lounges has views across Strangford Lough towards the Mountains of Mourne. Breakfast is a particularly good selection of home-made and local produce, served around a communal table.

Facilities 3 en suite (2 fmly) ⊗ TVB tea/coffee ✗ Cen ht ch fac No coaches Riding 🏇 **Prices** S £45-£50; D £70-£80✳ **Parking** 15 **Notes** Closed 24-26 Dec

Premier Collection

◆◆◆◆◆

GH Ballynester House ◇

1a Cardy Rd, Greyabbey BT22 2LS
☎ 028 4278 8386 📠 028 4278 8986
e-mail rc.davison@virgin.net
Dir A20 S from Newtownards to Greyabbey, or A20 N from Portaferry to Greyabbey, signed at Greyabbey rdbt

Please note that this establishment has recently changed hands. Nestling in the rolling hills above Strangford Lough, this stylish, modern house provides a peaceful haven. Smart day rooms make the most of the super views, and hearty breakfasts are served in the bright dining room. Richly furnished bedrooms include a host of thoughtful extras.

Facilities 3 en suite (1 fmly) (3 GF) ⊗ TVB tea/coffee ✗ Cen ht No coaches **Prices** S £30; D £50✳ **Parking** 10

PORTAFERRY

MAP 01 D5

◆◆◆◆ 🍽

GH The Narrows

8 Shore Rd BT22 1JY ☎ 028 4272 8148 📠 028 4272 8105
e-mail reservations@narrows.co.uk
Dir A20 to shore & left, The Narrows on left

Please note that this establishment has recently changed hands. The stylish guest house has a delightful quayside location on the shores of Strangford Lough. The bedrooms have modern facilities, and the contemporary day rooms include an appealing restaurant and the new Ruffians Bar. There is also a function room with panoramic views.

Facilities 13 en suite (3 fmly) (2 GF) ⊗ in bedrooms ⊗ in dining room TVB tea/coffee Direct dial from bedrooms ✗ Licensed Lift Cen ht Dinner Last d 9.15pm **Conf** Max 50 Thtr 50 Class 24 Board 24 **Parking** 5

CO FERMANAGH

ENNISKILLEN   MAP 01 C5

◆◆◆◆

GH Arch House Tullyhona Farm Guest House ◇

Marble Arch Rd, Florencecourt BT92 1DE
☎ 028 6634 8452
e-mail tullyguest60@hotmail.com
web www.archhouse.com
Dir *A4 from Enniskillen towards Sligo, 2.5m onto A32, right at NT sign for Florence Court*

This delightful house nestles in a tranquil country setting very close to the Marble Arch Caves and Florence Court. The refurbished bedrooms are stylish, and Tullyhona's restaurant is open for all-day breakfasts, as well as a range of traditional evening meals.

Facilities 4 en suite (4 fmly) ⊗ TVB Direct dial from bedrooms Cen ht TVL Riding Farm tours Trampoline Table tennis Badminton Dinner Last d 6.30pm **Prices** S £25-£30; D £46-£48✳ **LB Conf** Max 70 Thtr 70 Class 50 **Parking** 8

◆◆◆◆

GH Dromard House ◇

Tamlaght BT74 4HR ☎ 028 6638 7250
e-mail dromardhouse@yahoo.co.uk
web www.dromardhouse.com
Dir *2m SE of Enniskillen on A4 Belfast road*

This popular, smartly presented house has its own woodland trail down to the shores of beautiful Lough Erne. The attractively decorated bedrooms, with separate access, are in a converted, spacious stable block. Hearty breakfasts are served in the main house. A cosy lounge area is also available.

Facilities 4 annexe en suite (1 fmly) ⊗ TVB tea/coffee ✳ Cen ht TVL No coaches Fishing Woodland trail, private jetties for coarse fishing **Prices** S £25; D £50 **Parking** 4 **Notes** Closed 24-26 Dec

◆◆◆◆

GH Willowbank House ◇

60 Bellvue Rd BT74 4JH
☎ 028 6632 8582 📠 028 6632 8582
e-mail joan@willowbankhouse.com
Dir *A4 from Enniskillen towards Belfast, 0.25m right after Killy Helvin Hotel signed Upper Lough Erne & Willowbank House, 2m on left*

This peacefully situated house commands an elevated position in attractive grounds just a short drive from the town. Bedrooms, all on the ground floor, vary in size and some are suitable for families. There is a comfortable lounge and substantial breakfasts are served in the conservatory dining room, overlooking the lake.

Facilities 5 en suite (2 fmly) (5 GF) ⊗ TVB tea/coffee ✳ Cen ht TVL No coaches **Prices** S £30-£35; D £50-£60 **LB Parking** 6 **Notes** Closed Xmas

◆◆◆

GH Aghnacarra House ◇

Carrybridge, Lisbellaw BT94 5HX
☎ 028 6638 7077 📠 028 6638 5811
e-mail normaensor@talk21.com
web www.guesthouseireland.com
Dir *5.5m SE of Enniskillen. A4 onto B514, left for Carrybridge, 500yds on right, signed at bridge*

Surrounded by spacious grounds, gardens and countryside on the shores of Lough Erne, this delightful modern extended house is a haven of peace and quiet. It is understandably very popular with anglers, who may fish from the grounds. Bedrooms are well maintained, and day rooms include an elegant lounge, bright dining room and a spacious bar and games room.

Facilities 7 en suite (2 fmly) (5 GF) ⊗ in 2 bedrooms ⊗ in dining room ⊗ in 1 lounge tea/coffee ✳ Licensed Cen ht TVL No children 10yrs No coaches Pool Table Games room Dinner Last d 10am **Prices** S £30; D £50✳ **LB Parking** 8 **Notes** Closed Nov-Mar

Ireland

CO LONDONDERRY

CASTLEDAWSON
MAP 01 C5

[U] ⬛

The Inn at Castle Dawson

47 Main St BT45 8AA ☎ 028 7946 9777 📠 028 7946 9888
e-mail info@theinnatcastledawson.co.uk
web www.theinnatcastledawson.co.uk
Dir Off Castledawson rdbt on A6

At the time of going to press the rating for this establishment had not been confirmed. Please check the AA website www.theAA.com for up-to-date information.

Facilities 12 en suite (6 GF) ⊗ in bedrooms ⊗ in dining room ⊗ in 1 lounge TVB Direct dial from bedrooms Cen ht TVL Golf 18 Fishing Riding Dinner Last d 9pm **Prices** S £44-£49.95; D £64-£79.95✶ LB **Conf** Max 20 Thtr 20 Class 20 Board 20 **Parking** 15

COLERAINE
MAP 01 C6

Premier Collection

♦♦♦♦♦

GH Greenhill House

24 Greenhill Rd, Aghadowey BT51 4EU
☎ 028 7086 8241 📠 028 7086 8365
e-mail greenhill.house@btinternet.com
web www.greenhill-house.co.uk
Dir A29 from Coleraine south for 7m, left onto B66 Greenhill Rd for 300yds. House on right, AA sign at front gate

Located in the tranquil Bann Valley, overlooking the Antrim Hills, this delightful Georgian house nestles in well-tended gardens with views to open rolling countryside. Public rooms are traditionally styled and include a comfortable lounge and an elegant dining room. The pleasant bedrooms vary in size and style and have a host of thoughtful extras.

Facilities 6 en suite (2 fmly) ⊗ TVB tea/coffee Direct dial from bedrooms ✖ Cen ht TVL **Prices** S £40; D £60 **Parking** 10 **Notes** Closed Nov-Feb

♦♦♦♦

GH Bellevue Country House

43 Greenhill Rd, Aghadowey BT51 4EU
☎ 028 7086 8797 📠 028 7086 8780
e-mail info@bellevuecountryhouse.co.uk
web www.bellevuecountryhouse.co.uk
Dir On B66 just off A29, 7m S of Coleraine

This fine country house, dating from 1840, stands in peaceful grounds. A variety of bedrooms are offered, including a family room and ground-floor accommodation, and there is also a comfortable drawing room. Generous breakfasts are freshly prepared and served around one large table.

Facilities 3 en suite (1 fmly) (1 GF) ⊗ TVB tea/coffee ✖ Cen ht TVL No coaches Fishing **Parking** 9 **Notes** Closed 24-25 Dec ⊗

♦♦♦♦ 🅐

GH Heathfield ◇

31 Drumcroone Rd, Killykergan BT51 4EB
☎ 028 295 58245 & 07745 209296
e-mail relax@heathfieldfarm.com
web www.heathfieldfarm.com
Dir On A29 Garvagh Coleraine road. 2m N of Garvagh and 7m S of Coleraine.

Facilities 3 en suite ⊗ TVB tea/coffee Cen ht TVL **Prices** S £28-£30✶ **Parking** 12

LONDONDERRY
MAP 01 C5

♦♦♦

GH Clarence House ◇

15 Northland Rd BT48 7HY
☎ 028 7126 5342 & 07786 801954 📠 028 7126 5377
e-mail clarencehouse@zoom.co.uk
web www.guesthouseireland.co.uk
Dir From Belfast A6 next to University opp fire station & Radio Foyle

This long-established, family-run guest house provides charming, well-equipped bedrooms. Traditionally styled day rooms include a spacious lounge and a smartly presented dining room where wholesome and generous meals are served.

Facilities 9 en suite (2 fmly) ⊗ FTV TVB tea/coffee Direct dial from bedrooms ✖ Licensed Cen ht TVL Dinner Last d 2pm **Prices** S £26.55-£40; D £53.10-£60

If you have to cancel a booking, let the proprietor know immediately

Ireland

CO TYRONE

DUNGANNON
MAP 01 C5

Premier Collection

◆◆◆◆◆ 🏠 🍴

GH Grange Lodge

7 Grange Rd BT71 7EJ ☎ 028 8778 4212 📠 028 8778 4313
e-mail grangelodge@nireland.com
Dir M1 junct 15, A29 towards Armagh, 1m Grange Lodge signed, 1st right & 1st entrance on right

Grange Lodge dates from 1698 and nestles in 20 acres of well-tended grounds. It continues to set high standards in hospitality and food, and excellent meals are served in the bright and airy extension. Home-baked afternoon teas can be enjoyed in the sumptuous drawing room.

Facilities 5 en suite ⊗ STV TVB tea/coffee Direct dial from bedrooms ✘ Licensed Cen ht TVL No children 12yrs No coaches Dinner Last d 1pm previous day **Prices** S £55-£59; D £79 **Conf** Max 30 **Parking** 12 **Notes** Closed 21 Dec-9 Jan

◆◆◆◆◆

GH Stangmore Country House

65 Moy Rd BT71 7DT ☎ 028 8772 5600 📠 028 8772 6644
e-mail info@stangmorecountryhouse.com
Dir M1 junct 15 signed Dungannon from the rdbt, B&B 250yds on left.

Facilities 5 en suite 4 annexe en suite (1 fmly) (2 GF) ⊗ STV TVB tea/coffee Direct dial from bedrooms ✘ Licensed Cen ht TVL Dinner Last d 8.30pm **Prices** S £60-£75; D £80-£100✱ LB **Conf** Max 40 Thtr 40 Class 25 Board 16 Del £79.95 ✱ **Parking** 40

◆◆◆◆

GH Millbrook Bed & Breakfast

46 Moy Rd BT71 7DT ☎ 028 8772 3715
e-mail info@millbrookonline.co.uk
Dir On A29 1m S of Dungannon, 0.25m N of M1 junct 15

This well-presented bungalow is situated just outside the town, close to main routes. Comfortable ground-floor bedrooms and a new lounge are complemented by a substantial, freshly prepared breakfast. The owners' natural hospitality is memorable.

Facilities 3 en suite (3 GF) ⊗ TVB tea/coffee ✘ Cen ht TVL No coaches **Prices** S fr £35; d fr £50✱ **Parking** 4 **Notes** 🐾

◆◆◆◆

GH Reahs Restaurant & Luxury Accommodation

24 Killyman Rd BT71 6DH
☎ 028 8772 5575 📠 028 8772 6676
Dir On B34, at lights on Northland Row-Circular Rd, Reahs on left

This smart house stands in a residential location close to the town centre. The bright, contemporary bedrooms have modern bathrooms and comfortable beds. Day rooms include a cosy lounge, and a sizeable restaurant where wide-ranging menus attract a local following.

Facilities 7 en suite (2 fmly) (5 GF) ⊗ in bedrooms ⊗ in dining room STV TVB tea/coffee Direct dial from bedrooms ✘ Licensed Cen ht TVL Dinner Last d 9.30pm **Parking** 14

How do I find the perfect place?

Discover new horizons with **AA**
Britain's largest travel publisher

REPUBLIC OF IRELAND

CO CARLOW

BAGENALSTOWN
MAP 01 C3

◆◆◆◆

GH Orchard Grove

Wells ☎ 059 9722140 & 086 8387438
e-mail orchardgrove@eircom.net
Dir On N9 halfway between Carlow & Kilkenny

Lovely gardens with a play area surround this child-friendly house, which offers comfortable bedrooms and evening meals by arrangement. Inclusive packages can be arranged, and the house is close to Goresbridge bloodstock sales, Gowran Racecourse, fishing, golf, and walking routes.

Facilities 4 annexe en suite (1 fmly) ⊗ TVB tea/coffee ✘ Cen ht TVL No coaches Pool Table Dinner Last d 3pm **Prices** S €45; D €70✱ LB **Parking** 8 **Notes** Closed Dec

Ireland

CARLOW

MAP 01 C3

Premier Collection

◆◆◆◆◆

GH Barrowville Town House

Kilkenny Rd ☎ 059 914 3324 🖷 059 914 1953
e-mail barrowvilletownhouse@eircom.net
web www.barrowvillehouse.com
Dir *N9 N into town, 50 metres before lights*

Marie and Randal Dempsey are the friendly owners of this elegant 18th-century house. Many of the very comfortable bedrooms are spacious. The public rooms include one with a grand piano. Barrowwilles' legendary breakfasts are served in the conservatory, which has a fruiting vine and overlooks well-tended gardens.

Facilities 7 en suite ⊗ STV TVB tea/coffee Direct dial from bedrooms ✈ Cen ht TVL No children 15yrs No coaches **Prices** S €55-€65; D €95-€100 **LB Parking** 11

◆◆◆◆

GH Carlow Guest House

Green Ln, Dublin Rd
☎ 059 913 6033 & 913 6034 🖷 059 913 6034
e-mail info@carlowguesthouse.com
Dir *N9 S into town, over 4 rdbts, house 0.6km on left before Statoil station*

This purpose-built guest house, just 5 minutes from the town centre, is attractively decorated and comfortably furnished. Public areas include a library, television lounge, and a conservatory-dining room where traditional, continental and vegetarian options are served. The smart bedrooms are furnished in pine. Off-road parking.

Facilities 13 en suite (2 fmly) (7 GF) ⊗ STV TVB tea/coffee Direct dial from bedrooms ✈ Cen ht TVL **Prices** S €45-€90; D €80-€120 **LB Parking** 20 **Notes** Closed 24-26 Dec

RATHVILLY

MAP 01 D3

◆◆◆◆ ❦

Baile Ricead *(S 845836)*

☎ 059 916 1120 Mrs Corrigan
e-mail minacorrigan@eircom.net
Dir *5km from Rathvilly. N9 S, left at Castle Inn, left next junct, 2nd right before Graney Bridge, left after water pump, house on bend*

This delightful farmhouse has comfortable bedrooms furnished to a good standard. There is a lounge, and conservatory-dining room that looks out across the delightful gardens to the Wicklow Mountains. Guests can use the barbecue in the garden.

Facilities 4 rms (2 en suite) (1 fmly) ⊗ TVB tea/coffee Cen ht TVL 66 acres mixed **Parking** 6 **Notes** Closed Nov-16 Mar

CO CLARE

BALLYVAUGHAN

MAP 01 B

Premier Collection

◆◆◆◆◆

GH Drumcreehy Guesthouse

☎ 065 7077377 🖷 065 7077379
e-mail info@drumcreehyhouse.com
Dir *1.5km from village centre on N67 Galway route*

Located on the outskirts of the village, the Drumcreehy has wonderful views of Galway Bay and the surrounding Burren landscape. The bedrooms are carefully decorated in traditional character and have modern conveniences, and the extensive breakfast menu features home baking and local produce. There are village pubs and restaurants nearby.

Facilities 10 en suite (2 fmly) (2 GF) ⊗ STV TVB Direct dial from bedrooms Cen ht **Prices** S €53-€100; D €74-€100 **Parking** 12

Premier Collection

◆◆◆◆◆

GH *Rusheen Lodge*

☎ 065 7077092 🖷 065 7077152
e-mail rusheen@iol.ie
Dir *On N67 1km from Ballyvaughan*

A charming house situated in the valley of The Burren, an area famous for it's Arctic and Alpine plants. The McCann family were founders of the famous Aillwee Cave nearby and have a wealth of local folklore. The bedrooms are spacious some with extra seating areas. Patio gardens lead from the cosy dining room.

Facilities 9 en suite (3 fmly) (3 GF) ⊗ STV TVB tea/coffee Direct dial from bedrooms ✈ Cen ht TVL **Parking** 12 **Notes** Closed mid Nov-mid Feb

continued

Ireland

♦♦♦♦

GH *Cappabhaile House*

Newtown ☎ 065 7077260 🖷 065 7077300
e-mail cappabhaile@oceanfree.net

Dir 1km outside Ballyvaughan towards Aillwee Cave

Cappabhaile House was recently built using local stone and natural materials, on a 5-hectare site on the outskirts of the village in the heart of The Burren. The hosts are happy to assist guests with planning walks and hill climbs, or with archaeological or botanical information. The spacious bedrooms are suitable for families and are very well appointed. Guests can relax in the comfortable lounge or enjoy a game of pool in the games room. An 18-hole pitch and putt course surrounds the house. An extensive breakfast menu is on offer, with some baking a speciality.

Facilities 8 en suite (4 fmly) ⊘ TVB tea/coffee Direct dial from bedrooms ✖ Cen ht TVL No coaches Pool Table 18 hole pitch & putt **Parking** 20 **Notes** Closed Nov-Feb

BUNRATTY   MAP 01 B3

♦♦♦♦

T&C Park House

Low Rd ☎ 061 369902 🖷 061 369903
e-mail parkhouse@eircom.net

Dir From N18 take Bunratty exit, turn left at castle, pass Folk Park. Park House 4th house on left

A purpose-built guest house with spacious bedrooms within walking distance of the castle. There is a lounge and a lovely garden. Mairead Bateman's home baking can be sampled on arrival.

Facilities 6 en suite (3 fmly) (2 GF) ⊘ STV TVB tea/coffee ✖ Cen ht **Prices** S €45-€50; D €65-€70✳ **Parking** 6 **Notes** Closed mid Dec-Jan

CORROFIN   MAP 01 B3

♦♦♦

T&C Fergus View

Kilnaboy ☎ 065 6837606 🖷 065 6837192
e-mail deckell@indigo.ie

Dir 3.2km N of Corofin towards Kilfenora, past ruins of Kilnaboy Church on left on R476

This fourth-generation family home is well located for touring the Burren area. The varied breakfast menu includes home baking.

Facilities 6 rms (5 en suite) (1 fmly) ⊘ ✖ Cen ht TVL No coaches **Prices** S €49-€51; D €72✳ **Parking** 8 **Notes** Closed mid Oct-mid Mar

---

DOOLIN   MAP 01 B3

Premier Collection

♦♦♦♦♦ 📖 🍽

GH Ballyvara House

Ballyvara ☎ 065 7074467 🖷 065 7074868
e-mail bvara@iol.ie

Dir 1st left after Cullinans Restaurant on right, 0.5km on left

Once a 19th-century farm cottage, Ballyvara House has been transformed into a stylish guest house. Public areas and the spacious bedrooms are furnished to a high standard. The house is set in 8 hectares of unspoiled countryside close to Doolin, which is famous for traditional music, pubs and ferrys to the Aran Islands. Dinner is served from Tuesday to Saturday.

Facilities 11 en suite (2 fmly) (5 GF) ⊘ STV TVB tea/coffee Direct dial from bedrooms ✖ Licensed Cen ht TVL ⚲ Pool Table Childrens outdoor playground Dinner Last d 9pm **Prices** S €55-€100; D €80-€150✳ **LB** **Parking** 10 **Notes** Closed Nov-Feb

♦♦♦ 🍽

GH Cullinan's Guest House ◈

☎ 065 7074183 🖷 065 7074239
e-mail cullinans@eircom.net

Dir In town centre at x-rds by McGanns Pub & O Connors Pub

This charming guest house and restaurant is situated in the village of Doolin. Bedrooms are attractive decorated and comfortable. Chef patron James features locally caught fresh fish on his dinner menu, along with steaks, lamb and vegetarian dishes and there is a popular Early Bird menu. Other facilities include a lounge, a patio, and gardens that run down to the River Aille.

Facilities 8 en suite (3 fmly) (3 GF) ⊘ TV3B tea/coffee Direct dial from bedrooms ✖ Cen ht TVL Dinner Last d 9pm **Prices** S €40-€70; D €60-€90✳ **Parking** 15

ENNIS   MAP 01 B3

♦♦♦♦

GH Fountain Court

Lahinch Rd ☎ 065 6829845 🖷 065 6845030
e-mail kyran@fountain-court.com

Dir 3.2km from Ennis on N85 on left

Set in 1.6 hectares of mature gardens on an elevated site close to the town, this comfortable guest house is run by the Carr family. The majority of bedrooms are spacious, carefully decorated and have many thoughtful extras, including four-poster beds. Guests can relax in the elegant lounge or on the terrace.

Facilities 18 en suite (4 fmly) ⊘ STV TVB tea/coffee Direct dial from bedrooms ✖ Licensed Cen ht **Prices** S €55-€60; D €76-€96✳ **LB** **Parking** 25 **Notes** Closed 10 Dec-7 Mar

Ireland

ENNIS continued

♦♦♦♦

GH *Cill Eoin House*

Killadysert Cross, Clare Rd
☎ 065 6841668 & 6828311 ▤ 065 6841669
e-mail cilleoin@iol.ie
web www.euroka.com/cilleoin/
Dir *Off N18 onto R473 Killadysert road, house 100 metres*

This smart purpose-built house stands a short distance from the town centre. It is attractively furnished and has well-equipped en suite bedrooms. The hospitable owner is always available to help guests.

Facilities 14 en suite (2 fmly) ⊗ TVB tea/coffee Direct dial from bedrooms Cen ht TVL ੦६ Dinner Last d 4pm **Parking** 14 **Notes** Closed 22 Dec-9 Jan

---

KILRUSH
MAP 01 B3

♦♦♦♦

T&C *Hillcrest View*

Doonbeg Rd ☎ 065 9051986 ▤ 065 9051900
e-mail ethnahynes@eircom.net
Dir *Off N67 Kilkee road, on Doonbeg road*

Within walking distance of the town centre and a short drive from the Killimer ferry, Hillcrest View has spacious and well-appointed bedrooms. There is a sitting-dining room with a breakfast conservatory, while patio seats look over the pretty garden.

Facilities 6 en suite (2 fmly) ⊗ STV TVB tea/coffee ✖ Cen ht TVL No coaches **Parking** 7

♦♦♦

T&C *Bruach-na-Coille*

Killimer Rd ☎ 065 9052250 ▤ 065 9052250
e-mail clarekilrush@hotmail.com
Dir *From Kilrush left at Shannon Side Insurance onto Moore St, right at Mace supermarket onto N67 Killimer Rd*

This house, overlooking Kilrush Forest, offers accommodation with views of the Shannon Estuary. All rooms are well equipped and you can look forward to a warm welcome, an enjoyable breakfast, and helpful information about the area.

Facilities 4 rms (2 en suite) (1 fmly) ⊗ TVB tea/coffee ✖ Cen ht TVL No coaches **Parking** 8 **Notes** Closed 25 Dec

♦♦♦

GH *Cois Na Sionna*

Ferry Junction, Killimer
☎ 065 9053073 & 087 2377285 ▤ 065 9053073
e-mail coisnasionna@eircom.net
Dir *On N67 at entrance to Killimer-Tarbert car ferry*

The bedrooms of this modern house offer good space and are bright and well appointed. There is a comfortable lounge and a traditional cooked breakfast is served in the dining room. A good base for visiting Clare and Kerry.

Facilities 4 en suite (3 fmly) ⊗ TVB tea/coffee ✖ Cen ht TVL No coaches **Prices** S €43-€50; D €60-€72✱ LB **Parking** 6

LAHINCH
MAP 01 B3

♦♦♦♦♦ 🏠 🍴

GH *Moy House*

☎ 065 708 2800 ▤ 065 708 2500
e-mail moyhouse@eircom.net
Dir *3.2km from Lahinch on Miltown Malbay Rd, signed from Lahinch*

This 18th-century house overlooks Lahinch's world-famous surfing beach and championship golf links. Individually designed bedrooms are decorated with luxurious fabrics and fine antique furniture. The elegant drawing room has an open turf fire and breathtaking views. The carefully prepared dinner menu has an emphasis on excellent seafood, and breakfast is noteworthy too.

Facilities 9 en suite (2 fmly) (4 GF) ⊗ TVB Direct dial from bedrooms ✖ Licensed Cen ht Dinner Last d 8.45pm **Prices** S €135-€165; D €160-€290 LB **Conf** Max 16 Board 16 **Parking** 30 **Notes** Closed 24 Dec-16 Jan

---

OGONNELLOE
MAP 01 B3

♦♦♦

GH *Lantern House*

☎ 061 923034 & 923123 ▤ 061 923139
e-mail phil@lanternhouse.com
Dir *From Birdhill N7 onto 463 to Ballina/Killalue, over bridge, right, house 9.5km on left*

Situated overlooking Lough Derg, in a very scenic setting, this comfortable house offers nicely furnished and decorated bedrooms, together with a popular restaurant. The well-tended gardens provide a marvellous view of the lake.

Facilities 6 en suite (6 GF) ⊗ TVB Direct dial from bedrooms ✖ Licensed Cen ht TVL No coaches Dinner Last d 9pm **Prices** S €40-€48; D €76-€90✱ **Parking** 25 **Notes** Closed Nov-Mar

---

SCARRIFF
MAP 01 B3

♦♦♦♦

GH *Clareville House*

Tuamgraney ☎ 061 922925 & 087 6867548
e-mail clarevillehouse@iri.com
Dir *On R352 in village adjacent to Scariff*

Situated in the centre of the pretty lakeside village of Tuamgraney this purpose-built bed and breakfast is attractively decorated. The spacious bedrooms are furnished to a high standard and the cosy guest sitting room and dining room are also well furnished. Ample off-road parking is available.

Facilities 4 en suite (4 fmly) ⊗ TVB tea/coffee ✖ Cen ht TVL No coaches Golf Riding **Prices** S €45-€50; D €70✱ **Parking** 8 **Notes** Closed 20-27 Dec

CO CORK

BANDON
MAP 01 B2

◆◆◆◆

T&C Glebe Country House

Ballinadee ☎ 021 4778294 ▤ 021 4778456
e-mail glebehse@indigo.ie
Dir Off N71 at Innishannon Bridge signed Ballinadee, 8km along river bank, left after village sign

This lovely guest house stands in well-kept gardens, and is run with great attention to detail. Antique furnishings predominate throughout this comfortable house, which has a lounge and an elegant dining room. An interesting breakfast menu offers unusual options, and a country-house style dinner is available by arrangement.

Facilities 4 en suite (2 fmly) ⊗ tea/coffee Direct dial from bedrooms Cen ht TVL No coaches outdoor badminton Dinner Last d noon **Prices** S €65-€70; D €100-€110 LB **Parking** 30 **Notes** Closed 1 Dec-3 Jan

BLARNEY
MAP 01 B2

Premier Collection

◆◆◆◆◆ 🖩

GH Ashlee Lodge

Tower ☎ 021 4385346 ▤ 021 4385726
e-mail info@ashleelodge.com
Dir 4km from Blarney on R617

Ashlee Lodge is a purpose-built guest house, situated in the village of Tower, close to Blarney and local pubs and restaurants. Bedrooms are decorated with comfort and elegance in mind, some with whirlpool baths, and one room has easier access. The extensive breakfast menu is memorable for Ann's home baking. You can unwind in the sauna or the outdoor hot tub. Transfers to the nearest airport and railway station can be arranged, and tee times can be booked at many of the nearby golf courses. AA Guest Accommodation of the Year for Ireland 2006.

Facilities 10 en suite (2 fmly) (6 GF) ⊗ STV TVB tea/coffee Direct dial from bedrooms Licensed Cen ht TVL Sauna Hot tub Dinner Last d 8.30pm **Prices** S €85-€125; D €140-€240 LB **Parking** 12

◆◆◆◆

T&C Blarney Vale House

Cork Rd ☎ 021 4381511
e-mail info@blarneyvale.com
Dir On R617 adjacent to golf driving range on approach to town

Ann and Ray Hennessy are the enthusiastic hosts at this dormer bungalow, located on an elevated position above Cork Rd and surrounded by landscaped gardens. Everything is of an excellent standard and a pleasant lounge is available.

Facilities 4 en suite (2 fmly) (1 GF) ⊗ TVB tea/coffee ✱ Cen ht **Parking** 9 **Notes** Closed Dec-Jan ⊠

◆◆◆◆

GH Killarney House

Station Rd ☎ 021 4381841 ▤ 021 4381841
e-mail info@killarneyhouseblarney.com
Dir From N20 onto R617, right after Blarney filling station turn right, 1km on Station Rd on right

A no-smoking house with four ground-floor bedrooms in a new extension, and two on the first floor. Caroline Morgan is a charming, attentive hostess whose comfortable house is very well appointed. There is a television lounge, drying facilities for wet gear, and off-road parking. Golf available nearby.

Facilities 6 en suite (2 fmly) (4 GF) ⊗ TVB tea/coffee ✱ Cen ht **Prices** S €45-€55; D €66-€76✱ LB **Parking** 8 **Notes** ⊠

◆◆◆◆

T&C White House

Shean Lower ☎ 021 4385338
e-mail info@thewhitehouseblarney.com
web www.thewhitehouseblarney.com
Dir On R617, Cork/Blarney road

Situated on an elevated position near to the town, with views of Blarney Castle, this carefully maintained bungalow lies in grounds. Bedrooms, with modern facilities, are well appointed and have comfortable armchairs. There is a television lounge and a breakfast room. A private car park is also available.

Facilities 6 en suite (1 fmly) ⊗ STV TVB tea/coffee ✱ Cen ht **Prices** S €45-€50; D €64-€74 **Parking** 7

◆◆◆

GH Muskerry Arms

☎ 021 4385200 ▤ 021 4381013
e-mail info@muskerryarms.com
Dir In village centre

Situated on the square in Blarney village, the Muskerry Arms offers very comfortable and spacious bedrooms with views of the famous Blarney Castle. There is a traditional style bar where food is served all day and music every night during high season. There is a cosy lounge and secure parking at the rear.

Facilities 11 en suite (1 fmly) ⊗ in 6 bedrooms ⊗ in dining room ⊗ in lounges STV TVB Direct dial from bedrooms ✱ Licensed Cen ht TVL Pool Table Dinner Last d 9pm **Parking** 20 **Notes** Closed Xmas

CLONAKILTY MAP 01 B2

◆◆◆◆

GH An Garran Coir

Rathbarry, Rosscarbery Coast Route
☎ 023 48236 📄 023 48236
e-mail angarrancoir@eircom.net
Dir *Signed at Maxol station in Clonakilty. 6.5km W of town off N71, 1.5km on right*

On the coast road to Rosscarbery, close to sandy beaches and the village, this comfortable farmhouse has lovely views. Some of the attractive bedrooms have jacuzzis, and there are farm walks and a garden with a tennis court. Breakfast and evening meal (by arrangement) include farm-grown products and home baking.

Facilities 5 en suite (2 fmly) ⊗ TVB tea/coffee ✻ Cen ht ⚲ Local leisure club available - rates negotiated Dinner Last d 3pm **LB Parking** 5

◆◆◆◆

GH Duvane

Ballyduvane ☎ 023 33129 📄 023 33129
e-mail www.duvanefarm@eir.com.net
Dir *2km SW from Clonakilty on N71*

This Georgian farmhouse is on the N71 Skibbereen road. Bedrooms are comfortable and include four-poster and brass beds. There is a lovely sitting room and dining room, and a wide choice is available at breakfast (dinner is available by arrangement). Local amenities include Blue Flag beaches, riding and golf.

Facilities 4 en suite (1 fmly) ⊗ TVB tea/coffee ✻ Cen ht TVL Fishing Pool Table ♨ Dinner Last d 4pm **Prices** S €45-€50; D €76-€80✳ **LB Notes** Closed Nov-Mar

◆◆◆◆ ♥

Kilkern House *(W 330342)*

Rathbarry ☎ 023 40643 📄 023 40643
Mrs O'Donovan
e-mail eleanorodonovan@eircom.net
Dir *Signed from N71, 3km west of Clonakilty*

The elevated position of Kilkern House provides superb views of Kilkern Lake and the sea from many of the comfortable rooms and breakfast room. Mrs Eleanor O'Donovan is always on hand to ensure a welcoming stay, and breakfast is a particular highlight.

Facilities 5 en suite ⊗ TVB tea/coffee ✻ Cen ht TVL ⚲ Fishing 120 acres **Parking** 5

◆◆◆◆ ♥

Springfield House *(W 330342)*

Kilkern, Rathbarry, Castlefreke
☎ 023 40622 📄 023 40622 Mr & Mrs Callanan
e-mail jandmcallanan@eircom.net
Dir *N71 from Clonakilty for Skibbereen, 0.5km left after Pike Bar & signed for 5km*

A Georgian-style farmhouse in a picturesque rural setting. Maureen and John Callanan are genuine and welcoming hosts, and their comfortable home has well-appointed bedrooms and lovely gardens. You are welcome to watch the cows being milked. Home cooking is a speciality, and dinner is available by arrangement.

Facilities 4 rms (3 en suite) (2 fmly) ⊗ TV3B ✻ Cen ht TVL 130 acres dairy/beef Dinner Last d 3pm **Parking** 8 **Notes** Closed 20-27 Dec

◆◆ ♥

Desert House ◇ *(W 390411)*

Coast Rd ☎ 023 33331 📄 023 33048 Mrs Jennings
e-mail deserthouse@eircom.net
Dir *1km E of Clonakilty. Signed on N71 at 1st rdbt, house 500 metres on left*

This comfortable Georgian farmhouse overlooks Clonakilty Bay and is within walking distance of the town. The estuary is of great interest to bird watching enthusiasts. It is a good base for touring west Cork and Kerry.

Facilities 5 rms (4 en suite) ⊗ in dining room ⊗ in lounges TVB tea/coffee Cen ht 100 acres dairy mixed **Prices** S €35-€40; D €60✳ **Parking** 10

COBH MAP 01 B2

◆◆◆◆

GH *Knockeven House*

Rushbrooke ☎ 021 4811778 📄 021 4811719
e-mail info@knockevenhouse.com
Dir *From N25 follow signs for Cobh. At Belvelly Bridge turn right, then left by garage and 1st right*

Set on an elevated site on the outskirts of Cobh, Knockeven House offers excellent standards of comfort and hospitality. The spacious rooms are carefully decorated and include many thoughtful extras. The lounge and dining rooms retain many original features and are relaxing.

Facilities 4 en suite ⊗ Direct dial from bedrooms ✻ Cen ht TVL **Parking** 10 **Notes** Closed Jan

CORK MAP 01 B2

Premier Collection

◆◆◆◆◆

GH Lancaster Lodge

Lancaster Quay, Western Rd
☎ 021 4251125 📄 021 4251126
e-mail info@lancasterlodge.com
Dir *By Jurys Hotel*

Situated just five minutes from the city centre, this modern guest house overlooks the River Lee. Public rooms include a spacious lounge and contemporary style restaurant. Bedrooms are spacious

continued

and feature an excellent range of facilites. Two ground-floor rooms have easier access. A wide choice is offered for breakfast.

Facilities 39 en suite (3 GF) ⊛ STV TVB tea/coffee Direct dial from bedrooms ✗ Lift Cen ht TVL **Prices** S € 90-€ 140; D € 120-€ 200 **Parking** 40 **Notes** Closed 22-26 Dec

GH Crawford House

Western Rd ☎ 021 4279000 🖹 021 4279927
e-mail info@crawfordguesthouse.com
Dir 0.8km from city on N22 Cork-Killarney road, opp University College

Two adjoining Victorian houses form this friendly guest house, close to the university and city centre. Refurbished in a contemporary style, the bedrooms have refreshing natural colour schemes. The attractive dining room and conservatory overlook a colourful patio. An interesting breakfast menu is available and there is ample secure parking.

Facilities 12 en suite (2 fmly) (1 GF) ⊛ STV TVB tea/coffee Direct dial from bedrooms ✗ Cen ht **Prices** S € 60-€ 120; D € 100-€ 120✱ **Parking** 12 **Notes** Closed 22 Dec-15 Jan

GH Garnish House

1 Aldergrove, Western Rd ☎ 021 4275111 🖹 021 4273872
e-mail garnish@iol.ie
Dir Opp Cork University College

A stay in Garnish House is memorable for its carefully appointed rooms, with an optional jacuzzi en suite, and the extensive breakfast menu. Only a 5-minute walk to the city centre, and convenient for the ferry and airport, the guest house has 24-hour reception for reservations, departures and late arrivals.

Facilities 13 en suite (4 fmly) (1 GF) ⊛ in 5 bedrooms ⊛ in dining room ⊛ in lounges STV TVB tea/coffee Direct dial from bedrooms ✗ Cen ht TVL No children No coaches **Prices** S € 70-€ 100; D € 110-€ 150 **Parking** 10

GH *Killarney Guest House*

Western Rd ☎ 021 4270290 🖹 021 4271010
e-mail killarneyhouse@iol.ie
Dir From N22 (Cork-Killarney), guest house opp University College

Mrs O'Leary is the welcoming owner of this well-equipped guest house, which stands near Cork University on the N22. The bedrooms all have televisions, telephones and tea and coffee facilities. A comfortable lounge is available, and there is parking to the rear of the house.

Facilities 19 en suite (3 fmly) ⊛ STV TVB tea/coffee Direct dial from bedrooms ✗ Cen ht TVL **Parking** 15 **Notes** Closed 24-26 Dec

GH *Lotamore House*

Tivoli ☎ 021 4822344 🖹 021 4822219
e-mail lotamore@iol.ie
Dir N8 Dublin-Cork, 1.5km from city pass Silversprings Hotel on left, continue on dual carriageway, house signed on left

An elegant Georgian residence, quietly set in 1.6 hectares on an imposing position overlooking Cork Harbour, just a short walk from the Jack Lynch Lee Tunnel and city centre. Public areas are inviting, with gracious reception rooms. The spacious bedrooms are comfortable and well equipped with modern facilities, many having fine views.

Facilities 18 en suite (2 fmly) (6 GF) ⊛ STV TVB Direct dial from bedrooms Cen ht **Conf** Max 40 Thtr 40 Class 25 Board 20 **Parking** 25 **Notes** Closed 21 Dec-6 Jan

♦♦♦

GH Abbeypoint House

Western Rd ☎ 021 4275526 & 4274091 🖹 021 4251955
e-mail info@abbeypoint.com
Dir From city centre on Washington St, pass Jury's Hotel, Western Rd on left. Over lights at UCC Gates, Abbeypoint on right

A Victorian red-brick house, located opposite the University College Cork and within walking distance of the city centre. Bedrooms vary in size, and all are well equipped. There is a set-down arrivals area at the front of the house and lock-up parking at the rear.

Facilities 8 en suite (5 fmly) ⊛ TVB tea/coffee Direct dial from bedrooms ✗ Cen ht TVL No coaches **Parking** 10 **Notes** Closed 23 Dec-2 Jan

Ireland

CORK continued

◆◆◆
GH Rose Lodge
Mardyke Walk, off Western Rd
☎ 021 4272958 📠 021 4274087
e-mail info@roselodge.net
Dir N22 from city centre, pass Jurys Hotel on left, right at University College gates, right again, Lodge on right

This family-run guest house is close to UCC and just a 10-minute walk from the city centre. The en suite bedrooms are well appointed, and there is a comfortable sitting room and an attractive breakfast room. Limited off-road parking is available.

Facilities 16 en suite (4 fmly) ⊗ in dining room ⊗ in lounges STV TVB tea/coffee Direct dial from bedrooms ✖ Cen ht TVL **Parking** 8

FERMOY   MAP 01 B2

Premier Collection

◆◆◆◆◆
T&C Ballyvolane House
Castlelyons ☎ 025 36349 📠 025 36781
e-mail info@ballyvolanehouse.ie
Dir N8 onto R628 & signed

An Italianate country house, originally built in 1728, which has a magnificent setting in parkland and well-known gardens (open to the public in May). The Greens are exceptionally friendly hosts. Public areas are spacious, and bedrooms are comfortable. Dinner is served around a fine table. There are three lakes, one stocked with brown trout.

Facilities 6 en suite ⊗ TVB tea/coffee ✖ Licensed Cen ht Fishing ◖ Dinner Last d noon **Prices** S € 125-€ 130; D € 160-€ 200 **Conf** Max 14 Thtr 14 Class 14 Board 14 Del from € 180 ✴ **Parking** 25 **Notes** Closed 23-31 Dec

GOLEEN   MAP 01 A1

◆◆◆◆
T&C Carraig-Mor House
Toormore Bay ☎ 028 28410 📠 028 28410
e-mail carraigmorhouse@eircom.net
Dir From Cork N71 to Ballydehob & R592 to Schull & onto Toormore, Carraig-Mor 2nd house on right past Altar Church

Situated on the West Cork coast between Schull and Goleen. Attractively decorated and offers comfortable bedrooms and a conservatory lounge where guests can relax and enjoy the views across Toormore Bay. Fresh local ingredients feature at breakfast and packed lunches can be provided. A 24-hour mini bus service is available for airport, ferry or pub collection. Off-season painting weekends with artist Dor Sievers can be arranged.

Facilities 5 en suite (2 fmly) ⊗ TVB tea/coffee ✖ Cen ht TVL No children 6yrs Dinner Last d noon **Parking** 8 **Notes** Closed 24-26 Dec

◆◆◆◆ 🛥
T&C Heron's Cove
The Harbour ☎ 028 35225 📠 028 35422
e-mail suehill@eircom.net
Dir By harbour in Goleen

There are charming views of the harbour, fast-flowing steam and inland hills from Hearn's Cove, at Ireland's most south-westerly point, near Mizen Head. The restaurant and wine bar is run by chef-patron Sue Hill, where the freshest fish and local produce feature. Bedrooms are comfortable, some with balconies overlooking the harbour.

Facilities 5 en suite (2 fmly) ⊗ STV TVB tea/coffee Direct dial from bedrooms ✖ Licensed Cen ht No coaches Dinner Last d 9.30pm **Prices** d fr € 80 **Parking** 10 **Notes** Closed Xmas & New Year

See advertisement on opposite page

KINSALE   MAP 01 B2

Premier Collection

◆◆◆◆◆
GH *Old Bank House*
11 Pearse St ☎ 021 4774075 📠 021 4774296
e-mail info@oldbankhousekinsale.com
Dir On main road into Kinsale from Cork Airport (R600). House on right at start of Kinsale, next to Post Office

Under the personal supervision of Marie and Michael Riese, this delightful Georgian house has been restored to its former elegance. The en suite bedrooms, with period furniture and attractive decor, combine charm with modern comforts. Sailing, deep sea fishing and horse riding can be arranged. Irish, French and German spoken.

Facilities 17 en suite (2 fmly) ⊗ STV TVB Direct dial from bedrooms ✖ Licensed Lift Cen ht No coaches **Notes** Closed Dec-27 Mar

Premier Collection

◆◆◆◆◆
GH Perryville House
☎ 021 4772731 📠 021 4772298
e-mail sales@perryville.iol.ie

This elegant Georgian house in the centre of the town offers spacious, well-equipped accommodation. The comfortable drawing rooms are carefully decorated and the buffet breakfast is a highlight of the Perryville experience. A non-smoking property.

Facilities 26 en suite ⊗ TV available Direct dial from bedrooms ✖ No children 12yrs No coaches **Prices** D fr € 255 **Parking** 10 **Notes** Closed Nov-Apr

◆◆◆◆
T&C *Rivermount House*

Knocknabinny, Barrells Cross
☎ 021 4778033 📠 021 4778225
e-mail rivermnt@iol.ie
Dir *3km from Kinsale. R600 W towards Old Head of Kinsale, right at Barrels Cross*

This charming house is surrounded by lovely gardens, a patio and a children's play area. Attractive bedrooms are well equipped and furnished to a high standard, and there is a fine, large sitting room with a sun lounge. Light meals and packed lunches can be provided on request. The house overlooks the River Bandon, near a superbly sited new golf course, the Old Head Golf Links. Sea angling and bicycle hire can be arranged.

Facilities 6 en suite (3 fmly) (2 GF) ⊗ TVB tea/coffee Direct dial from bedrooms 🐾 Cen ht TVL No coaches **Parking** 10 **Notes** Closed Dec-Jan

◆◆◆◆
T&C Chart House Luxury Accommodation

6 Denis Quay ☎ 021 4774568 📠 021 4777907
e-mail charthouse@eircom.net
Dir *Off Pier Rd between Actons & Trident hotels onto Denis Quay, last house on right*

This 1790 Georgian house was once a sea captain's residence. It has been lovingly restored and the comfortable bedrooms are furnished with period pieces, while two have jacuzzis. There is a cosy lobby lounge and a dining room where Mary O'Connor serves delicious breakfasts, including home-made breads. Afternoon tea and coffee are served on arrival. Being in a gourmet capital, dinner reservations can be arranged and golfing and touring trips organised.

Facilities 3 en suite ⊗ STV TVB Direct dial from bedrooms 🐾 Cen ht No children **Prices** D € 110-€ 170✲ **Notes** Closed Xmas

◆◆◆◆
GH Friar's Lodge

5 Friars St
☎ 086 289 5075 & 021 4777384 📠 021 4774363
e-mail mtierney@indigo.ie
Dir *In town centre next to parish church*

This new, purpose built property near the Friary, has been developed with every comfort in mind. Located on a quiet street with parking to the rear. A very good choice is offered from the breakfast menu.

Facilities 18 en suite (2 fmly) (4 GF) ⊗ in 4 bedrooms ⊗ in dining room ⊗ in lounges STV TV available tea/coffee Direct dial from bedrooms Licensed Lift Cen ht **Prices** S € 60-€ 80; D €90-€ 140 **Parking** 20 **Notes** Closed Xmas

◆◆◆◆ 🛏
GH Harbour Lodge

Scilly ☎ 021 4772376 📠 021 4772675
e-mail relax@harbourlodge.com
Dir *Enter Kinsale on R600. Take 1st left to Scilly. At Spaniard Bar turn right, follow road towards coast*

This well-appointed house has superb views of Kinsale harbour and marina. Hospitality is excellent and breakfast is a particular treat with locally made herb sausages and homemade preserves. Your host, Raoul, also runs a popular restaurant in the town.

Facilities 9 en suite (9 fmly) (4 GF) ⊗ STV TVB Direct dial from bedrooms 🐾 Licensed Cen ht TVL Dinner Last d noon **Prices** S € 120; D € 165-€ 240✲ **LB Parking** 9

◆◆◆◆
GH Long Quay House

Long Quay ☎ 021 4774563 & 4773201 📠 021 4774563
e-mail longquayhouse@eircom.net
Dir *On right after entering town centre from R600, before Super Valu supermarket. House covered in Virginia Creeper*

Centrally located overlooking the inner harbour and yacht marina, Long Quay House is a restored Georgian house with very comfortable bedrooms and a large conservatory lounge. Local amenities include sailing, fishing, golf and sandy beaches.

Facilities 8 en suite (2 fmly) (1 GF) ⊗ TVB Direct dial from bedrooms 🐾 Cen ht TVL No coaches **Prices** S € 50-€ 85; D € 70-€ 130✲ **Notes** Closed 15 Nov-26 Dec

Ireland

KINSALE continued

◆◆◆◆

T&C The Old Presbytery

43 Cork St ☎ 021 4772027 🖷 021 4772166
e-mail info@oldpres.com
Dir *From Cork Rd to end of Pearse St, turn left, 1st right & 1st right again, establishment on right opp parish church*

This charming house, situated on a quiet street in the centre of the town, offers an elegant lounge and a delightful breakfast room. Bedrooms are traditional, with pine furnishings, brass beds and interesting memorabilia. One bedroom has external access via a staircase and is very peaceful. Sailing and sea fishing are available and there are plenty of excellent restaurants nearby. Booking is advised.
Facilities 6 en suite (1 fmly) (1 GF) ⊘ STV TVB tea/coffee Direct dial from bedrooms ✕ Cen ht TVL No coaches **Prices** S €70-€ 120; D €90-€ 160✳ **Parking** 6 **Notes** Closed Dec-14 Feb

◆◆◆◆

T&C Waterlands

Cork Rd ☎ 021 4772318 & 087 2767917 🖷 021 4774873
e-mail info@collinsbb.com
Dir *R600 to Kinsale, turn off at Welcome to Kinsale sign, Waterlands signed, turn right, house 140 metres*

This house, located on an elevated position, provides luxury accommodation. A south-facing conservatory breakfast room overlooks the picturesque gardens and offers an extensive breakfast menu. The comfortable, well-decorated en suite bedrooms have electric blankets, hairdryers and clock radios.
Facilities 4 en suite (2 fmly) ⊘ TVB tea/coffee ✕ Cen ht TVL No coaches **Prices** S €50-€60; D €64-€76 **Parking** 10 **Notes** Closed Dec-Feb

◆◆◆◆

GH Woodlands House B&B

Cappagh ☎ 021 4772633 🖷 021 4772649
e-mail info@woodlandskinsale.com
Dir *R605 NW from Kinsale, pass St Multoses Church, 0.5km on left*

Situated on a height overlooking the town, about a 10-minute walk away on the Bandon road, this new house offers great comfort and the personal attention of Veronica & Brian Hosford. Rooms are individually decorated, some with views towards the harbour. Breakfast is a particular pleasure, featuring home-made breads and preserves.
Facilities 6 en suite (1 fmly) (2 GF) ⊘ TVB tea/coffee Direct dial from bedrooms ✕ Cen ht TVL **Prices** S €50-€80; D €70-€ 100 **Parking** 8 **Notes** Closed 16 Nov-Feb

◆◆◆

GH The White House

Pearse St, The Glen ☎ 021 4772125 🖷 021 4772045
e-mail whitehse@indigo.ie
Dir *In town centre*

Centrally located among the narrow, twisting streets of Kinsale, this guest house dates from 1850. A welcoming hostelry with a

continued

comfortable bar, a choice of bistro or restaurant for dining, and a convenient car park at the rear.
Facilities 10 en suite (2 fmly) ⊘ STV TVB tea/coffee Direct dial from bedrooms ✕ Licensed Cen ht Dinner Last d 10pm **Prices** S €55-€95; D € 100-€ 150✳ **LB Notes** Closed 24-25 Dec

MALLOW MAP 01 B2

◆◆◆◆

T&C Greenfield House

Navigation Rd ☎ 022 50231 & 08723 63535
e-mail greenfieldhouse@hotmail.com
Dir *N20 at Mallow rdbt onto N72 Killarney road, last house 300 metres on left*

A purpose-built house, designed and furnished to the highest standards. Large, airy rooms look out over open country and all are luxuriously appointed with quality en suite facilities. Situated within walking distance of the town centre, station and Cork Racecourse. Parking facilities.
Facilities 6 en suite (3 fmly) (3 GF) ⊘ STV TVB tea/coffee ✕ Cen ht TVL **Parking** 10

◆◆◆◆

T&C *Oaklands House*

Springwood, Killarney Rd ☎ 022 21127 🖷 022 21127
e-mail oaklands@eircom.net
Dir *Off N72 Killarney road at railway bridge, signed*

Situated in a quiet residential area on the edge of town, Winifred O'Donovan's home is inviting and attractively decorated throughout. The atmosphere is particularly tranquil, with a dining room overlooking the lovely gardens where guests can enjoy Winifred's cooking. The dining room has recently been extended to provide a conservatory where breakfast is served
Facilities 4 en suite (1 fmly) ⊘ STV TVB tea/coffee ✕ Cen ht TVL **Parking** 6 **Notes** Closed Nov-Mar

SCHULL MAP 01 B1

Premier Collection

◆◆◆◆◆

T&C *Rock Cottage*

Barnatonicane ☎ 028 35538 🖷 028 35538
e-mail rockcottage@eircom.net
Dir *9.5km from Schull towards Goleen, at Toormore onto R591, 2.5km entrance on left*

This Georgian hunting lodge, built on the edge of Dunmanus Bay and stands in 7 hectares of grounds. It offers comfort, style and quality and a friendly welcome. The food is good, (breakfast is a real feast) and the inviting bedrooms are comfortable. Sitting on the terrace, overlooking the fields and farm animals is most relaxing.
Facilities 3 en suite (2 fmly) ⊘ in bedrooms ⊘ in dining room TVB tea/coffee ✕ Licensed Cen ht TVL No children 10yrs No coaches Dinner Last d 24hrs prior **Parking** 10

SHANAGARRY
MAP 01 C2

Premier Collection

♦♦♦♦♦

GH Ballymaloe House

☎ 021 4652531 🖷 021 4652021
e-mail res@ballymaloe.ie
Dir *On L35 from Midleton, 3km beyond Cloyne on Ballycotton road*

This charming country house is on a 162-hectare farm, part of the Geraldine estate. Bedrooms range from one within the old castle walls, to some in the main house and yet more in the courtyard buildings. All are well appointed to high standards. Much of the food on offer in the restaurant is produced on the farm. There is a craft shop on the estate.

Facilities 22 en suite 10 annexe en suite (2 fmly) (3 GF) ⊗ Direct dial from bedrooms 🛏 Licensed Cen ht TVL ⚓ Golf 7 ⚒ ⚐ Children's sand pit Dinner Last d 9pm **Prices** S €120-€175; D €210-€300 ✳ **LB**
Conf Max 25 Thtr 25 Class 25 Board 12 Del from €100 ✳ **Parking** 30
Notes Closed 23-26 Dec

SKIBBEREEN
MAP 01 B2

♦♦♦

T&C Ilenroy House ◇

10 North St ☎ 028 22751 & 22193 🖷 028 23228
e-mail ilenroyhouse@oceanfree.net
Dir *90 metres from main street on N71 Clonakilty road*

Conveniently situated in the centre of Skibbereen town this well maintained house has comfortable bedrooms that are equipped to a high standard. This is an excellent base from which to tour South West Cork and the Islands.

Facilities 5 en suite ⊗ in dining room STV TVB tea/coffee Direct dial from bedrooms 🛏 Cen ht **Prices** S €35-€50; D €60-€70 ✳

YOUGHAL
MAP 01 C2

Premier Collection

♦♦♦♦♦

GH *Ahernes*

163 North Main St ☎ 024 92424 🖷 024 92733
e-mail ahernes@eircom.net

In the same family since 1923, Ahernes offers a warm welcome, with turf fires and a traditional atmosphere. Spacious bedrooms are furnished to the highest standard and include antiques and modern facilities. There is a restaurant, well known for its daily-changing menu of the freshest seafood specialities, in addition to a cosy drawing room.

Facilities 13 en suite (2 fmly) (3 GF) ⊗ TVB Direct dial from bedrooms 🛏 Licensed Cen ht Dinner Last d 9.30pm **Conf** Max 20 Thtr 20 Class 20 Board 12 **Parking** 20 **Notes** Closed 23-29 Dec

---

CO DONEGAL

BALLYSHANNON
MAP 01 B5

♦♦♦♦

GH Dún Na Sí

Bundoran Rd ☎ 071 985 2322
e-mail dun-na-si@oceanfree.net
Dir *0.4km from Ballyshannon on N50 Bundoran road, next to Donegal Parian China showrooms*

A smart purpose-built guest house set back from the road and within walking distance of the town. The spacious bedrooms are comfortable and well equipped, and one of the two ground-floor rooms is suitable for the less mobile.

Facilities 7 en suite (2 fmly) (2 GF) ⊗ STV TVB tea/coffee Direct dial from bedrooms 🛏 Cen ht **Prices** S €40-€45; D €64-€70 ✳
Parking 15

CARRIGANS
MAP 01 C5

♦♦♦♦

T&C Mount Royd Country Home

☎ 074 914 0163 🖷 074 914 0400
e-mail jmartin@mountroyd.com
Dir *Off N14 onto R236*

Set in lovely mature gardens in the pretty village and 6km from Derry, the Mount Royd is an attractive creeper-clad house. The River Foyle runs along the back boundary. The friendly Martins have brought hospitality to new heights - nothing is too much trouble for them. Breakfast is a feast of choices. Bedrooms are very comfortable, with lots of personal touches.

Facilities 4 en suite (1 fmly) (1 GF) ⊗ STV TVB tea/coffee 🛏 Cen ht TVL No children 12yrs **Parking** 7 **Notes** Closed Jan rs Nov-Feb ⊛

DONEGAL
MAP 01 B5

♦♦♦♦

GH The Arches Country House

Lough Eske ☎ 074 972 2029 🖷 074 972 2029
e-mail archescountryhse@eircom.net
Dir *5km from Donegal. Signed off N15, 300 metres from garage,*

Located on an elevated site overlooking Lough Eske, this fine house is set amid beautifully manicured lawns. Each of the bedrooms shares the spectacular view, as do the breakfast room and comfortable lounge. A warm welcome is assured from the McGinty family.

Facilities 6 en suite (3 fmly) (2 GF) ⊗ TVB tea/coffee 🛏 Cen ht TVL **Prices** S €45-€50; D €60-€65 ✳ **Parking** 10

Ireland

DONEGAL continued

♦♦♦♦

T&C Ardeevin ◇

Lough Eske, Barnesmore ☎ 074 972 1790 📠 074 972 1790
e-mail seanmcginty@eircom.net
Dir N15 Derry road from Donegal for 5km, left at junction after garage for Ardeevin & Lough Eske & signs for Ardeevin

This homely house has a lovely location high above Lough Eske and with superb views of lake and mountain. Well-appointed bedrooms have en suite facilities.

Facilities 6 en suite (2 fmly) (2 GF) ⊘ STV FTV TVB tea/coffee ✱ Cen ht TVL No children 9yrs **Prices** S €42-€45; D €65-€70 **Parking** 10 **Notes** Closed Dec-mid Mar ⊛

♦♦♦♦

GH Ard Na Breatha

Drumrooske Middle
☎ 074 972 2288 & 086 842 1330 📠 074 974 0720
e-mail info@ardnabreatha.com
Dir From town centre onto Killybegs road, 2nd right, sharp right after shop

This new, family-run guest house is just a short drive from the town centre. Bedrooms are all well-appointed and very comfortable, with plans for an additional lounge under way. Evening meals are served in the popular restaurant at weekends and during high season, but can be arranged for residents at other times.

Facilities 6 en suite (1 fmly) (3 GF) ⊘ TVB tea/coffee Direct dial from bedrooms Licensed Cen ht Dinner Last d 9.30pm **Conf** Thtr 30 Class 40 Board 20 Del from €90 ✳ **Parking** 16 **Notes** Closed 24-27 Dec, 13 Jan-13 Feb

LETTERKENNY   MAP 01 C5

♦♦♦♦

GH *Ballyraine Guest House*

Ramelton Rd ☎ 074 912 4460 & 912 0851 📠 074 912 0851
e-mail ballyraineguesthouse@eircom.net
Dir N13 onto R245

This purpose-built guest house, 5km from the town centre, is well located for touring the Fanad and Inishowen Peninsula. Bedrooms are spacious and pleasantly decorated, some are suitable for families. There is a comfortable lounge and an attractive breakfast room.

Facilities 8 en suite (1 fmly) (2 GF) ⊘ STV TVB tea/coffee Direct dial from bedrooms ✱ Cen ht TVL **Parking** 12

♦♦♦

GH *Larkfield B&B*

Drumnahoe ☎ 074 912 1478 & 086 0621263
e-mail philomena21478@hotmail.com
Dir 1st left past Clanree Hotel. Signed N13 towards Letterkenny

This house offers quite and comfortable accommodation on the outskirts of Letterkenny. Mrs McDaid is a welcoming host and can advise on places to visit and restaurants for enjoyable evening meals. A good base for touring the Giant's Causeway and Glenveagh National Park.

Facilities 3 rms (2 en suite) (1 fmly) (3 GF) ⊘ TVB tea/coffee ✱ Cen ht TVL No coaches **Parking** 4 **Notes** Closed 21 Dec-2 Jan

CO DUBLIN

DUBLIN   MAP 01 D4
See also **Howth**

Premier Collection

♦♦♦♦♦

GH Aberdeen Lodge

53 Park Av, Ballsbridge ☎ 01 2838155 📠 01 2837877
e-mail aberdeen@iol.ie
Dir From city centre onto Merrion road towards Sydney Parade Dart station, 1st left onto Park Av

This particularly fine early Edwardian house stands on one of Dublin's most prestigious roads near to the Embassy suburb and DART or bus

continued

Ireland

to accesses the city centre. Bedrooms are very well equipped, some with four-poster beds, and there is a relaxing comfortable lounge and the breakfast room has lovely views of the colourful garden.

Facilities 16 en suite (8 fmly) ⊗ STV TVB tea/coffee Direct dial from bedrooms ✗ Licensed Cen ht **Prices** S €90-€ 120; D €120-€ 160 LB **Conf** Max 50 Thtr 50 Class 40 Board 40 **Parking** 16

◆◆◆◆◆

GH *Brownes Hotel*

22 St Stephen's Green ☎ 01 6383939 📄 01 6383900
e-mail info@brownesdublin.com
Dir N side of St Stephen's Green, beside Shelbourne Hotel

Situated overlooking St Stephen's Green, in the heart of the city this 18th-century Georgian house offers bedrooms that are decorated and furnished with comfort and luxury in mind. Browns Brasserie serves continental cuisine with emphasis on Irish beef and seafood. There is a private dining room and conference room, parking is available in near by car parks.

Facilities 11 en suite (1 fmly) ⊗ in 8 bedrooms ⊗ in dining room ⊗ in lounges STV TVB Direct dial from bedrooms ✗ Licensed Lift Cen ht No coaches Dinner Last d 10.30pm **Conf** Max 60 Thtr 60 Class 44 Board 25

◆◆◆◆◆

GH Blakes Townhouse

50 Merrion Rd, Ballsbridge ☎ 01 6688324 📄 01 6684280
e-mail blakestownhouse@iol.ie
Dir Merrion Rd S to Ballsbridge, Blakes opp RDS Convention Centre

This luxurious house has been refurbished to a very high standard. Some of the spacious, air-conditioned bedrooms have four-poster beds, others have balconies overlooking the gardens, plus all the expected facilities. Parking available.

Facilities 13 en suite (1 fmly) ⊗ STV TVB tea/coffee Direct dial from bedrooms ✗ Licensed Cen ht No coaches **Prices** S €90-€ 120; D €120-€ 160✳ LB **Parking** 6

◆◆◆◆◆

GH Glenogra

64 Merrion Rd, Ballsbridge ☎ 01 6683661 📄 01 6683698
e-mail info@glenogra.com
Dir Opp Royal Dublin Showgrounds & Four Seasons Hotel

This fine brick house is situated in the pleasant suburb of Ballsbridge opposite the RDS and close to the city centre. Bedrooms are comfortably appointed with many thoughtful extras. There is an elegant drawing room and dining room with a rear garden where there is limited parking.

Facilities 13 en suite (1 fmly) ⊗ STV TVB tea/coffee Direct dial from bedrooms ✗ Cen ht TVL No coaches **Prices** S €79-€ 99; D € 109-€ 139✳ LB **Parking** 10 **Notes** Closed 21 Dec-5 Jan

◆◆◆◆◆

GH Harrington Hall

69-70 Harcourt St ☎ 01 4753497 📄 01 4754544
e-mail harringtonhall@eircom.net
web www.harringtonhall.com
Dir St Stephens Green via O Connell St, in Earlsfort Ter pass National Concert Hall & right onto Hatch St, right onto Harcourt St

The restored Georgian house is on a one-way street, adjoining St Stephen's Green in the centre of the city. The spacious bedrooms and bathrooms are very comfortable and include two junior suites with galleried bedroom areas, and a full suite. A lovely plasterwork ceiling adorns the luxurious dining room. Elevator, porter service and parking.

Facilities 28 en suite (3 fmly) (3 GF) ⊗ STV TVB tea/coffee Direct dial from bedrooms ✗ Licensed Lift Cen ht **Conf** Max 20 Thtr 20 Class 6 Board 12 **Parking** 8

Ireland

DUBLIN continued

Premier Collection

♦♦♦♦♦
GH Merrion Hall
54-56 Merrion Rd, Ballsbridge
☎ 01 6681426 📠 01 6684280
e-mail merrionhall@iol.ie
Dir From city centre towards Dun Laoghaire Port, Ballsbridge 1.6km on main route, premises between British & US embassies

This elegant house in Ballsbridge is convenient to Royal Dublin Society and Lansdowne Rd Stadium. Reception rooms are spacious, and the breakfast room overlooks the gardens. The air-conditioned bedrooms are well appointed and some rooms have balconies. Limited off-road parking is available.

Facilities 28 en suite (4 fmly) (4 GF) ⊘ STV TVB tea/coffee Direct dial from bedrooms ⚓ Licensed Lift Cen ht **Prices** S €90-€120; D €120-€160 **LB Conf** Max 50 Thtr 50 Class 40 Board 40 Del from €149 ✳ **Parking** 10

Premier Collection

♦♦♦♦♦
GH Pembroke Town House
90 Pembroke Rd, Ballsbridge
☎ 01 6600277 📠 01 6600291
e-mail info@pembroketownhouse.ie
Dir After Trinity College onto Nassan St & Northumberland Rd, onto lane to right of service station before lights, house 200 metres on left

Close to the city centre, three Georgian houses have been converted to make a comfortable guest house. The marble-tiled foyer, inviting lounge, and the friendly and attentive staff all combine to provide a welcoming atmosphere. The well-appointed bedrooms vary in style and some have a mezzanine. Secure parking is available behind the house.

Facilities 48 en suite (4 fmly) (10 GF) ⊘ in 30 bedrooms ⊘ in dining room ⊘ in lounges TVB tea/coffee Direct dial from bedrooms ⚓ Licensed Lift Cen ht TVL **Prices** S €165; D €260 **LB Conf** Max 10 Board 10 **Parking** 20 **Notes** Closed 22 Dec-2 Jan

Book as early as possible, particularly in the peak holiday period

♦♦♦♦
GH *Raglan Lodge*
10 Raglan Rd, Ballsbridge ☎ 01 6606697 📠 01 6606781
Dir From city centre, at American Embassy left onto Elgin Rd, left at rdbt onto Raglan Rd

A charming Victorian lodge, dating from 1861, situated on a tree-lined residential road in the suburb of Ballsbridge, close to the US Embassy, the RDS centre and with easy access to the city centre. Owner Helen Moran puts great effort into ensuring guest comfort. The elegant drawing room invites relaxation around the fire, while breakfast is served in the cosy dining room. The bedrooms are spacious and well equipped.

Facilities 7 en suite (4 fmly) ⊘ in 4 bedrooms ⊘ in dining room STV TVB tea/coffee Direct dial from bedrooms Cen ht TVL No coaches **Parking** 12 **Notes** Closed 20 Dec-6 Jan, Etr week, last week Oct

♦♦♦♦
GH *Abrae Court*
9 Zion Rd, Rathgar ☎ 01 4922242 📠 01 4923944
e-mail abrae@eircom.net
Dir Junct Orwell Rd & Rathgar Rd

Abrae Court is a redbrick Victorian house built in 1864. It combines original features with modern comforts. The bedrooms are attractively decorated and well appointed, and there is a spacious guest sitting room with an open fire.

Facilities 14 en suite (2 fmly) ⊘ in 9 bedrooms ⊘ in dining room ⊘ in lounges STV TVB tea/coffee Direct dial from bedrooms ⚓ Cen ht Sightseeing tours available **Parking** 9

♦♦♦♦
GH Charleville Lodge
268/272 North Circular Rd, Phibsborough
☎ 01 8386633 📠 01 8385854
e-mail info@charlevillelodge.ie
web www.charlevillelodge.ie
Dir N from O Connell St to Phibsborough, left fork at St Peter's Church, guest house 250 metres on left

Situated close to the city centre near Phoenix Park, this elegant terrace of Victorian houses has been restored to a high standard. The two interconnecting lounges are welcoming and the smart dining room offers a choice of breakfasts. Bedrooms are very comfortable with pleasant decor, and there is a secure car park.

Facilities 30 en suite (2 fmly) (4 GF) ⊘ in 20 bedrooms ⊘ in dining room ⊘ in lounges STV TVB Direct dial from bedrooms ⚓ Cen ht TVL **LB Conf** Max 20 Thtr 20 Class 20 Board 20 **Parking** 18 **Notes** Closed 21-26 Dec

◆◆◆◆
GH *Eliza Lodge*

23/24 Wellington Quay, Temple Bar
☎ 01 6718044 📠 01 6718362
e-mail info@dublinlodge.com

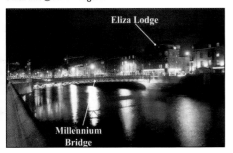

Very smart accommodation in a completely refurbished building situated at the foot of the Millennium Bridge. Inviting, comfortable bedrooms are well equipped, and there is a lounge with a hospitality centre, and a fully licensed restaurant.

Facilities 18 en suite (2 fmly) ⊗ STV TVB tea/coffee Direct dial from bedrooms ✗ Licensed Lift Cen ht TVL **Notes** Closed 23 Dec-2 Jan

◆◆◆◆
GH Glenshandan Lodge ◇

Dublin Rd, Swords ☎ 01 8408838 📠 01 8408838
e-mail glenshandan@eircom.net

Family and dog-friendly house, where the hospitable owners are attentive and offer good facilities including e-mail access. Bedrooms are comfortable and one room has easier access. Secure parking available. Close to pubs, restaurants, golf, airport and the Kennel Club.

Facilities 9 en suite (5 fmly) (5 GF) ⊗ in 8 bedrooms ⊗ in dining room TVB tea/coffee Cen ht TVL ch fac **Prices** S € 25-€ 65; D € 70-€ 90 **LB Conf** Max 20 **Parking** 10 **Notes** Closed Xmas/New Year

◆◆◆◆
GH Kilronan House

70 Adelaide Rd ☎ 01 4755266 📠 01 4782841
e-mail info@dublinn.com
Dir Next to National Concert Hall, Conrad Hotel, Eye & Ear Hospital

Located a 5-minute walk from St Stephen's Green, this fine house has comfortable well-equipped rooms that vary in size. The smart breakfast room is personally overseen by the hospitable Terry Masterson. Limited secure parking is available.

Facilities 12 en suite (1 fmly) ⊗ TVB tea/coffee Direct dial from bedrooms ✗ Cen ht TVL **Parking** 8

◆◆◆◆
GH Trinity Lodge

12 South Frederick St ☎ 01 6170900 📠 01 6170999
e-mail trinitylodge@eircom.net
Dir From N end of Grafton St onto Nassau St, pass Dawson St, next right

This listed Georgian house has been restored and converted to provide excellent accommodation right in the heart of the city centre. Bedrooms are beautifully appointed to a high standard with many thoughtful extras including a personal safe. Close to Trinity College and main shopping area.

Facilities 16 en suite (5 fmly) (1 GF) ⊗ STV TVB tea/coffee Direct dial from bedrooms ✗ Cen ht No coaches **Prices** S € 120-€ 150; D € 160-€ 250✳ **Notes** Closed 22-28 Dec

◆◆◆
T&C *Aran House*

5 Home Farm Rd, Drumcondra
☎ 01 8367395 📠 01 8367395
e-mail aranhouse@eircom.net
Dir From city centre towards airport/Drumcondra road. Past St Patrick's College and Cat & Cage pub. 1st left after Skylon Hotel

This comfortable, red-brick terrace house is just off the main airport road close to pubs and on a bus route to the city centre. The attractive dining room is an appropriate setting for delicious breakfasts and there is a cosy guest sitting room.

Facilities 4 en suite (2 fmly) ⊗ TVB tea/coffee Cen ht TVL **Notes** Closed Nov-Feb ⊛

If the freedom to smoke or be in a non-smoking atmosphere is important to you, check the rules when you book

Ireland

Ireland

DUBLIN continued

♦♦♦

GH Ardagh House

1 Highfield Rd, Rathgar ☎ 01 4977068 🖹 01 4973991
e-mail enquiries@ardagh-house.ie
Dir S of city centre through Rathmines

Ardagh House has been refurbished and upgraded by Mary and Willie Doyle, and some of the comfortable, airy en suite rooms look over the attractive rear garden.

Facilities 19 en suite (4 fmly) (1 GF) ⊛ STV TVB tea/coffee Direct dial from bedrooms ✝ Cen ht TVL Discounted rates at local leisure centre
Prices S €60-€90; D €90-€140 **Parking** 20 **Notes** Closed 22 Dec-3 Jan

♦♦♦

T&C Clifden Guest House

32 Gardiner Pl ☎ 01 8746364 🖹 01 8746122
e-mail bnb@indigo.ie
Dir From N end of O'Connell St, around 3 sides of Parnell Sq, exit at church onto Gardiner Row, through lights. House 4th on right

This city centre house is just a short walk from O'Connell St, and close to amenities. Facilities include a comfortable sitting room, cheerfully appointed breakfast room and a car park at the rear of the house.

Facilities 14 en suite (4 fmly) ⊛ in dining room ⊛ in lounges STV TVB tea/coffee Direct dial from bedrooms ✝ Cen ht TVL No coaches
Parking 12

♦♦♦

T&C Pairc na Bhfuiseog

55 Lorcan Crescent, Santry ☎ 01 8421318 🖹 01 8421318
e-mail rpjd@eircom.net
Dir N1 Dublin Airport, Swords Rd to Santry, over flyover, sharp left at rdbt, to top of road. Right onto Lorcan Crescent

An extended, modern semi-detached house, very nicely appointed throughout, with excellent en suite facilities. Convenient for Dublin Airport, ferries and city centre. The owners Ronald and Colette Downey provide a homely atmosphere and lots of local information.

Facilities 4 rms (3 en suite) (1 fmly) (1 GF) ⊛ STV TVB ✝ Cen ht No coaches **Parking** 4 **Notes** Closed 21 Dec-1 Jan

♦♦♦

GH St Aiden's Guesthouse

32 Brighton Rd, Rathgar
☎ 01 4902011 & 4906178 🖹 01 4920234
e-mail staidens@eircom.net
Dir M50 junct 11, towards city centre, premises 3rd left after lights in Terenure

A fine Victorian house situated in a residential tree-lined road just 15 minutes from the city centre. The well-proportioned reception rooms are comfortable and relaxing, and a hospitality trolley is available. Bedrooms vary from spacious family rooms to snug singles, and all have modern comforts.

Facilities 8 en suite (2 fmly) ⊛ STV TVB tea/coffee Direct dial from bedrooms ✝ Cen ht ch fac **Parking** 4

♦♦

GH Antrim Arms Guest House

27 Upper Drumcondra Rd ☎ 01 8375356 🖹 01 8378769
e-mail info@antrimarmsguesthouse.com
Dir N1 to Dublin city, at the end of N1, after 1.6km onto Drumcondra Rd, house next to Skylon Hotel

This fine, detached house is a 10-minute drive from Dublin Airport, the ferry port and the city centre. The attractive bedrooms, which vary in size, include some large family rooms and one room adapted for easier access. There is also a comfortable lounge and a dining room.

Facilities 24 en suite (3 fmly) (3 GF) ⊛ in 6 bedrooms ⊛ in dining room ⊛ in lounges TVB tea/coffee Cen ht TVL No children 16yrs
Parking 17 **Notes** Closed 22 Dec-3 Jan

GH Butlers Town House

44 Lansdowne Rd, Ballsbridge
☎ 01 6674022 🖹 01 6673960
e-mail info@butlers-hotel.com

At the time of going to press the rating for this establishment had not been confirmed. Please check the AA website www.theAA.com for up-to-date information.

Facilities 20 en suite ⊛ in bedrooms ⊛ in dining room ⊛ in lounges STV TVB Direct dial from bedrooms ✝ Licensed No coaches
Parking 14 **Notes** Closed 22 Dec-8 Jan

HOWTH   MAP 01 D4

♦♦♦♦

T&C Inisradharc

Balkill Rd ☎ 01 8322306
e-mail harbour_view@msn.com
Dir Off R105 past Howth Yacht Club onto Abbey St, bear right of church (in middle of road), house 0.4km up hill on right

Set in a charming fishing village with lovely views of the harbour and Dublin Bay. The breakfast room also has fine views and there is a spacious television lounge. Well-kept gardens surround the property. Convenient to Dublin airport, ferry port and 20 minutes by DART to city centre.

Facilities 3 en suite (1 fmly) (3 GF) ⊛ TVB tea/coffee ✝ Cen ht TVL No children 4yrs No coaches **Prices** D €72-€80 **Parking** 3
Notes Closed 12 Dec-8 Jan

LUSK   MAP 01 D4

♦♦♦

T&C Brookfield Lodge

Blakescross ☎ 01 8430043 🖹 01 8430177
e-mail trishb@indigo.ie
Dir M1, R132 Donabate/Skerries for 3km, pass Esso station, at junct R132-N1 & R129

Set in extensive gardens, this modern bungalow offers first-class hospitality and spacious, well-appointed rooms. Breakfasts are served in a conservatory-style dining room and there is also a comfortable lounge.

Facilities 3 en suite (2 fmly) ⊛ STV TVB tea/coffee ✝ Cen ht TVL
Parking 10 **Notes** Closed 24-26 Dec

RUSH   MAP 01 D4

◆◆◆◆

GH Sandyhills Bed & Breakfast

Sandyhills ☎ 01 843 7148 & 086 242 3660 ▤ 01 843 7148
e-mail mary@sandyhills.ie
Dir *Exit M1 onto N1, turn right to Lusk on R127. Take 2nd exit to Lusk village signed Corrs Ln/Sandyhills*

Set just a stroll from the sea and the village of Rush and just within easy reach of Dublin Airport. Sandyhills has spacious bedrooms, well equipped with thoughtful extra facilities. Breakfast is a special treat featuring local produce and Mary Buckley's preserves and freshly baked cakes and breads. There is a cosy sitting room and a lovely garden with secure car parking.

Facilities 5 en suite (2 fmly) (2 GF) ◎ TVB Direct dial from bedrooms ✘ Cen ht No coaches **Prices** S €65; D €110✳ LB **Parking** 20

CO GALWAY

CARNA (CARNA)   MAP 01 A4

◆◆◆◆

T&C Hillside House B&B

Kylesalia, Kilkieran ☎ 095 33420 ▤ 095 33624
e-mail hillsidehouse@oceanfree.net
Dir *Off N59 at Maam Cross or Recess onto R340 or follow coast road from Galway R336*

At the foot of Mordan Mountain, this house is a good touring base. Bedrooms are comfortable, there are lovely gardens and secure parking. Snack service available. Near fishing and beach.

Facilities 4 en suite (4 fmly) ◎ STV TVB tea/coffee ✘ Cen ht TVL No coaches **Parking** 8 **Notes** Closed Oct-Mar

CLIFDEN   MAP 01 A4

Premier Collection

◆◆◆◆◆ ⊜

GH *Byrne's Mal Dua House & Restaurant*

Galway Rd ☎ 095 21171 & 0800 904 7532 ▤ 095 21739
e-mail info@maldua.com
Dir *From Galway on N59, establishment on right 1km from Clifden. From Westport on N59, left at T-junct in town, then 1km*

Set in the outskirts of Clifden, this house offers a relaxed atmosphere of luxury, with a warm welcome the proprietors. An excellent dinner and breakfast is served in the delightful dining room, which overlooks the lovely garden. Spacious bedrooms are individually decorated with thoughtful extras. Guided tours, bicycles and fishing tackle are available for hire.

Facilities 14 en suite (2 fmly) (3 GF) ◎ STV TVB tea/coffee Direct dial from bedrooms ✘ Licensed Cen ht TVL ⏚ Bicycles & fishing rods for rent Last d 9pm **Conf** Max 30 **Parking** 20 **Notes** Closed 20-26 Dec

◆◆◆◆

GH Buttermilk Lodge

Westport Rd ☎ 095 21951 ▤ 095 21953
e-mail buttermilklodge@eircom.net
Dir *N59 from Galway. Right at Esso Station onto Westport Rd, Lodge 400 metres from junct on left. From Westport, Lodge on right, 100 metres after Clifden sign*

Expect carefully decorated and appointed bedrooms, four have luxury bath en suite and the remainder with shower en suite, along with many personal touches at this large house on the edge of town. Cathriona and Patrick O'Toole are welcoming hosts who offer fresh baking, tea and coffee on arrival.

Facilities 11 en suite (2 fmly) (4 GF) ◎ STV FTV TVB Direct dial from bedrooms ✘ Cen ht No children 5yrs farm visits with sheep & Connemara ponies **Prices** S €45-€70; D €70-€100 LB **Parking** 14 **Notes** Closed 3 Jan-1 Mar

◆◆◆◆ ✿

Ardmore House *(L 589523)*

Sky Rd ☎ 095 21221 ▤ 095 21100 Mr & Mrs Mullen
e-mail info@ardmore-house.com
web www.ardmore-house.com
Dir *5km W of Clifden. From Clifden signs for Sky Rd, pass bank onto the Abbey Glen Castle, house signed*

Ardmore is set among the wild scenery of Connemara between hills and the sea. Bedrooms are attractively decorated and the house is very comfortable throughout. A pathway leads from the house to the coast.

Facilities 6 en suite (3 fmly) (6 GF) ◎ STV TVB tea/coffee ✘ Cen ht 25 acres **Parking** 8 **Notes** Closed Oct-Mar ⊜

◆◆◆◆

GH *Dun Ri Guest House*

Hulk St ☎ 095 21625 ▤ 095 21635
e-mail dunri@anu.ie
Dir *N59 into Clifden, left before Statoil service station, signed*

This large, guest house stands in a quiet street close to the town centre. All the rooms are furnished to the same high standard and are equipped with modern comforts. Guests enjoy the amenity of a comfortable lounge and a separate dining room.

Facilities 10 en suite (2 fmly) ◎ in bedrooms ◎ in dining room STV TVB Direct dial from bedrooms ✘ Cen ht TVL No children 4yrs **Parking** 10 **Notes** Closed 3 Nov-Feb

◆◆◆◆ ✿

Faul House ◇ *(L 650475)*

Ballyconneely Rd
☎ 095 21239 ▤ 095 21998 Mrs Conneely
e-mail info@ireland.com
Dir *1.5km from town right at Connemara Pottery & signed*

A fine modern farmhouse stands on a quiet and secluded road overlooking Clifden Bay. It is smart and comfortable with large en suite bedrooms, all well furnished and with good views.

Facilities 6 en suite (3 fmly) (3 GF) ◎ TVB tea/coffee ✘ Cen ht TVL 28 acres sheep ponies ducks hens goats **Prices** D €33-€37 **Parking** 10 **Notes** Closed Nov -17 Mar ⊜

Ireland

CLIFDEN continued

♦♦♦♦

T&C Mallmore House

Ballyconneely Rd ☎ 095 21460
e-mail info@mallmorecountryhouse.com
Dir *1.5km from Clifden towards Ballyconneely, turn right at Connemara Pottery*

A charming Georgian-style house set in 14 hectares of woodland overlooking Clifden Bay, close to the Rock Glen Hotel. Alan and Kathy Hardman have restored the house with parquet flooring and some favourite antiques, while turf fires providing warmth and atmosphere.

Facilities 6 en suite (2 fmly) (6 GF) ⊗ TVB tea/coffee ✗ Cen ht No coaches 35 acres of mature woodland **Prices** D €64-€70✳ **Parking** 15 **Notes** Closed Oct-mid Mar 🐾

♦♦♦

GH *Ben View House*

Bridge St ☎ 095 21256 📄 095 21226
e-mail benviewhouse@ireland.com
Dir *Enter town on N59, opp Esso filling station*

This town-centre house offers good quality accommodation at a moderate cost, and is a good touring base.

Facilities 10 rms (9 en suite) (3 fmly) ⊗ in 2 bedrooms ⊗ in dining room ⊗ in lounges TV9B tea/coffee ✗ Cen ht TVL

♦♦♦ 🐾

Dan O'Hara's Farmhouse ◊ (L 730495)

Lettershea ☎ 095 21246 & 21808 📄 095 22098 Mr & Mrs M Walsh
e-mail danohara@eircom.net
Dir *Signed on N59 Galway-Clifden road, 8km from Clifden, next to Connemara Heritage Centre*

This smart country residence is part of the Connemara Heritage and History Centre, situated on a 81-hectare traditional working farm in the foothills of the Twelve Pins Mountains. Bedrooms are attractively decorated with pine furnishings and good facilities. There's a tea room, craft shop, comfortable sitting room, patio garden and a large car park.

Facilities 4 en suite (1 fmly) ⊗ STV TVB tea/coffee Direct dial from bedrooms ✗ Lift Cen ht TVL Fishing Sauna 200 acres mixed **Prices** S €42-€45; D €64-€70✳ **LB Parking** 30 **Notes** Closed Nov-Mar

CRAUGHWELL   MAP 01 B3

♦♦♦♦♦

GH St Clerans Manor House

☎ 091 846555 📄 091 846752
e-mail info@stclerans.com
Dir *N6 to Loughrea, take Athenry exit off rdbt and turn left after 6km, follow signs for St Clerans*

A delightful 18th-century Georgian manor house set in 45 acres. Previously owned by film director, John Houston, it is now owned by US TV personality, Merv Griffin. Bedrooms and public areas have been lovingly restored to a high standard of luxury and comfort. Local produce and Oriental influences feature nightly on the dinner menu. Coarse fishing, riding and croquet are available in the grounds. A helicopter pad and personalised chauffeur driven tours are available.

Facilities 12 en suite (2 fmly) (2 GF) ⊗ STV FTV TVB Direct dial from bedrooms Licensed TVL No coaches Fishing ♨ Dinner Last d 9pm **Prices** S €325-€525; D €325-€525✳ **LB Parking** 15 **Notes** Closed 24-29 Dec

GALWAY   MAP 01 B3

♦♦♦♦♦ 🏠

T&C Killeen House

Killeen, Bushypark ☎ 091 524179 📄 091 528065
e-mail killeenhouse@ireland.com
Dir *On N59 halfway between Galway & Moycullen*

This charming 19th-century house stands in 10 hectares of grounds stretching down to the shore of the Lough Corrib. The interior is beautifully appointed with antique furnishings, hand-woven carpets, fine linen and silver. Bedrooms reflect the character of the house and are individually furnished in the different eras. Guests have use of two-reception room and a breakfast room overlooking the garden.

Facilities 6 en suite (1 fmly) (1 GF) ⊗ in dining room ⊗ in lounges STV TVB tea/coffee Direct dial from bedrooms ✗ Lift Cen ht No children 12yrs No coaches **Prices** S €110-€150; D €150-€190 **Parking** 6 **Notes** Closed 23-28 Dec

Ireland

♦♦♦♦
T&C Almara House
2 Merlin Gate, Merlin Park, Dublin Rd
☎ 091 755345 & 086 2451220 ▤ 091 771585
e-mail matthewkiernan@eircom.net
Dir *3.2km E of Galway on R338 near Corrib Great Southern Hotel.
Signs for Merlin Park from junct N6 & N18*

Located in the eastern outskirts of Galway city, this attractive guest house offers well-appointed bedrooms with lots of thoughtful extras and wireless Internet access. Breakfast features Marie Kiernan's home baking. Almara House is well located for the Institute of Technology and off-road parking is available.

Facilities 4 en suite (1 fmly) ⊗ STV TVB tea/coffee ✖ Cen ht TVL No children 4yrs **Prices** S €45-€60; D €70-€100 **LB** **Parking** 8 **Notes** Closed 20-30 Dec

♦♦♦♦
GH Ardawn House
31 College Rd ☎ 091 568833 & 564551 ▤ 091 563454
e-mail ardawn@iol.ie
Dir *Galway East exit off dual-carriageway near Galway, signs for city centre, 1st guest house on right after Galway greyhound track*

This friendly family-run guest house is close to the city centre shops, pubs and restaurants. Breakfast is a feature here and includes home baking and a range of dishes. Bedrooms are comfortable and well furnished.

Facilities 8 en suite (2 fmly) ⊗ STV TVB Direct dial from bedrooms ✖ Cen ht No children 12yrs **Prices** S €50-€100; D €85-€150✳ **LB** **Parking** 8 **Notes** Closed 21-26 Dec

♦♦♦♦
T&C Atlantic Heights
2 Cashelmara, Knocknacarra Cross, Salthill
☎ 091 529466 & 528830
e-mail info@atlanticheightsgalway.com
web www.atlanticheightsgalway.com
Dir *2km W of city centre. 1km from Salthill promenade in upper Salthill on R336*

Enthusiastic hosts Robbie and Madeline Mitchell take great pride in their fine balconied house with views of Galway Bay. The bedrooms have many thoughful extras, and the extensive breakfast menu, served late if required, features home baking. Laundry service available.

T&C Atlantic Heights

Facilities 6 en suite (3 fmly) ⊗ STV TVB tea/coffee Direct dial from bedrooms Cen ht **Prices** S €40-€80; D €70-€100 **LB** **Parking** 6 **Notes** Closed Nov-Mar

♦♦♦♦
GH *Corrib Haven Guest House*
107 Upper Newcastle
☎ 091 524171 & 524711 ▤ 091 582414
e-mail corribhaven@eircom.net
Dir *From Galway on N59, follow signs for Clifden until Westwood House Hotel on left side of T-junct. Turn right at junct, Corrib Haven on right*

Situated on the N59 route to Connemara and close to Galway University and the city centre. Bedrooms are well appointed and there is a lounge and a dining room. Ample off-road parking is available.

Facilities 9 en suite (3 GF) ⊗ STV TVB Direct dial from bedrooms ✖ Cen ht TVL No children 4yrs **Parking** 13 **Notes** Closed 14 Dec-10 Jan

♦♦♦♦
GH *Marian Lodge Guest House*
Knocknacarra Rd, Salthill Upper
☎ 091 521678 ▤ 091 528103
e-mail celine@iol.ie
Dir *From Galway to Salthill on R336, through Salthill, 1st right after Spinnaker Hotel onto Knocknacarra Rd*

The large modern house is only 50 metres from the seafront. The fully equipped bedrooms have orthopedic beds and en suite facilities. There is also a lounge and separate breakfast room available.

Facilities 6 en suite (4 fmly) ⊗ STV TVB tea/coffee Direct dial from bedrooms ✖ Cen ht TVL No children 3yrs **Parking** 10 **Notes** Closed 23-28 Dec

continued

Ireland

GALWAY continued

◆◆◆
T&C *Four Seasons*
23 College Rd ☎ 091 564078 🖹 091 569765
e-mail 4season@gofree.indigo.ie
Dir From E or S take exit motorway, follow signs for Galway City East, then city centre. 5th house on right after sports ground/greyhound track

This comfortable house adjacent to the city centre is the family home of Eddie and Helen Fitzgerald who will immediately make you feel at home and help you with itineraries, sight seeing and will recommend restaurants for evening meals.

Facilities 5 en suite 2 annexe en suite (3 fmly) ⊗ in 3 bedrooms ⊗ in dining room ⊗ in lounges STV TVB tea/coffee ✖ Cen ht TVL **Parking** 7

LETTERFRACK   MAP 01 A4

◆◆◆◆
T&C Kylemore House
☎ 095 41143 🖹 095 41143
e-mail kylemorehouse@eircom.net
Dir Off N59 from Galway onto R344 at Recess

Standing on the shores of Lake Kylemore, protected by the Twelve Pins Mountains, this comfortable house has fishing rights on three lakes in a very scenic area of Connemara. Owner Mrs Naughton takes pride in her cooking and serves evening meals by arrangement.

Facilities 6 en suite (1 fmly) (1 GF) ⊗ tea/coffee Licensed Cen ht TVL No children 10yrs Fishing Boat hire for fishing Dinner Last d 4pm **Prices** D €68-€76 **Parking** 8 **Notes** Closed Nov-Feb

OUGHTERARD   MAP 01 B4

◆◆◆
T&C *Lakeland Country House*
Portacarron Bay ☎ 091 552121 & 552146 🖹 091 552146
e-mail mayfly@eircom.net
Dir Off N59 20 mins from Galway take 2nd right after Oughterard Golf Club sign. From Maam Cross through Oughterard, pass Gateway Hotel next left, house on lake shore

Situated on the shores of the lough, this comfortable house offers a spacious television lounge, and a fine dining room with views across the water. Fishing and boat trips can be arranged, and dinner is available.

continued

Facilities 9 rms (8 en suite) (3 fmly) ⊗ in bedrooms ⊗ in dining room tea/coffee ✖ Licensed Cen ht TVL Fishing **Parking** 20 **Notes** Closed 10 Dec-16 Jan

ROUNDSTONE   MAP 01 A4

◆◆◆◆
GH Eldons
☎ 095 35933 & 35942 🖹 095 35722

This guest house is situated in the picturesque village overlooking Roundstone Harbour with the Twelve Pins mountain range in the background. Bedrooms are carefully furnished and vary in size, the annexe rooms being the more spacious with seating areas. The home-cooked breakfasts served in the charming dining room are an appealing start to the day. Ann Conneely and her hospitable staff can assist to plan tours throughout Connemara.

Facilities 19 en suite (4 fmly) ⊗ TVB tea/coffee Direct dial from bedrooms ✖ Licensed Lift Cen ht TVL **Notes** Closed 5 Nov-15 Mar

◆◆◆◆
T&C Ivy Rock House
Letterdyfe ☎ 095 35872 🖹 095 35959
e-mail ivyrockhouse@eircom.net

Overlooking Bertraghboy Bay this house has been decorated to a high standard and provides comfortable accommodation. Public rooms include two adjoining reception rooms and a first-floor sitting room with spectacular views. Bedrooms are well appointed. There are good restaurants nearby.

Facilities 6 en suite (4 fmly) (3 GF) ⊗ TV4B ✖ Cen ht TVL Riding locally Last d 3pm **Prices** S €48-€50; D €60-€65✶ LB **Parking** 10 **Notes** Closed Oct-Mar

SPIDDAL (AN SPIDÉAL)   MAP 01 B3

◆◆◆◆
T&C Ardmor Country House ◇
Greenhill ☎ 091 553145 & 553596 🖹 091 553596
e-mail ardmorcountryhouse@yahoo.com
Dir On R336 coast road from Galway, 1km W of Spiddal

There are superb views of Galway Bay and the Aran Islands from this beautifully appointed luxury home. Bedrooms are spacious and there are relaxing lounges, a well-stocked library and delightful gardens.

Facilities 7 en suite (4 fmly) ⊗ TVB tea/coffee ✖ Cen ht TVL **Prices** S €40-€50; D €64-€70✶ **Parking** 20 **Notes** Closed Jan-Feb ⬚

◆◆◆◆
T&C Tuar Beag
Tuar Beag ☎ 091 553422 🖹 091 553010
e-mail tuarbeagbandb@eircom.net
Dir On R336 coast road on W edge of Spiddal

Tuar Beag is a prominent house, much extended from the 19th-century cottage where four generations of the proprietor's family grew up. The original stone walls and fireplace have been retained and the house now offers excellent accommodation overlooking Galway Bay and the Aran Islands. Breakfast is a notable feature.

continued

Facilities 6 en suite (6 fmly) ⊗ TVB tea/coffee ✱ Cen ht TVL
No children 2yrs **Prices** S €60; D €56–€70 **Parking** 20 **Notes** Closed
16 Nov-Jan 🐾

CO KERRY

BALLYBUNION
MAP 01 A3

Premier Collection

◆◆◆◆◆

GH *Cashen Course House*

Golf Links Rd ☎ 068 27351 🖷 068 28934
e-mail golfstay@eircom.net
Dir 200 metres from Ballybunion Golf Club

Overlooking the Cashen links, this spacious, purpose-built house
offers comfortable well-appointed bedrooms. A warm welcome is
assured from the O'Brien family who are on hand to advise and assist
with tee bookings. A baby grand piano is a feature of the inviting
lounge. Drying facilities are available.

Facilities 9 en suite (3 fmly) (3 GF) ⊗ STV TVB Direct dial from
bedrooms ✱ Cen ht TVL Golf 2 golf courses opposite **Parking** 12
Notes Closed Nov-Feb

CAHERDANIEL
(CATHAIR DÓNALL)
MAP 01 A2

◆◆◆◆

T&C Derrynane Bay House

☎ 066 9475404 & 08723 43974 🖷 066 9475436
e-mail dbhouse@eircom.net
Dir 1km on Waterville side of Caherdaniel village on N70
overlooking Derrynane Bay

Set back from the main road, this meticulously maintained house is
on an elevated position with views over Derrynane Bay. Carefully
furnished throughout, there is a comfortable sitting and dining room
and attractive bedrooms. The owner is very welcoming and offers a
good breakfast menu. Walking, water sports, good beaches, fishing
and golf are all nearby.

Facilities 6 rms (5 en suite) (1 pri facs) (2 fmly) (4 GF) ⊗ STV FTV
TVB tea/coffee Direct dial from bedrooms ✱ Cen ht TVL No coaches
Dinner Last d noon **Prices** S €45–€55; D €72–€75 **Parking** 10
Notes Closed Nov-23 Dec rs 30 Dec-15 Mar

◆◆

GH *The Scarriff Inn*

☎ 066 9475132 🖷 066 9475425
e-mail scarrif1@aol.com

There are spectacular views from all bedrooms in this family-run
house situated half-way around the Ring of Kerry. Seafood is a feature
of the restaurant, and bar facilities are available with a selection of
snacks throughout the day.

Facilities 6 en suite (6 GF) ⊗ STV TVB Direct dial from bedrooms ✱
Licensed Cen ht **Parking** 30 **Notes** Closed Nov-Apr Civ Wed 100

CASTLEGREGORY
MAP 01 A2

Premier Collection

◆◆◆◆◆

T&C *Shores Country House*

Conor Pass Rd, Cappatigue
☎ 066 713 9196 & 713 9195 🖷 066 713 9196
e-mail theshores@eircom.net
Dir N86/R560 through Stradbally village, continue 1.6km, house on
left

This charming house has panoramic views from its elevated position.
Bedrooms and public rooms are all individually decorated to a very
high standard. An interesting home-cooked dinner is available Monday
to Friday, and features local and seasonal produce.

Facilities 6 en suite (1 fmly) ⊗ STV TVB tea/coffee Direct dial from
bedrooms ✱ Licensed Cen ht TVL Library Dinner Last d 5pm
Parking 8 **Notes** Closed mid Nov-mid Feb 🐾

◆◆◆◆

T&C Sea-Mount House
Bed & Breakfast

Cappatigue, Conor Pass Rd
☎ 066 7139229 🖷 066 7139229
e-mail seamount@unison.ie
Dir On Conor Pass road, 2.4km W of Stradbally, overlooking
Brandon Bay

Located on the Conor Pass road between Tralee and Dingle, this
friendly house has great views of Brandon Bay. It is a good base for
exploring the Dingle Peninsula. The cosy sitting areas and bedrooms
make the most of the views, a great way to enjoy home baking and
welcome tea on arrival.

Facilities 3 en suite (1 fmly) (2 GF) ⊗ TVB tea/coffee ✱ Cen ht TVL
No coaches **LB** **Parking** 5 **Notes** Closed Dec-Apr

◆◆◆

GH *Beenoskee B & B*

Cappateige, Conor Pass Rd
☎ 066 7139263 🖷 066 7139263
e-mail beenoskee@eircom.net
Dir 1km W of Stradbally village on left

Beenoskee derives its name from the mountain that forms the
backdrop of this hospitable house. Many of the bedrooms and the
breakfast room have a spectacular view of Tralee Bay. An extensive
breakfast menu is provided in this non-smoking house, and dinner is
available by arrangement.

Facilities 5 en suite (5 GF) ⊗ TVB tea/coffee ✱ Cen ht TVL Dinner
Last d 2pm **Parking** 6

Ireland

CASTLEGREGORY continued

◆◆◆

T&C Griffin's Palm Beach Country House ◇

Goulane, Conor Pass Rd ☎ 066 7139147 📠 066 7139073
e-mail griffinspalmbeach@eircom.net
Dir 1.5km from Stradbally village

This farmhouse is a good base for exploring the Dingle Peninsula and unspoiled beaches. The comfortable bedrooms have fine views over Tralee Bay, and the delightful garden can be enjoyed from the dining room and sitting room. Mrs Griffin offers a warm welcome and her home baking is a feature on the breakfast menu.

Facilities 8 rms (6 en suite) (2 pri facs) (3 fmly) (1 GF) ⊗ tea/coffee Cen ht TVL ch fac **Prices** S € 40-€ 45; D € 80-€ 90✱ **Parking** 10
Notes Closed Nov-Feb

CASTLEMAINE

MAP 01 A2

◆◆◆ ▶

Murphys Farmhouse (R8801005)

Boolteens ☎ 066 976 7337 📠 066 976 7839 Mrs Murphy
e-mail info@murphysfarmhouse.com
Dir From Castlemaine village onto Dingle Rd (R561), B&B signed.

The elevated position of this long established house offers marvellous views of Dingle Bay. Bedrooms are very comfortable, and a choice of two lounges is available for guests, where one can expect a warm welcome from Mrs. Mary Murphy, whose family also own a traditional pub nearby, where dinner is served.

Facilities 14 en suite (5 fmly) (6 GF) ⊗ TVB tea/coffee ✗ Cen ht TVL 30 acres Dairy Dinner Last d 1pm **Prices** D € 56-€ 66✱ **LB** **Parking** 16

CLOGHANE (AN CLOCHÁN)

MAP 01 A2

◆◆ ▭

GH O'Connors Guesthouse

☎ 066 713 8113 📠 066 713 8270
e-mail oconnorsguesthouse@eircom.net
Dir In village centre

Situated in a lovely village close to Castlegregory, the long-established, family-run house has a traditional bar and restaurant, and some of the bedrooms look over the bay and mountains.

Facilities 9 en suite (6 fmly) (2 GF) ⊗ tea/coffee Direct dial from bedrooms ✗ Licensed Cen ht TVL Dinner Last d 8.30pm
Prices S € 45-€ 60; D € 70-€ 100✱ **LB** **Parking** 20 **Notes** Closed Nov-Feb

---

DINGLE (AN DAINGEAN)

MAP 01 A2

◆◆◆◆◆

GH Emlagh House

☎ 066 9152345 📠 066 9152369
e-mail info@emlaghhouse.com
Dir Pass filling station at E entrance to town, turn left & house ahead

Impressive Georgian-style house on the outskirts of Dingle where attention to detail and luxury combine to make a stay memorable. The stylish drawing room and dining room overlook the harbour. Bedrooms and bathrooms are individually decorated to a high standard with antique furniture, ground floor rooms have private patios. Breakfasts are very special here and make good use of fresh local produce.

Facilities 10 en suite (1 fmly) (4 GF) ⊗ STV TVB Direct dial from bedrooms ✗ Licensed Lift Cen ht No children 8yrs
Prices S € 115-€ 165; D € 180-€ 300 **LB** **Parking** 20 **Notes** Closed 5 Nov-10 Mar

◆◆◆◆◆ ▦

GH Milltown House

☎ 066 9151372 📠 066 9151095
e-mail info@milltownhousedingle.com
Dir 1.5km W of Dingle on Slea Head road, cross Milltown Bridge and turn left

Situated on a sea channel to the west of Dingle town, the house has been elegantly refurbished and has a warm inviting atmosphere, the Kerry family making guests feel really welcome. Bedrooms have attractive decor and are well appointed. There is also a cosy sitting room leading to a conservatory breakfast room.

Facilities 10 en suite (1 fmly) (3 GF) ⊗ STV TVB tea/coffee Direct dial from bedrooms ✗ Cen ht No children 5yrs No coaches
Prices S € 90-€ 125; D € 110-€ 160 **Parking** 10 **Notes** Closed 29 Oct-27 Apr

◆◆◆◆◆

GH Castlewood House

The Wood ☎ 066 915 2788 📠 066 915 2110
e-mail castlewoodhouse@eircom.net
Dir R559 from Dingle, 0.5km from Aquarium

Located at the western edge of the town, Castlewood House has been recently built to a high specification. Each of the individually designed bedrooms is very comfortable and well equipped. There is lift access to the upper floor and a spa bath in each en suite. Both the sitting room and breakfast rooms make the most of the beautiful views.

Facilities 12 en suite (3 fmly) (4 GF) ⊗ STV TVB tea/coffee Direct dial from bedrooms ✗ Lift Cen ht **Prices** S € 75-€ 130; D € 98-€ 180✱ **Parking** 15 **Notes** Closed 4-27 Dec, 4 Jan-4 Feb

◆◆◆◆◆

GH *Dingle Benners Hotel*

Main St ☎ 066 9151638 📄 066 9151412
e-mail info@dinglebenners.com
Dir In town centre

Located in the centre of the town with parking to the rear, this long-established property has a relaxed, traditional character. Bedrooms are well equipped and come in two styles, in the original house and in a more-recent block. Food is available in the popular bar.

Facilities 52 en suite (29 fmly) (9 GF) ⊗ STV TVB tea/coffee Direct dial from bedrooms ✖ Licensed Lift Cen ht TVL Dinner Last d 9pm **Conf** Max 50 Board 20 **Parking** 32 **Notes** Closed 23-26 Dec

◆◆◆◆◆ ⊜

GH *Gormans Clifftop House & Restaurant*

Glaise Bheag, Ballydavid ☎ 066 9155162 📄 066 9155003
e-mail info@gormans-clifftophouse.com
Dir From Dingle harbour to rdbt W of town, over rdbt signed An Feothanach to coast, keep left at junct

This traditional house-fronted is in a superb location overlooking Smerwick Harbour and the vastness of the Atlantic beyond. The Gorman family offer marvellous hospitality and the food is excellent. Lounges and restaurant enjoy stunning views. The comfortable bedrooms are most inviting, and one is adapted for the less mobile.

Facilities 9 en suite (2 fmly) (5 GF) ⊗ TVB tea/coffee Direct dial from bedrooms ✖ Licensed Cen ht Bicycles for hire Dinner Last d 8.30pm **Parking** 15 **Notes** Closed 24-26 Dec rs Nov-Feb

◆◆◆◆◆

GH Heatons Guest House

The Wood ☎ 066 9152288 📄 066 9152324
e-mail heatons@iol.ie
Dir 0.6km beyond marina

A family-run guest house located on the waterfront and near the town. Most bedrooms have views of Dingle Bay and are very comfortable and well appointed. Guests can also enjoy the views and relax in the spacious foyer lounge. The breakfast room is brightly decorated and offers an impressive carte.

Facilities 16 en suite (2 fmly) (5 GF) ⊗ STV TVB tea/coffee Direct dial from bedrooms ✖ Cen ht No children 8yrs **Prices** S € 55-€ 99; D € 90-€ 134 **Parking** 16 **Notes** Closed 5 Jan-1 Feb

◆◆◆◆

T&C *Alpine Guesthouse*

Mail Rd ☎ 066 9151250 📄 066 9151966
e-mail alpinedingle@eircom.net
Dir On right on N86 at entrance to town

On the edge of Dingle, this large, attractive three-storey guest house is run by the O'Shea family, who maintain excellent standards. The elegantly furnished bedrooms have large, spacious bathrooms. There is a private car park, and the guest house is just two minutes walk from the town centre.

Facilities 10 en suite (3 fmly) ⊗ STV TVB tea/coffee Direct dial from bedrooms ✖ Cen ht TVL No coaches **Parking** 15

◆◆◆◆

T&C Bambury's Guest House

Mail Rd ☎ 066 9151244 📄 066 9151786
e-mail info@bamburysguesthouse.com
Dir On N86 on left entering Dingle, past Shell Station

Set on the edge of Dingle, this pink house is eyecatching on the outside and attractive on the inside with pretty decor and comfortable appointments. There is a cosy lounge and a spacious dining room. En suite bedrooms are excellent with pine furnishings, pottery lamps, tea/coffee trays and big showers.

Facilities 12 en suite (1 fmly) (3 GF) ⊗ STV TVB tea/coffee Direct dial from bedrooms ✖ Cen ht TVL No children 4yrs **Parking** 12

◆◆◆

T&C *Dingle Heights*

Ballinaboola ☎ 066 9151543
e-mail dingleheights@hotmail.com
Dir 1km up main street to hospital, 180 metres 2nd B&B on right

Set high overlooking Dingle Bay, this house features comfortable, well-appointed accommodation and the charming hospitality of owner Mrs Fitzgerald.

Facilities 4 en suite (4 fmly) ⊗ in bedrooms ⊗ in dining room ⊗ in 1 lounge ✖ Cen ht TVL **Parking** 10 **Notes** ⊜

◆◆◆ ✙

Hurleys Farm (Q 392080)

An Dooneen, Kilcooley ☎ 066 9155112 Ms Mary Hurley
e-mail andooneen@eircom.net
Dir 11km W of Dingle town on Ballydavid-Muirioch road

Hurley's Farm is tucked away behind the church in Kilcooley, 1.5km from the beach and sheltered by Mount Brandon, a popular place for hill walkers. Accommodation includes a cosy TV room, dining room and comfortable en suite bedrooms, graced by some special pieces of high quality furniture. The whole area is rich in early historic and prehistoric relics: ogham stones, ring forts and the famous dry-stone masonry 'beehive' huts.

Facilities 4 en suite (2 GF) ⊗ ✖ Cen ht TVL 32 acres mixed **Parking** 6 **Notes** Closed Nov-Mar ⊜

KENMARE

MAP 01 B2

◆◆◆◆◆

T&C *Sallyport House*

Glengarriff Rd ☎ 064 42066 🖹 064 42067
e-mail port@iol.ie
Dir 400 metres S on N71

A superbly refurbished house, built for the Arthur family in 1932 and still owned by the family. Set in grounds and luxuriously appointed, the house is just a short walk from the town. Guests will appreciate the tranquil atmosphere of a house which has attractively decorated bedrooms, furnished with antiques, including a four-poster room. The comfortable sitting room has a roaring fire during the winter.

Facilities 5 en suite (2 fmly) STV TVB tea/coffee Direct dial from bedrooms Cen ht No children 10yrs **Parking** 10 **Notes** Closed Nov-Mar

◆◆◆◆

GH Davitts ◇

Henry St ☎ 064 42741 🖹 064 42757
e-mail info@davitts-kenmare.com
Dir On N22 (Cork-Killarney rd) at Kenmare junct (R569). In town centre

This town-centre guest house has been decorated to a high standard. The spacious, well-appointed bedrooms are decorated in a contemporary style, and there is a cosy sitting room on the first floor. Davitt's Restaurant is at street level, a popular venue to meet friends and locals and enjoy the varied menu.

Facilities 11 en suite (1 fmly) STV TVB Direct dial from bedrooms Licensed Cen ht TVL Dinner Last d 9.45pm **Prices** S €40-€60; D €76-€90✳ **Parking** 4 **Notes** Closed 1-14 Nov & 24-26 Dec

◆◆◆◆

T&C *Harbour View*

Castletownbere Rd, Dauros ☎ 064 41755 🖹 064 42611
e-mail maureenmccarthy@eircom.net
Dir From Kenmare towards Glengurriffe, onto Castletownbere Haven road 571, 1st right after bridge, Harbour View 6.5km on left on seashore

This charming house is situated on the seashore, with lovely views of Kenmare Bay and the mountains beyond. Maureen McCarthy is a cheerful, caring hostess with infectious enthusiasm, and her attention to detail is evident throughout the comfortable bedrooms. The breakfast menu includes fresh and smoked seafood and the home baking is excellent.

Facilities 4 en suite (3 fmly) in 1 bedrooms in dining room STV TVB tea/coffee Cen ht TVL Dinner Last d 8pm **Parking** 6 **Notes** Closed Nov-Feb

◆◆◆◆

GH *Sea Shore Farm Guest House*

Tubrid ☎ 064 41270 & 41675 🖹 064 41270
e-mail seashore@eircom.net
Dir 1.6km from Kenmare on N70 Ring of Kerry road. Signed at junct N70 & N71

Overlooking Kenmare Bay on the Ring of Kerry road, this modern farm guest house is close to town and has spacious bedrooms, ground-floor rooms open onto the patio and have easier access. Guests are welcome to enjoy the farm walks through the fields to the shore and salmon and trout fishing on a private stretch of the Roughty River. There is a comfortable sitting room and dining room and a delightful garden.

Facilities 6 en suite (2 fmly) (2 GF) TVB tea/coffee Direct dial from bedrooms Cen ht Private shore **Parking** 10 **Notes** Closed 15 Nov-Feb

◆◆◆◆

GH Virginia's Guesthouse

36 Henry St ☎ 064 41021 & 086 3720625
e-mail virginias@eircom.net
Dir In town centre

Virginia's is a well-presented house on the right as you drive towards the town green. Sharing an entrance with Mulcahy's Restaurant, the bedrooms are on the upper floors and are very comfortable. Breakfast features home-baked breads.

Facilities 8 en suite (1 fmly) STV TVB Direct dial from bedrooms Cen ht No children 12yrs **Prices** S €50-€75; D €70-€120 LB **Notes** Closed 20-25 Dec

◆◆◆

GH *Ashberry Lodge*

Ring of Kerry Rd (N70) ☎ 064 42720 & 42727
e-mail ashberry@iolfree.ie
Dir 2km from town centre. Off Kenmare N71 onto N70 Ring of Kerry, house on left after Kenmare Bay Hotel

This comfortable, family-run guest house is situated within walking distance of the town of Kenmare, the pretty garden has a pond and amply off-street parking. Bedrooms are spacious and well appointed, the sitting room and dining room are attractively decorated. An interesting breakfast menu is offered.

Facilities 8 en suite (1 fmly) (3 GF) TVB tea/coffee Direct dial from bedrooms Cen ht **Parking** 10 **Notes** Closed 24-25 Dec

If you have to cancel a booking, let the proprietor know immediately

KILGARVAN

MAP 01 B2

◆◆◆◆

T&C *Birchwood*

Church Ground ☎ 064 85473 ▤ 064 85570
e-mail birchwood1@eircom.net
Dir 50 metres E of Kilgarvan on R569

Birchwood stands in extensive gardens facing a natural forest and backed by the Mangerton Mountains, an area ideal for hill-walking and touring. The MacDonnells are caring hosts in this tranquil location who offer comfortable and attractively decorated bedrooms. Dinner is available, and the nearby Rivers Roughty and Slaheny provide good salmon and trout fishing.

Facilities 5 en suite (3 fmly) ⊗ TVB tea/coffee ✱ Cen ht TVL Fishing Dinner Last d 6.30pm **Parking** 6 **Notes** ✆

KILLARNEY

MAP 01 B2

Premier Collection

◆◆◆◆◆

GH Earls Court House

Woodlawn Junction, Muckross Rd
☎ 064 34009 ▤ 064 34366
e-mail info@killarney-earlscourt.ie
Dir Left at lights on Muckross Rd, Earls Court House 100 metres on left

A distinctive yellow building, contemporary in design and purpose-built, with the added facility of balconies adjoining most bedrooms. Elegance and luxury can be seen in the decor and the antique furnishings throughout the house. There is a comfortable lounge where rich fabrics have been used to create a setting for relaxation.

Facilities 24 en suite (3 fmly) ⊗ STV TVB tea/coffee Direct dial from bedrooms Licensed Lift Cen ht TVL ch fac **Prices** S €65-€100; D €100-€135 **LB** **Parking** 24 **Notes** Closed 13 Nov-11 Feb rs 6 Nov-28 Feb (group bookings 8+ only)

Premier Collection

◆◆◆◆◆ 🛏

GH Kathleen's Country House

Tralee Rd ☎ 064 32810 ▤ 064 32340
e-mail info@kathleens.net
Dir 1.6km N of town centre on N22

The modern, purpose-built guest house stands in lovely gardens amid scenic countryside. The family-run, luxury accommodation is a good touring centre. Bedrooms are furnished with antique pine and have excellent bathrooms, while the five sitting rooms all have different views. Breakfast is served in the elegant dining room overlooking the gardens.

Facilities 17 en suite (2 fmly) (2 GF) ⊗ STV TVB tea/coffee Direct dial from bedrooms ✱ Licensed Cen ht No children 3yrs ⚘ Reflexology, Massage aromatherapy **Prices** S €60-€120; D €100-€140 **LB** **Parking** 20 **Notes** Closed mid Oct-mid Mar

Premier Collection

◆◆◆◆◆ 🛏

GH *Fairview Guest House*

College St ☎ 064 34164 ▤ 064 71777
e-mail info@fairviewkillarney.com
Dir Off College St

This purpose-built guest house is situated in the town centre and close to the railway station. Great attention to detail has been taken in the furnishing and design to ensure guest comfort. The building is equipped with a lift and some rooms have easier access.

Facilities 18 en suite (1 GF) ⊗ in 17 bedrooms ⊗ in dining room ⊗ in lounges STV TVB tea/coffee Direct dial from bedrooms ✱ Lift Cen ht TVL jacuzzi suites available **Parking** 11

Ireland

Always confirm details with the establishment when booking

continued

KILLARNEY continued

Premier Collection

♦♦♦♦♦ ⊜

GH Foleys Town House

22/23 High St ☎ 064 31217 ▤ 064 34683
e-mail info@foleystownhouse.com
Dir In town centre

Charming individually designed bedrooms are a feature of this well-established house, which has good parking facilities and a comfortable lounge. Family owned and run by Carol Hartnett who is also the chef in the adjoining restaurant that specialises in seafood.

Facilities 28 en suite ⊘ in 12 bedrooms ⊘ in dining room ⊘ in lounges STV TVB tea/coffee Direct dial from bedrooms ✹ Licensed Lift Cen ht TVL Dinner Last d 10.30pm **Prices** S €70-€90; D €118-€130 **LB** **Parking** 60 **Notes** Closed 6 Nov-16 Mar

Premier Collection

♦♦♦♦♦

GH Old Weir Lodge

Muckross Rd ☎ 064 35593 ▤ 064 35583
e-mail oldweirlodge@eircom.net
Dir On Muckross Rd, 500 metres from Killarney

Welcoming, purpose-built Tudor-style lodge, set in attractive gardens. Maureen loves to cook and home-baking is a feature of the breakfasts; evening meals, are also available by arrangement. Dermot will help with leisure activities such as boat trips on the Killarney Lakes or golf and fishing. The comfortable bedrooms are equipped to a high standard and there is a delightful sitting room overlooking the gardens. There is also a drying room and ample off-road parking.

continued

Facilities 30 en suite (7 fmly) (6 GF) ⊘ in 12 bedrooms ⊘ in dining room ⊘ in lounges STV TVB tea/coffee Direct dial from bedrooms ✹ Licensed Lift Cen ht TVL Dinner Last d 8pm **Prices** S €60-€90✱ **Parking** 30 **Notes** Closed 23-26 Dec

♦♦♦♦

T&C Applecroft House

Woodlawn Rd ☎ 064 32782
e-mail applecroft@eircom.net
Dir N71 from Killarney on Muckross road for 500 metres, left at Shell filling station, onto Woodlawn Rd, signed 500 metres on left

Applecroft is a family home tucked away in a residential area, with beautiful landscaped gardens. Bedrooms are spacious and there is great attention to detail in the decoration. Guests can relax in the lounge or on the patio. The breakfast room overlooks the garden.

Facilities 5 en suite (2 fmly) ⊘ in bedrooms ⊘ in dining room ⊘ in 1 lounge STV TVB ✹ Cen ht TVL **Parking** 5 **Notes** Closed Dec-Feb

♦♦♦♦

GH Ashville

Rock Rd ☎ 064 36405 ▤ 064 36778
e-mail info@ashvillekillarney.com
Dir On N22 from Cork and Tralee, and from Limerick on N21

This inviting house is just a stroll from the town centre and near the the N22 Tralee road. Bedrooms are comfortably furnished and there is a pleasant relaxing sitting room and dining room. There is a private car park and tours can be arranged.

Facilities 10 en suite (3 fmly) (4 GF) ⊘ STV FTV TVB tea/coffee Direct dial from bedrooms ✹ Cen ht TVL **Prices** S €50-€90; D €70-€110 **LB** **Parking** 13 **Notes** Closed Nov-1 Mar

♦♦♦♦

T&C Crystal Springs

Ballycasheen ☎ 064 33272 & 35518 ▤ 064 35518
e-mail crystalsprings@eircom.net
Dir From Killarney town turn right off Cork Rd at 1st lights & Texaco. Left onto Rookery Rd, to end & Crystal Springs is across road at T-junct

This luxurious house is on the outskirts of the town and the garden runs down to the River Flesk. It overlooks a historic mill and is close to the mountains, lakes, golf courses and Killarney National Park. Bedrooms are attractively decorated and well equipped and there is a charming lounge and dining room where delicious breakfasts are served.

continued

T&C Crystal Springs

Facilities 7 en suite (3 fmly) (3 GF) ⊗ in bedrooms ⊗ in dining room ⊗ in 1 lounge STV TVB tea/coffee Direct dial from bedrooms ✗ Cen ht TVL Fishing Dinner Last d 3pm **Parking** 14

◆◆◆◆

T&C Killarney Villa

Mallow Rd ☎ 064 31878 📠 064 31878
e-mail killarneyvilla@ie-post.com
web www.killarneyvilla.com
Dir *N22 E from Killarney, over 1st rdbt, continue after 2nd rdbt on N22 & N72 for 2km, feft signed Mallow, Villa 300 metres*

This luxurious country home has a rooftop conservatory where complimentary beverages are available. It is situated on the outskirts of the town within easy reach of the beautiful Killarney lakes and mountains. Bedrooms are very comfortable and well equipped, and there is a lovely dining room where a variety of dishes are available at breakfast while enjoying the delightful garden.

Facilities 6 en suite ⊗ STV TVB tea/coffee ✗ Cen ht TVL
Prices S €45-€55; D €74-€90 LB **Parking** 20 **Notes** Closed Nov-Etr 🐾

◆◆◆◆

GH *Kingfisher Lodge*

Lewis Rd ☎ 064 37131 📠 064 39871
e-mail kingfisherguesthouse@eircom.net
Dir *Dublin link straight through 1st rdbt. Right at next rdbt towards town centre, Lodge on left*

This welcoming, family-run modern guest house, situated within walking distance of the town centre, has comfortable well-appointed bedrooms. A delicious breakfast is served in the attractively decorated dining room and there is also a relaxing lounge. A drying room is available for fishing and wet gear. Golf, walking and fishing trips can be arranged.

Facilities 10 en suite (1 fmly) (2 GF) ⊗ TVB tea/coffee Direct dial from bedrooms ✗ Cen ht TVL No coaches Walking, fishing, golf trips can be organised **Parking** 11 **Notes** Closed 15 Dec-Jan

◆◆◆◆

GH Redwood

Tralee Rd ☎ 064 34754 & 087 299 8924 📠 064 34178
e-mail redwd@indigo.ie
Dir *N22 N from Killarney, Redwood 3.2km from Cleeny rdbt on left*

Set in landscaped grounds 4km from the town centre, this is a very comfortable house. Bedrooms are well furnished, and the lounge and dining rooms are very spacious with picture windows framing the garden. A good choice is offered at breakfast.

Facilities 6 en suite (3 fmly) (2 GF) ⊗ STV TVB tea/coffee ✗ Cen ht
Prices S €46-€65; D €66-€82 LB **Parking** 6

◆◆◆◆

T&C Shraheen House

Ballycasheen, Off Cork Rd (N22)
☎ 064 31286 📠 064 37959
e-mail info@shraheenhouse.com
Dir *On Ballycasheen-Woodlawn road, 1.6km off N71 at lights*

The large modern house stands in extensive grounds on a quiet road. The bedrooms are all well equipped and have attractive soft furnishings. The quiet gardens and the pleasant sun lounge are very relaxing. Within easy reach of three golf courses or local fishing.

Facilities 6 en suite (2 fmly) (3 GF) ⊗ STV TVB tea/coffee ✗ Cen ht TVL **Prices** S €45-€55; D €64-€74 **Parking** 8 **Notes** Closed Dec-Jan 🐾

KILLORGLIN   MAP 01 A2

◆◆◆◆◆ 🛏 🍴

T&C *Carrig House Country House & Restaurant*

Caragh Lake ☎ 066 9769100 📠 066 9769166
e-mail info@carrighouse.com

A warm and friendly atmosphere combined with a range of relaxing lounges to make a visit to Carrig House a truly memorable event. The house is in excellent condition, nestled among very well kept gardens by the shore of the lake. The spacious bedrooms are all individually decorated and many have superb views of the lake, as does the dining room, where delicious evening meals are available. The hospitality shown by hosts Mary and Frank and their team makes one not want to leave.

Facilities 16 en suite ⊗ in bedrooms ⊗ in dining room Direct dial from bedrooms Licensed Cen ht TVL No children 8yrs No coaches Fishing 🎣 Dinner Last d 9.15pm **Parking** 20 **Notes** Closed Oct-Feb

continued

Ireland

KILLORGLIN continued

◆◆◆◆

T&C *The Grove Lodge*

Killarney Rd
☎ 066 9761157 & 08720 73238 ▤ 066 9762330
e-mail groveldg@iol.ie
Dir 800 metres from Killorglin Bridge on Killarney road-N72

A lovely riverside house extended and developed to a high standard, with all the rooms en suite and fully equipped. Mrs Foley is an enthusiastic host who likes to please her guests and for those who just want to relax there is a patio seating area in the garden by the river.

Facilities 10 en suite (4 fmly) (4 GF) STV TVB tea/coffee Direct dial from bedrooms ✖ Cen ht Fishing **Parking** 15 **Notes** Closed 22-30 Dec

◆◆◆ ✔

Dromin Farmhouse *(V 806902)*

Milltown Post Office ☎ 066 9761867 Mrs Foley
e-mail drominfarmhouse@yahoo.com
Dir 3km from Killorglin and Milltown. Turn off N70 1km from Killorglin at sign after factory. House straight on, 2km

Set on a sheep and cattle farm with fantastic mountain views, this elevated bungalow is near to local beaches, golf, fishing and horse riding. A television lounge is available and babysitting can be arranged. Evening meals are served, but reservations are appreciated.

Facilities 4 en suite (2 fmly) (4 GF) TVB tea/coffee ✖ Cen ht TVL 42 acres dairy sheep Dinner Last d noon **Prices** D €60-€65✳
Parking 10 **Notes** Closed Nov-16 Mar

◆◆◆ ✔

Hillview Farmhouse *(V 800908)*

☎ 066 9767117 ▤ 066 9767910 Ms Stephens
e-mail dstephens@eircom.net
Dir On N70 between Killorgin and Milltown

This working dairy and sheep farmhouse is good base for touring Dingle and the Ring of Kerry. There are comfortable bedrooms, a cosy lounge, and a dining room where Dorothea Stephens' home baking is a speciality.

Facilities 4 en suite (3 fmly) (2 GF) ✖ Cen ht TVL 100 acres Mixed **Parking** 8 **Notes** Closed Nov-Feb

◆◆◆

T&C *O'Regan's Country Home & Gardens*

Bansha ☎ 066 9761200 ▤ 066 9761200
e-mail jeromeoregan@eircom.net
Dir 1.6km from Killorglin on N70, turn right, beside Killorglin golf club

This dormer bungalow is set in colourful-award-winning gardens just off the N70, adjacent to Killorglin Golf Club. The bedrooms are comfortable, there is an inviting breakfast room, and the lounge overlooks the beautiful garden.

Facilities 4 rms (3 en suite) (1 fmly) TVB tea/coffee ✖ Cen ht TVL Last d noon **Parking** 8 **Notes** Closed Dec-Feb ⊠

TAHILLA
MAP 01 A2

◆◆◆◆

GH *Tahilla Cove Guesthouse*

☎ 064 45204 ▤ 064 45104
e-mail tahillacove@eircom.net
Dir 8km E of Sweem, off N70 Ring of Kerry road

Set in a 5-hectare seashore estate overlooking Kenmare Bay, Tahilla Cove has lawns and terraces that sweep down to the water's edge, where there is a private pier. The comfortable and well-appointed bedrooms are located in two houses and most have views of the bay. The Waterhouse family take pride in cooking with fresh local produce and dinner is available. This is a good base for golfing, hill walking, fishing and bathing.

Facilities 3 en suite 6 annexe en suite (4 fmly) in dining room STV TVB tea/coffee Direct dial from bedrooms Licensed Cen ht TVL No coaches Dinner Last d 9.30am **Parking** 20 **Notes** Closed Nov-Etr rs Tue & Wed evenings

TRALEE
MAP 01 A2

◆◆◆◆

T&C Brianville Guesthouse

Clogherbrien, Fenit Rd ☎ 066 7126645 ▤ 066 7126645
e-mail michsmit@gofree.indigo.ie
Dir R558 Tralee-Fenit road, 2km from Tralee

This welcoming large yellow bungalow, situated on the road to Fenit on the outskirts of Tralee, is within easy reach of beaches, golf and the Aqua Dome. Bedrooms vary in size and are attractively furnished with hand-crafted pine. Breakfast is served in the bright sitting/dining room overlooking the well-tended garden.

Facilities 5 en suite (1 fmly) ⊗ STV TVB tea/coffee ✖ Cen ht TVL **Parking** 10

◆◆◆◆ ✔

Heatherville Farm *(Q 816118)*

Blennerville
☎ 066 7121054 & 08761 77456 ▤ 066 7121054
Mrs Kerins
e-mail heatherville@eircom.net
Dir Off N86 Dingle Rd at Blennerville, premises 0.8km on left

A luxury modern farmhouse just off the Tralee to Dingle road. Mrs Hanna Kerins and her daughter, Ann, extend a warm welcome to their guests and ensure their comfort. Close to the restored Blennerville Windmill and steam railway.

Facilities 6 en suite (2 fmly) (4 GF) ⊗ TVB tea/coffee ✖ Cen ht TVL 40 acres Beef **Parking** 8 **Notes** Closed Nov-Feb

◆◆◆

GH *Tralee Townhouse*

1-2 High St ☎ 066 7181111 ▤ 066 7181112
e-mail traleetownhouse@eircom.net

Located in the town centre, close to pubs, restaurants and Splash World, this friendly guest house offers well-equipped bedrooms with a lift to all floors. Guests can relax in the comfortable lounge and

continued

Ireland

Eleanor Collins serves a variety of breakfast dishes and home baked breads.

GH Tralee Townhouse

Facilities 19 en suite (2 fmly) ⊗ in 9 bedrooms ⊗ in dining room STV TVB tea/coffee Direct dial from bedrooms ✗ Lift Cen ht TVL
Notes Closed 24-28 Dec

CO KILDARE

ATHY   MAP 01 C3

Premier Collection

♦♦♦♦♦

T&C Coursetown Country House

Stradbally Rd ☎ 059 8631101 ▤ 059 8632740
e-mail coursetown@hotmail.com
Dir *N78 at Athy onto R428, 3km from Athy*

This charming Victorian country house stands on a 100-hectare tillage farm and bird sanctuary. It has been extensively refurbished, and all bedrooms are furnished to the highest standards. Convalescent or disabled guests are especially welcome, and Iris and Jim Fox are happy to share their knowledge of the Irish countryside and its wildlife.

Facilities 5 en suite (1 GF) ⊗ TVB tea/coffee Direct dial from bedrooms Cen ht TVL No children 12yrs No coaches **Prices** D €110-€120 **Parking** 22 **Notes** Closed 15 Nov-15 Mar

NEWBRIDGE   MAP 01 C3

♦♦♦♦

GH Annagh Lodge

Naas Rd ☎ 045 433518 ▤ 045 433538
e-mail annaghlodge@eircom.net
Dir *0.8km NE of town centre on R445*

Annagh Lodge is an attractive house within walking distance of the town. Derna and Noel Wallace are very hospitable and their house is carefully decorated. The smart bedrooms are vary in size, and one room is designed for easier access. There is a relaxing conservatory, sun deck, television lounge and ample off-road parking.

Facilities 9 en suite (4 fmly) (9 GF) ⊗ TVB tea/coffee Direct dial from bedrooms ✗ Cen ht TVL **Prices** S €50-€80; D €100-€160✷ **Parking** 14

CO KILKENNY

GRAIGUENAMANAGH   MAP 01 C3

♦♦♦♦

GH Brandon View

Ballyling Lower ☎ 059 9724625 ▤ 059 9724625

With panoramic views of Brandon Hill, this purpose-built family home is a good base for touring south-east Ireland. Helen Doyle and her family offer a true welcome to their home, where bedrooms are comfortable and well appointed. Breakfast is served in the conservatory, and refreshments are available in the lounge.

Facilities 5 rms

KILKENNY   MAP 01 C3

♦♦♦♦

GH Butler House

Patrick St ☎ 056 7765707 & 7722828 ▤ 056 7765626
e-mail res@butler.ie
Dir *In centre near Kilkenny Castle*

Once the dower house of Kilkenny Castle, this fine Georgian building fronts onto the main street with secluded gardens at the rear, through which you stroll to have full breakfast in Kilkenny Design Centre. A continental breakfast is served in bedrooms, which feature contemporary decor. There is a comfortable foyer lounge and conference-banqueting suites.

Facilities 13 en suite (4 fmly) ⊗ STV TVB tea/coffee Direct dial from bedrooms ✗ Cen ht No coaches Dinner Last d 10pm
Prices S €80-€155; D €120-€200 **LB Conf** Max 120 Thtr 120 Class 40 Board 40 Del from €140 ✷ **Parking** 24 **Notes** Closed 24-29 Dec

♦♦♦♦

GH Laragh House

Smithsland North, Waterford Rd
☎ 056 7764674 ▤ 056 7703605
e-mail info@laraghhouse.com

This newly built guest house is conveniently situated on the outskirts of the mediaeval city of Kilkenny at the roundabout for Waterford N10. Bedrooms are comfortably furnished, some with four poster beds and Jacuzzi baths, two are on the ground floor. The guest sitting room and breakfast room are contemporary in design and smartly decorated. There is off street parking available.

Facilities 8 en suite ⊗ TV available tea/coffee Direct dial from bedrooms ✗ Cen ht **Prices** D €80-€90✷

Ireland

CO LAOIS

PORTLAOISE MAP 01 C3

Premier Collection

◆◆◆◆◆ 🍴

T&C *Ivyleigh House*

Bank Pl, Church St ☎ 0502 22081 📠 0502 63343
e-mail dinah@ivyleigh.com
Dir Opp town centre multi-storey car park

This refurbished Georgian house, just off the main street and close to
the railway station, is a haven of calm and luxury. The elegant drawing
rooms are complemented by a fine dining room where Dinah
Campion's superb breakfasts are served. Particularly comfortable beds
are dressed with excellent cotton in well-appointed bedrooms.

Facilities 6 en suite ⊗ tea/coffee Direct dial from bedrooms 🐾 Cen ht
TVL No children 8yrs No coaches **Parking** 6 **Notes** Closed 20 Dec-4 Jan

◆◆◆

T&C O'Sullivan Guesthouse

8 Kelly Ville Park ☎ 0502 22774 📠 0502 80863
Dir In town centre opp County Hall car park

This family-run semi-detatched house on the edge of the town offers a
homely atmosphere. The en suite bedrooms are comfortable and
secure parking is available.

Facilities 6 en suite (1 fmly) (2 GF) ⊗ in dining room ⊗ in lounges STV
TVB 🐾 Cen ht TVL **Prices** S €60; D €85✳ **LB** **Parking** 8 **Notes** 🐾

CO LIMERICK

ADARE MAP 01 B3

◆◆◆◆

T&C Berkeley Lodge

Station Rd ☎ 061 396857 📠 061 396857
e-mail berlodge@iol.ie
Dir In village centre

Situated just off the main street of this pretty village, Berkeley Lodge
offers comfortable, well equipped and carefully decorated
accommodation. The lounge leads on to an attractive conservatory-
style breakfast room, which offers an extensive menu.

Facilities 6 en suite (2 fmly) (1 GF) ⊗ TVB tea/coffee 🐾 Cen ht TVL
Prices S €58-€60; D €70✳ **Parking** 6

◆◆◆◆

GH Carrigane House

Rienroe ☎ 061 396778
e-mail carrigane.house@oceanfree.net
Dir Off N21 rdbt 0.4km NE of Adare onto Croom road, 2nd house on
right

Guests can be assured of a warm welcome at this purpose-built house
set in grounds. A relaxing lounge is available, while breakfast is a
particular treat. Ample parking to the front of the building.

Facilities 6 en suite (3 fmly) (1 GF) ⊗ TVB tea/coffee 🐾 Cen ht TVL
Prices S €50; D €65✳ **Parking** 10 **Notes** Closed 15 Dec-10 Jan 🐾

GLIN MAP 01 B3

Premier Collection

◆◆◆◆◆ 🍴 🛏

GH Glin Castle

☎ 068 34173 & 34112 📠 068 34364
e-mail knight@iol.ie
Dir Up Glin village Main St & 1st right

Glin Castle was built in the 18th century and stands in a 202-hectare
estate with formal gardens overlooking the Shannon estuary. The
Knight of Glin has a famous collection of Irish prints and antiques,
which furnish the elaborate reception rooms and sumptuous
bedrooms. Family portraits hang in the dining room, and the dinner
menu includes fruit and vegetables from the walled garden and
quality local produce.

Facilities 15 en suite ⊗ STV TVB Direct dial from bedrooms 🐾
Licensed Cen ht TVL No children 10yrs No coaches ९ ♫ Dinner Last
d 9.30pm **Prices** S €280-€440; D €280-€440✳ **LB** **Conf** Max 20
Thtr 20 Class 20 Board 20 Del from €180 **Parking** 20 **Notes** Closed
30 Nov-1 Mar

KILMALLOCK　　　　　MAP 01 B2

Premier Collection

◆◆◆◆◆ ❦

Flemingstown House *(R 629255)*

☎ 063 98093 ▤ 063 98546 Mrs Sheedy-King
e-mail info@flemingstown.com
Dir On R512 Kilmallock-Fermoy route, 3.2mm from Kilmallock

A lovely 18th-century farmhouse which has been modernised to provide stylish en suite facilities throughout. Public rooms include a comfortably furnished sitting room with antiques, and a dining room with beautiful stained glass windows. At breakfast much of the produce comes from the owners' own farm. Dinner is available by arrangement. The area is excellent for walkers, riders, anglers and golfers.

Facilities 5 en suite (2 fmly) ⊗ TVB tea/coffee ✖ Cen ht No children 8yrs Riding 125 acres mixed Dinner Last d noon **Parking** 20
Notes Closed Nov-Jan

LIMERICK　　　　　MAP 01 B3

◆◆◆

GH Clifton House

Ennis Rd ☎ 061 451166 ▤ 061 451224
e-mail michaelpowell@eircom.net
Dir On N18 towards Shannon Airport, opp Woodfield House Hotel

Providing well-equipped, attractive and very comfortable bedrooms has been the aim of the refurbishment of Michael and Mary Powell's guest house. Complimentary tea and coffee are available in the spacious, relaxing lounge.

Facilities 16 en suite ⊗ in dining room STV TVB Direct dial from bedrooms ✖ Cen ht TVL **Parking** 22 **Notes** Closed 21 Dec-2 Jan

◆◆◆

GH *Old Quarter Lodge*

Denmark St ☎ 061 315320 ▤ 061 316995
e-mail lodge@oldquarter.ie
Dir One-way system to front of Arthurs Quay shopping centre, left at lights onto Denmark St, next to church

The refurbished Old Quarter Lodge is in the city centre. Bedrooms vary in size and are carefully decorated, and suites and family rooms are available. The breakfast room and sitting room are on the first floor, and there is a bar and cafe within the building.

Facilities 26 en suite (2 fmly) ⊗ STV TVB tea/coffee Direct dial from bedrooms ✖ Licensed Cen ht TVL **Conf** Max 30 Thtr 30 Board 20
Notes Closed 24 Dec-1 Jan

CO LONGFORD

LONGFORD　　　　　MAP 01 C4

◆◆◆◆ ❦

Longford Country House − Cumiskeys

(N 173808)

Ennybegs ☎ 043 23320 ▤ 043 23516 Ms Cumiskey
e-mail info@longfordcountryhouse.com
web www.longfordcountryhouse.com
Dir 3rd exit off 2nd rdbt on N4 Longford bypass, 5km, left at x-rds after Old Forge pub, 2nd house on right

A hospitable, Tudor-style house. The parlour has a wrought-iron spiral stairway to the library loft, as well as a cosy sitting room with turf fire and a dining room where dinner is served by arrangement. Other facilities include a games room and pitch and putt. Self-catering cottages are also available.

Facilities 6 rms (5 en suite) (2 fmly) ⊗ FTV TVB tea/coffee ✖ Cen ht TVL Pitch & putt course Games room Aromatherapy Dinner Last d noon
LB **Parking** 20

CO LOUTH

CARLINGFORD　　　　　MAP 01 D4

Premier Collection

◆◆◆◆◆

T&C *Beaufort House*

Ghan Rd ☎ 042 9373879 ▤ 042 9373878
e-mail michaelcaine@beauforthouse.net
Dir On shore of Carlingford Lough, S of East Pier of harbour

Situated in a pretty village on Carlingford Lough, this charming guest house has spacious, well-equipped bedrooms and comfortable public rooms. An interesting breakfast menu includes fresh fish as well as traditional fare and home baking. Dinner is available for large parties by arrangement.

Facilities 5 en suite (2 fmly) (1 GF) ⊗ TVB tea/coffee Direct dial from bedrooms ✖ Licensed Cen ht TVL No coaches ⚓ Yacht charter and sailing school Dinner Last d 8pm **Conf** Max 20 Board 20 **Parking** 20

DUNDALK　　　　　MAP 01 D4

◆◆◆◆

T&C Rosemount

Dublin Rd ☎ 042 935878 ▤ 042 9335878
e-mail maisieb7@eircom.net
Dir On N1 2km S of Dundalk

This handsome bungalow stands in beautiful gardens on the southern outskirts of the town close to Dundalk IT College. The nicely furnished bedrooms are attractively decorated and have many thoughtful extras. There is also a comfortable lounge and ample parking.

Facilities 6 annexe en suite (4 fmly) (6 GF) ⊗ TVB tea/coffee ✖ Cen ht TVL **Parking** 8 **Notes** 🐾

Ireland

CO MAYO

ACHILL ISLAND
MAP 01 A4

◆◆◆◆

GH Gray's Guest House

Dugort ☎ 098 43244 & 43315
Dir 11km NW of Achill Sound. Off R319 to Doogort

This welcoming guest house is in Doogort, on the northern shore of Achill Island, at the foot of the Slievemore mountains. There is a smart conservatory and various lounges, the cosy bedrooms are well appointed, and dinner is served nightly in the cheerful dining room. A self-contained villa, ideal for families, is also available.

Facilities 5 en suite 10 annexe en suite (4 fmly) (2 GF) ⊗ TVB tea/coffee Licensed Cen ht TVL Pool Table 🎱 Table tennis Dinner Last d 6pm **Prices** S €61; D €110✳ **Parking** 30 **Notes** Closed 25 Dec-1 Jan

◆◆◆

T&C Lavelles Seaside House ◇

Dooega ☎ 098 45116 & 01 2828142
e-mail celialavelle@eircom.net
Dir R319 NW from Achill Sound, 4km turn left to Dooega

Friendliness and good food are offered at this comfortable guest house close to the beach. Facilities include a lounge, breakfast room, and a traditional pub where seafood is available during the high season. The more-spacious bedrooms are in the new wing.

Facilities 14 en suite (5 fmly) ⊗ tea/coffee 🐾 Licensed Cen ht TVL Dinner Last d 4.30pm **Prices** S €40-€45; D €60-€80✳ **LB** **Parking** 20 **Notes** Closed 2 Nov-mid Mar rs Dinner served Jul/Aug only

CASTLEBAR
MAP 01 B4

◆◆◆

GH Lough Lannagh Holiday Village

Old Westport Rd ☎ 094 902 7111 ▤ 094 902 7295
e-mail llv@eircom.net
Dir N5 around Castlebar. 3rd rdbt, 2nd exit. Next left, past playground 1st building on right

Lough Lannagh is in a delightful wooded area within walking distance of Castlebar. There is a conference centre, fitness centre, tennis, table tennis, laundry and drying facilities, a private kitchen, and many activities for children. Bedrooms are well appointed and breakfast is served in the Café. Dinner is available by appointment for groups.

continued

Facilities 24 en suite (24 fmly) (12 GF) ⊗ in 20 bedrooms ⊗ in dining room ⊗ in lounges TVB Direct dial from bedrooms 🐾 Cen ht TVL ⚲ Sauna Gymnasium Steam room, table tennis, child activities Jul-Aug Dinner **Prices** S €55; D €80✳ **LB** **Conf** Max 100 Thtr 100 Class 54 Board 34 **Parking** 24 **Notes** Closed 15 Dec-8 Jan

CONG
MAP 01 B4

Premier Collection

◆◆◆◆◆ ⊜

T&C Ballywarren House

Ballymacgibbon North, Cross
☎ 094 954 6989 ▤ 094 954 6989
e-mail ballywarrenhouse@eircom.net
Dir R334 Headford-Ballinrobe route, onto R346 at Cross, 1.2km down Cong Rd on right

Diane and David Skelton's long history of excellent hospitality continues at Ballywarren, a fine house set in grounds in a scenic area. Reservations for Diane's excellent dinners are advised.

Facilities 3 en suite ⊗ TVB Direct dial from bedrooms 🐾 Licensed Cen ht No children 14yrs No coaches Fishing 🎣 Dinner Last d 9am **Prices** S €98-€136; D €124-€148 **Parking** 4

WESTPORT
MAP 01 B4

◆◆◆◆

GH Augusta Lodge

Golf Links Rd ☎ 098 28900 ▤ 098 28995
e-mail info@augustalodge.ie
web www.augustalodge.ie
Dir N5 from Westport towards Newport, 1st house on left

This comfortable house close to the town centre is a haven for golfers. Bedrooms are well appointed, as are the relaxing lounge and breakfast room, which are decorated with golf memorabilia. There is a putting green on site and tee time can be arranged at Wesport and other courses.

Facilities 10 en suite (2 fmly) (3 GF) ⊗ STV TVB tea/coffee Direct dial from bedrooms 🐾 Cen ht TVL ♨ **Prices** S €45-€60 **LB** **Parking** 14 **Notes** Closed 23-27 Dec

◆◆◆◆

T&C Carrabaun House

Carrabaun, Leenane Rd ☎ 098 26196 ▤ 098 28466
e-mail carrabaun@anu.ie
Dir On N59 S. Leave Westport town, 1.6km pass Maxol station on left, house 200 metres

Friendly hosts, attractively furnished bedrooms and stunning views are all features here. Pilgrimage mountain Croagh Patrick, and Clew Bay beneath, are framed by picture windows in the sitting and dining rooms. There is private parking, and gardens surround the house.

Facilities 6 en suite (6 fmly) (1 GF) ⊗ TVB tea/coffee 🐾 Cen ht TVL **Prices** S €45-€50; D €66✳ **Parking** 12 **Notes** Closed 16-31 Dec

♦♦♦ ✔

Bertra House ◇ (L 903823)

Thornhill, Murrisk ☎ 098 64833 🖨 098 64833 Mrs Gill
e-mail bertrahse@eire.net
Dir W of Wesport off R335 near Croagh Patrick

This attractive bungalow overlooks the Blue Flag Bertra beach. Four bedrooms are en suite and the fifth its own bathroom. Breakfast is generous and Mrs Gill offers tea and home-baked cakes on arrival in the cosy lounge.

Facilities 5 rms (4 en suite) (3 fmly) (5 GF) ⊗ TVB tea/coffee ✖ Cen ht TVL 42 acres beef and sheep **Prices** S €40-€43; D €60-€65✳
LB **Parking** 7

♦♦♦

GH *Linden Hall*

Altamount St ☎ 098 27005
e-mail lindenhall@iol.ie
Dir Opp Hastings/EMO garage towards rail station

This spacious house lies in the heart of Westport and is within walking distance of restaurants, pubs and shops. Bedrooms are comfortable and well furnished. Breakfast is served in the ground-floor dining room. There is good on-street parking. The property is non-smoking throughout.

Facilities 4 en suite (3 fmly) ⊗ TVB tea/coffee ✖ Cen ht **Notes** ⊛

CO MEATH

NAVAN   MAP 01 C4

♦♦♦♦

T&C Killyon

Dublin Rd ☎ 046 907 1224 🖨 046 907 2766
e-mail info@killyonguesthouse.ie
Dir On N3, River Boyne side, opp Ardboyne Hotel

This luxurious house has fine views over the River Boyne from its balcony. Comfortable, well-appointed bedrooms and an inviting attractive lounge make this a popular place to stay. Owner Mrs Fogarty offers a wide range of home cooking.

Facilities 6 en suite (1 fmly) (1 GF) ⊗ STV TVB Direct dial from bedrooms ✖ Cen ht TVL Fishing **Prices** S €45-€50; D €70-€80✳ **Parking** 10

CO OFFALY

BIRR   MAP 01 C3

♦♦♦♦

GH Aaron House

Kinnitty ☎ 057 913 7040 🖨 057 913 7040
e-mail bgrimes@oceanfree.net
Dir 0.4km from Kinnitty Castle gate

This well-designed house is in the delightful village of Kinnitty, close to Kinnitty Castle. Bedrooms are spacious and stylishly furnished, and one ground-floor room has easier access. Guests can help themselves to

continued

tea or coffee in the cosy sitting room. Home-cooked breakfasts are an appealing star to the day and Betty Grimes is happy to advise on local tours.

Facilities 5 en suite (2 fmly) (1 GF) ⊗ TVB tea/coffee Direct dial from bedrooms ✖ Cen ht TVL **Prices** S €60; D €75✳ **Parking** 10

CO SLIGO

BALLYSADARE   MAP 01 B5

♦♦♦

T&C Seashore House

Lisduff ☎ 071 916 7827 🖨 071 916 7827
e-mail seashore@oceanfree.net
Dir 2.5m from village. N4 onto N59 W at Ballisadore, 4km Seashore signed, 0.6km right to house

An attractive dormer bungalow in a quiet seashore location. A comfortable lounge with open turf fire and sunny conservatory dining room looking out over attractive landscaped gardens to sea and mountain scenery. Bedrooms are attractively appointed and comfortable, and there is also a tennis court and bicycle storage.

Facilities 5 rms (4 en suite) (2 fmly) (3 GF) ⊗ STV TVB ✖ Cen ht TVL No children ◟ Solarium Bird watching facility **Prices** S €45-€55; D €75✳ LB **Parking** 6

INISHCRONE   MAP 01 B5

Premier Collection

♦♦♦♦♦

GH *Seasons Lodge*

Bartragh ☎ 096 37122
e-mail dermot@seasonslodge.ie
Dir Beside Enniscrone Golf Club

The modern guest house is next to Enniscrone Golf Course and close to the famous seaweed baths and a lovely beach. The spacious bedrooms are fitted to a high standard, are all on the ground floor and have access to the garden. There is a relaxing sitting and dining room where breakfast is served. Proprietor Dermot O'Regan is happy to arrange golf or tours.

Facilities 4 en suite (2 fmly) (4 GF) ⊗ STV TVB Direct dial from bedrooms ✖ Cen ht TVL No children 8yrs No coaches **Parking** 10
Notes Closed Dec-Jan

SLIGO   MAP 01 B5

♦♦♦

T&C *Aisling*

Cairns Hill ☎ 071 916 0704 🖨 071 916 0704
e-mail aislingsligo@eircom.net
Dir N4 to Sligo, right at 1st lights, S from Sligo past Esso service station, left at lights

This well-cared for modern bungalow stands only a short distance from the town centre. Bedrooms offer all modern comforts and there is a pleasant sitting room with a dining area, where at breakfast time guests can enjoy mountain views.

Facilities 5 rms (3 en suite) (2 fmly) (5 GF) ⊗ STV TVB ✖ Cen ht TVL No children 6yrs **Parking** 6 **Notes** Closed 24-28 Dec

Ireland

TOBERCURRY
MAP 01 B4

◆◆◆

T&C *Cruckawn House*

Ballymote/Boyle Rd ☎ 071 918 5188 ▤ 071 918 5188
e-mail cruckawn@esatclear.ie

Dir *300 metres off N17 on R294, on right, overlooking golf course*

Overlooking the golf course, just a short walk from the town centre, Cruckawn House offers friendly hospitality. The dining room adjoins the comfortable sun lounge, and there is also a television lounge. Salmon and coarse fishing, riding and mountain climbing are all available nearby and the area is renowned for traditional Irish music.

Facilities 5 en suite (2 fmly) ⊗ in bedrooms ⊗ in dining room ⊗ in 1 lounge TVB ✖ Cen ht TVL Golf 9 Gymnasium Pool Table ⚓ Game & coarse fishing, bike hire Dinner Last d 6pm **Parking** 8 **Notes** Closed Nov-Feb

CO TIPPERARY

BALLYKISTEEN
MAP 01 B3

◆◆◆◆

GH Ballykisteen Lodge B&B

☎ 062 33403 ▤ 062 33711
e-mail ballykisteenlodge@oceanfree.net

Dir *3km from Tipperary on N24 opp Tipperary Racecourse*

The well-presented guest house stands next to the racecourse and Ballykisteen Golf Centre and offers attractive bedrooms and a sitting room. Breakfast features home baking and a variety of freshly cooked dishes, and is served in the cosy dining room that looks over a delightful garden.

Facilities 4 en suite (3 fmly) ⊗ TVB tea/coffee ✖ Cen ht TVL No coaches **Prices** S €50-€55; D €70-€80✳ LB **Parking** 10

BANSHA
MAP 01 C3

◆◆◆◆ ❦

Bansha House (R 962320)

☎ 062 54194 ▤ 062 54215 Mr & Mrs Marnane
e-mail banshahouse@eircom.net

Dir *Off N24 in Bansha opp Statoil filling station*

A Georgian atmosphere on 40 hectares of farmland, where brood mares and foals roam freely. Riding can be arranged at the nearby

continued

Equestrian Centre. This comfortable house is noted for its excellent home baking, and the hosts are friendly and hospitable. Dinner is available by request.

Facilities 8 rms (5 en suite) (1 fmly) (2 GF) ⊗ ✖ Licensed Cen ht TVL Fishing Riding 100 acres horses cattle Dinner Last d 7pm **Parking** 10 **Notes** Closed 21-31 Dec

CASHEL
MAP 01 C3

◆◆◆◆

GH *Aulber House*

Golden Rd ☎ 062 63713 & 087 6314720 ▤ 062 63715
e-mail beralley@eircom.net

Dir *From Cashel on N74. Last house on left*

A newly built guest house, set in landscaped gardens just a 5-minute walk from the Rock of Cashel and town centre. Spacious bedrooms are thoughtfully furnished and equipped, and include one fitted for the less mobile. Relax by the open fire in the sitting room, or enjoy views of the surrounding countryside and the Rock from the first-floor lounge.

Facilities 12 en suite (2 fmly) (3 GF) ⊗ STV TVB tea/coffee Direct dial from bedrooms ✖ Cen ht TVL **Parking** 20 **Notes** Closed 23 Dec-2 Jan

◆◆◆◆ ⌨

GH Baileys Guesthouse & Restaurant

Main St ☎ 062 61937 ▤ 062 63957
e-mail info@baileys-ireland.com

Dir *In town centre*

The listed town-centre building dates from 1709 and has been carefully restored to its original splendour. It now offers modern comforts in bedrooms of varying size, with a relaxing lounge and very good restaurant.

Facilities 19 en suite (2 fmly) ⊗ STV FTV TVB Direct dial from bedrooms ✖ Licensed Lift Cen ht ⌨ Sauna Gymnasium Dinner Last d 9.30pm **Prices** S fr €80; D €180 LB **Parking** 19 **Notes** Closed 24-28 Dec

See advertisement on opposite page

♦♦♦♦
T&C Thornbrook House ◇

Dualla Rd ☎ 062 62388 📠 062 61480
e-mail thornbrookhouse@eircom.net
web www.thornbrookhouse.com
Dir *1st right after tourist office onto Friar St, left after church onto R691, house 1km on right*

Visitors to Thornbrook will relish the combined skills of the Kennedys. Mary runs this attractively appointed bungalow with great attention to detail, while the superbly landscaped gardens are the handiwork of Willie Kennedy. Comfortable lounge and bedrooms, ample parking.

Facilities 5 rms (3 en suite) (1 fmly) (5 GF) ⊘ TVB tea/coffee ✖ Cen ht **Prices** S €40-€55; D €60-€72 **Parking** 8 **Notes** Closed Nov-Mar

♦♦♦
T&C Ashmore House

John St ☎ 062 61286 📠 062 62789
e-mail info@ashmorehouse.com
Dir *Off N8 in town centre onto John St, house 100 metres on right*

Ashmore House is set in a pretty walled garden in the town centre with an enclosed car park. Guests have use of a large sitting and dining room, and bedrooms come in a variety of sizes from big family rooms to a more compact double.

Facilities 5 en suite (2 fmly) ⊘ STV TVB tea/coffee ✖ Cen ht TVL Dinner Last d 24hrs notice **Parking** 10

DUNDRUM
MAP 01 C3

♦♦♦♦
GH *Weston's Lot*

Grovelawn ☎ 062 71915 📠 062 71915
e-mail info@westonslot
Dir *Off R505 at Dundrum House Hotel, house 300 metres on right*

Set in a quiet rural setting opposite woodland, this house offers very relaxing and comfortable accommodation. A newly built property, near the local golf course and close to Dundrum House Hotel, where a warm welcome is guaranteed.

Facilities 5 rms (5 pri facs) ⊘ TVB tea/coffee ✖ Licensed Cen ht TVL **Conf** Max 14 Board 14 Del from €60 ✳ **Parking** 10

If the freedom to smoke or be in a non-smoking atmosphere is important to you, check the rules when you book

NENAGH
MAP 01 B3

♦♦♦♦
T&C Ashley Park House

☎ 067 38223 & 38013 📠 067 38013
e-mail margaret@ashleypark.com
Dir *6.5km N of Nenagh. Off N52 across lake, signed on left & left under arch*

The attractive, colonial style farmhouse was built in 1770. Set in gardens that run down to Lake Ourna, it has spacious bedrooms with quality antique furnishings. Breakfast is served in the dining room overlooking the lake, and dinner is available by arrangement. There is a delightful walled garden, and a boat for the fishing on the lake available.

Facilities 5 en suite (3 fmly) ⊘ TVB tea/coffee Licensed Cen ht TVL ch fac Golf 18 Fishing Snooker Dinner Last d 9pm **Prices** S €50-€55; D €90-€110✳ **Conf** Max 30 Board 30 **Parking** 30 **Notes** Civ Wed 90 ⌨

Ireland

NENAGH continued

◆◆◆

T&C *Williamsferry House*

Fintan Lalor St ☎ 067 31118 🖷 067 31256
e-mail williamsferry@eircom.net
Dir *From Limerick into Nenagh, over 3 rdbts, right at Centra foodstore on corner*

This refurbished house is situated close to local amenities, including water sports and cruising on the River Shannon. There is a comfortable television lounge and a breakfast room, and two of the bedrooms are on the ground floor.

Facilities 6 en suite (3 GF) ⊘ TVB tea/coffee ✗ Cen ht TVL
Parking 10 **Notes** Closed Xmas/New Year 🐾

THURLES   MAP 01 C3

Premier Collection

◆◆◆◆◆ ⊜

GH *Inch House Country House & Restaurant*

☎ 0504 51348 & 51261 🖷 0504 51754
e-mail inchhse@iol.ie
Dir *6.5km NE of Thurles on R498*

This lovely Georgian house was built in 1720 and the Egan family has restored the property. The elegant drawing room ceiling is particularly outstanding among the grand public rooms, and the spacious bedrooms are delightfully appointed. Reservations are essential in the fine restaurant, where an imaginative choice of freshly prepared dishes using local produce are on offer.

Facilities 5 en suite (2 fmly) ⊘ TVB tea/coffee Direct dial from bedrooms ✗ Licensed Cen ht TVL Dinner Last d 9.30pm **Parking** 40

Premier Collection

◆◆◆◆◆

T&C The Castle

Two Mile Borris ☎ 0504 44324 🖷 0504 44352
e-mail b&b@thecastletmb.com
Dir *7km W of Thurles. On N75 200 metres W of Twomileborris at Castle*

Pierce and Joan are very welcoming hosts. Their fascinating house, sheltered by a 16th-century tower house, has been in the Duggan

family for 200 years. Bedrooms are comfortable and spacious, there is a relaxing lounge, and the dining room overlooks the delightful garden. Golf, fishing, hill walking, and traditional pubs and restaurants are all nearby. Dinner is available by arrangement.

Facilities 4 en suite (3 fmly) ⊘ TVB tea/coffee ✗ Cen ht TVL
No coaches ॰ Fishing Pool Table ⅃⅃ Dinner Last d 11am
Prices S €48-€60; D €76-€100 **LB** **Conf** Max 40 **Parking** 30

◆◆◆◆

GH *Abbeyvale House B & B*

Cashel Rd, Holy Cross ☎ 0504 43032 🖷 0504 43032
e-mail info@abbeyvalehouse.com
Dir *On N8 at Horse & Jockey turn right, then 1st left to Holycross. Left towards Cashel House opp Abbey Tavern pub*

This new, purpose-built house is at the edge of the historic village of Holycross. Bedrooms are well appointed, comfortable and painted in muted colours. Breakfast is served in a conservatory dining room that adjoins a cosy lounge.

Facilities 4 en suite (1 fmly) (1 GF) ⊘ TVB tea/coffee ✗ Cen ht ch fac No coaches Fishing Riding Snooker Sauna Jacuzzi, Tanning Dinner Last d 2pm **Conf** Max 14 Board 14 **Parking** 8 **Notes** 🐾

TIPPERARY   MAP 01 C3

◆◆◆

GH Ach-na-Sheen House ◇

Clonmel Rd ☎ 062 51298 🖷 062 80467
e-mail gernoonan@eircom.net
Dir *In town centre*

This large, modern bungalow, only a 5-minute walk from main street of Tipperary, offers sound accommodation.

Facilities 8 en suite (5 fmly) (6 GF) ⊘ STV TVB tea/coffee ✗ Cen ht
Prices S €40-€50; D €68-€84 **Parking** 13 **Notes** Closed 11 Dec-8 Jan

CO WATERFORD

ARDMORE   MAP 01 C2

◆◆◆◆

GH *Newtown Farm Guesthouse*

Grange ☎ 024 94143 & 086 2600799 🖷 024 94143
e-mail newtownfarm@eircom.net
Dir *On N25 Dungarvan-Youghal road, left at Flemings pub*

Guests can be sure of a warm welcome at this comfortable modern farmhouse. Bedrooms look out over the dairy farm, and guests are welcome to stroll about, looking at the animals and farm activities. There is a play area for children, and home baking is a feature. Close to a variety of beaches and golf courses.

Facilities 6 annexe en suite (3 fmly) ⊘ in bedrooms ⊘ in dining room STV TVB tea/coffee Direct dial from bedrooms Cen ht TVL ॰ Snooker Pool Table Last d 6pm **Parking** 12 **Notes** Closed Dec-Feb

continued

BALLYMACARBRY — MAP 01 C2

Premier Collection

◆◆◆◆◆ ❦

Glasha Farmhouse (S1104106)

Glasha ☎ 052 36108 ▤ 052 36108 Mr & Mrs O'Gorman
e-mail glasha@eircom.net
Dir Signed off R671 between Clommel & Dungarvan

Excellent accommodation and a warm welcome are assured at this comfortable country house. Two of the bedrooms are on the ground floor and all rooms are individually styled with smart furnishings and lots of personal touches. Home-cooking is a speciality and trout fishing is available on the river which runs through the grounds.

Facilities 8 en suite (5 fmly) (2 GF) ⊗ TVB tea/coffee ✗ Cen ht TVL Fishing 150 acres dairy Dinner Last d 5.30pm **Parking** 10 **Notes** Closed 20-27 Dec

Premier Collection

◆◆◆◆◆

GH Hanoras Cottage

Nire Valley ☎ 052 36134 & 36442 ▤ 052 36540
e-mail hanorascottage@eircom.net
Dir From Clonmel or Dungarvan R672 to Ballymacarbry, at Melodys Bar turn into Nire Valley, establishment by river bridge beside church

Nestling in the beautiful Nire Valley, Hanora's Cottage offers spacious bedrooms with jacuzzis. Lounge areas are very comfortable and the award winning restaurant serves fresh local produce. Mrs Wall's breakfasts are a real feast and deserve to be savoured at leisure.

Facilities 10 en suite ⊗ TVB tea/coffee Direct dial from bedrooms ✗ Licensed Cen ht TVL No children No coaches Conservatory with hot spa tub Dinner Last d 8.30pm **Parking** 15 **Notes** Closed Xmas wk rs Sun

CAPPOQUIN — MAP 01 C2

Premier Collection

◆◆◆◆◆

GH Richmond House

☎ 058 54278 ▤ 058 54988
e-mail info@richmondhouse.net
Dir On N72, 1km from Cappoquin on Dungarvan road

An 18th-century Georgian country house with an award-winning restaurant and private parkland. Set in the heart of the Blackwater Valley, this splendid building has been carefully restored and is a good location for fishing, golfing and walking holidays. Each room is inviting with antique pieces to suit each room and modern comforts.

Facilities 9 en suite (2 fmly) ⊗ TVB tea/coffee Direct dial from bedrooms ✗ Licensed Cen ht Dinner Last d 9pm **Parking** 40 **Notes** Closed 23 Dec-20 Jan

DUNGARVAN — MAP 01 C2

Premier Collection

◆◆◆◆◆ ❦

The Castle Country House (S 192016)

Millstreet, Cappagh
☎ 058 68049 ▤ 058 68099 Mrs Nugent
e-mail castlefm@iol.ie
Dir 13km NW of Dungarvan. Off N72 onto R671 N to Millstreet

This delightful house is in the west wing of a 15th-century castle. Guests are spoiled by host Joan Nugent who loves to cook and hunt out antiques for her visitors to enjoy. She is helped by her husband Emmett who enjoys showing off his high-tech dairy farm and is a fount of local knowledge. Bedrooms are spacious and enjoy lovely views. There is a river walk and a beautiful garden to relax in.

Facilities 5 en suite (1 fmly) ⊗ TVB tea/coffee Licensed Cen ht Fishing Farm tour 200 acres dairy & beef Dinner Last d 5pm **Parking** 11 **Notes** Closed Dec-Feb

Premier Collection

◆◆◆◆◆

GH Powersfield House

Ballinamuck West ☎ 058 45594 ▤ 058 45550
e-mail powersfieldhouse@cablesurf.com
Dir R672 from Dungarvan for Killarney/Clonmel, 2nd left, 1st house on right

Eunice Powers' warm welcome is matched by her cooking skills, charming bedrooms and very high standards. Her Georgian-style residence is set in grounds, and the comfortable sitting room is the venue for afternoon tea or drinks beside the fire.

Facilities 6 en suite (3 fmly) (1 GF) ⊗ in bedrooms ⊗ in dining room STV TVB Direct dial from bedrooms ✗ Licensed Cen ht Dinner Last d 8pm **Conf** Max 20 Thtr 20 Class 12 Board 12 **Parking** 12

Premier Collection

◆◆◆◆◆ ▤ ❦

Sliabh gCua Farmhouse (S 191057)

Touraneena, Ballinamult ☎ 058 47120 Mrs Cullinan
e-mail breedacullinan@sliabhgcua.com
Dir Off R672, 15km NW from Dungarvan. Farmhouse signed left 1km

This creeper-clad farmhouse, set in landscaped grounds, is a sign of the warm welcome offered by the Cullinan family. Rooms are comfortably appointed, each with two views of the gardens. Breakfast is a particular delight, with bread baked each morning and a great selection of fruits.

Facilities 4 en suite (1 fmly) ⊗ tea/coffee ✗ Cen ht TVL Pool Table 200 acres dairy beef arable forestry **Parking** 6 **Notes** Closed Nov-Mar ▤

DUNGARVAN continued

◆◆◆◆

GH *An Bohreen*

Killineen West ☎ 051 291010 ▤ 051 291011
e-mail mulligans@anbohreen.com
Dir N25 NE from Dungarvan, 9.5km left, house 0.4km

A purpose-built bungalow, commanding panoramic views over Dungarvan Bay and the Commeragh Mountains. Bedrooms are comfortable and individually decorated, two have balconies. Contemporary, open-plan public areas take advantage of the wonderful scenery. The Mulligans are passionate about their business, Ann cooking each evening, (booking advised) and home baking is her speciality. Jim will organise trips and make bookings for golf at the many nearby Championship courses.

Facilities 4 en suite (4 GF) ⊘ ✖ Licensed Cen ht TVL No children 12yrs No coaches Horse drawn carriage rides Dinner Last d 10am **Parking** 6 **Notes** Closed Nov-mid Mar

◆◆◆◆ ▤ ✤

Gortnadiha Lodge *(X 259890)*

Ring ☎ 058 46142 Ms Harty
e-mail gortnadihalodge@eircom.net
Dir N25 onto R674 to Ring, 1.5km 1st left, 400 metres on right

Set on an elevated site overlooking Dungarvan Bay at the edge of the Gaeltacht, the Irish language speaking region, this modern house if very comfortably furnished with antiques. Breakfast is an extensive menu served at a large mahogany table in a very relaxing room with lovely views of the garden.

Facilities 3 rms TV1B tea/coffee Cen ht TVL **Prices** S € 45; D € 80 **Notes**

DUNMORE EAST   MAP 01 C2

◆◆◆◆

GH The Beach Guest House

Lower Village ☎ 051 383316 ▤ 051 383319
e-mail beachouse@eircom.net
Dir R684 from Waterford into Dunmore East, 1st left after filling station to sea wall, house on left

This purpose-built guest house is family run and centrally placed facing the beach in this picturesque village. No two bedrooms are alike but all share high standards of comfort and quality with a wealth of thoughtful extras. Expect a delicious breakfast served in the conservatory-style dining room, and relax in the lounge or on the patio.

Facilities 7 en suite (1 fmly) (1 GF) ⊘ TVB tea/coffee Direct dial from bedrooms ✖ Cen ht TVL No children 6yrs No coaches **Prices** S € 45-€ 60; D € 80-€ 90✳ **LB** **Parking** 11 **Notes** Closed Nov-Feb

TRAMORE   MAP 01 C2

◆◆◆◆

T&C *Glenorney*

Newtown ☎ 051 381056 ▤ 051 381103
e-mail glenoney@iol.ie
Dir On R675 opp Tramore Golf Club

A beautifully spacious and luxurious home with spectacular views of Tramore Bay, located opposite a championship golf course. Great attention has been paid to detail and there is an extensive breakfast menu. Bedrooms are carefully decorated and the lounge is comfortably furnished. There is also a sun room, patio and garden.

Facilities 6 en suite (2 fmly) (3 GF) ⊘ TVB tea/coffee Direct dial from bedrooms ✖ Cen ht TVL **Parking** 6 **Notes** Closed Xmas

◆◆◆◆

GH *Beach Haven House*

Tivoli Ter ☎ 051 390208 ▤ 051 330971
e-mail beachhavenhouse@eircom.net
Dir From Waterford R675 into Tramore, over 1st rdbt, house 200 metres on left

This newly renovated purpose-built house is well positioned on the main road to Tramore town. The distinctive split-level building offers a range of bedrooms all fitted to a high standard. The owners are very hospitable and go to great lengths to ensure a comfortable stay. Breakfast choices include some American-style options.

Facilities 8 en suite (4 fmly) ⊘ TVB tea/coffee Direct dial from bedrooms ✖ Cen ht TVL No coaches **Parking** 9 **Notes** Closed 26 Dec-Feb

◆◆◆◆

T&C *Cliff House*

Cliff Rd ☎ 051 381497 & 391296 ▤ 051 381497
e-mail hilary@cliffhouse.ie
Dir Off R675, left at Ritz thatched pub

A comfortable and spacious home with panoramic views of Tramore Bay and secure private parking. All bedrooms are decorated to a high standard, with modern facilities, and most rooms have sea views. The extensive breakfast menu offers many delicious choices. This is a good base for touring, and future developments include rooms with private balconies overlooking the bay.

Facilities 6 en suite (3 fmly) (3 GF) ⊘ STV TVB tea/coffee ✖ Cen ht TVL No children 6yrs **Parking** 10 **Notes** Closed 20 Dec-Jan

WATERFORD   MAP 01 C2

Premier Collection

◆◆◆◆◆ ♥

Foxmount Country House (S 659091)

Passage East Rd, Dunmore Rd
☎ 051 874308 ▤ 051 854906 Mrs Kent
e-mail info@foxmountcountryhouse.com
Dir *From Waterford onto Dunmore East road, 2.5km left fork towards Passage East for 0.8km, right at next T-junct*

This charming 17th-century country house is set on a busy dairy farm amid beautiful lawns and gardens with screening trees and a hard tennis court. Carefully modernised, it offers en suite bedrooms and attentive service from the charming hostess. The farm and gardens provide most of the raw materials for the carefully prepared evening meals.

Facilities 5 en suite (1 fmly) ⊛ ✳ Cen ht TVL ⚲ Table tennis 200 acres dairy **LB** **Parking** 6 **Notes** Closed early Nov-early Mar ⊛

Premier Collection

◆◆◆◆◆

T&C *Sion Hill House & Gardens*

Sion Hill, Ferrybank ☎ 051 851558 ▤ 051 851678
e-mail sionhill@eircom.net
Dir *Near city centre on N25 Rosslare route*

Situated close to the city, this 18th-century residence has extensive peaceful gardens, which include a walled garden, a meadow and woodlands. Flanked by two pavillions, the house has been refurbished to provide two fine reception rooms and comfortable en suite bedrooms. The friendly owners like to mix with their guests, as the visitors' book shows.

Facilities 4 en suite (4 fmly) ⊛ STV TVB tea/coffee ✳ Cen ht TVL No coaches **Parking** 16 **Notes** Closed mid Dec-early Jan

◆◆◆◆

GH Diamond Hill Country House

Diamond Hill, Slieverue ☎ 051 832855 ▤ 051 832254
e-mail info@staydiamondhill.com
Dir *2km from Waterford off N25 to Rosslare*

Extensive refurbishment has been carried out to a very high standard at this friendly house. These include spacious new bedrooms, comfortable lounges and a private car park. Diamond Hill is a welcoming home with lovely gardens and a sun terrace.

Facilities 17 en suite (6 fmly) (9 GF) ⊛ STV TVB tea/coffee Direct dial from bedrooms ✳ Cen ht TVL Dinner Last d 8pm **Prices** S €40-€50; D €35-€45✳ **Parking** 20 **Notes** Closed 22-27 Dec

◆◆◆◆

GH *The Coach House*

Butlerstown Castle, Butlerstown, Cork Rd
☎ 051 384656 ▤ 051 384751
e-mail coachhse@iol.ie
Dir *N25 from Waterford Crystal Factory towards Cork, 5km left at x-rds, Coach House signed, next left, house on right*

Built in 1870 as the coach house to Butlerstown Castle, this comfortable house has been skilfully refurbished. There is a fine lounge and the bedrooms are well equipped and furnished in traditional pine; a sauna is available.

Facilities 7 en suite (1 fmly) ⊛ TVB tea/coffee Direct dial from bedrooms ✳ Licensed Cen ht No coaches Sauna **Parking** 15 **Notes** Closed Nov-Apr

◆◆◆

T&C Belmont House

Belmont Rd, Rosslare Rd, Ferrybank
☎ 051 832174 ▤ 051 832174
e-mail belmonthouse@eircom.net
Dir *2km from Waterford on N25 to Rosslare road*

The dormer bungalow is convenient for the Waterford Glass Factory, golf clubs and the city centre. There are tea and coffee facilities in the sitting room and the dining room looks out across the garden to the countryside beyond. Bedrooms are comfortably furnished.

Facilities 6 rms (4 en suite) ⊛ ✳ Cen ht TVL No children 7yrs **Prices** S €50-€65; D €64-€70✳ **Parking** 6 **Notes** Closed Nov-Apr ⊛

CO WESTMEATH

ATHLONE   MAP 01 C4

◆◆◆◆

T&C Shelmalier House ◇

Cartontroy, Retreat Rd
☎ 090 647 2245 & 647 2145 ▤ 090 647 3190
e-mail shelmalier@eircom.net
Dir *2km E of town centre*

Shelmalier is a modern house in a residential area, set in well-kept gardens. The decor is very attractive, and bedrooms offer good quality furnishings and facilities. There is a comfortable lounge and a breakfast room.

Facilities 7 en suite (2 fmly) (1 GF) ⊛ STV TVB tea/coffee Direct dial from bedrooms ✳ Cen ht TVL Sauna Hot tub **Prices** S €42-€45; D €64-€68✳ **LB** **Parking** 10 **Notes** Closed 20 Dec-Jan

Ireland

continued

HORSELEAP
MAP 01 C4

◆◆◆◆ ✔

Woodlands Farm (N 286426)
Streamstown ☎ 044 26414 Mrs Maxwell
Dir N6 N onto R391 at Horseleap, farm signed 4km

This very comfortable and charming farmhouse has a delightful setting on a 48-hectare farm. The spacious sitting and dining rooms are very relaxing, and there is a hospitality kitchen where tea and coffee are available at all times.

Facilities 5 rms (4 en suite) (1 pri facs) (2 fmly) (2 GF) ⊗ in bedrooms ⊗ in dining room ⊗ in 1 lounge Cen ht TVL 120 acres mixed Last d 5pm **Parking** available **Notes** ⊠

MULLINGAR
MAP 01 C4

◆◆◆◆

T&C Hilltop Country House
Delvin Rd, Rathconnell ☎ 044 9348958
e-mail casean@tinet.ie
Dir Off N4 Mullingar bypass onto N52 towards Delvin, Hilltop signed 1km

This charming country house stands in glorious gardens, where flowers and shrubs fill every available space, the creative work of owner Sean Casey. South facing, the house has elevated reception rooms adjacent to an attractive patio garden, comfortable en suite bedrooms with good showers, and an excellent breakfast menu. Dymphna and Sean Casey will do everything possible to ensure happy visits to their home.

Facilities 5 en suite ⊗ STV TVB tea/coffee ✖ Cen ht TVL No children 15yrs No coaches **Prices** S €45; D €70 **LB** **Parking** 6 **Notes** Closed Nov-Mar

CO WEXFORD

BALLYHACK
MAP 01 C2

◆◆◆◆

T&C Marsh Mere Lodge
☎ 051 389186
e-mail stay@marshmerelodge.com
Dir R733 to Ballyhack

This charming house, a short walk from the Ballyhack ferry, embodies relaxation and comfort. Each bedroom has an individual character and afternoon tea is served on the sunny verandah overlooking King's Bay and Waterford harbour.

Facilities 4 en suite (2 GF) ⊗ ✖ Cen ht TVL Pony trap rides available on request **Parking** 5

CAMPILE
MAP 01 C2

Premier Collection

◆◆◆◆◆

T&C Kilmokea Country Manor & Gardens
Great Island ☎ 051 388109 🖷 051 388776
e-mail kilmokea@eircom.net
Dir R733 from New Ross to Campile, right before village for Great & Kilmokea Gardens

An 18th-century stone rectory, recently restored. Nestling in wooded gardens (open to the public), where peacocks wander and trout fishing is available on the lake. Comfortable bedrooms and public rooms are richly furnished, and a country-house style dinner is served nightly (booking essential). Take breakfast in the conservatory and tea overlooking the beautiful gardens.

Facilities 4 en suite 2 annexe en suite (1 fmly) (2 GF) ⊗ tea/coffee Direct dial from bedrooms Licensed Cen ht TVL 🖾 ❄ Fishing Sauna Gymnasium ⌦ jacuzzi, aromatherapy treatments Dinner Last d 8.30pm **Prices** S €115-€160; D €180-€260✴ **LB** **Conf** Thtr 40 Class 30 Board 25 **Parking** 20

ENNISCORTHY
MAP 01 D3

◆◆◆◆

T&C Lemongrove House ◇
Blackstoops ☎ 05392 36115 🖷 05392 36115
e-mail lemongrovehouse@iolfree.ie
Dir 1km N of Enniscorthy at rdbt on N11

A large house set on an elevated site surrounded by gardens. Lemongrove House offers en suite bedrooms which are all individually decorated in warm, cheerful colour schemes, and there is a comfortable sitting room and breakfast room. Plenty of parking.

Facilities 9 en suite (3 fmly) (5 GF) ⊗ STV TVB tea/coffee Direct dial from bedrooms ✖ Cen ht TVL **Prices** S €35-€50; D €66-€80 **LB** **Parking** 12 **Notes** Closed 20-31 Dec

GOREY
MAP 01 D3

Premier Collection

♦♦♦♦♦

Woodlands Country House *(T 163648)*

Killinierin ☎ 0402 37125 🖹 0402 37125 Ms O'Sullivan
e-mail info@woodlandscountryhouse.com
Dir *Signed 5km N of Gorey off N11*

The 1836 country house stands in extensive mature gardens with a courtyard of stone buildings. The O'Sullivan family offer warm hospitality (and home-made scones on arrival). Three rooms have balconies.

Facilities 6 en suite (3 fmly) STV FTV TVB tea/coffee Licensed Cen ht TVL Pool Table Children's play room, large garden 8 acres mixed **Prices** S €65; D €100-€120 LB **Parking** 10 **Notes** Closed Oct-Apr

♦♦♦♦

T&C Hillside House

Tubberduff ☎ 053 9421726 🖹 053 9422567
e-mail hillsidehouse@eircom.net
Dir *N11 from Dublin, left 1.5km after Toss Byrnes pub, signed Hillside House*

A pristine house with pretty garden set in a lovely rural location commanding panoramic views of mountains and the sea, only 3km from Ballymoney beach. Ann Sutherland is a good cook, providing a variety of home baking. The reception rooms are spacious, bedrooms are very comfortable and attractively decorated.

Facilities 6 en suite (4 fmly) (4 GF) STV TVB tea/coffee Licensed Cen ht TVL **Prices** S €40-€50; D €70-€80 LB **Parking** 6 **Notes** Closed 20-28 Dec

KILMUCKRIDGE
MAP 01 D3

♦♦♦♦

T&C *Ballygarran House*

Ballygarran ☎ 053 30164 🖹 053 30490
e-mail info@ballygarranhouse.com
Dir *R742 N into village, right, house at top*

A friendly welcome awaits guests at this lovely parochial house. A new extension contains bedrooms and receptions rooms, and imaginative decor and comfort features throughout. Breakfast is a feast and evening meals are available by arrangement. There are restaurants, pubs, an award-winning beach, and five golf courses nearby.

Facilities 6 en suite (1 fmly) TVB Cen ht TVL No coaches Dinner **Parking** 12 **Notes** Closed 20 Dec-3 Jan

NEW ROSS
MAP 01 C3

♦♦♦

T&C Woodlands House

Carrigbyrne ☎ 051 428287 🖹 051 428287
e-mail woodwex@eircom.net
Dir *On N25 New Ross-Wexford route, 0.4km from Cedar Lodge Hotel towards New Ross*

Commanding panoramic views, this is a recently rerfurbished bungalow with pretty gardens. It is only a 30-minute drive to Rosslare Harbour. Snacks are available, and dinner by arrangement. Bedrooms vary in size, though all are very comfortable. There is a guest sitting room.

Facilities 4 en suite (4 GF) TVB tea/coffee Cen ht No children 5yrs No coaches Dinner Last d 10am **Prices** S €38-€47.50; D €70-€75* LB **Parking** 6

ROSSLARE HARBOUR
MAP 01 D2

Premier Collection

♦♦♦♦♦

GH Churchtown House

☎ 053 32555 🖹 053 32577
e-mail info@churchtownhouse.com
Dir *N25 onto R736 at Tagoat, turn between Cushens pub & church, house 0.8km on left*

This charming house stands in mature grounds between Rosslare Strand and the harbour. Hosts Patricia and Austin Cody are very welcoming and have spent much time in restoring their home. The individually decorated bedrooms are very comfortable, and dinner following sherry is served in the lounge at 8pm.

Facilities 12 en suite (1 fmly) (5 GF) TVB Direct dial from bedrooms Licensed Cen ht TVL No coaches Dinner Last d noon **Prices** S €75-€95; D €110-€160 LB **Parking** 14 **Notes** Closed Nov-Feb

continued

Ireland

Ireland

ROSSLARE HARBOUR continued

◆◆◆◆

T&C *Oldcourt House*

☎ 053 33895 & 086 3742568
e-mail oldcrt@gofree.indigo.ie
Dir Off N11 at St Patrick's Church, establishment 700yds on left

An impressively large modern house on the quiet shoreside road overlooking Rosslare Bay, just 200 metres beyond Hotel Rosslare, and convenient for the car ferry, beaches and golf courses. The en suite bedrooms are large, airy and furnished to a high standard. There is a comfortable lounge and separate dining room. An ideal base for small golfing parties.

Facilities 6 en suite ⊗ in bedrooms ⊗ in dining room STV TVB ✕ Cen ht TVL **Parking** 10 **Notes** Closed Dec-Feb

◆◆◆

T&C *The Light House*

Main Rd ☎ 053 33214 📠 053 33214

A contemporary bungalow set in grounds, The Light House is convenient for ferry users or for the beach and golf club. There is a television lounge and breakfast room in addition to the bedrooms, all of which have excellent en suite shower rooms.

Facilities 4 en suite (4 GF) ⊗ TVB tea/coffee ✕ Cen ht TVL No children 18yrs **Parking** 6 **Notes** Closed Oct-Feb 🐾

WEXFORD
MAP 01 D3
See also **Kilmuckridge**

◆◆◆◆ 🍷

GH *Clonard House*

Clonard Great ☎ 053 43141 📠 053 43141
e-mail info@clonardhouse.com
Dir N25 onto R733 SW for 0.5km, 1st left, 1st entrance on left

This charming, well-maintained Georgian farmhouse is furnished with many well-chosen period pieces. The attractive sitting room has a large open fire and many of the bedrooms have four-poster beds and great views.

Facilities 9 en suite (4 fmly) ⊗ TVB ✕ Cen ht **Parking** 10 **Notes** Closed Nov-Feb

◆◆◆◆ 🐾

Killiane Castle *(T 058168)*

Drinagh ☎ 053 9158885 📠 053 9158885
Mr & Mrs Mernagh
e-mail killianecastle@yahoo.com
Dir Off N25 between Wexford & Rosslare

Set in pastureland, this guest house stands next to a 13th-century castle. The comfortable sitting and dining rooms are on the ground floor, and there is also a hospitality area where tea and coffee are available at all times. There are hard tennis courts in the grounds.

Facilities 8 en suite (2 fmly) ⊗ TVB ✕ Licensed Cen ht TVL ✎ 🎱 ⛳ Driving range 100 acres dairy Last d noon **Prices** S €65; D €100 **Parking** 8 **Notes** Closed Dec-Feb

◆◆◆◆

T&C *Maple Lodge*

Castlebridge ☎ 053 59195 & 59062 📠 053 59195
e-mail sreenan@eircom.net
Dir 5km N of Wexford. On R741 N on outskirts of Castlebridge, pink house on left

This imposing house, set in extensive mature gardens, is in a peaceful location close to Curracloe Beach. Eamonn and Margaret Sreenan offer warm hospitality in their comfortable home. There is a varied breakfast menu offered and and secure parking in the grounds.

Facilities 4 en suite (2 fmly) ⊗ STV TVB ✕ Cen ht TVL No children 10yrs No coaches **Parking** 5 **Notes** Closed mid Nov-mid Mar

◆◆◆◆

T&C **Rathaspeck Manor**

Rathaspeck ☎ 053 41672
Dir Signed on N25, near Johnstone Castle

Standing in grounds that feature an 18-hole par-3 golf course, this Georgian country house is 0.8km from Johnstone Castle. The comfortable, spacious bedrooms are en suite and the public rooms are appointed with period furnishings.

Facilities 5 en suite (3 fmly) (2 GF) ⊗ in dining room ⊗ in lounges TVB tea/coffee ✕ Cen ht TVL No children 10yrs No coaches Golf 18 ⛳ **Prices** S €80; D €140 **Parking** 8 **Notes** Closed 8 Nov-Jun 🐾

◆◆◆◆

GH *Slaney Manor*

Ferrycarrig ☎ 053 20051 & 20144 📠 053 20510
e-mail slaneymanor@eircom.net
Dir On N25, 0.8km W of N11 junct

This attractive manor house stands in 24 hectares of woodland overlooking the River Slaney. Restored by the owners, the house retains many fine features. The elegant, high-ceilinged drawing room and dining room have views of the river, and four-poster beds feature in all bedrooms. The rooms in the converted coach house can be reserved on a room only basis for those travelling on the Rosslare ferry.

Facilities 8 en suite (2 fmly) ⊗ TVB tea/coffee Direct dial from bedrooms ✕ Licensed Lift Cen ht TVL Dinner Last d noon **Parking** 30 **Notes** Closed Xmas wk

CO WICKLOW

ARKLOW
MAP 01 D3

◆◆◆

GH **Koliba Country Home**

Beech Rd, Avoca ☎ 0402 32737 📠 0402 32737
e-mail koliba@eircom.net
Dir N11 onto R772 into Arklow, right at Rover garage, house 3km on right

Situated halfway between Avoca and Arklow, this recently renovated house has panoramic views of the Vale of Avoca. Each cosy room is individually decorated. Rose and Brendan are very hospitable hosts and ensure a warm welcome.

continued

Facilities 4 en suite (4 fmly) (4 GF) ⊛ TVB tea/coffee ✱ Cen ht TVL
No coaches **Parking** 8 **Notes** Closed Nov-Mar

ASHFORD
MAP 01 D3

◆◆◆◆ 🌐 🍽 ✜

Ballyknocken House & Cookery
School (T 246925)

☎ 0404 44627 📠 0404 44696 Mrs Fulvio
e-mail cfulvio@ballyknocken.com
Dir N11 S into Ashford, right after Texaco station, house 5km on right

This charming Victorian farmhouse stands in the foothills of the
Wicklow Mountains. Catherine Fulvio is an enthusiastic hostess and
reservations are necessary for dinner, which includes imaginative,
freshly prepared dishes using produce from the garden and farm. The
smart bedrooms are comfortable, and the farm buildings have been
converted into a cookery school.

Facilities 7 en suite (1 fmly) ⊛ TVB tea/coffee Direct dial from
bedrooms ✱ Licensed Cen ht ❀ 350 acres sheep Dinner Last d noon
Prices S €69-€95; D €118-€124✳ **LB Conf** Max 80 Thtr 80 Class 50
Board 30 **Parking** 8 **Notes** Closed Dec & Jan

AVOCA
MAP 01 D3

◆◆◆◆

GH Sheepwalk House & Cottages

Beech Rd ☎ 0402 35189 📠 0402 35789
e-mail sheepwalk@eircom.net
web www.sheepwalk.com
Dir 2m from Avoca. Off N11 at Arklow/Redcross junct towards Avoca

An 18th-century Georgian house with lovely views across Arklow Bay. The
cosy bedrooms are equipped with every thoughtful extra, and guests can
breakfast in the informal sun lounge with sea views. Owner Jim McCabe
is a mine of information on golfing, shooting and fishing holidays.

Facilities 6 en suite ⊛ TVB tea/coffee ✱ Cen ht No coaches
Parking 12 **Notes** Closed Nov-14 Mar

◆◆◆

T&C *Cherrybrook Country Home*

☎ 0402 35179 & 08761 05027 📠 0402 35765
e-mail cherrybandb@eircom.net
Dir N11 S to Arklow, follow signs for Vale & Avola

Set in the village made famous by the television series Ballykissangel,
Cherrybrook has fine gardens with a barbeque area. It is a well-
continued

presented house with a lounge and dining room. Bedrooms are
attractively decorated. Evening meals are available by arrangement.

Facilities 5 en suite (2 fmly) (3 GF) ⊛ TVB tea/coffee ✱ Cen ht TVL
No children 13yrs **Parking** 5

BRAY
MAP 01 D3

◆◆◆◆◆

GH Pine Cottage

Windgates ☎ 01 2872601 📠 01 2872667
web homepage.eircom.net/~pinecottagebb
Dir N11 exit Bray South for Greystones, 1st left after golf club

Set on the tranquil southern slopes of Bray Head, with stunning views
of Little Sugar Loaf mountain, this smartly designed cottage has
spacious new bedrooms are and a particularly comfortable lounge.
This is a good base for playing the many nearby golf courses.

Facilities 3 en suite (3 GF) ⊛ in bedrooms ⊛ in dining room TVB ✱
Cen ht No children 10yrs No coaches **Prices** S €55-€60; D €80-€90
Parking 7 **Notes** Closed Nov-Feb 🐾

◆◆◆

T&C *Woodville*

Ballywaltrim Ln ☎ 01 2863103 📠 01 2863103
e-mail catherik@gofree.indigo.ie
Dir N11 from Dublin onto M11, 3rd exit signed Bray, 1st exit off rdbt,
right (as if going into filling station), follow cul-de-sac sign to bottom
of hill

An attractively designed bungalow, tucked away at the end of a cul de
sac, to the south of Bray town and convenient for the ferry port of
Dun Laoghaire. Bedrooms are comfortable and well appointed. The
relaxing lounge has a hostess trolley with tea and coffee. The garden is
well maintained and there is ample parking with a security gate.

Facilities 4 en suite (1 fmly) ⊛ TVB ✱ Cen ht TVL No children 3yrs
No coaches **Parking** 6 **Notes** Closed 15 Dec-7 Jan

DUNLAVIN

MAP 01 C3

◆◆◆◆◆ 🏛

GH Rathsallagh House

☎ 045 403112 📄 045 403343
e-mail info@rathsallagh.com
Dir 10.5km after end of M9 left signed Dunlavin, house signed 5km

Surrounded by its own 18-hole championship golf course this delightful house was converted from Queen Ann stables in 1798 and now has the new addition of spacious and luxurious bedrooms with conference and leisure facilities. Food is country-house cooking at its best, and there is a cosy bar and comfortable drawing room to relax in. Close to Curragh and Punchestown racecourses.

Facilities 17 en suite 12 annexe en suite (11 GF) ⊗ FTV TVB tea/coffee
Direct dial from bedrooms ✖ Licensed Cen ht TVL No children 12yrs
Golf 18 ✎ Snooker Sauna 🏋 ⅃ Jacuzzi / Beauty treatments / Steam
Room Dinner Last d 9pm **Prices** S €185-€270; D €270-€320✳ LB
Conf Max 160 Thtr 150 Class 75 Board 40 Del from €265 ✳
Parking 150

◆◆◆◆ ❦

Tynte House *(N 870015)*

☎ 045 401561 📄 045 401586 Mr & Mrs Lawler
e-mail info@tyntehouse.com
Dir N81 at Hollywood Cross, right at Dunlavin, follow finger signs for Tynte House, past market house in town centre

The 19th-century farmhouse stands in the square of this quiet country village. The friendly hosts have carried out a lot of restoration resulting in comfortable bedrooms and a relaxing guest sitting room. Breakfast is high light of a visit to this house, which features Caroline's home baking.

Facilities 7 en suite (2 fmly) ⊗ in 2 bedrooms ⊗ in dining room
⊗ in lounges TVB tea/coffee Direct dial from bedrooms Cen ht TVL ch
fac Golf 18 ✎ Pool Table Playground Games room 200 acres arable beef
Dinner Last d noon **Prices** S €44-€54; D €70-€90 LB **Parking** 16
Notes Closed 16 Dec-9 Jan

GLENDALOUGH

MAP 01 D3

◆◆◆◆

T&C Pinewood Lodge

☎ 0404 45437 📄 0404 45437
e-mail pinewoodlodge@eircom.net
Dir R756 from Laragh to Glendalough, 2nd house on right after school & church

Set in large grounds and bordered by forests, Pinewood Lodge is comfortable and well appointed. The bedrooms are attractively decorated and there is a spacious lounge and a breakfast room. There are pubs and restaurants nearby.

Facilities 6 en suite (3 fmly) (4 GF) ⊗ tea/coffee ✖ Cen ht TVL
No children 4yrs No coaches **Prices** S €55; D €75 **Parking** 10

KILTEGAN

MAP 01 D3

◆◆◆◆◆

T&C Barraderry House

☎ 059 647 3209 📄 059 647 3209
e-mail jo.hobson@oceanfree.net
Dir 0.5m from Kiltegan. N81 onto R747, 7km on right

A granite gateway is the entrance to this restored Georgian house. The drawing room is next to the television study, and breakfast is served in the dining room. Light evening meals can be booked in advance. The bedrooms are all furnished in keeping with the period of the house and have en suite bathrooms.

Facilities 4 en suite (2 fmly) ⊗ TVB tea/coffee ✖ Cen ht TVL
Prices S €50-€60; D €100-€120 LB **Conf** Max 8 **Parking** 12
Notes Closed mid Dec-mid Jan

RATHDRUM MAP 01 D3

♦♦♦

GH *Avonbrae Guesthouse*

☎ 0404 46198 📠 0404 46198
e-mail info@avonbrae.com
Dir 180 metres from village on Laragh Rd

Lovely rose gardens surround this peaceful rural retreat in the Wicklow Hills. Owner Paddy Geoghegan has spent the last few years refurbishing the house to a very high standard. Bedrooms, with pine furniture, are attractively decorated, and there is a charming sitting room and a spacious dining room.

Facilities 7 rms (6 en suite) (2 fmly) ⊗ tea/coffee Direct dial from bedrooms Licensed Cen ht TVL No coaches 🔄 ❊ Games room, table tennis Dinner Last d noon **Parking** 7 **Notes** Closed Nov-Mar

ROUNDWOOD MAP 01 D3

♦♦♦♦ ❧

Wicklow Way Lodge (O 165013)

Old Br ☎ 01 2818489 📠 01 2818189 Ms Kilnan
e-mail wicklowwaylodge@eircom.net
Dir From Roundwood signs for Lough Dan 4km, at T-junct onto Glenndalough road for 300 metres

Nestling on a mountainside amid spectacular scenery, this house is part of a sheep farm beside the Wicklow Mountains National Park and

continued

on the popular Wicklow Way long-distance path. There are spacious bedrooms, some with balconies, and the comfortable dining room and sitting room share the views. Convenient for Glendalough and many golf courses.

Facilities 5 en suite (1 fmly) (1 GF) TVB tea/coffee ✖ Cen ht 95 acres Sheep **Parking** available **Notes** Closed Dec-Jan

WICKLOW MAP 01 D3

♦♦♦♦ ❧

Kilpatrick House (T2257808)

Redcross ☎ 0404 47137 & 087 6358325 📠 0404 47866
Mr & Mrs Kingston
e-mail info@kilpatrickhouse.com
Dir 13km S, 3.2km off N11, signed from Jack Whites pub

This elegant 18th-century Georgian residence set on a beef and tillage farm just off the N11 north of Arklow. Bedrooms are carefully furnished and thoughtfully equipped. Dinner is available on request and the extensive breakfast menu includes Shirley's home baking and country produce. Close to Brittas Bay, there is a choice of golf courses and horse riding.

Facilities 4 rms (3 en suite) (1 pri facs) (2 fmly) ⊗ TVB tea/coffee ✖ Cen ht TVL ❊ Fishing 250 acres beef & arable Dinner Last d 10am **Prices** S €50; D €75 **Parking** 20 **Notes** Closed 6 Nov-Mar

Ireland

County Maps

England

1 Bedfordshire
2 Berkshire
3 Bristol
4 Buckinghamshire
5 Cambridgeshire
6 Greater Manchester
7 Herefordshire
8 Hertfordshire
9 Leicestershire
10 Northamptonshire
11 Nottinghamshire
12 Rutland
13 Staffordshire
14 Warwickshire
15 West Midlands
16 Worcestershire

Scotland

17 City of Glasgow
18 Clackmannanshire
19 East Ayrshire
20 East Dunbartonshire
21 East Renfrewshire
22 Perth & Kinross
23 Renfrewshire
24 South Lanarkshire
25 West Dunbartonshire

Wales

26 Blaenau Gwent
27 Bridgend
28 Caerphilly
29 Denbighshire
30 Flintshire
31 Merthyr Tydfil
32 Monmouthshire
33 Neath Port Talbot
34 Newport
35 Rhondda Cynon Taf
36 Torfaen
37 Vale of Glamorgan
38 Wrexham

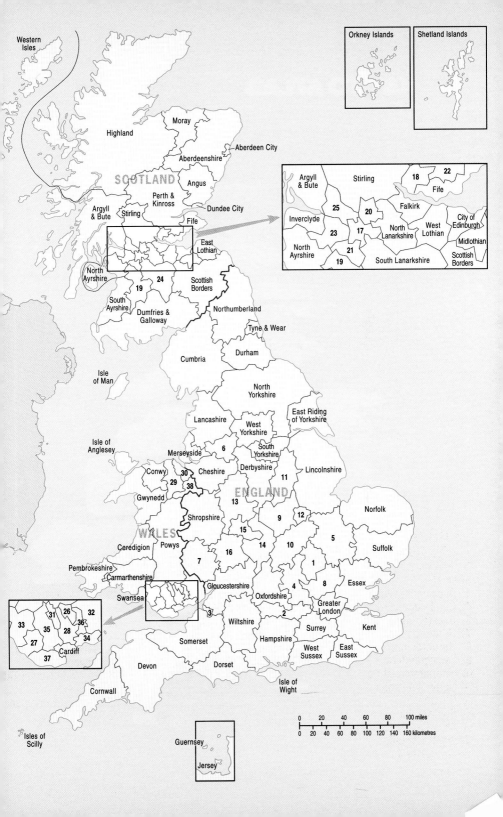

KEY TO ATLAS

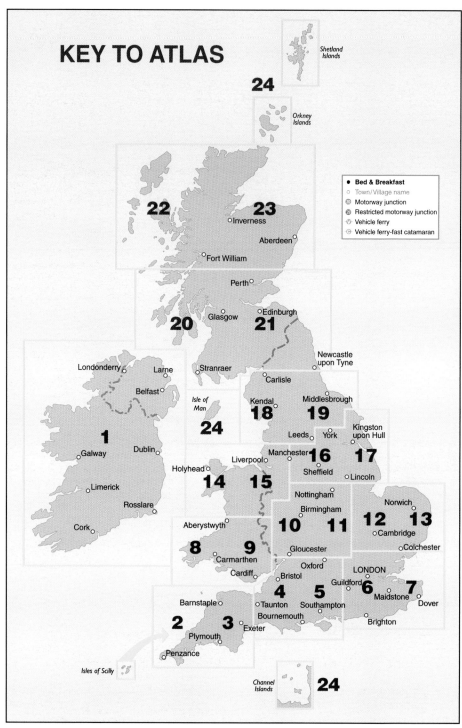

Shetland Islands
24

Orkney Islands

22

23
Inverness

Aberdeen

Fort William

Perth

20
Glasgow
Edinburgh
21

- Bed & Breakfast
- Town/Village name
- Motorway junction
- Restricted motorway junction
- Vehicle ferry
- Vehicle ferry-fast catamaran

Newcastle upon Tyne

Londonderry
Larne
Stranraer
Carlisle

Belfast
Isle of Man
Kendal
Middlesbrough
18
19

Leeds
York
Kingston upon Hull

1
Galway
Dublin
Liverpool
Manchester
16
17

Holyhead
Sheffield
Lincoln

Limerick
14
15
Nottingham

Rosslare
Birmingham
Norwich

Cork
Aberystwyth
10
11
12
13
Cambridge

8
9
Gloucester
Colchester

Carmarthen
Oxford
LONDON

Cardiff
Bristol
Guildford
6
7

Barnstaple
4
5
Maidstone
Dover

2
3
Taunton
Southampton

Bournemouth
Brighton

Plymouth
Exeter

Penzance

Isles of Scilly

Channel Islands
24

© Automobile Association Developments Limited 2006

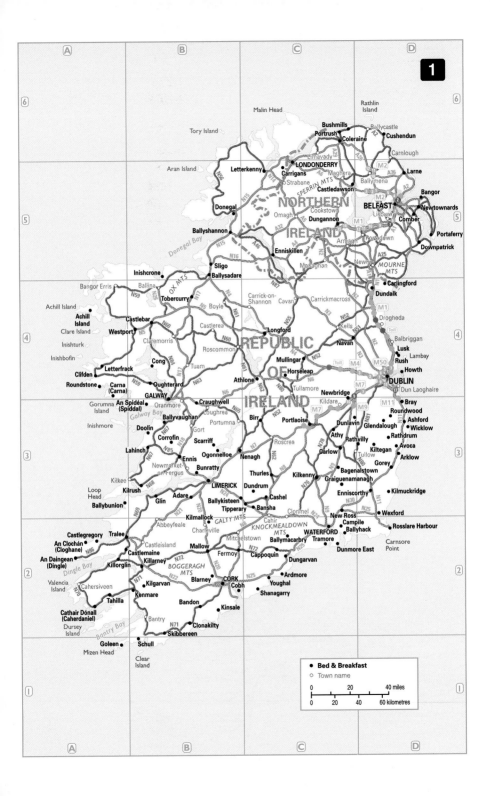

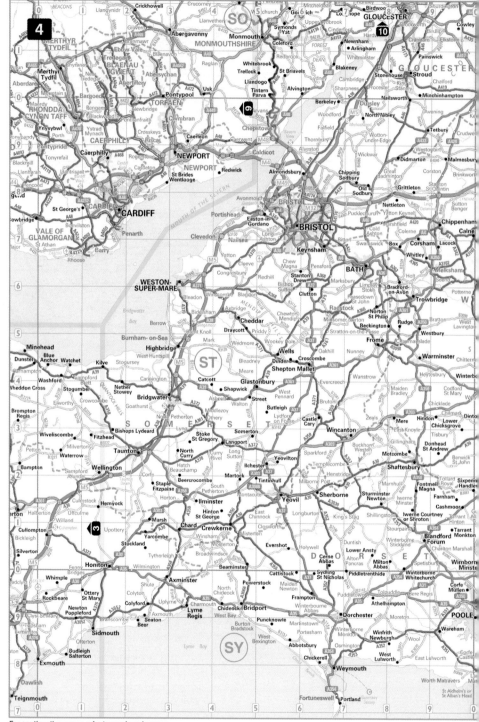

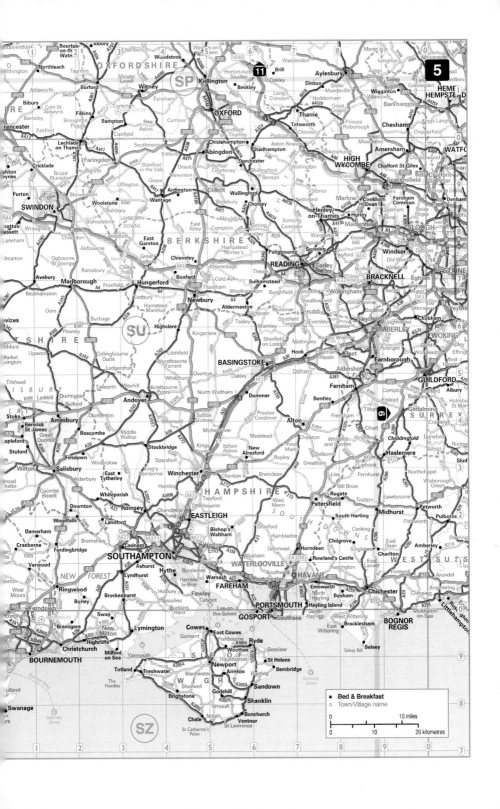

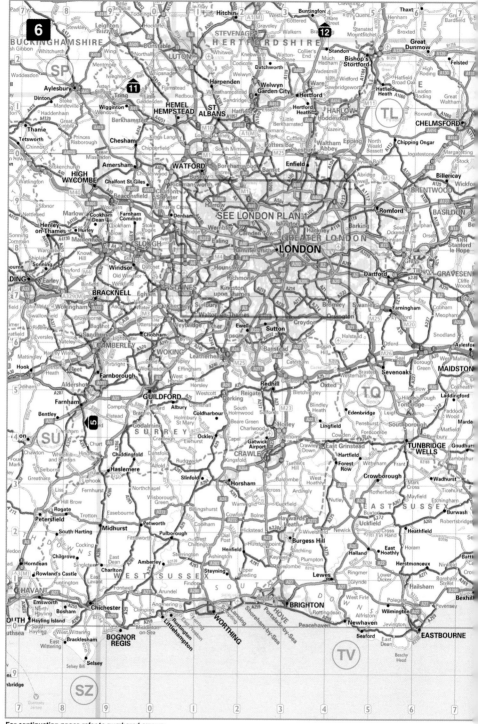

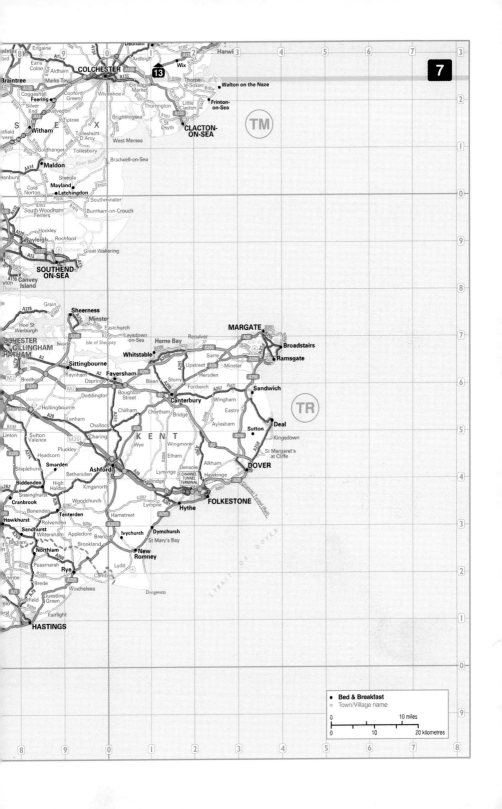

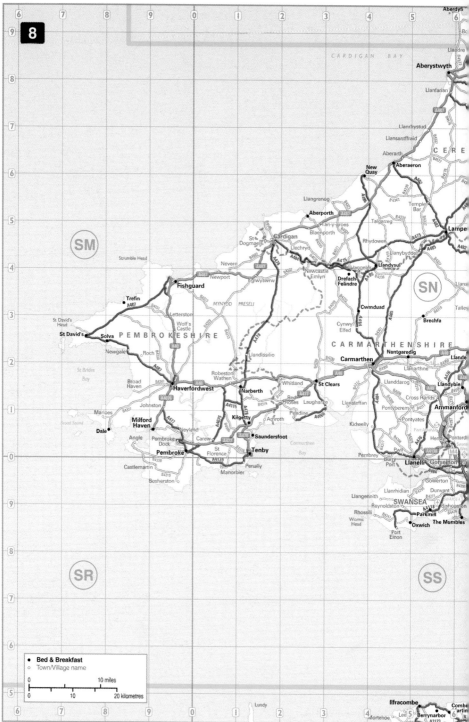

Bed & Breakfast
○ Town/Village name

0		10 miles
0	10	20 kilometres

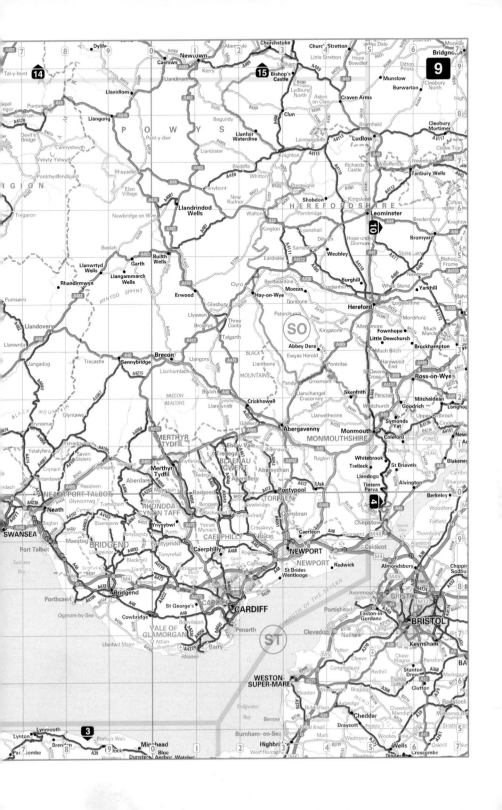

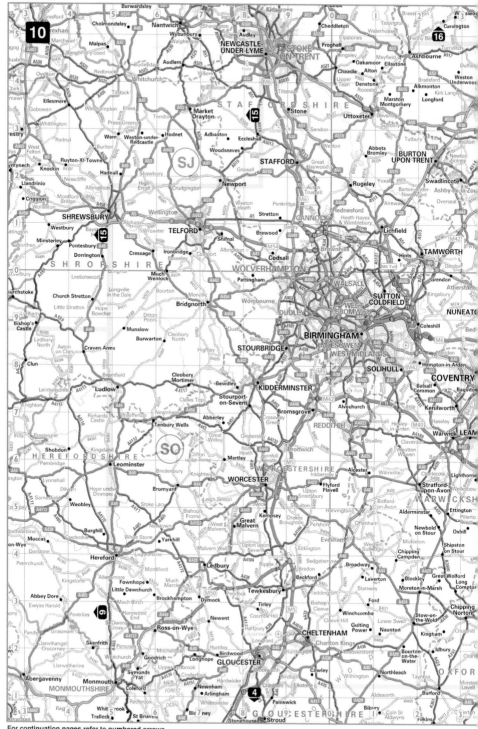

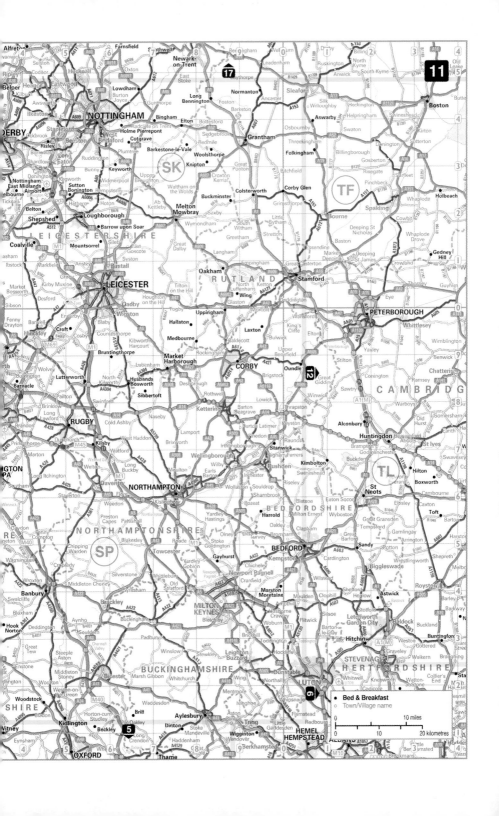

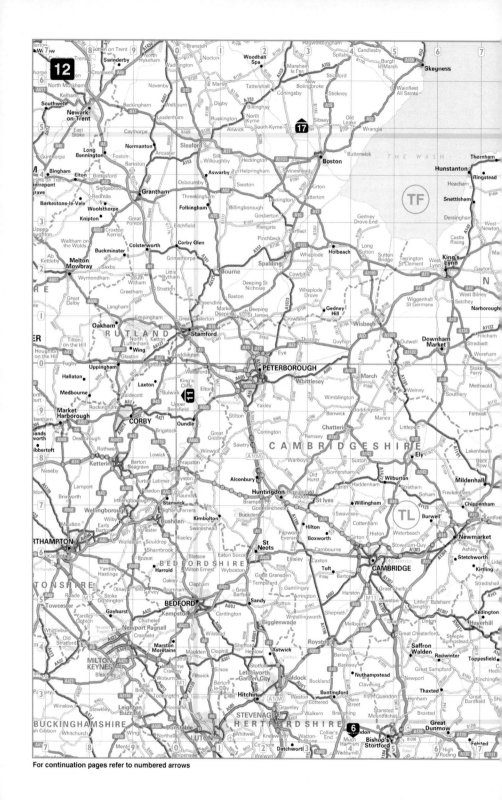

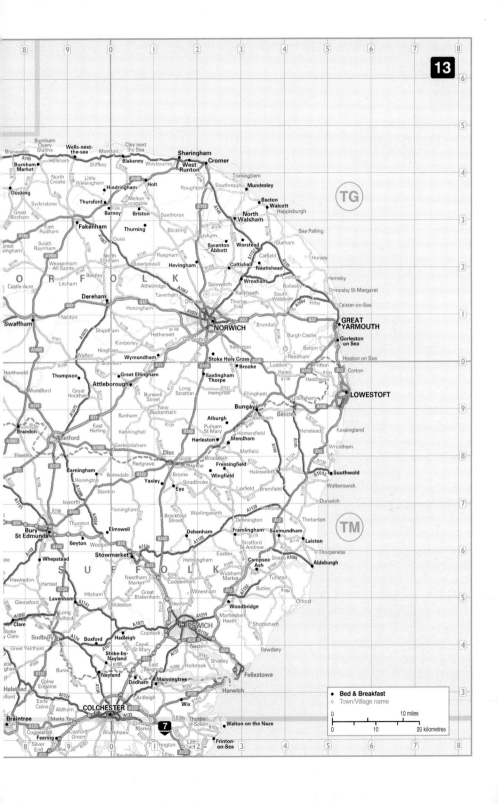

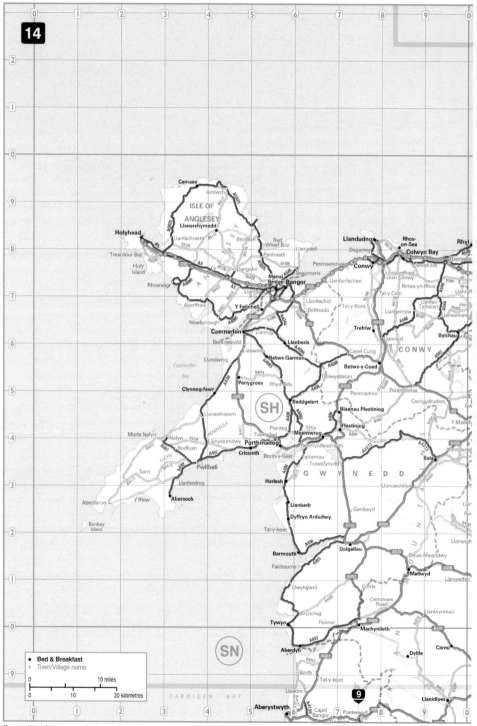

14

For continuation pages refer to numbered arrows

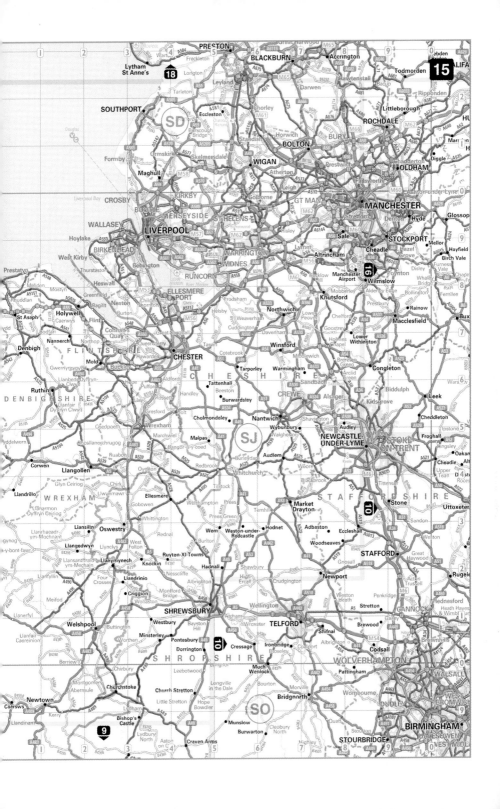

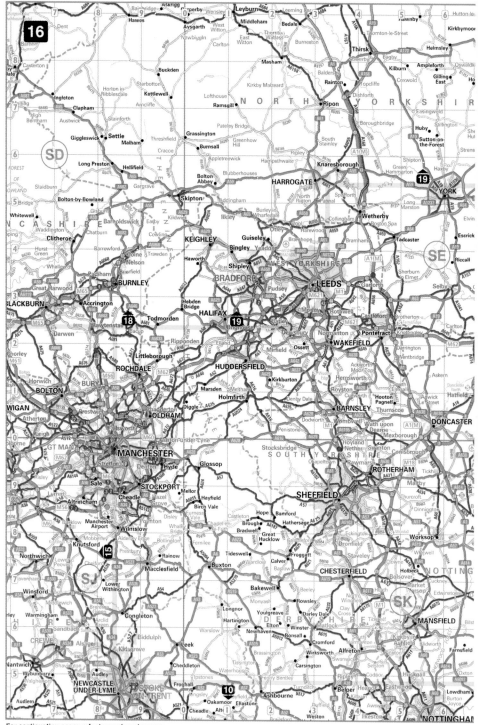

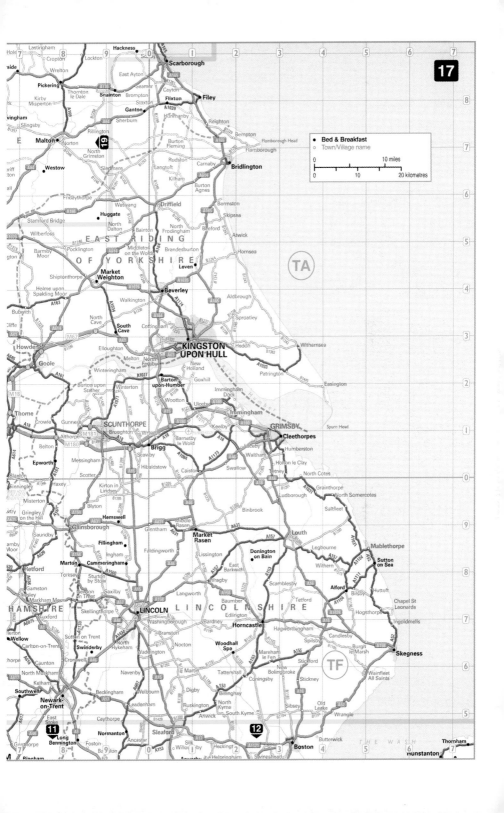

For continuation pages refer to numbered arrows

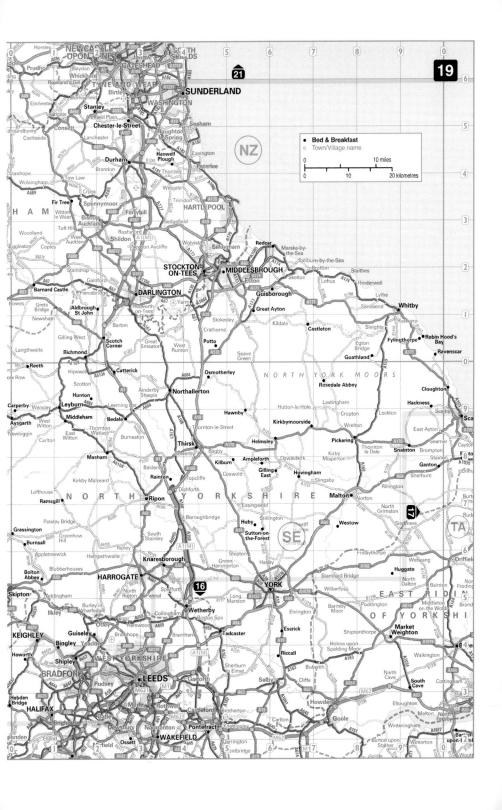

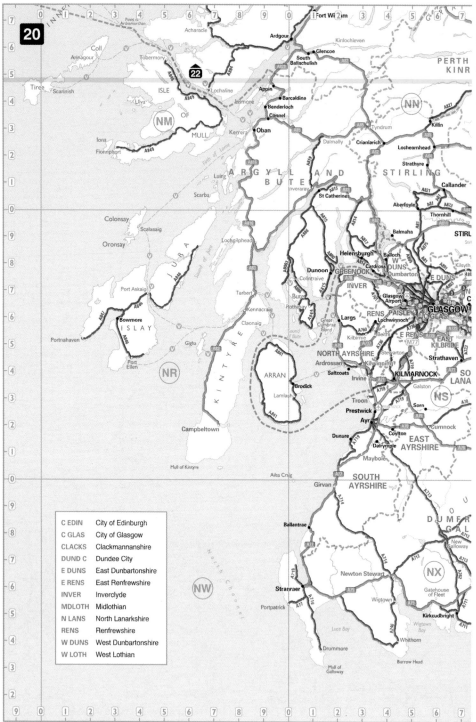

C EDIN	City of Edinburgh
C GLAS	City of Glasgow
CLACKS	Clackmannanshire
DUND C	Dundee City
E DUNS	East Dunbartonshire
E RENS	East Renfrewshire
INVER	Inverclyde
MDLOTH	Midlothian
N LANS	North Lanarkshire
RENS	Renfrewshire
W DUNS	West Dunbartonshire
W LOTH	West Lothian

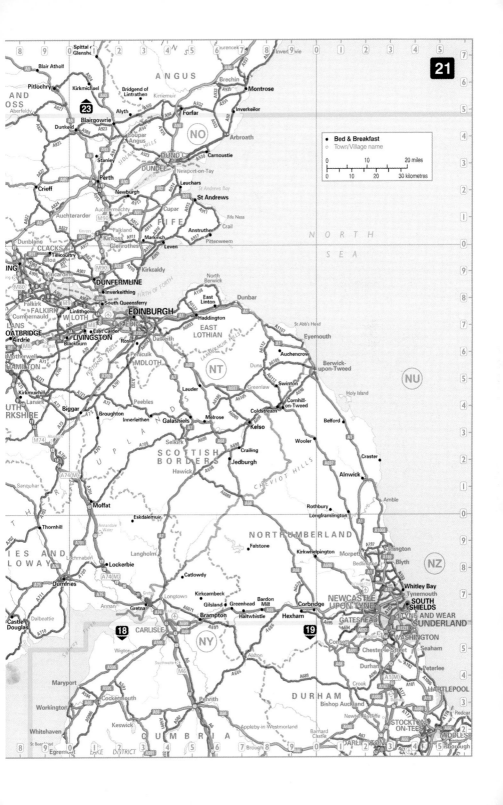

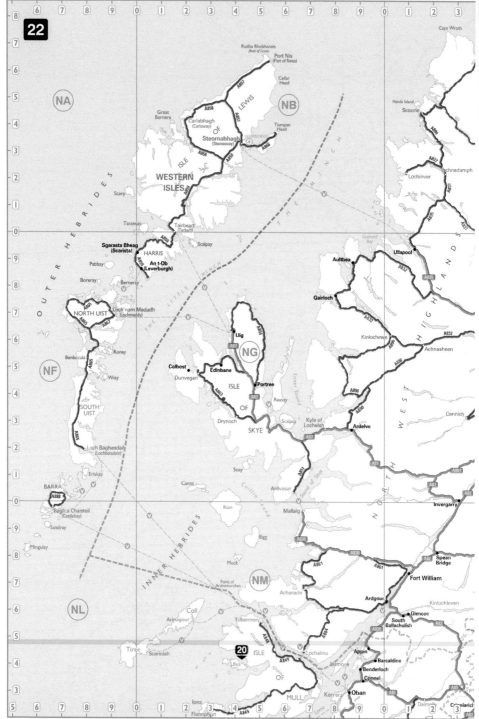

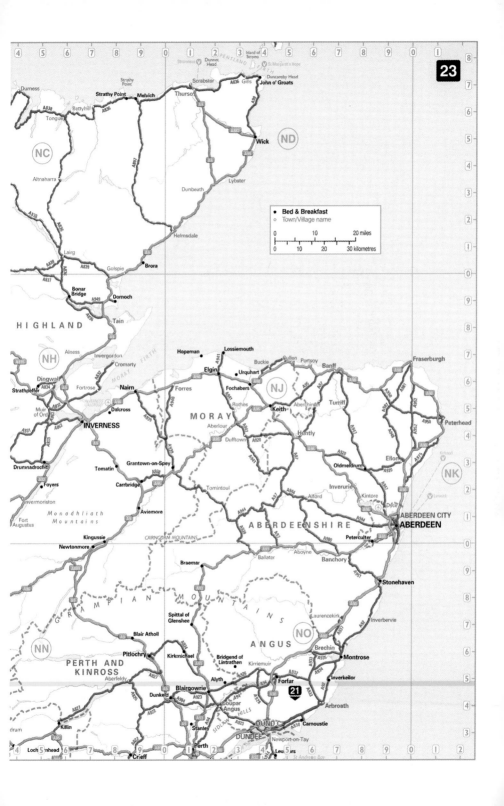

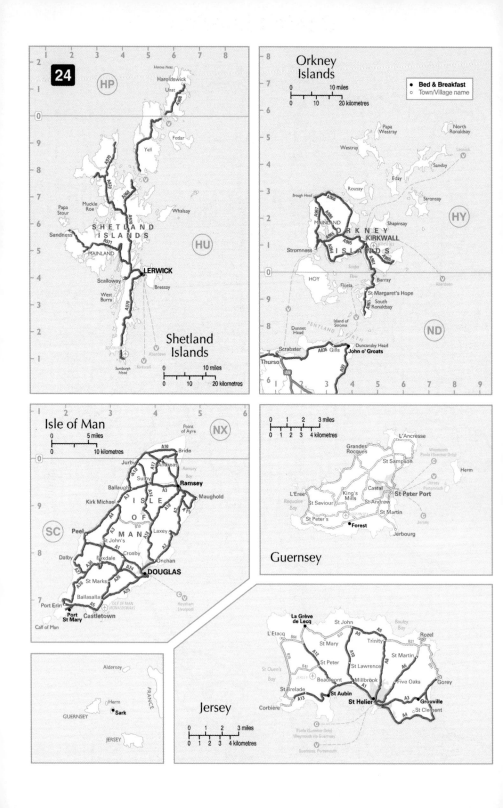

24

HP

Hermes Ness
Haroldswick
Unst
A968

Fetlar

Yell
A968
A970

Muckle Roe
Papa Stour
A970
Whalsay
A971
SHETLAND ISLANDS
HU
Sandness
A971
MAINLAND
LERWICK
Scalloway
Bressay
West Burra
A970

Shetland Islands

0   10 miles
0   10   20 kilometres

Sumburgh Head
Aberdeen
Kirkwall

Orkney Islands

0   10 miles
0   10   20 kilometres

● Bed & Breakfast
○ Town/Village name

Papa Westray
North Ronaldsay
Westray
Sanday
Eday
Rousay
Stronsay
HY
Brough Head
A967
A965
MAINLAND
ORKNEY
Shapinsay
KIRKWALL
A966
A965
Stromness
A960
A961
ISLANDS
Scapa
HOY
Flow
Burray
Flotta
St Margaret's Hope
Island of Stroma
South Ronaldsay
ND
Dunnet Head
PENTLAND FIRTH
Aberdeen
Scrabster
Gills
Duncansby Head
Thurso
A836
John o' Groats
A99

Isle of Man

0   5 miles
0   10 kilometres

Point of Ayre
NX
A10
Bride
Jurby
Andreas
Ramsey Bay
Sulby
Ballaugh
Ramsey
Kirk Michael
A3
ISLE
Maughold
A18
A2
A1
OF
SC
Peel
A1
MAN
St John's
Crosby
Laxey
Dalby
A3
Foxdale
B10
Onchan
A5
St Marks
A25
A24
DOUGLAS
A36
Ballasalla
A5
Port Erin
ISLE OF MAN (RONALDSWAY)
Port St Mary
Castletown
Heysham Liverpool
Calf of Man

---

0   1   2   3 miles
0   1   2   3   4 kilometres

L'Ancresse
Grandes Rocques
St Sampson
Herm
L'Eree
Weymouth Poole (Summer Only)
King's Mills
Castel
St Peter Port
Jersey Portsmouth
St Saviour
St Andrew
Rocquaine Bay
St Peter's
St Martin
Jersey
Forest
Jerbourg

Guernsey

Alderney
Herm
FRANCE
Sark
GUERNSEY
JERSEY

La Grève de Lecq
St John
Bouley Bay
L'Etacq
B44
St Mary
A9
Trinity
Rozel
B33
B41
St Peter
A10
St Martin
A6
St Ouen's Bay
A12
St Lawrence
Five Oaks
Beaumont
Millbrook
Gorey
St Brelade
A1
St Aubin
A3
Grouville
Corbière
A13
St Helier
St Clement
A4

Jersey

0   1   2   3 miles
0   1   2   3   4 kilometres

Poole (Summer Only)
Weymouth via Guernsey
Guernsey, Portsmouth

Central London

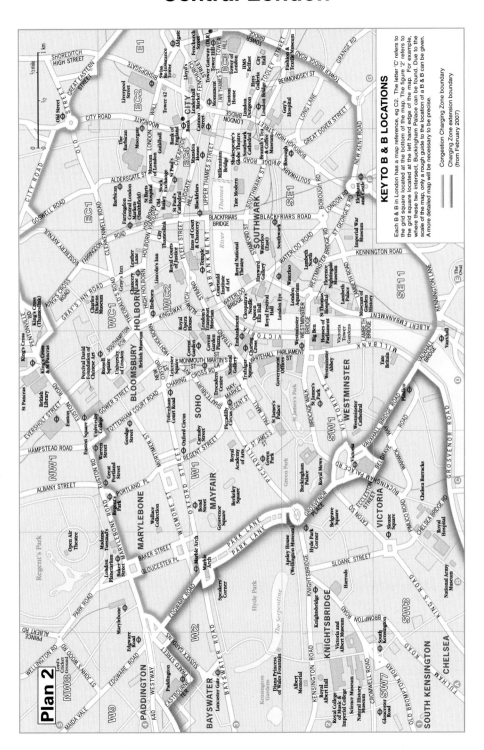

Plan 2

KEY TO B & B LOCATIONS

Each B & B in London has a map reference, eg C2. The letter 'C' refers to the grid square located at the bottom of the map. The figure '2' refers to the grid square located at the left hand edge of the map. For example, where these two intersect, Buckingham Palace can be found. Due to the scale of the map, only a rough guide to the location of a B & B can be given. A more detailed map will be necessary to be precise.

— — — Congestion Charging Zone boundary

——— Charging Zone extension boundary (from February 2007)

Index of locations

Index

Index

Index

Index

Picture credits

The Automobile Association wishes to thank the following picture libraries for their assistance in the preparation of this book:

Front cover: ©TongRo Image Stock / Alamy; 1 Photodisc; 3tr Photodisc; 3br AA World Travel Library/J Welsh; 3bc AA World Travel Library/S Day; 3bl AA World Travel Library/S Day; 4tr AA World Travel Library/R Moss; 6tl AA World Travel Library/M Birkitt; AA World Travel Library; 7tr Photodisc; 7b Stockbyte; 9tr Photodisc; 10tl AA World Travel Library/M Bikitt; 10b Stockbyte; 11tl Photodisc; 11tr Photodisc; 12tl AA World Travel Library/M Birkitt; 12tll Photodisc; 12tc AA World Travel Library/C Jones; 13tl AA World Travel Library/D Forss; 13tcl AA World Travel Library/P Enticknap; 13tcr Stockbyte; 13tr Stockbyte; 13trr Photodisc; 14tl AA World Travel Library/M Birkitt; 15tl AA World Travel Library/S Day; 15tr Photodisc; 23 AA World Travel Library/S L Day; 610 AAWorld Travel Library/ J Smith; 673 AA World Travel Library/I Burgum; 723 AA World Travel Library/S Whitehorne.

Every effort has been made to trace the copyright holders, and we apologise in advance for any accidental errors. We would be happy to apply the corrections in the following edition of this publication.

Notes

Notes

Notes

Notes

Notes

Notes

Notes

Please send this form to:

Editor, The B&B Guide
Lifestyle Guides
The Automobile Association
Fanum House
Basingstoke RG21 4EA

e-mail: lifestyleguides@theAA.com

Reader's Report Form

Use this form to recommend any guest house, farmhouse or inn you have stayed at that is not already in the Guide.

If you have any comments about your stay at an establishment listed in the Guide, please let us know, as feedback from readers helps to keep our Guide accurate and up to date. If you have a complaint during your stay, we recommend that you discuss the matter with the establishment.

Please note that the AA does not undertake to arbitrate between you and the establishment, to obtain compensation, or to engage in protracted correspondence.

Date:

Your name (block capitals)

Your address (block capitals)

....
....
....
....

e-mail address:

Comments (please include the name & address of the establishment)

....
....
....
....
....
....
....
....
....
....
....
....
....
....

(please attach a separate sheet if necessary)

Please tick here if you DO NOT wish to receive details of AA offers or products ☐

PTO

Reader's Report Form

	YES	NO
Have you bought this Guide before?	☐	☐

What other accommodation, restaurant, pub or food guides have you bought recently?

....

....

Why did you buy this Guide? (circle all that apply)

holiday   short break   business travel   special occasion

overnight stop   conference   other...

How often do you stay in B&Bs? (circle one choice)

more than once a month   once a month   once in 2-3 months

once in six months   once a year   less than once a year

Which of these factors are most important when choosing a B&B?

price   location   awards/ratings   service

décor/surroundings   previous experience   recommendation

Other:...

Did you read the editorial feature in the Guide? ....

Do you use the location atlas?...

What parts of the guide do you find the most useful when choosing somewhere to stay?

Diamond rating   description   photo   advertisement

Please suggest any improvements to the guide?

....

....

....

....

Thank you for returning this form